About Aspen Law & Business
Legal Education Division

With a dedication to preserving and strengthening the long-standing tradition of publishing excellence in legal education, Aspen Law & Business continues to provide the highest quality teaching and learning resources for today's law school community. Careful development, meticulous editing, and an unmatched responsiveness to the evolving needs of today's discerning educators combine in the creation of our outstanding casebooks, course-books, textbooks, and study aids.

Aspen Law & Business
A Division of Aspen Publishers, Inc.
A Wolters Kluwer Company
www.aspenpublishers.com

PROBLEMS, CASES, AND MATERIALS ON EVIDENCE

Third Edition

ERIC D. GREEN
Professor of Law
Boston University

CHARLES R. NESSON
William F. Weld Professor of Law
Harvard University

PETER L. MURRAY
Robert Braucher Visiting Professor of Law from Practice
Harvard University

ASPEN LAW & BUSINESS
A Division of Aspen Publishers, Inc.
Gaithersburg   New York

Permissions
Aspen Law & Business
1185 Avenue of the Americas
New York, NY   10036

Printed in the United States of America.

ISBN-0-7355-1983-8

2 3 4 5 6 7 8 9 0

Library of Congress Cataloging-in-Publication Data

Green, Eric D., 1946-
    Problems, cases, and materials on evidence / Eric D. Green, Charles R. Nesson, Peter L. Murray. — 3rd ed.
      p. cm.
    Includes index.
    ISBN 0-7355-1983-8
    1. Evidence (Law) — United States — Cases. I. Nesson, Charles R.
II. Murray, Peter L.   III. Title.

KF8934.G73   2001
347.73'6 — dc21

00-053594

Problems, Cases, and Materials
on Evidence

To my evidence teachers: John Doar, Leonard Boudin, William Matthew Byrne, Jr., and my students.

C.R.N.

To Carmin, Jessica, Eli, Rebecca, Nick, and Eliza.

E.D.G.

To Samuel and Margaret, born September 25, 2000.

P.L.M.

Summary of Contents

Contents

CHAPTER VII   Privileges   601

CHAPTER VIII Opinions, Scientific Proof, and Expert Testimony 753

CHAPTER IX   Authentication and Identification: Writings, Photographs, Voices, and Real Evidence   945

Preface

Nearly twenty years have passed since the First Edition of this book was published in 1984. This time period has seen extraordinary developments, both in the law of evidence and in the technology of teaching and publication of legal materials. At the time of publication of the First Edition, conventional printed books represented the only feasible means for law teachers to write, collect, arrange, and communicate pedagogical information to their students. Now the Internet provides law teachers with exciting new options for the collection and presentation of all forms of teaching materials.

The Evidence Web Site

In the world of 20 years ago, a law teacher planning a course on Evidence had to select among published casebooks and teaching texts offered by a handful of law publishers. Deviation from the materials provided by the authors of the published texts involved distribution of multiple handouts and supplements. This was laborious and expensive. Teachers had to content themselves largely with the selections and the order of the authors whose materials had been published.

Present-day digital technology permits teachers to make available to their students via the World Wide Web any choice of law teaching materials in any order. Web sites rather than printed casebooks define law school course syllabi and provide the selected reading materials. For several years, some of the co-authors of this book and many colleagues across the country have relied on the World Wide Web to disseminate some or all of the reading materials utilized by students in their courses.

Recognizing the potential of the Web to provide law teachers with practically unlimited access to legal resources and the ability of different law teachers to select and assemble these resources in different orders for different courses, the authors of this book have developed an experimental "Green, Nesson & Murray Evidence Web Site" which is main-

tained on the Web server at the Harvard Law School. The site may be
accessed at

www.law.harvard.edu/publications/evidenceiii/index.html.

All of the cases, problems, and other materials appearing in this Third
Edition as well as a large amount of additional material that may be of
some use to Evidence teachers, students, and practitioners can be found
on the Web site. The Web site includes the complete text of the Federal
Rules of Evidence along with topical indices and sample course syllabi
linked to cases, materials, and problems from the site. Colleagues are
invited to make free use of the Evidence Web site to gain electronic
access to Evidence teaching materials and to construct their own Web
based courses linked to the site. Practitioners and students are invited
to use the site as a source of Evidence materials, problems, and syllabi.
Colleagues, practitioners, and students are all invited to submit to the
authors comments on the Web site as well as materials for posting. The
Web site is a work in process. The authors' aim is to create and maintain
an ever-developing digital resource for the study and teaching of the
law of evidence.

No law teacher is any longer confined to the selections of teaching
materials provided by textbook authors. Digital technology and the
World Wide Web make it possible for all Evidence teachers to select
their own teaching materials, be they cases, problems, articles, or commentary, and make them available in their own special order to their
own students. The "value added" by a conventional evidence book such
as this one is the convenience to students and teacher alike of having a
selection of materials appropriate for teaching a law school course in a
standard, portable, easy-to-read printed form. We submit the selection
of materials in this Third Edition as representing our choice from the
vast amount of material that is now easily available in electronic form.
We have ordered these materials in a way we have found effective for a
basic one-semester, three- or four-credit course on Evidence. We have
added commentary, questions, problems, and transition designed to
make the materials selected to be pedagogically meaningful.

Approach of the Third Edition

This book may be used as books have been traditionally used in the past,
as the primary or sole source of materials for a course on Evidence; or
it may be used as a convenient printed version of materials which are
also made available to the students via a course Web site or in other
electronic form.

The Third Edition, much like the First and Second Editions, focuses on the law of Evidence as embodied in the Federal Rules of Evidence. Our goal is twofold: first, to provide materials from which students can draw a practical understanding of how the Federal Rules work in court. Students are entitled to expect this from any basic Evidence course. This objective has caused us to keep in mind the perspective of the trial lawyer working with the rules in court. On the other hand, we have not attempted to compile a book on trial skills and tactics, a task better left to the trial practice teachers and scholars.

Our second objective is to expose the underlying principles, policy choices, epistemological assumptions, and jurisprudential values on which the Federal Rules are based. The system of evidence in any society is itself evidence about the nature of that society and its concept of justice. Examining the philosophy of proof of the Federal Rules would be a worthwhile task in and of itself, but we also believe that it is impossible to achieve a working understanding of the rules without an appreciation of the spirit, reason, and policy that underlie them. These considerations have caused us to keep in mind the perspective of the draftsman, scholarly critic, and reformer, to point out the psychological and ethical dimensions of the rules, and to draw as often as we can on the positive tension between the practical and philosophical aspects of the Rules.

Departing from our practice in the first two editions, we have not included the text of any of the Federal Rules of Evidence in this edition. Experience with the first two editions convinced us that selective incorporation of the rules in the casebook deprived the selected Rules of their context in the set of Rules as a whole. Reproducing all of the Rules and the Advisory Committee Notes or legislative history in the casebook would add unduly to its bulk. The book should therefore be used in connection with the annual paperback Supplement, which contains the text of all of the Federal Rules of Evidence as enacted, several proposed, but not enacted, Federal Rules, the Advisory Committee Notes and selections from the legislative history, and the California Rules of Evidence.

We have not attempted to compile a comprehensive treatise on Evidence or even a textbook that covers every subject that an Evidence instructor might want to teach. Rather than follow the traditional approach of including full coverage of every possible Evidence topic—an approach that requires each instructor to pick and choose from a mass of material—we have chosen instead to include only what we feel is most important and teachable in a basic three- or four-hour course. This book, then, is the course we teach (in a four-hour format). We recognize that our selective approach runs the risk of excluding treatment of issues and problems held dear by others. We take comfort, however, in the expectation that such instances will be few and in the knowledge that it is now easier than ever before for law teachers to supplement written texts with additional materials and distribute those materials via electronic means.

This book mixes the case and problem approaches. It is used by its authors in the context of a multimedia course. We regard Evidence as a difficult subject to teach and think it wise to use the most effective pedagogical materials to put the subject across. Cases alone are inadequate. In many parts of the course, it is impossible to find concise, well-analyzed, well-written cases. All too often lawyers relegate Evidence issues to the back of their briefs, and judges decide Evidence questions barely concealing their result-orientation. Attempts to build principled analytical discussions on such material necessarily suffer.

The problem approach presents a good alternative. Problems can capture evidence issues concisely and can be organized to facilitate a point-to-point developmental discussion. They can challenge and motivate students to formulate their own solutions rather than rely on the analysis of a judicial opinion. After all, a problem is only a case without a judicial answer attached to it. But problems, too, have their pitfalls. They place a heavy burden on students to think about the issues before class and to try to work out answers, sometimes to the unanswerable. This, in moderation, is stimulating. But confronting students with too many problems can dampen motivation and give students a sense of being lost in a maze of questions, thereby risking that most feared of all pedagogical questions—"Who cares?"

We try to capture the best of the case and problem methods emphasizing one or the other approach where the subject matter dictates a choice and using textual material whenever we feel it will provide a clearer or deeper understanding of an important issue. In the chapters on confrontation and privilege we rely mostly on cases. In these areas doctrinal analysis is profitable—important aspects of the law have been developed in U.S. Supreme Court opinions in which theory, though well explored, remains unclear. The chapters on relevance and hearsay rely heavily on problems because the concepts are best taught by working through a large number of factual situations.

The book is organized around the Federal Rules of Evidence for two reasons. First, focus on a single system of rules is a great aid in teaching and far more coherent for students than is shuttling among common law rules and various state model and uniform codes. Interrelationships among provisions can be understood, the varying philosophical objectives of the original draftsmen and of those who revised the Rules can be explored, and the reasons stated in support of the Rules can be examined. Second, the Federal Rules are relevant to all students, no matter where they choose to practice. A majority of the states have revised their own rules to conform to the Federal Rules, thus making the Federal Rules truly a model code. Students should, therefore, have a complete set of the rules and legislative history as a separate reference book.

From our many years of teaching, we have a deep appreciation of the seamless nature of the law of Evidence and a sympathetic understanding of teachers' doubts about the most effective sequence of topics. The technological constraints of a printed and bound book give a rigidity of structure, which is somewhat artificial. We invite colleagues to vary the sequence of topics to suit their own priorities and methodologies and point out the unique capabilities of the Web site to facilitate such reorganizations.

The topical organization of this edition is one with which we feel comfortable. We begin with relevance because it is the cornerstone of the entire system—more so than ever under the Federal Rules. Chapter I explores the basic concept of relevance in the context of trial proof and the related doctrines of conditional relevancy, prejudice, and probability evidence. We have included textual material from philosophy and the social sciences here because the most advanced analyses of how people think and draw conclusions from data about uncertain events—i.e., what goes on at a trial—come from these disciplines.

Chapters II (Categorical Rules of Exclusion) and III (Evidence of Character) are a logical extension of Chapter I because the basic principles involved are those of relevance and prejudice. In this Third Edition, we have departed from the approach of the Second Edition, where we treated character evidence for truthfulness of a witness along with character evidence relevant to a substantive element of a case. Chapter III of this edition focuses on proof of character when relevant to an element of the case (Rules 404 and 405). We now treat evidence of character of a witness for truthfulness (Rules 608 and 609) with the other material on examination and impeachment of credibility in Chapter IV. This approach may better preserve the conceptual frameworks of the different uses of character evidence. However, as some of the cases demonstrate, even experienced judges sometimes have trouble understanding the difference between proof of a particular character trait relevant to the litigated event and proof of credibility. Teachers who prefer to teach the two types of character evidence in combination may continue to follow the order of the First and Second Editions.

The rules governing the examination of witnesses and evidence relevant to credibility of witnesses are the subject of Chapter IV. Section A covers a number of the more technical aspects of this process including competency of witnesses; the form, scope, and limits of direct and cross-examination; and the functions of judge and jury. An informal survey of evidence teachers reveals conflicting opinions as to when to teach this material and how much time to devote to it. Thus, Chapter IV, Section A, represents a compromise and should be treated like any compromise—an attempt at an imperfect but broadly acceptable solution.

The balance of Chapter IV addresses the issue of credibility and impeachment of witnesses and the use of evidence of character in the process.

Chapters V and VI treat the related problems of hearsay, confrontation, and compulsory process, from Raleigh's case through the latest attempts to demonstrate that the rule against hearsay should be abolished. These chapters lead naturally to the problem of privileges, the subject of Chapter VII. In that chapter, however, we are mostly concerned with uncovering the rationale for the present system of privileges. A major part of this chapter deals with how lawyers handle "hot stuff," such as a smoking gun, compromising tax records, or proof of illegal corporate payments, and thus affords an opportunity to consider the relationship between evidence and a lawyer's professional responsibility. We have included in this edition new material on the psychotherapist-patient privilege, an area of Evidence law which is experiencing rapid development.

Chapter VIII deals with the relatively self-contained topics of opinion, expert testimony, and scientific proof. It has been substantially expanded from prior editions to reflect the importance and difficulty of the issues surrounding expert testimony and some of the significant recent developments in this area. This chapter attempts to highlight the systematic problem of providing responsible adjudications of issues which are beyond the technical competence of the decision makers.

Chapter IX focuses on writings and real evidence—authenticity and proof of contents. Either or both of Chapters VIII and IX could be discussed out of turn without losing the coherence of the course as it is organized in the book. We have placed these topics near the end of the book because we feel it is preferable to teach them on a secure base of understanding of relevance, hearsay, and confrontation. Also, should the teacher or student find at the end of the term that time pressures require that some choices be made, it seems more important to us that the topics of the earlier chapters be given thorough treatment.

Strictly speaking, Chapter X does not deal with evidence at all but with the rules relating to what effect evidence is given. This material on allocation of burdens of proof, presumptions, and inferences could be considered at any point in the course. Logically, it should probably be the first chapter on the theory that relevance and all the other rules of proof depend on who has the burden of proof, what the standard of proof is, and how devices such as presumptions, inferences, and judicial comment affect the burden and standard of proof. Our experience indicates, however, that effective pedagogy does not follow logic on this point, chiefly because of the complexity of the subject matter. This material is difficult enough for most students at the end of the

course; to attempt it at the beginning of the course would be counter-
productive.

Teaching Aids

We use a variety of audiovisual materials in connection with this book.
A set of excellent Evidence films was produced to be used with the first
edition of the book. These films were made under the direction of Eric
Saltzman and Charles Nesson by the Harvard Evidence Film Project with
the support of the National Endowment for the Humanities and, at
inception, the Committee on Legal Professional Responsibility. Each
film functions as the visual statement of a case. They are not didactic;
indeed, often they depict lawyers and judges doing things wrong. Their
function is to raise provocative questions, to bring a sense of the courtroom into class, to portray lawyers and judges operating in a courtroom
context, and to reveal the varieties of tactics and styles that often go
unseen in courses using only traditional teaching materials. We have
had great success in using these films (now videos) in our classes, but
they are no longer distributed by the publisher. However, video versions
circulate in the evidence underground and teachers who are interested
can pursue the authors for sources of these classics.

Better yet, teachers now have available to them a wide array of video
material depicting actual trials. For example, videotapes of noteworthy
trials are available from Court TV in edited and unedited versions. We
use these tapes in our classes and find them to be even more realistic
and have better production values than earlier films. We encourage
teachers to consider supplementing the book with such materials, but
recognizing that some teachers may not want to take the time to show
films, we have designed the book so that it can be used independently
of them.

Over the last several years we have also become aware of the value of
computer-aided instruction in the teaching of Evidence. The Harvard
Educational Technology Center, 1 Holmes Hall, Harvard Law School,
Cambridge, MA 02138 (www.law.harvard.edu/Administrative_Services/
edtech/index.html) has developed a number of computer-video inter-
active exercises, which provide effective drill on the operation of the
Rules of Evidence in realistic simulated trial contexts. During the course
of the semester our students are assigned to perform three or four these
exercises, at computer terminals in groups of two or three. Feedback
from students and their apparent comfort and confidence in applying
the Rules have been highly positive. Simpler text-based computer learn-

ing exercises are available from the Center on Computer-Assisted Legal Instruction (CALI) (www.cali.org/index.html).

Acknowledgments and Thanks

The original impetus for the First Edition of this book was a general dissatisfaction with the materials then available for teaching Evidence and a belief that our own problem-oriented, Federal Rules-based approach would be an improvement. We submit this Third Edition with the positive experience of nearly two decades of use of prior editions and in the hope that the revisions and additions in this new edition will keep the book up-to-date and make it more useful, with or without the Web site.

Creating the various editions of this book to date has required more time and effort than we imagined. Without the help of many other people, this work never could have been accomplished.

First among those without whose ideas, inspiration, and support this book would not have been possible is the late James H. Chadbourn, the junior authors' teacher and the senior author's colleague at the Harvard Law School. In addition to having been during the formative period of our scholarly lives "the dean of living Evidence scholars" — a term Professor Chadbourn once used to describe his mentor, Professor Maguire—Professor Chadbourn was the source for many of the problems and cases in this book. His rationalization of the law of evidence and pedagogical approach to the subject matter so thoroughly inform this work that it is impossible to acknowledge his imprint in each specific instance.

Next, we must acknowledge our debt to the scholars and treatise and textbook writers who have preceded us. Although we cannot claim direct lineage through Chadbourn, Maguire, Morgan, and Wigmore back to James Bradley Thayer, any incremental advance by this book on what has come before is largely attributable to the advantage we have had in being exposed to the efforts, ideas, and experiments of our predecessors, ancient and modern.

A special debt of gratitude is also owed to Professor Ann Althouse of the University of Wisconsin, whose critique of the First Edition of this book has greatly increased the authors' awareness of and sensitivity to the perspective of women students to issues of evidence law and their presentation in this work. Her article, The Lying Woman, the Devious Prostitute, and Other Stories From the Evidence Casebook, 88 Northwestern Law Review 914 (1994), has led to significant revisions in both the Second Edition and this Third Edition. Thanks also to Professor Rose Zoltec-Jick for her perceptive comments and suggestions on these and other issues.

We would like to mention especially Margaret Berger, Edward Cleary, George Fisher, Richard Field, Edward J. Imwinkelried, John Kaplan, Richard Lempert, John Mansfield, Roger Park, Mark Pettit, Stephen Saltzburg, Eleanor Swift, Peter Tillers, Laurence Tribe, John Waltz, and Jack Weinstein as colleagues who have inspired us with their work in evidence.

We also would like to thank the following student research assistants for their help in researching, editing, and criticizing drafts of the book as it developed: Joel Africk, Frances Bermanzohn, Gerri Bridgman, Jill Daniels, Amber Eck, Emily Joselson, Tina Klein-Baker, Mary Perry, Vanessa Place, Carmin Reiss, Daniel Rubinstein, Lisa Schwartz, and Harvey Shapiro. Special thanks to Ksenya Medvedev for her work on the Evidence Web site. Thanks also to several classes of Boston University School of Law and Harvard Law School students who allowed us to experiment on them with drafts of these materials and have provided helpful feedback on the first two editions.

Finally, the authors would like to thank their families for their faith, forbearance, and support, without which we would be destitute.

Eric D. Green
Charles R. Nesson
Peter L. Murray

December 2000

Acknowledgments

We are grateful to the following sources for permission to reprint excerpts of their work:

R. Allen, Structuring Jury Decisionmaking in Criminal Cases: A Unified Constitutional Approach to Evidentiary Devices, 94 Harv. L. Rev. 321 (1980). Copyright © 1980 by the Harvard Law Review Association. Reprinted by permission.

Ann Althouse, The Lying Woman, The Devious Prostitute, and Other Stories from the Evidence Casebook, Nw. U. L. Rev. (1994). Copyright © 1994. Excerpts reprinted with permission of the author.

American Bar Association, Model Code of Professional Responsibility, Ethical Consideration 4-1. Excerpted from the Model Code of Professional Responsibility, copyright © 1986 by the American Bar Association, National Center for Professional Responsibility. Reprinted by permission. Copies of ABA Ethics Opinions are available from Service Center, American Bar Association, 750 North Lake Shore Drive, Chicago, IL 60611-4497. Copies of ABA Model Code of Professional Responsibility (1986) are available from Member Services, American Bar Association, 750 North Lake Shore Drive, Chicago, IL 60611-4497, 1-800-285-2211.

American Bar Association, Standards Relating to the Administration of Criminal Justice: The Defense Function, Lawyer-Client Relationship 109-112 (1974). Copyright © 1976 by the American Bar Association. Reprinted by permission.

A.J. Ayer, The Legacy Of Hume, in Probability and Evidence 3-6 (1972). Copyright © 1972 by the Columbia University Press. Reprinted by permission of Columbia University Press and Palgrave.

Edward W. Cleary, Presuming and Pleading: An Essay on Juristic Immaturity, 12 Stan. L. Rev. 5 (1959). Copyright © 1959 by the Board of Trustees of the Leland Stanford Junior University. Reprinted by permission.

L.J. Cohen, The Probable and the Provable 77-81 (1977). Copyright © 1977 by Oxford University Press. Reprinted by permission.

Irving M. Copi, Introduction To Logic © 1961. Adapted by permission of Prentice-Hall, Inc., Upper Saddle River, NJ.

Charles R. Nesson, Reasonable Doubt and Permissive Inference: The Value of Complexity, 92 Harv. L. Rev. 1187 (1979). Copyright © 1979 by the Harvard Law Review Association. Reprinted by permission.

Charles R. Nesson, Rationality, Presumptions and Judicial Comment: A Response to Professor Allen, 94 Harv. L. Rev. 1574 (1981). Copyright © 1979 by the Harvard Law Review Association. Reprinted by permission.

Peter Neufeld and Barry Scheck, Better Ways to Find the Guilty, June 6, 2000. Copyright © 2000 by The New York Times. Used with permission.

Note, The Theoretical Foundation of the Hearsay Rules, 93 Harv. L. Rev. 1786 (1980). Copyright © 1980 by the Harvard Law Review Association. Reprinted by permission.

Roger Park, McCormick on Evidence and the Concept of Hearsay: A Critical Analysis Followed by Suggestions to Law Teachers, 65 Minn. L. Rev. 423 (1981). Copyright © 1981 by the University of Minnesota Law Review. Reprinted by permission.

Bertrand Russell, The Problems of Philosophy. Copyright © 1912 by the Oxford University Press. Reprinted by permission.

Peter W. Tague, Perils of the Rulemaking Process: The Development, Application, and Unconstitutionality of Rule 804(b)(3)'s Penal Interest Exception, 69 Geo. L.J. 851 (1981). Copyright © 1981 by the Georgetown University Law Journal. Reprinted by permission.

J. Tanford and A. Bocchino, Rape Victim Shield Laws and the Sixth Amendment, 128 U. Pa. L. Rev. 544 (1981). Copyright © 1981 by the University of Pennsylvania Law Review. Reprinted by permission.

Laurence H. Tribe, Trial by Mathematics: Precision and Ritual in the Trial Process, 84 Harv. L. Rev. 1329 (1971). Copyright © 1971 by the Harvard Law Review Association. Reprinted by permission.

Laurence H. Tribe, Triangulating Hearsay, 87 Harv. L. Rev. 957 (1974). Copyright © 1974 by the Harvard Law Review Association. Reprinted by permission.

Joseph R. Tybor, Perjury Case Goes to the Dogs After Shadow Cast on Witness, National Law Journal, Sept. 14, 1980. Copyright © 1980, the National Law Journal. Reprinted with permission.

John Wigmore, A Student's Textbook on the Law of Evidence 10-12 (1935). Copyright © 1935 by the Foundation Press. Reprinted by permission.

George F. Will, DNA, the Death Penalty and Horrifying Mistakes, April 6, 2000. © 2000, The Washington Post Writers Group. Reprinted with permission.

Special Notice

Many of the problems in this book are based on real cases. In some instances, names and facts have been changed for educational purposes. In such event, there is no intent to represent the facts of the problem as real. Citations to cases on which problems are based are omitted in most cases in order to stimulate original thinking.

Problems, Cases, and Materials
on Evidence

CHAPTER I

Relevance

Scholars would no doubt differ sharply if asked to state the function of the law of evidence. Perhaps the simplest description is the most accurate and would be most likely to obtain the concurrence of judges, lawyers, and scholars: The function of the law of evidence is to specify (1) what types of information may be considered by the triers of fact in our law courts so that they may ascertain facts of importance to the determination of the dispute before the court, (2) in what forms this information may be communicated to the triers of fact, and (3) to some extent, what the judge, advocates, and triers of fact can do with this information.

Admittedly, this description of the function of the law of evidence says nothing about what *values* are important in determining the form and content of information to be considered by the triers of fact. Scholars, judges, philosophers, lawyers, and students debate how the goals of truth, justice, order, or certainty affect the rules of evidence. Rationality is a logical starting point for the study of the subject of evidence, and relevance—rationality's operational construct—has long been treated as a fundamental foundational concept. As James Bradley Thayer stated in his Preliminary Treatise on Evidence 264-265 (1898):

> There is a principle — not so much a rule of evidence as a presupposition involved in the very conception of a rational system of evidence . . . which forbids receiving anything irrelevant, not logically probative. . . .
>
> There is another precept which should be laid down as preliminary, in stating the law of evidence; namely, that unless excluded by some rule or principle of law, all that is logically probative is admissible. This general admissibility, however, of what is logically probative is not, like the former principle, a necessary presupposition in a rational system of evidence; there are many exceptions to it. Yet, in order to attain a clear conception of the law, it is important to notice this also as being a fundamental proposition.

But rationality may itself be a concept with roots in politics, race, gender, class, and culture. What does relevance mean in the law courts?

Thayer despaired of finding a test of relevancy in the law, referring simply to "logic and general experience, assuming that the principles of reasoning are known to its judges and ministers." Id. at 265.

Logic, the lessons of experience (i.e., precedent), and principles of reasoning are all components of relevance as that term is employed in law. As Wigmore pointed out, "the Anglo-American system of jury-trial rules of evidence . . . is *not* a pure *science* of logical proof." A Student's Textbook on the Law of Evidence 5 (1935). Some special considerations distinguishing the rules of proof in law courts from scientific or logical proof are identified by Wigmore (id. at 10-12, emphasis added):

> (a) In the first place, . . . the *materials* for inference are peculiar. In the scientist's laboratory, the phenomena of chemistry, biology, botany, physics, and the like, are the chief material. But in a law court the chief material consists of human conduct in its infinite varieties, and of everyday phenomena of streets, buildings, trucks, barrels, pistols, and the like, which have no interest usually for the scientist. . . .
>
> (b) In the second place, the scientist is not much hampered, as a court is, by limitations of *time* and *place*. A scientist can wait till he finds the data he wants; and he can use past, present, and future data; and he can go anywhere to get them. . . .
>
> But a judicial trial must be held at a fixed time and place, and the decision must be then made, once for all. Most of the data are distant, and in the past. Many can never be re-found or revived. These limitations seriously hamper the inquiry. The only compensating advantage is that a tribunal can compel the production of data, if available, from any citizen within the jurisdiction, while the scientist cannot do this.
>
> (c) In the third place, the tribunal deals with data presented by *parties in dispute*. Thus, human nature being what it is, there is a constant risk of fraud and bias. This makes it specially difficult for the tribunal to obtain and to valuate the evidence. . . .
>
> (d) In the fourth place, the judicial trial takes place under dramatic conditions of *emotional disturbance*. The disputant and defiant parties are present; their witnesses and other friends sense the antagonism. The spectators make it a public drama. Everyone is keyed up. Surprise, sympathy, contempt, ridicule, anger — all these emotions are latent. Even the most honest and disinterested witness feels the mental strain. . . .
>
> (e) And finally, the tribunal, whether judge alone or with a jury, consists of *laymen*. In a laboratory, the scientist, whatever his field, is trained in valuing the data of his special branch. But in a court room even the judge himself is not a specialist in the science of proof. The substantive law, and the law of procedure, form the main part of his equipment. And, under our system of frequent judicial change, the judge rarely has an opportunity to become a specialist in the valuing of evidence. Hence he needs the guidance of a certain set of conventional rules, based on the prior recorded experience of other judges.

In this country, the history of the law of evidence over the past century has been largely one of a movement *away* from a detailed set of legal relevance rules and in the direction of fewer but more general rules favoring admissibility of all logically relevant evidence, except where the trial judge, exercising discretion, determines that fairness or considerations of time or dangers of confusion favor exclusion. The Federal Rules of Evidence contain three basic rules of relevance (Rules 401, 402, and 403), buttressed by one additional housekeeping rule (Rule 104(b)) and supplemented by nine specific exclusionary rules designed for special, recurring situations (Rules 404-412). Rules 407-411 are discussed in Chapter II. Rules 404-406 and 412 (together with Rules 608 and 609) are treated separately in Chapter III because of the special problems associated with the use of character evidence and evidence relating to the credibility of a witness.

As you consider the material in this chapter, reflect on what "relevance" means and on whether its meaning has been captured by the definitions and limitations of the rules. Reflect also on the desirability and feasibility of formulating more specific "guiding rules" of relevancy. Has the trend toward general rules of relevance been taken too far in the Federal Rules or not yet far enough? Is the definition of "relevant evidence" in the Federal Rules too loose? Do the rules give too much discretion to the trial judge? Do they allow too much to get before the jury? Should the nine specific rules of exclusion be eliminated and their coverage subsumed within the three basic rules?

A. Materiality

Problem: King Solomon's Judgment (adapted from I Kings 3:16)

Then two women came to the king, and stood before him. The one woman said, "Oh, my lord, this woman and I dwell in the same house; and I gave birth to a child while she was in the house. Then on the third day after I was delivered, this woman also gave birth; and we were alone; there was no one else with us in the house, only we two were in the house. And this woman's son died in the night, because she lay on it. And she arose at midnight, and took my son from beside me, while I slept, and laid it in her bosom, and laid her dead son in my bosom.

"When I rose in the morning to nurse my child, behold, it was dead; but when I looked at it closely in the morning, behold, it was not the child that I had borne." But the other woman said, "No, the living child is mine, and the dead child is yours." The first said, "No, the dead child is yours, and the living child is mine." Thus they spoke before the king.

Then the king said, "The one says, 'This is my son that is alive, and your son is dead'; and the other says, 'No, but your son is dead and my son is the living one.'" And the king said, "Bring me a sword." So a sword was brought before the king. And the king said, "Divide the living child in two, and give half to the one, and half to the other."

Then the woman whose son was alive said to the king, because her heart yearned for her son, "Oh, my lord, give her the living child, and by no means slay it." But the other said, "It shall be neither mine nor yours; divide it." Then the king answered and said, "Give the living child to the first woman, and by no means slay it; she is its mother."

And all Israel heard of the judgment which the king had rendered; and they stood in awe of the king, because they perceived that the wisdom of God was in him, to render justice.

What was the relevance of the evidence on which Solomon relied? Is it possible that this "wisest" of all judgments was based on irrelevant evidence? Would a modern appellate court uphold a judgment based on such evidence if the appellate court were not convinced that the trial judge was divinely inspired?

In thinking about this problem, consider the following: Relevance is a relational concept. You cannot tell whether something is relevant without knowing what it is you are trying to decide. Thus, the most important question about any item of evidence is "What is this evidence offered to prove?" Or, to use Rule 401's terms, what is the "fact . . . of consequence"?

It looks as if Solomon were deciding who was the real mother. But the evidence, namely the differing responses of the two women to the prospect of the child's being killed, seems quite ambiguous when judged in terms of its probative value on the question of which woman is the real mother. One can easily imagine further facts about the two women and the child that would affect our view of the significance of their responses. Suppose there was evidence that one of the women was a brutal child-hater who already had more children than she wanted, while the other was a person who opposed all forms of killing and who had been trying for years to bear a child. Would this evidence be relevant? How would it cut? A brutal child-hater who already had more children than she wanted might prefer to have the king kill the baby rather than see it go to her hated, lying neighbor. Perhaps the neighbor was indeed a saintly person who had wanted a child for years and, when she found her baby dead, had pulled a switch—but then repented when she saw that the king was about to kill the baby. Is it possible that Solomon concluded that he could not decide who the natural mother was and therefore based his decision on a quite different ground, namely, who would be the better mother?

But if Solomon were deciding not who was the *real* mother, but who would be the *better* mother, we have little question about the relevance

[handwritten annotations: Materiality - whether the evidence being offered relates to the issue in the case ↳ who is the natural mother? *]*

of the women's responses, and Solomon's judgment exudes wisdom. The relevance of the evidence thus depends on what issue actually is being decided.

Suppose that Solomon knew just what he was doing: He wanted to act in the best interests of the child, and he was convinced that he would best serve the interests of the child by awarding custody of the child to the kind and generous woman—the "better" mother as opposed to the natural mother. Moreover, suppose further that he knew that a "best interests of the child" standard would be a radical departure from Hebraic tradition, likely to be highly controversial, perhaps even unpopular enough to lead his subjects to question his wisdom. Was it wise for Solomon to portray his judgment as one about who was the natural mother? By doing so, Solomon avoided many hard problems with the "best interests of the child" standard. What, for example, would stop a third woman from saying that she would be an even better mother to the child, or the natural mother from saying, "since when is it the law of Israel that you can take babies away from their real mothers?"

Do we think less of Solomon if we imagine that he saw all of this and consciously engaged in deception? Should the lawgiver always communicate his laws and judgments forthrightly, or are there circumstances in which we, knowing the full picture, would condone and perhaps even approve a bit of distortion in how we adjudicate a controversy in order to affect how our adjudication of the controversy is perceived by the populace? Is this the wisdom of real politics or a path to self-deception and corruption? In any event, what do these issues reveal about the logic of relevance in courts? If logic is not the only component of relevance in law courts, what other values does the concept of relevance serve?

Another view of the Solomon story sees it as a demonstration of ruthless, brutal male power exercised over powerless women who are stereotyped into the good woman, cowed and deferring to male authority, and the bad woman, strong enough to resist superior male power even when it seems hopeless and irrational. See A. Althouse, Beyond King Solomon's Harlots: Women in Evidence, 65 So. Cal. L. Rev. 1265 (1992). Althouse's alternative explanation of the biblical story (versions of which exist in many other cultures) is that it is a fiction designed to legitimize Solomon's attempt to make a transition from military conqueror to legitimate sovereign by demonstrating the wisdom of his judgment, but that, in fact, it does just the opposite if closely examined. Althouse argues that it is at least a reasonable interpretation that the first woman

yielded to the king when he flaunted his physical power and authority. The Other, whom history brands the bad, selfish woman, resists power, continues to assert her claim, and stands on principle, even in the face of a great loss. We can read the Other woman's statement as an outcry against injustice and brutality, a breakdown of reason. Indeed, the Other's comment comes only after the ["good"] One's concession of the child and thus does not appear to be a product of reason. If the Other were truly cold and calculating, she could have simply kept her silence and received the child. . . .

[B]ald power transmutes into the appearance of reason! The king lifts a murderous sword, and we manage to perceive it as a coup of reason, attributing to him not ruthless brutality, but amazing and modern wisdom. . . .

The notion that the Other saw through him and called his bluff, only to be penalized for upstart counterwisdom, or that she understood the cruelty of power, and despaired, remains submerged. We accept as supreme wisdom, as "the wisdom of God," a process by which a powerful man tricks two powerless women and sorts them into two piles: the good and the bad, the motherly and the unmotherly, the truthful and the lying. "Reason" here (and the very beginning of law) takes the form of a simplistic rule stating that proper mothers are selfless and sacrificing, a rule applied through the emotional torture of making the alleged mother believe in the imminent death of her baby and waiting to see what she happens to blurt out.

Id.

Does Professor Althouse's interpretation of Solomon's judgment suggest yet a deeper function for the rules of relevance and materiality, functions that go to the very sources of power and authority in society? Moreover, does the use of such archetypical myths, even as subjects of critical discussion, itself perpetuate the stereotypes and power structures that dominant members of society want to preserve, as Althouse suggests? Id. See also A. Althouse, The Lying Woman, the Devious Prostitute, and Other Stories from the Evidence Casebook, 88 Nw. U.L. Rev. 914 (1994).

King Solomon found the women's reactions to his proposal not only "relevant" to the decision he was required to make, in that they tended to make the facts on which the decision was based more likely than those facts would have been in the absence of their reactions, but also "sufficient" to support the decision rendered. In the trial of cases in court these two concepts are often separated. "Relevance," namely the tendency to make a fact of consequence to the decision sought more or less likely, is usually assessed at the time evidence is proffered. The court's job at that time is to determine whether the evidence will be "admitted" to be considered by the fact finder along with all the other evidence offered and to be offered during the trial. The issue of sufficiency comes up in a jury trial on a motion for a directed verdict at the close of the evidence. At that time, the court must decide whether the evidence "admitted" is "sufficient" as a matter of law to support all potential outcomes sought. If the judge determines that the evidence in support of a particular outcome is not "sufficient," it is the duty of the judge to direct a verdict against that outcome. The standard of sufficiency of evidence to support various outcomes, that is, how much evidence is required to support a potential jury verdict or factfinding by the judge, varies according to jurisdiction and cause of action and is not addressed in the Federal Rules of Evidence. The low standard of sufficiency of evidence often required to support a verdict of a jury and the lack of effective oversight over the jury's reasoning processes can mean that with key bits of evidence admissibility can become almost synonymous with sufficiency.

TANNER v. UNITED STATES
483 U.S. 107 (1987)

Justice O'CONNOR delivered the opinion of the Court.

[Tanner and Conover were convicted on various counts of mail fraud.] The day before petitioners were scheduled to be sentenced, Tanner filed a motion, in which Conover subsequently joined, seeking continuance of the sentencing date, permission to interview jurors, an evidentiary hearing, and a new trial. According to an affidavit accompanying the motion, Tanner's attorney had received an unsolicited telephone call from one of the trial jurors, Vera Asbul. Juror Asbul informed Tanner's attorney that several of the jurors consumed alcohol during the lunch breaks at various times throughout the trial, causing them to sleep through the afternoons. The District Court continued the sentencing date, ordered the parties to file memoranda, and heard argument on the motion to interview jurors. The District Court concluded that juror testimony on intoxication was inadmissible under Federal Rule of Evidence 606(b) to impeach the jury's verdict. The District Court invited petitioners to call any nonjuror witnesses, such as courtroom personnel, in support of the motion for new trial. Tanner's counsel took the stand and testified that he had observed one of the jurors "in a sort of giggly mood" at one point during the trial but did not bring this to anyone's attention at the time. . . .

While the appeal of this case was pending before the Eleventh Circuit, petitioners filed another new trial motion based on additional evidence of jury misconduct. In another affidavit, Tanner's attorney stated that he received an unsolicited visit at his residence from a second juror, Daniel Hardy. Despite the fact that the District Court had denied petitioners' motion for leave to interview jurors, two days after Hardy's visit Tanner's attorney arranged for Hardy to be interviewed by two private investigators. The interview was transcribed, sworn to by the juror, and attached to the new trial motion. In the interview Hardy stated that he "felt like . . . the jury was on one big party." Hardy indicated that seven of the jurors drank alcohol during the noon recess. Four jurors, including Hardy, consumed between them "a pitcher to three pitchers" of beer during various recesses. Of the three other jurors who were alleged to have consumed alcohol, Hardy stated that on several occasions he observed two jurors having one or two mixed drinks during the lunch recess, and one other juror, who was also the foreperson, having a liter of wine on each of three occasions. Juror Hardy also stated that he and three other jurors smoked marijuana quite regularly during the trial. Moreover, Hardy stated that during the trial he observed one juror ingest cocaine five times and another juror ingest cocaine two or three times. One juror sold a quarter pound of marijuana to another juror during the trial, and took marijuana, cocaine and drug paraphernalia into the courthouse. Hardy noted that some of the jurors were falling asleep during the trial, and that one of the jurors described himself to Hardy as "flying." Hardy stated that before he visited Tanner's attorney at his residence, no one had contacted him concerning the jury's conduct, and Hardy had not been offered anything in return for his statement. Hardy said that he came forward "to clear my conscience" and "[b]ecause I felt . . . that the people on the jury didn't have no business being on the jury. I felt . . . that Mr. Tanner should have a better opportunity to get somebody that would review the facts right."

The District Court, stating that the motions "contain supplemental allegations which differ quantitatively but not qualitatively from those in the April motions," denied petitioners' motion for a new trial. The Court of Appeals for the Eleventh Circuit affirmed. 772 F.2d 765 (1985). We granted certiorari, 479 U.S. —, 107 S. Ct. 397, 93 L. Ed. 2d 351 (1986), to consider whether the District Court was required to hold an evidentiary hearing, including juror testimony, on juror alcohol and drug use during the trial. . . . Petitioners argue that the District Court erred in not ordering an additional evidentiary hearing at which jurors would testify concerning drug and alcohol use during the trial. Petitioners assert that, contrary to the holdings of the District Court and the Court of Appeals, juror testimony on ingestion of drugs or alcohol during the trial is not barred by Federal Rule of Evidence 606(b). Moreover, petitioners argue that whether or not authorized by Rule 606(b), an evidentiary hearing including juror testimony on drug and alcohol use is compelled by their Sixth Amendment right to trial by a competent jury.

By the beginning of this century, if not earlier, the near-universal and firmly established common-law rule in the United States flatly prohibited the admission of juror testimony to impeach a jury verdict. See 8 J. Wigmore, Evidence §2352, pp.696-697 (McNaughton rev. ed. 1961) (common-law rule, originating from 1785 opinion of Lord Mansfield, "came to receive in the United States an adherence almost unquestioned"). Exceptions to the common-law rule were recognized only in situations in which an "extraneous influence," Mattox v. United States, 146 U.S. 140, 149, 13 S. Ct. 50, 53, 36 L. Ed. 917 (1892), was alleged to have affected the jury. In *Mattox,* this Court held admissible the testimony of jurors describing how they heard and read prejudicial information not admitted into evidence. The Court allowed juror testimony on influence by outsiders in Parker v. Gladden, 385 U.S. 363, 365, 87 S. Ct. 468, 470, 17 L. Ed. 2d 420 (1966) (bailiff's comments on defendant), and Remmer v. United States, 347 U.S. 227, 228-230, 74 S. Ct. 450, 450-452, 98 L. Ed. 654 (1954) (bribe offered to juror). See also Smith v. Phillips, 455 U.S. 209, 102 S. Ct. 940, 71 L. Ed. 2d 78 (1982) (juror in criminal trial had submitted an application for employment at the District Attorney's office). In situations that did not fall into this exception for external influence, however, the Court adhered to the common-law rule against admitting juror testimony to impeach a verdict. McDonald v. Pless, 278 U.S. 264, 35 S. Ct. 783, 59 L. Ed. 1300 (1915); Hyde v. United States, 225 U.S. 347, 384, 32 S. Ct. 793, 808, 56 L. Ed. 1114 (1912).

Lower courts used this external/internal distinction to identify those instances in which juror testimony impeaching a verdict would be admissible. The distinction was not based on whether the juror was literally inside or outside the jury room when the alleged irregularity took place; rather, the distinction was based on the nature of the allegation. Clearly a rigid distinction based only on whether the event took place inside or outside the jury room would have been quite unhelpful. For example, under a distinction based on location a juror could not testify concerning a newspaper read inside the jury room. Instead, of course, this has been considered an external influence about which juror testimony is admissible. See United States v. Thomas, 463 F.2d 1061 (C.A.7 1972). Similarly, under a rigid locational distinction jurors could be regularly required to testify after the verdict as to whether they heard and comprehended the judge's instructions, since the charge to the jury takes place outside the jury room. Courts wisely have treated allegations of a juror's inability to hear or comprehend at trial as an internal matter. See Government of the Virgin Islands v. Nicholas, 759 F.2d 1073 (C.A.3 1985); Davis v. United States, 47 F.2d 1071 (C.A.5 1931) (rejecting juror testimony impeaching verdict, including testimony that jurors had not heard a particular instruction of the court).

Most significant for the present case, however, is the fact that lower federal courts treated allegations of the physical or mental incompetence of a juror as "internal" rather than "external" matters. In United States v. Dioguardi, 492 F.2d 70 (C.A.2 1974), the defendant Dioguardi received a letter from one of the jurors soon after the trial in which the juror explained that she had "eyes and ears that . . . see things before [they] happen," but that her eyes "are only partly open" because "a curse was put upon them some years ago." Id., at 75. Armed with this letter and the opinions of seven psychiatrists that the letter suggested that the juror was suffering from a psychological disorder, Dioguardi sought a new trial or in the alternative an evidentiary hearing on the juror's competence. The District Court denied the motion and the

Court of Appeals affirmed. The Court of Appeals noted "[t]he strong policy against any post-verdict inquiry into a juror's state of mind," id., at 79, and observed: "The quickness with which jury findings will be set aside when there is proof of tampering or external influence . . . parallel the reluctance of courts to inquire into jury deliberations when a verdict is valid on its face. . . . Such exceptions support rather than undermine the rationale of the rule that possible internal abnormalities in a jury will not be inquired into except 'in the gravest and most important cases.'" Id., at 79, n.12, citing McDonald v. Pless, supra, 238 U.S., at 269, 35 S. Ct., at 785. The court of appeals concluded that when faced with allegations that a juror was mentally incompetent, "courts have refused to set aside a verdict, or even to make further inquiry, unless there be proof of an adjudication of insanity or mental incompetence closely in advance . . . of jury service," or proof of "a closely contemporaneous and independent post-trial adjudication of incompetency." 492 F.2d, at 80. . . .

The Court's holdings requiring an evidentiary hearing where extrinsic influence or relationships have tainted the deliberations do not detract from, but rather harmonize with, the weighty government interest in insulating the jury's deliberative process. See Smith v. Phillips, 455 U.S. 209, 102 S. Ct. 940, 71 L. Ed. 2d 78 (1982) (juror in criminal trial had submitted an application for employment at the District Attorney's office); Remmer v. United States, 347 U.S. 227, 74 S. Ct. 450, 98 L. Ed. 654 (1954) (juror reported attempted bribe during trial and was subjected to investigation). The Court's statement in *Remmer* that "[t]he integrity of jury proceeding must not be jeopardized by unauthorized invasions," id., at 229, 74 S. Ct., at 451, could also be applied to the inquiry petitioners seek to make into the internal processess of the jury.

There is little doubt that post-verdict investigation into juror misconduct would in some instances lead to the invalidation of verdicts reached after irresponsible or improper juror behavior. It is not at all clear, however, that the jury system could survive such efforts to perfect it. Allegations of juror misconduct, incompetency, or inattentiveness, raised for the first time days, weeks, or months after the verdict seriously disrupt the finality of the process. . . . Moreover, full and frank discussion in the jury room, jurors' willingness to return an unpopular verdict, and the community's trust in a system that relies on the decisions of laypeople would all be undermined by a barrage of post verdict scrutiny of juror conduct. See Note, Public Disclosures of Jury Deliberations, 96 Harv. L. Rev. 886, 888-892 (1983). . . . [P]etitioners argue that substance abuse constitutes an improper "outside influence" about which jurors may testify under Federal Rule of Evidence 606(b). In our view the language of the Rule cannot easily be stretched to cover this circumstance. However severe their effect and improper their use, drugs or alcohol voluntarily ingested by a juror seems no more an "outside influence" than a virus, poorly prepared food, or a lack of sleep. . . .

Justice MARSHALL, with whom Justice BRENNAN, Justice BLACKMUN, and Justice STEVENS join, dissenting in part.

Every criminal defendant has a constitutional right to be tried by competent jurors. This Court has long recognized that "[d]ue process implies a tribunal both impartial and mentally competent to afford a hearing," Jordan v. Massachusetts, 225 U.S. 167, 176, 32 S. Ct. 651, 652, 56 L. Ed. 1038 (1912), "a jury capable and willing to decide the case solely on the evidence before it." Smith v. Phillips, 455 U.S. 209, 217, 102 S. Ct. 940, 946, 71 L. Ed. 2d 78 (1982). If, as is charged, members of petitioners' jury were intoxicated as a result of their use of drugs and alcohol to the point of sleeping through material portions of the trial, the verdict in this case must be set aside. In directing district courts to ignore sworn allegations that jurors engaged in gross and debilitating misconduct, this Court denigrates the precious right to a competent jury. Accordingly, I dissent from that part of the Court's opinion. . . .

Despite the seriousness of the charges, the Court refuses to allow petitioners an opportunity to vindicate their fundamental right to a competent jury. The Court holds that petitioners are absolutely barred from exploring allegations of juror misconduct and incompetency through the only means available to them—examination of the jurors who have already voluntarily come forward. The basis for the Court's ruling is the mistaken belief that juror testimony concerning drug and alcohol abuse at trial is inadmissible under Federal Rule of Evidence 606(b) and is contrary to the policies the Rule was intended to advance.

I readily acknowledge the important policy considerations supporting the common-law rule against admission of jury testimony to impeach a verdict, now embodied in Federal Rule of Evidence 606(b): freedom of deliberation, finality of verdicts, and protection of jurors against harassment by dissatisfied litigants. See, e.g., McDonald v. Pless, 238 U.S. 264, 267-268, 35 S. Ct. 783, 784-785, 59 L. Ed. 1300 (1915); Advisory Committee's Notes on Fed. Rule Evid. 606(b), 28 U.S.C. App., p.700. It has been simultaneously recognized, however, that "simply putting verdicts beyond effective reach can only promote irregularity and injustice." Ibid. If the above-referenced policy considerations seriously threaten the constitutional right to trial by a fair and impartial jury, they must give way. See Parker v. Gladden, 385 U.S. 363, 87 S. Ct. 468, 17 L. Ed. 2d 420 (1966); Mattox v. United States, 146 U.S. 140, 13 S. Ct. 50, 36 L. Ed. 917 (1892).

In this case, however, we are not faced with a conflict between the policy considerations underlying Rule 606(b) and petitioners' Sixth Amendment rights. Rule 606(b) is not applicable to juror testimony on matters unrelated to the jury's deliberations. By its terms, Rule 606(b) renders jurors incompetent to testify only as to three subjects: (i) any "matter or statement" occurring during deliberations; (ii) the "effect" of anything upon the "mind or emotions" of any juror as it relates to his or her "assent to or dissent from the verdict"; and (iii) the "mental processes" of the juror in connection with his "assent to or dissent from the verdict." Even as to matters involving deliberations, the bar is not absolute.

It is undisputed that Rule 606(b) does not exclude juror testimony as to matters occurring before or after deliberations. See 3 D. Louisell & C. Mueller, Federal Evidence §290, p.151 (1979); cf. Note, Impeachment of Verdicts by Jurors — Rule of Evidence 606(b), 4 Wm. Mitchell L. Rev. 417, 431, n.88 (1978). But, more particularly, the Rule only "operates to prohibit testimony as to certain conduct by the jurors which has no verifiable manifestations," 3 J. Weinstein & M. Berger, Weinstein's Evidence ¶606[04], pp. 606-28 (1985); as to other matters, jurors remain competent to testify. See Fed. Rule Evid. 601. Because petitioners' claim of juror misconduct and incompetency involves objectively verifiable conduct occurring prior to deliberations, juror testimony in support of the claims is admissible under Rule 606(b). . . .

Even if I agreed with the Court's expansive construction of Rule 606(b), I would nonetheless find the testimony of juror intoxication admissible under the Rule's "outside influence" exception. As a common sense matter, drugs and alcohol are outside influences on jury members. Commentators have suggested that testimony as to drug and alcohol abuse, even during deliberations, falls within this exception. "[T]he present exception paves the way for proof by the affidavit or testimony of a juror that one or more jurors became intoxicated during deliberations. . . . Of course the use of hallucinogenic or narcotic drugs during deliberations should similarly be provable." 3 Louisell & Mueller, Federal Evidence, §289, pp.143-145 (footnote omitted). See 3 Weinstein & Berger, Weinstein's Evidence, supra, ¶606[04], pp.606-29-606-32 ("Rule 606(b) would not render a witness incompetent to testify to juror irregularities such as intoxication . . . regardless of whether the jury misconduct occurred within or without the jury room"). The Court suggests that, if these are outside influences, "a virus, poorly prepared food, or a lack of sleep" would also qualify. Distinguishing between a virus, for example, and a narcotic drug is a matter of line-drawing. Courts are asked to make these sorts of distinctions in numerous contexts; I have no doubt they would be capable of differentiating between the intoxicants involved in this case and minor indispositions not affecting juror competency. . . .

The Court acknowledges that "post verdict investigation into juror misconduct would in some instances lead to the invalidation of verdicts reached after irresponsible or improper juror behavior," but maintains that "[i]t is not at all clear . . . that the jury system could survive such efforts to perfect it." Petitioners are not asking for a perfect jury. They are seeking to determine whether the jury that heard their case behaved in a manner consonant with the minimum requirements of the Sixth Amendment. If we deny them this opportunity, the jury system may survive, but the constitutional guarantee on which it is based will become meaningless.

I dissent.

Problem: The Pizza

In a proceeding under the state Worker's Compensation Act, claimant George Smith alleges and introduces evidence that as he was operating a lathe his shirt sleeve caught in the machinery and his hand was severely injured. In defense, the employer's insurance carrier offers the testimony of a co-worker, White, that at the time of the accident Smith was eating a pizza and had looked away from his work momentarily to reach for a napkin. Smith's counsel objects to White's testimony. How should the judge rule? Why?

To be relevant, facts must be "of consequence to the determination of the action" (i.e., "material"). Rule 401. One must know the legal issues in a case before one can say whether evidence about a fact is "of consequence to the action." Therefore, when answering any question about the materiality aspect of relevance, one must understand the elements of the cause of action and the defenses in the case. But sometimes it is not so easy to determine the issues in a case, even upon examination of the pleadings, substantive law, and other evidence presented. The law is constantly in flux. New theories of liability are continuously being created while familiar theories are modified, discarded, or disguised. In court, the judge may ask counsel for an explanation of what she is trying to prove with particular evidence. The message behind the judge's question is that relevance is a relational concept; in law, relevance has no abstract meaning, but rather is dependent on the nature of the case. The lawyer had better have a firm idea of the theory of her case when she responds.

Problem: The Unopened Drum of Paint

Action to recover from the manufacturer, *D,* the price of a drum of waterproof roof paint. As proof of breach of *D*'s ten-year warranty, *P* offers evidence that she used another drum of the same brand of paint six months earlier and that shortly after she purchased the drum in issue, but before she opened it, the paint from the earlier drum allowed leaks and also ruined the roof shingles to which it had been applied. Should *P*'s offer of proof be accepted?

The operative substantive law sometimes can be understood only by understanding the actual, as opposed to the ostensible, rules of relevance that define it.

The material issue appears to be whether the second drum of paint is defective. On that issue the evidence that the first drum was defective is hardly probative. Before concluding that the second drum is defective, one would want to know at least whether the first drum caused the roof leaks and, if so, why? Was there a defect in the paint formula, poor ingredients, or an error in preparation, handling, or storage? Without more information on these points, is it sound to conclude that because the first drum may have been bad, the second drum is bad? Does it seem more likely that *D* would customarily sell bad paint under a ten-year warranty or that it occasionally sells a bad drum? Certainly, if a dissatisfied buyer must prove that her can of paint is defective in order to prevail, the offered evidence would not be sufficient for the plaintiff to survive a motion for a directed verdict.

Yet even if *D* showed that the second drum came from an entirely different batch of paint, this plaintiff might still win. How could this be so? If *P* wins, the court could be generating a new substantive rule of law that when a customer has been harmed by a defect in a company's warranted product, the customer can get her money back on all similar products that she had purchased prior to notice of the product failure. The theory on which this new rule of substantive law might be based is that the company breached not only its product warranty but its trust relation to that customer, a relationship that would only be reestablished if the customer were to make a further purchase after she became aware of the defect in the first can of paint.

Thus, if the issue is whether the second drum is bad, the evidence in question is of tenuous value. But if the issue is whether *P* should get her money back regardless of whether the second drum is good or bad, so long as she bought the second drum before her roof started leaking and after applying paint from the first drum, the offered evidence is very probative. Understood on this basis, a subtle, but undoubtedly substantive, rule of law is revealed behind what would otherwise be a doubtful evidentiary ruling. Once the new substantive rule is recognized, the relevance question is easy; indeed, they are one and the same thing. The concept of relevance defines the substantive concept, and vice versa.

Problem: Time Travel to Old Salem

Assume that you have set the controls of your time machine for Salem, Massachusetts, 1686. You arrive in a strange society prone to beliefs and superstitions about witches, goblins, warlocks, and the Devil.

Shortly before your arrival, two women and a man who reside in the settlement have been accused by leading elders of practicing witchcraft. According to local practice, they have been placed in the stockade until they can be tried in the Salem manner. In Salem at that time, those accused of witchcraft are given two options. One option is to submit to a trial, which consists of tying the accused to a board and dunking the person in a "pure" pond while the deacon recites the Lord's Prayer three times. If the accused survives the dunking, the purity of the accused's soul is vindicated and he or she is set free; if the accused does not survive, guilt and sentence are simultaneously announced. No one recalls any acquittals as a result of this process. Alternatively, the accused can accept banishment from the colony, which means exile to the western wilderness. Once banished, no one has ever been seen again.

Impressed by your mechanized mode of transportation, the Salem elders ask you to preside over the trial of the three accuseds. You agree on the condition that the trials be conducted by what we now think of as modern trial procedures. The elders agree but insist that the jurors be selected from among their ranks. At trial, the deacon serving as prosecutor seeks to present evidence that prior to your arrival the three accuseds refused to submit to trial by dunking.

Should this proof be admitted? Is it logically relevant? Why should anything be kept from the trier of fact?

Relevance depends not only on what one is trying to prove but also on the starting assumptions one makes about the nature of the world. But whose starting assumptions? Do we see the problem of "relevance" from the point of view of the victim, the defendant, the jury, the supposedly much more "knowing" judge, or any particular political or social group?

The evidence, though based on superstition, is relevant to the defendants' guilt if the defendants (1) believed in dunking as a valid test and (2) believed that they were witches or warlocks (whatever that meant in old Salem). But the evidence would be irrelevant if the defendants had no faith in the fairness and accuracy of the dunking procedure, and instead feared it would kill them whether they were guilty or not. You might recognize the relevance of the evidence yet nevertheless want to exclude it because you understand the superstition and do not want a conviction (apparently) based upon it. The jurors, believing the superstition, may assume that the defendants also believed it and avoided the dunking because of their guilt. Or the jurors may accept the proposition that the defendants put no faith in the dunking test, and consider this a form of heresy itself indicative of the defendants' guilt.

If, after recognizing the different points of view and seeing how they lead to different concepts of relevance, we conclude that we can't figure out by any abstract logic which concept of relevance is the "true" one for the system, then we may be led to conclude that the operative concept of relevance in the system is a reflection of the underlying social, political, and economic interests the system is serving. If this is true, it poses a profound problem, not subject to simple answer, that forces us to think about what the objectives of the legal system are, who is meant to be affected by its judgments, and what are the means by which the effects are produced. At bottom, we must ask what advantages, if any, the common law system of trial has over the trial by ordeal. We believe, from our present vantage point, that the current adversary process more accurately determines truth. But how culture-bound is this belief? Reconsider the judgment of Solomon in light of these questions.

B. Logical Relevance

H. HART & J. McNAUGHTON, EVIDENCE AND INFERENCE IN THE LAW
in Evidence and Inference 48, 50-51 (Lerner ed. 1959)

The central difficulty in a discussion of evidence and inference in the law is that the law has no single technique for connecting its conclusions with supporting data. The problems are highly varied, and techniques of decision vary correspondingly. A unified account of "evidence and inference in the law" is thus impossible. . . .

I. THE AFTER-THE-EVENT DETERMINATION OF ADJUDICATIVE FACTS

The first type of problem we have chosen is the simplest. It is the problem presented when a tribunal is called upon to apply a legal direction of undisputed content to a disputed state of fact. Ordinarily, such a direction will be a legal "rule" in the technical sense. Such a rule can be defined as an authoritative general directory which requires for its application only a determination of the happening or non-happening of physical or mental events. In logical terms, the rule is a special kind — a "prescriptive" kind — of major premise; the conclusion follows if the propositions comprising the minor premise are proved. While such a minor premise may include a proposition that something is likely to happen in the future, generally the problem is one of determining historical facts.

ILLUSTRATIVE CASES

Here are typical examples of simple undisputed-law, disputed-fact cases:

(1) A man is charged with murder. The rule made relevant by the facts of the case may be that any sane person who with malice afore-thought kills another person shall be put to death. The facts are such that there are no difficult questions of definition, say, of "sane" or of "malice aforethought." The only question is whether it was the defendant who fired the fatal shot. (2) A man is sued for breach of warranty. The rule made applicable by the facts of the situation may be that any person who sells goods to another which are not up to the seller's representations shall, provided the buyer gives prompt notice of the defect, pay the buyer a sum of money equal to the difference between the value of the goods promised and of those delivered. The facts raise no doubts as to the exact meaning of the rule. The only issue is whether the goods delivered were as represented by the seller. (3) A large estate is to be distributed. The relevant rule may be that two-thirds of the estate of any person dying without a will shall be divided equally among his children. There are no close questions requiring the law of descent to be clarified. The only question is whether the claimant is or is not one of the children of the deceased.

In such simple situations the resemblances of the law's problems to the problems of other disciplines in dealing with evidence are perhaps at their maximum. And yet the problems are quite different.

NOTE: ON PRINCIPLES OF REASONING

As Wigmore and Thayer point out, the study of evidence begins with the study of logic, a branch of epistemology. The following excerpts should provide a brief but basic understanding of the most important terms and processes.

1. The uses and limits of inductive proof. A.J. Ayer confronts us with the logical problem of induction.

A.J. AYER, HUME'S FORMULATION OF THE PROBLEM OF INDUCTION FROM THE LEGACY OF HUME, IN PROBABILITY AND EVIDENCE 3-6 (1972):   A rational man is one who makes a proper use of reason: and this implies, among other things, that he correctly estimates

the strength of evidence. In many instances, the result will be that he is
able to vindicate his assertions by adducing other propositions which
support them. But what is it for one proposition to support another? In
the most favourable case, the premises of an argument entail its conclusion, so that if they are true the conclusion also must be true. It would
seem, however, that not all our reasoning takes the form of deductive
inference. In many cases, and most conspicuously when we base an un-
restricted generalisation on a limited set of data, we appear to run beyond our evidence: that is, we appear not to have a logical guarantee
that even if our premises are true, they convey their truth to the conclusion. But then what sort of inference are we making, and how can it
be justified? These questions have not proved easy to answer, and their
difficulty creates what philosophers call the problem of induction.

The attention which has been paid to this problem is primarily due
to the work of David Hume; and it is worth taking some trouble to
restate Hume's argument since, for all its essential simplicity, it has often
been misunderstood. Hume starts from the assumption that we can have
reason to believe in the truth of any proposition concerning an empirical matter of fact only in so far as we are able to connect the state of
affairs which it describes with something that we now perceive or remember. Let us assign the neutral term "data" to what one perceives at
a given moment or what one then remembers having previously perceived, leaving aside the question what these data are. On any theory of
perception, their range will be very limited. Then Hume maintains that
one will have reason to believe in the existence of anything which is not
a datum, at the time in question, only if one has reason to believe that
it is connected with one's data in a law-like fashion. He puts this rather
misleadingly by saying that "all reasonings concerning matters of fact
seem to be founded on the relation of cause and effect." He then raises
the question whether our belief in the existence of these law-like connections can ever be rationally justified, and he offers a proof that it
cannot.

This proof may be set out in nine stages, as follows:

(i) An inference from one matter of fact to another is never demonstrative. This is not to say that when the inference is fully set out the
conclusion does not follow validly from the premises—there is no question but that "q" does follow from "p" and "if p then q"—but rather that
what one may call the guiding principle of the inference, the proposition "if p then q," when based on a supposed factual connection between
the events referred to by "p" and "q," is always an empirical proposition,
and as such can be denied without contradiction. Hume's way of putting
this, or one of his many ways of putting this, is to say that "knowledge
of the relation of cause and effect is not, in any instance, attained by
reasonings a priori, but arises entirely from experience."

(ii) There is no such thing as a synthetic necessary connection between events. These are not, of course, the terms in which Hume puts it, but this is what it comes to. No matter what events A and B are, if A is presented to us in some spatio-temporal relation to B, there is nothing in this situation from which we could validly infer, without the help of other premisses, that events of the same type as A and B are connected in the same way on any other occasion. There is no such thing as seeing that A *must* be attended by B, and this not just because we lack the requisite power of vision but because there is nothing of this sort to be seen. No sense can be given to a "must" of this type.

(iii) So the only ground that we can have for believing, in a case where A is observed by us and B not yet observed, that B does exist in such and such a spatio-temporal relation to A is our past experience of the constant conjunction of As and Bs.

(iv) But clearly the inference from the premiss "Events of the type A and B have invariably been found in conjunction," or to put it more shortly, "All hitherto observed As bear the relation R to Bs," to the conclusion "All As bear the relation R to Bs," or even to the conclusion "This A will have the relation R to some B," is not formally valid. There is what we may call an inductive jump.

(v) To make it valid an extra premiss is needed assuring us that what has held good in the past will hold good in the future. Hume's formulation of this principle in the Treatise of Human Nature is "that instances of which we have had no experience, must resemble those of which we have had experience, and that the course of nature continues always uniformly the same."

(vi) But if all our reasonings about matters of fact are founded on this principle, we have no justification for them unless the principle itself is justifiable. But what justification could it have? There can be no demonstrative argument for it. It is clearly not a logical truth. In Hume's own words "we can at least conceive a change in the course of nature; which sufficiently proves that such a change is not absolutely impossible."

(vii) Even if the principle cannot be demonstrated, perhaps we can at least show it to be probable. But a judgement of probability must have some foundation. And this foundation can lie only in our past experience. The only ground we can have for saying that it is even probable that the course of nature continues uniformly the same is that we have hitherto found this to be the case. But then we are arguing in a circle. To quote Hume again, "probability is founded on the presumption of a resemblance betwixt those objects of which we have had experience, and those of which we have had none; and therefore it is impossible that this presumption can arise from probability."

(viii) The same objection would apply to any attempt to by-pass the general principle of the uniformity of nature and argue that inferences from one matter of fact to another, though admittedly not demonstrative, can nevertheless be shown to be probable. Again, this judgement of probability must have some foundation. But this foundation can lie only in our past experience. And so we have to assume the very principle that we are trying to by-pass, and the same objections arise.

(ix) We must, therefore, admit that since the inferences on which we base our beliefs about matters of fact are not formally valid, and since the conclusions to which they lead cannot be shown without circularity even to be probable, there is no justification for them at all. We just have the habit of making such inferences, and that is all there is to it. Logically, we ought to be complete skeptics, but in practice we shall continue to be guided by our natural beliefs.

Bertrand Russell presents two vivid examples of the force and limits of inductive reasoning.

B. RUSSELL, ON INDUCTION, IN THE PROBLEMS OF PHILOSOPHY 60-69 (1912):   Let us take as an illustration a matter about which none of us, in fact, feel the slightest doubt. We are all convinced that the sun will rise to-morrow. Why? Is this belief a mere blind outcome of past experience, or can it be justified as a reasonable belief? It is not easy to find a test by which to judge whether a belief of this kind is reasonable or not, but we can at least ascertain what sort of general beliefs would suffice, if true, to justify the judgement that the sun will rise to-morrow, and the many other similar judgements upon which our actions are based.

It is obvious that if we are asked why we believe that the sun will rise to-morrow, we shall naturally answer, "Because it always has risen every day." We have a firm belief that it will rise in the future, because it has risen in the past. If we are challenged as to why we believe that it will continue to rise as heretofore, we may appeal to the laws of motion: the earth, we shall say, is a freely rotating body, and such bodies do not cease to rotate unless something interferes from outside, and there is nothing outside to interfere with the earth between now and to-morrow. Of course it might be doubted whether we are quite certain that there is nothing outside to interfere, but this is not the interesting doubt. The interesting doubt is as to whether the laws of motion will remain in operation until to-morrow. If this doubt is raised, we find ourselves in the same position as when the doubt about the sunrise was first raised.

The *only* reason for believing that the laws of motion will remain in operation is that they have operated hitherto, so far as our knowledge of the past enables us to judge. It is true that we have a greater body of evidence from the past in favour of the laws of motion than we have in favour of the sunrise, because the sunrise is merely a particular case of fulfillment of the laws of motion, and there are countless other partic-

Try another:

> Once upon a time in a faraway land, the king wanted his son to marry the smartest young woman in the kingdom. All women were tested. Three tied with the highest possible score. The king seated these three women at a round table. He asked them to close their eyes, which they did. He then announced that he was placing a beanie on each of their heads, positioned in such a way that, when they opened their eyes, each would be able to see the beanies on the heads of the other two but would not see the beanie on her own head. The king told the young women that the beanies might be either red or white. "When you open your eyes, you are to raise your right hand if you see one or more red beanies. When you deduce the color of the beanie on your own head, lower your hand and rise. Now, open your eyes." The king had, in fact, placed red beanies on each of the three women's heads. All three raised their hands. After ten seconds, one of them lowered her hand, rose, and explained her deduction that she was wearing a red beanie.

How did she do it?

3. Proof in the law courts. Proof in law differs from proof in logic because the functions of law and logic differ.

G. JAMES, RELEVANCY, PROBABILITY AND THE LAW, 29 CALIF. L. REV. 689 (1941): Dean Wigmore, recognizing this priority of logic, discusses the form of argument involved in the use of circumstantial evidence. . . .
Wigmore does not deny that in every instance proof must be based upon a generalization connecting the evidentiary proposition with the proposition to be proved. Conceding this, he argues that the generalization may as well be tacitly understood as expressed, that "the transmutation [from the inductive to the deductive form] is useless, because the Court's attention is merely transferred from the syllogism as a whole to the validity of the inference contained in the major premise." Yet it is precisely in this transfer of attention that the value of the transmutation lies. The author's own examples illustrate the point. In the case of the repaired machinery we are told: "'People who make such repairs [after an accident] show a consciousness of negligence; *A* made such repairs; therefore, *A* was conscious of negligence.'" Before this deductive proof can be evaluated, ambiguity must be eliminated from the major premise. By "people" shall we understand "some people" or "all people"? If the argument is intended to read, "Some people who make such repairs show consciousness of negligence; *A* made such repairs; therefore, *A* was conscious of negligence," it contains an obvious logical fallacy. If intended to read, "All people who make such repairs show consciousness of negligence; *A* made such repairs; therefore, *A* was conscious of negligence," it is logically valid. However, few could be found to accept the premise that all persons who repair machinery after an

accident show consciousness of guilt; that is, that no single case could be found of one who, confident of his care in the past, nevertheless made repairs to guard against repetition of an unforeseeable casualty or to preserve future fools against the consequence of their future folly. Here the result of transmuting a proposed direct inference into deductive form is discovery that it is invalid—at least in the terms suggested.

The other proposed argument is equally interesting: "'Men's fixed designs are probably carried out; A had a fixed design to kill B; therefore, A probably did kill B.'" Once one attempts to deal, in a quasi-syllogistic form, not with certainties but with probabilities, additional opportunities for fallacy are presented. Suppose that it is argued: "Most As are X, B is an A, therefore B is probably X"; or "Nine-tenths of all As are X, B is an A, therefore the chances are nine to one that B is X." Neither of these arguments is logically valid except upon the assumption that As may be treated as a uniform class with respect to the probability of their being X. This can be because there really is no way of subdividing the class, finding more Xs in one sub-class than in another, or because no subdivision can be made in terms of available data. Suppose that nine-tenths of all people in the world have dark eyes. If absolutely all one knew about B was that he was a person, it would be an apparent nine-to-one chance that B had dark eyes. But if one knew B to be a Swede, the percentage of dark eyes in the total population of the world would no longer be important. One would want to know about the proportion of dark-eyed Swedes, which might differ from the ratio among humans generally. Similarly in Wigmore's example. We know that we are interested in the probability of execution of a fixed design of a particular kind: to commit murder. There may be variation in the probability of execution of fixed designs on various subjects. As an initial criticism, therefore, the primary generalization should be "Men's fixed designs to kill are probably carried out." In this form we have a valid, quasi-syllogistic argument based upon the limited data available. Still, is the premise sound?

"Men's fixed designs to kill are probably carried out," as a major premise in this argument, must mean that they are carried out more often than not. While the word "probable" can be used in other senses, its meaning here is clear. Hence one would conclude from the single datum that A had a fixed design to kill B, no other evidence being offered, that more likely than not A actually did kill B. But when this argument was presented to a group of law students and teachers, only one was willing to accept the indicated conclusion. Several would accept it if supported by adequate evidence that B had been intentionally killed by some one. Others refused to accept it without still further evidence connecting A with B's death, or at the very least evidence that B had no other enemies. Moreover, there was less hesitancy in accepting the argument in its "inductive" form. Once the generalization was made explicit, and particularly after discussion of the meaning of "probably" as there used, doubts as to the propriety of the inference arose or sharpened. The demonstration, however "valid," is no better than its major premise, and the more one considers this premise the less reliable it looks. Certainly a permitted inference should rest upon some more easily acceptable law.

Of course, it does not follow that a proposed inference is improper because it can be shown not to follow on the basis of one possible generalization, or because another — which by the rules of logic would validate the inference — is unacceptable. There may be a third law, as yet unexpressed, which would justify the inference and at the same time be commonly accepted as true. And it may be very important to find the valid and accurate link, since the form of the link will control the form of the conclusion.

Persons who are unwilling to agree that men's fixed designs (at least in case of murder) are "probably" carried out — or, even conceding the fact of murder, that proof of A's fixed design to kill B establishes A, more likely than not, as B's killer—still agree that somehow this bit of evidence does have some tendency to indicate A's guilt. What form of general statement can reconcile these views? Perhaps something like this: "Men having such a fixed design are more likely to kill than are men not having such a fixed design." Those who contend that even fixed designs to kill are more often abandoned or thwarted than carried out can and doubtless will still concede that enough such designs are carried to execution so that the percentage of murderers is higher among persons entertaining such a fixed design than among the general public. Obviously this proposed generalization does not lead us from A's fixed design to kill B to the conclusion that A probably did kill B. There is nothing disturbing in this. This conclusion simply does not follow from the evidence of design. The error was in the original "direct induction." In fact, no useful conclusion about A's guilt can be drawn from design or intent alone. On the basis of an acceptable generalization we are able only to place A in a class of persons in which the incidence of murder is greater than among the general public. We cannot now say that A is probably guilty, but we can say that *the apparent probability of his guilt is now greater than before the evidence of design was received.* This is logical relevancy — the only logical relevancy we can expect in dealing with practical affairs where strict demonstration is never possible. The advantage of the transmutation into deductive (though not strictly syllogistic) form is that we know to what degree of proof we have attained, and do not overstate our results.

Which kind of reasoning is more powerful—deductive or inductive? Do trials lend themselves to one kind of proof more than the other?

Deductive reasoning, if valid, is extremely powerful — in fact, it is air-tight. Inductive reasoning always requires an inductive leap. Yet as the excerpts above point out, all deductive reasoning requires induction in formulating the major premise, so all legal reasoning is inductively based at some point in time.

Note in the problem "The Unopened Drum of Paint" how changing the substantive rule also changes the mode of reasoning from inductive to deductive. If the issue is whether the second drum is defective, evidence as to the quality of the first drum can only be used inductively. But if the issue is whether P purchased a second drum of paint prior to notice that a drum of the same kind of paint caused leaks in her roof, then evidence that the first drum of paint was defective supports a deductive argument. When does the inductive reasoning take place in this situation? With which part of the deductive process is the law of evidence primarily concerned?

Problem: The Burned Butt

Auto accident tort action. D, by cross-examination, unsuccessfully sought to force from P the admissions that he was driving under the influence of liquor and at the time of the accident was attempting to light a cigarette. D also sought to testify that two days after the accident and after P's demolished vehicle had been removed ten miles from the scene of the accident, she found a slightly burned cigarette on the floorboard of P's vehicle. Should D's testimony be admitted? Why?

Does the presence of a slightly burned cigarette in P's car "prove" that P was trying to light a cigarette at the time of the accident, or even that P was smoking at the time? Does this evidence alone make it more probable than not that P is even a smoker? Even if the butt had been found on the floorboard of P's car immediately after the accident and before anyone else would have had a chance to drop the butt there, would it necessarily make any of those propositions more probable than not? But is this the test of relevance adopted by the Federal Rules? Under Rule 401, the test is: Does the offered evidence have any tendency to make the existence of any fact that is of consequence more or less probable than it would be without the evidence? But who judges the probabilities? And how? For most evidentiary questions of relevance there is no objective probabilistic frequency data. Probability must therefore refer to possible subjective assessments by judge or jury.

Problem: Beer Cans in the Car

Charge: driving while intoxicated. At trial, the arresting officer testifies that she stopped D for speeding. While writing out a speeding ci-

people have different views.

tation, she observed a beer can on the seat next to *D*. The prosecution offers the beer can as evidence.

Should the beer can be admitted? Does it make any difference whether (1) the beer can is half empty, (2) the beer can is open and completely empty, or (3) the beer can is full and unopened?

For each situation, (1) the can half empty, (2) the can completely empty, and (3) the can unopened, we can imagine different stories that are consistent with guilt or innocence. The empty can: *D* had just polished it off, or it had been in *D*'s car for a week. The unopened can: *D* had not been drinking at all, or *D* had already drunk five cans of a six-pack, throwing the empties out the window, and *D* had only one left. The half-empty can seems different: We feel pretty sure from its presence that *D* was drinking at a time proximate to the accident, but how much? If only half a can, it is unlikely that *D* was drunk, but if *D* were chugging beers down, as people who drink beer while driving a car might be thought to do, then the half-empty can may show that *D* was drinking too much. It at least shows that *D* is the kind of person who drinks beer in a car while driving.

With regard to the empty or the unopened can, does the presence of the can make a material issue more or less probable? Probable in what sense? Evidently, more probable in the minds of the factfinders. But what factfinders? There may be six or twelve of them, and they may have different views about the way the world works. It seems as if "probable" means that if somehow we could run time backwards and count all past events in which people had an unopened or an empty can in their car, and then could somehow know the percentage of these occasions on which the driver was drinking to excess, then we could say whether the presence of either the full or the empty can made the issue of drinking to excess more or less probable in this case. But of course we cannot know these things. We have only the roughest ideas about such things, and each of us may have a different idea based on our own different life experience.

But because we do not know which of two possibilities, one consistent with innocence, one consistent with guilt, is the more "probable," does that mean that we should assume equal possibility and therefore irrelevance? We have no basis for assuming equal probability except our ignorance. In other words, if we could somehow make the fanciful count described above and arrive at rigorous frequency data about the mutual occurrence of drunkenness and the presence of an unopened beer can in the car, it would be exceedingly unlikely that the presence of the beer can would indicate an equal probability of drunkenness and sobriety, or fail at all to correlate with drunkenness as compared with drivers who had no beer cans in the car.

Whether the beer can makes a material issue more or less probable is largely indeterminate, since it depends on the individual perception of the world of the person making the judgment. If reasonable people can and do differ on the question of whether offered evidence makes the existence of the fact sought to be proved more or less likely than without it, what should the judge do? Who provides the relevant measure? The judge or a "reasonable jury"? What should the trial judge or a reviewing court take into account or bring to bear in making relevancy judgments? Logic? Experience? Local idiosyncrasies?

C. Conditional Relevance

Here we meet one of the mysteries in the law of evidence, the problem of conditional relevance. In the problem "Time Travel to Old Salem," the relevance of the evidence about the accused persons refusing to be dunked was arguably relevant if they believed in the efficacy of the dunking process. What about the "if"? Who decides the "if" question, the judge or jury, and must it be decided before a determination can be made about the relevance of the evidence of refusal? To generalize the question, it seems that the relevance of any item of information will depend on assumptions about other information. What assumptions can a jury make? What evidence must there be to support the assumptions? And won't we face the same questions of conditional relevance with respect to the evidence offered to support the assumptions? Does Rule 401 provide an adequate answer to these questions?

Problem: The Rim

A 1989 Ford and a 1991 Chevy collide at an intersection in the country. The owner of the Ford (*F*) claims that the owner of the Chevy (*C*) was speeding and did not slow down for the intersection. *F*'s investigator found a rim from a headlight in a field 200 feet from the point of impact. *F* has an expert witness prepared to testify that in order for the headlight rim to have been thrown 200 feet the Chevy had to be going at least 75 mph. *F* puts the investigator on the stand; she testifies to finding the rim, specifies the precise spot where she found it, and identifies the rim she found. *F* then offers the rim in evidence. What ruling? How will the judge go about deciding?

Suppose *F* tells the judge about his intention to call the expert and outlines the testimony expected from the expert?

Does *F* need a witness first who can identify the rim as having come from a 1991 Chevy? From *C*'s 1991 Chevy? Suppose *C* contests this proof with a witness who claims that the rim is from a 1987 Caddy? What ruling? By what procedure and by what standard does the judge go about deciding?

Federal Rule 104(b) speaks of "[w]hen the relevancy of evidence depends upon the fulfillment of a condition of fact." Does the relevancy of the rim depend upon a condition of fact?

Imagine the investigator when she first goes to the scene of this accident. She walks in the surrounding fields looking for evidence that will help her figure out what happened. She picks up a popsicle stick in the field. Is it relevant? She cannot imagine any connection it could have to the accident and discards it: irrelevant. She picks up a headlight rim. Is it relevant? She can imagine connections to the accident. She also recognizes that it might turn out to have nothing to do with the accident. Is it relevant? From her point of view, knowing what she knows at that time, it is relevant to what she is doing. She puts it in a plastic bag and adds it to the assemblage of evidence the significance of which she will explore further in trying to figure out what happened. The rim may, of course, turn out to be irrelevant, but only in a different context in which she knows things she does not know out there in the field.

Relevance thus has something to do with what we *don't* know: If we can imagine a coherent story about what happened that includes the types of evidence in question, then until we exclude that story from the possible, the evidence is relevant in the sense of Rule 401. Our investigator in the field considers the headlight relevant even though the connecting link she imagines at the time may seem very farfetched.

The idea of conditional relevance in Rule 104(b) addresses the degree of "farfetchedness" of the connecting link. Unlike the investigator who can do further searches, the jurors will be limited to the evidence presented at the trial. If evidence is offered that connects to a possible conclusion about what happened by a link that is too farfetched, even considering all the rest of the evidence that will be offered, then the connecting link has failed the test of Rule 104(b), and the evidence will be excluded.

The judge, unlike the investigator, can ask counsel what the evidence is being offered to prove and what evidence exists to link the offered material to the issues in the case. This allows the judge to assess the degree of farfetchedness of the line of inference counsel presents in suggesting the relevance of the evidence to a material issue in the case. This judgment—in the words of the rule, whether evidence is sufficient to support a finding—embraces the idea that some lines of inference are unacceptably speculative while others are acceptably rational. The line between these two concepts is as elusive as the "reasonable person." The task for the judge, though, is clear. The judge screens the evidence offered by counsel so that the resulting assemblage of evidence consists of everything a reasonable person should consider in trying to figure out what happened. In performing this screening function, should the court be influenced by the nature of the proof or the function it will play at trial? For example, should the line between the "unacceptably speculative" and "acceptably rational" shift depending on the centrality of the proof to the key fact issues in the case or on its likely impact on the jury?

ROMANO v. ANN & HOPE FACTORY OUTLET, INC.
417 A.2d 1375 (R.I. 1980)

KELLEHER, J. This is a products-liability case in which Pio Romano, father of the minor plaintiff, Rayna Romano, instituted an action in Superior Court to recover for her personal injuries. The 1973 suit alleged that Rayna received permanent injuries when she fell from a bicycle purchased from the defendant, Ann & Hope Factory Outlet, Inc. (Ann & Hope), on August 8, 1970. The Romanos contend that the bicycle's defectively designed coaster brake precipitated Rayna's injuries. . . .

The allegedly defective bicycle, a twenty-inch boy's model "Oxford" bicycle with a banana seat and high-rise handlebars, was purchased preassembled by Rayna's grandparents for her younger brother, John. The braking mechanism bore the inscription "Sturmey-Archer '69." At the time of their purchase, Rayna's grandparents received no maintenance instructions. Although Rayna and her older brother, Pio, already owned bicycles, each youngster customarily rode whichever bicycle was closest at hand. Testimony revealed that the "Oxford" bicycle functioned satisfactorily for just over a year.

On September 9, 1971, Rayna, then seven years old, mounted the "Oxford" bicycle and started down the steep hill on which the Romano home was located. The Romanos lived in Cranston on Bellevue Drive. As Rayna rode down the street, she applied the brakes "half-way" in order to keep the bicycle speed under control, but as she approached a bend in the road, the brakes failed, causing the bike to strike a curb at the foot of the hill. As a result of the impact, Rayna flew over the handlebars and hit a tree. She was hospitalized for extensive periods of time for a variety of injuries, including a fractured skull. . . .

Throughout this litigation the Romanos have claimed that the defect [in the braking mechanism] was a plastic fixture consisting of an oil cap which is attached to the top of a narrow tube. The entire fixture measures approximately one-quarter of an inch in length. The fixture is fitted into a hole found on the hub of the rear wheel. The brake chamber is lubricated by lifting the cap and letting the oil flow down the tube into the chamber. Hereafter we shall refer to the plastic fixture as the "plastic cap."

For the most part, maintenance of the "Oxford" was the responsibility of Rayna's older brother, Pio. He told the jury that prior to Rayna's unfortunate descent the plastic cap was missing from the "Oxford." Pio could not be specific as to the time when he first noticed the cap's absence. The Romanos have argued with great vigor that the trial justice committed reversible error when he prohibited their expert, Leonard Mandell (Mandell), from telling the jury that a plastic cap should never have been used because the cap could not be securely threaded into the hub's oil hole because the cap's plastic threads were destroyed once they were turned against the metal threads of the oil hole. If permitted, Mandell was prepared to tell the jury that the lack of this cap allowed debris to enter the brake chamber and oil to escape from the chamber —two conditions which, in Mandell's opinion, caused the brake failure.

In April of 1973, Mandell, a consulting engineer with a master of science degree in mechanical engineering, conferred with the Romanos at their home. As a result of their meeting, he took the bicycle to his laboratory where it was photographed and tested. Unfortunately, by the time the case was reached for trial in September 1977, the bicycle, together with Mandell's detailed notes regarding his investigation of the internal braking mechanism, had disappeared. According to Mandell, the bicycle was either taken when his office and laboratory were repeatedly burglarized sometime after September 1974, or it was "released somehow." Notwithstanding the unavailability at trial of the bicycle and the notes, Mandell was prepared to testify concerning the condition of the internal braking mechanism when he dismantled it in April of 1973.

The attorney for Ann & Hope objected to the admission of Mandell's testimony on the ground that a proper foundation had not been laid. He asserted that the 1973 findings would be irrelevant to the condition of the bicycle at the time of the 1971 descent unless accompanied by proof that the bicycle remained unchanged during the intervening twenty months. The Romanos thereupon attempted to establish "no substantial change" in the condition of the bicycle through the testimony of Bart Costerus (Costerus), a mechanical engineer who had examined the Romano bicycle in September 1971. The bicycle was in his possession for approximately three to four weeks. He tested the braking power using a braking force of fifty pounds, Rayna's approximate weight at the time of the accident. Costerus noted that the plastic lubrication cap was missing from the hole in the rear brake hub assembly when he received the bicycle. He testified further that he neither disassembled nor lubricated the braking mechanism.

Costerus first tested the brakes on a hill in Attleboro whose contour was similar to the Bellevue Drive slope. Costerus had attached to the right pedal blocks of steel which approximated Rayna's weight at the time she was injured. The engineer, who weighed 175 pounds, would sit on the banana seat of the "Oxford" and let the bicycle roll down the hill. As the bicycle began to pick up speed, Costerus would keep his feet up in the air, and the fifty-pound weight would cause the right pedal to turn downward and thereby activate the brake. Costerus employed this technique, making some forty descents, thirty-five in Attleboro and five in Cranston on Bellevue Drive. At no time, he reported, was there a "total loss of braking power."

Other testimony also revealed that after Rayna was injured, the bicycle was stored in a basement workroom of the Romano home untouched until Rayna's father delivered it to Costerus for inspection and testing in September 1971. A few weeks later, Rayna's father picked up the bicycle from Costerus and returned it to the basement of the Romano home. Again, it remained there unused until April 1973 when Mandell acquired it for further testing.

Arguing that the tests conducted by Costerus in and of themselves could have deformed the brake's mechanism, the defense attorneys continued to object to Mandell's proffered testimony regarding his observations of the brake's inner workings. The trial justice sustained the objections. The Romanos made several offers of proof intending to establish that the test runs made by Costerus did not deplete the amount of lubricant in the braking system and that evaporation of the oil in the interim between the accident and Mandell's testing was insignificant. The trial justice rejected a final offer of proof by the Romanos relative to the presence within the braking system of dirt and debris which allegedly was sufficient to cause a brake failure. Thereafter, unconvinced that the Romanos had established the necessary similarity of braking conditions, the trial justice directed a verdict. . . .

On appeal, the Romanos argue that in excluding the testimony of their expert, Mandell, the trial justice effectively precluded testimony on the issues of defective design and proximate cause, thus making a directed verdict inevitable. They argue further that the trial justice applied an erroneous standard of admissibility in excluding the testimony of their expert. According to the Romanos, the issue of whether the condition of the brake chamber remained unchanged between the date of the accident and its subsequent examination by Mandell was a question for the jury and not for the trial justice. To support their positions, the Romanos urge us to adopt the standard of "conditional relevancy." Under this theory, all the evidence would have been submitted to the jury who would then decide, under proper instruction, whether the condition of the brake had changed substantially from September 1971 to April 1973. As authority for this proposition they rely primarily upon Fed. R. Evid. 104(b). . . . The standard of admissibility "has been variously referred to as 'some evidence' or 'prima facie' evidence. The important point is that the preliminary fact can be decided by the judge against the proponent only where the jury could not reasonably find the preliminary fact to exist." 21 Wright & Graham, Federal Practice and Procedure §5054 at 269 (1977). The Romanos argue that inasmuch as a prima facie showing of no substantial change was made through uncontradicted testimony, the issue should have been submitted to the jury.

Stated differently, the Romanos contend that because the relevancy of Mandell's examination of the brake's innards depended upon proof of another conditionally relevant preliminary fact—"no substantial change"—both should have been for the jury to decide.

At the outset, we note that the acceptance of Rule 104(b) has been considerably less than universal. . . . One leading treatise considers proof of preliminary questions of fact as "one of the most complex, as well as most common, of evidentiary concepts." It suggests that "'laying a foundation' for the admissibility of evidence . . . is easier to do if you do not think too much about what you are doing. Thus, Rule 104 may be a provision that is best ignored." 21 Wright & Graham, Federal Practice and Procedure §5052 at 248 (1977). Another legal pundit, after a lengthy discussion highly critical of the conditional relevancy doctrine, concludes that Rule 104(b) is "an obstacle course for judge and jury alike." He declares that it is "based on incorrect analysis; it confuses the issues, invites errors, and should be repealed." Ball, The Myth of Conditional Relevancy, 1977 Ariz. St. L.J. 295, 325. Professor Ball argues that there is "no need to create a special rule to serve as a rescue apparatus to save the law of evidence from . . . mythical dangers." Id. at 310. The greater danger, he asserts, is that "once codifiers embark on this false trail, they will find a problem of 'conditional relevancy' behind every tree and will employ their rescue apparatus in a way which will confuse the jury and muddle the administration of the evidence rules far more than letting matters alone would have done." Id. at 310-11.

We are not prepared to embrace the doctrine of conditional relevancy as it is set forth in the rule. Indeed, we question how clearly the demarcation between the respective roles of judge and jury would be delineated under the rule. Professors Wright and Graham summarize commentary regarding the viability of Rule 104(b): "In short, about the only good thing that commentators have found in jury determination of preliminary questions is that it is likely to amount to a de facto repeal of the rules of evidence." 21 Wright & Graham, Federal Practice and Procedure §5052 at 249 (1977).

We have not as yet adopted the Federal Rules in this jurisdiction. Instead, we prefer to rely upon our vintage rule that the trial justice must exercise discretion regarding the admissibility of evidence when there has been an objection of irrelevancy. A ruling made under these circumstances would not be reversible error unless the trial justice abused his discretion to the prejudice of the objecting party. On review of the record, we do not find that he abused his discretion. . . .

Accordingly, we hold that the trial justice did not commit reversible error in excluding the testimony on the issues of defective design and causation because, as a matter of discretion, he concluded that the condition of the brake when examined by the Romanos' expert in 1973 was not substantially the same as it had been on September 9, 1971, the day Rayna was injured. Here, Mandell was prepared to testify that the 1971 malfunction was due to a lack of oil and the presence of dust in the brake's chamber. However, having in mind that there was no evidence in regard to the temperature in the area where the bicycle was stored during the twenty-month hiatus between Costerus's forty descents and Mandell's inspection, the trial justice was obviously dubious about how much of the dirt found by Mandell came about as a result of Costerus's experiments, and he was also unsure that the oil level in the brake chamber was the same in 1973 as it had been on the evening when the bicycle plunged down Bellevue Drive.

On this record and in light of the views expressed herein, we cannot fault the trial justice's refusal to allow Mandell to testify concerning the findings he made as a result of his 1973 examination of the coaster-brake portion of the "Oxford."

Accordingly, the plaintiffs' appeal is denied and dismissed, the judgment appealed from is affirmed, and the case is remanded to the Superior Court.

Do you agree with the court's analysis of Rule 104(b)? Is there an approach under the Federal Rules, other than the one rejected by the court, that would reach the same result that the Rhode Island court reached? Under either approach, what principle is to guide the trial judge in her exercise of discretion?

Romano illustrates the connection between the concept of relevance and the functional question of what is going to be done with the evidence. It also demonstrates another problem with the Rules' concept of conditional relevancy. In this case, given that credibility is for the jury to decide, there seems to be evidence sufficient to support a finding that the condition of the brake chamber remained unchanged between the date of the accident and its subsequent inspection by the expert, Mandell. The problem is that the judge does not believe this evidence and wants to make this judgment rather than leave it to the jury, as Rule 104(b) provides. The court thus rejects the approach of Rule 104 because it believes that under Rule 104, the trial court would have had to admit the evidence. Instead, the court follows Rhode Island's vintage rule under which relevancy issues are within the court's discretion.

In refusing to admit Mandell's observations about the condition of the brakes in 1973 on grounds of relevance, the judge is aware that they are a predicate for Mandell's expert testimony about the design of the braking mechanism, particularly the supposed defect of using a plastic cap for the oil hole. Whether the accident was caused by a brake failure, whether brake failure was caused by dirt in the oil hole, whether the dirt got into the oil hole because the plastic cap came off the hole, whether the cap came off the hole because it was plastic—all these connections are extremely tentative. Given the sympathetic position of the plaintiff, the mysterious disappearance of the bicycle, and the deep pockets of the defendant, the judge undoubtedly worried that the structure of inference was too fragile to carry the case to the jury. Yet if the question is asked, "Could reasonable persons, taking all issues of credibility in favor of the plaintiff, conclude that the condition of the bicycle had not materially changed between the time of the accident and the time of Mandell's tests?" the answer would seem to be "yes." That is the appropriate question under Rule 104(b).

Experimental evidence problems similar to the problem posed in *Romano* arise often. The issue generally is whether the experiment was conducted under conditions substantially similar to the real event in dispute. An example is People v. Terry, 38 Cal. App. 3d 432 (1974), where *D* was charged with robbery of a finance company at 4:30 P.M. on a Wednesday. *D* pleaded an alibi and testified that at 4:45 P.M. of the day in question he was at a certain bar some distance from the finance company office. The prosecution called a police officer to testify that three months after the robbery, on a Thursday, he drove an unmarked police car from the finance company office to the bar. The police officer testified that he left at 4:30 P.M., drove on the freeway at the speed limit, and arrived at the bar at 4:43 P.M. *D*'s objection on grounds of irrelevancy was overruled. The court held that despite the fact that the officer made the trip on a Thursday three months later, conditions were substantially similar. Thus, the evidence was relevant.

These cases call for a careful balancing based on the facts of the particular case. But under the approach of the Federal Rules, this balancing is supposed to be done for the most part by the jury. As long as the evidence passes the minimum threshold of Rules 104(b) and 401, differences between the conditions that were obtained at the time of the experiment and at the real event should go to weight, not admissibility. As *Romano* demonstrates, however, the cases reveal considerable reluctance on the part of judges to lower the barriers to experimental evidence of this sort.

The concept of "conditional relevance" is embodied in several of the Federal Rules of Evidence. Rule 602, requiring personal knowledge on the part of the witness as a prerequisite to admissible testimony and Rule 901, requiring that documents and tangible evidence be shown to be "authentic" before admission in evidence, are thought to pose specialized issues of conditional relevance.

Recently the whole construct of "conditional relevance" has come under severe scholarly criticism. Starting with Professor Ball's, The Myth of Conditional Relevancy, 14 Ga. L. Rev. 435 (1980), a parade of successive law review articles have savaged, debunked, defended, and reinterpreted the notion of conditional relevance. The following excerpt from one of these articles suggests that "conditional relevance" is merely a manifestation of the court's policy in favor of receiving the best and most complete evidence available.

DALE A. NANCE, CONDITIONAL RELEVANCE REINTERPRETED
70 B.U. L. Rev. 447 (1990)

The cornerstone of modern evidence law is relevance. Its rationalist tones may not engender the passion of notions like prejudice, due process, or even privilege. Yet its theoretical and practical importance cannot be denied. For example, the heart of the Federal Rules of Evidence, Rule 402, codifies the two fundamental principles of the common law of admissibility: the presumptive admissibility of relevant evidence and the inadmissibility of irrelevant evidence. Relevance is *the* threshold admissibility issue, applicable to every piece of evidence offered. Moreover, identification of the mode of relevance is usually the prelude to proper application of other exclusionary rules. Much turns, then, upon the question of relevance.

As relevance gained ascendancy in the law of evidence, so did the notion that the relevance of evidence can be "conditional," in the sense of depending upon a favorable finding of fact.[2] This view, explained by reference to common-sensical examples, has provided an important source of exclusionary authority. Conditional relevance is said to underlie a wide variety of common-law decisions. Accordingly, it also appears in several places in modern codifications.

However, the notion of conditional relevance has recently been subjected to powerful theoretical criticism.[3] It is argued that the idea rests upon a conceptual mistake, at least in terms of the examples by which it is regularly illustrated. Describing relevance as conditional in these examples simply misconceives the requirement of relevance. So convincing is this argument that conditional relevance now seems unable

2. Among commentators the idea can be traced primarily to the work of Edmund Morgan. The seminal article is Morgan, Functions of Judge and Jury in the Determination of Preliminary Questions of Fact, 43 Harv. L. Rev. 165 (1929).

3. The principal source of this criticism is the late Vaughn Ball. See Ball, The Myth of Conditional Relevancy, 14 Ga. L. Rev. 435 (1980).

to bear the weight as an explanatory device that it had confidently assumed. The upshot of the criticism is that we should abandon the notion entirely.

If this is correct, then either the judicial decisions thought to be based upon conditional relevance must be rejected as mistakes, or alternative explanatory vehicles must be found. This article reflects a mixed evaluation. It will be argued that many judicial decisions exemplifying conditional relevance, including decisions that have come to be explained in such terms even though they were not decided in such terms, have been following, however inartfully, distinguishable principles and policies. Moreover, there is an identifiable core of good sense in these principles and policies, a residual force to the conditional relevance idea. A reinterpretation of the doctrine will be offered to account for this residue.

This is an important project. Several long-accepted and practically important rules of evidence—notably, the requirements that documents be authenticated, that out-of-court speakers be identified, and that testimony reflect personal knowledge—are now said to be based upon the notion of conditional relevance. Again, if that notion is not serviceable, viable substitutes are needed, or a major revision of evidence law may be in order. Here, too, this article will take a mixed course, suggesting a modified interpretive stance based upon the residual force of conditional relevance.

A major thesis of this article is that the "best evidence principle"— the principle that parties should present to the tribunal the best reasonably available evidence on a disputed factual issue—is the vehicle that explains the residual force of conditional relevance. It does not explain *every* application of that idea found in cases, statutes, and secondary literature. In the end, we must be prepared to acknowledge some mistakes in this area, especially since the apparent plausibility of conditional relevance has led to its general acceptance. What can be said, however, is that the best evidence principle accounts for the residue of authority that may *justifiably* entail the exclusion of evidence.

This thesis has wide-ranging implications, since conditional relevance problems, as conventionally understood, are ubiquitous. In a recent federal criminal case, for example, the United States Supreme Court resolved a conflict among the circuits concerning the admissibility of evidence of alleged prior similar acts by the defendant.[7] The decision came after years of dispute over an issue of considerable importance to the criminal justice system, one generally thought to be far afield from the problem of relevance. However, the Court's opinion relies heavily upon framing the admissibility issue as one of conditional relevance. If the theory presented here is correct, it has significant ramifications for

7. Huddleston v. United States, 485 U.S. 681 (1988).

the propriety of a decision that portends substantially increased practical importance for that concept.

Part I of the article will present the basic idea of conditional relevance and lay out in simple yet improved terms the criticism that has cast severe doubt upon it. Part II will reexamine the principal authorities relied upon to support the doctrine, in order to discover what they are really about. Part III will test the suggested reconstruction by looking at those well-established doctrines that have come to be assimilated into the concept of conditional relevance and by examining certain problems of statutory interpretation that are raised by the theory advocated here. This examination will lead to consideration of the Supreme Court decision mentioned above. The Conclusion will recapitulate the practical and theoretical significance of a "best evidence" interpretation of conditional relevance.

I. THE PRESENT THEORETICAL IMPASSE

Evidence is said to be conditionally relevant if its relevance depends upon the satisfaction of a factual condition:

> [I]t often happens that upon an issue as to the existence of fact C, a combination of facts A and B will be highly relevant, but either without the other will have no significance.[8]

In such situations, the basic requirement of relevance means that the admissibility of evidence of either fact A or fact B must be conditioned upon some form of showing of the other. Unavoidably, evidence as to one must be introduced first, so administration of the trial requires the flexibility of allowing the proponent to "connect up" later with evidence of the other. Rule 104(b) of the Federal Rules of Evidence thus expresses the requirement in these terms:

> When the relevancy of evidence depends upon the fulfillment of a condition of fact, the court shall admit it upon, or subject to, the introduction of evidence sufficient to support a finding of the fulfillment of the condition.

Significantly, Rule 104(b) does not specify when relevance is conditional, but only what to do with a conditional relevance issue once it arises. For clues to the identification of such problems, one must look to the examples provided in the notes of the advisory committee that drafted the rules. One standard example (hereinafter the "notice hypothetical") is presented as follows:

---

8. E. Morgan, Basic Problems of Evidence 45 (1963). In his original article, Morgan expressed the point this way: "It often happens, however, that a fact, irrelevant in itself, will have great probative value in conjunction with another fact." Morgan, supra note 2, at 166.

[W]hen a spoken statement is relied upon to prove notice to X, it is without probative value unless X heard it.

* * *

The judge makes a preliminary determination whether the foundation evidence is sufficient to support a finding of fulfillment of the condition. If so, the item is admitted. If after all the evidence on the issue is in, pro and con, the jury could reasonably conclude that fulfillment of the condition is not [*sic*] established, the issue is for them. If the evidence is not such as to allow a finding, the judge withdraws the matter from their consideration.

The clear, if poorly articulated, intention is that a "finding" by the appropriate standard of proof (such as a preponderance of the evidence) of "fulfillment of the condition" means, in the context of the example, a finding that X heard the spoken statement. If so, this seemingly sensible doctrine is mistaken.

The reason, stated in terms of the example, is that the trier of fact need not make, and ought not be required to make, a "finding" on the question of whether the utterance was heard unless evidence of the utterance is the only evidence of notice presented. Of course, one must evaluate the *likelihood* that it was heard, but even if, from all the evidence presented, there is only a small probability that X heard the spoken statement, it is still some evidence of notice that, together with the other evidence, may warrant a finding of notice. This follows directly from the liberally inclusive concept of relevance now employed. Specifically, Federal Rule 401 provides:

> "Relevant evidence" means evidence having any tendency to make the existence of any fact that is of consequence to the determination of the action more probable or less probable than it would be without the evidence.

Suppose, for example, there were a hundred such utterances, independently made. The trier of fact might reasonably conclude that it is unlikely that X heard any particular utterance and yet also reasonably conclude that it is very likely that X heard *at least one* of them. More realistically, and more generally, there could be evidence of a variety of events, different in nature and weakly probative taken severally, that taken in combination make the existence of notice very likely but do not make it likely that the particular utterance was heard.

Indeed, even a "finding" of notice may be unnecessary, depending upon the applicable substantive law. If notice is merely an evidentiary proposition, rather than an ultimate proposition in the case, then the ultimate proposition toward which evidence of notice is directed may be found to be true notwithstanding insufficient evidence to warrant a finding of notice. In such a case, the evidence of notice must be considered together with other evidence that pertains to the ultimate prop-osition. The point is simply that the trier must make a *finding*, by the appropriate standard of proof, only as to the ultimate propositions in the case, not as to intermediate evidentiary propositions contained within inferential chains.

If, from all the evidence, one were certain that X did *not* hear the utterance, then the evidence thereof, taken in context, would have no probative value as to notice. One might then rightly speak of "condi-tional irrelevance." But such certainty is rarely to be found in a litigated case, and in any event it would license a ruling of inadmissibility (whether in advance or after the fact on a motion to strike) in many fewer cases than the prevailing doctrine of conditional relevance theo-retically prescribes. Under the conventional doctrine, any proposition that, if *known with certainty* to be false, would render the proffered evi-dence irrelevant (such as the proposition that X heard the utterance), is a proposition that must be proven true in order for the evidence properly to be considered by the trier of fact. *Any* item of evidence is vulnerable to such hypothesized conditions. Indeed, the only limit on the number of conditioning facts pertaining to each proffer is one's imagination.

This is not to say that hypothesized conditions are always useless con-structs. Quite the contrary, it is often helpful to ask whether evidence is relevant given certain assumed factual propositions, propositions about which the trier of fact will have to make judgments in the course of its decision-making. As long as the assumption *favors* relevance, it generates a necessary (but not sufficient) condition for admissibility. For example, one might ask whether the evidence of the utterance made to X in the notice hypothetical would be relevant on the favorable assumption that X heard it. That is, did the content of the utterance have anything to do with the matter about which X is claimed to have had notice? Here, the point is that the evidence of the utterance may be irrelevant, and therefore inadmissible, even if the utterance was heard. As suggested above, one can also ask whether the utterance would be relevant on the assumption that its content appropriately con-cerns the underlying matter being litigated. This assumption, implicit in the notice hypothetical as given, points one to the question of whether the utterance was heard and understood. Either way, this an-alytical device must not be confused with the conventional notion of conditional relevance. The probabilistic character of the tests of rele-vance generated thereby remains fundamentally at odds with the con-ventional theory.

One is moved to conclude that the concept of conditional relevance either simply confuses the standards for sufficiency with those for ad-missibility or else serves some function distinct from spelling out the logical implications of the basic requirement of relevance. This conclusion is confirmed by another standard hypothetical (hereinafter the "agency hypothetical"), presented by the drafters of the California Evidence Code:

> [I]f P sues D upon an alleged agreement, evidence of negotiations with A is inadmissible *because irrelevant* unless A is shown to be D's agent; but the evidence of negotiations with A is admissible if there is evidence sufficient to sustain a finding of the agency.[20]

This supposed application is even worse than the previous hypothetical, or rather what makes it erroneous is more transparent. Unlike the notice hypothetical, here the conditioning fact is one upon which a finding must be made by the trier of fact. The ultimate factual propositions that P must prove include A's agency for D as well as the agreement between P and A. To be relevant, an item of evidence need only tend to prove, or disprove, *one* of these propositions, or some other ultimate proposition in the case. The adequacy of proof as to the others is of no consequence in making that determination. Conditioning the admissibility of evidence of one of these propositions upon prior or subsequent presentation of evidence sufficient to support a finding of the other makes no more sense than conditioning the presentation of evidence of one element of a negligence cause of action (such as negligent conduct) upon the prior or subsequent introduction of sufficient evidence to support findings on the other elements (such as cause in fact and compensable injury).

The conflation of admissibility and sufficiency is blatant in this and similar hypotheticals. Of course, if a proponent cannot present sufficient evidence to support a finding on one of the essential elements of the proponent's cause of action or affirmative defense, then presentation of evidence on the other elements becomes *pointless*. It is perhaps understandable that evidence pointless in this sense would be excluded as "irrelevant." This usage finds some superficial support in the language by which relevance is now defined, since those other essential elements are no longer "of consequence to the determination of the action" as required by Rule 401. However, properly speaking, the "facts of consequence," known at common law as the "material" facts, are determined by the substantive law invoked by the parties' claims, as modified by any stipulations or other judicial admissions, not by the adequacy of proof that is adduced on those material facts. Thus, the only apparent justification for such a rule of conditional admissibility is

20. Cal. Evid. Code §403(a) assembly committee comment ("Section 350—Relevancy") (emphasis added). Section 403 is the Code's analogue to Fed. R. Evid. 104(b).

to save the tribunal from the consideration of a frivolous claim by insisting that counsel assure that sufficient evidence on the other ultimate issues will be presented in due course.

The foregoing criticism of the standard examples of conditional relevance is fully generalizable. Before concluding, however, that conditional relevance is simply a mistaken idea, one ought to reexamine how it came to be. In fact, the doctrine in its modern form, attributable largely to the work of Edmund Morgan, is more liberal in the admission of evidence than the doctrine sporadically invoked prior to its existence. In older cases raising the kinds of problems posed by the previous hypotheticals, some courts would employ a standard that required the judge to determine the existence of the conditioning fact. In our notice hypothetical, for example, the trial judge would have had to determine whether or not X heard the spoken statement. Professor Morgan offered the insight that employment of such a standard unwisely extended the procedure properly employed for determinations of preliminary facts affecting the application of other exclusionary rules, like the hearsay prohibition and its exceptions. Recognizing the loss of valuable evidence that such a standard entails, without the concomitant advantages that attend the judicial administration of the more technical "competency" rules, he argued successfully for a liberal standard like that of the Federal Rules. Thus, for example, to admit evidence of the statement, the court need only determine that there is evidence "sufficient to support a finding" that X heard the statement.

Morgan's efforts were salutary, but he did not go far enough, at least if the modern critique is right. Of course, if we ignore the prescribed *results* in the hypotheticals used to exemplify conditional relevance, then the standard expressed in provisions like Federal Rule 104(b) can be rendered formally compatible with the liberal modern definition of relevance. This is accomplished by accepting that the only "condition of fact" upon which "the relevancy of evidence depends" is the existence of a non-zero probability for each "conditioning" proposition of fact, that is, each proposition that affects the *probative value* of the original evidence in such a way that the evidence is logically relevant only if the probability of that fact being true is non-zero. In terms of the notice hypothetical, this would mean that the evidence should be excluded if the judge does not believe that a reasonable jury could find there to be a non-zero probability that X heard the statement. This construction would convert the doctrine into what was described above as one of "conditional irrelevance."

The test has been stated in a seemingly double negative form for a reason. One should not ignore the case in which it cannot reasonably be said *either* that there exists a non-zero probability of a conditioning proposition *or* that there exists a zero probability of that proposition.

This is just a special case of the general class of situations in which the probative value of the original evidence is unknown. See infra note 28.

Such a reading of Rule 104(b) would reduce the frequency of exclusions under the conditional relevance idea. Indeed, it would render the doctrine virtually a dead letter.[30] Before we embrace this result, it is wise to reconsider the judicial decisions that gave rise to the hypotheticals discussed above and other cases in which conditional relevance has been used as a rationale, or *post hoc* explanation, of a ruling on the admissibility of evidence. This is the purpose of the next Part. . . .

D. THE BEST EVIDENCE PRINCIPLE

In a previous article, I argued that much of the law of evidence is animated by a general principle that parties should present to the tribunal at trial the best reasonably available evidence on a disputed factual issue, "best" being measured in terms of the probative value of evidence to a rational trier of fact. The existence of a well-functioning adversary system, with developed discovery techniques, was said to provide a significant, but limited, privilege as against the prima facie duty imposed by this principle on each litigant. Many long-standing rules of admissibility in Anglo-American law, as well as other procedural rules, were explained as responses to the imperatives of this principle and to actual or perceived imperfections of the adversary process as measured thereby.

The thesis presented here is that the "conditional relevance" doctrine, *to the extent it is justifiable,* instantiates the best evidence principle. In some cases, like *Gila Valley,* it functions to require the proponent to present useful information about the "conditioning" event that is reasonably available to the proponent. The ruling reminds the proponent that this information should be presented so that the trier can accurately assess the probative value of the proffered evidence. In such cases, therefore, the doctrine would be described more felicitously as a doctrine of "conditional probative value" than as one of "conditional relevance." Failure to distinguish between relevance and probative value has

30. There is one class of situations of considerable practical importance where the concept of conditional relevance may have significance on nearly its own terms. Evidence may be proffered that has probative value *entirely unknown,* at least to an ordinary reasonable trier of fact. See Lempert, Modeling Relevance, 75 Mich. L. Rev. 1021, 1029-30 (1977). For example, a paternity plaintiff might offer evidence that a certain chemical compound, unfamiliar in common discourse, is found in the blood of both the child and the defendant. In this situation, it may be sensible to say that the evidence is conditionally relevant, its relevance (and probative value) depending upon the presentation of further information. Cf. Ball, supra note 3, at 463-65 (recognizing this possibility, but denying that Rule 104(b) applies because the additional information needed is not a "fact condition" but a generalization connecting evidenced facts with ultimate issues).

plagued not only the conventional theory of conditional relevance, but also the rare attempts to confront and resolve its paradoxical implications.

One should bear in mind that it is not the contingent quality of probative value alone which generates an exclusionary rule, for almost all evidence is subject to such contingency. It is, rather, the combination of such contingency with a variety of factors concerning access to the additional evidence and the comparative appropriateness of the exclusionary remedy. The result is still "conditional admissibility," but for an entirely different reason. The reason ultimately derives its force from what I have called the "expansionary" dimension of the best evidence principle. That is, the purpose is to "expand" the evidentiary package considered by the trier of fact as to a factual matter that the proponent has chosen to inject into the case. Exclusion of evidence as initially proffered does not, in this context, arise from its being irrelevant or *tainted,* but rather from its being *inexcusably incomplete* standing alone. The remedy is compatible with the discretionary power of the trial court to exclude evidence when its probative value is substantially outweighed by the danger of misleading the trier of fact, especially (but not only) when a suspicion is raised that the reasonably available—but missing—evidence would be unfavorable to the proponent. . . .

III. TESTING THE THEORY

In the first section of this Part, we will examine certain long-established doctrines that have come to be viewed as special cases of conditional relevance to see if they can survive the recent undermining of the conventional wisdom. The second section will consider the interpretational problem posed by a best evidence reconstruction of conditional relevance amid statutory language explicitly designed to reflect the conventional view. The final section will examine the recent Supreme Court decision that has given new significance to conditional relevance outside the contexts of its usual application.

A. COGNATE DOCTRINES

Among the doctrines that have come to be assimilated with conditional relevance are those of *authentication* and *identification.* They are expressed in Federal Rule 901 in this oblique fashion:

> The requirement of authentication or identification as a condition precedent to admissibility is satisfied by evidence sufficient to support a finding that the matter in question is what its proponent claims.

This was explained by the drafters in the following terms:

[T]his requirement of showing authenticity or identity falls in the category of relevancy dependent upon fulfillment of a condition of fact. . . .

Elsewhere, the drafters gave the following standard example:

[I]f a letter purporting to be from Y is relied upon to establish an admission by him, it has no probative value unless Y wrote or authorized it.

Once again, one can plainly see the error in this argument, for the document *is* relevant (provided of course the admission therein is itself relevant) unless one knows for certain that Y did *not* write or authorize it. Indeed, it is commonly noted that ordinary experience attributes relevance to documents without authentication of the type required in the law courts. By itself, the document may not be *sufficient* to support a finding of an admission by Y, were such a finding necessary in the case, but that is a different matter. As described in connection with the notice hypothetical, the mistake can be traced to the erroneous assumption that such a finding must be made by the trier of fact in all cases.

Nevertheless, there is a valid inclination to demand that the proponent tell the tribunal where this document was obtained, whether someone observed its signing, and so forth. Why? Because such evidence, helpful in the assessment of the probative value of the document, very likely exists. There is no reason to accept, without an excuse unlikely to be available, the proffer of a document or any tangible evidence unless the proponent explains, to the best of its ability, the connection of the evidence to the case. So, arguably, the litigant should be required, as a condition for admitting the evidence, to present by way of sponsoring witnesses, subject to cross-examination, the information apparently or presumably available that will assist the trier of fact in evaluating the thing proffered. To require the opponent to discern the basis of the connection through discovery, and to present such information during the next principal phase of the evidentiary presentations, would only be a confusing waste of time. . . .

These points are illustrated by a well-known case concerning identification of the author of a letter. In Coleman v. McIntosh,[175] plaintiff sued for breach of contract to marry. Defendant offered in evidence an unaddressed, unsigned love letter, contained in an envelope addressed to a named third person and postmarked over a year after the alleged breach, in which the writer implicitly denied having been engaged to defendant. Defendant attempted to support the admission of the letter by his own testimony identifying the handwriting as that of plaintiff. Plaintiff denied having written the letter, but equivocated about know-

175. 184 Ky. 370, 211 S.W. 872 (1919).

ing the apparent addressee. The trial court denied admission of the letter, and a verdict was rendered for plaintiff. The Court of Appeals of Kentucky reversed on the ground that this evidence should have been admitted. In making this ruling, the appellate court reviewed the circumstances surrounding the letter and held that "if the letter was genuine, and there was sufficient evidence to make this a question for the jury, the letter was admissible provided it contained statements otherwise relevant to the facts in issue." The court had no difficulty identifying statements in the letter that were relevant on the assumption of authenticity.

. . . It is not difficult to see the best evidence principle in operation here. One might wonder, for example, whether the trial court's concerns that generated the challenged exclusion related to the absence of testimony from the addressee of the letter, who very likely would know, better than defendant, who had written it. Similarly, one might wonder how the letter came to be in the hands of defendant. Explanation of these matters would go far to dispel concerns about fraud or mistake.

A similar explanation applies to another important doctrine, the firsthand knowledge requirement, expressed in Federal Rule 602 in the following terms:

> A witness may not testify to a matter unless evidence is introduced sufficient to support a finding that he has personal knowledge of the matter.

Again, we are told that "the rule is in fact a specialized application of the provisions . . . on conditional relevancy." And again, we must reject this explanation if it is to be taken literally. Suppose that a witness in a homicide case takes the stand and simply declares under oath that she knows who the killer is and that it is the defendant. There can be no doubt that this testimony is relevant, at least if the identity of the killer is contested. Surprisingly, some sophisticated modern commentators continue to reject this conclusion. To make the point plain, if we know nothing besides the fact of the testimonial identification by a competent witness, there is some *a priori* probability that the witness is basing the testimony on direct observation, some probability that it is based on the hearsay statements of others, and some probability that the witness is making the whole thing up. As long as we are not *certain* that she is either making it up or basing it on completely unreliable hearsay, or a combination of the two, we should conclude that it is more likely that defendant committed the crime given the testimony than it would be without the testimony. The presence of such potential testimonial defects is unlikely *a priori*, so the identification is relevant.

The law's refusal to admit the testimony, absent a showing of personal knowledge, cannot be grounded simply on the exclusion of irrelevant evidence. Nevertheless, admission is properly conditioned upon the presentation of evidence as to *how* the witness "knows" the identity of the culprit. The reasons are that (i) it is important to explore this in order to give the identification its proper weight, and (ii) the witness very likely knows, probably better than anyone else, how the witness came to have the claimed knowledge. We may rightly expect that this information be divulged, and it is not implausible to use inadmissibility as the sanction for the failure of the proponent to do so. If such disclosure shows the testimony to be based upon thin air, then a case of conditional irrelevance is encountered. The effect of disclosure may also be to reveal the applicability of another exclusionary rule, particularly the hearsay rule or the lay opinion rule. What is left, if anything, after these constraints are satisfied will be the information that is the product of the witness's first-hand observations. . . .

B. THE PROPONENT'S BURDEN

It has already been noted that the "sufficient to support a finding" standard, traceable directly to Morgan's arguments, presents significant interpretational problems once conditional relevance is disarmed as an explanatory device. The appearance of the standard in modern statutory rules of authentication and personal knowledge, as well as general conditional relevance, does suggest that these rules have *something* in common, and it has been argued what that something is. However, situations may arise in which the proponent's presentation of all reasonably demandable information on the conditioning fact is still considered insufficient "to support a finding" of the fulfillment of the condition by some specified standard such as a preponderance of the evidence. Conversely, evidence "sufficient to support a finding" under such a standard may be presented without presenting all reasonably demandable information on the conditioning fact. This is especially likely if the preponderance standard is interpreted as "more likely than not." So there is some apparent discontinuity between the best evidence principle and the nominally prevailing standard.

On the other hand, it would not be inappropriate to view this language as creating a flexible standard, one that depends on the availability of information. Contrary to the usual assumption, what is sufficient for a "finding" with regard to a fact that merely affects the probative value of other evidence need not be measured by one of the standards that govern sufficiency of the evidence with regard to the ultimate issues in the case. Moreover, even in ordinary rulings on sufficiency with respect to ultimate factual issues, the courts have considered the availability of further evidence as a factor in gauging a party's satisfaction of the burdens of production or persuasion. . . .

Of course, these problems of interpreting the "sufficient to support a finding" standard would seem to disappear if one accepts at face value the recent criticism of conditional relevance. If there are no cases of conditional relevance, then there are no preliminary fact determinations to be made under Rule 104(b). It must be remembered that Rule 104(b) is not itself an exclusionary rule, but rather a standard for resolving preliminary fact questions arising under other rules. It is naturally thought and clearly intended that the exclusionary rule in question is Rule 402, which provides for the exclusion of irrelevant evidence. The thrust of the best evidence principle is obviously closer to the exclusion of misleading evidence and evidence that is a waste of time, as authorized most prominently by Rule 403. One could, therefore, leave the best evidence principle to be honored by way of the latter rule, with preliminary questions, such as the reasonable availability of further information, resolved under Rule 104(a). The varying probative value of proffered evidence as well as missing evidence of facts that condition probative value of the proffer would then be accommodated readily under the weighing test of Rule 403.

Clearly, this resolution is not available for the personal knowledge requirement, since Rule 602 itself states an exclusionary rule. The existence of a distinct exclusionary rule here may be appropriate, given the variety of functions served by the personal knowledge requirement. A more difficult problem is presented by the authentication/identification requirement associated with Rule 901. That rule does not itself state an exclusionary rule, but merely provides a standard — the same as in Rule 104(b) — for the proponent to meet in satisfying a requirement presumably imposed elsewhere. Again, the pertinent exclusionary rule is supposed to be the exclusion of irrelevant evidence under Rule 402. It would be too incompatible with the detailed legislative provisions of Article IX of the Federal Rules to interpret Rule 901 as applicable to virtually none of the normal cases of documentary and other tangible evidence obviously contemplated by that Article. Consequently, the standard remains to be construed in the flexible manner suggested above, notwithstanding that the exclusionary rule giving rise to its employment must be either Rule 403 or one simply implicit in Rule 901. An important question to be explored, then, is which issues fall within Article IX, and which are left to be dealt with under Rule 403 and its procedural counterpart, Rule 104(a). This, however, must be left as a topic for another day. . . .

CONCLUSION

The probabilistic criticism of the conventional doctrine of conditional relevance is now well known, at least among academicians. It has led to the suggestion that the doctrine be abolished entirely. Others have echoed the criticism but balked at abolition for largely unarticulated reasons. No doubt there is skepticism about a change that would seem to undermine such well-accepted doctrines as authentication and personal knowledge. The best evidence principle offers an escape from this dilemma by shifting judicial energy away from attempts to apply the illusive concept of conditional relevance, and toward a pragmatic effort to identify situations in which the proponent should come forth with more information about the proffered (relevant) evidence as a condition of admissibility. The extent to which the doctrines now assimilated under the rubric of conditional relevance make sense is attributable to that principle. It rests upon considerations not of the logic of relevance, but rather of a protective evidentiary principle. In some cases the purpose of this reinterpreted doctrine of conditional relevance is to encourage the presentation of additional evidence rather than to exclude that which is originally proffered. Here, the doctrine can be seen as a manifestation of the expansionary dimension of the best evidence principle, enforced by an exclusionary rule. In other cases, where the probative value of the original proffer is slight without more, exclusion upon failure to present further information may also be simply an effort to avoid a waste of the time and energy of the tribunal, manifesting the contractionary dimension of the best evidence principle.

Of course, in the former case, the interference with the proponent's chosen proof strategy raises issues about the significance of the adversary process. The questions that can be asked in each instance are: Why not leave the exploration of the additional information to cross-examination or other treatment by the opponent of the original proffer? And, if intervention is necessary, should it take the form of an exclusionary rule?

Four responses are in order. First, the fact that the law retains the requirements of "conditional relevance," authentication, identification, and personal knowledge attests to the perceived irrelevancy or inadequacy of the adversary process in this regard. Second, such perceptions of *irrelevancy* may be well-grounded in the fundamental principle that one ought to do the right thing, even if failure to do so is harmless in a material sense. The "right thing" is to back up the inference that a proponent asks the trier of fact to make, with information reasonably available to the proponent. Third, such perceptions of *inadequacy* may be well grounded in at least four considerations: (i) the proponent's comparative ease of access to the further information; (ii) the presentation of ancillary information affecting probative value at a time more convenient to the trier's evaluation of the weight of the evidence in question; (iii) the prompt uncovering of other technical objections to admission; and (iv) the avoidance of waste of time and energy that would result from delayed discovery that an item of evidence is of so little probative value as to justify exclusion on that basis. Finally, assuming some form of intervention is necessary, reason does not necessarily contradict the historical view of the judiciary that the exclusionary sanction offers significant hope of obtaining the best evidence without sacrificing the advantages of judicial passivity associated with the adversary process.

Whether the authority for exclusion is judicial discretion under provisions like Rule 403, or some implicit authority to be derived from provisions like Rule 104(b), these are the factors that need to be considered in ruling on an objection framed in conditional relevance terms. In particular, when all that can reasonably be expected of a proponent is provided, and the resulting package of evidence has more than *de minimis* probative value, there is no basis for exclusion under the best evidence principle. Given the availability of discretion to exclude for prejudice or confusion of the issues, as well as various devices for monitoring the sufficiency of the evidence, there is no need for any further operation of a doctrine of conditional relevance.

The reinterpretation of conditional relevance offered here confirms an important aspect of relevance: its rationalist tone. In vogue, now and then, is seeing in the trial of disputes all manner of social functions other than the accurate determination of legally operative facts. The best evidence principle, on the other hand, draws upon a rich intellectual and professional heritage, of which Professor Morgan's work is a valued part, that recognizes and addresses the realities of the courtroom and the importance of assuring that contested factual claims are resolved as accurately as is possible within the resource constraints that circumscribe litigation. Insofar as one looks to the heretofore underexplored realm of juridical meanings in the doctrine of conditional relevance, there is every reason to think that this kind of rationalism thrives in the law of evidence.

D. Prejudice and Probative Value

J. THAYER, A PRELIMINARY TREATISE ON EVIDENCE 266 (1898): [W]e must not fall into the error of supposing that relevancy, logical connection, real or supposed, is the only test of admissibility; for so we should drop out of sight the chief part of the law of evidence. When we have said (1) that, without any exception, nothing which is not, or is not supposed to be, logically relevant is admissible; and (2) that, subject to many exceptions and qualifications, whatever is logically relevant is admissible; it is obvious that, in reality, there are tests of admissibility other than logical relevancy. Some things are rejected as being of too slight a significance, or as having too conjectural and remote a connection; others, as being dangerous, in their effect on the jury, and likely to be misused or overestimated by that body; others, as being impolitic, or unsafe on public grounds; others, on the bare ground of precedent. It is this sort of thing, as I said before, the rejection on one or another practical ground, of what is really probative, which is the characteristic thing in the law of evidence; stamping it as the child of the jury system.

Problem: A Picture Is Worth a Thousand Words

Defendant, Jack Lopinson, is charged with having secured the murder of his estranged wife, Judith, and his partner and accountant, Joseph Malito, whose bullet-ridden bodies were found early one morning in the basement office of defendant's Philadelphia restaurant, Dante's Inferno. Defendant's explanation was that the restaurant had been held up by an unknown man, who had fatally shot Judith and Joseph and wounded Lopinson.

At trial, the state calls Dr. Marvin Aronson, the County Medical Examiner, to testify to what he observed at Dante's the morning of the crime. As part of Dr. Aronson's testimony the state offers eight color slides of the crime scene. The defense objects. As part of the state's offer of proof Dr. Aronson testifies that the slides will aid him in describing to the jury the scene and the cause of death. Specifically, the state contends that the slides are offered for the following purposes:

(1) To show the scene of the murders—that is, where the murders were committed;

(2) To show the location of the dead bodies;

(3) To show the position and condition of the bodies and the posture of the bodies in relationship to other things in the room;

(4) To show the location, nature, character, and extent of the wounds inflicted and where each wound was in relationship to the other;

(5) To show the location of the points of entry of the bullets into the bodies; to show distinctly the existence of powder burns and the residue of gun powder around the wounds; to show that the injuries were to the vital parts of the bodies;

(6) To show the cause of death of the two victims—that is, to show the severity and the violence of the assault; and

(7) To aid the doctor in giving his testimony to the jury.

The defense contends that the prejudicial effect of the slides outweighs their probative worth and offers to stipulate to the cause of death. The state refuses the offered stipulation.

How should the court rule? How should the court go about deciding how to rule?

UNITED STATES v. YAHWEH BEN YAHWEH
792 F. Supp. 104 (S.D. Fla. 1992)

ROETTGER, J. ORDER. Violent crime cases are the exception in federal courts. The instant case is arguably the most violent case ever tried in a federal court: the indictment charges the sixteen defendants on trial with 14 murders by means such as beheading, stabbing, occasionally by pistol shots, plus severing of body parts such as ears to prove the worthiness of the killer. Plus, they are charged with arson of a slumbering neighborhood by molotov cocktails with the perpetrators under orders to wait outside the innocent victims' homes wearing ski masks and brandishing machetes to deter the victims from fleeing the flames.

In the course of the trial, the Government sought to introduce into evidence medical examiners' photographs of the victims. Defendants objected to the admission of these photographs into evidence on the grounds that the photographs were not relevant pursuant to Fed. R. Evid. 401 and prejudicial in effect pursuant to Fed. R. Evid. 403. Specifically, the Defendants contend that the size of the photographs, which are roughly 30 × 40 inches, were designed to inflame the passions of the jury.

The relevance of these photographs is without question. Photographs of homicide victims are relevant in showing the identity of the victim, the manner of death, the murder weapon, or any other element of the crime. In addition to identifying the victims and the means of death, the photographs in this case corroborate the testimony of witnesses, Lloyd Clark, Ricardo Woodside and Robert Rozier, whose credibility is central to the government's case.

With reference to the beating of Aston Green, Lloyd Clark testified that he "saw somebody jump on his [Aston Green's] chest." Further, Ricardo Woodside testified that there were "people jumping up and down on his chest. . . ." Government Exhibit 7 shows the outline of a footprint on the chest of Aston Green. Dr. Charles Wetli, the medical examiner who performed the autopsy on Aston Green, stated that this injury was consistent with someone jumping on the deceased's chest.

Ricardo Woodside testified concerning the decapitation of Aston Green. He estimated that he heard approximately fifteen to thirty "chops" as if a knife was coming down on flesh. He also heard the attention-riveting statement: "Damn. This blade is dull." This testimony at first seemed incredible. However, it was corroborated by Government Exhibit 9. This exhibit clearly shows that a number of "chops" were necessary for the decapitation.

Prior to the admission of Exhibits 7 & 9 in the enlarged size, this court reviewed the same photographs in the 8″ × 10″ size. The latter did not show the detail necessary to corroborate the witnesses' testimony. The footprint could not be seen clearly on the 8″ × 10″ of Exhibit 7 and the number of lacerations on the top of Aston Green's torso were not clearly visible on the 8″ × 10″ of Exhibit 9. Discussing the enlargements of Aston Green, Dr. Wetli testified, and the court concurs, that 8″ × 10″ photographs did not reveal the contusions on the deceased's face, the machete marks on the neck or the footprint on the chest. The enlarged photographs clearly show the footprint and that numerous "chops" were necessary for the decapitation.

Relevant evidence can be excluded pursuant to Fed. R. Evid. 403 if "its probative value is substantially outweighed by the danger of unfair prejudice. . . ." The subject matter of the photographs in question — decapitation, slit throat, removed ears, repeated stabbing, and gun shot wounds — is both difficult to view as well as disturbing and distasteful. However, so were the crimes alleged. Murder, particularly "murder most foul" by methods such as decapitation or stabbing and the removal of body parts, is inherently offensive. However, these exhibits are not flagrantly or deliberately gruesome depictions of the crimes.[2]

After careful review of the exhibits and the medical examiners' testimony and objections, the court found no distortion, exercised its discretion and overruled the objections.

In United States v. McRae, 593 F.2d 700 (5th Cir. 1979), the Fifth Circuit held that:

> Relevant evidence is inherently prejudicial; but it is only unfair prejudice, substantially outweighing probative value, which permits exclusion of relevant matter under Rule 403. Unless trials are to be conducted on scenarios, on unreal facts tailored and sanitized for the occasion, the application of Rule 403 must be cautious and sparing. . . . It is not designed to permit the court to "even out" the weight of evidence, to mitigate a crime. . . . Id. at 707.

Defendants argue that the gruesome or prejudicial effect of the photographs are heightened by the size of the photographs. . . . Defense counsel argued that an analytical chart could show specifically where injuries occurred and the extent of the injuries. In comparing the utility of an enlarged photograph as opposed to a chart, Dr. Wetli responded "[b]ecause the picture is much better than a diagram and my words. . . . [It] just depicts exactly what it is, what is there. . . . If you want a jury to have a true understanding of what I saw and how it matches up, not just with those marks but other photographs as well as what I presume will be other evidence entered, therefore the complete picture that is going to be given, then the pictures are extremely helpful." Further, he stated "diagrams will misstate the issue in that there is no blood and instruments and so forth; but the truth is the truth and the injuries are there."

Displaying an enlarged photograph while the medical examiner tes-

---

2. The Court notes that the Government has made an effort to limit the introduction of gruesome evidence. Although permissible under United States v. De Parias, 805 F.2d 1447 (11th Cir. 1986), the Government chose not to introduce the autopsy photographs of the decomposed body of Lyle Bellinger. The Government also represents that it has the severed ear of the victim, Raymond Kelly, but it was not offered. This is not to suggest that these would have been admissible if offered.

tified to facts illustrated in the photograph enabled all members of the jury simultaneously to follow the witness' testimony. Having seen many juries in trials struggle with a witness' presentation when 8" × 10" photographs are used, it is clearly easier for the jury to capture the substance of the testimony without straining to view the photograph. For twenty years, this court has stood by the jury box to observe as witnesses testified in front of the jury box concerning exhibits being published to the jury there. In this court's view the larger 30" × 40" pictures were the right size to illustrate and clarify the witness' testimony; in fact, even the 16" × 20" size was inadequately small by comparison.

The probative value of the enlarged autopsy photographs substantially outweighs the danger of unfair prejudice and therefore the objections to the photographs are overruled. Although enlargements may magnify certain wounds, they have by no means distorted the nature of the wounds in this case. This court has attempted to keep the photographs to about life-size. However, in certain instances larger blow ups have been permitted as necessary to illustrate the medical examiner's testimony, such as with reference to severed ears and a severed trachea and carotid artery. Even with an enlargement larger than life-size, the court found the enlargement did not distort the subject. Additionally, arguments as to size cut both ways. Photographs many times smaller than life-size do minimize the wounds inflicted, but, as was the case with the footprint in Exhibit 7, may not accurately reflect injuries which were present.

OLD CHIEF v. UNITED STATES
117 S. Ct. 644 (1997)

Justice SOUTER delivered the opinion of the Court.

Subject to certain limitations, 18 U.S.C. §922(g)(1) prohibits possession of a firearm by anyone with a prior felony conviction, which the government can prove by introducing a record of judgment or similar evidence identifying the previous offense. Fearing prejudice if the jury learns the nature of the earlier crime, defendants sometimes seek to avoid such an informative disclosure by offering to concede the fact of the prior conviction. The issue here is whether a district court abuses its discretion if it spurns such an offer and admits the full record of a prior judgment, when the name or nature of the prior offense raises the risk of a verdict tainted by improper considerations, and when the purpose of the evidence is solely to prove the element of prior conviction. We hold that it does.

In 1993, petitioner, Old Chief, was arrested after a fracas involving at least one gunshot. The ensuing federal charges included not only assault with a dangerous weapon and using a firearm in relation to a crime of violence but violation of 18 U.S.C. §922(g)(1). This statute makes it unlawful for anyone "who has been convicted in any court of, a crime punishable by imprisonment for a term exceeding one year" to "possess in or affecting commerce, any firearm. . . ."

The earlier crime charged in the indictment against Old Chief was assault causing serious bodily injury. Before trial, he moved for an order requiring the government "to refrain from mentioning—by reading the Indictment, during jury selection, in opening statement, or closing argument—and to refrain from offering into evidence or soliciting any testimony from any witness regarding the prior criminal convictions of the Defendant, except to state that the Defendant has been convicted of a crime punishable by imprisonment exceeding one (1) year." . . . He said that revealing the name and nature of his prior assault conviction would unfairly tax the jury's capacity to hold the Government to its burden of proof beyond a reasonable doubt on current charges of assault, possession, and violence with a firearm, and he offered to "solve the problem here by stipulating, agreeing and requesting the Court to instruct the jury that he has been convicted of a crime punishable by imprisonment exceeding one (1) year." App. 7. He argued that the offer to stipulate to the fact of the prior conviction rendered evidence of the name and nature of the offense inadmissible under Rule 403 of the Federal Rules of Evidence, the danger being that unfair prejudice from that evidence would substantially outweigh its probative value. He also proposed this jury instruction:

> The phrase "crime punishable by imprisonment for a term exceeding one year" generally means a crime which is a felony. The phrase does not include any state offense classified by the laws of that state as a misdemeanor and punishable by a term of imprisonment of two years or less and certain crimes concerning the regulation of business practices.
>
> [I] hereby instruct you that Defendant JOHNNY LYNN OLD CHIEF has been convicted of a crime punishable by imprisonment for a term exceeding one year. App. 11.

The Assistant United States Attorney refused to join in a stipulation, insisting on his right to prove his case his own way, and the District Court agreed, ruling orally that, "If he doesn't want to stipulate, he doesn't have to." . . . At trial, over renewed objection, the Government introduced the order of judgment and commitment for Old Chief's prior conviction. This document disclosed that on December 18, 1988, he "did knowingly and unlawfully assault Rory Dean Fenner, said assault resulting in serious bodily injury," for which Old Chief was sentenced to five years' imprisonment. . . . The jury found Old Chief guilty on all counts, and he appealed.

The Ninth Circuit addressed the point with brevity: "Regardless of the defendant's offer to stipulate, the government is entitled to prove a prior felony offense through introduction of probative evidence. . . . Under Ninth Circuit law, a stipulation is not proof, and, thus, it has no place in the FRE 403 balancing process. . . . Thus, we hold that the district court did not abuse its discretion by allowing the prosecution to introduce evidence of Old Chief's prior conviction to prove that element of the unlawful possession charge."

We granted Old Chief's petition for writ of certiorari because the Courts of Appeals have divided sharply in their treatment of defendants' efforts to exclude evidence of the names and natures of prior offenses in cases like this. . . . We now reverse the judgment of the Ninth Circuit.

II

A

As a threshold matter, there is Old Chief's erroneous argument that the name of his prior offense as contained in the record of conviction is irrelevant to the prior-conviction element, and for that reason inadmissible under Rule 402 of the Federal Rules of Evidence. Rule 401 defines relevant evidence as having "any tendency to make the existence of any fact that is of consequence to the determination of the action more probable or less probable than it would be without the evidence." Fed. Rule Evid. 401. To be sure, the fact that Old Chief's prior conviction was for assault resulting in serious bodily injury rather than, say, for theft was not itself an ultimate fact, as if the statute had specifically required proof of injurious assault. But its demonstration was a step on one evidentiary route to the ultimate fact, since it served to place Old Chief within a particular sub-class of offenders for whom firearms possession is outlawed by §922(g)(1). A documentary record of the conviction for that named offense was thus relevant evidence in making Old Chief's §922(g)(1) status more probable than it would have been without the evidence.

Nor was its evidentiary relevance under Rule 401 affected by the availability of alternative proofs of the element to which it went, such as an admission by Old Chief that he had been convicted of a crime "punishable by imprisonment for a term exceeding one year" within the meaning of the statute. The 1972 Advisory Committee Notes to Rule 401 make this point directly:

"The fact to which the evidence is directed need not be in dispute. While situations will arise which call for the exclusion of evidence offered to prove a point conceded by the opponent, the ruling should be made on the basis of such considerations as waste of time and undue prejudice (see Rule 403), rather than under any general requirement that evidence is admissible only if directed to matters in dispute." Advisory Committee's Notes on Fed. Rule Evid. 401.

If, then, relevant evidence is inadmissible in the presence of other evidence related to it, its exclusion must rest not on the ground that the other evidence has rendered it "irrelevant," but on its character as unfairly prejudicial, cumulative or the like, its relevance notwithstanding.

B

The principal issue is the scope of a trial judge's discretion under Rule 403, which authorizes exclusion of relevant evidence when its "probative value is substantially outweighed by the danger of unfair prejudice, confusion of the issues, or misleading the jury, or by considerations of undue delay, waste of time, or needless presentation of cumulative evidence." Fed. Rule Evid. 403. Old Chief relies on the danger of unfair prejudice.

1

The term "unfair prejudice," as to a criminal defendant, speaks to the capacity of some concededly relevant evidence to lure the factfinder into declaring guilt on a ground different from proof specific to the offense charged. . . . So, the Committee Notes to Rule 403 explain, "'Unfair prejudice' within its context means an undue tendency to suggest decision on an improper basis, commonly, though not necessarily, an emotional one." Advisory Committee's Notes on Fed. Rule Evid. 403. . . .

Such improper grounds certainly include the one that Old Chief points to here: generalizing a defendant's earlier bad act into bad character and taking that as raising the odds that he did the later bad act now charged (or, worse, as calling for preventive conviction even if he should happen to be innocent momentarily). As then-Judge Breyer put it, "Although . . . 'propensity evidence' is relevant, the risk that a jury will convict for crimes other than those charged—or that, uncertain of guilt, it will convict anyway because a bad person deserves punishment—creates a prejudicial effect that outweighs ordinary relevance." United States v. Moccia, 681 F.2d 61, 63 (CA1 1982). Justice Jackson describes how the law has handled this risk:

> Courts that follow the common-law tradition almost unanimously have come to disallow resort by the prosecution to any kind of evidence of a defendant's evil character to establish a probability of his guilt. Not that the law invests the defendant with a presumption of good character, Greer v. United States, 245

U.S. 559, 62 L. Ed. 469, 38 S. Ct. 209, but it simply closes the whole matter of character, disposition and reputation on the prosecution's case-in-chief. The state may not show defendant's prior trouble with the law, specific criminal acts, or ill name among his neighbors, even though such facts might logically be persuasive that he is by propensity a probable perpetrator of the crime. The inquiry is not rejected because character is irrelevant; on the contrary, it is said to weigh too much with the jury and to so overpersuade them as to prejudge one with a bad general record and deny him a fair opportunity to defend against a particular charge. The overriding policy of excluding such evidence, despite its admitted probative value, is the practical experience that its disallowance tends to prevent confusion of issues, unfair surprise and undue prejudice.

Michelson v. United States, 335 U.S. 469, 475-476, 93 L. Ed. 168, 69 S. Ct. 213 (1948) (footnotes omitted).

Rule of Evidence 404(b) reflects this common law tradition by addressing propensity reasoning directly: "Evidence of other crimes, wrongs, or acts is not admissible to prove the character of a person in order to show action in conformity therewith." Fed. Rule Evid. 404(b). There is, accordingly, no question that propensity would be an "improper basis" for conviction and that evidence of a prior conviction is subject to analysis under Rule 403 for relative probative value and for prejudicial risk of misuse as propensity evidence. . . .

As for the analytical method to be used in Rule 403 balancing, two basic possibilities present themselves. An item of evidence might be viewed as an island, with estimates of its own probative value and unfairly prejudicial risk the sole reference points in deciding whether the danger substantially outweighs the value and whether the evidence ought to be excluded. Or the question of admissibility might be seen as inviting further comparisons to take account of the full evidentiary context of the case as the court understands it when the ruling must be made. This second approach would start out like the first but be ready to go further. On objection, the court would decide whether a particular item of evidence raised a danger of unfair prejudice. If it did, the judge would go on to evaluate the degrees of probative value and unfair prejudice not only for the item in question but for any actually available substitutes as well. If an alternative were found to have substantially the same or greater probative value but a lower danger of unfair prejudice, sound judicial discretion would discount the value of the item first offered and exclude it if its discounted probative value were substantially outweighed by unfairly prejudicial risk. As we will explain later on, the judge would have to make these calculations with an appreciation of the offering party's need for evidentiary richness and narrative integrity in presenting a case, and the mere fact that two pieces of evidence might go to the same point would not, of course, necessarily mean that only one of them might come in. It would only mean that a judge applying Rule

403 could reasonably apply some discount to the probative value of an item of evidence when faced with less risky alternative proof going to the same point. Even under this second approach, as we explain below, a defendant's Rule 403 objection offering to concede a point generally cannot prevail over the Government's choice to offer evidence showing guilt and all the circumstances surrounding the offense.

The first understanding of the rule is open to a very telling objection. That reading would leave the party offering evidence with the option to structure a trial in whatever way would produce the maximum unfair prejudice consistent with relevance. He could choose the available alternative carrying the greatest threat of improper influence, despite the availability of less prejudicial but equally probative evidence. The worst he would have to fear would be a ruling sustaining a Rule 403 objection, and if that occurred, he could simply fall back to offering substitute evidence. This would be a strange rule. It would be very odd for the law of evidence to recognize the danger of unfair prejudice only to confer such a degree of autonomy on the party subject to temptation, and the Rules of Evidence are not so odd.

Rather, a reading of the companions to Rule 403, and of the commentaries that went with them to Congress, makes it clear that what counts as the Rule 403 "probative value" of an item of evidence, as distinct from its Rule 401 "relevance," may be calculated by comparing evidentiary alternatives. The Committee Notes to Rule 401 explicitly say that a party's concession is pertinent to the court's discretion to exclude evidence on the point conceded. Such a concession, according to the Notes, will sometimes "call for the exclusion of evidence offered to prove [a] point conceded by the opponent. . . ." Advisory Committee's Notes on Fed. Rule Evid. 401. . . . As already mentioned, the Notes make it clear that such rulings should be made not on the basis of Rule 401 relevance but on "such considerations as waste of time and undue prejudice (see Rule 403). . . ." The Notes to Rule 403 then take up the point by stating that when a court considers "whether to exclude on grounds of unfair prejudice," the "availability of other means of proof may . . . be an appropriate factor." Advisory Committee's Notes on Fed. Rule Evid. 403. . . . The point gets a reprise in the Notes to Rule 404(b), dealing with admissibility when a given evidentiary item has the dual nature of legitimate evidence of an element and illegitimate evidence of character: "No mechanical solution is offered. The determination must be made whether the danger of undue prejudice outweighs the probative value of the evidence in view of the availability of other means of proof and other facts appropriate for making a decision of this kind under 403." Advisory Committee's Notes on Fed. Rule Evid. 404. . . . Thus the notes leave no question that when Rule 403 confers discretion by providing that evidence "may" be excluded, the discretionary judgment may be informed not only by assessing an evidentiary item's twin tendencies, but by placing the result of that assessment alongside similar assessments of evidentiary alternatives. . . .

2

In dealing with the specific problem raised by §922(g)(1) and its prior-conviction element, there can be no question that evidence of the name or nature of the prior offense generally carries a risk of unfair prejudice to the defendant. That risk will vary from case to case, for the reasons already given, but will be substantial whenever the official record offered by the government would be arresting enough to lure a juror into a sequence of bad character reasoning. Where a prior conviction was for a gun crime or one similar to other charges in a pending case the risk of unfair prejudice would be especially obvious, and Old Chief sensibly worried that the prejudicial effect of his prior assault conviction, significant enough with respect to the current gun charges alone, would take on added weight from the related assault charge against him.

The District Court was also presented with alternative, relevant, admissible evidence of the prior conviction by Old Chief's offer to stipulate, evidence necessarily subject to the District Court's consideration on the motion to exclude the record offered by the Government. Although Old Chief's formal offer to stipulate was, strictly, to enter a formal agreement with the Government to be given to the jury, even without the Government's acceptance his proposal amounted to an offer to admit that the prior-conviction element was satisfied, and a defendant's admission is, of course, good evidence. See Fed. Rule Evid. 801(d)(2)(A).

Old Chief's proffered admission would, in fact, have been not merely relevant but seemingly conclusive evidence of the element. The statutory language in which the prior-conviction requirement is couched shows no congressional concern with the specific name or nature of the prior offense beyond what is necessary to place it within the broad category of qualifying felonies, and Old Chief clearly meant to admit that his felony did qualify, by stipulating "that the Government has proven one of the essential elements of the offense." As a consequence, although the name of the prior offense may have been technically relevant, it addressed no detail in the definition of the prior-conviction element that would not have been covered by the stipulation or admission. Logic, then, seems to side with Old Chief.

3

There is, however, one more question to be considered before deciding whether Old Chief's offer was to supply evidentiary value at least equivalent to what the Government's own evidence carried. In arguing that the stipulation or admission would not have carried equivalent value, the Government invokes the familiar, standard rule that the prosecution is entitled to prove its case by evidence of its own choice, or, more exactly, that a criminal defendant may not stipulate or admit his way out of the full evidentiary force of the case as the government chooses to present it. The authority usually cited for this rule is Parr v. United States, 255 F.2d 86 (CA5), cert. denied, 358 U.S. 824, 3 L. Ed. 2d 64, 79 S. Ct. 40 (1958), in which the Fifth Circuit explained that the "reason for the rule is to permit a party 'to present to the jury a picture of the events relied upon. To substitute for such a picture a naked admission might have the effect to rob the evidence of much of its fair and legitimate weight.'" 255 F.2d at 88 (quoting Dunning v. Maine Central R. Co., 91 Me. 87, 39 A. 352, 356 (1897)).

This is unquestionably true as a general matter. The "fair and legitimate weight" of conventional evidence showing individual thoughts and acts amounting to a crime reflects the fact that making a case with testimony and tangible things not only satisfies the formal definition of an offense, but tells a colorful story with descriptive richness. Unlike an abstract premise, whose force depends on going precisely to a particular step in a course of reasoning, a piece of evidence may address any number of separate elements, striking hard just because it shows so much at once; the account of a shooting that establishes capacity and causation may tell just as much about the triggerman's motive and intent. Evidence thus has force beyond any linear scheme of reasoning, and as its pieces come together a narrative gains momentum, with power not only to support conclusions but to sustain the willingness of jurors to draw the inferences, whatever they may be, necessary to reach an honest verdict. This persuasive power of the concrete and particular is often essential to the capacity of jurors to satisfy the obligations that the law places on them. Jury duty is usually unsought and sometimes resisted, and it may be as difficult for one juror suddenly to face the findings that can send another human being to prison, as it is for another to hold out conscientiously for acquittal. When a juror's duty does seem hard, the evidentiary account of what a defendant has thought and done can accomplish what no set of abstract statements ever could, not just to prove a fact but to establish its human significance, and so to implicate the law's moral underpinnings and a juror's obligation to sit in judgment. Thus, the prosecution may fairly seek to place its evidence before the jurors, as much to tell a story of guiltiness as to support an inference of guilt, to convince the jurors that a guilty verdict would be morally reasonable as much as to point to the discrete elements of a defendant's legal fault. ....

But there is something even more to the prosecution's interest in resisting efforts to replace the evidence of its choice with admissions and stipulations, for beyond the power of conventional evidence to support allegations and give life to the moral underpinnings of law's claims, there lies the need for evidence in all its particularity to satisfy the jurors' expectations about what proper proof should be. Some such demands they bring with them to the courthouse, assuming, for example, that a charge of using a firearm to commit an offense will be proven by introducing a gun in evidence. A prosecutor who fails to produce one, or some good reason for his failure, has something to be concerned about. "If [jurors'] expectations are not satisfied, triers of fact may penalize the party who disappoints them by drawing a negative inference against that party." Saltzburg, A Special Aspect of Relevance: Countering Negative Inferences Associated with the Absence of Evidence, 66 Calif. L. Rev. 1011, 1019 (1978) (footnotes omitted). Expectations may also arise in jurors' minds simply from the experience of a trial itself. The use of witnesses to describe a train of events naturally related can raise the prospect of learning about every ingredient of that natural sequence the same way. If suddenly the prosecution presents some occurrence in the series differently, as by announcing a stipulation or admission, the effect may be like saying, "never mind what's behind the door," and jurors may well wonder what they are being kept from knowing. A party seemingly responsible for cloaking something has reason for apprehension, and the prosecution with its burden of proof may prudently demur at a defense request to interrupt the flow of evidence telling the story in the usual way.

In sum, the accepted rule that the prosecution is entitled to prove its case free from any defendant's option to stipulate the evidence away rests on good sense. A syllogism is not a story, and a naked proposition in a courtroom may be no match for the robust evidence that would be used to prove it. People who hear a story interrupted by gaps of abstraction may be puzzled at the missing chapters, and jurors asked to rest a momentous decision on the story's truth can feel put upon at being asked to take responsibility knowing that more could be said than they have heard. A convincing tale can be told with economy, but when economy becomes a break in the natural sequence of narrative evidence, an assurance that the missing link is really there is never more than second best.

4

This recognition that the prosecution with its burden of persuasion needs evidentiary depth to tell a continuous story has, however, virtually no application when the point at issue is a defendant's legal status, dependent on some judgment rendered wholly independently of the concrete events of later criminal behavior charged against him. As in this case, the choice of evidence for such an element is usually not between eventful narrative and abstract proposition, but between propositions of slightly varying abstraction, either a record saying that conviction for some crime occurred at a certain time or a statement admitting the same thing without naming the particular offense. The issue of substituting one statement for the other normally arises only when the record of conviction would not be admissible for any purpose beyond proving status, so that excluding it would not deprive the prosecution of evidence with multiple utility; if, indeed, there were a justification for receiving evidence of the nature of prior acts on some issue other than status (i.e., to prove "motive, opportunity, intent, prepation, plan, knowledge, identity, or absence of mistake or accident," Fed. Rule Evid. 404(b)), Rule 404(b) guarantees the opportunity to seek its admission. Nor can it be argued that the events behind the prior conviction are proper nourishment for the jurors' sense of obligation to vindicate the public interest. The issue is not whether concrete details of the prior crime should come to the jurors' attention but whether the name or general character of that crime is to be disclosed. Congress, however, has made it plain that distinctions among generic felonies do not count for this purpose; the fact of the qualifying conviction is alone what matters under the statute. . . . The most the jury needs to know is that the conviction admitted by the defendant falls within the class of crimes that Congress thought should bar a convict from possessing a gun, and this point may be made readily in a defendant's admission and underscored in the court's jury instructions. Finally, the most obvious reason that the general presumption that the prosecution may choose its evidence is so remote from application here is that proof of the defendant's status goes to an element entirely outside the natural sequence of what the defendant is charged with thinking and doing to commit the current offense. Proving status without telling exactly why that status was imposed leaves no gap in the story of a defendant's subsequent criminality, and its demonstration by stipulation or admission neither displaces a chapter from a continuous sequence of conventional evidence nor comes across as an officious substitution, to confuse or offend or provoke reproach.

Given these peculiarities of the element of felony-convict status and of admissions and the like when used to prove it, there is no cognizable difference between the evidentiary significance of an admission and of the legitimately probative component of the official record the prosecution would prefer to place in evidence. For purposes of the Rule 403 weighing of the probative against the prejudicial, the functions of the competing evidence are distinguishable only by the risk inherent in the one and wholly absent from the other. In this case, as in any other in which the prior conviction is for an offense likely to support conviction on some improper ground, the only reasonable conclusion was that the risk of unfair prejudice did substantially outweigh the discounted probative value of the record of conviction, and it was an abuse of discretion to admit the record when an admission was available. What we have said shows why this will be the general rule when proof of convict status is at issue, just as the prosecutor's choice will generally survive a Rule 403 analysis when a defendant seeks to force the substitution of an admission for evidence creating a coherent narrative of his thoughts and actions in perpetrating the offense for which he is being tried.

The judgment is reversed, and the case is remanded to the Ninth Circuit for further proceedings consistent with this opinion.

Justice O'CONNOR, with whom The Chief Justice, Justice SCALIA, and Justice THOMAS join, dissenting.

The Court today announces a rule that misapplies Federal Rule of Evidence 403 and upsets, without explanation, longstanding precedent regarding criminal prosecutions. I do not agree that the Government's introduction of evidence that reveals the name and basic nature of a defendant's prior felony conviction in a prosecution brought under 18 U.S.C. §922(g)(1) "unfairly" prejudices the defendant within the meaning of Rule 403. Nor do I agree with the Court's newly minted rule that a defendant charged with violating §922(g)(1) can force the Government to accept his concession to the prior conviction element of that offense, thereby precluding the Government from offering evidence on this point. I therefore dissent.

I

Rule 403 provides that a district court may exclude relevant evidence if, among other things, "its probative value is substantially outweighed by the danger of unfair prejudice." Certainly, Rule 403 does not permit the court to exclude the Government's evidence simply because it may hurt the defendant. As a threshold matter, evidence is excludable only if it is "unfairly" prejudicial, in that it has "an undue tendency to suggest decision on an improper basis." Advisory Committee's Note on Fed. Rule Evid. 403. . . . The evidence tendered by the Government in this case — the order reflecting petitioner's prior conviction and sentence for assault resulting in serious bodily injury, in violation of 18 U.S.C. §1153 and 18 U.S.C. §113(f) — directly proved a necessary element of the §922(g)(1) offense, that is, that petitioner had committed a crime covered by §921(a)(20). Perhaps petitioner's case was damaged when the jury discovered that he previously had committed a felony and heard the name of his crime. But I cannot agree with the Court that it was unfairly prejudicial for the Government to establish an essential element of its case against petitioner with direct proof of his prior conviction.

The structure of §922(g)(1) itself shows that Congress envisioned jurors' learning the name and basic nature of the defendant's prior offense. Congress enacted §922(g)(1) to prohibit the possession of a firearm by any person convicted of "a crime punishable by imprisonment for a term exceeding one year." Section 922(g)(1) does not merely prohibit the possession of firearms by "felons," nor does it apply to all prior felony convictions. Rather, the statute excludes from §922(g)(1)'s coverage certain business crimes and state misdemeanors punishable by imprisonment of two years or less. §921(a)(20). Within the meaning of §922(g)(1), then, "a crime" is not an abstract or metaphysical concept. Rather, the Government must prove that the defendant committed a particular crime. In short, under §922(g)(1), a defendant's prior felony conviction connotes not only that he is a prior felon, but also that he has engaged in specific past criminal conduct.

Even more fundamentally, in our system of justice, a person is not simply convicted of "a crime" or "a felony." Rather, he is found guilty of a specified offense, almost always because he violated a specific statutory prohibition. For example, in the words of the order that the Government offered to prove petitioner's prior conviction in this case, petitioner "did knowingly and unlawfully assault Rory Dean Fenner, said assault resulting in serious bodily injury, in violation of Title 18 U.S.C. §§1153 and 113(f)."... That a variety of crimes would have satisfied the prior conviction element of the §922(g)(1) offense does not detract from the fact that petitioner committed a specific offense. The name and basic nature of petitioner's crime are inseparable from the fact of his earlier conviction and were therefore admissible to prove petitioner's guilt. ...

The Court never explains precisely why it constitutes "unfair" prejudice for the Government to directly prove an essential element of the §922(g)(1) offense with evidence that reveals the name or basic nature of the defendant's prior conviction. It simply notes that such evidence may lead a jury to conclude that the defendant has a propensity to commit crime, thereby raising the odds that the jury would find that he committed the crime with which he is currently charged. With a nod to the part of Rule 404(b) that says "evidence of other crimes, wrongs, or acts is not admissible to prove the character of a person in order to show action in conformity therewith," the Court writes:

"There is, accordingly, no question that propensity is an 'improper basis' for conviction and that evidence of a prior conviction is subject to analysis for probative value and for prejudicial risk of misuse as propensity evidence."

A few pages later, it leaps to the conclusion that there can be "no question that evidence of the name or nature of the prior offense carries a risk of unfair prejudice to the defendant."

Yes, to be sure, Rule 404(b) provides that "evidence of other crimes, wrongs, or acts is not admissible to prove the character of a person in order to show action in conformity therewith." But Rule 404(b) does not end there. It expressly contemplates the admission of evidence of prior crimes for other purposes, "such as proof of motive, opportunity, intent, preparation, plan, knowledge, identity, or absence of mistake or accident." The list is plainly not exhaustive, and where, as here, a prior conviction is an element of the charged offense, neither Rule 404(b) nor Rule 403 can bar its admission. The reason is simple: In a prosecution brought under §922(g)(1), the Government does not submit evidence of a past crime to prove the defendant's bad character or to "show action in conformity therewith." It tenders the evidence as direct proof of a necessary element of the offense with which it has charged the defendant. To say, as the Court does, that it "unfairly" prejudices the defendant for the Government to establish its §922(g)(1) case with evidence showing that, in fact, the defendant did commit a prior offense misreads the Rules of Evidence and defies common sense. . . .

II

The Court also holds that, if a defendant charged with violating §922(g)(1) concedes his prior felony conviction, a district court abuses its discretion if it admits evidence of the defendant's prior crime that raises the risk of a verdict "tainted by improper considerations.". . . Left unexplained is what, exactly, it was about the order introduced by the Government at trial that might cause a jury to decide the case improperly. The order offered into evidence (which the Court nowhere in its opinion sets out) stated, in relevant part:

> And the defendant having been convicted on his plea of guilty of the offense charged in Count II of the indictment in the above-entitled cause, to-wit: That on or about the 18th day of December 1988, at Browning, in the State and District of Montana, and on and within the exterior boundaries of the Blackfeet Indian Reservation, being Indian country, JOHNNY LYNN OLD CHIEF, an Indian person, did knowingly and unlawfully assault Rory Dean Fenner, said assault resulting in serious bodily injury, in violation of Title 18 U.S.C. §§1153 and 113(f).

The order went on to say that petitioner was sentenced for a term of 60 months' imprisonment, to be followed by two years of supervised release.

Why, precisely, does the Court think that this item of evidence raises the risk of a verdict "tainted by improper considerations"? Is it because the jury might learn that petitioner assaulted someone and caused serious bodily injury? If this is what the Court means, would evidence that petitioner had committed some other felony be admissible, and if so, what sort of crime might that me? Or does the Court object to the order because it gave a few specifics about the assault, such as the date, the location, and the victim's name? Or perhaps the Court finds that introducing the order risks a verdict "tainted by improper considerations" simply because the §922(g)(1) charge was joined with counts charging petitioner with using a firearm in relation to a crime of violence, in violation of 18 U.S.C. §924(c), and with committing an assault with a dangerous weapon, in violation of 18 U.S.C. §1153 and 18 U.S.C. §113(c)(1988 ed.)? Under the Court's nebulous standard for admission of prior felony evidence in a §922(g)(1) prosecution, these are open questions.

More troubling still is the Court's retreat from the fundamental principle that in a criminal prosecution the Government may prove its case as it sees fit. . . . A jury is as likely to be puzzled by the "missing chapter" resulting from a defendant's stipulation to his prior felony conviction as it would be by the defendant's conceding any other element of the crime. . . . It may well be that the prosecution needs "evidentiary depth to tell a continuous story" in order to prove its case in a way a jury will accept. . . . But that is by no means the only or the most important reason that a defendant may not oblige the Government to accept his concession to an element of the charged offense. The Constitution requires a criminal conviction to rest upon a jury determination that the defendant is guilty of every element of the crime of which he is charged beyond a reasonable doubt. . . . Further, a defendant's tactical decision not to contest an essential element of the crime does not remove the prosecution's burden to prove that element. . . . At trial, a defendant may thus choose to contest the Government's proof on every element; or he may concede some elements and contest others; or he may do nothing at all. Whatever his choice, the Government still carries the burden of proof beyond a reasonable doubt on each element.

It follows from these principles that a defendant's stipulation to an element of an offense does not remove that element from the jury's consideration. The usual instruction regarding stipulations in a criminal case reflects as much: "When the attorneys on both sides stipulate or agree as to the existence of a fact, you may accept the stipulation as evidence and regard that fact as proved. You are not required to do so, however, since you are the sole judge of the facts.". . . Obviously, we are not dealing with a stipulation here. A stipulation is an agreement, and no agreement was reached between petitioner and the Government in this case. Does the Court think a different rule applies when the defendant attempts to stipulate, over the Government's objection, to an element of the charged offense? . . . Because the Government bears the burden of proof on every element of a charged offense, it must be accorded substantial leeway to submit evidence of its choosing to prove its case. . . .

The Court manufactures a new rule that, in a §922(g)(1) case, a defendant can force the Government to accept his admission to the prior felony conviction element of the offense, thereby precluding the Government from offering evidence to directly prove a necessary element of its case. I cannot agree that it "unfairly" prejudices a defendant for the Government to prove his prior conviction with evidence that reveals the name of basic nature of his past crime. Like it or not, Congress chose to make a defendant's prior criminal conviction one of the two elements of the §922(g)(1) offense. Moreover, crimes have names; a defendant is not convicted of some indeterminate, unspecified "crime." Nor do I think that Federal Rule of Evidence 403 can be read to obviate the well accepted principle, grounded in both the Constitution and in our precedent, that the Government may not be forced to accept a defendant's concession to an element of a charged offense as proof of that element. I respectfully dissent.

Problem: Photos of the Decedent

EVANSVILLE SCHOOL CORP. v. PRICE 208 N.E.2d 689 (Ind. 1965): This action was commenced by Alfred Price, father of Alfred Lee Price (deceased), against the Evansville School Corporation, to recover damages for wrongful death allegedly sustained as the result of the decedent, Alfred Lee Price, being injured while a spectator attending a baseball game at Bosse Field in the City of Evansville, Indiana. The boy, age 11, was struck on the head with a baseball on May 27, 1960, and died as a result of said injuries on May 29, 1960. . . .

At the trial the appellee offered in evidence a color photograph depicting the deceased youth lying in his casket, after preparation by a mortician, and prior to internment. The photograph shows the white satin interior of the casket and that portion of the body exposed to public view. The decedent's face bears a deep tan, and he is clothed in a white sport coat and a blue shirt open at the neck. The photograph is not gruesome, nor does it depict any physical markings, wounds, defects or other bodily abnormalities. The appellant objected to the admission of the photo.

How would you argue the relevancy and admissibility, or the irrelevancy and inadmissibility, of the photograph? How should the court rule?

E.   Problems in Circumstantial Proof

Problem: Silk Stockings

PEOPLE v. ADAMSON, 27 Cal. 2d 478, 165 P.2d 3 (1946), Aff'd, 332 U.S. 46 (1947): [Defendant was charged with murder and burglary. He pleaded not guilty and was tried and convicted of murder and one count of burglary. The defendant did not testify at trial and produced no witnesses.]

The body of Stella Blauvelt, 64 years of age, was found on the floor of her Los Angeles apartment on July 25, 1944. The evidence indicated that she died on the afternoon of the preceding day. . . .

[The defendant admitted that Stella Blauvelt was murdered but contended that the evidence was not sufficient to identify him as the perpetrator.]

The tops of three women's stockings identified as having been taken from defendant's room were admitted in evidence. . . . The stocking parts were not all of the same color. At the end of each part, away from what was formerly the top of the stocking, a knot or knots were tied. When the body of the deceased was found, it did not have on any shoes or stockings. There was evidence that on the day of the murder the deceased had been wearing stockings. The lower part of a silk stocking with the top part torn off was found lying on the floor under the body. No part of the other stocking was found. There were other stockings in the apartment, some hanging in the kitchen and some in drawers in a dressing alcove, but no other parts of stockings were found. None of the stocking tops from defendant's room matched with the bottom part of the stocking found under the body. . . .

How should you go about analyzing the relevance of the stocking evidence in this case? What methodology should you employ in deciding relevance in general?

Suppose that the prosecution rests its case after proving the discovery and condition of the body and introducing the stocking evidence, over the defendant's objection. Defendant then moves for a directed verdict. If the court grants defendant's motion, are the rulings on the admissibility of the stocking evidence and the motion for a directed verdict compatible? Consider the court's opinion:

To be admissible, evidence must tend to prove a material issue in the light of human experience. The stocking tops found in defendant's room were relevant to identify defendant because their presence on his dresser and in a drawer thereof among other articles of wearing apparel with a knot or knots tied in the end away from what was formerly the top of the stocking indicates that defendant had some use for women's stocking tops. This interest in women's stocking tops is a circumstance that tends to identify defendant as the person who removed the stockings from the victim and took away the top of one and the whole of the other. Although the presence of the stocking tops in defendant's room was not by itself sufficient to identify defendant as the criminal, it constituted a logical link in the chain of evidence. Evidence that tends to throw light on a fact in dispute may be admitted. The weight to be given such evidence will be determined by the jury. (the jury finder)

It is contended that the admission of the stocking tops deprived defendant of a fair trial and therefore denied him due process of law.

The judgments and the order denying a new trial are affirmed.

Evidence concerning the defendant carries with it a greater risk of prejudice than evidence from the scene of the crime. Even though the stocking tops do not match the bottoms, they tend to show that the defendant had a use for stocking tops. Apparently, so did the killer. A person investigating this crime would clearly be interested in the stocking tops found in the defendant's room. In Rule 401's terminology, the presence of the stocking tops makes it more likely that Adamson was the killer than had the stockings not been found. Thus, the evidence is relevant. The problem is that the evidence may seem much more relevant than it is, and therefore may be prejudicial.

Two points can be made about the risk of overvaluing evidence about the defendant. First, a trial differs in a crucial way from an investigation. At the outset of an investigation, everyone is suspect. The investigation consists of a process of narrowing down the universe of suspects. It involves false starts and blind alleys. If successful, the investigation narrows to a single person, who is prosecuted. By contrast, at the outset of a trial there is only one suspect, the defendant. Evidence concerning the defendant that appears to connect him to the scene may seem to be more significant than it really is because it appears in a context that excludes the rest of the possible suspects. This is much less true for evidence found at the scene of the crime, and therefore the relevance of evidence at the scene of the crime is subjected to much less rigorous scrutiny than evidence concerning the defendant. Put another way, evidence from the scene of the crime would come to the attention of anyone who was trying to figure out what happened. Evidence about the defendant may come to the attention of the factfinder only because the defendant has been selected by the prosecutor as the person to be charged.

Second, questions about the foundation necessary to make evidence admissible are directly related to questions about how much we are willing to rely on the corrective nature of the adversary process to ensure that evidence is accorded its proper probative value. For example, once convinced that the stocking tops were minimally relevant under a Rule

401 standard, the judge could leave it to the defense to fill out the context to offset any tendencies of the evidence to mislead. But this subjects the process, perhaps unnecessarily and unwisely, to risks of inadequate defense representation.

Is the potential for prejudice in the admission of the stocking tops found in the defendant's room diminished (or their probativeness increased) if the prosecution also offers proof that the defendant's fingerprints were found on the windowsill of Stella's apartment?

Note that *Adamson*, in the Supreme Court of the United States, became the vehicle for Justice Black's first great incorporation opinion.

Problem: Seven T-Shirts

D was charged with having committed an assault in Langley Park, a Baltimore suburb, on June 11, 1966. He was arrested in November 1966 and brought to trial in May 1967. At trial, the victim testified that he had been assaulted in Langley Park by a man wearing a tight black ski mask who emitted a strong, unpleasant body odor. The arresting officer testified that at the time of arrest, *D* was wearing seven T-shirts, each dirtier and smellier than the one before. The prosecution offered the seven T-shirts into evidence.

Should *D*'s objection to this evidence be sustained? Are the T-shirts admissible? What is their relevance? If there were no additional evidence beyond that set forth above, should the judge direct a verdict in favor of the defendant?

Problem: Bombs, Bats, and Hammers

Consider these three cases together. Is the offered evidence relevant in any of them? Should it be admitted? Should its admission depend on anything else?

(1) Charge: assault with intent to commit murder. The state introduces evidence that the victim began to open an inner screen door of his trailer and an explosion took place. The state also introduces evidence that *D* had borrowed a clothespin from his friend the day before the explosion. The prosecution calls an expert on bombs and offers to have the expert testify using a model bomb to illustrate how a triggering device could detonate a charge of dynamite. The triggering device used in the model is a clothespin. The expert will testify that a clothespin was only one of a number of devices that might have been used to trigger the bomb and that the expert did not know what device was actually used. The expert will testify that a clothespin was used for the model only because it was easily available. *D* objects to the expert's use of the

model and of the clothespin trigger and explains that he used the borrowed clothespin to attach a map to his car's dashboard. (When D was arrested in his car, a map was attached to the dashboard in this manner.)

(2) Charge: murder in the first degree. M.O.: battering the victim with a blunt instrument. The state's evidence establishes that the victim had over 20 fresh wounds on his body, some of which were consistent with injury inflicted by a blunt instrument such as a baseball bat or rolling pin, others that could have been made by the claws of a hammer, and some by the rounded head of a hammer. The murder occurred in the home shared by D and the victim. W, a friend of the defendant, testifies that, on the day the beating occurred, she found a baseball bat and a hammer under the bed in the room in which the body was found. W also testifies that she saw another person bring a second bat from the rear of the house to the bedroom. Both bats and the hammer had been removed from the house and disposed of by other persons. The prosecution produces a bat and a hammer. W testifies that they closely resemble the ones she found under the bed. The prosecutor offers the bat and hammer in evidence. D objects that the items are irrelevant and unduly prejudicial.

(3) Charge: murder in the first degree. M.O.: blows to the head during an alleged attempted robbery. A pathologist testifies that death was caused by chop wounds to the skull and brain from some sharp and heavy instrument such as a hatchet or meat cleaver. No murder weapon was found.

D was employed as a construction worker on a cleanup crew. The construction job involved dry-wall construction, in which a dry-wall hammer is generally used. Such a hammer has one round flat surface and one very sharp hatchet-like edge. The prosecution offers evidence that the victim's wounds could have been caused by blows from a dry-wall hammer. It was never shown that D ever had a dry-wall hammer, but a framing hammer was found in D's car. The prosecutor borrows a dry-wall hammer from a worker in the courthouse. This hammer is identified, shown to the jury, and offered as evidence on the theory that it is illustrative of the testimony of various witnesses. D objects on grounds of irrelevancy and prejudice.

The evidence of these problems is fundamentally different from the direct testimonial evidence of a witness on the stand and the "real" evidence in *Adamson, Stone,* and the T-shirt case. The clothespin, baseball bat, and hammer are all "demonstrative" evidence. (Wigmore proposed "autoptic profferance" as the more precisely descriptive term for such evidence.) In each case, there is no contention that the exhibit was actually used in the commission of the crime, or that the defendant had any connection with such evidence. Admission of such evidence thus must rest on some theory different from that used to admit the stocking tops, condoms, and T-shirts. The theory that supports the admission of this kind of evidence is that it aids the witness in describing what the witness saw or in explaining what happened.

The key issue usually is what foundation must be laid before use of the evidentiary aid will be allowed. Such exhibits can create a big impression on jurors, who may lose sight of the fact that the exhibit was not actually used in the real event.

How much leeway should a party have in choosing whether to prove a fact with a picture, a demonstration, or a real object when the testimony of a competent witness could prove the same? Recall the *Lopinson* case. When is real evidence necessary to prove a fact? What is the effect of choosing one form of proof over another?

These questions involve sensitive considerations of probative value, prejudice, reliability, and, often, strategic choice. By and large, our adversary system employs a free market approach to the choice of evidence: Parties are free to prove a fact with any kind of evidence they like. But this free market is restrained by various rules of exclusion that limit parties' choice in certain circumstances. The rule requiring the production of the original document in certain cases (Rule 1002) is one example. Why do we have such a system? What are its advantages and disadvantages? An alternative system would contain a master list of types of evidence with a hierarchy of preference. In each case, the "higher" or "better" type of evidence would have to be used. This, no doubt, would promote certainty, but at great cost.

Problem: Flight as Circumstantial Evidence

Charge: murder. The state offers evidence that, prior to her arrest, *D* attempted to flee and conceal her identity. This evidence is offered on the theory that it constitutes proof of *D*'s consciousness of guilt. *D* objects on the ground of irrelevancy and offers to prove that the more plausible inferences to be drawn from her attempted flight were her belief that a warrant for her arrest on an unrelated charge was outstanding, her fear of being arrested for narcotics hidden in her car, and the fact that she had violated her parole.

Disregarding any hearsay problems, which are discussed further in the chapter on hearsay, should the evidence be admitted?

Problem: Non-Flight as Circumstantial Evidence

Charge: robbery. *D* offers evidence that while being transported before trial from one city to another, he and the transporting officer stopped at a restaurant for a meal. *D*'s handcuffs were removed, but he made no attempt to flee. The prosecutor objects on the grounds of irrelevancy. *D* contends that failure to flee when an opportunity is presented is proof of an innocent frame of mind that, in turn, leads to an inference that he had acted in conformity with that state of mind and had not committed the offense charged.

Should the evidence be admitted? Is it relevant? What is the standard of probative worth that evidence must meet to be admissible?

These problems present situations where evidence connected with the individual singled out for suspicion, rather than evidence found at the scene of the crime or connected to the scene, is used to link the individual with the crime. In addition (and unlike the problems in the previous section where the evidence was tangible), these problems require the factfinder to delve inside the mind of the accused to make the link between the individual's state of mind and his or her actions.

In the flight case, the chain of inferences that must be made for the evidence to be relevant is the following: The accused departed suddenly and unexpectedly, and therefore she fled; the defendant fled because she was conscious of her guilt and afraid of being apprehended; the defendant was conscious of her guilt and afraid of being apprehended because she was guilty. These inferences may not be valid in every case. A sudden and unexpected departure may be for reasons other than flight from a crime. Even if a person flees from the scene of a crime, it may not be because she thinks herself to be guilty. She may be afraid that she will be unjustly accused. Or she may not want to get involved as a witness. And even if the person flees because she thinks she is guilty, the person may in fact not be guilty under the law. Moreover, flight looks bad. There is a strong possibility that the jury may make all the connections in the chain of inferences and regard the evidence of flight as more probative of guilt than it really is. In fact, it is possible that evidence of flight may be enough to eliminate a large area of doubt that would otherwise have resulted in a verdict of acquittal.

UNITED STATES v. SILVERMAN
861 F.2d 571 (9th Cir. 1988)

ALARCON, Circuit Judge:

David Silverman appeals from his conviction for conspiracy to distribute a controlled substance (cocaine), possession with intent to distribute a controlled substance (cocaine), interstate travel in aid of racketeering, and aiding and abetting. . . .

[H]e contends that the district court erred in instructing the jury that a defendant's concealment of his identity from government agents would support an inference of guilt of the charged offenses. He asserts that because the concealment in this case occurred two months after the last act committed in the course of the alleged conspiracy and because the agents did not disclose the charges against him, no inference of guilt is justified. . . .

[The prosecution's case consisted primarily of the testimony of Willard, under a plea agreement, that he had purchased cocaine from the defendant's sister, Pearl, on three occasions in May and June 1983. Willard testified that each of these purchases involved private airplane flights from Reno to Van Nuys, California with Pearl. Upon landing, Pearl would make a phone call, arrange for a cab from the airport, and return to the airport in a few hours with the cocaine. On one of these occasions, Willard testified, Pearl returned to the airport in a car driven by a man who looked like the defendant. Cab company records corroborated that Pearl had taken cabs on the dates in question to locations at or near her brother David Silverman's residence in Woodland Hills.]

The final piece of evidence relied upon by the Government to connect David Silverman to the conspiracy was his evasive conduct when three agents of the Drug Enforcement Administration (DEA) called at his home. One of the DEA agents testified that on August 23, 1983, at about 4:00 P.M., she and her fellow officers knocked on the door of the residence at 22601 Waterbury, Woodland Hills, California. David Silverman opened the door in response. The officers identified themselves as DEA agents and stated that they wanted to ask David Silverman some questions. Although the DEA agents knew that a warrant for the arrest of David Silverman had been issued, they did not then disclose this information to him. The man at the door replied that David Silverman was not home. The DEA agents left a phone number, requesting that David Silverman be informed that he should contact one of them when he returned.

Soon thereafter, the DEA agents were advised through a radio transmission that someone at 22601 Waterbury had contacted the DEA office. The DEA agents returned to the residence. David Silverman again appeared at the door. He falsely identified himself, claiming to be Jim Walker. The DEA agents then, for the first time, disclosed "that there was a warrant for Mr. Silverman's arrest." The DEA agents then stated that David Silverman should contact the DEA as soon as possible. The record contains no evidence that the DEA agents ever informed David Silverman of the charges contained in the warrant or the relationship of the alleged crimes to his sister or to violations of the narcotics laws.

As the DEA agents were driving away from the area, their supervisor contacted them by radio and stated that an attorney had advised him that David Silverman was willing to turn himself in at a later date. David

Silverman surrendered voluntarily two days later. As a result of his voluntary surrender, the district court reduced the bail by two-thirds. . . .

Flight instructions* are valid only if there is evidence sufficient to support a chain of unbroken inferences from the defendant's behavior to the defendant's guilt of the crime charged. The Fifth Circuit has described this requirement clearly, explaining that four inferences must be justified: "(1) from the defendant's behavior to flight; (2) from flight to consciousness of guilt; (3) from consciousness of guilt to consciousness of guilt concerning the crime charged; and (4) from consciousness of guilt concerning the crime charged to actual guilt of the crime charged." United States v. Myers, 550 F.2d 1036, 1049 (5th Cir. 1977), cert. denied, 439 U.S. 847, 99 S. Ct. 147, 58 L. Ed. 2d 149 (1978). . . .

The inference from proof of an unfocused consciousness of guilt to consciousness of guilt concerning the crime charged has proven especially problematic. Flight and concealment of identity can be consistent with innocence, or with guilt of misconduct unknown to the Government. Accordingly, we must evaluate flight instructions by looking for facts that support the inference from flight to a consciousness of guilt of the specific crime charged. For example, we consider whether the defendant knew the police suspected him of a particular crime. We also consider whether the defendant fled immediately after the crime.

Under the totality of the circumstances in the present case, we find that it was error to give an instruction on flight. David Silverman's concealment of his identity lacked sufficient connection to the criminal acts for which he was charged. Although we agree with the Government that it is reasonable to infer from the fact that David Silverman concealed his identity that he was conscious that he was suspected of some wrongdoing, the Government has offered no evidence from which it can be inferred that he was conscious of guilt of any cocaine-related offense. There is no evidence in the record that David Silverman was aware of his sister's criminal conduct or that the DEA agents informed him during their visits that he was suspected of having committed any cocaine-related crime. For all the evidence shows, he might have been

---

*The trial court instructed the jury as follows:

The intentional concealment of a defendant after the commission of a crime, or after he is accused of a crime that has been committed, is not of course sufficient in itself to establish his guilt; but it is a fact which, if proved, may be considered by the jury in light of all other evidence in the case, in determining guilt or innocence. Whether or not evidence of concealment shows a consciousness of guilt, and the significance to be attached to any such evidence, are matters exclusively within the province of the jury.

In your consideration of the evidence of concealment you should consider that there are many reasons for this which are fully consistent with innocence. These may include fear of being apprehended, unwillingness to confront the police, or reluctance to appear as a witness. Let me suggest also that a feeling of guilt does not necessarily reflect actual guilt.

The jury will always bear in mind that the law never imposes upon a defendant in a criminal case the burden or duty of calling any witness or producing any evidence.

concealing his identity because he was conscious of having committed a drug-related offense unknown to the Government. Moreover, uncontradicted evidence suggests that David Silverman concealed his identity in order to make arrangements through his attorney to surrender voluntarily rather than face possible arrest at his residence. As noted above, his cooperation with the Government in surrendering voluntarily resulted in a two-thirds reduction in bail.

Further, David Silverman's concealment of his identity occurred two months after Pearl's last trip to Van Nuys and the last criminal act committed in furtherance of the alleged conspiracy. This two-month delay, coupled with the absence of any showing by the Government that David Silverman was aware of the nature of the charges against him at the time he concealed his identity, renders any inference of guilt from such concealment improper. . . .

WALLACE, J., dissenting:

. . . I must . . . dissent from the majority's holding that the district court erred in instructing the jury that it may infer guilt from Silverman's attempt to conceal his identity from the DEA agents who attempted to question him at his home. The majority concludes that Silverman's concealment of his identity lacked sufficient connection to the criminal acts with which he was charged for a jury to infer his guilt. I disagree. I do not believe we have held, as the majority suggests, either that a defendant's attempt at concealment must immediately follow his last criminal act or that a defendant must be aware of the particular charges against him. Rather, our cases indicate that we have used a more flexible approach in determining whether the defendant's behavior supports an inference of guilt. In so holding, we have also flatly rejected the argument that the government must prove that the defendant was "aware of the crime for which he was sought." I see no need to depart from this "totality of the circumstances" approach in the case before us. There was sufficient evidence that Silverman's evasive conduct was prompted by fear of apprehension for the jury to infer his guilt. The jury was properly instructed and could determine whether the inference should be drawn in light of the other evidence before it.

Moreover, even if we were (mistakenly, I suggest) to adopt a test requiring either "immediate" evasive conduct or a showing that the defendant had some knowledge that he was suspected of criminal activity that prompted his arrest, I believe that such a test has been satisfied here. While it is true that Silverman did not attempt to conceal his identity until two months after Pearl's last trip to Van Nuys, this fact does not necessarily indicate that an "immediacy" test is not met in the present case. Silverman had no reason to conceal his identity at the time of that transaction — the drug enforcement agents did not approach him at that time and he had no reason to fear that he was suspected of involvement in the drug conspiracy. However, Silverman did "immedi-

ately" attempt to conceal his identity when questioned by drug enforcement agents at his residence. Silverman instinctively reacted to the
possibility of apprehension by concealing his identity, which is all that
is required to demonstrate "immediacy."

In addition, the majority's assertion that Silverman's attempt at concealment occurred after a "two-month delay" is erroneous. Silverman
was not charged merely with isolated acts of supplying cocaine. He was
charged with an ongoing conspiracy. It is difficult to ascertain when his
"last criminal act" occurred. Where, as here, the "criminal act" is an
ongoing affair, an act of concealment which occurs during or within a
reasonable time after the conspiracy and which is directed toward law
enforcement agents investigating the crime clearly satisfies a requirement that the conduct be "immediate" to the crime.

I must also disagree with the majority's conclusion that no evidence
suggests that Silverman knew of the accusations against him. Silverman
did not know, to be sure, that he ultimately would be charged with
conspiring to deal cocaine in violation of federal law. It is fair to say that
most criminals are similarly ignorant about the particular charges they
will face, if caught. For this reason, it does not make sense to require
that a defendant know of the particular accusations against him as a
prerequisite to finding that his evasive conduct supports an inference
of guilt of the crime charged. Rather, it is sufficient that the defendant
have reason to believe he is suspected of the criminal activity that ultimately led to his arrest.

While it is possible, as the majority maintains, that Silverman's evasive
conduct was prompted by fear that he was suspected of some other drug-
related conduct, we have never conditioned the admissibility of flight
evidence on the government's ability to rule out every hypothetical suggested by the defendant. Every instance of flight is susceptible to more
than one interpretation. A person caught fleeing from a store or bank
in which an armed robbery has taken place is free to argue to the jury
that he was merely an innocent bystander concerned for his safety. However, the possibility that a flight has an innocent explanation has never
been a bar to its admissibility.

Applying the proper standard to the present case, it is clear that Silverman's evasive conduct was prompted by fear that he was suspected
of involvement in drug-related activities. Silverman attempted to conceal his identity the moment he had reason to believe that he was suspected of involvement in the cocaine conspiracy, that is, when the DEA
officials confronted him at his residence. It is significant that Silverman
again gave a false identity later that afternoon, after the agents left a
message with him to call the DEA to answer some questions. The agents
in question were not local police officers, but *Drug Enforcement Agency*
officials, who identified themselves as such. Their presence at Silverman's residence, their expressed interest in questioning Silverman, and

their return to his residence later that day, surely indicated to Silverman that he was suspected of involvement with illegal drugs, and by the federal government, at that.

In conclusion, Silverman's attempt to conceal his identity from DEA officers, when viewed in light of other evidence suggesting his guilt, clearly is sufficient to support the inference that Silverman was conscious of his guilt concerning the activity that led to his arrest, even under the majority's ill-advised new rule. I must therefore disagree with the majority's conclusion that the district court erred in instructing the jury that it might infer guilt from Silverman's false statements to the DEA agents.

JENKINS v. ANDERSON
447 U.S. 231 (1980)

Mr. Justice POWELL delivered the opinion of the Court.

The question in this case is whether the use of prearrest silence to impeach a defendant's credibility violates either the Fifth or the Fourteenth Amendments to the Constitution.

On August 13, 1974, the petitioner stabbed and killed Doyle Redding. The petitioner was not apprehended until he turned himself in.

The petitioner testified that his sister and her boyfriend were robbed by Redding and another man during the evening of August 12, 1974. The petitioner, who was nearby when the robbery occurred, followed the thieves a short distance and reported their whereabouts to the police. According to the petitioner's testimony, the next day he encountered Redding, who accused him of informing the police of the robbery. The petitioner stated that Redding attacked him with a knife, that the two men struggled briefly, and that the petitioner broke away. On cross-examination, the petitioner admitted that during the struggle he had tried "[t]o push that knife into [Redding] as far as [he] could," but maintained that he had acted solely in self-defense.

During the cross-examination, the prosecutor questioned the petitioner about his actions after the stabbing:

Q. And I suppose you waited for the Police to tell them what happened?
A. No, I didn't.
Q. You didn't?
A. No.
Q. I see. And how long was it after this day that you were arrested, or that you were taken into custody?

After some discussion of the date on which petitioner surrendered, the prosecutor continued:

Q. When was the first time that you reported the things that you have told us in Court today to anybody?

A. Two days after it happened.

Q. And who did you report it to?

A. To my probation officer.

Q. Well, apart from him?

A. No one.

Q. Who?

A. No one but my—

Q. (Interposing): Did you ever go to a Police Officer or to anyone else?

A. No, I didn't.

Q. As a matter of fact, it was two weeks later, wasn't it?

A. Yes. . . .

At trial the prosecutor attempted to impeach the petitioner's credibility by suggesting that the petitioner would have spoken out if he had killed in self-defense. The petitioner contends that the prosecutor's actions violated the Fifth Amendment as applied to the States through the Fourteenth Amendment. The Fifth Amendment guarantees an accused the right to remain silent during his criminal trial and prevents the prosecution from commenting on the silence of a defendant who asserts the right. Griffin v. California, 380 U.S. 609, 614 (1965). In this case, of course, the petitioner did not remain silent throughout the criminal proceedings. Instead, he voluntarily took the witness stand in his own defense.

This Court's decision in Raffel v. United States, 271 U.S. 494 (1926), recognized that the Fifth Amendment is not violated when a defendant who testifies in his own defense is impeached with his prior silence. [T]he *Raffel* Court concluded that the defendant was "subject to cross-examination impeaching his credibility just like any other witness." Grunewald v. United States, 353 U.S. 391, 420 (1957).

It can be argued that a person facing arrest will not remain silent if his failure to speak later can be used to impeach him. But the Constitution does not forbid "every government-imposed choice in the criminal process that has the effect of discouraging the exercise of constitutional rights." The "'threshold question is whether compelling the election impairs to an appreciable extent any of the policies behind the rights involved.'" Chaffin v. Stynchcombe, 412 U.S., at 32, quoting Crampton v. Ohio, decided with McGautha v. California, 402 U.S. 183, 213 (1971). The *Raffel* Court explicitly rejected the contention that the possibility of impeachment by prior silence is an impermissible burden upon the exercise of Fifth Amendment rights. "We are unable to see that the rule that [an accused who] testified . . . must testify fully, adds in any substantial manner to the inescapable embarrassment which the accused must experience in determining whether he shall testify or not." 271 U.S., at 499.

This Court similarly defined the scope of the Fifth Amendment protection in Harris v. New York, 401 U.S. 222 (1971). There the Court held that a statement taken in violation of *Miranda* may be used to impeach a defendant's credibility. Rejecting the contention that such impeachment violates the Fifth Amendment, the Court said: "Every criminal defendant is privileged to testify in his own defense, or to refuse to do so. But that privilege cannot be construed to include the right to commit perjury. . . . Having voluntarily taken the stand, petitioner was under an obligation to speak truthfully and accurately, and the prosecution here did no more than utilize the traditional truth-testing devices of the adversary process." Id., at 225.

In determining whether a constitutional right has been burdened impermissibly, it also is appropriate to consider the legitimacy of the challenged governmental practice. Attempted impeachment on cross-examination of a defendant, the practice at issue here, may enhance the reliability of the criminal process. Use of such impeachment on cross-examination allows prosecutors to test the credibility of witnesses by asking them to explain prior inconsistent statements and acts. A defendant may decide not to take the witness stand because of the risk of cross-examination. But this is a choice of litigation tactics. Once a defendant decides to testify, "[t]he interests of the other party and regard for the function of the courts of justice to ascertain the truth become relevant, and prevail in the balance of considerations determining the scope and limits of the privilege against self-incrimination." Brown v. United States, 356 U.S. 148, 156 (1958).

Thus, impeachment follows the defendant's own decision to cast aside his cloak of silence and advances the truth-finding function of the criminal trial. We conclude that the Fifth Amendment is not violated by the use of pre-arrest silence to impeach a criminal defendant's credibility.

The petitioner also contends that use of pre-arrest silence to impeach his credibility denied him the fundamental fairness guaranteed by the Fourteenth Amendment. We do not agree. Common law traditionally has allowed witnesses to be impeached by their previous failure to state a fact in circumstances in which that fact naturally would have been asserted. 3A Wigmore, Evidence §1042, at 1056 (Chadbourn rev. 1970). Each jurisdiction may formulate its own rules of evidence to determine when prior silence is so inconsistent with present statements that impeachment by reference to such silence is probative. For example, this Court has exercised its supervisory powers over federal courts to hold that prior silence cannot be used for impeachment where silence is not probative of a defendant's credibility and where prejudice to the defendant might result.[5]

Only in Doyle v. Ohio, 426 U.S. 610, did we find that impeachment by silence violated the Constitution. In that case, a defendant received the warnings required by Miranda v. Arizona, 384 U.S. 436, 467-473, when he was arrested for selling marihuana. At that time, he made no statements to the police. During his subsequent trial, the defendant testified that he had been framed. The prosecutor impeached the defendant's credibility on cross-examination by revealing that the defendant remained silent after his arrest. The State argued that the prosecutor's actions were permissible, but we concluded that "the Miranda decision compels rejection of the State's position." Miranda warnings inform a person that he has the right to remain silent and assure him, at least implicitly, that his subsequent decision to remain silent cannot be used against him. Accordingly, "'it does not comport with due process to permit the prosecution during the trial to call attention to his silence at the time of arrest and to insist that because he did not speak about the facts of the case at that time, as he was told he need not do, an unfavorable inference might be drawn as to the truth of his trial testimony.'"

In this case, no governmental action induced petitioner to remain silent before arrest. The failure to speak occurred before the petitioner was taken into custody and given Miranda warnings. Consequently, the fundamental unfairness present in Doyle is not present in this case. We hold that impeachment by use of prearrest silence does not violate the Fourteenth Amendment.

Our decision today does not force any state court to allow impeachment through the use of pre-arrest silence. Each jurisdiction remains free to formulate evidentiary rules defining the situations in which silence is viewed as more probative than prejudicial. We merely conclude that the use of prearrest silence to impeach a defendant's credibility does not violate the Constitution. The judgment of the Court of Appeals is affirmed.

Mr. Justice MARSHALL, with whom Mr. Justice BRENNAN joins, dissenting.

Today the Court holds that a criminal defendant's testimony in his own behalf may be impeached by the fact that he did not go to the

5. Mr. Justice Marshall contends that the petitioner's prearrest silence is not probative of his credibility. In this case, that is a question of state evidentiary law. In federal criminal proceeding the relevance of such silence, of course, would be a matter of federal law. See United States v. Hale, 422 U.S., at 181.

authorities before his arrest and confess his part in the offense. The decision thus strikes a blow at two of the foundation stones of our constitutional system: the privilege against self-incrimination and the right to present a defense.

The Court's decision today is extraordinarily broad. It goes far beyond a simple holding that the common-law rule permitting introduction of evidence of silence in the face of accusation or in circumstances calling for a response does not violate the privilege against self-incrimination. For in this case the prosecution was allowed to cast doubt on an accused's testimony that he acted in self-defense by forcing him to testify that he did not go to the police of his own volition, before he had been indicted, charged, or even accused of any offense, and volunteer his version of the events.

The Court's holding that a criminal defendant's testimony may be impeached by his prearrest silence has three patent—and, in my view, fatal—defects. First, the mere fact of prearrest silence is so unlikely to be probative of the falsity of the defendant's trial testimony that its use for impeachment purposes is contrary to the Due Process Clause of the Fourteenth Amendment. Second, the drawing of an adverse inference from the failure to volunteer incriminating statements impermissibly infringes the privilege against self-incrimination. Third, the availability of the inference for impeachment purposes impermissibly burdens the decision to exercise the constitutional right to testify in one's own defense.

The use of prior silence for impeachment purposes depends, as the majority recognizes, on the reasonableness of an inference that it is inconsistent with the statements that are to be impeached. If the defendant's prior silence does not make it more likely that his trial testimony was false, the evidence is simply irrelevant. Such an inference cannot fairly be drawn from petitioner's failure to go to the police before any charges were brought, admit that he had committed a homicide, and offer an exculpatory explanation.

In order for petitioner to offer his explanation of self-defense, he would necessarily have had to admit that it was he who fatally stabbed the victim, thereby supplying against himself the strongest possible proof of an essential element of criminal homicide. It is hard to imagine a purer case of self-incrimination. Since we cannot assume that in the absence of official warnings individuals are ignorant of or oblivious to their constitutional rights, we must recognize that petitioner may have acted in reliance on the constitutional guarantee. In fact, petitioner had most likely been informed previously of his privilege against self-incrimination, since he had two prior felony convictions. One who has at least twice before been given the *Miranda* warnings, which carry the implied promise that silence will not be penalized by use for impeachment purposes, Doyle v. Ohio, 426 U.S. 610 (1976), may well remember the rights of which he has been informed, and believe that the promise is still in force. Accordingly, the inference that petitioner's conduct was inconsistent with his exculpatory trial testimony is precluded. . . .

Moreover, other possible explanations for silence spring readily to mind. It is conceivable that a person who had acted in self-defense might believe that he had committed no crime and therefore had no call to explain himself to the police. Indeed, all the witnesses agreed that after the stabbing the victim ran across the street and climbed a flight of stairs before collapsing. Initially, at least, then, petitioner might not have known that there was a homicide to explain. Moreover, petitioner testified that he feared retaliation if he went to the police. One need not be persuaded that any of these possible explanations represents the true reason for petitioner's conduct to recognize that the availability of other plausible hypotheses vitiates the inference on which the admissibility of the evidence depends. . . .

The Court implies that its decision is consistent with the practice at common law; but at common law silence is admissible to contradict subsequent statements only if the circumstances would naturally have called for a response. For example, silence was traditionally considered a tacit admission if a statement made in the party's presence was heard and understood by the party, who was at liberty to respond, in circumstances naturally calling for a response, and the party failed to respond. Silence was not considered an admission if any of the prerequisites were absent, for in such a case the failure to speak could be explained other than as assent. Similarly, failure to assert a fact could be used for impeachment if it would have been natural, under the circumstances, to assert the fact. But the authority cited by the majority in support of this proposition, makes it clear that the rule cannot be invoked unless the facts affirmatively show that the witness was called on to speak, circumstances which are not present in this case. As we have previously observed, "[i]n most circumstances silence is so ambiguous that it is of little probative force." United States v. Hale, supra, at 176.

Since petitioner's failure to report and explain his actions prior to his arrest was not probative of the falsity of his testimony at trial, it was fundamentally unfair and a deprivation of due process to allow the jury to draw from that silence an inference that his trial testimony was false. . . .

The use of pre-arrest silence for impeachment purposes also violates the privilege against self-incrimination secured by the Fifth and Fourteenth Amendments.

[Separate opinions by Justices Stewart and Stevens are omitted.]

Problem: Anything You Don't Say Will Be Used Against You

Weir is charged with the murder of Buchanan. The evidence is that in the course of a fight in a nightclub parking lot, Buchanan pinned Weir to the ground. Buchanan then jumped to his feet and shouted that he had been stabbed; he ultimately died from stab wounds. Weir immediately left the scene and did not report the incident to the police. At trial, Weir admitted stabbing Buchanan, but testified that he acted in self-defense and that the stabbing was accidental. This trial testimony was the first time Weir offered an exculpatory version of the events. On cross-examination, the prosecutor asked Weir why, when arrested, he had failed to offer this exculpatory version of what happened or to reveal the location of the knife used in the stabbing. On Weir's objection to this line of questioning, what ruling and why? Should the court's ruling depend on whether Weir had been given his *Miranda* warnings?

Consider the relationship between relevance analysis and constitutional analysis. Does one logically precede the other? On what basis is Marshall dissenting in *Jenkins?* As a matter of state or federal evidentiary law, see footnote 5 to the majority's opinion in *Jenkins*; is such evidence of evasion or suppression or destruction of evidence always relevant, and when does the danger of prejudice substantially outweigh its probativeness? See United States v. Hale, 422 U.S. 171 (1975), and Fletcher v. Weir, 455 U.S. 603 (1982). See also Nesson, Incentives to Spoliate Evidence in Civil Litigation: The Need for Vigorous Judicial Action, 13 Cardozo L. Rev. 793 (1991).

Problem: Missing Evidence

Charge: prescribing a narcotic to persons not under treatment for a pathology. The state seeks to introduce evidence that during the preliminary hearing the clerk permitted Dr. *D* to examine the exhibits and later discovered that the prescriptions were missing. Pieces of the prescriptions were subsequently found floating in a toilet bowl in the courthouse rest room. *D* objects on grounds of relevancy.

What ruling and why? What chain of inferences does the prosecution want the jury to create in considering this evidence?

SMITH v. SUPERIOR COURT (ABBOTT FORD)
151 Cal. App. 3d 491, 198 Cal. Rptr. 829 (1984)

KLEIN, J.

Phyllis and Jay Smith (the Smiths) petitioned this court for a writ of

mandate, seeking relief from the sustaining of the demurrer of Abbott
Ford, Inc. (Abbott Ford), real party in interest, to one crucial cause of
action without leave to amend.

Because we conclude that the eighth count stated a cause of action
for intentional spoliation of evidence, significantly prejudicing the
Smiths' opportunity to obtain damages for their injuries, the alternative
writ is to be discharged and the trial court directed to overrule the
demurrer.

FACTS

On September 10, 1981, at about 6:10 A.M., Phyllis Smith was driving
her car southbound on California Avenue in West Covina. Ramsey
Sneed (Sneed) was driving a 1979 Ford van northbound on California
Avenue, at the approximate same time and place when the left rear
wheel and tire flew off of the van and crashed into the windshield of
Phyllis Smith's vehicle. The impact caused pieces of glass to strike her
in the eyes and face, resulting in permanent blindness in both eyes and
impairment of her sense of smell.

Abbott Ford was the dealer that customized the van with "deep dish
mag wheels" before it sold the van to Sneed. Immediately after the accident, the van was towed to Abbott Ford for repairs.

On or about September 25, 1981, Abbott Ford agreed with the
Smiths' counsel to maintain certain automotive parts (physical evidence), pending further investigation. Thereafter, Abbott Ford destroyed, lost or transferred said physical evidence, making it impossible
for the Smiths' experts to inspect and test those parts in order to pinpoint the cause of the failure of the wheel assembly on the van.

PROCEDURE

The second amended complaint contained an eighth cause of action
entitled "Tortious Interference with Prospective Civil Action By Spoliation of Evidence," stated against Abbott Ford. The prayer also sought
exemplary damages. The seventh and ninth causes of action for breach
of contract/promissory estoppel and negligence respectively were also
concerned with the loss of the physical evidence.

The seventh cause of action specifically alleged that after the accident, Abbott Ford promised the Smiths' counsel that it "would maintain
securely in their care, possession, custody and control for later examination and testing by Plaintiffs' technical experts the left rear tire and
wheel, lug bolts, lug nuts and brake drum which these Defendants [Ab-
bott Ford] had removed from Defendant['s] van."

It was further alleged that Abbott Ford knew that such physical evidence would be essential proof in a civil action to be brought by the

Smiths, and that Abbott Ford knew or should have known that the Smiths would be induced to rely upon its promise by forebearing from seeking a temporary restraining order to compel it to maintain the evidence securely. . . .

The damage alleged was the "significant prejudice" of the Smiths' opportunity to obtain compensation for their grievous physical and emotional injuries.

Abbott Ford demurred to the seventh and eighth causes of action on the grounds they failed to state a cause of action. In sustaining the demurrer only as to the eighth cause of action without leave to amend, the trial court ruled that such an intentional tort did not exist. The Smiths thereafter filed a petition for writ of mandate to direct the trial court to allow this cause of action.

DISCUSSION

1. "NEW AND NAMELESS TORTS ARE BEING RECOGNIZED CONSTANTLY"

Prosser instructs us that:

New and nameless torts are being recognized constantly, and the progress of the common law is marked by many cases of first impression, in which the court has struck out boldly to create a new cause of action, where none had been recognized before. The intentional infliction of mental suffering, . . . the invasion of [the] right of privacy, the denial of [the] right to vote, the conveyance of land to defeat a title, the infliction of prenatal injuries, the alienation of the affections of a parent, . . . to name only a few instances, could not be fitted into any accepted classifications when they first arose, but nevertheless have been held to be torts. The law of torts is anything but static, and the limits of its development are never set. *When it becomes clear that the plaintiff's interests are entitled to legal protection against the conduct of the defendant, the mere fact that the claim is novel will not of itself operate as a bar to a remedy.*

(Emphasis added; Prosser, Torts (4th ed. 1971) §1, pp.3-4.)

The common thread woven into all torts is the idea of unreasonable interference with the interests of others.

(Emphasis added; id., at p.6.)

California has long recognized "[f]or every wrong there is a remedy" (Civ. Code, §3523), and has allowed for new torts through the legislative and judicial process. (4 Witkin, Summary of Cal. Law (8th ed. 1974) Torts §10, p.2310.) Legal protection has been afforded recently in the area of wrongful birth (Stills v. Gratton (1976) 55 Cal. App. 3d 698, 127 Cal. Rptr. 652) and wrongful life (Turpin v. Sortini (1982) 31 Cal. 3d 220, 182 Cal. Rptr. 337, 643 P.2d 954).

In light of the foregoing, we believe that a new tort may be appro-

priate to cover the intentional spoliation of evidence, since it meets the
criteria spelled out by Prosser and recognized by case law.

a. *The Supreme Court Appears to Have Recognized a Negligence Cause of
Action for Failure to Preserve Evidence for Prospective Civil Litigation*

Abbott Ford argued that not only is there no tort of "intentional
interference with prospective civil action by spoliation of evidence," but
also that there is a failure on the part of the California courts to recognize a cause of action in negligence for the same activity. However, a
recent California Supreme Court case appears to recognize an injured
party's right to such a cause of action. The recent Supreme Court opinion in Williams v. State of California (1983) 34 Cal. 3d 18, 192 Cal. Rptr.
233, 664 P.2d 137, indicates that a negligence cause of action could be
stated, provided a duty exists on the part of the defendant.

In *Williams*, the plaintiff alleged that she was injured when a piece of
heated brake drum from a passing truck flew into her windshield and
struck her in the face before coming to rest on the rear seat of her
automobile. An officer came to her assistance. The plaintiff also alleged
that the officer assumed the responsibility of investigating the accident
and that this investigation was so negligently carried out that it "virtually
destroy[ed] any opportunity on plaintiff's part to obtain compensation
for the severe injuries and damages she suffered from any other
defendants."

While the *Williams* court found that the mere stopping to aid a mo-
torist does not in itself create a special relationship which would give
rise to a duty and that Williams therefore had not pled a cause of action,
the court granted Williams leave to amend her complaint, implying that
if she were able to allege a duty, she might be able to state a cause of
action for failure to preserve evidence for civil litigation.

Significantly, Abbott Ford did not demur to the cause of action for
negligent spoliation of evidence which is still viable in the trial court.

b. *The Intentional Tort Cause of Action*

Abbott Ford contends that a cause of action for an intentional tort
of spoliation of evidence is precluded under California statutory and
case law, because a penal statute has in effect preempted the field.

Penal Code section 135 states:

> Every person who, knowing that any book, paper, record, instrument in writ-
> ing, or other matter or thing, is about to be produced in evidence upon any trial,
> inquiry, or investigation whatever, authorized by law, willfully destroys or con-
> ceals the same, with intent thereby to prevent it from being produced, is guilty
> of a misdemeanor.

Agnew v. Parks (1959) 172 Cal. App. 2d 756, 766, 343 P.2d 118, interpreted the crime set forth in section 135 as an "obstruction of justice" for which only the state can prosecute, and held that there is no civil cause of action available to the party harmed.

In *Agnew*, the plaintiff had already received several favorable medical malpractice verdicts, and subsequently sued certain members of the County Medical Association "For Damages for Conspiracy to Obstruct the Orderly Prosecution of a Civil Action and for Concerted Refusal to Deal." She alleged that these members conspired to thwart her prior malpractice action against a physician by threatening other members of the association to prevent their testifying in her behalf, that they recommended a biased member as an expert, and that they concealed eighteen X-rays of her injuries. The *Agnew* court denied the perjury, subornation of perjury and evidence concealment causes of action.

The *Agnew* court observed that there must be an end to civil litigation, and the plaintiff had had the opportunity at an earlier trial to bring the claim of perjury to the attention of the original court. The court held that the alleged new cause of action would have involved essentially a relitigation of matters already adjudicated.

The disallowance of such duplicative causes of action after completion of the trial is solidly grounded on the impermissibility of making collateral attacks on the findings of a court and the desire to end litigation.

However, the situation in the instant case is vastly different procedurally. The Smiths' case has not yet gone to trial, and therefore, no collateral estoppel issue exists. Furthermore, if the Smiths are not allowed to maintain their intentional spoliation of evidence action at this juncture, if and when they attempt to bring this same action after the trial as the plaintiff in *Agnew* did, they may be met with the same estoppel theory.

Another rationale on which *Agnew* is predicated and is inapposite here is that perjury and subornation of perjury are not answerable in civil actions. Although the court was correct in its statement that "no civil right can be predicated upon a *mere* violation of a criminal statute," in some cases the same act may be both a crime against the state and a tort against an individual. In such an instance, because the interests invaded are not the same, and the objects to be accomplished by the two suits are different, there may be both a criminal prosecution and a civil tort action for the same offense. . . .

Even though it is clear that some acts can give rise to both tort and criminal liability, Abbott Ford contends that *Agnew* precludes civil action for intentional spoliation of evidence under section 135 because like false testimony and perjury, it is a form of obstruction of justice and is therefore a wrong against the public rather than against an individual plaintiff. We find this reasoning only partially sound.

False testimony and subornation of perjury occur during the trial and do adversely affect the public at large by interfering with the judicial process as well as impacting on an individual plaintiff. Here, the destruction of the Smiths' physical evidence took place before the trial ever began, and the Smiths seek compensation for the alleged intentional destruction of important evidence to be used in the *forthcoming* litigation. Granted intentional spoliation of evidence is a form of obstruction of justice, it has a devastating effect on a potential plaintiff and could prevent such a plaintiff even seeking justice in a court of law.

Furthermore, Abbott Ford is mistaken in its assumption that section 135 provides a sufficient deterrent. While Agnew v. Parks, supra, 172 Cal. App. 2d at p.766, 343 P.2d 118 states that "[c]oncealing or withholding documentary evidence is made a felony by section 135, Penal Code," it is now only a misdemeanor. (§135.) If crucial evidence could be intentionally destroyed by a party to a civil action who thereby stands to gain substantially monetarily by such destruction, the effect of a misdemeanor would be of minimal deterrence.

A recent *criminal* case held that there is no criminal offense under section 135 unless there is proof "that [a] law enforcement investigation in fact had started and/or that law enforcement was or would be looking for the particular item." (People v. Prysock (1982) 127 Cal. App. 3d 972, 1000, 180 Cal. Rptr. 15.)

In Agnew v. Parks, supra, plaintiff's *civil* cause of action for acts violative of the language of section 135 was disallowed. We know of no reported prosecution under section 135 — adopted in 1872 — and Abbott Ford cites us to none, for destroying or concealing documentary evidence relevant only to *prospective civil action.*

Neither section 135 nor *Agnew* prevents the recognition of intentional spoliation of evidence for prospective civil litigation as a tort.

2. CERTAINTY OF DAMAGES

The most troubling aspect in allowing a cause of action for intentional spoliation of evidence is the requisite tort element of damages proximately resulting from defendant's alleged act. Here, the underlying product liability case has not yet gone to trial and it is possible that the Smiths could prove their case through other means and recover damages.

We appreciate that one who has suffered a legally recognized injury is usually entitled to an award of damages. However, a plaintiff must not only establish the fact of damages with reasonable certainty, but must also prove the amount of damages with reasonable certainty. . . .

There are many interests which the law seeks to protect wherein damages cannot be proved with certainty. In wrongful death and personal injury cases, amounts of future earnings are uncertain, but are still recoverable. Likewise, in cases of patent or trademark infringement, damages may be difficult to estimate but nevertheless damage awards are sustained. Further, in tort actions such as libel, slander and invasion of privacy, substantial damages are awarded without any proof of economic harm or even emotional distress.

Deterrence is an important policy consideration for allowing the maintenance of suits when damages cannot be shown with certainty. . . .

Turning again to the instant situation, the Smiths' complaint alleged only that the loss or destruction of the physical evidence had "significantly prejudiced" their case. In a products liability action, doubtless the Smiths suffered "some" damage in the preparation of their case against Abbott Ford. At this point, the amount of damages is uncertain. It may be that the Smiths have pleaded their damages with as much certainty as the nature of the claim will allow.

While intentional spoliation of evidence has not been recognized as a tort heretofore, we conclude that a prospective civil action in a product liability case is a valuable "probable expectancy" that the court must protect from the kind of interference alleged herein. (Prosser, op. cit. supra, §130, at p. 950.) . . .

Further, we are cognizant of all the obvious and the sound practical reasons for allowing the Smiths' cause of action for intentional spoliation of evidence to be heard at the same time as their cause of action for personal injury—needless duplication of effort, two trials involving much the same evidence, time and expense imposed on litigants and the judicial system, and a jury uniquely equipped to determine how the Smiths were harmed.

CONCLUSION

Public policy dictates that the Smiths' interests in their prospective civil litigation are entitled to legal protection against Abbott Ford's alleged intentional spoliation of evidence, even though their damages cannot be stated with certainty.

Problem: Neither a Borrower nor a Lender Be

Action of debt on a note. *D* denied that he owed *P* any money, alleging that the note was a forgery. Several witnesses testified for *P* that the signature on the note was the handwriting of *D*. *D* then introduced several witnesses who testified that he was not in the country on the date of the note and several samples of his signature for the jury to compare with the signature on the note. *P* then called *W*, who offered to testify that *D* asked *W* to loan him money both before and after the date of the note.

Should *W*'s evidence be received? What is the inference that *P* wants the court to draw from *W*'s testimony? How would you articulate this inference in deductive form? Is this evidence "direct" or "circumstantial"? Would *W*'s testimony be more or less relevant if he did not lend *D* money? Would the evidence be more or less cogent if *W*'s testimony was that *D* sought to borrow from him the same sum for which the note to *P* was subsequently given? Would *W*'s testimony be more or less relevant if *P* introduced two additional witnesses to testify that *D* also sought to borrow money from them, or that *D* was a pauper?

If the defense offers a receipt for payment of the note, what should plaintiff's response be?

Problem: Double Indemnity

HARTENSTEIN v. NEW YORK LIFE INSURANCE CO., 113 N.E.2d 712 (Ohio Ct. App. 1952):   Mrs. Irma L. Hartenstein, as the beneficiary of a life insurance policy issued upon the life of her husband, Alfred D. Hartenstein, sued the New York Life Insurance Company to recover double indemnity provided for in the policy for death . . . from bodily injury effected solely through external, violent and accidental means [but not from suicide].

[Plaintiff alleged that on November 16 her husband was in his car at a railroad crossing and was struck and killed by a locomotive. The insurance company claimed that the husband committed suicide.]

The testimony of the several persons who were near the scene of the tragedy and witnessed the conduct and activity of the insured was that the insured drove his automobile on an improved highway to a point several hundred feet from a well-marked main line, four-track railroad crossing and then parked for "fifteen or twenty minutes." . . . Several automobiles at about this time came to the crossing and stopped to give way to a forty-car loaded Baltimore and Ohio freight train, which was approaching at a speed of approximately 40 miles an hour. While the warning lights were flashing, and the train's whistle was blowing, the insured drove his car away from its parked position, passed around the several automobiles ahead, which had been stopped for the train, hesitated momentarily at the boundary of the crossing, and then proceeded slowly to the track upon which the train was approaching, where the automobile came to a stop. In a "matter of seconds" the inevitable collision occurred, and the insured was thrown from his car to the side of the tracks, while the train continued on through the crossing, carrying the automobile on the front of the engine. Death followed quickly. In addition to the warning signals, there is evidence that the train could be plainly seen in the broad light of the day by all who approached the crossing.

After introduction of the above evidence, the defendant moves for a nonsuit at the close of the plaintiff's case. Defendant argues that the evidence shows, as a matter of law, that the insured committed suicide. What ruling and why?

During the trial, additional evidence was offered to show that at the time of his death the insured was the secretary of a local lodge. As secretary he received dues, and it was his duty to deposit this money in a local bank. Several weeks before his death an annual audit of these funds was commenced by the lodge, and it was revealed that while the secretary's books showed $23,401.76 on hand, the reconciliation with the bank indicated $13,607.76 in the account. Should such evidence have been admitted? What is its relevance? Does its relevance require an inference to be piled on another inference?

Should there be a rule against piling an inference on an inference? If not, should each intermediate inference have to be established to some degree of certitude (e.g., a preponderance) before the evidence will be admitted?

At common law, many jurisdictions followed a rule that prohibited "an inference on an inference." Rhode Island, for example, prohibited "pyramiding of inferences," see Waldman v. Shipyard Marina, 102 R.I. 366, 230 A.2d 841 (1967), but in more recent years interpreted this to mean that "an inference may rest upon a prior inference that has been established to the exclusion of all other reasonable inferences." The defense in the Claus van Bulow attempted murder case, 475 A.2d 995 (R.I. 1984), cited the Rhode Island cases pronouncing this rule as the first cases in its appellate brief.

Does the codification of the rules of evidence (Rhode Island Rules 401-403 are virtually identical to the federal rules) abolish the "no inference on an inference" rule and any similar rules that impose a threshold level of proof on an intermediate inference in a chain of inferences? Or does the discredited "no inference on an inference" rule live on in a different form through strict application of the concept of conditional relevance in Rule 104(b)?

F.   Relevance and Statistical Probability

PEOPLE v. COLLINS
68 Cal. 2d 319, 438 P.2d 33, 66 Cal. Rptr. 497 (1968)

SULLIVAN, J. We deal here with the novel question whether evidence of mathematical probability has been properly introduced and used by the prosecution in a criminal case. While we discern no inherent incompatibility between the disciplines of law and mathematics and intend no general disapproval or disparagement of the latter as an auxiliary in the general fact-finding processes of the former, we cannot uphold the technique employed in the instant case. As we explained in detail, infra, the testimony as to mathematical probability infected the case with fatal error and distorted the jury's traditional roles of determining guilt or innocence according to long-settled rules. Mathematics, a veritable sorcerer in our computerized society, while assisting the trier of fact in the search for truth, must not cast a spell over him. We conclude that on the record before us defendant should not have had his guilt determined by the odds and that he is entitled to a new trial. We reverse the judgment.

A jury found defendant Malcolm Ricardo Collins and his wife defendant Janet Louise Collins guilty of second degree robbery. Malcolm appeals from the judgment of conviction. Janet has not appealed.

On June 18, 1964, about 11:30 A.M. Mrs. Juanita Brooks, who had been shopping, was walking home along an alley in the San Pedro area of the City of Los Angeles. She was pulling behind her a wicker basket carryall containing groceries and had her purse on top of the packages. She was using a cane. As she stooped down to pick up an empty carton, she was suddenly pushed to the ground by a person whom she neither saw nor heard approach. She was stunned by the fall and felt some pain. She managed to look up and saw a young woman running from the scene. According to Mrs. Brooks the latter appeared to weigh about 145 pounds, was wearing "something dark," and had hair "between a dark blond and a light blond," but lighter than the color of defendant Janet Collins' hair as it appeared at trial. Immediately after the incident, Mrs. Brooks discovered that her purse, containing between $35 and $40 was missing.

About the same time as the robbery, John Bass, who lived on the street at the end of the alley, was in front of his house watering his lawn. His attention was attracted by "a lot of crying and screaming" coming from the alley. As he looked in that direction, he saw a woman run out of the alley and enter a yellow automobile parked across the street from him. He was unable to give the make of the car. The car started off immediately and pulled wide around another parked vehicle so that in the narrow street it passed within 6 feet of Bass. The latter then saw that it was being driven by a male Negro, wearing a mustache and beard. At the trial Bass identified defendant as the driver of the yellow automobile. However, an attempt was made to impeach his identification by his admission that at the preliminary hearing he testified to an uncertain identification at the police lineup shortly after the attack on Mrs. Brooks, when defendant was beardless.

In his testimony Bass described the woman who ran from the alley as a Caucasian, slightly over 5 feet tall, of ordinary build, with her hair in a dark blonde ponytail, and wearing dark clothing. He further testified that her ponytail was "just like" one which Janet had in a police photograph taken on June 22, 1964.

On the day of the robbery, Janet was employed as a housemaid in San Pedro. Her employer testified that she had arrived for work at 8:50 A.M. and that defendant had picked her up in a light yellow car[2] about 11:30 A.M. On that day, according to the witness, Janet was wearing her hair in a blonde ponytail but lighter in color than it appeared at trial.[3]

There was evidence from which it could be inferred that defendants had ample time to drive from Janet's place of employment and participate in the robbery. Defendants testified, however, that they went directly from her employer's house to the home of friends, where they remained for several hours. . . .

At the seven-day trial the prosecution experienced some difficulty in establishing the identities of the perpetrators of the crime. The victim could not identify Janet and had never seen defendant. The identification by the witness Bass, who observed the girl run out of the alley and get into the automobile, was incomplete as to Janet and may have been weakened as to defendant. There was also evidence, introduced by the defense, that Janet had worn light-colored clothing on the day in question, but both the victim and Bass testified that the girl they observed had worn dark clothing.

In an apparent attempt to bolster the identifications, the prosecutor called an instructor of mathematics at a state college. Through this witness he sought to establish that, assuming the robbery was committed by a Caucasian woman with a blonde ponytail who left the scene accompanied by a Negro with a beard and mustache, there was an overwhelming probability that the crime was committed by any couple answering such distinctive characteristics. The witness testified, in substance, to the "product rule," which states that the probability of the joint occurrence of a number of *mutually independent* events is equal to the product of the individual probabilities that each of the events will occur.[8] *Without presenting any statistical evidence whatsoever in support of the probabilities for the factors selected,* the prosecutor then proceeded to have the witness

2. Other witnesses variously described the car as yellow, as yellow with an off-white top, and yellow with an egg-shell white top. The car was also described as being medium to large in size. Defendant drove a car at or near the times in question which was a Lincoln with a yellow body and a white top.

3. There are inferences which may be drawn from the evidence that Janet attempted to alter the appearance of her hair after June 18. Janet denies that she cut, colored or bleached her hair at any time after June 18, and a number of witnesses supported her testimony.

8. In the example employed for illustrative purposes at the trial, the probability of rolling one die and coming up with a "2" is $1/6$, that is, any one of the six faces of a die has one chance in six of landing face up on any particular roll. The probability of rolling two "2's" in succession is $1/6 \times 1/6$, or $1/36$, that is, on only one occasion out of 36 double rolls (or the roll of two dice), will the selected number land face up on each roll or die.

assume[9] probability factors for the various characteristics which he deemed to be shared by the guilty couple and all other couples answering to such distinctive characteristics.[10]

Applying the product rule to his own factors the prosecutor arrived at a probability that there was but one chance in 12 million that any couple possessed the distinctive characteristics of the defendants. Accordingly, under this theory, it was to be inferred that there could be but one chance in 12 million that defendants were innocent and that another equally distinctive couple actually committed the robbery. Expanding on what he had thus purported to suggest as a hypothesis, the prosecutor offered the completely unfounded and improper testimonial assertion that, in his opinion, the factors he had assigned were "conservative estimates" and that, in reality, "the chances of anyone else besides these defendants being there, . . . having every similarity, ... is somewhat like one in a billion."

Objections were timely made to the mathematician's testimony on the grounds that it was immaterial, that it invaded the province of the jury, and that it was based on unfounded assumptions. The objections were "temporarily overruled" and the evidence admitted subject to a motion to strike. When that motion was made at the conclusion of the direct examination, the court denied it, stating that the testimony had been received only for the "purpose of illustrating the mathematical probabilities of various matters, the possibilities for them occurring or reoccurring."

Both defendants took the stand in their own behalf. They denied any knowledge of or participation in the crime and stated that after Malcolm called for Janet at her employer's house they went directly to a friend's

---

9. His argument to the jury was based on the same gratuitous assumptions or on similar assumptions which he invited the jury to make.

10. Although the prosecutor insisted that the factors he used were only for illustrative purposes — to demonstrate how the probability of the occurrence of mutually independent factors affected the probability that they would occur together — he nevertheless attempted to use factors which he personally related to the distinctive characteristics of defendants. In his argument to the jury he invited the jurors to apply their own factors, and asked defense counsel to suggest what the latter would deem as reasonable. The prosecutor himself proposed the individual probabilities set out in the table below. Although the transcript of the examination of the mathematics instructor and the information volunteered by the prosecutor at that time create some uncertainty as to precisely which of the characteristics the prosecutor assigned to the individual probabilities, he restated in his argument to the jury that they should be as follows:

Characteristic	Individual Probability
A. Partly yellow automobile	1/10
B. Man with mustache	1/4
C Girl with ponytail	1/10
D. Girl with blond hair	1/3
E. Negro man with beard	1/10
F. Interracial couple in car	1/1000

In his brief on appeal defendant agrees that the foregoing appeared on a table presented in the trial court.

house in Los Angeles where they remained for some time. According to this testimony defendants were not near the scene of the robbery when it occurred. Defendants' friend testified to a visit by them "in the middle of June" although she could not recall the precise date. Janet further testified that certain inducements were held out to her during the July 9 interrogation on condition that she confess her participation. . . .

As we shall explain, the prosecution's introduction and use of mathematical probability statistics injected two fundamental prejudicial errors into the case: (1) The testimony itself lacked an adequate foundation both in evidence and in statistical theory; and (2) the testimony and the manner in which the prosecution used it distracted the jury from its proper and requisite function of weighing the evidence on the issue of guilt, encouraged the jurors to rely upon an engaging but logically irrelevant expert demonstration, foreclosed the possibility of an effective defense by an attorney apparently unschooled in mathematical refinements, and placed the jurors and defense counsel at a disadvantage in sifting relevant fact from inapplicable theory.

We initially consider the defects in the testimony itself. As we have indicated, the specific technique presented through the mathematician's testimony and advanced by the prosecutor to measure the probabilities in question suffered from two basic and pervasive defects—an inadequate evidentiary foundation and an inadequate proof of statistical independence. First, as to the foundational requirement, we find the record devoid of any evidence relating to any of the six individual probability factors used by the prosecutor and ascribed by him to the six characteristics as we have set them out in footnote 10, ante. To put it another way, the prosecution produced no evidence whatsoever showing, or from which it could be in any way inferred, that only one out of every ten cars which might have been at the scene of the robbery was partly yellow, that only one out of every four men who might have been there wore a mustache, that only one out of every ten girls who might have been there wore a ponytail, or that any of the other individual probability factors listed were even roughly accurate.[12]

The bare, inescapable fact is that the prosecution made no attempt to offer any such evidence. Instead, through leading questions having perfunctorily elicited from the witness the response that the latter could not assign a probability factor for the characteristics involved,[13] the pros-

12. We seriously doubt that such evidence could ever be compiled since no statistician could possibly determine after the fact which cars, or which individuals, "might" have been present at the scene of the robbery; certainly there is no reason to suppose that the human and automotive populations of San Pedro, California, include all potential culprits—or, conversely, that all members of these populations are proper candidates for inclusion. Thus the sample from which the relevant probabilities would have to be derived is itself undeterminable. (See generally, Yaman, Statistics, An Introductory Analysis (1964), ch. I.)

13. The prosecutor asked the mathematics instructor: "Now, let me see if you can be of

ecutor himself suggested what the various probabilities should be and
these became the basis of the witness' testimony (see fn. 10, ante). It is
a curious circumstance of this adventure in proof that the prosecutor
not only made his own assertions of these factors in the hope that they
were "conservative" but also in later argument to the jury invited the
jurors to substitute their "estimates" should they wish to do so. We can
hardly conceive of a more fatal gap in the prosecution's scheme of
proof. A foundation for the admissibility of the witness' testimony was
never even attempted to be laid, let alone established. His testimony
was neither made to rest on his own testimonial knowledge nor presented by proper hypothetical questions based upon valid data in the
record. (See generally: 2 Wigmore on Evidence (3d ed. 1940) §§478,
650-652, 657, 659, 672-684; McCormick on Evidence, pp.19-20; State v.
Sneed (1966) 76 N.M. 349, 414 P.2d 858.) In the *Sneed* case, the court
reversed a conviction based on probabilistic evidence, stating: "We hold
that mathematical odds are not admissible as evidence to identify a defendant in a criminal proceeding *so long as the odds are based on estimates,
the validity of which have [sic] not been demonstrated.*" (Italics added.) (414
P.2d at p.862.)

But, as we have indicated, there was another glaring defect in the
prosecution's technique, namely an inadequate proof of the statistical
independence of the six factors. No proof was presented that the characteristics selected were mutually independent, even though the witness
himself acknowledged that such condition was essential to the proper
application of the "product rule" or "multiplication rule." To the extent
that the traits or characteristics were not mutually independent (e.g.,
To the extent that the traits or characteristics were not mutually independent (e.g., Negroes with beards and men with mustaches obviously
represent overlapping categories[15]), the "product rule" would inevitably
yield a wholly erroneous and exaggerated result even if all of the individual components had been determined with precision. (Siegel, Non-
parametric Statistics for the Behavioral Sciences (1956) 19; see generally
Harmon, Modern Factor Analysis (1960).)

In the instant case, therefore, because of the aforementioned two

---

some help to us with some independent factors, and you have some paper you may use. Your
specialty does not equip you, I suppose, to give us some probability of such things as a yellow
car as contrasted with any other kind of car, does it? . . . I appreciate the fact that you can't
assign a probability for a car being yellow as contrasted to some other car, can you?" A. "No,
I couldn't."

15. Assuming arguendo that factors B and E (see fn. 10, ante), were correctly estimated,
nevertheless it is still arguable that most Negro men with beards also have mustaches (exhibit
3 herein, for instance, shows defendant with both a mustache and a beard, indeed in a hirsute
continuum); if so, there is no basis for multiplying 1/4 by 1/10 to estimate the proportion of
Negroes who wear beards and mustaches. Again, the prosecution's technique could never be
meaningfully applied, since its accurate use would call for information as to the degree of
interdependence among the six individual factors. Such information cannot be compiled,
however, since the relevant sample necessarily remains unknown.

defects—the inadequate evidentiary foundation and the inadequate proof of statistical independence—the technique employed by the prosecutor could only lead to wild conjecture without demonstrated relevancy to the issues presented. It acquired no redeeming quality from the prosecutor's statement that it was being used only "for illustrative purposes" since, as we shall point out, the prosecutor's subsequent utilization of the mathematical testimony was not confined within such limits.

We now turn to the second fundamental error caused by the probability testimony. Quite apart from our foregoing objections to the specific technique employed by the prosecution to estimate the probability in question, we think that the entire enterprise upon which the prosecution embarked, and which was directed to the objective of measuring the likelihood of a random couple possessing the characteristics allegedly distinguishing the robbers, was gravely misguided. At best, it might yield an estimate as to how infrequently bearded Negroes drive yellow cars in the company of blonde females with ponytails.

The prosecution's approach, however, could furnish the jury with absolutely no guidance on the crucial issue: *Of the admittedly few such couples, which one, if any, was guilty of committing this robbery?* Probability theory necessarily remains silent on that question, since no mathematical equation can prove beyond a reasonable doubt (1) that the guilty couple *in fact* possessed the characteristics described by the People's witnesses, or even (2) that only *one* couple possessing those distinctive characteristics could be found in the entire Los Angeles area.

As to the first inherent failing we observe that the prosecution's theory of probability rested on the assumption that the witnesses called by the People had conclusively established that the guilty couple possessed the precise characteristics relied upon by the prosecution. But no mathematical formula could ever establish beyond a reasonable doubt that the prosecution's witnesses correctly observed and accurately described the distinctive features which were employed to link defendants to the crime. (See 2 Wigmore on Evidence (3d ed. 1940) §478.) Conceivably, for example, the guilty couple might have included a light-skinned Negress with bleached hair rather than a Caucasian blonde; or the driver of the car might have been wearing a false beard as a disguise; or the prosecution's witnesses might simply have been unreliable.[16]

The foregoing risks of error permeate the prosecution's circumstantial case. Traditionally, the jury weighs such risks in evaluating the credibility and probative value of trial testimony, but the likelihood of

16. In the instant case, for instance, the victim could not state whether the girl had a ponytail, although the victim observed the girl as she ran away. The witness Bass, on the other hand, was sure that the girl whom he saw had a ponytail. The demonstration engaged in by the prosecutor also leaves no room for the possibility, although perhaps a small one, that the girl whom the victim and the witness observed was, in fact, not the same girl.

human error or of falsification obviously cannot be quantified; that likelihood must therefore be excluded from any effort to assign a *number*
to the probability of guilt or innocence. Confronted with an equation
which purports to yield a numerical index of probable guilt, few juries
could resist the temptation to accord disproportionate weight to that
index; only an exceptional juror, and indeed only a defense attorney
schooled in mathematics, could successfully keep in mind the fact that
the probability computed by the prosecution can represent, *at best,* the
likelihood that a random couple would share the characteristics testified
to by the People's witnesses—*not necessarily the characteristics of the actually
guilty couple.*

As to the second inherent failing in the prosecution's approach, even
assuming that the first failing could be discounted, the most a mathematical computation could *ever* yield would be a measure of the probability that a random couple would possess the distinctive features in
question. In the present case, for example, the prosecution attempted
to compute the probability that a random couple would include a
bearded Negro, a blonde girl with a ponytail, and a partly yellow car;
the prosecution urged that this probability was no more than one in 12
million. Even accepting this conclusion as arithmetically accurate, however, one still could not conclude that the Collinses were probably *the*
guilty couple. On the contrary, as we explain in the Appendix, the prosecution's figures actually imply a likelihood of over 40 percent that the
Collinses could be "duplicated" by at least one other couple who might
equally have committed the San Pedro robbery. Urging that the Collinses be convicted on the basis of evidence which logically establishes
no more than this seems as indefensible as arguing for the conviction
of X on the ground that a witness saw either X or X's twin commit the
crime.

Again, few defense attorneys, and certainly few jurors, could be expected to comprehend this basic flaw in the prosecution's analysis. Conceivably even the prosecutor erroneously believed that his equation
established a high probability that *no* other bearded Negro in the Los
Angeles area drove a yellow car accompanied by a ponytailed blonde.
In any event, although his technique could demonstrate no such thing,
he solemnly told the jury that he had supplied mathematical proof of
guilt.

Sensing the novelty of that notion, the prosecutor told the jurors that
the traditional idea of proof beyond a reasonable doubt represented
"the most hackneyed, stereotyped, trite, misunderstood concept in criminal law." He sought to reconcile the jury to the risk that, under his "new
math" approach to criminal jurisprudence, "on some rare occasion . . .
an innocent person may be convicted." "Without taking that risk," the
prosecution continued, "life would be intolerable . . . because . . . there
would be immunity for the Collinses, for people who chose not to be

employed to go down and push old ladies down and take their money and be immune because how could we ever be sure they are the ones who did it?"

In essence this argument of the prosecutor was calculated to persuade the jury to convict defendants whether or not they were convinced of their guilt to a moral certainty and beyond a reasonable doubt. Undoubtedly the jurors were unduly impressed by the mystique of the mathematical demonstration but were unable to assess its relevancy or value. Although we make no appraisal of the proper applications of mathematical techniques in the proof of facts, we have strong feelings that such applications, particularly in a criminal case, must be critically examined in view of the substantial unfairness to a defendant which may result from ill conceived techniques with which the trier of fact is not technically equipped to cope. We feel that the technique employed in the case before us falls into the latter category. . . .

[W]e think that under the circumstances the "trial by mathematics" so distorted the role of the jury and so disadvantaged counsel for the defense, as to constitute in itself a miscarriage of justice. . . . The judgment against defendant must therefore be reversed. . . .

APPENDIX

If "Pr" represents the probability that a certain distinctive combination of characteristics, hereinafter designated "C," will occur jointly in a random couple, then the probability that C will *not* occur in a random couple is $(1 - \mathrm{Pr})$. Applying the product rule (see fn. 8, ante), the probability that C will occur in none of N couples chosen at random is $(1 - \mathrm{Pr})^N$, so that the probability of C occurring in *at least one* of N random couples is $[1 - (1 - \mathrm{Pr})^N]$.

Given a particular couple selected from a random set of N, the probability of C occurring in that couple (i.e., Pr), multiplied by the probability of C occurring in none of the remaining $N-1$ couples (i.e., $(1 - \mathrm{Pr})^{N-1}$), yields the probability that C will occur in the selected couple and in no other. Thus the probability of C occurring in any particular couple, and in that couple alone, is $[(\mathrm{Pr}) \times (1 - \mathrm{Pr})^{N-1}]$. Since this is true for each of the N couples, the probability that C will occur in precisely *one* of the N couples, without regard to which one, is $[(\mathrm{Pr}) \times (1 - \mathrm{Pr})^{N-1}]$ added N times, because the probability of the occurrence of one of several mutually exclusive events is equal to the sum of the individual probabilities. Thus the probability of C occurring in *exactly one* of N random couples (any one, but only one) is $[(N) \times (\mathrm{Pr}) \times (1 - \mathrm{Pr})^{N-1}]$.

By subtracting the probability that C will occur in *exactly one* couple from the probability that C will occur in *at least one* couple, one obtains the probability that C will occur in *more than one* couple: $[1 - (1 -$

$\text{Pr})^N] - [(N) \times (\text{Pr}) \times (1 - \text{Pr})^{N-1}]$. Dividing this difference by the probability that C will occur in at least one couple (i.e., dividing the difference by $[1 - (1 - \text{Pr})^N]$) then yields *the probability that C will occur more than once in a group of N couples in which C occurs at least once.*

Turning to the case in which C represents the characteristics which distinguish a bearded Negro accompanied by a ponytailed blonde in a yellow car, the prosecution sought to establish that the probability of C occurring in a random couple was 1/12,000,000 — i.e., that Pr = 1/12,000,000. Treating this conclusion as accurate, it follows that, in a population of N random couples, the probability of C occurring *exactly once* is $[(N) \times (1/12{,}000{,}000) \times (1 - 1/12{,}000{,}000)^{N-1}]$. Subtracting this product from $[1 - (1 - 1/12{,}000{,}000)^N]$, the probability of C occurring in at least one couple, and dividing the resulting difference by $[1 - (1 - 1/12{,}000{,}000)^N]$, the probability that C will occur in *at least one* couple, yields the probability that C will occur more than once in a group of N random couples of which at least one couple (namely, the one seen by the witnesses) possesses characteristics C. In other words, the probability of *another* such couple in a population of N is the quotient A/B, where A designates the numerator $[1 - (1 - 1/12{,}000{,}000)^N] - [(N) \times (1/12{,}000{,}000) \times (1 - 1/12{,}000{,}000)^{N-1}]$, and B designates the denominator $[1 - (1 - 1/12{,}000{,}000)^N]$.

N, which represents the total number of all couples who might conceivably have been at the scene of the San Pedro robbery, is not determinable, a fact which suggests yet another basic difficulty with the use of probability theory in establishing identity. One of the imponderables in determining N may well be the number of N-type couples in which a single person may participate. Such considerations make it evident that N, in the area adjoining the robbery, is in excess of several million; as N assumes values of such magnitude, the quotient A/B computed as above, representing the probability of a second couple as distinctive as the one described by the prosecution's witnesses, soon exceeds 4/10. Indeed, as N approaches 12 million, this probability quotient rises to approximately 41 percent. We note parenthetically that if 1/N = Pr, then as N increases indefinitely, the quotient in question approaches a limit of $(e-2)/(e-1)$, where "e" represents the transcendental number (approximately 2.71828) familiar in mathematics and physics.

Hence, even if we should accept the prosecution's figures without question, we would derive a probability of over 40 percent that the couple observed by the witnesses could be "duplicated" by at least one other equally distinctive interracial couple in the area, including a Negro with a beard and mustache, driving a partly yellow car in the company of a blonde with a ponytail. Thus the prosecution's computations, far from establishing beyond a reasonable doubt that the Collinses were the couple described by the prosecution's witnesses, imply a very substantial likelihood that the area contained *more than one* such couple, and that a couple *other* than the Collinses was the one observed at the scene of the robbery. (See generally: Hoel, Introduction to Mathematical Statistics (3d ed. 1962); Hodges & Leymann, Basic Concepts of Probability and Statistics (1964); Lindgren & McElrath, Introduction to Probability and Statistics (1959).)

Do you agree with the result in *Collins?* With all the reasons the court gives for reversing the conviction? Would the same circumstantial evidence that was introduced in *Collins,* but without the probability testimony and argumentation, be sufficient to sustain defendant's conviction? Should probability evidence of the sort introduced in *Collins* and *Sneed* be admitted if the foundational problems—the size of the sample, the establishment of realistic individual probabilities, and the certainty of mutual independence—can be overcome? Can these problems ever be overcome? Could the court take judicial notice of individual probabilities?

For more on the use of probability theory in trials and in the *Sneed* and *Collins* cases in particular see P. Tillers & E. Green, Probability and Inference in the Law of Evidence (1988); Finkelstein & Fairley, A Bayesian Approach to Identification Evidence, 83 Harv. L. Rev. 489 (1970); Tribe, Trial by Mathematics: Precision and Ritual in the Legal Process, 84 Harv. L. Rev. 1329 (1971); Finkelstein & Fairley, The Continuing Debate over Mathematics in the Law of Evidence: A Comment on "Trial by Mathematics," 84 Harv. L. Rev. 1801 (1971); Tribe, A Further Critique of Mathematical Proof, 84 Harv. L. Rev. 1810 (1971); Note, Evidence, etc., 1967 Duke L.J. 665. See also Kaplan, Decision Theory and the Factfinding Process, 20 Stan. L. Rev. 1065 (1968).

SMITH v. RAPID TRANSIT, INC.
317 Mass. 469, 58 N.E.2d 754 (1945)

SPALDING, Justice. The decisive question in this case is whether there was evidence for the jury that the plaintiff was injured by a bus of the defendant that was operated by one of its employees in the course of his employment. If there was, the defendant concedes that the evidence warranted the submission to the jury of the question of the operator's negligence in the management of the bus. The case is here on the plaintiff's exception to the direction of a verdict for the defendant.

These facts could have been found: While the plaintiff at about 1:00 A.M. on February 6, 1941, was driving an automobile on Main Street, Winthrop, in an easterly direction toward Winthrop Highlands, she observed a bus coming toward her which she described as a "great big, long, wide affair." The bus, which was proceeding at about forty miles an hour, "forced her to turn to the right," and her automobile collided with a "parked car." The plaintiff was coming from Dorchester. The department of public utilities had issued a certificate of public convenience or necessity to the defendant for three routes in Winthrop, one of which included Main Street, where the accident occurred, and this was in effect in February, 1941. "There was another bus line in operation in Winthrop at that time but not on Main Street." According to the defendant's timetable, buses were scheduled to leave Winthrop Highlands for Maverick Square via Main Street at 12:10 A.M., 12:45 A.M., 1:15 A.M., and 2:15 A.M. The running time for this trip at that time of night was thirty minutes.

The direction of a verdict for the defendant was right. The ownership of the bus was a matter of conjecture. While the defendant had the sole franchise for operating a bus line on Main Street, Winthrop, this did not preclude private or chartered buses from using this street; the bus in question could very well have been one operated by someone other than the defendant. It was said in Sargent v. Massachusetts Accident Co., 307 Mass. 246, 250, 29 N.E.2d 825, 827, that it is "not enough that mathematically the chances somewhat favor a proposition to be proved; for example, the fact that colored automobiles made in the current year outnumber black ones would not warrant a finding that an undescribed automobile of the current year is colored and not black, nor would the fact that only a minority of men die of cancer warrant a finding that a particular man did not die of cancer." The most that can be said of the evidence in the instant case is that perhaps the mathematical chances somewhat favor the proposition that a bus of the defendant caused the accident. This was not enough. A "proposition is proved by a preponderance of the evidence if it is made to appear more likely or probable in the sense that actual belief in its truth, derived from the evidence, exists in the mind or minds of the tribunal notwithstanding any doubts that may still linger there." Sargent v. Massachusetts Accident Co., 307 Mass. 246, 250, 29 N.E.2d 825, 827. . . .

Exceptions overruled.

Problem: License Plate Roulette

Personal injury action by *P* against Lawton's Supermarket. *P* was run down at an intersection in Lincoln, Massachusetts, by a truck with a Massachusetts license plate with five characters, the first three characters being "LAW"; *P* did not see the last two characters on the license plate. At trial, evidence is presented that Lawton's owns four trucks whose license plates read "LAW01" to "LAW04" and that Lawton's trucks were on the road making deliveries at the time of the accident. Lawton's introduces evidence that there are two other trucks with Massachusetts license plates that read "LAW — —," one garaged in the neighboring town of Lexington and one in Springfield, 100 miles away.

What is the probability that the truck that hit *P* belongs to Lawton's? Should the statistical evidence be admitted? Is the evidence sufficient to support a verdict for *P*?

Problem: Blue Bus

P is negligently run off the road into a parked car by a blue bus. *P* is prepared to prove that *D* operates four-fifths of all the blue buses that use the route. What effect, if any, should such proof be given?[1]

L.J. COHEN, THE PROBABLE AND THE PROVABLE
77-81 (1977)

THE DIFFICULTY ABOUT NEGATION

Consider, for example, a case in which it is common ground that 499 people paid for admission to a rodeo, and that 1,000 are counted on the seats, of whom *A* is one. Suppose no tickets were issued and there can be no testimony as to whether *A* paid for admission or climbed over the fence. So by any plausible criterion of mathematical probability there is a .501 probability, on the admitted facts, that he did not pay. The mathematicist theory would apparently imply that in such circumstances the rodeo organizers are entitled to judgement against *A* for the admission-money, since the balance of probability (and also the difference between prior and posterior probabilities) would lie in their favor. But it seems manifestly unjust that *A* should lose his case when there is an agreed mathematical probability of as high as .499 that he in fact paid for admission.

Indeed, if the organizers were really entitled to judgement against *A*, they would presumably be equally entitled to judgement against each person in the same situation as *A*. So they might conceivably be entitled to recover 1,000 admission-moneys, when it was admitted that 499 had actually been paid. The absurd injustice of this suffices to show that there is something wrong somewhere. But where? . . .

An important part of the trouble seems to be that, if standards of proof are interpreted in accordance with a theory of probability that has a complementational principle for negation, the litigants are construed as seeking to divide a determinate quantity of case-merit, as it

1. This problem is based on Tribe, Trial by Mathematics: Precision and Ritual in the Legal Process, 84 Harv. L. Rev. 1329, 1341 (1971).

were, between them. Such an interpretation treats it as an officially accepted necessity that the merit of the loser's case in a civil suit varies
inversely with that of the winner's, and this generates paradox where
proof is allowed on the mere balance of the two probabilities. Nor can
we say then as lawyers sometimes do say in practice that the defendant's
case is equally good on the facts in both of two similar lawsuits, while
the plaintiff's case is better in one than the other. But we can say this
quite consistently, and avoid the paradox, if we abandon any complementational principle for negation. We may then suppose litigants to
be taking part in a contest of case-strength or case-weight, rather than
dividing a determinate quantity of case-merit. The only possibility of
injustice that is then officially countenanced is the possibility that one
side may not have put forward as strong a case as it could. But where
that happens it is the fault of the litigant or of his lawyers or witnesses,
not of the legal system. . . . [I]f standards of juridical proof are interpreted in terms of inductive, rather than mathematical, probabilities
this is precisely what follows.

The point under discussion has not gone unnoticed in the courts. A
Massachusetts judge once remarked

> It has been held not enough that mathematically the chances somewhat fa-
> vour a proposition to be proved; for example, the fact that coloured automobiles
> made in the current year outnumber black ones would not warrant a finding
> that an undescribed automobile of the current year is coloured and not black.
> . . . After the evidence has been weighed, that proposition is proved by a pre-
> ponderance of evidence if it is made to appear more likely or probable in the
> sense that actual belief in its truth, derived from the evidence, exists in the mind
> or minds of the tribunal notwithstanding any doubts that may still linger there.[4]

In other words, the standard of proof in civil cases is to be interpreted
in terms leading one to expect that, after all the evidence has been
heard, a balance of probability in favor of a certain conclusion will produce belief in the truth of that conclusion among reasonable men. So
we need a concept of probability that admits a threshold for rational
acceptance, or moderate belief, which is quite distinct from the threshold for belief beyond reasonable doubt.

Problem: Conjunction

Assume that a probabilistically-minded jury, having heard and
weighed the evidence, concludes that the likelihood that the defendant

---

4. Lummus, J., in "Sargent v. Massachusetts Accident Co.," 307 Mass. 246, 29 N.E.2d 825,
827 (1940) quoted by V.C. Ball, "The moment of truth: probability theory and the standards
of proof," in Essays on Procedure and Evidence ed. T.G. Rondy Jr. and R.N. Covington (1961),
p. 95.

was negligent is .6, the likelihood that the defendant caused the plaintiff's injury is .6, and that the evidence of negligence is entirely independent of the evidence of causation. Should the jury decide for the plaintiff or for the defendant?

Problem: Prison Yard

In an enclosed yard are 25 identically dressed prisoners and a prison guard. The sole witness is too far away to distinguish features. He sees the guard, recognizable by his uniform, trip and fall, apparently knocking himself out. The prisoners huddle and argue. One breaks away from the others and goes to a shed in the corner of the yard to hide. The other 24 set upon the fallen guard and kill him. After the killing, the hidden prisoner emerges from the shed and mixes with the other prisoners. When the authorities later enter the yard, they find the dead guard and the 25 prisoners.

The prosecutor indicts one of the prisoners—call him prisoner #1. If the only evidence at trial is the testimony of the distant witness, is prisoner #1 entitled to a directed verdict of acquittal?

Suppose, in addition, that the prosecutor calls prisoner #2 as a witness for the prosecution, and prisoner #2 testifies that it was he who disassociated himself from the others and hid in the shed. Is prisoner #1 now entitled to a directed verdict of acquittal?

The *Collins* case, Cohen's gate-crasher hypothetical, and the foregoing Problems raise the issue of what effect, if any, mathematical or probabilistic proof should be given. In application, this issue must be broken down into two main questions. The first question is whether mathematical proof should be admitted at all. If so, there are subsidiary questions: What should the factfinder be told about it? In what form? One might ask this same question from a quite different perspective: Is it possible to utilize *any* proof that is *not* probabilistic? The second main question is: To what extent may probabilistic and mathematical models be used as standards on which to base a criminal conviction or civil judgment? This question deals with the *sufficiency* of proof to sustain a verdict.

C. NESSON, THE EVIDENCE OR THE EVENT? ON JUDICIAL PROOF AND THE ACCEPTABILITY OF VERDICTS
98 Harv. L. Rev. 1357 (1985)

Many decision-theory modes suggest that factfinders should base their decisions on the laws of probability in order to minimize the costs of erroneous judicial decisions. These models ignore the judicial function of generating acceptable verdicts which reflect and project substantive legal rules. . . . A court must generate an acceptable account of what actually happened as a predicate to imposing a sanction for violation of a substantive legal rule. . . . Many procedural and structural mechanisms of the legal system serve to enhance the acceptability of judicial verdicts. . . . The goal of generating acceptable verdicts is not met simply by choosing the verdict that is most probably accurate. Acceptable verdicts and probable verdicts might appear to coincide, given that one obvious way to gain public acceptance is to search for truth. But the correlation between probability and acceptability is not exact: a probable verdict may not be acceptable, and an acceptable verdict may not be probable.

Cases of naked statistical proof present the most provocative example of probable verdicts that are unacceptable. In these cases, the evidence suggests a sufficiently high numerical probability of liability, but the absence of deference-inducing mechanisms in the judicial process is such that the public is unable to view a verdict against the defendant as a statement about what actually happened. The statistical nature of the evidence precludes both acceptance of the verdict against the defendant and internalization of the underlying norms.

Decision theorists have tried, with great difficulty, to accommodate the blue bus case in their models. The logic of the standard decision-theory model holds that the plaintiff is entitled to win because he has shown, much more probably than not, that a bus owned by the Blue Bus Company ran him off the road. But most decision theorists have suggested that courts should grant a directed verdict to the defendant. The problem for the decision theorists, then, has been to explain their answer to the blue bus hypothetical without having to abandon their theory.

Professor Tribe has attempted to solve the decision theorists' problem. He has asserted that verdicts are based on subjective probability assessments. Although the plaintiff's objective proof indicates an 80% likelihood that the defendant's bus caused him to be injured, a juror is not bound to believe this probability. The very tenuousness of the plaintiff's evidence, Tribe argues, may cause the juror to feel some skepticism about the plaintiff's case. This skepticism may be enough to reduce the juror's subjective probability assessment of the defendant's liability to less than 50%. The juror presumably believes that if the defendant's bus really had forced the plaintiff off the road, the plaintiff would have had better proof; all told, the odds are less than fifty-fifty that it was the defendant's bus.

Tribe's argument explains how a juror might find against the plaintiff, but the actual cases involving the blue bus hypothetical do not pose that problem. Plaintiffs in such cases would almost certainly lose by directed verdict; the evidence would never reach the jury. Tribe's argument explains why a court should refuse to grant a directed verdict to the plaintiff, but his analysis does not explain why the judge should throw the plaintiff out of court. The jurors could arrive at a subjective probability higher than 50%; no objective evidence *compels* a juror to drop his subjective probability so drastically that the plaintiff must lose. The logic of Tribe's argument leads to the conclusion that the case should reach the jury, and the jury's verdict should be upheld, no matter which way it comes out.

Other commentators have rationalized granting a directed verdict against the plaintiff on the ground that any other result would impose too large a burden on the defendant. If a court held the Blue Bus Company liable in this case, courts would have to hold the company liable in all similar cases, even though it was responsible for only 80% of them. Some decision theorists consider this result unfair to the defendant company, even though the alternative of awarding nothing to all such plaintiffs hardly seems fairer. Others consider the result economically inefficient. Richard Posner, for example, argues that granting an award to the plaintiff—and to all similarly situated plaintiffs—would dislocate the market: it would disproportionately burden defendants like the Blue Bus Company and subsidize their smaller competitors. Because these competitors would then have little incentive to drive carefully, accident rates would increase. Simple application of a more-probable-than-not rule would not maximize utility. Posner would thus apply a special rule of proof in cases like the blue bus case, a requirement that the plaintiff offer some evidence of liability in addition to the statistical information. In effect, Posner's call for additional evidence reflects a need for a judicial mechanism that will induce deference to the jury's decision and thus promote an acceptable verdict.

Proportionate Damages.—One obvious alternative to a directed verdict for the defendant in the blue bus case would be to make the Blue Bus Company pay 80% of the plaintiff's damages. This solution responds to both the economic and fairness arguments advanced by decision theorists. It requires the company to pay in total (in this and all similar cases) for no more than the damage it probably caused over the long run. Forcing the Blue Bus Company to pay 80% of the damages in all such cases might still cause economic dislocation if the company's competitors had to pay nothing. This dislocation could be avoided, however, by requiring competitors to pay their proportionate shares as well. If there were a 20% probability that a defendant caused the plaintiff's damages, then the defendant would pay 20%. The transaction costs of litigating claims might suggest some minimal percentage (or dollar) threshold for liability, but it would surely not be as high as 50%. Requiring the Blue Bus Company's competitors to pay their fair share would give the plaintiff full recovery and properly balance the relative economic impact of the damage awards on the bus industry.

This proportionate-award approach could be applied to all cases in which the jury is uncertain of the facts on which a defendant's liability is predicated, including cases not based on statistical evidence. If the jury, after hearing a mass of conflicting evidence in a negligence case, is 40% certain that the defendant acted negligently, then the proportionate award approach would require the defendant to pay an award of 40% of the total actual damages, instead of paying nothing.

The proportionate-award approach addresses the concerns of the decision theorists so well that a question arises as to why our legal system is so firmly committed to the all-or-nothing rule. The answer is that a proportionate award projects a substantive legal rule that differs from the rule projected by an award of full damages. The former might project a behavioral message that differs from the message the court would convey by the standard application of the rule. Courts have resisted the proportionate-award approach because in most cases they have not desired to project the new legal rule and the new behavioral message that would accompany such an award.

The blue bus case illustrates this proposition. A court faced with such a case might choose to apportion damages according to the probability that the bus company injured the plaintiff. But a proportionate award against the company would not exemplify the basic negligence rule and its behavioral norm. The award would instead project a very different and seemingly perverse legal rule: courts will hold the defendant liable, notwithstanding the possibility that he committed no wrong, if the nature of his activity places him within a class of suspect persons. The behavioral norm embodied in this rule is not one of care and safety. In response to the rule, the Blue Bus Company might attempt to minimize exposure to liability by running fewer buses, rather than by trying to drive more carefully; the verdict sends a message about the volume of business, rather than one about safety standards. Indeed, proportionate awards of this kind make safety precautions more difficult to justify in economic terms. Thus, judicial hesitation to award proportionate damages in cases like the blue bus case may well arise, in part, from a reluctance to project the legal rule and behavioral message that would accompany such an award.

Courts have awarded proportionate damages, however, when such awards would convey desirable behavioral norms. In Summers v. Tice, for example, the plaintiff sued two hunters who had negligently fired in his direction. The court held that in the absence of any evidence as to which hunter had actually shot the plaintiff, the hunters were jointly liable for the plaintiff's injury. Similarly, in Sindell v. Abbott Laboratories, plaintiffs brought a class action against manufacturers of the drug DES. The court held that in the absence of evidence as to which manufacturers had made the product that caused the plaintiffs' injuries, each manufacturer was liable for the proportion of the judgment represented by its share of the DES market.

These cases are distinguishable from the blue bus hypothetical. In the hypothetical, only one bus company was negligent, and there is no basis for determining which one. A verdict that the defendant is liable would project the substantive rule that one need not act negligently to be liable. In *Summers* and *Sindell*, all of the defendants acted negligently, even though one cannot know which defendant actually caused the injury. The legal rule that these cases project is that when we do not know the identity of the person who caused an injury, we will award damages against all negligent parties in proportion to their probable responsibility for the specific harm. The rule and its behavioral message seem sensible enough. In *Summers* and *Sindell*, the courts imposed liability because the defendants acted wrongly, the courts thereby projected a message about the result of wrongful activity. . . .

The outcomes of the cases turn on substantive issues that relate to the effects of generating new legal rules. In *Summers* and *Sindell*, the courts generated a new definition of what was relevant to a finding of liability and thus generated a new rule of substantive law. Whether the courts generated a good rule depends on one's assessment of the rule and of the process of judicial lawmaking. Casting these issues as problems of proof serves only to obscure them. The cases concern changing the elements of the substantive legal rule; the problem of proof is simply that of generating acceptable conclusions about those elements.

Although the traditional logic of proof rules can inhibit judicial efforts to find liability when the evidence is merely statistical, we should recognize that courts can nevertheless find liability and generate new substantive law by redefining the elements of the legal rule and the sanction so they reflect the statistical nature of the evidence. The current reluctance of the judicial system to impose liability in such situations cannot be overcome by changing the grammar of proof, because this grammar is essential to achieving the projection and affirmation of the law's behavioral norms. Instead, reform must come, and should be welcomed, by bringing about changes in the factual elements that must be proved. An instinctive reaction against probabilistic proof should not constrain efforts to restructure substantive law by changing the rules that govern what must be proved.

GEORGE F. WILL, DNA, THE DEATH PENALTY AND HORRIFYING MISTAKES
Washington Post, April 6, 2000

"Don't you worry about it," said the Oklahoma prosecutor to the defense lawyer. "We're gonna needle your client. You know, lethal injection, the needle. We're going to needle Robert."

Oklahoma almost did. Robert Miller spent nine years on death row, during six of which the state had DNA test results proving that his sperm was not that of the man who raped and killed the 92-year-old woman. The prosecutor said the tests only proved that another man had been with Mr. Miller during the crime. Finally, the weight of scientific evidence got Mr. Miller released and another man indicted.

You could fill a book with such hair-curling true stories of blighted lives and justice traduced. Three authors have filled one. It should change the argument about capital punishment and other aspects of U.S. criminal justice. Conservatives, especially, should draw this lesson from the book: Capital punishment is a government program, so skepticism is in order.

Horror, too, is a reasonable response to what Barry Scheck, Peter Neufeld and Jim Dwyer demonstrate in "Actual Innocence: Five Days to Execution and Other Dispatches From the Wrongly Convicted." You will not soon read a more frightening book. It is a catalogue of appalling miscarriages of justice, some of them nearly lethal. Their cumulative weight compels the conclusion that many innocent people are in prison and some innocent people have been executed.

Mr. Scheck and Mr. Neufeld (both members of O.J. Simpson's "dream team" of defense lawyers) founded the pro-bono Innocence Project at the Benjamin N. Cardozo School of Law in New York to aid persons who convincingly claim to have been wrongly convicted. Mr. Dwyer, winner of two Pulitzer Prizes, is currently a columnist for the New York Daily News. Their book is a heartbreaking and infuriating compendium of stories of lives ruined by:

Mistaken identifications by eyewitnesses or victims, which contributed to 84 percent of the convictions overturned by the Innocence Project's DNA exonerations.

Criminal investigations, especially of the most heinous crimes, that become "echo chambers" in which, because of the normal craving for retribution, the perceptions of prosecutors and jurors are shaped by what they want to be true.

The sinister culture of jailhouse snitches, who earn reduced sentences by fabricating "admissions" by fellow inmates to unsolved crimes.

Incompetent defense representation.

The list of ways that the criminal justice system misfires could be extended, but some numbers tell the most serious story: In the 24 years since the resumption of executions under Supreme Court guidelines, about 620 have occurred, but 87 condemned persons—one for every seven executed—had their convictions vacated by exonerating evidence. In eight of these cases, and in many more exonerations not involving death row, DNA evidence was conclusive.

One inescapable inference from these numbers is that some of the 620 persons executed were innocent. Which is why, after the exoneration of 13 prisoners on death row in Illinois since 1987, Governor George Ryan, a Republican, has imposed a moratorium on executions.

Two powerful arguments for capital punishment are that its deterrent effect saves lives and it enhances society's valuation of life by expressing proportionate anger at murder. But that valuation is lowered by careless or corrupt administration of capital punishment, which "Actual Innocence" powerfully suggests is intolerably common.

PETER NEUFELD & BARRY SCHECK, BETTER WAYS TO FIND THE GUILTY
N.Y. Times, June 6, 2000

We know eyewitnesses sometimes make mistakes. Snitches tell lies. Confessions are coerced or fabricated. Racism trumps the truth. Defense lawyers sleep through trials. Prosecutors and police tell fibs.

Never have these flaws been more starkly exposed than in the last decade, when DNA has freed scores of wrongly convicted people and kept thousands of the wrongly accused out of jail. For the most part, the lessons have been ignored. Of all the statistics tallied by the system, not one shows the number of innocent people sent to prison. Oversight is fundamental for any system in which life or liberty is at stake. We have mechanisms to investigate plane crashes, deaths in hospitals and collapses of buildings. Only the criminal justice system exempts itself from accountability for its mistakes.

Among the bright exceptions to the indifference to accountability is Gov. George Ryan of Illinois, who followed his landmark moratorium on executions with appointment of a commission to find out why 13 men were wrongly sent to death row. New York's governor, George Pataki, has proposed that a committee review all convictions overturned on DNA evidence.

Their findings should be used to make it harder for innocent people to wind up in prison. And to make it easier for these people to get out, Congress should pass the Innocence Protection Act, which would give inmates the right to DNA tests to prove innocence and would require the preservation of evidence after conviction. Remember, though, that DNA solves crimes only when there is biological evidence.

The quality of old-fashioned evidence can be improved. Eyewitnesses will produce fewer false identifications and just as many correct ones, social scientists say, if police follow a few simple techniques that cut down guessing by witnesses and hints by detectives. False confessions can be curbed by requiring that all interrogations be recorded on tape, as is already done in Minnesota, Alaska, Ireland and Britain.

Convicting an innocent person not only commits a terrible injustice, but leaves a guilty criminal on the streets. Every state and every American has an interest in doing all we can to prevent it from happening.

NOTE—DNA EVIDENCE

Recent advances in science's ability to obtain, identify, and compare human DNA have revolutionized the field of identification evidence. More prevalent than blood, more easily obtainable than fingerprints, and now more reliable than either blood or prints or a host of other human traces offered for identification (for example, hair follicles, bite marks, scars, tattoos, or voiceprints), DNA evidence now makes it possible to inculpate or exculpate a suspect in a rape, assault, or murder case, prove or disprove paternity, or establish the *corpus delicti* to a scientific probability never before possible. This powerful tool, however, presents many problems when it is applied to a particular case. Some of these are familiar forensic problems such as reliability in the gathering and handling of the evidence by investigatory authorities, laboratories, and prosecutors. Others derive from the scientific nature of the evidence, the involvement of experts, and the probabilistic basis for the probative value of the evidence. As advances in DNA techniques and testing continue, and as more is understood about the assumptions and probabilistic underpinnings of the science, courts face increasing challenges to harness the positive potential of this evidentiary genie while avoiding the dangers of misapplication or over valuation of DNA proof.

J. McKENNA, J. CECIL & P. COUKOS, "REFERENCE GUIDE ON FORENSIC DNA EVIDENCE"
in Reference Manual on Scientific Evidence (Federal Judicial Center 1994)

DNA analysis is based on well-established principles of the wide genetic variability among humans and the presumed uniqueness of an individual's genetic makeup (identical twins excepted). Laboratory techniques for isolating and observing the DNA of human chromosomes have long been used in nonforensic scientific settings. The forensic application of the technique involves comparing a known DNA sample obtained from a suspect with a DNA sample obtained from the crime scene, and often with one obtained from the victim. Such analyses typically are offered to support or refute the claim that a criminal suspect contributed a biological specimen (e.g., semen or blood) collected at a crime scene. For example, an analyst may testify on the basis of a report that includes the following:

> Deoxyribonucleic acid (DNA) profiles for [the specific sites tested] were developed from specimens obtained from the crime scene, from the victim, and

from the suspect. Based on these results, the DNA profiles from the crime scene match those of the suspect. The probability of selecting at random from the population an unrelated individual having a DNA profile matching the suspect's is approximately 1 in 200,000 in Blacks, 1 in 200,000 in Whites, and 1 in 100,000 in Hispanics.

An objection to this sort of testimony usually comes before the court when the defense moves to exclude the testimony and the report. Such a motion can be made before or during trial, depending on circumstances and the court's rules regarding *in limine* motions. Before the Supreme Court's decision in Daubert v. Merrell Dow Pharmaceuticals, Inc., such disputes often were aired in hearings devoted to determining whether the theory and techniques of DNA identification were generally accepted by the relevant scientific community and so satisfied the *Frye* standard. Since *Daubert*, general acceptance remains an issue but only one of several a court may consider when DNA evidence is offered. Frequently disputed issues include the validity of applying the standard RFLP (restriction fragment length polymorphism) technique to crime samples, the proper interpretation of test results as showing a match, and the appropriate statistical determination of the probability of a co-incidental match. . . .

RFLP analysis is based on the observable variability of human genetic characteristics. Human genetic information (one's genome) is encoded primarily in chromosomal DNA, which is present in most body cells. Except for sperm and egg cells, each DNA-carrying cell contains 46 chromosomes. Forty-four of these are arranged in homologous pairs of one autosome (nonsex chromosome) inherited from the mother and one autosome from the father. The cells also carry two sex chromosomes (an X from the mother and either an X or a Y from the father). Chromosomal DNA sequences vary in length and are made up of four organic bases (adenine (*A*), cytosine (*C*), thymine (*T*), and guanine (*G*)). *A* pairs only with *T*; *C* pairs only with *G*. These sequences of base pairs are arranged in long chains that form the twisted double helix, or ladder structure, of DNA. Thus, if the bases on one side of the helix or ladder are represented as CATAGAT, the complementary side would be GTATCTA.

Most DNA-carrying cells in a human contain the same information encoded in the approximately 3.3 billion base pairs per set of chromosomes in each cell. More than 99% of the base pairs in human cells are the same for all individuals, which accounts for the many common traits that make humans an identifiable species. The remaining base pairs (about 3 million) are particular to an individual (identical twins excepted), which accounts for most of the wide variation that makes each person unique.

A gene (characteristic DNA sequence) is found at a particular site, or locus, on a particular chromosome. For instance, a gene for eye color is found at the same place or locus on the same chromosome in every individual. Normal individuals have two copies of each gene at a given locus—one from the father and one from the mother. A locus on the DNA molecule where all humans have the same genetic code is called *monomorphic*. However, genes vary. An individual may receive the genetic code for blue eyes from his or her mother and the genetic code for brown eyes from his or her father. An alternative form of a gene is known as an *allele*. A locus where the allele differs among individuals is called *polymorphic*, and the difference is known as a *polymorphism*.

Although some polymorphisms have been found to govern what makes individuals observably distinct from one another (e.g., eye color), others serve no known function. Among these noncoding DNA regions are some in which certain base pair sequences repeat in tandem many times (e.g., CATCATCAT . . . paired with GTAGTAGTA . . .). This is known as a *Variable Number of Tandem Repeats*, or a VNTR. The number of base pairs and the sequence of pairs vary from locus to locus on one chromosome and from chromosome to chromosome. RFLP analysis allows scientists to determine the size of a repetitive sequence. Because the length of these sequences (sometimes called band size) of base pairs is highly polymorphic, although not necessarily unique to an individual, comparison of several corresponding sequences of DNA from known (suspect) and unknown (forensic) sources gives information about whether the two samples are from the same source. . . .

First, DNA is extracted from an evidence sample collected at the crime scene. Second, it is digested by a restriction enzyme that recognizes a particular known sequence called a restriction site and cuts the DNA there. The result is many DNA fragments of varying sizes. Third, digested DNA from the crime sample is placed in a well at the end of a lane in an agarose gel, which is a gelatin-like material solidified in a slab about five inches thick. Digested DNA from the suspect is placed in another well on the same gel. Typically, control specimens of DNA fragments of known size, and, where appropriate, DNA specimens obtained from a victim, are run on the same gel. Mild electric current applied to the gel slowly separates the fragments in each lane by length, as shorter fragments travel farther than longer, heavier fragments. This procedure is known as *gel electrophoresis*.

Fourth, the resulting array of fragments is transferred for manageability to a sheet of nylon by a process known as *Southern blotting*. Either during or after this transfer, the DNA is denatured ("unzipped") by heating, separating the double helix into single strands. The weak bonds that connect the two strands are susceptible to heat and salinity. The double helix can be unzipped or denatured without disrupting the chain on either side. Fifth, a probe—usually with a radioactive tag—is applied to the membrane. The probe is a single strand of DNA that hybridizes with (binds to) its complementary sequence when it is applied to the samples of denatured DNA. The DNA locus identified by a given probe is found by experimentation, and individual probes often are patented by their developers. Different laboratories may use different probes (i.e., they may test for alleles at different loci). Where different probes are used, test results are not comparable.

Finally, excess hybridization solution is washed off, and the nylon membrane is placed between at least two sheets of photographic film. Over time, the radioactive probe material exposes the film where the biological probe has hybridized with the DNA fragments. The result is an *autoradiograph*, or an *autorad*, a visual pattern of bands representing specific DNA fragments. An autorad that shows two bands in a single lane indicates that the source is heterozygous for that locus (i.e., he or she inherited a different allele from each parent). If the autorad shows only one band, the person may be homozygous for that allele (i.e., each parent contributed the same variant of the gene). Together, the two alleles make up the person's genotype (genetic code) for the specific locus associated with the probe.

Once an appropriately exposed autorad is obtained, the probe is washed from the membrane, and the process is repeated with different probes that bind to different sequences of DNA. Three to five probes are typically used, the number depending in part on the amount of testable DNA recovered from the crime sample. The result is a set of autorads, each of which shows the results of one probe. . . . Illustrations of the results of all probes depict an overlay of multiple films or the results from a multilocus probe.

If the two DNA samples are from the same source, and if the laboratory procedures are conducted properly, hybridized DNA fragments of approximately the same length should appear at the same point in the suspect and evidence specimen lanes. If, on visual inspection, the DNA band patterns for the suspect and the evidence sample appear to be aligned on the autorad, this impression is verified by a computerized measurement. If the two bands fall within a specified length, or match window (e.g., ± 2.5% of band length), a match is declared for that probe or allele. For forensic purposes, a match means that the patterns are consistent with the conclusion that the two DNA samples came from the same source. Taken together, the results of the probes form the DNA profile. . . .

If a profile match is declared, it means only that the DNA profile of the suspect is consistent with that of the source of the crime sample. The crime sample may be from the suspect or from someone else whose profile, using the particular probes involved, happens to match that of the suspect. Expert testimony concerning the frequency with which the observed alleles are found in the appropriate comparison population is necessary for the finder of fact to make an informed assessment of the incriminating value of this match.[55]

---

55. Statistical testimony concerning the likelihood of a DNA profile matching by coincidence is necessary to assess the probative value of the matching profile. . . . See People v. Barney, 8 Cal. App. 4th 798, 817 (Cal. Ct. App. 1992) ("The statistical calculation step is the

The frequency with which an individual allele occurs in the comparison population is taken to be the probability of a coincidental match on that allele. These individual probabilities of a coincidental match are combined into an estimate of the probability of a coincidental match on the entire profile. This estimate is interpreted as the probability that a person selected at random from a comparison population would have a DNA profile that matches that of the crime sample. The probability estimate typically provided by a forensic expert cannot be interpreted strictly as the probability that an examiner will declare a match when the samples are actually from different sources. That probability is affected by other factors, the most important of which is the chance of laboratory error.

Differences in scientific opinion arise with respect to two main issues: (1) the appropriate method for computing the estimated probability of a coincidental match of a DNA profile; and (2) the selection of an appropriate comparison population. These issues are addressed below.

A.   WHAT PROCEDURE WAS USED TO ESTIMATE THE PROBABILITY THAT
     THE INDIVIDUAL ALLELES MATCH BY COINCIDENCE?

Ascertaining an allele's frequency in a given population is essentially an empirical exercise. A sample of individuals is drawn from the designated population, their DNA is examined with genetic probes used in forensic analysis, and a table of frequencies is developed. For example, the FBI has constructed frequency tables using a fixed-bin method, in which standardized size markers are used to define boundaries of bins into which are sorted the fragment sizes observed in a sample population. . . .

Assumptions of classical population genetics are used to estimate the probability that a person chosen at random from the specified population would exhibit the same genotype as the suspect's. The greater the probability of such a coincidental match, the lower the incriminating value of the evidence.

---

pivotal element of DNA analysis, for the evidence means nothing without a determination of the statistical significance of a match of DNA patterns."); D. H. Kaye, The Forensic Debut of the National Research Council's DNA Report: Population Structure, Ceiling Frequencies and the Need for Numbers, 34 Jurimetrics J. 369, 381 (1994) ("As a legal matter, a completely unexplained statement of a 'match' should be inadmissible because it is too cryptic to be weighed fairly by the jury, . . . [H]ow to present to a jury valid scientific evidence of a match is a legal rather than a scientific issue falling far outside the domain of the general acceptance test and the helds of statistics and population genetics. Thus, it would not be 'meaningless' to inform the jury that two samples match and that this match makes it more probable, in an amount that is not precisely known, that the DNA in the samples comes from the same person."). But see United States v. Martinez, 3 F.3d 1191, 1199 (8th Cir. 1993) (ruling that admitting evidence of a DNA profile match without evidence concerning the statistical probability of a coincidental match was not reversible error where defendant stipulated that statistical evidence was not required), cert. denied, 114 S. Ct. 734 (1994).

B.   HOW WERE THE PROBABILITY ESTIMATES FOR COINCIDENTAL
MATCHES OF INDIVIDUAL ALLELES COMBINED FOR AN OVERALL
ESTIMATE OF A COINCIDENTAL MATCH OF THE ENTIRE DNA PROFILE?

One of the most difficult and contentious issues in forensic use of DNA evidence is how to estimate the probability that two DNA profiles match by chance. This issue has become especially difficult in federal courts since the Supreme Court's decision in *Daubert.* . . .

What follows is a description of two techniques for estimating the probability of a coincidental match: the *product rule technique* and the *modified ceiling principle technique,* which was recommended by the NRC (National Research Council of the National Academy of Sciences) committee. The probability estimates can vary widely depending on the technique used.

1.   Product Rule Technique

The product rule technique offers the most straightforward method of computing the probability of a matching DNA profile. To compute the probability of a random occurrence of a specific pattern of alleles in a DNA profile, the analyst multiplies the separate estimated probabilities of a random occurrence of each allele in the comparison population. When these individual probabilities are multiplied, the estimated probability of a distinctive pattern occurring at random may be less than one in several hundred thousand.

The probability estimate resulting from the multiplication assumes that the individual alleles identified by genetic probes are independent of each other. If the probabilities of the individual alleles are not independent (i.e., if certain alleles are likely to occur together in a person), multiplying the individual allele frequencies may underestimate or overestimate the true probability of matching alleles in the chosen population and thereby misstate the incriminating value of the evidence. Critics of the product rule technique contend that in some ethnic subpopulations the alleles identified by commonly used genetic probes are not independent, and that using a broad-based comparison population is therefore inappropriate. They prefer estimation techniques that do not require analysts to assume the independence of individual alleles in large comparison populations.

2.   Modified Ceiling Principle Technique

The method recommended by the NRC committee involves conservative interpretations of existing population data. As a preliminary test, the laboratory should examine its population database to determine if it contains a sample that matches the profile of the multiple alleles of the crime sample. If no match is found across multiple genetic probes, the expert reports that "the DNA pattern was compared to a database containing N individuals from the population and no match was observed." This is an extremely conservative approach that yields probative information but does not give the factfinder any information concerning the probability of finding a matching profile by chance in the larger population.

The NRC committee has proposed a modified ceiling principle technique, which takes advantage of the computation techniques of population genetics but which includes adjustments that the committee believes make it an "appropriately conservative" approach. Although it noted that recent empirical studies have detected no evidence of a departure from independence within or across commonly used genetic probes, the NRC committee chose "to assume for the sake of discussion that population substructure may exist and provide a method for estimating population frequencies in a manner that adequately accounts for it." . . .

The NRC committee recommends that two adjustments be made to population frequencies derived from existing data to permit conservative estimates of the likelihood of a coincidental matching profile. First, the 95% upper confidence limit for the estimated allele frequency is computed for each of the existing population samples (Black, White, Native American, etc.). This upper bound of the confidence interval is intended to accommodate the uncertainties in current population sampling. Second, the largest of these upper confidence limit estimates, or 10%, whichever is greater, is used to compute the joint probability of a coincidental match on the DNA profile of the crime sample. A lower bound of 10% is intended to address concerns that current population data sets may be substructured in unknown ways that would yield misleading estimates of a coincidental matching profile for members of subpopulations. The resulting probabilities then are multiplied as in the product rule computations. The upper confidence limit from among the existing samples, or a 10% lower bound, is used to provide a probability estimate that errs, if at all, in a conservative direction (i.e., that is more favorable to a suspect).

C. WHAT IS THE RELEVANT COMPARISON POPULATION FOR ESTIMATING THE PROBABILITY OF A COINCIDENTAL ALLELIC MATCH?

Disputes over the appropriate comparison population have focused on cases in which the product rule technique has been used. The extent to which the product rule technique may underestimate the probability of a coincidental match has been hotly disputed by population geneticists and other scholars. The dispute centers on disagreements over the adequacy of commonly used comparison populations and the role of racial and ethnic subpopulations in probability estimation. Specifying the appropriate comparison population may be of considerable importance, as the estimates of a coincidental match can vary greatly depending on the population selected. For example, the prevalence of certain alleles may vary greatly across races—some alleles are common in Black populations and infrequent in White populations, and vice versa. If a DNA profile for a Black suspect is compared with frequency estimates based on a White population, the estimated likelihood of a chance match may be in error by some unknown amount. Similarly, if a DNA profile of a member of a subpopulation with a distinct frequency distribution of alleles is compared with frequency estimates based on an inappropriate larger population, an error of unknown magnitude may result. Concern over accuracy of estimates of a coincidental match has focused attention on the assumptions used in selecting a comparison population and the scientific validity of the methods used to estimate the probability of a coincidental match.

*1.   Is the Comparison Population Consistent with the Population
      of Possible Sources of the DNA?*

If the modified ceiling principle technique is not used, an appropriate comparison population must be designated. Such a designation is guided by the characteristics of the population of individuals who might have been the source of the sample. For example, if a rape victim saw her assailant and described him as White, and there is no more information to implicate a member of a specific subpopulation or group, the comparison population should be those who appear to be White and who were in a position to commit the assault. Comparisons based on members of populations or subpopulations who appear to be non-White therefore would be inappropriate. Similarly, where there is no information indicating the race or ethnicity of the perpetrator, the comparison population should be designated by the characteristics of those in a position to commit the assault. The race or ethnicity of the suspect is irrelevant.

In other cases, however, the pool of alternative suspects may be limited to members of a distinct isolated community or a specific ethnic subgroup. This circumstance has arisen in federal courts where the defendant was a member of a Native American tribe and the crime occurred on the tribal reservation. The typical databases of allele frequencies used for probability estimation address broader population groups, such as Blacks, Whites, Native Americans, Hispanics from the southeastern United States, and Hispanics from the southwestern United States. The extent to which broad racial and cultural comparison populations must correspond to the characteristics of the suspect population turns on the extent to which the distribution of alleles tested for in the forensic analysis differs for the suspect population and the comparison database. This remains a disputed issue among scientists. Difficulty in resolving this issue was responsible, in part, for the NRC committee's recommending a technique that does not require the designation of a suspect population.

2. *Does the Comparison Population Conform to Characteristics that Allow the Estimation of the Joint Occurrence of Matching Alleles by Multiplication of the Probabilities of the Individual Alleles?*

The comparison population must conform to assumptions that underlie the technique used to compute the estimate of a coincidental match, or at least conform sufficiently that minor deviations are of little consequence in computing the probability estimates. The computation of the probability of a random match by the product rule technique is based on the assumption that the individual alleles of the DNA profile are independent of one another. According to the principles of population genetics, the independence of alleles may be assumed only where the comparison population mixes freely and mates randomly (with respect to the alleles) such that the distribution of alleles within the comparison population is homogeneous. If the comparison population does not conform to these assumptions, the alleles may not be independent, and the computation of probability estimates may be incorrect.

Opponents of the product rule technique argue that it is inappropriate to use broad racial and cultural characteristics to specify the comparison population, because in reality such groups do not mix freely with respect to relevant genes. Broad racial groups, they argue, disguise subpopulations that would be more appropriate for comparison. More specifically, opponents charge that use of broad racial groups violates the assumption of independence justifying the multiplication of the separate probabilities assigned to each probe. For example, a White comparison group that includes diverse ethnic groups (e.g., persons of Polish, Italian, or Irish descent) may mask differences in the distribution of alleles among subgroups. Opponents charge that no meaningful estimate of the probability of a particular DNA profile can be developed without specifying a suitable subpopulation that meets the demanding assumptions of the product rule technique. When alleles are not independent, as when a comparison group contains a substructure, the product rule technique may underestimate the probability that the forensic and suspect DNA patterns match by coincidence.

Proponents of the product rule technique acknowledge that some substructuring may exist in the comparison populations typically used; but they argue that it is inappropriate to apply the assumption strictly and that the probability estimates generally are accurate in spite of violations of the strict assumption regarding the absence of substructuring. Furthermore, proponents claim that the conservative features of the fixed-bin method more than compensate for any underestimation. The NRC committee notes that what little empirical evidence existed at the time of its report appeared to support this contention. . . .

. . . [F]ederal courts are at odds with a number of state courts that have considered explicitly the NRC report, cited the modified ceiling principle technique with favor, and expressed the hope that it will gain general acceptance in the scientific community. Unlike the federal courts that have addressed the issue, many of the state courts continue to follow variations of the *Frye* standard and look to the NRC report as expressing a consensus of scientific opinion. Yet, while some state courts have embraced the modified ceiling principle technique, a portion of the scientific community has questioned its scientific validity. The possibility of a convergence of scientific opinion around the ceiling principle technique seems remote, and the NRC plans to impanel another committee to consider scientific criticisms of the technique and more recent research.

Although DNA evidence is potentially admissible in every American jurisdiction, judges are struggling with the question of how the results of DNA analysis should be presented to juries. Compare the approaches of the following three courts. . . .

COMMONWEALTH v. DANA A. DAGGETT, 416 Mass. 347, 622 N.E.2d 272 (1993): LIACOS, C.J. The defendant, Dana A. Daggett, was convicted of murder in the first degree by reason of extreme atrocity or cruelty. The principal claim of error the defendant makes is that evidence of tests performed on the victim's deoxyribonucleic acid (DNA) and DNA extracted from blood in the trunk of the defendant's automobile and blood found at the plant where defendant worked was improperly admitted at trial. . . .

. . . the Commonwealth offered evidence of DNA testing by Cellmark Diagnostics laboratory (Cellmark) to prove that the blood found on the chair and the table in the plant, and on the mat in the trunk of the defendant's automobile, was the victim's blood. At trial, the Commonwealth's expert witnesses testified to the process of DNA comparison testing and concluded that it was "highly likely" (or some other nonnumerical term) that the blood found on the chair, the table, and in the trunk came from the victim. . . .

At the time of the *Frye* hearing, and at the time of trial, this court had not yet issued its opinions in Commonwealth v. Lanigan, 413 Mass. 154, 596 N.E.2d 311 (1992), and Commonwealth v. Curnin, 409 Mass. 218, 565 N.E.2d 440 (1991). In both of those cases, we held that evidence of DNA testing was inadmissible because the methods used by Cellmark to calculate the statistical probability of a random match were not generally accepted by the relevant scientific community.[2] Lanigan, supra at 163. Curnin, supra at 227. The same assumptions underlying the statistical calculations made in those cases were relied on in this case. Thus, the conclusions reached by the Commonwealth's experts suffer from the flaws that were exposed in Curnin and Lanigan.[4]

STATE OF MINNESOTA v. TROY BRADLEY BLOOM, 516 N.W.2d 159 (Minn. 1994): KEITH, Chief Justice.   Agreeing with the state on the central issue in each of three separate criminal appeals decided today, we hold, first, that the National Research Council's recent adoption of the conservative "interim ceiling method" for computation of the probability that a randomly selected person would have the same DNA profile as that of a sample of bodily fluids found at a crime scene justifies the creation of a DNA exception to the rule against the admission of statistical probability evidence in criminal prosecutions to prove identity; second, that if the evidentiary foundation provided by the proponent of the evidence is sufficient, a properly qualified expert may express the

---

2. Recent cases from other jurisdictions confirm what we noted in *Curnin*, supra at 222 n.7, i.e., the importance to courts and to the scientific community of a valid statistical analysis of the likelihood of a match. See People v. Axell, 235 Cal. App. 3d 836, 866-867 (1991) (match means little without data on probability; calculation of statistical probability an integral part of process); Fishback v. State, 851 P.2d 884, 893 & n.18 (Colo. 1993) (match unaccompanied by statistical significance "essentially meaningless"); State v. Vandebogart, 135 N.H. 365, 381-382 (1992) (match "virtually meaningless" without statistical probability expressing frequency). Likewise, the National Research Council's April, 1992, report entitled DNA Technology in Forensic Science (NRC Report), stresses that: "To say that two patterns match, without providing any scientifically valid estimate (or, at least, an upper bound) of the frequency with which such matches might occur by chance, is meaningless." NRC Report at S-8.

4. The fact that the Commonwealth presented the evidence to the jury in nonnumerical terms does not alter this result. The Commonwealth has cited no authorities and presented no testimony either at the *Frye* hearing or at trial that the use of such terms is generally accepted by the scientific community in evaluating the significance of a match. Although the Commonwealth's experts testified that, in their opinions, evidence of a match indicated that the source of the samples was "highly likely" (or some other such phrase), no one testified that such characterizations alleviate the concerns the scientific community has voiced regarding the evaluation of matches. See State v. Cauthron, 120 Wash. 2d 879, 907, 846 P.2d 502 (1993) (testimony of non-statistical opinion presented insufficient because it did not include the background probability information). See also State v. Alt, 504 N.W.2d 38, 52 (Minn. Ct. App. 1993), and materials cited ("Nonstatistical opinion testimony . . . would not correctly reflect the nature of the DNA test results. . . . The scientific community considers the statistical frequency important in interpreting DNA test results, but does not consider the opinion of a match to be significant").

The concurrence mischaracterizes this opinion when it states, post at _____, "I do not agree that the DNA evidence offered by the Commonwealth in this case was inadmissible because the Commonwealth's experts' testimony concerning the background probability that the DNA matches in question were false was not presented numerically." The point is not that this court should require a numerical frequency, but that the scientific community clearly does. If the relevant scientific community generally accepted some nonnumerical expression of statistical frequency, then this court would likely accept it as well. See Commonwealth v. Beausoleil, 397 Mass. 206, 218-219, 490 N.E.2d 788 (1986). There was simply no evidence presented below that indicated that this might be the case, and, as the cases cited above illustrate, there is a substantial indication to the contrary.

opinion that, to a reasonable degree of scientific certainty, the defendant is (or is not) the source of the bodily evidence found at the crime scene.

These appeals give this court an opportunity to revisit an issue that recently has been the focus of considerable controversy in the scientific community. The issue is not, as some have put it, the admissibility of DNA identification evidence in criminal prosecutions but the form that the presentation of that evidence takes. . . .

One of the concerns expressed in our cases, which we discuss in detail later, has been that admission of the random match probability figure will confuse jurors. There is a chain of inferences that the jurors must make in order to get from the starting point, the testimony as to the probability of a random match, to the conclusion that the defendant is the perpetrator of the crime. Those inferential steps include: match report—true match—source—present at scene—perpetrator. See Jonathan J. Koehler, Error and Exaggeration in the Presentation of DNA Evidence at Trial, 34 Jurimetrics 21 (1993). Errors may occur at each step: . . .

Since it may be pointless to expect ever to reach a consensus on how to estimate, with any degree of precision, the probability of a random match and that, given the great difficulty in educating the jury as to precisely what that figure means and does not mean, it might make sense to simply try to arrive at a fair way of explaining the significance of the match in a verbal, qualitative, non-quantitative, nonstatistical way. . . .

Notwithstanding this, and notwithstanding the fact that the intense debate continues concerning the most reliable, accurate way of estimating random match probability and the proper role of statistical evidence in criminal trials, we now conclude, based on all the circumstances, including the very conservative nature of the probability figures obtained using the NRC's approach, that a DNA exception to the rule against admission of quantitative, statistical probability evidence in criminal prosecutions to prove identity is justified. Accordingly, any properly qualified prosecution or defense expert may, if evidentiary foundation is sufficient, give an opinion as to random match probability using the NRC's approach to computing that statistic.

We also conclude that, in an appropriate case, where there is an underlying statistical foundation for such an opinion, a properly qualified expert should be allowed to say more than that the DNA test results merely are consistent with the defendant's being the source of the physical evidence left behind by the assailant. . . .

We have concluded that the DNA expert should be allowed to express the opinion that there is a "match" between the defendant's DNA profile and that left by the assailant at the scene or on the victim. The strength of the expert's opinion is something the jury should be told;

it will depend in part on the degree of the expert's confidence in the opinion and in part on the underlying statistical foundation for the opinion. We also agree with Professor Kreiling that the expert should be allowed to phrase the opinion this way: that given a reliable multi-locus match, the probability that the match is random or coincidental is extremely low. . . .

The expert should not, of course, be allowed to say that a particular profile is unique. . . . Nor should the expert be allowed to say that defendant is the source to the exclusion of all others or to express an opinion as to the strength of the evidence. But should a properly qualified expert, assuming adequate foundation, be allowed to express an opinion that, to a reasonable scientific certainty, the defendant is (or is not) the source? We believe so. In reaching this conclusion, we merely are saying, as we intended all along, that the admissibility in a criminal trial of qualitative expert opinion testimony on DNA identification techniques be governed by the same basic rules of admissibility that historically have applied to qualitative expert opinion testimony based on other scientific identification techniques. See, e.g., State v. Rean, 353 N.W.2d 562, 564 (Minn. 1984) (where there was expert opinion testimony that it was "highly probable" that shoe prints found at scene were made by defendant's shoes).

We believe that allowing this sort of verbal, qualitative, non-statistical presentation of the underlying statistical evidence will lead to more agreement among reputable experts at trials and may decrease the likelihood of there being a battle of experts (over the reliability of the random match probability figure), with one expert cancelling out or discrediting the other.

THE PEOPLE, v. RALPH EDWARDS BARNEY, 8 Cal. App. 4th 798 (Cal. App. 1992): CHINN, J.   These two appeals challenge the admissibility of deoxyribonucleic acid (DNA) analysis evidence. The primary claim is that DNA analysis is a new scientific technique which does not meet the test of general acceptance prescribed by People v. Kelly (1976) 17 Cal. 3d 24 [130 Cal. Rptr. 144, 549 P.2d 1240] and Frye v. United States (D.C. Cir. 1923) 293 Fed. 1013. . . .

C. GENERAL ACCEPTANCE AND STATISTICAL ANALYSIS

This brings us to the heart of these appeals, the question whether the third step of DNA analysis—the determination of a match's *statistical significance*—has received general scientific acceptance. . . .

The appellate court in *Axell* addressed the statistical issues presented here, albeit before publication of the Science articles. The court concluded that "since a match between two DNA samples means little without data on probability, the calculation of statistical probability is an integral part of the process and the underlying method of arriving at that calculation must pass muster under *Kelly-Frye*." (People v. Axell, supra, 235 Cal. App. 3d at pp. 866-867.)

We agree. The statistical calculation step is the pivotal element of DNA analysis, for the evidence means nothing without a determination of the statistical significance of a match of DNA patterns. . . . It is the expression of statistical meaning, stated in terms of vanishingly small match probabilities, that makes the evidence so compelling. To say that the frequency of Howard's DNA pattern is 1 in 200 million in the Black population is tantamount to saying his pattern is totally unique, and thus *only* he could have been the source of the crime scene bloodstains that did not match those of the victim.

To end the *Kelly-Frye* inquiry at the matching step, and leave it to jurors to assess the current scientific debate on statistical calculation as a matter of weight rather than admissibility, would stand *Kelly-Frye* on its head. We would be asking jurors to do what judges carefully avoid — decide the substantive merits of competing scientific opinion as to the reliability of a novel method of scientific proof. We cannot reasonably ask the average juror to decide such arcane questions as whether genetic substructuring and linkage disequilibrium preclude use of the Hardy-Weinberg equation and the product rule, when we ourselves have struggled to grasp these concepts. The result would be predictable. The jury would simply skip to the bottom line — the only aspect of the process that is readily understood—and look at the ultimate expression of match probability, without competently assessing the reliability of the process by which the laboratory got to the bottom line. This is an instance in which the method of scientific proof is so impenetrable that it would "'. . . assume a posture of mystic infallibility in the eyes of a jury . . . .' [Citation.]" . . . It is the task of scientists — not judges, and not jurors — to assess reliability. "'The requirement of general acceptance in the scientific community assures that *those most qualified to assess the general validity of a scientific method will have the determinative voice . . . .*'"

Might the statistical calculation step be distinguished from the processing and matching steps for *Kelly-Frye* purposes on the ground that only the first two steps produce novel scientific evidence while the third step is merely interpretative? Again, such an approach would subvert *Kelly-Frye*. The evidence produced by DNA analysis is not merely the raw data of matching bands on autoradiographs but encompasses the ultimate expression of the statistical significance of a match, in the same way that polygraph evidence is not merely the raw data produced by a polygraph machine but encompasses the operator's ultimate expression of opinion whether the subject is telling the truth. Were we to terminate the *Kelly-Frye* inquiry short of the interpretative steps in new methods of scientific proof, *Kelly-Frye* would lose much of its efficacy as a tool of "considerable judicial caution" and of an "essentially conservative nature" that is "deliberately intended to interpose a substantial obstacle to the unrestrained admission of evidence based upon new scientific principles." (People v. Kelly, supra, 17 Cal. 3d at p. 31.)

4. GENERAL SCIENTIFIC ACCEPTANCE

. . .

We do not write on an entirely clean slate. The admissibility of DNA analysis evidence has been litigated in many forums in the past few years. The statistical calculation dispute, however, has not been judicially examined until quite recently.

The few published decisions exploring the question of general acceptance on this point are in conflict. One court, applying the *Frye* standard, concluded there is currently no general acceptance as to the statistical calculation process, and thus DNA analysis evidence is inadmissible. (Com. v. Curnin (1991) 409 Mass. 218, 221-227 [565 N.E.2d 440, 442-445]; see also Caldwell v. State (1990) 260 Ga. 278 [393 S.E.2d 436, 444] [laboratory's statistical evidence inadmissible because state failed to show data bases were in Hardy-Weinberg equilibrium]; State v. Schwartz (Minn. 1989) 447 N.W.2d 422, 428-429 [exclusion of statistical probability evidence necessary because of potentially exaggerated impact on jury].) Another court concluded otherwise under an amplified *Frye* standard, adopting a magistrate's finding that it is "more likely than not" there is general acceptance as to statistical calculation, although the magistrate acknowledged that "[s]cientists of indisputable national and international repute and stature . . . took diametrically opposed views on the issue of general acceptability, and those views reflected the division of opinion on the merits of the underlying scientific disagreements." (U.S. v. Yee, supra, 134 F.R.D. at p. 206; see also U.S. v. Jakobetz, supra, 955 F.2d at pp. 791-800 [upholding finding of reliability under relaxed admissibility standard less stringent than *Frye*]; Prater v. State (1991) 307 Ark. 180 [820 S.W.2d 429, 439] [upholding admission under non-*Frye* standard based on trial evidence, but noting that statistical calculation "is not a closed issue"].)

The appellate court in *Axell* found general acceptance as to statistical calculation based on testimony by Kenneth K. Kidd (one of the co-authors of the Chakraborty-Kidd article in *Science*) and another geneticist. The court concluded, "the prosecution showed that the method used by Cellmark in this case to arrive at its data base and statistical probabilities was generally accepted in the scientific community." (People v. Axell, supra, 235 Cal. App. 3d at p. 868.)

Whatever the merits of the prior decisions on the statistical calculation process — including *Axell* — the debate that erupted in *Science* in December 1991 changes the scientific landscape considerably, and demonstrates indisputably that there is no general acceptance of the current process. It has become irrelevant how *Axell* addressed this issue at the time of the decision's filing in October 1991. The situation is somewhat analogous to a "change in the attitude of the scientific community" which undermines a previously correct judicial determination of general acceptance. (People v. Kelly, supra, 17 Cal. 3d at p. 32.) Simply put, *Axell* has been eclipsed on this point by subsequent scientific developments. In reaching a conclusion different from that in *Axell*, we do not express disagreement with *Axell*'s reasoning at the time, but rather have progressed to a point on the continuum of scientific debate which neither the *Axell* court nor the two trial courts in the present cases could have anticipated.

5.   THE EFFECT OF NO GENERAL ACCEPTANCE

The Lewontin-Hartl article in *Science* concludes with a famous query: "What Is To Be Done?" (Lewontin & Hartl, supra, at p. 1749; see Lenin, What Is To Be Done? (1902).) We confront the same question. More specifically, must the absence of general scientific acceptance as to the current statistical calculation aspect of DNA analysis result in total exclusion of DNA evidence?

DNA analysis is a powerful forensic tool by any standard, and a role for it in the process of criminal justice is inevitable. Even Lewontin and Hartl concede its potential: "Appropriately carried out and correctly interpreted, DNA typing is possibly the most powerful innovation in forensics since the development of fingerprinting in the last part of the 19th century." (Lewontin & Hartl, supra, at p. 1746.)

Clearly, a match of DNA patterns is a matter of substantial significance. (See NRC rep., supra, at p. 74 ["a match between two DNA patterns can be considered strong evidence that the two samples came from the same source"].) The statistical dispute is restricted to the *extent* of that significance. There must be some common ground, some sufficiently conservative method of determining statistical significance, as to which there is general scientific agreement. (See Caldwell v. State, supra, 260 Ga. 278 [393 S.E.2d at pp. 443-444] [laboratory's calculation of 1 in 24 million held inadmissible, but expert witness's "more conservative" calculation of 1 in 250,000 held admissible].)

The NRC report on DNA analysis appears to point the way to such common ground. The report proposes a method of statistical calculation which accounts for the possibility of population substructuring, eliminates ethnicity as a factor in the calculation process, and permits the use of the product rule while ensuring that probability estimates are appropriately conservative. The report proposes a "ceiling frequency" approach, in which DNA samples from 15 to 20 homogeneous populations will be analyzed for allele frequencies. In subsequent analysis of the DNA of a suspect or crime scene sample, each allele will be assigned the highest frequency that appears in the tested populations, or 5 percent, whichever is greater. These frequencies will then be multiplied together using the product rule. (NRC rep., supra, at pp. 12-13, 82-83, 95, 134.) . . .

These proposals, however, do not solve the problem in the present cases. The DNA evidence admitted in *Howard* and *Barney* included frequency estimates based on statistical calculations which have not received general scientific acceptance. Even though the trial courts in these cases could not have anticipated the controversy that subsequently arose in the scientific community, this was still error, and no amount of after-the-fact fine tuning of the statistical calculation process can cure the error. The error infects the underlying match evidence, which is incomplete without an interpretation of its significance. (See NRC rep., supra, at p. 74.) Thus, we have no alternative but to hold that the DNA analysis evidence was inadmissible under *Kelly-Frye,* for want of general scientific acceptance of the statistical calculation process employed in these cases.

The question now at hand is whether the interim and future methods of statistical calculation proposed by the NRC report will be generally accepted by population geneticists. If, as appears likely, this question is answered in the affirmative in a future *Kelly-Frye* hearing, then DNA analysis evidence will be admissible in California.

Which approach, that of the Massachusetts, the Minnesota, or the California court, makes the most sense? How should a DNA expert explain the significance of a DNA match to the jury? What is the difference between DNA evidence and the kind of evidence that the court ruled inadmissible in People v. Collins?

CHAPTER II

Categorical Rules of Exclusion

Many of the problems and cases in Chapter I illustrate the notion embodied in Rule 403 that the trial judge may exclude relevant and otherwise admissible evidence if its probative value is "substantially outweighed by the danger of unfair prejudice, confusion of the issues, or misleading the jury" or by considerations of institutional efficiency.

The frequent recurrence of certain potentially prejudicial situations has prompted the development of a number of categorical exclusionary rules that supplement Rule 403's general and discretionary weighing of prejudicial effect and probative value. For example, Rules 404 and 405 exclude evidence of the character of an accused in a criminal case when offered solely to prove his propensity for criminal acts. These rules are discussed in Chapter III below. Rule 407 excludes evidence of subsequent remedial measures when offered to prove negligence; Rule 408 excludes settlement offers and negotiations when offered to prove liability. Rule 409 excludes evidence showing one party's payment of another's medical expenses when offered to prove liability. Rule 410 generally excludes evidence of a subsequently withdrawn guilty plea or of a plea of nolo contendere. Rule 411 excludes evidence of liability insurance to prove negligence. Rule 412 excludes from most cases evidence of a rape victim's past sexual conduct to prove the elements of a rape charge or defense. Rules 413-415, passed by Congress several years after the original Rules of Evidence were adopted, go in the opposite direction to grant admission of evidence of prior sexual misconduct by a defendant in a prosecution for sexual assault or child molestation, which would otherwise be excluded by one of the exclusionary rules. Rules 412-415 are discussed along with Rules 404-406 in Chapter III below.

The exclusionary rules by and large represent policy choices that were previously obscured under the common law concept of "legal relevancy," which has been much criticized and is in general disrepute today. The question remains, however, whether the categorical rules of exclusion may be individually justified on specific policy grounds or on

generalized relevancy determinations. To answer this we must explore
the policy underlying each rule and our thinking about what evidence
is probative in specific situations, such as rape trials. Once the possible
policy justifications for each rule have been analyzed, the question remains whether these categorical rules are necessary to accomplish their
objectives. Is it not possible for all of the policy concerns reflected by
these rules to be considered and properly weighed under Rule 403?
What are the advantages of having special rules for these situations in
addition to a general prejudice rule? What disadvantages are there?
Again, would it be preferable to leave the development of the law in
these areas to judicial elaboration in applying Rule 403 rather than have
Congress frame detailed rules? Would a middle road be preferable? For
example, should the rules specify what types of evidence are generally
excluded but permit exceptions when the evidence in a given case is
particularly necessary, probative, or free from prejudice? What factors
are relevant in evaluating the efficacy of particular exclusionary rules?

Most of these categorical exclusionary rules exclude evidence if offered for one purpose but do not exclude the evidence if it is offered
for other purposes. For example, evidence of subsequent remedial measures, inadmissible to prove negligence, may be introduced to prove
"ownership, control, or feasibility of precautionary measures, if controverted, or impeachment." Similarly, evidence of settlement offers, excluded by Rule 408 on the issue of liability, may be used to show that a
witness has a stake in the outcome of the case (bias). Even when evidence cannot be introduced for any permissible purpose, attorneys
sometimes suggest it to the jury in various ways that are possibly improper and unethical. If evidence within the reach of one of these categorical rules were offered by your opponent under a permissible
purpose exception, or if you were aware that it was going to be suggested
to the jury improperly, how would you go about keeping it out? If it got
in anyhow, how would you attempt to counteract its prejudicial effect?
As a judge in this situation, what limiting instructions would you give?
How effective are limiting instructions in these situations? Evidence that
is purportedly excluded by these rules nevertheless often gets before
the jury; to what extent does this affect your view on the wisdom of
having these rules?

A. Subsequent Remedial Measures

Problem: Locking the Barn Door

(1) Pedestrian *P1* v. *D* Construction Company for personal injuries
sustained when *P1* was struck by *D*'s crane while *P1* was walking on the

sidewalk past *D*'s construction site. At trial, *P1* offers evidence that the day after the accident *D*'s superintendent posted a safety rule reading as follows:

EFFECTIVE IMMEDIATELY

When operating a crane or any other equipment on this job within 10 feet of a sidewalk or street, a lookout must be posted to watch for pedestrians and other traffic.

By Order of the Superintendent

Is this evidence admissible?

(2) Pedestrian *P2* v. *D* Construction Company for personal injuries sustained when *P2* was struck by *D*'s crane while *P2* was walking on the sidewalk past *D*'s construction site, in the same place *P1* had been struck. At trial, *P2* offers evidence of the posted safety policy, which was posted the day *before* his accident. Admissible?

The traditional American common law rule has been to deny admissibility to subsequent remedial measures when offered to show fault. This rule has been embodied in Federal Rule of Evidence 407. The Advisory Committee's Note to Rule 407 concedes that under a liberal theory of relevancy, the fact that the posting of the safety sign is equally consistent with injury by mere accident or through contributory negligence would not support exclusion, since the inference of negligence is still a possible one from the posting of the sign. Rather than relying on non-relevancy as a ground of exclusion, the Advisory Committee bases Rule 407 "on a social policy of encouraging people to take, or at least not discouraging them from taking, steps in furtherance of added safety."

The rule against evidence of subsequent remedial measures has come under criticism. During the more than two decades during which the Federal Rules of Evidence have been in effect, many states have come to enact their own Rules of Evidence based on the Federal Rules. Two states, Maine and Rhode Island, adopted counterparts to FRE 407 that are exactly contrary to the federal rule and preexisting state law. The Maine and Rhode Island Rules 407 provided:

When, after an event, measures are taken which, if taken previously, would have made the event less likely to occur, evidence of the subsequent measures is admissible.

The Advisors' Note to Maine Rule 407 stated:

The public policy behind the rule against admissibility was that it would deter repairs. This rationale is unpersuasive today. In some instances subsequent repairs may be evidence of culpability. In other instances quite the contrary is the fact. Despite this departure from prior authority, it is still open to trial judge under Rule 403 to exclude such evidence if he believes its probative value is substantially outweighed by danger of unfair prejudice, confusion of issues, or misleading the jury. A situation where the change is effectuated for reasons unrelated to the hazard would be a clear case for such exclusion. . . .

It should be emphasized that although evidence of subsequent remedial measures is admitted, it remains for the jury to decide whether the standard of reasonable care has been satisfied. Proof that such measures were taken clearly does not compel a finding that the previous condition reflected culpable conduct.

The Commentary to Maine Rule 407 indicated that one of the reasons for admitting evidence of subsequent remedial measures is that when the evidence is admitted for other purposes the policy behind the rule barring admission — to avoid discouraging repairs — is largely defeated. Limiting instructions to consider the evidence only for the limited purpose of showing ownership, control, or feasibility of precautionary measures is unlikely to be effective. More fundamentally, however, the Commentary contends that the assumption that a defendant will not take corrective action because he knows that it might be used against him is not persuasive. A defendant as knowledgeable and as cold-blooded as the exclusionary rule suggests would probably be aware of the many exceptions, which would make it risky to refrain from making needed repairs. Enlightened self-interest would often lead defendants to make repairs despite the possibility of evidence of such action being received on the issue of fault. This would surely seem true of a structural change by a national manufacturer. Field & Murray, Maine Evidence (4th Ed.) 159. The Rhode Island Commentary is similar.

The federal rule has also been criticized on both evidentiary and substantive grounds as constituting an unwarranted federal intrusion into an area traditionally reserved to state regulation. See Schwartz, The Exclusionary Rule on Subsequent Repairs—A Rule in Need of Repair, 7 Forum 1 (1971); Wellborn, The Federal Rules of Evidence and the Application of State Law in Federal Cases, 55 Tex. L. Rev. 371 (1977). As to this issue, see the *Rioux* case, page 140, below.

During the codification and ratification of the Rhode Island Rules of Evidence, no rule was more controversial than RIRE 407. The proposed rule, which reversed the federal rule and existing state law to make evidence of subsequent remedial measures expressly admissible, was strenuously opposed by the defense bar and insurers.

In Maine, political opposition to the rule of admissibility on the part of insurers and municipal defendants ultimately resulted in legislation in 1995 repealing Maine Rule 407 as originally adopted by the Maine Supreme Judicial Court and substituting language tracking the federal version. This leaves Rhode Island as the sole American jurisdiction with a Rule 407 expressly granting admissibility to evidence of subsequent remedial measures.

Problem: Farmer Brown's Wagon

Farmer Brown has sued Joe Deer Co. for designing, manufacturing, and selling a defective farm wagon. Plaintiff's evidence at trial has tended to prove that while running a corn chopper with a farm wagon attached to catch the corn, the brackets that help support the wheels on one side of the farm wagon broke off and caused the wagon to collapse, injuring the plaintiff. Plaintiff's theory is that the wagon, which he purchased fifteen years before the accident, should have lasted at least twenty-five years, and that Deer should be liable because it did not notify plaintiff prior to the accident that it had developed stronger brackets since plaintiff's purchase.

At trial, plaintiff offers evidence that after plaintiff had purchased his wagon and before the accident Deer had redesigned the support brackets to make them stronger. Deer not only used the stronger brackets in new wagons, it also sold the new stronger brackets to farmers who needed to replace the brackets on their wagons. Deer notified its dealers of such parts but did not notify the farmers directly. Plaintiff also has experts who will testify that the stronger brackets on the modification would not have broken as the original weaker ones did.

Deer objects to the admission of this evidence under Rules 407, 402, and 403. Deer's witnesses will testify that the redesign of the inner and outer brackets was incidental to the redesign of the lubrication system (not an issue in Brown's accident) and was not related to any accidents or known problems with the brackets. Deer concedes that it would have been feasible to design and manufacture the brackets in the new, stronger way when the plaintiff's farm wagon was manufactured. Deer states that it did not notify the farmers of the subsequent modifications because there had been no problem with the original brackets in any of the more than 12,000 farm wagons sold.

What ruling on plaintiff's offer and why? What are the policy arguments for exclusion or admission of this evidence?

Problem: The Dismissed Employee

P v. *D* Company for personal injuries sustained by *P* when struck by a *D* Company truck driven by *D*'s driver, *E*. At trial, *P* offers evidence that *D* fired *E* one month after the accident. Admissible?

Problem: The D-Craft 184 Crash

P v. *D* Aircraft Company for damages for the death of *P*'s husband, *H,* who perished when the plane he was flying—a twin-engine "D-Craft 184"—crashed for no apparent reason on a clear day. The theory of *P*'s case, which she plans to present through expert testimony, is that the fuel tanks on the D-Craft 184, located in the wings, feed fuel to the engines through a "gravitational flow" system that is susceptible to centrifugal force when the fuel tanks are only partially full and the plane is in a steep curve or dive. *P*'s expert will testify that the centrifugal force causes the delivery of fuel to the engine from the tank on the wing on the inside of the curve to be momentarily interrupted. When this happens the inside engine stalls, causing the other engine to jerk the plane around in the opposite direction. The force of this resulting pull reverses the forces on the fuel tanks, causing the second engine to stall. *P*'s expert will testify that when this condition occurs, even an experienced test pilot would be lucky to bring the plane back under control and prevent a crash. *P* has other evidence that tends to suggest that the crash may have happened in this way.

P's attorney learns through pretrial discovery that *D* Aircraft Company plans to call an expert on light plane design to testify that the "gravitational flow" fuel system is safe for twin-engine planes of the "184" series. *P*'s attorney also learns that shortly after the accident, *D* Aircraft Company replaced the gravitational flow fuel system in its 184s with an electronic-pump system.

Is any of this admissible? How should the attorneys for *P* and *D* Aircraft Company structure their examination of the witnesses to put in as much favorable evidence as they can and keep out as much unfavorable evidence as possible?

Problem: Third-Party Repairs

P was injured when his car was struck by *D*'s train while crossing *D*'s railroad tracks. After the accident, the State Highway Department installed signal lights at the crossing. *P* sues *D.* At trial, *P* offers evidence of the Highway Department's remedial measures. *D* objects. What ruling and why?

———————————

The repair in this case was not made by the defendant but by a third party. Is evidence of the repair relevant to the dangerous nature of the crossing, which the railroad could have done something about? Is the policy of encouraging potential defendants to make repairs applicable in cases where the repairs are made by someone other than the defendant?

Problem: The Exploding Pinto

P bought a Ford Pinto. Four years after *P* bought the Pinto, her car exploded into flames after a rear-end collision, and *P* was badly burned.

P brings suit against Ford alleging that the Pinto was dangerously designed because the location of the rear fuel tank was such that even in a minor rear-end collision the tank would easily be pierced and explode.

(1) At the trial, *P* offers evidence that Ford knew of accidents in which the fuel tank had exploded under minimum impact but had not changed the design to protect against this. Admissible to prove negligence? Gross negligence?

(2) Ford offers evidence in its defense that it had carefully studied accidents in which the fuel tank had ruptured and had purposefully *not* changed the design of its cars. Further, Ford offers evidence that Chrysler had placed the fuel tank in a similar position in its cars of the same model years as the Pintos that had exploded and that Chrysler had not changed its design either. Admissible?

Is the threat of exposure to future lawsuits for negligence and gross negligence enough to cause most defendants, especially large manufacturing companies, to take precautionary measures and make repairs after accidents without regard to the evidentiary effect of those repairs?

Ford's failure to change the design of the fuel tank to protect against rupture, after it had notice of a possible defect in the design, could be admissible against it to show gross negligence and establish a claim for punitive damages. Arguably, this threat should be sufficient to cause Ford to take corrective action, if indeed corrective action should be taken. Thus, in many situations the public policy reason behind Rule 407 may be invalid.

But what about the individual defendant? In the classic case in which a chunk of ice falls off a homeowner's roof striking a pedestrian below, will the future admissibility of evidence that the homeowner placed a barrier on his roof cause the homeowner not to erect the barrier? Answers to this question are speculative and subjective. There are no data that test the crucial assumption on which the rule is based — that the future admissibility of such evidence will deter individuals from taking corrective action. It seems equally plausible that most individuals are not even aware of the rule excluding evidence of subsequent remedial measures and that individual behavior is unlikely to be affected by this rule. But critics have no more data to back up this belief than do the supporters of the current rule (mostly insurance companies and large manufacturers). For a skeptical comment on the effect of such rules on behavior, see Epstein, The Social Consequences of Common Law Rules, 95 Harv. L. Rev. 1717 (1982).

Problem: The Aluminum Gear Box

P v. *D* Equipment Manufacturing Company for personal injuries sustained by *P* when the vehicle in which she was driving left the road and plunged into a canyon. *P*'s complaint alleged that the aluminum gear box had failed. The claim was based on a theory of strict liability and breach of warranty. At trial, *P* offered evidence that aluminum was inappropriate for the gear box and that after the accident *D* changed from aluminum to malleable iron in producing the gear box. On *D*'s objection, what ruling and why?

Whether FRE 407 excludes evidence of subsequent remedial repairs in strict product liability cases was not clearly answered by the language of the rule as originally formulated. Congress amended Rule 407 in 1997 to attempt to make it clear that the exclusionary effect of Rule 407 would not depend on whether liability was premised on negligence or strict liability. As you consider the application of this rule to various fact situations and the policy behind the rule, does the stated policy of Rule 407 apply with equal force to all cases in which the rule language can be invoked? Compare Robbins v. Farmers Union Grain Terminal Association, 552 F.2d 788 (8th Cir. 1977), with Werner v. Upjohn Co., 628 F. 2d 848 (4th Cir. 1980) to see how two federal circuits came to opposite conclusions on the applicability of the policy of Federal Rule 407 to claims of strict liability.

These cases also raise issues of the scope of the exception to Rule 407 for showing the feasibility of precautionary measures. Another interesting case raising the issue of feasibility of precautionary measures is Anderson v. Malloy, 700 F.2d 1208 (8th Cir. 1983). Plaintiff was attacked in her motel room. She sued defendant motel owners for negligently failing to provide safe lodging. Plaintiff claimed on appeal that the trial court erroneously excluded evidence that, after the attack, defendants installed safety chains and peepholes in the doors of the rooms.

The Eighth Circuit found that defendants had affirmatively controverted feasibility of the safety devices by testifying that such devices only provided a false sense of security. The court noted that "[w]hether something is feasible relates not only to actual possibility of operation and to its cost and convenience, but also to its ultimate utility and success." The court held that defendants' testimony that the safety chains and peepholes provided a false sense of security implied not only that the devices would fail to provide security, but also that they would create a lesser level of security if installed. Plaintiff was entitled to rebut these inferences by showing that the devices were feasible. Further, plaintiff could impeach defendants' credibility by introducing evidence that the safety measures taken after the attack were those that defendants testified could not be used successfully.

The issue of whether and when evidence of subsequent remedial measures will deter people from taking safety measures usually produces much heat and little light. Neither side in this debate can offer data on whether the exclusionary rule affects the primary conduct of the mass producer of goods or only serves as a shield against potential liability. With the evidence supporting the policy in such a wee state, why not simply apply general principles of relevancy? In most cases, this will result in admission of evidence of subsequent remedial measures. But see Bizzle v. McKesson Corp., 961 F.2d 719 (8th Cir. 1992), upholding admissibility of evidence of recall of a walking cane in a strict products liability, negligence, and breach of warranty case pursuant to the Eighth Circuit's approach to such issues, but affirming exclusion of the evidence in the particular case under Rule 403.

Problem: Recall Letters

Plaintiff Harry Hazelton sues Defendant Snow-King Snowmobile Company and its local dealer, Ames Outdoor Recreation, Inc., for personal injuries sustained when his Snow-King snowmobile suddenly accelerated rapidly, went out of control, and hit a stone wall. He alleges that the throttle became stuck in the open position because of a defect in the design or construction of the throttle linkage cable.

Six months before the accident in which Harry was injured Snow-King Snowmobile had issued a "Customer Notice" advising owners of certain models of Snow-King snowmobiles (including Harry's) of a slight tendency for the throttle linkage to stick, which could be dangerous in certain situations, and requesting each owner to bring his machine to an authorized Snow King dealer for free installation of a replacement throttle linkage assembly.

As Harry's lawyer, what use can you make of this recall letter as evidence in Harry's case? Assume that it can be proved that Harry received a copy of this letter when it was issued and Snow King offers it on the issue of Harry's contributory or comparative negligence. What ruling, and why?

Now assume that the letter was issued after Harry's accident, but before the present suit was brought. Is the ruling different? Should it be?

RIOUX v. DANIEL INTERNATIONAL CORP.
582 F. Supp. 620 (D. Me. 1984)

CARTER, J.

The Defendant, Daniel International Corporation, filed on January 12, 1984, a motion in limine seeking a pretrial ruling pursuant to Fed. R. Evid. 407 as to the admissibility in the course of Plaintiff's case in chief, or in rebuttal, of evidence relevant to showing any change of method used by the Defendant, Daniel International Corporation, to secure vertical concrete pipe risers after the occurrence of the accident in question in this case. . . .

Daniel has moved "[t]hat pursuant to F.R. Evid. 407 Plaintiff and/or Third-Party Defendant be prohibited from offering evidence related to any methods used by the Defendant to secure vertical pipe risers after the death of Paul Rioux." The Plaintiff and Third-Party Defendant oppose this motion on the basis of two principal contentions: (1) that questions concerning the admissibility of such evidence should be governed by the provision of the Maine Rule of Evidence (Me. R. Evid. 407) and not by the provisions of the Federal Rule, and (2) that even if the Maine Rule does not apply, the evidence in question will be relevant to issues as to which it is properly admissible under the provisions of the second sentence of the Federal Rule.

The factual context of these contentions is that this is a wrongful death action arising out of the death of Paul A. Rioux on a construction site in Rumford, Maine on September 10, 1979. The decedent was an employee of Commercial Concrete Corporation. Defendant Daniel was the general contractor on the project. The decedent was killed when he was struck on the head by a falling section of concrete-filled steel pipe. The pipe was part of a vertical concrete piping system being used to pour concrete on the upper levels of a structure which Daniel was erecting. The Plaintiff contends that Daniel had the duty and responsibility of properly erecting and maintaining the vertical piping and that the piping fell because it was inadequately supported. It is represented that prior to the occurrence of this accident, Daniel supported the vertical concrete pipe risers with the use of rope attachments to the structure of the building. After the accident, it is asserted, Daniel changed its method of securing these vertical risers by performing this function with welded U-bolts. The Plaintiff intends to introduce into evidence these subsequent "remedial" changes in the method of placing and securing the vertical risers. Plaintiff contends that such evidence is relevant to show negligence or other culpable conduct on the part of Daniel in connection with the collapse of the riser here causing injury.

In deciding the issues raised here, the Court must conduct two inquiries. First, it must determine whether the Maine or the Federal Rule of Evidence applies in this case. If the Maine Rule applies, it is clear that the evidence is admissible for the broader purpose asserted by Plaintiff and Commercial. Should the Court, however, determine that the Maine Rule does not apply, then it must consider whether the evidence is admissible under the second sentence of Fed. R. Evid. 407, which permits the utilization of evidence of subsequent measures where it is relevant to genuine factual issues other than those of the negligence or culpable conduct of a party in connection with the establishment of liability for an event. These inquiries will be addressed in the order just stated.

A

This action was initiated in this Court by a Complaint filed herein on January 21, 1980. The jurisdiction of this Court is based upon diversity of citizenship between the Plaintiff and the Defendants. The Plaintiff and Commercial argue that Rule 407 of the Maine Rules of Evidence applies to all counts of the Complaint in this diversity-based action. That rule allows subsequent remedial measures to be admitted into evidence for the purpose of proving negligence or culpability. Rule 407 of the Federal Rules of Evidence specifically precludes admission of evidence of subsequent remedial measures for the purpose of proving negligence or culpability; it does allow, however, the evidence to be presented for other purposes such as proving feasibility or control. The Maine Rule 407 allows evidence of subsequent remedial measures to be admitted for purposes of showing negligence, or other liability creating culpable conduct, on the basis of a deliberate policy decision. Plaintiff and Commercial argue that the Maine Rule 407 must be applied because this is a diversity action in which state substantive law applies, and that state law for such purpose includes the provisions of Maine Rule 407 with its distinctly substantive, policy-based, connotations. . . .

Since the adoption of the Federal Rules of Evidence, distinguished commentators have taken the position that even in diversity cases the federal law of evidence applies in actions tried in federal court. Thus, Professors Wright, Miller and Cooper state:

> Of all the procedural and quasi procedural rules that are applied in the federal courts, the Federal Rules of Evidence are *least* affected by the *Erie* doctrine. The governing principle is easily stated. If a [Federal] rule of evidence covers a disputed point of evidence, the Rule is to be followed, *even in diversity cases,* and state law is pertinent only if and to the extent the Rule makes it so.

C. Wright, A. Miller & E. Cooper, 19 Federal Practice and Procedure, §4512 at 190 (1982) (emphasis added). See also 10 Moore's Federal Practice, §57 (1982).

In the keystone case of Hanna v. Plumer, 380 U.S. 460 (1965), the United States Supreme Court upheld the application of Rule 4(d)(1) of the Federal Rules of Civil Procedure in federal trial proceedings despite the argument that Massachusetts law under *Erie* should control the adequacy of service of process in a diversity case. Although the application of the Federal Rule would be "outcome determinative," the Court noted that Rule 4(d)(1) had been recommended by the Advisory Committee to the Federal Rules and promulgated by the Supreme Court, subject to the review of Congress. In this situation, the Advisory Committee, the Supreme Court, and Congress had made an initial determination that the rule in question was procedural and, therefore, within the proper province of Congress and the courts to promulgate. Thus, according to the Court in that case:

> When a situation is covered by one of the Federal Rules, the question facing the court is a far cry from the typical, relatively unguided *Erie* choice: the court has been instructed to apply the Federal Rule, and can refuse to do so only if the Advisory Committee, this Court and Congress erred in their prima facie judgment that the Rule in question transgresses neither the terms of the Enabling Act nor constitutional restrictions.

Id. at 471. The Court found that Congress has the power to promulgate rules for application in federal courts:

> For the constitutional provision for a federal court system (augmented by the Necessary and Proper Clause) carries with it congressional power to make rules governing the practice and pleading in those courts, which in turn includes a power to regulate matters which, though falling within the uncertain area between substance and procedure, are rationally capable of classification as either.

Id. at 472. In this case, to hold that a state rule of evidence supplants a federal evidentiary rule even if it were promulgated by the use of the same procedure as is utilized in the case of the Federal Rules of Civil Procedure would be, in essence, to hold that the Federal Rule exceeds the power of Congress to promulgate it because it cannot "rationally" be classified as procedural. It is significant to note that no federal rule of procedure or evidence has *ever* been struck down as exceeding Congress' constitutional power.[6]

This Court is satisfied that the Hanna v. Plumer test applies to the Federal Rules of Evidence as well as to the Federal Rules of Civil Pro-

---

6. The Hanna v. Plumer test for evaluating the Federal Rules of Civil Procedure under *Erie* was unanimously reaffirmed recently by the Supreme Court in Walker v. Armco Steel Corp., 446 U.S. 740 (1980). Indeed, in *Walker* the Court states that the Federal Rules of Civil Procedure are not to be construed narrowly to avoid conflict with state rules: "The Federal Rules should be given their plain meaning. If a direct collision with state law arises from that plain meaning, then the analysis developed in Hanna v. Plumer applies." 446 U.S. at 750, n.9. There could be no more direct conflict than in the case at bar. Federal Rule of Evidence 407 explicitly prohibits the introduction of evidence of subsequent remedial repairs to prove negligence or culpable conduct while Maine Rule of Evidence 407 explicitly permits the introduction of that evidence for that purpose.

cedure. E.g., Gibbs v. State Farm Mutual Ins. Co., 544 F.2d 423, 428 n.2 (9th Cir. 1976). The actual circumstances of the promulgation of the Federal Rules of Evidence make it even more compelling that the same result be obtained by the application of the Hanna v. Plumer test to those Rules. After the Rules were drafted by the Advisory Committee, the Supreme Court reported the new Rules to Congress under the Rules Enabling Act, 28 U.S.C. §2072. Because the new Rules were controversial, Congress intervened, rewrote the Rules where Congress deemed such rewriting appropriate, and then enacted them as so rewritten directly. Congress placed no reliance on either the Rules Enabling Act or the Rules of Decision Act, 28 U.S.C. §1652. See Rules of Evidence, Pub. L. 93-595, 88 Stat. 1926 (1974). The effect of this enactment is clear:

> Because the Rules of Evidence were enacted directly by Congress, their validity vis-à-vis state law and the principles of the *Erie* doctrine stands on even firmer ground than that of the Rules of Civil Procedure. They are not subject to the Rules of Decision Act or (unlike the Rules of Civil Procedure) to the Rules Enabling Act. Their validity is governed solely by the Constitution, but since all of the Evidence Rules can rationally be viewed as rules of procedure (the constitutional standard announced in Hanna v. Plumer), they all clearly are constitutional.

C. Wright, A. Miller & E. Cooper, supra, §4512 at 192-93 (footnotes omitted). . . .

It is to be noted that in enacting the Federal Rules of Evidence, Congress paid considerable deference to state evidentiary practice by explicitly incorporating state evidentiary practice where Congress thought that to be warranted. See, e.g., Fed. R. Evid. 302, 501, and 601. In addition, Congress did not alter such "substantive" state rules of evidence as the parol evidence rule, the collateral source rule, and the Statute of Frauds. See C. Wright, A. Miller & E. Cooper §4512 at 194-95. However, in Rule 407 Congress did enact a uniform rule governing the admission of evidence of subsequent remedial measures and that rule must be followed unless it can be shown to be unconstitutional because it cannot "rationally" be considered procedural under the *Hanna* test. Federal Rule 407, as enacted by Congress, is the identical rule drafted by the Advisory Committee and reported to Congress by the Supreme Court. Compare 56 F.R.D. 183, 225 (1973) with Pub. L. 93-595. Thus, this Court would have to hold in order to supplant that rule with the Maine Rule of opposite effect not only that Congress exceeded its constitutional power in promulgating the rule, but that it did so upon the considered recommendation of the Advisory Committee and of the Supreme Court. To date, all of the published judicial discussions of which this Court is aware on this issue have concluded that Rule 407 of the Federal Rules of Evidence should be applied to state claims tried by a federal court deriving its jurisdiction from the diversity of citizenship of the parties.

See [Grenada Steel Industries, Inc. v. Alabama Oxygen Co., Inc., 695 F.2d 883 (5th Cir. 1983)]; Oberst v. International Harvester Co., 640 F.2d 863, 867-68 n.2 (7th Cir. 1980) (Swygert, J., concurring and dissenting in part) (dictum).

Accordingly, the Court is satisfied that Federal Rule 407 governs the admissibility of evidence of subsequent remedial measures in this diversity case and that the Court may not supplant that rule by applying the provisions of Maine Rule 407.

B. Settlement Offers and Payment of Medical Expenses

Problem: Nice Guy

(1) Cars driven by *D* and *P* collide at an intersection controlled by a traffic signal. Each alights from his car, and the following dialogue ensues:

D: Why didn't you stop for the light? See what you've done?

P: What do you mean, "*you* stop for the light"? I had the green. Oh, my car. And my neck is hurt. Ohh . . .

D: Well, maybe it turned on me in the intersection. Let's not make a big deal of this. Maybe we can handle this ourselves.

P: Ohh, my neck . . . and my back . . . ohhh . . .

D: Now wait a minute, let's talk this over. I'm sorry I ran the light. Here, how's about if I give you this, ah, $100, for the fender, and, ah, here's another $100 for your neck—go get a massage or something. Let's forget about it—how about it?

P sues *D* for $750,000 for personal injuries and property damage. Is any of the above admissible?

(2) During pretrial discovery, *P*'s lawyer takes *D*'s deposition. After four hours of testimony, *D*, who is represented by counsel, says:

D: Now, look, you guys — I've had enough of this. Let's go off the record. This isn't going anywhere. Even if the case goes to trial it will take five years to get there, and who knows if *P* will get a cent? Even if he wins, he isn't going to get more than my liability coverage provides. How much were *P*'s medical bills? $2,300? Here's a check for that amount plus $1,700 for his time. If he signs this release, it's his.

P rejects these terms. At trial how much of this is admissible?

Federal Rule 408 excludes not only compromises and offers to compromise but also accompanying conduct and statements when offered to prove liability. This rule represents a departure from the traditional view that statements of fact made during compromise negotiations are admissible unless phrased in a formalistic, hypothetical fashion. See, e.g., State v. Stevens, 248 Minn. 309, 80 N.W.2d 22 (1965).

The same protection that is afforded statements of fact during compromise negotiations is denied to statements made in connection with the furnishing of medical expenses (Rule 409). The Advisory Committee's Note to Rule 409 says that the difference in treatment "arises from fundamental differences in nature. Communication is essential if compromises are to be effected, and consequently broad protection of statements is needed. This is not so in cases of payments or offers or promises to pay medical expenses, where factual statements may be expected to be incidental in nature." Is this explanation unconvincing?

Sometimes it is hard to distinguish between an admission and an offer to compromise. Despite attempts to liberalize the rule, it can still be a trap for the unwary. Is this claim in dispute as to either validity or amount? Is this an attempt to compromise a claim? D's statement, "Maybe we can handle this ourselves," could be interpreted as an attempt at informal dispute resolution, and, likewise, his comment, "let's talk this over." Moreover, although he seems to be conceding liability when he states, "Well, maybe it turned on me in the intersection" and "I'm sorry I ran the light," he does seem to be negotiating the amount of liability. If the purpose of the rule is to promote compromises and to eliminate the necessity of a formal announcement such as "Now we are in settlement negotiations," the court should adopt a liberal attitude as to when informal dealings and compromise negotiations begin. On the other hand, this evidence is extremely probative. In fact, admissions are so probative that they get special treatment under the hearsay rule (Rule 801), personal knowledge requirement (Rule 602), and various other rules of evidence (e.g., Rule 1007).

Further complicating this problem is that D's statement might be construed as evidence of offering or promising to pay medical, hospital, or similar expenses occasioned by an injury. Although such evidence is not admissible to prove liability, the Advisory Committee's Note to Rule 409 provides that *statements* not a part of the act of paying medical expenses are not covered by the rule and hence would be admissible. If Rule 409 applied, the evidence that D offered $100 for a neck massage might not be admissible, but the statements about the light turning on him in the intersection and his running the light would probably be admissible.

Given the reliability of such statements, and the lack of data showing that parties in this situation will not attempt to informally resolve matters without the protection of an exclusionary rule, should such statements be admissible?

D's outburst at deposition also raises the issue of whether the claim is disputed. But the claim is undoubtedly disputed in the pleadings, and

D appears to be negotiating the amount of his liability. This statement, even though an outburst, still seems like more of a compromise negotiation than the informal dealing in the street. Moreover, given the setting, its probativeness is diminished. It is common knowledge that litigants having their deposition taken have a strong incentive to buy peace and that this may be the motivating cause of the offer.

Problem: Threatening Letters

D Manufacturing Company recently received a letter from *P* Technology, Inc., accusing *D* of infringing three *P* patents on computerized credit authorization systems. *P* has a reputation as a vigorous enforcer of its patents. Indeed, *P* is currently involved in a fierce patent infringement action on the same patents against *C* Manufacturing Company, a competitor of *D*. The letter invited *D* to take a license for future use at a fee ($5,000,000) that might reflect damages for past infringement. *D* makes and sells credit authorization systems but utilizes technology developed by its employees. Nevertheless, *D*'s general counsel asked a patent attorney to look into *P*'s charge and draft a reply. Before he mails the reply, the general counsel would like your advice as to the effect on any subsequent patent infringement litigation of sending such a letter. The draft letter reads as follows:

Dear *P* Technology, Inc.:

This is in response to your letter of February 16 regarding U.S. Patent Nos. 3,212,062, 3,407,388, and 3,498,069.

We have reviewed these patents and considered our need for a license under them in light of our present and future products. We have concluded that we have no need for a license under any of these patents at this time. However, to show our good faith, we would be willing to take a fully paid license of these patents at a nominal rate ($50,000 to $100,000 range), if accompanied by a general release for past acts.

Please let us have your response within 10 days.

> Sincerely,
> (*Signature*)
> General Counsel,
> *D* Manufacturing Company

The legislative history indicates that the House Committee was very concerned that factual admissions might be excluded under Rule 408. Its amendment to require that parties protect themselves from future use of their statements by couching them in hypothetical form was opposed by the Senate Committee and ultimately rejected in conference. However, as finally enacted, the rule only excludes evidence relating to a claim that is disputed as to either validity or amount. Moreover, the Advisory Committee's Note to this rule states that the rule does not apply "when the effort is to induce a creditor to settle an admittedly due amount for a lesser sum. McCormick §252."

Is *D*'s general counsel trying to induce *P* Technology to accept a lesser sum for an amount that is due? Is *P* Technology's claim the liquidated sum-certain type of claim that the Advisory Committee's Note seems to have in mind? Will the prudent lawyer still use cautionary qualifying language referring to Rule 408 when negotiating?

Problem: The Plot Thickens

P, a passenger in *O*'s car, sues *D* for injuries resulting when *O*'s car collided with *D*'s car. *P* seeks to introduce evidence of a settlement reached between *D* and *Q*, another passenger in *O*'s car. *D* objects. What ruling and why? What other information might be useful in making this ruling?

Does Rule 408 also exclude evidence of completed compromises? Why?

Doesn't the relevance of this evidence depend on the amounts at issue in the two suits, particularly the amount at issue in the earlier *Q v. D* lawsuit and the amount of the settlement between *Q* and *D*? For example, if *Q*'s lawsuit against *D* sought $100 damages, and *P* seeks $1,000,000 damages, and *D* settled with *Q* for $50, the *Q-D* settlement would not be very probative to prove liability of *D* to *P*. In this situation, the most likely explanation for *D*'s settlement with *Q* would be his desire to buy peace in the more insignificant cases so that he can focus his attention on defending the larger suit by *P*. However, if the situation were reversed, that is, *D* had settled with *Q* for hundreds of thousands of dollars and *P* sought to introduce that evidence in his lawsuit against *D* for a few hundred dollars, the *D-Q* settlement would be more probative.

Exclusion of completed settlements, when offered against the party to the settlement, rests more firmly on the ground of promotion of the public policy favoring the compromise and settlement of disputes than it does on notions of relevancy.

Problem: Thicker Still

P, a passenger in *O*'s car, was injured when the car collided with a taxi driven by *D*. *P* sues *D*. *D* seeks to introduce evidence of settlements between *D* and *O*, where *O* agreed to pay for damages to *D*'s vehicle, and between *P* and *O*, wherein *O* paid *P* an undisclosed amount for *P*'s injuries. What ruling and why?

Even when evidence of a completed settlement is not offered against a party, can it be excluded under Rule 408 if offered to prove "invalidity of the claim or its amount"?

In this case, in contrast to the problem "The Plot Thickens," *D* seeks to introduce evidence of a settlement between himself and the driver (*O*) of the car in which *P* was riding, wherein *O* agreed to pay for damage done to *D*'s vehicle. The inference that *D* would like the jury to draw from this evidence is that *O*'s payment to *D* for property damage constitutes an implied admission that *O* was at fault in the accident. *D* also seeks to introduce evidence of *P*'s earlier settlement with *O*, the driver of the vehicle in which *P* was riding. The inference *D* would like the jury to draw from this evidence is twofold—that *O* admitted his fault by paying *P* and that *P* has already been compensated, at least in part, for his injuries. In many states, joint tortfeasor law may require settlements with co-defendants to be revealed to the jury upon the trial of nonsettling defendants. How would such a provision of state law be reconciled with Rule 408 in a diversity case in federal court?

Problem: Even Thicker

Plaintiffs sued *D* Manufacturing Company, its accountants, and seven of its officers and employees for various security violations in connection with a public offering of *D*'s stock. Two of the individual defendants, Jones and Smith — corporate officers — cross-claimed against the corporation, seeking indemnification for expenses incurred in defending the action. Under applicable state law, a corporate officer is entitled to indemnification for reasonable attorneys' fees and expenses, "to the extent he has been successful on the merits in a proceeding where his action as an officer allegedly violated the law." During the pretrial phase of the case, cross-claimants obtained voluntary dismissals, with prejudice, of the actions against them. As part of the arrangement, Jones made a payment to the plaintiffs of $35,000. Smith made no payment.

At the trial of the indemnification claims the issue is whether Jones and Smith were "successful on the merits" in the main case. On this point, the officers offer the dismissals. The corporation offers proof of Jones's $35,000 payment and an affidavit of an attorney for the plaintiffs in the main case regarding the settlement of the plaintiffs' claims against Smith and Jones. Is any of this admissible?

Rule 408's exceptions to the exclusion of evidence of compromises are exemplary rather than exclusive. Where evidence is offered for "another purpose," other than proving liability or validity of the claim or its amount, it may be admissible.

In this case, evidence of the settlement between Smith and Jones and the plaintiffs in the primary case is offered on the issue of whether they have been "successful on the merits" within the meaning of the applicable state law. Interpretations of the state law is a matter for the state court. However the statute is defined, the evidence of the settlements between Jones and Smith and the plaintiffs in the primary case may be relevant to that determination.

In this case, the state policy in applying the provisions of its corporate indemnification law may conflict with the policy underlying Rule 408 in promoting the settlement of disputes. Is there a way to avoid this conflict?

The rule excludes evidence of a compromise only on the issues of the amount or validity of the claim that is the subject of the compromise. Since the "claims" in the primary case and in the indemnification case are distinct, could one contend that the compromise negotiations were being used for "another purpose" and were not inadmissible under Rule 408?

Problem: Mediation

Wife and Husband are participating in court-ordered mediation concerning the custody and support of their children in connection with their divorce case. During one of the mediation sessions Husband expostulates, "When this nightmare is over, you won't be seeing anything of me! I never want to speak to you again!" At the trial one of the issues is whether there should be joint or separate custody of the parties' children. Wife calls the mediator as a witness to testify to Husband's outburst. What ruling and why?

Although Rule 408 does not explicitly refer to mediation many of the policy justifications for excluding statements made in the course of negotiations would apply to statements made in mediation. Are there differences that would justify different treatment of statements made in mediation? Are there limited purposes or issues on which statements in mediation should be admitted? Maine's version of Rule 408 has been amended to prohibit admission of statements made during court-ordered divorce mediation for any purpose.

Problem: Civil Settlements and Criminal Cases

D is prosecuted for violation of a Price Control Act in selling *P* a car at a price above the legal limit. The act premises criminal liability on a showing of willfulness, whereas civil liability exists for merely negligent violations. Testimony at trial shows that salesperson *S*, employed by *D*, actually made the sale. Liability therefore turns on whether *D* directed or acquiesced in *S*'s overcharging of *P*, the prosecutrix. The prosecution offers evidence of an offer made by *D* to *P* to refund the overcharge. *D* objects.

What ruling and why? What other information might the judge want to have before making this decision? What other policies besides that in favor of extrajudicial settlement of disputes are relevant in this context?

Criminal liability requires willfulness. Civil liability exists for merely negligent violations. Even if *D*'s offer to *P* to refund the overcharge could be constituted as an admission of civil liability, it would only constitute an admission of negligent supervision of *S*. This is not relevant in a criminal case where willfulness must be shown. Thus, not only are all of the policy reasons of Rule 408 present, there is the additional relevancy problem caused by the difference in standards of liability in the civil and criminal cases. Moreover, the general public policy reason underlying Rule 408 is stronger when it encourages settlement of civil cases without prejudice to possible criminal violations. In the reverse situation, the existence of the nolo contendere plea reflects this policy. See Rule 410(2).

C.   Pleas and Related Statements

Plea negotiations in criminal cases present many of the same policy considerations as do party negotiations in civil disputes. Full and frank discussions are fostered if the parties (particularly the defendant) need not fear that statements made in an effort to resolve the criminal prosecution will reappear in evidence in a current or future civil matter or another criminal case. Federal Rule 410 embodies this policy and restricts admissibility of prior pleas of nolo contendere, of later-withdrawn guilty pleas, and of offers and statements in plea negotiations. A question is whether the scope of the rule language matches the scope of the policy which it is intended to implement.

Problem: Plea Bargain

D was arrested on heroin distribution charges by DEA Agent *A,* who gave him *Miranda* warnings. *D* then informed *A* that he had cooperated with the government in the past and would be willing to do so in the future. In the course of this conversation, *D* made incriminating statements relating to the crime for which he had been arrested. Later that day, *D* met in a pre-arraignment conference with Assistant United States Attorney *B* and had a similar conversation. After his arraignment, *D* returned to DEA headquarters with a lawyer to meet with *A. D* again offered to cooperate, and *A* suggested that *D* contact Agent *C. D* thereafter contacted *C,* offered to cooperate, and made some incriminatory statements. At no time during any of these conversations did *D* explicitly offer to plead guilty or request a concession from the government.

Which parts, if any, of the conversations related above should be excluded under Rule 410? What additional information might assist you in making this determination?

Problem: Is Turnabout Fair Play?

D is charged with the sale of a controlled substance—heroin. At trial, *D* calls *W,* who was formerly the Assistant United States Attorney in charge of the case but is now in private practice. Through *W, D*'s attorney seeks to show that *W* offered *D* the opportunity to plead to possession, rather than sale, in exchange for *D*'s testimony against others. The prosecution objects. What ruling and why?

A criminal conviction based on a jury verdict may have collateral estoppel effect if offered against the defendant in a subsequent civil action. A guilty plea, however, constitutes only an admission and is not conclusive. The distinction between these situations is that the guilty plea does not result in a full adversarial presentation of the issues in the case. It may reflect only a compromise, such as to pay a fine rather than to litigate. Thus, fairness to civil litigants and the policy favoring expeditious administration of criminal justice combine in most jurisdictions to prohibit the application of collateral estoppel to guilty pleas. See Teitelbaum Furs, Inc. v. Dominion Ins. Co., 58 Cal. 2d 601, 25 Cal. Rptr. 559, 375 P.2d 439, cert. denied, 372 U.S. 966 (1962).

Pleas of nolo contendere go one step further — they are not even admissible. Rule 410(2). This is a long-standing rule. See FDIC v. Cloonan, 165 Kan. 68, 193 P.2d 656 (1948). The policy behind this exclusion is to provide an option whereby all the effects of a criminal conviction may be obtained but the pleading party may avoid an admission of guilt that can be used against him in a subsequent case.

The primary problem under Rule 410 is distinguishing admissible confessions or admissions (see Rule 801(d)(2)) from statements immunized under Rule 410. This problem was even more acute under the initial version of Rule 410, which was not tied to F. R. Crim. P. 11 nor limited to statements made in the course of plea discussions with an attorney for the prosecuting authority. Rule 410 was amended in 1979 to limit its application to these situations.

Under the current rule, one still must decide when statements or conduct by the defendant or the government official suffice to justify characterizing discussions as "plea discussions." Also, there is a pervasive relevancy question. In looking at evidence of statements arguably covered by the rule, one must be careful to understand the purposes for which plea-bargaining statements are offered, keeping in mind the realities of the plea-bargaining process.

UNITED STATES v. MEZZANATTO
513 U.S. 196 (1995)

Justice THOMAS delivered the opinion of the Court.

Federal Rule of Evidence 410 and Federal Rule of Criminal Procedure 11(e)(6) provide that statements made in the course of plea discussions between a criminal defendant and a prosecutor are inadmissible against the defendant. The court below held that these exclusionary provisions may not be waived by the defendant. We granted certiorari to resolve a conflict among the Courts of Appeals, and we now reverse.

I

On August 1, 1991, San Diego Narcotics Task Force agents arrested Gordon Shuster after discovering a methamphetamine laboratory at his residence in Rainbow, California. Shuster agreed to cooperate with the agents, and a few hours after his arrest he placed a call to respondent's pager. When respondent returned the call, Shuster told him that a friend wanted to purchase a pound of methamphetamine for $13,000. Shuster arranged to meet respondent later that day.

At their meeting, Shuster introduced an undercover officer as his "friend." The officer asked respondent if he had "brought the stuff with him," and respondent told the officer it was in his car. The two proceeded to the car, where respondent produced a brown paper package containing approximately one pound of methamphetamine. Respondent then presented a glass pipe (later found to contain methamphetamine residue) and asked the officer if he wanted to take a "hit." The officer indicated that he would first get respondent the money; as the officer left the car, he gave a prearranged arrest signal. Respondent was arrested and charged with possession of methamphetamine with intent to distribute. . . .

On October 17, 1991, respondent and his attorney asked to meet with the prosecutor to discuss the possibility of cooperating with the Government. The prosecutor agreed to meet later that day. At the beginning of the meeting, the prosecutor informed respondent that he had no obligation to talk, but that if he wanted to cooperate he would have to be completely truthful. As a condition to proceeding with the discussion, the prosecutor indicated that respondent would have to agree that any statements he made during the meeting could be used to impeach any contradictory testimony he might give at trial if the case proceeded that far. Respondent conferred with his counsel and agreed to proceed under the prosecutor's terms.

Respondent then admitted knowing that the package he had attempted to sell to the undercover police officer contained methamphetamine, but insisted that he had dealt only in "ounce" quantities of methamphetamine prior to his arrest. Initially, respondent also claimed that he was acting merely as a broker for Shuster and did not know that Shuster was manufacturing methamphetamine at his residence, but he later conceded that he knew about Shuster's laboratory. Respondent attempted to minimize his role in Shuster's operation by claiming that he had not visited Shuster's residence for at least a week before his arrest. At this point, the Government confronted respondent with surveillance evidence showing that his car was on Shuster's property the day before the arrest, and terminated the meeting on the basis of respondent's failure to provide completely truthful information.

Respondent eventually was tried on the methamphetamine charge and took the stand in his own defense. He maintained that he was not involved in methamphetamine trafficking and that he had thought Shuster used his home laboratory to manufacture plastic explosives for the CIA. He also denied knowing that the package he delivered to the undercover officer contained methamphetamine. Over defense counsel's objection, the prosecutor cross-examined respondent about the inconsistent statements he had made during the October 17 meeting. Respondent denied having made certain statements, and the prosecutor called one of the agents who had attended the meeting to recount the prior statements. The jury found respondent guilty, and the District Court sentenced him to 170 months in prison.

A panel of the Ninth Circuit reversed, over the dissent of Chief Judge Wallace. 998 F.2d 1452 (1993). The Ninth Circuit held that respondent's agreement to allow admission of his plea statements for purposes of impeachment was unenforceable and that the District Court therefore erred in admitting the statements for that purpose. We granted certiorari because the Ninth Circuit's decision conflicts with the Seventh Circuit's decision in United States v. Dortch, 5 F.3d 1056, 1067-1068 (1993).

II

Federal Rule of Evidence 410 and Federal Rule of Criminal Procedure 11(e)(6) (Rules or plea-statement Rules) are substantively identical. Rule 410 provides: ["]Except as otherwise provided in this rule, evidence of the following is not, in any civil or criminal proceeding, admissible against the defendant who . . . was a participant in the plea discussions: . . . (4) any statement made in the course of plea discussions with an attorney for the prosecuting authority which do not result in a plea of guilty. . . .["]

The Ninth Circuit noted that these Rules are subject to only two express exceptions, neither of which says anything about waiver, and thus concluded that Congress must have meant to preclude waiver agreements such as respondent's. In light of the "precision with which these rules are generally phrased," the Ninth Circuit declined to "write in a waiver in a waiverless rule."

The Ninth Circuit's analysis is directly contrary to the approach we have taken in the context of a broad array of constitutional and statutory provisions. Rather than deeming waiver presumptively unavailable absent some sort of express enabling clause, we instead have adhered to the opposite presumption. . . . A criminal defendant may knowingly and voluntarily waive many of the most fundamental protections afforded by the Constitution. Likewise, absent some affirmative indication of Congress' intent to preclude waiver, we have presumed that statutory provisions are subject to waiver by voluntary agreement of the parties. . . .

The presumption of waivability has found specific application in the context of evidentiary rules. Absent some "overriding procedural consideration that prevents enforcement of the contract," courts have held that agreements to waive evidentiary rules are generally enforceable even over a party's subsequent objections. Courts have "liberally enforced" agreements to waive various exclusionary rules of evidence. . . .

Indeed, evidentiary stipulations are a valuable and integral part of everyday trial practice. Prior to trial, parties often agree in writing to the admission of otherwise objectionable evidence, either in exchange for stipulations from opposing counsel or for other strategic purposes. Both the Federal Rules of Civil Procedure and the Federal Rules of Criminal Procedure appear to contemplate that the parties will enter into evidentiary agreements during a pretrial conference. During the course of trial, parties frequently decide to waive evidentiary objections, and such tactics are routinely honored by trial judges. . . .

III

Because the plea-statement Rules were enacted against a background presumption that legal rights generally, and evidentiary provisions specifically, are subject to waiver by voluntary agreement of the parties, we will not interpret Congress' silence as an implicit rejection of waivability. Respondent bears the responsibility of identifying some affirmative basis for concluding that the plea-statement Rules depart from the presumption of waivability.

Respondent offers three potential bases for concluding that the Rules should be placed beyond the control of the parties. We find none of them persuasive.

A

Respondent first suggests that the plea-statement Rules establish a "guarantee [to] fair procedure" that cannot be waived. Brief for Respondent 12. We agree with respondent's basic premise: there may be some evidentiary provisions that are so fundamental to the reliability of the fact-finding process that they may never be waived without irreparably "discredit[ing] the federal courts." [Citations omitted.] But enforcement of agreements like respondent's plainly will not have that effect. The admission of plea statements for impeachment purposes enhances the truth-seeking function of trials and will result in more accurate verdicts. [Citations omitted.] Under any view of the evidence, the defendant has made a false statement, either to the prosecutor during the plea discussion or to the jury at trial; making the jury aware of the inconsistency will tend to increase the reliability in the verdict without risking institutional harm to the federal courts. . . .

Rules 410 and 11(e)(6) "creat[e], in effect, a privilege of the defendant," and, like other evidentiary privileges, this one may be waived or varied at the defendant's request. The Rules provide that statements made in the course of plea discussions are inadmissible "against" the defendant, and thus leave open the possibility that a defendant may offer such statements into evidence for his own tactical advantage. Indeed, the Rules contemplate this result in permitting admission of statements made "in any proceeding wherein another statement made in the course of the same . . . plea discussions has been introduced and the statement ought in fairness be considered contemporaneously with it." Thus, the plea-statement Rules expressly contemplate a degree of party control that is consonant with the background presumption of waivability.

B

Respondent also contends that waiver is fundamentally inconsistent with the Rules' goal of encouraging voluntary settlement. See Advisory Committee Notes on Fed. Rule Evid. 410 (purpose of Rule is "promotion of disposition of criminal cases by compromise"). Because the prospect of waiver may make defendants "think twice" before entering into any plea negotiation, respondent suggests that enforcement of waiver agreements acts "as a brake, not as a facilitator, to the plea-bargain process." The Ninth Circuit expressed similar concerns, noting that Rules 410 and 11(e)(6) "aid in obtaining th[e] cooperation" that is often necessary to identify and prosecute the leaders of a criminal conspiracy and that waiver of the protections of the Rules "could easily have a chilling effect on the entire plea bargaining process." According to the Ninth Circuit, the plea-statement Rules "permit the plea bargainer to maximize what he has 'to sell'" by preserving "the ability to withdraw from the bargain proposed by the prosecutor without being harmed by any of his statements made in the course of an aborted plea bargaining session."

We need not decide whether and under what circumstances substantial "public policy" interests may permit the inference that Congress intended to override the presumption of waivability, for in this case there is no basis for concluding that waiver will interfere with the Rules' goal of encouraging plea bargaining. The court below focused entirely on the defendant's incentives and completely ignored the other essential party to the transaction: the prosecutor. Thus, although the availability of waiver may discourage some defendants from negotiating, it is also true that prosecutors may be unwilling to proceed without it. Prosecutors may be especially reluctant to negotiate without a waiver agreement during the early stages of a criminal investigation, when prosecutors are searching for leads and suspects may be willing to offer information in exchange for some form of immunity or leniency in sentencing. In this "cooperation" context, prosecutors face "painfully delicate" choices as to "whether to proceed and prosecute those suspects against whom the already produced evidence makes a case or whether to extend leniency or full immunity to some suspects in order to procure testimony against other, more dangerous suspects against whom existing evidence is flimsy or nonexistent." Because prosecutors have limited resources and must be able to answer "sensitive questions about the credibility of the testimony" they receive before entering into any sort of cooperation agreement, prosecutors may condition cooperation discussions on an agreement that the testimony provided may be used for impeachment purposes. If prosecutors were precluded from securing such agreements, they might well decline to enter into cooperation discussions in the first place and might never take this potential first step toward a plea bargain.

Indeed, as a logical matter, it simply makes no sense to conclude that mutual settlement will be encouraged by precluding negotiation over an issue that may be particularly important to one of the parties to the transaction. A sounder way to encourage settlement is to permit the interested parties to enter into knowing and voluntary negotiations without any arbitrary limits on their bargaining chips. To use the Ninth Circuit's metaphor, if the prosecutor is interested in "buying" the reliability assurance that accompanies a waiver agreement, then precluding waiver can only stifle the market for plea bargains. A defendant can "maximize" what he has to "sell" only if he is permitted to offer what the prosecutor is most interested in buying. And while it is certainly true that prosecutors often need help from the small fish in a conspiracy in order to catch the big ones, that is no reason to preclude waiver altogether. If prosecutors decide that certain crucial information will be gained only by preserving the inadmissibility of plea statements, they will agree to leave intact the exclusionary provisions of the plea-statement Rules.

In sum, there is no reason to believe that allowing negotiation as to waiver of the plea-statement Rules will bring plea bargaining to a grinding halt; it may well have the opposite effect. Respondent's unfounded policy argument thus provides no basis for concluding that Congress intended to prevent criminal defendants from offering to waive the plea-statement Rules during plea negotiation.

c

Finally, respondent contends that waiver agreements should be forbidden because they invite prosecutorial overreaching and abuse. Respondent asserts that there is a "gross disparity" in the relative bargaining power of the parties to a plea agreement and suggests that a waiver agreement is "inherently unfair and coercive." Because the prosecutor retains the discretion to "reward defendants for their substantial assistance" under the Sentencing Guidelines, respondent argues that defendants face an "'incredible dilemma'" when they are asked to accept waiver as the price of entering plea discussions.

The dilemma flagged by respondent is indistinguishable from any of a number of difficult choices that criminal defendants face every day. The plea bargaining process necessarily exerts pressure on defendants to plead guilty and to abandon a series of fundamental rights, but we have repeatedly held that the government "may encourage a guilty plea by offering substantial benefits in return for the plea." . . .

The mere potential for abuse of prosecutorial bargaining power is an insufficient basis for foreclosing negotiation altogether. "Rather, tradition and experience justify our belief that the great majority of prosecutors will be faithful to their duty." . . . Instead, the appropriate response to respondent's predictions of abuse is to permit case-by-case inquiries into whether waiver agreements are the product of fraud or coercion. We hold that absent some affirmative indication that the agreement was entered into unknowingly or involuntarily, an agreement to waive the exclusionary provisions of the plea-statement Rules is valid and enforceable.

IV

Respondent conferred with his lawyer after the prosecutor proposed waiver as a condition of proceeding with the plea discussion, and he has never complained that he entered into the waiver agreement at issue unknowingly or involuntarily. The Ninth Circuit's decision was based on its per se rejection of waiver of the plea-statement Rules. Accordingly, the judgment of the Court of Appeals is reversed.

It is so ordered.

[Concurring opinion by Justice GINSBURG omitted.]

Justice SOUTER, with whom Justice STEVENS joins, dissenting.

This case poses only one question: did Congress intend to create a personal right subject to waiver by its individual beneficiaries when it adopted Rule 410 of the Federal Rules of Evidence and Rule 11(e)(6) of the Federal Rules of Criminal Procedure, each Rule providing that statements made during plea discussions are inadmissible against the defendant except in two carefully described circumstances? The case raises no issue of policy to be settled by the courts, and if the generally applicable (and generally sound) judicial policy of respecting waivers of rights and privileges should conflict with a reading of the Rules as reasonably construed to accord with the intent of Congress, there is no doubt that congressional intent should prevail. Because the majority ruling is at odds with the intent of Congress and will render the Rules largely dead letters, I respectfully dissent. . . .

D. Proof of Insurance

ST. PIERRE v. HOUDE
269 A.2d 538 (Me. 1970)

WEBBER, J. — Plaintiff's action for recovery of damages suffered in an automobile accident resulted in a jury verdict of $5,000. Liability was admitted and trial was on damages only.

In the course of his argument to the jury, counsel for the defendant stated:

> Now, I say this to you, and I believe this is correct, that Mrs. Houde is liable. *She will have to pay the damages out of her own pocket*, and that is proper, but it is damages that are properly chargeable to this case.

Plaintiff's attorney then interrupted the argument and entered his objection. Colloquy ensued in the absence of the jury in the course of which plaintiff's counsel contended the statement was not the truth and was improper argument suggestive to the jury that defendant was not insured. It was not disputed that defendant was in fact covered by liability insurance. The presiding Justice, weighing the alternative methods by which the prejudicial effect of the statement might be corrected, first concluded that any attempted instruction to the jury would be inadequate. He then offered to permit defendant's counsel to retract the statement in further argument to the jury. This counsel declined to do. Thereupon the presiding Justice ruled that the plaintiff might elect either to have a mistrial or to state the true fact to the jury. This ruling is challenged on appeal.

Plaintiff's attorney elected not to request a mistrial but to undertake correction of the misstatement in his concluding argument to the jury. In the course of his statement to the jury, plaintiff's counsel said:

> And although the law is very clear in this state, the precedent and the practice before this bar, that it matters not from what source funds are obtained to pay a judgment that is awarded, although that is the practice and the law, you will recall full well that only some ten minutes ago, or so, Mr. Marshall stood before this bar and addressed this very jury, and he said to you substantially and in effect, as best I can quote him, that any judgment which you render, and a judgment you must render against his client, in the case in point, that any judgment you render must be paid for out of the pocket of the defendant. You will remember his words. And now I am authorized, with the approval of the presiding justice here, to say to you here and now that the statement that Mr. Marshall made to you, which I have just quoted, is not true in fact.

An objection was then noted by defendant's counsel. Plaintiff's counsel then continued:

> So my last, concluding statement to you is, members of the panel, that I have just made the statement to you that the judgment which you will render, will not be taken out of the pocket of the defendant.

Defendant's counsel in the absence of the jury immediately moved for a mistrial. The presiding Justice, deeming that the defendant's counsel had opened the door, denied the motion. This ruling is the object of the defendant's second point of appeal.

The plaintiff had special damages of $364, lost no wages and had no permanent injuries. As her third point of appeal, defendant asserts that a verdict of $5,000 six months after the accident was excessive and must have been the product of prejudice engendered by the trial incidents above described.

The rule has long been established that in cases where the wealth or poverty of a party is not a proper issue in the case, references by counsel to these matters constitute improper argument. The impropriety of mentioning insurance or the lack of it in such cases has its origin in that rule. The guidelines were made crystal clear in the case of Deschaine v. Deschaine (1958) 153 Me. 401, 406, 140 A.2d 746, 748, wherein we said:

> The reasons for excluding reference to poverty or wealth of parties are equally applicable in the case of insurance. In Mizula and Cherepowitch v. Sawyer, 130 Me. 428, at page 430, 157 A. 239, at page 239, an automobile accident case, the Court said: "The special motion presents a peculiar situation. It appears that counsel for Sawyer, in closing the case to the jury, dwelt on her age and limited financial ability. Just exactly what he said is not agreed upon, but very plainly his argument was irrelevant, improper, and prejudicial. References to the wealth or poverty of parties, unless the issues involved make such references admissible, may constitute reversible error."

We leave the rule as it has existed since at least 1897; that is to say, insurance in negligence cases is immaterial, prejudicial and not admissible. Sawyer v. J. M. Arnold Shoe Co., supra [90 Me. 369, 38 A. 333]. The rule obviously applies with equal force to arguments of counsel."

We add only that words used by counsel which by clear implication suggest the presence or absence of insurance, even though the word itself may not be used, can be violative of the rule and constitute improper argument. Such was the case here. Plaintiff's counsel did not sleep upon his rights as was the case in Patterson v. Rossignol (Me. 1968) 245 A.2d 852. He moved promptly by way of objection and requested some appropriate relief from prejudice. It thus became the duty of the presiding Justice, in the exercise of a sound discretion, to determine the prejudicial effect of the argument and what corrective measures might be taken.

Several courses of conduct are open to consideration in such circumstances, all of which were weighed by the presiding Justice here. He may conclude that a retraction by the counsel whose argument has created the problem may suffice. A counsel who has, perhaps by inadvertence, misstated a fact will often welcome the opportunity to select the words by means of which the misstatement is corrected. The trial court may conclude that an appropriate instruction to the jury will or will not effectively remove the risk of prejudice. He is in a peculiarly advantageous position to gauge the impact of the offending language. He has heard the tone and inflection of counsel—he has seen the visible re-action of the jury, if any, as the words were spoken—in short, he has the benefit of sensory reactions which cannot be transmitted through printed pages to the reviewing court. In the instant case we find no abuse of discretion on the part of the Justice below either when he concluded that an instruction to the jury would not adequately protect the rights of the plaintiff, or when he offered defendant's counsel an opportunity to retract.

The presiding Justice may in such a case permit opposing counsel to offer counter argument or make a corrective statement if there is good reason to believe that such a method is best adapted to assure a fair and just verdict. See *Mizula* and Cherepowitch v. Sawyer, supra. He may on request of the aggrieved party, or upon his own motion if the circum-stances so require, order a mistrial.

In the instant case the Justice below considered all possible alterna-tives. He took into account the fact that the door should not be opened to defendants to gain successive mistrials which could effectively prevent plaintiffs from securing final judgments. He had no request from plain-tiff's counsel that a mistrial be granted. Under the peculiar and difficult circumstances then existing, we are satisfied that it was proper for the Justice below to conclude that he should not order a mistrial *sua sponte* but should permit plaintiff's counsel to include a correction with re-spect to the misstated fact in his argument to the jury. So also, there was no error in denying defendant's motion. Counsel for the defendant had unfortunately opened the door and, having declined to make the necessary correction himself, could not be heard to complain if it was then fairly made by his opponent, so worded as to stay within limits imposed by the Court.

As a further ground of appeal, the defendant contends that the evi-dence will not support the verdict which therefore must be set aside as grossly excessive. We recognize that this issue must be treated entirely apart from issues related to the improper argument of defense counsel. The Court cannot sustain an excessive verdict merely in order to express condemnation of the conduct of counsel in the trial of a case no matter how vigorously the Court may disapprove of that conduct. Accordingly, we have examined the evidence, viewing it in the light most favorable to the plaintiff, to ascertain whether the verdict exceeds permissible limits.

At this point we are confronted by a partial and what seems to us inadequate record. If we consider such factors as special damages in the amount of only $364, no hospitalization, no lost wages and no perma-nent injuries, the verdict appears to be clearly excessive. On the other hand, we glean from the briefs that there was other evidence, omitted from the record on appeal, as for example the entire testimony of the plaintiff himself, which might have cast further light on the extent and continuation of plaintiff's pain and suffering. We are not furnished any explanation as to why the appellee did not designate additional portions of the record under M.R.C.P., Rule 74 if they were essential to a full review, but under the exceptional circumstances of this case we are unwilling to risk possible injustice to the plaintiff by ordering remittitur.

We conclude that as the case is now postured the verdict cannot stand. We further conclude that fairness and justice will be best assured by a new jury trial in an atmosphere freed of possible sources of prejudice which, in spite of the best efforts of the presiding Justice, may have affected the verdict. Since liability is admitted, there will be no occasion to try that issue.

Appeal sustained. New trial ordered on damages only.

The approach of the Maine Supreme Judicial Court in St. Pierre v. Houde represents the traditional view as to admissibility of information about the insured or uninsured status of the parties to civil litigation. This view was embodied in Federal Rule 411. The Federal Rule, however, takes pains to point out that while evidence of insurance may not be admissible on the issue of fault, it may be admissible for another purpose, such as to show that the insured exercised "control" over premises, or was in an agency relationship with the person maintaining the insurance.

In the view of the Maine Supreme Judicial Court, information about a party's insured status is potentially highly prejudicial in that such information would make it likely that the jury might decide the case based on considerations other than the legal rules of liability as charged by the court. Is this true in the current day and age, when liability insurance is commonplace, and most juries, if they think about the matter at all, would assume that most defendants are covered?

Problem: The Deep Pocket Approach

(1) *P* v. *D* Company for workers compensation. While he was working at a pressing machine at *D* Company, his employer, *P*'s arm became caught in the machine and eventually had to be amputated. During *P*'s cross-examination of *W,* the general manager of the *D* Company plant, *P*'s attorney asks *W* if *D* Company carries insurance against such accidents and, if so, in what amount. The attorney for *D* Company objects. What ruling and why? Now assume that *P* is required to prove negligence on the part of *D* in the maintenance of the machine. Would your ruling be different? Why?

(2) During the cross-examination of Dr. *X*, another witness for *D* Company who is called as an expert to testify on the operation and maintenance of the presses, *P*'s attorney asks *X* if he has been retained by the Casualty Insurance Company. *D* Company's attorney objects. *P* makes an offer of proof that if allowed to testify, Dr. *X* will state that he has been retained by the Casualty Insurance Company and, further, that Casualty has insured *D* Company for losses of this sort up to $3,000,000. What ruling and why?

A recurring problem with the categorical rules of exclusion is that they all provide that the prohibited evidence may be admitted if offered for other purposes. For example, Rule 411 does not require the exclusion of evidence of insurance when offered to prove agency, ownership, or control, or bias or prejudice of a witness. Moreover, prohibited evidence is often suggested to the jury by clever attorneys in various tricky ways even when it cannot be introduced for any admissible purpose. This, of course, raises ethical as well as practical questions. How do attorneys go about getting evidence of facts excluded by these rules before the jury? If evidence within the reach of these categorical rules is offered by an opponent and admitted over objection under a permissible purpose exception or is suggested to the jury improperly, how does one counteract its prejudicial effect? What limiting instructions should a judge give? How effective are they in these situations? How does the fact that evidence that is purportedly excluded by these rules nevertheless often gets before the jury affect your view on the wisdom of having these rules? If evidence of insurance is relevant to an issue other than "whether a person acted negligently or otherwise wrongfully," but the issue is of little importance or the evidence is of little probative force, can the court exclude the evidence under Rule 403?

Consider these trial practice problems:

(1)   You represent the plaintiff in a medical malpractice case. You want to get in evidence that defendant is insured up to $10,000,000. How do you do it (ethically)?

(2)   You represent the defendant in the same case. You want to get in evidence that the defendant has no insurance. What do you do (ethically)?

(3)   In the same case, you represent the defendant, who has no insurance. If the plaintiff somehow floats the suggestion that the defendant is insured, what do you do?

(4)   You represent the plaintiff in a negligence action against a supermarket. Plaintiff slipped and fell in the aisles. How do you (ethically) get in evidence that the supermarket changed from a wax floor polish to the non-skid variety a week after the accident?

Problem: Hit and Run

D is accused of leaving the scene of an accident. The testimony at his trial shows that, upon leaving work, *P* discovered her parked car to be dented along the side; *W* testifies that he saw *D*'s car skid, thump *P*'s parked car, and then drive away. *D* admits skidding toward *P*'s car but denies striking it. At trial, *D* offers to prove that he is covered by insurance for such damage. *P* objects. What ruling and why?

Problem: Absence of Coverage

P v. *D* Company for damages. While in *D* Company's employ, *P* was directing the backing up of a *D* Company truck that "jerked back" and crushed *P*'s arm against a loading dock. At trial, *P*'s attorney asks *P* on direct examination whether he received any workers' compensation benefits. *D* objects. During *D*'s case-in-chief, *D*'s attorney asks *W*, the president of *D* Company, whether *D* Company is insured for claims such as these. *P* objects. In each case the answer would be "no." How should the court rule?

In an age in which workers' compensation liability insurance is widely assumed to exist, is the rule excluding evidence of lack of insurance unfair to those who do not have such coverage?

In this case, both *P* and *D* seek to introduce evidence of lack of insurance in order to counter an assumption that such insurance exists. In *P*'s case, he is concerned that the jury will think that he has already been paid workers' compensation benefits, when in fact he has waived them in order to sue. In *D*'s case, the company is concerned that the jury will assume that any damages assessed against *D* will be paid by a faceless insurance company and therefore come in with a high verdict.

Strict application of the rule would exclude any mention of the presence or absence of coverage. This ostrichlike approach may create more problems than it solves.

The rule against evidence of insurance is one aspect of the "collateral source rule," which developed out of late nineteenth century tort law occasioned by the growing number of cases involving accidents in the workplace. See Seller, The Collateral Source Rule and Personal Injury Damages: The Irrelevant Principle and the Functional Approach, 58 Ky. L.J. 36, 38 (1969). The question is whether the collateral source rule and the evidentiary exclusion of insurance coverage or noncoverage have outlasted the social and economic conditions that precipitated their development. Seller argues that the increase in insurance and social benefit payments for injuries makes the rule obsolete.

There are three factual settings in which the issue of insurance or lack of it may arise in a civil trial. The first situation is where the defendant seeks to introduce proof that the plaintiff has received medical or other payments under either an insurance policy or workers' compensation from the employer or from another "collateral" source. In this situation, the goal of the defense is to show that the plaintiff has not been economically harmed as severely as claimed because these collateral payments have, in effect, mitigated the actual monetary damages sustained. Until recently, nearly all states prohibited the defendant from introducing such evidence.

The collateral source rule has been defended on the ground that a wrongful defendant should not benefit from the fact that the plaintiff has prudently acquired insurance because that would allow the defendant to receive a windfall from his immoral and wrongful actions. This argument reflects a view that the defendant should pay for harm that he has caused because he was a "wrongdoer." Also, many early cases employing the collateral source rule were brought by victims of industrial accidents. "People paid their medical bills out of private funds as savings, or a member of the family paid for them. Recovery of such sums from the defendant was justified as a recovery for 'out-of-pocket' loss, and the phrase was accurate." Seller, supra, at 39. In such cases, evidence of these collateral sources for payment of medical bills was excluded because it was irrelevant to the question of liability and the amount of damages it would take to make the injured party whole, including expenses paid by the injured party or his family. Given the choice of perhaps overcompensating the individual plaintiff for his injuries or providing the defendant with a windfall, the law favored the injured party and, in effect, punished the defendant.

This justification for the collateral source rule seems to be at odds with the modern trend in tort law toward allocating risk and compensating victims irrespective of fault. Today, liability insurance is available to all who wish to procure it. Insurance is available not only for liability, but also to cover medical bills, loss of earnings while incapacitated, and other damages that might accrue from an accident; social insurance, which may cover many accident-related expenses, is more prevalent. Few individuals are not somehow covered by medical insurance or a social benefit policy that will, in some way, pay all or a portion of the victim's expenses and, perhaps, lost wages as well. Therefore, collateral source payments (other than a loan or gift by a family member) are no longer irrelevant to the issue of what damages it will take to make the plaintiff whole.

A second justification for the rule against allowing evidence of insurance in particular and for the collateral source rule in general is based on a concern of prejudice on the issue of liability. Some courts fear that if evidence of collateral source payments were allowed, the jury would be more apt to find for the defendant on liability and not merely reduce the damages. "Most courts now recognize that the introduction of evidence of collateral source benefits can affect not only the question of damages, but the issue of liability as well." Seller, supra, at 55. The United States Supreme Court has cautioned trial courts in their use of collateral source evidence on the grounds that the jury is prone to misuse it if allowed in. See Eichel v. New York Central R.R. Co., 375 U.S. 253, 255 (1963) (the likelihood of misuse by the jury of evidence of disability payments to the plaintiff clearly outweighs any probative value of the evidence). Critics, however, contend that this is speculation and that it is hard to predict how a jury would use the evidence, especially when carefully instructed by the court. In Goldstein v. Gontarz, 364 Mass. 800, 813 (1979), the case on which the problem "Absence of Coverage" is based, the Massachusetts Supreme Court said that it is wrong for courts to base a rule on what it thinks a jury will assume.

There has been some erosion of the collateral source rule in recent years. For example, many states now permit evidence of collateral source payments in medical malpractice trials to combat what were perceived to be the high awards in such cases. Additionally, some states allow evidence of collateral income for the purpose of showing a plaintiff lost no time from work because of an alleged injury or to prove a motive for malingering.

The second situation in which evidence of insurance may arise is when the plaintiff seeks to introduce evidence that the defendant is insured for the loss. The third situation is simply the flip-side of the second—the defendant attempts to show that he has no insurance. The almost universal view of jurists is that such evidence tends to cause juries to decide cases emotionally rather than rationally, and that insurance or the lack of it has little, if any, probative value and is simply irrelevant. See Goldstein v. Gontarz, 364 Mass. 800, 809 (1979), citing King v. Starr, 43 Wash. 2d 115, 119-121 (1953); Socony Vacuum Oil Co. v. Marvin, 313 Mich. 528, 538-540 (1946); McCormick, Evidence (2d ed.) §201, pp.481-482 (1972); Appleman, Insurance Law and Practice §12838 (1962). The concern is that if the plaintiff shows the defendant has insurance and is thus adequately protected from financial liability for the accident, a jury will bring in a verdict (perhaps exaggerated in amount) for the plaintiff because the insurance company, which can afford it, will pay rather than the defendant. Goldstein v. Gontarz, supra, at 808.

In the first part of the Absence of Coverage problem and Goldstein v. Gontarz, 364 Mass. 800 (1974), we have the obverse of the flip-side. In *Goldstein*, in his opening statement, plaintiff's attorney stated that plaintiff did not take workers' compensation benefits and that the only way he could assert his rights was in court. This was also elicited on direct examination of the plaintiff, and plaintiff's counsel repeated this suggestion in his closing statement. The court held that the repeated reference to lack of workers' compensation was designed to prejudice the jury and ordered a new trial. The court stated, "Exposing juries to such information is condemned because it is not itself probative of any relevant proposition and is taken to lead to undeserved verdicts for plaintiffs and exaggerated awards which juries will readily land on faceless insurance companies supposedly paid for taking the risk." 364 Mass. at 808.

Wouldn't the same reasoning apply to *D* Company's reference to the effect that there is no insurance coverage for the accident? Juries are apt to misuse this evidence by deciding for the defendant simply because he cannot afford to pay the damages resulting from the accident. "Such statements are tantamount to a plea of poverty, not only irrelevant but prejudicial in that they might influence juries toward giving defendants compassionate but strictly unmerited relief from personal liability." Id. at 809. Consequently, *D* Company's reference that there is no insurance protection for the loss is impermissible and constitutes reversible error if found to have prejudiced the jury.

Despite the *Goldstein* court's reversal of the award for plaintiff, Justice Kaplan's opinion in that case suggests that today a more flexible approach to evidence of insurance coverage should be adopted, especially where a defendant does not have insurance and a jury is likely to assume he does:

> We are aware that the rules against introduction of matters of insurance coverage or the like have come under attack. Critics point out that, except as they guard against more or less explicit appeals to juries based simply on the presence or absence of coverage, the rules are not very effective in keeping the subject away from the triers.
>
> It is not possible to set up secure bulkheads against hints about insurance, especially as some information concerning it may be admissible as probative of a relevant proposition, say "control" or credibility of a particular witness. When the information is thus relevant, it may still be excluded on the ground that its prejudicial effect outweighs its probative value, but such judgments are delicate and may invite appeal. Again, even when the trial record is barren of any mention of the censored subjects, they may insinuate themselves into the case through casual assumptions about the prevalence of liability insurance or the availability of workmen's compensation. It is sometimes said that jurors are so prone to assume that workmen's compensation has been received for industrial accidents that a plaintiff who has not in fact received an award should be entitled to have that information given to the jurors in order to right the balance in their minds. On similar reasoning, if it be true that jurors assume that defendants generally carry liability insurance, then they should be told when a given defendant is not in fact covered. Cf. 29 Am. Jur. 2d, Evidence, §405 (1967). In this view, even the

amounts of the awards or the dollar limits of the liability insurance might also
be candidates for disclosure.

Id. at 812.

Professor McCormick agrees. He is one of the most outspoken critics
of the traditional rule. His criticism is based both on the absence of
theoretical justification for the rule and on the practical point that such
evidence often is insinuated to the jury anyhow. McCormick, Evidence
§201, at 981 (2d ed.).

Despite the academic criticism, in virtually all jurisdictions such evidence is inadmissible. However, in practice courts tend to reverse only
if the references to insurance were flagrant and the trial court failed to
cure with instructions. For example, in Woodward v. Wilbur, 54 R.I. 60,
63-64 (1963), the Rhode Island Supreme Court held it was within the
sound discretion of the trial judge to allow the plaintiff to cross-examine
the defense's expert witness to elicit the fact that the witness worked for
insurance companies. Recently, Rhode Island has continued the trend
of leaving the casual reference to a judge's discretion. In Cochrane v.
Dube, 114 R.I. 149, 152-153 (1975), the Rhode Island Supreme Court
held "that the mere mention of insurance in the course of a trial is not
per se a ground for passing the case." The more flexible approach
adopted by the Rhode Island Supreme Court in recent years has edged
its law closer to a Rule 403 approach. Under a Rule 403 approach, the
admissibility of evidence of insurance would depend on a weighing of
its probativeness and its prejudicial quality. This approach delegates
more power and discretion to the trial court than does Rule 411. Under
Rule 411, a judge may feel compelled to declare a mistrial any time a
reference to insurance is made by either counsel, despite the fact that
Rule 103(a) provides that "error may not be predicated upon a ruling
which admits or excludes evidence unless a substantial right of the party
is affected." Under a Rule 403 approach, a trial court could exclude the
evidence if the judge finds it to be either irrelevant or highly prejudicial,
but otherwise permit it. Only repeated, flagrant references would warrant a mistrial.

Under a Rule 403 approach, which would permit evidence of insurance or the lack of it in some cases, there is the problem of *how* the
evidence should be admitted. In Goldstein v. Gontarz, Justice Kaplan
suggested:

> What emerges from consideration of the decisions and the critical writing is
> that attention to a procedure for advance deliberation may prove helpful. When
> it appears that the question of the mention of coverage will arise in a serious
> way, counsel where feasible should consult beforehand with the judge as to how

the matter should be handled. Such discussions may well take place at pre-trial conference. . . . In many cases, minimizing or excluding reference to the subject during trial, and neutralizing any effect on the jury by a proper charge, will be a sound course. In some cases the better course may be to have the facts as to coverage frankly disclosed to the jury, again with appropriate commentary. Preferably the disclosure, as well as the commentary, should be by the judge. Unannounced unilateral forays by counsel in the course of trial, as in the present case, are perilous and should be avoided.

364 Mass. at 814.

Rhode Island adopted an alternative formulation of Rule 411 incorporating this approach:

RIRE 411. Liability Insurance

Evidence that a person was or was not insured against liability is not admissible upon the issue whether he acted negligently or otherwise wrongfully. This rule does not require the exclusion of evidence of insurance against liability when offered for another purpose, such as proof of agency, ownership, or control, bias or prejudice of a witness, or when the court determines that in the interest of justice evidence of insurance or lack of insurance should be permitted. A party intending to offer evidence of insurance or the lack of it should make an offer of proof of such evidence out of the hearing of the jury. If the court determines that such evidence should be disclosed, in the exercise of its discretion the court may direct that such evidence be disclosed to the jury by the court or by the parties in a manner best calculated to serve the interest of justice and avoid prejudice, confusion and waste of time.

CHAPTER III

Evidence of Character

This chapter explores the rules relating to proof of character. When trying to determine whether a person did something, most people believe that it is often helpful (relevant) to know whether he or she is the *kind of person* who would do such a thing. This is evidence of character used to prove action "in conformity therewith," in the phrase of Rule 404(a). Although perhaps relevant, evidence about a person's character raises severe problems of prejudice. Learning that a defendant is a confirmed thief, for example, might make it seem more likely that he was guilty of theft in the specific instance being litigated. However, it could also reduce the jury's concern about mistakenly finding the defendant guilty, thereby altering the effective standard of proof.

Opening the subject of character to proof also risks wasting time with marginally relevant evidence. How better to show someone's character (and thereby to show action in conformity therewith) than to introduce evidence about those episodes of the person's past life that most effectively reveal his character? Yet to expand the focus of the trial from the litigated event to include a variety of other factual episodes in the life of the defendant or witness is to vastly expand the scope of inquiry.

These considerations—prejudice and waste of time—leading to constraints on proving character, however, are opposed by considerations of fairness to a defendant who wants to prove his innocence by showing that he is *not* the sort of person who would commit such a crime. Such evidence also might waste some time, but this is a weak objection both from the viewpoint of a defendant trying to prove himself innocent and from that of the state trying to justify incarcerating the defendant.

These cross-currents are typical of those that swirl around the issues of character. The result at common law was an elaborate set of rules that sometimes permitted proof of character and sometimes barred it.

Yet another aspect of character comes into play at trial and has itself also generated a seemingly complex set of rules: whether a person who is testifying as a witness is truthful or deceitful. Because the process of finding facts through the testimony of live witnesses is so integral to the trial process, the law places a high priority on getting to the factfinder as much evidence as is reasonably useful about the reliability of the witness's testimony. This includes information about whether the witness was in a position to observe the events about which he is testifying (*first-hand knowledge*), how well he observed them (*perception*), how well he remembers the events (*memory*), how clearly he is reporting the events (*narration*), and how *honest* he is in reporting whatever he perceived and remembers. The requirement that the witness have first-hand knowledge about the events to which he testifies is treated in a separate rule (Rule 602). The qualities of perception, memory, and narration are the subjects of standard cross-examination, and do not seem to raise any issues of proof of character as that term is generally used in evidence. The question of the honesty of a witness does raise what most people would consider important questions of character. Many people (hence, many factfinders) believe that this aspect of character, which in court is called "credibility," has some enduring consistency in an individual, and that when a judge or jury has to figure out the most believable story from conflicting witness testimony about who did what to whom on some date in the past, it is useful to know something about the tendency of the differing witnesses to tell the truth or to lie. Accordingly, the rules allow in certain instances, and in very specific ways, proof of a witness's character for truth-telling as opposed to, for the moment, the witness's character for breaching contracts, robbing banks, killing, raping, or whatever the trial is actually about. The common law developed a separate system of rules for proof of character for credibility that were just as elaborate as the rules for proving character to show action in conformity therewith on the occasion of the event in litigation. Proof of character of a witness for the purpose of impeaching or rehabilitating the witness's credibility will be discussed in the next chapter on witnesses and their testimony.

Although the rules relating to (1) proof of character to show action in conformity therewith on the occasion of the event in litigation and (2) proof of character for credibility are separate as a matter of origin, policy, and location in the Federal Rules, the problems presented by these two sets of rules sometimes become complicated because a person's character for truth-telling (credibility) may be closely connected with the aspects of a person's character that are more directly related to the episode that is the subject of the trial. For example, when the defendant in a criminal fraud trial takes the witness stand and denies that she made any material misrepresentation, her character for truthfulness may be relevant to whether she is the kind of person who would commit fraud (i.e., did she lie to the victims—the event in litigation) as well as to whether she is a credible witness (i.e., is she lying to the factfinder now as she testifies). In contrast, in a common barroom brawl assault and battery case, it is much harder to see a connection between the defendant's character for peacefulness (the aspect of character that relates to the event in litigation) and his character for truthfulness (when he takes the witness stand, is he a credible witness).

The common law rules attempted to maintain a major distinction between evidence of character offered to prove action in conformity therewith *on the occasion of the litigated event* (did he do it?) and evidence of the character of a witness to show action in conformity therewith *while testifying at trial* (is he lying?). Moreover, in instances where character could be proved, the common law rules often constrained the method of proof, insisting on time-saving but perhaps ineffective modes of proof in some instances, allowing effective but perhaps inefficient modes in others. Character to show action in conformity therewith could be proved, if at all, only by evidence of reputation, not by evidence of the specific acts in the person's life. By contrast, when a person's character was itself the subject of litigation (for example, in libel suits), proof could be by specific acts.

Justice Jackson, in Michelson v. United States, 335 U.S. 469 (1948), page 235, below, described the character rules as "archaic, paradoxical and full of compromises and compensations by which an irrational advantage to one side is offset by a poorly reasoned counter privilege to the other." But he hesitated to tinker with the structure. "To pull one misshapen stone out of the grotesque structure," he said, "is more likely simply to upset its present balance between adverse interests than to establish a rational edifice."

The drafters of the Federal Rules had the opportunity to propose a complete overhaul; they chose not to. The overall structure remains an elaborate compromise, keyed to considerations of prejudice and remoteness. It is sensitive to the differing functions of civil and criminal litigation, to the differing interests of prosecution and defense, and to the differing contests of direct and cross-examination. Three years after the promulgation of the Federal Rules, Congress did make a major change, specifically barring proof of character of the victim in sexual assault cases in most instances, but again with many specific and some very general exceptions, qualifications, and procedural requirements (Rule 412). Again, in 1996 Congress amended the character evidence rules applicable to sexual assault and child molestation cases, in this case specifically to permit one kind of proof of the defendant's character—by proof of prior acts of sexual assault or child molestation. But even these major changes have not prompted any deep reevaluation of the overall structure of the character rules. A 1990 amendment of the rule relating to impeachment of a witness's credibility by showing the prior convictions of the witness (Rule 609) does attempt to clear up some of the problems that arise when the defendant and the witness are one and the same and proof of character for credibility implicates character to prove action in conformity therewith, but the basic common law structure remains unchanged and just as difficult for courts and lawyers to navigate through as ever.

The approach we have taken to these issues in this edition[1] is first to examine the basic propensity rule (Rule 404) in the criminal context to see where it applies and where it does not apply (although it looks as though maybe it should). We next look at the methods of proving character when it is allowed to be proven (Rule 405), and how proof of character or similar kinds of proof are used in civil cases. We next turn to the issue of habit, which is generally thought to consist of specific character traits etched so deeply in a person as to be unconscious or nearly so, and which is given its own evidence rule (Rule 406). Habit is a good testing ground for our understanding of character proof generally. Finally, we turn to the special problem of proof of character in sexual assault cases, the subject of Rules 412-415.

Having completed analysis of proof of character to show action in conformity therewith, we then turn to the vexing problem of trying to keep separate the management of proof of character to prove action in conformity therewith and proof of character for credibility when nearly everyone in the courtroom is equally confused about what is going on, and the appeals court is left to figure out what happened and whether it was error. However, our detailed consideration of proof of a witness's character for honesty and truthfulness will be deferred until the following chapter when we consider witness competency and credibility in general.

As you explore and try to integrate Rules 404, 405, 406, 412-415 consider whether Justice Jackson's eloquent description is fair. Is the structure of these rules both grotesque and irrational, or merely grotesque?

A. The Propensity Rule

PEOPLE v. ZACKOWITZ
254 N.Y. 192, 172 N.E. 466 (1930)

CARDOZO, C.J. On November 10, 1929, shortly after midnight, the defendant in Kings county shot Frank Coppola and killed him without

---

1. In the second edition we treated character evidence relevant to substantive issues in the trial and character evidence relevant only to witness credibility in the same section of the casebook. The third co-author joining the original authors in this edition has convinced us to treat character evidence relevant only to witness credibility in the section of the casebook on competence, examination, and impeachment of witnesses.

justification or excuse. A crime is admitted. What is doubtful is the degree only.

Four young men, of whom Coppola was one, were at work repairing an automobile in a Brooklyn street. A woman, the defendant's wife, walked by on the opposite side. One of the men spoke to her insultingly, or so at least she understood him. The defendant, who had dropped behind to buy a newspaper, came up to find his wife in tears. He was told she had been insulted, though she did not then repeat the words. Enraged, he stepped across the street and upbraided the offenders with words of coarse profanity. He informed them, so the survivors testify, that "if they did not get out of there in five minutes, he would come back and bump them all off." Rejoining his wife, he walked with her to their apartment house located close at hand. He was heated with liquor which he had been drinking at a dance. Within the apartment he induced her to tell him what the insulting words had been. A youth had asked her to lie with him, and had offered her $2. With rage aroused again, the defendant went back to the scene of the insult and found the four young men still working at the car. In a statement to the police, he said that he had armed himself at the apartment with a .25-caliber automatic pistol. In his testimony at the trial he said that this pistol had been in his pocket all the evening. Words and blows followed, and then a shot. The defendant kicked Coppola in the stomach. There is evidence that Coppola went for him with a wrench. The pistol came from the pocket, and from the pistol a single shot, which did its deadly work. The defendant walked away and at the corner met his wife who had followed him from the home. The two took a taxicab to Manhattan, where they spent the rest of the night at the dwelling of a friend. On the way the defendant threw his pistol into the river. He was arrested on January 7, 1930, about two months following the crime.

At the trial the vital question was the defendant's state of mind at the moment of the homicide. Did he shoot with a deliberate and premeditated design to kill? Was he so inflamed by drink or by anger or by both combined that, though he knew the nature of his act, he was the prey to sudden impulse, the fury of the fleeting moment? People v. Caruso, 246 N.Y. 437, 446, 159 N.E. 390. If he went forth from his apartment with a preconceived design to kill, how is it that he failed to shoot at once? How to reconcile such a design with the drawing of the pistol later in the heat and rage of an affray? These and like questions the jurors were to ask themselves and answer before measuring the defendant's guilt. Answers consistent with guilt in its highest grade can reasonably be made. Even so, the line between impulse and deliberation is too narrow and elusive to make the answers wholly clear. The sphygmograph records with graphic certainty the fluctuations of the pulse. There is no instrument yet invented that records with equal certainty the fluctuations of the mind. At least, if such an instrument exists, it was not working at midnight in the Brooklyn street when Coppola and the defendant came together in a chance affray. With only the rough and ready tests supplied by their experience of life, the jurors were to look into the workings of another's mind, and discover its capacities and disabilities, its urges and inhibitions, in moments of intense excitement. Delicate enough and subtle is the inquiry, even in the most favorable conditions, with every warping influence excluded. There must be no blurring of the issues by evidence illegally admitted and carrying with it in its admission an appeal to prejudice and passion.

Evidence charged with that appeal was, we think, admitted here. Not only was it admitted, and this under objection and exception, but the changes were rung upon it by prosecutor and judge. Almost at the opening of the trial the people began the endeavor to load the defendant down with the burden of an evil character. He was to be put before the jury as a man of murderous disposition. To that end they were allowed to prove that at the time of the encounter and at that of his arrest he had in his apartment, kept there in a radio box, three pistols and a tear-gas gun. There was no claim that he had brought these weapons out at the time of the affray, no claim that with any of them he had discharged the fatal shot. He could not have done so, for they were all of different caliber. The end to be served by laying the weapons before the jury was something very different. The end was to bring persuasion that here was a man of vicious and dangerous propensities, who because of those propensities was more likely to kill with deliberate and premeditated design than a man of irreproachable life and amiable manners. Indeed, this is the very ground on which the introduction of the evidence is now explained and defended. The district attorney tells us in his brief that the possession of the weapons characterized the defendant as "a desperate type of criminal," a "person criminally inclined." The dissenting opinion, if it puts the argument less bluntly, leaves the substance of the thought unchanged. "Defendant was presented to the jury as a man having dangerous weapons in his possession, making a selection therefrom and going forth to put into execution his threats to kill." The weapons were not brought by the defendant to the scene of the encounter. They were left in his apartment where they were incapable of harm. In such circumstances, ownership of the weapons, if it has any relevance at all, has relevance only as indicating a general disposition to make use of them thereafter, and a general disposition to make use of them thereafter is without relevance except as indicating a "desperate type of criminal," a criminal affected with a murderous propensity.

We are asked to extenuate the error by calling it an incident; what was proved may have an air of innocence if it is styled the history of the crime. The virus of the ruling is not so easily extracted. Here was no passing reference to something casually brought out in the narrative of the killing, as if an admission had been proved against the defendant that he had picked one weapon out of several. Here in the forefront of the trial, immediately following the statement of the medical examiner, testimony was admitted that weapons, not the instruments of the killing, had been discovered by the police in the apartment of the killer; and the weapons with great display were laid before the jury, marked as exhibits, and thereafter made the subject of animated argument. Room for doubt there is none that in the thought of the jury, as in that of the district attorney, the tendency of the whole performance was to characterize the defendant as a man murderously inclined. The purpose was not disguised. From the opening to the verdict, it was flaunted and avowed.

If a murderous propensity may be proved against a defendant as one of the tokens of his guilt, a rule of criminal evidence, long believed to be of fundamental importance for the protection of the innocent, must be first declared away. Fundamental hitherto has been the rule that character is never an issue in a criminal prosecution unless the defendant chooses to make it one. Wigmore, Evidence, vol. 1, §§55, 192. In a very real sense a defendant starts his life afresh when he stands before a jury, a prisoner at the bar. There has been a homicide in a public place. The killer admits the killing, but urges self-defense and sudden impulse. Inflexibly the law has set its face against the endeavor to fasten guilt upon him by proof of character or experience predisposing to an act of crime. The endeavor has been often made, but always it has failed. At times, when the issue has been self-defense, testimony has been admitted as to the murderous propensity of the deceased, the victim of the homicide, but never of such a propensity on the part of the killer. The principle back of the exclusion is one, not of logic, but of policy. There may be cogency in the argument that a quarrelsome defendant is more likely to start a quarrel than one of milder type, a man of dangerous mode of life more likely than a shy recluse. The law is not blind to this, but equally it is not blind to the peril to the innocent if character is accepted as probative of crime. "The natural and inevitable tendency of the tribunal—whether judge or jury—is to give excessive weight to the vicious record of crime thus exhibited, and either to allow it to bear too strongly on the present charge, or to take the proof of it as justifying a condemnation irrespective of guilt of the present charge." Wigmore, Evidence, vol. 1, §194, and cases cited.

A different question would be here if the pistols had been bought in expectation of this particular encounter. They would then have been admissible as evidence of preparation and design. A different question would be here if they were so connected with the crime as to identify the perpetrator, if he had dropped them, for example, at the scene of the affray. They would then have been admissible as tending to implicate the possessor (if identity was disputed), no matter what the opprobrium attached to his possession. Different, also, would be the question if the defendant had been shown to have gone forth from the apartment with all the weapons on his person. To be armed from head to foot at the very moment of an encounter may be a circumstance worthy to be considered, like acts of preparation generally, as a proof of preconceived design. There can be no such implication from the ownership of weapons which one leaves behind at home.

The endeavor was to generate an atmosphere of professional criminality. It was an endeavor the more unfair in that, apart from the suspicion attaching to the possession of these weapons, there is nothing to mark the defendant as a man of evil life. He was not in crime as a business. He did not shoot as a bandit shoots in the hope of wrongful gain. He was engaged in a decent calling, an optician regularly employed, without criminal record, or criminal associates. If his own testimony be true, he had gathered these weapons together as curios, a collection that interested and amused him. Perhaps his explanation of their ownership is false. There is nothing stronger than mere suspicion to guide us to an answer. Whether the explanation be false or true, he should not have been driven by the people to the necessity of offering it. Brought to answer a specific charge, and to defend himself against it, he was placed in a position where he had to defend himself against another, more general and sweeping. He was made to answer to the charge, pervasive and poisonous even if insidious and covert, that he was a man of murderous heart, of criminal disposition. . . .

The judgment of conviction should be reversed, and a new trial ordered.

POUND, J. (dissenting). . . .
Nearly two months after the killing of Coppola, the police entered defendant's home in connection with his arrest and found there concealed in a box in the radio three revolvers and a tear-gas bomb, together with a supply of cartridges suitable for use both in the revolvers and the bomb. Defendant had in his confession, which was received without objection, admitted that he had these weapons in his possession at the time of the killing. The .25-caliber automatic was not among them. Defendant says that he threw it away after he shot Coppola. The people, as a part of their principal case, introduced these articles in evidence over defendant's objection and exception. This is the only ruling by which the question of error in law is presented on this appeal. No objection was made to the summation by the district attorney nor to any specific instructions by the court. The possession of these dangerous weapons was a separate crime. Penal Law, §1897. The broad question is whether it had any connection with the crime charged. The substantial rights of the defendant must be protected. Where the penalty is death, we may grant a new trial if justice requires it, even though no exception was taken in the court below. Code Cr. Proc. §528.

The people may not prove against a defendant crimes not alleged in the indictment committed on other occasions than the crime charged as aiding the proofs that he is guilty of the crime charged unless such proof tends to establish (1) motive; (2) intent; (3) absence of mistake or accident; (4) a common scheme or plan embracing the commission of two or more crimes so related to each other that proof of the one tends to establish the other; (5) the identity of the person charged with the commission of the crime on trial. These exceptions are stated generally and not with categorical precision and may not be all-inclusive. None of them apply here, nor were the weapons offered under an exception to the general rule. They were offered as a part of the transaction itself. The accused was tried only for the crime charged. The real question is whether the matter relied on has such a connection with the crime charged as to be admissible on any ground. If so, the fact that it constitutes another distinct crime does not render it inadmissible. The rule laid down in the *Molineux* case [People v. Molineux, 168 N.Y. 264 (1901)] has never been applied to prevent the people from proving all the elements of the offense charged, although separate crimes are included in such proof. Thus in this case no question is made as to the separate crime of illegal possession of the weapon with which the killing was done. It was "a part of the history of the case" having a distinct relation to and bearing upon the facts connected with the killing.

As the district attorney argues in his brief, if defendant had been arrested at the time of the killing, and these weapons had been found on his person, the people would not have been barred from proving the fact, and the further fact that they were near by in his apartment should not preclude the proof as bearing on the entire deed of which the act charged forms a part. Defendant was presented to the jury as a man having dangerous weapons in his possession, making a selection therefrom, and going forth to put into execution his threats to kill; not as a man of a dangerous disposition in general, but as one who, having an opportunity to select a weapon to carry out his threats, proceeded to do so. . . .

The judgment of conviction should be affirmed.

How would you state the general rule, as relied on by Chief Justice Cardozo, regarding proof of character by the prosecution in criminal cases? Is such evidence excluded because it is irrelevant? Would it have made any difference in this case if Zackowitz had taken the other guns with him to the affray? Why? Would it have made any difference if Zackowitz had been convicted of illegally possessing the other guns? Why? How would you state the rule as relied upon by Justice Pound? Would Pound's rationale for admitting the "other guns" evidence annihilate the propensity rule? With which statement and application of the rule do you agree?

Problem: A Return to the Scene of the Crime

Charge: theft of valuable documents, coins, and case from the heavy metal safe in Attorney *A*'s office on June 1. Modus operandi: opening the combination lock and absconding with the contents.

At *D*'s trial the state offers to prove that on May 1, *D* broke into Attorney *A*'s office, opened the safe, and stole some bonds from the safe. *D* objects on the basis of the propensity rule.

What ruling and why? If *D*'s objection is overruled, what type of limiting charge should *D* request?

The first clause of Rule 404(a) contains the basic rule excluding evidence of character used as circumstantial proof of action in conformity therewith. Note carefully the limited scope of this exclusion. It recites the traditional propensity rule as applied by Chief Justice Cardozo in *Zackowitz*, but, as Justice Pound's dissent shows, the same evidence that one judge believes is barred by the propensity rule another judge may believe is relevant for a nonpropensity, admissible purpose. To understand why this is so, it is important to understand the particular chain of inferences that is barred by the propensity rule so that one can then understand the permitted use of evidence that looks, sounds, and feels like character evidence but is admissible.

The following outlines the specific chain of inferences prohibited by Rule 404(a)'s propensity rule:

a.   Character evidence leads the factfinder to infer that the actor in question possessed a certain character
b.   The factfinder infers that a person with the proven trait of character is more likely to have acted in a way associated with that character trait.

Evidence is *not* barred by Rule 404(a)'s propensity rule if the evidence is relevant to a material issue in a way that does *not* require an inferential connection through character (the middle step in the example above). In addition to restating the basic propensity rule of Rule 404(a), Rule 404(b) gives some generic examples of how evidence that is similar to the proof barred by Rule 404(a) when used to link up the impermissible chain of inferences through character might be admissible when used in a different way — that is, not used to prove a trait of character and, from that trait, an issue in the case. To take the Return to the Scene of the Crime problem as an example, the evidence of the prior crime is directly relevant to show the defendant's knowledge—one of the possibly permissible uses of prior crimes, wrongs, or acts listed in 404(b)—of the location and the combination of the safe, and perhaps also some expectation that there might be some valuable booty in the safe worth going after. The evidence may also show something about the defendant's character, but to make use of the evidence to prove knowledge, is it necessary to make the inference about the defendant's character?

However, it is not quite right to say that the evidence of the prior theft is made admissible under Rule 404(b). As a matter of analysis, Rule 404(b) is superfluous. The kinds of evidence it describes, when used for the purposes it describes, if relevant under Rule 401, would be admissible under Rule 402 unless excluded under some specific rule of exclusion or in the court's discretion under Rule 403's balancing test. Actually, Rule 404(a) does all the exclusionary work of the propensity rule when character is used circumstantially to prove action in conformity therewith, and 404(b) adds nothing except clarification of when the propensity rule does not apply because propensity is not being proved (some clarification!).

In fact, Rule 404(b) often causes confusion because its examples of permitted use of character-type evidence are sometimes mistaken as an exhaustive list of when such evidence is permitted. Notice the vital words, "other purposes, such as" in the second sentence of Rule 404(b). These words cover a universe of proof and permissible purposes as compared to the limited scope of Rule 404(a)'s exclusion.

We have not dealt adequately yet with what happens when proof of other crimes, acts, or wrongs is offered for some purpose other than proving action in conformity therewith (propensity), such as knowledge of the combination of a safe from which money is stolen, but the evidence, if believed, might also say something about the person's thieving character (propensity). A skeptical mind would recognize that we dismissed this problem too superficially. Indeed, courts frequently must struggle with this problem, and it is not always easy to resolve. Professor Imwinkelried reports that Rule 404(a) has generated more published opinions than any other subsection of the Federal Rules. The Use of Evidence of an Accused's Uncharged Misconduct to Prove Mens Rea, 51 Ohio St. L.J. 575, 576 (1990). Sound resolution of this problem requires a clear understanding of the scope and purpose of Rules 401, 402, and 403, Rule 404's subsections, and Rule 105 (the rule of limited admissibility).

As with most complex problems, it helps to have a theory. Starting with Rule 404(a), the applicable specific rule of exclusion, the chain of inferences goes as follows:

    a. Evidence of another event or of the actor's reputation—for example evidence that the defendant
       i. previously stole something;
      ii. has a reputation as a bully;
     iii. previously assaulted someone;
    b. Finding that the actor has a particular trait of character — for example that the defendant is
       i. dishonest;
      ii. violent;
     iii. assaultive;
    c. Finding that the actor has acted in some way material to the present case—for example that the defendant
       i. stole in this case;
      ii. hit someone in this case;
     iii. assaulted the victim in this case.

However, the chain of inferences using the same or similar proof and recited as examples of possibly permissible proof in Rule 404(b), and that is not barred by Rule 404(a), can be shown as follows:

    a. Evidence that the defendant stole, assaulted, killed;
    b. Finding that the defendant had a motive, plan, knowledge, M.O.

A comparison of these chains of inference makes it clear that the crucial issue is the route of the trip from evidence that the defendant has previously stolen to the conclusion that he stole in the charged case. If the route goes through character (defendant is a thief), the evidence is barred by Rule 404(a); if the route goes through some other issue (defendant knew the combination of the safe), the evidence is not excluded by Rule 404(a), even though the factfinder may also conclude that defendant is a thief (the "superfluous inference" in "non-propensity" use of character evidence and the "prohibited inference" when used as a link in a chain of inferences to get from the evidence of the prior theft to evidence of guilt of the crime charged).

Note that the analysis so far says only that the evidence of the prior theft, when offered to start the permissible chain of inferences, is not excluded. What makes it admissible? Not the propensity rule of 404(a), which is a rule of exclusion, or even Rule 404(b), which, as we have said, is merely a statement elaborating what is not made inadmissible by Rule 404(a). To be admissible, the evidence must be independently relevant under Rules 401 and 402 for some purpose other than merely proving propensity. But how does the court guard against misuse by the factfinder of the very same evidence to start the impermissible chain of inferences?

This is where Rules 105 and 403 come into play. The doctrine of limited admissibility of Rule 105 provides that "when evidence which is admissible . . . for one purpose but not admissible . . . for another purpose is admitted, the court, upon request, shall restrict the evidence to its proper scope and instruct the jury accordingly." Thus, the first possibility when character-type evidence can be used by the trier of fact impermissibly as well as permissibly is for the court to admit the evidence and give an instruction to the jury directing it to use the evidence only for the permitted purpose.

What kind of limiting instruction should the court give the jury? In the problem "Return to the Scene of the Crime," the limiting instruction would go something like this:

> The defendant is on trial only for the crime charged. The jury may consider the evidence offered only as showing knowledge of the location and combination of the safe, and not for the fact that the defendant commits criminal acts, or that the defendant may have broken into the safe before. You have to decide whether the defendant committed the specific crime charged on the day in question, not other crimes on other days.

If you were representing the defendant, from a tactical standpoint would you want the judge to say this to the jury? Could mentioning what is prohibited suggest that very use to the jury?

Despite its questionable efficacy, the admission with a limiting instruction is what usually occurs when evidence of other crimes, wrongs, or acts is offered and objected to under Rule 404. In fact, this occurs so often that the very limited scope of exclusion of the propensity rule might be clearer if Rule 404 were turned around (as it is in several state rules), so that it said:

> Evidence of other crimes, wrongs or acts which tend to prove any material fact is admissible, subject to Rule 403, unless its *sole* purpose is to show that the accused has a criminal propensity.

Another possibility when dealing with evidence that is not excluded by the propensity rule but might be used by the factfinder impermissibly as well as permissibly is to apply Rule 403's balancing test to the evidence. But the question must be asked whether Rule 403 applies to evidence dealt with by Rule 404. It is in answering this question that the difference between seeing Rule 404 as a limited rule of exclusion rather than a rule of admissibility becomes important. Consider for a moment whether your answer to the question of the applicability of Rule 403 to evidence of other crimes, acts, or wrongs would be different if the second sentence of Rule 404(b) said, "It is admissible as proof of motive, opportunity, intent, preparation, plan, knowledge, identity, or absence of mistake or accident." If such evidence is not made admissible by Rule

404(b), but rather is admissible because it is relevant (Rule 401) and not excluded by Rule 404(a), applying the Rule 403 balancing step appears unremarkable. This is the logic that produces the "two-step" analysis. See the *Danzey, Huddleston,* and *Beechum* cases, below.

Problem: Res Gestae

(1) Charge: violation of federal firearms statute by unlawfully receiving a firearm transported interstate after *D* had previously been convicted of a crime punishable by more than one year in prison. At trial, *W,* a druggist, testified for the prosecution that *D* had entered his pharmacy with a prescription that *W* recognized as forged. When *W* asked *D* to remain in the store so the police could check the prescription, *D* bolted, and *W* gave chase. During the chase, *D* dropped the drugs and gun over the side of a wall. *D* objected to the evidence of the alleged forged prescription.

(2) Charge: illegal sale of narcotics. At trial a state narcotics agent is offered by the prosecution to testify that he and another agent had visited *D*'s house together and that each had purchased a can containing some substance, which the agents believed was marijuana. *D* objects to the testimony concerning the sale to the other agent.

Remember the words "other purposes, such as" in Rule 404(b). Evidence may be admitted when it is necessary to tell the whole story of the events in issue at trial, even though the evidence tends to show the commission of other crimes or a criminal character. Such "res gestae" evidence is one example of the nonapplication of the general propensity rule that is not listed in the illustrations specified by Rule 404(b).

The evidence of the forged prescription in (1) must be admitted so that the jury can understand the facts central to the gun possession charge. Without the evidence, the prosecution's case is virtually unintelligible. The term "res gestae" has been used to describe this "exception" to Rule 404(a), even though there is no explicit mention of it in 404(b). The case for admission of the "other sale" evidence under the "res gestae" exception is weaker in (2). The purchase of marijuana by one agent can be understood as a "complete story" without reference to the contemporaneous purchase by the second narcotics agent. However, if *D* raises the defense of entrapment, evidence of the second sale becomes directly relevant to rebut the entrapment defense on the issue of predisposition. This is analogous to a defendant's opening the door to character evidence by raising the issue.

Chief Justice Cardozo alludes to the res gestae exception in *Zackowitz* when he states, "Different, also, would be the question if the defendant had been shown to have gone forth from the apartment with all the weapons on his person. To be armed from head to foot at the very moment of an encounter may be a circumstance worthy to be considered, like acts of preparation generally, as proof of preconceived design." Yet Cardozo cautions against unthinking use of res gestae: "what was proved may have an air of innocence if it is styled the history of the crime."

There is often an overlap between res gestae evidence and evidence of preparation or plan. Res gestae goes to all acts that are necessary to fill in the factual context of the crime charges. These facts may be happenstance, or they may be criminal in nature and reflect poorly on the defendant. Either way, they are independently relevant for descriptive purposes. In contrast, evidence of preparation and plan is admissible because specific inferences highly pertinent to the crime charged follow from the very existence of preparation or plans.

Often the distinction between res gestae and preparation evidence is blurred. The hypothetical posed by Cardozo in *Zackowitz* is an example. The crucial issue in *Zackowitz* was the state of mind of the defendant at the moment of the homicide. If the defendant had been carrying all of his weapons, this fact would be an inextricable part of understanding the whole event, that is, res gestae. At the same time, the fact of carrying these weapons is evidence of preparation from which a trier of fact can make inferences specifically about premeditation (state of mind) by the defendant. Had state of mind not been an issue, admission of the evidence of the guns could not have been justified on this basis, but this information probably would still be needed to describe the whole picture.

Problem: Money or Death

Charge: robbery of the First National Bank in City *A* on June 1. Modus operandi: handing the teller a note with a death threat on it that says, "Money or death: The choice is yours," accompanied by pictures of a dead body under the word "death" and a live, smiling person under the word "money." At trial the state offers to prove through the teller of the First Federal Bank in City *B* that on February 1 he was robbed in the same manner by *D*—that is, that he was handed a deposit slip with the very same death threat written on it. The state also offers several other bank tellers from different banks to testify similarly.

D objects to the tellers' testimony. What ruling and why?

Evidence establishing a distinctive modus operandi may be admitted for the purpose of showing identity even though it also shows a criminal character.

Evidence of the prior crime is relevant to show that it was the defendant who committed the robbery being tried. The defendant's modus operandi is so distinctive that it marks his work like a signature (like the mark of Zorro). Because the evidence bears on identity without any logical necessity either to draw a conclusion about the defendant's character or to reason from his character to a conclusion that he acted in conformity therewith, the evidence is not barred by the propensity rule.

Whether the evidence passes the "second step" admissibility barrier of Rule 403 is a tougher question. What if the defendant is not contesting the issue of identity? Should the prosecution be prevented from using such evidence until the defendant makes clear that he is disputing identification? What if the defendant has never been convicted of the previous crime or has been tried for the previous crime and acquitted? Should there be some minimum standard of proof for showing that the defendant did in fact commit the previous crime? Should evidence relating to crimes for which the defendant has been acquitted be barred altogether? This issue is discussed in *Huddleston* and *Dowling,* below, but first we must examine the question of how probative the proof of identity must be before it can be accepted as proof of a distinctive modus operandi.

UNITED STATES v. TRENKLER
61 F.3d 45 (1st Cir. 1995)*

STAHL, Circuit Judge. Following a lengthy criminal trial, a jury convicted defendant Alfred Trenkler of various charges stemming from a bomb explosion in Roslindale, Massachusetts ("the Roslindale bomb"). On appeal, Trenkler challenges the admission of evidence relating to his participation in a prior bombing that occurred five years earlier in Quincy, Massachusetts ("the Quincy bomb"). Trenkler also assigns error to two evidentiary rulings admitting evidence derived from a computer database that purported to establish that Trenkler built both the Quincy and the Roslindale bombs and several out-of-court statements [*] made by a fellow participant in the bombing. After careful review, we affirm.

I.   BACKGROUND

On October 28, 1991, a bomb exploded at the Roslindale home of Thomas L. Shay ("Shay Sr."), killing one Boston police officer and severely injuring another. The two officers, members of the Boston Police Department Bomb Squad, had been dispatched to Shay Sr.'s home to investigate a suspicious object located in Shay Sr.'s driveway. Shay Sr.

---

*The authors thank Professor George Fisher, Stanford Law School, for this case, which has replaced a less apposite case in the prior editions.

had earlier reported that, while backing his 1986 Buick Century into the street the day before, he had heard a loud noise emanating from beneath the floorboard of his automobile. Shay Sr. added that, subsequently, he found the suspicious object resting near the crest of his driveway.

Following the explosion, a massive investigation ensued involving a variety of federal, state and local law-enforcement agencies. On June 24, 1993, this investigation culminated with the return of a three-count indictment charging Trenkler and Thomas A. Shay ("Shay Jr."), Shay Sr.'s son, with responsibility for the Roslindale bombing. Trenkler filed a successful severance motion, and the government tried the two defendants separately. Shay Jr. was tried first, and a jury convicted him on counts of conspiracy and malicious destruction of property by means of explosives.

At Trenkler's trial, the thrust of the government's case was that Trenkler had built the Roslindale bomb for Shay Jr. to use against his father. To establish Trenkler's identity as the builder of the bomb, the government offered, inter alia, evidence that Trenkler had previously constructed a remote-control device, the Quincy bomb, which exploded in Quincy, Massachusetts, in 1986. The government contended that unique similarities in design, choice of components, and overall modus operandi between the two bombs compelled the conclusion that Trenkler had designed and built both devices. Prior to trial, the government filed a motion in limine seeking to admit the "similarity" evidence. Following a day-long evidentiary hearing, the district court ruled the evidence admissible, finding that it was relevant on the issues of identity, skill, knowledge, and intent. Although Trenkler did not testify at trial, his counsel stipulated at the evidentiary hearing that Trenkler had built the Quincy bomb.

1986 QUINCY BOMB

Trenkler constructed the Quincy bomb in 1986 for a friend, Donna Shea. At the time, Shea was involved in a dispute with the owners of the Capeway Fish Market and she wanted the bomb to use as a means to intimidate them. At her request, Trenkler assembled a remote-control, radio-activated explosive device. The device was later attached to the undercarriage of a truck belonging to the Capeway Fish Market and detonated in the middle of the night. The resulting bomb blast caused no injuries and little property damage.

In building the Quincy bomb, Trenkler used as the explosive material a military flash simulator typically utilized to mimic gunfire in combat exercises. To provide remote-control capabilities, Trenkler employed a radio-receiver he had removed from a small toy car. Trenkler wrapped the bomb in duct tape and attached a large donut-shaped speaker magnet to enable the bomb to adhere to the undercarriage of the truck. Other components Trenkler used included a "double throw" toggle switch, four AA batteries, two six-volt batteries, an electric relay, solder, various wires, and a slide switch.

Testimony at trial established that Trenkler purchased some of the electrical components for the Quincy bomb from a Radio Shack store. On one occasion, Trenkler sought to obtain needed components by sending Shea's eleven-year-old nephew into a Radio Shack store with a list of items to purchase while Trenkler remained waiting outside. Shea's nephew, however, was unable to find all of the items, and Trenkler eventually came into the store to assist him.

1991 ROSLINDALE BOMB

The government contended that Trenkler built the Roslindale bomb at Shay Jr.'s request. At trial, the government offered evidence about Trenkler's relationship with Shay Jr., dating back at least two years prior to the Roslindale bombing. Several witnesses, including Trenkler's business partner, reported seeing the two together on different occasions in 1990 and 1991. Shay Jr.'s address book included an entry for Trenkler listing his current pager number. Moreover, Trenkler's roommate at the time of the Roslindale bombing testified that, during September and October of 1991, Shay Jr. left several voice-mail messages on the pager for Trenkler.

Testimony from government investigators and Shay Sr. established that the Roslindale bomb was a remote-control, radio-activated device with an explosive force supplied by two or three sticks of dynamite connected to two electrical blasting caps. A black wooden box weighing two or three pounds and measuring approximately eight- to ten-inches long, five- to six-inches wide and one- to two-inches deep housed the bomb. A large donut-shaped magnet and several smaller round magnets attached to the box were used to secure the device to the underside of Shay Sr.'s automobile. Other components used in the construction of the bomb included duct tape, a "single throw" toggle switch, four AA batteries, five nine-volt batteries, a Futaba radio receiver, solder, various wires, and a slide switch.

According to the government's experts and Shay Sr., the bomb was originally attached to the undercarriage of Shay Sr.'s automobile directly beneath the driver's seat. The government's explosives expert testified that if the bomb had exploded while still attached to the car, it probably would have killed or at least seriously injured any individual sitting in the driver's seat.

The government also asserted that Trenkler used Shay Jr. to purchase the electronic components used in the bomb. In support of this assertion, the government introduced a sales receipt for a toggle switch purchased in October 1991 at a Radio Shack store located across the street from where Trenkler, at the time, was installing a satellite dish. Agents from the Bureau of Alcohol, Tobacco and Firearms ("ATF") recovered from the debris of the Roslindale bomb a switch identical to the one purchased. Shay Jr. admitted purchasing the switch during a taped television interview, portions of which the government introduced at trial. Furthermore, a sales clerk at the Radio Shack testified that, prior to purchasing the switch, the person who bought it had browsed in the store for several minutes, appearing to shop for items written on a list. The sales clerk also testified that he recalled seeing Trenkler in the store on two or three occasions during the fall of 1991.

Both the government and Trenkler elicited testimony from their respective explosives experts explaining the similarities and differences between the two bombs. Both experts testified at length concerning the electronic designs, the choice of components and the method of construction. The government's expert opined that the two incidents shared many similar traits and characteristics, evincing the "signature" of a single bomb maker. He further stated that he had no doubt "whatsoever" that the same person built both bombs. Trenkler's expert, on the other hand, stated that too many dissimilarities existed to conclude that the same person built both bombs. Moreover, Trenkler's expert testified that the similarities that existed lacked sufficient distinguishing qualities to identify the two bombs as the handiwork of a specific individual.

EXIS COMPUTER DATABASE EVIDENCE

To support the inference that Trenkler built both bombs, the government offered testimony both at the pretrial hearing and at trial concerning information retrieved from an ATF computer database of explosives and arson incidents. Stephen Scheid, an Intelligence Research Specialist with ATF, testified that the database, known as EXIS, contains information taken from reports submitted to ATF by various federal, state and local law-enforcement agencies. Scheid further testified that he had been personally responsible for maintaining the database since 1977. Scheid stated that he reviews submitted incident reports, culling from them information describing the characteristics of each bombing or arson episode. Scheid added that he then encodes the extracted information on a standardized worksheet, which he or a data-entry person in turn uses to enter the information into the database.

Scheid testified that, through the use of a computer program, he then produces investigatory leads by retrieving all incidents entered in the database that are listed as possessing a specific component or characteristic. Scheid further testified that, in an effort to identify the builder of the Roslindale bomb, he performed a series of computer queries, focusing on characteristics of the Roslindale bomb. This series of inquiries narrowed the field of reported incidents in the database from 40,867 to seven.[6] The seven remaining incidents included both the Roslindale and Quincy bombs. Scheid stated that he subsequently conducted a manual analysis of the remaining incidents and was able to identify several additional characteristics common to only the Roslindale and Quincy bombs.

Scheid also testified that the report of the Quincy bomb did not come to his attention through normal procedures. Scheid did not receive information about the 1986 Quincy bomb, nor enter any information pertaining to it into the EXIS database, until after the Roslindale incident in 1991.

OTHER TRIAL EVIDENCE

[The court discusses other evidence admitted at the trial tending to prove Trenkler's guilt.]

The jury returned a guilty verdict on all counts of the indictment. Subsequently, the district court sentenced Trenkler to concurrent terms of life imprisonment on the counts of receipt of explosive materials and attempted malicious destruction of property by means of explosives and sixty months on the count of conspiracy. Trenkler now appeals.

II. DISCUSSION

On appeal, Trenkler assigns error to the admission of the Quincy bomb evidence, contending primarily that the incident was not sufficiently similar to the Roslindale bomb to be relevant on the issue of identity, and to the admission of the EXIS database-derived evidence that the government used to prove the similarity of the two bombs. . . .

A. QUINCY BOMBING EVIDENCE

We begin with Trenkler's contention that the district court erred in admitting the evidence of the Quincy bombing.

---

6. The computer queries and the total number of resulting incidents are listed below. The queries are successive.

All incidents in database	40,867
Bombings and attempted bombings	14,252
Involving cars and trucks	2,504
Under vehicles	428
Remote-control	19
Using magnets	7

1. *Fed. R. Evid. 404(b): Other Act Evidence*

In general, Rule 404(b) proscribes the use of other bad-act evidence solely to establish that the defendant has a propensity towards criminal behavior. Rule 404(b)'s proscription, however, is not absolute: the rule permits the use of such evidence if it bears on a material issue such as motive, knowledge or identity. In this Circuit, we have adopted a two-part test for determining the admissibility of Rule 404(b) evidence. E.g., United States v. Williams, 985 F.2d 634, 637 (1st Cir. 1993). First, the district court must determine whether the evidence has some "special relevance" independent of its tendency simply to show criminal propensity. E.g., United States v. Guyon, 27 F.3d 723, 728 (1st Cir. 1994). Second, if the evidence has "special relevance" on a material issue, the court must then carefully conduct a Rule 403 analysis to determine if the probative value of the evidence is not substantially outweighed by the danger of unfair prejudice. . . . As with most evidentiary rulings, the district court has considerable leeway in determining whether to admit or exclude Rule 404(b) evidence. Accordingly, we review its decision only under the lens of abuse of discretion. . . .

2. *Identity*

The government offered the evidence of the Quincy bomb, which Trenkler admitted building, primarily to prove that Trenkler also built the Roslindale bomb. The government contends that the evidence of the Quincy bomb has "special relevance" on the issue of identity because the numerous similarities surrounding the Quincy and Roslindale incidents compel the conclusion that the same individual built both bombs. Trenkler, on the other hand, argues that the Quincy incident is too dissimilar to be relevant on the issue of identity, and even if it has some relevance, the risk of unfair prejudice that it poses far outweighs its probative value. We agree with the government that the Quincy bomb evidence has "special relevance" on the issue of identity and that the district court did not abuse its considerable discretion in admitting it.

a. Rule 404(b) Evidence: Special Relevance

When, as in this case, Rule 404(b) evidence is offered because it has "special relevance" on the issue of identity, we have required, as a prerequisite to admission, a showing that there exists a high degree of similarity between the other act and the charged crime. . . . Indeed, the proponent must demonstrate that the two acts exhibit a commonality of distinguishing features sufficient to earmark them as the handiwork of the same individual. . . . This preliminary showing is necessary because

[a] defendant cannot be identified as the perpetrator of the charged act simply because he has at other times committed the same commonplace variety of crim-

inal act except by reference to the forbidden inference of propensity. The question for the court[, therefore, must be] whether the characteristics relied upon are sufficiently idiosyncratic to permit an inference of pattern for purposes of proof.

United States v. Pisari, 636 F.2d 855, 858-59 (1st Cir. 1981) (internal quotations and citations omitted) (emphasis added).

Resolving whether the prior act is sufficiently similar to the charged offense to have "special relevance" on the issue of identity, however, is essentially an issue of "preliminary" or "conditional" fact. In other words, the prior act has no tendency to prove the perpetrator's identity — i.e., it is not relevant — unless the proponent can first establish the conditional fact: that the two acts are sufficiently idiosyncratic to support the inference that they are the handiwork of the same individual. The admissibility of evidence whose relevance turns on the resolution of a conditional fact is governed by Fed. R. Evid. 104(b). See Huddleston v. United States, 485 U.S. 681, 689, 99 L. Ed. 2d 771, 108 S. Ct. 1496 (1988). . . . Moreover, in determining whether the Government has introduced sufficient evidence to meet Rule 104(b), the trial court neither weighs credibility nor makes a finding that the Government has proved the conditional fact by a preponderance of the evidence. The court simply examines all the evidence in the case and decides whether the jury could reasonably find the conditional fact . . . by a preponderance of the evidence. *Huddleston,* 485 U.S. at 690. Thus, as here, when a party seeks to admit Rule 404(b) evidence to establish identity, the district court must condition its admission on a showing that the shared characteristics of the other act and the charged offense are sufficiently idiosyncratic that a reasonable jury could find it more likely than not that the same person performed them both.

Trenkler contends that the array of similarities between the two incidents amounts to no more than a collection of "prosaic commonalit[ies that] cannot give rise to an inference that the same person was involved in both acts without reference to propensity." United States v. Garcia-Rosa, 876 F.2d 209, 225 (1st Cir. 1989). . . . However, in resolving whether the evidence supports an inference that the two incidents are "sufficiently idiosyncratic," we have cautioned that "an exact match is not necessary." . . . The test must focus on the "totality of the comparison," demanding not a "facsimile or exact replica" but rather the " 'conjunction of several identifying characteristics or the presence of some highly distinctive quality.' " . . . In this case, we think the balance of the evidence tilts sufficiently towards admission to satisfy the first step of the Rule 404(b) analysis. Accordingly, we believe that the district court did not abuse its discretion in determining that the numerous similarities in components, design, and technique of assembly, combined with the similar modus operandi and the closeness of geographic proximity between the two events, sufficiently support the inference that the same person built both bombs.

We begin by noting that the government's explosives expert, Thomas Waskom, testified that his analysis of the similarities shared by the two incidents left him with no doubt "whatsoever" that the same individual built both bombs. Our own review of the record reveals that the two bombs did indeed share a number of similar components and characteristics. Both bombs were remote-controlled, radio-activated, electronic explosive devices. Both were homemade mechanisms, comprising, in general, electronic components easily purchased at a hobby store. Both had similar, though not identical, firing and fusing circuits with separate battery power supplies for each. Both had switches in their fusing circuits to disconnect the radio receivers. To energize their respective radio receivers, both devices utilized similar power supplies, consisting of four AA batteries. Both employed many similar components such as batteries, duct tape, toggle switches, radio receivers, antennas, solder, electrical tape, and large round speaker magnets. Moreover, both used a distinctive method (i.e., twisting, soldering, and taping) to connect some, though not all, of the wires used. Though we hardly find any of these factors by themselves to be "highly distinctive," the coalescence of them is fairly persuasive. Indeed, even Trenkler's expert witness, Denny Kline, testified at the pretrial hearing that, in light of these similarities, "there is a possibility, a probability, that maybe there is a connection between the maker of these two bombs." (Emphasis added.)

Accordingly, we believe some significance is properly attributed to the simple fact that both incidents are bombings. A bombing, in and of itself, is, arguably, a fairly distinctive method for intimidating or killing an individual. . . . In addition, both incidents involved not simply bombs, but remote-control bombs that were placed underneath automotive vehicles.

In both instances, the bombs were constructed and used to benefit a friend of the builder. Trenkler built the Quincy bomb for Donna Shea to use to intimidate the owners of the Capeway Fish Market, and the evidence supported the inference that the person who constructed the Roslindale bomb built it for Shay Jr. to use against his father. Furthermore, in both instances the builder attempted to conceal his or her participation by using a third party to purchase the electronic components used in the explosive device. In 1986, Trenkler initially waited in his car while sending Donna Shea's nephew into the electronics store with a list to purchase the needed components. Similarly, the evidence supports the inference that the builder of the Roslindale bomb used Shay Jr. to purchase the needed components. Finally, the fact that both bombings occurred within a relatively close geographic proximity must be given some weight in the analysis.

In United States v. Pisari, 636 F.2d 855 (1st Cir. 1981), we reversed the district court's decision to admit evidence of a prior robbery solely on the issue of identity, where the only similarity between it and the charged offense was that a knife was used. Similarly, in *Garcia-Rosa,* 876 F.2d at 224-25, we refused to sanction the admission of a prior drug transaction where the only characteristic linking it to the charged drug deal was the characteristic exchange of a sample of drugs prior to the sale. In *Garcia-Rosa,* we held that a single "prosaic commonality" was insufficient "to give rise to an inference that the same person was involved in both acts without reference to propensity." Id. at 225. See also United States v. Benedetto, 571 F.2d 1246, 1249 (2d Cir. 1978) (no signature where shared characteristic is merely "a similar technique for receiving the cash: the passing of folded bills by way of a handshake").

In the present case, however, the government presented more than a single "prosaic commonality." Indeed, the government propounded a laundry list of similarities in design, component selection, construction and overall modus operandi. On the other hand, Trenkler offered a fairly impressive list of differences between the two incidents. In the absence of one or more highly distinctive factors that in themselves point to idiosyncracy, we must examine the combination of all the factors. Had Trenkler been unable to point to any significant differences, we suspect he would have had little chance in establishing an abuse of discretion in allowing the evidence. Similarly, had the government found but three or four common characteristics to establish sufficient similarity, we doubt that the admission of the evidence would have been granted or sustained. Here, in the middle, with substantial evidence on either side and conflicting expert opinions, could a reasonable jury have found it more likely than not that the same person was responsible for both bombs? We think the answer is yes. . . .

b.   Rule 404(b) Evidence: Probative Value and Unfair Prejudice

Resolving that the district court did not abuse its discretion in determining that a rational jury could infer that it was more likely than not that the same person built both bombs, however, does not end the analysis. We must also review the trial court's determination that the probative value of the evidence was not substantially outweighed by the risk of unfair prejudice. Several factors weigh heavily in this balancing, such as the government's need for the evidence, . . . the strength of evidence establishing the similarity of the two acts, . . . the inflammatory nature of the evidence, and the degree to which it would promote an inference based solely on the defendant's criminal propensity. . . .

We believe the district court acted well within its broad discretion in admitting the evidence. First, the evidence was important to the government's case. The evidence that Trenkler had built the Quincy bomb corroborated David Lindholm's testimony, identifying Trenkler as the builder of the Roslindale bomb. Second, although the evidence of sim-

ilarity could have been more compelling, it was nonetheless substantial:
Indeed, the government's explosives expert testified that he had no
doubt "whatsoever" that the same person designed and constructed
both bombs.

On the other hand, we disagree with the district court that the evidence did not pose any risk of unfair prejudice. As with all "bad act"
evidence, there is always some danger that the jury will use the evidence
not on the narrow point for which it is offered but rather to infer that
the defendant has a propensity towards criminal behavior. Nonetheless,
outside the context of propensity, the evidence was not unduly inflammatory. The Quincy bomb did not kill or injure any individual and
caused little property damage. Moreover, the district court minimized
any risk of unfair prejudice by carefully instructing the jury not to use
the evidence of the Quincy bombing to infer Trenkler's guilt simply
because he was a bad person or because the fact he had a built a bomb
in the past made it more likely he had built the bomb in this case. In
sum, we believe that the district court did not abuse its discretion in
determining that the probative value of the Quincy bomb evidence was
not substantially outweighed by the risk of unfair prejudice.[19] . . .

For the foregoing reasons, we affirm Trenkler's conviction.

TORRUELLA, Chief Judge (Dissenting). In my view, the erroneous admission in this case of evidence derived from the EXIS computer database violated the defendant's Sixth Amendment right to confront
witnesses against him. Contrary to my brethren, I do not believe that
this error was harmless beyond a reasonable doubt. I therefore dissent.

I . . .

The majority also alludes to a potentially more pernicious problem
concerning the EXIS-derived evidence. The majority notes that the database entry for the Roslindale incident lists approximately twenty-two
characteristics describing that incident, but Scheid, inexplicably, chose

19. Trenkler also contends that the district court abused its discretion in admitting the
Quincy bomb evidence to prove knowledge, skill, and intent. With respect to the issues of
knowledge and skill, we find little merit in Trenkler's argument. Obviously, the fact that Trenkler had in the past built a remote-control bomb has some relevance on whether he possessed
the skill and knowledge necessary to build the Roslindale bomb. See United States v. Latorre,
922 F.2d 1, 8 (1st Cir. 1990), cert. denied, 502 U.S. 876, 116 L. Ed. 2d 175, 112 S. Ct. 217
(1991). Furthermore, because the evidence was otherwise admissible to show identity, allowing
the government to use it to show skill and knowledge, posed no additional risk of unfair
prejudice. Trenkler's contention with respect to intent stands on firmer ground. We have
some difficulty comprehending (and the government does not clearly articulate) any theory
of "special relevance" tending to show intent that does not depend heavily on an inference of
propensity. See United States v. Lynn, 856 F.2d 430, 436 (1st Cir. 1988) (error to admit evidence on intent where inference depends on propensity). Nonetheless, because the evidence
was properly admitted to show identity, knowledge and skill, any error in its admission to show
intent is harmless. See *Benavente Gomez*, 921 F.2d at 386 (harmless error if it is "highly probable"
the error did not contribute to the verdict).

only to query ten of those characteristics.[34] . . . The majority notes that there is nothing to suggest that these ten characteristics are more important to a bomb-signature analysis than any of the other characteristics not chosen. Scheid offers no reason why he chose to query only certain generic characteristics instead of the more specific characteristics of the Roslindale bomb, which would be more evincing of a "signature." For example, the Quincy device would not have been a match if Scheid had queried any of the following characteristics of the Roslindale bombing: Futaba antenna, Rockstar detonator, use of dynamite, nails, glue, 6-volt battery, slide switch, paint, magazine page, or black electrical tape. The majority leaves the implication unspoken. I will not be so discreet. The obvious implication is that Scheid chose the particular characteristics in an attempt to find a match with the Quincy device. This implication is enforced by the fact that, according to Scheid's own testimony, the Quincy incident was not entered into the database until after the Roslindale incident. That is, government agents brought the Quincy bombing to Scheid's attention when they asked him to investigate the Roslindale bombing. . . .

As I see it, there are three related reasons why admission of the EXIS evidence cannot be considered harmless beyond a reasonable doubt. First, it is clear to me that the district court relied on the improper EXIS evidence in its decision to allow the government to present evidence of the Quincy incident to the jury to prove identity under Rule 404(b).

At the hearing on its motion in limine to admit evidence of the Quincy incident under Fed. R. Evid. 404(b), the government presented the testimony of Scheid, regarding the EXIS computer analysis, and the testimony of the government's bomb expert, Waskom, who testified that, in his opinion, the Quincy and Roslindale devices were so similar that they must have been built by the same person. In turn, Trenkler presented expert testimony that the devices were too different for anyone to be able to determine if they were built by the same person. After hearing this evidence, the district court concluded that "the similarities [between the two incidents] are sufficient to admit the evidence under the rules established . . . by the First Circuit."

The majority states that, based upon its review of the record, it is convinced that the EXIS-based evidence "was not a critical factor in the district court's decision to admit the Quincy bomb evidence for purposes of identity. The EXIS-derived evidence was merely cumulative,

34. The queried characteristics were 1) bombings and attempted bombings; 2) involving cars or trucks; 3) with bomb placed under the car or truck; 4) using remote-control; and magnets. EXIS listed seven incidents which included these characteristics. Scheid testified that he then performed a manual query of the seven incidents using other characteristics of the Roslindale bombing. He checked the other incidents to see if they involved 1) duct tape; soldering; 3) AA batteries; 4) a toggle switch; and 5) round magnets. Scheid did not check all 14,252 bombings and attempted bombings for these latter characteristics, only the seven.

corroborating the testimony of the government's explosives expert."
Supra pp. 39-40. Yet the record demonstrates that the district court
judge thought otherwise when she decided to admit evidence of the
1986 Quincy incident. In her oral opinion on the government's motion,
the district court judge began by summarizing the testimony of Waskom,
and then stated: "Adding to this evidence, the statistical evidence from
the EXIS system, I am persuaded that the two devices are sufficiently
similar to prove that the same person built them, and thus relevant to
the issues in this case." (emphasis added). The district court judge did
not say that the EXIS evidence "corroborated" Waskom's testimony. She
stated that, when she adds the EXIS evidence to Waskom's testimony,
she becomes convinced that the two devices are sufficiently similar. It
is plain that the district court judge relied on the EXIS evidence to form
the critical final link between the two devices. Indeed, in arguing its
motion, the government chose to first present the EXIS evidence and
then to present the Waskom testimony, suggesting that it intended the
latter to corroborate the former. The district court's erroneous determination that the EXIS evidence was admissible led not only to the jury
hearing that evidence, but also to the jury hearing Waskom's testimony
with respect to the two incidents. I cannot agree, therefore, that admission of this evidence was harmless beyond a reasonable doubt.

The second reason that admission of the EXIS evidence cannot be
considered harmless is that this type of "scientific" evidence is too misleading, too powerful, and has too great a potential impact on lay jurors,
to be disregarded as harmless.

The EXIS-derived evidence was, in the best case scenario, unintentionally misleading, and, in the worst case scenario, deliberately skewed.
Scheid testified that, in entering information about the Quincy incident
into the EXIS database, he relied solely on a laboratory report prepared
in 1986 by investigators from the Massachusetts Department of Public
Safety. This report does not state that the Quincy device was attached
to the underside of the Capeway truck. Rather, it refers only to an "explosion on truck." Somebody must have given Scheid further information about the Quincy explosion because he entered "under vehicle" as
a characteristic of the Quincy incident. The majority acknowledges
these facts but, inexplicably, makes no comment. These facts are important for three reasons. First, they illustrate the fallibility of the underlying reports. How many of the other 14,232 reports had similar
defects? Second, they illustrate how easily one wrong or incomplete
entry can affect a query result. If Scheid had actually followed the report,
the Quincy incident would not have matched the Roslindale bombing
because Scheid's query entry was for a bomb "under vehicle." Finally,
these facts indicate that the EXIS test was skewed (whether intentionally
or unintentionally) to find a match between the Quincy and Roslindale
incidents.

The EXIS-derived evidence is also misleading because it focuses the jury's attention on the trees instead of the forest. By focusing on similar minor aspects between the two devices—e.g., duct tape, magnets and soldering—the majority completely brushes aside the fact that the central and most important ingredient in the two devices is fundamentally different. The central ingredient in a bomb, one would think, is the explosive content (in much the same way that the central ingredient in a high-performance car is the engine). The Roslindale bomb used two to three sticks of dynamite — a very powerful explosive. The Quincy device used an M-21 Hoffman artillery simulator, which is a device used by the military to simulate, in a safe fashion, the flash and noise of artillery. The simulator is, in effect, a firecracker-like device; it has nowhere near the strength of dynamite. In stark contrast to dynamite, a simulator is not designed to cause physical or property damage. Indeed, while the Roslindale device created an explosion large enough to kill, the Quincy device caused no visible damage to the truck it was placed under. Equating the two devices is like equating a BB gun with a high caliber rifle.

The misleading nature of the EXIS-derived statement is compounded by the nature of its source, and the way in which it was presented to the jury. Not only is it rank hearsay evidence, it is hearsay evidence wrapped in a shroud of "scientific" authenticity. This is not a paid government expert testifying that, in his opinion, the two devices were built by the same person; this is a computer declaring that the two devices were built by the same person. Computers deal in facts, not opinions. Computers are not paid by one side to testify. Computers do not have prejudices. And computers are not subject to cross-examination. Moreover, the chart of the EXIS queries performed by Scheid, and the printouts of the results of those queries, were introduced into evidence and presented as exhibits to the jury. Consequently, the jury had this misleading, physical evidence with them in the jury room during deliberations. Does it not stand to reason that the lay juror will accord greater weight to a computer's written findings than to the testimony of a government expert witness? The common-sense answer is, of course. . . .

V

A horrible crime was committed in which one police officer was killed and another seriously injured. Society rightfully demands that the guilty be apprehended, tried, and punished. But the distinguishing feature of our legal system is that even those charged with grotesque crimes are guaranteed certain constitutional rights intended to ensure that they receive a fair trial. Unfortunately, and with all due respect to my brethren, I believe the defendant's right to a fair trial was violated when the government was permitted to introduce the highly prejudicial evidence derived from the EXIS computer database. Because this error so severely violated defendant's Sixth Amendment right to confront the witnesses against him, and because the remainder of the evidence against him was not "overwhelming," I dissent.

Do you agree that the defendant's modus operandi was a sufficiently distinctive method of making bombs as to rise to a level of "signature quality" identity evidence? What about the role of the computer to "match" the two incidents? Isn't it always possible to select several features of any activity that are likely be the similar when the activity is repeated, even by different actors? Which attributes, either alone, or in conjunction with others, are really as unique as a "signature"?

An interesting variation on this problem occurs when a defendant attempts to introduce evidence of other similar crimes by someone else to prove that the case on trial is a case of mistaken identity. The Colorado Supreme Court has adopted the position that similar offense evidence when introduced by the defendant is subject to a case-by-case test of admissibility. People v. Flowers, 644 P.2d 917 (Colo. 1981). In *Flowers,* defendant was convicted of first-degree sexual assault and sought to introduce evidence of nine other sexual assaults in the same locality within five months of his alleged assault. The defendant wanted to offer testimony from detectives that each of the victims was unable to identify the defendant from a line-up as her assailant and to call a forensic serologist to testify that seminal fluid recovered from one of the sexual assault victims excluded the defendant as the assailant. The court upheld the district court's determination that the details of the other crimes were not distinctive enough to represent the "signature" of a single individual but were features common to most sexual assaults.

It is interesting to note the nonsymmetrical application of the Rule 403/404 two-step approach. For example, in *Flowers* if the semen had matched and the defendant had been positively identified for one of the prior neighborhood assault cases, such evidence might have been admitted if the government could point to some "unique" characteristics shared by the assaults.

If the two-step approach is to be applied nonsymmetrically when evidence of other crimes is offered exculpatorily by the defendant, which way should the scales of admissibility tilt?

COMMONWEALTH v. JEWETT
392 Mass. 558, 467 N.E.2d 155 (1984)

Lynch, J.

The defendant was convicted of rape and was sentenced to a term of thirty-five to fifty years at the Massachusetts Correctional Institution,

Walpole. He filed a timely appeal from this conviction. The defendant also filed a motion for a new trial, which the trial judge denied. A notice of appeal from this denial was filed, and this was consolidated with the appeal from the defendant's conviction.

After a decision by the Appeals Court reversing the judgment of the Superior Court, Commonwealth v. Jewett, 17 Mass. App. 354 (1984), we granted the Commonwealth's application for further appellate review. We reach the same result.

We summarize the facts, based upon the findings of the trial judge in response to a motion to suppress the identification of the defendant. On October 31, 1979, the victim was alone at her mother's home in Newton. About 8 P.M., she heard noises outside which sounded as if her cat were fighting with another animal. She decided to go outside and investigate. She walked out the front door and around the porch to the rear of the house. Hearing the noises continuing from some point beyond the rear yard, she walked down a path into the woods for a short distance. She came to a clearing in the woods, and, although the noises continued, she decided to turn back. As she was turning, the victim was grabbed from behind, dragged from the path, thrown down and raped. The episode lasted no more than five minutes; at the sound of a rustling nearby, the victim's assailant fled on foot.

Although it was dark at the time of the incident, there was evidence that the victim was able to see her assailant's face adequately on account of light from a nearby MBTA train station and a warehouse, and because it was a clear night with some moonlight. Soon after the incident, the police were called and they went to the victim's home. They showed her an array of about twenty photographs, and from this she selected the defendant's picture as being the one she "thought" was that of her assailant. However, she stated that she "would like to see" the man in person so as to confirm her initial impression. On November 19, 1979, the victim again picked the defendant's picture out of a smaller array of about nine color photographs. Again, she declined to state that she was "positive" that the picture she selected was that of her assailant. Finally, three months after the incident, the victim attempted an in-person identification of her attacker. On February 1, 1980, the defendant was in the Newton District Court on another matter. The victim walked around the courtroom and identified the defendant as her assailant.

The defendant has consistently maintained a defense of mistaken identity. Through the testimony of a number of witnesses, he introduced evidence that at the time of the incident he and a friend were driving to or waiting at a railroad station located a number of miles from the victim's home, for the purpose of meeting a train carrying their girl friends. However, the Commonwealth placed emphasis on the fact that during the course of the defendant's trip to the station, he and his companion stopped at a restaurant located within one mile of the victim's residence. They left the restaurant about 8 P.M.

Identification was, essentially, the sole issue at trial, with the defendant's alibi defense being weighed against the victim's testimony. . . .

The Commonwealth argues that the trial judge correctly refused to permit the defendant to introduce testimony by a victim (hereafter, victim B) of a sexual assault five days before the incident at issue. Victim B, a teenager one year younger than the victim in the instant case (hereafter, victim A or the victim), was walking to school along a "short cut" path in a neighboring town (Watertown) when she was attacked. She, like victim A, was grabbed from behind and thrown to the ground, and as in the instant case her assailant fled on foot when startled by a noise along the path (in this case, a group of children). Acting on information provided by the Newton police department, the Watertown police included the same photograph of the defendant in the array shown to victim B. As with victim A, although victim B tentatively suggested that the defendant's photograph could be that of her attacker, she stated that she could not positively confirm this fact unless she saw him in person. On November 19, 1979, victim B viewed twenty to twenty-five people in the Newton District Court and identified the defendant as the person who had assaulted her. She stated that she was "85% positive" of this fact. However, on November 26, 1979, the charges against the defendant in victim B's case were dropped on the prosecutor's recommendation, since on the day of the incident the defendant was a voluntary in-patient at the treatment center at the Massachusetts Correctional Institution, Bridgewater, and therefore could not have been in Watertown.[35]

At trial, the defendant's counsel explained these facts to the judge in some detail, and proposed to call victim B as a witness and to introduce the dismissed complaint in evidence, in support of his theory of misidentification on the part of victim A. His offer of proof was cut off by the judge, and his request to introduce the evidence denied.[36] The

---

35. Consistent with his misidentification theory, the defendant has also asked us to consider evidence of a third sexual assault which occurred two days before the assault on victim B, and for which the defendant was charged as the assailant on the basis of a similar photographic identification. Unlike the case involving victim B, this case went to trial and resulted in the defendant's acquittal, probably due to evidence showing that the defendant could not have been at the location of the incident (Newton) at the time when it occurred. However, this third incident was neither raised by the defendant at trial nor until more than one and one-half years later, in the context of an amended motion for new trial. We therefore decline to consider it as a basis for this appeal.

36. The exchange between defendant's counsel and the trial judge consisted of the following:

Defense Counsel: It's my understanding there was a young lady . . . in Watertown who accused Mr. Jewett of raping her on the 26th of October, 1979, five days before this offense. She went to the Newton District Court, identified him there, looked at the very same pictures

defendant argues that this ruling deprived him of the ability to present a defense, misidentification — an especially serious deprivation considering that the prosecution's entire case hinged on the accuracy of victim A's identification. The defendant argues that the judge's action was error, and that therefore he is entitled to a new trial. We agree. . . .

"Just as an accused has the right to confront the prosecution's witnesses for the purpose of challenging their testimony, he has the right to present his own witnesses to establish a defense. This right is a fundamental element of due process of law." Washington v. Texas, 388 U.S. 14, 19 (1967). This broad right has given rise to a rule allowing a defendant to introduce evidence that another person recently committed a similar crime by similar methods, since such evidence tends to show that someone other than the accused committed the particular crime.

No positive rule of law other than normal considerations of relevancy stands in the way of the admission of misidentification evidence. "Although the decision of a trial judge to admit or reject evidence of other crimes ordinarily will not be disturbed, that decision is not absolute and may be set aside if justice requires a different result." Commonwealth v. Keizer, [377 Mass. 264, 267 (1979)]. In the instant case, justice does require the admission of the proffered evidence concerning possible misidentification of the defendant, due to the similarity of the circumstances and the importance of the identification in this case. The same photograph of the defendant was used in both initial identifications. This was not a coincidence; the Newton police had focused on the defendant as a suspect and had notified the Watertown police of their suspicions. In addition, the incidents share many similarities. There was a close correspondence of time and location; the incidents happened within one week of each other in neighboring towns. Both involved assaults on individuals of roughly the same age, consisting of a sudden and brief attack from behind, followed by a quick departure on foot. Both victims experienced similar difficulties in making a firm identification based on only a photograph, and each refused to say that she was "positive" that her assailant was the defendant until she could view him in person.

We agree with the Appeals Court that the defendant need not "demonstrate the same degree of similarity [between incidents] which the Commonwealth must demonstrate when seeking to introduce such evi-

---

that had been introduced in evidence here, and positively identified him from both the pictures and the in-court identification. Subsequent to that, when Mr. Jewett was brought into . . . Waltham District Court, before that probable cause hearing, it was shown to the Commonwealth that Mr. Jewett was locked up on the 26th of October at M.C.I. Bridgewater. As a result of that fact he was incarcerated on the date this supposedly happened. That complaint was dismissed. I want to bring the girl in here, the complaint introduced in evidence, to show that—

The Judge: That is denied and your exception is noted.

dence to establish the defendant's guilt." Commonwealth v. Jewett, 17 Mass. App. 354, 358 n.4 (1984). When a defendant offers exculpatory evidence regarding misidentification, prejudice ceases to be a factor, and relevance should function as the admissibility standard.

We have little doubt of the relevancy of the evidence proffered by the defendant, and reject the Commonwealth's argument that it was merely collateral. While it is true that the extent to which collateral matters may be made the subject of inquiry at trial is largely within the sound discretion of the trial judge, we have also said that "[w]here . . . identification was an important issue, the defendant undoubtedly had the right to show that . . . [the victim's] identification of him was unreliable." Commonwealth v. Franklin, 366 Mass. 284 (1974), quoting from Commonwealth v. Roselli, 335 Mass. 38, 40 (1956). Here, the prosecution's case relied upon the victim's identification of her assailant and the defendant's case consisted wholly of a rebuttal of this identification by means of an alibi and evidence of misidentification. Under these circumstances, evidence of a prior misidentification occurring in a similar incident and based upon the same photograph of the defendant was probative on the only contested issue and should not have been excluded.

The Commonwealth's related argument that inclusion of evidence regarding victim *B*'s misidentification would amount to an impermissible attempt to impeach victim *A*'s credibility is also wide of the mark. Victim *B*'s mistaken selection has no bearing on victim *A*'s credibility. The purpose for which evidence is offered is determinative of its relevancy, and here evidence of victim *B*'s misidentification was *not* offered for impeachment. Instead, the evidence was offered "for the purpose of direct testimony to establish a defense" of mistaken identity, and to this end it was relevant. . . .

Judgment reversed.

REX v. SMITH
11 Cr. App. R. 229, 84 L.J.K.B. 2153 (1915)

Appeal on points of law against a conviction for murder before Scrutton, J. at the Central Criminal Court. The appellant was indicted for the murder of Bessie Munday, who was discovered dead in her bath at Herne Bay on the 12th July 1912. The appellant had gone through a ceremony of marriage with the deceased, his own wife being then alive. At the trial of the appellant on the charge of murder evidence was given that subsequent to the death of Bessie Munday two other women named Alice Burnham and Margaret Elizabeth Lofty had both died in their baths under nearly the same circumstances as those which occurred in the case of Bessie Munday. In both of these subsequent cases the appellant had gone through a ceremony of marriage. The appellant was convicted at the Central Criminal Court of the murder of Bessie Munday and sentenced to death. The contention on behalf of the appellant is that the evidence was not admissible on examination in chief. It was admitted as evidence of a system of murder.

LORD READING, C.J. The principles of law governing the admission of evidence of this nature have been often under the consideration of this court and depend chiefly on the statement of the law in the case of Makin v. Attorney-General for New South Wales (sup.), where Lord Herschell says:

> It is undoubtedly not competent for the prosecution to adduce evidence tend-
> ing to show that the accused has been guilty of criminal acts other than those
> covered by the indictment, for the purpose of leading to the conclusion that the
> accused is a person likely from his criminal conduct or character to have com-
> mitted the offence for which he is being tried. On the other hand, the mere fact
> that the evidence adduced tends to show the commission of other crimes does
> not render it inadmissible if it be relevant to an issue before the jury, and it may
> be so relevant if it bears upon the question whether the acts alleged to constitute
> the crime charged in his indictment were designed or accidental, or to rebut a
> defence which would otherwise be open to the accused.

In the present case the prosecution tendered evidence relating to the other two women, and it was admitted by the judge as tending to show that the act charged was committed with design.

The second point taken is that even assuming that evidence of the other two women was admissible, the prosecution should not have been allowed to give evidence beyond the fact that the two women were found dead in their baths. Obviously for the reasons given in dealing with the first point, it would not have been of any assistance to cut short the evidence in this way. We think that the prosecution were entitled to give, and the judge rightly admitted, evidence of the circumstances relating to the deaths of the two women.

Appeal dismissed.

Evidence of other similar happenings that might be only marginally probative if considered in isolation can become highly probative when considered in conjunction. The logic that applies is called the "doctrine of chances." The Brides in the Baths is the classic case showing lack of accident under the doctrine of chances. Considering each episode in isolation, it is hard to say whether the defendant killed his bride or whether she slipped and fell. But when the same apparent accident occurs repeatedly, the likelihood is that it is being caused to happen.

Professor Imwinkelried, The Use of Evidence of an Accused's Uncharged Misconduct to Prove Mens Rea, 51 Ohio St. L.J. 575, 586-588 (1990), explains how the doctrine of chances supports admissibility of defendant's other crimes without violating the propensity rule:

United States v. Woods is the paradigmatic case. In *Woods,* the accused stood trial for infanticide. The victim had died of cyanosis. The accused claimed that the suffocation was accidental. To rebut the accused's claim, the prosecutor offered evidence that over a twenty-five year period, children in the accused's custody had experienced twenty cyanotic episodes. The defense objected to the admission of the testimony on the ground that the testimony amounted to impermissible evidence of the accused's bad character. However, the prosecution rejoined that the testimony was relevant on a noncharacter theory, that is, the doctrine of chances. . . .

. . . Under both the doctrine [of chances] and the character theory [of the propensity rule], the trier of fact begins at the same starting point, the evidence of the accused's uncharged crimes. However, when the trier engages in character reasoning, the initial decision facing the trier is whether to infer from the evidence that the accused has a personal bad character. In contrast, under the doctrine of chances, the trier need not focus on the accused's subjective character. Under the doctrine of chances, the initial decision facing the trier is whether the uncharged incidents are so numerous that it is objectively improbable that so many accidents would befall the accused. The decision is akin to the determination the trier must make in a tort case when the plaintiff relies on *res ipsa loquitur.* In the tort setting, the trier must decide whether objectively the most likely cause of the plaintiff's injury is the defendant's negligent act. In the present setting, the trier must determine whether the more likely cause of the victim's injury is the act of another human being.

Assume *arguendo* that statistics compiled by the United States Public Health Service indicate that during a twenty-five year period, only two percent of American children experienced an accidental cyanotic episode. Contrast that figure with the incidence of cyanotic episodes experienced by the children in Ms. Woods' custody. Suppose, for example, that during the same twenty-five year period, twenty percent of those children had cyanotic episodes. The frequency of the episodes among those children far exceeds the national average for such episodes. The episodes are so recurrent among those children that it is objectively implausible to assume that all those episodes were accidental. Either one or some of those episodes were caused by human intervention, or Ms. Woods is one of the most unlucky people alive. . . .

. . . [T]he doctrine is distinguishable from a character reasoning theory in terms of the pertinent policies. The probative dangers posed by the doctrine differ to a marked degree from the risks raised by a character theory.

One risk raised by a character theory is that at least at a subconscious level, the jury will be tempted to punish the accused for uncharged misdeeds. That risk is acute under a character theory because the theory forces the jury to concentrate on the accused's personal character or disposition. The jurors must consciously address the question of the type of person the accused is. There is no need for the jurors to grapple with that question under the doctrine of chances. There is an undeniable possibility that on their own motion, the jurors may advert to the question. However, unlike a character theory, the doctrine of chances does not compel the jurors to focus on the accused's subjective disposition. Consequently, the nature of the initial inferential step under the doctrine significantly reduces the risk of a decision on an improper basis.

The second probative danger raised by a character theory is that the jury will overvalue the probative worth of the item of evidence. Although general character has only slight or small relevancy to the issue of the accused's conduct on a specific occasion, we fear that the jurors will treat character as a reliable predictor of conduct. There is less risk of overestimation of probative value under the doctrine of chances. The doctrine invites the trier to compare the accused's experience with statistical data or the trier's knowledge of everyday, human experience. We commonly accept the trier's knowledge of "the ways of the world" as a trustworthy basis for legal reasoning. That knowledge is one of the bases for the *res ipsa loquitur* doctrine; and the jury instructions in many jurisdictions specifically encourage jurors to employ that knowledge as a basis for resolving factual disputes.

Since the theory of relevance [under the doctrine of chances] is distinguishable from the forbidden theory . . . , prosecutors may properly rely on the doctrine of chances as a noncharacter theory for satisfying Rule 404(b). However, the courts should not admit uncharged misconduct evidence as a matter of course whenever the prosecutor asserts that the evidence is relevant under the doctrine of chances to prove the *actus reus*. Rather than accepting the prosecutor's argument as *ipse dixit*, the courts should carefully evaluate the evidence to ensure that the prosecutor has established the factual predicate for invoking the doctrine.

What is the "factual predicate for invoking the doctrine"?

TUCKER v. STATE
82 Nev. 127, 412 P.2d 970 (1966)

THOMPSON, J. On May 7, 1957, Horace Tucker telephoned the police station and asked a detective to come to the Tucker home in North Las Vegas. Upon arrival the detective observed that Tucker had been drinking, was unshaven, and looked tired. Tucker led the detective to the dining room where one, Earl Kaylor, was dead on the floor. Kaylor had been shot several times. When asked what had happened, Tucker said that he (Tucker) had been sleeping in the bedroom, awakened, and walked to the dining room where he noticed Kaylor lying on the floor. Upon ascertaining that Kaylor was dead, Tucker telephoned the police station. He denied having killed Kaylor. A grand jury conducted an extensive investigation. Fifty-three witnesses were examined. However, an indictment was not returned as the grand jury deemed the evidence inconclusive. No one, including Tucker, has ever been charged with that killing.

On October 8, 1963, Horace Tucker telephoned the police and asked a sergeant to come to the Tucker home in North Las Vegas; that there was an old man dead there. Upon arrival the sergeant noticed that Tucker had been drinking. The body of Omar Evans was dead on the couch in the living room. Evans had been shot. Tucker stated that he (Tucker) had been asleep, awakened, and found Evans dead on the couch. Subsequently Tucker was charged with the murder of Evans. A jury convicted him of second degree murder and the court pronounced judgment and the statutory sentence of imprisonment for a term of "not less than 10 years, which term may be extended to life."

At trial, over vehement objection, the court allowed the state to introduce evidence of the Kaylor homicide. The court reasoned that the circumstances of the deaths of Kaylor and Evans were sufficiently parallel to render admissible evidence of the Kaylor homicide to prove that Tucker intended to kill Evans, that the killing of Evans was part of a common scheme or plan in Tucker's mind, and also to negate any defense of accidental death. These limited purposes, for which the evidence was received and could be considered by the jury, were specified by court instruction as required by case law. We rule that evidence of the Kaylor homicide was not admissible for any purpose and that prejudicial error occurred when the court permitted the jury to hear and consider it. . . .

Whenever the problem of evidence of other offenses confronts a trial court, grave considerations attend. The danger of prejudice to the defendant is ever present, for the jury may convict now because he has escaped punishment in the past. Nor has the defendant been advised that he must be prepared to meet extraneous charges. Indeed, as our system of justice is accusatorial rather than inquisitorial, there is much to be said for the notion that the prosecution must prove the defendant guilty of the specific crime charged without resort to past conduct. Thus when the other offense sought to be introduced falls within an exception to the rule of exclusion, the trial court should be convinced that the probative value of such evidence outweighs its prejudicial effect. The reception of such evidence is justified by necessity and, if other evidence has substantially established the element of the crime involved (motive, intent, identity, absence of mistake, etc.), the probative value of showing another offense is diminished, and the trial court should rule it inadmissible even though relevant and within an exception to the rule of exclusion.

In the case at hand we need not consider whether evidence of the Kaylor homicide comes within one of the exceptions to the rule of exclusion, because the first requisite for admissibility is wholly absent— namely, that the defendant on trial committed the independent offense sought to be introduced. There is nothing in this record to establish that Tucker killed Kaylor. Anonymous crimes can have no relevance in deciding whether the defendant committed the crime with which he is charged. Kaylor's assailant remains unknown. A fortiori, evidence of that crime cannot be received in the trial for the murder of Evans.

We have not before had occasion to discuss the quantum of proof needed to establish that the defendant on trial committed the separate offense sought to be introduced. Here there was only conjecture and suspicion, aroused by the fact that Kaylor was found dead in Tucker's home. We now adopt the rule that, before evidence of a collateral offense is admissible for any purpose, the prosecution must first establish by plain, clear and convincing evidence, that the defendant committed that offense. Fundamental fairness demands this standard in order to preclude verdicts which might otherwise rest on false assumptions. . . .

Reversed and remanded for new trial.

What quantum of proof of other crimes should be required when the state seeks to admit such proof under one of the exceptions to the general rule of exclusion? What is "plain, clear and convincing evidence"? Is it more than a preponderance? How much more? As much as proof beyond a reasonable doubt? Is defendant's connection with the other crime a jury question or a question for the judge? Does it matter which exception to the propensity rule is called into play? What do the Federal Rules provide on this question?

What effect should acquittal of a charge of an alleged prior crime have on the admissibility of evidence of that prior crime when it is offered to show a common scheme or plan at a subsequent trial on another offense? Are res judicata or double jeopardy principles applicable? Does it depend on the quantum of proof of the prior crime chosen as the standard for proof of prior crimes under the propensity rule exceptions?

HUDDLESTON v. UNITED STATES
485 U.S. 681 (1988)

Chief Justice REHNQUIST delivered the opinion of the Court.

Petitioner, Guy Rufus Huddleston, was charged with one count of selling stolen goods in interstate commerce, 18 U.S.C. §2315, and one count of possessing stolen property in interstate commerce, 18 U.S.C. §659. The two counts related to two portions of a shipment of stolen Memorex video cassette tapes that petitioner was alleged to have possessed and sold, knowing that they were stolen.

The evidence at trial showed that a trailer containing over 32,000 blank Memorex video cassette tapes with a manufacturing cost of $4.53 per tape was stolen from the Overnight Express yard in South Holland, Illinois, sometime between April 11 and 15, 1985. On April 17, 1985, petitioner contacted Karen Curry, the manager of the Magic Rent-to-Own in Ypsilanti, Michigan, seeking her assistance in selling a large number of blank Memorex video cassette tapes. After assuring Curry that the tapes were not stolen, he told her he wished to sell them in lots of at least 500 at $2.75 to $3.00 per tape. Curry subsequently arranged for the sale of a total of 5,000 tapes, which petitioner delivered to the various purchasers—who apparently believed the sales were legitimate.

There was no dispute that the tapes which petitioner sold were stolen; the only material issue at trial was whether petitioner knew they were stolen. The District Court allowed the Government to introduce evidence of "similar acts" under Rule 404(b), concluding that such evidence had "clear relevance as to [petitioner's knowledge]." The first piece of similar act evidence offered by the Government was the testimony of Paul Toney, a record store owner. He testified that in February 1985, petitioner offered to sell new 12" black and white televisions for $28 a piece. According to Toney, petitioner indicated that he could obtain several thousand of these televisions. Petitioner and Toney eventually traveled to the Magic Rent-to-Own, where Toney purchased 20 of the televisions. Several days later, Toney purchased 18 more televisions.

The second piece of similar act evidence was the testimony of Robert Nelson, an undercover FBI agent posing as a buyer for an appliance store. Nelson testified that in May 1985, petitioner offered to sell him a large quantity of Amana appliances—28 refrigerators, 2 ranges, and 40 icemakers. Nelson agreed to pay $8,000 for the appliances. Petitioner was arrested shortly after he arrived at the parking lot where he and Nelson had agreed to transfer the appliances. A truck containing the appliances was stopped a short distance from the parking lot, and Leroy Wesby, who was driving the truck, was also arrested. It was determined that the appliances had a value of approximately $20,000 and were part of a shipment that had been stolen.

Petitioner testified that the Memorex tapes, the televisions, and the appliances had all been provided by Leroy Wesby, who had represented that all of the merchandise was obtained legitimately. Petitioner stated that he had sold 6,500 Memorex tapes for Wesby on a commission basis. Petitioner maintained that all of the sales for Wesby had been on a commission basis and that he had no knowledge that any of the goods were stolen.

In closing, the prosecution explained that petitioner was not on trial for his dealings with the appliances or the televisions. The District Court instructed the jury that the similar acts evidence was to be used only to establish petitioner's knowledge, and not to prove his character. The jury convicted petitioner on the possession count only.

A divided panel of the United States Court of Appeals for the Sixth Circuit initially reversed the conviction, concluding that because the Government had failed to prove by clear and convincing evidence that the televisions were stolen, the District Court erred in admitting the testimony concerning the televisions. 802 F.2d 874 (1986).[1] The panel subsequently granted rehearing to address the decision in United States v. Ebens, 800 F.2d 1422 (C.A.6 1986), in which a different panel had held: "Courts may admit evidence of prior bad acts if the proof shows by a preponderance of the evidence that the defendant did in fact commit the act." On rehearing, the court affirmed the conviction. "Applying the preponderance of the evidence standard adopted in *Ebens,* we cannot say that the district court abused its discretion in admitting evidence of the similar acts in question here." 811 F.2d 974, 975 (1987) (per curiam). The court noted that the evidence concerning the televisions was admitted for a proper purpose and that the probative value of this evidence was not outweighed by its potential prejudicial effect.

We granted certiorari to resolve a conflict among the Courts of Appeals as to whether the trial court must make a preliminary finding before "similar act" and other Rule 404(b) evidence is submitted to the jury. We conclude that such evidence should be admitted if there is sufficient evidence to support a finding by the jury that the defendant committed the similar act.

Federal Rule of Evidence 404(b) — which applies in both civil and criminal cases—generally prohibits the introduction of evidence of extrinsic acts that might adversely reflect on the actor's character, unless that evidence bears upon a relevant issue in the case such as motive, opportunity, or knowledge. Extrinsic acts evidence may be critical to the establishment of the truth as to a disputed issue, especially when that issue involves the actor's state of mind and the only means of ascertaining that mental state is by drawing inferences from conduct. The actor in the instant case was a criminal defendant, and the act in question was "similar" to the one with which he was charged. Our use of these terms is not meant to suggest that our analysis is limited to such circumstances.

Before this Court, petitioner argues that the District Court erred in admitting Toney's testimony as to petitioner's sale of the televisions.

The threshold inquiry a court must make before admitting similar acts evidence under Rule 404(b) is whether that evidence is probative of a material issue other than character. The Government's theory of relevance was that the televisions were stolen, and proof that petitioner had engaged in a series of sales of stolen merchandise from the same suspicious source would be strong evidence that he was aware that each of these items, including the Memorex tapes, was stolen. As such, the sale of the televisions was a "similar act" only if the televisions were

---

1. "[T]he government's only support for the assertion that the televisions were stolen was [petitioner's] failure to produce a bill of sale at trial and the fact that the televisions were sold at a low price."

stolen. Petitioner acknowledges that this evidence was admitted for the proper purpose of showing his knowledge that the Memorex tapes were stolen. He asserts, however, that the evidence should not have been admitted because the Government failed to prove to the District Court that the televisions were in fact stolen.

Petitioner argues from the premise that evidence of similar acts has a grave potential for causing improper prejudice. For instance, the jury may choose to punish the defendant for the similar rather than the charged act, or the jury may infer that the defendant is an evil person inclined to violate the law. Because of this danger, petitioner maintains, the jury ought not to be exposed to similar act evidence until the trial court has heard the evidence and made a determination under Federal Rule of Evidence 104(a) that the defendant committed the similar act. Rule 104(a) provides that "[p]reliminary questions concerning the qualification of a person to be a witness, the existence of a privilege, or the admissibility of evidence shall be determined by the court, subject to the provisions of subdivision (b)." According to petitioner, the trial court must make this preliminary finding by at least a preponderance of the evidence.

We reject petitioner's position, for it is inconsistent with the structure of the Rules of Evidence and with the plain language of Rule 404(b). Article IV of the Rules of Evidence deals with the relevancy of evidence. Rules 401 and 402 establish the broad principle that relevant evidence — evidence that makes the existence of any fact at issue more or less probable — is admissible unless the Rules provide otherwise. Rule 403 allows the trial judge to exclude relevant evidence if, among other things, "its probative value is substantially outweighed by the danger of unfair prejudice." Rules 404 through 412 address specific types of evidence that have generated problems. Generally, these latter Rules do not flatly prohibit the introduction of such evidence but instead limit the purpose for which it may be introduced. Rule 404(b), for example, protects against the introduction of extrinsic act evidence when that evidence is offered solely to prove character. The text contains no intimation, however, that any preliminary showing is necessary before such evidence may be introduced for a proper purpose. If offered for such a proper purpose, the evidence is subject only to general strictures limiting admissibility such as Rules 402 and 403.

Petitioner's reading of Rule 404(b) as mandating a preliminary finding by the trial court that the act in question occurred not only superimposes a level of judicial oversight that is nowhere apparent from the language of that provision, but it is simply inconsistent with the legislative history behind Rule 404(b). The Advisory Committee specifically declined to offer any "mechanical solution" to the admission of evidence under 404(b). Advisory Committee's Notes on Fed. Rule Evid. 404(b), 28 U.S.C. App., p.691. Rather, the Committee indicated that the trial court should assess such evidence under the usual rules for admissibility: "The determination must be made whether the danger of undue prejudice outweighs the probative value of the evidence in view of the availability of other means of proof and other factors appropriate for making decisions of this kind under Rule 403." Ibid; see also S. Rep. No. 93-1277, p. 25 (1974) ("[I]t is anticipated that with respect to permissible uses for such evidence, the trial judge may exclude it only on the basis of those considerations set forth in Rule 403, i.e. prejudice, confusion or waste of time").

Petitioner's suggestion that a preliminary finding is necessary to protect the defendant from the potential for unfair prejudice is also belied by the Reports of the House of Representatives and the Senate. The House made clear that the version of Rule 404(b) which became law was intended to "plac[e] greater emphasis on admissibility than did the final Court version." H.R. Rep. No. 93-650, p.7 (1973). The Senate echoed this theme: "[T]he use of the discretionary word 'may' with respect to the admissibility of evidence of crimes, wrongs, or other acts is not intended to confer any arbitrary discretion on the trial judge." S. Rep. No. 93-1277, at 24. Thus, Congress was not nearly so concerned with the potential prejudicial effect of Rule 404(b) evidence as it was with ensuring that restrictions would not be placed on the admission of such evidence.

We conclude that a preliminary finding by the court that the Government has proved the act by a preponderance of the evidence is not called for under Rule 104(a).[3] This is not to say, however, that the Government may parade past the jury a litany of potentially prejudicial similar acts that have been established or connected to the defendant only by unsubstantiated innuendo. Evidence is admissible under Rule 404(b) only if it is relevant. "Relevancy is not an inherent characteristic of any item of evidence but exists only as a relation between an item of evidence and a matter properly provable in the case." Advisory Committee's Notes on Fed. Rule Evid. 401, 28 U.S.C. App., p.688. In the Rule 404(b) context, similar act evidence is relevant only if the jury can reasonably conclude that the act occurred and that the defendant was the actor. See United States v. Beechum, 582 F.2d 898, 912-913 (C.A.5 1978) (en banc). In the instant case, the evidence that petitioner was selling

---

3. Petitioner also suggests that in performing the balancing prescribed by Federal Rule of Evidence 403, the trial court must find that the prejudicial potential of similar acts evidence substantially outweighs its probative value unless the court concludes by a preponderance of the evidence that the defendant committed the similar act. We reject this suggestion because Rule 403 admits of no such gloss and because such a holding would be erroneous for the same reasons that a preliminary finding under Rule 104(a) is inappropriate. We do, however, agree with the Government's concession at oral argument that the strength of the evidence establishing the similar act is one of the factors the court may consider when conducting the Rule 403 balancing.

the televisions was relevant under the Government's theory only if the jury could reasonably find that the televisions were stolen.

Such questions of relevance conditioned on a fact are dealt with under Federal Rule of Evidence 104(b). . . .

In determining whether the Government has introduced sufficient evidence to meet Rule 104(b), the trial court neither weighs credibility nor makes a finding that the Government has proved the conditional fact by a preponderance of the evidence. The court simply examines all the evidence in the case and decides whether the jury could reasonably find the conditional fact—here, that the televisions were stolen—by a preponderance of the evidence. The trial court has traditionally exercised the broadest sort of discretion in controlling the order of proof at trial, and we see nothing in the Rules of Evidence that would change this practice. Often the trial court may decide to allow the proponent to introduce evidence concerning a similar act, and at a later point in the trial assess whether sufficient evidence has been offered to permit the jury to make the requisite finding. If the proponent has failed to meet this minimal standard of proof, the trial court must instruct the jury to disregard the evidence.

We emphasize that in assessing the sufficiency of the evidence under Rule 104(b), the trial court must consider all evidence presented to the jury. "[I]ndividual pieces of evidence, insufficient in themselves to prove a point, may in cumulation prove it. The sum of an evidentiary presentation may well be greater than its constituent parts." Bourjaily v. United States, 483 U.S. 171, 107 S. Ct. 268, 93 L. Ed. 2d 246 (1987). In assessing whether the evidence was sufficient to support a finding that the televisions were stolen, the court here was required to consider not only the direct evidence on that point—the low price of the televisions, the large quantity offered for sale, and petitioner's inability to produce a bill of sale—but also the evidence concerning petitioner's involvement in the sales of other stolen merchandise obtained from Wesby, such as the Memorex tapes and the Amana appliances. Given this evidence, the jury reasonably could have concluded that the televisions were stolen, and the trial court therefore properly allowed the evidence to go to the jury.

We share petitioner's concern that unduly prejudicial evidence might be introduced under Rule 404(b). See Michelson v. United States, 335 U.S. 469, 475-476, 69 S. Ct. 213, 218-219, 93 L. Ed. 168 (1948). We think, however, that the protection against such unfair prejudice emanates not from a requirement of a preliminary finding by the trial court, but rather from four other sources: first, from the requirement of Rule 404(b) that the evidence be offered for a proper purpose; second, from the relevancy requirement of Rule 402 — as enforced through Rule 104(b); third, from the assessment the trial court must make under Rule

403 to determine whether the probative value of the similar acts evidence is substantially outweighed by its potential for unfair prejudice, see Advisory Committee's Notes on Fed. Rule Evid. 404(b), 28 U.S.C. App., p.691; S. Rep. No. 93-1277, at 25; and fourth, from Federal Rule of Evidence 105, which provides that the trial court shall, upon request, instruct the jury that the similar acts evidence is to be considered only for the proper purpose for which it was admitted.

Affirmed.

DOWLING v. UNITED STATES
493 U.S. 342 (1990)

Justice WHITE delivered the opinion of the Court.

At petitioner's trial for various offenses arising out of a bank robbery, testimony was admitted under Rule 404(b) of the Federal Rules of Evidence, relating to an alleged crime that the defendant had previously been acquitted of committing. We conclude that neither the Double Jeopardy nor the Due Process Clause barred the use of this testimony.

On the afternoon of July 8, 1985, a man wearing a ski mask and armed with a small pistol robbed the First Pennsylvania Bank in Frederiksted, St. Croix, Virgin Islands, taking over $7,000 in cash from a bank teller, approximately $5,000 in cash from a customer, and various personal and travelers' checks. The culprit ran from the bank, scurried around in the street momentarily, and then commandeered a passing taxi van. While driving away from the scene, the robber pulled off his ski mask. An eyewitness, who had slipped out of the bank while the robbery was taking place, saw the maskless man and at trial identified him as petitioner, Reuben Dowling. Other witnesses testified that they had seen Dowling driving the hijacked taxi van outside of Frederiksted shortly after the bank robbery.

Following his arrest, Dowling was charged with the federal crimes of bank robbery, 18 U.S.C. §2113(a), and armed robbery, §2113(d), and with various crimes under Virgin Islands law. Dowling pleaded not guilty to all charges. Dowling's first trial ended with a hung jury. He was tried again and convicted, but the Third Circuit reversed this conviction on appeal. Government of Virgin Islands v. Dowling, 814 F.2d 134 (1987). After a third trial, Dowling was convicted on most of the counts; the trial judge sentenced him to 70 years imprisonment.

During petitioner's third trial, the Government over petitioner's objection called a woman named Vena Henry to the stand. Ms. Henry testified that a man wearing a knitted mask with cutout eyes and carrying a small handgun had, together with a man named Delroy Christian, entered her home in Frederiksted approximately two weeks after the First Pennsylvania Bank robbery. Ms. Henry testified that a struggle ensued and that she unmasked the intruder, whom she identified as Dowling. Based on this incident, Dowling had been charged under Virgin Islands law with burglary, attempted robbery, assault, and weapons offenses, but had been acquitted after a trial held before his third trial in the bank robbery case.

The Government assertedly elicited Henry's testimony for two purposes. First, it believed that Henry's description of Dowling as wearing a mask and carrying a gun similar to the mask worn and the gun carried by the robber of the First Pennsylvania Bank strengthened the Government's identification of Dowling as the bank robber. Second, the Government sought to link Dowling with Delroy Christian, the other man who entered Henry's home. The day before the bank robbery, Dowling had borrowed a white Volkswagen from a friend. At Dowling's trial for the First Pennsylvania Bank robbery, a police officer testified that, shortly before the bank robbery, she and her partner had come upon Christian and another man parked in a white Volkswagen in front of the bank with the car door open into the street; Christian was in the backseat. The officers told the two men to close the door, and the men drove away to the north. The police followed the Volkswagen for about a mile and, shortly thereafter, received a radio message that the bank had been robbed. The Government's theory was that Christian and his friend were to drive the getaway car after Dowling robbed the bank.

Before opening statements, the Government disclosed its intention to call Ms. Henry and explained its rationale for doing so, relying on Rule 404(b) of the Federal Rules of Evidence, which provides that evidence of other crimes, wrongs, or acts may be admissible against a defendant for purposes other than character evidence. After a hearing, the District Court characterized the testimony as highly probative circumstantial evidence and ruled that it was admissible under Rule 404(b). When Henry left the stand, the District Court instructed the jury that petitioner had been acquitted of robbing Henry, and emphasized the limited purpose for which Henry's testimony was being offered. The court reiterated that admonition in its final charge to the jury.

On appeal, the Third Circuit determined that the District Court should not have admitted Henry's testimony, but nevertheless affirmed Dowling's conviction. Relying on its decision in United States v. Keller, 624 F.2d 1154 (1980), the court held that petitioner's acquittal of the charges arising out of the incident at Henry's home collaterally estopped the Government from offering evidence of that incident at petitioner's trial for the First Pennsylvania Bank robbery.

Alternatively, the Court of Appeals ruled that the evidence was inadmissible under the Federal Rules of Evidence. The court noted that we had recently held in Huddleston v. United States that "[i]n the Rule 404(b) context, similar act evidence is relevant only if the jury can reasonably conclude that the act occurred and that the defendant was the actor." The Third Circuit found Henry's testimony inadmissible under Rule 404(b) because "when the prior act sought to be introduced was the subject of an acquittal by a jury, a second jury should not be permitted to conclude 'that the act occurred and that the defendant was the actor.' " The court also relied on Rule 403 of the Federal Rules of Evidence because, in the Third Circuit's opinion, the danger of unfair prejudice outweighed the probative value of Henry's testimony.

The Third Circuit, however, held that the admission of Henry's testimony was harmless because it was highly probable that the error did not prejudice the petitioner. . . . We granted certiorari to consider Dowling's contention that Henry's testimony was inadmissible under both the Double Jeopardy and the Due Process Clauses of the Fifth Amendment.

There is no claim here that the acquittal in the case involving Ms. Henry barred further prosecution in the present case. The issue is the inadmissibility of Henry's testimony.

In Ashe v. Swenson, 397 U.S. 436, 90 S. Ct. 1189, 25 L. Ed. 2d 469 (1970), we recognized that the Double Jeopardy Clause incorporates the doctrine of collateral estoppel. In that case, a group of masked men had robbed six men playing poker in the basement of a home. The State unsuccessfully prosecuted Ashe for robbing one of the men. Six weeks later, however, the defendant was convicted for the robbery of one of the other players. Applying the doctrine of collateral estoppel which we found implicit in the Double Jeopardy Clause, we reversed Ashe's conviction, holding that his acquittal in the first trial precluded the State from charging him for the second offense. We defined the collateral estoppel doctrine as providing that "when an issue of ultimate fact has once been determined by a valid and final judgment, that issue cannot again be litigated between the same parties in any future lawsuit." Ashe's acquittal in the first trial foreclosed the second trial because, in the circumstances of that case, the acquittal verdict could only have meant that the jury was unable to conclude beyond a reasonable doubt that the defendant was one of the bandits. A second prosecution was impermissible because, to have convicted the defendant in the second trial, the second jury had had to have reached a directly contrary conclusion.

Dowling contends that, by the same principle, his prior acquittal precluded the government from introducing into evidence Henry's testimony at the third trial in the bank robbery case. We disagree because, unlike the situation in Ashe v. Swenson, the prior acquittal did not determine an ultimate issue in the present case. This much Dowling concedes, and we decline to extend Ashe v. Swenson and the collateral estoppel component of the Double Jeopardy Clause to exclude in all circumstances, as Dowling would have it, relevant and probative evidence that is otherwise admissible under the Rules of Evidence simply because it relates to alleged criminal conduct for which a defendant has been acquitted.

For present purposes, we assume for the sake of argument that Dowling's acquittal established that there was a reasonable doubt as to whether Dowling was the masked man who entered Vena Henry's home with Delroy Christian two weeks after the First Pennsylvania Bank robbery. But to introduce evidence on this point at the bank robbery trial, the Government did not have to demonstrate that Dowling was the man who entered the home beyond a reasonable doubt: the Government sought to introduce Henry's testimony under Rule 404(b), and, as mentioned earlier, in Huddleston v. United States we held that "[i]n the Rule 404(b) context, similar act evidence is relevant only if the jury can reasonably conclude that the act occurred and that the defendant was the actor." Because a jury might reasonably conclude that Dowling was the masked man who entered Henry's home, even if it did not believe beyond a reasonable doubt that Dowling committed the crimes charged at the first trial, the collateral estoppel component of the Double Jeopardy Clause is inapposite.

Our decision is consistent with other cases where we have held that an acquittal in a criminal case does not preclude the government from relitigating an issue when it is presented in a subsequent action governed by a lower standard of proof. In United States v. One Assortment of 89 Firearms, 465 U.S. 354, 104 S. Ct. 1099, 79 L. Ed. 2d 361 (1984), for example, we unanimously agreed that a gun owner's acquittal on a charge of dealing firearms without a license did not preclude a subsequent in rem forfeiture proceeding against those firearms, even though forfeiture was only appropriate if the jury in the forfeiture proceeding concluded that the defendant had committed the underlying offense. Because the forfeiture action was a civil proceeding, we rejected the defendant's contention that the government was estopped from relitigating the issue of the defendant's alleged wrongdoing: "[The acquittal did] not prove that the defendant is innocent; it merely proves the existence of a reasonable doubt as to his guilt. . . . [T]he jury verdict in the criminal action did not negate the possibility that a preponderance of the evidence could show that [the defendant] was engaged in an unlicensed firearms business. . . . It is clear that the difference in the relative burdens of proof in the criminal and civil actions precludes the application of the doctrine of collateral estoppel."

We thus cannot agree that the Government was constitutionally barred from using Henry's testimony at the bank robbery trial, and for the same reasons we find no merit in the Third Circuit's holding that the common-law doctrine of collateral estoppel in all circumstances bars the later use of evidence relating to prior conduct which the government failed to prove violated a criminal law.

Even if we agreed with petitioner that the lower burden of proof at the second proceeding does not serve to avoid the collateral estoppel component of the Double Jeopardy Clause, we agree with the Government that the challenged evidence was nevertheless admissible because Dowling did not demonstrate that his acquittal in his first trial represented a jury determination that he was not one of the men who entered Ms. Henry's home. In Ashe v. Swenson, we stated that where a previous judgment of acquittal was based on a general verdict, courts must " 'examine the record of [the] prior proceeding, taking into account the pleadings, evidence, charge, and other relevant matter, and conclude whether a rational jury could have grounded its verdict on an issue other than that which the defendant seeks to foreclose from consideration." ' 397 U.S., at 444, 90 S. Ct., at 1194 (citation omitted). The Courts of Appeals have unanimously placed the burden on the defendant to demonstrate that the issue whose relitigation he seeks to foreclose was actually decided in the first proceeding. . . . We see no reason to depart from the majority rule in this case. . . .

There are any number of possible explanations for the jury's acquittal verdict at Dowling's first trial. As the record stands, there is nothing at all that persuasively indicates that the question of identity was at issue and was determined in Dowling's favor at the prior trial; at oral argument, Dowling conceded as much. As a result, even if we were to apply the Double Jeopardy Clause to this case, we would conclude that petitioner has failed to satisfy his burden of demonstrating that the first jury concluded that he was not one of the intruders in Ms. Henry's home.

Besides arguing that the introduction of Henry's testimony violated the Double Jeopardy Clause, petitioner also contends that the introduction of this evidence was unconstitutional because it failed the due process test of "fundamental fairness." We recognize that the introduction of evidence in circumstances like those involved here has the potential to prejudice the jury or unfairly force the defendant to spend time and money relitigating matters considered at the first trial. The question, however, is whether it is acceptable to deal with the potential for abuse through nonconstitutional sources like the Federal Rules of Evidence, or whether the introduction of this type of evidence is so extremely unfair that its admission violates "fundamental conceptions of justice." United States v. Lovasco, 431 U.S. 783, 790, 97 S. Ct. 2044, 2048, 52 L. Ed. 2d 752 (1977). . . . Petitioner lists four reasons why, according to him, admission of Henry's testimony was fundamentally unfair. First, petitioner suggests that evidence relating to acquitted conduct is inherently unreliable. We disagree: the jury in this case, for example, remained free to assess the truthfulness and the significance of Henry's testimony, and petitioner had the opportunity to refute it. Second, Dowling contends that the use of this type of evidence creates a constitutionally unacceptable risk that the jury will convict the defendant on the basis of inferences drawn from the acquitted conduct; we believe that the trial court's authority to exclude potentially prejudicial evidence adequately addresses this possibility.

Third, petitioner claims that the exclusion of acquitted conduct evidence furthers the desirable goal of consistent jury verdicts. We, however, do not find any inconsistency between Dowling's conviction for the First Pennsylvania Bank robbery and his acquittal on the charge of robbing Ms. Henry for the obvious reason that the jury's verdict in his second trial did not entail any judgment with respect to the offenses charged in his first. In any event, inconsistent verdicts are constitutionally tolerable. See Standefer v. United States, 447 U.S. 10, 25, 100 S. Ct. 1999, 2008, 64 L. Ed. 2d 689 (1980). Fourth, petitioner argues that the introduction of Henry's testimony in this case contravenes a tradition that the government may not force a person acquitted in one trial to defend against the same accusation in a subsequent proceeding. We acknowledge the tradition, but find it amply protected by the Double Jeopardy Clause. We decline to use the Due Process Clause as a device for extending the double jeopardy protection to cases where it otherwise would not extend.

Because we conclude that the admission of Ms. Henry's testimony was constitutional and the Court of Appeals therefore applied the correct harmless-error standard, we affirm the judgment of the Court of Appeals.

It is so ordered.

Justice BRENNAN, with whom Justice MARSHALL and Justice STEVENS join, dissenting. . . .

The question in this case is whether the criminal collateral estoppel doctrine should apply when the Government seeks to introduce in a subsequent trial evidence relating to a prior criminal offense for which the defendant has been acquitted. Before a jury can consider facts relating to a prior criminal offense as proof of an element of the presently charged offense, the jury must conclude by a preponderance of the evidence "that the act occurred and that the defendant was the actor." Huddleston v. United States. To the extent that the acquittal of the prior offense determined either of those factual issues in the defendant's favor, the introduction of this evidence imposes on the defendant the burden of relitigating those facts and thereby increases the likelihood of an erroneous conviction on the charged offense. Thus, I would extend the collateral estoppel doctrine to preclude the Government from introducing evidence which relies on facts previously determined in the defendant's favor by an acquittal.

The Court refuses to apply the collateral estoppel doctrine in this case for two reasons. First, it asserts that petitioner failed to carry his burden of proving that the issue on which he sought to foreclose relitigation was decided in his favor by the first acquittal. More importantly, the Court refuses to apply the collateral estoppel doctrine when facts underlying a prior acquittal are used as evidence of another offense. Both the Court's conclusions are inconsistent with the purposes of the collateral estoppel rule.

The Court first asserts that petitioner did not prove that the issue on which he sought to foreclose relitigation "was actually decided in the first proceeding." The Court's summary conclusion that the defendant should bear the burden of proof when invoking the collateral estoppel doctrine fails to serve the purposes of the doctrine and the Double Jeopardy Clause in general. Since the doctrine serves to protect defendants against governmental overreaching, the Government should bear the burden of proving that the issue it seeks to relitigate was not decided in the defendant's favor by the prior acquittal. As we noted in *Ashe,* because criminal verdicts are general verdicts, it is usually difficult to determine the precise route of the jury's reasoning and the basis on which the verdict rests. By putting the burden on the defendant to prove what issues were "actually decided," the Court essentially denies the protection of collateral estoppel to those defendants who affirmatively contest more than one issue or who put the Government to its burden of proof with respect to all elements of the offense. . . .

Even assuming that petitioner was properly required to bear the burden of proof, I conclude that petitioner carried it in this case. Vena Henry testified that petitioner had entered her home wearing a mask and carrying a gun but that, after a struggle in which she pulled off the mask, he ran away. There is every reason to believe that the jury rested its verdict on the belief that petitioner was not present in the Henry home. Petitioner was charged with such a wide array of offenses relating to the Henry incident that no other conclusion is "rationally conceivable." *Ashe,* 397 U.S., at 445, 90 S. Ct., at 1195. For example, if the jury had acquitted petitioner of attempted robbery because he lacked the requisite intent, it would still have found him guilty of a weapons offense. Neither the comments of the trial judge in this trial that petitioner had not "seriously contested" the issue of identity in the Henry trial but had stated a general defense, nor the prosecutor's statement in this case that petitioner's codefendant in the Henry trial had admitted being in the house, provides a sufficient basis on which to conclude that the issue of identity was not resolved in petitioner's favor by the acquittal. Thus, if collateral estoppel applies to the evidentiary use of facts, the Government should not have been allowed to introduce Henry's testimony.

The Court holds, however, that collateral estoppel does not apply when facts previously found in a defendant's favor are later introduced as evidence of a second offense. The Court excepts from the normal rule of criminal collateral estoppel those situations when the jury can

consider the facts under a lower standard of proof in the second proceeding than in the first trial. The Court endorses this exception without any consideration of the purposes underlying the collateral estoppel
doctrine; it is not surprising that the Court's holding reflects an unrealistic view of the risks and burdens imposed on the defendant when
facts relating to a prior offense for which defendant has been acquitted
are introduced in a subsequent criminal proceeding.

As the Court notes, we have held that an acquittal in a criminal case
does not bar subsequent civil forfeiture actions for the same transaction
because the acquittal "merely proves the existence of a reasonable doubt
as to [the defendant's] guilt." . . . However, those forfeiture cases involved civil remedial measures rather than criminal punishment. . . . We
have never before applied such reasoning to a successive criminal prosecution in which the Government seeks to punish the defendant and
hinges that punishment at least in part on a criminal act for which the
defendant has been acquitted. Indeed, in *Ashe* we indicated to the contrary: " 'It is much too late to suggest that [collateral estoppel] is not
fully applicable to a former judgment in a criminal case, . . . because
the judgment may reflect only a belief that the Government had not
met the higher burden of proof exacted in such cases for the Government's evidence as a whole. . . .' " We have always recognized a distinction between governmental action intended to punish and that which
is not, see, e.g., United States v. Halper, 490 U.S. 435, 109 S. Ct. 256,
102 L. Ed. 2d 244 (1989) (Double Jeopardy Clause implicated when
civil fine is punitive); United States v. Salerno, 481 U.S. 739, 746-747,
107 S. Ct. 2095, 2101, 95 L. Ed. 2d 697 (1987) (upholding Bail Reform
Act as regulatory rather than punitive measure). Thus, it would be consistent to hold that the collateral estoppel doctrine applies in the criminal (or quasi-criminal) context and not in the civil; when the
Government seeks to punish a defendant, the concern for fairness is
much more acute. Whenever a defendant is forced to relitigate the facts
underlying a prior offense for which he has been acquitted, there is a
risk that the jury erroneously will decide that he is guilty of that offense.
That risk is heightened because the jury is required to conclude that
the defendant committed the prior offense only by a preponderance of
the evidence.

The fact that the prior offense is used as evidence of the presently
charged offense raises concerns about the reliability of the jury's ultimate conclusion that the defendant committed the presently charged
offense. These concerns stem in large part from the inherent danger
of evidence relating to an extrinsic criminal offense. First, "[o]ne of the
dangers inherent in the admission of extrinsic offense evidence is that
the jury may convict the defendant not for the offense charged but for
the extrinsic offense. This danger is particularly great where . . . the
extrinsic activity was not the subject of a conviction; the jury may feel

the defendant should be punished for that activity even if he is not guilty of the offense charged." United States v. Beechum, 582 F.2d 898, 914 (C.A.5 1978) (en banc) (citations omitted). Alternatively, there is the danger that the evidence "may lead [the jury] to conclude that, having committed a crime of the type charged, [the defendant] is likely to repeat it." Ibid. Thus, the fact that the defendant is forced to relitigate his participation in a prior criminal offense under a low standard of proof combined with the inherently prejudicial nature of such evidence increases the risk that the jury erroneously will convict the defendant of the presently charged offense.

The Court's only response is that the defendant is free to introduce evidence to rebut the contention that he committed the prior offense. This response, of course, underscores the flaw in the Court's reasoning: introduction of this type of evidence requires the defendant to mount a second defense to an offense for which he has been acquitted. That the facts relating to the prior offense are used only as evidence of another crime does not reduce the burden on the defendant; he is still required to defend against the prior charges. Moreover, because of the significance a jury may place on evidence of a prior criminal offense, presenting a defense against that offense may be as burdensome as defending against the presently charged offense. Finally, since the lower standard of proof makes it easier for the jury to conclude that the defendant committed the prior offense, the defendant is essentially forced to present affirmative evidence to rebut the contention that he committed that offense.

The Court today adds a powerful new weapon to the Government's arsenal. The ability to relitigate the facts relating to an offense for which the defendant has been acquitted benefits the Government because there are many situations in which the defendant will not be able to present a second defense because of the passage of time, the expense, or some other factor. Indeed there is no discernible limit to the Court's rule; the defendant could be forced to relitigate these facts in trial after trial. . . .

UNITED STATES v. BEECHUM
582 F.2d 898 (5th Cir. 1978), cert. denied, 440 U.S. 920 (1979)

TJOFLAT, J. This case comes before the court en banc for reconsideration of this circuit's doctrine on the admissibility of offenses extrinsic to a defendant's indictment to prove his criminal intent.[1] That doctrine,

1. We shall use the term "extrinsic offense" to denote an "offense" for which the defendant is not charged in the indictment that is the subject of the case sub judice. Commentators and cases have referred to such offenses as "prior" or "similar" offenses. We choose to avoid the connotations carried by these more commonly used terms for the following reasons.

deriving in part from the case of United States v. Broadway, 477 F.2d 991 (5th Cir. 1973), requires that the essential physical elements of the extrinsic offense include those of the offense charged and that each of these elements be proved by plain, clear, and convincing evidence. We are here called upon to determine the effect of the recently enacted Federal Rules of Evidence on this doctrine, an issue expressly reserved in a number of our cases decided prior to the panel opinion in this case. The panel hearing this case was of the opinion, Judge Gee dissenting, that *Broadway* and its progeny survived intact the enactment of the rules. United States v. Beechum, 555 F.2d 487, 504-08 (5th Cir. 1977). With deference to the panel, we must disagree.

A jury convicted Orange Jell Beechum, a substitute letter carrier for the United States Postal Service, of unlawfully possessing an 1890 silver dollar that he knew to be stolen from the mails, in violation of 18 U.S.C. §1708 (1976). To establish that Beechum intentionally and unlawfully possessed the silver dollar, the Government introduced into evidence two Sears, Roebuck & Co. credit cards found in Beechum's wallet when he was arrested. Neither card was issued to Beechum, and neither was signed. The Government also introduced evidence indicating that the cards had been mailed some ten months prior to Beechum's arrest to two different addresses on routes he had serviced. The propriety of the admission of this evidence is the primary issue in this appeal. . . .

The Government indicted Beechum on one count for unlawfully possessing the silver dollar. Argument at the preliminary hearing indicated that the primary issue in the case would be whether Beechum harbored the requisite intent to possess the silver dollar unlawfully. Defense counsel, by motion in limine heard in the absence of the jury, sought to exclude the credit cards as irrelevant and prejudicial. The court overruled the motion, in part on the basis that the cards were relevant to the issue of intent.

In its case in chief, the Government introduced the credit cards and explained the circumstances surrounding their obtention. . . .

In anticipation that Beechum would claim that he sought to turn in the silver dollar, the Government called to the stand Beechum's super-

---

The principles governing extrinsic offense evidence are the same whether that offense occurs before or after the offense charged. The term "prior offense" is therefore unnecessarily restrictive and misleading.

"Similar offense" is a phrase that assumes the conclusion that extrinsic offenses are admissible only if similar to the offense charged. Although in a technical sense this is true, the common connotations of the word are misleading. The meaning and significance of similarity depends on the issue to which the extrinsic offense evidence is addressed. Therefore, to avoid an ambiguous application of the term, we shall speak of similarity only when its meaning is clear in the context.

We use the term "offense" to include "other crimes, wrongs, or acts," as set forth in Fed. R. Evid. 404(b). Our analysis applies whenever the extrinsic activity reflects adversely on the character of the defendant, regardless whether that activity might give rise to criminal liability.

visor, Mr. Cox. Cox testified that he was in the view of Beechum on several occasions, and, indeed, that he had taken mail directly from Beechum.

At the close of the Government's case in chief, the defense moved for a directed verdict of acquittal, alleging that the Government had failed to come forward with sufficient evidence "to establish that Mr. Bonner [sic] possessed the silver dollar with a requisite specific intent that the government is required to establish in this case."

The defense argued that the Government had failed to demonstrate that the credit cards were unlawfully taken from the mail or that Beechum possessed the cards without authorization. The motion was overruled.

At this time defense counsel indicated to the court that Beechum would take the stand and would testify "as to matters concerning the offense for which he is charged," but that he would invoke the fifth amendment as to any questions concerning the credit cards. The defense sought a ruling that the Government be precluded from asking Beechum any question about the cards; the rationale was that the defendant should not be required to invoke his fifth amendment privilege in the presence of the jury. The court declined so to limit the prosecution and indicated that Beechum would have to invoke the amendment in response to the questions he did not wish to answer.

On direct examination Beechum testified that the silver dollar fell out of the mailbox as he was raking out the mail and that he picked it up and placed it first in his shirt pocket, and later (after it had fallen out) in his hip pocket, where he claimed to keep his change. Beechum also testified that, upon return to the postal station, he intended to turn in the silver dollar to Cox but that he could not find Cox. Beechum also stated that he was not leaving the station when he was arrested. No mention was made of the credit cards.

On cross-examination the Government asked Beechum if the credit cards were in his wallet when he was arrested. Defense counsel objected on the basis that inquiry about the cards was outside the scope of cross-examination, and the court overruled the objection. On reassertion of the question, Beechum invoked his fifth amendment rights, but the prosecutor continued questioning on the subject of the cards. This occasioned repeated invocation of the fifth amendment by Beechum and vehement objection by defense counsel. Eventually, Beechum did admit to stating shortly after his arrest that the inspector could "answer his own questions" when the inspector quizzed him about the cards and that the only credit cards he had were his own. . . .

A.   SCOPE OF CROSS-EXAMINATION

Beechum took the stand at trial to explain his possession of the silver dollar. He claimed that he came upon it innocently when he collected the mail from the box in which the test letter was placed. He testified that he placed the coin in his hip pocket, with the rest of his change, after it fell out of his shirt pocket. Beechum explained that he searched for his supervisor, Cox, so that he could properly relinquish the coin but that Cox was nowhere to be found. Clearly, Beechum was saying that he did not intend to possess the coin unlawfully because he obtained it innocently and intended to give it to the proper authority.

At the time of his arrest, however, Beechum was carrying in his wallet the credit cards of two other persons. If Beechum wrongfully possessed these cards, the plausibility of his story about the coin is appreciably diminished. Therefore, assuming that it could be established that the cards were wrongfully possessed by Beechum, they were relevant to the issue of Beechum's intent to commit the crime for which he was charged. Fed. R. Evid. 401.

The scope of proper cross-examination is set forth in Fed. R. Evid. 611(b), which provides as follows:

> *Scope of cross-examination.* Cross-examination should be limited to the subject matter of the direct examination and matters affecting the credibility of the witness. The court may, in the exercise of discretion, permit inquiry into additional matters as if on direct examination.

Implicit in the rule is that all evidence relevant to the subject matter of direct examination is within the scope of cross-examination. See McCormick, Evidence §30, at 57-58 (2d ed. 1972). Of course, this is not to say that all such relevant evidence is admissible, for the rules themselves embody policies that exclude evidence even though relevant. E.g., Fed. R. Evid. 403, 404(b). Unless, however, one of these exclusionary policies acts to prohibit the introduction of the credit cards, they are admissible as within the scope of cross-examination because they are relevant to the issue of intent, an issue placed squarely in contention by Beechum's testimony. Moreover, that Beechum did not refer to the cards on direct examination does not render inquiry about them irrelevant and therefore does not preclude the Government's inquiries about them.

B.   REPEATED INVOCATION OF THE FIFTH AMENDMENT

At the close of the Government's case in chief, defense counsel sought a ruling that the prosecutor be prohibited from questioning Beechum about the credit cards because Beechum intended to assert the fifth amendment as to any such questions. The court denied the motion, but Beechum took the stand to profess his innocence despite the court's ruling. As promised, when the prosecutor asked Beechum about the cards, he invoked the fifth amendment. The prosecutor continued to question Beechum concerning the cards, and Beechum continued to assert the privilege. The defense claims this to have created undue prejudice before the jury. We cannot agree.

It is an inveterate principle that a defendant who takes the stand waives his fifth amendment privilege against self-incrimination at least to the extent of cross-examination relevant to issues raised by his testimony. E.g., Brown v. United States, 356 U.S. 148, 155-56 (1958); Powers v. United States, 223 U.S. 303 (1912); United States v. Pate, 357 F.2d 911, 915 (7th Cir. 1966). Whether a defendant waives the privilege to the full scope of cross-examination permissible under the Federal Rules is an issue we need not determine. As we shall show, however, the cross-examination in this case comes well within the scope of matters that a defendant is deemed to waive when he takes the stand. The rationale behind this waiver rule is of equal pertinence to the extrinsic offense issue in this case; therefore, we briefly explicate that rationale below.

Truth is the essential objective of our adversary system of justice. Of course, the search for truth is in certain instances subordinated to higher values. Indeed, the privilege against self-incrimination ordinarily represents such a value. But where the defendant takes the stand to offer his version of the facts, "the interests of the [Government] and regard for the function of courts of justice to ascertain the truth become relevant, and prevail in the balance of considerations determining the scope and limits of the privilege against self-incrimination." Brown v. United States, 356 U.S. 148, 156 (1958). To allow a defendant to testify with impunity on matters he chooses and in a manner he chooses is a "positive invitation to mutilate the truth a party offers to tell." Id.; accord, Fitzpatrick v. United States, 178 U.S. 304, 316 (1900). The defendant therefore is deemed to waive the privilege, at least with respect to matters about which he testifies, and the Government is entitled to subject his testimony to the acid test of adverse cross-examination.

Here, Beechum sought to attain precisely what the waiver rule seeks to prohibit. His objective was to testify that he intended to give the silver dollar to his supervisor without having to explain the possession of two credit cards not belonging to him. In this, he was largely successful. Had the Government been allowed to ask Beechum about the credit cards, he would have had to explain why he would turn in the coin but keep the cards. Any answer would have borne directly on the issue of intent, and the jury was entitled to consider such highly probative testimony.

The questions the Government sought to ask Beechum concerned matters within the letter and the spirit of the waiver rule. The court below erroneously permitted Beechum to invoke the fifth amendment and avoid response. Not satisfied with this, Beechum contends that he was unduly prejudiced by having to assert the amendment repeatedly. He claims that the prejudice was aggravated because the Government knew that the questions would evoke the assertion of the privilege. We find these contentions without merit.

It is impermissibly prejudicial for the Government to attempt to influence the jury by calling a witness it knows will invoke the fifth amendment. United States v. Ritz, 548 F.2d 510 (5th Cir. 1977); United States v. Maloney, 262 F.2d 535 (2d Cir. 1959). Moreover, where the government witness indicates beforehand that he will invoke the privilege, the court may properly refuse to allow him to testify before the jury. United States v. Lacouture, 495 F.2d 1237 (5th Cir.), cert. denied, 419 U.S. 1053 (1974). But this is not such a case. Here the *defendant* took the stand, knowing full well that the Government would inquire about the cards because the court had refused to prohibit that inquiry. Any prejudice deriving from the invocation of the privilege is therefore attributable to Beechum's decision to testify. Indeed, Beechum can hardly complain; if the court had ruled correctly and not allowed him to invoke the fifth amendment, he could have refused to respond only on peril of contempt. See United States v. Brannon, 546 F.2d 1242, 1247 (5th Cir. 1977). Moreover, in that instance the Government would have been entitled to comment on Beechum's refusal to answer, see Caminetti v. United States, 242 U.S. 470 (1917), notwithstanding the prohibition on such comment where the privilege is properly invoked. Griffin v. California, 380 U.S. 609 (1965). Beechum achieved essentially what he desired, refusal to testify concerning the cards, without subjection to contempt or comment. He surely cannot successfully claim undue prejudice on this basis.

C. The Extrinsic Offense

At the time of his arrest, Beechum possessed a silver dollar and two credit cards, none of which belonged to him. The only contested issue concerning the silver dollar was whether Beechum intended to turn it in, as he claimed, or to keep it for himself. Apparently, he had possessed the credit cards for some time, perhaps ten months, prior to his arrest. The obvious question is why would Beechum give up the silver dollar if he kept the credit cards. In this case, the Government was entitled to an answer.

It is derogative of the search for truth to allow a defendant to tell his story of innocence without facing him with evidence impeaching that story. A basic premise of our adversary system of justice is that the truth is best attained by requiring a witness to explain contrary evidence if he can. As we have seen, for this reason the defendant who chooses to testify waives his fifth amendment privilege with respect to relevant cross-examination. This is not to say that merely by taking the stand a defendant opens himself to the introduction of evidence that is relevant solely to his propensity to commit bad acts or crimes. But where the defendant testifies to controvert an element of the Government's case, such as intent, to which the extrinsic offense is highly relevant, the integrity of the judicial process commands that the defendant be faced with that offense.

In this case, the jury was entitled to assess the credibility of Beechum's explanation but was deprived of the most effective vehicle for determining the veracity of Beechum's story when the judge erroneously allowed Beechum to invoke the fifth amendment and avoid the critical question on cross-examination. The Government was relegated to the inferences the jury might draw from the credit cards themselves and the additional evidence relating to them. . . .

. . . The directly applicable rule is Fed. R. Evid. 404(b). The rule follows the venerable principle that evidence of extrinsic offenses should not be admitted solely to demonstrate the defendant's bad character. Even though such evidence is relevant, because a man of bad character is more likely to commit a crime than one not, the principle prohibits such evidence because it is inherently prejudicial. See, e.g., Michelson v. United States, 335 U.S. 469, 475-76 (1948). Without an issue other than mere character to which the extrinsic offenses are relevant, the probative value of those offenses is deemed insufficient in all cases to outweigh the inherent prejudice. Where, however, the extrinsic offense evidence is relevant to an issue such as intent, it may well be that the evidence has probative force that is not substantially outweighed by its inherent prejudice. If this is so, the evidence may be admissible.

What the rule calls for is essentially a two-step test. First, it must be determined that the extrinsic offense evidence is relevant to an issue other than the defendant's character. Second, the evidence must possess probative value that is not substantially outweighed by its undue prejudice and must meet the other requirements of Rule 403. See Rule 404(b) Other Crimes Evidence: The Need for a Two-Step Analysis, 71 Nw. U.L. Rev. 636 (1976). . . .

As we have stated, the central concern of rule 403 is whether the probative value of the evidence sought to be introduced is "substantially outweighed by the danger of unfair prejudice." . . . One of the dangers inherent in the admission of extrinsic offense evidence is that the jury may convict the defendant not for the offense charged but for the extrinsic offense. . . . The touchstone of the trial judge's analysis in this context should be whether the Government has proved the extrinsic offense sufficiently to allow the jury to determine that the defendant possessed the same state of mind at the time he committed the extrinsic offense as he allegedly possessed when he committed the charged offense. Forcing the Government to "overpersuade" the jury that the defendant committed an offense of substantial similarity engenders excessive and unnecessary prejudice. . . .

Probity in this context is not an absolute; its value must be determined with regard to the extent to which the defendant's unlawful intent is established by other evidence, stipulation, or inference. It is the incremental probity of the evidence that is to be balanced against its potential for undue prejudice. Thus, if the Government has a strong case on the intent issue, the extrinsic offense may add little and consequently will be excluded more readily. If the defendant's intent is not contested, then the incremental probative value of the extrinsic offense is inconsequential when compared to its prejudice; therefore, in this circumstance the evidence is uniformly excluded. In measuring the probative value of the evidence, the judge should consider the overall similarity of the extrinsic and charged offenses. If they are dissimilar except for the common element of intent, the extrinsic offense may have little probative value to counterbalance the inherent prejudice of this type of evidence. Of course, equivalence of the elements of the charged and extrinsic offenses is not required. But the probative value of the extrinsic offense correlates positively with its likeness to the offense charged.[20] Whether the extrinsic offense is sufficiently similar in its physical elements so that its probative value is not substantially outweighed by its undue prejudice is a matter within the sound discretion of the trial judge. The judge should also consider how much time separates the extrinsic and charged offenses: temporal remoteness depreciates the probity of the extrinsic offense.

We shall now apply the precepts we have set forth to the facts of this case. As we have demonstrated above, the credit card evidence is relevant to Beechum's intent with respect to the silver dollar. That Beechum possessed the credit cards with illicit intent diminishes the likelihood that at the same moment he intended to turn in the silver dollar. If there is sufficient evidence to establish that Beechum wrongfully possessed the credit cards, the requirement of the first step under rule 404(b), that the evidence be relevant to an issue other than propensity, is met. This is so even if the evidence were insufficient for a finding that the cards were stolen from the mail. As we have said, relevancy is established once the identity of the significant state of mind is established. The similarity of the physical elements of the extrinsic and charged offenses is a measure of probity.

The standard for determining whether the evidence is sufficient for a finding that Beechum wrongfully possessed the credit cards is provided by rule 104(b): whether the evidence would support such a finding by the jury. We think the evidence in the record clearly supports a finding that Beechum possessed the credit cards with the intent not to relinquish them to their rightful owners. Beechum possessed the credit

20. It is true as well that the more closely the extrinsic offense resembles the charged offense, the greater the prejudice to the defendant. The likelihood that the jury will convict the defendant because he is the kind of person who commits this particular type of crime or because he was not punished for the extrinsic offense increases with the increasing likeliness of the offenses. Of course, it is true that this prejudice is likely to be less when the extrinsic activity is not of a criminal nature. . . .

cards of two different individuals. Neither card had been signed by the person to whom it was issued. When asked about the cards, Beechum answered first that the only cards he had were his own. When confronted with the credit cards, which were obviously not his own, Beechum responded that they had never been used. He refused to respond further because the inspector "had all the answers." The logical inference from this statement is that Beechum was attempting to mitigate his culpability, having been caught red-handed. The undisputed evidence indicated that he could have possessed the cards for some ten months. The jury would have been wholly justified in finding that Beechum possessed these cards with the intent permanently to deprive the owners of them. This is all the rules require the court to determine to establish the relevancy of the extrinsic offense evidence.

We move now to the second step of the rule 404(b) analysis, the application of rule 403. The incremental probity of the extrinsic offense evidence in this case approaches its intrinsic value. Indeed, the posture of this case and the nature of the Government's proof with respect to the intent issue present perhaps the most compelling circumstance for the admission of extrinsic offense evidence. From the very inception of trial, it was clear that the crucial issue in the case would be Beechum's intent in possessing the silver dollar. He took the stand to proclaim that he intended to surrender the coin to his supervisor. The issue of intent was therefore clearly drawn, and the policies of justice that require a defendant to explain evidence that impugns his exculpatory testimony were in full force. As we have seen, these policies dictate that a defendant waive his fifth amendment privilege against self-incrimination as to cross-examination relevant to his testimony. Where a privilege so central to our notions of fairness and justice yields to the search for truth, we should not lightly obstruct that quest. The credit card evidence bore directly on the plausibility of Beechum's story; justice called for its admission.

That the posture of this case demanded the admission of the credit card evidence is reinforced by the nature of the Government's proof on the issue of intent apart from that evidence. This proof consisted of the following. The Government called Cox, Beechum's supervisor, who testified that Beechum had had several opportunities to surrender the coin to him. Beechum denied this, and called two fellow employees who testified that Beechum had asked them if they had seen Cox. Absent the credit card evidence, the issue would have been decided wholly by the jury's assessment of the credibility of these witnesses. The Government, therefore, did not make out such a strong case of criminal intent that the credit card evidence would have been of little incremental probity. In fact, the credit card evidence may have been determinative.

Having examined at length the circumstances of this case, we conclude that the credit card evidence meets the requirements of rule 403.

Therefore, the conditions imposed by the second step of the analysis under rule 404(b) have been met, and the extrinsic offense evidence in this case was properly admitted at trial.

GOLDBERG, J., with whom GODBOLD, SIMPSON, MORGAN and RONEY, JJ., join, dissenting: . . .

Another problem with the majority's interpretation of the vague language in Rule 404(b) is that it conflicts with the specific language in Rules 608 and 609. Suppose, for example, that Beechum had been convicted of fraudulent use of credit cards 10 years before his trial for the coin theft. Under Rule 609, if Beechum took the stand his credibility could be impeached with evidence of the prior conviction only if the probative value of the prior offense *substantially* outweighed its prejudicial impact on the jury. If the conviction had been more recent than 10 years ago, then the test would be a simple weighing of probativeness and prejudice.

Next, suppose that the evidence of the prior offense were clear and convincing, but that the defendant had never been convicted for it. In this case, Rule 608 would forbid *any* admission of the evidence of the prior offense except for what could be elicited from the defendant on the stand. If the defendant chose to exercise his Fifth Amendment right of silence, then no evidence of the prior offense could reach the jury.

Now, finally, consider the result under the majority's reading of Rule 404(b). Here the evidence of a prior offense is independently admissible to the jury,[6] as long as its probative value is not substantially outweighed by its prejudicial impact. The prior offense need not be proved beyond a reasonable doubt, as in Rule 609, nor even clearly and convincingly, as might be the case under Rule 608, but rather only to the minimal Rule 104 standard, i.e. where a reasonable jury might find the defendant committed the crime. This leads to a bizarre anomaly. According to the majority, the government under Rule 404(b) can submit with ease prejudicial, flimsy evidence of an extrinsic offense, but under Rule 609, where the crime was proved beyond a reasonable doubt, the admissions standards are much stricter. Under Rule 608, the evidence is inadmissible entirely except from the defendant's own mouth, even if the evidence of the other crime is clear and convincing, or established beyond a reasonable doubt.[7] You might say then that, for purposes of

6. That is, the government can submit it directly to the jury, whether or not the defendant takes the stand, and does not have to elicit it from the defendant on the stand, as in Rule 608.

7. The majority might try to explain this by asserting that impeachment evidence of a criminal defendant is generally less probative of guilt than evidence of an element of the crime, such as intent. We find this argument less than convincing. Inferring intent in one crime from the defendant's behavior in a totally unrelated crime seems to us at least as tenuous and unprobative as evidence that a defendant is lying on the stand. The 609/404 distinction is especially flimsy where the defendant is testifying about his intent. Where extremely tenuous

admitting extrinsic offense evidence, the majority of this court may at times presume a defendant guilty until he is proven guilty beyond a reasonable doubt, at which point the court may begin presuming him innocent. . . .

United States v. Beechum illustrates the often indistinct distinction between character evidence offered for the purpose of proving an element of the crime charged, i.e. Beechum's intent in possessing the dollar coin, and evidence tending to cast doubt on the truthfulness of a witness's testimony, i.e. Beechum's testimony that he did not intend to keep the silver dollar. It is sometimes helpful to ask why the evidence of the prior act tends to make us disbelieve the defendant's testimony. Is it because the evidence of prior acts tends to make it less likely in the informed judgment of the jury that events could have transpired as asserted by the defendant? Knowing that Beechum had hung on to the credit cards for several months, is it harder to believe that he in fact had the intention to return the coin? Or does the knowledge of the prior events make us less likely to believe the testimony because we think that a person who would commit such acts is less likely to be truthful than someone who had not. Does the knowledge that Beechum had taken the credit cards make him less trustworthy as a witness in our views so that we would view whatever he said with some suspicion? One can say that if the factfinder's tendency is to consider the evidence with respect to the likelihood of the facts asserted, the admissibility of the evidence should be analyzed under Rule 404. If the factfinder would use the evidence of prior actions to discredit the actor as a later witness, the admissibility of the evidence should be analyzed under Rule 608. And if both kinds of inferences are likely, the evidence must be analyzed under both rules and the jury appropriately instructed. If the prior acts evidence tends to make whatever the witness is asserting on the stand so incredible that the factfinder concludes that he is lying on the stand, and hence disbelieves this or other testimony as that of a liar, both chains of inference are at work. The 404-type inference makes us disbelieve the facts asserted as inconsistent in our experience with the prior acts evidence. Beechum's assertion that he intended to return the coin could be found to be incredible in light of his retention of the credit cards. The jury's consequent assessment of Beechum as a liar comes

---

evidence is involved, we see little difference between trying to prove that the defendant is lying, and trying to prove that what he is saying is a lie.

Moreover, probativeness is a factor taken into account in the balancing process itself. If impeachment evidence is inherently less probative, then this can be fully reflected by its weight in the balancing test itself without also requiring that the test be weighted specially against the evidence.

not from the prior acts, but from his present testimony, which cannot be reconciled with the prior acts. This assessment as a liar may not only color the jury's appraisal of his testimony about his intent with the coin, it may also carry over to impeach his testimony on other topics. At this point we have the chain of reasoning regulated by Rule 608.

Problem: "A Nice Piece of Change"

Action by a real estate broker, Leon Easerly, for his brokerage commission. New York's statute of frauds excepted real estate brokers' oral agreements for commission from the normal requirement that such contracts be in writing. Easerly claims that Letwin, the defendant, orally commissioned him to negotiate the purchase of a shopping center owned by a Mr. Odessa. At trial Easerly testifies that after he persuaded Odessa to accept Letwin's offer for the property, hence earning his commission, Letwin backed out of the deal. Letwin claims that he never made any arrangement with Easerly. Moreover, Letwin's lawyer has discovered that in the last two years Easerly has brought eight very similar lawsuits against others in the New York area, all based on alleged oral contracts.

During the direct examination Easerly testifies that Letwin promised him, "Leon, don't worry. Listen, you put that deal over, and there's going to be a nice piece of change for you."

On cross-examination Letwin's lawyer tries to bring out these eight previous lawsuits and in an offer of proof states that the trial transcripts of them show Easerly claiming that at the critical moment the prospective buyer or seller said, "There's a nice piece of change in it for you."

Should defendant's offer of proof be accepted? What factors militate for and against receiving evidence of the eight other lawsuits?

Does the evidence relate, first, to proving an element of the acts at issue in the case (intent in *Beechum;* plan, preparation, or modus operandi in the brokerage case) and then, second, depending on what you conclude happened, to credibility? Or is the evidence in the problem "A Nice Piece of Change" pure credibility evidence? This case is harder than *Beechum*, because Easerly's M.O. (if one concludes he is perpetrating a scam) involves false testimony in court. Exposing this is very close to exposing him as a liar—Rule 608/609 material.

Thus, this offer of evidence can be approached as either similar acts evidence or evidence of credibility. Viewed as similar acts evidence, it may be relevant under Rule 401 in a way that is roughly equivalent to Rule 404(b) evidence of a plan or modus operandi (the Brides in the *Baths* case). The striking similarity of Easerly's past testimony makes the evidence highly probative. The question is whether the jury can use this evidence without making any inferences about Easerly's general character, so that any propensity considerations are a by-product that can be dealt with through a Rule 105 limiting instruction. Under the two-step analysis, this evidence would also be subject to a determination under Rule 403 that its probative value was not outweighed by waste of time, confusion, or prejudice.

The evidence would, on this theory, be offered to prove what happened on the occasion of the litigated event, and not for the purpose of attacking Easerly's credibility. This would mean that Letwin would be permitted to offer proof of the prior incidents regardless of whether Easerly took the stand, and would be able to prove the prior incidents with extrinsic proof (that is, by offering transcripts of Easerly's prior testimony and by calling the other real estate men whom Easerly had allegedly bilked). Of course, whether or not the prior incidents should have been admitted on this theory involves a similar acts analysis that would be extremely time-consuming and confusing—hence the reluctance of most judges to allow it.

Suppose that the judge ruled that the evidence of the prior incidents was *not* admissible on this theory because proof of the prior incidents would be extraordinarily time consuming and would tend to confuse the issues and lead the jury astray. Testimony about the prior suits could also be properly elicited on cross-examination under Rule 608 to attack the credibility of the witness, subject to the discretion of the trial judge. The theory of the doctrine of chances applies to testing the witness's credibility, and hence the form of proof would be much more efficient —simply question and answer with the witness without extrinsic proof.

Why only questions and answers on cross-examination? Rule 608(b) disallows introduction of extrinsic evidence of specific instances of conduct of a witness when attacking credibility. Thus, Easerly's prior allegations might be inquired into on cross-examination, but the transcripts of his prior testimony and the testimony of his other victims could not be introduced. This rule against extrinsic evidence is motivated by a desire to restrict the amount of time spent on issues collateral to the trial at hand. While a trial transcript makes the offer of proof less troublesome since it is unlikely that Easerly would claim he did not make the statements attributed to him, not all cases are so simple. Even in this case, however, there are many potential problems. For example, what if Easerly won some of the prior suits and lost some?

B.   Exceptions to the Propensity Rule

MICHELSON v. UNITED STATES
335 U.S. 469 (1948)

JACKSON, J. In 1947 petitioner Michelson was convicted of bribing a federal revenue agent. The Government proved a large payment by accused to the agent for the purpose of influencing his official action. The defendant, as a witness on his own behalf, admitted passing the money but claimed it was done in response to the agent's demands, threats, solicitations, and inducements that amounted to entrapment. It is enough for our purposes to say that determination of the issue turned on whether the jury should believe the agent or the accused.

On direct examination of defendant, his own counsel brought out that, in 1927, he had been convicted of a misdemeanor having to do with trading in counterfeit watch dials. On cross-examination it appeared that in 1930, in executing an application for a license to deal in second-hand jewelry, he answered "No" to the question whether he had theretofore been arrested or summoned for any offense.

Defendant called five witnesses to prove that he enjoyed a good reputation. Two of them testified that their acquaintance with him extended over a period of about thirty years and the others said they had known him at least half that long. A typical examination in chief was as follows:

Q: Do you know the defendant Michelson?
A: Yes.
Q: How long do you know Mr. Michelson?
A: About 30 years.
Q: Do you know other people who know him?
A: Yes.
Q: Have you had occasion to discuss his reputation for honesty and truthfulness and for being a law-abiding citizen?
A: It is very good.
Q: You have talked to others?
A: Yes.
Q: And what is his reputation?
A: Very good.

These are representative of answers by three witnesses; two others replied, in substance, that they never had heard anything against Michelson.

On cross-examination, four of the witnesses were asked, in substance, this question: "Did you ever hear that Mr. Michelson on March 4, 1927, was convicted of a violation of the trademark law in New York City in regard to watches?" This referred to the twenty-year-old conviction about which defendant himself had testified on direct examination. Two of them had heard of it and two had not.

To four of these witnesses the prosecution also addressed the question the allowance of which, over defendant's objection, is claimed to be reversible error: "Did you ever hear that on October 11, 1920, the defendant, Solomon Michelson, was arrested for receiving stolen goods?"

None of the witnesses appears to have heard of this.

The trial court asked counsel for the prosecution, out of presence of the jury, "Is it a fact according to the best information in your possession, that Michelson was arrested for receiving stolen goods?" Counsel replied that it was, and to support his good faith exhibited a paper record which defendant's counsel did not challenge.

The judge also on three occasions warned the jury, in terms that are not criticized, of the limited purpose for which this evidence was received.[3]

Defendant-petitioner challenges the right of the prosecution so to cross-examine his character witnesses. The Court of Appeals held that it was permissible. The opinion, however, points out that the practice has been severely criticized and invites us, in one respect, to change the rule.[4] Serious and responsible criticism has been aimed, however, not

3. In ruling on the objection when the question was first asked, the Court said:

". . . I instruct the jury that what is happening now is this: the defendant has called character witnesses, and the basis for the evidence given by those character witnesses is the reputation of the defendant in the community, and since the defendant tenders the issue of his reputation the prosecution may ask the witness if she has heard of various incidents in his career. I say to you that regardless of her answer you are not to assume that the incidents asked about actually took place. All that is happening is that this witness' standard of opinion of the reputation of the defendant is being tested. Is that clear?"

In overruling the second objection to the question the Court said:

"Again I say to the jury there is no proof that Mr. Michelson was arrested for receiving stolen goods in 1920, there isn't any such proof. All this witness has been asked is whether he had heard of that. There is nothing before you on that issue. Now would you base your decision on the case fairly in spite of the fact that that question has been asked? You would? All right."

The charge included the following:

"In connection with the character evidence in the case I permitted a question whether or not the witness knew that in 1920 this defendant had been arrested for receiving stolen goods. I tried to give you the instruction then that that question was permitted only to test the standards of character evidence that these character witnesses seemed to have. There isn't any proof in the case that could be produced before you legally within the rules of evidence that this defendant was arrested in 1920 for receiving stolen goods, and that fact you are not to hold against him; nor are you to assume what the consequences of that arrest were. You just drive it from your mind so far as he is concerned, and take it into consideration only in weighing the evidence of the character witnesses."

4. Footnote 8 to that court's opinion reads as follows:

"Wigmore, Evidence (3d ed. 1940) §988, after noting that 'such inquiries are almost universally admitted,' not as 'impeachment by extrinsic testimony of particular acts of misconduct,' but as means of testing the character 'witness' grounds of knowledge,' continues with these comments: 'But the serious objection to them is that practically the above distinction—

alone at the detail now questioned by the Court of Appeals but at common-law doctrine on the whole subject of proof of reputation or character. It would not be possible to appraise the usefulness and propriety of this cross-examination without consideration of the unique practice concerning character testimony, of which such cross-examination is a minor part.

Courts that follow the common-law tradition almost unanimously have come to disallow resort by the prosecution to any kind of evidence of a defendant's evil character to establish a probability of his guilt. Not that the law invests the defendant with a presumption of good character, but it simply closes the whole matter of character, disposition and reputation on the prosecution's case-in-chief. The state may not show defendant's prior trouble with the law, specific criminal acts, or ill name among his neighbors, even though such facts might logically be persuasive that he is by propensity a probable perpetrator of the crime. The inquiry is not rejected because character is irrelevant; on the contrary, it is said to weigh too much with the jury and to so overpersuade them as to prejudge one with a bad general record and deny him a fair opportunity to defend against a particular charge. The overriding policy of excluding such evidence, despite its admitted probative value, is the practical experience that its disallowance tends to prevent confusion of issues, unfair surprise and undue prejudice.

But this line of inquiry firmly denied to the State is opened to the defendant because character is relevant in resolving probabilities of guilt. He may introduce affirmative testimony that the general estimate of his character is so favorable that the jury may infer that he would not be likely to commit the offense charged. This privilege is sometimes valuable to a defendant for this Court has held that such testimony

---

between rumors of such conduct, as affecting reputation, and the fact of it as violating the rule against particular facts — cannot be maintained in the mind of the jury. The rumor of the misconduct, when admitted, goes far, in spite of all theory and of the judge's charge, towards fixing the misconduct as a fact upon the other person, and thus does three improper things, — (1) it violates the fundamental rule of fairness that prohibits the use of such facts, (2) it gets at them by hearsay only, and not by trustworthy testimony, and (3) it leaves the other person no means of defending himself by denial or explanation, such as he would otherwise have had if the rule had allowed that conduct to be made the subject of an issue. Moreover, these are not occurrences of possibility, but of daily practice. This method of inquiry or cross-examination is frequently resorted to by counsel for the very purpose of injuring by indirection a character which they are forbidden directly to attack in that way; they rely upon the mere putting of the question (not caring that it is answered negatively) to convey their covert insinuation. The value of the inquiry for testing purposes is often so small and the opportunities of its abuse by underhand ways are so great that the practice may amount to little more than a mere subterfuge, and should be strictly supervised by forbidding it to counsel who do not use it in good faith.'

"Because, as Wigmore says, the jury almost surely cannot comprehend the judge's limiting instruction, the writer of this opinion wishes that the United States Supreme Court would tell us to follow what appears to be the Illinois rule, i.e., that such questions are improper unless they relate to offenses similar to those for which the defendant is on trial. See Aiken v. People, 183 Ill. 215, 55 N.E. 695; cf. People v. Hannon, 381 Ill. 206, 44 N.E.2d 923."

alone, in some circumstances, may be enough to raise a reasonable doubt of guilt and that in the federal courts a jury in a proper case should be so instructed.

When the defendant elects to initiate a character inquiry, another anomalous rule comes into play. Not only is he permitted to call witnesses to testify from hearsay, but indeed such a witness is not allowed to base his testimony on anything but hearsay. What commonly is called "character evidence" is only such when "character" is employed as a synonym for "reputation." The witness may not testify about defendant's specific acts or courses of conduct or his possession of a particular disposition or of benign mental and moral traits; nor can he testify that his own acquaintance, observation, and knowledge of defendant leads to his own independent opinion that defendant possesses a good general or specific character, inconsistent with commission of acts charged. The witness is, however, allowed to summarize what he has heard in the community, although much of it may have been said by persons less qualified to judge than himself. The evidence which the law permits is not as to the personality of defendant but only as to the shadow his daily life has cast in his neighborhood. This has been well described in a different connection as "the slow growth of months and years, the resultant picture of forgotten incidents, passing events, habitual and daily conduct, presumably honest because disinterested, and safer to be trusted because prone to suspect. . . . It is for that reason that such general repute is permitted to be proven. It sums up a multitude of trivial details. It compacts into the brief phrase of a verdict the teaching of many incidents and the conduct of years. It is the average intelligence drawing its conclusion." Finch, J., in Badger v. Badger, 88 N.Y. 546, 552.

While courts have recognized logical grounds for criticism of this type of opinion-based-on-hearsay testimony, it is said to be justified by "overwhelming considerations of practical convenience" in avoiding innumerable collateral issues which, if it were attempted to prove character by direct testimony, would complicate and confuse the trial, distract the minds of jurymen and befog the chief issues in the litigation.

Another paradox in this branch of the law of evidence is that the delicate and responsible task of compacting reputation hearsay into the "brief phrase of a verdict" is one of the few instances in which conclusions are accepted from a witness on a subject in which he is not an expert. However, the witness must qualify to give an opinion by showing such acquaintance with the defendant, the community in which he has lived and the circles in which he has moved, as to speak with authority of the terms in which generally he is regarded. To require affirmative knowledge of the reputation may seem inconsistent with the latitude given to the witness to testify when all he can say of the reputation is that he has "heard nothing against defendant." This is permitted upon assumption that, if no ill is reported of one, his reputation must be good.

But this answer is accepted only from a witness whose knowledge of defendant's habitat and surroundings is intimate enough so that his failure to hear of any relevant ill repute is an assurance that no ugly rumors were about.

Thus the law extends helpful but illogical options to a defendant. Experience taught a necessity that they be counterweighted with equally illogical conditions to keep the advantage from becoming an unfair and unreasonable one. The price a defendant must pay for attempting to prove his good name is to throw open the entire subject which the law has kept closed for his benefit and to make himself vulnerable where the law otherwise shields him. The prosecution may pursue the inquiry with contradictory witnesses to show that damaging rumors, whether or not well-grounded, were afloat—for it is not the man that he is, but the name that he has which is put in issue. Another hazard is that his own witness is subject to cross-examination as to the contents and extent of the hearsay on which he bases his conclusions, and he may be required to disclose rumors and reports that are current even if they do not affect his own conclusion. It may test the sufficiency of his knowledge by asking what stories were circulating concerning events, such as one's arrest, about which people normally comment and speculate. Thus, while the law gives defendant the option to show as a fact that his reputation reflects a life and habit incompatible with commission of the offense charged, it subjects his proof to tests of credibility designed to prevent him from profiting by a mere parade of partisans.

To thus digress from evidence as to the offense to hear a contest as to the standing of the accused, at its best opens a tricky line of inquiry as to a shapeless and elusive subject matter. At its worst it opens a veritable Pandora's box of irresponsible gossip, innuendo and smear. In the frontier phase of our law's development, calling friends to vouch for defendant's good character, and its counterpart—calling the rivals and enemies of a witness to impeach him by testifying that his reputation for veracity was so bad that he was unworthy of belief on his oath—were favorite and frequent ways of converting an individual litigation into a community contest and a trial into a spectacle. Growth of urban conditions, where one may never know or hear the name of his next-door neighbor, have tended to limit the use of these techniques and to deprive them of weight with juries. The popularity of both procedures has subsided, but courts of last resort have sought to overcome danger that the true issues will be obscured and confused by investing the trial court with discretion to limit the number of such witnesses and to control cross-examination. Both propriety and abuse of hearsay reputation testimony, on both sides, depend on numerous and subtle considerations difficult to detect or appraise from a cold record, and therefore rarely and only on clear showing of prejudicial abuse of discretion will Courts of Appeals disturb rulings of trial courts on this subject.

Wide discretion is accompanied by heavy responsibility on trial courts to protect the practice from any misuse. The trial judge was scrupulous to so guard it in the case before us. He took pains to ascertain, out of presence of the jury, that the target of the question was an actual event, which would probably result in some comment among acquaintances if not injury to defendant's reputation. He satisfied himself that counsel was not merely taking a random shot at a reputation imprudently exposed or asking a groundless question to waft an unwarranted innuendo into the jury box.

The question permitted by the trial court, however, involves several features that may be worthy of comment. Its form invited hearsay; it asked about an arrest, not a conviction, and for an offense not closely similar to the one on trial; and it concerned an occurrence many years past.

Since the whole inquiry, as we have pointed out, is calculated to ascertain the general talk of people about defendant, rather than the witness' own knowledge of him, the form of inquiry, "Have you heard?" has general approval, and "Do you know?" is not allowed. [Note the change in FRE 105.—Eds.]

A character witness may be cross-examined as to an arrest whether or not it culminated in a conviction, according to the overwhelming weight of authority. This rule is sometimes confused with that which prohibits cross-examination to credibility by asking a witness whether he himself has been arrested.

Arrest without more does not, in law any more than in reason, impeach the integrity or impair the credibility of a witness. It happens to the innocent as well as the guilty. Only a conviction, therefore, may be inquired about to undermine the trustworthiness of a witness.

Arrest without more may nevertheless impair or cloud one's reputation. False arrest may do that. Even to be acquitted may damage one's good name if the community receives the verdict with a wink and chooses to remember defendant as one who ought to have been convicted. A conviction, on the other hand, may be accepted as a misfortune or an injustice, and even enhance the standing of one who mends his ways and lives it down. Reputation is the net balance of so many debits and credits that the law does not attach the finality to a conviction, when the issue is reputation, that is given to it when the issue is the credibility of the convict.

The inquiry as to an arrest is permissible also because the prosecution has a right to test the qualifications of the witness to bespeak the community opinion. If one never heard the speculations and rumors in which even one's friends indulge upon his arrest, the jury may doubt whether he is capable of giving any very reliable conclusions as to his reputation.

In this case the crime inquired about was receiving stolen goods; the trial was for bribery. The Court of Appeals thought this dissimilarity of offenses too great to sustain the inquiry in logic, though conceding that it is authorized by preponderance of authority. It asks us to substitute the Illinois rule which allows inquiry about arrest, but only for very closely similar if not identical charges, in place of the rule more generally adhered to in this country and in England. We think the facts of this case show the proposal to be inexpedient.

The good character which the defendant had sought to establish was broader than the crime charged and included the traits of "honesty and truthfulness" and "being a law-abiding citizen." Possession of these characteristics would seem as incompatible with offering a bribe to a revenue agent as with receiving stolen goods. The crimes may be unlike, but both alike proceed from the same defects of character which the witnesses said this defendant was reputed not to exhibit. It is not only by comparison with the crime on trial but by comparison with the reputation asserted that a court may judge whether the prior arrest should be made subject of inquiry. By this test the inquiry was permissible. It was proper cross-examination because reports of his arrest for receiving stolen goods, if admitted, would tend to weaken the assertion that he was known as an honest and law-abiding citizen. The cross-examination may take in as much ground as the testimony it is designed to verify. To hold otherwise would give defendant the benefit of testimony that he was honest and law-abiding in reputation when such might not be the fact; the refutation was founded on convictions equally persuasive though not for crimes exactly repeated in the present charge.

The inquiry here concerned an arrest twenty-seven years before the trial. Events a generation old are likely to be lived down and dropped from the present thought and talk of the community and to be absent from the knowledge of younger or more recent acquaintances. The court in its discretion may well exclude inquiry about rumors of an event so remote, unless recent misconduct revived them. But two of these witnesses dated their acquaintance with defendant as commencing thirty years before the trial. Defendant, on direct examination, voluntarily called attention to his conviction twenty years before. While the jury might conclude that a matter so old and indecisive as a 1920 arrest would shed little light on the present reputation and hence propensities of the defendant, we cannot say that, in the context of this evidence and in the absence of objection on this specific ground, its admission was an abuse of discretion.

We do not overlook or minimize the consideration that "the jury almost surely cannot comprehend the judge's limiting instruction," which disturbed the Court of Appeals. The refinements of the evidentiary rules on this subject are such that even lawyers and judges, after study and reflection, often are confused, and surely jurors in the hurried and unfamiliar movement of a trial must find them almost unintelligible. However, limiting instructions on this subject are no more difficult to comprehend or apply than those upon various other subjects; for example, instructions that admissions of a co-defendant are to be limited to the question of his guilt and are not to be considered as evidence against other defendants, and instructions as to other problems in the trial of conspiracy charges. A defendant in such a case is powerless to prevent his cause from being irretrievably obscured and confused; but, in cases such as the one before us, the law foreclosed this whole confounding line of inquiry, unless defendant thought the net advantage from opening it up would be with him. Given this option, we think defendants in general and this defendant in particular have no valid complaint at the latitude which existing law allows to the prosecution to meet by cross-examination an issue voluntarily tendered by the defense.

We end, as we began, with the observation that the law regulating the offering and testing of character testimony may merit many criticisms. England and some states have overhauled the practice by statute. But the task of modernizing the long-standing rules on the subject is one of magnitude and difficulty which even those dedicated to law reform do not lightly undertake.

The law of evidence relating to proof of reputation in criminal cases has developed almost entirely at the hands of state courts of last resort, which have such questions frequently before them. This Court, on the other hand, has contributed little to this or to any phase of the law of evidence, for the reason, among others, that it has had extremely rare occasion to decide such issues, as the paucity of citations in this opinion to our own writings attests. It is obvious that a court which can make only infrequent sallies into the field cannot recast the body of case law on this subject in many, many years, even if it were clear what the rules should be.

We concur in the general opinion of courts, textwriters and the profession that much of this law is archaic, paradoxical and full of compromises and compensations by which an irrational advantage to one side is offset by a poorly reasoned counterprivilege to the other. But somehow it has proved a workable even if clumsy system when moderated by discretionary controls in the hands of a wise and strong trial court. To pull one misshapen stone out of the grotesque structure is more likely simply to upset its present balance between adverse interests than to establish a rational edifice.

The present suggestion is that we adopt for all federal courts a new rule as to cross-examination about prior arrest, adhered to by the courts of only one state and rejected elsewhere. The confusion and error it would engender would seem too heavy a price to pay for an almost imperceptible logical improvement, if any, in a system which is justified, if at all, by accumulated judicial experience rather than abstract logic.

The judgment is affirmed.

Rule 404 states when proof of character may be admitted. Rule 405 attempts to set forth the form such proof may take. How do Rules 403, 404, and 405 relate to each other? How does the question of *when* proof of character can be made relate to the question of *what form* such proof should take? What form of character evidence — reputation, opinion, or specific prior acts — is most probative? Most prejudicial? Most desirable from an objective viewpoint? Do you feel that the use of such evidence can be confined to its permissible purposes by instructions to the jury?

In federal court what type of character evidence may be introduced for purposes other than impeaching a witness's credibility:

(1) By the prosecution as part of its case-in-chief;

(2) By the accused as part of its case-in-chief;

(3) By the prosecution on cross-examination of defendant's witnesses;

(4) By the prosecution to rebut the accused's case-in-chief;

(5) By the accused to rehabilitate its case after attack by the prosecution; and

(6) In a civil case, by either side?

What are the reasons and policies behind these rules?

Is the "Illinois rule," discussed in the *Michelson* case, an improvement on the federal rule? Why not exclude character evidence — good and bad — regardless of who offers it, when its only purpose is to prove the evil or saintly character of the accused? Or should all the rules of exclusion and exception be replaced with one rule giving the trial judge discretion, similar to Rule 403? What should the standard of review be on appeal of these issues under the present system or a modified system?

Problem: Proof of the Defendant's Good Character

Charge: robbery.

(1) At *D*'s trial the state calls *W1*, a teller at the bank, who identifies *D* as the robber. The state next calls *W2* and proposes that *W2* testify that he is familiar with *D*'s reputation in the community and that *D*'s reputation is one of a thieving, embezzling, bunko artist. On *D*'s timely objection, what ruling and why? Does the objection call into play the propensity rule?

(2) Assume that *D*'s objection to *W2*'s testimony is sustained and the prosecution rests. *D* calls witness *W3* to testify to *D*'s reputation in the

community as an honest, quiet person. On the district attorney's timely objection, what ruling and why? Does the objection call into play the propensity rule? Should it?

(3) Suppose the district attorney's objection is overruled. *W3* testifies as proposed. On cross-examination may the district attorney ask *W3*—over *D*'s objection—whether *W3* has heard that last year *D* swindled the widow Brown?

(4) After *W3* is through testifying and *D* has presented the rest of her case, should the state be allowed to reopen its case to offer proof of *D*'s prior arrest for armed robbery? Why?

Problem: Proof of the Defendant's Violent Character

Charge: murder by strangulation, bludgeoning, stabbing, and burning.

(1) As part of the state's case-in-chief the district attorney offers the testimony of witness *A* to testify that for the past twenty years she has lived in the same town as *D* and that she knows *D*'s reputation in the community to be that of a vicious bully and troublemaker, prone to violence and breaches of the peace. *D* objects to *A*'s testimony. What ruling and why?

(2) Suppose that *D*'s objection to *A*'s testimony is sustained. The district attorney next offers witness *B* to testify that on May 1, a year ago, *D* committed an armed robbery of *B*. *D* objects to *B*'s testimony. What ruling and why?

(3) Suppose that *D*'s objection to *B*'s testimony is sustained. The district attorney introduces a certified record of *D*'s conviction for armed robbery of *B* one year ago. Should this evidence be admitted over *D*'s objection?

(4) Suppose that *D*'s objection to proof of his prior conviction, on the grounds that the evidence is irrelevant, incompetent, immaterial, and prejudicial, is overruled and the evidence is admitted. *D* is convicted. On appeal, the judgment is affirmed by the state supreme court, which holds that such evidence is admissible to show *D*'s propensity as a habitual criminal, thus affecting the degree of punishment. *D*'s petition for a writ of certiorari to the United States Supreme Court is granted. Has *D* been deprived of due process of law?

Problem: The Mayor

Action against the *D* Tribune for libel, with federal jurisdiction based on diversity of citizenship. *P* alleges that *D* published an article referring to him as "the most corrupt mayor we have had in a long time."

At trial, *D* offers evidence that *P* has been twice convicted of taking bribes and that *P*'s net worth has increased to $20 million during the last 5 years while P has served as the full-time mayor at a salary of $50,000 per year. *P* objects. What ruling and why?

Problem: Child Custody

P and *D* are suing each other for divorce. At issue is the custody and visitation of the couple's two children. Each asserts that she or he is the more fit parent for the children and seeks to prove that the other is unfit as a parent. What kinds of evidence of the "character" of *P* or *D* as a parent can the judge receive to assist her in deciding these issues? How about the following?

a. Evidence that *P* threw a canoe from the roof of the family car to the ground in an angry rage after a quarrel with *D*?
b. Evidence that *D* has the reputation in the community as a conscientious and caring parent?
c. The opinion of one of the children's teachers that *P* is a thoughtful and capable parent?
d. Evidence that on one occasion prior to the trial *D* left one of the children (aged four) alone in an unlocked automobile outside the Post Office for five minutes?

Eloquent as is Justice Jackson's opinion in *Michelson,* he makes the rules relating to proof of character seem even more arbitrary than they are. As *Michelson* and the three problems that follow demonstrate, the rules present a balance between how central proof of character is to the litigation and how much time it takes to prove character. The most compelling way to prove character is by proving a person's specific acts, yet this form of proof can be extremely time consuming. The rules permit this form of proof when character is an essential element of the case. When character is not an essential issue, the rules bar this time-consuming form of proof, limiting proof of character to the less compelling but far more time-efficient forms of reputation and opinion testimony. Thus, Rules 404 and 405 express particularized judgments of the general balance between probity and "confusion of the issues, . . . waste of time, or needless presentation of cumulative evidence" set out in Rule 403. The balance is sometimes struck in favor of total exclusion of character evidence (e.g., in civil cases for purposes of proving what happened on the occasion of the litigated event, as opposed to use of character in attacking the credibility of witnesses). Sometimes, the balance is struck in favor of admissibility (e.g., proof of a defendant's good character in a criminal case) but with the form of proof limited to short-cut second-rate forms of proof, or in favor of admissibility with no restriction on the form of proof (e.g., when character is an essential element of a claim or defense).

The holding of *Michelson* has been codified in the second sentence of Rule 405(a): "On cross-examination, inquiry is allowable into relevant specific instances of conduct." The reasoning behind this approach is that when a defendant introduces evidence of his own good character, in effect he makes the very propensity argument that the prosecution is forbidden from using. This is the accused's choice. The defendant uses reputation evidence to persuade the jury that he is not the kind of person who would commit an act such as the one he is charged with committing. But once raised, the prosecution may not only attack the pertinent character or propensities of the defendant (Rule 404(a)(1)) by calling its own character witness (first sentence of Rule 405(a)), it may also attack the witness attesting to the defendant's good reputation. The attack is either on the witness's knowledge or standards or both. In practice, this response is not very limited since the prosecution may ask questions about virtually any "relevant specific instances of conduct" of the defendant that the prosecutor has a good faith reason for believing occurred.

Problem: Battered Spouse Syndrome

Defendant is on trial for murder. The evidence is that defendant's husband was shot twelve times as he stood in the shower. Defendant does not contest the commission of the act, but pleads self-defense.

Defendant's proof consists of a number of witnesses who will testify that for many years the decedent, a heavy drinker, continually abused the defendant, both physically and psychologically. Defendant also plans to call an expert psychologist who will testify that the defendant suffered from the abused spouse syndrome. The psychologist will also testify that one of the symptoms of abuse spouse syndrome is a constant and frequently triggered fear of further abuse at the hands of the abuser and that in the present case this fear could have caused defendant ultimately to kill the decedent in self-defense. Should this evidence be admitted?

STATE v. CONLOGUE
474 A.2d 167 (Me. 1984)

GLASSMAN, J.—The defendant Christopher Conlogue was convicted by a jury in the Superior Court, Franklin County, of aggravated assault,

17-A M.R.S.A. §208(1983). On appeal from the judgment, he assigns numerous claims of error. Since we find the presiding justice committed reversible error in excluding certain testimony offered by the defendant tending to show the crime had been committed by another person, we sustain the appeal and vacate the judgment of conviction.

I

During the summer of 1981, the defendant and Patricia Easler lived at a camp in Chesterville with Ms. Easler's three young children. Donna Dill, who visited the camp on August 6, 1981, observed what she believed to be abusive treatment of the 1½–year-old Tina Easler by the defendant, and alerted the Department of Human Services. . . .

On September 29, 1981, a joint indictment was returned against the defendant and Patricia Easler, charging each with aggravated assault. Patricia Easler subsequently agreed to plead guilty to a charge of endangering the welfare of a child, 17-A M.R.S.A. §554(1983), and to testify against the defendant, in return for a dismissal of the aggravated assault charge. . . .

The defendant's trial began on October 25, 1982, in the Superior Court, Franklin County. After the State rested, the defendant moved for dismissal. . . . The jury returned a verdict on October 28, 1982, finding the defendant guilty of recklessly causing serious bodily injury to Tina Easler. The defendant's motion for judgment notwithstanding the verdict was denied.

The defendant appeals, assigning error . . . to several evidentiary rulings made by the presiding justice. . . .

II.   EVIDENTIARY RULINGS

The admissibility of evidence is left to the sound discretion of the presiding justice. Generally, the determination of relevance and the determination that the probative value of evidence is outweighed by its danger of unfair prejudice are reviewed on appeal only for an abuse of that discretion. . . .

4.   EXCLUSION OF PROFFERED TESTIMONY

The defendant argues the exclusion of certain testimony of Dr. Lambert and three defense witnesses was erroneous. We agree.

On direct examination by the State, Dr. Lambert testified as to his training and experience with the treatment and diagnosis of child injuries, his training under Dr. Kempe, an international specialist and author of a treatise on "The Battered Child Syndrome," and the acceptance of the battered child syndrome as a diagnosis not only in Franklin County, but in the State of Maine. Dr. Lambert also testified as to the nature and extent of Tina Easler's injuries and his diagnosis of Tina as an "abused battered child."

On cross-examination the doctor testified Patricia Easler told him it was she who had injured Tina. The defendant, out of the presence of the jury, through testimony of Dr. Lambert, then made an offer of proof that Patricia Easler had also told Dr. Lambert she had been an abused child, the details of such abuse, and the doctor's opinion that, consistent with his experience and the teachings and treatise of Dr. Kempe, abused children often become abusive parents. The trial justice deemed this testimony inadmissible as violative of M.R.Evid. 404(a).[1]

The court also ruled inadmissible the testimony of three defense witnesses who, in offers of proof, indicated they would testify they were former neighbors of Patricia Easler and had seen her physically abuse her two older children. The court cited M.R.Evid. 404(a) as grounds for exclusion of this evidence. The defendant argues the exclusion of this testimony prevented him from pursuing a defense strategy of showing that Patricia Easler's confession had been true, and her later recantation false.

We have previously recognized the right of a criminal defendant "in appropriate circumstances . . . to introduce evidence to show that another person committed the crime or had the motive, intent, and opportunity to commit it." State v. LeClair, 425 A.2d 182, 187 (Me. 1981). . . . In other words, evidence tending to implicate another person, and deflect guilt from the defendant, must be admitted if it is of sufficient probative value to raise a reasonable doubt as to the defendant's culpability. As we stated in *LeClair*, "[T]he court should allow the defendant 'wide latitude' to present all the evidence relevant to his defense, unhampered by piecemeal rulings on admissibility." . . .

The presiding justice erred in his determination that M.R.Evid. 404(a) prohibited the introduction of this testimony. The medical testimony concerning battered child syndrome, and the eyewitness testimony of Patricia Easler's three former neighbors cannot fairly be called "character evidence" within the meaning of the rule. Field & Murray, Maine Evidence describes character as a "generalized description of one's disposition, or of one's disposition in respect to a general trait, such as honesty, temperance, or peacefulness." §406.1 at 75. The rationale behind the rule limiting inquiry into the character of a witness is to ensure the trial remains focused on the guilt or innocence of the accused, and "avoids surprise, waste of time, and confusion, and makes

---

1. M.R.Evid. 404(a) provides, in pertinent part:

(a) Character evidence generally. Evidence of a person's character or a trait of his character is not admissible for the purpose of proving that he acted in conformity therewith on a particular occasion, except: . . .

(2) Character of witness. Evidence of the character of a witness, as provided in Rules 607, 608 and 609.

the task of being a witness somewhat less unpleasant." M.R.Evid. 608 advisors' note.

Such considerations supporting the rule make it obvious that it is not the rule's purpose to preclude the introduction of evidence such as here offered by the defendant. Patricia Easler told the jury she had confessed, then retracted that confession when faced with the loss of her children in the subsequent District Court proceeding; she also told the jury she had been indicted with the defendant, and was allowed to plead guilty to a lesser charge in exchange for her later testimony against the defendant; Detective Lesson's testimony informed the jury that Patricia Easler had herself been an abused child. In these circumstances, any evidence the defendant could adduce which would tend to prove the truthfulness of Easler's confession, and thereby raise a reasonable doubt as to the defendant's own guilt, should have been admitted for the jury's consideration.

The medical testimony of the State's expert witness concerning battered child syndrome, offered after the jury had heard evidence that Patricia Easler had been an abused child, tended only to rehabilitate her retracted confession. In State v. Anaya, 438 A.2d 892 (Me. 1981), we held the trial court abused its discretion in excluding testimony concerning battered wife syndrome, offered by the defendant to support her claim of self-defense. We decided testimony as to how the syndrome may have been manifested in the defendant's behavior may have given the jury reason to believe that her conduct was consistent with her theory of self-defense. . . . Similarly, in the instant case, a description of battered child syndrome and the likelihood that Patricia's own history of child abuse would predispose her to abuse her own child, would have allowed the jury to weigh the credibility of Patricia's confession against the credibility of her later retraction. The defendant was improperly denied the opportunity to have the jury consider the credibility, based on all available evidence, of Patricia Easler's recantation of her confession to the crime with which the defendant was charged. . . .

Judgment vacated. Remanded to the Superior Court for further proceedings consistent with the opinion herein.

SCOLNIK, Justice, with whom MCKUSICK, Chief Justice, joins, dissenting.
. . . I must dissent, however, as to part II(4). In my view, the proffered testimony was not only inadmissible pursuant to M.R.Evid. 404, but it also was an improper method of proof under M.R.Evid. 405. For these reasons, I find no error in the trial court's exclusion of the evidence and would affirm the judgment of the Superior Court.

While a defendant may prove any fact or circumstance tending to show that someone else committed the crime, such evidence is inadmissible unless it clearly links the other person to the commission of the crime. . . . Character evidence, however, merely creates a conjectural inference or suspicion as to another's guilt and therefore is inadmissible. . . .

Generally, evidence of a person's character is not admissible for the purpose of proving that he "acted in conformity therewith on a particular occasion." M.R.Evid. 404(a). Rule 404 renders inadmissible evidence of the character of third persons, "even if the ultimate purpose of proof of another's character is to exculpate the accused." 22 C. Wright & K. Graham, Federal Practice and Procedure §5236, at 385(1978). . . . A defendant is also precluded from introducing evidence of a rape victim's reputation for chastity in support of a claim of consent. In each situation, the evidence, although relevant, is excluded because it has only "slight probative value and is likely to be highly prejudicial, so as to divert attention from what actually occurred.". . .

Rule 404 may be viewed as a concrete application of the balancing of the probative value of character evidence against countervailing dangers of prejudice, confusion, distraction, and delay. The rule itself concludes that the probative value of character evidence is always outweighed by the danger of prejudice, confusion, distraction and delay. . . . When the defendant, in an attempt to raise a reasonable doubt as to his own guilt, seeks to introduce character evidence of a third person, the evidence is no more probative and no less likely to confuse the issues, divert the jury, and waste time, than any other time when character evidence is sought to be introduced.

In the present case, both the medical testimony that abused children often become abusive parents and the testimony of former neighbors as to prior acts of child abuse is evidence of a trait of Patricia Easler's character. See State v. Lagasse, 410 A.2d at 542 (evidence that the decedent regularly beat his wife was character evidence). This testimony was offered for the sole purpose of furnishing a basis for an inference that (1) Patricia Easler is an abusive parent and (2) on the particular occasion in question, she acted in conformity with her character. Because it is difficult logically to justify the drawing of such a chain of inferences, the trial justice, in excluding this evidence, was in full compliance with the letter and spirit of Rule 404.

Even if not subject to exclusion under Rule 404, the proffered character testimony was inadmissible for its failure to satisfy the requirements of Rule 405. With one exception, character must be proved by evidence of reputation M.R.Evid. 405(a). Proof may be made by evidence of specific instances of conduct only in those situations in which character is an essential element of a charge, claim or defense. M.R.Evid. 405(b). Dr. Lambert's testimony was not evidence of Patricia Easler's reputation. In fact, it was not even proof of what her character was but rather what it might possibly have been. Nor was it evidence of specific instances of her conduct. At most, it demonstrated that Patricia Easler was herself the victim of abusive conduct engaged in by others as a result of which expert witnesses deemed it probable that her victimization caused her to develop a child abusing character trait.

The testimony of the former neighbors to specific instances of Patricia Easler's conduct is also defective under Rule 405. Because her disposition to abuse her children is not an element of a charge, claim or defense, her character may be proved only by reputational evidence.

The Court's position which erroneously concludes that the proffered testimony is not character evidence cannot alternatively be justified by its assertion that the evidence is admissible for the purpose of impeaching the credibility of Patricia Easler's recantation of her confession. Impeachment by character evidence is governed by Rule 608. . . . This rule is limited to evidence probative of the truthfulness or untruthfulness of the witness. Patricia Easler's alleged character trait for child abuse has no bearing on her character for veracity. . . . Therefore, the evidence was also inadmissible for the purpose of impeaching her credibility.

Furthermore, the Court's reliance on State v. Anaya, 438 A.2d 892 (Me. 1981), is misplaced. In *Anaya,* we found it an abuse of the trial court's discretion to exclude, pursuant to M.R.Evid. 403, expert testimony regarding battered wife syndrome, when such evidence was offered to support the defendant's claim of self-defense or provocation to mitigate or justify her conduct. Its purpose was to show the psyche of battered wives and that the defendant's perceptions and behavior at the time of the killing were consistent with those exhibited by women who suffered repeated physical abuse at the hands of their husbands or lovers. This testimony supported the defendant's contention that she was indeed fearful of her abuser despite the fact that she continued to live with him. Thus, evidence of battered wife syndrome was admissible, not to prove conduct, but rather for the purpose of showing her mental perceptions to assist the jury in determining whether in such a state of mind she acted reasonably to protect herself from another beating. It was not evidence of character. Its admission contravened none of the rules of evidence and was governed exclusively by the general rules of relevance.

In the present case, however, the attempted use of evidence of battered child syndrome was totally dissimilar to the use of battered wife syndrome evidence found permissible in *Anaya.* The sole purpose of evidence of the vicious cycle where abused children grow up to become abusive parents was to allow the jury to infer that because Patricia Easler was an abused child, she was an abusive parent, and to further infer, that she abused her child, Tina, on the particular occasion in question. As earlier demonstrated, evidence for this purpose is inadmissible under the Maine Rules of Evidence.

Accordingly, the trial justice correctly excluded the evidence. In striving to achieve the worthy goal of affording a criminal defendant every exculpatory nuance, we are not free to stretch the rules to permit in substance and method the kind of "character evidence" which was offered in this case.

I would affirm the judgment.

Though proof of character may have its place in criminal cases, is there any reason for its use in civil cases?

Problem: Tit for Tat

Rip Rapper v. Shawn Pend for damage allegedly occurring as a result of Pend's assault and battery on Rapper at the Beverly Hills Disco on July 14. Defendant's answer alleges that plaintiff was the aggressor and pleads self-defense.

(1) As part of his case-in-chief Rapper offers evidence of his reputation for peacefulness. Admissible?

(2) As part of his case-in-chief Rapper offers evidence of Pend's reputation as a bully, fighter, and all-around troublemaker. Admissible?

(3) Suppose that the evidence offered in (1) and (2) is excluded and that as part of his case-in-chief defendant offers evidence of his good reputation. Admissible? Suppose defendant also offers evidence of plaintiff's bad reputation. Admissible?

(4) Suppose the court excludes all the evidence offered above except defendant's good reputation evidence. On rebuttal may plaintiff offer evidence of defendant's bad reputation or of his own good reputation?

CRUMPTON v. CONFEDERATION LIFE INSURANCE CO.
672 F.2d 1248 (5th Cir. 1982)

BROWN, Circuit Judge.

Vicki Crumpton, the beneficiary of an accidental death policy, sued Confederation Life Insurance Co. (Confederation) for the benefits under the policy. From a jury verdict and judgment in favor of the beneficiary, Confederation appeals. The asserted error [is the] improper admission of prejudicial evidence of the character of the insured. . . .

The facts in this suit on an insurance policy are unusual for that genre of cases. The insured, Titus Crumpton (Crumpton), was shot by Joanne Petton, a neighbor who lived just a little more than a block away. While Confederation's defense to the policy was that Crumpton's death was not accidental, the focus of the trial was on the alleged rape of Ms. Petton by the deceased insured. Thus we find it necessary briefly to summarize the circumstances claimed to have led to Crumpton's death.

On the afternoon of November 8, 1978, Ms. Petton, a housewife with

three children, was allegedly raped and beaten in her home by Crumpton. The assailant apparently threatened to kill Petton's children if she
informed the police or anyone about the rape. Ms. Petton did report
the incident to the police five days later, on the morning of November
13, 1978, stating that the attack had occurred on the morning of November 8 and that she could not identify her assailant. Between the
time of the alleged rape and her report to the police, Ms. Petton did
inform her parents and her husband, but she never revealed to her
husband that the assailant had made threats against her. On November
13, Ms. Petton was also examined by her physician who found multiple
bruises on Petton's body "more consistent with a sex assault than just
would be a general beating of some sort."

At approximately 9 P.M. on November 13, 1978 Ms. Petton asked her
husband to pick up some medication at the drug store. After he left,
Ms. Petton then delivered to her next door neighbor a sealed envelope
containing a handwritten note stating "Mr. Crumpton attacked and
raped me in afternoon not morning." Subsequently, Ms. Petton, with a
pistol in her possession, went out to the garage at which time she observed Crumpton standing out on the street. Apparently, he proceeded
toward her so she pulled out the gun and, without any verbal warning,
shot Crumpton at close range.

Titus Crumpton was insured by Confederation as part of a group
policy obtained by his employer to cover accidental death and dismemberment. The policy, in the amount of $150,000, designated Vicki
Crumpton as the beneficiary. The policy provided benefits for accidental death, defined as "death resulting from . . . accidental bodily injury
visible on the surface of the body or disclosed by an autopsy."

Vicki Crumpton brought this suit seeking recovery of the proceeds
of this policy, claiming that her father, Titus Crumpton, died of gunshot
wounds inflicted by another person. Confederation, while admitting
that Crumpton was insured under the policy, denied coverage, asserting
that Crumpton's death did not result from an accidental bodily injury
within the meaning of the policy. Specifically, Confederation, while not
disputing the death, contended that Crumpton had raped his neighbor
who fatally shot him in the belief that he had returned to inflict further
harm on her or her children. For this reason, Confederation asserted
that Crumpton should have anticipated that his actions would result in
bodily injury, and thus death was not accidental under the meaning of
the policy.

The beneficiary denied that the rape occurred or alternatively asserted that Crumpton could not reasonably have anticipated his death
five days after the rape. The case was tried to a jury to whom one special
interrogatory was submitted: "Did plaintiff Vicki Crumpton prove by a
preponderance of the evidence that the bodily injuries of T.B. Crumpton which resulted in his death were accidental"? The jury responded

that "Plaintiff did prove." The District Court entered judgment awarding the beneficiary the benefits under the policy as well as statutory
penalties and attorney's fees. Confederation appeals.

Confederation's primary assertion of error concerns the admission
by the District Court of evidence regarding Crumpton's character. Prior
to trial, Confederation by motion in limine sought an order prohibiting
the admission into evidence of "any fact regarding or relating to T.B.
Crumpton's character or reputation in the community." This motion
was denied by the District Court judge who found that under the peculiar fact circumstances Crumpton's character was at issue. Also, the
District Court determined that the evidence would be admissible in a
criminal case under F.R. Evid. 404(a), which rule, although appearing
to apply only to criminal cases, should properly apply to the type of case
at hand.

At the trial Vicki Crumpton called as witnesses several persons who
testified to Crumpton's "character." The witnesses included the pastor
of a church, who testified that Crumpton did not have a violent temper,
did not use profanity, and did not make passes at women; the church
secretary who testified similarly; a "good friend" who testified that
Crumpton did not use profanities or make obscene gestures or indecent
proposals to women, was not violent, and did not drink; Crumpton's
sister-in-law who testified similarly; and the beneficiary who testified that
her father was not violent and did not use threats.

Confederation contends that the admission of this testimony not only
violated F.R. Evid. 404 but was also prejudicial, constituting "virtually
the only direct evidence adduced to satisfy the Beneficiary's burden. . . ." The propriety of the admission of evidence of character depends in part on the purpose for which that evidence is offered.
Generally this type of evidence is offered for one of two purposes:
(1) when a person's possession of a particular character trait is an operative fact in determining the legal rights and liabilities of the party
and thus is one of the ultimate issues in the case, or (2) to prove circumstantially that a person acted in conformity with his character on a
particular occasion.

The use of character evidence for the first purpose above is generally
referred to as "character at issue." When used for such a purpose, it is
not within the scope of F.R. Evid. 404 which applies instead to the second use, that of showing that the person acted in conformity with his
character. F.R. Evid. 404(a) governs the admission of character evidence
when used for the circumstantial purpose and generally excludes such
evidence unless within one of the three exceptions. These exceptions
are admission of character evidence to prove action in conformity with
character of the accused, of a victim in certain circumstances, and of a
witness. With these exceptions, character evidence is generally excluded
because it is viewed as having slight probative value and yet may be very

prejudicial. Where character is part of the ultimate issue of a case, F.R. Evid. 404(a) is not relevant.

The District Court also found that even if F.R. Evid. 404(a) were applicable, the evidence of character would be admissible under the exceptions. While Rule 404(a) generally applies to criminal cases, the unusual circumstances here place the case very close to one of a criminal nature. The focus of the civil suit on the insurance policy was the issue of rape, and the resulting trial was in most respects similar to a criminal case for rape. Had there been a criminal case against Crumpton, evidence of his character that was pertinent would have been admissible. We do not view the notes of the Advisory Committee as contravening this interpretation. . . .

The argument is made that circumstantial use of character ought to be allowed in civil cases to the same extent as in criminal cases, i.e., evidence of good (nonprejudicial) character would be admissible in the first instance, subject to rebuttal by evidence of bad character. . . . The difficulty with expanding the use of character evidence in civil cases is set forth by the California Law Revision Commission. . . . Character evidence is of slight probative value and may be very prejudicial. It tends to distract the trier of fact from the main question of what actually happened on the particular occasion. It subtly permits the trier of fact to reward the good man to punish the bad man because of their respective characters despite what evidence in the case shows actually happened.

While the Committee's notes reject the expanded use of character evidence in civil cases, we do not view this as determinative of the circumstances of this case, which while actually civil, in character is akin to a criminal case. By implication, when evidence would be admissible under Rule 404(a) in a criminal case, we think that it should also be admissible in a civil suit where the focus is on essentially criminal aspects, and the evidence is relevant, probative, and not unduly prejudicial.

Affirmed.

GINTER v. NORTHWESTERN MUTUAL LIFE INSURANCE CO.
576 F. Supp. 627 (E.D. Ky. 1984)

BERTELSMAN, J.

This matter is before the court on a motion for a pretrial evidentiary ruling on the question of whether character evidence is admissible in a civil case under F.R. Ev. 404(a).

This is an action by the beneficiary of a life insurance policy against the insurance company which issued the policy. There is no dispute that the plaintiff's deceased husband took out a policy on his life with the defendant insurance company and that the premiums were properly paid. However, the insurance company defends on the ground that there were material omissions from the application. More particularly, the insurance company contends that the insured decedent failed to disclose that he was under treatment by a psychiatrist for depression. Plaintiff responds that the application was completely answered and that any inaccuracies were not a material consideration in the issuance of the policy.

The plaintiff in the pending motion has requested a ruling from the court that evidence is admissible from witnesses who would testify that the deceased insured was a man of good character who would be unlikely to submit a fraudulent or erroneous application.

After careful consideration, the court concludes that it is the intention of Rule 404(a) to exclude evidence of a character trait in civil cases, except where character itself is an element of the claim or defense, as in cases involving defamation.

A leading text states that the following was the situation prior to the adoption of the Federal Rules of Evidence.

> The common law relaxed its ban upon evidence of character to show conduct to the extent of permitting the accused to open the door by producing evidence of his good character. This was a special dispensation to criminal defendants whose life or liberty were at hazard. Should the same dispensation be accorded to the party in a civil action who has been charged by his adversary's pleading or proof with a criminal offence involving moral turpitude? The peril of judgment here is less, and most courts have declined to pay the price in consumption of time and distraction from the issue which the concession entails. A growing minority, however, has been impressed with the serious consequences to the party's standing, reputation and relationships which such a charge, even in a civil action, may bring in its train, and has followed the criminal analogy, by permitting the party to introduce evidence of his good reputation for the trait involved in the charge. The balance of expediency is a close one.

McCormick on Evidence, §192 at 459-60 (2d Ed. 1972). . . .

It may be noted that the text [of FRE 404] does not specifically state that evidence of a relevant character trait is not admissible in civil cases. Nevertheless, this result seems to be implicit by the use of the terms "accused," "prosecution," "victim," and "crime."

Plaintiff argues that certain recent decisions militate against the conclusion that the rule of exclusion of character trait evidence from civil cases is absolute.

Most particularly, plaintiff cites Crumpton v. Confederation Life Insurance Company, 672 F.2d 1248 (5th Cir. 1982). This was a case somewhat similar to the case at bar. In *Crumpton,* the appellate court affirmed the admission of evidence of a peaceable character of an insured who had been shot to death. Whether or not the death was "accidental" within the meaning of the policy depended on whether the insured had approached the woman who shot him with the intent to molest her. . . .

The court advanced several grounds for admitting the evidence, one of which was that it felt that the decedent's character was at issue. The court also stated, however, that it felt that "the unusual circumstances here placed the case very close to one of a criminal nature." 672 F.2d at 1253. Therefore, the court held that evidence would be admissible even if character were not in issue. . . .

> Thus by implication, when evidence would be admissible under Rule 404(a) in a criminal case, we think that it should also be admissible in a civil suit where the focus is on essentially criminal aspects, and the evidence is relevant, probative, and not unduly prejudicial.

Id.

With respect, this court must disagree with the *Crumpton* decision. It seems beyond peradventure of doubt that the drafters of F.R. Ev. 404(a) explicitly intended that all character evidence, except where "character is at issue" was to be excluded. After an extensive review of the various points of view on this issue, the Advisory Committee expressly stated, "[i]t is believed that those espousing change (from the view of excluding character evidence in civil cases) have not met the burden of persuasion." This language leads to the inevitable conclusion that the use in Rule 404(a) of terms applicable only to criminal cases was not accidental. . . .

This court believes that the language of the rule, as originally drafted by the Advisory Committee and ultimately approved by Congress, has the effect of a statute in excluding the proffered evidence here, even though the case may be considered as analogous to a criminal prosecution. (Here some of the elements of mail fraud or larceny by trick are arguably present.) The court regards itself as not having any discretion in this matter by reason of the explicit language of the rule, since it is clear that this case is not one where character is at issue.

Therefore, the preliminary motion seeking admissibility of the evidence must be denied. The proffered evidence will be excluded at trial.

Problem: The Acrobatic Driver

On June 1, at the intersection of Walden and Thoreau Streets, *A,* a pedestrian, was hit by *B*'s car and killed. *B* entered Walden Street from the south. There is a stop sign controlling such traffic at the corner. Shortly after the accident *B* died of injuries unrelated to the accident.

P, the executor of *A*'s estate, sues *D,* the executor of *B*'s estate, for damages due to *B*'s alleged negligence. The issue is whether *B* stopped at the stop sign. At trial, *P* proposes to have *W1* testify that he once saw *B* drive the wrong way down a one-way street, that he once saw *B* blow his horn in a hospital quiet zone, and that he once saw *B* steer with his feet in heavy traffic. *P* also proposes to have *W2* testify that he is familiar with *B*'s reputation for driving and that his reputation is that of a reckless daredevil.

Is the proffered testimony of *W1* or *W2* relevant? Is it admissible in a Federal Rules jurisdiction? Should such evidence be admitted? If you were *P*'s attorney, how would you try to get this evidence in?

PHINNEY v. DETROIT UNITED RAILWAY CO.
232 Mich. 399, 205 N.W. 124 (1925)

SHARPE, J. A highway, running north and south, crosses the line of defendant's railway almost at right angles at the village of Atlas, in Genesee county. On Sunday, February 20, 1921, about 2 o'clock in the afternoon, John H. Densmore was driving a Ford roadster, going north, on the highway. With him in the car were his wife, his child, Odessa, and Florence Phinney, the wife of plaintiff. Defendant has a small station house at Atlas, located about 50 feet east of the highway. About 1,300 feet east of the crossing, defendant's track makes a long sweeping curve to the south. One of defendant's limited interurban cars, going west, not scheduled to stop at Atlas, collided with the roadster driven by Densmore at the crossing. As a result of the collision, the three adults were killed, and the child was injured.

Plaintiff, as administrator of his wife's estate, brings this action to recover the loss sustained, due to her death. The cause was submitted to the jury, who found for the defendant. Plaintiff reviews the judgment entered by writ of error. . . .

Edward Elford, who was in the employ of the defendant as a conductor on an interurban car at the time of the accident, and had been so employed for several years prior thereto, was asked, "What would be the proper thing to do to stop it as quickly as possible in case of an emergency?" An objection to the question asked was sustained. Error is assigned thereon.

Hinkley, called for cross-examination, had testified that he first saw the automobile when his car was 800 or 900 feet from the crossing; that the station house afterwards obstructed his view, and he next saw it when it was about 50 feet from the crossing and his car about 250 or 300 feet therefrom; that he made no special effort to stop until within 100 feet from the crossing, and that he then applied the brakes with full force; that he did "not sound the foot gong, or reverse the motor, nor apply the sand on the wheels"; that he had theretofore sounded the usual crossing whistle; that he considered the application of the air (emergency) brake the safer way to quickly stop his car; that at that time he was going from 35 to 40 miles an hour. He admitted that on a former trial of this case he had testified that he had not applied the brakes until his car was within 35 or 40 feet from the crossing, and, on being asked, "That is right, is it?" answered, "Yes, sir." . . .

Error is assigned on the refusal of court to permit plaintiff's counsel to show by Elford and other employees of the defendant that Hinkley had the reputation of being a reckless motorman. The authorities cited by counsel in support of his contention that this evidence was admissible are cases in which employees were injured through the negligence of a fellow servant. We think they have no application to the facts here presented. The jury were concerned only with the manner in which Hinkley drove his car and the effort he made to stop it at the time of the collision.

Why was Elford's testimony as to the motorman's reputation for recklessness excluded? Would evidence of specific acts of recklessness have been admissible?

DALLAS RAILWAY & TERMINAL CO. v. FARNSWORTH
148 Tex. 584, 227 S.W.2d 1017 (1950)

Action for damages on account of injuries suffered by respondent, Mrs. Letta M. Farnsworth, when struck by petitioner's streetcar immediately after she had alighted from it.

Respondent, a widow, fifty-two years of age, became a passenger, together with her thirty year old daughter and three year old grandson, on petitioner's streetcar to travel from South Lamar Street to the corner of Elm and St. Paul Streets, a distance estimated by the operator of the streetcar to be approximately one mile and by respondent approximately three or four miles. Traveling east on Elm Street, the car stopped when it arrived at St. Paul Street. At that place the car tracks do not extend farther on Elm Street, but turn to the left and north on St. Paul Street. Although respondent had been a passenger on streetcars in Dallas and in other places oftentimes over many years, she had never been on a streetcar on Elm Street and did not know that the car turned to the left at St. Paul Street, and did not look at the tracks ahead of the car, and she had never observed that the rear end of a streetcar would swing out as the car went around a curve and did not know that it would.

Eight or ten passengers alighted from the streetcar at its front door.

According to respondent's testimony all of the others were ahead of respondent, her daughter and grandchild, respondent being the last passenger to alight. She testified that just as she stepped off the streetcar step within the safety zone the traffic light which she was facing and in the direction that she intended to go, that is, to the south, changed to red, and that before she had time to take a step, almost instantaneously, she was struck and knocked down by the streetcar.

The operator of the streetcar testified that as he closed the door of the car immediately before starting he looked to his right, saw that the door was clear, and saw no one within reach of the door or within reach of the overhang of the streetcar, and that there was no one "at the point of my front door within the overswing zone"; and that after he closed the door and started the streetcar he never looked back to his right or to the back of the streetcar, his attention being given to watching the traffic traveling west on Elm Street and the pedestrians who were crossing St. Paul Street. His testimony shows that he knew nothing about the accident until he had traveled to the end of the line and returned to Elm and Ervay Streets, where he was told of it by the company's supervisor.

Respondent was permitted to testify, over objections, that when she entered the streetcar on Lamar Street the operator started the car before she could get to a seat and was in a great hurry, that he stopped at Lamar and Young Streets and passengers "scarcely got off before he started," and that the same was true at Lamar and Main Streets. This testimony when first considered may appear to be forbidden by the general rule that "when the question is whether or not a person has been negligent in doing or in failing to do a particular act, evidence is not admissible to show that he has been guilty of a similar act of negligence or even habitually negligent upon a similar occasion." The reason for the rule is the fundamental principle that evidence must be relevant to the facts in issue in the case on trial and tend to prove or disprove those facts, evidence as to collateral facts not being admissible. There are some modifications of the general rule as applied to particular cases. It has been said that evidence of similar transactions or *conduct on other occasions* is not competent to prove the commission of a particular act charged "*unless the acts are connected in some special way, indicating a relevancy beyond mere similarity in certain particulars.*"

Should the evidence of the operator's prior conduct be admitted? Can this case be reconciled with *Phinney*? What does the court have in mind by "unless the acts are connected in some special way, indicating a relevancy beyond mere similarity in certain particulars''? Does the admissibility of evidence of similar occurrences in civil cases depend on the way counsel packages it?

Problem: The Why Concert

On December 1, 1978, Peter, age fifteen, was killed at the Cincinnati Riverfront Coliseum. Peter had gone to the Coliseum to attend a concert by The Why, a rock-and-roll group. He and ten others were killed when the crowd trampled them to death.

P, Peter's father, has brought a wrongful death diversity action in federal court against *D1*, the owner of the Coliseum, and *D2*, the promoter of the concert. *P*'s complaint alleges that the defendants were negligent in overselling general admission tickets and in failing to control the crowd of ticketholders waiting to get in and that the defendants' negligence caused Peter's death. Specifically, *P* alleges that the defendants sold more tickets than there were seats, did not admit the gathered crowd of ticketholders in a timely and orderly manner, and failed to provide sufficient access, security, and crowd control. Both defendants have filed general denials and affirmatively pleaded contributory negligence and assumption of the risk.

At trial, *P* calls *W* to testify that she has been to twelve rock concerts at the Coliseum in the past year. She says that at every concert there was a mad scramble for general admission tickets, a press of people outside the doors until they opened a half-hour or so before the scheduled starting time of the concert, and once the doors opened a violent rush for the best seats and standing room.

Should *W*'s testimony be accepted?

CLARK v. STEWART
126 Ohio St. 263, 185 N.E. 71 (1933)

STEPHENSON, J. The action was for personal injuries alleged to have been caused by the negligence of the son of the defendant, who at the time was agent for his father, and, while acting within the scope of his employment while operating an automobile, negligently struck plaintiff from the rear, causing the injuries of which he complains.

The first theory of the petition sought to invoke the doctrine of respondeat superior. There were six averments of negligence. There was an additional averment in the petition to the effect that defendant's son at the time of the collision and injury was of about the age of seventeen years and was an inexperienced, careless, reckless and incompetent driver, which fact was well known to the defendant, and that the defendant was careless and negligent in entrusting his motor vehicle to his son on a public highway. This is followed by the averments of earning capacity, injury, damage, and prayer for recovery.

Defendant in answering plaintiff's amended petition admits that, on the date claimed by plaintiff, his son was operating a motor vehicle as his agent and that there was a collision between the motor vehicle and the person of the plaintiff. He proceeds with the affirmative statement that the injuries sustained by plaintiff on said occasion were caused solely by plaintiff's negligence and carelessness, in the particulars therein set out.

It is claimed that error was infused into the case when counsel for plaintiff called the defendant for cross-examination under the statute and propounded the following questions:

Q: Before January 5, 1931, how many automobile accidents had Walter Stewart had? (Defendant objects.)

And thereupon court recessed for a few minutes, the court first admonishing the jury. . . . And thereupon after the jury returned to the court room the objection was sustained. To all of which the plaintiff excepted.

Q: Had you ridden with Walter when he drove the car?
A: Yes, sir.
Q: You have ridden with him when he drove the car sixty miles an hour, haven't you?
A: No, sir.
Q: Ever ride with him when he run into another car?
A: No, sir.
Q: Were you with him when he—
Mr. Elliott: I object and I think this question is for the purpose of getting around the ruling of the court.

Mr. Harlan, in behalf of plaintiff, objected to misconduct of counsel.

Q: Were you riding with Walter in the latter part of May, 1930, when he was traveling very fast and ran into an automobile at Flenner's Corner? (Defendant objects; overruled; defendant excepts.)
A: Why he never ran into anybody at Flenner's Corner.
Q: (Stenographer reads question.)
A: No, I wasn't.
Q: You make the statement he never ran into any one, how do you know?
A: If he broke the machine or damaged the machine I would know it, wouldn't I?
Q: Didn't he break the machine up some at Flenner's Corner in May, 1930? (Defendant objects; overruled; defendant excepts.)
Q: You say you ought to know if he had damaged the car any—isn't it a matter of fact, don't you know it, that he did? (Defendant objects; overruled; defendant excepts.)
A: No, he didn't.

Q: Didn't he have an accident there and damage your car and didn't David Clark himself bring Walter home?

A: No, he brought the other boy home. This wasn't Walter. This was Roy. The accident didn't happen at Flenner's Corner, either.

Q: It was about at Flenner's Corner, wasn't it?

A: No, the fellows took the machine to Flenner's Corner to have it fixed.

Q: It was in the neighborhood of Flenner's Corner, wasn't it?

A: No.

Q: Where did it happen?

A: In front of Jake Stout's.

Q: That is farther on towards Excello from where you live?

A: Yes, sir.

Q: You say that wasn't Walter?

A: No, it wasn't Walter.

Q: Where is the other boy?

A: At home.

Q: How old is he?

A: Nineteen.

Q: Was that the boy David Clark brought home?

A: Yes, sir.

Q: Wasn't it Walter?

A: No.

Q: Now you say you ought to know if Walter ever had the car broken up, let's see if you know. Didn't he run into somebody at Matson's Corner and have the car broken up? (Defendant objects.)

Court: He may answer if he knows. (Defendant excepts.)

Q: (Stenographer reads question.)

A: Not as I know of.

Q: Not that you know of?

A: Not my car.

Q: Well, whose car was it?

A: I don't know.

Q: Sir?

A: He was driving the milk route for his brother and was coming out of the road and somebody ran into him, that is all.

Q: Were you there?

A: No.

Q: When you say somebody ran into him, then you have no personal knowledge of that, have you—no personal knowledge, have you?

A: Well I heard them talking about it. . . . (Plaintiff moves to strike out answer; answer stricken out.)

Q: Now the automobile that he was driving that you refer to at Matson's Corner, wasn't that yours?

A: No, sir.

Q: That was another son's?
A: Yes, sir.
Q: Was that Roy's?
A: No, sir, William's. . . .
Q: Was Walter driving your car and ran into another car, just outside of Monroe? (Defendant objects; overruled; defendant excepts.). . . .
Q: Don't you know Walter had the reputation of driving fifty or sixty miles an hour? (Defendant objects.)
Court: He may answer yes or no, as to whether he knows. (Defendant excepts.)
A: He did not have that reputation.
Q: Do you have any personal knowledge of his running into other automobiles? (Defendant objects; overruled; defendant excepts.)
A: Well, I know he never ran into any other automobiles.

Was the cross-examination proper? What objections would you make to it? Why? Is proof of character or prior occurrences ever proper in civil cases? When? Compare Rule 405.

Problem: The Soo Line Smash

On a fine August day, Timmy and his dog, Laddie, were walking along defendant Soo Line's railroad tracks when a Soo Line freight train approached. Laddie did not heed the warning whistle, and Timmy jumped back into the path of the oncoming train to rescue his dog. Laddie was unhurt, but Timmy sustained serious damages when struck by the train. Timmy's parents sued the Soo Line for negligence in the operation of its train.

At trial, plaintiffs offered evidence of a recent U.S. Department of Transportation Assessment report that Soo Line had a comparatively high system-wide accident rate.

What ruling and why?

EXUM v. GENERAL ELECTRIC CO.
819 F.2d 1158 (D.C. Cir. 1987)

MIKVA, Circuit Judge: Appellant Reginald Exum suffered first- and second-degree burns while using a french fryer designed and marketed by General Electric ("GE"). He sued the company under several theories, the most important of which for purposes of this appeal is negligent design. At the close of Exum's case, the trial court directed a verdict for General Electric. Exum contends in this appeal that the trial court erroneously excluded ... evidence of similar accidents. ...

Mr. Exum was 19 years old and a new employee at a Wendy's franchise on June 10, 1983, the date of the accident giving rise to this suit. One of Exum's duties was filtering the hot grease used in his employer's GE Model 811 french fryer (the "Model 811"). This task required Exum to lift a six-pound pan containing 15 pounds of grease at a temperature of 350 degrees and pour the grease through a paper cone filter into a second pan placed on the floor.

Exum is asthmatic and carries with him a pressurized asthma inhaler. As he poured the grease through the filter, the inhaler dropped from his shirt pocket into the scalding liquid. An explosion occurred, and Exum was burned and scarred on his face, neck, and chest. ...

The premise of Exum's negligent design theory was that the Model 811 is an obviously and unreasonably dangerous machine. At trial, Exum hoped to show that the company was unreasonable to market an industrial french fryer requiring the use of two open pans when a safer fryer with a closed filtration system could have been created by installing an inexpensive manual siphon. In support of this theory, Exum sought to introduce evidence of other cases in which young employees of Wendy's had been burned seriously while filtering grease with the Model 811. The trial court first made a tentative decision to admit evidence of these other incidents, but ultimately it excluded the evidence. The court reasoned that all but one of the other cases were not sufficiently similar to Mr. Exum's to be relevant, because they did not involve an employee's accidentally dropping an object into the grease. The court excluded the remaining case on the rationale that because it occurred after Exum's accident, it could not be used to show either notice or dangerousness. ...

Our analysis of District of Columbia law also leads us to disagree with the trial court's evidentiary rulings. Exum offered about 15 case files detailing incidents in which young employees were burned while filtering grease with the Model 811. In one of the cases, the victim, like Exum, had dropped an object in the grease; the other incidents involved slightly different and sundry fact patterns—for example, spillages.

Exum argued that the evidence was admissible on either of two theories. First, the other incidents tended to show that the Model 811 is dangerous. Second, the incidents put GE on notice of the dangerousness of its design. The trial court found that the prior incidents were not relevant under either theory. We may reverse that ruling only for abuse of discretion.

In appraising the relevancy of similar incidents in product liability cases, courts have required the other incidents to be "substantially similar" to the case at bar. How substantial the similarity must be is in part a function of the proponent's theory of proof. "If dangerousness is the issue, a high degree of similarity will be essential. On the other hand, if the accident is offered to prove notice, a lack of exact similarity of conditions will not cause exclusion provided the accident was of a kind which should have served to warn the defendant." 1 Weinstein & Berger, Weinstein's Evidence §401[10], at 401-66-67.

There is without doubt a high degree of similarity between Exum's case and the incident in which a Wendy's employee was injured by dropping an object into the hot grease in the Model 811. In fact, the court excluded that case not on substantial similarity grounds but because it occurred after June 10, 1983, the date of Exum's accident. However, although subsequent incidents cannot be introduced to prove the manufacturer had notice, they are relevant to show dangerousness. It therefore was an abuse of discretion not to admit evidence of this particular incident.

The other incidents appear relevant to show both dangerousness and notice. In order to determine whether the Model 811 was negligently designed and marketed, a jury would have to balance " 'the likelihood of harm, and the gravity of harm if it happens, against the burden of precaution which would be effective to avoid the harm.' " The similar incidents could have aided the jury in its calculations of one side of the balance — the likelihood and the gravity of harm arising from the use of the Model 811. Cf. Bailey v. Southern Pacific Transportation Co., 613 F.2d 1385 (5th Cir. 1980) (admission of evidence of prior train collisions; fact that they occurred at different times in the day and involved cars going in the opposite direction were factors going to the weight of the evidence); Kehm v. Procter & Gamble Mfg. Co., 724 F.2d 613 (8th Cir. 1983) (evidence of consumer complaints held relevant to show dangerousness of tampon over manufacturer's objection that the complaints didn't refer to symptoms of toxic shock syndrome). Since the incidents are admissible on a dangerousness theory, they are, a fortiori, also admissible under a theory of notice, which imposes a less rigorous requirement of similarity. Certainly these other accidents were "of a kind which should have served to warn" GE of the risks of an open system fryer. . . .

C. Character and Habit

The difficulty with the propensity rule (and it is a difficulty) is figuring out what is meant by "character." Rule 406, like Rule 404(b), provides an indication of the difficulty. Both rules are logically superfluous. They complement Rule 404(a) but logically add nothing to it except five examples of evidence that is not barred by the propensity rule. Practically speaking, however, both rules help to delineate what the propensity rule is *not* intended to exclude. Rule 404(b), as we have argued above, restates the basic rule of 404(a) and gives a non-exhaustive list of illustrations of what is not covered.

Rule 406 declares that evidence of habit or of the routine practice of an organization is relevant to prove action in conformity therewith. This is an odd declaration. In and of itself, this declaration would not distinguish habit or routine practice from character evidence. Character evidence is relevant to prove action in conformity therewith; Rule 404(a) does not declare such evidence irrelevant but rather "inadmissible," and does so because the relevance of character evidence to show general propensity is outweighed by its potential for prejudice and waste of time. What Rule 406 should say (and what everyone understands it as saying) is that evidence of habit and routine practice is not "inadmissible" by reason of the propensity rule of 404(a). Why? Because "habit" is different from "character," and therefore evidence of habit is not made inadmissible by the general propensity rule of Rule 404(a). Admissibility of relevant evidence of habit and routine practice is not admissibility of evidence of "character."

All of which sets the stage for trying to say, again, what "character" is. McCormick says, "character is a generalized description of one's disposition, or of one's disposition in respect to a general trait such as honesty, temperance, or peacefulness." (McCormick §162, quoted in the Advisory Committee's Note to Rule 406.) Generality seems to be the key: A disposition sufficiently general to encompass many different kinds of specific behavior is what is meant by character. One can manifest "peacefulness" or "honesty" in many ways. One can manifest a disposition to climb steps two at a time only by climbing steps two at a time. Exclusion of proof of a person's "character" for the purpose of proving that "he acted in conformity therewith on a particular occasion" is meant to exclude proof of a general disposition that could encompass a wide variety of conforming actions when offered to prove that one particular action conformed. Habit is a disposition that manifests itself by a narrow range of behavior. This is the key distinction between habit and routine practice on the one hand and character on the other, and it is for this reason that habit and routine are not encompassed by the concept of "character" within the meaning of Rule 404(a).

Much of the confusion created by the so-called character rules would be eliminated if terminology were more precise. The term "character evidence," when used to describe what is excluded by the propensity rule, should not be applied to evidence of specific acts that is independently relevant.

This leads us to a conceptual view of habit and character evidence that, while not recognized explicitly in the cases, we believe best explains the actual treatment of such evidence by the courts and rules drafters. In our view, it is crucial to understanding the propensity rule to see that Rules 404(b) and 406, while giving some examples of what is not character proof, leave an undefined middle. One cannot define what is included within the propensity rule simply by determining what is not included under Rules 404(b) and 406. Rather, it is crucial to develop an affirmative understanding of the boundaries of the propensity rule and to see that if evidence is not covered by the propensity rule, its admissibility is determined solely by the basic relevance considerations of Rule 403.

Try applying this approach to the next three problems. Does it help?

Problem: The Careless Smoker

Action for damages by garage owner *P* against *D*, the administrator of the estate of *S*, who was burned to death in a fire in *P*'s garage. *P*'s complaint claims that *S* went to sleep in his car while smoking a cigarette, which ignited the seats in *S*'s car and touched off a general conflagration that burned *P*'s garage to the ground. *S*'s body was found in his car in the smoldering remains of the garage. At trial, *P* offers evidence of three previous fires caused by *S*'s smoking and falling asleep.

Is such evidence relevant? Is it admissible? Is it evidence of habit or character?

Problem: Smoking v. Speeding

Action for damages and personal injuries received by *P* when the car that *P* was driving collided with *D*'s car at 7:30 P.M. on Saturday, June 1, at an intersection controlled by a traffic light. *P* claims that she was proceeding through a green light when *D*'s car struck her from the right. *D* claims that *P* ran a yellow light and that *D* had the green light while in the intersection. There were no eyewitnesses to the accident other than the drivers.

At the trial, *D* offers the testimony of *P*'s roommate, *W*, a hostile witness, that on the night in question, *P* was on her way to a movie and that *P* generally smoked several marijuana cigarettes immediately before or on the way to movies. *P* offers evidence showing that *D* has been cited eight times in the past two years for going through red lights and that three of those citations were given after automobiles driven by *D* had been involved in collisions with other vehicles.

Is any of this evidence admissible? Why?

Problem: The Acrobatic Driver—A Reprise

In the problem of the acrobatic but reckless driver above, suppose *P* offers *W3* to testify that he worked at a gas station on the corner of Walden and Thoreau Streets, that he has serviced *B*'s car and knows it is a standard-shift automobile, and that in all the times he saw *B* drive through the Walden/Thoreau intersection, he never saw *B* come to a full stop at the stop sign. Rather, *B* always would spurt through the intersection without downshifting to first gear.

Is *W3*'s testimony relevant? Is it admissible? What is the difference between *W3*'s proposed testimony and *W1*'s and *W2*'s proposed testimony? Would your decision as to whether any of the witnesses' testimony should be admitted be affected by the presence or absence of eyewitnesses to the collision between *B*'s car and *A*? Should it be?

Repetition of an act does not in itself constitute a "habit." But merely because the various similar occurrences do not constitute proof of habit does not mean that they are automatically inadmissible. In each case, one must ask is the evidence relevant? If it is relevant, then is it evidence of character because of its generality, or of similar acts that reveal a specific disposition that manifests itself in a narrow way? If the latter, how would the admissibility of the evidence be decided under Rule 403?

If the act does not amount to a habit, it might yet fall into a middle ground of prior similar acts that neither clearly qualify as admissible habit under Rule 406 nor clearly are inadmissible under the general propensity Rule of 404(a). What then? There would seem to be no other choice but to decide the issue of the admissibility of similar acts that fall into this middle ground on a case-by-case basis under Rule 403.

In the context of the problem "The Careless Smoker," in which there is apparently very little other evidence of causation and no serious potential for prejudice stemming from the nature of the acts in question, the evidence of the prior instances in which *S* caused fires by falling asleep while smoking should be admitted, although a trial judge who refused to admit this evidence would undoubtedly not be reversed.

In applying Rule 403, it sometimes happens that the nature of prior similar acts (whether or not they amount to habit) may raise substantial problems of prejudice. Does this occur in the case of the careless smoker?

What about the problem "Smoking v. Speeding"? *P*'s practice of smoking marijuana before going to movies concerns a specific pattern of behavior, not offered for purposes of showing *P*'s general character. The proof shows a particular propensity to act in a given way in a given context. For this reason, the evidence may not be excluded by the general propensity rule of FRE 404(a), but whether it is admissible is another question.

P's practice of smoking marijuana before going to movies is not easily described as a habit. There is a volitional aspect to smoking marijuana that resists the "habit" label, which, in this context at least, suggests "addiction." The evidence is, therefore, not clearly covered by Rule 406.

Thus, this is another example of evidence of similar acts that falls in the middle ground between character and habit, the admissibility of which must be determined under Rule 403.

There would not seem to be a serious problem of "waste of time" in the proof of these similar acts (and that is often the most serious problem). However, there is a substantial risk here that the factfinder would decide the case based on a prejudice against pot smokers and not on the basis of the best assessment of what actually happened. Either way, do you think that the trial judge will be reversed however she rules?

What about *D* in the problem "Smoking v. Speeding"? *P*'s evidence that *D* has been cited eight times in two years for going through red lights is offered to show that he has a propensity to run red lights and therefore that it is more likely that he ran the red light in this case. This is a fairly specific behavior pattern, quite different, for example, from proof that *D* was negligent or reckless in a variety of ways while driving. Compare the *Phinney* and *Farnsworth* cases again.

Compare Example 1

D was stopped for
  running red lights $\longrightarrow$ *D* has a propensity $\longrightarrow$ *D* ran the red light
  eight times in   to run red lights   in this case
  two years

with Example 2

D was ticketed for
  going 80 MPH $\longrightarrow$ *D* has a propensity $\longrightarrow$ *D* ran the red light
D was cited for drunk   to drive recklessly   in this case
  driving
D drove with his feet

In the second example in the chart there is a wide variety of behavior that manifests the character trait; thus the propensity is general. In the first example, the propensity is much more specific, and therefore the proof based on the similar act logic is much more probative.

Is the propensity specific enough to take it out from under the general propensity rule of FRE 404(a)? The range from the general to the specific obviously runs a spectrum: There is no bright line of demarcation. General propensity is at one end; habit is at the other. There is considerable variety possible in the contexts and conditions under which red lights could be run, and no contention that *D* automatically runs all of them. It is easy to imagine an even more specific propensity (i.e., "habit") with respect to running red lights.

The evidence of *D* running red lights is an example of evidence in the middle ground between character (general propensity) and habit (a very specific propensity), the admissibility of which is determined neither by Rule 404(a) nor by Rule 406, but which must be determined under Rule 403.

In making the Rule 403 balance, the trial judge should weigh the following:

1.   There is a risk that the jury will find against *D* simply because the three accidents he has been in show that he is a menace on the road, regardless of whether he was the one at fault in this one.
2.   Eight citations in two years show a tremendous penchant for running red lights; if *D* was cited eight times there must have been additional hundreds of times when he was not caught, and neither accidents nor being caught deters him.
3.   The proof of the prior acts can be made with the citations, which is both efficient and reliable.

Finally, what about the acrobatic driver? How one packages evidence may well determine whether the evidence will qualify as habit evidence. *W3*'s testimony is highly relevant and concerns sufficiently "habitual" behavior to be admitted as evidence of habit. The testimony shows that *B* invariably went through the intersection without stopping. The testimony implies that this behavior was so regular that *B* never stopped.

The difference between this testimony and the testimony of *W1* and *W2* is that this testimony is narrower, validated by more observations, and more specifically relevant because it concerns the same location as the accident and deals directly with not stopping at the sign. This specifically may mean the difference between admission and exclusion. Note in the next case how careful organizational policies and procedures (not to mention good lawyering) can turn Rule 406 into an effective shield against liability.

MEYER v. UNITED STATES
464 F. Supp. 317 (D. Colo. 1979)

FINESILVER, J.

I

As the wife of a serviceman, plaintiff was an eligible patient at the Family Dental Clinic and on March 29, 1974, she was seen by Kent L.

Aitkin, D.D.S. After his examination, Dr. Aitkin advised her that she needed several fillings and recommended extraction of her upper and lower third molars (wisdom teeth). He advised her that the teeth were impacted and absent removal she would have trouble in the future. She was already experiencing distress and pain from the molars. These molars are the end back teeth and generally are not functional either in concert or alone.

Plaintiff returned to the clinic on April 12, 1974, at which time two right third molars were removed by Dr. Aitkin. Packing was placed in the extracted areas. She was allowed to return home with the packing in place, additional replacement packing, medications, prescriptions for pain and infection, and instructions on care at home.

Later that same evening (or in the early morning hours), plaintiff had a coughing spell and was unable to swallow apparently because of residual bloody and boney fragments resulting from the operation. She was seen in the emergency room at Fitzsimons Army Medical Center and received a prescription that offered her relief. She returned home.

Shortly thereafter she experienced numbness to the right side of the tongue and right gum line.

On April 26, 1974, she was seen again by Dr. Aitkin at the clinic who noted that healing was proceeding in regular fashion. He informed her that her complaints of numbness to the tongue, right gum and partial impairment of sensation were temporary and would return in a matter of months. He also noted this condition was normal in some molar extractions.

Thereafter she was seen by Dr. Jones, an oral surgeon attached to Lowry Air Force Base. She was advised that the loss of sensation and numbness could dissipate in eighteen months, and failure to do so might mean permanent loss of lingual sensation to the right side of the mouth and, in that event, she should consult a lawyer. This suit was filed in January of 1977, following earlier filing of an administrative claim.

It is unrefuted that at this time plaintiff suffers from numbness, permanent loss of sensation and loss of taste in the right front quadrant of her tongue, and right front gum.

Plaintiff related that her injury as a result of nerve damage manifests itself in her inability to taste bland foods, lack of taste differentiation on the right side of the tongue, numbness to this area and to the right gum, and a tendency to stutter. Anxiety over the condition, she contends, makes her unsure of her speech and this has affected her progress and effectiveness as a banking executive for a savings and loan banking facility.

Dentists agree that the lingual nerve has been damaged. Causation of the nerve damage and question of informed consent are matters in dispute.

II

Dr. Aitkin, a dentist in general practice, had specialized dental surgical experience during his three year military service and surgical rotation at each of three duty stations. He had a three month training period in dental surgery at Fort Hood and like periods in Vietnam and in a V.A. residency dental program in California. He related that he had previously performed numerous extractions of third molars in military service and on a weekly basis at the Family Dental Clinic.

Dr. Aitkin does not recollect the various surgical procedures undertaken by him in treating the plaintiff nor the exact conversation he had with plaintiff prior to surgery. His testimony was based in part on his recollection refreshed by the patient's dental chart. He also based his testimony on his habit, custom, and treating routine followed over a considerable period of time.

III

Prior to the extraction procedure, Dr. Aitkin reviewed the x-rays of the teeth in question and in his opinion they were sufficient for the surgical procedure. He administered three injections of novocaine to deaden the pain. The top molar was removed without incident. The lower third molar presented more difficulty because of its mesial angular impaction. He cut a small flap in the lower right gum proximate to the lower molar, observed the impacted molar, removed the bone over the tooth by use of dental instruments, and sectioned and surgically removed the molar. The flap was sutured and area cleansed. Additional injections of novocaine were administered during the operative period. There is no evidence that the lingual nerve was visible to Dr. Aitkin during the operation. The evidence is clear that the nerve may be located along the gum line or elsewhere in the jaw. The nerve is frequently hidden, and the exact location not discernible. In his opinion, x-rays of the molars and locations of roots are of no assistance in knowing where the lingual nerve is situated. The preponderance of the evidence supports this view.

IV

One issue in the case is that of informed consent. Plaintiff testified that she did not receive advice and warnings by Dr. Aitkin as to potential risks of the surgical procedure including possible nerve damage, and had she been so advised she may have declined to go through with the operation.

Dr. Aitkin testified that his habit and custom since dental school, during his three year military service and extending to his association at the Family Dental Clinic, was to give standard advice to patients about extraction of third molars. He advised patients as to the need for the extraction, potential for nerve damage from extraction of the molars including loss of sensation or taste, and general details of the extraction procedure. He generally gave the advice to the patient when he first diagnosed the need for the extraction, although, from his custom, it could come at any time prior to the surgical procedure.

While the testimony is in conflict, we find (a) that plaintiff was informed that as a result of the extractions there was a possibility of damage to the nerves that were proximately located in the area of the molars and roots, and (b) she fully and voluntarily consented to the extraction and medical procedure.

We find that Dr. Aitkin's habit and custom, and routine of advising patients of potential risk as a result of molar extraction was present with plaintiff and he acted in conformity with that long established habit and custom.

We further find that Dr. Aitkin advised plaintiff in a general way of the common and potential risks of extraction of the lower third molar, as shown by his habit, custom and routine, and corroborated by dental assistants Mugele and Smith. He thus complied with a dentist's or physician's duty under Colorado law to inform a patient in a general way as to procedures to be followed in the operation and potential risks. . . .

In the context of Rule 406, habit is a person's or organization's practice of handling a particular kind of situation with a specific type of conduct. Habit is one's regular response to a repeated specific situation. McCormick on Evidence §195 (2d ed. 1972). In similar fashion, an organization's regularity of action is within the purview of Rule 406.

Habit in modern usage is described as "a tendency to act in a certain way or to do a certain thing; usual way of acting; custom; practice. . . ." World Book Dictionary (1974 ed.).

In the instant action there is substantial evidence establishing that the principal actor (Dr. Aitkin) routinely and regularly informed dental patients of the potential risks involved in extraction of third molars. His testimony is supported by two chair-side dental assistants (Mugele and Smith) neither of whom heard the testimony of the other (sequestration pursuant to Rule 615, Fed. R. Evid. was in force during the trial).

D. Character Evidence in Sexual Assault Cases

S. ESTRICH, REAL RAPE
1-7, 42-56 (1987)

In May 1974 a man held an ice pick to my throat and said: "Push over, shut up, or I'll kill you." I did what he said, but I couldn't stop crying. When he was finished, I jumped out of my car as he drove away.

I ended up in the back seat of a Boston police car. I told the two officers I had been raped by a man who came up to the car door as I was getting out in my own parking lot (and trying to balance two bags of groceries and kick the car door open). He took the car, too.

They asked me if he was a crow. That was their first question. A crow, I learned that day, meant to them someone who is black. That was the year the public schools in Boston were integrated.

They asked me if I knew him. That was their second question. They believed me when I said I didn't. Because, as one of them put it, how would a nice (white) girl like me know a crow?

Now they were really listening. They asked me if he took any money. He did; but though I remember virtually every detail of that day and night, I can't remember how much. It doesn't matter. I remember their answer. He did take money; that made it an armed robbery. Much better than a rape. They got right on the radio with that.

We went to the police station first, not the hospital, so I could repeat my story (and then what did he do?) to four more policemen. When we got there, I borrowed a dime to call my father. They all liked that.

By the time we went to the hospital, they were really on my team. I could've been one of their kids. Now there was something they'd better tell me. Did I realize what prosecuting a rape complaint was all about? Did I think I could handle it, I seemed like a nice girl, what a defense lawyer could do . . .

Late that night, I sat in the Police Headquarters looking at mug shots. I was the one who had insisted on going back that night. My memory was fresh. I was ready. They had four or five to "really show" me; being "really shown" a mug shot means exactly what defense attorneys are afraid it means. But it wasn't any one of them. After that, they couldn't help me very much. One shot looked familiar until my father realized that the man had been the right age ten years before. It was late. I didn't have a great description of identifying marks or the like: no one had ever told me that if you're raped, you should not shut your eyes and cry for fear that this really is happening, but should keep your eyes open and focus so you can identify him when you survive. After an hour of looking, I left the police station. They told me they'd get back in touch. They didn't.

A clerk called one day to tell me that my car had been found minus all its tires and I should come sign a release and have it towed — no small matter when you don't have a car to get there and are slightly afraid of your shadow. The women from the rape crisis center called me every day, then every other day, then every week. The police detectives never called at all.

At first, being raped is something you simply don't talk about. Then it occurs to you that people whose houses are broken into or who are mugged in Central Park talk about it *all* the time. Rape is a much more serious crime. If it isn't my fault, why am I supposed to be ashamed? If I'm not ashamed, if it wasn't "personal," why look askance when I mention it? . . .

In many respects I am a very lucky rape victim, if there can be such a thing. Not because the police never found him: looking for him myself every time I crossed the street, as I did for a long time, may be even harder than confronting him in a courtroom. No, I am lucky because everyone agrees that I was "really" raped. When I tell my story, no one doubts my status as a victim. No one suggests that I was "asking for it." No one wonders, at least out loud, if it was really my fault. No one seems to identify with the rapist. His being black, I fear, probably makes my account more believable to some people, as it certainly did with the police. But the most important thing is that he was a stranger; that he approached me not only armed but uninvited; that he was after my money and car, which I surely don't give away lightly, as well as my body. As one person put it: "You really didn't do anything wrong."

Had the man who raped me been found, the chances are relatively good that he would have been arrested and prosecuted and convicted. Stranger rape is prosecuted more frequently, and more successfully, than many violent crimes. And the punishment on conviction tends to be substantial. In some states, until very recently, it could have been death. Not without costs for me, to be sure: under the best circumstances, prosecuting a rape case has unique costs for the victim. And many jurisdictions have made it harder still, by imposing unique obstacles in rape cases, from the requirement that the victim's testimony be corroborated by other evidence to the requirement that she resist her attacker to the inquiry into her sexual past. But although the requirements were theoretically imposed in all cases, victims like me surely fared best. We could count on prosecutors to take our cases more seriously, on juries to be more sympathetic, and on courts to manipulate the doctrinal rules to protect a conviction.

But most rape cases are not as clear-cut as mine, and many that are, like mine, simply are never solved. It is always easier to find the man when the woman knows who he is. But those are the men who are least likely to be arrested, prosecuted, and convicted. Those are the cases least likely to be considered real rapes.

Many women continue to believe that men can force you to have sex against your will and that it isn't rape so long as they know you and don't beat you nearly to death in the process. Many men continue to act as if they have that right. In a very real sense, they do. That is not what the law says: the law says that it is rape to force a woman "not your wife" to engage in intercourse against her will and without her consent. But while husbands have always enjoyed the greatest protection, the protection of being excluded from rape prohibitions, even friends and neighbors have been assured sexual access. What the law seems to say and what it has been in practice are two different things. In fact, the law's abhorrence of the rapist in stranger cases like mine has been matched only by its distrust of the victim who claims to have been raped by a friend or neighbor or acquaintance.

The latter cases are cases of "simple rape." The distinction between the aggravated and simple case is one commonly drawn in assault. It was applied in rape in the mid-1960s by Professors Harry Kalven and Hans Zeisel of the University of Chicago in their landmark study of American juries. Kalven and Zeisel defined an aggravated rape as one with extrinsic violence (guns, knives, or beatings) or multiple assailants or no prior relationship between the victim and the defendant. A simple rape was a case in which none of these aggravating circumstances was present: a case of a single defendant who knew his victim and neither beat her nor threatened her with a weapon. They found that juries were four times as willing to convict in the aggravated rape as in the simple one. And where there was "contributory behavior" on the part of the woman—where she was hitchhiking, or dating the man, or met him at a party—juries were willing to go to extremes in their leniency toward the defendant, even in cases where judges considered the evidence sufficient to support a conviction for rape.

Juries have never been alone in refusing to blame the man who commits a "simple rape." Three centuries ago the English Lord Chief Justice Matthew Hale warned that rape is a charge "easily to be made and hard to be proved, and harder to be defended by the party accused, tho' never so innocent." If it is so difficult for the man to establish his innocence, far better to demand that a woman victim prove hers; under Hale's approach, the one who so "easily" charges rape must first prove her own lack of guilt. That has been the approach of the law. The usual procedural guarantees and the constitutional mandate that the government prove the man's guilt beyond a reasonable doubt have not been considered enough to protect the man accused of rape. The crime has been defined so as to require proof of actual physical resistance by the victim, as well as substantial force by the man. Evidentiary rules have been defined to require corroboration of the victim's account, to penalize women who do not complain promptly, and to ensure the relevance of a woman's prior history of unchastity.

Men have written for decades about women's rape fantasies—about our supposed desire to be forcibly ravished, to "enjoy" sex without taking responsibility for it, to be passive participants in sexual ecstacy which, when we are spurned in the relationship or caught in the act and forced to explain, we then call "rape." That was Hale's concern. It ignores the burdens and humiliation of prosecuting a rape case. It converts the harmless fantasy of some women that a favorite movie star would not take "no" for an answer into a dangerous stereotype that all women wish to be ignored and treated like objects by any man we know.

Yet if the female rape fantasy is open to challenge, and I think it is, the law of rape stands as clear proof of the power and force of a male rape fantasy. The male rape fantasy is a nightmare of being caught in the classic, simple rape. A man engages in sex. Perhaps he's a bit aggressive about it. The woman says no but doesn't fight very much. Finally, she gives in. It's happened like this before, with other women, if not with her. But this time is different: she charges rape. There are no witnesses. It's a contest of credibility, and he is the accused "rapist."

It is important to note that the male rape fantasy is not a nightmare about all rapes, and all women, but only about some; the law of rape has focused its greatest distrust not on all victims, but only on some. The formal prohibitions of the statutes do not distinguish between the stranger and the neighbor, between the man who climbs in the car and the one offered a ride home. The requirements of force and resistance and corroboration and fresh complaint have been formally applicable in every case, regardless of the relationship between victim and defendant. In practice, distinctions have always been drawn. It is in the male fantasy cases—the "simple" cases in which the unarmed man rapes the woman he knows—that these rules have been articulated and applied most conscientiously to punish the victims and protect male defendants. And it is in those cases that prosecutors, courts, and juries continue to enforce them in practice. . . . The rules governing the proof of rape are the perfect complement to the courts' definition of the crime itself. Here as well unique requirements were imposed; and here as well the requirements placed the heaviest burden of proof on cases of simple rape in potentially appropriate situations.

A simple rape might be reversed because the victim did not adequately resist, but it could as easily be reversed on the grounds that her testimony was not corroborated. In many jurisdictions corroboration was technically required in all rape cases. But, as with resistance, the absence of corroborating evidence was most critical where the case turned on questions of attitude (that is, the meaning of "no") or where the woman's story was considered incredible or inculpatory. Limits on a defense counsel's ability to ask questions or present evidence about a woman's sexual past might be upheld in a stranger case, but never in a simple rape. A delay in reporting a simple rape—a delay which empirical evidence, let alone the humiliation of pursuing a rape complaint, suggests is common and understandable—was proof to the common law courts, at least in the cases of simple rape, that the woman should not be believed. As for juries, it was never enough for them to be told that they could convict only on proof that established guilt beyond a reasonable doubt. Courts insisted that they be told, in Hale's own words, to focus their distrust on these women victims.

The reform of these rules has been a primary goal of feminist efforts in recent years, and for good reasons. The rules all too often resulted in the victim's being violated a second time — by the criminal justice system. Formally, most of these rules have now been repealed. In practice, many of them are still applied, if not quite as often in the opinions of the appellate courts, then in the day-to-day workings of the system.

I am interested in these evidentiary rules not so much as an example of the law of evidence gone awry, but for the light they shed on how the crime of rape has been understood in the courts. Here, as with the definition of the crime itself, the underlying theme is distrust of women; that distrust is always focused on rape complaints in appropriate relationships; and the evidentiary rules, like the resistance requirement, serve to enforce the "no means yes" philosophy of social relations and to assure men broad sexual access in appropriate situations.

The requirement that the victim's testimony be corroborated in order to support a conviction was, in its heyday, formally applied in a significant minority of American jurisdictions. In practice, it continues to be a critical factor in determining the disposition of rape charges even today. The justification for the formal rule was, quite explicitly, that women lie. As the Columbia Law Review explained in the late 1960s: "Surely the simplest, and perhaps the most important, reason not to permit conviction for rape on the uncorroborated word of the prosecutrix is that that word is very often false. . . . Since stories of rape are frequently lies or fantasies, it is reasonable to provide that such a story, in itself, should not be enough to convict a man of a crime." The writer felt no need to cite a single authority for the long-held, if never-tested, proposition that women frequently lie, voluntarily exposing themselves to the potential humiliation of a rape prosecution.

Rhetorically a number of courts agreed. Without the corroboration rule, "every man is in danger of being prosecuted and convicted on the testimony of a base woman, in whose testimony there is no truth." The corroboration rule is required because of the "psychic complexes" of "errant young girls and women coming before the court," which take the form "of contriving false charges of sexual offences by men." "If proof of opportunity to commit the crime were alone sufficient to sustain a conviction, no man would be safe." Corroboration is required because "sexual cases are particularly subject to the danger of deliberately false charges, resulting from sexual neurosis, phantasy, jealousy, spite, or simply a girl's refusal to admit that she consented to an act of which she is now ashamed."

In practice, the corroboration requirement tended to be applied by these courts more flexibly than their rhetoric suggests. Sometimes they insisted on corroboration of every detail: not only the fact of intercourse, but force, resistance, and the identity of the defendant. Sometimes little or no corroboration was required. The plausibility of the victim's story was determinative. If her testimony was "credible," it might support conviction even if largely or wholly uncorroborated; where it was "inherently incredible, or . . . contrary to human experience or to usual human behavior," the corroboration requirement mandated reversal of the conviction.

The corroboration requirement was an almost perfect complement to the resistance requirement, both in principle and in application. One is as hard pressed to find the convictions of men who jump from behind bushes reversed for lack of corroboration as for lack of resistance, even if they leave no bruises. These accounts are rarely considered so "inherently incredible" as to be reversed for lack of corroboration. Complaints of simple rape are another matter. The "inherently incredible" standard, clearly rooted in Hale's distrust, made corroboration most important precisely in the cases where resistance was most likely to be demanded. . . .

The evidentiary rules relating to the relevance of a woman's sexual past have been even more controversial than the corroboration requirement. Perhaps the most often quoted justification for the admission of such evidence is that of New York's highest court in 1838: "Will you not more readily infer assent in the practiced Messalina, in loose attire, than in the reserved and virtuous Lucretia?" Where there was evidence that the woman was a "common prostitute," another court emphasized: "It would be absurd, and shock our sense of truth, for any man to affirm that there was not a much greater probability in favor of the proposition that a common prostitute had yielded her assent to sexual intercourse than in the case of the virgin of uncontaminated purity." But it was not necessary that the woman be a prostitute; "no impartial mind can resist the conclusion that a female who had been in the recent habit of illicit intercourse with others will not be so likely to resist as one spotless and pure."

For these courts and many others unchastity was relevant both to the issue of consent and to the woman's credibility as a witness (that is, whether her testimony could be believed). Some courts restricted evidence of the victim's sexual relations with men other than the defendant to testimony of general reputation; witnesses could be asked if the victim had a "bad" reputation for chastity in the community. Others allowed cross-examination, and even direct evidence, relating to "specific immoral and unchaste acts," so long as not too remote in time. When the woman took the stand to testify, defense counsel could cross-examine her as to the details of any of these past relations with other men. In some states the men themselves might be called as witnesses. As the Nebraska Supreme Court explained it in 1949, evidence of past specific acts must be available, "not only for the purpose of being considered by the jury in deciding the weight and credibility of [the victim's] testimony generally, but for the purpose of inferring the probability of consent and discrediting her testimony relating to force or violence used by the defendant in accomplishing his purpose and her claimed resistance thereto." The court termed this the "modern realist rule," and "the better one." It certainly was the better one for the male defendant.

In a general sense, the belief that a woman's sexual past is relevant to her complaint of rape reflects, as does the resistance requirement, the law's punitive celebration of female chastity and its unwillingness to protect women who lack its version of virtue. Wigmore, the leading commentator on the law of evidence, so distrusted women who complained of rape that he proposed a requirement that the unchaste complainant be subject to a mandatory psychiatric evaluation before her testimony could be presented to a jury. According to him:

> [Rape complainants'] psychic complexes are multifarious, distorted partly by inherent defects, partly by diseased derangements or abnormal instincts, partly by bad social environment, partly by temporary physiological or emotional conditions. . . . The unchaste . . . mentality finds incidental but direct expression in the narration of imaginary sex incidents of which the narrator is the heroine or the victim. On the surface the narration is straight-forward and convincing.

Even apart from Wigmore's extreme proposal, the risks of painful humiliation for the sexually experienced victim were enormous. And the likelihood of convicting the defendant after the humiliation of the victim was questionable. Sociological studies have found significant correlations between victim chastity and the perceived seriousness of the rape. Holding all other facts constant, the rape of an experienced woman is viewed as a less serious assault. Courts have long been aware of the danger of prejudice based on sexual history, but in a different way: they have never been as willing to allow similar inquiries into a male defendant's sexual history, precisely because of the prejudice which might be occasioned in the mind of the jury.

But, again as with the resistance requirement, distinctions have always been drawn in these cases, based on the type of rape and the type of relationship. Where the defendant is a stranger-in-the-bushes, courts have upheld convictions even if the trial judge exercised his discretion to limit the evidence of a woman's sexual history. But where it is a simple rape by someone the victim knows, let alone someone with whom she has previously been intimate, limits on questioning almost routinely led to reversals of convictions. Past acts of intercourse with *this* defendant have always been considered relevant evidence of consent. The influential Model Penal Code automatically downgrades the severity of the offense where there is a past relationship of intimacy. Under this approach, the existence of a prior relationship is not only relevant evidence but is itself an issue of fact which must affirmatively be found by the jury.

A defendant who had engaged in a continuing relationship with the victim might assume that his passive partner was consenting on the occasion she later claimed was rape, and justly complain that his actions could not fairly be judged apart from their prior relationship. But cases like that are unlikely to result in the filing of charges in the first instance, let alone a discretionary decision by a trial judge to exclude this evidence, let alone a conviction of rape—at least absent extraordinary force. . . .

The more common issue in the appellate cases relates to evidence of a woman's past sexual relations with men *other* than the defendant. Procedurally these cases take the form of appeals by convicted defendants challenging the trial court's exclusion of such evidence. The question is whether the trial court's decision to exclude requires reversal of the conviction. When the defendant is a stranger, particularly an armed stranger, courts seldom reverse. The stated reason is that consent is not an issue. Thus, the same court that held evidence of a prior relationship between victim and defendant, "regardless of how false," to be admissible, has also held that "where want of consent is not an issue, as where accused denies the act charged, evidence of the female's want of chastity is immaterial and inadmissible."

The most common justification for upholding the exclusion of evidence of a woman's sexual past—that consent is not at issue—does not fully explain the pattern of results. There are some simple rape cases where consent is also not at issue because the defendant, like the stranger in the aggravated case, denies having had intercourse with the victim. But evidence of her sexual history has still been considered so important that its exclusion justifies reversal: for example, by finding it to be relevant to testimony as to the severity of the alleged injury. By the same token, there are cases of aggravated rape where the defendant nonetheless claims consent as a defense and the court still affirms the conviction notwithstanding the exclusion of evidence. In those cases little or no weight is given to the relevance of the evidence of consent; instead, one finds courts emphasizing the brutal nature of the attack or the corroborating proof or the existence of a confession, albeit contested. Of course consent is not the only issue to which sexual history evidence is considered relevant; the woman's (dubious) credibility is always mentioned and often stressed when courts are ordering the admission of such evidence. In the aggravated rape cases where exclusion is upheld, the credibility issue is rarely even mentioned. What explains the cases best is not whether consent is raised as a technical defense, but whether the court sees reason to doubt or suspect the woman. If there is no reason to distrust, there is also no reason to humiliate.

Where there is reason to distrust—where the man is not a stranger and the relationship not inappropriate—the opportunity to humiliate is required as a matter of law. . . .

If a defendant knew of a woman's sexual history, an argument might be made that such knowledge is relevant to determining what he thought at the time of intercourse, whether he believed that she was consenting to his advances. Even in that case one might conclude that the prejudice of the evidence exceeded its very limited probative value. But the admission of evidence of a woman's sexual history was not limited to cases where the defendant himself knew his victim's reputation or history. The defendant lucky enough to find out, albeit later, that his victim was sexually experienced could and would try to hide behind that fact at trial, if she was willing even to proceed to trial. The decision to admit such evidence rested, in the first place, with the trial court. For the appellate courts it represented another opportunity to give explicit meaning to the distinction between the trusted victim of the stranger rape and the suspect victim of simple rape. For many of these courts the requirement of humiliation, like the requirement of resistance, was limited to the latter.

The cautionary instruction is a final example of the institutionalization of the law's distrust of women victims through rules of evidence and procedure. Juries are always told that they must be convinced beyond a reasonable doubt of the defendant's guilt. In rape cases, since the nineteenth century they have also been told, sometimes in Hale's own words, that they must be especially suspicious of the woman victim. In a fairly typical version of the instruction, the jury is told "to evaluate the testimony of a victim or complaining witness with special care in view of the *emotional involvement* of the witness and the *difficulty of determining the truth* with respect to alleged sexual activities carried out in private." All women who are forced to have sex therefore have an "emotional involvement" in the event and are not to be totally trusted in their recounting of it. The force of the instruction is, not unintentionally I think, likely to be greatest in those cases where there is some prior "involvement," if not emotion, between the man and the woman.

Each of the rules discussed in this chapter, and particularly the patterns of their application in the appellate courts, can be seen as a response to a man's nightmarish fantasy of being charged with simple rape. The requirement that the woman resist, as strictly applied in the nonstranger cases, provides men the needed notice that sex is unwelcome. The requirement of corroboration, again applied most strictly in the "improbable cases," prevents a simple credibility contest. The requirement of fresh complaint limits the woman's freedom to turn on her former friend or lover or neighbor after she has been spurned or discovers she is pregnant. Even after all of this, the cautionary instruction reminds the jury of the unfair and vulnerable position in which the man finds himself and the suspicion women deserve in such cases.

It is important to understand that this male rape fantasy is not just a nightmare about women. It is also a nightmare about juries, and about the unwillingness or inability of prosecutors and judges to exercise their discretion to dismiss unfounded complaints. For if juries were not distrusted, then they could be expected to recognize the "ambivalent" woman without the corroboration requirement, let alone the resistance requirement; to take into account the absence of a fresh complaint as one factor to be considered in judging her credibility; and certainly to resolve the issues presented without the necessity of a cautionary instruction.

The nightmare is not merely that women are confused and ambivalent to begin with and filled with vengeance and deceit after the fact, but that the passions of the men on the jury (prior to the 1970s it was constitutional to discriminate against women in jury duty) may be so inflamed by the violation of rape that they will rush to judgment. It is "because the crime of rape arouses emotions as do few others," because of "the respect and sympathy naturally felt by any tribunal for a wronged female," and because "public sentiment seems preinclined to believe a man guilty of any illicit sexual offense he may be charged with" that appellate courts and statute writers must perform their watchdog functions.

The male fantasy has never been substantiated by an empirical study. From all we know, the nightmare case is highly unlikely even to be reported to the police, let alone prosecuted; trials which are no more than credibility contests between the victim and the defendant are virtually nonexistent; and juries tend to be biased against the prosecution in rape cases, particularly in simple, non-stranger cases. Convictions in the absence of "aggravating circumstances" are extremely rare.

Far from challenging that bias, common law judges have given it the force of law. By adopting and enforcing the most insulting stereotypes of women victims of simple rapes, they have enshrined distrust of women in the law, legitimated the male fantasy, and ensured that rape trials would indeed be *real* nightmares—for the women victims.

The rules governing character in sexual assault cases have been substantially clarified and revised in the last few decades. Traditionally, evidence of prior sexual behavior of the victim could be admitted on several grounds. The porosity of the character evidence rules with respect to the prior sexual history of a victim-witness in a sexual assault case allowed defense counsel aggressively to cross-examine prosecuting victim-witnesses on these matters and essentially put them on trial in the manner described by Professor Estrich. This state of affairs tended to discourage many victims of sexual assault from coming forward to report the crime and assist in its prosecution.

In recent years, this sensitive subject matter has been regulated by legislative changes in the Federal Rules of Evidence and by statute and court rules in many states. Rule 412 (originally adopted in 1978) and its numerous state "rape shield law" counterparts severely restricts admissibility of evidence of the prior sexual behavior of a victim of sexual assault or other misconduct. This new rule represents a legislative resolution of some of the issues raised by Professor Estrich, above. Traditionally, evidence of prior sexual assaults by the defendant was subject to exclusion when its only relevance was as evidence of a propensity for sexual misconduct. However, in the mid-1990s, Congress enacted new Rules 413–415 to make evidence of the defendant's prior sexual misconduct expressly admissible in a criminal prosecution or civil action for sexual assault or child molestation.

As you consider the difficult issues raised by this kind of criminal activity and its effective prosecution in the problems and cases which follow, please keep some of the following questions in mind.

How does proof of character in sexual assault cases differ from proof of character under Rules 404-406?

Is there a logical, experiential, or policy justification for treating evidence of the prior conduct of a defendant in a sexual assault case differently from such evidence in other criminal cases? Is evidence rendered admissible by Rules 413-415 subject to exclusion under Rule 403? If so, under what conditions?

When, if ever, should evidence of the prior conduct of a prosecuting witness in a sexual assault case be admitted? Are restrictions on this sort of proof in sexual assault cases based only on considerations of relevance, or do the modern rape-victim shield statutes (such as Rule 412) also create a *privilege* for the sexual assault victim, similar to other privileges, that operates to exclude possibly relevant evidence? If the rape-victim shield statutes are based on considerations of relevance, whose notion of relevance is incorporated in the statutes — that of women? men? the average person? reformers? feminists? "enlightened" legislators seeking to bar "the information jurors would tend to use to perpetuate stereotyped and prejudiced views about women"?

J. TANFORD & A. BOCCHINO, RAPE VICTIM SHIELD LAWS AND THE SIXTH AMENDMENT
128 U. Pa. L. Rev. 544, 544-549, 550-551 (1980)

In the last few years, forty-six jurisdictions have made efforts to protect rape victims from the humiliation of public disclosure of the details of their prior sexual activities. In most states the legislatures have passed shield laws restricting a criminal defendant's ability to present to the jury evidence of past sexual history. In one instance, the same result has been reached by an appellate court ruling. Late in 1978, the United States Congress followed this trend and enacted rule 412 of the Federal Rules of Evidence. While these laws vary in scope and procedural details, they share the features of declaring an end to the presumptive admissibility of such evidence and of restricting the situations in which a defendant will be allowed to bring the victim's sexual history to the attention of the jury. Almost unanimously, the literature of the last few years has encouraged these laws and attempted to justify any adverse consequences to the defendant by claiming that the state's interest in protecting rape victims is sufficiently important to overcome any constitutional objections. The changing moral climate in this country and the increasing leniency about sexual relationships outside of marriage, it is usually argued, have discredited the old rationale that the unchastity of a woman has a material bearing on whether she has really been raped.

The new laws do not, however, merely end an antiquated rule of evidence; they establish a new rule in some cases as extreme as the old one. Statutes such as rule 412 create a presumption that the sexual history of a rape victim will never be admissible, except when compelled by due process because of overwhelming probative value. It is, of course, difficult to argue with the position that the old rule of automatic admissibility should have been eliminated. It is not as easy to say that it is wise or consistent with the rights of a criminal defendant automatically to prevent introduction of evidence of a rape victim's sexual history.

The premise of the first part of this Article is that evidence of a rape victim's sexual history may be probative of an issue material to determining the guilt of a defendant charged with rape. Later sections of the Article will discuss particular circumstances in which such evidence is relevant and necessary to the effective presentation of the accused's defense. Initially, this Article will evaluate the new rules in light of the sixth amendment rights of a defendant to confront the witnesses against him and to produce witnesses in his favor. . . .

II.   HISTORICAL PERSPECTIVES

At common law, the rules governing the use of a rape complainant's sexual history provided that such evidence was always admissible. Three elements combined to create the rule of admissibility. The first was the fear of false charges brought by vindictive women. Sir Matthew Hale, Lord Chief Justice of the King's Bench, stated that rape "is an accusation easily to be made . . . and harder to be defended by the party accused, tho, never so innocent." Second was the concept that chastity was a character trait. If a woman could be shown to be unchaste by nature, then it could be inferred that she had consented to sex with the defendant. Third was the belief that premarital sex was immoral. Acts of previous illicit sexual relations, like other acts of moral turpitude, could thus be used to impeach the credibility of the complaining witness in a rape case.

The fear expressed by Sir Matthew Hale, that it is difficult to defend against fabricated rape charges, pervaded the early writings justifying the need for sexual history evidence.

> The unchaste (let us call it) mentality finds . . . expression in the narration of imaginary sex incidents of which the narrator is the heroine or the victim. On the surface the narration is straightforward and convincing. The real victim, however . . . is the innocent man; for the respect and sympathy naturally felt by any tribunal for a wronged female helps to give easy credit to such a plausible tale.

To protect these innocent men, juries were usually instructed to scrutinize closely the testimony of a rape complainant: "Where the complaining witness and the defendant are the only witnesses, a charge of rape is one which, generally speaking, is easily made, and once made, difficult to disprove. Therefore, I charge you that the law requires that you examine the testimony of the prosecuting witness with caution." Dean Wigmore went so far as to urge that all women who brought rape charges undergo psychiatric examination before being allowed to testify in order to weed out charges stemming from sexual fantasy, rather than fact.

Whatever the situation may have been in times past, it is difficult to argue today that the danger of false charges is greater for rape than for any other kind of crime. If anything, the statistics show just the opposite. Rape is one of the most under-reported crimes. In addition, rape allegations are carefully screened in most instances to assure that only legitimate cases go to trial. For no other category of crime is the scrutiny by the police and prosecutor closer.

Most states today do *not* have a rule automatically allowing the use in rape trials of testimony about a woman's "character" for chastity. Not long ago, however, courts reasoned that most women were virtuous by nature and that an unchaste woman must therefore have an unusual character flaw. This character trait had caused her to consent in the past (when, obviously, a "normal" woman would never have consented) and made it likely that she would consent repeatedly. Because consent was a defense to rape, evidence that was thought to show a propensity towards sexual relations was always admissible to suggest consent in the particular instance. Courts and legislatures have adapted to the times and have realized that a woman who is unchaste — or in modern parlance, who has had extramarital sexual relationships—is no more likely to consent indiscriminately than is a chaste woman.

Another problem that led to dissatisfaction with viewing sexual history as evidence of character was the manner of proof. Character is usually proved by testimony about a person's reputation and less often by opinion testimony or by evidence of specific acts. Thus, in rape cases, the defendant was entitled to introduce testimony about the sexual reputation of the victim and could often have a witness testify to his opinion of the woman's chastity. Even if there is some probative value in showing that a rape victim is casual in her selection of sexual partners, the least accurate way of doing so is by evidence of her reputation or the opinion of one witness perhaps lacking any personal knowledge.

Sensing the inherent weaknesses of relying on the character-evidence rationale for admitting sexual history evidence, some courts attempted to justify it on the ground that it impeached the complainant's credibility. This reasoning assumes that promiscuity is a form of dishonesty, and that, as in the case of other acts affecting honesty, promiscuity lessens the witness's credibility. This effort to justify admitting evidence of sexual history is seriously flawed. First, the cases offering this explanation limited the inference to women. Promiscuous men could not be similarly impeached. Second, only women who brought rape charges were open to this kind of impeachment. Female prosecuting witnesses who charged defendants with other types of crimes, such as robbery, could never be impeached by their prior sexual history. . . .

III. THE MODERN RESPONSE

Much of the debate about rape victim shield laws has centered on the attempt to define precisely those situations in which fairness and due process demand that the defendant be allowed to introduce sexual history evidence. Professor Berger has written a comprehensive article defining seven particular types of evidence that, subject to judicial findings of relevance and fairness, the defendant ought to be allowed to introduce.[41] Other writers have argued that a man accused of rape may delve into the victim's sexual history in far fewer instances.[42] . . .

41. (1) Evidence of the complainant's sexual conduct with the defendant; (2) evidence of specific instances of conduct to show that someone other than the accused caused the physical condition (semen, pregnancy, disease) allegedly arising from the act; (3) evidence of a distinctive pattern of conduct closely resembling the defendant's version of the encounter, to prove consent; (4) evidence of prior sexual conduct known to the defendant (presumably by reputation) tending to prove that he believed complainant was consenting; (5) evidence showing a motive to fabricate the charge; (6) evidence that rebuts proof offered by the state on victim's sexual conduct; and (7) evidence as the basis for expert testimony that the complainant fantasized the act. Berger, [Man's Trial, Woman's Tribulation: Rape Cases in the Courtroom, 77 Colum. L. Rev. 90,] 98-99 [1977].

42. E.g., Ordover, [Admissibility of Patterns of Similar Sexual Conduct: The Unlamented Death of Character for Chastity, 63 Cornell L. Rev. 90, 110-118 (1979)] (distinctive patterns of behavior under similar circumstances); Note, California Rape Evidence Reform: An Analysis of Senate Bill 1678, 26 Hastings L.J. 1551, 1572 (1975) (only when victim's testimony is sole incriminating evidence); [Evelyn Sroufe, Evidence—Admissibility of the Victim's Past Sexual Behavior Under Washington's Rape Evidence Law,] 52 Wash L. Rev. 1011, 1023, 1027-33 (1977) (bias and relations with the defendant only).

VII. CONCLUSION

A state is constitutionally prohibited from enacting a rape victim shield law that limits a defendant's ability to introduce otherwise admissible evidence. The sixth amendment rights of confrontation and compulsory process guarantee exactly this: no person accused of a crime may be denied the right to introduce evidence when the probative value outweighs the prejudicial effect. The state and federal governments may not legislate to alter the rules of evidence so as to place unusual and new burdens on the accused's ability to defend himself. Testing rape victim shield laws against this federal constitutional standard finds many of them defective.

Because sexual history evidence is potentially relevant in some rape cases, those statutes that contain absolute prohibitions, whether against all such evidence or only certain classes or uses of evidence, certainly cannot be reconciled with the sixth amendment. Shield laws also run afoul of the Constitution when they alter the traditional standard for the admissibility of evidence. The sixth amendment guarantees incorporate a federal constitutional standard for the admission and exclusion of evidence offered by the accused, and the states cannot, therefore, require the evidence offered by rape defendants to satisfy a stricter standard.

There is, however, nothing wrong with requiring that the relevance of sexual history evidence be determined before trial, by employing the traditional standard of probative value weighed against prejudicial effect. To the extent that shield statutes limit the accused from unfairly attacking the morality of a rape victim, they are unobjectionable. To the extent that such statutes require that rape victims be treated no differently from other witnesses and that sexual conduct testimony be treated the same as any other evidence, they are certainly valid. A statute that seeks to correct past abuses and to change the old rule automatically admitting evidence of the rape victim's morality is laudatory. No valid constitutional reason justifies singling out rape complainants for different treatment. But fairness to rape victims and control over potentially prejudicial testimony can also be accomplished by a pretrial determination of the relevance of sexual history evidence. A valid shield law should thus read:

> Evidence of specific instances of the victim's sexual conduct, opinion evidence of the victim's sexual conduct, and reputation evidence of the victim's sexual conduct may be admitted . . . only if, and only to the extent that, the judge finds that the evidence is material to a fact at issue in the case and that its inflammatory or prejudicial nature does not outweigh its probative value.
>
> If the defendant proposes to ask any question concerning [such evidence], either by direct examination or cross-examination of any witness, the defendant must inform the court out of the hearing of the jury prior to asking any such

question. After this notice, the court shall conduct an in camera hearing . . . to determine whether the proposed evidence is admissible.

Times change, and the prevailing morality changes with them. The move for equality of women has made us aware of the abuse of rape victims in the criminal justice system. Although steps have appropriately been taken towards protecting them, they have in many instances come at the expense of rights guaranteed the accused. While a rape defendant should have no greater right to present evidence than other defendants and should not be allowed to sidetrack the search for truth by introducing irrelevant testimony about the sexual mores of the complainant, the sixth amendment guarantees that he will not be prevented from eliciting testimony relevant to his defense. Shield laws must be tested against his established rights to confront his accusers and to present his own defense. If these laws are found wanting, they must be struck down and rewritten to assure that the desire to protect rape victims does not unconstitutionally hinder the ability of the accused to defend himself.

As the questions in the text introducing this section suggest, we believe that the Rule 412 protection afforded victims in sexual assault cases to prevent evidence of their prior sexual activities cannot always be justified solely on relevance grounds, at least as that term is defined in Rule 401. Nor can this protection be justified by the familiar prejudice considerations of Rules 403, 404, 405, or 609, because these rules are concerned primarily with prejudice to the accused, not to witnesses against the accused. Possibly, exclusion of relevant sexual history could be justified in some cases on grounds that evidence of the victim's prior sexual history (1) misleads the jury, (2) confuses the issues, or (3) wastes time—other 403 grounds for exclusion of relevant evidence. But exclusion on these bases would be on a case-by-case, not a per se, basis.

The rape-victim shield law is predicated on assertions about relevance. There is some tendency for people to think about the concept of relevance as logical and objective. It is important, however, to recognize that concepts of relevance are very much dependent on one's point of view. See the Time Travel to Old Salem Problem above. The law of sexual assault has unquestionably been dominated by conceptions of relevance derived from centuries of development by male judges. The shield laws assert a different concept of relevance, stemming from a different point of view. It is precisely this difference in point of view that makes discussion of the problem in this section both intense and interesting.

The shield statutes, including Rule 412, which was enacted after the adoption of the Federal Rules in 1975, can also be thought of as creating a privilege for the victims of sexual assaults. As with other privileges (see the chapter on Privileges below), the sexual assault victim's privilege may work to exclude evidence that is relevant. And, again like other privileges, the sexual assault victim's privilege can be conceptualized in terms of privacy or instrumental utilitarianism.

The shield statutes are strongly grounded in privacy and respect for the integrity of the victim. Details of a person's sexual life lie close to the heart of the privacy considerations articulated by Krattenmaker and Westin. See Chapter VII(A) below. The statutes also are strongly grounded on utilitarian objectives: Without the privilege, victims will be hesitant to come forward and press charges, or guilty defendants will go unpunished because they succeed in playing on the jury's prejudices by putting the victim on trial. In either case, dangerous criminals will not be brought to justice, which endangers society.

Had Rule 412 only eliminated use of propensity logic as it related to actions of a rape victim, the statute would have created no serious constitutional problems. Propensity logic—that is, the use of character to prove action on a specific occasion in conformity with character—is pretty thin stuff. Its marginal relevance partially accounts for the limitations on its use in Rules 404(a) and 405. By contrast, Rule 404(b) emphasizes that there are situations in which proof of specific instances of conduct may be highly relevant to some material issue although the proof may also show character. Rule 404(b) deals with situations in which the logical line of inference does not go through character.

However, by purporting to bar evidence of past instances of the victim's sexual behavior for virtually all purposes, Rule 412 went well beyond the elimination of propensity logic. Rule 412 eliminated as well virtually all relevant uses of specific instances of the victim's past sexual behavior, even though the inference to be drawn from proof of such instances bears on a material issue without explicitly going through character. In this sense, Rule 412 may be thought of as having eliminated 404(b)-type uses of past conduct as well as 404(a)-type uses. Defendants may contend that these uses may be highly relevant in a particular case, and therefore their elimination raises serious questions of violation of the defendant's right to present his defense. Compare the statutory proposal of Professor Berger above. She articulates a number of situations in which past specific instances of the sexual conduct of the victim would be highly relevant. Unlike Rule 404(b), however, Professor Berger's statute would provide a limited and exclusive number of affirmative justifications for admissibility rather than (like Rule 404(b)) a series of examples in which a general rule of exclusion does not logically apply.

Professor Althouse is critical of Tanford and Bocchino's analysis and of the absence of balancing material in the previous edition of this casebook. She states:

Even if rights trump competing concerns, there remains a preliminary question as to the content of those rights. Moreover, one could question the meaning given to rights, perhaps on the ground that the rights that law has embraced over the years express the concerns of men. By labeling women's concerns mere "indignities" or offenses to "sensibilities" and men's concerns "rights," the article can sweep women's concerns aside with the seemingly neutral principle that rights must prevail.

The article excerpt also asserts that the defendant's perspective "must" be taken, but this requirement lies unexamined. In the ordinary development of the meaning of rights, the needs of the criminal justice system, the interests of victims, and the values of society play a substantial role. Moreover, many have argued that the law of rape has taken the male perspective to an inordinate degree and thus reflects a deep-seated antagonism to women.

See Althouse, Nw. U.L. Rev., supra, citing, among others, S. Estrich, Real Rape; C. MacKinnon, Toward a Feminist Theory of the State (1989); and S. Brownmiller, Against our Will (1975).

Susan Brownmiller studies male sexual violence against females regardless of age or sexual orientation from prehistoric and biblical times through today; this definitive treatment examines violence in war, riots, and pogroms; religious, racial, and ethnic persecutions; slavery, gangs, and prison; and in myth, fantasy, and even heroic glorification. Brownmiller's central thesis: "From prehistoric times to the present . . . rape has played a critical function. It is nothing more or less than a conscious process of intimidation by which *all men* keep *all women* in a state of fear. Brownmiller builds a powerful case based on massive and wide-ranging accounts and data of the systematized use of rape as a tool of intimidation, control, and power by men against women. Seen in this light, supposedly "neutral" rules of evidence, as applied in the antiseptic atmosphere of the halls of justice, take on a new hue.

In Sexual Violence: Our War Against Rape (1993), Linda A. Fairstein, an assistant district attorney in New York and for over 15 years the director of that city's Sex Crimes Prosecution Unit, recounts numerous successful, and some unsuccessful, prosecutions for rape. Fairstein points out that the success of her unit was dramatically increased by the elimination of the corroboration requirement in New York and by the enactment of a rape-victim's shield law. Fairstein states:

> Allowing unlimited questioning about a victim's proper sexual history worked against her in at least two ways. At trial in the courtroom, it diverted the jury from the issue of the defendant's guilt by trying the witness for her "promiscuity." And even worse, it worked to keep many survivors from participating in the legal process and subjecting themselves to debasing and humiliating treatment. Before the introduction of the so-called rape shield laws, then, many witnesses simply refused to expose themselves to such mistreatment.

Id. at 122. According to Fairstein, even the threat of the use of a victim's prior sexual history can be seen as a tool that permits rape to go unpunished. Thus, from Brownmiller's perspective, evidence rules that permit such inquiry can be seen as part of a system of domination, intimidation, and condoned violence by men against women.

With these considerations in mind, is it so clear, as Tanford and Bocchino state, that the exclusion of evidence by rape-shield statutes that do not apply to all witnesses violates the Constitution?

COMMONWEALTH v. GOUVEIA
371 Mass. 566, 358 N.E.2d 1001 (1976)

BRAUCHER, J. The defendant appeals from convictions of rape and an unnatural act, and argues two assignments of error: (1) exclusion of evidence of prior sexual intercourse by the victim, and (2) denial of his motion for a mistrial after the prosecutor in his closing argument asserted that there was no evidence to refute the victim's testimony as to what happened when she and the defendant were alone together. We hold that there was no error in excluding evidence of prior sexual acts between the victim and a person other than the defendant. . . . We therefore affirm the convictions.

The case for the Commonwealth consisted almost entirely of the testimony of the victim, which we summarize. She was nineteen years old and lived and worked in Billerica. On the evening of Saturday, August 25, 1973, she drove her automobile to a bar in Lowell and had two or three drinks with friends and with a young man whom she met there and who invited her to a family birthday party. She drove him to the party, a few minutes away, arriving about 11:30 to 12 P.M., and found approximately thirty people there. About a half hour later, she felt sick and she and her escort went out and got into the back seat of her car. He passed out, she vomited, and she discovered that her wallet and car keys were missing. She got out of the car and spoke to others who said they would look for the car keys.

At this point the defendant, whom she did not know, suggested that she could lie down in his van, parked nearby, and she did so. She was there for about two hours, during which time several men looked in, and one made sexual advances which she repulsed. Finally, the defendant got into the van and committed the crimes charged. After ten or fifteen minutes the defendant "gave up"; she put her jeans back on; and she went back to her car, leaving her underwear in the van. She rolled up the windows and locked the doors of her car, and a woman came over and screamed at her. Others were standing around. Later the defendant came back, said the woman was going to beat her up, and offered to give her "a ride to get out of there." They got into the van, and he drove her to within a quarter of a mile of her home. He gave her the wrong name of the street where the party was, and he falsely said the van was not his. She noted the license number and wrote it down when she arrived home about 5:15 A.M.

About 7 or 7:30 A.M. she called a friend, and he drove her to Lowell to look for her car. The same morning, after searching without success, they went to the Lowell police department. She gave the police the license number of the van and learned the defendant's name. About a week later the police recovered her car, and her wallet was found in a mailbox.

The defendant stipulated that he was at the party with his van, and that he drove the victim home. The escort, six women, and the husband of one of them testified for the defendant. All the witnesses were related to the escort by blood or marriage and all but one testified that they had known the defendant for many years. He did not testify.

In September, 1975, the defendant was convicted of both rape and an unnatural act, and was sentenced to nine to twelve years for rape and to a lesser concurrent sentence for an unnatural act. An appeal to the Appellate Division of the Superior Court resulted in concurrent sentences of three to five years. The defendant appealed pursuant to G.L. c. 278, §§33A-33G, and we allowed the parties' joint application for direct appellate review, which focused on the admissibility of evidence of prior sexual acts by a rape victim.

1. *Evidence of prior sexual acts.* The victim testified on direct examination that she was outside in the back seat of her car with her escort about two hours before the crimes took place. On cross-examination she said that she was talking to him, and that he kissed her and "attempted to make a pass" at her, "and that was it." She denied having sexual intercourse with him, but the judge sustained an objection to the question and instructed the jury to disregard it. She denied that she was undressed.

Defense witnesses testified that the victim and her escort were in the back seat of her car, and that he passed out and was carried into the house. They testified that both the victim and her escort were completely undressed, and two of them testified to obscene behavior on her part. Several also testified that she got out of the car wholly or partly undressed and walked down the street. The judge excluded questions whether she and her escort engaged in sexual intercourse.

The defendant accepts our general rule that in a rape case, although evidence of a general reputation for unchastity may be admitted, evidence of instances of prior intercourse of the victim with persons other than the defendant is inadmissible. Commonwealth v. Gardner, 350 Mass. 664, 668, 216 N.E.2d 558 (1966), and cases cited. But he argues that the rule should be limited to cases where it is "justified on the ground that collateral questions relating to those specific events would prolong the trial and divert the attention of the trier of fact from the issues." Commonwealth v. McKay, 363 Mass. 220, 227, 294 N.E.2d 213,

218 (1973). Here, he says, the prior act was close in time and nature to the crimes charged, and it was therefore admissible . . . to prove her consent. . . .

On the issue of consent, we stand by the principle that "the victim's consent to intercourse with one man does not imply her consent in the case of another." Commonwealth v. McKay, supra, 363 Mass. at 227, 294 N.E.2d at 218. At least in the circumstances here, a prior consent close in time and place might negate rather than create such an implication of subsequent consent. We need hardly add that the defendant had no right to appeal to the jury on the basis that by her conduct the victim had forfeited any claim to protection from rape.

The defendant further complains that proof of the victim's "obscene and public actions, short of intercourse, . . . strongly and erroneously implied to the jury that no such intercourse did occur," and that subsequent consent to intercourse with the defendant therefore seemed "most improbable." It is at least equally likely that the jury disbelieved the defense testimony, or that they thought, as we do, that prior consent was irrelevant to subsequent consent. In any event, the evidence of "obscene and public actions" was all introduced by the defendant, and he is in no position to complain.

The defendant argues that if our rule excludes the "demonstrably relevant evidence" offered in this case, "merely to protect the dignity of the witness," it denies the defendant his right to a fair trial and violates the United States Constitution. We have said enough to indicate that no relevant evidence was excluded. We do not regard the protection of the dignity of witnesses as illegitimate. See Commonwealth v. Bailey, 348 N.E.2d 746 (1976). But that is not the purpose of the rule here considered. . . .

The defense position was that the alleged victim had open sex with her escort, whom she had met for the first time that night, that she acted obscenely at the party, that she willingly accepted the defendant's invitation to lie down in the back of his van, that she consented to sex with the defendant, that she willingly accepted a ride home from the defendant, and that she claimed she was raped only when she could not find her car and needed to enlist the help of the police in finding it. The defendant's claim is that the alleged victim's sexual conduct with her escort was an integral part of the overall picture of what happened on that night—the res gestae.

Justice Braucher aggressively asserts that the exclusion of the victim's prior sexual acts is based entirely on relevance grounds. (See the last line of the opinion as edited.) This is the way in which the rape-victim shield law is framed, and provides a good opportunity for pointing out again that relevance is not an objective logical concept but rather depends very much on the point of view of the person making the relevance assessment. Do you agree with Justice Braucher? What if there were evidence offered that the alleged victim had had sexual intercourse with several others at the party who visited her in the back of the van? Would the relevance of the evidence be any greater?

Problem: Prostitution, Rape, or Both?

D and *V* met at a bar, then went to a hotel room and engaged in sexual intercourse. *V* asserts that their acquaintance was strictly a social one, and that she was raped. *D* claims that *V* offered him sexual favors in return for money, that they made a deal for $50, that when it came time to pay he had only $20 with him and that *V* thereupon became enraged and accused him of rape.

How should the court rule on the following offers of evidence?

a. *D*'s testimony about conversations with *V* concerning sex for money earlier in the evening:

b. Testimony by others that they had engaged in prior transactions of prostitution with *V*.

c. Evidence that *V* had been prosecuted and twice convicted of prostitution before the encounter with *D*.

d. Evidence that *V* had a reputation as a prostitute in the community in which both *D* and *V* lived.

Although it would be likely that *D* would be permitted to testify about the circumstances of his encounter with *V*, the inference from such proof that "*V* is a prostitute" and hence likely to have behaved in a particular way would likely run afoul of the policy of Rule 412. Other kinds of evidence supporting this inference would almost certainly be banned by that rule. Of course, just because *V* is a prostitute does not mean that she is incapable of being raped. However, the fact of her being picked up in a bar and going to a hotel room, coupled with proof that she was a prostitute, would indicate that she had made a bargain to engage in sex, thereby consenting. This distinguishes this problem from the situation in the *Gouveia* case and makes the proof of her prior sexual behavior much more pertinent here.

In Commonwealth v. Joyce, 382 Mass. 222 (1981), the Massachusetts Supreme Judicial Court held that it was reversible error to exclude evidence under the Massachusetts rape-victim shield statute that the victim had twice previously been charged with prostitution. In *Joyce*, the court held that the evidence was admissible not to show that the victim was a prostitute and that it was more likely that she had consented to sex with the defendant, but rather to show that the victim's allegations against the defendant might have been motivated by her desire to avoid further prosecution against her. Professor Althouse points out:

> While it is plausible that a prostitute might engage in extortion with a threat of false report, actually carrying out the threat seems quite farfetched. Further, given the discretion exercised by the police in deciding which rape claims to report and by the prosecutor in determining which cases to file, it seems wildly unlikely that arrest and prosecution would result.

See Althouse, Nw. U.L. Rev., supra.

Prosecutor Fairstein reports that, in her experience, unfortunately Althouse's first point is not correct but, even more unfortunately, the second point is:

> It is unlikely that any occupation or lifestyle exposes a woman to the threat of assault and gratuitous violence as constantly and completely as prostitution. Every year we see scores of "working girls" who have been victimized by assailants who are confident that these women will be unable to go to the police for help since they live outside the law.
>
> The questions most often posed in this regard are: "Can a prostitute be raped?" "Isn't she assuming that risk by the very nature of her work?" "Isn't it impossible to convict a rapist of forcing a prostitute to have sex with him? That's what she was going to do anyway."
>
> There are jurisdictions in this country in which these women are denied protection of the law, which is a rather shocking commentary on societal views of both women and rape. In 1991, for example, a journalist published a report that the police in Oakland, California, had closed more than two hundred reports of sexual assault—those made by prostitutes and drug addicts—without a single interview or follow-up investigation. The cases were simply "unfounded"—police jargon for saying that no crime ever occurred. It was only when the news story about their failure to examine the complaints appeared that the police were forced to reopen the many cases.
>
> Similarly, in a Southern California community the same year, police closed all rape reports made by prostitutes and addicts by placing them in a file stamped "NHI"—No Human Involved. It is astounding to see in how many towns and cities this travesty is tolerated. In New York, and in other urban areas where prostitution flourishes despite its illegal status and accompanying risks, the police know full well the reality of the situation and generally are responsive to such complaints.
>
> Are there ever false reports, and don't these cases cause serious credibility problems for juries? The answer to both questions is sometimes.
>
> The most obvious kind of problem in complaints made by prostitutes is what police call "fare beat" cases. This is somewhat analogous to the individuals who jump a turnstile in a subway station to avoid buying a token and paying the fare. They are guilty of a crime called theft of services. They have cheated the system by not paying the fare as the rest of us must—hence they are "fare beaters." . . .
>
> In "fare beat" cases no rape has occurred; there has been no force, no threat,

no violence — as the woman usually admits . . . the next morning. There has, instead, been a theft of her services. The sexual act was consensual but the woman was defrauded of her fee. It is obviously critical to identify these cases and get them out of the system — they *do* jaundice law enforcement workers who have much more important things to do than chase down false reports.

That issue aside, the rape and sexual assault of prostitutes illustrate better than any other kind of victimization that these crimes are *not* about sex. The availability of commercial sexual partners in a place like Manhattan is, sadly, limitless. The prices are correspondingly very low — almost every kind of act is for sale for less than the price of a meal at McDonald's. But as everyone who understands the history of this behavior recognizes, prostitutes are victims of rapists whose motives are degradation and humiliation, control and possession, anger and hatred, intimidation and terrorization. These women desperately need the protection of the law and yet are too frequently denied access to the system of justice.

Danny Minella, by the age of twenty-eight, appeared to be a model citizen in the small Westchester village in which he had been raised. He had achieved the rank of Life Scout during his high school days, gone on to a prestigious college before returning home to help his immigrant parents run their thriving retail clothing business, and served in the community as an auxiliary police officer.

In September 1983, a prostitute working on West Forty-third Street was propositioned by a handsome young man driving a Lincoln Continental. Her pimp, several doorways down the sidewalk, nodded his approval and Ginger, the prostitute, negotiated a price and tucked the thirty dollars the driver handed her into her boot before she got into the front passenger seat. They drove around the corner to Tenth Avenue, which Ginger expected, but she did not expect to see the gun that her "date," as she called the driver, removed from beneath his seat and held against her head.

From his back pocket, the driver then produced a pair of handcuffs, attaching one circle to Ginger's wrist and the other to the steering wheel. Holding the gun directly to the side of the anguished woman's head, he told her he was going to play Russian roulette with her and commanded her to suck his penis. When he had ejaculated, he calmly lowered the gun, unzipped Ginger's knee-high boots to remove the several hundred dollars she had made that evening, uncuffed her, and let her out by the side of the car in her bare feet. He told her there was no point in reporting to anyone what had happened since he himself was a police officer.

By the time Ginger walked back to her usual corner, she was determined to go to the Midtown South Precinct and make a formal complaint. She knew her pimp had recorded the plate number as she entered the car, and she knew the fancy Continental even had a small brass plate on the dashboard that said "Danny." She knew that some of the cops who had locked her up in the past would believe her this time since she had never cried wolf before. But her pimp disagreed. He saw no need to call police attention to either of them, and said that if the same driver came back, he'd take care of the guy himself.

During a period of five weeks, Danny made repeated forays into the midtown strip. He became bolder and bolder, cocking his gun and actually pulling the trigger as he sodomized and raped his cuffed victims on the front seat of his car. On one occasion, after blindfolding the young woman he had lured in, he drove her to a storefront in Westchester, took her down to the basement stockroom, and attacked her there, before driving her halfway back to Manhattan and throwing her out on the side of the parkway.

He had claimed four victims by this time, two of whom had gone to the police, described their plight, and given the partial license plate they had remembered. The midtown cops, well aware of the vulnerability of these women, were looking for the Lincoln every night between midnight and four A.M. And so were the pimps, because word had spread on the street. On October 11, 1983, at one in the morning, Ginger spotted the car and Danny cruising the Deuce (as Forty-second Street is known in the trade). She ran to a pay phone to call 911, fearful that her pimp would attempt to take Danny on himself and be shot to death.

Two patrol cars were on the scene immediately and one group of cops recognized Ginger. She repeated her story and the officers confronted Danny, whom she identified face-to-face. When the cops searched him, they found a switchblade in his pocket and a loaded semiautomatic gun under the car seat, next to a pair of handcuffs and a magazine clip with seven more live rounds.

The following morning, after all of his victims had identified him in a lineup, he was placed in a police car for the ride downtown to central booking. One of the detectives leaned his head in the front window to tell the cop, "Take the paperwork to Fairstein's office—she'll write up the case." Minella groaned, "You can't take me there." Nobody paid any attention to him, but when the cop walked into my office with the arrest report, the problem was immediately apparent. I had known Danny Minella and his family all of my life. His parents were fine, decent people who had worked a lifetime to establish a successful retail business and raise a family. I had gone to school with their sons and shopped in their store. I didn't want to see Danny any more than he wanted to see me.

I assigned the case to one of my senior colleagues, Peggy Finerty. She indicted Minella for the series of rapes and robberies. Months later, the case actually went to trial—I think Minella and his lawyer both believed that the women would never show up, or in the alternative, that jurors would neither care about them nor believe their testimony. He was convicted on all counts and sentenced to a term of nine to eighteen years in state prison. The morning after the verdict, when Peggy called to tell the women that the rapist had been found guilty, one of them said to her, "God bless America! Where else could a prostitute be raped and be believed in a court of law. Thank you." . . .

The vulnerability to violence of the women who live on the street—whether they are prostitutes or drug addicts, or merely homeless or mentally ill—is extraordinarily greater than that of those with a more sheltered lifestyle. The criminal justice system must be made accessible to every woman who is victimized, no matter how unsavory or unappealing the circumstances under which the attack occurs.

Fairstein, supra, at 171-177.

Problem: Explanation for Pregnancy

At *D*'s trial for sexual assault of *V, V* testifies that *D* raped her and that she became pregnant as a result. *D* seeks to prove *V*'s prior consensual sexual activity with X on the theory that V became pregnant by X and then falsely accused D of rape to provide an alternate explanation for the pregnancy. Would the following proffered evidence be admissible?:

a. cross examination questions asking V whether she had engaged in sexual intercourse with X?
b. testimony by X that he had engaged in sexual intercourse with V?
c. DNA evidence that V's unborn child was not the child of D?

In some sexual assault cases, evidence of the victim's sexual activity with others is admissible.

Rule 412(b)(2)(A) provides that evidence of the victim's past sexual behavior with persons other than the accused is admissible on the issue of whether the accused was the source of semen or injury. This contemplates the situation where medical evidence offered by the prosecution shows that semen or injuries were found on the victim, and the defendant's response is that he was not their source.

The rule does not address the pregnancy situation presented by the problem. Are the situations similar so that the exception should apply?

If this evidence is not admissible by logical extension of Rule 412(b)(2)(A), should it be admitted under Rule 412(b)(1)? (Constitutionally required?) The accused may argue that to exclude this evidence would be to deny D the opportunity to present the core of his defense. Moreover, this evidence does not go to V's general sexual character; rather, it goes to her motive in accusing D of rape. Thus, it could be argued that it is independently relevant, like evidence of motive that is held admissible under Rule 404(b) in other types of cases as not implicating the propensity rule. Do you agree? What other facts would you want to know before deciding?

STATE v. JACQUES
558 A.2d 706 (Me. 1989)

ROBERTS, J.: Gerald Jacques was convicted after a jury trial in Superior Court of two charges of gross sexual misconduct against two children. 17-A M.R.S.A. §253 (Supp. 1988). Before trial, the State brought a motion in limine asking the court to exclude any evidence of each child victim's past sexual behavior. The State had furnished to the defense evidence that both victims were subjected to sexual abuse by persons other than Jacques. The court ruled that such prior sexual activity would not be admissible regardless of the potential relevance of that evidence. At trial the victims, a girl aged 5 and a boy aged 10, testified that Jacques had sexually abused them. Although it is undisputed that both children had been sexually abused by others, the trial court prevented cross-examination of the victims concerning other sources of sexual abuse. Jacques challenges that ruling on appeal. We vacate the convictions.

The past sexual behavior of a victim is generally not admissible under M.R. Evid. 412. The purpose of the Rule is to prevent a trial from becoming a trial of the victim, rather than the accused. Field & Murray, *Maine Evidence* §412.1, at 140 (2d ed. 1987). The limitation protects the State's strong and legitimate interest in preventing the victims of sex offenses from being further victimized at trial. Id.

Evidence of sexual abuse by others would fall within the scope of the Rule and, if the only consideration were to prevent testimony about past sexual behavior or abuse, the court's ruling would be correct.[2] However, the State's legitimate interest in protecting victims of sexual abuse is neither absolute nor paramount. See, M.R. Evid. 412 advisory committee's note to 1983 amend., Me. Rptr., 449-458 A.2d LXX, LXXI, Field & Murray §412, at 138 (all evidence of sexual behavior offered for any purpose not necessarily inadmissible, examination as to prior sexual behavior is admissible to impeach or for "some other proper purpose" (emphasis added)). The State's interest must be weighed against the defendant's constitutional right of effective cross-examination and to present a proper defense.

Although the wording of M.R. Evid. 412 is not as clear as it might be, the Advisory Committee Note is explicit that "evidence constitutionally required to be admitted" overrides the exclusion in the text of Rule 412. Me. Rptr., 449-458 A.2d LXX; cf., Davis v. Alaska, 415 U.S. 308, 39 L. Ed. 2d 347, 94 S. Ct. 1105 (1974) (state's interest in protecting juvenile offender does not take precedence over defendant's right to effectively cross-examine). The advisory committee note gives as an example the instance where the prosecution "opens the door" "by offering evidence of the victim's lack of sexual experience or chastity on direct." Field & Murray §412, at 139.

Where the victim is a child, as in this case, the lack of sexual experience is automatically in the case without specific action by the prosecutor. A defendant therefore must be permitted to rebut the inference a jury might otherwise draw that the victim was so naive sexually that she could not have fabricated the charge. A number of jurisdictions with similar rules permit the admission of evidence of prior sexual activity for the limited purposes of rebutting the jury's natural assumption concerning a child's sexual innocence and of protecting the defendant's

---

2. We reject, as providing insufficient protection to victims, the defendant's proposed interpretation of "sexual behavior" to apply only to a victim's "volitional sexual behavior."

rights.[3] In a case decided prior to the adoption of M.R. Evid. 412, we relied on just such an analysis to vacate a conviction where evidence of prior sexual activity had been excluded. State v. Davis, 406 A.2d 900 (Me. 1979). Additionally, in State v. Albert, 495 A.2d 1242 (Me. 1985) we implied that, notwithstanding Rule 412, evidence of prior sexual abuse might be admissible if offered for the purpose of challenging the jury's assumption of children's innocence, subject to limitations of relevance under Rule 403. Id. at 1244. See Field & Murray §412.2, at 142.

Jacques offered the evidence of other abuse for two purposes. He wished to show the circumstances in which he was first accused by the victims and, recognizing the jury's natural assumption that children are innocent of sexual matters, to rebut the inference that he was responsible for their unusual sexual knowledge. The court prevented the defense from exploring that source of the victims' sexual knowledge by cross-examination concerning other abuse. In addition, Jacques was prevented from exploring the timing and other circumstances of the victims' complaints against him in relation to complaints against others. See State v. True, 438 A.2d 460, 464 (Me. 1981); State v. Walton, 432 A.2d 1275, 1277 (Me. 1981).

These rulings curtailed Jacques's effort to generate doubt as to his participation in abuse of the children. The court might, within its discretion under M.R. Evid. 403 and 611, limit the scope of cross-examination of the victims. . . . The ruling in limine, however, went further than the victims' testimony. The court refused to allow inquiry into any evidence of other abuse, including the childrens' earlier statements that others had abused them. That ruling clearly deprived Jacques of his right to present an effective defense.

Judgments vacated.

Jacques is an example of a judicially created exception to Rule 412 designed to safeguard the right of the accused to a fair trial. Does the constitution require that evidence of the prior sexual history of a victim or other witness be admitted despite Rule 412 if the accused can articulate a non-propensity relevance of this evidence? Is there a threshold of probative value which must be surmounted to invoke the constitutional "exception" to Rule 412? Does the approach taken by the court in Jacques carve a hole in the rule that could threaten the rule itself? For a thoughtful discussion of these developments in the context of child abuse prosecutions, see Lipez, "The Child Witness in Sexual Abuse

---

3. See, e.g., Commonwealth v. Ruffen, 399 Mass. 811, 507 N.E.2d 684 (1987); State v. Peterson, 35 Wash. App. 481, 667 P.2d 645 (1983); State v. Carver, 37 Wash. App. 122, 678 P.2d 842 (1984); State v. Baker, 127 N.H. 801, 508 A.2d 1059 (1986).

Cases in Maine: Presentation, Impeachment and Controversy," 42 Maine L. Rev. 283 (1990).

Problem: False Accusation?

Charge: sexual asault. M.O.: victim put in fear of serious bodily harm but no physical injury other than the sexual contact. Defense: consent. You are defense counsel. In pretrial investigation, you learn that in the past two years the victim has accused five other men of sexual assault. In four cases, she subsequently withdrew her accusations, and in the other case the accused was acquitted by the jury in one-half hour after a five-day trial. You have been informed by an expert psychologist that the victim is a pathological liar. How would you introduce evidence of the prior accusations at defendant's trial? As prosecutor, what would you argue to exclude the evidence? Should such evidence be admitted? As a judge how would you rule?

Is evidence of prior (probably false) allegations of rape evidence of an alleged victim's past sexual behavior? If this problem were analyzed under the Federal Rules—pre-Rule 412—the result would be that the examination would be allowed and the defendant should be permitted to prove the prior false allegations of sexual assault. The limitations of Rule 608 would not apply because the evidence is not offered to prove the witness's general propensity for untruthfulness.

Does Rule 412 change this result? Should the concept of "past sexual behavior" be interpreted to encompass past false allegations? If it were to be interpreted so as to exclude proof of past false allegations of rape, then the bar of the statute could be unconstitutional. Under the familiar doctrine of limited admissibility (see *Jacques* above) such evidence would not necessarily be barred by Rule 412, even though it may also reveal something about the victim's past sexual conduct. But *should* it be barred?

Professor Althouse points out:

> Students should know that the failure to report rape is far more common than false report. Indeed, if students [considered] the pressures and motivations affecting a person thinking of calling the police, they might see that the reasons for declining to report a rape far exceed those for falsely reporting.
>
> [The False Accusation? problem] obscures all the difficulties encountered by the prosecution in giving weight to a rape victim's testimony and overcoming jurors' disinclination to convict for rape.

See Althouse, Nw. U.L. Rev., supra. Prosecutor Fairstein agrees:

The rarest circumstance in the field of sexual assault crimes—but by far the most pernicious—is that of false reporting. . . . It is hard to imagine what forces would drive someone to contemplate making such a claim, no less to carry out the entire deception. Aside from any ethical compunction, the stigma of being a victim is still a deterrent for many legitimate victims, as is the possibly rigorous path of a survivor through law enforcement agencies and medical protocols.

Fairstein, supra, at 217. Fairstein, does, however, describe two actual cases of false report and alludes to many more. She states that "most law enforcement officials equate the amount of false reporting of sex offenses with that of every other category of crime, at approximately 5 percent of the total number of reports." Id. at 229.

Problem: Victim's Rights/Defendant's Rights

The California Constitution was amended in June 1982 to include "The Victims' Bill of Rights," one section of which is as follows:

> *Right to Truth-in-Evidence.* Except as provided by statute hereafter enacted by a two-thirds vote of the membership in each house of the Legislature, relevant evidence shall not be excluded in any criminal proceeding, including pretrial and post conviction motions and hearings, or in any trial or hearing of a juvenile for a criminal offense, whether heard in juvenile or adult court. Nothing in this section shall affect any existing statutory rule of evidence relating to privilege or hearsay, or Evidence Code Sections 352, 782 or 1103. Nothing in this section shall affect any existing statutory or constitutional right of the press.

(Calif. Const. Art. I, §28(d).)

The Evidence Code sections not affected are §352, a provision like FRE 403 permitting a balancing of probity against prejudice; §782, California's rape-victim shield statute; and §1103, a provision equivalent to FRE 404(a)(2), authorizing the use of evidence regarding the character of the victim of a crime to prove the conduct of the victim.

How would the Victim's Bill of Rights, if it were applicable, affect the Federal Rules?

COMMONWEALTH v. STOCKHAMMER
409 Mass. 867, 570 N.E.2d 992 (1991)

GREANEY, J. The defendant was convicted of rape, and assault with intent to commit rape, after a jury-waived trial in the Superior Court. The defendant appealed, and we transferred the case to this court on our own motion.

The defendant claims error in: (1) the denial of his motions for required findings of not guilty and a new trial based on the weight of the evidence; (2) the preclusion by the judge of cross-examination of the complainant regarding a specific basis for bias and motive to lie; and (3) the denial of his motion for an order authorizing counsel to examine certain treatment records of the complainant. The motions for required findings and for a new trial on the basis of the weight of the evidence were correctly denied. We agree with the defendant, however, that the judge should not have curtailed the cross-examination of the complainant as he did, and that counsel for both sides should have access to the complainant's treatment records. Accordingly, we reverse and remand the case for a new trial.

Both the complainant and the defendant testified that intercourse had occurred, but the evidence in most other respects was highly contradictory. . . .

Restriction on cross-examination. Pursuant to G.L. c.233, §21B (the rape-shield statute), the defendant filed a pretrial motion in limine requesting a ruling on the admissibility of testimony relating to sexual activity of the complainant. The sexual activity that the defendant referred to was intercourse with the defendant in the weeks following April 19, 1988, and intercourse with her boy friend before and after April 19. The defendant argued in the motion that this testimony was admissible on the issues of consent, bias, and motive to falsify.

During the cross-examination of the complainant, at the point where defense counsel desired to probe the areas covered in the motion, the judge held a sidebar conference and questioned counsel about the evidence. Counsel stated that the testimony concerning the complainant's sexual relationship with her boy friend would support an inference that the complainant was involved in an ongoing relationship with him at the time of the alleged rape. The complainant was motivated to lie about what had happened between herself and the defendant, defense counsel argued, because acknowledgment of a sexual relationship with the defendant could alienate the boy friend. The judge ruled that counsel could inquire whether the complainant had a sexual relationship with the boy friend before April, 1988, but that he could not pursue the issue beyond that.

Based on this conference, defense counsel put the authorized question to the complainant, as well as questions relating to the possible reaction of her boy friend and other friends to the knowledge that the complainant had intercourse with the defendant. Counsel then attempted to move to the topic of the reaction of the complainant's parents to the knowledge that the complainant had been sexually active with her boy friend. The prosecutor objected; the court sustained the objection, and then refused the defendant's offer of proof.[3] The defen-

---

3. *Defense Counsel:* "Did you tell your parents [that prior to April 19th 1988 you had a sexual relationship with your boy friend]?"

dant argues that the judge erred in precluding cross-examination designed to uncover evidence that the complainant was biased and motivated to lie because she did not want her parents to learn that she was sexually active. We agree with the defendant that the judge's restriction on cross-examination was reversible error.

"Because bias is intimately related to credibility, a defendant has the right to cross-examine a prosecution witness in order to reveal bias." "A judge may not restrict cross-examination of a material witness by foreclosing inquiry into a subject that could show bias or prejudice [or motive to lie] on the part of the witness." "If a defendant believes that the judge improperly restrained his cross-examination of a witness, the defendant must demonstrate that the judge abused his discretion and that he was prejudiced by such restraint."

The principles protecting a defendant's right to cross-examination are particularly important when the charge is rape, because " '[t]he right to cross-examine a complainant in a rape case to show a false accusation may be the last refuge of an innocent defendant.' " For this reason, rape convictions have been reversed on a number of occasions because of rulings by trial judges prejudicially infringing on the right to cross-examine the complainant.

In this case, the defense was consent. The evidence in many ways was contradictory, and, even looking only at the complainant's testimony, in some respects was inconsistent with an allegation of rape. Thus, the complainant's credibility was of critical importance. Defense counsel intended to elicit from the complainant that her parents strongly disapproved of premarital sex, and that she was afraid to how they would react to the knowledge that she was sexually active.

If counsel had succeeded in eliciting testimony to this effect, it would have been most helpful to the defendant's case. Such evidence would

---

The Judge: "Excuse me."
The Prosecutor: "Objection."
The Judge: "Sustained."
Defense Counsel: "Did you tell your parents, as of April 19th 1988, that you had a sexual relationship with [your boy friend]?"
The Judge: "No, I've already said that's sustained, counsel."
Defense Counsel: "Oh, I'm sorry."
The Judge: "That's beyond the scope of what I said you could have."
Defense Counsel: "May I approach the sidebar about that your Honor?"
The Judge: "No."
Defense Counsel: "May I state for the record—"
The Judge: "No, counsel, we reviewed at the sidebar what you could go over. You did not mention that and you're not going to do it now, that's the end of it."
"Had you done that, I would have reviewed it at that time. At this point in time I rule it's unnecessary. You may proceed."
Defense Counsel: "At the sidebar, your Honor, I mentioned—"
The Judge: "Counsel, please, the next question."
Defense Counsel: "Very well, your Honor."

support the inference that the complainant had reason to lie in addition to her concern that her boy friend might learn that she had sex with the defendant. The testimony that counsel hoped to elicit would have supported the inference that the complainant was motivated to lie to prevent her parents from learning that she was sexually active. This would have amounted to a separate and discrete basis of impeachment of the complainant's credibility.

Testimony to this effect also would have had the additional persuasive effect of explaining some of the complainant's rather curious behavior after the alleged rape occurred. For example, fear of parental reaction would tend to explain why the complainant swore her classmate and childhood friend (who presumably knew the complainant's parents) to silence after reporting to the classmate that she had been raped. The same fear also would tend to explain why the complainant waited nine months to report the incident to her parents, and did not do so until her hand was forced by the anonymous caller who spoke with her father. Thus, relying on the admitted testimony about the relationship with her boy friend, and the excluded testimony about the views of the complainant's parents on premarital sex, defense counsel could have argued that the complainant lied initially to preserve her relationship with her boy friend, and continued to lie later (after she and her boy friend had broken up) to preserve her relationship with her parents. Because of the judge's ruling, however, counsel was unable to make this argument. . . .

In sum, the judge prevented counsel from pursuing on cross-examination a line of inquiry that was not violative of rape-shield strictures and that could have established that the complainant was biased and has a specific reason to lie about what had happened between her and the defendant. This reason to lie, if proved, would have been unrelated to other possible reasons that the complainant may have had to dissemble, and it was not provable through other evidence admitted at trial. Therefore, and in view of the conflicting nature of the evidence of the defendant's guilt, we cannot say that the introduction of this evidence would not have had a material effect on the outcome of the trial. A new trial is necessary.

Examination by counsel of the complainant's treatment records. After the trial, defense counsel learned for the first time (as did the prosecutor) of the complainant's treatment at the New York Hospital. The defendant promptly moved for postconviction relief in part on the ground that the complainant had failed to provide the court with a full and accurate account of the sources of her treatment records. The judge ordered that the records of the New York Hospital treatment be produced. The defendant then moved for "appropriate relief" concerning the New York Hospital records. In this motion, the defendant argued that an in camera inspection of the records by the judge might not adequately protect his right to a fair trial, and he requested that the records be made available to the Commonwealth and the defendant for inspection. After a hearing and review of the records in camera, the judge denied both motions.

Citing his rights under the Massachusetts Declaration of Rights to confrontation, compulsory process, and a fair trial, the defendant argues that his counsel should be permitted to examine the records of the complainant's treatment at the New York Hospital and with the Greenwich, Connecticut, social worker. The Commonwealth contends in response that the desired records are privilege and that the defendant's rights were adequately protected by the judge's in camera review of the records. We discuss this issue now for purposes of the retrial.

The United States Supreme Court has held that, where a criminal defendant desires access to privileged records of the confidential communications of the complaining witness, the interests of the defendant and the State in a fair trial are fully protected by an in camera review of those records by the trial judge. This holding does not necessarily answer the question before us, however, because, in the past, "on similar facts, we have reached different results under the State Constitution from those that were reached by the Supreme Court of the United States under the Federal Constitution." Thus, in Commonwealth v. Clancy, 402 Mass. 664 (1988), we rejected the defendant's argument — predicated solely on Federal constitutional principles — that he was entitled to examine the medical records of the chief prosecution witness. At the same time, we reserved the question whether the result would be the same under the Massachusetts Declaration of Rights. . . .

The Federal standard requiring only an in camera review by the trial judge of privileged records requested by the defendant rests on the assumptions that trial judges can temporarily and effectively assume the role of advocate when examining such records; and that the interests of the State and complainant in the confidentiality of the records cannot adequately be protected in any other way. Neither assumption withstands close scrutiny.

As to the first assumption, the United States Supreme Court has said that "'it [is] extremely difficult for even the most able and experienced trial judge under the pressures of conducting a trial to pick out all of the [information] that would be useful in impeaching a witness.' . . . Nor is it realistic to assume that the trial court's judgment as to the utility of material for impeachment . . . would exhaust the possibilities. In our adversary system, it is enough for judges to judge. The determination of what may be useful to the defense can properly and effectively be made only by an advocate." We have expressed a similar concern: "The danger lurking in the practice of . . . in camera review [of privileged documents] by the trial judge is a confusion between the roles of trial judge and the defense counsel. The judge is not necessarily in the best position to know what is necessary to the defense." . . .

Regarding the second assumption, we are not convinced that the interests of the State and the complaining witness in preserving the confidentiality of communications to psychotherapists and social workers can only be protected by an in camera review procedure. Trial judges have broad discretion to control the proceedings before them. There is no reason why they cannot take steps to insure that breaches of confidentiality attending discovery are limited only to those absolutely and unavoidably necessary to the preparation and presentation of the defendant's defense. For example, judges could allow counsel access to privileged records only in their capacity as officers of the court. Admission of or reference to any such information at trial could be conditioned on a determination (made after an in camera hearing) that the information counsel seeks to use is not available from any other source. Protective orders (enforced by the threat of sanctions) requiring counsel and other necessary participants in the trial not to disclose such information could be entered. Although these procedures would result in counsel for the defendant and the Commonwealth, rather than just the judge, viewing privileged records, if careful precautions in the order of those described above are taken, such breaches of confidentiality need not be any more intrusive or harmful than those attending in camera review of records by the judge alone. . . .

Balanced against these qualified privileges are important State constitutional rights of the defendant. Because we have said that, in appropriate circumstances, even absolute statutory privileges (nonconstitutionally based) must yield to a defendant's constitutional right to use privileged communications in his defense, we are not persuaded that allowing counsel access to the treatment records at issue in this case would do great violence to the less firmly based policies represented by §§20B and 135. In these circumstances, those policies must give way to the defendant's need to examine the complainant's treatment records.

Accordingly, we conclude that, under art. 12 of the Massachusetts Declaration of Rights, counsel for the defendant is entitled to review the records of the complainant's treatment at the New York Hospital and with the Greenwich, Connecticut, social worker to search for evidence of bias, prejudice, or motive to lie. On remand, the judge shall determine the circumstances under which counsel for the defendant and the Commonwealth shall review the records. The judge then shall conduct an in camera hearing concerning the admissibility of any information in the records that counsel may wish to use at trial. In his discretion, the judge also shall enter any orders that are deemed appropriate to ensure that the information contained in the records will not be disclosed beyond the defendant's need to prepare and present his defense.

One additional point bears mention. Because victims of sexual crimes are likely to suffer a "depth and range of emotional and psychological disturbance . . . not felt by the victims of most other crimes," the public interest lies in assisting victims of sexual crimes to recover from injuries. The policy of the Commonwealth is in accord. We therefore remind lawyers and judges that the mere fact that such a victim sought counseling may not be used for impeachment purposes.

The judgments are reversed, and the verdicts set aside. The case is remanded for a new trial.

So ordered.

Stockhammer is another case where the court was faced with a conflict between policies of protection of victims of sexual assault and policies of affording defendants every opportunity to contest the state's proof of guilt and prove their innocence. Permitting inquiry on cross-examination into the alleged victim's concern about her parents' reactions to her sexual activity with anyone does not seem to be directly barred by Rule 412 as long as evidence of the activity itself is admissible. However, the embarrassment and discomfort to the witness from such an examination would likely be similar to that involved with an examination about the sexual activity itself. Certainly, a victim who thought that she might have to undergo such an examination might well be deterred from coming forward to report a sexual assault. And would a victim of sexual assault be encouraged to counseling concerning a sexual assault by the knowledge that the records of the therapy would be accessible to the lawyer for the defendant and might be admissible at the trial? Do you agree with the Massachusetts court that considerations of fundamental fairness require that this conflict be resolved in favor of the defendant?

Problem: The Beach Party

Spring weekend at the Kenneally beachfront compound in Florida. William Kenneally Smits, a twenty-four-year-old member of the family on vacation from medical school, is holding a weekend party. During the course of the weekend, dozens of revelers come and go, engaging in drinking, dancing, swimming, and other amusements while at the compound. At 4:00 A.M. Sunday morning Patricia Doe appears at the local police station to report that she has been sexually assaulted by Smits at the compound. At Smits' subsequent trial for rape, Smits admits to sexual intercourse with Doe but contends that it was consensual. Smits seeks to offer evidence that Doe voluntarily engaged in sex with another guest that weekend while at the compound. The prosecution seeks to offer evidence that Smits sexually attacked another female guest that weekend at the compound. Assuming the proper notice and objections, what rulings and why?

BRIAN C. MOONEY, FLORIDA v. WILLIAM KENNEDY SMITH
Boston Globe, July 24, 1991

With the filing of a simple two-page document in court Monday, the Palm Beach rape case against William Kennedy Smith has moved from the tabloids to the legal journals.

By attempting to introduce evidence of unrelated but allegedly similar assaults by Smith in the past, lead prosecutor Moira Lasch has invoked a controversial rule.

Judge Mary Lupo, who is presiding over the Smith case, must balance Smith's right to a fair trial and the prosecution's ability to use a potentially devastating tool. In Florida, it is called the Williams Rule and allows prosecutors to offer evidence of prior acts similar to those alleged in the pending case as circumstantial proof of motive, intent, preparation or method of operation. The rule, however, may not be used solely to prove bad character or a propensity to commit a particular crime. . . .

Smith is accused of sexual battery, Florida's equivalent of rape, on a Florida woman at the Kennedy family estate on Easter weekend. Lasch's office on Monday said it would seek to introduce testimony from three women from New York and Washington, alleging that Smith raped one three years ago and tried to rape the other two in 1988 and 1983. Smith, who has pleaded not guilty in the pending case, was not charged in any of the other incidents.

The Florida rule dates to 1959 when the state Supreme Court decided the case of Ralph Williams, who was found guilty of raping a woman in her car after evidence that he was involved in a similar incident in the same St. Petersburg parking lot six weeks earlier. . . . The rule was made part of the state's code of evidence in 1979 and is patterned after a similar federal rule of evidence. . . .

LARRY TYE & IRENE SEGE, FLORIDA v. WILLIAM KENNEDY SMITH
Boston Globe, July 24, 1991

On first appearance, William Kennedy Smith is a disarmingly charming young man, but alone with a woman, he can become "animal-like," "violent" and a "sicko," according to statements made public yesterday from three women who say Smith assaulted them in recent years. . . .

EXCERPTS FROM THE STATEMENTS

The following are excerpts from the statements made by the three women who, according to prosecutors, were sexually attacked by William Kennedy Smith before the Palm Beach case. The boldface text is a Globe summary of the transcript.

From a woman who says she was attacked in 1983 at the home of Smith's parents in New York City:

After a party, Smith offers to let the woman stay in the guest room of his parents' home, which is nearby. She says he directed her to the guest room.

"One moment he was standing in front of me, talking with me, saying good-night and the next minute he . . . tackled me onto the bed . . . that I was standing next to and was trying to kiss me, and had his body completely cover mine, and had me pinned on the bed, and from there . . . he continued to try to kiss me and put his hands on me. . . .

"I was resisting it every moment. I was not in any way relaxed. My . . . entire body was focused on getting him off of me, which must have made it kind of difficult for him to continue. It was a constant struggle." . . .

Smith then apologizes, she says.

"For a moment I actually thought he means it, and it was just a mistake somehow and it'll be OK. But that was just for a brief moment because he immediately did the same thing again. Almost as if it was a repeat performance." . . .

The woman is asked if she recalled him saying anything at that point.

"Just to be quiet. To shut up. But that's the only thing I remember.

"I also remember being really scared and thinking this is really a messed-up situation, and this is really a nightmare and I want to get out of here." . . .

The next day she called Max Kennedy, Smith's cousin, who was then her boyfriend.

"I called Max the next day and I said your cousin Willie attacked me, I met your cousin Willie last night and he attacked me and he's a sicko and called him some names and, you know, expected some sympathy and some reaction, I don't know exactly what." . . .

The woman later broke up with Max Kennedy, but when she heard of the Palm Beach incident, she said they spoke by telephone.

"He said, 'It sounds like Willie really has a problem,' and he apologized again to me.

"He did say that it . . . it had been hard for him because, you know, people [slight pause] it was hard for his family at that particular moment because people were perceiving them as 'you sick rapists,' and that it was a . . . it was a tough time for his family." . . .

The woman said she had been reluctant to go to police at the time.

"I frankly thought that nobody would think it was too much of a big deal because I hadn't been actually raped and because I . . . Max was minimizing it. I started to do the same.

"I also thought that nobody would believe me, being, you know, considering who . . . who the people were involved." . . .

Why has she come forward now?

"Well, it's just been really on my mind and, it's got a lot to . . . it's complicated, I . . . it has to do with the fact that I didn't do anything at the time when I was assaulted and I . . . that makes me feel kind of powerless and I wish that I could have done something and this is something that possibly will be an action that . . . that will have some . . . some impact on this case in Florida.

"I mean it's my obligation to support her by you know, doing what I can to. . . ."

SECOND STATEMENT

From a woman who says she was sexually attacked by Smith in 1988 at his Washington apartment:

"I went over to get my purse. He handed me the drink that we had been drinking. I put it back down. We were on the back side of the couch. At that point without any warning he grabbed me by my wrists . . . threw me over the couch, and I landed on the floor on my back pinned to the floor by the wrist with him on top of me.

"I felt like if I struggled he probably wouldn't have let me up . . . whereas if I treated him like a normal person that didn't have any . . . any violent tendencies that he might indeed act like a normal person and let me up.

"I was frightened. I thought that if I didn't somehow talk this fellow out of it that I was going to be raped." . . .

She did not report the incident to police.

"Because I know how powerful his family is and he does seem to be such an upstanding medical student." . . .

Why come forward now?

"Several reasons, one being that I saw him in the media from what I felt was sources being portrayed as such a wonderful gentlemanly scholarly dedicated, you know, physician and I just didn't feel that was true."

THIRD STATEMENT

From a woman who says Smith raped her in 1988, at his apartment in Washington, after the two had been at a party together:

"It was one of those parties that just the whole house got kind of trashed from all the people . . . there were so many people in the house . . . there was beer on the floor . . . that kind of thing . . . and then I don't know . . . I got pretty drunk.

"I just thought he was going to be a gentleman and let me sleep in his bed . . . I mean that's really what I thought and I didn't even think anything . . . I mean it's a king-size bed . . . it was a huge bed so I wouldn't of even of thought anything of it if he had slept next to me you know.

"I was about to lie down and . . . and he like took off my shorts and I thought he was . . . I still thought . . . I mean at that point I began to get a little scared but I kind of said you know stop it . . . I just want to go to sleep . . . leave me alone and I don't know, he started getting just more and more aggressive and . . . and . . . I didn't know what to do.

"I began to realize he wasn't going to take no for an answer.

"I can't even describe the fear I mean it was . . . it was like . . . I felt so out of control.

"I realized I . . . I can't . . . I have to go along with this . . . I can't fight at this point . . . that this . . . he's going to hurt me and I could see it in his face . . . he was such a . . . ferocious . . . almost animal-like kind of look to him . . . it was just horrible.

"He said stop fighting or stop it . . . you know . . . that kind of thing.

"I sort of passed out at some point in the middle of it . . . . I . . . I just don't even remember.

"When he took off his clothes, he reached over to the dresser and pulled out a condom." . . .

After charges that Smith raped a Florida woman became public this year, Smith . . .

"Did try to call me through friends. . . .

"I just didn't want to talk to him . . . I think I would have gotten sick if I had spoken with him."

Did other Kennedy family members or friends try to contact her?

"No. Unless his lawyer counts." . . .

Why didn't she press charges in 1988?

"I had been advised by a lawyer at the time not to press charges, not to do anything and . . . and the Kennedys you know, you'll never win."
. . .

She came forward now, she said, because . . .

"If he wins or loses, that message is going to go across to college campuses and to other people and if . . . if he gets away with it . . . then the message is going to be clear that this is OK."

WILLIAMS v. FLORIDA

110 So. 2d 654 (Fla. Sup. Ct. 1959)

THORNAL, J. Appellant Ralph Williams, who was defendant below, seeks reversal of a judgment of conviction and sentence to death in the electric chair pursuant to a jury verdict finding him guilty of the crime of rape. Several points for reversal are assigned but the principal question which challenges our detailed consideration is the alleged error of the trial judge in the allowance of certain similar factual evidence which tended to establish a collateral crime.

On December 18, 1957, the 17-year old prosecutrix parked her family automobile on a parking lot known as "the second parking space" in the vicinity of Webb's City in St. Petersburg. She did some shopping and returned to her car between 9 and 9:30 P.M. She testified that after she had driven the car a short distance the appellant suddenly reached over from the back seat of the car and stabbed her in the chest with an ice pick. He next leaped over into the driver's seat. She stated that he then forced her to keep her head down on the front seat as he drove. The sum of the gruesome details, according to her testimony, was that appellant drove her around the city of St. Petersburg, threatening to kill her if she did not submit to his wishes. Consistent with the threats he criminally assaulted her sexually on two separate occasions. The testimony is that appellant finally stopped the car and departed. The prosecutrix reached her home in a hysterical condition around 11 P.M. She was taken to a hospital where medical examination confirmed the sexual assault as well as the severe ice pick wound in her chest.

Appellant, who testified in his own behalf, did not deny having had sexual relations with the prosecutrix. His sole defense was that his relationship with her was attained with her consent. He related in sum that he had made her acquaintance in July, 1957. He stated that from time to time he had had conversations with the prosecutrix; that he had a date with her the early part of December, 1957, and again on December 17, 1957, during all of which time, he testified, he was employed by Webb's City. During these prior dates, according to appellant's testimony, he had sexual relations with the prosecutrix with her consent.

According to his version, the gruesome details of the fatal night related by the prosecutrix did not occur. He defends his position by testifying that he met the prosecutrix pursuant to prior arrangement and that his sexual relationships with her on that night were accomplished with her consent and without threat. The ice pick incident is explained away by his statement that he stopped the car suddenly while the prosecutrix had the ice pick in her hand threatening to do him harm in the event that he fulfilled a previously announced intention of severing his relationship with her.

The State completely devastated most of the defensive contentions offered by the appellant. It was established by representatives of Webb's City that he had not worked for that business since August of 1957. Williams had testified that he regularly met the prosecutrix at Webb's City while he was employed there during November and December of that year. On the particular occasions when he was supposed to have had prior dates with the prosecutrix in December, the testimony, without dispute, establishes that she could not have been where he said she was. The opinion of the doctor who examined her was unequivocal to the effect that the young woman had never had sexual relations prior to the night when the jury found that she was abused by the appellant.

In the ultimate, the jury chose to believe the witnesses who testified for the State and rendered a verdict of guilty without a recommendation of mercy. The trial judge entered a judgment of guilt. As required by law the supreme penalty was prescribed. Reversal of this judgment is now sought.

We are . . . confronted with a problem which has required . . . comprehensive analysis and research. It will be recalled that the prosecutrix testified that she left her automobile on the "second parking space" near Webb's City at about 7:30 P.M. on the night in question. To this we should add the testimony of a deputy sheriff who arrested the appellant the following day. He stated that Williams advised him on this occasion that when he saw the automobile he thought it was his brother's and crawled in the back to take a nap. At the time of his arrest, appellant did not relate to the officer his subsequent story of extensive sexual relations with the prosecutrix. He did this from the witness stand later and then denied having made the statement with reference to climbing in the back of the car under the erroneous impression that it was his brother's automobile.

As a part of its case in chief, the State offered, and the trial judge allowed, the testimony of one Judy Baker, aged 16, and one Kirk, a law enforcement officer, regarding an incident which occurred on November 5, 1957, approximately six weeks prior to the attack on the prosecutrix. The testimony of these two witnesses simply was that on the earlier date Miss Baker had parked her car at approximately the same hour and on the same parking lot as did the prosecutrix on the night of December 18, 1957. Upon returning to her car sometime later with parcels purchased in Webb's City, Judy Baker opened the door and saw the head of a man on the floor in the back of the car. Fortunately for her she screamed and two auxiliary policemen came to the rescue. The occupant of the back of the car ran. Immediate pursuit resulted in the apprehension of the appellant Ralph Williams, who was identified as the occupant of the back of Miss Baker's automobile. He later testified at police headquarters that he had mistaken the car for his brother's automobile and had crawled into the back of it to take a nap. The Baker automobile was a black Plymouth of a model several years earlier than the green Buick which was driven by prosecutrix.

As pointed out above the trial judge permitted this testimony but at the time admonished the jury that it was to be taken as bearing upon the question of identity, intent, "the plan or design only" and was limited to that. The appellant takes the position that error was committed in admitting into evidence this testimony regarding the involvement of appellant in a similar factual situation which had occurred six weeks before the matter in issue but which had a tendency to reveal the commission of a collateral criminal act involving another person and unrelated by parties, facts, time or circumstances to the crime laid in the indictment. The sum of the position of the appellant on this point is that the evidence was totally irrelevant and that it tended to establish a collateral crime to the undue prejudice of the appellant in the minds of the jury. The State takes the position that the evidence was relevant to identify the appellant, to show a plan or method of operation whereby this particular appellant created his opportunities for assaulting young white girls and finally tended to offset the anticipated defense of consent.

We could dispose of the problem by brief reference to a limited number of cases which appear to sustain what has been broadly described as "an exception" to an asserted rule which excludes collateral similar fact evidence that tends to point up the commission of a separate crime. However, we think we should not be content with such a cursory disposition of the problem. Our research and analysis of the historical development of the applicable rule of evidence suggest that considerable confusion has been the product of numerous divergent points of view. It is therefore appropriate, for the future guidance of the bar and the trial courts, that we analyze the rule and in the ultimate revive the original precedents so that in the future the correct rule of evidence may be applied in its proper setting.

Let us begin with a reminder that we here deal with so-called similar fact evidence which tends to reveal the commission of a collateral crime. Our initial premise is the general canon of evidence that any fact relevant to prove a fact in issue is admissible into evidence unless its admissibility is precluded by some specific rule of exclusion. Viewing the problem at hand from this perspective, we begin by thinking in terms of a rule of admissibility as contrasted to a rule of exclusion. With regard to similar fact evidence, illustrated by that in the case at bar, those who would exclude it invoke the principles of undue prejudice, collateral issues and immateriality. In so doing it appears to us that they disregard the basic principle of the admissibility of all relevant evidence having probative value in establishing a material issue.

The rule governing the admissibility of similar fact evidence finds its antecedents, of course, in many of the English cases. Prior to the middle of the Nineteenth Century, the English judges themselves engaged in numerous semantic gymnastics in an effort to simplify a rule of admissibility of this type of evidence. As a result of these early decisions, confusion followed until Regina v. Geering (1849) 18 L.J.M.C. 215, which established the general rule that similar fact evidence is admissible if relevant to a fact in issue even though it also points to the commission of a separate crime. The rule is subject to the lone exception that such evidence is inadmissible if its sole relevancy is to establish a bad character on the part of the accused. The bad character exception to the rule of admissibility had been clearly announced in the early case of Rex v. Cole cited in Phillips, Law of Evidence (1st ed.) 69-70. The English rule as finally formulated in Regina v. Geering, supra, was subsequently reaffirmed and emphatically recognized by Makin v. Attorney General of New South Wales [1894] A.C. 57. The case last cited is generally recognized as the English judicial progenitor of the correctly stated rule. With regard to this type of evidence, therefore, the rule which has been followed in England for more than a hundred years is a broad rule of admissibility of all relevant evidence except as to character or propensity, and subject only to specific exclusions or exceptions which are few.

In this form the English rule was transplanted in Florida during the latter part of the Nineteenth Century. Our own court started with the rule of admissibility so long as the evidence was relevant except for the purpose of degrading the character of the accused. However, as the cases multiplied and developed, we inclined toward announcing the rule in terms of exceptions to a broad rule of exclusion rather than in terms of a broad rule of admissibility. For example, it has been not uncommon for this court to state that collateral similar facts pointing to the commission of another crime are not admissible except to show motive or intent or design and the like.

Our own cases over the past fifty years have tended to convert the original rule of admissibility into a rule of exclusion with innumerable exceptions. We thereby have allowed relevant evidence as an "exception" to a broad rule excluding all other evidence. The result simply is that once again the exceptions have become the rule. In actuality we are merely applying the basic canon of relevancy in each particular case in order to determine whether certain specific evidence is or is not admissible. Otherwise stated, if the evidence appears to be relevant to a material fact in issue, we have customarily found an exception with which to clothe it with admissibility. On the other hand, if the collateral similar fact evidence lacks relevancy to a fact in issue, we have come to announce that such evidence is not admissible, there being no exception within which it could fall in order to make it relevant.

The objectionable feature of this approach is that seemingly the fundamental principle of logical relevancy is abandoned. In its place is substituted a search for an exception under which the evidence becomes admissible, but which will be discovered only if out of the infinite variety of human activities a case has arisen in which some court had held it so. . . .

In the immediate case at bar we think the evidence regarding the Judy Baker incident was clearly admissible because it was relevant to several of the issues involved. It definitely had probative value to establish a plan, scheme or design. It was relevant to meet the anticipated defense of consent. At the time when it was offered in the presentation of the State's main case it had a substantial degree of relevance in order to identify the accused. Finally, it was relevant because it demonstrated a plan or pattern followed by the accused in committing the type of crime laid in the indictment.

In view of our analysis of the precedents and for the future guidance of the bench and bar, the rule which we have applied in affirming this conviction simply is that evidence of any facts relevant to a material fact in issue except where the sole relevancy is character or propensity of the accused is admissible unless precluded by some specific exception or rule of exclusion. This rule we hold applies to relevant similar fact evidence illustrated by that in the case at bar even though it points to the commission of another crime. The matter of relevancy should be carefully and cautiously considered by the trial judge. However, when found relevant within the limits of the stated rule, such evidence should be permitted to go to the jury. . . .

Finding no error and finding as we do that the ends of justice do not demand a new trial, the judgment under attack is affirmed. Affirmed.

Williams v. Florida illustrates the traditional rule of non-admissibility of the defendant's prior sexual misconduct and one of the numerous exceptions to that rule. For many years, prosecutors have successfully offered evidence of the defendant's prior sexual misconduct with the victim witness and with others, both charged and uncharged, for limited purposes under the provisions of Rule 404(b) and its state analogues. This kind of evidence was often admitted as demonstrating the accused's "knowledge," "intent," or "relationship with the victim." Although such proof would be subject to limiting instructions, its impact in favor of the prosecution would often be significant. For a discussion of evidence of prior sexual misdeeds offered for limited purposes in a state jurisdiction with evidence rules patterned on the Federal Rules of Evidence, see, Field and Murray, Maine Evidence-2000 Edition (Lexis 1999) §404.5.

In September 1994, Congress passed the Violent Crime Control and Enforcement Act, which included several proposed amendments to the Federal Rules of Evidence. New Rules 413, 414, and 415 provide that in criminal cases in which the defendant is accused of an offense of sexual assault or child molestation, or in a civil case in which a claim for damages or other relief is predicated on a party's alleged commission of conduct constituting an offense of sexual assault or child molestation, "evidence of the defendant's commission of another offense or offenses of sexual assault (or child molestation) is admissible, and may be considered for its bearing on any matter to which it is relevant." The effective date of the new rules was deferred pending receipt of comments from the Judicial Conference. In February 1995, the Judicial Conference transmitted to Congress a report criticizing Rules 413-415 and proposing different rules in their stead. Congress did not follow the recommendation of the Judicial Conference and present Rules 413-415 became effective on July 9, 1995.

On their face these new rules would appear to alter the existing rules relating to evidence of other similar acts in sexual assault cases, even to the extent of allowing evidence of such acts to show the accused's propensity for the crime charged. One issue that arose early was the extent evidence made admissible by the new rules would also be subject to a balancing test under Rule 403. Another question is how the prior offense is to be proved? Is a conviction for the other offense of sexual assault or child molestation that is sought to be admitted necessary, or do the words "defendant's commission" permit introduction of evidence of uncharged or charged but acquitted offenses? Does the different treatment accorded prior offenses of sexual assault or child molestation implicate the defendant's constitutional rights to due process and equal protection of the laws?

UNITED STATES v. GUARDIA
135 F.3d 1326 (10th Cir. 1998)

Tacha, Circuit Judge.

On September 5, 1996, a federal grand jury in New Mexico returned an indictment charging defendant David Guardia with two counts of sexual abuse in violation of 18 U.S.C. §2242(2)(A). In addition, the grand jury charged the defendant under the Assimilative Crimes Statute, 18 U.S.C. §13, with two counts of criminal sexual penetration in violation of N.M. Stat. Ann. §30-9-11(E) (Michie Supp. 1997) and two counts of battery in violation of N.M. Stat. Ann. §30-3-4 (Michie 1978). These charges arose from the defendant's allegedly improper behavior during gynecological exams he performed at Kirtland Air Force Base in October and November of 1995. Dr. Guardia moved in limine to exclude evidence proffered by the United States under Federal Rule of Evidence 413. The district court granted Dr. Guardia's motion, finding under Federal Rule of Evidence 403 that the risk of jury confusion substantially outweighed the probative value of the Rule 413 evidence. See United States v. Guardia, 955 F. Supp. 115 (D. N.M. 1997). This appeal followed. We exercise jurisdiction under 18 U.S.C. §3731 and affirm.

BACKGROUND

The indictment is based upon the complaints of two alleged victims who contend that Dr. Guardia sexually abused them in the course of gynecological procedures that he conducted at Kirtland. Both complainants, Carla G. and Francesca L., allege that during an examination Dr. Guardia engaged in . . . contact that exceeded the bounds of medically appropriate examination techniques and constituted sexual abuse. Francesca L. alleges that Dr. Guardia demonstrated the sexual nature of his conduct by stating "I love my job" during the examination. In addition, Carla G. alleges that Dr. Guardia called her at home and performed other acts suggesting his sexual interest in her. Neither of the examinations occurred in the presence of a chaperon.

In addition to offering the testimony of Carla G. and Francesca L., the government moved to introduce, under Rule 413, the testimony of four women who allege that Dr. Guardia abused them during gynecological examinations in a manner similar to the alleged abuse of Carla G. and Francesca L. For example, two of the four additional witnesses also complained of excessive . . . contact, and one complained of similarly suggestive comments. On the other hand, the testimony of Carla G. and Francesca L. differs significantly in some respects from the testimony of the Rule 413 witnesses. For instance, one of the witnesses complains that Dr. Guardia improperly touched her breasts, not her pelvic area. Another complains of the defendant's use of a medical instrument, not his hands. Chaperons were present during the examination of two of the four Rule 413 witnesses. All six women had extraordinary gynecological problems that appeared to require different courses of treatment and examination.

After considering the nature and content of the testimony proffered under Rule 413, the district court applied Rule 403 and excluded the evidence. The government appeals the district court's determination.

DISCUSSION

Congress recently enacted Federal Rule of Evidence 413, along with Rules 414 and 415, as part of the Violent Crime Control and Law Enforcement Act of 1994, Pub. L. No. 103-322, tit. XXXII, §320935(a), 108 Stat. 1796, 2136 (1994). This case presents important questions regarding the way in which Rule 413 interacts with Rule 403. The latter rule gives trial courts discretionary authority to exclude certain evidence when the prejudicial value of the evidence substantially outweighs its probative value. See Fed. R. Evid. 403.

We review legal interpretations of the federal rules of evidence de novo. See Reeder v. American Economy Ins. Co., 88 F.3d 892, 894 (10th Cir. 1996). In this appeal, we first define the requirements for admission of evidence under Rule 413. We then conclude, following United States v. Meacham, 115 F.3d 1488 (10th Cir. 1997), that Rule 403 applies to evidence introduced under Rule 413. Finally, we explain how the Rule 403 balancing test should proceed. We conclude that the district court made no error of legal interpretation in this case. Having so found, we review the court's Rule 403 decision for an abuse of discretion, see United States v. Davis, 40 F.3d 1069, 1076 (10th Cir. 1994), and find none.

I.   REQUIREMENTS OF RULE 413

Rule 413 provides in pertinent part:

> In a criminal case in which the defendant is accused of an offense of sexual assault, evidence of the defendant's commission of another offense or offenses of sexual assault is admissible, and may be considered for its bearing on any matter to which it is relevant.

Fed. R. Evid. 413(a). Thus, evidence offered under Rule 413 must meet three threshold requirements before a district court can admit it. A district court must first determine that "the defendant is accused of an offense of sexual assault." Id.; . . . The district court implicitly recognized these requirements in its hearing on the motion in limine and in its written opinion. See United States v. Guardia, 955 F. Supp. 115, 117, 119 (D. N.M. 1997); Tr. of Mot. Hr'g, December 30, 1996, passim.

The third requirement, applicable to all evidence, is that the evidence be relevant. See Fed. R. Evid. 402 ("Evidence which is not relevant is not admissible."). The rules define relevant evidence as evidence that "has any tendency to make the existence of any fact that is of consequence to the determination of the action more probable or less probable than it would be without the evidence." Fed. R. Evid. 401. A defendant with a propensity to commit acts similar to the charged crime is more likely to have committed the charged crime than another. Evidence of such a propensity is therefore relevant. See Old Chief v. United States, 519 U.S. 172, 136 L. Ed. 2d 574, 117 S. Ct. 644, 650 (1997) ("Propensity evidence is relevant. . . .") (citations and internal quotation marks omitted); Michelson v. United States, 335 U.S. 469, 475-76, 93 L. Ed. 168, 69 S. Ct. 213 (1948) (noting the "admitted probative value" of propensity evidence).

In most cases, though not in Rule 413 cases, the court must exclude propensity evidence despite its acknowledged relevance. Rule 404(b) prohibits the use of prior acts of a person "to prove the character of a person in order to show action in conformity therewith." Fed. R. Evid. 404(b). Under Rule 413, however, evidence of a defendant's other sexual assaults may be admitted "for its bearing on any matter to which it is relevant." Fed. R. Evid. 413 (emphasis added). Thus, Rule 413 supersedes Rule 404(b)'s restriction and allows the government to offer evidence of a defendant's prior conduct for the purpose of demonstrating a defendant's propensity to commit the charged offense. . . .

We turn now to the court's relevance finding in this particular case. We will not upset the court's determination that evidence is relevant absent a clear abuse of discretion. See United States v. Alexander, 849 F.2d 1293, 1301 (10th Cir. 1988). If believed, the Rule 413 evidence in this case would demonstrate that the defendant has a propensity to take advantage of female patients by touching them in a salacious manner and making comments while doing so. Because the defendant's propensity is to engage in conduct which closely matches that alleged in this case, the evidence is probative of his guilt. The district court implicitly recognized the relevance of this evidence by acknowledging that it contains some, albeit limited, probative value to the government's case. . . . We find no abuse of discretion. The evidence proffered in this case, therefore, satisfies Rule 413's three threshold requirements.

II.   THE APPLICABILITY OF RULE 403

The district court also properly concluded that the Rule 403 balancing test applies to evidence submitted under Rule 413. This conclusion is a legal determination that we review de novo. . . . Rule 403 allows a district court to exclude evidence "if its probative value is substantially outweighed by the danger of unfair prejudice" or other enumerated considerations, including confusion of the issues or undue delay. Fed. R. Evid. 403. Rule 403 applies to all evidence admitted in federal court, except in those rare instances when other rules make an exception to it. See, e.g., Fed. R. Evid. 609(a)(2) (mandating that prior conviction of a witness be admitted for impeachment purposes if prior crime involved dishonesty).

The wording of Rule 413 has led some commentators to infer that it creates an exception for itself to the Rule 403 balancing test. See Guardia, 955 F. Supp. at 117 (noting scholarly debate). Rule 413 states that evidence meeting its criteria "is admissible." Fed. R. Evid. 413. Rule 412, on the other hand, which also allows evidence of prior sexual behavior, states that certain evidence "is admissible, if otherwise admissible under these rules." Fed. R. Evid. 412(b) (emphasis added). One could assume from this fact that because the emphasized clause does not appear in Rule 413, Congress intended to make the introduction of Rule 413 evidence mandatory rather than subject to the discretion of the trial judge under Rule 403. See Judicial Conference of the United States, Report of the Judicial Conference on the Admission of Character Evidence in Certain Sexual Misconduct Cases, 159 F.R.D. 51, 53 (1995) (noting that the advisory committee believed the above position to be "arguable").

The other rules, however, demonstrate that the difference between Rule 412 and Rule 413 is not significant. Most importantly, Rule 402, the rule allowing admission of all relevant evidence and a rule to which the 403 balancing test undoubtedly applies, contains language no more explicit than that in Rule 413. The rule states simply that "all relevant evidence is admissible." Fed. R. Evid. 402 (emphasis added). Furthermore, when the drafters of the federal rules of evidence alter the 403 balancing test or make it inapplicable to certain evidence, they use language much more explicit than that found in Rule 413. See, e.g., Fed. R. Evid. 609(a)(2) (stating that convictions involving dishonesty "shall be admitted" for impeachment purposes); Fed. R. Evid. 609(a)(1) (requiring court to find that the probative value of a prior conviction outweighs its prejudicial effect on the accused).

Thus, in United States v. Meacham, 115 F.3d 1488, 1495 (10th Cir. 1997), we found that evidence proffered under Rule 414, which concerns prior acts of child molestation and uses language identical to Rule 413, is subject to Rule 403 balancing. See also United States v. Sumner, 119 F.3d 658, 661 (8th Cir. 1997) (concluding that Rule 403 applies to Rule 414); United States v. Larson, 112 F.3d 600, 604-05 (2d Cir. 1997) (same). Following *Meacham,* and for the above reasons, we hold that the 403 balancing test applies to Rule 413 evidence.

III. THE 403 BALANCING TEST AND RULE 413

In accordance with the above, after the district court resolves the three threshold issues, including a finding that the proffered evidence is relevant, it must proceed to balance the probative weight of the Rule 413 evidence against "the danger of unfair prejudice, confusion of the issues, or misleading the jury, or . . . considerations of undue delay, waste of time, or needless presentation of cumulative evidence." Fed. R. Evid. 403. We hold that a court must perform the same 403 analysis that it does in any other context, but with careful attention to both the significant probative value and the strong prejudicial qualities inherent in all evidence submitted under 413.

A. *Legal Principles*

Rule 413 marks a sea change in the federal rules' approach to character evidence, a fact which could lead to at least two different misapplications of the 403 balancing test. First, a court could be tempted to exclude the Rule 413 evidence simply because character evidence traditionally has been considered too prejudicial for admission. Cf. Old Chief v. United States, 519 U.S. 172, 136 L. Ed. 2d 574, 117 S. Ct. 644, 651 (U.S. 1997) (stating that Rule 404(b) merely "reflects . . . common law tradition"). Second, a court could perform a restrained 403 analysis because of the belief that Rule 413 embodies a legislative judgment that propensity evidence regarding sexual assaults is never too prejudicial or confusing and generally should be admitted. See United States v. Le-Compte, 131 F.3d 767, 1997 WL 781217, at *2 (8th Cir. 1997).

We find both interpretations illogical. With regard to the first position, we note that this court refrains from construing the words and phrases of a statute—or entire statutory provisions—in a way that renders them superfluous. . . . Rule 413 allows for evidence that otherwise would be excluded to be admitted. If Rule 413 evidence were always too prejudicial under 403, Rule 413 would never lead to the introduction of evidence. Therefore, Rule 413 only has effect if we interpret it in a way that leaves open the possibility of admission.

This interpretation harmonizes with the Supreme Court's comment in *Old Chief* and similar statements in the advisory committee's notes to Rules 401 and 403 that the ban on character evidence is merely an application of Rule 403 to a recurring issue. See *Old Chief*, 117 S. Ct. at 651. All of the rules in Article IV of the Federal Rules of Evidence, not just Rule 404, are "concrete applications [of Rules 402 and 403] evolved for particular situations." Fed. R. Evid. 403 advisory committee's note. The fact that Congress created Rule 413 can only mean that Congress intended to partially repeal the "concrete application" found in 404(b) for a subset of cases in which Congress found 404(b)'s rigid rule to be inappropriate. That conclusion is not surprising, given the fact that propensity evidence has a unique probative value in sexual assault trials and that such trials often suffer from a lack of any relevant evidence beyond the testimony of the alleged victim and the defendant. See Mark A. Sheft, Federal Rule of Evidence 413: A Dangerous New Frontier, 33 Am. Crim. L. Rev. 57, 69-70 (1995). Rule 413 is a refinement, and it exemplifies the type of evolution of Rules 402 and 403 that one can expect to find in Article IV.

While Rule 413 removes the per se exclusion of character evidence, courts should continue to consider the traditional reasons for the prohibition of character evidence as "risks of prejudice" weighing against admission. For example, a court should, in each 413 case, take into account the chance that "a jury will convict for crimes other than those charged—or that, uncertain of guilt, it will convict anyway because a bad person deserves punishment." *Old Chief*, 117 S. Ct. at 650 (citations and internal quotation marks omitted). A court should also be aware that evidence of prior acts can have the effect of confusing the issues in a case. See Michelson v. United States, 335 U.S. 469, 476, 93 L. Ed. 168, 69 S. Ct. 213 (1948). These risks will be present every time evidence is admitted under Rule 413. See United States v. Patterson, 20 F.3d 809, 814 (10th Cir. 1994) ("Evidence of prior bad acts will always be prejudicial."). The size of the risk, of course, will depend on the individual case.

With regard to the second potential misapplication of Rule 413, the government urges us to approve a lenient 403 balancing test. We agree that Rule 413, like all other rules of admissibility, favors the introduction of evidence. See 140 Cong. Rec. H8968-01, H8991 (Aug. 21, 1994) (statement of S. Molinari) ("The presumption is in favor of admission."), quoted in United States v. Enjady, 134 F.3d 1427, 1998 U.S. App. LEXIS 737 (10th Cir. 1998). Rule 413, however, contains no language that supports an especially lenient application of Rule 403. Furthermore, courts apply Rule 403 in undiluted form to Rules 404(a)(1)-(3), the other exceptions to the ban on propensity evidence. Those rules allow a criminal defendant to use character evidence of himself, his victim, or in limited circumstances, of other witnesses, in order to "prove action in conformity therewith." Fed. R. Evid. 404(a)(1-3). Like Rule 413, these rules carve out exceptions to Rule 404(a) and reflect a legislative judgment that certain types of propensity evidence should be admitted. Courts have never found, however, that because the drafters made exceptions to the general rule of 404(a), they tempered 403 as well. . . .

Similarly, under Rule 404(b), evidence of a person's prior acts can be used for other purposes other than proving character. Despite Rule 404(b)'s legislative judgment in favor of admission, Rule 403 applies with all its vigor to Rule 404(b) evidence. See Huddleston v. United States, 485 U.S. 681, 687-88, 99 L. Ed. 2d 771, 108 S. Ct. 1496 (1988) (noting that rules of admissibility in Article IV are subject to "general strictures . . . such as Rules 402 and 403").

When balancing Rule 413 evidence under 403, then, the district court should not alter its normal process of weighing the probative value of the evidence against the danger of unfair prejudice. In Rule 413 cases, the risk of prejudice will be present to varying degrees. Propensity evidence, however, has indisputable probative value. That value in a given case will depend on innumerable considerations, including the similarity of the prior acts to the acts charged, . . . , the closeness in time of the prior acts to the charged acts, see id., the frequency of the prior acts, the presence or lack of intervening events, . . . and the need for evidence beyond the testimony of the defendant and alleged victim. Because of the sensitive nature of the balancing test in these cases, it will be particularly important for a district court to fully evaluate the proffered Rule 413 evidence and make a clear record of the reasoning behind its findings. . . .

B. Balancing in the Present Case

The decision to exclude evidence under Rule 403 is within the sound discretion of the trial court, and will be reversed only upon a showing of a clear abuse of that discretion. . . . During the motion hearing and in its written decision, the district court made clear that its overriding, if not exclusive, concern was the danger that the proffered testimony would confuse the issues in the case, thereby misleading the jury. The district court properly exercised its discretion in determining that the potential for confusion of the issues substantially outweighed the probative value of the proffered testimony.

We must consider the trial court's ruling in light of the unusual nature of this case. This trial undoubtedly will focus upon whether the manner in which Dr. Guardia examined the complaining patients was medically appropriate. Unlike other sexual assault cases, resolution of credibility issues alone will not enable the jury to decide whether Dr. Guardia's act was proper. Rather, the jury will be required to evaluate expert testimony regarding the medical propriety of each examination to determine whether Dr. Guardia acted within the scope of his patients' consent.

Because so much depends upon the medical propriety of Dr. Guardia's conduct towards Carla G. and Francesca L., the fact that Dr. Guardia treated the four additional witnesses under similar but distinct circumstances creates a substantial risk of jury confusion. Admission of the testimony would transform the trial of two incidents into the trial of six incidents, each requiring description by lay witnesses and explanation by expert witnesses. The subtle factual distinctions among these incidents would make it difficult for the jury to separate the evidence of the uncharged conduct from the charged conduct. See 23 Charles Alan Wright & Kenneth W. Graham, Jr., Federal Practice and Procedure, §5412, at 273 (Supp. 1997) (noting the potential for confusion when Rule 413 evidence is admitted).

Expert testimony explaining the propriety of Dr. Guardia's conduct as to each witness would exacerbate the risk of confusion by multiplying conflicting and overlapping testimony. Although the evidence proffered under Rule 413 is probative of Dr. Guardia's disposition and supports the testimony of the complaining witnesses, we cannot conclude that the district court exceeded the bounds of permissible choice by excluding the evidence under the circumstances of this case.

Finally, we reject the government's contention that the district court erred by failing to engineer a method of presenting the evidence to minimize the risk of jury confusion. In Hill v. Bache Halsey Stuart Shields Inc., 790 F.2d 817, 826-27 (10th Cir. 1986), we held that the district court abused its discretion under Rule 403 because it excluded evidence that had a high probative value even though its prejudicial effect could have been minimized through a "less elaborate" method of presentation. In this case, however, the evidence that the district court excluded is not realistically susceptible to any less elaborate presentation than that proposed by the government. Thus, the district court did not abuse its discretion by failing to require such a presentation.

CONCLUSION

Evidence must pass several hurdles before it can be admitted under Rule 413. First, the defendant must be on trial for "an offense of sexual assault." Second, the proffered evidence must be of "another offense of . . . sexual assault." Third, the trial court must find the evidence relevant — that is, the evidence must show both that the defendant had a particular propensity, and that the propensity it demonstrates has a bearing on the charged crime. Fourth and finally, the trial court must make a reasoned, recorded finding that the prejudicial value of the evidence does not substantially outweigh its probative value.

In this case, the district court's colloquy with the attorneys at the motion hearing and the court's written decision reflect its thoughtful consideration of both the relevance of the Rule 413 evidence and the policies behind Rule 403. Given the deference due district courts in making Rule 403 determinations, we find that the district court did not abuse its discretion in concluding under Rule 403 that the risk of jury confusion substantially outweighed the probative value of the Rule 413 evidence proffered by the government. Therefore, the decision of the district court is AFFIRMED.

CHAPTER IV

Competency, Examination, and Credibility of Witnesses

The preceding chapters have already demonstrated the importance of understanding and being able to use the mechanics of proof—the rules relating to examination of witnesses, introduction of exhibits, making of objections, offers of proof, the record on appeal, and functions of judge, jury, appeals court, and advocate. The evidence rules that govern these functions may be thought of as the courtroom rules of the road. Like the rules of the highway, they tell you *how* to get where you want to go, not *where* you want to go; like driving rules, they should be learned so thoroughly that conforming to them becomes automatic.

The approach we have chosen in this book is to integrate the problems associated with these more mechanical or procedural rules with the substantive subjects of relevancy, hearsay, privileges, experts, and writings. We deliberately have constructed problems and chosen cases in the other chapters to highlight procedural problems as they arise in specific evidentiary contexts. This integrated approach emphasizes the connections between the procedural and substantive aspects of evidence and also replicates the world in which such rules are applied.

Nonetheless, it seems worthwhile to focus separately on the rules of the road, as this section does, albeit in a somewhat abbreviated manner. Segregating and considering the procedural rules in a variety of substantive contexts reveals that they are not as mechanical as they first seem; they often present important policy choices that implicate fundamental values. Both perspectives—the integrated and the isolated—are valuable.

This section takes a closer look at examination of witnesses, particularly the purposes of cross-examination, the limits of permissible cross-examination, and the form and scope of both direct and cross-examination.

Cross-examination, as the trial lawyers claim, is an art that the student cannot begin to master in an introductory course in evidence. Our much more modest goal is to impart an understanding of the basic rules and an appreciation for the potential of the method.

When considering the specific issues posed by the problems and cases in this section, reflect on the larger questions associated with the federal rules of the road. What values do these rules serve? Accuracy? Efficiency? Fairness? Certainty? What do these rules reveal about the drafters' views of the competency and proper role of the jury and the trial judge? What image of the adversary system do these rules reveal? How would you improve the system?

We proceed from the rules of the road for examining and cross-examining witnesses into the overall subject of credibility of witnesses and the somewhat intricate rules governing how a lawyer may challenge the witness's character for truthfulness. We will thus be returning to the concept of "character evidence," but in a different and more limited context, the context of the witness as a reliable source of information for the trial.

A.   Competency of Witnesses

The common law had very strict rules about who was qualified to testify in court. Parties were deemed incompetent as witnesses because of the natural inclination of humans to stretch the truth in their own self-interest. Similarly, spouses were held incompetent under the doctrine of *coverture* as a natural extension of the disqualification for *interest*. Felons were disqualified for *infamy* on the grounds that any person convicted of a serious crime was not worthy of belief. Witnesses who could not swear their belief in an omnipotent God who saw and immediately rewarded falsehood with a severe sanction were disqualified for *irreligion*. This requirement was subsequently relaxed to require only a belief in a God who rewarded and punished truth and falsity in the hereafter, and then relaxed further to require only a belief in God.

With all these disqualifications, it was sometimes difficult to find anyone with any first-hand knowledge of the relevant event to testify. A not too far-fetched example:

Time: early nineteenth century. Place: the Four Horseshoes Inn, a country pub at Madingley, Cambridgeshire. Present in the pub are Peter, Peter's wife, Mary, David, Lawrence, and Kevin, the tavern keeper. A brawl breaks out between Peter and David, and Peter later brings an action of assault against David. Lawrence, it develops, is a convicted felon, and when Kevin is called to the witness stand at trial, he states that he is an agnostic.

Who could testify to what happened in the pub? No one. Peter and David were incompetent because of their interest. Mary was incompetent by reason of coverture, Lawrence by reason of infamy, and Kevin on account of his irreligion.

The common law system gradually gave way to the modern approach of Rules 601 and 602, which allow anyone to be a witness who has personal knowledge of facts relevant to the case and can communicate them in some manner.

What, if anything, is left of the common law disqualifications for interest, coverture, infamy, and irreligion? Most of the concerns expressed by these concepts have been relegated to reliance on cross-examination to bring out the infirmities of witness testimony, but some vestiges remain. The "Dead Man's Rule" in some state jurisdictions prevents a party from testifying in a lawsuit when death has stilled the tongue of his opponent. In diversity cases, such rules may continue to have validity in federal court. See Rule 601. Spouses today have a privilege not to testify against each other. In certain circumstances, felons may have their criminal record brought out to impeach their credibility. And Rule 603 requires that witnesses still must swear or affirm that they will testify truthfully.

In considering the problems in this section, keep in mind that competency of witnesses under the Federal Rules boils down to a question of the capacity of the witness to testify—especially the capacity of the witness to be cross-examined. Analysis of all of the problems raising issues of competency of the witness should start with the question "Can this witness be cross-examined sufficiently so that the factfinder can appraise the witness's testimony fairly and accurately?" Answering this question requires consideration of whether the witness can understand, communicate, and appreciate the obligation to testify truthfully to a sufficient level such that the factfinder can make some rational use of the testimony. Thus, any impairment of memory, narrative ability, or appreciation of the difference between reality and fantasy must be weighed by the trial judge, who makes the determination of competency of witnesses under Rule 104(a), against the cost of loss of the evidence entirely if the witness is deemed so impaired she is not allowed to testify. One of the factors the court should take into account is the ability of jurors to recognize any impairment of the witness's testimonial capacities and make their own assessment and, if necessary, discount the reliability of the evidence. Courts also generally recognize that the ability of a witness to be vigorously cross-examined is a subjective ideal that may never be attained in the eyes of the cross-examining lawyer, and that this ideal standard must sometimes yield to pragmatic considerations.

Problem: The Intoxicated Informer

Charge: sale of a proscribed substance, to wit, heroin, to *I*. The state introduces evidence to show that *I*, a known heroin addict, was given $300 by the police to purchase heroin from *D* at *D*'s barber shop. The state calls *I* as its first witness. *D* objects to any testimony from *I* on the grounds that *I* is incompetent to be a witness by virtue of drug use. The trial court conducts an in-chambers hearing on the question. *D* calls *P*, a psychiatrist, who testifies that the use of LSD may confuse one's perception, thereby impairing the capacity to perceive or remember one's observations. *P*'s opinion is based on her experience with LSD users, whom she has found to have a history of suffering blackouts, although she has not personally interviewed *I*. *I* admits to excessive use of drugs, including LSD, but denies ever passing out, freaking out, or having loss of memory from the use of LSD.

What ruling and why? Is there a minimum threshold of the ability of the witness to observe, remember, relate, and appreciate the obligation of telling the truth that the witness must cross before he will be allowed to testify?

Problem: Little Archie, The Child Witness

On June 1, 1981, a male child is born to Mr. and Mrs. *P*. The child is normal and named Archie. On June 1, 1984, Archie suffers multiple punctures of his leg in a playground injury. No one saw what happened. The punctures could have been made by a dog's teeth, nails in the sandbox board, or any number of other things. Archie's parents claim that *D*'s dog is the culprit. On June 15, 1984, *P* sues *D*. At trial beginning July 15, 1984, Archie is called to testify. *D*'s objection to calling Archie as a witness is sustained. *P* takes a voluntary nonsuit, and the case is dismissed. On December 15, 1984, *P* refiles his complaint. *D* answers. There are many continuances. Finally, the trial is held in 1990 before the same judge who presided at the first trial. Archie is called as the first witness.

D's objection to calling Archie as a witness is overruled. Are the two rulings compatible?

Problem: The Aphasic Witness

Action for damages for personal injuries arising out of a collision between *P*'s car and *D*'s bus. The accident took place in November 1990 at the intersection of Oak Park Avenue and Madison Street. This intersection is controlled by traffic lights. At trial, the issue is who ran the traffic light. Prior to the accident, *P* had been a healthy, active 35-year-old policeman. He was taken unconscious from the scene of the accident, suffering from a head injury. When *P* regained consciousness, it was found that he had lost the power of reason and speech; restraints were needed to control him. Two weeks later, his condition was slightly improved, and he was sent home, but at the time of trial the injuries still affected his ability to speak coherently and intelligently. He could answer only simple questions. On direct examination, *P* gave his name, address, age, and the day and year of the accident but was unable to say the month in which the accident took place. He was able to testify that the accident took place at the Oak Park Avenue and Madison Street intersection and that there were traffic lights there. Further direct testimony was as follows:

Q: What street were you driving on when the accident happened?
A: Oak Park and Madison Street.
Q: Were there any traffic lights at Oak Park and Madison Street?
A: Yes.
Q: What direction were you going?
A: South.
Q: Now what was the color of the light as you approached and reached the intersection?
A: Green.
Q: What happened as you were going over? Tell the jury what happened.
A: Green and amber, amber and bus struck.
Q: What happened as you were going over the crossing?
A: I get hit.
Q: You got hit?
A: Yes.
Q: By what?
A: A bus.
Q: What do you next remember after that?
A: I don't remember.

There was no objection to *P*'s competency at this point.

The cross-examination required twenty pages of transcript. In response to defense counsel's questions, *P* could not say where he had been going. His answers often lacked consistency. He would testify differently to the same question. Sometimes, his answers were incoherent and meaningless; however, some answers were corroborated by other credible evidence. At the conclusion of the cross-examination, *D* objected and moved to strike *P*'s direct and cross-examination. The judge conducted a voir dire on the issue. Medical experts testified that *P* understood the questions put to him but that his speech was impaired and that his mental condition made him unable to repeat simple phrases or frame his responses. The experts testified that *P* could answer single-word questions correctly for a while but that he would tire and become confused. This condition was diagnosed as "aphasia"—the inability to coordinate thoughts and use words to express them.

How should the judge rule? Should the direct and cross-examination be stricken on the grounds that the witness is incompetent to testify, or should the evidence go to the jury for whatever weight it decides to give it?

Problem: Communication by Motion

Charge: theft of personal property from the person in an amount not exceeding $150. M.O.: taking a ring from the finger of the victim while she slept in her bed in a nursing home. At trial, the victim of the crime was incompetent to testify. The principal witness against *D* was the victim's roommate, *W*, an elderly lady who could not speak but who, according to medical testimony, had normal hearing. *W* could answer the questions put to her only by raising her right knee if the answer to the question were "yes" and by remaining still if the answer were "no." In this manner, *W* testified that she was the roommate of the victim, that she knew *D*, and that *D* was the person who came into the room of the victim and the witness late at night and took the ring from the victim's finger.

Defense counsel objected to *W*'s testimony on grounds of competency. What ruling and why?

Problem: The Medium Is the Message

Should a witness who is unable to speak be permitted to testify if the only way the witness can communicate is through another person, such as a medium, who claims to be able to apprehend in some way the witness's answers to questions and to translate them? If the medium is sworn to interpret the witness's answers correctly, should the mute witness be allowed to testify? See People v. Walker, 69 Cal. App. 475, 231 P. 572 (1924); I. Disraeli, Curiosities of Literature, chapters on "Literary Impostures" and "Literary Forgeries," cited in J. Maguire, J. Weinstein, J. Chadbourn & J. Mansfield, Evidence 265 (1973). See also Hamisi s/o Salum v. R. (1951) 18 E.A.C.A. 217 (Kenya), discussed in P. Durand, Evidence for Magistrates 94 (1969).

Problem: "You Feel Very Sleepy . . ."

Charge: murder in the first degree. Evidence for the state tended to show that Wilma Norris was the employer of Linda Lingle. The cause of death in each instance was a bullet wound in the back of the head.

The principal prosecution witness, Barbara Kiser, testified, "Sometimes I knew that I saw the defendant kill them and sometimes I really knew I hadn't seen him; I just know I couldn't remember." At her request, she had been hypnotized a few weeks prior to trial. She testified, "When I was under hypnosis I was able to actually go back to that day five years ago and just relive the whole morning and see the whole day like it was right now, everything was fresh. I remember now that I saw those women being shot by Roger McQueen [the defendant]."

Defense counsel were given a tape of the hypnosis procedure the day before trial. It was not offered in evidence. The hypnotist was not called as a witness either by the state or the defense. The record contains no testimony concerning the hypnotic procedure or what the witness related while under hypnosis.

Defendant contended at trial that Kiser had killed Norris and Lingle and objected to Kiser's testimony on the grounds that it was false and the result of her pretrial hypnosis.

Did the court err in allowing Kiser's testimony? How would you cross-examine or otherwise defend against hypnotically recollected evidence?

PEOPLE v. HUGHES
59 N.Y.2d 523, 453 N.E.2d 484, 466 N.Y.S.2d 255 (1983)

WACHTLER, J.

The primary question on this appeal concerns the admissibility of a rape victim's testimony when she has undergone hypnosis sometime prior to trial for the purpose of refreshing or restoring her memory of the incident. The trial court held that the pre-trial use of hypnosis did not affect the admissibility of the victim's testimony but only presented a credibility question for the jury. The Appellate Division reversed and ordered a new trial. The court held that hypnosis has not been generally accepted in the scientific community as a reliable method of restoring memory and that therefore the victim's posthypnotic recollections should have been suppressed. The court noted however that on the new trial the victim could testify concerning events recalled prior to hypnosis. The prosecutor has appealed.

I

On the evening of May 19, 1978 a man broke into the victim's Syracuse apartment, dragged her from her bed and raped her in the yard behind her home. During the attack she was choked and beaten. On June 8, 1978 the defendant was arrested and subsequently indicted for rape, assault and burglary in connection with the incident.

Prior to trial the defendant moved to suppress the victim's identification. In support of the application he noted that the victim's hospital records indicated that she was unable to recall what happened. It was also noted that after her release from the hospital the police had arranged for her to be hypnotized by a psychologist and under hypnosis she apparently was able to identify the defendant as her assailant. The defendant contended that hypnosis "has as its core and implementation a suggestibility" and that the victim's identification was therefore unduly suggestive as a matter of law. In the alternative he requested a hearing pursuant to United States v. Wade, 388 U.S. 218.

The trial court granted the motion to the extent of ordering that a hearing be held. That court adopted what it found to be the general, if not universal, rule throughout the country at that time, that "hypnotically induced recollection, is not inadmissible as a matter of law." The trial court held however that "where the hypnosis is conducted by or in conjunction with or under the direction of law enforcement personnel, it is clearly an identification proceeding within the meaning of CPL 710.30 and 710.20." The court thus ordered a hearing ["]to determine whether, under the totality of the circumstances, the procedures used were so impermissibly suggestive as to give rise to the very substantial likelihood of irreparable misidentification."

Following that decision the defendant asserted as an additional ground for suppression, a contention that the hypnosis had impaired his right of confrontation. He stated: "Once the hypnosis was held, as the victim cannot separate the result of the hypnosis from the independent recollection, there could never be a right of cross-examination at that point."

The testimony at the hearing shows that in 1978 the victim lived with her husband and four-year-old son in a two-story house occupied by several families. The victim and her family occupied one of two apartments on the second floor; the defendant and his female companion, Dianne, occupied the other. The two couples were well acquainted, having resided in the same building for some time. On occasion Dianne babysat for the victim's son. Indeed several times the defendant himself had done so.

The victim's husband worked at a nearby factory. On Friday, May 19, 1978, he worked the evening shift beginning at 6 P.M. When he returned from work shortly after 2 o'clock on Saturday morning he found his wife lying on the landing between the two apartments. She was not wearing any clothes and her body was covered with bruises, dirt and grass. She said that she had been raped.

The victim's husband called the police and she was taken to a local hospital where she remained for several days. Immediately following her admission she was sent for a time to the intensive care unit when it was determined that her blood pressure was low and she was having difficulty breathing. She was diagnosed as suffering from traumatic injuries, particularly to her head and neck. The laboratory reports also indicate that she had been sexually attacked.

The victim originally gave no information to the authorities. An officer who arrived at the scene testified that she was hysterical and incoherent. At the hospital she refused to see Officer George Rendle, the investigator assigned to the case, when he attempted to interview her in the intensive care unit. Later in the day she informed him that she did not know what happened. She made similar responses when questioned by hospital personnel. However, when her sister visited her and asked on several occasions who had done this to her she finally stated: "I saw Kirk." Kirk is the defendant's first name.

On that same day Officer Rendle had independently concluded that the defendant was the prime suspect after making inquiries in the neighborhood and learning from another officer that the defendant had recently been arrested and charged with a rape committed in April. That afternoon he questioned the defendant at police headquarters located in the Public Safety Building in Syracuse. At that time the officer noticed and photographed scratches on the defendant's back. The defendant also made a potentially incriminating statement which was subsequently suppressed on the ground that he had not been advised of all of his rights. Later the officer went to the defendant's apartment where Dianne turned over certain items of clothing belonging to the defendant. That evening the victim's husband saw a photograph of the defendant in Officer Rendle's file and learned that the police suspected the defendant of the rape. However at the officer's request he agreed not to inform his wife of this.

On May 22, Officer Rendle returned to the hospital with Officer Denise Banazek and found the victim more responsive. He testified that on this occasion the victim told him that on the night of the attack she put her son to bed early and went to bed herself sometime before 9 o'clock. She left the door unlocked for her husband who did not have his key. She next recalled someone grabbing her by the throat and dragging her down a flight of stairs. She also recalled that there was another person outside talking to her attacker. This other person did not hurt her and ran away while the attack on her continued. She said that her attacker wore eyeglasses and had smooth hair which was not very long.

On May 24, Officer Rendle spoke to the victim again, this time at her sister's home. The officer testified that during this interview she stated "it wasn't clear, things were not quite clear but [she] kept remembering Kirk. She stated this occurred while she was in the hospital and her head stopped spinning." They also discussed hypnosis and the victim agreed to try anything that would help her recall the man who had attacked her. That same day the officer called Dr. Jay M. Land, a clinical psychologist in private practice, and told him that he was investigating a rape or assault in which the victim could not identify her attacker. He also indicated that there was a suspect but at the doctor's request did not identify him or reveal any of the details of the investigation. The psychologist agreed to meet with the victim and an appointment was made for the interview. Sometime prior to that meeting the victim's husband told her that the police suspected the defendant of the rape.

The first hypnotic session took place at the Public Safety Building on June 7. A preliminary meeting between Dr. Land, the victim and her husband was not recorded. The remainder of the session, lasting approximately an hour and a half, was recorded on video tape. At the victim's request her husband was present. Officer Rendle and the officer operating the recording equipment also attended. In response to one of Dr. Land's questions before the induction, the victim stated that she knew the police had a suspect but she hoped it wasn't the defendant. Dr. Land then proceeded to hypnotize her and asked her to imagine that she was watching a television on which she could see what had occurred in her room on the night of May 19. This proved unsuccessful and she was awakened. However she agreed to try again, was again placed in a hypnotic state and this time identified the defendant as her attacker. When she was awakened she recalled identifying the defendant and confirmed the identification. At that point the recording equipment was turned off. She was asked several questions by Officer Rendle and gave him an affidavit identifying the defendant as the man who had raped and beaten her.

Subsequently the victim read in the newspapers about the possible effects of prehypnotic suggestions and decided to consult a psychiatrist, Dr. Goldfarb, to make sure she was not being forced to remember something that was not true. That led to three meetings with Dr. Goldfarb, all of which were recorded on audio tape. At the first meeting on June 20 she informed the psychiatrist that she had been attacked and raped and was attempting to recall a man's name. She also told him that she had been hypnotized and that some information had "come out" during that session and she wanted to find out whether it was true. During that meeting Dr. Goldfarb hypnotized her but she could only remember someone's hand around her throat and mouth and nothing beyond that.

On June 24, Dr. Goldfarb again placed her under hypnosis but encountered the same "block." He then suggested that they use sodium pentothal, a so-called "truth-serum." She agreed and an appointment was made for July 11.

Before her next meeting with Dr. Goldfarb, the victim was again hypnotized by Dr. Land on June 27. However at this session, which was recorded on audio tape, she could not remember any more than she had at the first session with Dr. Land.

On July 11, Dr. Goldfarb administered sodium pentothal to the victim at St. Joseph's Hospital. While under the influence of this drug she recalled being raped outdoors by the defendant. She also recalled that the defendant's brother was present and attempted to talk the defendant out of it. On July 22, she told Officer Rendle that the defendant's brother was the second man in the backyard.

At the hearing the People also called several neighbors for the purpose of corroborating the victim's recollections. Anna De Pasquale, who resided in the house adjoining the victim's, testified that she was sitting on her porch at about 10 o'clock on the evening of May 19 when she saw the defendant arrive home. Mrs. De Pasquale's daughter, Ann Brown, recalled that at approximately 10:15 that evening, while she was upstairs reading, she heard a child "really screaming" in the victim's house, and then heard a woman shouting "what are you doing here. What do you want, get out." A few minutes later she heard a thumping noise "like something going" down the stairs, followed by a child crying: "Mommy, where are you?" Shirley Thompson, a neighbor residing directly across the street, also heard a child crying and saw him in the window of the victim's apartment calling for his mother. She then saw the child come downstairs, look around and return upstairs. Shortly after 11 o'clock, while Mrs. Thompson was standing on the sidewalk in front of her home, she saw the defendant emerge from the alleyway next to his home and proceed up the stairs. These neighbors had all resided in the neighborhood for several years and were acquainted with the defendant.

After the hearing the court filed a written opinion in which it concluded that the People had shown by clear and convincing evidence that the hypnotic procedures employed by Dr. Land were not impermissibly suggestive under the totality of the circumstances. Recognizing the suggestibility of the person who has been hypnotized, and the potential for abuse, the hearing court adopted an extensive set of safeguards to be followed by the police and the hypnotist whenever there is a possibility that the person undergoing hypnosis may be later called to testify at trial. The court held that "although not each of these safeguards was adhered to strictly and a few not at all . . . there was substantial compliance such that the defendant's rights were adequately protected." The court also stated that all facts given during the session should be corroborated as far as possible because "all professionals agree that no examiner can be certain that the responses of the subject are free from confabulation" or can be considered reliable without independent verification. On this point the court concluded that the neighbors' testimony as well as the statement the victim made to her sister in the hospital "although circumstantial in nature, tends to verify the accuracy of the hypnotically aided recall."

At the trial the victim testified to the events as recalled both prior to and following the various hypnotic sessions and identified the defendant as her attacker. The jury found the defendant guilty of rape, burglary and assault.

The Appellate Division reversed in an opinion in which a majority of the court found that the trial court's decision "runs counter to the thrust of recent holdings in other jurisdictions that such evidence should not be permitted" unless it satisfies the criterion for the admission of scientific proof. The majority concluded: "From our reading of recent decisions in the field and of recognized authorities we are persuaded that hypnotically produced testimony is not generally accepted in the scientific community as reliable and that it should therefore, be inadmissible." However, as noted, the majority also indicated that upon the new trial the victim would not be precluded from testifying to facts recalled prior to the first hypnotic procedure. One Justice dissented on the ground that hypnotically refreshed recollections should be admissible when corroborated by other evidence, and concluded that in this case there was sufficient corroboration.

II

Although hypnosis has long been regarded with suspicion or disapproval as one of the dark arts, it is now recognized as a procedure having a scientific basis, not fully understood but proven capable of producing useful or beneficial results in limited contexts. It has frequently been employed to check compulsive habits, alleviate pain and, less frequently, to perform operations without anesthesia. It is also employed with some regularity in the diagnosis and treatment of mental disorders including amnesia (9 Encyclopaedia Britannica, Macropaedia [1981] Hypnosis, p.133). In the 1950's hypnosis was formally acknowledged by the major medical associations as an accepted procedure for medical use (see Council on Mental Heath, Medical Use of Hypnosis, 168 JAMA 186, 187; Cheek & Le Cron, Clinical Hypno-therapy [1968], p.19).

In recent years it has also been used to obtain leads in criminal investigations. Hypnosis has been credited with furnishing the crucial lead, a license plate number, in a California case involving the kidnapping of 26 children from a school bus. It was also reported as instrumental in another celebrated case involving the murder of a cellist at the Metropolitan Opera in New York (see Hypnotism v. Crime: A Powerful Weapon or an Abused Tool?, New York Times, Oct. 14, 1980, col. 1). Its failures understandably have received less attention, but it is clear from the scientific journals which study and report on the phenomenon, that the use of hypnosis in criminal investigations produces at best mixed results. Nevertheless law enforcement authorities are increasingly resorting to hypnosis to obtain leads, particularly in cases where traditional police procedures have been fruitless. In fact many law enforcement agencies are now having officers trained in the use of hypnosis, who are sometimes referred to as members of the Svengali Squad.

The latest, and most controversial development, involves the attempt by litigants to introduce hypnotically induced statements as evidence in civil and, more commonly, criminal trials. The suitability of utilizing hypnotic results in legal proceedings has not been endorsed by scientific experts. On the contrary their response essentially has been either to condemn the practice or caution that it be used very sparingly and then only under limited and controlled circumstances.

The basic problem with admitting hypnotically generated statements or recollections in evidence is that hypnosis is an inherently suggestive procedure. In fact suggestion is the method or mechanism used to induce the hypnotic state. Of course the power of suggestion does not affect all people to the same extent and, indeed, has little or no effect on some. It is recognized, however, that the hypnotic subject will be affected to some degree in three primary respects.

First, a person who has been hypnotized becomes increasingly susceptible to suggestions consciously or unconsciously planted by the hypnotist or others present during the session. The place at which the procedure is employed and the purpose for conducting it may also suggest or affect the outcome.

Second, the subject himself may confabulate, that is imagine incidents to fill memory gaps, by for instance imagining that he has experienced something he has simply heard from others. He may also intentionally fabricate events perceived to be beneficial to himself or those conducting the hypnotic session.

Third, a person who has recalled an incident under hypnosis will experience an increased confidence in his subsequent recollection of that incident.

These effects have been demonstrated under experimental conditions. In one series of experiments, involving age regression, hypnotic subjects were able to recall, with great detail and convincing manner, events or incidents from their childhood which upon investigation often proved to be totally unfounded. A more dramatic illustration is provided by experiments with age progression in which the hypnotized persons recalled, with equal specificity and conviction, events which "happened" in the future. In these instances the defects in hypnotically induced recollection were easily detected by reference to known facts. When such verification is not available, there is no currently accepted method for scientifically determining the reliability of hypnotically induced recollection.

These are points on which all of the experts who testified at the hearing in this case agreed and, as indicated, they are supported by the literature on the subject. Indeed the Executive Council of the Society for Clinical and Experimental Hypnosis has formally adopted the following resolution:

> Because we recognize that hypnotically aided recall may produce either accurate memories or at times may facilitate the creation of pseudo memories, or fantasies that are accepted as real by subject and hypnotist alike, we are deeply troubled by the utilization of this technique among the police. It must be emphasized that there is no known way of distinguishing with certainty between actual recall and pseudo memories except by independent verification.

(27 Int. J. of Clinical & Experimental Hypnosis 452.)

In the clinical setting where the goal is to relieve distress, and not compile an accurate account of a past event, the inherent suggestibility of the hypnotic procedure is generally beneficial to the patient. In criminal investigations the fact that a hypnotized witness may furnish a false lead is hardly beneficial but often worth the time needed to pursue it if no other leads are available. Scientific experts have no general objection to the investigative use of hypnosis provided the posthypnotic recollections are used only as leads to other evidence which then serves to solve or prove the crime. The potential unreliability of the hypnotic statements will be resolved or rendered moot as soon as the lead has been investigated. But the side effects of hypnosis cannot be so easily discounted if the hypnotically induced statements are later sought to be introduced at trial.

III

Although this is the first case to present the issue to this court, it has been extensively litigated in other jurisdictions both State and Federal. Most of the cases are of recent origin and as the decisions of the lower courts in this case indicate, the results have been diverse. . . .

The cases which have produced disagreement are, like the one now before us, cases in which hypnosis has been employed to refresh or restore the memory of a witness to events which might have been forgotten, overlooked or, occasionally, even repressed following a traumatic event. In these cases the evidence offered at trial is not the actual statements made by the witness while under hypnosis, but the witness's present recollection which, in theory, has simply been refreshed by hypnosis sometime prior to trial. And like the present case, the evidence is usually offered by the prosecutor in a case where hypnosis has been employed sometime prior to trial in an effort to restore or enhance the recollection of a victim or witness to a crime in order to aid the investigation or provide testimony for trial.

The initial reaction in other jurisdictions was to treat hypnotically refreshed recollections as no different from recollections refreshed in other legally acceptable ways. The first court to confront the problem was the Maryland Court of Special Appeals which in the 1969 case of Harding v. State, 5 Md. App. 230, 246 A.2d 302, cert. den. 395 U.S. 949, held that the use of hypnosis for this purpose affected only the weight of the evidence not its admissibility. That decision was based on the testimony of a single expert who stated that he "seriously doubt[ed]" that a person's recollections during hypnosis might be affected by suggestions made by others. The court observed (5 Md. App. at p.246, 246 A.2d 302) that "some authorities warn that fancy can be mingled with fact," but the court made no effort to determine which view prevailed in the scientific community. In fact the *Frye* test for the admissibility of scientific evidence was not adopted in Maryland until 10 years later (Reed v. State, 283 Md. 374, 391 A.2d 364). Following its adoption, the court which had initiated the *Harding* rule reexamined it and overruled it (see Polk v. State, 48 Md. App. 382, 427 A.2d 1041; Collins v. State, 52 Md. App. 186, 447 A.2d 1272). By that time it had become evident that the view expressed by the expert in *Harding* was not shared by scientific experts specializing in hypnosis.

Until 1980 the *Harding* rule had been uniformly, almost automatically, followed in other jurisdictions and still commands a majority. In the last few years, however, most courts considering the problem for the first time have applied the *Frye* test, but differ as to its consequences.

The New Jersey Supreme Court, noting that hypnosis is a scientifically accepted technique for treating amnesia, has held that the risk of suggestibility inherent in the procedure may be minimized if a series of standards or safeguards, proposed by various experts, are observed by those administering the hypnosis (see, e.g., State v. Hurd, 86 N.J. 525, 432 A.2d 86). In that case however, the court held the hypnotically refreshed recollection inadmissible because the hypnotic session had not been conducted in accordance with the prescribed standards (see, also, State v. Beachum, 97 N.M. 682, 643 P.2d 246, adopting the *Hurd* standards and holding that the trial court did not abuse its discretion in excluding posthypnotic recollections or in admitting those recalled prior to hypnosis).

Other courts have more broadly held that hypnotically refreshed recollection fails the *Frye* test because at the present time hypnosis is not generally accepted as a reliable method of restoring memory. They consider the proposed standards ineffective or judicially unworkable (see, e.g., People v. Gonzalez, 108 Mich. App. 145, 310 N.W.2d 306; Commonwealth v. Nazarovitch, 496 Pa. 97, 436 A.2d 170; State v. Palmer,

210 Neb. 206, 313 N.W.2d 648; Commonwealth v. Kater, 388 Mass. 519, 447 N.E.2d 1190, 1196) and note that there is no scientifically accepted method for determining whether the subject himself has fabricated or confabulated the events recalled under hypnosis. These courts hold that events recalled after hypnosis should not be admitted at trial but that the witness may be permitted to testify to events recalled prior to hypnosis. This view has been characterized as the "emerging consensus" (State v. Wren, 425 So. 2d 756, 760 [La.]).

The most extreme view thus far adopted in the other jurisdictions is that a witness who has been hypnotized is "contaminated" and is incompetent to testify, even to events recalled prior to hypnosis. It is reasoned that merely excluding the posthypnotic recollections does not completely eliminate the impact of the hypnotic session because the added confidence the witness has obtained remains and may hinder effective cross-examination. The logical purity of the rule is illusory. It has been applied to exclude the testimony of the victim and presumably other prosecution witnesses, but has not been carried so far as to preclude a defendant from testifying on his own behalf if he had previously employed hypnosis to refresh his recollection. Thus complete logical extension of this rule has been checked when logic would conflict with principles more important in the administration of criminal justice. This view was initiated by the Arizona Supreme Court (State v. Menna, 128 Ariz. 226, 624 P.2d 1274). It was later adopted by the Supreme Court of California (People v. Shirley, 31 Cal. 3d 18, 181 Cal. Rptr. 243, 641 P.2d 775) at about the same time Arizona abandoned it in favor of the rule permitting a witness to testify to prehypnotic recollection (State ex rel. Collins v. Superior Ct., 132 Ariz. 180, 644 P.2d 1266). At the present time the former Arizona rule is followed only in California.

Some States have rejected both the *Frye* test as well as the old *Harding* rule, that hypnotically refreshed recollections raise only questions of credibility, preferring a case-by-case approach which focuses on the suggestibility of the particular hypnotic session and the reliability of the recollections under the totality of the circumstances (see, e.g., State v. Armstrong, 110 Wis. 2d 555, 329 N.W.2d 386). The *Harding* rule itself has gained few adherents in the last few years, principally in cases where hypnosis contributed little or nothing to the witness's initial recollections (Chapman v. State, 638 P.2d 1280 [Wyo.]; Pearson v. State, 441 N.E.2d 468 [Ind.]; State v. Wren, 425 So. 2d 756 [La.], supra).

In short the law is in a state of flux and there is no rule which will entirely satisfy all the demands of logic, policy and practicality.

IV

The prosecutor urges that the *Harding* rule is still the most appropriate one to apply to recollections refreshed by hypnosis. He notes that the testimony will come from a lay witness and not an expert claiming scientific endorsement for the procedure employed. This, he contends, should eliminate the primary difficulty with scientific proof, namely that the jury or fact finder may be unduly impressed with the scientific and presumably reliable basis for the evidence presented. He also notes that the rules of evidence generally permit a witness to testify from present recollection even when the recollection has been refreshed in ways which have not met with scientific approval. Although he recognizes that the use of hypnosis to refresh recollection is relatively new and unusual he urges that it is no worse than the other methods currently accepted in the law.

In essence then the prosecutor urges that we extend the rules relating to refreshed recollection and give a more restricted reading to the rule governing the admissibility of scientific proof. However, the current trend of the law, when dealing with suggestive or scientific procedures relating to eyewitness testimony, particularly in this State has been to take the opposite course.

It is now clear that the police cannot refresh a witness's recollection by use of a suggestive pretrial identification procedure, and that such practices might violate the defendant's right to due process (Stovall v. Denno, 388 U.S. 293, 302). The Supreme Court has also held that the defendant has a right to counsel at identification proceedings occurring after the commencement of the criminal action (United States v. Wade, 388 U.S. 218, supra). These rules were prompted by increased judicial sensitivity to the fact that "[t]he influence of improper suggestion upon identifying witnesses probably accounts for more miscarriages of justice than any other single factor — perhaps it is responsible for more such errors than all other factors combined" (Wall, Eye-Witness Identification in Criminal Cases, p.26, quoted in United States v. Wade, supra, at p.229). The vagaries of eyewitness identification have long been a concern of this court which has on occasion gone further than the Federal Constitution requires in order to further minimize the risk of mistaken identification (see, e.g., People v. Adams, 53 N.Y.2d 241, 440 N.Y.S.2d 902, 423 N.E.2d 379).

Similarly, when presented with scientific evidence purporting to gauge the credibility of participants or witnesses to a criminal incident, we have established a very high level of reliability, tantamount to certainty, as a predicate for its admissibility (People v. Leone, 25 N.Y.2d 511, 307 N.Y.S.2d 430, 255 N.E.2d 696). Although ordinary scientific proof need not meet such a demanding standard, the increased certitude has been found appropriate when the fallibility of the scientific procedure might directly affect the fact finder's assessment of eyewitness credibility (People v. Allweiss, 48 N.Y.2d 40, 50, 421 N.Y.S.2d 341, 396 N.E.2d 735).

Hypnotically refreshed recollections pose analogous problems. Because hypnosis is an inherently suggestive procedure, its use by the police to obtain an identification or details concerning a crime may, if impermissibly suggestive, violate the defendant's constitutional rights. The constitutional cases usually deal with identifications by strangers. The principles, however, would also seem to be applicable to cases, such as this one, in which the parties were well acquainted but the victim or witness experienced some difficulty in describing the event or making an identification because of the circumstances under which the crime was committed. The constitutional restrictions aimed at curtailing improperly suggestive police procedures, would not apply to hypnosis employed by private individuals without any police involvement. The common-law rules of evidence, on the other hand, are not so limited in their application and do not require an element of State action. We do not rely on the constitutional questions for the resolution of this case.

Contrary to the prosecutor's contention, hypnosis is not comparable to the other methods of refreshing recollection long accepted at common law. Indeed if the prosecutor's point were well taken there would be no need, when the other means were available, to employ hypnosis. One of the legally endorsed techniques for reviving a witness's recollection would do just as well. What distinguishes hypnosis is the fact that suggestion is an essential and inseparable part of the process which alters a witness's consciousness and makes him more prone to suggestion and to recall events inaccurately than he would in a normal state of consciousness. In fact, it is a scientific process and the recollections it generates must be considered as scientific results. Certainly a layman could not assess those results without expert guidance and might be unduly impressed by the witness's enhanced recollections if he mistakenly viewed them as the result of normal recall.

The question then is whether the results are generally accepted as reliable in the scientific community. Because hypnosis is only intended to restore memory loss, and not to gauge the truth of the subject's statements, it would seem that the proper inquiry is whether hypnosis has gained general acceptance in the scientific community as a reliable means of restoring recollection. It is evident, however, that at the present time hypnosis has not achieved that status. As noted it has been scientifically demonstrated that it produces recollections which may contain a mixture of accurate recall, fantasy or pure fabrication in unknown quantities.

The standards adopted by the trial court in the case now before us (see, also, State v. Hurd, 86 N.J. 525, 432 A.2d 86, supra) although proposed by leading experts would only provide a partial solution even if strictly followed.[33] The primary purpose of those standards is to govern

33. In *Hurd* the court adopted six standards or guidelines proposed by Dr. Orne in the trial court, which may be briefly summarized as follows: (1) the hypnotic session should be con-

the conduct of the police and the hypnotist so as to minimize or hopefully eliminate the possibility of suggestion coming from those parties. This, however, is not the major problem. As one commentator has observed: "The greatest variable in the hypnosis of an individual is the individual himself." No procedures have yet been devised for eliminating the common risk that the subject himself is more likely to confabulate or fantasize to fill in gaps in his memory as a result of the hypnotic process. Nor is there any scientific method for detecting this type of "recollection," absent objective external verification of the statements generated by the hypnotic session.

We note that even if we had found that the proposed standards provided an effective means of insuring reliable recall under hypnosis, they could not be said to have been adequately met in this case. The information provided by the police to the hypnotist concerning the crime was not furnished in writing or otherwise recorded. Police officers, as well as the victim's husband, were present at the initial hypnotic session when the victim made her first positive identification of the defendant. Indeed, the hypnotic session was not held in a neutral setting, but at the police headquarters. In addition, and most significantly, the victim knew that the police had a suspect and knew that it was the defendant because her husband had informed her of this sometime prior to the first hypnotic session.

Neither can it be said that there was any objective verification of the victim's recollections. This, of course, was not a classic case where the police had no suspect and needed to employ hypnosis in order to obtain leads for further investigation. There is no showing on the record that the hypnotic sessions with the victim provided any leads or information which the police did not already possess. Indeed it appears that the victim's recollections under hypnosis had the opposite effect of confirming or validating the suspicions of the police, to which she was unfortunately privy.

In sum, the Appellate Division correctly held that the defendant is entitled to a new trial because the trial court should not have permitted the victim to testify to events recalled after the hypnotic sessions. However, since there must be a new trial, we note our agreement with those courts which have concluded that the pretrial use of hypnosis does not necessarily render the witness incompetent to testify to events recalled prior to being hypnotized.

---

ducted by a psychiatrist or psychologist experienced in the use of hypnosis; (2) he or she should be independent, not regularly employed by either party; (3) any information given to the hypnotist should be recorded; (4) before inducing hypnosis the hypnotist should obtain a detailed description of the facts the subject presently recalls, and should avoid influencing the description; (5) all contacts between the hypnotist and the subject should be recorded; (6) only the hypnotist and the subject should be present during any phase of the hypnotic session.

As indicated, hypnosis has proven to be a useful and apparently essential investigative tool for generating leads in cases where normal police procedures have proven inadequate, although its use to confirm police suspicions, or prepare a witness for trial is more dubious and is not to be encouraged. It also appears that hypnosis has become a fairly standard course of medical treatment for amnesia resulting from traumatic events, including witnessing or being victimized by a criminal act. A criminal trial for rape or assault would present an odd spectacle if the victim was barred from saying anything, including the fact that the crime occurred, simply because he or she submitted to hypnosis sometime prior to trial to aid the investigation or obtain needed medical treatment. Even in cases dealing with the frailties of eyewitness identification some allowance must be made for practicalities.

When confronted with suggestive pretrial identifications it has not been found necessary to preclude the witness from making an in-court identification on the basis of recollections prior to the suggestive procedure, if it is found as a fact that he can do so without relying on the improperly made identification. A similar procedure would seem to be appropriate in cases involving the pretrial use of hypnosis.

The major difficulty, of course, is that a witness who has been hypnotized acquires an increased confidence in his recollections, presumably greater than the witness who has experienced a suggestive identification, which could inhibit the defendant's right of cross-examination. The problem is greatest when the hypnotist suggests to the person under hypnosis that a certain event occurred or that the person will recall everything when he returns to the normal state of consciousness. Absent such suggestions it appears that the degree of confidence gained through hypnosis depends upon the individual's belief in the ability of hypnosis to yield the truth, the degree to which he has been hypnotized and the extent to which those administering the hypnosis have observed the standards recommended by the experts. Indeed in some cases where the witness was quite confident in his initial recollections and hypnosis was employed unsuccessfully to yield additional details, there may be little or no impairment of the defendant's power to cross-examine. In any event these are questions which the trial court should resolve at a pretrial hearing.

It would appear that two aspects of the matter warrant inquiry and resolution at the pretrial state—the extent of the witness's prehypnotic recollection (which would establish the boundaries of admissible testimony) and whether the hypnosis was so impermissibly suggestive as to require exclusion of in-court testimony with respect to such prehypnotic recollection. Little reported authority is available as a basis on which to prescribe guidelines for such inquiry and resolution. Experience and determination on a case-by-case basis will be required before procedural standards can be properly enunciated with any degree of definiteness.

As to the scope and content of the prehypnotic recollection of the witness, it would seem that evidence, testimonial and documentary, which is material to the determination thereof should be received at the pretrial hearing, without rigid application of the hearsay rule. The proof to establish the extent of the witness's unaided recollection of the particular criminal transaction will necessarily vary from case to case and will depend on what procedures were followed and what events occurred before the hypnosis. To the extent practicable full opportunity should be afforded counsel to test the probative worth of the proof offered.

With respect to the hypnosis itself, detailed proof should be introduced as to the precise procedures that were followed in the particular instance, including measures taken to reduce the risk of impermissible suggestiveness. At this point the standards or guidelines proposed by the experts for the conduct of hypnotic sessions in connection with criminal investigations may be pertinent. Here, too, experience will be the best teacher, and it would be inappropriate in this case to undertake the formulation of rigid guidelines.

Because of the unique and sometimes unfathomable consequences of hypnosis, the People should assume the burden of demonstrating by clear and convincing proof that the testimony of the witness as to his or her prehypnotic recollection will be reliable and that there has been no substantial impairment of the defendant's right of cross-examination. If the witness is held to be competent to testify, the defendant, of course, has the option at trial of introducing proof with respect to the hypnotic procedures followed as well as expert testimony concerning the potential effect of the hypnosis on the witness's recollections. And since there is general agreement in the scientific community that a witness who has been hypnotized usually acquires some measure of confidence in events recalled under hypnosis, the court should charge the jury to that effect if the defendant requests it. In our view these measures represent a reasonable accommodation between the legitimate uses of hypnosis and the defendant's right of confrontation.

In the present case where the trial court erroneously concluded that hypnosis was a reliable means of refreshing a witness's recollection, it was not necessary for the court to consider, or the People to address, the separate question as to whether the witness's prehypnotic recollections were unduly influenced by the hypnotic sessions. Thus on the retrial the court should consider the issue at a pretrial hearing.

For the reasons stated, the defendant is entitled to a new trial to be held in accordance with this opinion, and the order of the Appellate Division should be affirmed.

What procedural protections would you recommend when such evidence enhanced by hypnotism is offered? Should a witness be permitted to testify in court while under hypnosis? Should a pretrial statement made by a witness while under hypnosis be admissible?

ROCK v. ARKANSAS
483 U.S. 44 (1987)

Justice BLACKMUN delivered the opinion of the Court.

The issue presented in this case is whether Arkansas' evidentiary rule prohibiting the admission of hypnotically refreshed testimony violated petitioner's constitutional right to testify on her own behalf as a defendant in a criminal case.

I

Petitioner Vickie Lorene Rock was charged with manslaughter in the death of her husband, Frank Rock, on July 2, 1983. A dispute had been simmering about Frank's wish to move from the couple's small apartment adjacent to Vickie's beauty parlor to a trailer she owned outside town. That night a fight erupted when Frank refused to let petitioner eat some pizza and prevented her from leaving the apartment to get something else to eat. When police arrived on the scene they found Frank on the floor with a bullet wound in his chest. Petitioner urged the officers to help her husband, and cried to a sergeant who took her in charge, "please save him" and "don't let him die." The police removed her from the building because she was upset and because she interfered with their investigation by her repeated attempts to use the telephone to call her husband's parents. According to the testimony of one of the investigating officers, petitioner told him that "she stood up to leave the room and [her husband] grabbed her by the throat and choked her and threw her against the wall and . . . at that time she walked over and picked up the weapon and pointed it toward the floor and he hit her again and she shot him."

Because petitioner could not remember the precise details of the shooting, her attorney suggested that she submit to hypnosis in order to refresh her memory. Petitioner was hypnotized twice by Doctor Betty Back, a licensed neuropsychologist with training in the field of hypnosis. Doctor Back interviewed petitioner for an hour prior to the first hypnosis session, taking notes on petitioner's general history and her recollections of the shooting. Both hypnosis sessions were recorded on tape. Petitioner did not relate any new information during either of the sessions, but, after the hypnosis, she was able to remember that at the time of the incident she had her thumb on the hammer of the gun, but had not held her finger on the trigger. She also recalled that the gun had discharged when her husband grabbed her arm during the scuffle. As a result of the details that petitioner was able to remember about the shooting, her counsel arranged for a gun expert to examine the handgun, a single action Hawes .22 Deputy Marshal. That inspection revealed that the gun was defective and prone to fire, when hit or dropped, without the trigger's being pulled.

When the prosecutor learned of the hypnosis sessions, he filed a motion to exclude petitioner's testimony. The trial judge held a pretrial hearing on the motion and concluded that no hypnotically refreshed testimony would be admitted. The court issued an order limiting petitioner's testimony to "matters remembered and stated to the examiner prior to being placed under hypnosis." At trial, petitioner introduced testimony by the gun expert, but the court limited petitioner's own description of the events on the day of the shooting to a reiteration of the sketchy information in Doctor Back's notes. The jury convicted petitioner on the manslaughter charge and she was sentenced to 10 years imprisonment and a $10,000 fine.

On appeal, the Supreme Court of Arkansas rejected petitioner's claim that the limitations on her testimony violated her right to present her defense. The court concluded that "the dangers of admitting this kind of testimony outweigh whatever probative value it may have," and decided to follow the approach of States that have held hypnotically refreshed testimony of witnesses inadmissible per se, Rock v. State, 288 Ark. 566, 573, 708 S.W.2d 78, 81 (1986). Although the court acknowledged that "a defendant's right to testify is fundamental," id., at 578, 708 S.W.2d, at 84, it ruled that the exclusion of petitioner's testimony did not violate her constitutional rights. Any "prejudice or deprivation" she suffered "was minimal and resulted from her own actions and not by any erroneous ruling of the court." Id., at 580, 708 S.W.2d, at 86. We granted certiorari to consider the constitutionality of Arkansas' per se rule excluding a criminal defendant's hypnotically refreshed testimony.

II

Petitioner's claim that her testimony was impermissibly excluded is bottomed on her constitutional right to testify in her own defense. At this point in the development of our adversary system, it cannot be doubted that a defendant in a criminal case has the right to take the witness stand and to testify in his or her own defense. This, of course, is a change from the historic common-law view, which was that all parties to litigation, including criminal defendants, were disqualified from testifying because of their interest in the outcome of the trial. The principal rationale for this rule was the possible untrustworthiness of a party's testimony. Under the common law, the practice did develop of permitting criminal defendants to tell their side of the story, but they were limited to making an unsworn statement that could not be elicited through direct examination by counsel and was not subject to cross-examination.

This Court in Ferguson v. Georgia, 365 U.S. 570, 573-582 (1961), detailed the history of the transition from a rule of a defendant's incompetency to a rule of competency. As the Court there recounted, it came to be recognized that permitting a defendant to testify advances both the " 'detection of guilt' " and " 'the protection of innocence,' " id., at 581, quoting 1 Am. L. Rev. 396 (1867), and by the end of the second half of the 19th century, all States except Georgia had enacted statutes that declared criminal defendants competent to testify. Congress enacted a general competency statute in the Act of Mar. 16, 1878, 20 Stat. 30, as amended, 18 U.S.C. §3481, and similar developments followed in other common-law countries. Thus, more than 25 years ago this Court was able to state:

> In sum, decades ago the considered consensus of the English-speaking world came to be that there was no rational justification for prohibiting the sworn testimony of the accused, who above all others may be in a position to meet the prosecution's case.

Ferguson v. Georgia, 356 U.S., at 582.

The right to testify on one's own behalf at a criminal trial has sources in several provisions of the Constitution. It is one of the rights that "are essential to due process of law in a fair adversary process." Faretta v. California, 422 U.S. 806, 819, n.15 (1975). The necessary ingredients of the Fourteenth Amendment's guarantee that no one shall be deprived of liberty without due process of law include a right to be heard and to offer testimony:

> A person's right to reasonable notice of a charge against him, and *an opportunity to be heard in his defense*—a right to his day in court—are basic in our system of jurisprudence; and these rights include, as a minimum, a right to examine the witnesses against him, to offer testimony, and to be represented by counsel.

(Emphasis added.) In re Oliver, 333 U.S. 257, 273 (1948). . . .

The right to testify is also found in the Compulsory Process Clause of the Sixth Amendment, which grants a defendant the right to call "witnesses in his favor," a right that is guaranteed in the criminal courts of the States by the Fourteenth Amendment. Washington v. Texas, 388 U.S. 14, 17-19 (1967). Logically included in the accused's right to call witnesses whose testimony is "material and favorable to his defense,"

United States v. Valenzuela-Bernal, 458 U.S. 858, 867 (1982), is a right to testify himself, should he decide it is in his favor to do so. In fact, the most important witness for the defense in many criminal cases is the defendant himself. There is no justification today for a rule that denies an accused the opportunity to offer his own testimony. Like the truthfulness of other witnesses, the defendant's veracity, which was the concern behind the original common-law rule, can be tested adequately by cross-examination. See generally Westen, The Compulsory Process Clause, 73 Mich. L. Rev. 71, 119-120 (1974).

Moreover, in Faretta v. California, 422 U.S., at 819, the Court recognized that the Sixth Amendment

> grants to the accused *personally* the right to make his defense. It is the accused, not counsel, who must be "informed of the nature and cause of the accusation," who must be "confronted with the witnesses against him," and who must be accorded "compulsory process for obtaining witnesses in his favor."

(Emphasis added.) Even more fundamental to a personal defense than the right of self-representation, which was found to be "necessarily implied by the structure of the Amendment," ibid., is an accused's right to present his own version of events in his own words. A defendant's opportunity to conduct his own defense by calling witnesses is incomplete if he may not present himself as a witness.

The opportunity to testify is also a necessary corollary to the Fifth Amendment's guarantee against compelled testimony. In Harris v. New York, 401 U.S. 222, 230 (1971), the Court stated: "Every criminal defendant is privileged to testify in his own defense, or to refuse to do so." Id., at 225. Three of the dissenting Justices in that case agreed that the Fifth Amendment encompasses this right:

> [The Fifth Amendment's privilege against self-incrimination] is fulfilled only when an accused is guaranteed the right "to remain silent unless he chooses to speak in the unfettered exercise of his own will." . . . The choice of whether to testify in one's own defense . . . is an exercise of the constitutional privilege.

Id., at 230, quoting Malloy v. Hogan, 378 U.S. 1, 8 (1964). (Emphasis removed.)

III

The question now before the Court is whether a criminal defendant's right to testify may be restricted by a state rule that excludes her post-hypnosis testimony. This is not the first time this Court has faced a constitutional challenge to a state rule, designed to ensure trustworthy evidence, that interfered with the ability of a defendant to offer testimony. In Washington v. Texas, 388 U.S. 14 (1967), the Court was confronted with a state statute that prevented persons charged as principals, accomplices, or accessories in the same crime from being introduced as witnesses for one another. The statute, like the original common-law prohibition on testimony by the accused, was grounded in a concern for the reliability of evidence presented by an interested party:

> It was thought that if two persons charged with the same crime were allowed to testify on behalf of each other, "each would try to swear the other out of the charge." This rule, as well as the other disqualifications for interest, rested on the unstated premises that the right to present witnesses was subordinate to the court's interest in preventing perjury, and that erroneous decisions were best avoided by preventing the jury from hearing any testimony that might be perjured, even if it were the only testimony available on a crucial issue.

(Footnote omitted.) Id., at 21, quoting Benson v. United States, 146 U.S. 325, 335 (1982).

As the Court recognized, the incompetency of a codefendant to testify had been rejected on nonconstitutional grounds in 1918, when the Court, refusing to be bound by "the dead hand of the common-law rule of 1789," stated:

> "[T]he conviction of our time [is] that the truth is more likely to be arrived at by hearing the testimony of all persons of competent understanding who may seem to have knowledge of the facts involved in a case, leaving the credit and weight of such testimony to be determined by the jury or by the court. . . ."

388 U.S., at 22, quoting Rosen v. United States, 245 U.S. 467, 471 (1918). The Court concluded that this reasoning was compelled by the Sixth Amendment's protections for the accused. In particular, the Court reasoned that the Sixth Amendment was designed in part "to make the testimony of a defendant's witnesses admissible on his behalf in court," 388 U.S., at 22.

With the rationale for the common-law incompetency rule thus rejected on constitutional grounds, the Court found that the mere presence of the witness in the courtroom was not enough to satisfy the Constitution's Compulsory Process Clause. By preventing the defendant from having the benefit of his accomplice's testimony, "the State *arbitrarily* denied him the right to put on the stand a witness who was physically and mentally capable of testifying to events that he had personally observed, and whose testimony would have been relevant and material to the defense." (Emphasis added.) Id., at 23.

Just as a State may not apply an arbitrary rule of competence to exclude a material defense witness from taking the stand, it also may not apply a rule of evidence that permits a witness to take the stand, but arbitrarily excludes material portions of his testimony. In Chambers v.

Mississippi, 410 U.S. 284 (1973), the Court invalidated a State's hearsay rule on the ground that it abridged the defendant's right to "present witnesses in his own defense." Id., at 302. Chambers was tried for a murder to which another person repeatedly had confessed in the presence of acquaintances. The State's hearsay rule, coupled with a "voucher" rule that did not allow the defendant to cross-examine the confessed murderer directly, prevented Chambers from introducing testimony concerning these confessions, which were critical to his defense. This Court reversed the judgment of conviction, holding that when a state rule of evidence conflicts with the right to present witnesses, the rule may "not be applied mechanistically to defeat the ends of justice," but must meet the fundamental standards of due process. Ibid. In the Court's view, the State in *Chambers* did not demonstrate that the hearsay testimony in that case, which bore "assurances of trustworthiness" including corroboration by other evidence, would be unreliable, and thus the defendant should have been able to introduce the exculpatory testimony. Ibid.

Of course, the right to present relevant testimony is not without limitation. The right "may, in appropriate cases, bow to accommodate other legitimate interests in the criminal trial process." Id., at 295. But restrictions of a defendant's right to testify may not be arbitrary or disproportionate to the purposes they are designed to serve. In applying its evidentiary rules a State must evaluate whether the interests served by a rule justify the limitation imposed on the defendant's constitutional right to testify.

IV

The Arkansas rule enunciated by the state courts does not allow a trial court to consider whether posthypnosis testimony may be admissible in a particular case; it is a per se rule prohibiting the admission at trial of any defendant's hypnotically refreshed testimony on the ground that such testimony is always unreliable. Thus, in Arkansas, an accused's testimony is limited to matters that he or she can prove were remembered *before* hypnosis. This rule operates to the detriment of any defendant who undergoes hypnosis, without regard to the reasons for it, the circumstances under which it took place, or any independent verification of the information it produced.

In this case, the application of that rule had a significant adverse effect on petitioner's ability to testify. It virtually prevented her from describing any of the events that occurred on the day of the shooting, despite corroboration of many of those events by other witnesses. Even more importantly, under the court's rule petitioner was not permitted to describe the actual shooting except in the words contained in Doctor Back's notes. The expert's description of the gun's tendency to misfire would have taken on greater significance if the jury had heard petitioner testify that she did not have her finger on the trigger and that the gun went off when her husband hit her arm.

In establishing its per se rule, the Arkansas Supreme Court simply followed the approach taken by a number of States that have decided that hypnotically enhanced testimony should be excluded at trial on the ground that it tends to be unreliable. Other States that have adopted an exclusionary rule, however, have done so for the testimony of *witnesses,* not for the testimony of a *defendant.* The Arkansas Supreme Court failed to perform the constitutional analysis that is necessary when a defendant's right to testify is at stake.

Although the Arkansas court concluded that any testimony that cannot be proved to be the product of prehypnosis memory is unreliable, many courts have eschewed a per se rule and permit the admission of hypnotically refreshed testimony. Hypnosis by trained physicians or psychologists has been recognized as a valid therapeutic technique since 1958, although there is no generally accepted theory to explain the phenomenon, or even a consensus on a single definition of hypnosis. See Council on Scientific Affairs, Scientific Status of Refreshing Recollection by the Use of Hypnosis, 253 J.A.M.A. 1918, 1918-1919 (1985) (Council Report). The use of hypnosis in criminal investigations, however, is controversial, and the current medical and legal view of its appropriate role is unsettled.

Responses of individuals to hypnosis vary greatly. The popular belief that hypnosis guarantees the accuracy of recall is as yet without established foundation and, in fact, hypnosis often has no effect at all on memory. The most common response to hypnosis, however, appears to be an increase in both correct and incorrect recollections. Three general characteristics of hypnosis may lead to the introduction of inaccurate memories: the subject becomes "suggestible" and may try to please the hypnosist with answers the subject thinks will be met with approval; the subject is likely to "confabulate," that is, to fill in details from the imagination in order to make an answer more coherent and complete; and, the subject experiences "memory hardening," which gives him great confidence in both true and false memories, making effective cross-examination more difficult. See generally M. Orne, et al., Hypnotically Induced Testimony, in Eye-witness Testimony: Psychological Perspectives 171 (G. Wells and E. Loftus, eds., 1985); Diamond, Inherent Problems in the Use of Pretrial Hypnosis on a Prospective Witness, 68 Calif. L. Rev. 313, 333-342 (1980). Despite the unreliability that hypnosis concededly may introduce, however, the procedure has been credited as instrumental in obtaining investigative leads or identifications that were later confirmed by independent evidence.

The inaccuracies the process introduces can be reduced, although perhaps not eliminated, by the use of procedural safeguards. One set of suggested guidelines calls for hypnosis to be performed only by a psychologist or psychiatrist with special training in its use and who is independent of the investigation. See Orne, The Use and Misuse of Hypnosis in Court, 27 Intl. J. Clinical & Experimental Hypnosis 311, 335-336 (1979). These procedures reduce the possibility that biases will be communicated to the hypersuggestive subject by the hypnotist. Suggestion will be less likely also if the hypnosis is conducted in a neutral setting with no one present but the hypnotist and the subject. Tape or video recording of all interrogations, before, during, and after hypnosis, can help reveal if leading questions were asked. Id., at 336. Such guidelines do not guarantee the accuracy of the testimony, because they cannot control the subject's own motivations or any tendency to confabulate, but they do provide a means of controlling overt suggestions.

The more traditional means of assessing accuracy of testimony also remain applicable in the case of a previously hypnotized defendant. Certain information recalled as a result of hypnosis may be verified as highly accurate by corroborating evidence. Cross-examination, even in the face of a confident defendant, is an effective tool for revealing inconsistencies. Moreover, a jury can be educated to the risks of hypnosis through expert testimony and cautionary instructions. Indeed, it is probably to a defendant's advantage to establish carefully the extent of his memory prior to hypnosis, in order to minimize the decrease in credibility the procedure might introduce.

We are not now prepared to endorse without qualifications the use of hypnosis as an investigative tool; scientific understanding of the phenomenon and of the means to control the effects of hypnosis is still in its infancy. Arkansas, however, has not justified the exclusion of *all* of a defendant's testimony that the defendant is unable to prove to be the product of prehypnosis memory. A State's legitimate interest in barring unreliable evidence does not extend to per se exclusions that may be reliable in an individual case. Wholesale inadmissibility of a defendant's testimony is an arbitrary restriction on the right to testify in the absence of clear evidence by the State repudiating the validity of all posthypnosis recollections. The State would be well within its powers if it established guidelines to aid trial courts in the evaluation of posthypnosis testimony and it may be able to show that testimony in a particular case is so unreliable that exclusion is justified. But it has not shown that hypnotically enhanced testimony is always so untrustworthy and so immune to the traditional means of evaluating credibility that it should disable a defendant from presenting her version of the events for which she is on trial.

In this case, the defective condition of the gun corroborated the details petitioner remembered about the shooting. The tape recordings provided some means to evaluate the hypnosis and the trial judge concluded that Doctor Back did not suggest responses with leading questions. Those circumstances present an argument for admissibility of petitioner's testimony in this particular case, an argument that must be considered by the trial court. Arkansas' per se rule excluding all post-hypnosis testimony infringes impermissibly on the right of a defendant to testify on his or her own behalf.

The judgment of the Supreme Court of Arkansas is vacated and the case is remanded to that court for further proceedings not inconsistent with this opinion.

It is so ordered.

Chief Justice REHNQUIST, with whom Justice WHITE, Justice O'CONNOR, and Justice SCALIA join, dissenting.

In deciding that petitioner Rock's testimony was properly limited at her trial, the Arkansas Supreme Court cited several factors that undermine the reliability of hypnotically induced testimony. Like the Court today, the Arkansas Supreme Court observed that a hypnotized individual becomes subject to suggestion, is likely to confabulate, and experiences artificially increased confidence in both true and false memories following hypnosis. No known set of procedures, both courts agree, can insure against the inherently unreliable nature of such testimony. Having acceded to the factual premises of the Arkansas Supreme Court, the Court nevertheless concludes that a state trial court must attempt to make its own scientific assessment of reliability in each case it is confronted with a request for the admission of hypnotically induced testimony. I find no justification in the Constitution for such a ruling.

In the Court's words, the decision today is "bottomed" on recognition of Rock's "constitutional right to testify in her own defense." While it is true that this Court, in dictum, has recognized the existence of such a right, see, e.g., Faretta v. California, 422 U.S. 806, 819, n.15 (1975), the principles identified by the Court as underlying this right provide little support for invalidating the evidentiary rule applied by the Arkansas Supreme Court.

As a general matter, the Court first recites, a defendant's right to testify facilitates the truth-seeking function of a criminal trial by advancing both the " 'detection of guilt' " and " 'the protection of innocence,' " quoting Ferguson v. Georgia, 365 U.S. 570, 581 (1961). Such reasoning is hardly controlling here, where advancement of the truth-seeking function of Rock's trial was the sole motivation behind limiting her testimony. The Court also posits, however, that "a rule that denies an accused the opportunity to offer his own testimony" cannot be upheld because, "[l]ike the truthfulness of other witnesses, the defendant's veracity . . . can be tested adequately by cross-examination." But the Court candidly admits that the increased confidence inspired by hypnotism makes "cross-examination more difficult," thereby diminishing an adverse party's ability to test the truthfulness of defendants such as Rock. Nevertheless, we are told, the exclusion of a defendant's testimony cannot be sanctioned because the defendant " 'above all others may be in a position to meet the prosecution's case,' " quoting Ferguson v. Georgia, supra, at 582. In relying on such reasoning, the Court apparently forgets that the issue before us arises only by virtue of Rock's memory loss, which rendered her less able "to meet the prosecution's case." Ibid.

In conjunction with its reliance on broad principles that have little relevance here, the Court barely concerns itself with the recognition, present throughout our decisions, that an individual's right to present evidence is subject always to reasonable restrictions. Indeed, the due process decisions relied on by the Court all envision that an individual's right to present evidence on his behalf is not absolute and must oftentimes give way to countervailing considerations. Similarly, our Compulsory Process Clause decisions make clear that the right to present relevant testimony "may, in appropriate cases, bow to accommodate other legitimate interests in the criminal trial process." Chambers v. Mississippi, 410 U.S. 284, 295 (1973); see Washington v. Texas, 388 U.S. 14, 22 (1967). The Constitution does not in any way relieve a defendant from compliance with "rules of procedure and evidence designed to assure both fairness and reliability in the ascertainment of guilt and innocence." Chambers v. Mississippi, supra, at 302. Surely a rule designed to exclude testimony whose trustworthiness is inherently suspect cannot be said to fall outside this description.

This Court has traditionally accorded the States "respect . . . in the establishment and implementation of their own criminal trial rules and procedures." 410 U.S., at 302-303; see, e.g., Marshall v. Lonberger, 459 U.S. 422, 438, n.6 (1983) ("[T]he Due Process Clause does not permit the federal courts to engage in a finely tuned review of the wisdom of state evidentiary rules"); Patterson v. New York, 432 U.S. 197, 201 (1977) ("[W]e should not lightly construe the Constitution so as to intrude upon the administration of justice by the individual States"). One would think that this deference would be at its highest in an area such as this, where, as the Court concedes, "scientific understanding . . . is still in its infancy." Turning a blind eye to this concession, the Court chooses instead to restrict the ability of both state and federal courts to respond to changes in the understanding of hypnosis.

The Supreme Court of Arkansas' decision was an entirely permissible response to a novel and difficult question. See National Institute of Justice, Issues and Practices, M. Orne et al., Hypnotically Refreshed Testimony: Enhanced Memory or Tampering with Evidence? 51 (1985). As an original proposition, the solution this Court imposes upon Arkansas may be equally sensible, though requiring the matter to be considered *res nova* by every single trial judge in every single case might seem to some to pose serious administrative difficulties. But until there is a much more general consensus on the use of hypnosis than there is now, the Constitution does not warrant this Court's mandating its own view of how to deal with the issue.

B.   Form and Scope of Examination of Witnesses

The method of presentation of witness testimony in Anglo-American trial procedure is by direct and cross-examination of the witness by the attorneys for the repective parties. Attorney examination of witnesses in the common law world is to be contrasted with procedure in jurisdictions from the civil law tradition, where witness testimony is primarily elicited by the judge, and where the lawyers' role is more supportive and suggestive. There are many who think that the civil law approach is more efficient and better calculated to develop an accurate picture of the witness's knowledge than the process of adversarial questioning familiar to lawyers and law students in England and its former colonies, including the United States. See, e.g., Langbein, "The German Advantage in Civil Procedure," 52 Chicago L. Rev. 823 (1985).

Under the American procedure, a party "calls" the witness to testify. Either party may call any accessible witness, including the opposite party. The one great exception to this rule is that the State cannot call the criminal defendant as a witness. The party calling the witness conducts the initial "direct examination." After the direct examiner has completed her initial inquiry the opponent has the opportunity to "cross-examine" the witness. Following cross-examination, the proponent of the witness may conduct redirect, after which there may be recross, and so forth.

Although usually most of the information relevant to the issues of a case is elicited during direct examination, it is cross-examination that often holds the most interest for lawyers and students. When thinking about cross-examination, it is important to keep in mind that its primary purpose is destructive—to destroy the credibility of the witness by suggesting that the witness did not perceive correctly, does not remember accurately what she saw, is not communicating accurately what she thinks she remembers she saw, or is lying. Thus, most cross-examination, when it is not eliciting new facts that the witness has not testified to on direct examination in order to help build the cross-examiner's case-in-chief or defense, attacks perception, memory, clarity, or sincerity. Sincerity is the most complex of these testimonial capacities and is itself often broken down into bias, prejudice, interest, and corruption.

Cross-examination is often spoken of by trial lawyers as the ultimate trial art—the most difficult skill for a lawyer to master, requiring years of practice, an intuitive grasp of human psychology, and understanding of the legal subject matter, the judge and jury's subjective needs and biases, and all of the information contained in the World Almanac (just in case the witness testifies on direct that he saw the crime committed in the moonlight on a night in which there was no moon). Young lawyers, however, often find that asking a nonobjectionable question on direct examination is a bigger problem.

Direct examination is also a matter of knowing what the foundational requirements are for the evidence you want to elicit, asking the questions in the proper order (starting with who the witness is and what her connection to the case happens to be) to establish the necessary foundation, and allowing the witness to tell her story.

Allowing the witness to tell her story makes not only good sense from an advocacy perspective, it is what the rules require. As the Advisory Committee's Note states, Rule 611(c) provides that leading questions should not be used on direct examination or with friendly witnesses on cross-examination. The rule is suggestive and comes down to letting the witness testify rather than ratify the lawyer's testimony in the form of questions to the witness. It is often useful to remember to ask "W" questions to avoid leading the witness: "Who?", "What?", "When?", "Where?", "How?" — the "W" is at the end — and, at times, even — despite the maxim—"Why?"

The cross-examination rule is also suggestive rather than mandatory. Rule 611(b) adopts a loose form of the rule of restrictive cross-examination, allowing great latitude to the trial judge and little scope for appellate scrutiny. This final rule is the product of legislative amendment—the original rule proposed by the Supreme Court was the wide-open rule of cross-examination. When reviewing the problems in this section, consider the advantages and disadvantages of the restrictive approach and the wide-open approach, as well as the practical problems in applying the final rule.

Problem: Direct Examination—Accident

Action for damages for personal injuries that allegedly occurred when *D* ran over *P* on June 1 while *P* was crossing the road. *D*'s answer denies the allegations of the complaint and pleads contributory negligence. At trial, the jury is sworn, counsel makes a brief opening statement, and *P* is called to the stand as plaintiff's first witness. The first question put to her is, "Where were you on June 1?" *D* objects. What ruling and why?

The next question is, "Did defendant drive his car into you on June 1?" *D* objects. What ruling and why?

Construct a direct examination of *P* that will avoid the mistakes plaintiff's attorney has made.

Problem: Direct Examination — Car Theft

Action for the alleged conversion by *D* on June 1 of a $5,000 car allegedly owned by *P*. *D*'s answer is a general denial of every allegation in the complaint. On direct examination of *P*, the first witness, the preliminary foundational questions are asked and answered, at which point *P*'s counsel asks the witness, "And when you returned from the store, you saw *D* driving your car away, didn't you?" *D* objects.

What ruling and why? What mistake has *P*'s attorney made? Construct a short segment of direct examination that would avoid the problem presented in this example.

Problem: Direct and Cross-Examination — High Sticking

Charge: aggravated assault and battery. Defendant: *D*, a professional hockey player for the out-of-town Brotherly Bullies. Victim: Kevin O'Casey, a loyal hometown fan. M.O.: striking O'Casey over the head with a hockey stick in the local arena on February 14. At *D*'s trial, O'Casey is the first prosecution witness and testifies on direct examination as to his name, age, employment, and so forth. The assistant D.A. next has a hockey stick marked as People's Exhibit A for identification. The direct examination continues:

Q: I show you what has been marked as People's Exhibit A for identification and ask you if you recognize it?
       (The witness does not answer.)
Q: Mr. *D* struck you with this, didn't he?
By defense counsel: Objection — leading question.

What ruling and why?
    Bobby Boor, a member of the local hockey club, is subpoenaed by the defense and testifies as its first witness. Following his direct testimony, he is cross-examined by the assistant D. A. as follows:

Q: Did you see anyone strike O'Casey?
A: Yes.
Q: Was it you?
A: No.
Q: It was the defendant, *D*, who struck him, wasn't it?
By defense counsel: Objection.

What ruling and why?

What standard should be used in deciding whether a question is an improper leading question? What are the practical or policy considerations for the rule prohibiting leading questions to a friendly witness? What is wrong with leading a friendly witness?

C. Cross-Examination and Witness Credibility

As you consider the problems and cases in this section, think first of all about the purpose of cross-examination. There is an old saying among trial lawyers, "If you can't think of the reason why you are asking a question on cross-examination, don't ask it!" Although the purpose of cross-examination is usually to undermine or discredit an adverse witness's testimony or to cast doubt on the witness's credibility, cross-examination is also used to develop facts of consequence omitted in the direct examination and merely to clarify potential misimpressions from the witness's direct testimony. Cross-examination need not be "cross"! As we will see, however, the most interesting evidentiary problems arise in the course of cross-examinations designed to cast doubt on or "impeach" the witness's credibility, that is to give rise to factually based arguments that the witness's direct testimony, or some part of it, should not be believed.

Problem: The B & G Bar and Grill

Malpractice damage action against surgeon *D* for the alleged negligent performance of a tonsillectomy on *P* on June 1, 1996, at 2 P.M. The specific negligent act alleged is operating while intoxicated. At trial, *P* offers *W*, a waitress at the B & G Bar and Grill, to testify that on June 1 at 1 P.M. *D* entered the bar, occupied the booth, and consumed several drinks. The cross-examination is as follows:

Q: What were the drinks that the defendant ordered?
A: Bloody Marys.
Q: How many drinks did he order?
A: A lot of drinks.
Q: What do you mean by "A lot of drinks"?
A: More than two.
Q: More than five?
A: Maybe—about that many.
Q: Did you see the drinks mixed?

A: No.
Q: Was the defendant alone?
A: No. There were people with him.
Q: How many?
A: Several—three or four.
Q: Men or women?
A: Men and women.
Q: How many men and how many women?
A: I don't know. There were some of each.
Q: Did defendant eat anything when he was there?
A: I don't know.
Q: How many customers were in the B & G while defendant was there?
A: Oh, it's a big place and very busy at that hour.
Q: How many?
A: Probably 50 or so.
Q: How many waitresses were there?
A: Well, there were just two of us on then, I think.
Q: Did you also take money and serve as a cashier?
A: Yes, except Harry at the bar took money there for drinks.
Q: So during the time defendant was in the bar you would be taking money and making change?
A: Yes.
Q: Who paid the tab for the drinks at defendant's table?
A: I can't remember.
Q: Have you ever had a disagreement with defendant over the service or anything else in the B & G?
A: Well, once he claimed to have given me a $20 bill when he had given me only a $10 bill, and we had some words over it.

What is the purpose of this cross-examination? What qualities of the witness are tested? What capacities and skills of the witness are impugned?

Consider the following from Kinsey v. State, 65 P.2d 1141 (Ariz. 1937):

> What is the purpose of cross-examination? Obviously it is to convince the triers of fact, in some manner, that the testimony of the witness is untrue, for if the cross-examiner accepts it as true, there will be no need nor desire for cross-examination. How, then, may the truthfulness of the evidence of a witness be attacked through cross-examination? It seems to us that all attacks thereon must be reduced to one of three classes: (a) Upon the honesty and integrity of the witness; (b) upon his ability to observe accurately at the time the incident occurred; and (c) upon his accuracy of recollection of the past events.

If one of the purposes of cross-examination is to destroy the credibility of the witness, what are the limits of acceptable attack?

BERGER v. UNITED STATES
295 U.S. 78 (1935)

Charge: conspiracy to utter counterfeit notes.

SUTHERLAND, J. . . . That the United States prosecuting attorney over-stepped the bounds of that propriety and fairness which should characterize the conduct of such an officer in the prosecution of a criminal offense is clearly shown by the record. He was guilty of misstating the facts in his cross-examination of witnesses; of putting into the mouths of such witnesses things which they had not said; of suggesting by his questions that statements had been made to him personally out of court, in respect of which no proof was offered; of pretending to understand that a witness had said something which he had not said and persistently cross-examining the witness upon that basis; of assuming prejudicial facts not in evidence; of bullying and arguing with witnesses; and in general, of conducting himself in a thoroughly indecorous and improper manner. We produce in the margin[1] a few excerpts from the

---

1. [The defendant (petitioner) was on the stand; cross-examination by the United States attorney]:

Q: The man who didn't have his pants on and was running around the apartment, he wasn't there?

A: No, Mr. Singer. Mr. Godby told me about this, he told me, as long as you ask me about it, if you want it, I will tell you, he told me "If you give this man's name out, I will give you the works."

Q: Give me the works?

A: No, Mr. Godby told me that.

Q: You are going to give me the works?

A: Mr. Singer, you are a gentleman. I have got nothing against you. You are doing your duty.

Mr. Wegman: You are not going to give Mr. Singer the works. Apparently Mr. Singer misunderstood you. Who made that statement?

The Witness: Mr. Godby says that.

Q: Wait a minute. Are you going to give me the works?

A: Mr. Singer, you are absolutely a gentleman, in my opinion, you are doing your duty here.

Q: Thank you very much. But I am only asking you are you going to give me the works?

A: I do not give anybody such things, I never said it.

Q: All right. Then do not make the statement.

Mr. Wegman: The witness said that Mr. Godby said that.

The Court: The jury heard what was said. It is not for you or me to interpret the testimony.

Q: I asked you whether the man who was running around this apartment . . . , was he there in the Secret Service office on the morning that you were arrested?

A: I didn't see him.

Q: I wasn't in that apartment, was I?

A: No, Mr. Singer.

Q: I didn't pull the gun on you and stick you up against the wall?

A: No.

Q: I wasn't up in this apartment at any time, as far as you know, was I?

A: As far as I know, you weren't.

Q: You might have an idea that I may have been there?

A: No, I should say not.

Q: I just want to get that part of it straight. . . .

Q: Was I in that apartment that night?

A: No, but Mr. Godby—

record illustrating some of the various points of the foregoing summary. It is impossible, however, without reading the testimony at some length, and thereby obtaining a knowledge of the setting in which the objectionable matter occurred, to appreciate fully the extent of the misconduct. The trial judge, it is true, sustained objections to some of the questions, insinuations and misstatements, and instructed the jury to

---

Q: Was Mr. Godby in that apartment?

A: No, but he has been there. . . .

Q: Do you include as those who may have been there the Court and all the jurymen and your own counsel?

A: Mr. Singer, you asked me a question. May I answer it?

Mr. Wegman: I object to the question.

The Witness: Are you serious about that?

The Court: I am not going to stop him because the question includes the Court. I will let him answer it.

Mr. Singer: I would like to have an answer to it.

The Witness: Mr. Singer, you asked me the question before—

The Court: You answer this question.

(Question repeated by the reporter.)

A: I should say not; that is ridiculous. . . .

Q: Now Mr. Berger, do you remember yesterday when the court recessed for a few minutes and you saw me out in the hall; do you remember that?

A: I do, Mr. Singer.

Q: You talked to me out in the hall?

A: I talked to you?

Q: Yes.

A: No.

Q: You say you didn't say to me out in the hall yesterday, "You wait until I take the stand and I will take care of you"? You didn't say that yesterday?

A: No; I didn't. Mr. Singer, you are lying.

Q: I am lying, you are right. You didn't say that at all?

A: No.

Q: You didn't speak to me out in the hall?

A: I never did speak to you outside since this case started, except the day I was in your office, when you questioned me.

Q: I said yesterday.

A: No, Mr. Singer.

Q: Do you mean that seriously?

A: I said no.

Q: That never happened?

A: No, Mr. Singer, it did not.

Q: You did not say that to me?

A: I did not.

Q: Of course, I have just made that up?

A: What do you want me to answer you?

Q: I want you to tell me I am lying, is that so? . . .

[No effort was later made to prove that any such statement had ever been made.]

Q: Did she say she was going to meet me for anything except business purposes?

A: No.

Q: If she was to meet me?

A: Just told me that you gave her your home telephone number and told her to call you up after nine o'clock in the evening if she found out anything about the case that you could help me with, that is what she told me.

Q: Even if that is so, what is wrong about that, that you have been squawking about all morning?

disregard them. But the situation was one which called for stern rebuke and repressive measures and, perhaps, if these were not successful, for the granting of a mistrial. It is impossible to say that the evil influence upon the jury of these acts of misconduct was removed by such mild judicial action as was taken.

A witness by the name of Goldie Goldstein had been called by the prosecution to identify the petitioner. She apparently had difficulty in doing so. The prosecuting attorney, in the course of his argument, said (italics added):

"Mrs. Goldie Goldstein takes the stand. She says she knows Jones, *and you can bet your bottom dollar she knew Berger.* She stood right where I am now and looked at him and was afraid to go over there, and when I waved my arm everybody started to holler, 'Don't point at him.' You know the rules of law. Well, it is the most complicated game in the world. I was examining *a woman that I knew knew Berger and could identify him,* she was standing right here looking at him, and I couldn't say, 'Isn't that the man?' Now, imagine that! But that is the rules of the game, and I have to play within those rules."

The jury was thus invited to conclude that the witness Goldstein knew Berger well but pretended otherwise; and that this was within the personal knowledge of the prosecuting attorney.

Again, at another point in his argument, after suggesting that defendants' counsel had the advantage of being able to charge the district attorney with being unfair, "of trying to twist a witness," he said:

"But, oh, they can twist the questions, . . . *they can sit up in their offices and devise ways to pass counterfeit money;* 'but don't let the Government touch me, that is unfair; please leave my client alone.'"

In what ways did the prosecuting attorney overstep the bounds of acceptable cross-examination? Would the same behavior by defense counsel be improper? When a lawyer is out to destroy the credibility of an opponent's witness who, let us assume, the lawyer believes is either lying or mistaken, how do you draw the line between permissible and impermissible attack

Problem: Cross-Examination — Charles Atlas

Charge: mayhem. Defendant: *D*—5'3", 90 pounds. Victim: Ali— 6'4", 230 pounds. At *D*'s trial, the first witness for the prosecution is the arresting officer, *O*. On cross-examination, defense counsel elicits facts concerning *D*'s size and weight and then asks, "Isn't it a fact that the evidence shows beyond a reasonable doubt that the defendant is too small to beat up the victim?"

The prosecution objects. What ruling and why?

Problem: Cross-Examination — When Did You Stop Beating . . . ?

Charge: murder. Defendant: *D*. Victim: Mr. *D*. M.O.: shotgun wound
to the body. Eyewitnesses: none. Defense: alibi. At trial the prosecution
makes out a prima facie case and rests. *D* takes the stand and on direct
questioning maintains her complete innocence. On cross-examination
the following questions are asked by the district attorney:

Q: What had your husband done to cause you to kill him? . . .
Q: Did you have any reason for taking that man's life that you said you
     loved? . . .
Q: Can you give the jury any reason why you shot your husband and
     killed him? . . .
Q: Did he threaten you? . . .
Q: Did he draw a gun? Just answer yes or no. . . .

Defense counsel objects to these questions. What ruling and why?

Problem: Opium

Charge: violation of Section 54 of the state penal code, which makes
it a crime for any person to manufacture, possess, control, sell, prescribe, administer, or dispense any narcotic drug except as provided
therein. The indictment alleges that on June 1 *D* did unlawfully manufacture, possess, and control a narcotic drug — to wit, opium. At trial,
the D.A. makes his opening statement, in which he says that the prosecution will prove that *D* purchased paregoric and then proceeded to
reduce it to opium. The first witness for the prosecution is *J.J.* His direct
examination is as follows:

Q: What is your name?
A: J.J.
Q: Where do you live?
A: 734 Boylston Street, Boston.
Q: Are you employed?
A: On June 1, 1980, *D* bought paregoric and reduced it to opium.
By defense counsel: Object and move to strike.

What ruling and why?

Problem: Hostile Witness

Personal injury action arising out of a collision between a truck
owned by *D* Company and operated by *D*'s employee, *S*, and the car in

which *P* was riding. At trial, *P*'s first witness is *S*. On direct examination, *S* is asked if he was in the employ of *D* and engaged in *D*'s employ at the time of the accident. Upon establishing *S*'s agency, *P* has no further questions for *S*. *D* asks S questions designed to elicit the following:

(1) That at the time the accident occurred *S* was detouring from his normal route in order to check in with his bookie;

(2) That *S* came to a full stop and waited for a green light before entering the intersection in which the accident occurred; and

(3) That *P* ran a red light and hit *S*.

On *P*'s objection, what ruling and why?

Problem: Death at the Awahnee

Civil action by *P* against *D* Insurance Company on an insurance policy issued by *D* on the life of *V*, naming *P* as the beneficiary. The policy covers only accidental death, expressly excluding death by suicide. At trial, *P*'s first witness is *C*, the caretaker of the Awahnee Hunting Lodge. *C* testifies that on December 31, 1999, she found *V*'s body near the lodge; *V*'s body was clad in hunting clothes and was warm and supple. Next to the body *C* found a double-barrel shotgun with one barrel discharged; there was a gaping wound in *V*'s chest. *C* is then excused by *P*.

At this point what alternative procedures could be followed by *D* to elicit further testimony from *C* that on December 25, she had Christmas dinner with *V* at the lodge, that *C* and *V* had many strong drinks, that *V* drank a lot but ate nothing, that *V* said he had advanced cancer and remarked, "As the century ends, so will I"?

Problem: The Powder-Puff Killer

On June 1 at 6 P.M. Mrs. *D*, wife of Dr. *D*, awakens from her nap and begins to dress and apply cosmetics for the opera. She opens her compact and takes out her powder-puff. Suddenly a spider emerges, springs on Mrs. *D*, bites her, and absconds. That night Mrs. *D* is in bed in pain and is feverish. Dr. *D* gives her a hypodermic injection. The injection may be Demerol or it may be air bubbles. Shortly after the injection Mrs. *D* dies. Dr. *D* is charged with premeditated murder by spider bite and air bubbles.

(1) At Dr. *D*'s trial the prosecution calls Dr. *T*, a toxicologist, as its first witness. On direct examination Dr. *T* states that upon testing the cadaver of Mrs. *D* for venom, he found spider venom. On cross-examination the following occurs:

Q: How much venom did you find?
A: About one-half cc.
Q: What kind?
A: Black widow.
Q: You also found traces of Demerol, didn't you?
By the D.A.: Objection.

What is the basis of the district attorney's objection? What ruling should the court make? Why?

(2) Suppose that after Dr. *T* is excused the prosecution calls *M*, Mrs. *D*'s mother. *M* testifies that she saw *D* open his wife's compact and put a spider into it. On cross-examination *M* is asked if she has made a will that disinherits Dr. *D*. The D.A. objects.

What ruling and why? What general rules concerning the scope of cross-examination may be derived from this example?

Problem: Showdown at the W-Q Ranch

Ejectment action by *P* against *D*. *P*'s complaint avers that he owns the W-Q Ranch and that *D* is wrongfully in possession. *P* prays for judgment giving possession of the W-Q Ranch to *P*. The former owner of the W-Q Ranch was Mr. Quarrels. Mr. Quarrels died New Year's Day, 2000. *P* is Mr. Quarrels's nephew; *D* is Mr. Quarrels's son. *D* claims as Mr. Quarrels's heir; *P* claims as Mr. Quarrels's grantee and claims that a document he possesses (Plaintiff's Exhibit *A*) is a deed whereby Mr. Quarrels granted the W-Q Ranch to *P* in fee simple absolute. Exhibit *A* is dated December 23, 1999. *D* has examined Exhibit *A* and claims that Mr. Quarrels's signature is spurious and that even if it is real the document was never delivered to take effect as a deed. At trial, *P* is the first witness. He testifies that on December 24, 1999, he received Exhibit *A* through the mail, was overjoyed, and said to himself, "Hooray for Uncle Q!" Plaintiff's second witness is Mr. *M*, the late Mr. Quarrels's secretary and manager of the W-Q Ranch. On direct examination, *M* testifies that on December 23 in Mr. Quarrels's study at the W-Q Ranch he saw Mr. Quarrels sign Exhibit *A*. On cross-examination, Mr. *M* is asked the following question:

Q: Isn't it true that on January 1, 2000, at the W-Q Ranch, you saw Exhibit *A* among the papers on Mr. Quarrels's desk?

(1) On *P*'s objection what ruling and why? What problem regarding the scope of cross-examination is presented by this example that has not been presented by the previous problems? If there should be a rule of restrictive cross-examination, how should it be applied when multiple

witnesses have testified and the question asked on cross-examination of a later witness (*W2*) is within the scope of questions asked on direct examination of a former witness (*W1*) but not within the scope of the direct examination of the witness on the stand (*W2*)?

(2) Suppose *P*'s objection is sustained. *M* then turns to the judge and says that he is most anxious to complete his testimony in the case and leave for Australia, where he has an impending business engagement. *D* proposes that he make *M* his witness and examine *M* then and there on the question of delivery of the deed. *P* objects. What should the court do? If the court accepts defendant's suggestion, how will the procedure differ from allowing *D* to put his questions regarding delivery of the deed to *M* on cross-examination? What types of questions will be permitted, or precluded, by following the procedure suggested by *D*?

D. Impeachment by Character Evidence

As discussed in the introduction to Chapter III, Rules 404, 405, and 406 deal with the use of character evidence to prove what happened on the occasion of the litigated event. Rules 608 and 609 deal with character evidence to show whether the witness is being untruthful at the time of trial. Rules 608 and 609 come into play only if and when the witness has testified.

1. Character and Credibility

Although Rules 608 and 609 deal with "is he lying" and not with "what happened," it is crucially important to understanding their operation to recognize that the inferential logic involved is propensity logic, just as was true with Rules 404, 405, and 406. Evidence is offered to show that the witness has the character of a liar, thereby to show that it is more likely that he is lying on this specific occasion—his testimony at trial.

This line of logic should be distinguished from evidence that contradicts the witness's story. For example, the defendant says he did not commit the crime for which he is charged. Other evidence shows that he did commit the crime. This evidence, if believed, shows that the defendant is a liar. Nonetheless, its initial relevance is to what happened, not to the defendant's credibility. Only after the factfinder has concluded what happened is it possible to draw a conclusion about the defendant's credibility, and it is a superfluous conclusion from which nothing follows.

In contrast, Rules 608 and 609 deal with evidence that bears on the witness's character as a truth-teller, from which an inference can follow as to whether the witness's testimony was true, from which an inference may be drawn about what happened.

Compare the chain of inferences in the two situations.

When a witness testifies, he is said to "put his credibility in issue." "Credibility" is a broad term that can be broken down into various component parts and subparts. When a witness testifies, he exposes his testimonial capacities. These are classically described as

1.   his perception,
2.   his memory,
3.   his ability to communicate clearly, and
4.   his sincerity.

If the witness perceived accurately, remembered well, communicated clearly, and testified honestly, then the factfinder can credit his testimony about what happened.

The constraints of Rule 608 and 609 apply *only* to evidence the relevance of which is to show the witness's *general* character for truthfulness or untruthfulness.

For example, the testimonial capacity of "sincerity" has both general and specific aspects. Used generally, "sincerity" refers to a person's regular disposition to be honest or not. But other aspects of sincerity may emerge in specific contexts. The witness may be *biased* in favor of one party or *prejudiced* against a party, or personally *interested* in the outcome or in some aspect of the litigation. These are influences that may affect the sincerity of the witness in the immediate litigation. He may, in other words, be a truth-teller in general yet have some particular reason to lie in the immediate case.

Or he may be a liar in general and thus likely to lie in this and any other case. This last is the aspect of credibility that involves reasoning from the witness's *general* character for truthfulness. This is the aspect of sincerity with which Rules 608 and 609 are concerned, just as Rule 404(a) is concerned with the defendant's *general* propensity for the trait in question.

All of the other aspects of sincerity that relate to a specific reason to lie in the immediate case—bias, prejudice, and interest—are wide open on cross-examination of a witness and may be proved by extrinsic proof, subject only to a Rule 403 balance, as with the "other purposes" referred to in Rule 404(b).

The same distinction between general propensity on the one hand and reasons specific to the immediate case on the other holds as well for the testimonial capacities other than sincerity. A witness may have a general propensity to misperceive. Rule 608 constrains efforts by counsel to show such general propensities. However, if there is some reason specific to the immediate case why the witness might have misperceived, Rule 608 imposes no restraint whatever in exploring it or in offering extrinsic proof to establish it. Thus, Rule 608 would constrain counsel's efforts to show that the witness has identified the wrong man in an earlier otherwise unrelated incident. (Counsel might, subject to the judge's discretion, be permitted to cross-examine about it, but could not put on extrinsic proof.) By contrast, counsel would not be constrained in any way by Rule 608 in proving that the witness normally wore eyeglasses but was not wearing them on the occasion of the litigated event.

For an interesting review of the character and credibility thicket, see Wydick, Character Evidence: A Guided Tour of the Grotesque Structure, 21 U.C. Davis L. Rev. 123 (1987). See also Davis, Evidence of Character to Prove Conduct: A Reassessment of Relevancy, 27 Crim. L. Bull. 504 (1991); Friedman, Character Impeachment Evidence: Psycho-Bayesian Analysis and a Proposed Overhaul, 38 U.C.L.A. L. Rev. 637 (1991).

Problem: The Worrisome Witness

D is accused of murdering *V* on June 1 between the hours of 9 and 11 P.M. at *V*'s home. The alleged motive is revenge for *V*'s ending their long-time business relationship. At trial *V*'s maid, Emma, gives scream-scram testimony for the prosecution: She heard *V* scream, she saw *D* scram. The defense is an alibi. The principal defense witness is *W*, who testifies that from 9 to 11 P.M. on June 1 she and *D* were at the office working together. In rebuttal the prosecution offers to prove through *C*, a cashier at Martin's Liquor Store, that on May 1 he saw *W* steal a case of Remy Martin by pretending it had been paid for when in fact it had not. *D* objects. What ruling and why?

Suppose that the prosecution offers to prove on cross-examination *W*'s conviction for grand larceny for a theft of a case of Remy Martin from Martin's and *D* objects. What ruling and why? What reasons are there to treat the two situations differently? If the prosecution introduces evidence of *W*'s prior conviction, should the defense in surre-buttal be allowed to elicit from *W* testimony that she was convicted but was framed and is really innocent?

Problem: Fracas at Fenway Park

Action for damages arising out of *D*'s alleged assault and battery on *P* on June 1 in the bleachers at Fenway Park. The complaint alleges that *D* struck *P* over the head with a Budweiser bottle while *P* was giving the

Yankee pitcher a standing ovation for striking out the heart of the Red
Sox batting order. The defense: self-defense.

(1) At trial, *P* offers the testimony of *A* that he was at the game with
P and that he saw *D* strike *P* over the head with a Budweiser bottle
without any provocation. *P* then offers the testimony of *B* that although
he was not at the game with *P* and *A*, he lives on the same street in the
Bronx as *A* and knows *A*'s reputation in the community for peace and
quietude to be good. *D* objects. What result and why?

(2) Suppose that *B*'s testimony is that he is familiar with *A*'s reputation in the community for truthfulness and veracity and that it is good.
D objects. What ruling and why?

(3) On cross-examination of *A*, defense counsel asks *A* whether he
has ever been convicted of possession of marijuana. *P* objects. What
ruling and why?

(4) On cross-examination of *A*, defense counsel asks *A* if he was convicted of perjury twelve years before. *P* objects. What ruling and why?

(5) Suppose that the objection to *B*'s testimony, set forth in (2),
above, was overruled. On cross-examination of *B*, defense counsel asks
B if he knows that *A* was convicted of perjury twelve years before. *P*
objects. What ruling and why? What if *B* is asked on cross-examination
whether he is aware that *A* was convicted of possession of marijuana?

(6) In rebuttal, *D* offers the testimony of *C* that eleven years ago *A*
filed a false 10K statement with the SEC. *P* objects. What ruling and why?

(7) Suppose that after *A* has been asked on cross-examination by
defense counsel whether he was previously convicted for perjury, or
after *C* testified to the false 10K statement, or after rebuttal reputation
testimony that *A*'s reputation in the community for truthfulness is bad,
B is recalled to the stand to testify to *A*'s reputation for truthfulness. *D*
objects. What ruling and why?

(8) Suppose that on cross-examination of *A*, *A* admits that he is *P*'s
brother. *P* then calls *B* to testify that *A*'s reputation for truthfulness and
veracity is good. *D* objects. What ruling and why?

(9) Suppose that as part of *A*'s direct examination, *A* testifies that in
the third inning he saw *D* drink three large beers. In rebuttal, *D* testifies
that in the third inning he had two cokes, three hot dogs, a box of
popcorn, two bags of peanuts, two pieces of pizza, and an ice cream,
but no beer. In surrebuttal, may *B* testify to *A*'s reputation for truthfulness and veracity?

2.   The Use of Prior Convictions

Rule 609 attempted to codify various common law rules permitting
a witness's credibility to be impeached by proof that the witness had

been convicted of a crime. As originally drafted, Rule 609 was the result of an elaborate political debate and compromise in the courts, the House, the Senate, and the Conference Committee. It is also an example of the evidence rules taking their own ostensible logic too seriously. Rule 609 held that the only reason for introducing prior convictions is for their probative value on the question of whether the defendant (who has taken the stand) is a liar. This logic played itself out in a categorization of crimes that supposedly reflect on the criminal's honesty as opposed to crimes that show his other qualities but do not relate to honesty.

Impeachment by prior crimes could alternatively be viewed as a practical counterbalance to the Fifth Amendment, allowing the prosecution minimal latitude in telling the factfinder about the background of a defendant who chooses to step out from behind the shield of the Fifth Amendment to assert his innocence. The defendant with a criminal record is thereby prevented from presenting himself to the jury as naively innocent. Many courts harbor this view of Rule 609.

The logic of this approach would forswear the idea that the sole function of introducing prior convictions is to prove by the nature of the prior crime that the defendant has a dishonest character. The harsh truth is that all defendants have an extremely powerful incentive to tell a story consistent with their innocence. Instead, the function of impeachment by prior crimes could be conceived more broadly: to give the factfinder some background about the defendant to provide a framework in which to judge the plausibility of the defendant's story of innocence.

The drafters compromised by throwing admissibility of prior crimes evidence into the lap of the trial judge who was to do one weighing under 609(a) for most crimes and a second weighing under 609(b) for vintage crimes. As a result, the debate continued in the courts with the rule serving, at best, as a guideline.

Because of continued criticism and debate over the scope and application of Rule 609, the Advisory Committee on the Federal Rules considered many requests for amendments to the rule. In 1990, several amendments were adopted, but many of the issues that troubled courts and practitioners were not resolved.

The 1990 amendment to Rule 609 did three major things. First, it deleted from the original rule the limitation that impeaching convictions may only be elicited during cross-examination. This amendment merely ratified the common practice of the witness's revealing on direct examination his convictions to "take the sting out" of the impeachment. Most courts of appeal had permitted this tactic under the old rule.

Second, the amendment removed an ambiguity in the rule concerning impeachment of witnesses other than a criminal accused, such as the plaintiff in a civil lawsuit. While the 1990 amendments were under submission to Congress, the Supreme Court held in *Green v. Rock Laundry Machine Co.*, 490 U.S. 504 (1989), that not only did Rule 609 permit a civil litigant to impeach an adversary's credibility with evidence of the adversary's prior felony convictions, but that the rules did *not* permit the trial court to exercise any discretion under Rule 403 to exclude the impeaching conviction evidence on grounds of prejudice. The majority opinion in *Green* reviewed the tortured legislative history of Rule 609 in detail and concluded that the admission of prior felony convictions (burglary) was mandatory in Green's product liability lawsuit for damages received when a machine he was operating at his car wash job tore off his right arm. The 1990 amendment confirms that witnesses in civil cases, as well as witnesses other than the accused in criminal cases, may be impeached by prior convictions, but it explicitly provides for a Rule 403 balancing of probativeness and prejudice (except for convictions involving dishonesty or false statement, which under Rule 609(a)(2) continue to be mandatorily admissible without any balancing in all cases).

Third, the rule retained the special balancing test for the criminal defendant who chooses to testify — in this case, the court must determine that the probative value of admitting the impeachment evidence outweighs its prejudicial effect to the accused (again, excepting convictions involving dishonesty or false statement) — but removed any ambiguity that this special balancing test was available to other defense witnesses.

Unfortunately, the 1990 amendment did not clarify the meaning of crimes involving "dishonesty or false statement," which must be admitted under 609(a)(2) even if their prejudicial effect outweighs their probative value. The Advisory Committee noted that "some cases raise a concern about the proper interpretation of the words 'dishonesty or false statement,'" but decided that the final Conference Report on the original rule "provides sufficient guidance to trial courts and that no amendment is necessary, notwithstanding some decisions that take an unduly broad view of 'dishonesty,' admitting convictions as for bank robbery or bank larceny." Thus, the amendments left this element of the debate over the logic of Rule 609 to the courts.

Finally, the drafters of the amendment also declined to add any language to the rule stating that when a prior conviction is offered under Rule 609, the probative value of the prior conviction is to be considered for *impeachment* only. The Advisory Committee concluded that this limitation was perfectly clear because of the title of the rule, its first sentence, and its placement among the impeachment rules.

It is interesting to count the different weighings that courts must keep straight when prior crimes impeachment evidence is offered. From the "most stringent" weighing to the least stringent weighing (i.e., no weighing permitted), they are:

juvenile adjudications (609(d))	generally not admissible, but if necessary for a fair determination of the issue of guilt, juvenile adjudications of witness other than the accused may be allowed if admissible against an adult
old convictions (609(b))	court must determine in the interest of justice that the probative value of the conviction supported by specific facts and circumstances substantially outweighs its prejudicial effect
accused's felony convictions (609(a)(1))	court must determine that the probative value of admitting evidence outweighs prejudice to the accused
witness other than accused (609(a)(1))	Rule 403 balance—admitted unless prejudice substantially outweighs probativeness
dishonesty or false statement (609(a)(2))	shall be admitted without weighing

Compare the language of Rule 609(a)(1) ("the probative value . . . outweighs its prejudicial effect to the accused") with the language of Rule 403 ("excluded if its probative value is substantially outweighed by the danger of unfair prejudice"). Assuming this different phraseology was purposeful, when a defendant witness is faced with a prior felony conviction not involving dishonesty or false statement, the presumption is in favor of exclusion. For the evidence to be admitted, the scale must just be tipped in favor of probativeness. If the conviction is older than ten years, there is a strong presumptive bar, and the scale must be tipped substantially in favor of probativeness before it is admitted. Finally, under the basic relevance rule (Rule 403), the information is allowed unless the scale is substantially in favor of prejudice; but once a conviction passes Rule 609(b)'s hurdle, this weighing is superfluous.

These differences can be visualized as loci on a continuum with a fulcrum that attempts to balance the desire for information with fairness. At the threshold relevance level, as much information as possible should be allowed to assist truth-finding; thus, there is a presumption in favor of admitting information (Rule 403). With felony/nondishonesty crimes of the accused, the desire for the information is still strong but the possibility of unfairness increases so the evidence will be admitted only if there is a showing that probativeness outweighs prejudice (Rule 609(a)(1)). When the information is that of a stale conviction, the desire for the information is lessened because of its weaker probative value and there is still a high potential for prejudice (though perhaps less so than with more recent convictions); thus, there is a strong presumption against admitting the evidence (Rule 609(b)).

Keeping these various standards straight is complicated enough, but the problem is compounded by the lack of any guidance in the rules about what factors courts should weigh in the exercise of discretion under any of these standards. Are the same factors applicable for each standard? What are the factors that go into the exercise of discretion under each standard?

Problem: Robbery of the Mom & Pop Spa

Charge: robbery on June 1, 1997, of the Mom & Pop Spa. M.O.: pointing a gun at Pop and absconding with the contents of the cash register. At trial on June 1, 1998, the state calls C, the Clerk of the Superior Court, to testify and authenticate as an exhibit certified records of D's prior convictions as follows:

(1)   Armed robbery, June 1, 1996;
(2)   Petty larceny, May 1, 1996;
(3)   Fraud, June 1, 1995;
(4)   Perjury, June 1, 1984; and
(5)   Perjury, June 1, 1968.

Which, if any, of these prior convictions are admissible?

The following cases illustrate efforts to apply Rule 609 in various situations. As you think about these cases ask yourself whether it is indeed possible to make a meaningful generalization in any rule about the probative value of prior criminal convictions on the likely truthfulness or untruthfulness of a witness.

UNITED STATES v. ALEXANDER
48 F.3d 1477 (9th Cir. 1995)

THOMPSON, Circuit Judge:

These are the consolidated appeals of defendants Gary Edward Alexander, Jonathan Harrington, Anthony F. Hicks and Willie James Harris. The defendants appeal their convictions for conspiracy to commit robbery, . . . armed bank robbery, . . . and use of a firearm during commission of a crime of violence. . . .

[D]efendant Hicks seeks reversal of his conviction on the ground that the district court erroneously admitted, for impeachment purposes, evidence of his prior drug and robbery convictions. . . . We affirm all convictions and all sentences.

FACTS

On January 24, 1992, four armed men — all wearing blue coveralls, gloves, and ski masks—burst into the First Interstate Bank in Victorville, California. They ordered everyone present in the bank to lie down, forced two of the bank's employees to open the vault, and emptied cash from the vault into a duffle bag. After taking the money, the robbers fled in a van. The total amount stolen was $331,951.

The police had been alerted to the robbery by a passerby. As a result, officers arrived at the scene in time to pursue the van as it left the bank. A high-speed chase ensued in which the occupants of the van fired several shots at the police.

Eventually, the van pulled into a K-Mart parking lot. The four robbers got out of the van and split up. Two of them got into a Camaro and the other two got into a Camry. The vehicles sped away in different directions, with the police in pursuit. The chase continued at speeds up to 110 miles per hour, with more shots being fired at the police from the fleeing vehicles.

Eventually, the Camaro stalled; defendants Harrington and Alexander were arrested inside the car. The Camry also came to a stop, but its occupants continued their flight on foot. After a brief chase, police arrested defendants Harris and Hicks a short distance from the abandoned Camry.

Remaining pertinent facts are discussed in relevant portions of the discussion that follows.

DISCUSSION

. . .

III.   ADMISSION OF PRIOR CONVICTIONS FOR IMPEACHMENT PURPOSES

Before trial, defendant Hicks filed a motion in limine to exclude evidence of his prior felony convictions for residential robbery and possession of rock cocaine for sale. The district court denied the motion, ruling that, if Hicks elected to testify, the evidence would be admissible for impeachment purposes, under Federal Rule of Evidence 609(a)(1), because its probative value outweighed its prejudicial effect.

At trial, Hicks chose to take the stand and present an alibi defense. He testified that he was in the vicinity of the arrests on the day of the robbery because he was scheduled to meet a friend there. He also said he ran away when he heard sirens and saw police cars because he was afraid of being arrested on two outstanding warrants for traffic violations. Purportedly for the same reason, he also gave the arresting officer a false name.

At the conclusion of his direct examination, Hicks again moved to exclude the evidence of his prior convictions. The district court adhered to its original ruling and denied the motion. On cross examination, the prosecution elicited testimony from Hicks regarding the nature and dates of both prior convictions.

Hicks contends the district court erred in allowing the jury to hear evidence of his prior convictions. With regard to his prior robbery conviction, he argues United States v. Brackeen, 969 F.2d 827, 830 (9th Cir. 1992) (en banc) (per curiam), stands for the proposition that a prior robbery conviction cannot be used to attack a defendant's credibility. We disagree. Federal Rule of Evidence 609(a) provides, in pertinent part, that evidence of prior convictions is admissible for purposes of attacking the credibility of a witness if the crime "(1) was [a felony], and the court determines the probative value of admitting this evidence outweighs its prejudicial effect to the defendant, or (2) involved dishonesty or false statement. . . ." Brackeen held only that, in this circuit, bank robbery is not per se a crime of dishonesty, and therefore prior robbery convictions are not admissible for impeachment purposes under Rule 609(a)(2). We did not foreclose in Brackeen the admission of a prior robbery conviction under the balancing test of Rule 609(a)(1).

Here, the government explicitly stated it intended to introduce both of Hick's prior convictions under Rule 609(a)(1), and the district court specifically ruled on that basis by applying the appropriate balancing test. If the district court did not abuse its discretion when it concluded Hicks's prior convictions were more probative of his credibility than prejudicial to his defense, the evidence of both of his prior convictions was properly admitted. United States v. Browne, 829 F.2d 760, 762 (9th Cir. 1987), cert. denied, 485 U.S. 991, 108 S. Ct. 1298, 99 L. Ed. 2d 508 (1988) (noting that a district court's decision to admit evidence of prior convictions is reviewed for an abuse of discretion).

In United States v. Cook, 608 F.2d 1175, 1185 n.8 (9th Cir. 1979) (en banc), cert. denied, 444 U.S. 1034, 100 S. Ct. 706, 62 L. Ed. 2d 670 (1980), overruled on other grounds, Luce v. United States, 469 U.S. 38, 105 S. Ct. 460, 83 L. Ed. 2d 443 (1984), we outlined five factors that should be considered in balancing the probative value of a prior con-

viction against its prejudicial impact for purposes of Rule 609(a)(1):
(1) the impeachment value of the prior crime; (2) the point in time of
conviction and the defendant's subsequent history; (3) the similarity
between the past crime and the charged crime; (4) the importance of
the defendant's testimony; and (5) the centrality of the defendant's
credibility. The government bears the burden of showing, based on
these factors, that the proffered evidence's probative value substantially
outweighs its prejudicial effect.

Hicks does not dispute that the first factor favors admission of both
his prior convictions. We have previously stated that "prior convictions
for robbery are probative of veracity." The same is true of prior convictions for drug offenses.

Hicks stipulates that both his prior crimes were sufficiently recent to
satisfy the second *Cook* factor. He was convicted of residential robbery,
and was sentenced to a four-year prison term, in 1987. Shortly after his
parole in 1988, he committed the drug offense, for which he received
another four-year prison sentence. Less than a year later, he was arrested
for the present crime. "By its terms, Rule 609 allows for admissibility of
such . . . prior conviction[s] even where the defendant has been released for up to ten years." *Browne*, 829 F.2d at 763. See Fed. R. Evid.
609(b).

Hicks concedes that, as to his prior drug offense, the third factor is
satisfied because the drug offense is sufficiently different from the present bank robbery. With regard to the prior residential robbery, the district court held that offense was similar to the charged bank robbery
and, therefore, the third factor weighed in favor of excluding it. However, we have held that even "a prior 'bank robbery conviction [is] not
inadmissable per se, merely because the offense involved was identical
to that for which [the defendant] was on trial.'" What matters is the
balance of all five factors.

Hicks contends that, contrary to the district court's determination,
the related fourth and fifth factors weigh against admission of his prior
convictions. He contends his trial testimony was not particularly important and his credibility was not central to the case, because other evidence corroborated his alibi defense. We disagree. When a defendant
takes the stand and denies having committed the charged offense, he
places his credibility directly at issue.

In United States v. Bagley, 772 F.2d 482, 488 (9th Cir. 1985), cert.
denied, 475 U.S. 1023, 106 S. Ct. 1215, 89 L. Ed. 2d 326 (1986), we held
that admission of the defendant's prior robbery convictions was an
abuse of the district court's discretion. But in that case we emphasized
"the record [was] devoid of any evidence that [the defendant] intended
to misrepresent his character or to testify falsely as to his prior criminal
record." Id. Here, Hicks testified he ran from the police because he was
afraid of being arrested on outstanding warrants for traffic violations.
This testimony could reasonably have misled the jury into believing that,

with the exception of some minor traffic infractions, Hicks had no previous trouble with the police. As we said in Cook:

> [I]t is not surprising that the [district] court was unwilling to let a man with a substantial criminal history misrepresent himself to the jury, with the government forced to sit silently by, looking at a criminal record which, if made known, would give the jury a more comprehensive view of the trustworthiness of the defendant as a witness.

Cook, 608 F.2d at 1187.

We conclude that the district court properly balanced all five Cook factors and did not abuse its discretion in permitting the government to impeach Hicks with evidence of his prior drug and residential robbery convictions. . . .

For the foregoing reasons, the convictions and sentences of all defendants are affirmed.

UNITED STATES v. ESTES
994 F.2d 147 (5th Cir. 1993)

Before HIGGINBOTHAM, SMITH, and DeMoss, Circuit Judges.
Per Curiam:

BACKGROUND

Ralph Edward Estes was convicted of being a felon in possession of a firearm and was sentenced to 180 months' imprisonment and three years' supervised release. The Government's chief witness was Deputy Douglas Yeager, who testified that he stopped Estes for a traffic violation and discovered the firearm in his possession. Prior to trial, the Government filed a motion in limine to exclude evidence of Deputy Yeager's prior state misdemeanor conviction for impersonating a public official. The conviction was approximately 12 years old. The Government sought to prevent Estes from making any reference to this conviction to impeach Yeager. Estes argued that Federal Rule of Evidence 609(b) gave the district court the discretion to admit the evidence. He argued that Yeager's conviction was extremely probative of his credibility and that its admission was necessary. . . .

OPINION

Estes argues that the district court erred in refusing to admit evidence of Yeager's prior conviction. He contends that the district court failed to perform the balancing test required by Fed. R. Evid. 609(b) and relied only on the age of the conviction as a basis for excluding the evidence. He contends that this conviction was probative of Yeager's credibility and was critical evidence because the evidence against him came exclusively from Yeager. He argues that the Government has failed to show any danger of prejudice from admission of this evidence. . . .

Fed. R. Evid. 609(a) allows a witness's credibility to be impeached by evidence of prior convictions punishable by death or imprisonment in excess of one year, provided the court determines that the probative value of the evidence outweighs its prejudicial effect. Fed. R. Evid. 609(b) provides that evidence of such convictions is not admissible if the conviction is more than ten years old, unless the court determines that the probative value of the conviction substantially outweighs its prejudicial effect.

The district court has broad discretion in its application of this rule, and when made, the weighing of probative value and prejudicial effect must be made on the record. This Court has stated that this requirement is mandatory rather than discretionary.

We read Rule 609(b) to say that the probative value of a conviction over ten years old is outweighed by its prejudicial effect. The general rule is inadmissibility. It is only when the court admits evidence of a conviction over ten years old that the court must engage in a balancing test on the record. . . .

Finally, we have serious doubt that the conviction was probably admissible anyway because it was not the type of conviction allowed to be used for impeachment under Fed. R. Evid. 609. The Government stated in its motion in limine that the conviction was a state misdemeanor for impersonating a public official. Estes has never disputed this assertion. Rule 609(a) provides that the conviction must be for a crime punishable by death or imprisonment in excess of one year. The crime of impersonating a public servant under Texas law is a Class A misdemeanor punishable by no more than one year.

For the foregoing reasons, we affirm the district court's ruling on the motion in limine.

UNITED STATES v. AMAECHI
991 F.2d 374 (7th Cir. 1993)

CUMMINGS, Circuit Judge.

On August 15, 1991, a suitcase arrived at John F. Kennedy Airport in New York from Lagos, Nigeria, addressed to one Doreen Bennett at the Children's Home and Aid Society in Joliet, Illinois. According to trial testimony, a letter and waybill attached to the outside of the suitcase indicated that it contained traditional Nigerian clothing sent to Bennett as thanks for a gift of bibles to the Elder Okezie, Christ Devian Church in Aba, Nigeria. A customs inspector at the airport opened the suitcase and found that it was indeed stuffed with clothes. However, the inspector smelled glue. He stripped away the inner shell of the suitcase to discover a plastic bag containing 431 grams of 91 percent pure heroin. It was stipulated at trial that this extraordinarily pure heroin, at $22,000 per ounce, was worth between $352,000 and $396,000. A day later another special agent flew to New York, picked up the suitcase and brought it to Chicago. He placed a radio transmitter inside the suitcase and exchanged the seized drugs with a similar package containing a less potent mixture of heroin. Four days later, posing as a delivery man, the agent dropped off the package to its addressee, Doreen Bennett, at the Children's Home. The radio transmitter went off ten minutes later, signaling that the suitcase had been opened, and agents entered the Children's Home where they discovered Bennett kneeling down in front of the open valise and beginning to peel back the lining.

Claiming to be ignorant of the illicit contents, Bennett agreed to cooperate with agents by delivering the suitcase to a friend: defendant Ihuoma R. Amaechi. She said it was Amaechi who had asked her to receive the package in the first place. According to Bennett, a case manager at the Children's Home, Amaechi asked her on August 1, 1989 for her business address so that he could send her flowers — which she never received. On August 13 he called her, said he would be out of town, and asked if she would accept a package of clothing from his church. She agreed reluctantly but when the suitcase arrived she was disconcerted that it was addressed to her and that it was a valise rather than a package. Bennett was actually on the phone with Amaechi when the suitcase arrived. He was so anxious to get hold of it that he offered her $50 if she would cancel a hair appointment she had scheduled that evening—apparently Amaechi had not gone out of town—and he explained that he would lose a sale if he did not get the clothing quickly to the buyer. Bennett arranged to meet Amaechi that night at a bar appropriately called LaMirage. Followed by the federal agents with whom Bennett had agreed to cooperate, she met Amaechi at the bar; Amaechi of course asked for the suitcase and Bennett told him it was in her automobile. After a drink she drove Amaechi to his car, and after transferring the suitcase to the trunk of his car, defendant was arrested.

Amaechi was indicted for attempting to possess with intent to distribute 523.2 grams of heroin. . . .

Ihuoma Amaechi was convicted after a jury trial and sentenced to 112 months in prison plus a life term of supervised release under 21 U.S.C. §841(a). . . .

Defendant also suggests that the court erred in excluding evidence of Doreen Bennett's conviction for shoplifting. Bennett pleaded guilty on April 19, 1989 in Cook County Circuit Court to stealing less than $150, a misdemeanor, and was sentenced to a three-month term of supervision. Federal Rule of Evidence 609 allows evidence of a witness's prior conviction for impeachment if, among other things, the punishment could have exceeded one year (Bennett's did not), or if the crime involves dishonesty or false statement no matter how long the sentence. It is difficult to see how this evidence prejudiced Amaechi since his defense was that he was framed by his half-brother; he did not dispute that he arranged with Bennett for her to receive a package of clothing. Thus Bennett's credibility as a witness did not bolster or undermine Amaechi's story so much as it helped the authorities evaluate Bennett's claim to be ignorant of the contents of the suitcase. In any event, Illinois law clearly contemplates that a sentence of supervision does not constitute a conviction for evidentiary purposes. Since Bennett's shoplifting did not result in a conviction, it may not be admitted to attack her credibility under Rule 609(a)(2).

The government also urges us to adopt the reasoning of nine circuits that shoplifting is not a crime of dishonesty unless committed in a fraudulent or deceitful manner. Shoplifting, of course, does involve dishonesty of a certain kind; the question is whether it involves the kind contemplated by Congress in drafting the Rules of Evidence — i.e., whether it indicates that a person may be more likely to commit perjury. The calculus underlying this realm of evidence law — that people who lie in other contexts are more likely to perjure themselves than people who steal — is empirically questionable on a number of levels. Some people who falsify forms, for example, would stop short of committing the crime of perjury, while many thieves may be incorrigible liars. Yet the drafters of the Rules of Evidence explicitly intended that Rule 609 be limited to crimes involving "some element of misrepresentation or other indication of a propensity to lie and excluding those crimes which, bad though they are, do not carry with them a tinge of falsification." Having made the initial questionable assumption that some people are more given to perjury than others based on past conduct, we agree with nine other circuits that to include shoplifting as a crime of dishonesty would swallow the rule and allow any past crime to be admitted for impeachment purposes. Therefore, we hold that petty shoplifting does not in and of itself qualify as a crime of dishonesty under Rule 609. The district judge correctly prohibited Amaechi's counsel from impeaching Bennett with her shoplifting conviction. . . .

The judgment is affirmed. . . .

UNITED STATES v. PAIGE
464 F. Supp. 99 (E.D. Pa. 1978)

NEWCOMER, J. The defendant pleaded guilty on October 19, 1970, to violating Title 18, United States Code, Section 659, that is, possession of goods of a value in excess of $100 stolen from a foreign shipment knowing that the goods were stolen. Pursuant to Rule 609(a)(1) of the Federal Rules of Evidence, he moves to prevent the government from impeaching his credibility by use of that conviction in the upcoming criminal trial of the above-captioned matter. . . .

. . . It is the government's burden to establish that the probative value of the prior conviction's use outweighs its prejudicial effect. United States v. Hayes, 553 F.2d 824 (2d Cir.), cert. denied, 434 U.S. 867 (1977). In this case, where the defendant is charged with the knowing receipt and concealment of stolen securities in violation of Title 18, United States Code, Section 2315, the government has failed to meet that burden.

To make the necessary determination under Rule 609(a)(1) the Court should take into account certain factors:

(1)   the impeachment value of the prior crime;
(2)   the point in time of the conviction and the witness's subsequent history;
(3)   the similarity between the past crime and the charged crime;
(4)   the importance of the defendant's testimony; and
(5)   the centrality of the credibility issue.

United States v. Mahone, 537 F.2d 922 (7th Cir.), cert. denied, 429 U.S. 1025 (1976). Upon balancing these factors in this case, the Court is convinced that evidence of the prior conviction should be excluded.

Although the defendant's prior crime reflects adversely to his honesty and integrity, the length of time between that conviction and the present trial lessens its probative value. Eight years ago he entered that plea and received a five year sentence which term was suspended but for one month. Since that time, he has not been convicted of any other crimes. Therefore, the defendant's subsequent criminal history and the prior conviction's age diminish its probative value.

On the other hand, the prior conviction's effect on the jury is likely to be extremely prejudicial. The prior crime and the presently charged crime are similar, sharing the common element of possession of stolen goods. Although the government argues that the "similarity in the crimes is the strongest argument in support of the use of this evidence," the law is directly the contrary. Similarity between the crimes weighs strongly in favor of exclusion. United States v. Seamster, 568 F.2d 188 (10th Cir. 1978); United States v. Hawley, 554 F.2d 50, n.6 (2d Cir. 1977); United States v. Hayes, supra. Revealing the prior conviction to the jurors may cause them to believe that if the defendant "did it before he probably did so this time." Gordon v. United States, 127 U.S. App. D.C. 343, 347, 383 F.2d 936, 940 (1967), cert. denied, 390 U.S. 1029

(1968). Because such use of the prior conviction would be highly prejudicial and improper, prior similar crimes generally are not admitted
unless strong reasons exist for disclosure.

In this case, it is especially important that the defendant feel free to
testify and this also weighs heavily against allowing the impeachment
use of the prior similar conviction. The government is likely to ask the
Court to instruct the jury that it may infer guilt from proof of the defendant's recent possession of stolen goods, if the defendant has failed
to explain such possession to the jury's satisfaction. This instruction is
usually given, and it practically shifts the burden to defendant to explain
his possession of the goods. For the defendant to do so, he probably
will have to testify. Thus, his defense will be prejudiced severely if he is
deterred from testifying from fear that he will be convicted on the basis
of a prior crime. Suggs v. United States, 129 U.S. App. D.C. 133, 391
F.2d 971 (1968). Therefore, as was recognized in Smith v. United States,
123 U.S. App. D.C. 259, 359 F.2d 243 (1966), justice requires that use
of the prior conviction be disallowed unless the government shows
strong justification. As the prior conviction's probative value is limited,
such justification has not been shown here.

Therefore, the motion will be granted.

UNITED STATES v. VALENCIA
61 F.3d 616 (8th Cir. 1995)

BOGUE, Senior District Judge.

Otoniel Maldonado Valencia (appellant) was charged by superseding
indictment with one count of conspiracy to possess with intent to distribute and to distribute cocaine HCl, three counts of distribution of
cocaine HCl, and one count of money laundering. Witnesss cooperating with the government gave testimony to the effect that appellant
was the California connection for various North Dakota drug dealers. A
jury returned guilty verdicts on all counts and appellant was subsequently sentenced by the district court to 240 months imprisonment.
For reversal he asserts error in the district court's admission of a prior
conviction under Fed. R. Evid. 609. . . .

For the reasons stated below, we affirm.

I. CONVICTION

Appellant first contends the district court erred when it admitted, for
impeachment purposes, a prior conviction of the appellant for unlawful
possession for sale and purchase for sale of a controlled substance. Previously, in its case in chief, the government had offered the prior con-

viction pursuant to Fed. R. Evid. 404(b). The district court denied the use of the previous conviction during the government's case in chief, finding that the balancing required under Fed. R. Evid. 403 militated against admission. Anticipating that the issue would likely arise later in the proceedings, the district court noted that

> I'm going to exclude this evidence in the government's case in chief as it is observed under 404(b) and my reasoning again is under 403 and I find within my judgment and my discretion that I believe this evidence, though it may be relevant, is highly prejudicial and this unfair prejudice substantially outweighs any probative value of the evidence as it is observed. Now as I've indicated this ruling applies to the offer of the evidence under 404(b). My ruling under 609 at least as the facts of this case presently stand would be different. . . .

Later in the trial the appellant testified in his own defense. On direct examination he admitted that he had a prior conviction for the possession of a controlled substance. On cross-examination, the government offered a certified copy of the appellant's prior conviction. The government believed the appellant attempted to "explain away or minimize his guilt on the prior conviction" on direct examination. Over the appellant's objection, the copy of the prior conviction was admitted under Fed. R. Evid. 609 for impeachment purposes.

Whether evidence of a prior conviction should be admitted is left to the discretion of the trial court. United States v. Swanson, 9 F.3d 1354, 1356 (8th Cir. 1993) (citing United States v. Reeves, 730 F.2d 1189, 1196 (8th Cir. 1984)). The standard of review on appeal is an abuse of discretion standard. Swanson, 9 F.3d at 1356.

The admission of prior bad acts evidence under Rule 404(b) is restricted by Rule 403 which states that otherwise relevant evidence may be excluded if its probative value is substantially outweighed by the danger of unfair prejudice. The appellant contends that Rule 609(a)'s internalized balancing test is stricter in terms of admissibility in that a prior conviction is not admissible against the accused for impeachment purposes unless the probative value of the evidence outweighs its prejudicial effect. Appellant's argument is that after finding that the prejudice of the prior conviction substantially outweighed the probative value under 404(b), the district court abused its discretion in admitting the same evidence under Rule 609, where it would be excluded if the prejudice merely outweighed its probative effect. We disagree.

First, it should be noted that we are not confronted with the district court's rulings in combination. No party has appealed the district court's Rule 404(b) decision excluding the prior conviction during the government's case in chief. Each ruling must be treated independently, divorced from prior rulings. We are faced solely with the ruling regarding whether the district court erred in admitting appellant's prior conviction for impeachment purposes under Rule 609. The appellant has offered no authority, and we have discovered none, which indicates that a ruling under 404(b) governs a decision or forecloses analysis in a later-presented Rule 609 question.

This lack of support for appellant's position is not surprising in that the respective rules operate in two completely different situations. In a criminal setting, evidence offered under Rule 404(b) is substantive evidence against the accused, i.e., it is part of the government's case offered to prove his guilt beyond a reasonable doubt. Rule 609 evidence on the other hand has to do with the accused's ability to tell the truth when testifying on his or her own behalf. While both rules speak of "probative value" and "prejudice," it is critical to note that evidence offered under the respective rules is probative as to different matters. The probative character of evidence under Rule 609 has to do with credibility of a witness, while 404(b) "probativeness" essentially goes to the question of whether or not the accused committed the crime charged. Any similarity or overlap in the standards of admissibility under the respective rules is irrelevant because the rules apply to completely distinct situations.

Having found the district court's earlier ruling under Rule 404(b) irrelevant in terms of the subsequent ruling under Rule 609, we turn to the specific ruling appealed. When he testified on direct examination, the appellant admitted that he had a prior conviction for possession of cocaine, but attempted to minimize his guilt regarding the prior conviction.[6] The government thereafter properly cross-examined the appellant in an effort to clarify the facts of the prior conviction and impeach his direct testimony. This cross-examination included the offer and receipt into evidence of a certified copy of the appellant's prior conviction. The appellant in effect opened the door for the government's cross-examination by attempting to explain away or minimize his guilt. Swanson, 9 F.3d at 1357 (citing United States v. Amahia, 825 F.2d 177, 180 (8th Cir. 1987)). Viewing the entire record before us, we cannot say that the prior conviction had no bearing on the case or that the district court abused its discretion in admitting the same. United States v. Sykes, 977 F.2d 1242, 1246 (8th Cir. 1992). . . .

III. CONCLUSION

Accordingly, we affirm the appellant's conviction and sentence.

---

6. Appellant testified to the effect that he was arrested and pled guilty to the possession charge, but the cocaine actually belonged to someone else.

3.   Rehabilitation of Credibility of Witnesses

When a witness's credibility has been attacked on cross-examination by other character witnesses, through prior inconsistent statements, or by specific contradiction, how and when may the witness's credibility be supported or restored? Consider the following problems.

Problem: Assault and Battery

Charge: assault and battery on *V*. At trial, *D* takes the stand and denies the assault.

(1) *D* calls *W* to testify that he is familiar with *D*'s reputation for truth and veracity and that *D*'s reputation is good. On the prosecution's objection, what ruling and why?

(2) *W* is asked to testify as to *D*'s reputation for peace and quietude. On the prosecution's objection, what ruling and why?

(3) In rebuttal, the prosecution shows that *D* was convicted of grand larceny nine years ago. In surrebuttal, *D* recalls *W* and puts the same question to him as in (1) about *D*'s reputation for truth and veracity. On the prosecution's objection, what ruling and why?

Problem: Impeachment by Specific Contradiction and Self-Contradiction

(1) Charge: murder in the first degree. M.O.: beating *D*'s father-in-law on November 27 and poisoning him on November 28, with death resulting on December 8. At *D*'s trial, the star witness for the prosecution is *S*, the sister of *D*'s husband. *S* testifies that at noon on November 27, in *D*'s house, she saw *D* beat her father over the head with a wrench and that on November 28, in *D*'s house, she saw *D* take pills from a bottle and give them to her father, who chugged them down. Later at the trial, *D* produces a witness, *J*, who testifies that on November 27 he was with *D* all day hunting, 200 miles away from *D*'s residence. How, if at all, does *J*'s testimony tend to impeach *S*?

(2) Suppose that *J*'s testimony is that on November 28 *S* told him that the day before she had seen someone beat her father over the head but that it was not *D*—it was someone else. How does the impeachment of *S* in (2) differ from that in (1)?

There are a number of ways to persuade a factfinder that the witness should not be believed. One way is to have a second witness testify to the first witness's bad reputation for truthfulness or give his opinion that the first witness is untruthful. This is an attack on character that can be met with a rehabilitating character witness. Another way is to have a second witness testify in a way that cannot be reconciled with the testimony of the witness being attacked. A third method is to introduce evidence that in the past the witness has made statements contradictory to her testimony at trial. The last two methods may or may not be deemed attacks on the character for truthfulness of the witness. If not, rehabilitation with good reputation evidence will not be allowed.

The Impeachment by Specific Contradiction . . . problem is an example of impeachment by specific contradiction. S's character for truthfulness has not been attacked directly. Nonetheless, the trial judge could consider the contradiction to be sharp and the issue to be sufficiently important to justify treating J's testimony as an attack on S's character for truthfulness, and allow rehabilitation.

In the second part of the same problem, S is being impeached by a prior inconsistent statement. In theory, such statements are admitted not for their truth, but to show that the witness tells different stories at different times and is, therefore, not to be believed. The prior inconsistent statement is a specific instance of conduct offered to show that the witness's present statements are unreliable. Depending on the facts of the case, this may amount to a general attack on the character of the witness for truthfulness, but it may only go to show that the witness is forgetful or biased in a manner that does not impugn the witness's general character for truthfulness.

Impeachment by prior inconsistent statements of the witness is governed by Rules 613, 801(d)(1)(A), and 804(b)(1) and by the common law *Hitchcock* rule relating to when an inconsistent statement can be proved by extrinsic proof. Rehabilitation by prior consistent statements is always allowed, but rehabilitation with a reputation witness will be allowed only if the court deems the prior inconsistent statement to be an attack on general character for veracity.

Mere contradiction of a witness is usually not enough to be considered an attack on character for truthfulness, but, depending on the case, it may be so considered. Compare the following problems.

Problem: Rehabilitation After Contradiction

Action for damages arising out of an automobile collision on June 1. Liability is conceded. The issue is whether P sustained neck and back injuries in the accident or whether the injuries are feigned. At trial, on direct examination, P testified that he did not go to see a doctor until two months after the collision because he did not have the money to pay a doctor. On cross-examination, it was brought out that P had a health and accident insurance policy that would have covered the cost of seeing a doctor and also that *P* was receiving a Veterans' Administration pension of $90 a month that could have been used to defray at least some of the cost. In rebuttal, *P* offered the testimony of a witness to testify to *P*'s good reputation for truth and veracity. On *D*'s objection, what ruling and why?

Problem: Red Light/Green Light

Action for damages arising out of the collision of *P*'s and *D*'s cars at the intersection of Commonwealth Avenue and Beacon Street. The issue is who had the green light. At trial, *P* calls *W1* who testifies that he saw the accident and that the light was green for *P* and red for *D*. In defense, *D* calls *W2* who testifies that he saw the accident and that the light was red for *P* and green for *D*. In rebuttal, *P* calls *W3* to testify to *W1*'s good reputation for truth and veracity. On *D*'s objection, what ruling and why?

4. Using Extrinsic Evidence of Character to Impeach Credibility

Proof of character for truthfulness as it affects witness credibility may be elicited through direct and cross-examination of the witness whose character is in question, by means of a document, or through the testimony of other witnesses. Understanding the rules of the road of direct and cross-examination, the offering of exhibits, and the making of objections and offers of proof is vital to this process. These subjects are covered by Rule 103 and the rules in Article VI of the Federal Rules of Evidence.

Proof of character for purposes of attacking witness credibility often involves the issue of whether and when "extrinsic evidence" (i.e., evidence other than that obtained by examination of the principal witness) of the witness's character ought to be allowed. The extrinsic evidence rule is prominent in this area because of the "collateral" nature of proof of character. There is always the danger that the focus of the trial will be diverted from the issues in the case to a fact scenario whose only relevance is that it is claimed to illuminate something about the character of truthfulness of a witness. In this sense the issues raised in the introduction to this chapter are simply placed in sharper focus when extrinsic evidence, rather than cross-examination, is offered to prove character or credibility.

Problem: Bijou Blues

Charge: violation of Dyer Act (interstate transportation of stolen vehicle). The principal prosecution witness, *W*, testifies that on June 1 *D* accosted him in Philadelphia, stole his car, and absconded across the Delaware River Bridge into Camden, New Jersey.

The cross-examination of W is as follows:

Q: Where did you have supper June 1?
A: The Philadelphia Hoagie House.
Q: What did you do after dinner?
A: Went to the movies.
Q: Where?
A: The Bijou.
Q: What did you see?
A: *Aladdin.*

As part of its case-in-chief, D calls M, the manager of the Bijou, to testify that on June 1 *A River Runs Through It* was playing at the Bijou. On the prosecution's objection, what ruling and why? Is M's testimony relevant to impeach W's credibility? What sort of impeachment is M's testimony? What considerations are important in deciding whether to sustain or overrule the objection? What is the appropriate standard of "collateralness" in deciding whether extrinsic impeachment evidence is admissible? Can any workable standard be articulated? Should there be *any* limit on the use of extrinsic impeachment evidence?

In Attorney-General v. Hitchcock, 1 Exch. 91, 99 (Eng. 1847), Chief Baron Pollock laid down the rule as follows:

> If the answer of a witness is [about] a matter which you would be allowed on your part to prove in evidence—if it have such a connection with the issue, that you would be allowed to give it in evidence—then it is a matter on which you may contradict him [with extrinsic evidence].

Is this a sound rule for determining when contradiction by extrinsic evidence should be allowed? Is it workable?

Problem: The Wind River Ranch

In the ejectment action over the Wind River Ranch, D's attorney asks W, P's witness, the following questions on cross-examination and receives the following answers.

Q: Is W your correct name?
A: Yes.
Q: Have you ever been known by another name?
A: No.
Q: What is your address?
A: 42 Russell Street.
Q: What do you do for a living now?
A: I am a teller at the Cooperative Bank.

In rebuttal, *D* offers to prove that *W* changed his name from *X* five years ago, lives on Pine Street, and works as a Fuller Brush man. *P* objects on the grounds that such evidence relates to a collateral matter not independently provable and thus is not provable by extrinsic evidence for impeachment purposes.

What ruling under the *Hitchcock* rule? Should this extrinsic evidence be admitted? See Rule 608.

Problem: Harry's Harborside

P, executor of *V*'s estate, v. *D* for damages for an alleged assault and battery by *D* on *V* on June 1 at 10 P.M. at Harry's Harborside Tavern, a rowdy sailors' bar in Revere, Massachusetts. At trial, *P*'s first witness is Harry. Harry testifies that on June 1 at around 10 P.M. in his bar he saw *D* splash *V*'s face with beer and then break a beer bottle over *V*'s head. On cross-examination the following occurs:

Q: Weren't you bitten by *D*'s dog on May 1?
By P's counsel: Objection — beyond the scope of the direct examination. (What ruling and why?)
A: No, I was not bitten by *D*'s dog on May 1.

In rebuttal, *D* offers *W*, who testifies that *D* was out fishing all day and night on June 1, and the testimony of *D, Jr.*, that on May 1 he saw Fang, the *D* family dog, bite Harry. *P*'s counsel objects to *D, Jr.*'s testimony. What ruling and why?

UNITED STATES v. ABEL
469 U.S. 45 (1984)

Justice REHNQUIST delivered the opinion of the Court.

A divided panel of the Court of Appeals for the Ninth Circuit reversed respondent's conviction for bank robbery. The Court of Appeals held that the District Court improperly admitted testimony which impeached one of respondent's witnesses. We hold that the District Court did not err, and we reverse.

Respondent John Abel and two cohorts were indicted for robbing a savings and loan in Bellflower, Ca., in violation of 18 U.S.C. §§2113(a) and (d). The cohorts elected to plead guilty, but respondent went to trial. One of the cohorts, Kurt Ehle, agreed to testify against respondent and identify him as a participant in the robbery.

Respondent informed the District Court at a pretrial conference that he would seek to counter Ehle's testimony with that of Robert Mills. Mills was not a participant in the robbery but was friendly with respondent and with Ehle, and had spent time with both in prison. Mills planned to testify that after the robbery Ehle had admitted to Mills that Ehle intended to implicate respondent falsely, in order to receive favorable treatment from the government. The prosecutor in turn disclosed that he intended to discredit Mills' testimony by calling Ehle back to the stand and eliciting from Ehle the fact that respondent, Mills, and Ehle were all members of the "Aryan Brotherhood," a secret prison gang that required its members always to deny the existence of the organization and to commit perjury, theft, and murder on each member's behalf.

Defense counsel objected to Ehle's proffered rebuttal testimony as too prejudicial to respondent. After a lengthy discussion in chambers the District Court decided to permit the prosecutor to cross-examine Mills about the gang, and if Mills denied knowledge of the gang, to introduce Ehle's rebuttal testimony concerning the tenets of the gang and Mills' and respondent's membership in it. The District Court held that the probative value of Ehle's rebuttal testimony outweighed its prejudicial effect, but that respondent might be entitled to a limiting instruction if his counsel would submit one to the court.

At trial Ehle implicated respondent as a participant in the robbery. Mills, called by respondent, testified that Ehle told him in prison that Ehle planned to implicate respondent falsely. When the prosecutor sought to cross-examine Mills concerning membership in the prison gang, the District Court conferred again with counsel outside of the jury's presence, and ordered the prosecutor not to use the term "Aryan Brotherhood" because it was unduly prejudicial. Accordingly, the prosecutor asked Mills if he and respondent were members of a "secret type of prison organization" which had a creed requiring members to deny its existence and lie for each other. When Mills denied knowledge of such an organization the prosecutor recalled Ehle.

Ehle testified that respondent, Mills, and he were indeed members of a secret prison organization whose tenets required its members to deny its existence and "lie, cheat, steal [and] kill" to protect each other. The District Court sustained a defense objection to a question concerning the punishment for violating the organization's rules. Ehle then further described the organization and testified that "in view of the fact of how close Abel and Mills were" it would have been "suicide" for Ehle to have told Mills what Mills attributed to him. Respondent's counsel did not request a limiting instruction and none was given.

The jury convicted respondent. On his appeal a divided panel of the Court of Appeals reversed. The Court of Appeals held that Ehle's rebuttal testimony was admitted not just to show that respondent's and Mills' membership in the same group might cause Mills to color his testimony; the court held that the contested evidence was also admitted to show that because Mills belonged to a perjurious organization, he must be lying on the stand. This suggestion of perjury, based upon a group tenet, was impermissible. . . . The court concluded that Ehle's testimony implicated respondent as a member of the gang; but since respondent did not take the stand, the testimony could not have been offered to impeach him and it prejudiced him "by mere association."

We hold that the evidence showing Mills' and respondent's membership in the prison gang was sufficiently probative of Mills' possible bias towards respondent to warrant its admission into evidence. Thus it was within the District Court's discretion to admit Ehle's testimony, and the Court of Appeals was wrong in concluding otherwise.

Both parties correctly assume, as did the District Court and the Court of Appeals, that the question is governed by the Federal Rules of Evidence. But the Rules do not by their terms deal with impeachment for "bias," although they do expressly treat impeachment by character evidence and conduct, Rule 608, by evidence of conviction of a crime, Rule 609, and by showing of religious beliefs or opinion, Rule 610. Neither party has suggested what significance we should attribute to this fact. Although we are nominally the promulgators of the Rules, and should in theory need only to consult our collective memories to analyze the situation properly, we are in truth merely a conduit when we deal with an undertaking as substantial as the preparation of the Fed. Rules of Evid. In the case of these Rules, too, it must be remembered that Congress extensively reviewed our submission, and considerably revised it. . . .

[I]t is permissible to impeach a witness by showing his bias under the Fed. Rules of Evid. just as it was permissible to do so before their adoption. In this connection, the comment of the Reporter for the Advisory Committee which drafted the Rules is apropos:

> In principle, under the Federal Rules no common law of evidence remains. "All relevant evidence is admissible, except as otherwise provided. . . ." In reality, of course, the body of common law knowledge continues to exist, though in the somewhat altered form of a source of guidance in the exercise of delegated powers.

Cleary, Preliminary Notes on Reading the Rules of Evidence, 57 Neb. L. Rev. 908, 915 (1978) (footnote omitted).

Ehle's testimony about the prison gang certainly made the existence of Mills' bias towards respondent more probable. Thus it was relevant to support that inference. Bias is a term used in the "common law of evidence" to describe the relationship between a party and a witness which might lead the witness to slant, unconsciously or otherwise, his testimony in favor or against a party. Bias may be induced by a witness' like, dislike, or fear of a party, or by the witness' self-interest. Proof of bias is almost always relevant because the jury, as finder of fact and weigher of credibility, has historically been entitled to assess all evidence which might bear on the accuracy and truth of a witness' testimony. The "common law of evidence" allowed the showing of bias by extrinsic evidence, while requiring the cross-examiner to "take the answer of the witness" with respect to less favored forms of impeachment.

Mills' and respondent's membership in the Aryan Brotherhood supported the inference that Mills' testimony was slanted or perhaps fabricated in respondent's favor. A witness' and a party's common membership in an organization, even without proof that the witness or party has personally adopted its tenets, is certainly probative of bias. . . . Mills' and respondent's membership in the Aryan Brotherhood was not offered to convict either of a crime, but to impeach Mills' testimony. Mills was subject to no sanction other than that he might be disbelieved. Under these circumstances there is no requirement that the witness must be shown to have subscribed to all the tenets of the organization. . . .

Respondent argues that even if the evidence of membership in the prison gang were relevant to show bias, the District Court erred in permitting a full description of the gang and its odious tenets. Respondent contends that the District Court abused its discretion under Federal Rules of Evidence 403, because the prejudicial effect of the contested evidence outweighed its probative value. In other words, testimony about the gang inflamed the jury against respondent, and the chance that he would be convicted by his mere association with the organization outweighed any probative value the testimony may have had on Mills' bias.

Respondent specifically contends that the District Court should not have permitted Ehle's precise description of the gang as a lying and murderous group. Respondent suggests that the District Court should have cut off the testimony after the prosecutor had elicited that Mills knew respondent and both may have belonged to an organization together. This argument ignores the fact that the *type* of organization in which a witness and a party share membership may be relevant to show bias. If the organization is a loosely knit group having nothing to do with the subject matter of the litigation, the inference of bias arising from common membership may be small or nonexistent. If the prosecutor had elicited that both respondent and Mills belonged to the Book of the Month Club, the jury probably would not have inferred bias even if the District Court had admitted the testimony. The attributes of the Aryan Brotherhood — a secret prison sect sworn to perjury and self-protection — bore directly not only on the *fact* of bias but also on the *source* and *strength* of Mills' bias. The tenets of this group showed that Mills had a powerful motive to slant his testimony towards respondent, or even commit perjury outright. . . .

Respondent makes an additional argument based on Rule 608(b).

That Rule allows a cross-examiner to impeach a witness by asking him about specific instances of past conduct, other than crimes covered by Rule 609, which are probative of his veracity or "character for truthfulness or untruthfulness." The Rule limits the inquiry to cross-examination of the witness, however, and prohibits the cross-examiner from introducing extrinsic evidence of the witness' past conduct.

Respondent claims that the prosecutor cross-examined Mills about the gang not to show bias but to offer Mills' membership in the gang as past conduct bearing on his veracity. This was error under Rule 608(b), respondent contends, because the mere fact of Mills' membership, without more, was not sufficiently probative of Mills' character for truthfulness. Respondent cites a second error under the same Rule, contending that Ehle's rebuttal testimony concerning the gang was extrinsic evidence offered to impugn Mills' veracity, and extrinsic evidence is barred by Rule 608(b). . . .

It seems clear to us that the proffered testimony with respect to Mills' membership in the Aryan Brotherhood sufficed to show potential bias in favor of respondent; because of the tenets of the organization described, it might also impeach his veracity directly. But there is no rule of evidence which provides that testimony admissible for one purpose and inadmissible for another purpose is thereby rendered inadmissible; quite the contrary is the case. It would be a strange rule of law which held that relevant, competent evidence which tended to show bias on the part of a witness was nonetheless inadmissible because it also tended to show that the witness was a liar.

We intimate no view as to whether the evidence of Mills' membership in an organization having the tenets ascribed to the Aryan Brotherhood would be a specific instance of Mills' conduct which could not be proved against him by extrinsic evidence except as otherwise provided in Rule 608(b). It was enough that such evidence could properly be found admissible to show bias.

The judgment of the Court of Appeals is reversed.

Problem: Cutting Through an Alibi

Charge: robbing a drug store using a knife. Several employees of the store identified *D*.

At the conclusion of the government's case, a bench conference is held in which the government urges that it be allowed to call Coombs, an undercover agent of the Bureau of Alcohol, Tobacco, and Firearms, who would testify that *D* had told him three months before the robbery that he had robbed a drug dealer, using a knife. The government theory, articulated in a memorandum of law for the court, is that the use of a knife in a prior crime is probative of appellant's identity under Rule

404(b)(2). The district court and counsel engage in the following colloquy:

Mr. Healy (prosecutor):   Essentially, that is my case. I submitted a memo . . .

The Court: I read the memo and I would say, in the interest of quitting while you are ahead, at the present time I will confine you to your case. I don't know what George has for a defense. You might try and get it in rebuttal, if it gets to that point.

Mr. Higgins (counsel for defendant):   Mine is strictly alibi, your Honor.

The Court: This business—I am sure you have a copy (indicating).

Mr. Higgins: I am going to be eating large chunks of the rug if he starts with that stuff.

The Court: It is arguably admissible. If you read the *Heatherton* [*sic*] and *Wright* cases [United States v. Eatherton, 519 F.2d 603 (1st Cir. 1975); United States v. Wright, 573 F.2d 681 (1st Cir. 1978)], it is arguably admissible. I won't say I won't let it come in, but for your direct case I don't think you need it at the moment. You have a pretty strong case and I suggest you quit while you are ahead. At the end of his case, if you want to take a shot at it and offer it, we will see about it then.

D then presents his case, testifying that he had been elsewhere at the time of the robbery. In the course of *D*'s cross-examination by the government, the relevant questions and answers are as follows:

Q: In late 1977, did you commit any robberies by knife?

A: In 1977? By knife? Did I commit any robberies?

Mr. Higgins: I object to that, your Honor.

The Witness: No.

The Court: He said no. All right.

The Witness: No. I didn't, wait a minute. 1977? Did I commit any robberies?

Q: Late 1977, any robberies by knife?

A: I—no. I have not committed any robberies by knife in 1977.

After the defendant presents his case, the government seeks once again to introduce Agent Coombs's testimony.

Mr. Healy: There were certain matters that I had written a memorandum on and I want to put out in my case in chief, and at this time there is one in particular, and that is my recollection of the defendant's testimony was that he denied . . .

The Court: Conducting a robbery in late 1977 by the use of a knife, and

you have a witness that is going to say he admitted that, and that is
admissible on the limited issue of his credibility.

Mr. Healy: Yes.

Mr. Higgins: Your Honor, please note my objection. It will be my position that that is so prejudicial as to warrant its exclusion; and,
further, that matter was not raised on direct.

The Court: It was raised on cross-examination, and the defendant's
credibility is crucial in this case where there is an alibi defense, and
there are Court of Appeals opinions indicating that when a defendant's testimony is critical that cross-examination is permissible on
the issue of credibility. I will take it with a limiting instruction that
I will give to the jury that it is admissible on the defendant's credibility. I will, of course, note your objection.

The prosecution then calls Agent Coombs:

Q: Sir, in what capacity did you meet the defendant?
A: I met him while I was working in an undercover capacity.
Q: Now, sir, did there come a time in September of 1977 when you
had a conversation with him concerning the possible robbery of a
drug dealer?
A: Yes.
Q: What, if any, conversation was that?
A: In, I believe it was in the beginning of September, he asked me if
I would be interested in assisting him in the robbery of a Puerto
Rican drug dealer in the City of Somerville.
Q: Did he state the drug dealer's name?
A: No.
Q: November 16, 1977, sir; did you see him on that day?
A: Yes.
Q: Did you have a conversation with him concerning that same drug
dealer?
A: Yes.
Q: And, sir, in substance, what did he say?
A: He basically said that he had robbed a Puerto Rican drug dealer by
the name of Vincente with a knife.

D is convicted. Was there error?

UNITED STATES v. PISARI
636 F.2d 855 (1st Cir. 1981)

COFFIN, C.J. On June 5, 1980 we issued our opinion in this case, reversing appellant's conviction and holding that rebuttal testimony of a gov-

ernment witness, Coombs, was improperly admitted, being admissible neither as independent proof of appellant's identity, Fed. R. Evid. 404(b), nor as impeachment by prior inconsistent statement. On August 4 we granted the government's petition for rehearing and withdrew our opinion. After receiving and considering new briefs from the parties, we arrive at the same result, a reversal, via a different analysis. . . .

The parties, the district court, and this court have been mistaken in various ways in their analysis of the admissibility of agent Coombs' statement. The district court, as noted, admitted the evidence as proof of a prior inconsistent statement relevant to the credibility of the defendant. The government defends the district court's admission of the evidence for impeachment purposes, or as a proper resort to Rule 404(b), the testimony tending to prove that defendant had committed an earlier "strikingly similar" crime and therefore was the person who committed the crime at bar. Appellant has attacked the testimony as constituting extrinsic evidence of specific conduct, in violation of Rule 608(b). He opposes the application of Rule 404(b), arguing that the testimony was not admitted on this basis and that in any event the evidence of misconduct was neither direct nor competent. As for the impeachment ground, appellant argues that defendant's denial of having engaged in robbery by knife is not necessarily inconsistent with his having falsely told the undercover agent that he had committed such an act. In our earlier opinion, we rejected both proffered grounds for admissibility on the rationale now understandably defended on rehearing by appellant.

In our rethinking of the admissibility of the Coombs testimony, we consider first the impeachment ground specifically relied on by the district court. The government has suggested the proper starting point for analysis by acknowledging that a denial on cross-examination which relates to a collateral matter cannot be disputed by extrinsic evidence, citing McCormick, Law of Evidence, ch. 56, §36 at 70 (2d ed. 1972). See also Saltzburg and Redden, Federal Rules of Evidence Manual, 390 (2d ed. 1977). As one treatise summarizes the test at common law,

> The test for collateralness proposed by Wigmore and endorsed by a number of federal courts [footnote omitted] is "Could the fact, as to which the prior self-contradiction is predicated, have been shown in evidence for any purpose independently of the self-contradiction?" In other words, the [prior inconsistent] statement may be proved if it relates to a matter which the examiner could have proven even if the witness had said nothing on the subject. 3 Weinstein's Evidence, ¶607[06], at 607-69, -70 (1978).

While at common law the test for collateralness was frequently mechanical, we are advised by commentators that: "The better approach —and one in accord with the structure of the federal rules—would be to eliminate mechanical application of the 'collateral' test in favor of the balancing approach mandated by Rule 403. Evidence at which the collateral test is primarily directed, which is relevant solely because it suggests that the witness may have lied about something in the past would generally be excluded because of its low probative value and its tendency to prejudice the jury. Evidence of higher probative value would be assessed in terms of its impact on the jury in light of the particular circumstances presented." Id. at 607-71 to -72.

The government assumes that the issue of collateralness is easily hurdled, because "[t]he identity of the perpetrator of a crime is always a relevant and material issue." That is, the government contends that the prior robbery of a drug dealer by appellant, having a knife as his weapon, is so "strikingly similar" to the robbery of the postal installation in the pharmacy presented in this case that it is probative that the same person, appellant, committed both crimes.

We think the government has underestimated the similarity necessary to justify, under Rule 404(b), the admission of evidence of other crimes to prove identity. Weinstein quotes McCormick as stating that evidence may be admitted:

> to prove other like crimes by the accused so nearly identical in method as to earmark them as the handiwork of the accused. Here much more is demanded than the mere repeated commission of crimes of the same class, such as repeated burglaries or thefts. *The device used must be so unusual and distinctive as to be like a signature.* (Emphasis in original.) Id. at 404-92, quoting McCormick, Evidence §157 (1954). . . .

Our own precedents allowing "other crimes as signature" evidence have involved the conjunction of several identifying characteristics or the presence of some highly distinctive quality. In United States v. Eatherton, 519 F.2d 603, 611 (1st Cir.), cert. denied, 423 U.S. 987 (1975), a gun and three ski masks taken from defendant corresponded in character and number to accessories used in a robbery a few days earlier. In United States v. Barrett, 539 F.2d 244, 248 (1st Cir. 1976), testimony that defendant possessed expertise in the operation of burglar alarms was admissible where, in the case at bar, a burglary had been facilitated by bypassing an alarm, "so distinctive a feature of the stamp burglary" that defendant's expertise "reinforced the evidence that linked him to the burglary."

In contrast, the only factor common to the postal installation burglary and the robbery about which agent Coombs quoted appellant was a knife. We have no idea whether the knives used on these occasions were either similar or distinctive. We have no clear idea of the propinquity of the events in time. In one case a store is the target of the crime; in the other, an individual is the target. In one case, there were two robbers; in the other, so far as we know, one. In this case the objects taken were drugs and money; we do not know whether drugs or money were taken in the other robbery. . . .

We are, in short, unable to make the determination that the elements of the offense revealed in agent Coombs' testimony and in the case at bar are so distinctive as to give rise to an inference that the same person was involved in both. The single fact that in committing a robbery, one invokes the threat of using a knife falls far short of a sufficient signature or trademark upon which to posit an inference of identity. We therefore conclude that, since agent Coombs' testimony, not being justified as evidence bearing on the identity of appellant, was addressed only to a collateral matter, it was improperly admitted as impeachment evidence. Our analysis also necessarily rules out any invocation of Rule 404(b) as an independent basis of admissibility. No other basis has been suggested, nor does any commend itself to us. . . .

Since we cannot say with certainty that the error was harmless, we must reverse. . . .

Reversed and remanded.

CHAPTER V

Hearsay

As the preceding chapter indicates, the device most heavily relied upon to promote reliable factfinding at trial is cross-examination. Other devices, rules, and limitations that are relied on to a lesser extent to promote accuracy include the oath and sanctions for its violation, competency limitations, the rule requiring first-hand knowledge, the Confrontation Clause of the Constitution, the relevancy rule, the prejudice rule, and the categorical rules of exclusion primarily found in Rules 404 through 412. These devices are designed to promote fair and accurate factfinding by deterring, excluding, or exposing false testimony of witnesses about *their own* perceptions of events relevant to the inquiry. The rule against hearsay, on the other hand, is designed to promote fair and accurate factfinding by excluding unreliable testimony by witnesses about *others'* (or their own previous) perceptions and statements.

The rule against hearsay is a historical product of the Anglo-American system of judicial resolution of disputes. Continental systems of adjudication seem to do nicely without this complex and difficult doctrine. What accounts for its development and persistence in Anglo-American jurisprudence? Traditional justifications for the rule usually focus on some of the peculiar characteristics of the Anglo-American trial system: (1) the adversarial presentation of proof (2) by live witnesses (3) before a lay factfinder. These justifications view the rule against hearsay as simply another device to promote reliable factfinding in a system of this design. The big question is, do the rule and its exceptions effectively and consistently fulfill this function?

A conceptual problem is posed by the traditional explanation for the rule against hearsay and its exceptions: When, if ever, may these other truth-promoting devices, rules, and limitations safely be dispensed with? Put another way, when should an in-court witness (or document) be allowed to relate the observation, statements, or beliefs of someone else who is not in court and thus not subject to the normal truth-promoting rules, policies, and procedures (especially cross-examination)? This is the realm of the rule against hearsay.

As Professor Morgan observed, consistency would require that the answer to the previous questions be "never." "Consistency, however, is not a characteristic of common law procedure. History, policy, and experience render impractical the application of the rules of formal logic." Morgan, Hearsay Dangers and the Application of the Hearsay Concept, 62 Harv. L. Rev. 177, 179 (1948). Moreover, some evidence that cannot be subjected to the normal truth-promoting devices may be superior to evidence that is subject to these devices. Furthermore, the choice is often between taking evidence as it is found—absent the normal safeguards applied to in-court testimony—or doing without it altogether. Thus, history, policy, experience, necessity, and perhaps logic convert the clearcut "never" into a confusing "sometimes."

Given the origins of the rule and the bases for its exceptions, application to concrete cases sometimes seems as much art as science. Nevertheless, it should be possible for students to develop an analytical approach to hearsay that (1) usually makes sense and (2) provides a methodology by which most hearsay problems can be quickly identified and resolved. The materials in this chapter are organized along the lines of the following suggested structure for dealing with hearsay problems:

1. Decide if the offered evidence raises a hearsay issue;
2. Decide if the offered evidence is hearsay. This involves consideration of
   a. What the evidence is offered to prove (relevancy);
   b. Whether the evidence is a "statement," that is, an oral or written assertion or nonverbal conduct intended as an assertion;
   c. Whether the statement was made by someone other than the witness testifying at the hearing;
   d. Whether the statement is offered to prove the truth of the matter asserted;
3. Decide if the evidence may be admitted for another, nonhearsay purpose;
4. If the evidence is hearsay, decide if the evidence fits within one of the many hearsay exceptions; and
5. Decide whether the evidence, even if it is not hearsay, ought to be excluded because of prejudice or constitutional considerations related to the policy behind the rule against hearsay.

The following problems and materials should stimulate students to consider the larger jurisprudential and policy questions raised by the hearsay doctrine. Does the hearsay doctrine promote the values it purports to serve? Is it based on valid assumptions about juror competence? Does it reflect a paternalistic, elitist view of society? Does the doctrine incorporate political, class, and cultural biases that are neither explicit nor fair? Has the rule become so bulky and complex that it creates more problems than it solves? Is the doctrine merely a "glass-bead game" for trial lawyers or a self-protective mechanism for courts? Should the rule and exceptions be replaced by a unitary rule that gives the trial judge discretion to admit hearsay for whatever it is worth if, on balance, the evidence is more probative than prejudicial?

In recent years there have been many attempts to "rationalize the rule against hearsay" and reform it from the ground up. For a critique of the modern approach to hearsay contained in the Federal Rules, see Note, The Theoretical Foundation of the Hearsay Rules, 93 Harv. L. Rev. 1786 (1980), at page 542, below. See also Park, A Subject Matter Approach to Hearsay Reform, 86 Mich. L. Rev. 51 (1987); Swift, A Foundation Fact Approach to Hearsay, 75 Cal. L. Rev. 1339 (1987); Swift, Abolishing the Hearsay Rule, 75 Cal. L. Rev. 495 (1987); Mueller, Post-Modern Hearsay Reform: The Importance of Complexity, 76 Minn. L. Rev. 367 (1992).

A. The Rule Against Hearsay

NOTE: THE TREASON TRIAL OF SIR WALTER RALEIGH

In a celebrated trial in 1603 Sir Walter Raleigh was accused of conspiracy to commit treason against the Crown by attempting to establish Arabella Stuart as queen of England. At his trial, the evidence consisted primarily of a sworn "confession" by Lord Cobham, Raleigh's alleged co-conspirator, before the Privy Council and a letter by Cobham. Raleigh asserted that Cobham had recanted his confession and protested its introduction:

> But it is strange to see how you press me still with my Lord Cobham, and yet will not produce him; . . . [H]e is in the house hard by, and may soon be brought hither; let him be produced, and if he will yet accuse me or avow this confession of his, it shall convict me and ease you of further proof.

Raleigh's Trial, 2 How. St. Tr. 16 (1603); 1 Jardine's Crim. Trials 418 (1832). The prosecution responded not by producing Cobham but by calling a boat pilot named Dyer, who testified that while in Lisbon a Portuguese gentleman told him, "Your king [James] shall never be crowned for Don Cobham and Don Raleigh will cut his throat before he come to be crowned." Raleigh protested this evidence on the ground that, "This is the saying of some wild Jesuit or beggarly priest; but what proof is it against me?" The prosecutor, Lord Coke, responded, "It must perforce arise out of some preceding intelligence and shews that your treason had wings." On this evidence, Raleigh was convicted and later executed. See 1 J. Stephen, A History of the Criminal Law of England 333-336 (1883); 9 Holdsworth, A History of English Law 216-217, 226-228 (1926); J. G. Phillimore, History and Principles of the Law of Evidence 157 (1850).

What do the testimonies of Lord Cobham and Dyer have in common? What infirmities, if any, does such evidence contain? Should such evidence be admissible in criminal or civil cases? Does it make a difference whether other probative, corroborative evidence is introduced by live witnesses who testify from their own observations? What values are implicated by the use of such evidence? Fairness? Reliability? Necessity? Individual integrity?

Outrage at the injustice done to Raleigh contributed to the development of the hearsay rules and the constitutional rights of confrontation and compulsory process. One of the puzzles of this subject is how hearsay, confrontation, and compulsory process interrelate.

It is crucial, in applying the hearsay rule, to understand the *purpose* for which the evidence is being offered. Is a statement being offered to prove the truth of the matter it asserts? Or to prove that the statement was made?

As you work through the following problems, consider carefully whether the "statement" in question is being offered to prove the truth of the matter asserted. Also consider whether the chain of inference for which the evidence is offered requires a trip through the mind of — and hence reliance on the testimonial capacities of — an out-of-court declarant. Who is the witness? Who is the declarant?

Problem: Arsenic and Hors d'Oeuvres

Time: Christmas Eve. Place: the *D* family house. The *D* family consists of Mr. and Mrs. *D* and Mrs. *D*'s aged, invalid father. As usual, *D* prepares pre-dinner drinks — martinis for his wife and father-in-law and a highball for himself. Since it is a special occasion, *D* also prepares hors d'oeuvres. But *D* does not eat any hors d'oeuvres himself. The next day his wife and father-in-law are found dead. An autopsy of the bodies and a chemical analysis of the martinis and hors d'oeuvres reveal traces of arsenic poisoning in the bodies, drinks, and food. *D* is charged with two counts of first-degree murder.

(1) At *D*'s trial, suppose that the prosecution proves the above and then calls *W*, a salesman in the local drugstore, to testify that on December 24 he sold *D* a tube of rat poison. On *D*'s objection, what ruling and why?

(2) Suppose the prosecution calls *S*, *W*'s sister, to testify that *W* told her on December 25 that *D* bought rat poison. On *D*'s objection, what ruling and why?

Problem: Murder at the Seaside Bistro

Charge: first-degree murder. M.O.: blowing *V*'s head off with a shotgun. Time: 10 A.M., June 1. The day after the murder Officer Kojak interviews *H*, the owner of the Seaside Bistro, in which the shooting occurred. In Kojak's presence, *H* prepares and signs a statement that says, "I saw *D* shoot *V*."

At *D*'s trial, the first witness is Kojak. Kojak identifies *H*'s written statement and says, "*H* is dead." *H*'s statement is offered. *D* objects. What ruling and why? Is *H*'s statement hearsay? If it is hearsay, should it be admitted nonetheless? If it is not hearsay, should it be excluded anyhow?

Problem: Assault on Massachusetts Avenue

Action for damages for assault. At trial, *P* testifies that she was driving down Massachusetts Avenue at 6 P.M. on June 1, and while she was stopped at a street light someone threw a brick through her car window. Although *P* did not see who hurled the brick, Andy, Bob, Cindy, and Dora were the only ones on the street at the time.

(1) *P* proposes to testify further that she stopped her car and Andy walked over to her and said, "Dora threw it, Lady." Dora objects. What ruling and why?

(2) Suppose that *P* proposes to testify that she stopped her car and asked Andy who threw the brick and Andy pointed to Dora. Dora objects. What ruling and why?

Problem: Murder in the Ajax Building

Time: June 1, 11:55 A.M. Place: room 1601 on the sixteenth floor of the Ajax Building. Room 1601 is a one-room office with one window. Outside the window on the ledge is a pigeon's nest containing freshly laid pigeon eggs. Several feet to the left of the window in room 1601 are two desks with typewriters and swivel chairs. There is also a copying machine several feet to the right of the window. At 11:59 A.M. there are four people in room 1601: Agnes, Belle, Claire, and David. Agnes and Belle are sitting in the swivel chairs at the two desks. Claire is standing on a chair at point C, leaning out the open window. David is at the copying machine.

At 12:01 P.M. Claire's body is in the street. There are three possible explanations for Claire's change in position: (1) There was an accident; (2) she committed suicide; or (3) a homicide has occurred. The state decides that the third explanation is the most likely and indicts and tries David for Claire's murder.

(1) At David's trial, the first witness for the prosecution is Scalpel, the coroner. Scalpel testifies that she took possession of Claire's body shortly after arriving on the scene. Scalpel then describes the condition of the body, including the results of an autopsy. Among other things, the autopsy revealed that Claire was not pregnant at the time of her death.

(2) The second witness for the prosecution is Nosey. Nosey testifies that she works in room 1500 in the Babbo Building, which is directly across the street from the Ajax Building. Room 1500 is on the fifteenth floor of the Babbo Building, which puts it slightly below room 1601 of the Ajax Building. Nosey testifies that from room 1500 of the Babbo Building she has a good view of the window of room 1601 of the Ajax Building. Nosey further testifies that shortly before noon on June 1 she had her back to the window of room 1500 of the Babbo Building. She heard a scream, turned, and saw a body falling. She looked up at the window and saw what appeared to be the face of a man at the window of room 1601 of the Ajax Building. If you were defense counsel in this case, what type of questions would you want to ask Nosey on cross-examination?

(3) The third witness for the prosecution at David's trial is Officer Kojak. Kojak testifies that he is a member of the municipal homicide squad. He was assigned to investigate Claire's death. As part of his investigation, Kojak spoke to Agnes at 6 P.M. on June 1. Kojak proposes to testify that during this conversation Agnes told him that David shoved Claire, who then fell to her death. Defendant objects. What ruling and why? Is Kojak's proposed testimony hearsay? Should it be admitted anyhow? If it is not hearsay, should it nonetheless be excluded?

(4) The fourth witness for the prosecution is Belle. Belle testifies that she was in room 1601 at the time Claire fell to her death and that she saw what happened. Belle further testifies that she was interviewed by Kojak at her home at 7 P.M. on June 1. Belle testifies that during that interview she told Kojak that David pushed Claire out the window. Defendant objects and moves to strike. What ruling and why? Is Belle's testimony hearsay? If it is hearsay, should it be admitted anyhow? If it is not hearsay, should it nonetheless be excluded?

(5) The prosecution offers as People's Exhibit *A* a document found face up on the copying machine in room 1601 immediately after Claire's fall. The document is identified and authenticated as being in Claire's handwriting. It states:

> David,
>   I will never give in to your pressure. Even though you may be the father of my unborn child, I will not be forced into an abortion that I don't want. I will have the baby and sue you for support.
>
> Claire

David objects to the admission of the exhibit. What ruling and why? Is Exhibit *A* hearsay? If it is hearsay, should it be admitted anyhow? If it is not hearsay, should it nonetheless be excluded?

R. PARK, McCORMICK ON EVIDENCE AND THE CONCEPT OF HEARSAY: A CRITICAL ANALYSIS FOLLOWED BY SUGGESTIONS TO LAW TEACHERS
65 Minn. L. Rev. 423 (1981)

Definitions of hearsay are commonly either assertion-oriented or declarant-oriented. An assertion-oriented definition focuses on whether an out-of-court assertion will be used to prove the truth of what it asserts, while a declarant-oriented definition focuses on whether the use of the utterance will require reliance on the credibility of the out-of-court declarant.

The exposition of the concept of hearsay in *McCormick* draws on both of these traditions. The book defines hearsay as follows:

> Hearsay evidence is testimony in court, or written evidence, of a statement made out of court, the statement being offered as an assertion to show the truth of matters asserted therein, and thus resting for its value upon the credibility of the out-of-court asserter.

Although this definition is essentially assertion-oriented, the final clause introduces a declarant-oriented aspect by stating that when an utterance is offered for its truth, then it rests for value on the declarant's credibility. The text immediately following the definition goes further, and indicates that when an assertion is *not* offered for its truth, then it does not depend for value on the declarant's credibility. Taken together, these passages in *McCormick* suggest that the assertion-oriented and declarant-oriented definitions are functionally equivalent.

This suggestion is misleading, since choice of one definition over the other can lead to different results. An utterance offered as a falsehood provides the most vivid example. Suppose that X is charged with committing a crime in Boston. The police talk to X's wife, who tells them that X was with her in Denver on the day in question. The wife's statement is demonstrably false, and the prosecution seeks to use it against X for the inference that X's wife lied because she knew him to be guilty. Under an assertion-oriented definition, the wife's statement is not hearsay because it is not offered to prove the truth of the matter asserted. Under a declarant-oriented definition, however, the statement would be hearsay because the trier's use of it requires reliance on the wife's powers of memory, perception, and narration.[11]

McCormick itself deems certain utterances nonhearsay even though they depend for value upon the declarant's credibility. For example, the book states that the utterance "Harold is the finest of my sons," offered to prove that the declarant was fond of Harold, is nonhearsay because it is not offered to show the truth of its assertion. Under a declarant-oriented definition, however, the utterance would be hearsay because it rests on the declarant's sincerity and narrative ability.[13]

L. TRIBE, TRIANGULATING HEARSAY
87 Harv. L. Rev. 957, 957-961 (1974)

While another elaborate argument for the reform of hearsay law might be in order, the purpose of this Comment is a more modest one. It will present a heuristic device which I believe can aid in the analysis of the hearsay rule and its exceptions by exposing the rule's structure and the underlying values at stake. The goal, in the first instance, is to assist

---

11. The wife might not have intended a cover-up; she may simply have been mistaken about the date of her husband's presence in Denver. Even if she intended to mislead the police because she believed her husband was guilty, her belief may have been based on a bare suspicion or an insane delusion. Alternatively, she may have misspoken, saying "June first" when she meant "July first." Thus, substantial reliance on her memory, perception, and narrative ability are required in order to reach the final inference that her husband is guilty. For examples of declarant-oriented definitions that would seem to classify the wife's utterance as hearsay, see R. Lempert & S. Saltzburg [A Modern Approach to Evidence 340-341 (1977)], at 340-45; Tribe [Triangulating Hearsay, 87 Harv. L. Rev. 957, 959 (1974)], at 959-60. See also Morgan [Hearsay Dangers and the Application of the Hearsay Concept, 62 Harv. L. Rev. 196-212 (1948)], at 218-19.

13. The utterance rests on the declarant's narrative ability because it loses value if the declarant meant to say "Arnold is the finest of my sons" or "Harold is the first of my sons." It rests on the declarant's sincerity because a deliberate lie about Harold's character, for example to his prospective employer, would undercut the inference that the declarant was especially fond of Harold. Another hearsay danger, ambiguity of inference, is also present because the declarant might genuinely believe that Harold is the finest, but might nevertheless be more fond of his youngest son Joe.

students of the law in understanding an otherwise complex area. No less important, by directing the attention of students, practitioners, and judges toward structure and policy and away from cookbook formulas of rule and exception, the device may dramatize the inconsistencies and oddities that pervade hearsay law. And that may be a first step to future reform.

I. THE TESTIMONIAL TRIANGLE

The basic hearsay problem is that of forging a reliable chain of inferences, from an act or utterance of a person not subject to contemporaneous in-court cross-examination about that act or utterance, to an event that the act or utterance is supposed to reflect. Typically, the first link in the required chain of inferences is the link from the act or utterance to the belief it is thought to express or indicate. It is helpful to think of this link as involving a "trip" into the head of the person responsible for the act or utterance (the declarant) to see what he or she was really thinking when the act occurred. The second link is the one from the declarant's assumed belief to a conclusion about some external event that is supposed to have triggered the belief, or that is linked to the belief in some other way. This link involves a trip out of the head of the declarant, in order to match the declarant's assumed belief with the external reality sought to be demonstrated.

The trier must obviously employ such a chain of inferences whenever a witness testifies in court. But the process has long been regarded as particularly suspect when the act or utterance is not one made in court, under oath, by a person whose demeanor at the time is witnessed by the trier, and under circumstances permitting immediate cross-examination by counsel in order to probe possible inaccuracies in the inferential chain. These inaccuracies are usually attributed to the four testimonial infirmities of ambiguity, insincerity, faulty perception, and erroneous memory. In the absence of special reasons, the perceived untrustworthiness of such an out-of-court act or utterance has led the Anglo-Saxon legal system to exclude it as hearsay despite its potentially probative value.

There exists a rather simple way of schematizing all of this in terms of an elementary geometric construct that serves to structure its several related elements. The construct might be called "the testimonial triangle." By making graphic the path of inferences, and by functionally grouping problems encountered along the path, the triangle makes it easier both to identify when a hearsay problem exists and to structure consideration of the appropriateness of exceptions to the rule that bars hearsay inferences.

The diagram is as follows:

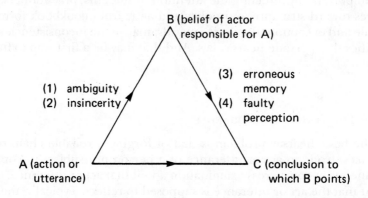

If we use the diagram to trace the inferential path the trier must follow, we begin at the lower left vertex of the triangle (*A*), which represents the declarant's (*X*'s) act or assertion. The path first takes us to the upper vertex (*B*), representing *X*'s belief in what his or her act or assertion suggests, and then takes us to the lower right vertex (*C*), representing the external reality suggested by *X*'s belief. When "A" is used to prove "C" along the path through "B," a traditional hearsay problem exists and the use of the act or assertion as evidence is disallowed upon proper objection in the absence of some special reason to permit it.

It is of course a simple matter to locate the four testimonial infirmities on the triangle to show where and how they might impede the process of utterance. To go from "A" to "B," the declarant's belief, one must remove the obstacles of (1) ambiguity and (2) insincerity. To go from "B" to "C," the external fact, one must further remove the obstacles of (3) erroneous memory and (4) faulty perception.

When it is possible to go directly from "A" to "C" with no detour through "B," there is no hearsay problem unless the validity of the trier's conclusion depends upon an implicit path through "B."[9] Suppose, for example, that the issue in a lawsuit is whether the Government took

9. An uncompromising behaviorist might insist that no detour through mental states is ever necessary because every trip from an act or utterance "A" to a conclusion "C" is reducible to a circumstantial inference about the statistical frequency with which "C" is present when "A" is present. There are difficulties with accepting the behaviorist perspective as a coherent one. See Chomsky, A Review of B.F. Skinner's Verbal Behavior, 35 Language 26 (1959); Chomsky, The Case Against B.F. Skinner, New York Review of Books, Dec. 30, 1971, at 18. But even if one does adopt such a perspective, it does not follow that the trier's way of using the evidence "A" will in fact mirror that perspective, for the trier is likely to reason about states of mind even if it is in some sense incorrect or unnecessary to do so. Moreover, the connection between "A" and "C" may well be such that the frequency with which the latter accompanies the former depends upon the actor's testimonial capacities so that, even from a behaviorist perspective, information about a declarant's use of language, tendency to lie, eyesight, and so forth, may increase or decrease the statistical correlation between the utterance and the fact reported.

adequate safety precautions in connection with the nuclear test at Amchitka in 1971. James Schlesinger, then Chairman of the Atomic Energy Commission, "told reporters at Elmendorf Air Force Base outside Anchorage that he was taking his wife . . . and daughters . . . with him [to the site of the Amchitka blast] in response to Alaska Gov. William E. Egan's invitation. Egan strongly disapprove[d] of the test." In these circumstances, the trip from "A," the Chairman's proposed travel with his family to the site of the blast, to "C," the conclusion that the blast was reasonably safe, may appear at first to be purely "circumstantial," but in fact that trip requires a journey into the Chairman's head and out again — a journey through the belief "B" suggested by his willingness to be near the blast with his family. The journey from "A" to "B" involves problems of possible ambiguity and of insincerity in that the Chairman was apparently seeking to dispel fears of danger, so that his act may not bespeak an actual belief in the test's safety. And the journey from "B" to "C" involves problems of memory and perception in that he may not have recalled all the relevant data and may have misperceived such data in the first instance, so that his belief in the test's safety, even if we assume the journey from "A" to "B" safely completed, may not correspond to the facts sought to be demonstrated. On both legs of the triangle, therefore, there are testimonial infirmities that cross-examination contemporaneous with the act "A" could help to expose.

By contrast, when the trier's inference can proceed from "A" directly to "C," the infirmities of hearsay do not arise. . . .

Problem: Hot Goods

Charge: knowingly receiving stolen goods (two diamond earrings) by D from Jenkens on June 1. At trial, the prosecution makes out a prima facie case and rests. D proposes to testify that Jenkens gave him the diamond earrings on June 1, told D that he had bought them as an anniversary gift for his wife, and asked him to keep them until Mr. and Mrs. Jenkens's anniversary on June 7, so that Jenkens could surprise his wife. D further testifies that he believed Jenkens. The D.A. objects. What ruling and why? Is D's proposed testimony hearsay? If it is hearsay, should it be admitted anyhow? If it is not hearsay, should it nonetheless be excluded?

Problem: Slander per Se

Action for defamation. At trial, P is the first witness. P proposes to testify that D said, in the presence of several people, "P is now and has always been a robber and thief." *D* objects. What ruling and why? Is *P*'s proposed testimony hearsay? If it is hearsay, should it be admitted anyhow? If it is not hearsay, should it nonetheless be excluded?

Problem: Speaking Out

Action for damages to *P*'s child, *C*, which allegedly occurred when *D* struck *C*, causing *C* to suffer permanent paralysis of her vocal chords. *D*'s answer is a general denial. In the second week of trial, *D* offers *W* to testify that the day before he heard *C* say, "I can speak." *P* objects. What ruling and why? What if *W* proposes to testify that he heard *C* say, "Don't step on a crack or you'll break your mother's back"?

Problem: "Palming Off"

P Knife Manufacturing Company v. *D* Knife Manufacturing Company for *D*'s alleged unfair methods of competition in "palming off" a knife made by *D* to look like *P*'s knife. *D* denies generally. At trial, *P* offers a letter it received from the National Business Gifts Company, a jobber of pocket knives, which states, "We did not find this knife in the catalogue but are sure you made it." The enclosed knife was manufactured by *D*. Admissible?

Problem: Summary Judgment

Federal court action against Los Angeles Police Department officers for an injunction and declaratory relief arising out of the search and seizure of certain items from the plaintiff, the Hollywood Free Paper. Plaintiff alleges that defendants' search and seizure violated the first and fourth amendments to the U.S. Constitution and the qualified journalist's privilege recognized by some members of the Supreme Court in Branzburg v. Hayes. In support of its motion for summary judgment, plaintiff submits an affidavit from Robert Woodstein, a reporter for the Washington Boast. Woodstein's affidavit states that press searches tend to chill confidential news sources in and out of government. The affidavit contains several examples in which Woodstein allegedly lost sources of his own after he was subpoenaed by the Attorney General and forced to disclose the identity of "Deep Throat," a source for a particularly sensitive story that died when the Attorney General's subpoena was served. Defendants object and move to strike the affidavits on the grounds of hearsay. What ruling and why?

Problem: Contractual Terms and Hearsay

Action for the purchase price of a television set bought by *D* from the Acme TV Company. *P*'s complaint alleges the following:

(1) Acme sold and delivered a television to *D* on June 1 on credit;
(2) *D* has failed to pay for the television in breach of the credit agreement;
(3) Acme assigned its claim to *P* on September 1;
(4) On September 15 *P* demanded payment from *D*; *D* refused; and
(5) *P*'s claim is now due and unpaid, whereby *P* demands judgment for the purchase price.

D's answer alleges that *P* is not the real party in interest. At trial, *P* testifies that on September 1 he proposed to Acme that Acme assign its claim to him and that Acme then executed a document marked Plaintiff's Exhibit 1 for identification. Exhibit 1 states: "Acme TV Company hereby assigns its claim against *D* to *P* for good and valuable consideration." *D* objects and moves to strike *P*'s testimony and to exclude Exhibit 1. What ruling and why?

Problem: The Dissatisfied Purchaser

P, administrator of Sucker's estate, v. Desert Land Co. for a return of the down payment made by Sucker on real estate located in the Mojave Desert, California, and sold by Desert. At trial, *P* offers two exhibits:

(1) *P1*, an advertisement from the New York Times for Mojave Garden Lots. The ad says, "Make a down payment to reserve your lot and pay later by installments. If you inspect your lot within 90 days and state your dissatisfaction to us and ask for your down payment back, it will be returned, no questions asked."

(2) *P2*, a letter from Sucker to Desert Land that says, "I have inspected my lot. I am dissatisfied. I demand my money back."

Defendant objects to the introduction of the exhibits. Are they hearsay? If so, should they be admitted anyhow? If not, should they be excluded anyhow?

Problem: The "Corn-Crib" Case

Plaintiff Hanson owned and leased a farm to Schrik. Under the lease, Schrik was to pay Hanson 2/5 of the corn grown in return for the use of the land. In other words, Schrik was a sharecropper. To obtain money for seed and fertilizer, Schrik gave a mortgage to defendant bank on his share of the crops. The bottom fell out of the corn market, and Schrik's tenant's mortgaged property was sold at auction by the bank with his permission. At this sale, a crib of corn containing 393 bushels was sold by the bank to defendant Johnson. Hanson contended that this corn was his share of the crop and thus that it had been converted by defendants.

In an effort to prove that the corn was part of his share, Hanson testified, over the objection of hearsay and self-serving, that when Schrik was about through husking corn he was on the farm and the tenant pointed out the corn in question and said: "Mr. Hanson, here is your corn for this year; this double crib here and this single crib here is your share for this year's corn; this belongs to you, Mr. Hanson." A bystander was called and against the same objection testified to having heard the talk in substantially the same language.

(1) Is plaintiff's proposed testimony hearsay? If it is, should it be admitted anyhow? If it is not, should it nonetheless be excluded?

(2) What if plaintiff called another bystander to testify that after the tenant had husked the corn, tenant said to the second bystander, out of the presence of Hanson, "This double crib here and this single crib here is Mr. Hanson's share for this year's corn; this belongs to him." Would this testimony be hearsay?

NOTE: WHEN CONDUCT PRESENTS HEARSAY PROBLEMS

As the Assault on Massachusetts Avenue problem demonstrates, hearsay issues arise when conduct is treated as an assertion. However, assume that the conduct is nonassertive. What hearsay problem does nonassertive conduct present?

In relying upon nonassertive conduct, the chain of inferences involves a trip through the mind of a nontestifying actor and conceptually presents hearsay problems. But Rule 801(a)(2) defines "statement" in a way that excludes such nonassertive conduct. Hence, nonassertive conduct is conceptually, but not legally, hearsay. Problems arise because it is sometimes difficult to grasp what is and what is not an "assertion"; conduct often has both communicative and noncommunicative purposes. Under Rule 801(a), conduct is not an assertion unless it is *intended* to communicate something. The Advisory Committee's Note to Rule 801(a) states that the burden is on the party claiming that an intention to assert existed; "ambiguous and doubtful cases will be resolved . . . in favor of admissibility."

Yet even when the conduct is clearly nonassertive, and thus not hearsay under the Federal Rules, the factfinder may still be relying on the testimonial capacities of the out-of-court actor. Further, "inferential assertions"—assertions about something other than the point for which the statement is offered—may be admissible as nonhearsay under the Federal Rules approach despite their dependence on the testimonial capacities of the out-of-court declarant. More than ever, to find one's way through this thicket, one must understand the purpose for which the statement is offered and the intention of the assertion or reason for the conduct.

J. FALKNOR, THE "HEAR-SAY" RULE AS A "SEE-DO" RULE: EVIDENCE OF CONDUCT
33 Rocky Mt. L. Rev. 133-138 (1960)

It is time to go to lunch. When you left home for the office in the morning it was raining and you brought your umbrella. Will you need it at lunchtime? You consult your secretary, she looks out the window, and tells you that you had better take your umbrella. If, in some subsequent litigation, the question should arise whether it was raining when you went out to lunch, would the secretary be permitted to testify that when she looked out she saw a number of passers-by with their umbrellas up? More precisely, would her testimony as to what she *saw* these people *do* be equated to what she would have *heard* them *say*, had she called out, asked them whether it was raining, and they had replied that it was?

Or, take another one: You drive up to signal-controlled intersection and pull up behind a large truck and trailer which has stopped at the near side of the intersection. The truck and trailer block your view of the traffic light. In a moment or so the truck moves ahead and you follow it. If, in subsequent litigation, the question arises whether the light had changed to green when you started up, may you testify, as tending to show that the light had changed, that the truck driver had moved ahead before you did? More precisely, would your testimony as to what you *saw* the truck driver *do*, be equated to what you would have *heard* him *say* had he, before moving ahead, called back to tell you that the light had changed?

Of course, if, in either of these supposititious situations, the conduct proposed to be shown is to be treated as merely equivalent to an assertion of the fact the evidence is offered to establish, we are in trouble with the hearsay rule. And by many cases (probably in most of those where the hearsay question has been identified and raised) evidence of extra-judicial conduct, relevant only as an "implied assertion" of the fact the evidence is offered to prove, is within the hearsay ban. Put otherwise, where evidence of non-verbal conduct is relevant only as supporting inferences from the conduct to the belief of the actor and thence to the truth of his belief, prevailing doctrine stigmatizes the evidence as hearsay, inadmissible unless accommodated within one of the exceptions to the rule. Thus, it seems quite correct to say that in situations of this sort, the "hear-say" rule actually operates as a "see-do" rule.

In the instances supposed, the conduct offered to be proven was completely "non-verbal"; but an identical problem arises where the conduct, although "verbal," is relevant, not as tending to prove the truth of what was said, but circumstantially, that is, as manifesting a belief in the existence of the fact the evidence is offered to prove. As a matter of fact the leading case equating an "implied" to an "express" assertion and thus stigmatizing the evidence as hearsay, concerned the admissibility, in a will contest, of evidence of the writing of a letter to the testator by the vicar of the parish about a matter of consequence, relevant not as evidence of the truth of anything in the letter, but as manifesting the vicar's apparent belief in the testator's mental competency as tending to prove competency.

And in a Texas case, where defendant was charged with stealing his grandmother's cow which he admittedly sold while she was away, his defense being that she had authorized him to sell the cow, evidence (offered by the prosecution) that on her return home she demanded of the purchaser the cow rather than the balance of the purchase price, was held inadmissible as hearsay; it amounted merely to her extra-judicial "implied" assertion that she had not authorized the sale. A similar question has arisen in prosecutions for the maintenance of a betting establishment when the prosecution has offered to prove incoming telephone calls, during the raid, by callers seeking to place bets. Here again, while the conduct sought to be shown is "verbal," relevancy does not depend on a direct hearsay use of the utterances but only upon acceptance of the calls as "implied" assertions of the character of the place to which the calls were directed.

The same problem arises with respect to evidence of "non-action" or "silence" when relevant as justifying inferences from the non-action of the individual to his apparent belief and thence to the truth of that belief. While there is a division of authority with respect to the applicability of the hearsay rule to evidence of this sort, it is undoubtedly correct to say that in most cases where the hearsay objection has been urged, it has been sustained. The typical case has to do with the admissibility, on an issue of the quality of goods, of evidence of the failure of other purchasers to complain.

In any of these situations, the hearsay objection is likely to be overlooked. This is especially so when the evidence concerns "nonverbal" conduct because the hearsay rule is almost always, in the abstract, phrased in terms of "statements" or "utterances" and the possible application of the rule to "conduct" may not be immediately apparent. And the same is true, although perhaps to a lesser degree, when the evidence is of "verbal" conduct relevant only circumstantially. Cases are legion consequently where the hearsay objection, with strong supporting authority, might have been raised but was not.

But ought the hearsay rule be deemed applicable to evidence of conduct? As McCormick has observed, the problem "has only once received any adequate discussion in any decided case," i.e., in Wright v. Tatham. . . . And even in that case the court did not pursue its inquiry beyond the point of concluding that evidence of an "implied" assertion would be inadmissible. But as has been pointed out more than once (although I find no *judicial* recognition of the difference), the "implied" assertion is, from the hearsay standpoint, not nearly as vulnerable as an express assertion of the fact which the evidence is offered to establish.

This is on the assumption that the conduct was "non-assertive"; that the passers-by had their umbrellas up for the sake of keeping dry, not for the purpose of telling anyone it was raining; that the truck driver started up for the sake of resuming his journey, not for the purpose of telling anyone that the light had changed; that the vicar wrote the letter to the testator for the purpose of settling the dispute with the latter, rather than with any idea of expressing his opinion of the testator's sanity. And in the typical "conduct as hearsay" case this assumption will be quite justifiable.

On this assumption, it is clear that evidence of conduct must be taken as freed from at least one of the hearsay dangers, i.e., mendacity. A man does not lie to himself. Put otherwise, if in doing what he does a man has no intention of asserting the existence or non-existence of a fact, it would appear that the trustworthiness of evidence of this conduct is the same whether he is an egregious liar or a paragon of veracity. Accordingly, the lack of opportunity for cross-examination in relation to his veracity or lack of it, would seem to be of no substantial importance. Accordingly, the usual judicial disposition to equate the "implied" to the "express" assertion is very questionable.

This is not to say that the "implied" assertion is completely free of hearsay infirmities or that cross-examination of the individual would not be helpful. His opportunity to observe the event or condition in question, the quality of the sense-impressions which he received, and of his recollection, are all matters which bear upon the trustworthiness of his conduct, and, ideally, these ought to be subject to being probed by cross-examination. Nonetheless, the absence of the danger of misrepresentation does work strongly in favor of by-passing the hearsay objection, at least where the evidence of conduct is cogently probative. And it will be, where the action taken was important to the individual in his own affairs, e.g., the action of the vicar in communicating with the testator, the action of the truck driver in moving ahead. . . .

Accordingly, it has sometimes been suggested, that the admissibility of evidence of non-assertive conduct should depend on a preliminary finding by the judge that the conduct was of a sort "as to give reasonable assurance of trustworthiness," that is to say, that it was of substantial importance to the actor in his own affairs. But for application in the "heat and hurry" of the trial, such a solution leaves a good deal to be desired. As Thayer observed, "we should have a system of evidence, simple, aiming straight at the substance of justice, not nice or refined in its details, not too rigid, easily grasped and easily applied."

The "simple, easily grasped and easily applied" rule, "not nice or refined in its details," would seem to be one which would eliminate completely the hearsay stigma from evidence of non-assertive conduct. Because such conduct is evidently more dependable than an assertion, there is rational basis for the differentiation. And there is a cogent practical argument for such a rule in the circumstance that experience has shown that very often, probably more often than not, and understandably, the hearsay objection to evidence of non-assertive conduct is overlooked in practice with the result that the present doctrine operates very unevenly.

Such is the solution proposed by the [Federal] Rules of Evidence. . . . Non-assertive conduct is excluded from the definition of hearsay. Precisely, a statement (so as to be subject to the hearsay ban) would include only "non-verbal conduct of a person intended by him as a substitute for words in expressing the matter stated." This, it seems clear, would operate to eliminate the hearsay stigma from evidence of conduct unless it appeared to the judge that what was done was done for the sake of asserting the fact the evidence is now offered to establish.

This does not mean that all non-assertive conduct would be provable. There would remain the question of relevancy; and even though the evidence appeared to possess some slight probative value, it would be subject to exclusion under Uniform Rule 45 if the judge concluded that probative value was "substantially out-weighed" by the "counter-factors" enumerated in that rule: that to receive the evidence would take more time than it is worth, that it would confuse the issues, mislead the jury, create undue prejudice or unfairly surprise the opponent. . . .

Problem: Captain Cook and Davey Jones

Action for loss of *P*'s goods when *D* Shipping Company's ship went down in calm waters off Liverpool. *P* alleges that *D*'s ship was not seaworthy. *D* generally denies. At trial, *D* offers evidence that Captain Cook, a sea captain with 30 years' experience, inspected every part of its ship before setting sail on it with his own family on board. *P* objects. What ruling and why? Is this evidence hearsay? If so, should it be admitted anyhow? If not, should it nonetheless be excluded?

Problem: Black Crepe

(1) Action against *D* Insurance Company to recover on a life insurance policy on Howard's life. The policy expired midnight May 31. Howard's death occurred the week of May 31, but there is a disputed issue

of fact as to whether death occurred prior to or after May 31. At trial, P calls White to testify that on the afternoon of May 31 he saw the doorway to Howard's house hung with black crepe and bedecked with white lilies.

(2) At trial, P calls Weir to testify that he saw Dr. Munroe, Howard's attending physician, examine Howard on May 31 and then pull the bed sheet up over Howard's head.

Problem: Hot Pursuit?

At 11:30 P.M. Dr. and Mrs. David Alberstrom returned to their suburban Washington home from a night at the opera. As Dr. Alberstrom entered the living room, he was attacked by a knife-wielding man coming from the dining room. Dr. Alberstrom and the stranger struggled for some minutes, but the intruder escaped, leaving the doctor wounded on the floor. Mrs. Alberstrom rushed to help her husband. She noticed that he had been stabbed and was bleeding. They got into their car to go to the hospital, with the doctor behind the steering wheel. Proceeding down the country road leading from the Alberstrom house, the doctor noticed a man running along the side of the road. As the car drew even with the man, it swerved sharply to the right, striking the man and coming to rest in a ditch at the side of the road. Dr. Alberstrom was slumped over the wheel unconscious. An ambulance called to the scene took both Dr. Alberstrom and the injured pedestrian to the hospital. Dr. Alberstrom died of his knife wounds without regaining consciousness. The pedestrian recovered from his injuries and was subsequently charged with attempted robbery and the murder of Dr. Alberstrom.

At defendant's trial the prosecution offers Mrs. Alberstrom's testimony to the above on the issue of the identity of the knife-wielding intruder. Defendant objects. What ruling and why? What result if Mrs. Alberstrom's proffered testimony included Dr. Alberstrom's exclaiming "That's him!" just before the car swerved into the defendant?

Problem: Ptomaine Poisoning at the Greasy Spoon

Action against the Greasy Spoon Restaurant. P claims she was served spoiled baked beans by the Greasy Spoon on June 1 and got ptomaine poisoning as a result. At trial, defendant offers to prove that the Greasy Spoon had a large pot of beans in the kitchen on June 1, that P was served from this pot, that at least 20 other Greasy Spoon patrons were served from the same pot, and that the Greasy Spoon received no other complaints. *P* objects. What ruling and why? What is the nature of the hearsay problem presented by this case? What result under the Federal Rules?

CAMERON v. WALTON-MARCH, INC.
No. 88-7279, 1990 U.S. Dist. LEXIS 4815 (E.D. Pa. Apr. 24, 1990)

DUBOIS, J.

This case is before the Court on the Motion of plaintiffs, Windell and Shirley Cameron, for a new Trial. For the reasons stated below, plaintiffs' Motion will be denied.

The case arises out of injuries to the hands of Windell Cameron, a trolley operator for Southeastern Pennsylvania Transportation Authority ("SEPTA"), allegedly caused by contact with a trolley bar which had been cleaned with Prime Time, a product of Walton-March, Inc. Plaintiffs' claim is based on the allegation that Walton-March, knowing of the dangerous propensities of its product, failed to adequately warn and instruct users to avoid contact with the product which remained on surfaces it was used to clean.

The case was tried before a jury which, on December 11, 1989, in response to Special Interrogatories, determined that the product, Prime Time, was not defective.

Plaintiffs' Motion for New Trial is based on three alleged trial errors, as follows:

1. The Court improperly admitted into evidence the testimony of Richard Cameron, an employee of Walton-March, regarding the alleged absence of prior complaints concerning Prime Time because Walton-March failed to lay a proper foundation. . . .

Plaintiffs tried the case under §402A of the Restatement (Second) of Torts, claiming that Walton-March's product, Prime Time, was defective. More specifically, plaintiffs claimed that the product was defective because it was not accompanied by proper warnings and instructions concerning its use. It was plaintiffs' contention that Windell Cameron's injury was caused by contact dermatitis, which, in turn, was caused by an allergic reaction to an ingredient or ingredients contained in Prime Time.

The case was submitted to the jury under the law set forth in Comment (j) to §402A of the Restatement (Second) of Torts. Pursuant to Comment (j), the jury was instructed that a defendant is entitled to assume that those persons with common allergies will be aware of them, and a defendant is not required to warn against them. On the other hand, the jury was charged that when a product contains ingredients to which a substantial number of the population is allergic and the ingredients are ones whose danger is not generally known to the public, a defendant is required to give warnings and instructions if the defendant has knowledge, or by the application of reasonable developed human skill and foresight, should have knowledge of the presence of the ingredient and the danger. There were no exceptions taken to that charge, and that charge is not implicated in plaintiffs' Motion for New Trial. . . .

Richard Cameron was the Customer Service Manager and former Sales Administration Manager of Walton-March, Inc. He testified that he had been continuously employed by Walton-March from November of 1982 through the present. In 1982 he was a Sales Administrator; in 1984 he was promoted to Sales Administration Manager; and in 1986 he became the Customer Service Manager. In all those positions, he said he was familiar with the manner in which Walton-March handled complaints relating to products, including complaints of health problems associated with the use of Prime Time, and the procedure for opening and maintaining files relating to such complaints.

Walton-March offered the testimony of Richard Cameron to establish that Walton-March had received no prior complaints of health problems associated with the use of Prime Time. Such evidence was offered on the question whether Prime Time contained ingredients to which a substantial number of the population was allergic.

Under the Federal Rules of Evidence, the absence of an entry made in the regular course of business is admissible to prove the non-occurrence or non-existence of the matter.

The only requirement for the use of evidence to prove the non-existence or non-occurrence of an event is the laying of a proper foundation. In order to lay a proper foundation it is not essential that the offering witness be the person who actually recorded the events. To the contrary, it is sufficient that the witness is able to testify with respect to the way in which the records were made and the fact that they were retained in the regular course of business.

During the trial, at the conclusion of a trial day, Richard Cameron's discovery deposition and video trial deposition were taken. The Court, after reading the deposition transcripts, concluded that a proper foundation had not been laid for the introduction of testimony concerning the absence of complaints about Prime Time, and accordingly, Mr. Cameron was required to testify in person. At that time, he testified that, during the period November of 1982 to the date of his testimony, he was familiar with the way in which Walton-March handled product complaints. In elaborating on that testimony, he explained that, after receipt of each complaint, a letter would be written by someone at Walton-March to the complaining customer, and a file was created. All communications regarding customer complaints were placed in the complaint files.

Richard Cameron testified that he had physical possession of the complaint files since about 1984, and that the complaint files, before and after that date, were kept in the regular course of business activity of Walton-March.

Based on Richard Cameron's testimony, the Court determined that a proper foundation had been laid and permitted Mr. Cameron to testify that, after reviewing all of the complaint files, he could find no reference to any complaints from any users of Prime Time or any other complaints relating to Prime Time.

Plaintiffs argue that Richard Cameron's testimony about the absence of prior complaints involving Prime Time should not have been received into evidence as proof of the safety of the product for two reasons. First, plaintiffs argue that defendant failed to establish that records of complaints were kept in the regular course of Walton-March's business. For the reasons stated above, I affirm the ruling that I made at trial in which I rejected this contention.

Second, plaintiffs argue that Richard Cameron's testimony about lack of prior complaints should have been excluded because Walton-March "neglected to prove that Prime Time was being used or came into contact with users in the same way that Mr. Cameron came into contact with Prime Time; i.e., rubbing his hands directly on a surface that probably was coated with Prime Time ingredients in their pure, undiluted form." The Court rejects plaintiffs' position. The evidence of lack of prior complaints was not offered to prove the safety of Prime Time as plaintiff suggests; rather, it was admitted as proof that a substantial number of the population are not allergic to the ingredients in the product. While substantial similarity of conditions of use of a product must be established in order to prove that prior complaints constituted motive of a dangerous or defective condition, it need not be established by the offering party when evidence of absence of prior complaints is introduced merely to show that a substantial number of the population is not allergic to any ingredients in the product. Furthermore, even if defendant had the burden of establishing similarity of circumstance, it met that burden. Defendant offered sufficient evidence to establish that trolley bars on SEPTA trolleys were regularly cleaned with Prime Time in the manner that the trolley bar at issue had been cleaned before Windell Cameron came into contact with it. See, e.g., Testimony of David Stumpo, Superintendent of Transit Car Maintenance for the Southeastern Pennsylvania Transportation Authority; Testimony of Robert Hughes, Shop Foreman for Southeastern Pennsylvania Transportation Authority. . . .

This case is before the Court on the Motion of plaintiffs, Windell and Shirley Cameron, for a New Trial. For the reasons stated below, plaintiffs' Motion will be denied.

The case arises out of injuries to the hands of Windell Cameron, a trolley operator. The Motion of plaintiffs for a New Trial is denied.

How would the Federal Rules treat this hearsay issue? What is the unstated hearsay problem in *Walton-March*?

Problem: "Thieves Will Out"

Charge: murder in the first degree. M.O.: shotgun blast in the face. Defense: alibi. At *D*'s trial the government calls *W* to testify that just before the shooting, the victim, *V*, handed him a slip of paper with *D*'s nickname and telephone number on it. *V* told *W* to call the police if *V* were not home by 3 P.M. the next day and give the police the slip of paper. *D* objects to *W*'s proposed testimony and to the introduction of the slip of paper. What ruling and why? Would the case for admission be stronger or weaker if the defense were self-defense or accident?

Problem: The Briefcase

Charge: Unlawful possession of a proscribed substance, to wit, marijuana. At *D*'s trial, the prosecution offers into evidence a briefcase found by the police at *D*'s office. According to the testifying officer, the briefcase contained more than one kilogram of marijuana. *D* works at the Acme Insurance Company. His office is a large open room with no dividers in which 25 people work at computer workstations. The only other evidence to link the briefcase to the defendant is the monogram on the briefcase consisting of the letters "WGM." The defendant's name is William G. Mellon. *D* objects to the introduction of the briefcase with the monogram on grounds of hearsay. What ruling and why?

B. Statements of a Party Opponent

This and the following sections explore the application of the rule against hearsay in situations where an out-of-court statement is offered for the truth of the matter it asserts. In this section, the out-of-court statement is that of a party or its agents; cross-examination of the declarant sometimes is not possible or practical, but if other conditions are satisfied, the statement is admitted. Why? Is it because such statements are inherently reliable? Because there is no "right" to cross-examination in such circumstances, or because there is no "need" to cross-examine? Note that many admissions are self-serving; also, that in many of these cases where the statement is that of a party's agent, the agent may not be available at trial to explain or deny the statement. Is an estoppel-like "game" theory of litigation at work in this area? What values would such a theory further?

Problem: He Who Laughs Last . . .

City *A* taxes real property on the basis of 100 percent of value. The city tax collector appraises Cheat's property at $100,000 and taxes it accordingly. Cheat files an abatement request stating that his property is worth only $50,000. Later, the state condemns Cheat's property under its power of eminent domain. The value of the property is disputed. The state claims the property is worth $50,000; Cheat claims it is worth $100,000.

(1) At the trial of this issue, the state offers Cheat's abatement request filing. Cheat objects. What ruling and why? If admitted, what is the reasoning on which the decision rests?

(2) Suppose the state claims the value of the property is $30,000. Cheat offers the abatement request filing. The state objects. What ruling and why?

(3) At trial Cheat offers the city tax assessment. The state objects. What ruling and why?

Problem: "If You're Gonna Get Hit, Get Hit by a Rolls"

D's Rolls-Royce strikes *P* while *P* is crossing the street in a crosswalk with the light. *D*'s chauffeur, *C*, who was in the Rolls at the time, and *P* are the only eyewitnesses. *P* has amnesia as a result of the accident and cannot remember what occurred. *P*, by his guardian, *G*, sues *D* for damages. The issue is *C*'s negligence *vel non*.

(1) At trial, *P* offers a letter by *D* properly authenticated, which says in part, "*C*'s negligence caused *P*'s injuries." *D* objects. What ruling and why?

(2) If *P* rests after the above and *D* moves for a nonsuit, what ruling and why?

(3) *P* also calls *W*, a bystander who ran up after the accident, to testify that *C* said to *P*, "I'm *D*'s chauffeur. It was all my fault. Don't worry, I'm sure that *D* will make this good." *D* objects. What ruling and why?

What indicia of reliability inhere in admissions? What justifications are there for permitting the use of hearsay admissions? Are these justifications sufficiently strong to override even nonhearsay limitations on the admission of evidence, such as the firsthand knowledge rule (Rule 602), the opinion rule (Rule 701), and the rule requiring the production of the original document (Rule 1002)? Why?

Problem: Silence as Statement

(1) *D*, the executor of *E*'s estate, is charged with secreting *E*'s assets, to wit, fifty $1,000 bills. *D* denies the existence of this money.

At *D*'s trial, the state calls *W* to testify that he was present at the meeting of *E*'s heirs on June 1 when *D* opened *E*'s wall safe. *W* will testify that he saw *D* rummage around in the safe and announce, "Nothing of value — just some one-dollar bills." *W* will further testify that *E*'s son, *S*, who was peering over *D*'s shoulder, responded, "Hey, those aren't one-dollar bills; they're one thousand-dollar bills" and that *D* was silent. *S* is dead. May *W* testify to *S*'s statement? If so, how should the court charge the jury?

(2) At trial, *O* is called to testify that on June 2 he arrested *D* for theft; on the way down to the station in the police cruiser *O* said to *D*, "So you thought you would get away with an easy 50 grand, did you? *D* was silent. Is *O*'s testimony admissible? Why?

(3) Charge: first-degree murder of *V.* Defense: self-defense. At trial the prosecution seeks to elicit testimony on cross-examination of *D* that *D* did not come forward to report the incident or his involvement in it to the police for two weeks. Would such evidence be hearsay? Would its introduction violate the Confrontation Clause, the Self-Incrimination Clause, the Due Process Clause, or the doctrine of Griffin v. California, 380 U.S. 609 (1965)? Should such evidence be admitted even if *D* does not take the stand?

FLETCHER v. WEIR
455 U.S. 603 (1982)

PER CURIAM.

In the course of a fight in a nightclub parking lot, Ronnie Buchanan pinned respondent Weir to the ground. Buchanan then jumped to his feet and shouted that he had been stabbed; he ultimately died from his stab wounds. Respondent immediately left the scene, and did not report the incident to the police.

At his trial for intentional murder, respondent took the stand in his own defense. He admitted stabbing Buchanan, but claimed that he acted in self-defense and that the stabbing was accidental. This in-court statement was the first occasion on which respondent offered an excul-

patory version of the stabbing. The prosecutor cross-examined him as
to why he had, when arrested, failed either to advance his exculpatory
explanation to the arresting officers or to disclose the location of the
knife he had used to stab Buchanan. Respondent was ultimately found
guilty by a jury of first degree manslaughter. The conviction was affirmed on appeal to the Supreme Court of Kentucky.

The United States District Court for the Western District of Kentucky
then granted respondent a writ of habeas corpus, and the Court of
Appeals for the Sixth Circuit affirmed. The Court of Appeals concluded
that respondent was denied due process of law guaranteed by the
Fourteenth Amendment when the prosecutor used his postarrest silence for impeachment purposes.[1] Although it did not appear from the
record that the arresting officers had immediately read respondent his
Miranda warnings, the court concluded that a defendant cannot be impeached by use of his postarrest silence even if no *Miranda* warnings
had been given. The court held that "it is inherently unfair to allow
cross-examination concerning post-arrest silence," and rejected the contention that our decision in Doyle v. Ohio, 426 U.S. 610 (1976), applied
only where the police had read *Miranda* warnings to a defendant. Because we think that the Court of Appeals gave an overly broad reading
to our decision in Doyle v. Ohio, supra, we reverse its judgment.

One year prior to our decision in *Doyle,* we held in the exercise of
our supervisory power over the federal courts that silence following the
giving of *Miranda* warnings was ordinarily so ambiguous as to have little
probative value. United States v. Hale, 422 U.S. 171 (1975). There we
said: "In light of the many alternative explanations for his pretrial silence, we do not think it sufficiently probative of an inconsistency with
his in-court testimony to warrant admission of evidence thereof." Id., at
180.

The principles which evolved on the basis of decisional law dealing
with appeals within the federal court system are not, of course, necessarily based on any constitutional principle. Where they are not, the
States are free to follow or to disregard them so long as the state
procedure as a whole remains consistent with due process of law. See
Cupp v. Naughten, 414 U.S. 141, 146 (1973). The year after our decision
in *Hale,* we were called upon to decide an issue similar to that presented
in *Hale* in the context of a state criminal proceeding. While recognizing
the importance of cross-examination and of exposing fabricated
defenses, we held in Doyle v. Ohio, supra, that because of the nature of

---

1. During cross-examination, the prosecutor also questioned respondent concerning his
failure prior to his arrest to report the incident to the police and offer his exculpatory story.
Relying on our decision in Jenkins v. Anderson, 447 U.S. 231 (1980), the Court of Appeals
correctly held that there was no constitutional impropriety in the prosecutor's use of respondent's pre-arrest silence for impeachment purposes.

Miranda warnings it would be a violation of due process to allow comment on the silence which the warnings may well have encouraged:

> [W]hile it is true that the *Miranda* warnings contain no express assurance that silence will carry no penalty, such assurance is implicit to any person who receives the warnings. In such circumstances, it would be fundamentally unfair and a deprivation of due process to allow the arrested person's silence to be used to impeach an explanation subsequently offered at trial.

Id., at 618 (footnote omitted).

The significant difference between the present case and *Doyle* is that the record does not indicate that respondent Weir received any *Miranda* warnings during the period in which he remained silent immediately after his arrest. The majority of the Court of Appeals recognized the difference, but sought to extend *Doyle* to cover Weir's situation by stating that "[w]e think an arrest, by itself, is governmental action which implicitly induces a defendant to remain silent." We think that this broadening of *Doyle* is unsupported by the reasoning of that case and contrary to our post-*Doyle* decisions.

In Jenkins v. Anderson, 447 U.S. 231, 239 (1980), a case dealing with pre-arrest silence, we said:

> Common law traditionally has allowed witnesses to be impeached by their previous failure to state a fact in circumstances in which that fact naturally would have been asserted. 3A J. Wigmore, Evidence §1042, p.1056 (Chadbourn rev. 1970). Each jurisdiction may formulate its own rules of evidence to determine when prior silence is so inconsistent with present statements that impeachment by reference to such silence is probative.

In *Jenkins*, as in other post-*Doyle* cases, we have consistently explained *Doyle* as a case where the government had induced silence by implicitly assuring the defendant that his silence would not be used against him. In Roberts v. United States, 445 U.S. 552, 561 (1980), we observed that the postconviction, presentencing silence of the defendant did not resemble "postarrest silence that may be induced by the assurances contained in *Miranda* warnings." In *Jenkins*, we noted that the failure to speak involved in that case occurred before the defendant was taken into custody and was given his *Miranda* warnings, commenting that no governmental action induced the defendant to remain silent before his arrest. Finally, in Anderson v. Charles, 447 U.S. 404, 407-408 (1980), we explained that use of silence for impeachment was fundamentally unfair in *Doyle* because "*Miranda* warnings inform a person of his right to remain silent and assure him, at least implicitly, that his silence will not be used against him. . . . *Doyle* bars the use against a criminal defendant of silence maintained after receipt of governmental assurances."

In the absence of the sort of affirmative assurances embodied in the *Miranda* warnings, we do not believe that it violates due process of law for a State to permit cross-examination as to postarrest silence when a defendant chooses to take the stand. A State is entitled, in such situations, to leave to the judge and jury under its own rules of evidence the resolution of the extent to which postarrest silence may be deemed to impeach a criminal defendant's own testimony. . . .

Problem: Omar the Disappearing Cat

Action for negligence of *D*, a veterinarian who owns the Deluxe Cat and Dog Sanitarium. *P*'s complaint alleges that his prize Persian cat, Omar, developed a neurosis in his declining years, so *P* sent him to *D*'s hospital on June 1 where *D* accepted Omar as a patient. *P*'s complaint further alleges that on June 2, as a result of *D*'s employees' negligence, Omar escaped and has not been seen since. *P* seeks $1 million in damages. *D*'s answer denies that he ever received Omar.

(1) At trial, *P* calls *M*, who testifes that she is now and was on June 1 the manager of *D*'s hospital. *M* is excused. *P* then testifies that Omar was his cat; that on June 1 he instructed his chauffeur, *C*, whose whereabouts are now unknown, to take Omar to *D*'s hospital; that on the evening of June 1 *P* stopped at *D*'s office and asked *M* if Omar had been checked in; that *M* replied, "Yes, and we are honored to have him." *D* objects. What ruling and why?

(2) Suppose that *M* does not testify as in (1) above but that *P* testifies that when he went by *D*'s hospital on the evening of June 1, the office was locked so he went across the street to a restaurant for dinner. At dinner *P* told his tablemate about Omar and his tablemate said, "Don't worry about Omar; he's snug in the cat hospital." *P* then said, "How do you know?" His tablemate replied, "It's my business to know; I'm *D*'s manager." *D* objects. What ruling and why?

Problem: P v. Greed Power & Light Company

On June 1 at 4 A.M., following two days of heavy rain, a flood wiped out the housing development at Rancho Mudslide. The cause of the flood was the collapse of the dam five miles upstream from the development. The dam was built and owned by the Greed Power & Light Company. *P*, individually and on behalf of the class of residents of Rancho Mudslide, has sued Greed for $5 million in actual property damages and $50 million in punitive damages, alleging that Greed was negligent in building and maintaining the dam.

The following evidentiary problems came to light at the pretrial conference. How would you resolve each of them?

(1) *P* proposes to call Meyer, the president of the Rancho Mudslide Homeowner's Association, to testify that on May 25 he was at the dam site and that an engineer who had been sent to repair a sluice said to him, "This repair won't do much good if there is a heavy rain. The whole system is bad."

(2) *P* proposes to call Harry, the engineer's husband, to testify that his wife told him when she came home from work on May 25 that "the repairs she had made would not do any good if there was a heavy rain because the whole system was bad."

(3) *P* proposes to call Clark Kent, a reporter for the Mudslide Muckraker, to testify that, upon learning of the catastrophe, he called up Rockeyfellow, the president of Greed, at 5 A.M. on June 1 for a reaction. Kent will testify that upon hearing what had happened, Rockeyfellow said, "Oh my God, the sluice system must have failed. We were negligent in maintaining it."

(4) *P* proposes to call Stoole, a Greed employee, to testify that a report by the Rancid Corporation, an outside consulting firm, prepared for the company ten years ago when the decision to build the dam was being made, states, "The soil at the suggested dam site is too porous. In case of heavy rain, there would be danger of collapse and flooding of the land downstream."

(5) *D* proposes to call Harbinger, its vice-president for public relations, to testify that eight years ago he sent a letter to all owners of land in the then-proposed Rancho Mudslide development, informing them that the proposed development lay in the path of any water discharge from the dam and that a property owner would be foolish and negligent to build a residence in that location.

MAHLANDT v. WILD CANID SURVIVAL & RESEARCH CENTER, INC.
588 F.2d 626 (8th Cir. 1979)

VAN SICKLE, J. This is a civil action for damages arising out of an alleged attack by a wolf on a child. The sole issues on appeal are as to the correctness of three rulings which excluded conclusionary statements against interest. Two of them were made by a defendant, who was also an employee of the corporate defendant; and the third was in the form of a statement appearing in the records of a board meeting of the corporate defendant.

On March 23, 1973, Daniel Mahlandt, then 3 years, 10 months, and 8 days old, was sent by his mother to a neighbor's home on an adjoining street to get his older brother, Donald. Daniel's mother watched him cross the street, and then turned into the house to get her car keys. Daniel's path took him along a walkway adjacent to the Poos' residence. Next to the walkway was a five foot chain link fence to which Sophie had been chained with a six foot chain. In other words, Sophie was free to move in a half circle having a six foot radius on the side of the fence opposite Daniel.

Sophie was a bitch wolf, 11 months and 28 days old, who had been born at the St. Louis Zoo, and kept there until she reached 6 months of age, at which time she was given to the Wild Canid Survival and Research Center, Inc. It was the policy of the Zoo to remove wolves from the Children's Zoo after they reached the age of 5 or 6 months. Sophie was supposed to be kept at the Tyson Research Center, but Kenneth Poos, as Director of Education for the Wild Canid Survival and Research Center, Inc., had been keeping her at his home because he was taking Sophie to schools and institutions where he showed films and gave programs with respect to the nature of wolves. Sophie was known as a very gentle wolf who had proved herself to be good natured and stable during her contacts with thousands of children, while she was in the St. Louis Children's Zoo.

Sophie was chained because the evening before she had jumped the fence and attacked a beagle who was running along the fence and yapping at her.

A neighbor who was ill in bed in the second floor of his home heard a child's screams and went to his window, where he saw a boy lying on his back within the enclosure, with a wolf straddling him. The wolf's face was near Daniel's face, but the distance was so great that he could not see what the wolf was doing and did not see any biting. Within about 15 seconds the neighbor saw Clarke Poos, about seventeen, run around the house, get the wolf off of the boy, and disappear with the child in his arms to the back of the house. Clarke took the boy in and laid him on the kitchen floor.

Clarke had been returning from his friend's home immediately west when he heard a child's cries and ran around to the enclosure. He found Daniel lying within the enclosure, about three feet from the fence, and Sophie standing back from the boy the length of her chain, and wailing. An expert in the behavior of wolves stated that when a wolf licks a child's face that it is a sign of care, and not a sign of attack; that a wolf's wail is a sign of compassion, and an effort to get attention, not a sign of attack. No witness saw or knew how Daniel was injured. Clarke and his sister ran over to get Daniel's mother. She says that Clarke told her, "a wolf got Danny and he is dying." Clarke denies that statement. The defendant, Mr. Poos, arrived home while Daniel and his mother were in the kitchen. After Daniel was taken in an ambulance, Mr. Poos talked to everyone present, including a neighbor who came in. Within an hour after he arrived home, Mr. Poos went to Washington University to inform Owen Sexton, President of Wild Canid Survival and Research Center, Inc., of the incident. Mr. Sexton was not in his office so Mr. Poos left the following note on his door:

> Owen, would you call me at home, 727-5080? Sophie bit a child that came in our back yard. All has been taken care of. I need to convey what happened to you. [Exhibit 11]

Denial of admission of this note is one of the issues on appeal.

Later that day, Mr. Poos found Mr. Sexton at the Tyson Research Center and told him what had happened. Denial of plaintiff's offer to prove that Mr. Poos told Mr. Sexton that, "Sophie had bit a child that day," is the second issue on appeal.

A meeting of the Directors of the Wild Canid Survival and Research Center, Inc., was held on April 4, 1973. Mr. Poos was not present at that meeting. The minutes of that meeting reflect that there was a "great deal of discussion . . . about the legal aspects of the incident of Sophie biting the child." Plaintiff offered an abstract of the minutes containing that reference. Denial of the offer of that abstract is the third issue on appeal.

Daniel had lacerations of the face, left thigh, left calf, and right thigh, and abrasions and bruises of the abdomen and chest. Mr. Mahlandt was permitted to state that Daniel had indicated that he had gone under the fence. Mr. Mahlandt and Mr. Poos, about a month after the incident, examined the fence to determine what caused Daniel's lacerations. Mr. Mahlandt felt that they did not look like animal bites. The parallel scars on Daniel's thigh appeared to match the configuration of the barbs or tines on the fence. The expert as to the behavior of wolves opined that the lacerations were not wolf bites or wounds caused by wolf claws. Wolves have powerful jaws and a wolf bite will result in massive crushing or severing of a limb. He stated that if Sophie had bitten Daniel there would have been clear apposition of teeth and massive crushing of Daniel's hands and arms which were not injured. Also, if Sophie had pulled Daniel under the fence, tooth marks on the foot or leg would have been present, although Sophie possessed enough strength to pull the boy under the fence.

The jury brought in a verdict for the defense.

The trial judge's rationale for excluding the note, the statement, and the corporate minutes, was the same in each case. He reasoned that Mr. Poos did not have any personal knowledge of the facts, and accordingly, the first two admissions were based on hearsay; and the third admission contained in the minutes of the board meeting was subject to the same objection of hearsay, and unreliability because of lack of personal knowledge. . . .

[T]he statement in the note pinned on the door is not hearsay, and is admissible against Mr. Poos. It was his own statement, and as such was clearly different from the reported statement of another. Example, "I was told that. . . ." It was also a statement of which he had manifested his adoption or belief in its truth. And the same observations may be made of the statement made later in the day to Mr. Sexton that, "Sophie had bit a child. . . ."

Are these statements admissible against Wild Canid Survival and Research Center, Inc.? They were made by Mr. Poos when he was an agent or servant of the Wild Canid Survival and Research Center, Inc., and they concerned a matter within the scope of his agency, or employment, i.e., his custody of Sophie, and were made during the existence of that relationship.

Defendant argues that Rule 801(d)(2) does not provide for the admission of "in house" statements: that is, it allows only admissions made to third parties.

The notes of the Advisory Committee on the Proposed Rules discuss the problem of "in house" admissions with reference to Rule 801(d)(2)(C) situations. This is not a (C) situation because Mr. Poos was not authorized or directed to make a statement on the matter by anyone. But the rationale developed in that comment does apply to this (D) situation. Mr. Poos had actual physical custody of Sophie. His conclusions, his opinions, were obviously accepted as a basis for action by his principal. See minutes of corporate meeting. As the Advisory Committee points out in its note on (C) situations:

> communication to an outsider has not generally been thought to be an essential characteristic of an admission. Thus a party's books or records are usable against him, without regard to any intent to disclose to third persons.

V Wigmore on Evidence §1557. Weinstein's discussion of Rule 801(d)(2)(D), states that:

> Rule 801(d)(2)(D) adopts the approach . . . which, as a general proposition, makes statement made by agents within the scope of their employment admissible. . . . Once agency, and the making of the statement while the relationship continues, are established, the statement is exempt from the hearsay rule so long as it relates to a matter within the scope of the agency.

After reciting a lengthy quotation which justifies the rule as necessary, and suggests that such admissions are trustworthy and reliable, Weinstein states categorically that although an express requirement of personal knowledge on the part of the declarant of the facts underlying his statement is not written into the rule, it should be. He feels that is mandated by Rules 805 and 403.

Rule 805 recites, in effect, that a statement containing hearsay within hearsay is admissible if each part of the statement falls within an exception to the hearsay rule. Rule 805, however, deals only with hearsay exceptions. A statement based on the personal knowledge of the declarant of facts underlying his statement is not the repetition of the statement of another, thus not hearsay. It is merely opinion testimony. Rule 805 cannot mandate the implied condition desired by Judge Weinstein.

Rule 403 provides for the exclusion of relevant evidence if its probative value is substantially outweighed by the danger of unfair prejudice, confusion of the issues, or misleading the jury, or by consideration of undue delay, waste of time, or needless presentation of cumulative evidence. Nor does Rule 403 mandate the implied condition desired by Judge Weinstein.

Thus, while both Rule 805 and Rule 403 provide additional bases for excluding otherwise acceptable evidence, neither rule mandates the introduction into Rule 801(d)(2)(D) of an implied requirement that the declarant have personal knowledge of the facts underlying his statement. So we conclude that the two statements made by Mr. Poos were admissible against Wild Canid Survival and Research Center, Inc.

As to the entry in the records of a corporate meeting, the directors as primary officers of the corporation had the authority to include their conclusions in the record of the meeting. So the evidence would fall within 801(d)(2)(C) as to Wild Canid Survival and Research Center, Inc., and be admissible. The "in house" aspect of this admission has already been discussed. Rule 801(d)(2)(D), supra.

But there was no servant, or agency, relationship which justified admitting the evidence of the board minutes as against Mr. Poos.

None of the conditions of 801(d)(2) cover the claim that minutes of a corporate board meeting can be used against a non-attending, non-participating employee of that corporation. The evidence was not admissible as against Mr. Poos.

There is left only the question of whether the trial court's rulings which excluded all three items of evidence are justified under Rule 403. He clearly found that the evidence was not reliable, pointing out that none of the statements were based on the personal knowledge of the declarant.

Again, the problem was faced by the Advisory Committee on Proposed Rules. In its discussion of 801(d)(2) exceptions to the hearsay rule, the Committee said:

> The freedom which admissions have enjoyed from technical demands of searching for an assurance of trustworthiness in some against-interest circumstances, and from the restrictive influences of the opinion rule and the rule requiring first hand knowledge, when taken with the apparently prevalent satisfaction with the results, calls for generous treatment of this avenue to admissibility.

28 U.S.C.A., Volume of Federal Rules of Evidence, Rule 801, p.527, at p.530. So here, remembering that relevant evidence is usually prejudicial to the cause of the side against which it is presented, and that the prejudice which concerns us is unreasonable prejudice; and applying the spirit of Rule 801(d)(2), we hold that Rule 403 does not warrant the exclusion of the evidence of Mr. Poos' statements as against himself or Wild Canid Survival and Research Center, Inc.

But the limited admissibility of the corporate minutes, coupled with the repetitive nature of the evidence and the low probative value of the minute record, all justify supporting the judgment of the trial court under Rule 403.

The judgment of the District Court is reversed and the matter remanded to the District Court for a new trial consistent with this opinion.

UNITED STATES v. HARRIS
914 F.2d 927 (7th Cir. 1990)

BAUER, Chief Judge.

This appeal from a conviction for armed bank robbery presents us with the interesting issue of whether an attorney's out-of-court statements may be offered against a defendant as the statements of an agent on behalf of his principal under Federal Rule of Evidence 801(d)(2)(D). Although there are significant policy concerns which must be considered before the admission of such statements, we believe these concerns are not seriously implicated under the facts of this case and therefore affirm.

On November 2, 1988, shortly after 11:00 in the morning, a young black male dressed in a green army jacket, camouflage pants, gray wool cap and dark sunglasses, and wearing a bandana across his face, robbed the Reliance Savings and Loan in Milwaukee, Wisconsin. The robbery was not especially creative. The man walked up to a teller's window, pulled out a gun and demanded money. The teller, Lisa Wick, handed the robber $505 in small bills from her drawer. Several of the bills were "bait money"—their serial numbers had been recorded to help identify any future use of the funds. The robber then fled from the building.

A few minutes later, Leslie Freeman, who lived a short distance from the savings and loan, encountered a young, black male standing in his garage. The man, who appeared extremely agitated, was holding a pair of camouflage pants and transferring a wad of bills from them into the pants he was wearing. The man spoke briefly with Freeman, then picked up a green Army jacket and the camouflage pants and left the garage. Freeman later identified Rickey Lee Harris, in a photo identification, as the man he discovered in his garage. That afternoon, Freeman and a Milwaukee police officer found the pants and the jacket, with some of the "bait money" in the jacket pocket, on Freeman's lawn. Other police officers found a pair of gloves, sunglasses, a gray wool cap, a green bandana and a knife in a baby carriage in Freeman's garage.

Five days after the robbery, on November 7, 1988, Milwaukee police arrested Rickey Lee Harris. After being taken to the station, Harris was given his *Miranda* warnings and informed of the evidence against him. Harris indicated that he would speak only with Special Agent Dan Craft, an FBI agent whom Harris apparently knew and trusted. When the agent arrived, Craft told Harris that he did not have to talk with him. Craft did not, however, re-read the formal *Miranda* rights. According to Craft and the Milwaukee police officers present at the time, Harris then confessed to the robbery of the Reliance Savings and Loan.

Harris was charged in the Eastern District of Wisconsin with one count of armed bank robbery in violation of 18 U.S.C. §2113(a), and a second count of using and carrying a firearm, in the commission of a crime of violence in violation of 18 U.S.C. §924(c). Prior to trial, John Carlson, Harris' court-appointed attorney asked for and received permission from the court to withdraw as defense counsel. The court then appointed Dennis Coffey to serve as Harris' attorney at trial. A three-day jury trial began on February 27, 1989. The jury returned a verdict of guilty on the count of bank robbery on March 1. The district court sentenced Harris to 266 months imprisonment. Harris filed a timely notice of appeal.

Harris raises several challenges to his conviction. Only one, however, merits extended discussion: whether the trial court erred by admitting into evidence the out-of-court statements of Harris' former attorney. The resolution of this issue turns, in part, upon the determination of whether an attorney may be considered the agent of his client for purposes of the Federal Rules of Evidence.

This rarely litigated legal issue comes to us as the result of an unfortunate gambit by Harris' first appointed counsel, John Carlson. Apparently, in an attempt to develop Harris' defense, Carlson had visited Leslie Freeman, the "garage eyewitness," at work and showed him pictures of Harris' brother, James. The defense's theory was that James had committed the robbery and fled to Freeman's garage, and that Rickey Harris was simply a victim of mistaken identity. Freeman, however, upon reviewing the pictures, did not think James looked anything like his brother, and was confident that Rickey Harris, not James, was the man he saw in his garage. Freeman indicated this to Carlson during the visit at Freeman's office. Though defense counsel continued to pursue this mistaken identity theory, any reference to Carlson's visit was carefully buried. During Freeman's cross-examination, however, defense counsel asked Freeman if he had been asked to look at photographs other than the ones included in the photograph line-up from which he identified Harris. Freeman asked if this included attorneys. Defense counsel responded "sure." Freeman then explained that a man identifying himself as John Carlson, Harris' attorney, had visited Freeman at work and showed him a picture of Harris' brother James. On re-direct examination, Freeman explained that he was confident that Rickey Harris, not James, was the person he had talked to in his garage. This testimony effectively crushed the defense's theory that James had committed the robbery.

The court permitted Freeman to testify about Carlson's statements, over defense counsel's vigorous objections, holding that Carlson was an agent of the defendant acting within the scope of his agency when he visited Freeman, and that therefore Carlson's statements were not hearsay under Fed. R. Evid. 801(d)(2)(D). On appeal, Harris now contends that this use of his former attorney's statements was reversible error.

... Under the traditional law of agency, the statements of an agent made in the course of the agency serve to bind the principal. Thus, such statements are presumably reliable in the absence of cross-examination because they are considered as if they were statements of the principal himself.

An attorney *may be* the agent of his client for purposes of Rule 801(d)(2)(D). The unique nature of the attorney-client relationship, however, demands that a trial court exercise caution in admitting statements that are the product of this relationship. As at least one circuit has noted, "the routine use of attorney statements against a criminal defendant risks impairment of the privilege against self-incrimination, the right to counsel of one's choice and the right to effective assistance of counsel." United States v. Valencia, 826 F.2d 169, 172 (2d Cir. 1987). Moreover, "the free use of prior [statments] may deter counsel from vigorous and legitimate advocacy" on behalf of his client. [United States v. McKeon, 738 F.2d 26, 32 (2d Cir. 1984).] Thus, a more exacting standard must be demanded for admission of statements by attorneys under Rule 801(d)(2)(D), "in order to avoid trenching upon other important policies."

Turning to facts of Harris' case, however, we are satisfied that these policies were not harmed by the admission of Carlson's statements. Carlson did withdraw as Harris' defense counsel, thus implicating the policies ... concerning the effective assistance of the counsel of one's choosing. Carlson's withdrawal cannot be linked to the possible use of these out-of-court statements. If anything, Carlson's absence is the likely result of his becoming a possible witness in Harris' trial due to his unsuccessful gambit. Whatever the reason, however, Harris was effectively represented at trial and Carlson's withdrawal predated any discussion of the use of these statements.

Beyond this, Carlson's statements did not impair Harris' privilege against self-incrimination. These statements, and the inferences drawn from them, undermined the defense's theory of mistaken identity. They did not, however, force Harris to take the stand to rebut them. Carlson was not relating confidential information about his client to Freeman. Instead, he was testing a theory on behalf of his client. Harris' rights under the fifth amendment were burdened by allowing this testimony only to the extent that any damaging piece of evidence generally forces a defendant to present a competing explanation to the jury. This does not, however, violate the privilege against self-incrimination.

Finally, allowing Carlson's statements to be presented to the jury did not impair "vigorous and legitimate advocacy" on Harris' behalf. The defense continued to present its theory of mistaken identity and the jury was free to accept this. They did not. Carlson gambled that Freeman would be confused by the picture of James Harris. He lost. Other attorneys will have to assess the risks of such a strategy in the future. We cannot say, however, that legitimate advocacy would be chilled by requiring lawyers to make such judgment calls. Effective advocacy requires strategic and tactical decisions at all levels of the criminal process. The fact that a lawyer's unsuccessful maneuver might be used against his client will not unduly chill legitimate advocacy.

Nor does such a result conflict with the Second Circuit's holdings in *McKeon* and *Valencia*. In *McKeon*, 738 F.2d 26, the court was concerned with the admission of certain statements made by defense counsel in a previous *trial* which were now inconsistent with the defendant's current theory of defense. Thus, the court in *McKeon* was faced with various concerns not present here, including forcing criminal defendants to face a "Hobson's choice" between limiting their defense arguments at a later trial to ones offered at an earlier trial, or having any later arguments impeached with earlier ones. *Valencia*, 826 F.2d 169, was concerned with informal statements made by a defense attorney to a prosecutor during an off-the-record discussion of the defendant's case. As a matter of policy we encourage such open discussions to encourage swift administration of trials. This policy concern is obviously not seriously implicated by the admission of statements elicited by an attorney on a gambit such as Carlson's visit to Freeman. We must also note that, these differences from our case aside, the Second Circuit has narrowed the reach of *McKeon* and *Valencia* in United States v. Arrington, 867 F.2d 122 (2d Cir. 1989), holding that despite the concerns raised about the use of attorney's out-of-court statements, no special procedures are required for the admission of such evidence.

Carlson was acting as an agent of his client when he interviewed Freeman. He was his counsel of record and his statements were made within the scope of that relationship. For purposes of Rule 801(d)(2)(D), therefore, these statements were technically not hearsay and were admissible against Harris. None of the policy concerns inherent in the lawyer-client relationship were infringed by admitting this evidence. Decisions on the admission of evidence are within the broad discretion of the trial judge, and we will only reverse such decisions upon a clear abuse of that considerable discretion. For purposes of determining whether the special policy concerns implicated by the admission of an attorney's statements as the agent of a client, we also must rely on the discretion of the trial judge and his or her close proximity to the parties involved. *Valencia*, 826 F.2d at 173. The admission of Carlson's out-of-court statements was not an abuse of this discretion.

Problem: Recall Letters

Action initiated by Mrs. *P*, administrator of Mr. *P*'s estate, for wrongful death of *P* allegedly caused by Dbilt Truck Company's negligence in the design, testing, and manufacture of the truck that *P* was driving when he died. The complaint also contains a count in strict liability based on Dbilt Truck Company's failure to give *P* timely warning as to the unsafe condition of the suspension system of the truck. Sixteen weeks after the accident, Mrs. *P* received the following letter, addressed to her deceased husband, from Dbilt Truck Company:

> This letter is sent to you pursuant to the requirement of the National Traffic and Motor Vehicle Safety Act. The rear suspension of your Dbilt truck/tractor . . . may contain a potentially hazardous condition.
>
> We have discovered that the combination of spring misalignment, improper maintenance, and pressure imbalance can cause overstressing of one spring resulting in a premature spring failure that can seriously affect vehicle control. You should make a simple visual inspection at once and have broken springs replaced immediately (at no charge). Regardless of the condition of these springs, federal law requires that an authorized Dbilt distributor perform certain adjustments and modifications to prevent the development of a hazardous condition.
>
> We apologize for the inconvenience this will cause you, but the seriousness of this situation cannot be overstated. We urge you to contact any authorized Dbilt distributor and make your vehicle available for this rework at the earliest possible time.

Dbilt Truck Company objects to the introduction of the recall letter on the grounds of hearsay and prejudice, pointing out that the recall campaign was instituted under the compulsion of the National Traffic and Motor Vehicle Safety Act, 15 U.S.C. §1401 et seq. What ruling and why?

Problem: The Rat Roommate

Charge: murder. On the issue of *D*'s intention to kill *V*, the prosecution, in rebuttal, puts a police officer, *W*, on the stand to testify that *R*, *D*'s roommate, after being fully warned of his rights, told *W*, "The night before the killing *D* said something about his planning to get *V*." *D* objects. What ruling and why?

Problem: Incident

Harry is robbed at knifepoint by two muggers as he leaves his favorite tavern one summer evening. After giving up his money, he and his buddies jump into a car and cruise the neighborhood, looking for the culprits. They spot some people in a vacant lot. Harry says, "That's them." The men pile out of the car and grab a young man and woman. During the struggle, the man says, "The girl made me do it." The woman says something that could be construed as a denial. Harry says, "He already told us you put him up to it."

If the state attempts to call Harry to testify to the man's statement at a trial of the woman, is the statement admissible? Why? Is the woman's response? Is Harry's response to the woman's statement?

NOTE: THE PROCEDURE OF ADMITTING EVIDENCE UNDER RULE 801(d)(2)(E): CO-CONSPIRATORS' STATEMENTS

Difficult procedural questions arise when statements of an alleged co-conspirator are offered against a defendant under Rule 801(d)(2)(E). Under the rule, such statements are admissible only if made during and in furtherance of the conspiracy. Thus, two preliminary question must be answered before the exception becomes applicable, (1) whether a conspiracy existed at the time the statement was made and (2) whether the statement was in furtherance of the conspiracy.

This question in turn raises several antecedent questions about the operation of the Federal Rules that were not clearly spelled out in the rules. For example, is the question of whether a conspiracy existed a question for the judge to determine under Rule 104(a), or is it a 104(b) question for the jury to determine like issues of conditional relevancy? If this question is a 104(b) issue, is the standard of proof of a conspiracy that must be satisfied before the hearsay is allowed any different from the standard of proof of conspiracy that the judge must apply if this is a 104(a) question? Regardless of whether this is a 104(a) or 104(b) issue, may the hearsay statement itself be considered on the preliminary issue of whether a conspiracy existed? If the court decides that the existence of a conspiracy is a 104(a) question, must it hear *all* the proof regarding existence or nonexistence of the conspiracy and make its decision as to whether a conspiracy existed before allowing in the hearsay statement whose admissibility depends on a finding of a conspiracy? If the court concludes that the existence of a conspiracy is a 104(b) issue, or if the court concludes it is a 104(a) issue but allows the hearsay evidence in before ruling on the preliminary issue of the existence of a conspiracy, and it turns out that the proof of the existence of a conspiracy is insufficient, what corrective options are available to the court?

Many cases raising these issues created a thriving appellate practice for criminal defense lawyers and prosecutors until in 1987 the Supreme

Court stepped into the fray. In Bourjaily v. United States, 483 U.S. 171 (1987), the Court held:

1. The existence of a conspiracy and the accused's participation in it are preliminary questions of fact that must be resolved by the Court under Rule 104(a);
2. When the preliminary facts are disputed, the offering party must prove them by a preponderance of the evidence (rejecting a higher standard and citing Lego v. Twomey, 401 U.S. 477, 488 (1972)); and
3. In determining whether a conspiracy exists and whether the defendant was a part of it, the court may "bootstrap," that is, may consider the hearsay statement itself sought to be admitted.

The Court declined to express an opinion on

1. The proper order of proof that trial courts should follow in an ongoing trial in making the preliminary factual determination of the existence of a conspiracy; and
2. Whether a preliminary finding of a conspiracy could be based *solely* on the contested hearsay statement.

Although seemingly clarifying many controversial issues, *Bourjaily* did little to stem the tide of appellate opinion-writing on Rule 801(d)(2)(E). However, in 1997 the Supreme Court revised Rule 801 to codify the holding in *Bourjaily* that the court could consider the out-of-court statement in making the preliminary determination on the existence of the conspiracy and to make it clear that the statement would not by itself be sufficient to establish these preliminary matters.

BOURJAILY v. UNITED STATES
483 U.S. 171 (1987)

Chief Justice REHNQUIST delivered the opinion of the Court.

Federal Rule of Evidence 801(d)(2)(E) provides, "A statement is not hearsay if ... [t]he statement is offered against a party and is ... a statement by a co-conspirator of a party during the course and in furtherance of the conspiracy." We granted certiorari to answer three questions regarding the admission of statements under Rule 801(d)(2)(E): (1) whether the court must determine by independent evidence that the conspiracy existed and that the defendant and the declarant were members of this conspiracy; (2) the quantum of proof on which such determinations must be based; and (3) whether a court must in each case examine the circumstances of such a statement to determine its reliability.

In May 1984, Clarence Greathouse, an informant working for the Federal Bureau of Investigation, arranged to sell a kilogram of cocaine to Angelo Lonardo. Lonardo agreed that he would find individuals to distribute the drug. When the sale became imminent, Lonardo stated in a tape-recorded telephone conversation that he had a "gentleman friend" who had some questions to ask about the cocaine. In a subsequent telephone call, Greathouse spoke to the "friend" about the quality of the drug and the price. Greathouse then spoke again with Lonardo, and the two arranged the details of the purchase. They agreed that the sale would take place in a designated hotel parking lot, and Lonardo would transfer the drug from Greathouse's car to the "friend," who would be waiting in the parking lot in his own car. Greathouse proceeded with the transaction as planned, and FBI agents arrested Lonardo and petitioner immediately after Lonardo placed a kilogram of cocaine into petitioner's car in the hotel parking lot. In petitioner's car, the agents found over $20,000 in cash.

Petitioner was charged with conspiring to distribute cocaine, in violation of 21 U.S.C. §846, and possession of cocaine with intent to distribute, a violation of 21 U.S.C. §841(a)(1). The Government introduced, over petitioner's objection, Angelo Lonardo's telephone statements regarding the participation of the "friend" in the transaction. The District Court found that, considering the events in the parking lot and Lonardo's statements over the telephone, the Government had established by a preponderance of the evidence that a conspiracy involving Lonardo and petitioner existed, and that Lonardo's statements over the telephone had been made in the course of and in furtherance of the conspiracy. Accordingly, the trial court held that Lonardo's out-of-court statements satisfied Rule 801(d)(2)(E) and were not hearsay. Petitioner was convicted on both counts and sentenced to 15 years. . . . We affirm.

Before admitting a co-conspirator's statement over an objection that it does not qualify under Rule 801(d)(2)(E), a court must be satisfied that the statement actually falls within the definition of the rule. There must be evidence that there was a conspiracy involving the declarant and the nonoffering party, and that the statement was made "in the course and in furtherance of the conspiracy." Federal Rule of Evidence 104(a) provides: "Preliminary questions concerning . . . the admissibility of evidence shall be determined by the court." Petitioner and respondent agree that the existence of a conspiracy and petitioner's involvement in it are preliminary questions of fact that, under Rule 104, must be resolved by the court. The Federal Rules, however, nowhere define

the standard of proof the court must observe in resolving these
questions.

We are therefore guided by our prior decisions regarding admissibility determinations that hinge on preliminary factual questions. We
have traditionally required that these matters be established by a preponderance of proof. Evidence is placed before the jury when it satisfies
the technical requirements of the evidentiary Rules, which embody certain legal and policy determinations. The inquiry made by a court concerned with these matters is not whether the proponent of the evidence
wins or loses his case on the merits, but whether the evidentiary Rules
have been satisfied. Thus, the evidentiary standard is unrelated to the
burden of proof on the substantive issues, be it a criminal case, see In
re Winship, 397 U.S. 358 (1970), or a civil case. See generally Colorado
v. Connelly, 479 U.S. 157 (1986). The preponderance standard ensures
that before admitting evidence, the court will have found it more likely
than not that the technical issues and policy concerns addressed by the
Federal Rules of Evidence have been afforded due consideration. As in
Lego v. Twomey, 404 U.S. 477, 488 (1972), we find "nothing to suggest
that admissibility rulings have been unreliable or otherwise wanting in
quality because not based on some higher standard." We think that our
previous decisions in this area resolve the matter. . . . Therefore, we hold
that when the preliminary facts relevant to Rule 801(d)(2)(E) are disputed, the offering party must prove them by a preponderance of the
evidence.[1]

Even though petitioner agrees that the courts below applied the
proper standard of proof with regard to the preliminary facts relevant
to Rule 801(d)(2)(E), he nevertheless challenges the admission of Lonardo's statements. Petitioner argues that in determining whether a conspiracy exists and whether the defendant was a member of it, the court
must look only to independent evidence — that is, evidence other than
the statements sought to be admitted. Petitioner relies on Glasser v.
United States, 315 U.S. 60 (1942), in which this Court first mentioned
the so-called "bootstrapping rule." The relevant issue in *Glasser* was
whether Glasser's counsel, who also represented another defendant,
faced such a conflict of interest that Glasser received ineffective assistance. Glasser contended that conflicting loyalties led his lawyer not to
object to statements made by one of Glasser's co-conspirators. The Gov-

---

1. We intimate no view on the proper standard of proof for questions falling under Federal
Rule of Evidence 104(b) (conditional relevancy). We also decline to address the circumstances
in which the burden of coming forward to show that the proffered evidence is inadmissible is
appropriately placed on the nonoffering party. See E. Cleary, McCormick on Evidence, §53,
p.136, n.8 (3d ed. 1984). Finally, we do not express an opinion on the proper order of proof
that trial courts should follow in concluding that the preponderance standard has been satisfied in an on-going trial.

ernment argued that any objection would have been fruitless because the statements were admissible. The Court rejected this proposition:

> [S]uch declarations are admissible over the objection of an alleged co-conspirator, who was not present when they were made, only if there is proof *aliunde* that he is connected with the conspiracy. . . . Otherwise, hearsay would lift itself by its own bootstraps to the level of competent evidence.

Id., at 74-75. The Court revisited the bootstrapping rule in United States v. Nixon, 418 U.S. 688 (1974), where again, in passing, the Court stated, "Declarations by one defendant may also be admissible against other defendants upon a sufficient showing, *by independent evidence,* of a conspiracy among one or more other defendants and the declarant and if the declarations at issue were in furtherance of that conspiracy." Id. Read in the light most favorable to petitioner, *Glasser* could mean that a court should not consider hearsay statements at all in determining preliminary facts under Rule 801(d)(2)(E). Petitioner, of course, adopts this view of the bootstrapping rule. *Glasser,* however, could also mean that a court must have *some* proof *aliunde,* but may look at the hearsay statements themselves in light of this independent evidence to determine whether a conspiracy has been shown by a preponderance of the evidence. The Courts of Appeals have widely adopted the former view and held that in determining the preliminary facts relevant to co-conspirators' out-of-court statements, a court may not look at the hearsay statements themselves for their evidentiary value.

Both *Glasser* and *Nixon,* however, were decided before Congress enacted the Federal Rules of Evidence in 1975. These Rules now govern the treatment of evidentiary questions in federal courts. Rule 104(a) provides: "Preliminary questions concerning . . . the admissibility of evidence shall be determined by the court. . . . In making its determination it is not bound by the rules of evidence except those with respect to privileges." Similarly, Rule 1101(d)(1) states that the Rules of Evidence (other than with respect to privileges) shall not apply to "[t]he determination of questions of fact preliminary to admissibility of evidence when the issue is to be determined by the court under rule 104." The question thus presented is whether any aspect of *Glasser's* bootstrapping rule remains viable after the enactment of the Federal Rules of Evidence.

Petitioner concedes that Rule 104, on its face, appears to allow the court to make the preliminary factual determinations relevant to Rule 801(d)(2)(E) by considering any evidence it wishes, unhindered by considerations of admissibility. That would seem to many to be the end of the matter. Congress has decided that courts may consider hearsay in making these factual determinations. Out-of-court statements made by anyone, including putative co-conspirators, are often hearsay. Even if they are, they may be considered, *Glasser* and the bootstrapping rule notwithstanding. But petitioner nevertheless argues that the bootstrapping rule, as most Courts of Appeals have construed it, survived this apparently unequivocal change in the law unscathed and that Rule 104, as applied to the admission of co-conspirator's statements, does not mean what it says. We disagree.

Petitioner claims that Congress evidenced no intent to disturb the bootstrapping rule, which was embedded in the previous approach, and we should not find that Congress altered the rule without affirmative evidence so indicating. It would be extraordinary to require legislative history to *confirm* the plain meaning of Rule 104. The Rule on its face allows the trial judge to consider any evidence whatsoever, bound only by the rules of privilege. We think that the Rule is sufficiently clear that to the extent that it is inconsistent with petitioner's interpretation of *Glasser* and *Nixon,* the Rule prevails.[2]

Nor do we agree with petitioner that this construction of Rule 104(a) will allow courts to admit hearsay statements without any credible proof of the conspiracy, thus fundamentally changing the nature of the co-conspirator exception. Petitioner starts with the proposition that co-conspirators' out-of-court statements are deemed unreliable and are inadmissible, at least until a conspiracy is shown. Since these statements are unreliable, petitioner contends that they should not form any part of the basis for establishing a conspiracy, the very antecedent that renders them admissible.

Petitioner's theory ignores two simple facts of evidentiary life. First, out-of-court statements are only *presumed* unreliable. The presumption may be rebutted by appropriate proof. See Fed. Rule Evid. 803(24) (otherwise inadmissible hearsay may be admitted if circumstantial guarantees of trustworthiness demonstrated). Second, individual pieces of evidence, insufficient in themselves to prove a point, may in cumulation prove it. The sum of an evidentiary presentation may well be greater

---

2. The Advisory Committee Notes show that the Rule was not adopted in a fit of absent-mindedness. The Note to Rule 104 specifically addresses the process by which a federal court should make the factual determinations requisite to a finding of admissibility:

If the question is factual in nature, the judge will of necessity receive evidence pro and con on the issue. The rule provides that the rules of evidence in general do not apply to this process. McCormick §53, p.123, n.8, points out that the authorities are "scattered and inconclusive," and observes:

"'Should the exclusionary law of evidence, "the child of the jury system" in Thayer's phrase, be applied to this hearing before the judge? Sound sense backs the view that it should not, and that the judge should be empowered to hear any relevant evidence, such as affidavits or other reliable hearsay.'" 28 U.S.C. App., p.681 (emphasis added).

The Advisory Committee further noted, "An item, offered and objected to, may itself be considered in ruling on admissibility, though not yet admitted in evidence." Ibid. (emphasis added). We think this language makes plain the drafters' intent to abolish any kind of bootstrapping rule. Silence is at best ambiguous, and we decline the invitation to rely on speculation to impart ambiguity into what is otherwise a clear rule.

than its constituent parts. Taken together, these two propositions demonstrate that a piece of evidence, unreliable in isolation, may become quite probative when corroborated by other evidence. A per se rule barring consideration of these hearsay statements during preliminary factfinding is not therefore required. Even if out-of-court declarations by co-conspirators are presumptively unreliable, trial courts must be permitted to evaluate these statements for their evidentiary worth as revealed by the particular circumstances of the case. Courts often act as factfinders, and there is no reason to believe that courts are any less able to properly recognize the probative value of evidence in this particular area. The party opposing admission has an adequate incentive to point out the shortcomings in such evidence before the trial court finds the preliminary facts. If the opposing party is unsuccessful in keeping the evidence from the factfinder, he still has the opportunity to attack the probative value of the evidence as it relates to the substantive issue in the case. See, e.g., Fed. Rule Evid. 806 (allowing attack on credibility of out-of-court declarant).

We think that there is little doubt that a co-conspirator's statements could themselves be probative of the existence of a conspiracy and the participation of both the defendant and the declarant in the conspiracy. Petitioner's case presents a paradigm. The out-of-court statements of Lonardo indicated that Lonardo was involved in a conspiracy with a "friend." The statements indicated that the friend had agreed with Lonardo to buy a kilogram of cocaine and to distribute it. The statements also revealed that the friend would be at the hotel parking lot, in his car, and would accept the cocaine from Greathouse's car after Greathouse gave Lonardo the keys. Each one of Lonardo's statements may itself be unreliable, but taken as a whole, the entire conversation between Lonardo and Greathouse was corroborated by independent evidence. The friend, who turned out to be petitioner, showed up at the prearranged spot at the prearranged time. He picked up the cocaine, and a significant sum of money was found in his car. On these facts, the trial court concluded, in our view correctly, that the Government had established the existence of a conspiracy and petitioner's participation in it.

We need not decide in this case whether the courts below could have relied solely upon Lonardo's hearsay statements to determine that a conspiracy had been established by a preponderance of the evidence. To the extent that *Glasser* meant that courts could not look to the hearsay statements themselves for any purpose, it has clearly been superseded by Rule 104(a). It is sufficient for today to hold that a court, in making a preliminary factual determination under Rule 801(d)(2)(E), may examine the hearsay statements sought to be admitted. As we have held in other cases concerning admissibility determinations, "the judge should receive the evidence and give it such weight as his judgment and experience counsel." United States v. Matlock, 415 U.S. 164 (1974). The courts below properly considered the statements of Lonardo and the subsequent events in finding that the Government had established by a preponderance of the evidence that Lonardo was involved in a conspiracy with petitioner. We have no reason to believe that the District Court's factfinding of this point was clearly erroneous. We hold that Lonardo's out-of-court statements were properly admitted against petitioner.

We also reject any suggestion that admission of these statements against petitioner violated his rights under the Confrontation Clause of the Sixth Amendment. That Clause provides, "In all criminal prosecutions, the accused shall enjoy the right . . . to be confronted with the witnesses against him." At petitioner's trial, Lonardo exercised his right not to testify. Petitioner argued that Lonardo's unavailability rendered the admission of his out-of-court statements unconstitutional since petitioner had no opportunity to confront Lonardo as to these statements. The Court of Appeals held that the requirements for admission under Rule 801(d)(2)(E) are identical to the requirements of the Confrontation Clause, and since the statements were admissible under the Rule, there was no constitutional problem. We agree.

While a literal interpretation of the Confrontation Clause could bar the use of any out-of-court statements when the declarant is unavailable, this Court has rejected that view as "unintended and too extreme." Ohio v. Roberts, 448 U.S. 56, 63 (1980). Rather, we have attempted to harmonize the goal of the Clause—placing limits on the kind of evidence that may be received against a defendant—with a societal interest in accurate factfinding, which may require consideration of out-of-court statements. To accommodate these competing interests, the Court has, as a general matter only, required the prosecution to demonstrate both the unavailability of the declarant and the "indicia of reliability" surrounding the out-of-court declaration. Id., at 65-66. Last Term in United States v. Inadi, 475 U.S. 387 (1986), we held that the first of these two generalized inquiries, unavailability, was not required when the hearsay statement is the out-of-court declaration of a co-conspirator. Today, we conclude that the second inquiry, independent indicia of reliability, is also not mandated by the Constitution.

The Court's decision in Ohio v. Roberts laid down only "a general approach to the problem" of reconciling hearsay exceptions with the Confrontation Clause. In fact, *Roberts* itself limits the requirement that a court make a separate inquiry into the reliability of an out-of-court statement. Because "'hearsay rules and the Confrontation Clause are generally designed to protect similar values,' California v. Green, and 'stem from the same roots,' Dutton v. Evans," we concluded in *Roberts* that no independent inquiry into reliability is required when the evidence "falls within a firmly rooted hearsay exception." Ibid. We think that the co-conspirator exception to the hearsay rule is firmly enough rooted in our jurisprudence that, under this Court's holding in *Roberts*, a court need not independently inquire into the reliability of such statements. Cf. Dutton v. Evans (reliability inquiry required where evidentiary rule deviates from common-law approach, admitting co-conspirators' hearsay statements made after termination of conspiracy). The admissibility of co-conspirators' statements was first established in this Court over a century and a half ago in United States v. Gooding, 12 Wheat. *460, 6 L. Ed. 693 (1827) (interpreting statements of co-conspirator as *res gestae* and thus admissible against defendant), and the Court has repeatedly reaffirmed the exception as accepted practice. . . . We think that these cases demonstrate that co-conspirators' statements, when made in the course and in furtherance of the conspiracy, have a long tradition of being outside the compass of the general hearsay exclusion. Accordingly, we hold that the Confrontation Clause does not require a court to embark on an independent inquiry into the reliability of statements that satisfy the requirements of Rule 801(d)(2)(E).[4]

The judgment of the Court of Appeals is affirmed.

Justice STEVENS, concurring. . . .

In my view, *Glasser* holds that a declarant's out-of-court statement is inadmissible against his alleged co-conspirators unless there is some corroborating evidence to support the triple conclusion that there was a conspiracy among those defendants, that the declarant was a member of the conspiracy, and that the statement furthered the objectives of the conspiracy. An otherwise inadmissible hearsay statement cannot provide the sole evidentiary support for its own admissibility—it cannot lift itself into admissibility entirely by tugging on its own bootstraps. It may, however, use its own bootstraps, together with other support, to overcome the objection.

In a conspiracy case, what effect does a "not guilty" verdict have on the admissibility of the acquitted co-conspirator's statements under Rule 801(d)(2)(E)? The problem can arise in this situation: At the joint trial of two defendants, *A* and *B*, *B*'s statements are admitted against *A* and *B* under Rule 801(d)(2)(E). Following *Bourjaily*, the court considered *B*'s statement itself in determining that a conspiracy existed and that the statement was in furtherance of the conspiracy. But *B* was acquitted; *A* was convicted. *A* argues on appeal that because the conspiracy count

4. We reject any suggestion that by abolishing the bootstrapping rule, the Federal Rules of Evidence have changed the co-conspirator hearsay exception such that it is no longer "firmly rooted" in our legal tradition. The bootstrapping rule relates only to the method of proof that the exception has been satisfied. It does not change any element of the co-conspirator exception, which has remained substantively unchanged since its adoption in this country.

would not be available on retrial, the prosecution would not be able to introduce *B*'s statement, and thus that the admission of *B*'s statement at the first trial was erroneous. Does the subsequent acquittal of the alleged co-conspirator retroactively render his statement inadmissible? See United States v. Carroll, 860 F.2d 500 (1st Cir. 1988), below.

C. Prior Statements of a Witness

The Federal Rules give special treatment to a witness's own prior out-of-court statements. One might think that, with the witness on the stand and subject to cross-examination, there would be no problem admitting the witness's own prior statements. And indeed, in some states all prior statements by a witness who testifies at the trial are either nonhearsay or are covered by a hearsay rule exception. There is no problem also when the prior statement is being offered as a prior inconsistent statement solely to impeach the witness's in-court testimony. There the truth of the prior statement is not relevant. The impeachment is based on the fact that the witness has told two different stories on two different occasions and hence may not be totally reliable.

The Federal Rules do not exempt all prior statements of a testifying witness from the ban of the rule against hearsay. The Rules permit only certain prior statements of a witness to be admitted as nonhearsay depending on the specific circumstances in which the prior statement was made and the purposes for which the prior statement is being offered at trial. Prior consistent statements are treated differently from prior inconsistent statements. Prior statements of identification are treated yet another way. And in all cases, the rules require one to distinguish carefully between the offer of a statement for its truth (under Rule 801) and its offer for impeachment purposes only (under Rule 613).

Under Rule 801(d)(1)(a), in order for prior inconsistent statements to be admitted as substantive evidence rather than for purposes of impeachment, they must be made under oath at a prior hearing and the declarant must testify at trial subject to cross-examination. Why shouldn't prior inconsistent statements not made under oath and subject to the penalty of perjury at trial be admitted as substantive evidence so long as the declarant is also the witness and available for cross-examination? This is the approach that the original Advisory Committee took to the subject. See also R.I. R. Evid. 801(d)(1). The legislative history that created the compromise that ultimately became Rule 801(d)(1) is set forth in the rules supplement. What procedural safeguards favor admitting such statements? Are hearsay concerns justified in such instances?

Problem: The Stolen BMW

P drives her new BMW home from the BMW dealer on June 1. She parks it in front of her house with the motor running while she goes in to pick up her running shoes. *P* notices some acquaintances — *W*, *D*, and *T*—standing on the sidewalk. *P* shouts to them to keep an eye on her new car. When *P* comes out of her house a minute later, the BMW is gone and so are *D* and *T*. *P* asks *W* where the car is. *W* says, "*D* took it."

P sues *D* for conversion of the BMW. *D*'s answer generally denies *P*'s allegations. At trial, *P* calls *W* and asks him if he saw who took the BMW. *W* says, "Yes, *T* took it." *P* then questions *W* about his June 1 statement to *P* that *D* took the BMW. *D*'s objection is overruled. *W* denies making the statement. *P* takes the stand and over *D*'s objection testifies to *W*'s June 1 statement. *P* rests her case. *D* moves for a nonsuit. If *D*'s motion is granted, what is the rationale for overruling his objections to the evidence but granting his motion? Compare Rules 607, 613, and 801(d)(1).

Problem: The "Forgetful" Witness

Charge: conspiracy to commit mail fraud. *D* was indicted with two alleged co-conspirators who pled guilty before defendant's trial. *W*, one of these co-conspirators, was called at *D*'s trial by the prosecution to testify to the details of *D*'s participation in the alleged mail fraud. But *W* testified that he could not remember these details. At this point, the prosecution sought to introduce *W*'s grand jury testimony on these points. *D* objected. On voir dire, *W* states that he does not remember making the statements attributed to him before the grand jury nor does he now remember the details of the alleged mail fraud.

(1) Are *W*'s prior statements before the grand jury "inconsistent"?
(2) Does testimony before the grand jury fall within 801(d)(1)(A)? Should it? Compare the limitations on the use of former testimony in Rule 804(b)(1). What does "other proceeding," as used in Rule 801(d)(1)(A), include?
(3) Would it make any difference to the admissibility of *W*'s grand jury testimony if *W* were present in the courtroom but was not called by the prosecution to testify? Should it?
(4) Is *W* "subject to cross-examination" concerning the grand jury testimony?
(5) Have *D*'s sixth amendment rights been violated?
(6) Would your analysis of any of the above questions be any different if instead of grand jury testimony the prosecution sought to introduce in this situation:

(a)   *W*'s testimony at a preliminary hearing at which he was actually cross-examined by *D*'s attorney; or

(b)   *W*'s statements to the arresting officer while in custody prior to indictment?

E. MORGAN, HEARSAY DANGERS AND THE APPLICATION OF THE HEARSAY CONCEPT
62 Harv. L. Rev. 177, 192-196 (1948)

There is one situation where the courts are prone to call hearsay what does not in fact involve in any substantial degree any of the hearsay risks. When the declarant is also a witness, it is difficult to justify classifying as hearsay evidence of his own prior statements. This is especially true where declarant as a witness is giving as part of his testimony his own prior statement. . . . The courts declare the prior statement to be hearsay because it was not made under oath, subject to the penalty for perjury or to the test of cross-examination. To which the answer might well be: "The declarant as a witness is now under oath and now purports to remember and narrate accurately. The adversary can now expose every element that may carry a danger of misleading the trier of fact both in the previous statement and in the present testimony, and the trier can judge whether both the previous declaration and the present testimony are reliable in whole or in part." To this Mr. Justice Stone of the Minnesota Supreme Court, speaking of evidence of prior contradictory statements, has framed this reply:

> The chief merit of cross-examination is not that at some future time it gives the party opponent the right to dissect adverse testimony. Its principal virtue is in its immediate application of the testing process. Its strokes fall while the iron is hot. False testimony is apt to harden and become unyielding to the blows of truth in proportion as the witness has opportunity for reconsideration and influence by the suggestions of others, whose interest may be, and often is, to maintain falsehood rather than truth.

He adds the "practical reasons" that receipt of such evidence would create temptation and opportunity to manufacture evidence and entrap witnesses, and would require admission of prior consistent statements. Why does falsehood harden any more quickly or unyieldingly than truth? What has become of the idea that truth is eternal and, though crushed to earth, will rise again? Isn't the opportunity for reconsideration and for baneful influence by others even more likely to color the later testimony than the prior statement? Furthermore, it must be remembered that the trier of fact is often permitted to hear these prior statements to impeach or rehabilitate the declarant-witness. In such event, of course, the trier will be told that he must not treat the statement as evidence of the truth of the matter stated. But to what practical effect? Wasn't Judge Swan right in saying, "Practically, men will often believe that if a witness has earlier sworn to the opposite of what he now swears to, he was speaking the truth when he first testified"? Do the judges deceive themselves or do they realize that they are indulging in a pious fraud? . . .

In these situations it is unquestionably true that the trier is being asked to treat the former utterance as if it were now being made by the witness on the stand. But whether or not the declarant at the time of the utterance was subject to all the conditions usually imposed upon witnesses should be immaterial, for the declarant is now present as a witness. If his prior statement is consistent with his present testimony, he now affirms it under oath subject to all sanctions and to cross-examination in the presence of the trier who is to value it. Perhaps it ought not to be received because unnecessary, but surely the rejection should not be on the ground that the statement involves any danger inherent in hearsay. If the witness testifies that all the statements he made were true . . . , then the only debatable question is whether he made the statement; and as to that the trier has all the witnesses before him, and has also the benefit of thorough cross-examination as to the facts which are the subject matter of the statement. If the witness denies having made any statement at all, the situation is but little different, for he will usually swear that he tried to tell the truth in anything that he may have said. If he concedes that he made the statement but now swears that it wasn't true, the experience in human affairs which the average trier brings to a controversy will enable him to decide which story represents the truth in the light of all the facts, such as the demeanor of the witness, the matter brought out on his direct and cross-examination, and the testimony of others. In any of these situations Proponent is not asking Trier to rely upon the credibility of any one who is not present and subject to all the conditions imposed upon a witness. Adversary has all the protection which oath and cross-examination can give him. Trier is in a position to consider the evidence impartially and to give it no more than its reasonable persuasive effect. Consequently there is no real reason for classifying the evidence as hearsay. . . .

WHITEHURST v. WRIGHT
592 F.2d 834 (5th Cir. 1979)

[Civil rights action under 42 U.S.C. §1983 against defendant city police officers.]

VANCE, J. Bernard Whitehurst was gunned down by Montgomery, Alabama police who mistook him for a suspect in a local robbery. The fatal shot was fired by police officer Donald Foster, who claims that Whitehurst shot first. Although none of the officers in the vicinity found a gun near the body, a detective subsequently called to the scene spotted a gun twenty-seven inches from the victim. It was later discovered that the gun had been confiscated by police in a drug raid occurring over one year prior to the Whitehurst shooting. . . .

IMPEACHMENT OF PLAINTIFF'S WITNESS

Mrs. Whitehurst contends that the trial court erroneously refused to allow her to impeach her own witness, in violation of Fed. R. Evid. 607. The witness, Detective Cecil Humphrey of the Montgomery Police Department, was called solely to establish whether he had fired the single spent round in the gun found next to Whitehurst's body. Humphrey denied that he had fired the gun, and Mrs. Whitehurst was aware that he would so testify. Nevertheless, she called him to the stand with the express purpose of impeaching him with an out of court statement made by Humphrey to his friend, Lt. J.C. Cunningham, to the effect that he had fired the gun.[6]

While it is now proper for a party to impeach his own witness, Fed. R. Evid. 607, "impeachment by prior inconsistent statement may not be permitted where employed as a mere subterfuge to get before the jury evidence not otherwise admissible." Here the statement made to Cunningham is hearsay and is generally inadmissible for substantive purposes. Fed. R. Evid. 801(c), 802.[7] Mrs. Whitehurst asserts on appeal that she would have called Lt. Cunningham "to establish Humphrey's role concerning the pistol firing. . . ." To use a prior inconsistent statement in that manner exceeds the scope of impeachment, and is an attempt to use hearsay evidence for substantive purposes. We do not believe that the rules of evidence espouse such a revolutionary approach to circumvent the traditional principles of hearsay. . . .

Do you agree with the court's conclusion? What arguments could you make for admissibility? Would the result be different if Detective Hum-

6. The following colloquy took place prior to the direct examination of Humphrey:

Mr. Watkins: . . . we expect the evidence to show that Mr. Humphrey actually retrieved the gun from the scene and has reported to a J.C. Cunningham that he checked the gun at that point, saw that it had not been fired and fired the gun, one round, so that the gun would appear to have been fired at some point between the time he retrieved the gun at the scene and the time he arrived with the gun at police headquarters.

Mr. Black [defense counsel]:   You deny that, don't you?

Mr. Humphrey: That's right, I don't know what he is talking about.

Mr. Watkins: Then we would like to call J.C. Cunningham behind him.

7. Because the statement was offered only for impeachment purposes, we make no determination as to its admissibility under Fed. R. Evid. §803(24). But cf. Fed. R. Evid. 801(d)(1)(A). . . .

phrey were named as a defendant in the case? If so, why should the result on the admissibility of this item of evidence turn on the formality of the pleadings? Would it make any difference if Detective Humphrey were dead? If so, why should this fortuity make a difference?

Problem: The Prosecution's Patsy

Charge: possession with intent to distribute heroin. At trial, *W*, who has pled guilty to a lesser charge in return for her cooperation, testifies against *D*. Her testimony includes references to *D*'s nephew's participation in the narcotics distribution scheme. On cross-examination, *D* is permitted to impeach *W* by introducing evidence that *W*'s grand jury testimony and her testimony at the trial of two other members of the ring did not include any reference to *D*'s nephew. On redirect, the government seeks to read portions of *W*'s prior grand jury testimony and the testimony from the two other trials that are consistent with the present testimony implicating *D* but that do not contain any references to *D*'s nephew. *D* objects. What ruling and why? Has *D* expressly or impliedly charged *W* with recent fabrication or improper influence or motive? If so, has the prosecution rebutted that charge?

TOME v. UNITED STATES
513 U.S. 150 (1995)

Justice KENNEDY delivered the opinion of the Court, except as to Part IIB.

Various federal Courts of Appeals are divided over the evidence question presented by this case. At issue is the interpretation of a provision in the Federal Rules of Evidence bearing upon the admissibility of statements, made by a declarant who testifies as a witness, that are consistent with the testimony and are offered to rebut a charge of a "recent fabrication or improper influence or motive." Fed. Rule Evid. 810(d)(1)(B). The question is whether out-of-court consistent statements made after the alleged fabrication, or after the alleged improper influence or motive arose, and admissible under the Rule.

I

Petitioner Tome was charged in a one-count indictment with the felony of sexual abuse of a child, his own daughter, aged four at the time of the alleged crime. The case having arisen on the Navajo Indian Reservation, Tome was tried by a jury in the United States District Court for the District of New Mexico, where he was found guilty. . . .

Tome and the child's mother had been divorced in 1988. A trial court awarded joint custody of the daughter, A.T., to both parents, but Tome had primary physical custody. In 1989 the mother was unsuccessful in petitioning the tribal court for primary custody of A.T., but was awarded custody for the summer of 1990. Neither parent attended a further custody hearing in August 1990. On August 27, 1990, the mother contacted Colorado authorities with allegations that Tome had committed sexual abuse against A.T.

The prosecution's theory was that Tome committed sexual assaults upon the child while she was in his custody and that the crime was disclosed when the child was spending vacation time with her mother. The defense argued that the allegations were concocted so the child would not be returned to her father. At trial A.T., then six and one half years old, was the Government's first witness. For the most part, her direct testimony consisted of one- and two-word answers to a series of leading questions. Cross-examination took place over a two trial days. The defense asked A.T. 348 questions. On the first day A.T. answered all the questions posed to her on general, background subjects.

The next day there was no testimony, and the prosecutor met with A.T. When cross-examination of A.T. resumed, she was questioned about the conversations but was reluctant to discuss them. Defense counsel then began questioning her about the allegations of abuse, and it appears she was reluctant at many points to answer. As the trial judge noted, however, some of the defense questions were imprecise or unclear. The judge expressed his concerns with the examination of A.T., observing there were lapses of as much as 40-55 seconds between some questions and the answers and that on the second day of examination the witness seemed to be losing concentration. The trial judge stated, "We have a very difficult situation here."

After A.T. testified, the Government produced six witnesses who testified about a total of seven statements made by A.T. describing the alleged sexual assaults: A.T.'s babysitter recited A.T.'s statement to her on August 22, 1990, that she did not want to return to her father because he "gets drunk and he thinks I'm his wife"; the babysitter related further details given by A.T. on August 27, 1990, while A.T.'s mother stood outside the room and listened after the mother had been unsuccessful in questioning A.T. herself; the mother recounted what she had heard A.T. tell the babysitter; a social worker recounted details A.T. told her on August 28, 1990 about the assaults; and three pediatricians, Drs. Kuper, Reich and Spiegel, related A.T.'s statements to them describing how and where she had been touched by Tome. All but A.T.'s statement to Dr. Spiegel implicated Tome. (The physicians also testified that their clinical examinations of the child indicated that she had been subjected to vaginal penetrations. That part of the testimony is not at issue here.)

A.T.'s out-of-court statements, recounted by the six witnesses, were offered by the Government under Rule 801(d)(1)(B). The trial court admitted all of the statements over defense counsel's objection, accepting the Government's argument that they rebutted the implicit charge that A.T.'s testimony was motivated by a desire to live with her mother. The court also admitted A.T.'s August 22nd statement to her babysitter under Rule 803(24), and the statements to Dr. Kuper (and apparently also to Dr. Reich) under Rule 803(4) (statements for purposes of medical diagnosis). The Government offered the testimony of the social worker under both Rules 801(d)(1)(B) and 803(24), but the record does not indicate whether the court ruled on the latter ground. No objection was made to Dr. Spiegel's testimony. Following trial, Tome was convicted and sentenced to 12 years imprisonment.

On appeal, the Court of Appeals for the Tenth Circuit affirmed, adopting the Government's argument that all of A.T.'s out-of-court statements were admissible under Rule 801(d)(1)(B) even though they had been made after A.T.'s alleged motive to fabricate arose. . . . The court recognized that some Circuits require that the consistent statements, to be admissible under the Rule, must be made before the motive or influence arose, in support of its balancing approach. Applying this balancing test to A.T.'s first statement to her babysitter, the Court of Appeals determined that although A.T. might have had "some motive to lie, we do not believe that it is a particularly strong one." The court held that the district judge had not abused his discretion in admitting A.T.'s out-of-court statements. It did not analyze the probative quality of A.T.'s six other out-of-court statements, nor did it reach the admissibility of the statements under any other rule of evidence.

We granted certiorari, and now reverse.

II

The prevailing common-law rule for more than a century before adoption of the Federal Rules of Evidence was that a prior consistent statement introduced to rebut a charge of recent fabrication or improper influence or motive was admissible if the statement had been made before the alleged fabrication, influence, or motive came into being, but it was inadmissible if made afterwards. . . . The question is whether Rule 801(d)(1)(B) embodies this temporal requirement. We hold that it does. . . .

A

Rule 801 provides:

(d) Statements which are not hearsay.—A statement is not hearsay if—

> (1) Prior statement by witness.—The declarant testifies at the trial or hearing and is subject to cross-examination concerning the statement, and the statement is . . .

> (B) Consistent with the declarant's testimony and is offered to rebut
> an express or implied charge against the declarant of recent fabrication
> or improper influence or motive.

Rule 801 defines prior consistent statements as nonhearsay only if they are offered to rebut a charge of "recent fabrication or improper influence or motive." Fed. Rule Evid. 801(d)(1)(B). Noting the "troublesome" logic of treating a witness' prior consistent statements as hearsay at all (because the declarant is present in court and subject to cross-examination), the Advisory Committee decided to treat those consistent statements, once the preconditions of the Rule were satisfied, as nonhearsay and admissible as substantive evidence, not just to rebut an attack on the witness' credibility. A consistent statement meeting the requirements of the Rule is thus placed in the same category as a declarant's inconsistent statement made under oath in another proceeding, or prior indentification testimony, or admissions by a party opponent. See Fed. Rule Evid. 801.

The Rules do not accord this weighty, nonhearsay status to all prior consistent statements. To the contrary, admissibility under the Rules is confined to those statements offered to rebut a charge of "recent fabrication or improper influence or motive," the same phrase used by the Advisory Committee in its description of the "traditiona[l]" common law of evidence, which was the background against which the Rules were drafted. Prior consistent statements may not be admitted to counter all forms of impeachment or to bolster the witness merely because she has been discredited. In the present context, the question is whether A.T.'s out-of-court statements rebutted the alleged link between her desire to be with her mother and her testimony, not whether they suggested that A.T.'s in-court testimony was true. The Rule speaks of a party rebutting an alleged motive, not bolstering the veracity of the story told.

This limitation is instructive, not only to establish the preconditions of admissibility but also to reinforce the significance of the requirement that the consistent statements must have been made before the alleged influence, or motive to fabricate arose. . . .

There may arise instances when out-of-court statements that postdate the alleged fabrication have some probative force in rebutting a charge of fabrication or improper influence or motive, but those statements refute the charged fabrication in a less direct and forceful way. Evidence that a witness made consistent statements after the alleged motive to fabricate arose may suggest in some degree that the in-court testimony is truthful, and thus suggest in some degree that the testimony did not result from some improper influence; but if the drafters of Rule 801(d)(1)(B) intended to countenance rebuttal along that indirect inferential chain, the purpose of confining the types of impeachment that open the door to rebuttal by introducing consistent statements becomes unclear. If consistent statements are admissible without reference to the time frame we find imbedded in the Rule, there appears no sound reason not to admit consistent statements to rebut other forms of impeachment as well. Whatever objections can be leveled against limiting the Rule to this designated form of impeachment and confining the rebuttal to those statements made before the fabrication or improper influence or motive arose, it is clear to us that the drafters of Rule 801(d)(1)(B) were relying upon the common-law temporal requirement.

The underlying theory of the Government's position is that an out-of-court consistent statement, whenever it was made, tends to bolster the testimony of a witness and so tends also to rebut an express or implied charge that the testimony has been the product of an improper influence. Congress could have adopted that rule with ease, providing, for instance, that "a witness' prior consistent statements are admissible whenever relevant to assess the witness's truthfulness or accuracy." The theory would be that, in a broad sense, any prior statement by a witness concerning the disputed issues at trial would have some relevance in assessing the accuracy or truthfulness of the witness's in-court testimony on the same subject. The narrow Rule enacted by Congress, however, cannot be understood to incorporate the Government's theory. . . .

The language of the Rule, in its concentration on rebutting charges of recent fabrication, improper influence and motive to the exclusion of other forms of impeachment, as well as in its use of wording which follows the language of the common-law cases, suggests that it was intended to carry over the common-law pre-motive rule.

B

Our conclusion that Rule 801(d)(1)(B) embodies the common-law premotive requirement is confirmed by an examination of the Advisory Committee Notes to the Federal Rules of Evidence. We have relied on those well-considered Notes as a useful guide in ascertaining the meaning of the Rules. . . .

The Notes disclose a purpose to adhere to the common law in the application of evidentiary principles, absent express provisions to the contrary. Where the Rules did depart from their common-law antecedents, in general the Committee said so. [Citations omitted.] The Notes give no indication, however, that Rule 801(d)(1)(B) abandoned the premotive requirement. The entire discussion of Rule 801(d)(1)(B) is limited to the following comment:

> Prior consistent statements traditionally have been admissible to rebut charges of recent fabrication or improper influence or motive but not as substantive evidence. Under the rule they are substantive evidence. The prior statement is

consistent with the testimony given on the stand, and, if the opposite party wishes to open the door for its admission in evidence, no sound reason is apparent why it should not be received generally.

Throughout their discussion of the Rules, the Advisory Committee Notes rely on Wigmore and McCormick as authority for the common-law approach. In light of the categorical manner in which those authors state the premotive requirement, it is difficult to imagine that the drafters, who noted the new substantive use of prior consistent statements, would have remained silent if they intended to modify the premotive requirement. . . . Here, we do not think the drafters of the Rule intended to scuttle the whole premotive requirement and rationale without so much as a whisper of explanation. . . .

"A party contending that legislative action changed settled law has the burden of showing that the legislature intended such a change." Nothing in the Advisory Committee's Notes suggests that it intended to alter the common-law premotive requirement.

C

The Government's final argument in favor of affirmance is that the common-law premotive rule advocated by petitioner is inconsistent with the Federal Rules' liberal approach to relevancy and with strong academic criticism, beginning in the 1940's, directed at the exclusion of out-of-court statements made by a declarant who is present in court and subject to cross-examination. This argument misconceives the design of the Rules' hearsay provisions. . . .

To be sure, certain commentators in the years preceding the adoption of the Rules had been critical of the common-law approach to hearsay, particularly its categorical exclusion of out-of-court statements offered for substantive purposes. General criticism was directed to the exclusion of a declarant's out-of-court statements where the declarant testified at trial. . . . As an alternative, they suggested moving away from the categorical exclusion of hearsay and toward a case-by-case balancing of the probative value of particular statements against their likely prejudicial effect. The Advisory Committee, however, was explicit in rejecting this balancing approach to hearsay:

> The Advisory Committee has rejected this approach to hearsay as involving too great a measure of judicial discretion, minimizing the predictability of rulings, [and] enhancing the difficulties of preparation for trial.

Advisory Committee's Introduction, at 771. Given the Advisory Committee's rejection of both the general balancing approach to hearsay, and of Uniform Rule 63(1), the Government's reliance on the views of those who advocated these positions is misplaced.

The statement-by-statement balancing approach advocated by the Government and adopted by the Tenth Circuit creates the precise dangers the Advisory Committee noted and sought to avoid: It involves considerable judicial discretion; it reduces predictability; and it enhances the difficulties of trial preparation because parties will have difficulty knowing in advance whether or not particular out-of-court statements will be admitted.

D

The case before us illustrates some of the important considerations supporting the Rule as we interpret it, especially in criminal cases. If the Rule were to permit the introduction of prior statements as substantive evidence to rebut every implicit charge that a witness' in-court testimony results from recent fabrication or improper influence or motive, the whole emphasis of the trial could shift to the out-of-court statements, not the in-court ones. The present case illustrates the point. In response to a rather weak charge that A.T.'s testimony was a fabrication created so the child could remain with her mother, the Government was permitted to present a parade of sympathetic and credible witnesses who did no more than recount A.T.'s detailed out-of-court statements to them. Although those statements might have been probative on the question whether the alleged conduct had occurred, they shed but minimal light on whether A.T. had the charged motive to fabricate. At closing argument before the jury, the Government placed great reliance on the prior statements for substantive purposes but did not once seek to use them to rebut the impact of the alleged motive. . . .

III

. . . Our holding is confined to the requirements for admission under Rule 801(d)(1)(B). The Rule permits the introduction of a declarant's consistent out-of-court statements to rebut a charge of recent fabrication or improper influence or motive only when those statements were made before the charged recent fabrication or improper influence or motive. These conditions of admissibility were not established here.

The judgment of the Court of Appeals for the Tenth Circuit is reversed, and the case is remanded for further proceedings consistent with this opinion.

It is so ordered.

[Concurring opinion by Justice Scalia and dissenting opinion by Justice Breyer omitted.]

Problem: Blind Justice

A blind man sitting at a bar feels someone trying to steal his wallet from his back pocket. He whirls on the thief and grabs him by his chest in a vice-like grip. "Call the police," he says to the bartender, who does so. Some minutes later a policeman arrives. The blind man, still holding the thief by the chest, hands the thief to the policeman, saying, "Here is the man who tried to steal my wallet." At trial of the thief for attempted larceny, the blind man tells this story. When the prosecutor asks him if he sees the thief in the courtroom, the blind man replies negatively. The prosecutor next calls the policeman who took the thief into custody. When the prosecutor asks him whether he sees the person he arrested in the courtroom, the policeman points to the defendant. The prosecutor then asks, "What did the blind man say to you when he delivered the defendant to you?" Defense counsel objects on grounds of hearsay. What ruling and why?

Problem: The Erring Eyewitness

Charge: armed robbery. At trial, *W*, an eyewitness, is asked to pick out the robber. She points to a U.S. Marshal seated in the courtroom. After the prosecutor recovers, he elicits testimony from *W* concerning *W*'s selection of a photograph of the alleged robber from a display of photographs conducted shortly after the robbery. The photograph was of the defendant. Defendant objects. What ruling and why? Does Rule 801(d)(1)(C) apply to photographic as well as corporeal out-of-court identifications? Does Rule 801(d)(1)(A)'s "under oath" limitation apply to prior identifications inconsistent with a later in-court identification? Is this a case of "inconsistency"? Should third-party testimony concerning an out-of-court identification by a witness be admissible if the witness cannot recall the prior identification?

D. Exceptions to the Hearsay Rule—Declarant Unavailable

The rule against hearsay is famous, or more aptly, notorious, for the number and intricacy of its exceptions. These many exceptions offer the resourceful lawyer many opportunities to get otherwise inadmissible hearsay evidence before the jury in some form or for some purpose. Some authorities believe that the hearsay exceptions have literally swallowed the rule itself.

Irving Younger, a famous lecturer on Evidence, at the point of his lecture where he was discussing hearsay often would exclaim in a booming stentorian voice, "Never!, Never! Never in the history of modern jurisprudence has any court ever been reversed for admitting hearsay!" When his lecture was delivered to groups of judges, however, there would inevitably be a few who would shake their heads, muttering, "That can't be true. . . . I was reversed for admitting hearsay . . ."

Regardless of whether Professor Younger's assertion is literally true, it cannot be disputed that the many hearsay rule exceptions allow in evidence much, if not most, of the material which would otherwise be excluded by operation of the rule itself.

As indicated at the outset of this chapter, the primary purpose of the Hearsay Rule is to safeguard the right of cross-examination as the primary guarantee of accuracy and reliability of information transmitted from persons with knowledge. The exceptions recognize the reality that requiring cross-examination of all information that could be useful at a trial might severely constrict the amount of information available to the judicial process. The hearsay exceptions are thus often employed to permit second-hand information where first-hand testimony is not available. The exceptions are crafted around circumstances surrounding the making of a statement that would indicate a degree of likely reliability. The two policy justifications for admitting hearsay statements, unavailability of the testimony in the usual form, and likely reliability based on the circumstances of the statement, often complement each other. That is, the more circumstantially reliable statements are often admitted without having to show necessity at all. Statements possessing less impressive circumstantial indications of reliability are often admitted only on a showing that the declarant is "unavailable" to testify in person at the trial.

1. Prior Testimony

Under Rule 804(b)(1), testimony given as a witness at another hearing may be used if the witness is unavailable at trial, if the party against whom the testimony is now offered had an opportunity to examine the witness whether through direct, cross- or re-direct examination. The tough issue, as the Advisory Committee's Note points out, is whether fairness allows imposing upon the party against whom is now offered the handling of the witness on the earlier occasion. If the parties are identical, then it seems fair to permit earlier testimony into evidence, and the balance of doing without the evidence altogether or doing with evidence that was once examined seems to tilt toward admission. If the parties (or issues) are different, however, is it fair to permit the use of former testimony, and is the preference for old evidence over no evidence? Under Rule 804(b)(1) the test is whether the party against whom the testimony is offered was a predecessor in interest. Under this approach, what factors should a court consider in determining whether a party in a later case is a predecessor in interest to a party in a former case? Should similarity of factual and legal issues count in assessing similarity of interest? The amount at stake?

Problem: Speaking from the Grave—The Dead Witness

(1) Action against *D* Supermarket for injuries allegedly sustained when *P* slipped and fell while shopping in the *D* store. *P* claims he slipped on ketchup from a broken bottle. *D* claims *P* slipped on a wad of tobacco from *P*'s mouth. *W*, a customer in the store who rushed to *P*'s aid while *P* was lying unconscious on the floor, is *P*'s first witness at trial. *W* testifies that she saw ketchup on the soles of *P*'s shoes after the fall. On cross-examination, defense counsel questions *W*'s perception, memory, and veracity but fails to make much progress. Verdict is for *P*, but when the jury is polled it is discovered that the panel consists of only 11 people. A mistrial is declared. On retrial, *P* introduces evidence that *W* is dead and calls *R*, the court reporter from the first trial, to testify that he remembers *W*'s former testimony and to relate it. *D* objects. What ruling and why?

What policies justify the use of former testimony of an unavailable witness? What are the dangers and drawbacks of the use of this type of evidence? What limitations should be imposed on the use of former testimony?

(2) *P*'s car collides with *D*'s car. *G* was a guest in *P*'s car. *W* witnessed the collision. At the trial of *P*'s action against *D*, *W* testifies for *P*. Later, at the trial of *G*'s action against *D*, *G* proves *W*'s death and offers a transcript of *W*'s former testimony from the first trial. *D* objects. What rulings and why?

(3) *P* is tried on a charge of arson. *W* testifies for the prosecution. Later, *P* sues *D* Insurance Company to recover for losses sustained in the fire. *D* Insurance Company proves *W*'s death and offers a transcript of *W*'s former testimony. *P* objects. What ruling and why?

What result if *W* had first testified in the civil action and his testimony was offered at a subsequent criminal trial?

(4) *P* is injured while alighting from the *D* Bus Company's bus. *P*'s husband, *H*, sues *D* for loss of his wife's services, claiming that *D*'s driver started driving the bus before *P* had completely alighted. At trial, *W* testifies for *D* that the bus did not move but that *P* tripped over her own feet. Later, *P* sues *D* for personal injuries. *D* proves *W*'s death and offers the transcript of *W*'s former testimony. *P* objects. What ruling and why?

(5) *P*'s car collides with *D*'s car, injuring bystander *W*. At the trial of *P*'s action against *D*, *D* testifies. Later, at the trial of *W*'s action against *P*, *W* proves *D*'s death and offers a transcript of *D*'s former testimony. *P* objects. What ruling and why?

Compare this problem with subparagraph 2, above. What additional information would you like to have in deciding this problem? In determining the admissibility of former testimony, should the trial judge place greater weight on similarity of factual issues in the two proceedings or on similarity of legal issues? To what extent should former testimony be excluded on the grounds that it related only to a collateral issue in the earlier proceeding?

2. Statements Against Interest

The rationale for Rule 804(b)(3) is that people are not likely to make statements damaging to themselves unless they believe them to be true and, thus, such statements retain sufficient trustworthiness to be admissible even though hearsay. Remember, however, that If the statement is that of a party, it comes in as an admission under Rule 803(d)(2) without any against-interest requirement.

Rule 804(b)(3) expands the traditional common law hearsay exception to render not only statements against pecuniary or proprietary interest admissible, but also statements that subject the declarant to civil or criminal liability and statements tending to expose the declarant to hatred, ridicule, or disgrace. The Advisory Committee states that only statements clearly against the declarant's interest at the time and in the circumstances at which they were made may be admitted into evidence. The comment points out that statements made to gain the favor of the prosecutor are not against interest. What is the standard for determining whether a co-conspirator's statement is made to gain the favor of a prosecutor? See United States v. Barrett, 539 F.2d 244 (1st Cir. 1976), and United States v. Pena, 527 F.2d 1356 (5th Cir. 1976).

Problem: The Fraudulent Transfers

Action on a promissory note and for fraudulent transfer of *D*'s assets, allegedly rendering him insolvent. *P*'s complaint seeks a money judgment for $10,000, the amount of the note, interest, and costs, and an order against *D* and *E*, setting aside a purported conveyance of Brownacre from *D* to *E*. *D*'s answer admits the debt to *P* and the conveyance to *E* but denies that the conveyance was made with any fraudulent intent or effect. At trial, *D* offers two witnesses:

(1) *W1*, Jr., to testify that his father, *W1*, Sr., is dead, that *W1*, Sr.'s estate is not yet settled, and that just before *W1*, Sr., died he said that he owed *D* $5,000.

(2) *W2*, Jr., to testify that his father, *W2*, Sr., is dead, that *W2*, Sr.'s estate is not yet settled, and that just before *W2*, Sr., died he said that he had secretly conveyed Goldacre to *D*.

What ruling and why on these offers? What policy considerations support admissibility? What policy considerations militate against admitting such evidence? What types of statements are covered by the exception for statements against interest? Where would you draw the line? What other elements must exist to invoke the exception?

Problem: The Speeding Chauffeur

Action for damages that allegedly occurred when *D*'s car collided with *B*'s car, swerved up on the sidewalk, and struck *P*, who was walking on the sidewalk. *D*'s car was driven by *D*, but *B*'s car was driven by his chauffeur, Jeeves, who was alone in the car. *D*'s answer denies he was negligent and alleges the accident was totally Jeeves's fault. At trial, *B* is unavailable. *D* offers *W* to testify that a month before trial *W* heard *B* say that Jeeves was driving so fast at the time of the accident that he ran a stop sign. *P* objects. What ruling and why?

P. TAGUE, PERILS OF THE RULEMAKING PROCESS: TE DEVELOPMENT, APPLICATION, AND UNCONSTITUTIONALITY OF RULE 804(b)(3)'S PENAL INTEREST EXCEPTION
69 Geo. L.J. 851, 862-863, 971 (1981)

The penal interest exception rests on the assumption that no one would knowingly implicate himself falsely in criminal conduct. Testing the validity of that assumption in a particular case involves at least six evidentiary questions. . . .

First, is a statement against a declarant's penal interest because of the "plain" meaning of the words spoken, the litigation effect of the statement, or the declarant's motivation to tell the truth? If a court concentrates on the words spoken, it probably will limit admissibility to confessions ("I am guilty of murdering Smith") or to explicit factual assertions ("I shot Smith"). If, however, the court analyzes the litigation effect of the statement, it might permit the introduction of opinions ("The defendant is not guilty"), statements whose relevance depends upon an inference ("I was present when Smith was shot"), or comments about the defendant's complicity related to the statement ("*X* and I, but not the defendant, committed the crime").

Second, must the statement have been "against interest" at the time the declarant made it? If a court admits only statements that are confessional in nature, it would focus on when the declarant made the statement. If, however, the court analyzes the litigation effect of the statement, its inquiry could encompass a greater time period.

Third, must the declarant have understood that his statement was "against interest"? Courts usually use a "reasonable man" inquiry because they condition admission on the declarant's unavailability to testify. If, however, at the moment he spoke or at some later point the declarant says that he understood the "against interest" nature of his statement, should a court reject the "reasonable man" test and focus instead on the declarant's apparent subjective understanding?

Fourth, must the statement substitute the declarant for the defendant as the culprit? If so, a court should exclude the statement if it is relevant only to the defendant's degree of culpability, not his innocence. A statement that exonerated the defendant of complicity in a crime committed by more than one person is similarly inadmissible because this kind of statement provides the Government with a reason to charge the declarant as well as the defendant.

Fifth, may the Government use the exception to introduce a statement that implicates both the declarant and the defendant? A Government-offered statement presents the same "collateral statement" problem as does the defense-offered statement in the fourth issue.

Sixth, must the proponent introduce other evidence to support the truthfulness of either the witness' report of the statement or the statement itself? Demanding corroborating evidence of either sort suggests uncertainty about the declarant's motivation or his sincerity. . . .

Five mechanical questions arise when the defendant offers a penal interest statement. First, should the judge or the jury decide if the statement satisfies the "against interest" tests of the rule's first sentence and the corroboration test of the rule's second sentence? Second, may the judge consider the trustworthiness of the reporting witness in deciding whether to admit the statement? Third, what is the defendant's burden of proof under the separate tests of the rule's first and second sentences? Fourth, what evidence may the judge consider in deciding whether to admit the statement? Finally, what evidence may the jury consider in deciding how to evaluate the declarant's statement? . . .

Problem: Thick as Thieves

Charge: murder of *V* on June 1 at the intersection of JFK Street and Massachusetts Avenue.

(1) At *D*'s trial, *D* offers, through *W*, the statement of Joe (now dead), "I killed *V*." Is Joe's statement admissible? Under what circumstances?

(2) Suppose instead that *D* offers a letter signed by Joe, dated June 5, stating "I killed *V*." After objection and on voir dire the prosecution offers the coroner to testify that on June 5 Joe committed suicide. Is the letter admissible?

(3) Suppose instead that *D* offers, through *W*, Joe's statement, "*D* is not guilty of killing *V*." Admissible?

(4) Suppose instead that *D* offers, through *W*, Joe's statement, "Frank and I killed *V*. *D* did not have anything to do with it." Admissible?

(5) Suppose the prosecution offers, through *W*, Joe's statement, "*D* and I killed *V*." Admissible?

The Supreme Court has indicated that there are constitutional limitations on a state's application of the declaration against interest exception to the hearsay rule in criminal cases when the declaration is offered by the defendant. See Green v. Georgia, 442 U.S. 95 (1979). Where do these limits fall?

3. Dying Declarations

The Federal Rules codify a common law hearsay exception for certain statements made by a person in belief of impending death. The rationale for this exception is necessity and the belief that impending death induces a person to speak the truth. For a hearsay statement to be admitted as a dying declaration, it must be made under a sense of "impending doom." This standard requires a subjective determination of the state of the declarant's mind at the time the statement was made. What evidence may be presented to prove the declarant's sense of doom —the statement itself, last rites, circumstantial evidence? The declarant need not die to admit the statement as a dying declaration—it is good enough if she thought she was going to die. The rule limits the admissibility of dying declarations in criminal cases to homicide cases and to the cause of circumstances of death. Why?

Problem: The Voice from the Grave

Charge: murder, first-degree. M.O.: shooting *V* with a handgun on June 1 and then escaping unseen. *V* is taken to the hospital and her condition deteriorates over the next five days. On June 6, in agony and gasping for breath, *V* says that her sister, *D*, shot her. *V* then dies. At *D*'s trial the D.A. offers *W*, who heard *V*'s declaration, to testify to its contents. *D* objects. What ruling and why?

What policy considerations generally support admitting such statements? In what respects are such statements similar to or different from admissions, declarations against interest, or excited utterances? Are they more or less reliable than declarations admitted under these other exceptions?

SHEPARD v. UNITED STATES
290 U.S. 96 (1933)

Mr. Justice CARDOZO delivered the opinion of the Court.

The petitioner, Charles A. Shepard, a major in the medical corps of the United States army, has been convicted of the murder of his wife, Zenana Shepard, at Fort Riley, Kansas, a United States military reservation. . . .

The crime is charged to have been committed by poisoning the victim with bichloride of mercury. The defendant was in love with another woman, and wished to make her his wife. There is circumstantial evidence to sustain a finding by the jury that to win himself his freedom he turned to poison and murder. Even so, guilt was contested and conflicting inferences are possible. The defendant asks us to hold that by the acceptance of incompetent evidence the scales were weighted to his prejudice and in the end to his undoing.

The evidence complained of was offered by the Government in rebuttal when the trial was nearly over. On May 22, 1929, there was a conversation in the absence of the defendant between Mrs. Shepard, then ill in bed, and Clara Brown, her nurse. The patient asked the nurse to go to the closet in the defendant's room and bring a bottle of whisky that would be found upon a shelf. When the bottle was produced, she said that this was the liquor she had taken just before collapsing. She asked whether enough was left to make a test for the presence of poison, insisting that the smell and taste were strange. And then she added the words, "Dr. Shepard has poisoned me."

The conversation was proved twice. After the first proof of it, the Government asked to strike it out, being doubtful of its competence, and this request was granted. A little later, however, the offer was renewed, the nurse having then testified to statements by Mrs. Shepard as to the prospect of recovery. "She said she was not going to get well; she was going to die." With the aid of this new evidence, the conversation already summarized was proved a second time. There was a timely challenge of the ruling.

She said, "Dr. Shepard has poisoned me." The admission of this declaration, if erroneous, was more than unsubstantial error. As to that the parties are agreed. The voice of the dead wife was heard in accusation of her husband, and the accusation was accepted as evidence of guilt. If the evidence was incompetent, the verdict may not stand.

Upon the hearing in this court the Government finds its main prop in the position that what was said by Mrs. Shepard was admissible as a dying declaration. This is manifestly the theory upon which it was offered and received. The prop, however, is a broken reed. To make out a dying declaration the declarant must have spoken without hope of recovery and in the shadow of impending death. The record furnishes no proof of that indispensable condition. So, indeed, it was ruled by all the judges of the court below, though the majority held the view that the testimony was competent for quite another purpose, which will be considered later on.

We have said that the declarant was not shown to have spoken without hope of recovery and in the shadow of impending death. Her illness began on May 20. She was found in a state of collapse, delirious, in pain, the pupils of her eyes dilated, and the retina suffused with blood. The conversation with the nurse occurred two days later. At that time her mind had cleared up, and her speech was rational and orderly. There was as yet no thought by any of her physicians that she was dangerously ill, still less that her case was hopeless. To all seeming she had greatly improved, and was moving forward to recovery. There had been no diagnosis of poison as the cause of her distress. Not till about a week afterwards was there a relapse, accompanied by an infection of the mouth, renewed congestion of the eyes, and later hemorrhages of the bowels. Death followed on June 15.

Nothing in the condition of the patient on May 22 gives fair support to the conclusion that hope had then been lost. She may have thought she was going to die and have said so to her nurse, but this was consistent with hope, which could not have been put aside without more to quench it. Indeed, a fortnight later, she said to one of her physicians, though her condition was then grave, "You will get me well, won't you?" Fear or even belief that illness will end in death will not avail of itself to make a dying declaration. There must be "a settled hopeless expectation" that death is near at hand, and what is said must have been spoken in the hush of its impending presence. . . .

The petitioner insists that the form of the declaration exhibits other defects that call for its exclusion, apart from the objection that death was not imminent and that hope was still alive. Homicide may not be imputed to a defendant on the basis of mere suspicions, though they are the suspicions of the dying. To let the declaration in, the inference must be permissible that there was knowledge or the opportunity for knowledge as to the acts that are declared. . . . The form is not decisive, though it be that of a conclusion, a statement of the result with the antecedent steps omitted. Wigmore, §1447. "He murdered me" does not cease to be competent as a dying declaration because in the statement of the act there is also an appraisal of the crime. One does not hold the dying to the observance of all the niceties of speech to which conformity is exacted from a witness on the stand. What is decisive is something deeper and more fundamental than any difference of form.

The declaration is kept out if the setting of the occasion satisfies the judge, or in reason ought to satisfy him, that the speaker is giving expression to suspicion or conjecture, and not to known facts. The difficulty is not so much in respect of the governing principle as in its application to varying and equivocal conditions. In this case, the ruling that there was a failure to make out the imminence of death and the abandonment of hope relieves us of the duty of determining whether it is a legitimate inference that there was the opportunity for knowledge. We leave that question open. . . .

Problem: Dying Declarations

Charge: homicide, first-degree. M.O.: striking *V* on the head with a tire iron at noon on June 1. *D* and *E* were the only two present at the scene of the crime. One of them did it. At 12:55 *V* is dying and knows it. Before he dies, *V* says that it was *D* who struck him. At noon on June 2, *E* has a heart attack. At 12:55, *E* is dying and knows it. Before he dies *E* says that it was he who struck *V* on June 1. At trial, the D.A. offers proof of *V*'s statement, and *D* offers proof of *E*'s statement. What rulings and why to timely objections to both offers?

Problem: Double Death

Action by *P*, executor of *V*'s estate, against *D* for *V*'s wrongful death. Evidence is introduced to show that *V* was struck in a crosswalk by a hit-and-run driver. *V* was taken to a hospital and her condition worsened. *V* knew death was imminent and shouted out, "It was that bastard *D* who hit me." The only auditor of this statement was *A*, another patient in the room with *V*. After *V*'s body was wheeled out of the room, the doctor told *A* his death was imminent. *A* then said to the doctor, "Before I die I must unburden myself. *V* told me that it was *D* who hit her." *A* then dies. At trial, *P* calls the doctor to testify to *A*'s statement. *D* objects. What ruling and why?

What rule would you propose for dying declarations? Would it be the same for civil and criminal cases? Should the admissibility of hearsay dying declarations depend upon the declarant's belief in an afterlife?

Problem: "Speak Up, Please"

Charge: murder of *V*. Dr. Jones is called to the stand by the prosecution. At *D*'s request the judge first listens to Dr. Jones's testimony out of the presence of the jury. Jones states that just before *V* died, Jones said to her, "You are very badly wounded," and that shortly thereafter

V mumbled, "*D* did it." The judge thinks that *V* probably knew she was dying but recognized that reasonable people might differ on that question. The judge also thinks that *V* probably did not say, "*D* did it," but rather mumbled something else which the doctor misunderstood, but the judge recognizes that reasonable persons might also differ on that. Defense counsel objects to Jones's being allowed to testify before the jury. What ruling and why?

E. Hearsay Exceptions—Availability of Declarant Immaterial

The Federal Rules of Evidence codify a number of exceptions to the hearsay rule which do not depend on the unavailability of the declarant to appear and testify at the trial. These exceptions can be thought to rest on better circumstantial guarantees of reliability than those statements that are admissible only if the declarant is unavailable. Or it could merely be that these exceptions were better known and accepted at common law when the Rules were initially adopted. We address these largely through a number of problems which illustrate how the exceptions work. As you do these problems, consider whether the circumstances supporting any applicable hearsay rule exceptions adequately substitute for cross-examination as a guarantee of truthfulness of the statement.

1. Present Sense Impressions, Excited Utterances, Statements of Current Physical or Mental Condition, Statements for Diagnosis or Treatment

Problem: Stage Fright

(1) Action for wrongful death of *V*. *D* denies generally. At trial, *P* calls *V*'s daughter, *G*, to testify that on June 1 she and *V* were riding in *V*'s carriage along a narrow country road, that she saw *D* come up behind the carriage on horseback, that she did not see anything thereafter because she ducked down on the floor of the carriage, and that after the carriage turned over *V* said to her, "That no-good *D* hit our horse with his whip." On *D*'s objection, what ruling and why?

(2) *P* also calls *B*, *V*'s butler, to testify that when *G* arrived home on June 1 she was distraught and speechless. *B* immediately gave her a brandy and made her lie down. Two hours later, *G* awoke and told *B* that *D* had whipped the horse and caused the carriage to turn over, killing *V*. On *D*'s objection, what ruling and why?

What considerations of reliability militate for admission of such statements? What considerations militate against admission? How would you frame a rule of law applicable generally to such declarations?

Problem: Stagger P

Action for damages allegedly sustained when *P* was struck by a car driven by *D*. Defense: contributory negligence. At trial, *D* calls *W* to testify that ten minutes before the accident *W* was at a bar with *P* and *Q*, that *P* got up to leave, and that *Q* said to *W*, "Look at *P* stagger. Man, is he smashed." *P* objects. What ruling and why? What factors militate for and against admission of this evidence?

Problem: Husband Harry

Action for damages arising out of a collision between cars driven by *P* and *D*. At trial, *P* calls *W*, a passenger in *D*'s car, to testify that just after the accident she called *D*'s husband, Harry, to inform him of the accident and that Harry said, "Oh, my goodness. It must have been our fault. We've known these brakes were bad for two weeks." On *D*'s objection, what ruling and why?

Problem: Snowmobile Crash

Action for damages *P* allegedly sustained on January 1 when *D* ran over *P* with his snowmobile while *P* was cross-country skiing. *D* denies hitting *P* and also that *P* suffered any injuries.

(1) At trial, *P* calls *W* to testify that he was a patient in the same room of the hospital to which *P* was taken and that the day after *P* was brought in, *P* said to *W*, "*D* ran over me with his snowmobile. I was in agony out on the trail, couldn't sleep last night, and now my legs are really throbbing." *D* objects. What ruling and why?

(2) Suppose that *P*'s statement was made to the attending hospital physician while *P* was being examined. May *W* testify to the statement? May the physician?

(3) Suppose that *P*'s statement was made to a second physician retained specially by *P*'s brother, a personal injury plaintiff's lawyer, to examine *P* in anticipation of his testifying against *D* at a future trial. May *W* testify to the statement? May this physician?

Rule 803(4) is premised on the patient's strong motivation to be truthful about information that will form the basis of his diagnosis and treatment. The exception applies to statements of present or past condition, medical history, and general causation, but not to statements as to fault. The extension of Rule 803(4) to cover statements made to nontreating physicians purely for the purpose of diagnosis in preparation for testifying at trial is one of the most radical extensions of the Federal Rules. It is highly questionable whether statements made in this context have any circumstantial guarantees of trustworthiness.

Problem: Strong Feelings and Future Plans

(1) Action for alienation of affections of *P*'s wife, *A*. At trial, *P* calls *W*, a former friend of *A*, to testify that *A* told her, "After one night with *D*, I realized how much I despise *P*." *D* objects. What ruling and why? If testimony is admitted, what should *D* do?

(2) Worker's compensation action by *W* seeking recovery against *D* for the death of her husband, *H*. The issue is whether the accident in which *H* perished occurred during the course of *H*'s employment. At trial, *W* offers evidence that shortly before going to the airport *H* made several statements that he had to go away on business. *D* objects. What ruling and why?

What difference do you see between these two problems in terms of the purposes for which the evidence is offered? What considerations support and militate against admitting the evidence in these situations? How would you frame a rule of law to cover both situations?

MUTUAL LIFE INSURANCE CO. v. HILLMON
145 U.S. 285 (1892)

GRAY, J. On July 13, 1880, Sallie E. Hillmon, a citizen of Kansas, brought an action against the Mutual Life Insurance Company, a corporation of New York, on a policy of insurance, dated December 10, 1878, on the life of her husband, John W. Hillmon, in the sum of $10,000, payable to her within sixty days after notice and proof of his death. On the same day the plaintiff brought two other actions, the one against the New York Life Insurance Company, a corporation of New York, on two similar policies of life insurance, dated respectively November 30, 1878, and December 10, 1878, for the sum of $5,000 each; and the other against the Connecticut Mutual Life Insurance Company, a corporation of Connecticut, on a similar policy, dated March 4, 1879, for the sum of $5,000.

In each case, the declaration alleged that Hillmon died on March 17, 1879, during the continuance of the policy, but that the defendant, though duly notified of the fact, had refused to pay the amount of the policy, or any part thereof; and the answer denied the death of Hillmon, and alleged that he, together with John H. Brown and divers other persons, on or before November 30, 1878, conspiring to defraud the defendant, procured the issue of all the policies, and afterwards, in March and April, 1879, falsely pretended and represented that Hillmon was dead, and that a dead body which they had procured was his, whereas in reality he was alive and hiding. . . .

At the trial the plaintiff introduced evidence tending to show that on or about March 5, 1879, Hillmon and Brown left Wichita in the State of Kansas in search of a site for a cattle ranch; that on the night of March 18 while they were in camp at a place called Crooked Creek, Hillmon was killed by the accidental discharge of a gun; that Brown at once notified persons living in the neighborhood; and that the body was thereupon taken to a neighboring town, where, after an inquest, it was buried. The defendants introduced evidence tending to show that the body found in the camp at Crooked Creek on the night of March 18 was not the body of Hillmon, but was the body of one Frederick Adolph Walters. Upon the question whose body this was, there was much conflicting evidence, including photographs and descriptions of the corpse, and of the marks and scars upon it, and testimony to its likeness to Hillmon and to Walters.

The defendants introduced testimony that Walters left his home at Fort Madison in the State of Iowa in March, 1878, and was afterwards in Kansas in 1878, and in January and February, 1879; that during that time his family frequently received letters from him, the last of which was written from Wichita; and that he had not been heard from since March, 1879. The defendants also offered the following evidence:

Elizabeth Rieffenach testified that she was a sister of Frederick Adolph Walters, and lived at Fort Madison; and thereupon, as shown by the bill of exceptions, the following proceedings took place:

> Witness further testified that she had received a letter written from Wichita, Kansas, about the 4th or 5th day of March, 1879, by her brother Frederick Adolph; that the letter was dated at Wichita, and was in the handwriting of her brother; that she had searched for the letter, but could not find the same, it being lost; that she remembered and could state the contents of the letter.
>
> Thereupon the defendants' counsel asked the question: "State the contents of that letter." To which the plaintiff objected, on the ground that the same is incompetent, irrelevant, and hearsay. The objection was sustained, and the defendants duly excepted. The following is the letter as stated by witness:

Wichita, Kansas

March 4th or 5th or 3d or 4th—I don't know—1879.

Dear Sister and all: I now in my usual style drop you a few lines to let you know that I expect to leave Wichita on or about March the 5th, with a certain

Mr. Hillmon, a sheep-trader, for Colorado or parts unknown to me. I expect to see the country now. News are of no interest to you, as you are not acquainted here. I will close with compliments to all inquiring friends. Love to all.

> I am truly your brother,
> Fred. Adolph Walters.

Alvina D. Kasten testified that she was twenty-one years of age and resided in Fort Madison; that she was engaged to be married to Frederick Adolph Walters; that she last saw him on March 24, 1878, at Fort Madison; that he left there at that time and had not returned; that she corresponded regularly with him, and received a letter from him about every two weeks until March 3, 1879, which was the last time she received a letter from him; that this letter was dated at Wichita, March 1, 1879, and was addressed to her at Fort Madison, and the envelope was postmarked "Wichita, Kansas, March 2, 1879"; and that she had never heard from or seen him since that time.

The defendants put in evidence the envelope with the postmark and address; and thereupon offered to read the letter in evidence. The plaintiff objected to the reading of the letter, the court sustained the objection, and the defendants excepted.

This letter was dated "Wichita, March 1, 1879," was signed by Walters, and began as follows:

> Dearest Alvina: Your kind and ever welcome letter was received yesterday afternoon about an hour before I left Emporia. I will stay here until the fore part of next week, and then will leave here to see a part of the country that I never expected to see when I left home, as I am going with a man by the name of Hillmon, who intends to start a sheep ranch, and as he promised me more wages than I could make at anything else I concluded to take it, for a while at least, until I strike something better. There is so many folks in this country that have got the Leadville fever, and if I could not of got the situation that I have now I would have went there myself; but as it is at present I get to see the best portion of Kansas, Indian Territory, Colorado, and Mexico. The route that we intend to take would cost a man to travel from $150 to $200, but it will not cost me a cent; besides, I get good wages. I will drop you a letter occasionally until I get settled down; then I want you to answer it. . . .

The court, after recapitulating some of the testimony introduced, instructed the jury as follows:

> You have perceived from the very beginning of the trial that the conclusion to be reached must practically turn upon the question of fact, and all the large volume of evidence, with its graphic and varied details, has no actual significance, save as the facts established thereby may throw light upon and aid you in an-

swering the question, whose body was it that on the evening of March 18, 1879, lay dead by the camp-fire on Crooked Creek? The decision of that question decides the verdict you should render.

The jury, being instructed by the court to return a separate verdict in each case, returned verdicts for the plaintiff against the three defendants respectively for the amounts of their policies, and interest, upon which separate judgments were rendered. The defendants sued out four writs of error, one jointly in the three cases as consolidated, and one in each case separately. . . .

The matter chiefly contested at the trial was the death of John W. Hillmon, the insured; and that depended upon the question whether the body found at Crooked Creek on the night of March 18, 1879, was his body, or the body of one Walters. . . .

A man's state of mind or feeling can only be manifested to others by countenance, attitude or gesture, or by sounds or words, spoken or written. The nature of the fact to be proved is the same, and evidence of its proper tokens is equally competent to prove it, whether expressed by aspect or conduct, by voice or pen. When the intention to be proved is important only as qualifying an act, its connections with that act must be shown, in order to warrant the admission of declarations of the intention. But whenever the intention is of itself a distinct and material fact in a chain of circumstances, it may be proved by contemporaneous oral or written declarations of the party.

The existence of a particular intention in a certain person at a certain time being a material fact to be proved, evidence that he expressed that intention at that time is as direct evidence of the fact, as his own testimony that he then had that intention would be. After his death, there can hardly be any other way of proving it; and while he is still alive, his own memory of his state of mind at a former time is no more likely to be clear and true than a bystander's recollection of what he then said, and is less trustworthy than letters written by him at the very time and under circumstances precluding a suspicion of misrepresentation.

The letters in question were competent, not as narratives of facts communicated to the writer by others, nor yet as proof that he actually went away from Wichita, but as evidence that, shortly before the time when other evidence tended to show that he went away, he had the intention of going, and of going with Hillmon, which made it more probable both that he did go and that he went with Hillmon, than if there had been no proof of such intention. In view of the mass of conflicting testimony introduced upon the question whether it was the body of Walters that was found in Hillmon's camp, this evidence might properly influence the jury in determining that question.

The rule applicable to this case has been thus stated by this court: "Wherever the bodily or mental feelings of an individual are material to be proved, the usual expression of such feelings are original and competent evidence. Those expressions are the natural reflexes of what it might be impossible to show by other testimony. If there be such other testimony, this may be necessary to set the facts thus developed in their true light, and to give them their proper effect. As independent, explanatory or corroborative evidence, it is often indispensable to the due administration of justice. Such declarations are regarded as verbal acts, and are as competent as any other testimony, when relevant to the issue. Their truth or falsity is an inquiry for the jury." Teachers Ins. Co. v. Mosley, 8 Wall. 397, 404, 405. . . .

Upon principle and authority, therefore we are of opinion that the two letters were competent evidence of the intention of Walters at the time of writing them, which was a material fact bearing upon the question in controversy; and that for the exclusion of these letters, as well as for the undue restriction of the defendants' challenges, the verdicts must be set aside, and a new trial had.

Should statements of a declarant that he intended to do a certain act be admissible to prove that another person did a subsequent act? For example, should V's statement that she was going out with defendant the night she was murdered be admissible to prove that the defendant went out with her?

Or in the *Hillmon* case, if it were disputed whether Hillmon went to Crooked Creek (which it was not), should Walters' letters be admissible on this issue? An example is United States v. Pheaster, 544 F.2d 353 (9th Cir. 1976), where evidence was offered in a kidnapping prosecution that shortly before he disappeared the victim said he was going to meet the defendant. Should such evidence be admitted to prove the defendant went to meet the victim? Compare the Advisory Committee Notes and the Report of the House Committee on the Judiciary, S. Rep. No. 1277, 93d Cong., 2d Sess., 120 Cong. Rec. 40069 (1974). Should the availability of the declarant be a factor in these situations?

Problem: Threats

Charge: murder of V. Defense: alibi. At trial, D calls W to testify that a week before V's death, O told W, "I hate V. Someday I'll kick V from here to Timbuktu." The prosecution objects. What ruling and why?

Problem: The Accusing Hand

Charge: murder. M.O.: poisoning patients in a Veterans' Administration hospital where D was a nurse. At D's trial the prosecution seeks to introduce a note written by a patient, now deceased, two hours after suffering a respiratory arrest allegedly caused by *D*. The patient's doctor testified that about two hours after the arrest he ascertained that the patient was resting comfortably and assured the patient he was out of danger. The doctor then asked if anyone had given him any medication just before the arrest. The patient responded by writing *D*'s name. On *D*'s objection, what ruling and why?

Should out-of-court statements of present memory or facts believed by the declarant ever be admitted to show that the remembered or believed fact previously existed? In other words, should the *Hillmon* exception, incorporated in Rule 803(3), point backward in time as well as forward?

In the *Shepard* case, discussed above on another point, the prosecution sought to introduce testimony through a nurse that the defendant's wife, the victim, had told her, "Dr. Shepard [the deceased's husband] has poisoned me." Admissible?

SHEPARD v. UNITED STATES
290 U.S. 96 (1933)

CARDOZO, J. . . . We pass to the question whether the statements to the nurse, though incompetent as dying declarations, were admissible on other grounds.

The Circuit Court of Appeals determined that they were. Witnesses for the defendant had testified to declarations by Mrs. Shepard which suggested a mind bent upon suicide, or at any rate were thought by the defendant to carry that suggestion. More than once before her illness she had stated in the hearing of these witnesses that she had no wish to live, and had nothing to live for, and on one occasion she added that she expected some day to make an end to her life. This testimony opened the door, so it is argued, to declarations in rebuttal that she had been poisoned by her husband. They were admissible, in that view, not as evidence of the truth of what was said, but as betokening a state of mind inconsistent with the presence of suicidal intent.

(a) The testimony was neither offered nor received for the strained and narrow purpose now suggested as legitimate. . . .

(b) Aside, however, from this objection, the accusatory declaration must have been rejected as evidence of a state of mind, though the purpose thus to limit it had been brought to light upon the trial. The defendant had tried to show by Mrs. Shepard's declarations to her friends that she had exhibited a weariness of life and a readiness to end it, the testimony giving plausibility to the hypothesis of suicide. Wigmore, Evidence §1726; Commonwealth v. Trefethen, 157 Mass. 180, 31

N.E. 961. By the proof of these declarations evincing an unhappy state of mind the defendant opened the door to the offer by the Government of declarations evincing a different state of mind, declarations consistent with the persistence of a will to live. The defendant would have no grievance if the testimony in rebuttal had been narrowed to that point. What the Government put in evidence, however, was something very different. It did not use the declarations by Mrs. Shepard to prove her present thoughts and feelings, or even her thoughts and feelings in times past. It used the declarations as proof of an act committed by someone else, as evidence that she was dying of poison given by her husband. This fact, if fact it was, the Government was free to prove, but not by hearsay declarations. It will not do to say that the jury might accept the declarations for any light that they cast upon the existence of a vital urge, and reject them to the extent that they charged the death to someone else. Discrimination so subtle is a feat beyond the compass of ordinary minds. The reverberating clang of those accusatory words would drown all weaker sounds. It is for ordinary minds, and not for psychoanalysis, that our rules of evidence are framed. They have their source very often in considerations of administrative convenience, of practical expediency, and not in rules of logic. When the risk of confusion is so great as to upset the balance of advantage, the evidence goes out. Thayer, Preliminary Treatise on the Law of Evidence, 266, 516; Wigmore, Evidence, §§1421, 1714.

These precepts of caution are a guide to judgment here. There are times when a state of mind, if relevant, may be proved by contemporaneous declarations of feeling or intent. Mutual Life Ins. Co. v. Hillmon, 145 U.S. 285, 295. . . .

The ruling in that case marks the high water line beyond which courts have been unwilling to go. It has developed a substantial body of criticism and commentary. Declarations of intention, casting light upon the future, have been sharply distinguished from declarations of memory, pointing backwards to the past. There would be an end, or nearly that, to the rule against hearsay if the distinction were ignored.

The testimony now questioned faced backward and not forward. This at least it did in its most obvious implications. What is even more important, it spoke to a past act, and more than that, to an act by some one not the speaker. Other tendency, if it had any, was a filament too fine to be disentangled by a jury.

The judgment should be reversed and the cause remanded to the District Court for further proceedings in accordance with this opinion. Reversed.

Is the *Shepard* rule logically persuasive? Should there be a general exception for the declaration of any unavailable or dead declarant? If the declaration is made prior to the commencement of the action in which it is offered? If the statement concerns a condition or event that had been recently perceived by the declarant and the declarant's recollection is shown to have been clear at the time? If the declaration is also shown to have been made in good faith, not in contemplation of pending or anticipated litigation, and not in response to the instigation of a person engaged in litigation? If the declaration relates to declarant's will? Various exceptions to the hearsay rule along this line have been proposed. Some have even been adopted. Compare Rule 803(1); deleted Rule 804(b)(2) and Advisory Committee Notes following.

Problem: 911 Call

Pierre Roberts is being tried for assault on Mary Jamison on June 11, 1998. On that day, Pierre and Mary lived together in Apartment 3 at 206 Brackett Street. Mary Jamison is not available to testify. A few days before the trial she disappeared along with her 5-year-old son, Christopher.

The State's Attorney offers the following in evidence:

1. Original 911 tape recording of emergency call received by the police on June 11, 1998, and testimony of the 911 operator that the police computer-telephone indicated that call came from 206 Brackett Street, Apt. 3 at 10:10 P.M. The voice is that of a child, "He's hitting her! He's hitting her! It's awful! Please help!" The police officer who responded to the call recognizes the voice on the tape recording as that of Christopher Jamison.

2. Testimony by a neighbor in Apt. 4 that at about 10:00 P.M. on June 11, 1998, Mary Jamison arrived at her apartment disheveled and panting with Christopher in her arms crying "I can't take it any more . . . he got drunk and beat me up. Chris called 911!"

3. Testimony by a doctor who examined Mary Jamison at the emergency room of the local hospital at about 10:30 P.M. on June 11, 1998, at the request of the police to document injuries and render any necessary treatment. (No medical treatment was actually rendered). "She told me that she had got into an argument with her boyfriend and that he hit her."

The defendant's attorney objects to each of these proffers as hearsay. What ruling and why?

Assume that each of these offers of evidence is admitted and that the State offers no other evidence. At the conclusion of the State's evidence the defendant's attorney moves for a directed verdict of acquittal. What ruling and why?

2. Two Processes of Proof: Refreshing Recollection and Past Recollection Recorded

There are often instances when witnesses are unable to remember certain details or even large parts of their expected testimony. When this occurs the lawyer may refresh the witness's recollection with either a leading question or with any object which will serve to prompt the witness's recollection. The object used to refresh the witness's recollection is not offered in evidence. It is merely a prompt to the witness. Most often the object used to refresh recollection will be a prior statement of the witness. However, it should be stressed that there is no requirement of authenticity or admissibility in evidence for objects which are used to refresh recollection. Once the witness's recollection has been refreshed, the witness testifies from memory like any other witness and may be cross-examined to test the witness's perception, memory, description, and sincerity. Rule 612 deals with the process of refreshing a witness's recollection and provides for safeguards against use of spurious material. The primary safeguard is that the opposing attorney is entitled to see whatever is being used to refresh a witness's recollection at the time it is used.

If it is not feasible to refresh a witness's recollection, a prior accurate statement by that witness can come in evidence as "past recollection recorded." Subsection 803(5) creates an exception to the hearsay rule for past recollection recorded. In this case, in contrast to the situation where the witness's memory is refreshed, there is very little cross-examination of the witness possible.

To qualify under Rule 803(5) a strange state of "quasi-unavailability" must exist — the witness must testify that the record was made or adopted when the matter was fresh in the declarant's memory and that it was accurate when made, but the witness must not be able to testify fully and accurately from memory alone. If the foundational requirements are met, courts usually permit the document to be read, but it does not become an exhibit unless offered by the adverse party.

Problem: Negligent Entrustment

Action against *D* Warehouse Company for negligence. In June 1989, Mrs. *P* prepared to sell her Cambridge house and move to Palo Alto.

She decided to sell some of her household furnishings, take some with her, and store the rest. Mrs. *P*'s maid, *M*, is put in charge of selecting things to be sold at a garage sale and packing what is not sold for storage. After the garage sale, *M* packs the unsold items in sealed boxes and makes a handwritten list of the contents of each box. The boxes are then delivered to the *D* Warehouse Company for storage. Ten years later, Mrs. *P* returns to Cambridge, claims the boxes, and is told they were destroyed by termites. At trial the only issue is the contents of the boxes. Compare these methods of proof:

(1) Mrs. *P* takes the stand and testifies to her 1989 instructions to *M*, her employee, and authenticates the handwriting on the lists as *M*'s. The lists are then offered in evidence. *D* objects.

(2) *M* takes the stand and testifies to the instructions she received in 1989 from Mrs. *P*, her employer, and how she carried out those instructions. When asked to specify the contents of the boxes, however, *M* says that she cannot remember what was put into the boxes. *P*'s attorney then shows *M* the lists. *M* studies the lists, testifies that she now remembers the contents of the boxes, and proceeds to specify the contents. *D* objects and moves to strike.

(3) The same as in (2) except that *M* testifies that even after looking at the lists she cannot remember what she put into the boxes. However, she does remember making the lists when she did the packing and that they were made accurately. The lists are then offered in evidence. *D* objects.

(4) Suppose that instead of *M*'s doing all the packing alone, Mrs. *P* helped her by packing each item in the boxes, stating orally what each item was and in which box it was put while *M* recorded the items on the lists. However, *M*, being fully occupied with making the lists, did not observe Mrs. *P* pack the items. At trial, Mrs. *P* and *M* testify to the above. Mrs. *P* cannot remember the items packed but does remember making the oral statements, which were accurate. *M* cannot remember what Mrs. *P* said but does remember taking down her statements and that her notes were accurate. *M* identifies the lists, and *P*'s attorney then reads the lists. *D* objects.

Which of these methods of proof will work? What reasons underlie the rules governing the use of past recollection recorded and refreshing recollection? What are the elements and procedures of each method? Compare Rules 803(5) and 612.

3. Business Records

The hearsay rule exceptions for records of a regularly conducted business activity derives from seventeenth-century "shop book" statutes, which enabled merchants to use the records of the time to prove their

routine business transactions in court. Indeed, without some kind of
rule authorizing proof by business records, it would be often very
clumsy, and sometimes impossible to prove business matters at all. The
conditions under which the exception applies vary to some extent from
jurisdiction to jurisdiction. The proponent of business records evidence
must show that the record proffered in evidence satisfies the conditions
of the exception before the record will be admitted. The process of
showing that an item of proffered evidence is likely authentic and fulfills
the requirements of admissibility (including, in cases of statements, at
least one hearsay rule exception) is called "laying the foundation" for
admission of the evidence. The business records exception appears in
Federal Rules of Evidence 803(6) and (7).

Problem: The Window Washers' Witnesses

Action by the P Window Washing Company against the D Tower Company for money allegedly due P for washing the windows on D's 100-
story skyscraper, the D Tower. D denies it owes P anything and disputes
that the work was ever done.

As P's attorney, you have found out that for a large tower like the D
Tower, P assigns a window washing foreman to each floor. Several window washers, grade one, and window washers' assistants, grade two, are
assigned to each foreman. As the washers and assistants wash a window,
they "tick off" a square representing the washed window on a form that
depicts the window arrangement for the floor on which they are working. At the end of the day, the foreman collects the forms and delivers
them to the area supervisor. There is usually an area supervisor for every
ten floors. The area supervisors tally the number of windows washed
and report this information to P's building manager. The manager
turns this information over to P's bookkeeping office, where the information is fed into P's data processing equipment. For billing purposes,
P's computer provides a biweekly printout of the number of windows
washed during that period.

You want to prove that P Window Washing Company washed 97,873
windows (the total shown by the computer printouts) on the D Tower
during the period in question. How do you go about it? What foundational and procedural considerations are there? Try preparing direct
examination(s) to get the proof in.

Compare Rule 803(5) and (6). How does the exception for business
records relate to the exception for recorded recollection? What are the
differences between the various formulations of the business records
exception to the hearsay rule? Why is an exception made for such records in the first place? Do these reasons suggest limits to the exception
based on type of business or record? Should the routineness of the

report or the motivations of the reporter affect the admissibility of such records?

Problem: Accident Reports

Action by *P* Plumbing & Heating Company for property damages to *P*'s vehicle, driven by its employee *E*, allegedly sustained in an accident with a *D* Bus Company bus driven by *D*'s employee, *F*. At trial, *P* offers a memo made by *E* one hour after the accident and filed at *P*'s office. The memo says that *F*'s bus ran a red light and struck *E*'s car broadside. *D* objects.

In its case, *D* offers an accident report on its standard form made out by *F* three hours after the accident, which claims *E* ran the light. *P* objects. What rulings and why?

Under Rule 803(6), the test for admitting business records is "trustworthiness" rather than "routineness." Generally, the routineness of business record-keeping promotes objectivity and accuracy. But as the lower court pointed out in Palmer v. Hoffman, 318 U.S. 109 (1943) (quoted in the Advisory Committee's Notes to Rule 803(6)), even when accident reports are routinely made, the circumstances cause them to be "dripping with motivations to misrepresent." While the motivation to falsify may be present even in the case of the grocer's account book, the making of a report *after* an event that is likely to be the subject of a *dispute* creates special trustworthiness problems. In this circumstance, the function of the report may be to prepare for litigation, not business.

Rule 803(6) addresses this problem by adding the proviso that evidence covered by the exception will be admitted "unless the source of information or the method or circumstances of preparation indicate lack of trustworthiness." This, in effect, gives the trial court discretion to exclude evidence otherwise within the letter of the exception.

PALMER v. HOFFMAN
318 U.S. 109 (1943)

Mr. Justice DOUGLAS delivered the opinion of the Court.

This case arose out of a grade crossing accident which occurred in Massachusetts. . . .

I

The accident occurred on the night of December 25, 1940. On December 27, 1940 the engineer of the train who died before the trial, made a statement at a freight office of petitioners where he was interviewed by an assistant superintendent of the road and by a representative of the Massachusetts Public Utilities Commission. See Mass. Gen. L. (1932) c.159, §29. This statement was offered in evidence by petitioners under the Act of June 20, 1936, 49 Stat. 1561, 28 U.S.C. §695. They offered to prove (in the language of the Act) that the statement was signed in the regular course of business, it being the regular course of such business to make such a statement. Respondent's objection to its introduction was sustained.

We agree with the majority view below that it was properly excluded.

We may assume that if the statement was made "in the regular course" of business, it would satisfy the other provisions of the Act. But we do not think that it was made "in the regular course" of business within the meaning of the Act. The business of the petitioners is the railroad business. That business like other enterprises entails the keeping of numerous books and records essential to its conduct or useful in its efficient operation. Though such books and records were considered reliable and trustworthy for major decisions in the industrial and business world, their use in litigation was greatly circumscribed or hedged about by the hearsay rule—restrictions which greatly increased the time and cost of making the proof where those who made the records were numerous. 5 Wigmore, Evidence (3d ed., 1940) §1530. It was that problem which started the movement towards adoption of legislation embodying the principles of the present Act. See Morgan et al., The Law of Evidence, Some Proposals for its Reform (1927) c.V. And the legislative history of the Act indicates the same purpose.

The engineer's statement which was held inadmissible in this case falls into quite a different category. It is not a record made for the systematic conduct of the business as a business. An accident report may affect that business in the sense that it affords information on which the management may act. It is not, however, typical of entries made systematically or as a matter of routine to record events or occurrences, to reflect transactions with others, or to provide internal controls. The conduct of a business commonly entails the payment of tort claims incurred by the negligence of its employees. But the fact that a company makes a business out of recording its employees' versions of their accidents does not put those statements in the class of records made "in the regular course" of the business within the meaning of the Act. If it did, then any law office in the land could follow the same course, since business as defined in the Act includes the professions. We would then have a real perversion of a rule designed to facilitate admission of records which experience has shown to be quite trustworthy. Any business by installing a regular system for recording and preserving its version of accidents for which it was potentially liable could qualify those reports under the Act. The result would be that the Act would cover any system of recording events or occurrences provided it was "regular" and though it had little or nothing to do with the management or operation of the business as such. Preparation of cases for trial by virtue of being a "business" or incidental thereto would obtain the benefits of this liberalized version of the early shop book rule. The probability of trustworthiness of records because they were routine reflections of the day to day operations of a business would be forgotten as the basis of the rule. Regularity of preparation would become the test rather than the character of the records and their earmarks of reliability acquired from their source and origin and the nature of their compilation. We cannot so completely empty the words of the Act of their historic meaning. If the Act is to be extended to apply not only to a "regular course" of a business but also to any "regular course" of conduct which may have some relationship to business, Congress not this Court must extend it. Such a major change which opens wide the door to avoidance of cross-examination should not be left to implication. Nor is it any answer to say that Congress has provided in the Act that the various circumstances of the making of the record should affect its weight not its admissibility. That provision comes into play only in case the other requirements of the Act are met.

In short, it is manifest that in this case those reports are not for the systematic conduct of the enterprise as a railroad business. Unlike payrolls, accounts receivable, accounts payable, bills of lading and the like these reports are calculated for use essentially in the court, not in the business. Their primary utility is in litigating, not in railroading.

It is, of course, not for us to take these reports out of the Act if Congress has put them in. But there is nothing in the background of the law on which this Act was built or in its legislative history which suggests for a moment that the business of preparing cases for trial should be included. In this connection it should be noted that the Act of May 6, 1910, 36 Stat. 350, 45 U.S.C. §38, requires officers of common carriers by rail to make under oath monthly reports of railroad accidents to the Interstate Commerce Commission, setting forth the nature and causes of the accidents and the circumstances connected therewith. And the same Act, 45 U.S.C. §40, gives the Commission authority to investigate and to make reports upon such accidents. It is provided, however, that

> Neither the report required by section 38 of this title nor any report of the investigation provided for in section 40 of this title nor any part thereof shall be admitted as evidence or used for any purpose in any suit or action for damages growing out of any matter mentioned in said report or investigation.

45 U.S.C. §41. A similar provision, 36 Stat. 916, 54 Stat. 148, 45 U.S.C. §33, bars the use in litigation of reports concerning accidents resulting from the failure of a locomotive boiler or its appurtenances. 45 U.S.C. §§32, 33. The legislation reveals an explicit Congressional policy to rule

out reports of accidents which certainly have as great a claim to objectivity as the statement sought to be admitted in the present case. We can hardly suppose that Congress modified or qualified by implication these long standing statutes when it permitted records made "in the regular course" of business to be introduced. Nor can we assume that Congress having expressly prohibited the use of the company's reports on its accidents impliedly altered that policy when it came to reports by its employees to their superiors. The inference is wholly the other way.

The several hundred years of history behind the Act (Wigmore, supra, §§1517-1520) indicate the nature of the reforms which it was designed to effect. It should of course be liberally interpreted so as to do away with the anachronistic rules which gave rise to its need and at which it was aimed. But "regular course" of business must find its meaning in the inherent nature of the business in question and in the methods systematically employed for the conduct of the business as a business. . . .

Problem: Loss Memos

Action by *P*, franchisee, against *D*, franchisor and supplier, for credit for inventory returned by *P* after termination of *P*'s franchise. At trial, *P* offers a list of inventory parts and their value that was compiled by *P* after the termination. *D* objects. What ruling and why?

Problem: Hospital Reports

D hit *P*, a small boy, when *P* ran out into the street. *D* picked up *P* and rushed him to *A* Hospital. In a suit for negligence by *P* against *D* arising from the accident, *P*'s lawyer calls the custodian of records of *A* Hospital and through him seeks to introduce a hospital report dated the day of the accident, reading as follows:

> *D* brought *P* to the emergency room stating that *D* had struck *P* with his car when *P* ran into the street. *D* stated that he tried to stop in time but his brakes were bad and he could not.

D's lawyer objects. What ruling and why?

Problem: Computer Records

Action by *P* Insurance Company against *D* Trucking Company for premiums allegedly owed under a retrospective liability policy. Under such a policy, the premium for each year is calculated on the basis of the loss experience for that year according to an elaborate, agreed-upon formula. A computer in *P*'s office stores this formula and the claims history for the year on its magnetic disc memory. At trial, *P* offers a printout of the computer's data and calculations to prove the amount due it. *D* objects. What ruling and why? What are the foundational requirements? Try preparing a direct examination to admit this evidence.

Problem: "Giving Them the Business"*

Civil action for collection on a debt. The plaintiff, Viza Credit Cards, alleges that defendant Dale Donner, a cardholder, owes it $1,172.87 in unpaid charges and additional financing charges for late payment. Donner claims to have paid the charges on time. At trial, Viza offers its billing records and computerized accounts and invoices under Rule 803(6) through the testimony of an account manager who describes the manner in which Viza compiles and keeps such records in the ordinary course of its business. Donner offers under Rule 803(6) the register from her and her husband's checking account, which shows a check having been written to Viza in the amount in question, and describes the manner in which the Donner family regularly makes and keeps such records. On objections to both offers, what rulings and why?

Would it make any difference if the Donners operated a small business selling woven mats out of their home and the charges and checks were on the account of the "Donner Woven Mat Company"?

SUPRUNIUK v. PETRIW
334 A.2d 857 (Me. 1975)

WEATHERBEE, J.: The parties to this controversy are Russian speaking farm owners of the Richmond area. The Plaintiff, John Supruniuk, seeks an order of specific performance of an agreement written by one of the Defendants, Ilija Petriw, in Russian, to sell the Plaintiff the Defendants' 100 acre farm. After the completion of testimony before a jury, the presiding Justice took the case from the jury and ordered the Defendants to convey the property to the Plaintiff upon payment by the Plaintiff of the agreed purchase price. The Defendants appealed. We sustain the appeal. . . .

THE UNDISPUTED FACTS

It is undisputed that the Defendant Mr. Petriw made known to the Plaintiff his desire to sell his farm and that after a discussion they agreed

---

*The idea for this problem comes from Kenneth Graham, "Q: What Happened to the Last Generation of [Hearsay] Reformers?" 1991 Hearsay Reform Conference Papers, U. Minn. Law School.

upon a purchase price of $6500.00. Mr. Petriw (who spoke only Russian) prepared an agreement written in the Russian language which the Plaintiff, Mr. Petriw, and Mr. Petriw's wife, Anastasia, also signed.[5] The Plaintiff was furnished with a copy of the deed which had conveyed the farm to the Defendants and he initiated procedures to obtain a loan from the Federal Housing Administration to enable him to complete the purchase, which was to be not later than July. Sometime after that Mr. Petriw decided that he did not wish to sell the farm to the Plaintiff and he told the Plaintiff that he would not complete the agreement.

THE DISPUTED FACTS

Mr. Petriw insists that the writing did not include all the terms of their agreement. He testified (through an interpreter) that he was to retain the right to live upon the farm until his death and that during Mr. Petriw's life the Plaintiff was to have the use of the farm as a depository for his chicken manure. He testified that the Plaintiff promised to give him a deposit of $200.00 *after the agreement was signed* and that the Plaintiff, who was also a dental technician, also promised to make him some dentures. He said the Plaintiff never made the impressions for the dentures or paid the $200.00.

Mr. Petriw said that the Plaintiff insisted, over Mr. Petriw's objections, that Mr. Petriw should be the one to write out their agreement in longhand. He said that the agreement which he wrote for their signatures did not contain the promise to make the dentures or the reservation of the life estate because

"He told me at the time of making the agreement that we would not write everything down because it would take too much time; we'll put in just the main points, and the rest we'll put in when we get ready to sign the main papers."

The Plaintiff testified that he paid the $200.00 deposit by check in hand. Mr. Petriw denies this. The Plaintiff says there was no agreement that he should make dentures for the Defendant nor any agreement

5. The following is a translation, accepted as accurate by the Plaintiff and Defendants, of the written agreement:

"AGREEMENT

I, Ilija Petriw, and my wife, Anastasia Petriw are selling one farm (approximately one hundred acres) which is located on Langdon Road, Richmond, Maine.

I, John Supruniuk, am buying this farm and I am paying two hundred dollars ($200.00) as my deposit and after the closing deal (approximately in July, not later) I shall pay the additional six thousand and three hundred dollars ($6,300.00).

We confirm this by signing:
1. Owners of the farm:
   Ilija Petriw
   Anastasia Petriw
2. The buyer of the farm *John Supruniuk*"

that a life estate was to be retained by the Defendant. The Plaintiff did say he told Mr. Petriw that Mr. Petriw could remain on the property for one year. The Plaintiff denies that he gave Mr. Petriw directions as to the contents of the written agreement. The Plaintiff testified that when his loan was approved by the F.H.A. and his money was available he went to Mr. Petriw and asked Mr. Petriw to go to an attorney's office to execute the deed to the plaintiff and that Mr. Petriw refused to go with him to complete the sale. The Plaintiff's testimony, given in imperfect English, leaves it unclear whether he actually tendered the balance of the purchase price to Mr. Petriw and it was refused or whether he only told Mr. Petriw that the money was available for payment as soon as the deed was executed and approved. Mr. Petriw denies that the Plaintiff came to him and asked him to go with him to the attorney's office to complete the transaction. He says that in June he met the Plaintiff who, "at that time . . . knew that [I] did not wish to sell the farm", and that "he shook my hand, and we parted as good friends".

[Discussion of other issues omitted.] . . .

THE PLAINTIFF'S CHECK BOOK

Inasmuch as this matter will probably be tried again, we feel that another claimed error should be discussed briefly. The Plaintiff offered, and the Court admitted, over the Defendants' objections, what the Plaintiff called "the journal book what I keep my records when I pay check to some people. . . . Each check when I write," and which the Defendants refer to as the Plaintiff's "check stubs". In fact, the exhibit is recognizable as a portion of a type of check book which provides a page on which may be recorded the check number, date, name of payee and amount of the several checks drawn (together with the balance remaining on deposit)—contrasting in form only with the familiar type of small book in which each check has a separate stub for the recording of such information.

The book contained the entry:

"553 5/10 Petriw & Anastasia 200 = 275.14 [balance]"

The exhibit was offered as an original record to prove the payment of the $200.00 "deposit". (The check—if one in fact was given—was never presented for payment.) Defendants argue that this journal is not admissible under the common law "shop-book rule" or under 16 M.R.S.A. §356,[5] and we agree. In construing that statute we have held

---

5. §356. Accounts admissible though hearsay or self-serving:

"An entry in an account kept in a book or by a card system or by any other system of keeping accounts shall not be inadmissible in any civil proceeding as evidence of the facts

that "memoranda made for the convenience or purposes of the one who made them" are not intended to be included under the exception. Other than that the Plaintiff was a farmer who needed to keep some record of such of his expenditures as were made by check, little else was established to show the regularity, objectivity, and reliability upon which this exception is founded.

It appears to us that the exhibit did not qualify for admission.

The entry will be: Appeal sustained. Remanded to the Superior Court for retrial.

Is the position taken by the Maine Supreme Court too strict? Isn't the entry in the checkbook at least some proof that a check was issued? Does it provide some corroboration of the plaintiff's assertion that the deposit check was written and delivered to Mr. Petriw? Do people generally manage their personal checkbooks in a way which would give the entries sufficient reliability to serve as proof in the absence of cross-examination?

4.   Public Records and Reports

A time-honored and often-cited exception to the rule against hearsay covers certain official documents and records. The Advisory Committee's Note states that "justification for the exception is the assumption that a public official will perform his duty properly and the unlikelihood that he will remember details independently of the record." This may be so, but beware hearsay from ordinary citizens within the official's report.

Even if a report qualifies under Rule 803(8)(B) on a matter "observed" pursuant to duty imposed by law as to which there was a duty to report or under Rule 803(8)(C) as "factual findings" resulting from an investigation, hearsay statements within the report have to qualify under an exception to be admissible. Rule 803(8)(C) "factual findings" necessarily must often be based on underlying hearsay, yet are admis-

---

therein stated because it is transcribed or because it is hearsay or self-serving, if the court finds that the entry was made in good faith in the regular course of business and before the beginning of the civil proceeding. The court in its discretion, before admitting such entry in evidence, may, to such extent as it deems practicable or desirable but to no greater extent than the law required before June 30, 1933, require the party offering the same to produce and offer in evidence the original entry, writing, document or account from which the entry offered or the facts therein stated were transcribed or taken, and to call as his witness any person who made the entry offered or the original or any other entry, writing, document or account from which the entry offered or the facts therein stated were transcribed or taken or who has personal knowledge of the facts stated in the entry offered."

sible. The rule deals with this problem by (1) excluding such reports in criminal cases when offered against the accused, and (2) by excluding such reports when "the sources of information or other circumstances indicate lack of trustworthiness." There is a difference, however, between admitting factual findings or observations of a public agency, even when based partially on hearsay, and straight reporting of a third party's hearsay statement, which would be admitted only if the reported statement came under another hearsay exception.

In the criminal context, Congress amended Rule 803(8)(B) specifically to exclude from the exception for public records and reports those matters observed by police officers. If reports of police officers also fall within the exception for records of regularly conducted activities (Rule 803(6)), should the same restrictions apply? Confrontation clause concerns exist no matter which exception is used.

Problem: Police Reports

Action for wrongful death of *P*'s intestate, killed when the bicycle the deceased was riding collided with *D*'s car. At trial, *D* offers an official report of the accident, filed by the first officer on the scene, which contains the observations of witnesses interviewed by the officer at the scene. *P* objects. What ruling and why?

JOHNSON v. LUTZ
253 N.Y. 124, 170 N.E. 517 (1930)

HUBBS, J. This action is to recover damages for the wrongful death of the plaintiff's intestate, who was killed when his motorcycle came into a collision with the defendants' truck at a street intersection. There was a sharp conflict in the testimony in regard to the circumstances under which the collision took place. A policeman's report of the accident filed by him in the station house was offered in evidence by the defendants under section 374-a of the Civil Practice Act, and was excluded. The sole ground for reversal urged by the appellants is that said report was erroneously excluded. . . .

. . . The memorandum in question was not made in the regular course of any business, profession, occupation, or calling. The policeman who made it was not present at the time of the accident. The memorandum was made from hearsay statements of third persons who happened to be present at the scene of the accident when he arrived. It does not appear when they saw the accident and stated to him what they knew, or stated what some other persons had told them.

The purpose of the Legislature in enacting section 374-a was to permit a writing or record, made in the regular course of business, to be received in evidence, without the necessity of calling as witnesses all of the persons who had any part in making it, provided the record was made as a part of the duty of the person making it, or on information imparted by persons who were under a duty to impart such information. The amendment permits the introduction of shopbooks without the necessity of calling all clerks who may have sold different items of account. It was not intended to permit the receipt in evidence of entries based upon voluntary hearsay statements made by third parties not engaged in the business or under any duty in relation thereto. It was said, in Mayor, etc., of New York City v. Second Ave. R. Co., 102 N.Y. 572, at page 581, 7 N.E. 905, 909, 55 Am. Rep. 839: "It is a proper qualification of the rule admitting such evidence that the account must have been made in the ordinary course of business, and that it should not be extended so as to admit a mere private memorandum, not made in pursuance of any duty owing by the person making it, or when made upon information derived from another who made the communication casually and voluntarily, and not under the sanction of duty or other obligation."

An important consideration leading to the amendment was the fact that in the business world credit is given to records made in the course of business by persons who are engaged in the business upon information given by others engaged in the same business as part of their duty.

> Such entries are dealt with in that way in the most important undertakings of mercantile and industrial life. They are the ultimate basis of calculation, investment, and general confidence in every business enterprise. Nor does the practical impossibility of obtaining constantly and permanently the verification of every employee affect the trust that is given to such books. It would seem that expedients which the entire commercial world recognizes as safe could be sanctioned, and not discredited, by courts of justice. When it is a mere question of whether provisional confidence can be placed in a certain class of statements, there cannot profitably and sensibly be one rule for the business world and another for the court-room. The merchant and the manufacturer must not be turned away remediless because the methods in which the entire community places a just confidence are a little difficult to reconcile with technical judicial scruples on the part of the same persons who as attorneys have already employed and relied upon the same methods. In short, courts must here cease to be pedantic and endeavor to be practical.

3 Wigmore on Evidence (1923) §1530, p.278.

The Legislature has sought by the amendment to make the courts practical. It would be unfortunate not to give the amendment a construction which will enable it to cure the evil complained of and accomplish the purpose for which it was enacted. In constructing it, we should not, however, permit it to be applied in a case for which it was never intended.

The judgment should be affirmed, with costs.

Problem: Aircrash

Action against *D* Airline Company for wrongful death of plaintiff's intestate, who perished in a crash of one of *D*'s planes. At trial, *P* offers the following on the issue of *D*'s negligence:

(1) The policy manual of the air traffic control tower at the airport controlling the plane at the time of the crash;

(2) The U.S. Meteorological Service records of the weather on the night of the crash; and

(3) The report of the FAA investigational team assigned to investigate and report on the cause of the crash. The report contains 356 pages of detailed findings and 56 pages of conclusions and recommendations. One of the report's conclusions is that the failure of the plane's operator to properly maintain the plane's radar equipment was a primary cause of the crash.

D objects to these offers. What rulings and why? What factors justify the receipt of such evidence or argue against its use?

BEECH AIRCRAFT CORP. v. RAINEY
488 U.S. 153 (1988)

Justice BRENNAN delivered the opinion of the Court.

In this case we address a longstanding conflict among the federal courts of appeal over whether Federal Rule of Evidence 803(8)(C), which provides an exception to the hearsay rule for public investigatory reports containing "factual findings," extends to conclusions and opinions contained in such reports. We also consider whether, on the facts of this case, the trial court abused its discretion in refusing to admit, on cross-examination, testimony intended to provide a more complete picture of a document about which the witness had testified on direct.

I

This litigation stems from the crash of a Navy training aircraft at Middleton Field, Alabama, on July 13, 1982, which took the lives of both pilots on board, Lieutenant Commander Barbara Ann Rainey and Ensign Donald Bruce Knowlton. The accident took place while Rainey, a Navy flight instructor, and Knowlton, her student, were flying "touch-and-go" exercises in a T-34C Turbo-Mentor aircraft, number 3E955. Their aircraft and several others flew in an oval pattern, each plane making successive landing/takeoff maneuvers on the runway. Following its fourth pass at the runway, 3E955 appeared to make a left turn prematurely, cutting out the aircraft ahead of it in the pattern and threatening a collision. After radio warnings from two other pilots, the plane banked sharply to the right in order to avoid the other aircraft. At that point it lost altitude rapidly, crashed, and burned.

Because of the damage to the plane and the lack of any survivors, the cause of the accident could not be determined with certainty. The two pilots' surviving spouses brought a product liability suit against petitioners Beech Aircraft Corporation, the plane's manufacturer, and Beech Aerospace Services, which serviced the plane under contract with the Navy. The plaintiffs alleged that the crash had been caused by a loss of engine power, known as "rollback," due to some defect in the aircraft's fuel control system. The defendants, on the other hand, advanced the theory of pilot error, suggesting that the plane had stalled during the abrupt avoidance maneuver. At trial, the only seriously disputed question was whether pilot error or equipment malfunction had caused the crash. Both sides relied primarily on expert testimony. One piece of evidence presented by the defense was an investigative report prepared by Lieutenant Commander William Morgan on order of the training squadron's commanding officer and pursuant to authority granted in the Manual of the Judge Advocate General. This "JAG Report," completed during the six weeks following the accident, was organized into sections labeled "finding of fact," "opinions," and "recommendations," and was supported by some 60 attachments. The "finding of fact" included statements like the following:

"13. At approximately 10:20, while turning crosswind without proper interval, 3E955 crashed, immediately caught fire and burned.

"27. At the time of impact, the engine of 3E955 was operating but was operating at reduced power." Among his "opinions" Lieutenant Commander Morgan stated, in paragraph five, that due to the deaths of the two pilots and the destruction of the aircraft "it is almost impossible to determine exactly what happened to Navy 3E955 from the time it left the runway on its last touch and go until it impacted the ground." He nonetheless continued with a detailed reconstruction of a possible set of events, based on pilot error, that could have caused the accident.[2]

---

2. Paragraph five reads in its entirety as follows: "Because both pilots were killed in the crash and because of the nearly total destruction of the aircraft by fire, it is almost impossible to determine exactly what happened to Navy 3E955 from the time it left the runway on its last touch and go until it impacted the ground. However, from evidence available and the information gained from eyewitnesses, a possible scenario can be constructed as follows:

"a. 3E955 entered the Middleton pattern with ENS Knowlton at the controls attempting to make normal landings.

"b. After two unsuccessful attempts, LCDR Rainey took the aircraft and demonstrated two landings 'on the numbers.' After getting the aircraft safely airborne from the touch and go, LCDR Rainey transferred control to ENS Knowlton.

The next two paragraphs stated a caveat and a conclusion: "6. Although the above sequence of events is the most likely to have occurred, it does not change the possibility that a 'rollback' did occur.

"7. The most probable cause of the accident was the pilots [*sic*] failure to maintain proper interval."

The trial judge initially determined, at a pretrial conference, that the JAG Report was sufficiently trustworthy to be admissible, but that it "would be admissible only on its factual findings and would not be admissible insofar as any opinions or conclusions are concerned." The day before trial, however, the court reversed itself and ruled, over the plaintiff's objection, that certain of the conclusions would be admitted. Accordingly, the court admitted most of the report's "opinions," including the first sentence of paragraph five about the impossibility of determining exactly what happened, and paragraph seven, which opined about failure to maintain proper interval as "[t]he most probable cause of the accident." On the other hand, the remainder of paragraph five was barred as "nothing but a possible scenario," and paragraph six, in which investigator Morgan refused to rule out rollback, was deleted as well.[3] ... Following a two-week trial, the jury returned a verdict for the petitioners. A panel of the Eleventh Circuit reversed and remanded for a new trial. 784 F.2d 1523 (C.A.11 1986). Considering itself bound by the Fifth Circuit precedent of Smith v. Ithaca Corp., 612 F.2d 215 (C.A.5 1980), the panel agreed with Rainey's argument that Federal Rule of Evidence 803(8)(C), which excepts investigatory reports from the hearsay rule, did not encompass evaluative conclusions or opinions. Therefore, it held, the "conclusions" contained in the JAG Report should have been excluded. One member of the panel, concurring specially, urged however that the Circuit reconsider its interpretation of Rule 803(8)(C). . . .

"c. Due to his physical strength, ENS Knowlton did not trim down elevator as the aircraft accelerated toward 100 knots; in fact, due to his inexperience, he may have trimmed incorrectly, putting in more up elevator.

"d. As ENS Knowlton was climbing to pattern altitude, he did not see the aircraft established on downwind so he began his crosswind turn. Due to ENS Knowlton's large size, LCDR Rainey was unable to see the conflicting traffic.

"e. Hearing the first call, LCDR Rainey probably cautioned ENS Knowlton to check for traffic. Hearing the second call, she took immediate action and told ENS Knowlton she had the aircraft as she initiated a turn toward an upwind heading.

"f. As the aircraft was rolling from a climbing left turn to a climbing right turn, ENS Knowlton released the stick letting the up elevator trim take effect causing the nose of the aircraft to pitch abruptly up.

"g. The large angle of bank used trying to maneuver for aircraft separation coupled with the abrupt pitch up caused the aircraft to stall. As the aircraft stalled and went into a nose low attitude, LCDR Rainey reduced the PCL (power control lever) toward idle. As she was rolling toward wings level, she advanced the PCL to maximum to stop the loss of altitude but due to the 2 to 4 second lag in engine response, the aircraft impacted the ground before power was available."

3. The record gives no indication why paragraph six was deleted. Neither at trial nor on appeal have respondents raised any objection to the deletion of paragraph six.

II

Federal Rule of Evidence 803 provides that certain types of hearsay statements are not made excludable by the hearsay rule, whether or not the declarant is available to testify. Rule 803(8) defines the "public records and reports" which are not excludable, as follows: "Records, reports, statements, or data compilations, in any form, of public offices or agencies, setting forth (A) the activities of the office or agency, or (B) matters observed pursuant to duty imposed by law as to which matters there was a duty to report, . . . or (C) in civil actions and proceedings and against the Government in criminal cases, factual findings resulting from an investigation made pursuant to authority granted by law, unless the sources of information or other circumstances indicate lack of trustworthiness." Controversy over what "public records and reports" are made not excludable by Rule 803(8)(C) has divided the federal courts from the beginning. In the present case, the Court of Appeals followed the "narrow" interpretation of Smith v. Ithaca Corp., 612 F.2d 215, 220-223 (C.A.5 1980), which held that the term "factual findings" did not encompass "opinions" or "conclusions." Courts of appeal other than those of the Fifth and Eleventh Circuits, however, have generally adopted a broader interpretation. For example, the Court of Appeals for the Sixth Circuit, in Baker v. Elcona Homes Corp., 588 F.2d 551, 557-558 (1978), cert. denied, 441 U.S. 933, 99 S. Ct. 2054, 60 L. Ed. 2d 661 (1979), held that "factual findings admissible under Rule 803(8)(C) may be those which are made by the preparer of the report from disputed evidence. . . ." The other courts of appeal that have squarely confronted the issue have also adopted the broader interpretation. We agree and hold that factually based conclusions or opinions are not on that account excluded from the scope of Rule 803(8)(C).

Because the Federal Rules of Evidence are a legislative enactment, we turn to the "traditional tools of statutory construction," INS v. Cardoza-Fonseca, 480 U.S. 421, 446, 107 S. Ct. 1207, 1221, 94 L. Ed. 2d 434 (1987), in order to construe their provisions. We begin with the language of the Rule itself. Proponents of the narrow view have generally relied heavily on a perceived dichotomy between "fact" and "opinion" in arguing for the limited scope of the phrase "factual findings." Smith v. Ithaca Corp., supra, contrasted the term "factual findings" in Rule 803(8)(C) with the language of Rule 803(6) (records of regularly conducted activity), which expressly refers to "opinions" and "diagnoses." "Factual findings," the court opined, must be something other than opinions. *Smith*, supra, at 221-222.

For several reasons, we do not agree. In the first place, it is not apparent that the term "factual findings" should be read to mean simply "facts" (as opposed to "opinions" or "conclusions"). A common definition of "finding of fact" is, for example, "[a] conclusion by way of reasonable inference from the evidence." Black's Law Dictionary 569 (5th ed. 1979). To say the least, the language of the Rule does not compel us to reject the interpretation that "factual findings" includes conclusions or opinions that flow from a factual investigation. Second, we note that, contrary to what is often assumed, the language of the Rule does not state that "factual findings" are admissible, but that "reports . . . setting forth . . . factual findings" are admissible. On this reading, the language of the Rule does not create a distinction between "fact" and "opinion" contained in such reports. . . .

That "provision for escape" is contained in the final clause of the Rule: evaluative reports are admissible "unless the sources of information or other circumstances indicate lack of trustworthiness." This trustworthiness inquiry—and not an arbitrary distinction between "fact" and "opinion"—was the Committee's primary safeguard against the admission of unreliable evidence, and it is important to note that it applies to all elements of the report. Thus, a trial judge has the discretion, and indeed the obligation, to exclude an entire report or portions thereof —whether narrow "factual" statements or broader "conclusions"—that she determines to be untrustworthy.[4]

Moreover, safeguards built in to other portions of the Federal Rules, such as those dealing with relevance and prejudice, provide the court with additional means of scrutinizing and, where appropriate, excluding evaluative reports or portions of them. And of course it goes without saying that the admission of a report containing "conclusions" is subject to the ultimate safeguard — the opponent's right to present evidence tending to contradict or diminish the weight of those conclusions.

Our conclusion that neither the language of the Rule nor the intent of its framers calls for a distinction between "fact" and "opinion" is strengthened by the analytical difficulty of drawing such a line. It has frequently been remarked that the distinction between statements of fact and opinion is, at best, one of degree:

"All statements in language are statements of opinion, i.e., statements of mental processes or perceptions. So-called 'statements of fact' are only more specific statements of opinion. What the judge means to say,

---

4. The Advisory Committee proposed a nonexclusive list of four factors it thought would be helpful in passing on this question: (1) the timeliness of the investigation; (2) the investigator's skill or experience; (3) whether a hearing was held; and (4) possible bias when reports are prepared with a view to possible litigation (citing Palmer v. Hoffman, 318 U.S. 109, 63 S. Ct. 477, 87 L. Ed. 645 (1943)). Advisory Committee's Notes on Fed. Rule Evid. 803(8), 28 U.S.C. App., p.725; see Note, The Trustworthiness of Government Evaluative Reports under Federal Rule of Evidence 803(8)(C), 96 Harv. L. Rev. 492 (1982). In a case similar in many respects to this one, the trial court applied the trustworthiness requirement to hold inadmissible a JAG Report on the causes of a Navy airplane accident; it found the report untrustworthy because it "was prepared by an inexperienced investigator in a highly complex field of investigation." Fraley v. Rockwell Intl. Corp., 470 F. Supp. 1264, 1267 (S.D. Ohio 1979). In the present case, the District Court found the JAG Report to be trustworthy. App. 35. As no party has challenged that finding, we have no occasion to express an opinion on it.

when he asks the witness to state the facts, is: 'The nature of this case requires that you be more specific, if you can, in your description of what you saw.'" W. King & D. Pillinger, Opinion Evidence in Illinois 4 (1942) (footnote omitted), quoted in 3 J. Weinstein & M. Berger, Weinstein's Evidence ¶701[01], p.701-6 (1988). See also E. Cleary, McCormick on Evidence 27 (3d ed. 1984) ("There is no conceivable statement however specific, detailed and 'factual,' that is not in some measure the product of inference and reflection as well as observation and memory"); R. Lempert & S. Saltzburg, A Modern Approach to Evidence 449 (2d ed. 1982) ("A factual finding, unless it is a simple report of something observed, is an opinion as to what more basic facts imply"). Thus, the traditional requirement that lay witnesses give statements of fact rather than opinion may be considered, "[l]ike the hearsay and original documents rules . . . a 'best evidence' rule." McCormick, Opinion Evidence in Iowa, 19 Drake L. Rev. 245, 246 (1970).

In the present case, the trial court had no difficulty in admitting as a factual finding the statement in the JAG Report that "[a]t the time of impact, the engine of 3E955 was operating but was operating at reduced power." Surely this "factual finding" could also be characterized as an opinion, which the investigator presumably arrived at on the basis of clues contained in the airplane wreckage. Rather than requiring that we draw some inevitably arbitrary line between the various shades of fact/opinion that invariably will be present in investigatory reports, we believe the Rule instructs us — as its plain language states — to admit "reports . . . setting forth . . . factual findings." The Rule's limitations and safeguards lie elsewhere: First, the requirement that reports contain factual findings bars the admission of statements not based on factual investigation. Second, the trustworthiness provision requires the court to make a determination as to whether the report, or any portion thereof, is sufficiently trustworthy to be admitted.

A broad approach to admissibility under Rule 803(8)(C), as we have outlined it, is also consistent with the Federal Rules' general approach of relaxing the traditional barriers to "opinion" testimony. Rules 702-705 permit experts to testify in the form of an opinion, and without any exclusion of opinions on "ultimate issues." And Rule 701 permits even a lay witness to testify in the form of opinions or inferences drawn from her observations when testimony in that form will be helpful to the trier of fact. We see no reason to strain to reach an interpretation of Rule 803(8)(C) that is contrary to the liberal thrust of the Federal Rules.

We hold, therefore, that portions of investigatory reports otherwise admissible under Rule 803(8)(C) are not inadmissible merely because they state a conclusion or opinion. As long as the conclusion is based on a factual investigation and satisfies the Rule's trustworthiness requirement, it should be admissible along with the other portions of the report. As the trial judge in this case determined that certain of the JAG

Report's conclusions were trustworthy, he rightly allowed them to be admitted into evidence. We therefore reverse the judgment of the Court of Appeals in respect of the Rule 803(8)(C) issue.

F.   Exceptions to the Hearsay Rule—The "Residuary Exception"

DALLAS COUNTY v. COMMERCIAL UNION ASSURANCE CO.
286 F.2d 388 (5th Cir. 1961)

WISDOM, J. This appeal presents a single question—the admissibility in evidence of a newspaper to show that the Dallas County Courthouse in Selma, Alabama, was damaged by fire in 1901. We hold that the newspaper was admissible, and affirm the judgment below.

On a bright, sunny morning, July 7, 1957, the clock tower of the Dallas County Courthouse at Selma, Alabama, commenced to lean, made loud cracking and popping noises, then fell, and telescoped into the courtroom. Fortunately, the collapse of the tower took place on a Sunday morning; no one was injured, but damage to the courthouse exceeded $100,000. An examination of the tower debris showed the presence of charcoal and charred timbers. The State Toxicologist, called in by Dallas County, reported the char was evidence that lightning struck the courthouse. Later, several residents of Selma reported that a bolt of lightning struck the courthouse July 2, 1957. On this information, Dallas County concluded that a lightning bolt had hit the building causing the collapse of the clock tower five days later. Dallas County carried insurance for loss to its courthouse caused by fire or lightning. The insurers' engineers and investigators found that the courthouse collapsed of its own weight. They reported that the courthouse had not been struck by lightning; that lightning could not have caused the collapse of the tower; that the collapse of the tower was caused by structural weaknesses attributable to a faulty design, poor construction, gradual deterioration of the structure, and overloading brought about by remodeling and the recent installation of an air-conditioning system, part of which was constructed over the courtroom trusses. In their opinion, the char was the result of a fire in the courthouse tower and roof that must have occurred many, many years before July 2, 1957. The insurers denied liability.

The County sued its insurers in the Circuit Court of Dallas County. As many of the suits as could be removed, seven, were removed to the United States District Court for the Southern District of Alabama, and were consolidated for trial. The case went to the jury on one issue: did lightning cause the collapse of the clock tower?

The record contains ample evidence to support a jury verdict either way. The County produced witnesses who testified they saw lightning strike the clock tower; the insurers produced witnesses who testified an examination of the debris showed that lightning did not strike the clock tower. Some witnesses said the char was fresh and smelled smoky; other witnesses said it was obviously old and had no fresh smoky smell at all. Both sides presented a great mass of engineering testimony bearing on the design, construction, overload or lack of overload. All of this was for the jury to evaluate. The jury chose to believe the insurers' witnesses and brought in a verdict for the defendants.

During the trial the defendants introduced a copy of the Morning Times of Selma for June 9, 1901. This issue carried an unsigned article describing a fire that occurred at two in the morning of June 9, 1901, while the courthouse was still under construction. The article stated, in part: "The unfinished dome of the County's new courthouse was in flames at the top, and . . . soon fell in. The fire was soon under control and the main building was saved. . . ." The insurers do not contend that the collapse of the tower resulted from unsound charred timbers used in the repair of the building after the fire; they offered the newspaper account to show there had been a fire long before 1957 that would account for charred timber in the clock tower.

As a predicate for introducing the newspaper in evidence, the defendants called to the stand the editor of the Selma Times-Journal who testified that his publishing company maintains archives of the published issues of the Times-Journal and of the Morning Times, its predecessor, and that the archives contain the issue of the Morning Times of Selma for June 9, 1901, offered in evidence. The plaintiff objected that the newspaper article was hearsay; that it was not a business record nor an ancient document, nor was it admissible under any recognized exception to the hearsay doctrine. The trial judge admitted the newspaper as part of the records of the Selma Times-Journal. The sole error Dallas County specifies on appeal is the admission of the newspaper in evidence.

In the Anglo-American adversary system of law, courts usually will not admit evidence unless its accuracy and trustworthiness may be tested by cross-examination. Here, therefore, the plaintiff argues that the newspaper should not be admitted: "You cannot cross-examine a newspaper."[1] Of course, a newspaper article *is* hearsay, and in almost all

---

1. This argument, a familiar one. rests on a misunderstanding of its origin and the nature of the hearsay rule. The rule is not an ancient principle of English law recognized at Runnymede. And gone is its odor of sanctity.

Wigmore is often quoted for the statement that "cross-examination is beyond any doubt the greatest legal engine ever invented for the discovery of truth." 5 Wigmore §1367 (3d ed.). In over 1200 pages devoted to the hearsay rule, however, he makes very clear that:

"[T]he rule aims to insist on testing all statements by cross-examination, *if they can be.* . . . No one could defend a rule which pronounced that all statements thus untested are worthless;

circumstances is inadmissible. However, the law governing hearsay is somewhat less than pellucid. And, as with most rules, the hearsay rule is not absolute; it is replete with exceptions. Witnesses die, documents are lost, deeds are destroyed, memories fade. All too often, primary evidence is not available and courts and lawyers must rely on secondary evidence. . . .

We turn now to a case, decided long before the Federal Rules were adopted, in which the court used an approach we consider appropriate for the solution of the problem before us. G. & C. Merriam Co. v. Syndicate Pub. Co., 2 Cir., 1913, 207 F. 515, 518, concerned a controversy between dictionary publishers over the use of the title "Webster's Dictionary" when the defendant's dictionary allegedly was not based upon Webster's Dictionary at all. The bone of contention was whether a statement in the preface to the dictionary was admissible as evidence of the facts it recited. Ogilvie, the compiler of the dictionary, stated in his

---

for all historical truth is based on uncross-examined assertions; and every day's experience of life gives denial to such an exaggeration. What the Hearsay Rule implies—and with profound verity — is that all testimonial assertions *ought to be* tested by cross-examination, as the best attainable measure; and it should not be burdened with the pedantic implication that they must be rejected as worthless if the test is unavailable." 1 Wigmore §8c. In this connection see Falknor, The Hearsay Rule and its Exceptions, 2 U.C.L.A.L. Rev. 43 (1954).

In The Introductory Note to Chapter VI, Hearsay Evidence, American Law Institute Model Code of Evidence (1942), Edmund M. Morgan, Reporter, it is pointed out that "the hearsay rule is the child of the adversary system." The Note continues:

"During the first centuries of the jury system, the jury based its decision upon what the jurors themselves knew of the matter in dispute and what they learned through the words of their fathers and through such words of these persons whom they are bound to trust as worthy. . . . Until the end of the sixteenth century hearsay was received without question.

". . . The opportunity for cross-examination is not a necessary element of a jury system, while it is the very heart of the adversary system.

". . . As the judges began their attempts to rationalize the results of the decisions dealing with evidence, they first relied upon the general notion that a party was obliged to produce the best evidence available, but no more. Had they applied this generally, hearsay would have been received whenever better evidence could not be obtained. Therefore the judges discovered a special sort of necessity in . . . exceptional cases . . . [making] the admissible hearsay less unreliable than hearsay in general. . . . [By 1840] it became the fashion to attribute the exclusion of hearsay to the incapacity of the jury to evaluate, and in the development of exceptions to the rule, courts have doubtless been influenced by this notion. . . . Modern textwriters and judges have purported to find for each exception some sort of necessity for resort to hearsay and some condition attending the making of the excepted statement which will enable the jury to put a fair value upon it and will thus serve as a substitute for cross-examination. A careful examination of the eighteen or nineteen classes of utterances, each of which is now recognized as an exception to the hearsay rule by some respectable authority, will reveal that in many of them the necessity resolves itself into mere convenience and the substitute for cross-examination is imperceptible. . . . In most of the exceptions, however, the adversary theory is disregarded. There is nothing in any of the situations to warrant depriving the adversary of an opportunity to cross-examine; but those rationalizing the results purport to find some substitute for cross-examination. In most instances one will look in vain for anything more than a situation in which an ordinary man making such statement would positively desire to tell the truth; and in some the most that can be claimed is the absence of a motive to falsify." For the history of the rule see 5 Wigmore, Evidence, §1364 (3rd ed.); 9 Holdsworth's History of English Law, 214 (1926).

preface that he used Webster's Dictionary as the basis for his own publication. The dictionary, with its preface, was published in 1850, sixty-three years before the trial of the case. Ogilvie's published statement was challenged as hearsay. Judge Learned Hand, then a district judge, unable, as we are here, to find a case in point, for authority relied solely on Wigmore on Evidence (then a recent publication), particularly on Wigmore's analysis that "the requisites of an exception of the hearsay rules are necessity and circumstantial guaranty of trustworthiness." Wigmore on Evidence, §§1421, 1422, 1690 (1st ed. 1913). Applying these criteria, Judge Hand held that the statement was admissible as an exception to the hearsay rule:

"Ogilvie's preface is of course an unsworn statement and as such only hearsay testimony, which may be admitted only as an exception to the general rule. The question is whether there is such an exception. I have been unable to find any express authority in point and must decide the question upon principle. In the first place, I think it fair to insist that to reject such a statement is to refuse evidence about the truth of which no reasonable person should have any doubt whatever, because it fulfills both the requisites of an exception to the hearsay rule, necessity and circumstantial guaranty of trustworthiness. Wigmore, §§1421, 1422, 1906. . . . Besides Ogilvie, everyone else is dead who ever knew anything about the matter and could intelligently tell us what the fact is. . . . As to the trustworthiness of the testimony, it has the guaranty of the occasion, at which there was no motive for fabrication." 207 F. 515, 518.

The Court of Appeals adopted the district court's opinion in its entirety.

The first of the two requisites is necessity. As to necessity, Wigmore points out this requisite means that unless the hearsay statement is admitted, the facts it brings out may otherwise be lost, either because the person whose assertion is offered may be dead or unavailable, or because the assertion is of such a nature that one could not expect to obtain evidence of the same value from the same person or from other sources. Wigmore, §1421 (3rd ed.). "In effect, Wigmore says that, as the word necessary is here used, it is not to be interpreted as uniformly demanding a showing of total inaccessibility of first-hand evidence as a condition precedent to the acceptance of a particular piece of hearsay, but that necessity exists where otherwise great practical inconvenience would be experienced in making the desired proof. (Wigmore, 3d Ed., Vol. V, sec. 1421; Vol. VI, sec. 1702). . . . If it were otherwise, the result would be that the exception created to the hearsay rule would thereby be mostly, if not completely, destroyed." United States v. Aluminum Co. of America, D.C. 1940, 35 F. Supp. 820, 823.

The fire referred to in the newspaper account occurred fifty-eight years before the trial of this case. Any witness who saw that fire with sufficient understanding to observe it and describe it accurately, would have been older than a young child at the time of the fire. We may reasonably assume that at the time of the trial he was either dead or his faculties were dimmed by the passage of fifty-eight years. It would have been burdensome, but not impossible, for the defendant to have discovered the name of the author of the article (although it has no by-line) and, perhaps, to have found an eyewitness to the fire. But it is improbable—so it seems to us—that any witness could have been found whose recollection would have been accurate at the time of the trial of this case. And it seems impossible that the testimony of any witness would have been as accurate and as reliable as the statement of facts in the contemporary newspaper article.

The rationale behind the "ancient documents" exception is applicable here: after a long lapse of time, ordinary evidence regarding signatures or handwriting is virtually unavailable, and it is therefore permissible to resort to circumstantial evidence. Thus, in Trustees of German Township, Montgomery County v. Farmers & Citizens Savings Bank Co., Ohio Com. Pl. 1953, 113 N.E.2d 409, 412, affirmed Ohio App., 115 N.E.2d 690, the court admitted as ancient documents newspapers eighty years old containing notices of advertisements for bids relating to the town hall: "Such exhibits, by reason of age, alone, and unquestioned authenticity, qualify as ancient documents." The ancient documents rule applies to documents a generation or more in age. Here, the Selma Times-Journal article is almost two generations old. The principle of necessity, not requiring absolute impossibility of total inaccessibility of first-hand knowledge, is satisfied by the practicalities of the situation before us.

The second requisite for admission of hearsay evidence is trustworthiness. According to Wigmore, there are three sets of circumstances when hearsay is trustworthy enough to serve as a practicable substitute for the ordinary test of cross-examination:

> Where the circumstances are such that a sincere and accurate statement would naturally be uttered, and no plan of falsification be formed; where, even though a desire to falsify might present itself, other considerations, such as the danger of easy detection or the fear of punishment, would probably counteract its force; where the statement was made under such conditions of publicity that an error, if it had occurred, would probably have been detected and corrected.

5 Wigmore, Evidence, §1422 (3rd ed.). These circumstances fit the instant case.

There is no procedural canon against the exercise of common sense in deciding the admissibility of hearsay evidence. In 1901 Selma, Alabama was a small town. Taking a common sense view of this case, it is inconceivable to us that a newspaper reporter in a small town would report there was a fire in the dome of the new courthouse—if there had been no fire. He is without motive to falsify, and a false report would have subjected the newspaper and him to embarrassment in the community. The usual dangers inherent in hearsay evidence, such as lack of memory, faulty narration, intent to influence the court proceedings, and plain lack of truthfulness are not present here. To our minds, the article published in the Selma Morning-Times on the day of the fire is more reliable, more trustworthy, more competent evidence than the testimony of a witness called to the stand fifty-eight years later.

We hold, that in matters of local interest, when the fact in question is of such a public nature it would be generally known throughout the community, and when the questioned fact occurred so long ago that the testimony of an eye-witness would probably be less trustworthy than a contemporary newspaper account, a federal court, under Rule 43(a), may relax the exclusionary rules to the extent of admitting the newspaper article in evidence. We do not characterize this newspaper as a "business record," nor as an "ancient document," nor as any other readily identifiable and happily tagged species of hearsay exception. It is admissible because it is necessary and trustworthy, relevant and material, and its admission is within the trial judge's exercise of discretion in holding the hearing within reasonable bounds.

Judgment is affirmed.

When the Federal Rules of Evidence were adopted an effort was made to codify all of the established exceptions to the hearsay rule known at the time. However, the question remained whether the new rules should leave open the possibility of further development of hearsay exceptions by operation of the common law. The drafters of the original Supreme Court version of the rules thought so and included "catchalls" in both Rules 803 and 804 (804(24) and 804(b)(5)) authorizing admission of "[a] statement not specifically covered by any of the foregoing exceptions but having comparable circumstantial guarantees of trustworthiness." Congress initially deleted the "catchalls" and then ultimately restored them in a somewhat more restrictive form with a requirement of advance notice and specific preliminary findings of necessity and probative quality. In 1997, the residuary exceptions in Rules 803 and 804 were combined and moved to new Rule 807 without change in operative language.

Problem: An Accusing Finger

The state offers the picture on page 510 (The Boston Globe, November 17, 1981, p.1) into evidence at a trial of the handcuffed man in the dark sweater for armed robbery. Is it hearsay? If so, does it fall within any exception of the hearsay rule? Does this depend on whether the guard lying on the stretcher is available? If the picture does not fall within any specific exception to the hearsay rule, should it nonetheless be admitted under the residual exceptions Rule 807?

Compare this case to the *Dallas County* case. Is this a stronger or weaker case for admission? Would admitting this picture violate the defendant's rights under the Confrontation Clause?

BROOKOVER v. MARY HITCHCOCK MEMORIAL HOSPITAL
893 F.2d 411 (1st Cir. 1990)

BOWNES, Circuit Judge.

Defendant-appellant Mary Hitchcock Memorial Hospital (Hospital) appeals from a jury verdict holding it liable in this diversity jurisdiction medical malpractice case. The case arose from a fall by a patient, Ronald Brookover (Ronald), in his room at the Hospital. Plaintiff-appellee Leroy E. Brookover is the parent and guardian of Ronald Brookover. There are two issues on appeal: the admission of statements under Fed. R. Evid. 801(d)(2)(D); and the admission of statements under Fed. R. Evid. 804(b)(5).

I. THE FACTS

The basic facts are uncontested. Ronald was age 36 at the time of the accident. When he was nine years old he was in an automobile accident and incurred injuries resulting in periodic epileptic seizures. As Ronald grew older his seizures became more severe and more difficult to control. These seizures included grand mal seizures that caused Ronald to convulse violently and lose consciousness and akinetic seizures that caused him to drop uncontrollably to the floor. Both types of seizures caused Ronald to fall on numerous occasions and resulted in injuries that included two fractured ankles, broken teeth and various bruises. Ronald is also mentally retarded.

After trying various methods to improve Ronald's condition, the Brookovers finally decided to try a corpus callosotomy, a surgical procedure in which the left and right hemispheres of the brain are separated. If successful, the operation reduces epileptic seizures significantly. The procedure requires two phases: the first is a partial dissection, the second phase completes the separation of the brain hemispheres.

Ronald was admitted to the Hospital in April of 1983 for the first phase of the corpus callosotomy. Ronald responded well to the first phase of the operation and returned to the Hospital in November of 1983 for the second phase. The operation was performed on November

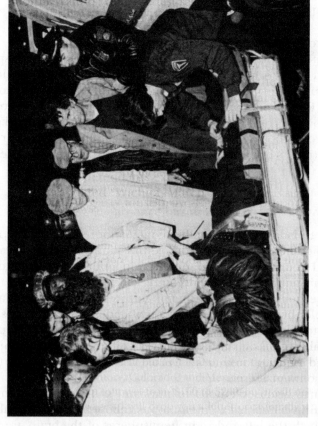

AN ACCUSING FINGER — While ambulance attendant straps him to stretcher, Brink's guard John McCann identifies John McGrath (hatless, second right) as man involved in $150,000 holdup in which McCann suffered gunshot wound. Suspect was arrested near scene of robbery outside First National Bank's Fields Corner office in Dorchester. Second suspect is sought. Page 20. GLOBE PHOTO BY GEORGE RIZER

Copyright © 1981 by The Boston Globe

10, 1983. On November 13, Ronald, who was not physically restrained, got out of his bed to go to the bathroom and fell, breaking his hip. Prior to getting out of bed Ronald had pressed his call bell for assistance, but no one came immediately.

A medical malpractice suit was brought by plaintiff for the injuries suffered by Ronald as a result of the fall. At trial there were two basic issues: whether the Hospital was negligent in not restraining Ronald to prevent him from getting out of bed; and, whether the Hospital's response time to Ronald's call for assistance was unreasonably slow. . . .

III.   Ronald's Statements to His Mother

After considering submitted memoranda as well as oral argument, the district court ruled that statements made by Ronald to his mother approximately eleven hours after his fall were admissible under the "catch-all" hearsay exception, Fed. R. Evid. 804(b)(5). On appeal, the Hospital contends that Ronald's hearsay statements did not meet the requirements of that exception and, therefore, should have been excluded. . . .

At the time of Ronald's fall one of the Hospital nurses, Nurse Kennedy, was in the adjacent room. She testified that she heard a loud thump against the wall in Ronald's room and immediately left to investigate. She discovered Ronald on the floor and asked him what had happened. Based on what Ronald told her and her personal observations, she made the following notation on Ronald's clinical record: "Found pt [patient] on floor—Apparently crawled out end of bed—trying to get to BR [bathroom]—had called for help but not a quick enough response."

Approximately eleven hours after Ronald's fall, his parents arrived at the hospital unaware of the previous night's events. After learning from the station nurse that Ronald had fallen, the Brookovers went to their son in his hospital room and asked him what had happened. Over the Hospital's objection, Mrs. Brookover testified as follows:

Mrs. Brookover: We ran into the room and we said, "Ron, what in the world's happened?" And he said, "Oh, Mother, I fell." He said, "I needed to go to the bathroom. I wanted to tinkle."
Attorney Felmly: Is that the way he describes going to the bathroom?
Mrs. Brookover: Yes. He said, "I put the call bell on," or the call light. He said, "I put the call bell on and I waited and I waited and no one came. I waited again and put the call bell on again two or three times." He'd keep a punching it he said. "And no one came to help me. And I called out, 'help! Help me!' and no one came." And he said, "Mother, I fell."

Attorney Felmly: Did he tell you how he managed to fall or how it came
    to be that he actually fell after trying to use the call button?
Mrs. Brookover: He showed me that he got out through the rails, the
    split rails. He was smaller than he is now. He told me, he said, "I
    got out through these rails, Mother. And I fell. I hit my head and
    I hit my leg." And he said, "The nurse came in finally when I fell
    and she was about mad at me. She bawled me out."

Following this testimony, Attorney Felmly showed Mrs. Brookover
Nurse Kennedy's notations, supra, and asked her, through a series of
questions, if the notations confirmed what Ronald had told her that
next morning. Mrs. Brookover testified that the two were consistent.

There was additional testimony directly on the question whether the
Hospital's response was tardy. Mrs. Brookover testified that a couple of
days after Ronald's fall:

> [Nurse Kennedy] came up in the hall, my husband and I was standing in the
> hall, and by Ron's room, and she said — she was crying and she said, "Mr. and
> Mrs. Brookover, I am so sorry. I just couldn't get to Ron. I was with another
> patient. We're so short-handed and I was with another patient and I couldn't get
> to Ron. The call light was on and I heard him call, but I couldn't get to him."

Nurse Kennedy, on direct examination, admitted apologizing to the
Brookovers but denied ever telling them that the Hospital was short-
staffed or that she had heard the call bell. On cross examination, Attorney Felmly brought out that in a deposition taken a year earlier,
Nurse Kennedy stated that she did not remember exactly what she had
told the Brookovers. . . .

A ruling on admissibility under the residual exceptions (Rules
803(24) and 804(b)(5)) is reviewed under the clearly erroneous standard. This standard gives considerable discretion to the trial court's
determination. Its ruling should not be disturbed "unless we have 'a
definite and firm conviction that the court made a clear error of judgment in the conclusion it reached based upon a weighing of the relevant
factors.'" United States v. Doe, 860 F.2d 488, 491 (1st Cir. 1988), cert.
denied, 490 U.S. 1049, 109 S. Ct. 1961, 104 L. Ed. 2d 430 (1989) (quoting, Page v. Barko Hydraulics, 673 F.2d 134, 140 (5th Cir. 1982)).

General guidance on the use of the residual hearsay exceptions is
found in the Senate Judiciary Committee Report. . . .

The Hospital has not challenged the unavailability of Ronald as a
witness. Nor has any question been raised about the requirement of
prior notice to the adverse party that the exception(s) will be invoked.
We assume, therefore, that it was met. The Hospital's main attack
against the admission of Ronald's statements as related by his mother
stems from the Rule's requirement that the statements have "equivalent
circumstantial guarantees of trustworthiness" to the other hearsay ex-

ceptions. The Hospital argues that because both Ronald and his mother are interested parties, because Ronald had a motive to fabricate and embellish the prior night events,[5] and because the statements lacked any contemporaneity with the event, Ronald's statements do not meet the "equivalent trustworthiness" requirement.

The case law on this issue reflects that the determination of equivalent trustworthiness is completely fact driven. In Furtado v. Bishop, 604 F.2d 80 (1st Cir. 1979), appellant objected to the introduction of a letter written by an attorney who had died by the time of trial. The trial judge admitted the letter pursuant to the residual exception on the basis that he knew the deceased to be an honorable man. This court questioned the judge's reason for admitting the letter, but found other additional indicia of reliability from its own examination of the record and upheld the admission. The court also stated that the weight to be given to the evidence was a matter for the jury to decide.

Here, the trial judge did not explicitly state what indicia of reliability and trustworthiness he relied on for admitting Mrs. Brookover's testimony. This was contrary to the admonition in the Senate Committee notes and it would have been helpful to us had he done so. On the other hand we know that the trial judge was the beneficiary of both written memoranda and oral argument on the issue. We must assume that he understood the requirements and limitations of the Rule. There is nothing in the Rule itself that requires explicit findings.

No single factor is dispositive on the issue of whether evidence should be admitted under the residual exception. The district judge must evaluate all of the factors and make a determination. In this case the judge made a careful decision after considering the arguments presented by both sides. Of course, Ronald's testimony would be the most probative on what happened in his room. The district judge also had the benefit of seeing Mrs. Brookover testify, and it was her credibility more than her son's that counted. In addition, the jury was able to evaluate the credibility of Mrs. Brookover's testimony and determine the weight it should be given.

Moreover, there is one strong, indeed almost irrefutable, indicia of reliability. The notes of Nurse Kennedy, which were clearly admissible and made within a short time after Ronald's fall corroborated what Mrs. Brookover testified Ronald told her eleven hours after the fall.[6] Nurse

5. Appellant contends that because Ronald functioned at a twelve year old level and had been told on numerous occasions not to get out of bed without help, it was likely that he would make up a story so he would not be blamed for what happened.

6. Our dissenting brother stresses that the eleven hour passage of time between Ronald's fall and his statement to his mother means that the statements were not contemporaneous. Although the length of time is not so short as to insure its reliability, it does not necessarily indicate inaccuracy. The amount of time that elapsed is just one of many factors that the district court judge considered in admitting the testimony. Courts have admitted statements under this exception that were made a much longer time after the incident than the one at

Kennedy wrote that she found Ronald on the floor, that he apparently crawled out of bed to get to the bathroom and significantly, "had called for help but not a quick enough response." Considering all the relevant factors we cannot say that "we have a definite and firm conviction that the court made a clear error of judgment" in admitting Mrs. Brookover's testimony. United States v. Doe, 860 F.2d at 491.[7]

BREYER, Circuit Judge (dissenting).

In order to admit into evidence the hearsay statement of an unavailable declarant under Fed. R. Evid. 804(b)(5)'s residual hearsay exception, a court must find "circumstantial guarantees" of the statement's "trustworthiness" that are "equivalent" to those found in the Rule's other exceptions for (1) former testimony subject to somewhat similar cross examination, (2) a statement made under belief of impending death, (3) a statement against interest, and (4) a statement of personal or family history. Fed. R. Evid 804(b)(1-4). See 4 J. Weinstein & M. Berger, Weinstein's Evidence ¶804(b)(5)[01], at 804-173 (1988) ("[T]he courts have admitted hearsay statements pursuant to Rule 804(b)(5) when a trustworthiness within the spirit of the Rule 804 class exceptions have been demonstrated.") [hereinafter Weinstein's Evidence]. Where can the court find such guarantees with respect to Ronald's statements, made to his mother the day following his accident, that he "put the call bell on," "waited and . . . waited," and "put the call bell on again two or three times" before he left the bed and fell?

The majority finds such a guarantee in hospital notes that Nurse Kennedy wrote, notes that say,

> Found pt on floor—apparently crawled out of end of bed—trying to get to BR —had called for help but not quick enough response.

These notes, however, do not indicate whether Nurse Kennedy meant the last phrase—"not quick enough response"—as evaluating the situation or as stating the obvious (that the response was not quick enough to prevent the fall), or, if the former, whether the evaluation is her own or Ronald's. No other corroborating evidence was ever introduced; on the contrary, Nurse Call testified that she arrived in Ronald's room "be-

---

issue here. See, e.g., United States v. Van Lufkins, 676 F.2d 1189 (8th Cir. 1982) (up to a week passed between the event and the hearsay statement to the witness) (cited with favor in United States v. Vretta, 790 F.2d 651, 659 (7th Cir. 1986); Furtado v. Bishop, 604 F.2d at 91 (affidavit admitted although written more than eight months after incident). In addition, the conversation at issue was the first time that the Brookovers were able to speak with Ronald after his fall.

7. Indeed, in light of the nurse's notations as to how the accident happened, it is hard to understand why Mrs. Brookover's testimony was offered.

tween 30 and 45 seconds" after hearing "Ron's bell go off" and found Nurse Kennedy already there. Where in this is there any special "guarantee" of "trustworthiness" for the relevant portion of Ronald's statement, the assertion of a significant lapse of time between his signalling for help and the nurses' response?

There is no special "guarantee" of "trustworthiness" in the fact that Ronald is retarded. He may not have been capable of understanding how his statement ("I waited and waited") might be used to show the hospital's liability, but he was perfectly capable of understanding that he was not supposed to get out of bed on his own, and he would seem as capable as anyone else of exaggerating the wait to disown his own fault. Cf. United States v. York, 852 F.2d 221, 226 (7th Cir. 1988) (excluding statements of fourteen year-old witness partly because he "had a motive to misrepresent the truth"); id. at 225 ("critical" factor in trustworthiness analysis is "whether the hearsay declarant had a motive to lie") (internal quotation marks omitted); United States v. Ferri, 778 F.2d 985, 991 (3d Cir. 1985) (same). Nor can one find a "guarantee" of "trustworthiness" in the timing of his statement, for he made it, not contemporaneous with the accident, but, rather, the next morning. Cf. United States v. Vretta, 790 F.2d 651, 659 (7th Cir. 1986) ("[C]lose proximity in time between the statement [describing the event] and the [event] itself lends support to the statement's trustworthiness.") And, I do not see how one can find a special "guarantee" in the fact that his mother testified that he was a very truthful person.

In fact, to permit admission of this statement simply because Nurse Kennedy's note provides some weak, and highly controverted, corroboration is to eliminate any legal requirement of special "trustworthiness." It is, in essence, to read the "residual" hearsay exception as allowing the district court to admit any hearsay for which it finds a special need. Such a reading seems wrong, see United States v. McCall, 740 F.2d 1331, 1342 (Widener, J., concurring) (where evidence of reliability is weak, "[m]ere unavailability . . . is an insufficient reason to justify the admissibility of [hearsay] statements"), for it is contrary to the intent of Congress. Indeed, the House of Representatives initially voted not to permit a residual hearsay exception precisely because it feared such a result. See House Comm. on the Judiciary, Report on Federal Rules of Evidence. The House withdrew its opposition only when the Senate narrowed the scope of the exception and instructed courts that it "intended that the residual hearsay exceptions will be used very rarely, and only in exceptional circumstances," Senate Comm. on the Judiciary, Report on Federal Rules of Evidence. The Senate Committee admonished courts applying 804(b)(5) to "exercise no less care, reflection and caution than the courts did under the common law in establishing the now-recognized exceptions to the hearsay rule." Failure by the lower court here to identify specific "guarantees" of the "trustworthiness" of

Ronald's statements suggests that the admission of these statements was not preceded by sufficient "reflection and caution."

I can find no case admitting hearsay under circumstances like those present here. *Furtado,* supra, which involved a lawyer's out-of-court statement made under oath, certainly does not. Nor do United States v. Carlson, 547 F.2d 1346 (8th Cir. 1976) and United States v. Murphy, 696 F.2d 282 (4th Cir. 1982), the other two cases cited by appellee. *Carlson* and *Murphy* both involved grand jury testimony which, at least in the case of *Murphy,* was supported by "strongly corroborative testimony and proof, some of which was unimpeachable." 696 F.2d at 286. Cases admitting hearsay under Rule 804(b)(5) involve substantially greater guarantees of reliability than those present here. See Weinstein's Evidence ¶804(b)(5)[01], at 804-173 n.3 (collecting cases). . . .

Since I believe the Federal Rules of Evidence do not permit admission of Ronald's hearsay statements and that their admission was not harmless, I must dissent.

Problem: Emergency Evidence

Charge: murder. Defense: alibi. At *D*'s trial the prosecution offers a tape recording of a telephone call received by the Boston Police Department 911 emergency operator at 1:09:40 P.M. on March 14. The conversation goes as follows:

Police operator: Police emergency.
Woman: Yes, please. Emergency at 295 Commonwealth Avenue, Apartment 2B.
Police operator: What's going on?
Woman: I was just stabbed.
Police operator: Do you need an ambulance?
Woman: Yes.

The prosecution also offers the testimony of *W*, a registered nurse. *W* will testify that he was apartment-hunting with a friend on March 14 on the second floor at 295 Commonwealth Avenue when he heard someone say, "Get a doctor." *W* looked into a room through a door left ajar and saw a woman lying face down on the floor. *W* asked the woman what happened, and she replied, "I've been stabbed." *W* then told the woman that he was going to call for help. The woman responded, "I've already called." After he called the police, *W* went back to the woman and asked her name. She said, "*V*." *W* then checked *V*'s back to determine if she had any injuries to her spine before turning her over and straightening her legs. At that point he could see bloodstains on the clothes. He pulled up the victim's sweater and blouse and exposed a wound just under her ribcage on her right side. *W* inquired whether the victim suffered from any health problems or allergies, and she answered "migraines" and "mushrooms." *W* had to repeat his questions. *V*'s responses were getting slower and weaker. She was getting paler. Her pulse was getting threadier and faster.

After getting a towel to place on *V*'s wound, *W* asked *V* if she could identify the assailant, and she replied, "Two men." Then *W* asked her how old they were, and *V* said, "In their 20s." *W* asked her their height. *V* said, "About 6 feet, 2 inches." *W* couldn't get any further information from *V*.

Shortly thereafter, a nurse and a doctor arrived at the apartment. *V* was lifted to a chair and a sheet was wrapped around her. *V*'s head flopped forward. At that point *W* felt that *V* would not make it. *V* died two hours later.

Is either the tape recording or *W*'s testimony admissible? If so, on what theory?

UNITED STATES v. BAILEY
439 F. Supp. 1303 (W.D. Pa. 1977)

TEITELBAUM, J. On June 9, 1976, the defendant, Milton Edward Bailey, was indicted by a Federal Grand Jury sitting in the Western District of Pennsylvania. The two-count indictment, alleging violations of Sections 2, 2113(a) and 2113(d) of Title 18, United States Code, charged the defendant with the February 6, 1975, armed robbery of the branch office of the Colony Federal Savings and Loan Office in Aliquippa, Pennsylvania.

Palm prints taken from the teller's counter at the bank were determined to be those of John Bernard Stewart. Stewart was indicted and on April 29, 1976, pursuant to a plea bargain, gave a written statement to the Federal Bureau of Investigation detailing the robbery and naming Milton Edward Bailey as his accomplice.[1]

A major issue at trial was identification. Four of the eyewitnesses to the robbery did not identify the defendant at trial and had made no pretrial photographic identification.[2] Two other eyewitnesses testified that they had picked the defendant's picture out of a pretrial photographic display and, in Court, they were only able to make a qualified identification of the defendant.

John Bernard Stewart, who at the time of his guilty plea to the instant

---

1. Ms. Caroline Thomas and Mrs. Regina Dorsey both testified that John Bernard Stewart was a friend of Milton Bailey.
2. Tellers Farinelli and Cavender were ordered to lie face down on the floor and they never even glimpsed the robber standing near the manager's desk. Likewise, the customer, Mr. Sylvester, was struck on the head from behind and had only the briefest opportunity, as he fell from his chair onto the floor, to see his assailant's face.

robbery had agreed to testify for the government, was called, out of the presence of the jury, as a witness. However, Stewart refused to testify despite an order of the Court to do so. In view of Stewart's refusal, the government moved, pursuant to Rule 804 of the Federal Rules of Evidence, to have Stewart's written statement admitted into evidence. The Court granted both counsel a day's recess to research the question of admissibility. After argument, the Court admitted the statement under Rule 804(b)(5). Thereafter, a defense counsel, having previously been given a copy of the statement, was given a three-day recess to prepare to meet the statement and was told additional time would be given if needed.

The detailed statement of John Bernard Stewart, which was read into evidence by Special Agent Preston of the Federal Bureau of Investigation, alleged that Stewart and the defendant, Bailey, using the defendant's girlfriend's car, drove to Aliquippa from Washington, D.C., the morning of the robbery, searched Aliquippa for an opportune bank to rob, drove to Pittsburgh, Pa. where they split up and met again in Washington, D.C., to divide the proceeds of the robbery.

Counsel, on cross-examination, was permitted to impeach Stewart by questioning Agent Preston about Stewart's prior criminal record and motive to lie.

Upon the foregoing testimony, the jury returned a verdict of guilty as to both counts of the indictment. Defendant has now moved for a new trial and/or judgment of acquittal.

ISSUE

The issue to be decided is whether the out-of-court statement of Stewart was properly admitted into evidence as a hearsay exception under Rule 804(b)(5) of the Federal Rules of Evidence, and, if so, whether its admissibility comports with the Sixth Amendment right to confront one's accusers.

EVIDENTIARY ADMISSIBILITY

Rule 804(b)(5) formulates a new "trustworthiness" exception to the hearsay rule. . . .

The first question to be asked is whether Stewart was "unavailable" within the ambit of 804(b)(5). The answer to this question is easily provided by 804(a)(2) which states:

(a) *Definition of unavailability.* "Unavailability as a witness" includes situations in which the declarant (2) persists in refusing to testify concerning the subject matter of his statement despite an order of the court to do so.

In the case sub judice, Stewart refused to testify in spite of an order of Court. Stewart, therefore, was clearly unavailable for purposes of application of the Federal Rules of Evidence in general and 804(b)(5) in particular.

We now turn to an examination of the specific requirements of admissibility under 804(b)(5).

The first requirement is that the statement offered be evidence of a material fact. All parties concede that identity was a material issue at trial.

The second requirement is that the statement be more probative on the point for which it is offered than any other evidence which the proponent can procure through reasonable efforts. This requirement was satisfied because no other person was able to provide the specific evidence as to identity that was furnished via Stewart's statement.

The third requirement is that the general purpose of the Rules and the interests of justice will be best served by admission of the statement into evidence. Stewart testified in his statement that defendant and he were driving the car that belonged to the mother of defendant's girlfriend. That particular car was in Aliquippa at the time of the robbery and those persons who robbed the bank used that car to flee.[5] Such a corroborating circumstance serves to guarantee the trustworthiness of the statement and mandates its admission in the interests of justice.

Additionally, the statement cannot be admitted under 804(b)(5) unless the adverse party knows of it sufficiently in advance of trial to be provided with a fair opportunity to meet it. The purpose of this notice requirement is to give the adverse party an adequate opportunity to prepare to contest the use of the statement. Although notice was not given to defense counsel prior to trial, the trial was recessed for three days to enable counsel to prepare to meet Stewart's statement and additional time was made available to him if necessary. The failure of pretrial disclosure occurred because Stewart's "unavailability" did not arise until trial when he refused to testify in defiance of this Court's Order. The government could not know whether Stewart would be unavailable to testify until after his refusal during trial. Thus, the notice requirement of 804(b)(5) was fulfilled in both spirit and purpose by recessing the proceedings. It is significant to note that defendant does not claim three days was insufficient for investigation or that he was prejudiced in any manner by the procedure utilized. Under the circumstances sub judice, Stewart's statement was properly admitted under Rule 804(b)(5).

[Discussion of Sixth Amendment right of confrontation is omitted.]

CONCLUSION

We have examined defendant's other contentions and find them to

---

5. One of the witnesses made a positive identification of the car as being the getaway vehicle.

be without merit. Defendant's motion for a new trial and/or judgment of acquittal is therefore denied. An appropriate Order will issue.

Do you agree with the district court's use of Rule 804(b)(5) in *Bailey*? If you represented the defendant, what counter arguments would you make to the Court of Appeals?

UNITED STATES v. BAILEY
581 F.2d 341 (3d Cir. 1978)

GIBBONS, Circuit Judge. . . . There is no doubt that Stewart's confession was a "written assertion," and thus a "statement" by Stewart, which the government offered at trial to prove the truth of the matters asserted in it. Thus it was hearsay under F.R. Evid. 801(c), and as such was inadmissible unless other rules permitted the statement to be admitted. F.R. Evid. 802.

At trial, the government argued that the confession of Stewart was admissible as a declaration against penal interest, pursuant to Fed. R. Evid. 804(b)(3). The court determined that the requirements of that section had not been met, since the statement had been made by Stewart while he was in custody and after he had been offered a bargain involving dismissal of one count of the indictment against him. The government has not pressed its argument on this point here, and we do not disagree with the trial court.

The trial court grounded the admissibility of the Stewart confession on Rule 804(b)(5) of the Federal Rules of Evidence. That rule is one of two "residual" exceptions to the hearsay rule, providing for the admission of evidence even when the traditional requirements for the admission of hearsay are not met.

Prior to the adoption of the Federal Rules of Evidence, the out-of-court confession involved in this case could not have been used against Bailey. Thus we must determine the extent to which the addition of the residual Rule of 804(b)(5) has broadened the trial court's discretion in admitting evidence.

The trial court is vested with discretion in its determination whether hearsay evidence afforded by a party meets the requirements of an exception set forth in the Federal Rules of Evidence. Our role, therefore, is to decide whether the trial court abused its discretion in determining that Stewart's confession met all requirements of Rule 804(b)(5).

To be admissible under Rule 804(b)(5), an out-of-court statement must meet the following requirements:

The declarant must be unavailable;

The statement must have circumstantial guarantees of trustworthiness equivalent to the first four exceptions in Rule 804(b);

The statement must be offered as evidence of a material fact;

The statement must be more probative on the point for which it is offered than any other evidence that the proponent reasonably can procure;

Introduction of the statement must serve the interests of justice and the purposes of the Federal Rules;

The proponent of the evidence to be offered must have given his adversary the notice required by the rule.

The history of Rule 804(b)(5) and its counterpart, Rule 803(24), indicates a congressional intention that the rules have a narrow focus. The initial "residual" rule for the introduction of hearsay not covered by one of the specific exceptions to the hearsay rule was phrased by the Advisory Committee as follows:

> A statement not specifically covered by any of the foregoing exceptions, but having comparable circumstantial guarantees of trustworthiness.

56 F.R.D. 183, 322 (1972).

After the rules were submitted to Congress, the House Judiciary Committee removed from both Rules 803 and 804 the residual exceptions on the grounds that the rules added too much uncertainty to the law of evidence.[7] The Senate Judiciary Committee reinstated the deleted Advisory Committee residual exceptions in a modified form. The Senate Committee noted its fear that without residual rules of admissibility for hearsay in certain instances, the established exceptions would be tortured in order to allow reliable evidence to be introduced. Further, the new proposed residual rules were drafted to apply only when certain exceptional guarantees of trustworthiness exist and when high degrees of probativeness and necessity are present.[8] The Senate Committee fur-

---

7. The committee noted that some leeway was provided for the courts by Rule 102, which could cover the anomalous situation calling for admission of hearsay not covered by an enumerated exception. Rule 102 states:

"These rules shall be construed to secure fairness in administration, elimination of unjustifiable expense and delay, and promotion of growth and development of the law of evidence to the end that the truth may be ascertained and proceedings justly determined."

The House Committee also stated that "if additional hearsay exceptions are to be created, they should be by amendments to the Rules, not on a case-by-case basis." H.R. Rep. No. 650, 93d Cong. 2d Sess. (1973), reprinted in [1974] U.S. Code Cong. & Admin. News, pp.7051, 7079.

8. The Committee cited as an appropriate example the case of Dallas County v. Commercial Union Assoc. Co., Ltd., 286 F.2d 388 (5th Cir. 1961). In that case, the court allowed into evidence a copy of a newspaper article describing a fire in a county courthouse fifty years prior to the collapse of the courthouse tower. The insurer offered this evidence in order to show that certain charred wood found in the ruins might not have been the product of lightning striking the courthouse and causing its collapse, as the county contended. The article, however,

ther stated that the residual exceptions were to be used only rarely, and in exceptional circumstances. The Senate Report cautioned that "[t]he residual exceptions are not meant to authorize major judicial revisions of the hearsay rules, including its present exceptions."

The House-Senate Conference Committee agreed to include the Senate residual rule with further modifications. Representative Dennis, one of the floor managers of the Federal Rules of Evidence bill, stated in the House debate preceding passage of the bill that the residual rules applied to situations "comparable to the ordinary hearsay exceptions." In his view, the residual rule did not purport to accomplish much at all regarding expansion of traditional rules of evidence. Thus, in reviewing the admissibility of evidence under Rule 804(b)(5), we must keep in mind its limited scope as intended by Congress.

Defendant does not contest the trial judge's finding that Stewart was unavailable, or that the confession was evidence of a material fact — Bailey's identification as one of the bank robbers. Bailey contends, however, that other elements of Rule 804(b)(5) were not satisfied.[11] Initially, he argues that the statement cannot be used against him since it was not until after trial had commenced that the government informed him that it would seek to have Stewart's statement introduced.

Before an out-of-court statement can be admitted pursuant to Rule 804(b)(5), the proponent of it must advise the adverse party his intention to use the statement, as well as the "particulars of it, including the name and address of the declarant." The proponent must give notice "sufficiently before trial . . . to provide the adverse party with a fair opportunity to meet [the statement]. . . ." The advance notice provision came into being during the House-Senate Conference on the proposed rules.

The debates in Congress and the statements of Rep. William Hungate (Chairman of the House Judiciary Committee Subcommittee on Criminal Justice) indicate some understanding that the requirement of advance notice was to be strictly followed.

We believe that the purpose of the rules and requirement of fairness to an adversary contained in the advance notice requirement of Rule

---

would have supported the insurer's proposition that the tower collapsed because of deterioration and disrepair. In allowing the evidence to be admitted, the court considered the inconceivability of the unknown reporter fifty years previously writing about a fire if one had not in fact occurred. See S. Rep. No. 1277, 93d Cong. 2d Sess. (1974) reprinted in [1974] U.S. Code Cong. & Admin. News at 7065-66.

11. One of Bailey's contentions is that Stewart's statement was not "more probative on the point for which it is offered than any other evidence which the proponent can procure through reasonable efforts." F.R. Evid. 804(b)(5)(B). We disagree. Although the government made an effort to place Bailey in the bank during the robbery through the identification testimony of prosecution witnesses, none were able to state positively that they recognized Bailey at trial as the second bank robber. We feel the trial judge did not abuse his discretion in resolving this issue.

803(24) and Rule 804(b)(5) are satisfied when, as here, the proponent of the evidence is without fault in failing to notify his adversary prior to trial and the trial judge has offered sufficient time, by means of granting a continuance, for the party against whom the evidence is to be offered to prepare to meet and contest its admission. . . .

Bailey also argues that Stewart's confession failed to meet the requirement that the evidence to be admitted pursuant to Rule 804(b)(5) must possess "guarantees of trustworthiness" equivalent to the other enumerated exceptions under Rule 804(b). We find this contention convincing.

The specific hearsay exceptions of Rule 804(b) include those for former testimony, dying declarations, statements against interest, and statements of family background or history. Each of these kinds of statements is admissible, though hearsay, because the circumstances in which the statements are made are indicative of a strong propensity for truthfulness (dying declarations), because there has been a previous opportunity for cross-examination (former testimony), or because the contents of the statements themselves are of such a nature that one reasonably would conclude that the speaker was telling the truth (statements against interest, statements of family history).[12]

The trial judge determined the reliability of the hearsay statement on the evidence that the bank robbers fled the crime in Bailey's girlfriend's car. Since the statement mentioned that Stewart and Bailey traveled to Aliquippa in the car, the trial judge held that Stewart's statement possessed sufficient indicia of reliability to justify its admission pursuant to 804(b)(5). We believe that the recitation of this single factor does not satisfy the requirement that the statement to be offered in evidence have "circumstantial guarantees of trustworthiness" equivalent to the other 804(b) exceptions. Indeed, if Stewart had borrowed the car from Bailey and had committed the robbery with another, the bargain he struck with the authorities provided him with the opportunity to sidetrack the investigation and protect his accomplice by naming Bailey, a plausible suspect, as his partner in the robbery.

We do not feel that the trustworthiness of a statement offered pursuant to the rule should be analyzed solely on the basis of the facts corroborating the authenticity of the statement. Since the rule is designed to come into play when there is a need for the evidence in order

---

12. As originally submitted to Congress, the proposed Federal Rules contained an additional exception for statements of recent perception. The House Committee, however, deleted this rule on the grounds that statements of the type encompassed within this exception did not bear "sufficient guarantees of trustworthiness to justify admissibility." We think that an awareness of Congress' deletion of proposed Rule 804(b)(2) provides some guidance in determining whether a statement offered under Rule 804(b)(5) possesses guarantees of trustworthiness equivalent to those 804(b) exceptions included in the final version of the federal rules.

to ascertain the truth in a case, it would make little sense for a judge, in determining whether the hearsay is admissible, tó examine only facts corroborating the substance of the declaration. Such an analysis in effect might increase the likelihood of admissibility when corroborating circumstances indicate a reduced need for the introduction of the hearsay statement. We do not believe that Congress intended that "trustworthiness" be analyzed in this manner. Rather, the trustworthiness of a statement should be analyzed by evaluating not only the facts corroborating the veracity of the statement, but also the circumstances in which the declarant made the statement and the incentive he had to speak truthfully or falsely. Further, consideration should be given to factors bearing on the reliability of the reporting of the hearsay by the witness.

In United States v. Medico, 557 F.2d 309 (2d Cir. 1977), the court held that circumstantial degrees of trustworthiness justified the admission of an unknown bystander's report of the license plate of a fleeing automobile used by escaping bankrobbers. The bystander shouted the numbers out from the street to another bystander, who was stationed next to the locked door of the bank. The bystander near the door relayed the information into the bank to an employee who transcribed the description and tag number of the car. In assessing the reliability of the hearsay, the court looked to the opportunity of the declarants to observe, the amount of time for the information to be relayed to the bank employee, and the potential for misidentification or fabrication, determining that the situation in which the statements were offered provided a guarantee of trustworthiness on a par with the enumerated 804(b) exceptions.

In United States v. Gomez, 559 F.2d 1271 (5th Cir. 1977), the court held that the grand jury testimony of a witness who had refused to take the stand at trial was not admissible, because the circumstances in which he gave his grand jury testimony did not measure up to the trustworthiness requirement of Rule 804(b)(5). In that case, the witness had been convicted and had been granted immunity in order to compel him to testify before the grand jury. Since the government had made the witness aware that he could be subjected to an unlimited number of contempt proceedings if he failed to testify, and since the witness was in fear of retaliation against himself and his family if he did testify, the court found that his responses to leading questions before the grand jury failed to pass the trustworthiness test of Rule 804(b)(5).[13]

---

13. In United States v. Carlson [547 F.2d 1346 (8th Cir. 1976)], the Eighth Circuit held admissible statements by a grand jury witness who refused to testify at trial. There the court focused on the fact that the declarant had been under oath at the time of making the statements, and that when informing the trial judge of his refusal to testify later, the declarant stated that he had told the truth to the grand jury. See also United States v. West, 574 F.2d 1131 (4th Cir. 1978) (trustworthiness found in deceased declarant's grand jury testimony

In this case, the circumstances under which Stewart provided his statement implicating Bailey do not inspire confidence in its reliability. First, as we have discussed, the statement was made during negotiations for reduction of charges lodged against Stewart. Secondly, the statements were made in a face-to-face meeting with two FBI agents. Further, the statement was not made under oath and its veracity had not been tested, certainly not by cross-examination. Finally, the fact relied upon by the trial judge as corroborating Stewart's confession, the identification of the car, does not provide a sufficient degree of reliability to justify the statement's introduction. Thus we feel that the trial judge's determination as to the trustworthiness of the statement was an abuse of his discretion, since the assertions in the statement and the circumstances in which the statement was given do not provide guarantees of trustworthiness equivalent to the other Rule 804(b) exceptions that serve as a benchmark for Rule 804(b)(5).

We also have grave doubts about the propriety of introducing Stewart's confession in light of clause (C) of 804(b)(5), which requires that "the general purpose of [the Federal Rules of Evidence] and the interests of justice will best be served by [the] admission of the statement into evidence." Although we do not reach the constitutional issue raised in this case, we are concerned with the relationship between the Confrontation Clause of the Sixth Amendment and the admissibility of this evidence under the Federal Rules of Evidence. In drafting the proposed rules submitted to Congress, the Advisory Committee provided leeway in order to insure that the rules did not collide with the Confrontation Clause. Thus, in analyzing the admissibility of evidence pursuant to Rule 804(b)(5), a court should exercise its discretion in order to avoid potential conflicts between confrontation rights and this hearsay exception.

The use of Stewart's confession at Bailey's trial raises difficult constitutional issues, and we have doubts whether, in light of the lack of cross-examination, the questionable reliability of the statement on the record before us, and the devastating impact of the statement, admission of this statement could pass constitutional muster. Thus, in evaluating the purpose of the rules under 804(b)(5)(C), the better course would have been for the trial judge to have exercised his discretion under the rules not to admit the evidence.

Although we have mentioned the values protected by the Confrontation Clause, we expressly do not base our decision to reverse Bailey's conviction on constitutional grounds. At present, the state of this aspect of the Sixth Amendment is unsettled, and its future path has been a

---

because close supervision of his activities as undercover informant rendered deception of agents "substantially impossible").

matter of some commentary. Our decision is based on the failure of Stewart's statement implicating Bailey to satisfy the requirements of Rule 804(b)(5).

The judgment of the district court will be reversed and remanded for a new trial.

UNITED STATES v. WEST
574 F.2d 1131 (4th Cir. 1978)

HAYNSWORTH, C.J. Calvin W. West, Floyd Lee Davis and Joseph Lee Dempsey appeal their convictions for distributing heroin and possessing heroin with the intent to distribute it. The most significant question presented is whether the admission of the grand jury testimony of Michael Victor Brown, who was slain prior to trial, was permissible under Rule 804(b)(5) of the Federal Rules of Evidence and the Confrontation Clause of the Sixth Amendment. We hold that it was.

The convictions challenged here are the product of an extensive Drug Enforcement Agency (DEA) investigation in which Brown played a vital role. Brown volunteered his assistance to the DEA while he was in jail on a drug charge and under a detainer for parole violation. He agreed to purchase heroin under police surveillance.

Each purchase was similar. Brown would contact West or Davis and arrange to purchase heroin. Twice the DEA monitored Brown's calls to West arranging heroin deals. It also monitored one phone call to Davis. On other occasions it seems that Brown simply notified the DEA that he had arranged a purchase.

Each time that the DEA agents received notice that Brown was about to make a purchase, they made arrangements for extensive surveillance. Before each purchase, DEA agents strip-searched Brown to make sure that he had no drugs, and they concealed a transmitter on him. They then searched his vehicle to be sure that it contained no drugs and gave Brown the money required for the anticipated purchase.

According to the government's evidence, on three occasions, Brown went to West, gave West money, and obtained heroin. Twice Brown went to Davis, gave Davis money and obtained heroin. On another occasion, Brown gave West money then accompanied him to meet Dempsey. West then gave Dempsey money and told Brown that they were to meet Dempsey at Griffin's home. Brown and West went to Griffin's home. Dempsey arrived, went to the open window of Brown's car and then entered Griffin's home and told Brown that everything was all right. Brown then returned to his car to find 30 capsules of heroin.

Each time, law enforcement officials observed Brown's movements and obtained photographs of Brown as he met with West and with Davis.

After each transaction Brown returned to the DEA office and surrendered the heroin that he had purchased and any money remaining.
Each time the agents searched Brown and his car to be sure that he
retained no contraband. Agent Scott then discussed with Brown the
events that had taken place and composed a detailed summary of what
had occurred, which Brown read, corrected and signed. After one of
the purchases Brown himself prepared a statement which Agent Scott
revised before Brown read, corrected and signed it. Each time, Scott
and Brown listened to the tapes from the body transmitter for audibility
and voice identification. By reviewing the tapes with Brown, Scott independently became able to identify the voices of the defendants.

On March 8, 1976, the defendants and others were indicted by a
grand jury, apparently without Brown's testimony. On March 16, Brown
appeared before a grand jury and testified under oath regarding his
knowledge of the drug traffic in Virginia's Tidewater area. The government attorney read the statements that Brown had signed and periodically asked Brown if they were correct.

As a result of his cooperation, Brown was released from jail, the pending drug charge against him was nol prossed, and the detainer for parole
violation was lifted. The DEA also gave Brown $855 for his personal use
so that he would not arouse suspicion and jeopardize his cover by being
without funds immediately after supposedly selling a large amount of
heroin.

On March 19 Brown was murdered in a manner suggestive of contract killers. Four bullets were fired into the back of his head while he
was driving his car. According to the government, at least four potential
government witnesses in this and related narcotics investigations have
been murdered after they had agreed to cooperate. But these defendants have not been charged with Brown's murder, and the government
did not offer any evidence to show that they were responsible for it.

On April 22, a week before the scheduled trial date, the government
notified the defendants, pursuant to Rule 804(b)(5) of the Federal
Rules of Evidence, that it intended to introduce Brown's grand jury
testimony at trial. It agreed to give defense counsel all of its evidence,
including Brown's arrest record, and transcripts of the tapes of Brown's
conversations with the defendants.

After a pre-trial hearing, the district court ruled that the grand jury
testimony was admissible under Rule 804(b)(5) because, under the circumstances, it was essential and trustworthy. It also gave the defense a
week's continuance after it announced that it would admit Brown's
grand jury testimony.

During the trial the government introduced the transcript of Brown's
grand jury testimony, the photographs, an expert on voice identification
and the heroin. It also played the tapes of Brown's conversations with
the defendants. Law enforcement agents testified about their observa-

tion of Brown's activities and corroborated Brown's highly detailed grand jury testimony. The government sought to introduce transcripts which it had prepared from the tapes from Brown's body transmitter. Although the district judge found that the transcripts were a fair representation of the taped conversations, he permitted the jury to see the transcripts only while they listened to the tapes and instructed the jurors to decide for themselves what the tapes said.

I

The defendants contend that the district judge erred in concluding that the transcript of Brown's grand jury testimony was admissible under Rule 804(b)(5). . . .

The defendants do not contend that the grand jury transcript fails to meet the criteria of clauses (A), (B) and (C). Instead, they focus upon the general requirement that the statement have "equivalent circumstantial guarantees of trustworthiness" as statements the admission of which is authorized by any of the preceding four paragraphs. They find a lack of trustworthiness in Brown's criminal record and their lack of any opportunity to cross-examine him. They point to legislative history indicating that Rule 804(b)(5) applies only where "exceptional circumstances" lend to the extra-judicial statement a degree of trustworthiness equivalent to that of evidence admissible under other §804(b) exceptions.

There were present very exceptional circumstances providing substantial guarantees of trustworthiness of Brown's grand jury testimony probably exceeding by far the substantial guarantees of trustworthiness of some of the other §804(b) hearsay exceptions. Before each contact by Brown with West, Davis or Dempsey, the agents took elaborate steps to assure themselves that Brown possessed no drugs or money other than the money supplied by the agents to effect the purchases. Except when he entered a building and became concealed from their view he was under constant surveillance, and photographs were taken when he was with one of the defendants. Moreover, his transmitter was broadcasting his conversations with the defendants, and a tape recorder preserved those conversations. Moreover, immediately after each purchase, he and one of the agents reviewed what Brown had done, said and observed, and a statement of it was prepared and corrected. The immediate transcription and verification of Brown's statements provide an additional guarantee other admissible hearsay statements lack. But the most impressive assurance of trustworthiness comes from the corroboration provided by the observations of the agents, the pictures they took and their recordings of the conversations. Brown had a criminal record, and he was seeking favors to avoid further incarceration, but the circumstances make deception of the agents inconceivable. The agents simply followed, photographed and recorded conversations to such an extent that deception by Brown was substantially impossible. Moreover, his interest in gaining favors to avoid further imprisonment gave him every incentive to be extremely accurate in his reports. He knew what the agents were doing to corroborate and verify his reports, and any attempted deception would only have been calculated to arouse the suspicion of the agents and to lose for Brown their favor.

The substantially contemporaneous sworn written statements by Brown were the basis of Brown's grand jury testimony. The corroborative circumstances and verification procedures lend to his grand jury testimony a degree of trustworthiness probably substantially exceeding that inherent in dying declarations, statements against interest, and statements of personal or family history, all of which are routinely admitted under §804(b)(2), (3) and (4).

Although Brown's grand jury testimony was not subject to immediate cross-examination, to a large extent what Brown said was corroborated by the observations of the agents. The agents did appear as witnesses and were subject to cross-examination about what they observed, including the possibility of mistake or prevarication by Brown, and their own roles in preparing Brown's statements. Moreover, defense counsel had Brown's criminal record and knew of his interest in gaining favor with the agents. They could, and did, present those bases of impeachment of Brown which might have been developed on cross-examination if Brown had been present to testify.

Under all of these circumstances, the absence of an opportunity to cross-examine Brown himself is of considerable less significance than in those cases involving statements against interest, statements of family history, or dying declarations.

Whether the circumstantial guarantees of trustworthiness of Brown's grand jury testimony are equivalent to those which arise from cross- or direct examination which underlies the former testimony exception of §804(b)(1), we need not determine. In this unusual case, those guarantees were probably greater, but the equivalent guarantee of trustworthiness requirement of §804(b)(5) is met if there is equivalency of any one of the preceding §804(b) exceptions. Clearly there is such equivalency with the exceptions we find in paragraphs 2, 3, and 4.

The defense lawyers were given every opportunity to attack Brown's credibility, and they fully utilized their opportunities. It may be of passing significance that the jury did not accept all that Brown said, for it acquitted two of the defendants implicated by him. That it convicted West, Davis and Dempsey suggests that it carefully considered the very substantial extent to which the corroborative evidence established their

guilt, either directly or through strong demonstration of the trustworthiness of Brown's testimony as to them. . . .

What was the unspoken assumption of the appellate court in its discussion of the various indicia of reliability attached to the statements of
the witness Brown? Is a strong accountability to one party, albeit the
government, the kind of circumstantial reliability that should justify dispensing with cross-examination?

In United States v. West, one senses from the opinion that the defendant may have played a role in the unavailability of the informant Brown
as a witness at trial. In 1997, the Supreme Court replaced subsection
(5) of Rule 804(b) (which had been incorporated in new Rule 807)
with a new Rule 804(b)(5) authorizing admission in evidence of a hearsay statement against a party that has "engaged or acquiesced in wrongdoing" that procured the unavailability of the declarant as a witness.
What guarantees of reliability do such statements possess which would
justify dispensing with cross-examination?

UNITED STATES v. GARNER
574 F.2d 1141 (4th Cir. 1978)

HAYNSWORTH, C.J. Convicted of drug related offenses arising out of the
alleged importation of substantial quantities of heroin from West Germany and Holland, the defendants complain primarily of the admission
in evidence of the grand jury testimony of an alleged co-conspirator
who declined to testify at the trial despite the best efforts of the trial
judge and his own lawyer to get him to do so.

I

Warren Robinson, the grand jury witness, had been indicted for offenses committed by him in connection with the importation of the
heroin. He had previously commenced serving a six year sentence imposed upon him for unrelated offenses, and he was under indictment
in New York for still other unrelated offenses. Faced with the possibility
that very heavy penalties might be imposed upon him if convicted under
this indictment, he entered into a plea agreement. The agreement was
that he would enter a plea of guilty to a two-count information, would
testify fully before a grand jury and in any ensuing criminal proceedings,
in exchange for which the government would dismiss the indictment.
There was no agreement respecting the disposition of the New York
charges.

Robinson entered his guilty pleas to the two counts in the information, and was sentenced to two successive five year terms to commence upon completion of his earlier six year sentence. He then appeared as a seemingly willing witness before a grand jury.

He told the grand jury that Garner had approached him with information that McKethan, an airline employee, had a source for large quantities of heroin in West Germany. Garner sought to enlist Robinson's participation in the importation of heroin from western Europe and its distribution in the metropolitan Washington area.

There followed a number of trips to West Germany and to Holland, where another source of supply had been developed with the assistance of their first contact. Robinson did not get his passport in time to make Garner's first trip, but he and Garner traveled together on two later ones, and he was told by the defendants of still later trips that they took. On one of the trips Garner and Robinson were accompanied by two young women who, traveling separately on the return trip, brought the heroin into the United States concealed in their girdles.

Before Garner and McKethan were brought to trial, Robinson indicated reluctance to testify at trial. This occasioned inquiry of him in an in camera proceeding before the trial opened. He then stated that in the absence of his lawyer he would not testify. His lawyer was summoned and advised him to testify, but to no avail. After the trial opened, though the court had granted him use immunity, and threatened him with a contempt citation if he refused, he persisted in his refusal to testify. In another in camera proceeding, Robinson indicated that he might answer questions put by defense counsel. The district court then ruled that, though he was "unavailable" as a witness within the meaning of Rule 804(b)(5) of the F.R. Evid., he was "available" for cross-examination by defense counsel. In the presence of the jury, Robinson stated that he knew Garner and McKethan and that his grand jury testimony was inaccurate. He answered some questions about European travel with answers which seemed to say that he knew nothing of any drug trafficking by Garner or McKethan. At other times he declined to answer, and his seeming disclaimers of knowledge may have been understood by the jury to be the equivalent of a refusal to testify. The transcript gives one the general impression not that the grand jury testimony was false but that, whatever pressures were brought upon him, the defendant was unwilling to testify, and particularly unwilling to say anything which would incriminate either of these defendants.

There is no explanation of this unwillingness. Cooperating former co-conspirators have sometimes been the victims of threats by their former associates facing trials. That Robinson was the victim of threats by either Garner or McKethan, however, can be no more than speculation. Robinson was in prison at the time, and he may have been the victim of the code that condemns a conspirator for testifying against his former associates.

II

In United States v. West, 4th Cir., 574 F.2d 1131, we have upheld the admission of sworn grand jury testimony, though not subject to cross-examination, when the witness was murdered in the interim between his grand jury testimony and the trial of the drug offenders. In that case, there was extraordinary corroboration of the grand jury testimony, for he had been wired for sound; his conversations had been recorded; he had been kept under close surveillance when not within buildings, and the officers who had watched and recorded his conversations were witnesses available for cross-examination.

In United States v. Carlson, 8th Cir., 547 F.2d 1346, a grand jury witness refused to testify at Carlson's trial because, he said, of threats directed to him by Carlson. That, too, was a drug offense case. There was substantial circumstantial corroboration of the grand jury testimony. Because of that, and a general affirmation by the witness at trial of his grand jury testimony, the Eighth Circuit held the grand jury testimony admissible under Rule 804(b)(5). As to the Confrontation Clause, it held that Carlson had waived his right, reasoning that Carlson should not be allowed to complain of the silence of the witness when he was the procurer of the silence. See Motes v. U.S., 178 U.S. 458.

On the other hand, in United States v. Gonzalez, 5th Cir., 559 F.2d 1271, the Fifth Circuit, in another drug offense case, held that the testimony of the grand jury witness was inadmissible. There the grand jury witness had been most reluctant to testify during his appearance before the grand jury, apparently torn between the possibility of injury to himself or his family if he testified and further imprisonment for contempt if he refused. Faced with these unpleasant alternatives, the pressure to testify may have prompted the witness falsely to identify the defendant as his employer, and the identity of the employer was entirely dependent upon the testimony of the witness.

Since we have canvassed this scene in *West*, we need not repeat it here. It is enough to recite that sworn grand jury testimony may be admitted under Rule 804(b)(5) when there are substantial guarantees of trustworthiness equivalent to those which warrant recognized exceptions to the hearsay rule. The admission of such sworn testimony is not a violation of the Confrontation Clause of the Constitution if it bears sufficient guarantees of reliability and the circumstances contain a sufficient basis upon which the jury may assess its trustworthiness. The distinction is illustrated by the strong indicators of reliability found in *West* and the absence of such indicators in *Gonzalez*. See also U.S. v. Rogers, 549 F.2d 490 (8th Cir. 1976), cert. denied, 431 U.S. 918 (1977).

Here there are strong indicators of reliability, and the jury had an ample basis upon which to determine the trustworthiness of the testimony.

One of the two young women who, according to Robinson's grand jury testimony, had accompanied Garner and him on their trip to Amsterdam beginning on October 15, 1974, was produced as a witness at the trial. She fully confirmed Robinson's grand jury testimony about the trip. She, Miss McKee, and a Miss Hallums, had accompanied Garner and Robinson to Amsterdam for the purpose of serving as couriers. While in Amsterdam, Miss McKee shared a hotel room with Robinson, while Miss Hallums shared another nearby room with Garner. After Garner and Robinson had procured the heroin, she testified, Robinson "blended" it into powder form and packaged it into two packages. This was done in a hotel room in which Garner and the two women were also present. Miss McKee "snorted" some of the heroin, and the men showed the girls how to conceal one package each in her girdle. The two girls then flew to Dulles, while the two men took another plane to New York, just as Robinson had testified. When the men got to Washington, Miss McKee testified she delivered the two packages of heroin to Garner, who was sitting on the passenger side of a car being driven by Robinson.

Moreover, there was irrefutable evidence of their travels. The United States introduced records of airline tickets, customs declarations, passport endorsements, and European hotel registrations. They show that McKethan made five trips to western Europe between mid-July 1974 and mid-March 1975. Garner made seven such trips in the same period. These records show that McKethan was in Amsterdam in early September 1974 when Robinson testified that he and Garner met him there and made their first contact with the Chinese supplier. McKethan and Garner were also in Copenhagen at the same time in December 1974 and apparently were traveling on the same flights to Copenhagen and Amsterdam in March 1975.

Moreover, the records show that Henry Thompson arrived at Dulles from Europe on September 4, 1974. Thompson was a member of the United States Armed Forces stationed in West Germany. He was McKethan's cousin. On his entry form he noted that he would be staying with McKethan and that McKethan was a person who would know his whereabouts. Robinson had testified that Garner had used Thompson, their initial heroin contact in Europe, as a courier after Garner's first trip, although the available records indicate that Thompson was on the same flight with Garner and Robinson returning from their first joint trip. Testifying from his recollection more than a year later, Robinson may have been confused about which trip Thompson made, but the record of Thompson's flight provides general corroboration of Robinson's testimony that he was used as a courier.

These travel records would contain no implication of guilt if the record contained any reasonable explanation of them consistent with innocence. If the defendants were stewards employed by Pan American Air Lines in international flights, their frequent European travels would contain no suggestion of wrongdoing. Suspicion would not attach if they were reputable international businessmen with branches in Holland, Denmark and the United States. For others of us, however, having no patent occasion for frequent European travel, the sudden onset of successive trips of short duration alone can raise suspicion as long as any reasonable explanation is lacking. As to Garner, there is no suggestion of any such explanation. McKethan testified, however, and attempted to offer one but, as a description of it will indicate, it may fairly be regarded as preposterous. The only believable explanation of the frequent trips is that offered by Robinson in his grand jury testimony, and the record of the trips strongly tends to corroborate the testimony.

McKethan was employed as a cargo handler by United Airlines in Washington National Airport. His airline employment, he testified, entitled him to very large discounts on airline fares, and he made his frequent trips to Frankfurt, Copenhagen, Amsterdam, and London mostly for pleasure. For a while he had a girlfriend in Copenhagen, a fact that Robinson had mentioned. He was also learning the "language of the pyramids" from a black African in Europe,[1] and he was busy making inquiries in Germany and Sweden about the importation into the United States of Mercedes-Benz automobiles and Swedish sheepskin jackets. He did not suggest how an airline cargo handler might finance such businesses, nor was any such business developed.

Robinson, in his grand jury testimony, did not suggest that McKethan was a part of the distribution business conducted jointly by Garner and Robinson for a number of months, and later separately by each, but did testify that McKethan was the one who initially suggested that he could put them in touch with Henry Thompson in Frankfurt as a source of supply. According to Robinson, he agreed to meet them in Frankfurt in September, but by the time Garner and Robinson arrived at Thompson's house, they were told by Thompson's girlfriend that she was to take them to Amsterdam. In Amsterdam they did meet McKethan and Thompson, who put them in touch with a Chinese supplier. According to Robinson, McKethan was paid some $10,000 for his part in arranging this source of supply for them. Later, Robinson had testified, McKethan agreed to meet Garner in Amsterdam, for the purpose of showing Garner how to avoid the thorough searches made of passengers flying out

---

1. According to McKethan, knowledge of this "lost language of the pyramids" would enable him to arrive eventually at "logical procedures of understanding." McKethan sought in Copenhagen "rhythm[s] of understanding."

of Amsterdam to the United States. This turned out to be no more than taking a train from Amsterdam to Copenhagen and flying from there to the United States. Afterwards McKethan complained to Robinson that Garner had not paid him the $7,000 he promised. Moreover, the joint trip by Garner and McKethan in March 1975, against this background, does not suggest that McKethan was off on an independent lark of his own.

McKethan did admit having received a payment of $3,500 from Robinson on one occasion, but he claimed that he had set up a grocery business for Robinson, though none of the stock was issued in Robinson's name, and the $3,500 was in payment for his services in setting up the grocery business.

McKethan's testimony does not tarnish the badges of reliability for Robinson's grand jury testimony. He offered innocent explanations of his frequent trips to Europe, but the jury was entitled to find the explanation incredible. The fact remains that the truthfulness of Robinson's grand jury testimony is strengthened by the testimony of Miss McKee and, particularly, by the airline tickets, customs declarations, passport endorsements, and hotel records. This is enough to satisfy the requirements of Rule 804(b)(5) and to avoid the bar of the hearsay rule. It also satisfies the requirements of the Confrontation Clause.

In this case, of course, Robinson did appear on the witness stand. Indeed, the defendants complain that this prejudiced their cases in the minds of the jurors, but the judge ordered the initial examination of Robinson in the presence of the jury in order that the jury would not be left with speculation about the reason for Robinson's absence, speculation which might have suggested inferences more hurtful to the defendants than Robinson's refusal to testify. He was presented for cross-examination only after Robinson had stated in an in camera hearing that he might answer the questions of defense counsel, and that he could not tell whether he would respond until they asked the questions. Though, as we have indicated earlier, the jurors may have taken Robinson's earlier disclaimers of knowledge as equivalent to a later explicit refusal to testify, they also may have received such disclaimers, with Robinson's statement that his grand jury testimony was inaccurate, as exculpatory. In any event, the jury saw and heard Robinson on the witness stand. What they saw and heard may have been of substantial assistance to the jury in assessing the truthfulness of his grand jury testimony. We do not hold, however, that this cross-examination under these difficult circumstances was adequate to meet the requirements of the Confrontation Clause. Cf. U.S. v. Insana, 423 F.2d 1165 (2d Cir.), cert. denied, 400 U.S. 841 (1970); U.S. v. Mingoia, 424 F.2d 710 (2d Cir. 1970). It is enough that the grand jury testimony was admissible because of its strong corroboration by the testimony of Miss McKee and the undeniable records. . . .

GARNER v. UNITED STATES
439 U.S. 936 (1978)

Certiorari denied.

Mr. Justice STEWART, with whom Mr. Justice MARSHALL joins, dissenting.

These petitioners contend that the admission into evidence at their trial of the grand jury testimony of an unavailable witness violated both the Federal Rules of Evidence and the Sixth Amendment. The Courts of Appeals have differed as to the admissibility of such evidence in similar cases. I would grant certiorari to resolve these questions.

The petitioners were convicted of conspiracy and substantive offenses stemming from their alleged importation of heroin. An alleged accomplice named Robinson was allowed to plead guilty to two lesser offenses in return for his testimony against the petitioners before a grand jury. The prosecution intended to rely heavily on Robinson's testimony at the petitioners' trial. Before the trial, however, Robinson stated that he would not testify. Although the court granted Robinson use immunity, he persisted in his refusal to testify. Over the petitioners' objections, the trial judge then admitted the transcript of Robinson's grand jury testimony under Fed. Rule Evid. 804(b)(5). After this transcript was read to the trial jury, Robinson did take the witness stand. He stated that he knew the petitioners and that his grand jury testimony had been false. The Court of Appeals characterized his comments as "giv[ing] one the general impression not that the grand jury testimony was false but that, whatever pressures were brought upon him, [he] was unwilling to testify, and particularly unwilling to say anything which would incriminate either of these defendants." 574 F.2d 1141, 1143 (1978). The grand jury testimony was the main support for the jury's guilty verdict against one of the petitioners, and an important part of the prosecution's case against the other.

A divided panel of the Court of Appeals for the Fourth Circuit affirmed the petitioners' convictions, concluding that neither the Federal Rules of Evidence nor the Confrontation Clause barred the admission of Robinson's grand jury testimony because it possessed "strong indicators of reliability." Id., at 1144. The Court of Appeals found that Robinson's story was corroborated by the testimony at the trial from another member of the alleged conspiracy and by documentary evidence of the petitioners' overseas travels.

Although they are not coextensive, the Confrontation Clause and the hearsay rule "stem from the same roots." Dutton v. Evans, 400 U.S. 74, 86 (1970). Considered under either the Sixth Amendment or the Federal Rules of Evidence, I have grave doubts about the admissibility of Robinson's grand jury testimony.

That the evidence was first given before a grand jury adds little to its reliability. In grand jury proceedings, the ordinary rules of evidence do not apply. Leading questions and multiple hearsay are permitted and common. Grand jury investigations are not adversary proceedings. No one is present to cross-examine the witnesses, to give the defendant's version of the story, or to expose weaknesses in the witnesses' testimony.

The only factor that generally makes grand jury testimony more trustworthy than other out-of-court statements is the fact that it is given under oath. The witnesses speak under the threat of prosecution for material false statements. But that usual indication of trustworthiness was missing here. Robinson recanted his grand jury testimony at the trial. By disclaiming under oath his earlier sworn statements, he put himself in a position where one of his two sworn statements had to be false. Without further proof, Robinson would appear to have violated federal law, and, after the petitioners' trial, the Government did, indeed, indict Robinson for violation of 18 U.S.C. §1623. The charges were dismissed only after he pleaded guilty to a contempt citation.

The Courts of Appeals are struggling with the problem of the admissibility of hearsay evidence not falling within one of the traditional exceptions to inadmissibility. The Fourth Circuit has taken a relatively liberal view of the admissibility of grand jury testimony, both in this case and in United States v. West, 574 F.2d 1131 (1978). In a similar situation the Fifth Circuit concluded that grand jury testimony was inadmissible. United States v. Gonzalez, 559 F.2d 1271 (1977). Before the adoption of the Federal Rules of Evidence, the Second Circuit held that the use of grand jury testimony in a situation like this violated both the hearsay rule and the Sixth Amendment. United States v. Fiore, 443 F.2d 112 (1971). The Eighth Circuit, in a case in which the grand jury witness had not recanted his testimony, allowed the grand jury testimony to be admitted. United States v. Carlson, 547 F.2d 1346 (1976).

While those cases may be factually distinguishable, the conflict in interpretation among the Circuits remains.[3] In some Circuits Rule 804(b)(5) is being used to admit grand jury testimony when the witness is unavailable at trial; in others, it is not. Here, the witness recanted his grand jury testimony under oath at the trial, yet it was the crucial evidence in these petitioners' convictions.

I would grant certiorari to determine the limits placed upon the admissibility of this kind of evidence by either the Federal Rules of Evidence or the Constitution.

Problem: Turnabout Is Fair Play

A defendant is being tried for a robbery committed by a lone gunman at three in the afternoon. Defense counsel gives appropriate notice of

---

3. It seems to me open to serious doubt whether Rule 804(b)(5) was intended to provide case-by-case hearsay exceptions, rather than only to permit expansion of the hearsay exceptions by categories.

his intention to use Rule 804(b)(5) and establishes that he served several subpoenas at declarant Smith's home. Smith has not responded, and the attorney states that he has no further knowledge of Smith's whereabouts.

At trial, defendant seeks to introduce a transcript of questions by his attorney and answers by Smith made shortly after the defendant's arrest. A notary, available for trial, administered an oath to Smith. The stenographer who made the transcript swears to its accuracy. The transcript contains Smith's assertions that defendant was with him the entire day, the two did various activities together, and defendant could not have been the robber because the defendant and Smith were watching television together at the time of the robbery.

The defense then produces the parish priest who confirms that Smith and the defendant attended Mass together, as Smith asserted. Bank records confirm Smith's assertion that the defendant deposited a check, and the bank's surveillance film establishes that Smith and the defendant were there together. People from a take-out-food restaurant remember Smith and the defendant. Television station logs corroborate Smith's description of the shows they watched together. A waitress testifies that Smith and the defendant ate dinner together that night.

Are Smith's out-of-court declarations admissible?*

Randolph Jonakait is critical of the Fourth Circuit's liberal use of Rule 804(b)(5) to admit the grand jury testimony of a witness who does not testify at trial. In analyzing the *West* and *Garner* cases, among others,[1] Jonakait states that the Fourth Circuit's interpretation of the residual exceptions "are not only stretching the boundaries of the specific exceptions, but are replacing the traditional hearsay structure with one explicitly rejected by the Rules' drafters. As a result, the fundamental hearsay framework adopted in the Federal Rules of Evidence is being subverted." Jonakait, The Subversion of the Hearsay Rule: The Residual Hearsay Exceptions, Circumstantial Guarantees of Trustworthiness, and Grand Jury Testimony, 36 Case W. Res. L. Rev. 431, 433 (1986).

The crucial error, according to Jonakait, is the Fourth Circuit's reliance on corroboration as the touchstone of admissibility under Rule 804(b)(5). Jonakait points out that grand jury testimony of a witness who is unavailable or refuses to testify at trial is generally inadmissible as former testimony (no cross-examination at the grand jury), state-

---

    1. See also United States v. Walker, 696 F.2d 277 (4th Cir. 1982), cert. denied, 464 U.S. 891 (1983); United States v. Murphy, 696 F.2d 282 (4th Cir. 1982), cert. denied, 461 U.S. 945 (1983); United States v. Thomas, 705 F.2d 709 (4th Cir.), cert. denied, 464 U.S. 890 (1983).

ments against interest (statements often an attempt to curry favor with the prosecution), co-conspirator's admission (not during and in furtherance of the conspiracy), or prior inconsistent statements (foundational requirement of trial cross-examination absent). Id. at 441-445. The court in *West* and *Garner* focused on the other testimony offered that tended to prove the fact of the defendants' guilt — details of the crimes — that were consistent with the declarants' grand jury testimony. But Jonakait finds that, in fact, the corroborating evidence was quite thin in *Garner* and in most of the other cases admitting the grand jury testimony, and that the court used that evidence selectively to show the truthfulness of portions of the grand jury testimony, ignoring the lack of corroboration of other facts as well as factors that tended to show its untrustworthiness. Id. at 451.

Jonakait argues that looking to corroboration of the declarant's grand jury testimony at the time of trial is wrong for five reasons. First, "it leads to the near routine admission of grand jury testimony," which conflicts with other hearsay provisions. Id. at 458-459. Second, it is inconsistent with the congressional intention that the residual exceptions would authorize the admission of hearsay "only in truly exceptional circumstances." Id. at 459. Third, the corroboration requirement is internally inconsistent with the necessity requirement of Rule 804(b)(5) — the "more probative than other reasonably obtainable evidence" requirement. The more corroboration, the less necessary is the hearsay. Id. at 459-460. Fourth, the corroboration requirement is difficult to justify under standard statutory construction doctrine because "corroborating circumstances" was used in Rule 804(b)(3) but not in Rule 804(b)(5). Presumably, Congress would have said "corroboration" in the latter if that is what it meant. Id. at 460. Fifth, it tempts courts to admit proscribed hearsay that is a "near-miss" of some other exception or exclusion. Jonakait argues that "near-misses" may be "covered" by an exception within the meaning of the opening words of the residual exceptions, that is, within the ambit of a specific exception, but not be admissible under the specific exception, and that the proper disposition of such evidence is exclusion, not admission if the evidence is corroborated. Id. at 461-462.

The correct approach to the residual exceptions, Jonakait argues, is similar to the approach of the specific exceptions. Direct reliability is not the test. Rather, "*circumstances* that assure reliability must be measured":

> When deciding whether hearsay falls within a traditional exception, the court only decides whether the circumstances surrounding the statement fit the exception's requirements. For example, before hearsay can be admitted as an excited utterance, the court has to decide whether the out-of-court statement was made "under the stress" of an exciting event. . . . The court evaluating such statements decides questions that are different from ones the jury must ultimately

determine. It rules on admissibility without ever considering whether it believes what the excited . . . declarant said.

Id. at 465.

Under this approach, and considering the circumstantial guarantees of trustworthiness of the other Rule 804 exceptions, Jonakait concludes that for evidence to be properly admissible under Rule 804(b)(5), one or more of the traditional hearsay dangers of memory, perception, narration, or sincerity must be eliminated or lessened comparable to the specific exceptions, and that "the guarantees of trustworthiness must exist at the time of the hearsay's making," not after hearing the other evidence at trial. Id. at 469-470.

Do you agree with Professor Jonakait's analysis? What result would application of Jonakait's analysis have on the *West* and *Garner* cases?

Problem: The Mystery of the Available Declarant

Charge: mail fraud and racketeering. Part of the prosecution's case is that *D*, the mayor of *A*, received bribes in exchange for favoring *B* Bus Company in its bid for the contract to bus *A* school children to and from school. The prosecution presented the testimony of *C*, a member of the city council, which had to recommend the contractor, that certain unidentified councilors had told him that the Mayor "would not mind" if the council recommended *B* Bus Company. *D* objects. The prosecution argues that the evidence is admissible under 803(24). What ruling and why?

Consider the different approaches advocated by the House and Senate committees to a residual hearsay exception in the legislative history to Rules 803(24) and 804(b)(5) (now Rule 807). Compare these views to the pre-Federal Rules view expressed by the court in *Dallas County* above and the results in *Bailey*, *West*, and *Garner*, above. Have these open-ended provisions "emasculated" the hearsay rules and undermined the rationale of codification? Have they introduced too much uncertainty in civil cases and exposed the defendant in criminal cases to Confrontation Clause violations? Or, on the other hand, are these exceptions an appropriate attempt to prevent ossification of the rules consistent with the policies on which the rules are based? Should the rule against hearsay, and its exceptions, be abolished?

The hearsay rules continue to generate a steady stream of academic and judicial attention, most of it critical. New calls for reform of the hearsay doctrine are heard every generation. One of the most recent revivalist meetings occurred in 1991 in Minnesota under the sponsorship of Roger Park, a leading "post-modernist reformer." The 1991 Minnesota Hearsay Reform Conference produced about five pounds of paper on the subject, ranging from Kenneth Graham, Jr's "Q. What Happened to the Last Generation of Reformers?" ("A. They all died."), Hearsay Conference Paper (1991), to Richard Friedman's Towards a Partial Economic, Game-Theoretic Analysis of Hearsay, 76 Minn. L. Rev. 723 (1992). Among all the commentators, Professor Park, Christopher Mueller, and Eleanor Swift have taken the point in the latest attack on the hearsay citadel.

Professor Mueller summarizes the modern attacks on hearsay as resting on four "powerful points":

(1) The doctrine excludes probative evidence of the kind that most of us rely on regularly in our daily lives.

(2) Juries are much better educated than they used to be and are sophisticated enough to evaluate hearsay. With modern juries, we run greater risks from excluding hearsay than admitting it.

(3) The exceptions make little sense, often excluding what should be admitted and admitting what should be excluded.

(4) The doctrine is too complicated and thus difficult to apply. See Christopher Mueller, Post-Modern Hearsay Reform: The Importance of Complexity, 76 Minn. L. Rev. 367 (1992).

Although agreeing with these criticisms at least in part, Mueller nonetheless finds much to value in the traditional approach to hearsay, even if this value was not explicitly recognized until recently by the "post-modernists." According to Mueller, the current structure is actually reasonably successful in incorporating a complex set of values, including reliability in factfinding and pretrial and trial process concerns that should distinguish the rules of proof in law courts from the rules by which individuals make fact-based decisions in other aspects of their lives. Id.

Park, A Subject Matter Approach to Hearsay Reform, 86 Mich. L. Rev. 51 (1987), advocates a distinction between the admissibility of hearsay in civil and criminal cases. According to Park, in civil cases hearsay that fits within an established exception should be admitted and other hearsay should be admitted on proper notice with no discretionary screening by the trial judge. In criminal cases, however, the "principal features" of the hearsay rule should be retained with some incremental changes tailored to particular criminal trial issues in order to protect the accused against "misuse of governmental power."

Professor Swift rejects both polar extremes in modern hearsay doctrine—categorical or class exceptions for "reliable" hearsay (the present system under the Federal Rules), including reform of the currently prescribed exceptions, and abolition of the rule and substitution of broadly gauged judicial discretion to admit good hearsay and exclude bad hearsay. The problem with the current hearsay regime, Swift says, is that it is both overinclusive and underinclusive in what it admits. Some hearsay is excluded that should be admitted because the notions of reliability on which the doctrine rests are too narrow; but some hearsay is admitted that should be excluded because of a lack of foundational information available to the trier of fact to assess candor, meaning, perception, and memory. On the other hand, Swift argues that, on the whole, the rule "buttresses the rationalist assumptions underlying adjudicative factfinding and implements the traditional assignment of comparative burdens borne by the parties." Rather than refine each exception or throw the whole artifice out on its ear, Swift argues that courts should admit hearsay if the proponent presents "foundation facts" that permit the jury to evaluate the hearsay intelligently. This would be accomplished through the testimony of a "process foundation witness" who would testify to the circumstances in which the declarant perceived, remembered, and spoke, and offer information about the candor of the declarant. (Provisions are made in Swift's approach for when such a witness cannot be obtained, but in many cases application of the Swift approach would force the proponent to call the declarant because only the declarant could present the foundation facts.) See Swift, A Foundation Fact Approach to Hearsay, 75 Cal. L. Rev. 1339, 1363 (1987); Swift, Abolishing the Hearsay Rule, 75 U. Cal. L. Rev. 495 (1987); Swift, The Hearsay Rule at Work: Has It Been Abolished De Facto by Judicial Decision?, 76 Minn. L. Rev. 473 (1992).

For the interested student of hearsay, there is no shortage of critical literature. Other recent work of interest includes Peter Tillers & David Schum, Hearsay Logic, 76 Minn. L. Rev. 813 (1992) (using "signal detection theory" to analyze the hearsay rule and its exceptions, it is impossible to substantiate the rationality or irrationality of the rule's "coarse legal categorizations," which therefore may be "a rule of thumb [that] is sometimes an efficient strategy for dealing with otherwise intractable complexity and subtlety"), id. at 857-858, and Carlson, Experts as Hearsay Conduits: Confrontation Abuses in Opinion Testimony, 76 Minn. L. Rev. 859 (1992) (advocating an "active role" for courts in reviewing the bases for expert testimony under Rule 703 to police for unauthenticated and unreliable "back-door" hearsay).

For the more radical approach to hearsay—abolish it—consider the following note.

NOTE, THE THEORETICAL FOUNDATION OF THE HEARSAY RULES
93 Harv. L. Rev. 1786, 1786-1807 (1980)

Why have centuries of jurisprudence given rise to a rule known mostly by its exceptions, a rule that allows many avenues of circumvention and whose violation is rarely cause for concern by appellate courts? For decades, a fierce polemic has raged over the rule against hearsay and its exceptions. . . . [T]his debate is totally misdirected because the participants appeal to principles that have never been critically examined and that are incapable of rationalizing the rule against hearsay in any form.

I.   Rationalizing the Rule Against Hearsay

A.   A General Model for Exclusion

Motivated by the assumption that a primary goal of our legal system is to achieve accurate case results, this Section will develop a framework that premises the exclusion of a relevant piece of evidence upon an expectation that the jury will erroneously assess the credibility of that evidence. To determine the extent to which the jury's assessment is erroneous, that assessment must be measured against some standard. Although ideally one would choose a standard of "truth," such a standard is, of course, impossible in principle to ascertain in the context of a trial. Instead, the framework will use the best alternative: the credibility that would be assigned to the evidence by "experts"—judges, attorneys, and academicians. This criterion will be referred to as "absolute reliability." Any relevant evidence, including hearsay, has at least some absolute reliability because the existence of infirmities and uncertainties of a piece of evidence only justifies *discounting* the weight given to the evidence rather than *ignoring* the evidence through exclusion. For example, even a statement by one known to be biased should not be ignored completely. With respect to hearsay, the existence of bias may be uncertain because there is no opportunity to cross-examine the declarant. Yet exclusion of such evidence would be inappropriate since the effect is to discount the evidence even more than if we were certain that the witness was biased.

If the jury's assessment is accurate by the standard of absolute reliability—that is, if the jury and the "expert" assessments coincide—the evidence should be admitted. When the jury cannot accurately assess the credibility of a piece of evidence, the error results in a gap between the jury's perception of the evidence and the absolute reliability of the evidence. Were the jury expected to *under*assess reliability, the controversy would not be over exclusion but over methods designed to increase the jury's reliance on the evidence. Exclusion is premised upon jury *over*assessment.

Any error that the jury commits in using the evidence to arrive at its verdict will depend upon the gap that remains at the conclusion of the trial—the residual gap—and not on the gap that existed after direct examination. Cross-examination and closing argument present opportunities to expose the weaknesses of testimony, improving the accuracy of the jury's assessment. Although with hearsay evidence cross-examination must be of the in-court witness instead of the declarant, there are still opportunities to expose weaknesses in the evidence. For example, if the evidence is ambiguous, cross-examination designed to reveal each of the possible meanings of the hearsay declaration would bring the weakness to the jury's attention. After these "remedies," the residual gap presumably would be smaller than the gap that existed immediately after direct examination. Such remedies vary, however, in their effectiveness and are limited in their range of potential application and by their strategic costs.

The concept of residual gap measures the expected jury error—the cost of admitting evidence. Credibility, judged by the standard of absolute reliability, measures the expected value of the evidence — the expected benefit from admission. A cost-benefit decision rule aimed at maximizing the accuracy of the result in a given case would exclude evidence when the expected error exceeds the expected value. This formula is analogous to rule 403 of the Federal Rules of Evidence which provides for the exclusion of relevant evidence when its prejudicial effect outweighs its probative value.

One way to examine the amount of error required to outweigh value, in order to justify exclusion, is to imagine a scale for recording assessments of the credibility of evidence. Zero would correspond to evidence given no credibility whatsoever; 100 to evidence believed with absolute certainty. Suppose the expert assessment (absolute reliability) of the evidence is above 50—for example, 51. Since the greatest value the jury could assign to the evidence is 100, the largest possible gap is 49. Thus, the expected value (51) exceeds the gap (at most 49) and the evidence should be admitted under the decision rule. Alternatively, consider a case where the expert assessment of value was 30 and the jury assessment was 61. The resulting gap of 31 exceeds the value of 30, barely justifying exclusion. Exclusion requires that the gap exceed the value of the evidence, and, as this second example indicates, this condition is fulfilled only if the jury assessment exceeds twice the value of the evidence.[13] The occurrence of this condition is unlikely since it requires the existence of factors that indicate to the experts in the legal profession that the credibility of some evidence is very low but that are so far beyond the comprehension of laypersons that juries still would assess the credibility as being quite high.[14]

13. More formally:

> Gap = Jury Perception — Absolute Reliability
> Absolute Reliability = Value

This implies	Gap = Jury Perception — Value
Therefore	Gap > Value
is equivalent to	Jury Perception — Value > Value
which yields	Jury Perception > 2 × Value
as an equivalent condition.	

14. Many commentators reject the claim that there is any significant jury misperception at all. . . . No attempt has been made to quantify the degree of overevaluation.

Given the range of efforts over the decades attempting merely to explain the hearsay rules and the difficulties in teaching the intricacies of the hearsay rules to law students, one might question the ability of the jury to evaluate hearsay evidence accurately. See Blackmore, Some Things About Hearsay: Article VIII, 6 Cap. U.L. Rev. 597, 597 (1977). It would be a mistake, however, to infer from the complexity of the hearsay rules that evaluation of most hearsay evidence is beyond the competence of a jury.

One qualification is necessary in the case of exceptionally unreliable hearsay evidence (for example, with a value of one on the 100 point scale) where it may be plausible that the jury

B. EXCLUSION ON THE GROUND THAT EVIDENCE IS HEARSAY

The process of determining the admissibility of a relevant piece of evidence by balancing its value against the residual gap between expected jury perception and absolute reliability is applicable to all types of evidence, and not just hearsay. Hearsay is distinguished from other evidence by the absence of the declarant. To justify the exclusion of evidence *because it is hearsay,* two conditions must be satisfied: (1) In the absence of the declarant (or when testimony is offered of the witness' own past statements), the gap must exceed value. (2) If the declarant is present (testifying to a current recollection of the events), the value must exceed the gap. If the first condition fails, there would be no reason to exclude. Without the second, exclusion would be justified even if the evidence were not hearsay. The second condition might fail, for example, when the exclusion of excited utterances is defended on the ground that the jury is not sufficiently aware of possible flaws in the declarant's perception. It is not, however, the hearsay character of this evidence that causes jury overassessment. Thus, that the evidence is an out-of-court declaration could not be asserted as the ground for exclusion.

Positions taken by those advocating reform of the rule against hearsay can readily be evaluated in the context of the framework just developed. For example, Judge Weinstein's well-known argument for more liberal admission of hearsay emphasizes the probative force (value) of hearsay, but provides no explicit analysis of the gap against which probative force must be balanced.[19] The implicit assumption necessary to justify his approach is that the reliability of hearsay is usually high enough (over 50 on the scale)[20] that insufficient room remains for a gap large enough

---

assessment would exceed twice the value (in this example, an assessment of three). Such evidence may be excluded because of the waste of time, Fed. R. Evid. 403, and in any event the impact of such slight error would be de minimis. Moreover, for evidence of such low credibility, it is not clear that the jury will usually overassess the evidence instead of giving it too little weight or ignoring it completely.

19. Weinstein, Alternatives [to the Present Hearsay Rules, 44 F.R.D. 375 (1967)] at 379-80; Weinstein, Probative Force [of Hearsay, 46 Iowa L. Rev. 331 (1961)] at 338-42. He only analogizes loosely to a balance similar to considerations of prejudice, Fed. R. Evid. 403; Weinstein, Probative Force, supra, at 338-39. Since the prejudice rule is already applicable to all evidence, his position for all practical purposes supports abolition of the rule against hearsay. However, his comment that "[t]he circumstantial proof of credibility which gave rise to the class exception may continue to be utilized in the particular case in assessing probative force," id. at 339, implies that his intention falls short of abolition. In any event, he provides no framework for the required balancing of value and jury overassessment. . . .

20. Actually, Judge Weinstein's approach could be justified if reliability were near or above 50. For example, if some evidence had only an absolute reliability of 45, admission would be proper for any jury perception below 90 — which arguably includes most cases — and the greatest possible net loss would be limited to 10, in the case where the jury gave full weight to the evidence (an assessment of 100). However, once these subtleties are combined with the argument of probative force, the justification for Judge Weinstein's approach should be more properly viewed as derived from the entire framework presented in this Note.

to outweigh the value of the hearsay. Some favor abolishing the rule against hearsay on the ground that juries comprehend the shortcomings of hearsay as well as the "experts" do, a challenge to the existence of any initial gap. Others supporting abolition believe that cross-examination or other techniques will alert the jury to the weaknesses of hearsay, an assertion that any initial gap is remediable. Unfortunately, one feature common to most discourse on hearsay is the absence of any in-depth examination of these assumptions concerning the characteristics of evidence and how they are perceived by jurors.

It is not surprising that neither abolition nor extensive liberalization has occurred since few in the legal profession believe that juries are fully as aware of hearsay dangers as "experts," few believe that remedies are completely effective in all cases, and few believe that the value of evidence is always so high that all prospects of jury error can be ignored. But what apparently has gone unnoticed is that justifying retention of the rule against hearsay simultaneously requires that juries are generally unaware of hearsay dangers, that remedies usually fail to reveal dangers to the jury, and that the value of hearsay rarely approaches an intermediate level of credibility (50 on the scale)—a level that would make it impossible for the jury's assessment of hearsay to exceed twice the expert assessment (value) of the evidence.

II. MISDIRECTION OF THE HEARSAY RULES: FAILURE ON THEIR OWN TERMS

A. THE MYSTERY OF THE AVAILABLE DECLARANT

Admissibility of hearsay where the declarant is available has received much attention in the literature and is addressed explicitly in the Federal Rules of Evidence.[27] In the context of considering the accuracy of the result in a given case, arguments over the admission of the hearsay of available declarants make little sense because in any given case application of either of the two extreme approaches (always exclude or always admit) leads to the same result. If the declarant is available, (1) exclusion would be of little consequence to the party needing the evidence since the declarant can be called directly, and (2) admission

---

27. The Federal Rules have two sets of exceptions — those for which availability of the declarant is immaterial and those for unavailable declarants. Fed. R. Evid. 803, 804. There is no across-the-board rule admitting the hearsay of available declarants. Thus, the Federal Rules go to great lengths to differentiate among the hearsay of available declarants in determining admissibility. See Advisory Comm. Note, Fed. R. Evid. 803.

The existence of rule 803(24) of the Federal Rules of Evidence is difficult to explain. If the declarant is unavailable, identical exception 804(b)(5) may be used; if the declarant is available, the criteria of the exception seem impossible to meet since "the statement [must be] more probative on the point for which it is offered than any other evidence which the proponent can procure through reasonable efforts." Fed. R. Evid. 803(24).

would not damage the position of a party fearing jury overvaluation of the hearsay since the declarant can be called for cross-examination, which allows the same impeachment possibilities that would have existed were the opponent to have called the declarant for direct examination. If exclusion is the general rule, some special treatment of hearsay of available declarants may be justified on grounds unrelated to fears of jury overvaluation. For example, business records might be admitted to save the time and expense of calling the five employees who each had a hand in processing the data. Nonetheless, the traditional discussion claiming to address the accuracy of case results persists with full force despite the fact that it has no bearing upon whether the hearsay of an available declarant should be admitted.[30] The remainder of this Part therefore implicitly considers only the unavailable declarant.

B. TRADITIONAL JUSTIFICATION FOR HEARSAY EXCEPTIONS

Exceptions to the rule against hearsay are traditionally justified on the grounds that some hearsay is particularly reliable or necessary. This Section will address the prominence of each criterion in the hearsay polemic, question the possibility and practicality of applying each consistently, and analyze shortcomings revealed by application of the framework developed in Part I.

1. Reliability. The most common and accepted characterization of the hearsay problem is that such evidence is not sufficiently reliable and that exceptions are made for categories of hearsay that exhibit additional guarantees of trustworthiness. This approach permeates the major treatises on evidence. The Federal Rules of Evidence demonstrate adherence to this view through the requirements for an exception under the residual clauses and more generally through the supporting analysis provided by the Advisory Committee. Perhaps the most famous of hearsay decisions, Dallas County v. Commercial Union Assurance Co., recognizes this principle, as does Chambers v. Mississippi, in which the Supreme Court examined the constitutional implications of the hearsay rules in criminal procedure. This view is pervasive in the contemporary debate over hearsay issues.

Focusing on reliability as a justification for admission ignores all but the first element (absolute reliability) of the framework developed in Part I. First, this traditional approach errs by failing to consider the

---

30. Exclusion serves to minimize the potential for manipulation when the decision not to call the available declarant may provide some strategic benefit. Also, it avoids disruption that might result from allowing the opponent to cross-examine the declarant immediately after direct examination of the witness testifying to the hearsay statement, possible surprise to the opponent if no notice is required, and placing burdens on the opponent to procure the declarant. . . .

jury's perception of reliability.[39] For example, a piece of hearsay evidence may be fairly reliable, yet the jury may still significantly overassess its credibility; on the other hand, some hearsay may have no circumstantial indicia of reliability, but all its defects may be obvious to any juror. The traditional approach would admit the former evidence, despite the danger of overassessment, and exclude the latter, though it poses no real threat. Second, Part I demonstrated the need for examining the potential to remedy defects in jury evaluation of hearsay and the likelihood that such defects would not arise had the declaration been testimony subject to cross-examination. It is not surprising that one overlooks these factors when focusing solely upon reliability since the importance of both factors becomes apparent only upon recognition that the central emphasis should be on jury perception. Most investigations look to the reliability of hearsay in a vacuum instead of focusing upon the reliability *gap*. Finally, examinations of the exceptions often ignore the value lost whenever evidence is excluded, against which the reliability gap must be balanced.

Current analyses are unpersuasive even in their attempts to identify which categories of hearsay are reliable. The reliability of hearsay is usually determined by examining the degree to which believing the evidence requires unsupported reliance upon the declarant's four testimonial capacities: narration, sincerity, memory, and perception. If circumstances indicate that no danger would result from reliance upon one or more of these capacities, an exception is sometimes said to be warranted. Yet it is not clear why the hearsay problem is "solved" when only one or two of the four defects have been removed. Analysis of an exception justified on the basis of circumstantial guarantees as to one capacity suggests that the three that remain unchecked present no significant ground for worry. After examination of several exceptions, each justified by guarantees as to a different capacity, one would conclude that *none* of the four capacities found wanting in circumstantial guarantees presents a significant problem. One might respond to this criticism by assuming that the degree to which the reliability gap exceeded

---

39. In other words, focus is upon absolute reliability instead of upon the reliability gap.

For analysis of the absolute reliability in isolation to provide the same result as a complete examination of the residual hearsay gap, the jury must always give full weight to hearsay evidence. In that event, any unreliability contributes to the reliability gap. But, if the jury gives the hearsay anything less than full weight, including the possibility of giving too little weight, the unreliability of the evidence overstates the warrant for exclusion. It is impossible for the jury always to give hearsay full weight when conflicting hearsay is presented by opposing parties. Similarly, it seems unlikely that it would give hearsay full weight when conflicting nonhearsay evidence on the issue is present since this implicitly assumes that the jury gives full weight to the dubious hearsay evidence while giving no weight to the other evidence, which may be of greater reliability. This makes the full weight assumption implausible regardless of how able one thinks jurors are. . . .

the value of the evidence was small enough that the incremental de-crease in the gap provided by the removal of one of the defects is suf-ficient to swing the balance in favor of admission. If that is the case, however, it seems curious that those implicitly making this assumption devote so much attention to determining which categories of hearsay should be admitted and which should be excluded. The assumption itself suggests that most questions regarding the admissibility of hearsay are nearly a tossup.

The above criticism would not prove embarrassing to those wishing to inquire into the reliability of hearsay if one capacity could be isolated as the most important, with exceptions being made solely when there exist circumstantial guarantees for that capacity. In fact, most advocates of exceptions do emphasize circumstantial guarantees for one capacity —the sincerity of the out-of-court declarant. Acceptance of the princi-ple that only appeals to sincerity can justify exceptions renders mean-ingless all current discussion of the other three capacities. More important, analysis within the framework of the first Part reveals how this justification backfires. Distinguishing hearsay from other evidence depends upon the testability of the hearsay declaration, assuming that it was offered as testimony in court. Few would doubt that cross-exami-nation effectively remedies defects in the other three capacities: it ex-poses and resolves ambiguity, it tests or refreshes memory, and it brings into question possible defects in perception. By contrast, cross-exami-nation may be less well suited to exposing insincerity. Studies of jury reaction to eyewitness testimony indicate that the jury does not function as an effective lie detector. Focus upon sincerity as the pivotal element could be justified if it is the most testable capacity; in fact, it may be the least. Alternatively, one might justify this focus on the ground that, al-though sincerity is less testable, sincerity problems occur far more fre-quently in the underlying population of potential hearsay evidence than do weaknesses in the other three capacities. This empirical assertion has not even been stated, much less proved, by those who appeal to circum-stantial indications of sincerity when arguing for exceptions. Without facing such empirical questions and defending one particular position, it is impossible to rationalize singling out sincerity as the most important capacity. The current approach of justifying hearsay exceptions by ap-peals to the circumstantial guarantees of testimonial capacities cannot be defended by isolating sincerity, in terms of testability or frequency of occurrence. Thus, the traditional formulation is without rational foundation. . . .

[T]he current method of justifying hearsay exceptions is the opposite of the proper approach. Instead of considering those testimonial ca-pacities for which there are circumstantial guarantees of trustworthi-ness, one should focus upon those capacities for which there are *not* such guarantees. For example, the current approach allows a hearsay exception for excited utterances because of their alleged sincerity. The reliability of such utterances is dubious, however, because the declarant's perception and narration may be impaired. Regardless of strong guarantees as to sincerity, the evidence may remain unreliable.

2. Necessity. Although Wigmore puts forth the principle of necessity as coequal with the principle of reliability for the purpose of justifying exceptions to the rule against hearsay, necessity is addressed far less frequently in specific analyses of exceptions, and its prominence in the literature seems to exceed its impact upon the rules of evidence. In the Federal Rules of Evidence, it is one of the many requirements for admission under the residual exceptions but does not appear explicitly elsewhere. Even though the principle seems central to the justification for some exceptions, such as dying declarations, the rules make no distinction between "necessary" and other uses of the evidence. . . .

Since necessity is a function of the other evidence available in a given case, it will be difficult to identify, a priori, any categories of hearsay—with the possible exception of dying declarations—that will be "necessary." Therefore, implementing the necessity principle involves according broad discretion to the trial judge. Even then, a circulatory problem arises within a single trial because the necessity of any evidence depends upon what other evidence is admitted. This difficulty is compounded by problems raised by the order of presentation, the difficulty of changing previous rulings, the potential for parties to manipulate the judge by failing to investigate or present other sources of evidence, and the sheer complexity of making rulings that depend upon the variety of possible configurations of other evidence in a given case. . . .

[T]wo polar cases reveal how the principle of necessity may be just as likely to favor exclusion as admission. First, where much other evidence or far more credible evidence is available, there is no *need* to let in hearsay that may mislead the jury. The very existence of the other or better evidence, however, implies that, even if the jury's error in evaluating the hearsay is large, its error in deciding the case will be small since that decision reflects its consideration of all the other evidence in combination with the hearsay. By contrast, in the second case, where there is little or no other evidence probative of the issue, the evidence is most valuable to the case as a whole. Assume that a significant reliability gap initially exists. Since that gap arises from the jury's overvaluation of the evidence in question, one would expect significant error to remain in the jury's determination of the ultimate issue because no other information intervened in its decision process. It is precisely when the unreliable evidence is highly probative and little other evidence is available that the greatest danger appears. Thus, the greater the need, the greater the danger, and the less the need, the less the danger.

The principle of necessity thus directs attention away from the individual piece of evidence and towards its impact on the case as a whole. The correlation between necessity and the value of evidence to the case as a whole has always been recognized. What is generally ignored is the correlation between necessity and the impact of jury error upon its ultimate decision; the less other evidence is available, the less will be the opportunity to remedy or mitigate the impact of jury error in evaluating the given piece of evidence.

A formal analysis of how the necessity of the evidence affects both its value and its danger reveals that, a priori, the implications of the necessity criterion for determining the admissibility of evidence are indeterminate. The expected jury error in processing the evidence to reach its ultimate decision and the value of the evidence both increase as necessity increases. This is illustrated in Figure 1. The amount and quality of other evidence is measured along the horizontal axis. The value of the evidence to the case as a whole—"Value"—and the expected error in the jury's decision resulting from admission—"Error"—are both measured along the vertical axis. For any category of hearsay, there are four possible cases. First, it is possible that error exceeds value for all degrees of necessity, justifying exclusion in all cases (illustrated in Figure 1). Second, value might exceed error for all degrees of necessity, justifying admission in all cases (Figure 2). In both cases the necessity of the evidence is irrelevant to the decision to admit or ex-

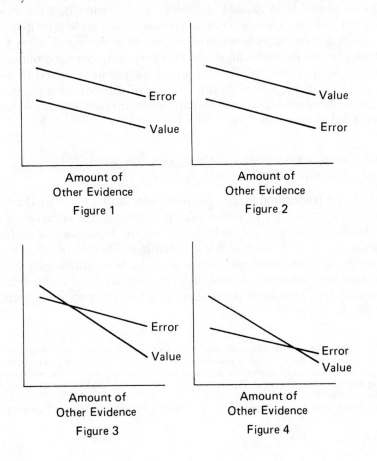

Amount of
Other Evidence

Figure 1

Amount of
Other Evidence

Figure 2

Amount of
Other Evidence

Figure 3

Amount of
Other Evidence

Figure 4

clude. A third possibility is that value declines more rapidly than does error as the amount and quality of other available evidence increases (i.e., as the necessity of the evidence in question decreases). In other words, where little other evidence is available, value outweighs error, and the evidence should be admitted; where much is available, error exceeds value, and the evidence should be excluded (Figure 3). The standard argument that necessity justifies the admission of hearsay assumes that this case is an accurate description of the world. The existence of a fourth case, however, indicates that the opposite result is equally plausible. This would occur if error is above value when little other evidence is available, justifying exclusion, but that error falls below value as more evidence is available, justifying admission (Figure 4). In both case three and case four, the admissibility decision when little other evidence is available will be the opposite of the ruling when much other evidence is available. Neither case is complete without specification of where that reversal occurs. For example, Figure 3 portrays a crossover where little other evidence on the issue is available, and in Figure 4 the crossover does not occur until far more evidence is available. In other words, one must determine how much other evidence must be available to change the decision. Asserting that the reversal occurs at *some* point is only a first step toward a workable principle either for discretionary implementation by judges or for application to the debate over the delineation of hearsay exceptions. No attempt has been made to support the implicit empirical judgment reflected by adherence to case three, to specify the location of the switching point, or to examine the significance of the gap between error and value for any given level of necessity.[66]

III.   Inconsistency of the Hearsay Rules with Judge-Jury Relations

Both the traditional analysis of hearsay examined in Part II and the framework presented in Part I take maximizing the accuracy of case results as the objective, thereby assuming the legitimacy of excluding hearsay on the grounds that it is unreliable or likely to be misperceived by juries. Yet one could use the same grounds to justify the exclusion of nonhearsay evidence, a result directly contrary to "the time-honored formula [that] credibility is a matter of fact for the jury, not a matter of law for the court."[67]

---

66. A priori, one can predict only that error and value decline as the quantity of other evidence increases; these declining functions need not be linear, as portrayed in Figures 1 to 4. Thus, combinations of cases three and four in general are possible, wherein the proper ruling alternates between admitting and excluding the hearsay evidence as the amount and quality of other available evidence increases.

67. Chadbourn, Bentham and the Hearsay Rule—A Benthamic View of Rule 63(4)(c) of

The Federal Rules of Evidence provide that "[a]lthough relevant, evidence may be excluded if its probative value is substantially outweighed by the danger of unfair prejudice." Under this structure, exclusion is justified by fears of how the jury will be influenced by the evidence. However, it is not traditional to think of hearsay as merely a subdivision of this structure, and the Federal Rules do not conceive of hearsay in that manner. Prejudice refers to the jury's use of evidence for inferences other than those for which the evidence is legally relevant; by contrast, the rule against hearsay questions the jury's ability to evaluate the strength of a *legitimate* inference to be drawn from the evidence. For example, were a judge to exclude testimony because a witness was particularly smooth or convincing, there would be no doubt as to the usurpation of the jury's function. Thus, unlike prejudices recognized by the evidence rules, such as those stemming from racial or religious biases or from the introduction of photographs of a victim's final state, the exclusion of hearsay on the basis of misperception strikes at the root of the jury's function by usurping its power to process quite ordinary evidence, the type of information routinely encountered by jurors in their everyday lives.

Even if one were to accept the coherence of the two principles of reliability and necessity, hearsay provisions based on them would remain inconsistent with the common understanding of the role played by the rules of evidence in our system of adjudication. Outside the hearsay context, it is not generally required that evidence be necessary in order to be admissible. Furthermore, exclusion of evidence because it is unreliable is grossly inconsistent with our usual view of the jury's ability to process evidence and to make inferences. In considering absolute reliability, which is germane to the weight that should be given to evidence, the rulemakers and treatise writers approach the hearsay problems from the wrong perspective: they exclude evidence that they would discount or disbelieve if *they* were sitting as trier of fact rather than considering which evidence should be kept from a trier of fact.

The practice of regularly admitting hearsay evidence for nonhearsay purposes further illustrates the inconsistency of the hearsay rules with traditional conceptions of the role of the jury. Even if the jury is instructed that such evidence may only be used for nonhearsay purposes,

the Uniform Rules of Evidence, 75 Harv. L. Rev. 932, 947 (1962); cf. Advisory Comm. Note, Fed. R. Evid. 104(b) ("If preliminary questions of conditional relevancy were determined solely by the judge, as provided in subdivision (a), the functioning of the jury as trier of fact would be greatly restricted and in some cases virtually destroyed.").

One condition argued to be necessary to rationalize the exclusion of evidence because it is hearsay was that the reliability gap would not exceed value had the evidence been in-court testimony. But acceptance of the legitimacy of the reliability gap/value balancing test formulation in fact suggests that any evidence that could not be effectively tested before the jury should be excluded.

the result will be little different than if the jury had been permitted to evaluate the evidence for the hearsay purpose as well. To have justified excluding the evidence as hearsay, the reliability gap must have exceeded the value of the evidence in its hearsay use. To justify reversal of that judgment, the value of the evidence in its nonhearsay use must be greater than the amount by which the gap had exceeded the value in its hearsay use. Yet this assumption is unwarranted since any nonhearsay use is considered sufficient to admit any evidence otherwise excluded by the rule against hearsay. Thus, when focusing upon nonhearsay uses of evidence, courts implicitly ignore the original justifications for the exclusion of hearsay, a result that is not surprising since those justifications conflict with the usual view of the role of the jury.

Though the rule against hearsay is formally applicable to bench trials, it is in fact little used in the absence of a jury. The appropriateness of applying the hearsay prohibition to bench trials has been questioned on the ground that the hearsay rules reflect a concern with attributes peculiar to the jury, a position flowing comfortably from the analysis that focuses on jury perception. A variety of techniques are employed that, in effect, permit the admission of hearsay in nonjury trials. It is not surprising that these techniques arose given that judges presiding without a jury undoubtedly found the inconsistency between the treatment of hearsay and other evidence too glaring to tolerate, reinforcing the conclusion that the hearsay rules and debate are in fact directed more toward issues of evaluation than toward questions of admission. These practices also demonstrate that exclusion cannot rationally be premised on the traditional ground of unreliability because this rationale makes no distinction between whether a jury or a judge is the trier of fact. De facto *consistency* within the nonjury setting highlights the *inconsistency* of the hearsay rules with other rules of evidence when the jury is present.

IV. THE HEARSAY RULES AS A MEANS OF ENHANCING THE SOCIAL
     ACCEPTANCE OF OUR SYSTEM OF ADJUDICATION

Some explanation is necessary for the continued reliance upon the traditional hearsay analysis given that all justifications for the rules both fail on their own terms and conflict with accepted notions of the role of the jury. This Part offers one possible explanation of how the traditional approach came to be and why it tends to survive.

Society needs to have confidence in the outcomes produced by its system of adjudication. Criminal law most clearly dramatizes this need; when we contemplate punishment that deprives one of liberty, property, or even life, the *perception* of fairness is essential to quiet our collective conscience. Social acceptance is a function of how the system is perceived, and not of how it actually performs. The hearsay rules, though incoherent when viewed from the [traditional] perspective, might seem more comprehensible when viewed from a cynical perspective, . . . as aimed at enhancing social acceptance by directly addressing society's perception of the system rather than the system's performance.

First, hearsay rules shield the system from possible embarrassment. Admitting hearsay generally creates the possibility that the declarant might later come forward to reveal that injustice resulted from the trier of fact's reliance on such evidence. Second, hearsay is distinctive in that its deficiencies can be observed readily by anyone outside the system. With other evidence, the jury functions as a "black box": its ability to observe demeanor, though limited in revealing truth, "justifies" deference to the jury's decision because the jury ostensibly has additional information that those absent could not possibly duplicate and those present could not fully communicate.

These two considerations indicate how a rule against hearsay enhances social acceptance by excluding evidence. Yet extensive exclusion of hearsay may itself diminish acceptance since we like to believe that the trier considers all relevant information in reaching its decision. Therefore, maximizing social acceptance implies that hearsay exceptions are appropriate where the danger of *exposing* error is less, whereas the Part I framework justifies exceptions where the danger of jury misperception is less.

The danger of exposing error is minimized by creating exceptions to the rule against hearsay when later contradictory statements from the declarant are unlikely to arise or would not prove embarrassing. The clearest illustration is the exception for dying declarations, the classic example of an exception of dubious validity by traditionally accepted criteria. Admissions by a party opponent would be allowed in evidence since "[a] party can hardly object that he had no opportunity to cross-examine himself or that he is unworthy of credence save when speaking under sanction of an oath." With respect to present sense impressions, excited utterances, and indications of the declarant's state of mind, the declarant's recollection of the events presented after a trial is no more and possibly less credible than the extrinsic (hearsay) evidence of the declarant's knowledge at the time of the incident. For business records and official public reports, the body responsible for the existence of the information is unlikely to surprise us later. Similarly, the admission of statements against interest by an unavailable declarant does not risk future embarrassment because declarants typically will not become available, and, even if one does, later contrary statements will not prove embarrassing. As these examples illustrate, the current pattern of hearsay exceptions seems quite rational as a reflection of the desire to enhance social acceptance by shielding the system from possible embarrassment.

The retention of rules excluding hearsay in non-jury trials despite widespread admission of hearsay in actual practice may also reflect the desire to promote social acceptance. Improperly admitted hearsay endangers the appearances of the system only if it appears that the trial court actually relied on the hearsay in making its decision. Current appellate practice, by invoking "the time-honored presumption that a trial judge does not utilize erroneously admitted evidence in rendering his verdict," preserves the appearance that such evidence was not a factor in the decision. The public's view of the courts may similarly decline if it appears that the trial judge is not considering admissible evidence. Appellate courts avoid this danger by inviting the trial judge to admit this evidence into the record. If the evidence in the record is disregarded by the trial judge, who believed it to be inadmissible,[100] the appellate court will still uphold the decision although the evidence was admissible, implicitly presuming that the evidence was considered in the decision.[101] This appellate procedure is supplemented by a veritable arsenal of weapons that increase the likelihood of upholding the admission of hearsay (and other evidence) by lower courts in both jury and nonjury settings. Since reliance on the hearsay is not explicit when any of these methods is used, the system's appearances are protected.

If this rationalization of the hearsay structure were the true explanation for its existence, one still would not expect it to be explicitly advanced in support of the hearsay rules since stating this rationalization is self-defeating; rules cannot successfully protect the appearances of a system if the rules are openly presented as serving that end. It seems implausible that the hearsay rules were consciously designed and subsequently modified to shelter the system from embarrassment and to preserve the jury's ability to function as a "black box." It seems plausible, however, that those operating within our system of adjudication would be motivated by a desire, perhaps subconscious, to feel that the system to which they have devoted their energy is worthy of society's acceptance as a system of justice.

Since the underlying purposes may remain subconscious and, in any event, could not be openly expressed, other justifications would be of-

100. The use of such evidence in reaching the decision would be contrary to the trial judge's belief that the evidence was inadmissible. This practice is inconsistent with conscientious judicial behavior and, in any event, will not be imputed by the appellate court; an error in fact may result though no error in law is admitted. Furthermore, if inadmissible evidence is to be entered into the record, trial judges will give less thought to questions of admissibility in the first instance, making ultimate reliance upon improper evidence more likely.

101. The result is effectively to exclude admissible evidence since the judge as trier of fact ignores it, but, as a consequence of the act of admitting the evidence into record, the judge's erroneous belief is insulated from review. In fact, an appellate ruling might be unnecessary since the evidence would have been admitted and there would not be any ruling by the lower court that the evidence was ignored. For example, the lower court may admit the evidence and simply make no mention of it in a finding of fact, directed verdict, or judgment notwithstanding the verdict. See Note, Improper Evidence in Nonjury Trials: Basis for Reversal?, 79 Harv. L. Rev. 407, 409-11 (1965).

fered in their place. These surrogate justifications would give rise to a set of rules that only approximately mirror the rules that would result if the actual objectives were openly admitted. After the process of adjusting and amending the proffered justifications to fit the desired objectives more closely, one would expect the resultant patchwork of rules to appear confused and complex, much as the hearsay rules are today.

The hypothesis that the hearsay rules are designed to protect appearances explains the prominence in the hearsay debate of absolute reliability instead of the reliability gap. Keeping hearsay evidence from the jury because it is unreliable both seems necessary to avoid exposure of error, since nothing prevents outside observers from perceiving the deficiency, and lends additional external credibility to trials by giving the impression that the process is cleansed of such questionable evidence. Because the broad interpretations given to hearsay exceptions and the limited appellate scrutiny are not readily apparent to those outside the system, they do not seriously threaten the appearance afforded by appealing to reliability. The strong superficial appeal of reliability as a criterion makes it easy to understand how dependence upon it might have arisen during the evolution of our rules of evidence and why this dependence continues even now. By contrast, suggesting that one focus upon jury error . . . directly presents the problem of the jury's inability to assess hearsay accurately, undermining any attempt to defend the system's appearances.

The principle of necessity is similarly attractive. Assurances that there is no other evidence probative on the issue shield the system from all sources of potential future embarrassment except from the hearsay declarant. Appeals to the criterion of necessity implicitly recognize the decline in value of the evidence as more evidence is available but overlook the decline in jury error. Both recognition of this shortcoming and attempts to rectify it necessarily direct attention to the jury's inability to evaluate hearsay.

This open recognition, which careful analysis of the reliability or the necessity criterion makes inevitable, engenders not merely suspicion about hearsay evidence but also a deep skepticism about the institution of trial by jury. Without the jury to insulate us from observing the inherent limitations upon factfinding, our system of adjudication is called into question. . . .

The social acceptance rationale should be rejected as a normative basis for the hearsay rules for another more compelling reason. . . . [W]e tend to hide the limitations of the jury as a trier of fact while promoting an almost mystic view of our system of justice. To accept that such an approach produces sound results entails unwarranted optimism —a belief that what exists, although we never examine it or admit its nature even to ourselves, is either for the best or will improve if left to itself, perhaps for another century of incoherent evolution. Even if the legal profession is fully aware of what is at issue, contrary to the indications, . . . there remain serious questions concerning whether it is appropriate for the profession to aim directly at social acceptance when making decisions about the course of adjudication on behalf of society at large. This secrecy also limits the range of our imagination when considering problems that continue to arise in the law of evidence and elsewhere. Finally, there are moral questions raised by acceptance of the framework of the current polemic: Can we continue to call our system "just" when we allow the signs of injustice to remain hidden from our own view?

V. CONCLUSION . . .

Since virtually all criteria seeking to distinguish between good and bad hearsay are either incoherent, inconsistent, or indeterminate, the only alternative to a general rule of admission would be an absolute rule of exclusion, which is surely inferior. More important, the assumptions necessary to justify a rule against hearsay — requiring that the jury's assessment of hearsay evidence, after possible remedies, generally exceed twice the value of the evidence — seem insupportable and, in any event, are inconsistent with accepted notions of the function of the jury. Therefore, the hearsay rules should be abolished.

CHAPTER VI

Hearsay and the Confrontation Clause

With the injustice of the Raleigh case as its inspiration, the Confrontation Clause was adopted as part of the Bill of Rights. The clause declares: "In all criminal prosecutions, the accused shall enjoy the right ... to be confronted with the witnesses against him." By its terms, the clause appears to give a criminal defendant an unequivocal right to confront and cross-examine his accusers. Reading the clause in this fashion would constitutionalize a clean "no hearsay" rule, a rule without exception that would bar the admission of hearsay accusations against criminal defendants. But a clean no-hearsay rule would exclude evidence that sensible judges and evidence scholars want factfinders to know about. Every hearsay exception purports to describe such a situation. Interpreting the Confrontation Clause to impose a clean no-hearsay rule at a constitutional level would wipe out all hearsay exceptions.

The Supreme Court has never been willing to take such a stringent view of the clause's requirement. Instead, the Court has decided that established exceptions to the hearsay rule—for example, dying declarations—should also be treated as exceptions to the constitutional confrontation requirement. Once the Court recognizes hearsay exceptions as exceptions to the confrontation requirement, however, where is the stopping point, and what is the theory? Must the Court go all the way, accepting any exception to the hearsay rule as also an exception to the constitutional right of confrontation? This is an ugly result. The hearsay rule, together with its exceptions, is a mind-boggling hodge-podge, a "rule" with more than twenty-five exclusions and exceptions (including a catch-all), really a set of rules without a clear underlying standard, hence a rule that does not express a coherent constitutional principle. Equating the right of confrontation with hearsay law would give us a constitutional rule that epitomizes legal technicality, subordinates the

Constitution to the rules of evidence, and lacks any clear bounds or coherent rationalization.

Both judges and commentators would dearly value a sensible, middle-ground interpretation of the Confrontation Clause, one that would distinguish confrontation from hearsay, leave hearsay law and its mess of exceptions to lower levels of common law elaboration, and reserve for the constitutional realm a general and sensible principle of justice to bound the outside limits of common law practice. But every attempt to find such a bounding principle has so far failed, ensnared in the tangle between confrontation and hearsay. Years of struggle with this problem by judges and evidence commentators have produced no satisfactory solution.

Wigmore, the great treatise-writer who laboriously identified the different forms of hearsay that courts had been admitting and categorized them into the framework of exceptions that is now represented in the Federal Rules of Evidence, offered the following rationalization for why hearsay exceptions are *not* unconstitutional:

> The theory of the hearsay rule . . . is that the many possible sources of inaccuracy and untrustworthiness which may lie underneath the bare untested assertion of a witness can best be brought to light and exposed, if they exist, by the test of cross-examination. But this test or security may in a given instance be superfluous; it may be sufficiently clear, in that instance, that the statement offered is free enough from the risk of inaccuracy and untrustworthiness, so that the test of cross-examination would be a work of supererogation.

5 J. Wigmore, Evidence sec. 1420, p.251 (J. Chadbourne rev. 1974).

In other words, Wigmore claims hearsay exceptions are constitutional because the statements admitted in evidence pursuant to them are supposedly so reliable that testing by cross-examination is superfluous. This seems utterly ridiculous. The hearsay exceptions by no stretch give complete assurance of the declarant's testimonial capacities. No trial lawyer would forego cross-examination, if given the opportunity. The very weakness of Wigmore's argument for the constitutionality of the hearsay exceptions suggests how difficult a detailed and focused analysis of their constitutionality would be against a standard giving criminal defendants a right to cross-examine all declarants against them.

For more than 100 years after the adoption of the Confrontation Clause there was no elaboration of it in the United States Supreme Court. Why was that? Because, prior to the establishment of intermediate appellate federal courts, there was no appeal of what might be considered "ordinary" trial errors. The jurisdiction of a trial court, in the sense of its power to try the case, might be tested. But the evidentiary rulings by judges presiding over cases within their jurisdiction became subject to appellate review only with the establishment by Congress of the Circuit Courts of Appeal.

The first Confrontation Clause case that came to the Supreme Court was Mattox v. United States, a retrial of a defendant convicted of murder on federal land. The conviction was based on the testimony of two eye-witnesses. Both the witnesses were present and were fully examined and cross-examined at the first trial. The defendants, however, successfully appealed (on grounds unrelated to confrontation problems) and obtained a new trial. By the time of the second trial, the two eye-witnesses were dead. Without the live witnesses at the second trial, the prosecutor introduced transcripts of testimony from the first trial. Whereupon the defendant made Raleigh's objection to the effect, "Would you convict an American on the basis of a piece of paper? I'm entitled by the Confrontation Clause to be confronted by the witnesses against me in this criminal case."

MATTOX v. UNITED STATES
156 U.S. 237 (1895)

Mr. Justice BROWN delivered the opinion of the court.

Upon the [second] trial it was shown by the government that two of its witnesses on the former trial . . . had since died, whereupon a transcribed copy of the reporter's stenographic notes of their testimony upon such trial, supported by his testimony that it was correct, was admitted to be read in evidence, and constituted the strongest proof against the accused. Both these witnesses were present and were fully examined and cross-examined on the former trial. It is claimed, however, that the constitutional provision that the accused shall "be confronted with the witnesses against him" was infringed, by permitting the testimony of witnesses sworn upon the former trial to be read against him. No question is made that this may not be done in a civil case, but it is insisted that the reasons of convenience and necessity which excuse a departure from the ordinary course of procedure in civil cases cannot override the constitutional provision in question. . . .

The primary object of the constitutional provision in question was to prevent depositions or ex parte affidavits, such as were sometimes admitted in civil cases, being used against the prisoner in lieu of a personal examination and cross-examination of the witness in which the accused has an opportunity, not only of testing the recollection and sifting the conscience of the witness, but of compelling him to stand face to face with the jury in order that they may look at him, and judge by his demeanor upon the stand and the manner in which he gives his testimony whether he is worthy of belief. There is doubtless reason for saying that the accused should never lose the benefit of any of these safeguards even by the death of the witness; and that, if notes of his testimony are permitted to be read, he is deprived of the advantage of that personal presence of the witness before the jury which the law has designed for his protection. But general rules of law of this kind, however beneficent in their operation and valuable to the accused, must occasionally give way to considerations of public policy and the necessities of the case. To say that a criminal, after having once been convicted by the testimony of a certain witness, should go scot free simply because death has closed the mouth of that witness, would be carrying his constitutional protection to an unwarrantable extent. The law in its wisdom declares that the rights of the public shall not be wholly sacrificed in order that an incidental benefit may be preserved to the accused.

We are bound to interpret the Constitution in the light of the law as it existed at the time it was adopted, not as reaching out for new guaranties of the rights of the citizen, but as securing to every individual such as he already possessed as a British subject—such as his ancestors had inherited and defended since the days of Magna Charta. Many of its provisions in the nature of a Bill of Rights are subject to exceptions, recognized long before the adoption of the Constitution, and not interfering at all with its spirit. Such exceptions were obviously intended to be respected. A technical adherence to the letter of a constitutional provision may occasionally be carried farther than is necessary to the just protection of the accused, and farther than the safety of the public will warrant. For instance, there could be nothing more directly contrary to the letter of the provision in question than the admission of dying declarations. They are rarely made in the presence of the accused; they are made without any opportunity for examination or cross-examination; nor is the witness brought face to face with the jury; yet from time immemorial they have been treated as competent testimony, and no one would have the hardihood at this day to question their admissibility. They are admitted not in conformity with any general rule regarding the admission of testimony, but as an exception to such rules, simply from the necessities of the case, and to prevent a manifest failure of justice. As was said by the Chief Justice when this case was here upon the first writ of error, (146 U.S. 140, 152), the sense of impending death is presumed to remove all temptation to falsehood, and to enforce as strict an adherence to the truth as would the obligation of an oath. If such declarations are admitted, because made by a person then dead, under circumstances which give his statements the same weight as if made under oath, there is equal if not greater reason for admitting testimony of his statements which were made under oath. . . .

The substance of the constitutional protection is preserved to the prisoner in the advantage he has once had of seeing the witness face to face, and of subjecting him to the ordeal of a cross-examination. . . .

Would the evidence have been admissible under the Federal Rules? Does argument by analogy to dying declarations prove too much? Does *Mattox* stand for the principle that all statements that are as reliable as dying declarations are admissible without violating the Confrontation Clause, at least if the witness is unavailable? Does the Court suggest that the Confrontation Clause covers only cases that present the danger of prosecutorial abuse inherent in the practice of proof by ex parte affidavit (such as the mode of proof used to convict Sir Walter Raleigh)?

No further significant development of Confrontation Clause theory occurred until 1965 when the Supreme Court incorporated the Clause against the states in Pointer v. Texas. This was part of Justice Black's ongoing incorporation campaign and was the focus of his attention in the opinion he wrote in Pointer. He interprets the Confrontation Clause as a powerful protector of the defendant's right to cross-examine. He pays no attention to how his approach to the Confrontation Clause affects the hearsay rule and its myriad exceptions.

POINTER v. TEXAS
380 U.S. 400 (1965)

Mr. Justice BLACK delivered the opinion of the Court. . . .

The petitioner Pointer and one Dillard were arrested in Texas and taken before a state judge for a preliminary hearing (in Texas called the "examining trial") on a charge of having robbed Kenneth W. Phillips of $375 "by assault, or violence, or by putting in fear of life or bodily injury," in violation of Texas Penal Code Art. 1408. At this hearing an Assistant District Attorney conducted the prosecution and examined witnesses, but neither of the defendants, both of whom were laymen, had a lawyer. Phillips as chief witness for the State gave his version of the alleged robbery in detail, identifying petitioner as the man who had robbed him at gunpoint. Apparently Dillard tried to cross-examine Phillips but Pointer did not, although Pointer was said to have tried to cross-examine some other witnesses at the hearing. Petitioner was subsequently indicted on a charge of having committed the robbery. Some time before the trial was held, Phillips moved to California. After putting in evidence to show that Phillips had moved and did not intend to return to Texas, the State at the trial offered the transcript of Phillips' testimony given at the preliminary hearing as evidence against petitioner. Petitioner's counsel immediately objected to introduction of the transcript, stating, "Your Honor, we will object to that, as it is a denial of the confrontment of the witnesses against the Defendant." Similar objections were repeatedly made by petitioner's counsel but were over-ruled by the trial judge, apparently in part because, as the judge viewed it, petitioner had been present at the preliminary hearing and therefore had been "accorded the opportunity of cross examining the witnesses there against him." The Texas Court of Criminal Appeals, the highest state court to which the case could be taken, affirmed petitioner's conviction, rejecting his contention that use of the transcript to convict him denied him rights guaranteed by the Sixth and Fourteenth Amendments. . . .

The Sixth Amendment is a part of what is called our Bill of Rights. In Gideon v. Wainright, [372 U.S. 335 (1963),] in which this Court held that the Sixth Amendment's right to the assistance of counsel is obligatory upon the States, we did so on the ground that "a provision of the Bill of Rights which is 'fundamental and essential to a fair trial' is made obligatory upon the States by the Fourteenth Amendment." 372 U.S., at 342. . . . We hold today that the Sixth Amendment's right of an accused to confront the witnesses against him is likewise a fundamental right and is made obligatory on the States by the Fourteenth Amendment.

It cannot seriously be doubted at this late date that the right of cross-examination is included in the right of an accused in a criminal case to confront the witnesses against him. And probably no one, certainly no one experienced in the trial of lawsuits, would deny the value of cross-examination in exposing falsehood and bringing out the truth in the trial of a criminal case. See, e.g., 5 Wigmore, Evidence §1367 (3d ed. 1940). The fact that this right appears in the Sixth Amendment of our Bill of Rights reflects the belief of the Framers of those liberties and safeguards that confrontation was a fundamental right essential to a fair trial in a criminal prosecution. Moreover, the decisions of this Court and other courts throughout the years have constantly emphasized the necessity for cross-examination as a protection for defendants in criminal cases. . . .

This Court has recognized the admissibility against an accused of dying declarations, Mattox v. United States, 146 U.S. 140, 151, and of testimony of a deceased witness who has testified at a former trial. Mattox v. United States, 156 U.S. 237, 240-244. Nothing we hold here is to the contrary. The case before us would be quite a different one had Phillips' statement been taken at a full-fledged hearing at which petitioner had been represented by counsel who had been given a complete and adequate opportunity to cross-examine. . . . Because the transcript of Phillips' statement offered against petitioner at his trial had not been taken at a time and under circumstances affording petitioner through counsel an adequate opportunity to cross-examine Phillips, its introduction in a federal court in a criminal case against Pointer would have amounted to denial of the privilege of confrontation guaranteed by the

Sixth Amendment. Since we hold that the right of an accused to be confronted with the witnesses against him must be determined by the same standards whether the right is denied in a federal or state proceeding, it follows that use of the transcript to convict petitioner denied him a constitutional right, and that his conviction must be reversed.

Reversed and remanded.

If cross-examination is the touchstone of confrontation, as it seems here, how can the use of dying declarations be rationalized? Were Phillips's statements under oath at the preliminary hearing less reliable than dying declarations?

After *Pointer,* the Supreme Court appeared to be on a path that would lead it inevitably to address the apparent conflict between the Confrontation Clause and the various hearsay exceptions. Would the Court do better with the issue than Wigmore? Could the Supreme Court actually rise to the challenge of making constitutional sense of the various hearsay exceptions?

Quite to the contrary, the Supreme Court simply shuffled the issue aside.

OHIO v. ROBERTS
448 U.S. 56 (1980)

Mr. Justice BLACKMUN delivered the opinion of the Court.

[The issue in this case, as in *Pointer,* involved an attempt to use the transcript of a witness's testimony from the preliminary hearing against the defendant at trial. The defendant had called the witness at the preliminary hearing and had examined her. The significance of the case rests on its strikingly summary (and partially ill-advised) doctrinal pronouncements, not on any fine parsing of the doctrine as applied to the facts of the case.] . . .

The Confrontation Clause operates in two separate ways to restrict the range of admissible hearsay. First, in conformance with the Framers' preference for face-to-face accusation, the Sixth Amendment establishes a rule of necessity. In the usual case (including cases where prior cross-examination has occurred), the prosecution must either produce, or demonstrate the unavailability of, the declarant whose statement it wishes to use against the defendant.

The second aspect operates once a witness is shown to be unavailable. Reflecting its underlying purpose to augment accuracy in the factfinding process by ensuring the defendant an effective means to test adverse evidence, the Clause countenances only hearsay marked with such trustworthiness that "there is no material departure from the reason of the general rule." Snyder v. Massachusetts, 291 U.S., at 107. . . . "It is clear from these statements, and from numerous prior decisions of this Court, that even though the witness be unavailable his prior testimony must bear some of these 'indicia of reliability.'"

The Court has applied this "indicia of reliability" requirement principally by concluding that certain hearsay exceptions rest upon such solid foundations that admission of virtually any evidence within them comports with the "substance of the constitutional protection." Mattox v. United States, 156 U.S., at 244. This reflects the truism that "hearsay rules and the Confrontation Clause are generally designed to protect similar values," California v. Green, 399 U.S., at 155, and "stem from the same roots," Dutton v. Evans, 400 U.S. 74, 86 (1970). It also responds to the need for certainty in the workaday world of conducting criminal trials.

In sum, when a hearsay declarant is not present for cross-examination at trial, the Confrontation Clause normally requires a showing that he is unavailable. Even then, his statement is admissible only if it bears adequate "indicia of reliability." Reliability can be inferred without more in a case where the evidence falls within a firmly rooted hearsay exception. In other cases, the evidence must be excluded, at least absent a showing of particularized guarantees of trustworthiness.

The ill-advised piece of Justice Blackmun's pronouncement involved his assertion that, "when a hearsay declarant is not present for cross-examination at trial, the Confrontation Clause normally requires a showing that he is unavailable." Reasonable as this sounds, it appears to undercut all of the hearsay exceptions listed in Rule 803. Recall that the hearsay rules class hearsay exceptions into two categories, the Rule 803 exceptions, for which the availability or unavailability of the declarant is irrelevant, and the Rule 804 exceptions, which require a demonstration of the declarant's unavailability as a condition to admissibility. Justice Blackmun's pronouncement would appear to establish a constitutional requirement to demonstrate the declarant's unavailability for all hearsay exceptions. Every indication from subsequent Supreme Court cases, as you will shortly see in White v. Illinois, is that this was simply a blunder.

The lasting and most far-reaching piece of the doctrinal framework was set in a single sentence: "Reliability can be inferred without more in a case where the evidence falls within a firmly rooted hearsay exception." With this one sentence statement of presumption Justice Blackmun dispenses with the problems that the Confrontation Clause might have been thought to pose to established hearsay exceptions (do you find this satisfying?), and narrows the need to make actual substantive

assessments of reliability to newly established, non-traditional exceptions. What kinds of exceptions are these?

IDAHO v. WRIGHT
497 U.S. 805 (1990)

Justice O'CONNOR delivered the opinion of the Court.

This case requires us to decide whether the admission at trial of certain hearsay statements made by a child declarant to an examining pediatrician violates a defendant's rights under the Confrontation Clause
of the Sixth Amendment.

I

Respondent Laura Lee Wright was jointly charged with Robert L.
Giles of two counts of lewd conduct with a minor under 16, in violation
of Idaho Code §18-1508 (1987). The alleged victims were respondent's
two daughters, one of whom was 5½ and the other 2½ years old at the
time the crimes were charged.

Respondent and her ex-husband, Louis Wright, the father of the
older daughter, had reached an informal agreement whereby each parent would have custody of the older daughter for six consecutive
months. The allegations surfaced in November 1986 when the older
daughter told Cynthia Goodman, Louis Wright's female companion,
that Giles had had sexual intercourse with her while respondent held
her down and covered her mouth, and that she had seen respondent
and Giles do the same thing to respondent's younger daughter. The
younger daughter was living with her parents — respondent and Giles
— at the time of the alleged offenses.

Goodman reported the older daughter's disclosures to the police the
next day and took the older daughter to the hospital. A medical examination of the older daughter revealed evidence of sexual abuse. One
of the examining physicians was Dr. John Jambura, a pediatrician with
extensive experience in child abuse cases. Police and welfare officials
took the younger daughter into custody that day for protection and
investigation. Dr. Jambura examined her the following day and found
conditions "strongly suggestive of sexual abuse with vaginal contact,"
occurring approximately two to three days prior to the examination. Id.
at 105, 106.

At the joint trial of respondent and Giles, the trial court conducted
a voir dire examination of the younger daughter, who was three years
old at the time of the trial, to determine whether she was capable of
testifying. The court concluded, and the parties agreed, that the
younger daughter was "not capable of communicating to the jury."

At issue in this case is the admission at trial of certain statements made by the younger daughter to Dr. Jambura in response to questions he asked regarding the alleged abuse. Over objection by respondent and Giles, the trial court permitted Dr. Jambura to testify before the jury as follows:

Q. [By the prosecutor] Now, calling your attention then to your examination of Kathy Wright on November 10th. What—would you describe any interview dialogue that you had with Kathy at that time? Excuse me, before you get into that, would you lay a setting of where this took place and who else might have been present?

A. This took place in my office, in my examining room, and, as I recall, I believe previous testimony I said that I recall a female attendant being present, I don't recall her identity. I started out with basically, "Hi, how are you," you know, "What did you have for breakfast this morning?" Essentially a few minutes of just sort of chitchat.

Q. Was there response from Kathy to that first—those first questions?

A. There was. She started to carry on a very relaxed animated conversation. I then proceeded to just gently start asking questions about, "Well, how are things at home," you know, those sorts. Gently moving into the domestic situation and then moved into four questions in particular, as I reflected in my records, "Do you play with daddy? Does daddy play with you? Does daddy touch you with his pee-pee? Do you touch his pee-pee?" And again we then established what was meant by pee-pee, it was a generic term for genital area.

Q. Before you get into that, what was, as best you recollect, what was her response to the question "Do you play with daddy?"

A. Yes, we play—I remember her making a comment about yes we play a lot and expanding on that and talking about spending time with daddy.

Q. And "Does daddy play with you?" Was there any response?

A. She responded to that as well, that they played together in a variety of circumstances and, you know, seemed very unaffected by the question.

Q. And then what did you say and her response?

A. When I asked her "Does daddy touch you with his pee-pee," she did admit to that. When I asked, "Do you touch his pee-pee," she did not have any response.

Q. Excuse me. Did you notice any change in her affect or attitude in that line of questioning?

A. Yes.

Q. What did you observe?

A. She would not—oh, she did not talk any further about that. She would not elucidate what exactly—what kind of touching was taking place, or how it was happening. She did, however, say that daddy does do this with me, but he does it a lot more with my sister than with me.

Q.   And how did she offer that last statement? Was that in response to a question or was that just a volunteered statement?

A.   That was a volunteered statement as I sat and waited for her to respond, again after she sort of clammed-up, and that was the next statement that she made after just allowing some silence to occur.

Id., at 121-123. On cross-examination, Dr. Jambura acknowledged that a picture that he drew during his questioning of the younger daughter had been discarded. Id., at 124. Dr. Jambura also stated that although he had dictated notes to summarize the conversation, his notes were not detailed and did not record any changes in the child's affect or attitude. Id., at 123-124.

The trial court admitted these statements under Idaho's residual hearsay exception, which provides in relevant part:

> Rule 803. Hearsay exceptions; availability of declarant immaterial.—The following are not excluded by the hearsay rule, even though the declarant is available as a witness. . . .
>
> (24) Other exceptions. A statement not specifically covered by any of the foregoing exceptions but having equivalent circumstantial guarantees of trustworthiness, if the court determines that (A) the statement is offered as evidence of a material fact; (B) the statement is more probative on the point for which it is offered than any other evidence which the proponent can procure through reasonable efforts; and (C) the general purposes of these rules and the interests of justice will best be served by admission of the statement into evidence.

Idaho Rule Evid. 803(24).

Respondent and Giles were each convicted of two counts of lewd conduct with a minor under 16 and sentenced to 20 years imprisonment. Each appealed only from the conviction involving the younger daughter. Giles contended that the trial court erred in admitting Dr. Jambura's testimony under Idaho's residual hearsay exception. The Idaho Supreme Court disagreed and affirmed his conviction. State v. Giles, 115 Idaho 984, 772 P.2d 191 (1989). Respondent asserted that the admission of Dr. Jambura's testimony under the residual hearsay exception nevertheless violated her rights under the Confrontation Clause. The Idaho Supreme Court agreed and reversed respondent's conviction. 116 Idaho 382, 775 P.2d 1224 (1989).

The Supreme Court of Idaho held that the admission of the inculpatory hearsay testimony violated respondent's federal constitutional right to confrontation because the testimony did not fall within a traditional hearsay exception and was based on an interview that lacked procedural safeguards. Id., at 385, 775 P.2d, at 1227. The court found

Dr. Jambura's interview tec   inadequate because "the questions and answers were not record   t videotape for preservation and perusal by the defense at or before trial; and, blatantly leading questions were used in the interrogation." Ibid. The statements also lacked trustworthiness, according to the court, because "this interrogation was performed by someone with a preconceived idea of what the child should be disclosing." Ibid. Noting that expert testimony and child psychology texts indicated that children are susceptible to suggestion and are therefore likely to be misled by leading questions, the court found that "[t]he circumstances surrounding this interview demonstrate dangers of unreliability which, because the interview was not [audio or video] recorded, can never be fully assessed." Id., at 388, 775 P.2d, at 1230. The court concluded that the younger daughter's statements lacked the particularized guarantees of trustworthiness necessary to satisfy the requirements of the Confrontation Clause and that therefore the trial court erred in admitting them. Id., at 389, 775 P.2d, at 1231. Because the court was not convinced, beyond a reasonable doubt, that the jury would have reached the same result had the error not occurred, the court reversed respondent's conviction on the count involving the younger daughter and remanded for a new trial. Ibid.

We granted certiorari, 493 U.S. 1040, 110 S. Ct. 833, 107 L. Ed. 2d 829 (1990), and now affirm.

II

The Confrontation Clause of the Sixth Amendment, made applicable to the States through the Fourteenth Amendment, provides: "In all criminal prosecutions, the accused shall enjoy the right . . . to be confronted with the witnesses against him."

From the earliest days of our Confrontation Clause jurisprudence, we have consistently held that the Clause does not necessarily prohibit the admission of hearsay statements against a criminal defendant, even though the admission of such statements might be thought to violate the literal terms of the Clause. See, e.g., Mattox v. United States, 156 U.S. 237, 243, 15 S. Ct. 337, 339, 39 L. Ed. 409 (1895); Pointer v. Texas, 380 U.S. 400, 407, 85 S. Ct. 1065, 1069, 13 L. Ed. 2d 923 (1965). . . .

In Ohio v. Roberts, we set forth "a general approach" for determining when incriminating statements admissible under an exception to the hearsay rule also meet the requirements of the Confrontation Clause. 448 U.S., at 65, 100 S. Ct., at 2538. We noted that the Confrontation Clause "operates in two separate ways to restrict the range of admissible hearsay." Ibid. "First, in conformance with the Framers' preference for face-to-face accusation, the Sixth Amendment establishes a rule of necessity. In the usual case . . . , the prosecution must either produce or demonstrate the unavailability of, the declarant whose statement it wishes to use against the defendant." Ibid. (citations omitted). Second, once a witness is shown to be unavailable, "his statement is admissible only if it bears adequate 'indicia of reliability.' Reliability can be inferred without more in a case where the evidence falls within a firmly rooted hearsay exception. In other cases, the evidence must be excluded, at least absent a showing of particularized guarantees of trustworthiness." Id., at 66, 100 S. Ct., at 2539. . . .

Applying the *Roberts* approach to this case, we first note that this case does not raise the question whether, before a child's out-of-court statements are admitted, the Confrontation Clause requires the prosecution to show that a child witness is unavailable at trial—and, if so, what that showing requires. The trial court in this case found that respondent's younger daughter was incapable of communicating with the jury, and defense counsel agreed. The court below neither questioned this finding nor discussed the general requirement of unavailability. For purposes of deciding this case, we assume without deciding that, to the extent the unavailability requirement applies in this case, the younger daughter was an unavailable witness within the meaning of the Confrontation Clause.

The crux of the question presented is therefore whether the State, as the proponent of evidence presumptively barred by the hearsay rule and the Confrontation Clause, has carried its burden of proving that the younger daughter's incriminating statements to Dr. Jambura bore sufficient indicia of reliability to withstand scrutiny under the Clause. The court below held that, although the trial court had properly admitted the statements under the State's residual hearsay exception, the statements were "fraught with the dangers of unreliability which the Confrontation Clause is designed to highlight and obviate." 116 Idaho, at 389, 775 P.2d, at 1231. The State asserts that the court below erected too stringent a standard for admitting the statements and that the statements were, under the totality of the circumstances, sufficiently reliable for Confrontation Clause purposes.

In *Roberts*, we suggested that the "indicia of reliability" requirement could be met in either of two circumstances: where the hearsay statement "falls within a firmly rooted hearsay exception," or where it is supported by "a showing of particularized guarantees of trustworthiness." 448 U.S., at 66, 100 S. Ct., at 2539. . . .

We note at the outset that Idaho's residual hearsay exception, Idaho Rule Evid. 803(24), under which the challenged statements were admitted, App. 113-115, is not a firmly rooted hearsay exception for Confrontation Clause purposes. Admission under a firmly rooted hearsay exception satisfies the constitutional requirement of reliability because of the weight accorded longstanding judicial and legislative experience in assessing the trustworthiness of certain types of out-of-court statements. . . . The residual hearsay exception, by contrast, accommodates ad hoc instances in which statements not otherwise falling within a recognized hearsay exception might nevertheless be sufficiently reliable to be admissible at trial. See, e.g., Senate Judiciary Committee's Note on Fed. Rule Evid. 803(24), 28 U.S.C. App., pp.786-787; E. Cleary, McCormick on Evidence §324.1, pp.907-909 (3d ed. 1984). Hearsay statements admitted under the residual exception, almost by definition, therefore do not share the same tradition of reliability that supports the admissibility of statements under a firmly rooted hearsay exception. . . .

The State in any event does not press the matter strongly and recognizes that, because the younger daughter's hearsay statements do not fall within a firmly rooted hearsay exception, they are "presumptively unreliable and inadmissible for Confrontation Clause purposes," *Lee*, 476 U.S., at 543, 106 S. Ct., at 2063, and "must be excluded, at least absent a showing of particularized guarantees of trustworthiness," *Roberts*, 448 U.S., at 66, 100 S. Ct., at 2539. The court below concluded that the State had not made such a showing, in large measure because the statements resulted from an interview lacking certain procedural safeguards. The court below specifically noted that Dr. Jambura failed to record the interview on videotape, asked leading questions, and questioned the idea with a preconceived idea of what she should be disclosing. See 116 Idaho, at 388, 775 P.2d, at 1230.

Although we agree with the court below that the Confrontation Clause bars the admission of the younger daughter's hearsay statements, we reject the apparently dispositive weight place by that court on the lack of procedural safeguards at the interview. Out-of-court statements made by children regarding sexual abuse arise in a wide variety of circumstances, and we do not believe the Constitution imposes a fixed set of procedural prerequisites to the admission of such statements at trial. The procedural requirements identified by the court below, to the extent regarded as conditions precedent to the admission of child hearsay statements in child sexual abuse cases, may in many instances be inappropriate or unnecessary to a determination whether a given statement is sufficiently trustworthy for Confrontation Clause purposes. . . . Although the procedural guidelines propounded by the court below may well enhance the reliability of out-of-court statements of children regarding sexual abuse, we decline to read into the Confrontation Clause a preconceived and artificial litmus test for the procedural propriety of professional interviews in which children make hearsay statements against a defendant.

The State responds that a finding of "particularized guarantees of trustworthiness" should instead be based on a consideration of the totality of the circumstances, including not only the circumstances surrounding the making of the statement, but also other evidence at trial that corroborates the truth of the statement. We agree that "particularized guarantees of trustworthiness" must be shown from the totality of the circumstances, but we think the relevant circumstances include only those that surround the making of the statement and that render the declarant particularly worthy of belief. This conclusion derives from the rationale for permitting exceptions to the general rule against hearsay: "The theory of the hearsay rule . . . is that the many possible sources of inaccuracy and untrustworthiness which may lie underneath the bare untested assertion of a witness can best be brought to light and exposed, if they exist, by the test of cross-examination. But this test or security may in a given instance be superfluous; it may be sufficiently clear, in that instance, that the statement offered is free enough from the risk of inaccuracy and untrustworthiness, so that the test of cross-examination would be a work of supererogation." 5 J. Wigmore, Evidence §1420, p.251 (J. Chadbourne rev. 1974). In other words, if the declarant's truthfulness is so clear from the surrounding circumstances that the test of cross-examination would be of marginal utility, then the hearsay rule does not bar admission of the statement at trial. The basis for the "excited utterance" exception, for example, is that such statements are given under circumstances that eliminate the possibility of fabrication, coaching, or confabulation, and that therefore the circumstances surrounding the making of the statement provide sufficient assurance that the statement is trustworthy and that cross-examination would be superfluous. See, e.g., 6 Wigmore, supra, §§1745-1764; 4 J. Weinstein & M. Berger, Weinstein's Evidence ¶803(2)[01] (1988); Advisory Committee's Note on Fed. Rule Evid. 803(2), 28 U.S.C. App., p.778. Likewise, the "dying declaration" and "medical treatment" exceptions to the hearsay rule are based on the belief that persons making such statements are highly unlikely to lie. See, e.g., *Mattox,* 156 U.S., at 244, 15 S. Ct., at 340 ("[T]he sense of impending death is presumed to remove all temptation to falsehood, and to enforce as strict an adherence to the truth as would the obligation of oath"); Queen v. Osman, 15 Cox Crim. Cas. 1, 3 (Eng. N. Wales Cir. 1881) (Lush, L.J.) ("[N]o person, who is immediately going into the presence of his Maker, will do so with a lie upon his lips"); Mosteller, Child Sexual Abuse and Statements for the Purpose of Medical Diagnosis or Treatment, 67 N.C.L. Rev. 257 (1989). "The circumstantial guarantees of trustworthiness on which the various specific exceptions to the hearsay rule are based are those that existed at the time the statement was made and do not include those that may be added by using hindsight." Huff v. White Motor Corp., 609 F.2d 286, 292 (C.A.7 1979).

We think the "particularized guarantees of trustworthiness" required for admission under the Confrontation Clause must likewise be drawn from the totality of circumstances that surround the making of the statement and that render the declarant particularly worthy of belief. Our precedents have recognized that statements admitted under a "firmly rooted" hearsay exception are so trustworthy that adversarial testing would add little to their reliability. . . . Because evidence possessing "particularized guarantees of trustworthiness" must be at least as reliable as evidence admitted under a firmly rooted hearsay exception, see *Roberts,* supra, at 66, 100 S. Ct., at 2539, we think that evidence admitted under the former requirement must similarly be so trustworthy that adversarial testing would add little to its reliability. . . .Thus, unless an affirmative reason, arising from the circumstances in which the statement was made, provides a basis for rebutting the presumption that a hearsay statement is not worthy of reliance at trial, the Confrontation Clause requires exclusion of the out-of-court statement.

The state and federal courts have identified a number of factors that we think properly relate to whether hearsay statements made by a child witness in child sexual abuse cases are reliable. See, e.g., State v. Robinson, 153 Ariz. 191, 201, 735 P.2d 801, 811 (1987) (spontaneity and consistent repetition); Morgan v. Foretich, 846 F.2d 941, 948 (C.A.4 1988) (mental state of the declarant); State v. Sorenson, 143 Wis. 2d 226, 246, 421 N.W.2d 77, 85 (1988) (use of terminology unexpected of a child of similar age); State v. Kuone, 243 Kan. 218, 221-222, 757 P.2d 289, 292-293 (1988) (lack of motive to fabricate). Although these cases (which we cite for the factors they discuss and not necessarily to approve the results that they reach) involve the application of various hearsay exceptions to statements of child declarants, we think the factors identified also apply to whether such statements bear "particularized guarantees of trustworthiness" under the Confrontation Clause. These factors are, of course, not exclusive, and courts have considerable leeway in their consideration of appropriate factors. We therefore decline to endorse a mechanical test for determining "particularized guarantees of trustworthiness" under the Clause. Rather, the unifying principle is that these factors relate to whether the child declarant was particularly likely to be telling the truth when the statement was made.

As our discussion above suggests, we are unpersuaded by the State's contention that evidence corroborating the truth of a hearsay statement may properly support a finding that the statement bears "particularized guarantees of trustworthiness." To be admissible under the Confrontation Clause, hearsay evidence used to convict a defendant must possess indicia of reliability by virtue of its inherent trustworthiness, not by reference to other evidence at trial. . . . A statement made under duress, for example, may happen to be a true statement, but the circumstances under which it is made may provide no basis for supposing that the declarant is particularly likely to be telling the truth—indeed, the circumstances may even be such that the declarant is particularly unlikely to be telling the truth. In such a case, cross-examination at trial would be highly useful to probe the declarant's state-of-mind when he made the statements; the presence of evidence tending to corroborate the truth of the statement would be no substitute for cross-examination of the declarant at trial.

In short, the use of corroborating evidence to support a hearsay statement's "particularized guarantees of trustworthiness" would permit admission of a presumptively unreliable statement by bootstrapping on the trustworthiness of other evidence at trial, a result we think at odds with the requirement that hearsay evidence admitted under the Confrontation Clause be so trustworthy that cross-examination of the declarant would be of marginal utility. . . .

Finally, we reject respondent's contention that the younger daughter's out-of-court statements in this case are per se unreliable, or at least presumptively unreliable, on the ground that the trial court found the younger daughter incompetent to testify at trial. First, respondent's contention rests upon a questionable reading of the record in this case. The trial court found only that the younger daughter was "not capable of communicating to the jury." Although Idaho law provides that a child witness may not testify if he "appear[s] incapable of receiving just impressions of the facts respecting which they are examined, or of relating them truly," Idaho Code §9-202 (Supp. 1989); Idaho Rule Evid. 601(a), the trial court in this case made no such findings. Indeed, the more reasonable inference is that, by ruling that the statements were admissible under Idaho's residual hearsay exception, the trial court implicitly found that the younger daughter, at the time she made the statements, was capable of receiving just impressions of the facts and of relating them truly. See App. 115. In addition, we have in any event held that the Confrontation Clause does not erect a per se rule barring the admission of prior statements of a declarant who is unable to communicate to the jury at the time of trial. See, e.g., *Mattox*, 156 U.S., at 243-244, 15 S. Ct., at 339-340; see also 4 Louisell & Mueller, supra, §486, pp.1041-1045. Although such inability might be relevant to whether the earlier hearsay statement possessed particularized guarantees of trustworthiness, a per se rule of exclusion would not only frustrate the truth-seeking purpose of the Confrontation Clause, but would also hinder States in their own "enlightened development in the law of evidence," *Evans*, 400 U.S., at 95, 91 S. Ct., at 222 (Harlan, J., concurring in result).

III

. . . We think the Supreme Court of Idaho properly focused on the presumptive unreliability of the out-of-court statements and on the suggestive manner in which Dr. Jambura conducted the interview. Viewing the totality of the circumstances surrounding the younger daughter's responses to Dr. Jambura's questions, we find no special reason for supposing that the incriminating statements were particularly trustworthy.

The younger daughter's last statement regarding the abuse of the older daughter, however, presents a closer question. According to Dr. Jambura, the younger daughter "volunteered" that statement "after she sort of clammed-up." Id., at 123. Although the spontaneity of the statement and the change in demeanor suggest that the younger daughter was telling the truth when she made the statement, we note that it is possible that "[i]f there is evidence of prior interrogation, prompting, or manipulation by adults, spontaneity may be an inaccurate indicator of trustworthiness." *Robinson*, 153 Ariz., at 201, 735 P.2d, at 811. Moreover, the statement was not made under circumstances of reliability comparable to those required, for example, for the admission of excited utterances or statements made for purposes of medical diagnosis or treatment. Given the presumption of inadmissibility accorded accusatory hearsay statements not admitted pursuant to a firmly rooted hearsay exception, *Lee*, 476 U.S., at 543, 106 S. Ct., at 2058, we agree with the court below that the State has failed to show that the younger daughter's incriminating statements to the pediatrician possessed sufficient "particularized guarantees of trustworthiness" under the Confrontation Clause to overcome that presumption.

The State does not challenge the Idaho Supreme Court's conclusion that the Confrontation Clause error in this case was not harmless beyond a reasonable doubt, and we see no reason to revisit the issue. We therefore agree with that court that respondent's conviction involving the younger daughter must be reversed and the case remanded for further proceedings. Accordingly, the judgment of the Supreme Court of Idaho is affirmed.

It is so ordered.

Justice KENNEDY, with whom the Chief Justice, Justice WHITE and Justice BLACKMUN join, dissenting.

. . . Given the principle, for cases involving hearsay statements that do not come within one of the traditional hearsay exceptions, that admissibility depends upon finding particular guarantees of trustworthiness in each case, it is difficult to state rules of general application. I believe the Court recognizes this. The majority errs, in my view, by adopting a rule that corroboration of the statement by other evidence is an impermissible part of the trustworthiness inquiry. The Court's apparent ruling is that corroborating evidence may not be considered in whole or in part for this purpose. This limitation, at least on a facial interpretation of the Court's analytic categories, is a new creation by the Court; it likely will prove unworkable and does not even square with the examples of reliability indicators the Court itself invokes; and it is contrary to our own precedents.

I see no constitutional justification for this decision to prescind corroborating evidence from consideration of the question whether a child's statements are reliable. . . .

Idaho v. Wright holds that corroborative evidence cannot be used to establish the reliability and hence the admissibility of nontraditional hearsay. What if nontraditional hearsay appears to have sufficient indicia of reliability considered by itself, but is contradicted by other evidence in a way that suggests its unreliability? Should the trial judge consider such contradictory evidence when assessing the hearsay's reliability?

How thin and contradicted can hearsay get and still be sufficient to sustain a conviction against a criminal defendant? Can a defendant be convicted on hearsay alone? Is the credibility of the person who reports a child's hearsay statements relevant in any way to the constitutional confrontation issue? Can the statements of a child who has been found to be incompetent because she does not remember accurately or appreciate the obligation to tell the truth ever be considered reliable enough to be admitted as nontraditional hearsay? Should such statements be admitted even if they fall within a traditional hearsay exception?

WHITE v. ILLINOIS
112 S. Ct. 736 (1992)

The CHIEF JUSTICE delivered the opinion of the court.

In this case we consider whether the Confrontation Clause of the Sixth Amendment requires that, before a trial court admits testimony under the "spontaneous declaration" and "medical examination" exceptions to the hearsay rule, the prosecution must either produce the declarant at trial or the trial court must find that the declarant is unavailable. The Illinois Appellate Court concluded that such procedures are not constitutionally required. We agree with that conclusion.

Petitioner was convicted by a jury of aggravated criminal sexual assault, residential burglary, and unlawful restraint. Ill. Rev. Stat., ch. 38, ¶¶12-14, 19-3, 10-3 (1989). The events giving rise to the charges related to the sexual assault of S.G., then four years old. Testimony at the trial established that in the early morning hours of April 16, 1988, S.G.'s babysitter, Tony DeVore, was awakened by S.G.'s scream. DeVore went to S.G.'s bedroom and witnessed petitioner leaving the room and petitioner then left the house. 6 Tr. 10-11. DeVore knew petitioner because petitioner was a friend of S.G.'s mother, Tammy Grigsby, id., at 27. DeVore asked S.G. what had happened. According to DeVore's trial testimony, S.G. stated that petitioner had put his hand over her mouth, choked her, threatened to whip her if she screamed and had "touch[ed] her in the wrong places." Asked by DeVore to point to where she had been touched, S.G. identified the vaginal area. Id., at 12-17.

Tammy Grigsby, S.G.'s mother, returned home about 30 minutes later. Grigsby testified that her daughter appeared "scared" and a "little hyper." Id., at 77-78. Grigsby proceeded to question her daughter about what had happened. At trial, Grigsby testified that S.G. repeated her claims that petitioner choked and threatened her. Grigsby also testified that S.G. stated that petitioner "put his mouth on her front part." Id., at 79. Grigsby also noticed that S.G. had bruises and red marks on her neck that had not been there previously. Id., at 81. Grigsby called the police.

Officer Terry Lewis arrived a few minutes later, roughly 45 minutes after S.G.'s scream had first awakened DeVore. Lewis questioned S.G. alone in the kitchen. At trial, Lewis' summary of S.G.'s statement indicated that she had offered essentially the same story as she had first reported to DeVore and to Grigsby, including a statement that petitioner had "used his tongue on her in her private parts." Id., at 110-112.

After Lewis concluded his investigation, and approximately four hours after DeVore first heard S.G.'s scream, S.G. was taken to the hospital. She was examined first by Cheryl Reents, an emergency room nurse, and then by Dr. Michael Meinzen. Each testified at trial and their testimony indicated that, in response to questioning, S.G. again provided an account of events that was essentially identical to the one she had given to DeVore, Grigsby, and Lewis.

S.G. never testified at petitioner's trial. The State attempted on two occasions to call her as a witness but she apparently experienced emotional difficulty on being brought to the courtroom and in each instance left without testifying. App. at 14. The defense made no attempt to call S.G. as a witness and the trial court neither made, nor was it asked to make, a finding that S.G. was unavailable to testify. 6 Tr. 105-106.

Petitioner objected on hearsay grounds to DeVore, Grigsby, Lewis, Reents, and Meinzen being permitted to testify regarding S.G.'s statements describing the assault. The trial court overruled each objection. With respect to DeVore, Grigsby, and Lewis the trial court concluded that the testimony could be permitted pursuant to an Illinois hearsay exception for spontaneous declarations. Petitioner's objections to Reents' and Meinzen's testimony was similarly overruled, based on both the spontaneous declaration exception and an exception for statements made in the course of securing medical treatment. The trial court also denied petitioner's motion for a mistrial based on S.G.'s "presence [and] failure to testify." App. 14.

Petitioner was found guilty by a jury, and the Illinois Appellate Court affirmed his conviction. It held that the trial court operated within the discretion accorded it under state law in ruling that the statements offered by DeVore, Grigsby and Lewis qualified for the spontaneous declaration exception and in ruling that the statements offered by Reents and Meinzen qualified for the medical examination exception. 198 Ill. App. 3d 641, 647, 657, 144 Ill. Dec. 722, 727-732, 555 N.E.2d 1241, 1246-1251 (1990). The court then went on to reject petitioner's Confrontation Clause challenge, a challenge based principally on language contained in this Court's decision in Ohio v. Roberts, 448 U.S. 56, 100 S. Ct. 2531, 65 L. Ed. 2d 597 (1980). It concluded that our later decision in United States v. Inadi, 475 U.S. 387, 106 S. Ct. 1121, 89 L. Ed. 2d 390 (1986), foreclosed any rule requiring that, as a necessary antecedent to the introduction of hearsay testimony, the prosecution must either produce the declarant at trial or show that the declarant is unavailable. The Illinois Supreme Court denied discretionary review, and we granted certiorari, 111 S. Ct. 1681, 114 L. Ed. 2d 76 (1991), limited to the constitutional question whether permitting the challenged testimony violated petitioner's Sixth Amendment Confrontation Clause right.

We consider as a preliminary matter an argument not considered below but urged by the United States as amicus curiae in support of respondent. The United States contends that petitioner's Confrontation Clause claim should be rejected because the Confrontation Clause's limited purpose is to prevent a particular abuse common in 16th and 17th century England: prosecuting a defendant through the presentation of ex parte affidavits, without the affiants ever being produced at trial. Because S.G.'s out-of-court statements do not fit this description, the United States suggests that S.G. was not a "witness against" petitioner within the meaning of the Clause. The United States urges this position, apparently in order that we might further conclude that the Confrontation Clause generally does not apply to the introduction of out-of-court statements admitted under an accepted hearsay exception. The only situation in which the Confrontation Clause would apply to such an exception, it argues, would be those few cases where the statement sought to be admitted was in the character of an ex parte affidavit, i.e., where the circumstances surrounding the out-of-court statement's utterance suggest that the statement has been made for the principal purpose of accusing or incriminating the defendant.

Such a narrow reading of the Confrontation Clause, which would virtually eliminate its role in restricting the admission of hearsay testimony, is foreclosed by our prior cases. The discussions in these cases, going back at least as far as Mattox v. United States, 156 U.S. 237, 15 S. Ct. 337, 39 L. Ed. 409 (1895), have included historical examination of the origins of the Confrontation Clause, and of the state of the law of evidence existing at the time the Sixth Amendment was adopted and later. . . . In *Mattox* itself, upon which the Government relies, the Court allowed the recorded testimony of a witness at a prior trial to be admitted. But, in the Court's view, the result was justified not because the hearsay testimony was unlike an ex parte affidavit, but because it came within an established exception to the hearsay rule. We think that the argument presented by the Government comes too late in the day to warrant reexamination of this approach.

We therefore now turn to petitioner's principal contention that our prior decision in *Roberts* requires that his conviction be vacated. In *Roberts* we considered a Confrontation Clause challenge to the introduction at trial of a transcript containing testimony from a probable-cause hearing, where the transcript included testimony from a witness not produced at trial but who had been subject to examination by defendant's counsel at the probable-cause hearing. In the course of rejecting the Confrontation Clause claim in that case, we used language that might suggest that the Confrontation Clause generally requires that a declarant either be produced at trial or be found unavailable before his out-of-court statement may be admitted into evidence. However, we think such an expansive reading of the Clause is negated by our subsequent decision in *Inadi*, supra.

In *Inadi* we considered the admission of out-of-court statements made by a co-conspirator in the course of the conspiracy. As an initial matter, we rejected the proposition that *Roberts* established a rule that "no out-of-court statement would be admissible without a showing of unavailability." 475 U.S., at 392, 106 S. Ct., at 1124. To the contrary, rather than establishing "a wholesale revision of the law of evidence" under the guise of the Confrontation Clause, ibid., we concluded that "*Roberts* must be read consistently with the question it answered, the authority it cited, and its own facts." Id., at 394, 106 S. Ct., at 1125. So understood, *Roberts* stands for the proposition that unavailability analysis is a necessary part of the Confrontation Clause inquiry only when the challenged out-of-court statements were made in the course of a prior judicial proceeding. Ibid.

Having clarified the scope of *Roberts,* the Court in *Inadi* then went on to reject the Confrontation Clause challenge presented there. In particular, we refused to extend the unavailability requirement established in *Roberts* to all out-of-court statements. Our decision rested on two factors. First, unlike former in-court testimony, co-conspirator statements "provide evidence of the conspiracy's context that cannot be replicated, even if the declarant testifies to the same matters in court," *Inadi*, 475 U.S., at 395, 106 S. Ct., at 1126. Also, given a declarant's likely change in status by the time the trial occurs, simply calling the declarant in the hope of having him repeat his prior out-of-court statements is a poor substitute for the full evidentiary significance that flows from statements made when the conspiracy is operating in full force. Ibid.

Second, we observed that there is little benefit, if any, to be accomplished by imposing an "unavailability rule." Such a rule will not work to bar absolutely the introduction of the out-of-court statements; if the declarant either is unavailable, or is available and produced for trial, the statements can be introduced. Id., at 396, 106 S. Ct., at 1126-1127. Nor is an unavailability rule likely to produce much testimony that adds meaningfully to the trial's truth-determining process. Ibid. Many declarants will be subpoenaed by the prosecution or defense, regardless of any Confrontation Clause requirement, while the Compulsory Process Clause and evidentiary rules permitting a defendant to treat witnesses as hostile will aid defendants in obtaining a declarant's live testimony. Id., at 396-398, 106 S. Ct., at 1126-1128. And while an unavailability rule would therefore do little to improve the accuracy of factfinding, it is likely to impose substantial additional burdens on the factfinding process. The prosecution would be required to repeatedly locate and keep continuously available each declarant, even when neither the prosecution nor the defense has any interest in calling the witness to the stand. An additional inquiry would be injected into the question of admissibility of evidence, to be litigated both at trial and on appeal. Id., at 398-399, 106 S. Ct., at 1127-1128.

These observations, although expressed in the context of evaluating co-conspirator statements, apply with full force to the case at hand. We note first that the evidentiary rationale for permitting hearsay testimony regarding spontaneous declarations and statements made in the course of receiving medical care is that such out-of-court declarations are made in contexts that provide substantial guarantees of their trustworthiness. But those same factors that contribute to the statements' reliability cannot be recaptured even by later in-court testimony. A statement that has been offered in a moment of excitement—without the opportunity to reflect on the consequences of one's exclamation—may justifiably carry more weight with a trier of fact than a similar statement offered in the relative calm of the courtroom. Similarly, a statement made in the course of procuring medical services, where the declarant knows that a false statement may cause misdiagnosis or mistreatment, carries special guarantees of credibility that a trier of fact may not think replicated by courtroom testimony. They are thus materially different from the statements at issue in *Roberts,* where the out-of-court statements sought to be introduced were themselves made in the course of a judicial proceeding, and where there was consequently no threat of lost evidentiary value if the out-of-court statements were replaced with live testimony.

The preference for live testimony in the case of statements like those offered in *Roberts* is because of the importance of cross examination, "the greatest legal engine ever invented for the discovery of truth." *Green,* 399 U.S., at 158, 90 S. Ct., at 1935. Thus courts have adopted the general rule prohibiting the receipt of hearsay evidence. But where proffered hearsay has sufficient guarantees of reliability to come within a firmly rooted exception to the hearsay rule, the Confrontation Clause is satisfied.

We therefore think that the out-of-court statements admitted in this case had substantial probative value, value that could not be duplicated simply by the declarant later testifying in court. To exclude such statements would be the height of wrong-headedness given that the Confrontation Clause has as a basic purpose the promotion of the " 'integrity of the factfinding process.' " Coy v. Iowa, 487 U.S. 1012, 1020, 108 S. Ct. 2798, 2802, 101 L. Ed. 2d 857 (1988) (quoting Kentucky v. Stincer, 482 U.S. 730, 736, 107 S. Ct. 2658, 2662, 96 L. Ed. 2d 631 (1987)). And as we have also noted, a statement that qualifies for admission under a "firmly rooted" hearsay exception is so trustworthy that adversarial testing can be expected to add little to its reliability. *Wright,* 497 U.S., at 820-821, 110 S. Ct., at 3149. Given the evidentiary value of such statements, their reliability, and that establishing a generally applicable unavailability rule would have few practical benefits while imposing pointless litigation costs, we see no reason to treat the out-of-court statements in this case differently from those we found admissible in *Inadi.* A contrary rule would result in exactly the kind of "wholesale revision" of the laws of evidence that we expressly disavowed in *Inadi.* We therefore see no basis in *Roberts* or *Inadi* for excluding from trial, under the aegis of the Confrontation Clause, evidence embraced within such exceptions to the hearsay rule as those for spontaneous declarations and statements made for medical treatment. . . .

For the foregoing reasons, the judgment of the Illinois Appellate Court is affirmed.

Justice THOMAS, with whom Justice SCALIA joins, concurring in part and concurring in the judgment.

The Court reaches the correct result under our precedents. I write separately only to suggest that our Confrontation Clause jurisprudence has evolved in a manner that is perhaps inconsistent with the text and history of the Clause itself. The Court unnecessarily rejects, in dicta, the United States' suggestion that the Confrontation Clause in general may not regulate the admission of hearsay evidence. The truth may be that this Court's cases unnecessarily have complicated and confused the relationship between the constitutional right of confrontation and the hearsay rules of evidence.

The Confrontation Clause provides simply that "[i]n all criminal prosecutions, the accused shall enjoy the right . . . to be confronted with the witnesses against him. . . ." U.S. Const., Amend. 6. It is plain that the critical phrase within the Clause for purposes of this case is "witnesses against him." Any attempt at unraveling and understanding the relationship between the Clause and the hearsay rules must begin with an analysis of the meaning of that phrase. Unfortunately, in recent cases in this area, the Court has assumed that all hearsay declarants are "witnesses against" a defendant within the meaning of the Clause, see, e.g., Ohio v. Roberts, 448 U.S. 56, 100 S. Ct. 2531, 65 L. Ed. 2d 597 (1980); Lee v. Illinois, 476 U.S. 530, 106 S. Ct. 2056, 90 L. Ed. 2d 514 (1986); Idaho v. Wright, 497 U.S. 805, 110 S. Ct. 3139, 111 L. Ed. 2d 638 (1990), an assumption that is neither warranted nor supported by the history or text of the Confrontation Clause.

There is virtually no evidence of what the drafters of the Confrontation Clause intended it to mean. See California v. Green, 399 U.S. 149, 176, n.8, 90 S. Ct. 1930, 1944, n.8, 26 L. Ed. 2d 489 (1970) (Harlan, J., concurring); Dutton v. Evans, 400 U.S. 74, 95, 91 S. Ct. 210, 222-223, 27 L. Ed. 2d 213 (1970) (Harlan, J., concurring in result); Baker, The Right to Confrontation, The Hearsay Rules, and Due Process—A Proposal for Determining When Hearsay May Be Used in Criminal Trials, 6 Conn. Law Rev. 529, 532 (1974). The strictest reading would be to construe the phrase "witness against him" to confer on a defendant the right to confront and cross-examine only those witnesses who actually appear and testify at trial. This was Wigmore's view: "The net result, then, under the constitutional rule, is that, so far as testimony is required under the hearsay rule to be taken infrajudicially, it shall be taken in a certain way, namely, subject to cross-examination — not secretly or ex parte away from the accused. The Constitution does not prescribe what kinds of testimonial statements (dying declarations or the like) shall be given infrajudicially—this depends on the law of evidence for the time being—but only what mode of procedure shall be followed—i.e., a cross-examining procedure—in the case of such testimony as is required by the ordinary law of evidence to be given infrajudicially." 5 J. Wigmore, Evidence §1397, p.159 (J. Chadbourn rev. 1974) (footnote omitted). The Wigmore view was endorsed by Justice Harlan in his opinion concurring in the result in Dutton v. Evans, supra, at 94, 91 S. Ct., at 222. It also finds support in the plain language of the Clause. As Justice Scalia recently observed: "The Sixth Amendment does not literally contain a prohibition upon [hearsay] evidence, since it guarantees the defendant only the right to confront the 'witness against him.' As applied in the Sixth Amendment's context of a prosecution, the noun 'witness'—in 1791 as today—could mean either (a) one 'who knows or sees any thing; one personally present' or (b) 'one who gives testimony' or who 'testifies,' i.e., '[i]n judicial proceedings, [one who] make[s] a solemn declaration under oath, for the purpose of establishing or making proof of some fact to a court.' 2 N. Webster, An American Dictionary of the English Language (1828). See also J. Buchanan, Linguae Britannicae Vera Pronunciatio (1757). The former meaning (one 'who knows or sees') would cover hearsay evidence, but is excluded in the Sixth Amendment by the words following the noun: 'witness against him.' The phrase obviously refers to those who give testimony against the defendant at trial." Maryland v. Craig, 497 U.S. [836, 865, 110 S. Ct. 3157, 3173, 111 L. Ed. 2d 666] (1990) (dissenting opinion). The difficulty with the Wigmore-Harlan view in its purest form is its tension with much of the apparent history surrounding the evolution of the right of confrontation at common law and with a long line of this Court's precedent, discussed below. For those reasons, the pure Wigmore-Harlan reading may be an improper construction of the Confrontation Clause.

Relevant historical sources and our own earlier decisions, nonetheless, suggest that a narrower reading of the Clause than the one given to it since 1980 may well be correct. In 16th-century England, magistrates interrogated the prisoner, accomplices, and others prior to trial. These interrogations were "intended only for the information of the court. The prisoner had no right to be, and probably never was, present." 1 J. Stephen, A History of the Criminal Law of England 221 (1883). At the trial itself, "proof was usually given by reading depositions, confessions of accomplices, letters, and the like; and this occasioned frequent demands by the prisoner to have his 'accusers,' i.e., the witnesses against him, brought before him face to face. . . ." Id., at 326. See also 5 Wigmore, supra, §1364, at 13 ("there was . . . no appreciation at all of the necessity of calling a person to the stand as a witness"; rather, it was common practice to obtain "information by consulting informed persons not called into court"); 9 W. Holdsworth, History of English Law 227-229 (3d ed. 1944). The infamous trial of Sir Walter Raleigh on charges of treason in 1603 in which the Crown's primary evidence against him was the confession of an alleged co-conspirator (the confession was repudiated before trial and probably had been obtained by torture) is a well-known example of this feature of English criminal procedure. See Pollitt, The Right of Confrontation: Its History and Modern Dress, 8 J. Pub. L. 381, 388-389 (1959); 1 Stephen, supra, at 333-336; 9 Holdsworth, supra, at 216-217, 226-228.

Apparently in response to such abuses, a common-law right of confrontation began to develop in England during the late 16th and early 17th centuries. 5 Wigmore, supra, §1364, at 23; Pollitt, supra, at 389-390. Justice Story believed that the Sixth Amendment codified some of this common law, 3 J. Story, Commentaries on the Constitution of the United States 662 (1833), and this Court previously has recognized the common-law origins of the right. See Salinger v. United States, 272 U.S. 542, 548, 47 S. Ct. 173, 175, 71 L. Ed. 398 (1926) ("The right of confrontation did not originate with the provision in the Sixth Amendment, but was a common-law right having recognized exceptions"). The Court consistently has indicated that the primary purpose of the Clause was to prevent the abuses which had occurred in England. See Mattox v. United States, 156 U.S. 237, 242, 15 S. Ct. 337, 339, 39 L. Ed. 409 (1895) ("The primary object of the [Confrontation Clause] was to prevent depositions or ex parte affidavits, such as were sometimes admitted in civil cases, being used against the prisoner in lieu of a personal examination and cross-examination of the witness . . ."); California v. Green, 399 U.S., at 156, 90 S. Ct., at 1934 ("It is sufficient to note that the particular vice that gave impetus to the confrontation claim was the practice of trying defendants on 'evidence' which consisted solely of ex parte affidavits or depositions secured by the examining magistrates, thus denying the defendant the opportunity to challenge his accuser in a face-to-face encounter in front of the trier of fact"); id., at 179, 90 S. Ct., at 1946 (Harlan, J., concurring) ("From the scant information available it may tentatively be concluded that the Confrontation Clause was meant to constitutionalize a barrier against flagrant abuses, trials by anonymous accusers, and absentee witnesses"); Dutton v. Evans, 400 U.S., at 94, 91 S. Ct., at 222 (Harlan, J., concurring in result) (the "paradigmatic evil the Confrontation Clause was aimed at" was "trial by affidavit").

There appears to be little if any indication in the historical record that the exceptions to the hearsay rule were understood to be limited by the simultaneously evolving common-law right of confrontation. The Court has never explored the historical evidence on this point. As a matter of plain language, however, it is difficult to see how or why the Clause should apply to hearsay evidence as a general proposition. As Justice Harlan observed:

"If one were to translate the Confrontation Clause into language in more common use today, it would read: 'In all criminal prosecutions, the accused shall enjoy the right to be present and to cross-examine the witnesses against him.' Nothing in this language or in its 18th-century equivalent would connote a purpose to control the scope of the rules of evidence. The language is particularly ill-chosen if what was intended was a prohibition on the use of any hearsay. . . ." Id., 400 U.S., at 95, 91 S. Ct., at 222-223 (opinion concurring in result).

The standards that the Court has developed to implement its assumption that the Confrontation Clause limits admission of hearsay evidence have no basis in the text of the Sixth Amendment. Ever since Ohio v. Roberts, 448 U.S. 56, 100 S. Ct. 2531, 65 L. Ed. 2d 597 (1980), the Court has interpreted the Clause to mean that hearsay may be admitted only under a "firmly rooted" exception, id., at 66, 100 S. Ct., at 2539, or if it otherwise bears "particularized guarantees of trustworthiness," ibid. See, e.g., Idaho v. Wright, 497 U.S., at 805, 110 S. Ct., at 3141; Bourjaily v. United States, 483 U.S. 171, 183, 107 S. Ct. 2775, 2782-2783, 97 L. Ed. 2d 144 (1987). This analysis implies that the Confrontation Clause bars only unreliable hearsay. Although the historical concern with trial by affidavit and anonymous accusers does reflect concern with the reliability of the evidence against a defendant, the Clause makes no distinction based on the reliability of the evidence presented. Nor does it seem likely that the drafters of the Sixth Amendment intended to permit a defendant to be tried on the basis of ex parte affidavits found to be reliable. Cf. U.S. Const., Art. III, §3 ("No person shall be convicted of Treason unless on the Testimony of two Witnesses to the same overt Act, or on Confession in open Court"). Reliability is more properly a due process concern. There is no reason to strain the text of the Confrontation Clause to provide criminal defendants with a protection that due process already provides them.

The United States, as amicus curiae, has suggested that the Confrontation Clause should apply only to those persons who provide in-court testimony or the functional equivalent, such as affidavits, depositions, or confessions that are made in contemplation of legal proceedings. This interpretation is in some ways more consistent with the text and history of the Clause than our current jurisprudence, and it is largely consistent with our cases. If not carefully formulated, however, this approach might be difficult to apply, and might develop in a manner not entirely consistent with the crucial "witnesses against him" phrase.

In this case, for example, the victim's statements to the investigating police officer might be considered the functional equivalent of in-court testimony because the statements arguably were made in contemplation of legal proceedings. Attempts to draw a line between statements made in contemplation of legal proceedings and those not so made would entangle the courts in a multitude of difficulties. Few types of statements could be categorically characterized as within or without the reach of a defendant's confrontation rights. Not even statements made to the police or government officials could be deemed automatically subject to the right of confrontation (imagine a victim who blurts out an accusation to a passing police officer, or the unsuspecting social-services worker who is told of possible child abuse). It is also not clear under the United States' approach whether the declarant or the listener (or both) must be contemplating legal proceedings. The United States devotes little attention to the application of its proposed standard in this case.

Thus, we are faced with a situation in which the text of the Sixth Amendment supports the Wigmore-Harlan view but history and our earlier cases point away from that strictest reading of the text. Despite this tension, I believe it is possible to interpret the Confrontation Clause along the lines suggested by the United States in a manner that is faithful to both the provision's text and history. One possible formulation is as follows: The federal constitutional right of confrontation extends to any witness who actually testifies at trial, but the Confrontation Clause is implicated by extrajudicial statements only insofar as they are contained in formalized testimonial materials, such as affidavits, depositions, prior testimony, or confessions. It was this discrete category of testimonial materials that was historically abused by prosecutors as a means of depriving criminal defendants of the benefit of the adversary process, see, e.g., Mattox v. United States, 156 U.S. 237, 242-243, 15 S. Ct. 337, 239-240, 39 L. Ed. 409 (1895), and under this approach, the Confrontation Clause would not be construed to extend beyond the historical evil to which it was directed.

Such an approach would be consistent with the vast majority of our cases, since virtually all of them decided before Ohio v. Roberts involved prior testimony or confessions, exactly the type of formalized testimonial evidence that lies at the core of the Confrontation Clause's concern. This narrower reading of the Confrontation Clause would greatly simplify the inquiry in the hearsay context. Furthermore, this interpretation would avoid the problem posed by the Court's current focus on hearsay exceptions that are "firmly rooted" in the common law. The Court has never explained the Confrontation Clause implications of a State's decision to adopt an exception not recognized at common law or one not recognized by a majority of the States. Our current jurisprudence suggests that, in order to satisfy the Sixth Amendment, the State would have to establish in each individual case that hearsay admitted pursuant to the newly created exception bears "particularized guarantees of trustworthiness," and would have to continue doing so until the exception became "firmly rooted" in the common law, if that is even possible under the Court's standard. This result is difficult to square with the Clause itself. Neither the language of the Clause nor the historical evidence appears to support the notion that the Confrontation Clause was intended to constitutionalize the hearsay rule and its exceptions. Although the Court repeatedly has disavowed any intent to cause that result, see, e.g., Idaho v. Wright, 497 U.S., at 806, 110 S. Ct., at 3141-3142; United States v. Inadi, 475 U.S. 387, 393, n.5, 106 S. Ct. 1121, 1125, n.5, 89 L. Ed. 2d 390 (1986); Dutton v. Evans, 400 U.S., at 86, 91 S. Ct., at 218; California v. Green, 399 U.S., at 155, 90 S. Ct., at 1933-1934, I fear that our decisions have edged ever further in that direction.

For the foregoing reasons, I respectfully suggest that, in an appropriate case, we reconsider how the phrase "witness against" in the Confrontation Clause pertains to the admission of hearsay. I join the Court's opinion except for its discussion of the narrow reading of this phrase proposed by the United States.

LILLY v. VIRGINIA
527 U.S. 116, 119 S. CT. 1887 (1999)

Justice STEVENS announced the judgment of the Court and delivered the opinion of the Court with respect to Parts I, II, and VI, and an opinion with respect to Parts III, IV, and V, in which Justice SOUTER, Justice GINSBURG, and Justice BREYER join.

The question presented in this case is whether the accused's Sixth Amendment right "to be confronted with the witnesses against him" was violated by admitting into evidence at his trial a nontestifying accomplice's entire confession that contained some statements against the accomplice's penal interest and others that inculpated the accused.

I

On December 4, 1995, three men—Benjamin Lee Lilly (petitioner), his brother Mark, and Mark's roommate, Gary Wayne Barker—broke into a home and stole nine bottles of liquor, three loaded guns, and a safe. The next day, the men drank the stolen liquor, robbed a small country store, and shot at geese with their stolen weapons. After their car broke down, they abducted Alex DeFilippis and used his vehicle to drive to a deserted location. One of them shot and killed DeFilippis. The three men then committed two more robberies before they were apprehended by the police late in the evening of December 5.

After taking them into custody, the police questioned each of the three men separately. Petitioner did not mention the murder to the police and stated that the other two men had forced him to participate in the robberies. Petitioner's brother Mark and Barker told the police somewhat different accounts of the crimes, but both maintained that petitioner masterminded the robberies and was the one who had killed DeFilippis.

A tape recording of Mark's initial oral statement indicates that he was questioned from 1:35 A.M. until 2:12 A.M. on December 6. The police interrogated him again from 2:30 A.M. until 2:53 A.M. During both interviews, Mark continually emphasized how drunk he had been during the entire spree. When asked about his participation in the string of crimes, Mark admitted that he stole liquor during the initial burglary and that he stole a 12-pack of beer during the robbery of the liquor store. Mark also conceded that he had handled a gun earlier that day and that he was present during the more serious thefts and the homicide.

The police told Mark that he would be charged with armed robbery and that, unless he broke "family ties," petitioner "may be dragging you right into a life sentence," App. 257. Mark acknowledged that he would be sent away to the penitentiary. He claimed, however, that while he had primarily been drinking, petitioner and Barker had "got some guns or something" during the initial burglary. Id. at 250. Mark said that Barker had pulled a gun in one of the robberies. He further insisted that petitioner had instigated the carjacking and that he (Mark) "didn't have nothing to do with the shooting" of DeFilippis. Id. at 256. In a brief portion of one of his statements, Mark stated that petitioner was the one who shot DeFilippis.

The Commonwealth of Virginia charged petitioner with several offenses, including the murder of DeFilippis, and tried him separately. At trial, the Commonwealth called Mark as a witness, but he invoked his Fifth Amendment privilege against self-incrimination. The Commonwealth therefore offered to introduce into evidence the statements Mark made to the police after his arrest, arguing that they were admissible as declarations of an unavailable witness against penal interest. Petitioner objected on the ground that the statements were not actually against Mark's penal interest because they shifted responsibility for the crimes to Barker and to petitioner, and that their admission would violate the Sixth Amendment's Confrontation Clause. The trial judge overruled the objection and admitted the tape recordings and written transcripts of the statements in their entirety. The jury found petitioner guilty of robbery, abduction, carjacking, possession of a firearm by a felon, and four charges of illegal use of a firearm, for which offenses he received consecutive prison sentences of two life terms plus 27 years. The jury also convicted petitioner of capital murder and recommended a sentence of death, which the court imposed.

The Supreme Court of Virginia affirmed petitioner's convictions and sentences. As is relevant here, the court first concluded that Mark's statements were declarations of an unavailable witness against penal interest; that the statements' reliability was established by other evidence; and, therefore, that they fell within an exception to the Virginia hearsay rule. The court then turned to petitioner's Confrontation Clause challenge. It began by relying on our opinion in White v. Illinois, 502 U.S. 346, 116 L. Ed. 2d 848, 112 S. Ct. 736 (1992), for the proposition that "'where proffered hearsay has sufficient guarantees of reliability to come within a firmly rooted exception to the hearsay rule, the Confrontation Clause is satisfied.'" 255 Va. 558, 574, 499 S.E.2d 522, 534 (1998) (quoting White, 502 U.S. at 356). The Virginia court also remarked:

> "Admissiblity into evidence of the statement against penal interest of an unavailable witness is a 'firmly rooted' exception to the hearsay rule in Virginia. Thus, we hold that the trial court did not err in admitting Mark Lilly's statements into evidence." Id. at 575, 499 S.E.2d at 534.
>
> "That Mark Lilly's statements were self-serving, in that they tended to shift principal responsibility to others or to offer claims of mitigating circumstances, goes to the weight the jury could assign to them and not to their admissibility." Id. at 574, 499 S.E.2d at 534.

Our concern that this decision represented a significant departure from our Confrontation Clause jurisprudence prompted us to grant certiorari. 525 U.S. — (1998). . . .

III

In all criminal prosecutions, state as well as federal, the accused has a right, guaranteed by the Sixth and Fourteenth Amendments to the United States Constitution, "to be confronted with the witnesses against him." U.S. Const., Amdt. 6; Pointer v. Texas, 380 U.S. 400, 13 L. Ed. 2d 923, 85 S. Ct. 1065 (1965) (applying Sixth Amendment to the States). "The central concern of the Confrontation Clause is to ensure the reliability of the evidence against a criminal defendant by subjecting it to rigorous testing in the context of an adversary proceeding before the trier of fact." Maryland v. Craig, 497 U.S. 836, 845, 111 L. Ed. 2d 666, 110 S. Ct. 3157 (1990). When the government seeks to offer a declarant's out-of-court statements against the accused, and, as in this case, the declarant is unavailable, courts must decide whether the Clause permits the government to deny the accused his usual right to force the declarant "to submit to cross-examination, the 'greatest legal engine ever invented for the discovery of truth.'" California v. Green, 399 U.S. 149, 158, 26 L. Ed. 2d 489, 90 S. Ct. 1930 (1970).

In our most recent case interpreting the Confrontation Clause, White v. Illinois, 502 U.S. 346, 116 L. Ed. 2d 848, 112 S. Ct. 736 (1992), we rejected the suggestion that the Clause should be narrowly construed to apply only to practices comparable to "a particular abuse common in 16th- and 17th-century England: prosecuting a defendant through the presentation of *ex parte* affidavits, without the affiants ever being produced at trial." Id. at 352. This abuse included using out-of-court depositions and "confessions of accomplices." *Green,* 399 U.S. at 157. Accord *White,* 502 U.S. at 361, 363 (noting that this rule applies even if the confession is "found to be reliable") (THOMAS, J., concurring in part and concurring in judgment). Because that restrictive reading of the Clause's term "witnesses" would have virtually eliminated the Clause's role in restricting the admission of hearsay testimony, we considered it foreclosed by our prior cases. Instead, we adhered to our general framework, summarized in Ohio v. Roberts, 448 U.S. 56, 65 L. Ed. 2d 597, 100 S. Ct. 2531 (1980), that the veracity of hearsay statements is sufficiently dependable to allow the untested admission of such statements against an accused when (1) "the evidence falls within a firmly rooted hearsay exception" or (2) it contains "particularized guarantees of trustworthiness" such that adversarial testing would be expected to add little, if anything, to the statements' reliability. Id. at 66.

Before turning to the dual *Roberts* inquiries, however, we note that the statements taken from petitioner's brother in the early morning of December 6 were obviously obtained for the purpose of creating evidence that would be useful at a future trial. The analogy to the presentation of *ex parte* affidavits in the early English proceedings thus brings the Confrontation Clause into play no matter how narrowly its gateway might be read.

IV

The Supreme Court of Virginia held that the admission of Mark Lilly's confession was constitutional primarily because, in its view, it was against Mark's penal interest and because "the statement against penal interest of an unavailable witness is a 'firmly rooted' exception to the hearsay rule in Virginia." 255 Va. at 575, 449 S.E.2d at 534. We assume, as we must, that Mark's statements were against his penal interest as a matter of state law, but the question whether the statements fall within a firmly rooted hearsay exception for Confrontation Clause purposes is a question of federal law. Accordingly, it is appropriate to begin our analysis by examining the "firmly rooted" doctrine and the roots of the "against penal interest" exception.

We have allowed the admission of statements falling within a firmly rooted hearsay exception since the Court's recognition in Mattox v. United States that the Framers of the Sixth Amendment "obviously intended to . . . respect" certain unquestionable rules of evidence in drafting the Confrontation Clause. Justice Brown, writing for the Court in that case, did not question the wisdom of excluding deposition testimony, *ex parte* affidavits and their equivalents. But he reasoned that an unduly strict and "technical" reading of the Clause would have the effect of excluding other hearsay evidence, such as dying declarations, whose admissibility neither the Framers nor anyone else 100 years later "would have [had] the hardihood . . . to question." *Ibid.*

We now describe a hearsay exception as "firmly rooted" if, in light of "longstanding judicial and legislative experience," Idaho v. Wright, it "rests [on] such [a] solid foundation that admission of virtually any evidence within [it] comports with the 'substance of the constitutional protection.'" Ohio v. Roberts (quoting *Mattox*). This standard is designed to allow the introduction of statements falling within a category of hearsay whose conditions have proven over time "to remove all temptation to falsehood, and to enforce as strict an adherence to the truth as would the obligation of an oath" and cross-examination at a trial. *Mattox.* In *White*, for instance, we held that the hearsay exception for spontaneous declarations is firmly rooted because it "is at least two centuries old," currently "widely accepted among the States," and carries "substantial guarantees of . . . trustworthiness . . . [that] cannot be recaptured even by later in-court testimony." Established practice, in short, must confirm that statements falling within a category of hearsay inherently "carry special guarantees of credibility" essentially equivalent to, or greater than, those produced by the Constitution's preference for cross-examined trial testimony.

The "against penal interest" exception to the hearsay rule—unlike other previously recognized firmly rooted exceptions—is not generally based on the maxim that statements made without a motive to reflect on the legal consequences of one's statement, and in situations that are exceptionally conducive to veracity, lack the dangers of inaccuracy that typically accompany hearsay. The exception, rather, is founded on the broad assumption "that a person is unlikely to fabricate a statement against his own interest at the time it is made." Chambers v. Mississippi, 410 U.S. 284, 299, 35 L. Ed. 2d 297, 93 S. Ct. 1038 (1973).

We have previously noted that, due to the sweeping scope of the label, the simple categorization of a statement as a "'declaration against penal interest' . . . defines too large a class for meaningful Confrontation Clause analysis." Lee v. Illinois, 476 U.S. at 544, n. 5. In criminal trials, statements against penal interest are offered into evidence in three principal situations: (1) as voluntary admissions against the declarant; (2) as exculpatory evidence offered by a defendant who claims that the declarant committed, or was involved in, the offense; and (3) as evidence offered by the prosecution to establish the guilt of an alleged accomplice of the declarant. It is useful to consider the three categories and their roots separately.

Statements in the first category—voluntary admissions of the declarant—are routinely offered into evidence against the maker of the statement and carry a distinguished heritage confirming their admissibility when so used. See G. Gilbert, Evidence 139-140 (1756); Lambe's Case, 2 Leach 552, 168 Eng. Rep. 379 (1791); State v. Kirby, 32 S.C. L. 155, 1 Strob. 155, 156 (1846); State v. Cowan, 29 N.C. 239, 246 (1847). Thus, assuming that Mark Lilly's statements were taken in conformance with constitutional prerequisites, they would unquestionably be admissible against him if he were on trial for stealing alcoholic beverages.

If Mark were a codefendant in a joint trial, however, even the use of his confession to prove his guilt might have an adverse impact on the rights of his accomplices. When dealing with admissions against penal interest, we have taken great care to separate using admissions against the declarant (the first category above) from using them against other criminal defendants (the third category).

In Bruton v. United States, 391 U.S. 123, 20 L. Ed. 2d 476, 88 S. Ct. 1620 (1968), two codefendants, Evans and Bruton, were tried jointly and convicted of armed postal robbery. A postal inspector testified that Evans had orally confessed that he and Bruton had committed the crime. The jury was instructed that Evans' confession was admissible against him, but could not be considered in assessing Bruton's guilt. Despite that instruction, this Court concluded that the introduction of

Evans' confession posed such a serious threat to Bruton's right to confront and cross-examine the witnesses against him that he was entitled to a new trial. The case is relevant to the issue before us today, not because of its principal holding concerning the ability or inability of the jury to follow the judge's instruction, but rather because it was common ground among all of the Justices that the fact that the confession was a statement against the penal interest of Evans did not justify its use against Bruton. As Justice White noted at the outset of his dissent, "nothing in that confession which was relevant and material to Bruton's case was admissible against Bruton." Id. at 138.

In the years since *Bruton* was decided, we have reviewed a number of cases in which one defendant's confession has been introduced into evidence in a joint trial pursuant to instructions that it could be used against him but not against his codefendant. Despite frequent disagreement over matters such as the adequacy of the trial judge's instructions, or the sufficiency of the redaction of ambiguous references to the declarant's accomplice, we have consistently either stated or assumed that the mere fact that one accomplice's confession qualified as a statement against his penal interest did not justify its use as evidence against another person. . . .

The second category of statements against penal interest encompasses those offered as exculpatory evidence by a defendant who claims that it was the maker of the statement, rather than he, who committed (or was involved in) the crime in question. In this context, our Court, over the dissent of Justice Holmes, originally followed the 19th-century English rule that categorically refused to recognize any "against penal interest" exception to the hearsay rule, holding instead that under federal law only hearsay statements against pecuniary (and perhaps proprietary) interest were sufficiently reliable to warrant their admission at the trial of someone other than the declarant. See Donnelly v. United States, 228 U.S. 243, 272-277, 57 L. Ed. 820, 33 S. Ct. 449 (1913). Indeed, most States adhered to this approach well into the latter half of the 20th century. See *Chambers,* 410 U.S. at 299 (collecting citations).

As time passed, however, the precise *Donnelly* rule, which barred the admission of other persons' confessions that exculpated the accused, became the subject of increasing criticism. Professor Wigmore, for example, remarked years after *Donnelly* that:

"The only practical consequences of this unreasoning limitation are shocking to the sense of justice; for, in its commonest application, it requires, in a criminal trial, the rejection of a confession, however well authenticated, of a person deceased or insane or fled from the jurisdiction (and therefore quite unavailable) who has avowed himself to be the true culprit. . . . It is therefore not too late to retrace our steps, and to discard this barbarous doctrine, which would refuse to let an innocent accused vindicate himself even by producing to the tribunal a perfectly authenticated written confession, made on the very gallows, by the true culprit now beyond the reach of justice."

5 J. Wigmore, Evidence §1477, pp. 289-290 (3d ed. 1940)....

Finally, in 1973, this Court endorsed the more enlightened view in *Chambers*, holding that the Due Process Clause affords criminal defendants the right to introduce into evidence third parties' declarations against penal interest—their confessions—when the circumstances surrounding the statements "provide considerable assurance of their reliability." 410 U.S. at 300. Not surprisingly, most States have now amended their hearsay rules to allow the admission of such statements under against-penal-interest exceptions. See 5 J. Wigmore, Evidence §1476; p. 352, and n.9 (J. Chadbourn rev. 1974); id. §1477, p. 360, and n.7; J. Wigmore, Evidence §§1476 and 1477, pp. 618-626 (A. Best ed. Supp. 1998). But because hearsay statements of this sort are, by definition, offered by the accused, the admission of such statements does not implicate Confrontation Clause concerns. Thus, there is no need to decide whether the reliability of such statements is so inherently dependable that they would constitute a firmly rooted hearsay exception.

The third category includes cases, like the one before us today, in which the government seeks to introduce "a confession by an accomplice which incriminates a criminal defendant." Lee, 476 U.S. at 544, n.5. The practice of admitting statements in this category under an exception to the hearsay rule—to the extent that such a practice exists in certain jurisdictions—is, unlike the first category or even the second, of quite recent vintage. This category also typically includes statements that, when offered in the absence of the declarant, function similarly to those used in the ancient *ex parte* affidavit system.

Most important, this third category of hearsay encompasses statements that are inherently unreliable. Typical of the groundswell of scholarly and judicial criticism that culminated in the *Chambers* decision, Wigmore's treatise still expressly distinguishes accomplices' confessions that inculpate themselves and the accused as beyond a proper understanding of the against-penal-interest exception because an accomplice often has a considerable interest in "confessing and betraying his co-criminals." 5 Wigmore, Evidence §1477, at 358, n.1. Consistent with this scholarship and the assumption that underlies the analysis in our *Bruton* line of cases, we have over the years "spoken with one voice in declaring presumptively unreliable accomplices' confessions that incriminate defendants." *Lee*, 476 U.S. at 541. See also *Cruz*, 481 U.S. at 195 (White, J., dissenting) (such statements "have traditionally been viewed with special suspicion"); *Bruton*, 391 U.S. at 136 (such statements are "inevitably suspect")....

It is clear that our cases consistently have viewed an accomplice's statements that shift or spread the blame to a criminal defendant as falling outside the realm of those "hearsay exceptions [that are] so trustworthy that adversarial testing can be expected to add little to [the statements'] reliability." *White,* 502 U.S. at 357. This view is also reflected in several States' hearsay law. Indeed, prior to 1995, it appears that even Virginia rarely allowed statements against the penal interest of the declarant to be used at criminal trials. See, e.g., Ellison v. Commonwealth, 219 Va. 404, 247 S.E.2d 685 (1978). That Virginia relaxed that portion of its hearsay law when it decided Chandler v. Commonwealth, 249 Va. 270, 455 S.E.2d 219 (1995), and that it later apparently concluded that all statements against penal interest fall within "a 'firmly rooted' exception to the hearsay rule in Virginia," 255 Va. at 575, 499 S.E.2d at 534, is of no consequence. The decisive fact, which we make explicit today, is that accomplices' confessions that inculpate a criminal defendant are not within a firmly rooted exception to the hearsay rule as that concept has been defined in our Confrontation Clause jurisprudence.

V

Aside from its conclusion that Mark's statements were admissible under a firmly rooted hearsay exception, the Supreme Court of Virginia also affirmed the trial court's holding that the statements were "reliable . . . in the context of the facts and circumstances under which [they were] given" because (i) "Mark Lilly was cognizant of the import of his statements and that he was implicating himself as a participant in numerous crimes" and (ii) "elements of [his] statements were independently corroborated" by other evidence offered at trial. Id. at 574, 499 S.E.2d at 534. See also App. 18 (trial court's decision). The Commonwealth contends that we should defer to this "fact-intensive" determination. It further argues that these two indicia of reliability, coupled with the facts that the police read Mark his *Miranda* rights and did not promise him leniency in exchange for his statements, demonstrate that the circumstances surrounding his statements bore "particularized guarantees of trustworthiness," *Roberts,* 448 U.S. at 66, sufficient to satisfy the Confrontation Clause's residual admissibility test.

The residual "trustworthiness" test credits the axiom that a rigid application of the Clause's standard for admissibility might in an exceptional case exclude a statement of an unavailable witness that is incontestably probative, competent, and reliable, yet nonetheless outside of any firmly rooted hearsay exception. When a court can be confident — as in the context of hearsay falling within a firmly rooted exception — that "the declarant's truthfulness is so clear from the surrounding circumstances that the test of cross-examination would be of marginal utility," the Sixth Amendment's residual "trustworthiness" test allows the admission of the declarant's statements. *Wright,* 497 U.S. at 820.

Nothing in our prior opinions, however, suggests that appellate courts should defer to lower courts' determinations regarding whether a hearsay statement has particularized guarantees of trustworthiness. To the contrary, those opinions indicate that we have assumed, as with other fact-intensive, mixed questions of constitutional law, that "independent review is . . . necessary . . . to maintain control of, and to clarify, the legal principles" governing the factual circumstances necessary to satisfy the protections of the Bill of Rights. Ornelas v. United States, 517 U.S. 690, 697, 134 L. Ed. 2d 911, 116 S. Ct. 1657 (1996) (holding that appellate courts should review reasonable suspicion and probable cause determinations *de novo*). We, of course, accept the Virginia courts' determination that Mark's statements were reliable for purposes of state hearsay law, and, as should any appellate court, we review the presence or absence of historical facts for clear error. But the surrounding circumstances relevant to a Sixth Amendment admissibility determination do not include the declarant's in-court demeanor (otherwise the declarant would be testifying) or any other factor uniquely suited to the province of trial courts. For these reasons, when deciding whether the admission of a declarant's out-of-court statements violates the Confrontation Clause, courts should independently review whether the government's proffered guarantees of trustworthiness satisfy the demands of the Clause. . . .

[T]he Commonwealth's asserted guarantees of trustworthiness fail to convince us that Mark's confession was sufficiently reliable as to be admissible without allowing petitioner to cross-examine him. That other evidence at trial corroborated portions of Mark's statements is irrelevant. We have squarely rejected the notion that "evidence corroborating the truth of a hearsay statement may properly support a finding that the statement bears 'particularized guarantees of trustworthiness.'" *Wright,* 497 U.S. at 822. In *Wright,* we concluded that the admission of hearsay statements by a child declarant violated the Confrontation Clause even though the statements were admissible under an exception to the hearsay rule recognized in Idaho, and even though they were corroborated by other evidence. We recognized that it was theoretically possible for such statements to possess "'particularized guarantees of trustworthiness'" that would justify their admissibility, but we refused to allow the State to "bootstrap on" the trustworthiness of other evidence. "To be admissible under the Confrontation Clause," we held, "hearsay evidence used to convict a defendant must possess indicia of reliability by virtue of its inherent trustworthiness, not by reference to other evidence at trial." *Ibid.*

Nor did the police's informing Mark of his *Miranda* rights render the circumstances surrounding his statements significantly more trustworthy. We noted in rejecting a similar argument in *Lee* that a finding that a confession was "voluntary for Fifth Amendment purposes . . . does not bear on the question of whether the confession was also free from any desire, motive, or impulse [the declarant] may have had either to mitigate the appearance of his own culpability by spreading the blame or to overstate [the defendant's] involvement" in the crimes at issue. 476 U.S. at 544. By the same token, we believe that a suspect's consciousness of his *Miranda* rights has little, if any, bearing on the likelihood of truthfulness of his statements. When a suspect is in custody for his obvious involvement in serious crimes, his knowledge that anything he says may be used against him militates against depending on his veracity.

The Commonwealth's next proffered basis for reliability—that Mark knew he was exposing himself to criminal liability—merely restates the fact that portions of his statements were technically against penal interest. And as we have explained, such statements are suspect insofar as they inculpate other persons. "That a person is making a broadly self-inculpatory confession does not make more credible the confession's non-self-inculpatory parts." *Williamson,* 512 U.S. at 599. Accord, *Lee,* 476 U.S. at 545. Similarly, the absence of an express promise of leniency to Mark does not enhance his statements' reliability to the level necessary for their untested admission. The police need not tell a person who is in custody that his statements may gain him leniency in order for the suspect to surmise that speaking up, and particularly placing blame on his cohorts, may inure to his advantage.

It is abundantly clear that neither the words that Mark spoke nor the setting in which he was questioned provides any basis for concluding that his comments regarding petitioner's guilt were so reliable that there was no need to subject them to adversarial testing in a trial setting. Mark was in custody for his involvement in, and knowledge of, serious crimes and made his statements under the supervision of governmental authorities. He was primarily responding to the officers' leading questions, which were asked without any contemporaneous cross-examination by adverse parties. Thus, Mark had a natural motive to attempt to exculpate himself as much as possible. Mark also was obviously still under the influence of alcohol. Each of these factors militates against finding that his statements were so inherently reliable that cross-examination would have been superfluous.

VI

Accordingly, the judgment of the Supreme Court of Virginia is reversed, and the case is remanded for further proceedings not inconsistent with this opinion.

It is so ordered.

Chief Justice REHNQUIST, with whom Justice O'CONNOR and Justice KENNEDY join, concurring in the judgment.

The plurality today concludes that all accomplice confessions that inculpate a criminal defendant are not within a firmly rooted exception to the hearsay rule under Ohio v. Roberts. It also concludes that appellate courts should independently review the government's proffered guarantees of trustworthiness under the second half of the *Roberts* inquiry. I disagree with both of these conclusions, but concur in the judgment reversing the decision of the Supreme Court of Virginia.

I

The plurality correctly states the issue in this case in the opening sentence of its opinion: Whether petitioner's Confrontation Clause rights were violated by admission of an accomplice's confession "that contained some statements against the accomplice's penal interest and others that inculpated the accused." The confession of the accomplice, Mark Lilly, covers 50 pages in the Joint Appendix, and the interviews themselves lasted about an hour. The statements of Mark Lilly which are against his penal interest—and would probably show him as an aider and abettor — are quite separate in time and place from other statements exculpating Mark and incriminating his brother, petitioner Benjamin Lilly, in the murder of Alexis DeFilippis.

Thus one is at a loss to know why so much of the plurality's opinion is devoted to whether a declaration against penal interest is a "firmly rooted exception" to the hearsay rule under Ohio v. Roberts. Certainly, we must accept the Virginia court's determination that Mark's statements as a whole were declarations against penal interest for purposes of the Commonwealth's hearsay rule. Simply labeling a confession a "declaration against penal interest," however, is insufficient for purposes of *Roberts*, as this exception "defines too large a class for meaningful Confrontation Clause analysis." Lee v. Illinois, 476 U.S. 530, 544, n. 5, 106 S. Ct. 2056 (1986). The plurality tries its hand at systematizing this class, but most of its housecleaning is unwarranted and results in a complete ban on the government's use of accomplice confessions that inculpate a codefendant. Such a categorical holding has no place in this case because the relevant portions of Mark Lilly's confession were simply not "declarations against penal interest" as that term is understood in the law of evidence. There may be close cases where the declaration against penal interest portion is closely tied in with the portion incriminating the defendant, see 2 J. Strong, McCormick on Evidence §319 (4th ed. 1992), but this is not one of them. Mark Lilly's statements inculpating his brother in the murder of DeFilippis are not in the least against Mark's penal interest. . . .

The plurality's blanket ban on the government's use of accomplice statements that incriminate a defendant thus sweeps beyond the facts of this case and our precedent, ignoring both the exculpatory nature of Mark's confession and the circumstances in which it was given. Unlike the plurality, I would limit our holding here to the case at hand, and decide only that the Mark Lilly's custodial confession laying sole responsibility on petitioner cannot satisfy a firmly rooted hearsay exception. . . .

CHAPTER VII

Privileges

A. Privileges in General

In Chapter II, we explored the fundamental rule of evidence that all relevant evidence is admissible and all irrelevant evidence is inadmissible. The premise on which this primary rule is based is that accurate factfinding in an adversary system of justice is promoted when the factfinder has all the information that bears on the issues in dispute. As we have seen, there are many exceptions to the primary rule. But virtually all the exceptions we have examined to this point have been justified on the grounds that the excluded evidence is likely to undermine the factfinding process because of the unreliability or prejudicial nature of the evidence or its capacity to mislead or confuse the factfinder. Concededly, some of the categorical rules of exclusion, such as Rules 407 to 412 (evidence of subsequent repairs, compromise offers, payment of medical expenses, pleas, liability insurance, and prior sexual history), are based at least in part on policy considerations not directly connected to the truth-promoting principle, but, as seen, the legitimacy of these rules is a matter of controversy, and there is strong pressure to eliminate some of them.

The evidentiary privileges are the most important set of rules that operate to exclude relevant, nonprejudicial, and nonconfusing evidence for reasons completely unrelated to the truth-promoting principle. Is there a unifying principle that justifies departure from the quest for truth in these instances? Or does the existing system of privileges simply reflect ad hoc policy judgments on specific issues or, more cynically, the relative power of various economic or social interests?

Our examination of this and other issues begins by considering some general philosophical questions raised by the nature and justification of privileges. These issues are explored more specifically in connection with the assertion of a reporter's privilege in the *Farber* case and juxtaposed with the privileges applicable to communications to clergy, psychotherapists, and lawyers. The remainder of the chapter pursues issues raised in the introductory section while treating in greater detail the two of the most frequently encountered traditional privileges—lawyer-client, husband-wife and a less traditional privilege which is becoming of greater significance—the psychotherapist-patient privilege.

On the conceptual level, it is interesting to observe how commentators' and judges' views on specific privileges seem to be colored by the underlying philosophical approach they take to the subject. These approaches range from the utilitarian, instrumental, or pragmatic view to the humanistic.

The classic utilitarian approach is Wigmore's. Starting from the premise that "the public is entitled to every man's evidence" and that exemptions from this rule are exceptional and to be discountenanced, Wigmore posits four conditions that must be fulfilled to justify a privilege:

> (1) The communications must originate in a *confidence* that they will not be disclosed.
>
> (2) This element of *confidentiality must be essential* to the full and satisfactory maintenance of the relation between the parties.
>
> (3) The *relation* must be one which in the opinion of the community ought to be sedulously *fostered.*
>
> (4) The *injury* that would inure to the relation by the disclosure of the communications must be *greater than the benefit* thereby gained for the correct disposal of litigation.

8 Wigmore, Evidence §§2191, 2192, 2285 (McNaughton rev. 1961). Note the dual focus in Wigmore's formula on the instrumental purpose of the communication and the cost/benefit effect on the litigation process.

In the *Nixon* tapes case, United States v. Nixon, 418 U.S. 683 (1974), the Supreme Court applied this utilitarian approach to the president's claim of a privilege for confidential presidential communications. In rejecting the President's claim of privilege in the specific case before it, the Court took pains to highlight the fundamental inconsistency between privileges and accuracy in the judicial process:

> But this presumptive privilege [for Presidential communications] must be considered in light of our historic commitment to the rule of law. This is nowhere more profoundly manifest than in our view that "the twofold aim [of criminal justice] is that guilt shall not escape or innocence suffer." Berger v. United States, 295 U.S., at 88. We have elected to employ an adversary system of criminal justice in which the parties contest all issues before a court of law. The need to develop all relevant facts in the adversary system is both fundamental and comprehensive.

The ends of criminal justice would be defeated if judgments were to be founded on a partial or speculative presentation of the facts. The very integrity of the judicial system and public confidence in the system depend on full disclosure of all the facts, within the framework of the rules of evidence. To ensure that justice is done, it is imperative to the function of courts that compulsory process be available for the production of evidence needed either by the prosecution or by the defense.

Only recently the Court restated the ancient proposition of law, albeit in the context of a grand jury inquiry rather than a trial, "That 'the public . . . has a right to every man's evidence,' except for those persons protected by a constitutional, common-law, or statutory privilege, United States v. Bryan, 339 U.S. [323, 331 (1950)]; Blackmer v. United States, 284 U.S. 421, 438 (1932). . . ." Branzburg v. Hayes, 408 U.S. 665, 688 (1972). The privileges referred to by the Court are designed to protect weighty and legitimate competing interests. Thus, the Fifth Amendment to the Constitution provides that no man "shall be compelled in any criminal case to be a witness against himself." And, generally, an attorney or a priest may not be required to disclose what has been revealed in professional confidence. . . . [T]hese exceptions to the demand for every man's evidence are not lightly created nor expansively construed, for they are in derogation of the search for truth. . . .

Nowhere in the Constitution, as we have noted earlier, is there any explicit reference to a privilege of confidentiality, yet to the extent this interest relates to the effective discharge of a President's powers, it is constitutionally based.

The right to the production of all evidence at a criminal trial similarly has constitutional dimensions. The Sixth Amendment explicitly confers upon every defendant in a criminal trial the right "to be confronted with the witnesses against him" and "to have compulsory process for obtaining witnesses in his favor." Moreover, the Fifth Amendment also guarantees that no person shall be deprived of liberty without due process of law. It is the manifest duty of the courts to vindicate those guarantees, and to accomplish that it is essential that all relevant and admissible evidence be produced.

In this case we must weigh the importance of the general privilege of confidentiality of Presidential communications in performance of the President's responsibilities against the inroads of such a privilege on the fair administration of criminal justice. The interest in preserving confidentiality is weighty indeed and entitled to great respect. However, we cannot conclude that advisers will be moved to temper the candor of their remarks by the infrequent occasions of disclosure because of the possibility that such conversations will be called for in the context of a prosecution.

On the other hand, the allowance of the privilege to withhold evidence that is demonstrably relevant in a criminal trial would cut deeply into the guarantee of due process of law and gravely impair the basic function of the courts. A President's acknowledged need for confidentiality in the communications of his office is general in nature, whereas the constitutional need for production of relevant evidence in a criminal proceeding is specific and central to the fair adjudication of a particular criminal case in the administration of justice. Without access to specific facts a criminal prosecution may be totally frustrated. The President's broad interest in confidentiality of communications will not be vitiated by disclosure of a limited number of conversations preliminarily shown to have some bearing on the pending criminal cases.

We conclude that when the ground for asserting privilege as to subpoenaed materials sought for use in a criminal trial is based only on the generalized interest in confidentiality, it cannot prevail over the fundamental demands of due process of law in the fair administration of criminal justice. The generalized assertion of privilege must yield to the demonstrated, specific need for evidence in a pending criminal trial.

418 U.S. at 708-713.

Some commentators have criticized Wigmore and the Supreme Court's approach as too narrowly based on an instrumental calculus that overvalues accuracy in the judicial process while undervaluing other important human values such as privacy, dignity, intimacy, anonymity, and individuality. Focusing on these humanistic values, Professor Alan Westin, Privacy and Freedom 31-39 (1967), has identified the following important functions furthered by privacy in communications in modern democratic societies:

> *personal autonomy:* privacy preserves social processes that safeguard one's "sacred individuality" . . . and permits "sheltered experimentation and testing of ideas";
>
> *emotional release:* privacy affords "relaxation . . . from the pressure of playing social roles, [creates an opportunity for people] to lay their masks aside for a rest [and obtain] respite from the emotional stimulation of daily life, [grants] protection . . . to minor non-compliance with social norms, [and allows one] to give vent to . . . anger at the system . . . without fear of being held responsible for such comments";
>
> *self-evaluation:* privacy is essential if one is to fulfill the individual's need "to integrate his experiences into a meaningful pattern and to exert his individuality on events" . . . and "process the information that is constantly bombarding [him]"; privacy also furthers "the proper timing of the decision to move from private reflection or intimate conversations to a more general publication of acts and thoughts";
>
> *limited and protected communications:* privacy is necessary for psychic self-preservation for men in the metropolis, "[providing] the opportunities . . . for sharing confidences and intimacies with those he trusts — spouse; the family; personal friends; and close associates at work."

Professor Thomas Krattenmaker, building mostly on Westin's catalogue of functions served by privacy in communications, is severely critical of the modern trend toward an instrumentalist view of privileges. In an analysis of the federal privilege rules proposed by the Supreme Court, Krattenmaker states:

> [I]n circumscribing personal testimonial privileges, the Rules would intrude severely and unwarrantably upon personal privacy and the individual's interest in freedom of expression. . . .

It is imperative to ascertain precisely what is meant by the concept of privacy in twentieth century America, what individual and societal benefits flow from public protections accorded privacy, whether recognition of interpersonal testimonial privileges does, indeed, substantially contribute to these ends, and whether less drastic means might produce whatever benefits privileges yield. In short, the central question is whether the simple device of excluding evidence at trial can be viewed as an important, well-designed adjunct of the right of privacy.

Privacy, in the sense that term is employed here, is not merely secrecy but also involves the voluntary and secure control one possesses over communication of information about oneself; a person locked in a closet against his will may have secrecy but is unlikely to be enjoying privacy. Simple secrecy is in no sense a valuable right. What makes privacy both a distinct concept and a valuable right is the fact that it is voluntary and that it includes a secured ability to control by oneself how much information about oneself is disseminated and the scope and circumstances of its communication.

The rejection of a claim of privilege destroys the claimant's control over the breadth of the audience receiving personal information as well as his control over the timing and conditions of its release. Clearly then, limitations on testimonial privileges are invasions of privacy.

Not every deprivation of privacy, of course, is socially deplorable or constitutionally objectionable. For example, mandatory examination of restaurant workers for the presence of communicable diseases robs such persons of voluntary control over information concerning one aspect of themselves, but that probably would not lead thoughtful people to conclude that such examinations should be abolished. Most people would agree that such a limited intrusion is outweighed by other social needs.

The question whether to protect an interest in privacy, then, necessarily must involve weighing matters of degree. Therefore, whether society should tolerate either a lesser intrusion upon privacy or an intrusion for certain weighty countervailing reasons must depend, in large measure, upon the importance to individuals and American society of the right of personal privacy as well as the precise nature of that right. At bottom it appears the Rules implicitly adopt an incredible topsy-turvy ranking of the relative strengths of governmental, corporate and individual claims to the right of privacy. . . .

The right of privacy is not simply a very important means to highly valued but distinct ends. Rather, privacy is further an end in itself—an essential condition of political liberty and our very humanity. Without the opportunities privacy provides for personal autonomy, emotional release, self-evaluation and limited and protected communications, individual political freedom as we know it would not flourish. Democracy requires both individual growth, creativity and responsibility, and an inner zone of personal security which the state cannot penetrate. Privacy provides both that zone of impenetrable individuality and the means by which public contributions can flow from responsible individual control over oneself. Privacy both protects private citizens from state control and permits full development of their public selves. . . .

Once care is taken to analyze the concept of privacy, its relationship to personal testimonial privileges is quite striking. Indeed, it is not a farfetched view that personal evidentiary privileges go to the heart of the modern American citizen's need for a right of privacy. For, to repeat, the essence of that right is control over, not the absence of, information. In this regard, privacy is a two-sided concept. People in society constantly are seeking a balance between personal secrecy and social participation. The principal contribution of this right of privacy is that it permits individuals to seek their own balance without being forced to choose between the extremes of total secrecy and total openness. For this reason, it is even more important to the preservation of a useful right of privacy that limited communication be possible than that full secrecy be available.

Testimonial privileges, through fostering this control, help to provide a context for the development of personal autonomy, emotional release, self-evaluation, and limited and protected communication. None of these ends is attainable solely by oneself; successful pursuit of any one of them apparently requires at least some disclosure to another, but that must occur in a situation which permits individual control over the breadth of disclosure. And, as further noted above, providing a means for attaining these ends is essential to the maintenance of democracy and the human condition.

Indeed, this need for controlled disclosure such as by privileged communication, touching as it does upon such fundamental conditions of our society, is supported not simply by considerations of privacy, but by similar and perhaps more familiar principles respecting the function of freedom of speech. For the social policies furthered by recognition of a right of personal privacy are in many instances similar to those protected by the theoretical underpinnings of freedom of speech. . . .

Proponents of testimonial privileges need not carry the burden of proving what factors influence behavior. Privileges also are important for other reasons as well. For in protecting those relatively few confidential utterances that do bear upon concrete litigation, the law protects all those that may. Moreover, the societal recognition of the right of privacy entailed in permitting a claim of personal privilege serves as an embodiment of the fundamental regard in which society does, and should, hold that right. Most important, however, is the simple fact that when a particular confidant's claim of privilege is upheld, so is his very right of privacy. That society cannot protect against all abridgments of that right makes it more, not less, imperative that privacy be preserved whenever possible. That we cannot guarantee the inviolability of every man's every attempt to strike his own balance between secrecy and participation does not mean judges should be unleashed to compel divulgence of every confidence they can discover. In short, our security and privacy is enriched substantially when a testimonial privilege, properly invoked, is given societal approval. . . .

The confidential communication that is part and parcel of the right of privacy may pass between parent and child or counsellor and client or roommate and roommate, as well as husband and wife or doctor and patient. Not only attorneys and their clients, but also judges and their clerks and legislators or administrators and their aides, may need the privilege if law is to be freely and fairly administered. Like the corporation's trade secret, such matters deserve a finer, more discriminating treatment than wholesale rejection in advance of every such claim of privilege, without regard to the necessity for the testimony or the availability of other techniques to better protect the interests of all litigants. Accordingly, a general, qualified privilege for confidential communications that pass between individuals intimately related or in a position of close personal trust should be adopted, modeled upon the trade secrets provision of rule 508.

Krattenmaker, Testimonial Privileges in Federal Courts: An Alternative to the Proposed Federal Rules of Evidence, 62 Geo. L.J. 61, 85-94 (1973). See also Louisell, Confidentiality, Conformity and Confusions: Privileges in Federal Court Today, 31 Tul. L. Rev. 101 (1956). Most European justice systems provide testimonial privileges in both the business and family contexts which are far more generous that their American counterparts. For instance, in Germany, a party has the right to prevent any close relative, including siblings, parents, grandparents, and children, from giving testimony in a civil or criminal case. See German Zivilprozessordnung, §383.

Krattenmaker's response was a typical reaction at one extreme to the Supreme Court's proposed rules on privileges, the most controversial of the proposed Federal Rules. Some of the criticism was based on clear-cut policy differences and focused on specific proposed privileges or the absence of others—for example, the lack of a reporter's privilege. Other criticism was more broadly based on separation of powers and federalism grounds, contending that it was for the legislature and not the courts to create rules of privilege and that in diversity cases state rather than federal rules should apply.

To prevent the controversy over the privilege rules from delaying the entire Federal Rules, Congress decided to delete all thirteen of the Court's proposed privilege rules (nine privileges and four ancillary rules) and to substitute a single rule, Rule 501, which did two things:

(1) It adopted the approach of Erie Railroad Co. v. Tompkins, 304 U.S. 64 (1938), by mandating that in federal court cases governed by state substantive law, state law as to privileges shall apply; and

(2) It provided that in cases governed by federal substantive law the principles of the common law shall apply, "as they may be interpreted by the courts of the United States in the light of reason and experience."

In short, the final version of the Federal Rules left the whole matter of privileges up in the air and the philosophical debate over the underlying justification for the recognition and nonrecognition of certain privileges no closer to a resolution.

Must one choose sides in this debate? Does either the instrumentalist or the humanistic approach by itself provide a satisfactory explanation for the recognized privileges and for the nonrecognition of seemingly similar but unprotected relationships? If not, perhaps it is because there is more than one type of privilege designed to accomplish more than one purpose.

Indeed, there seem to be at least two distinct types of privileges. A rudimentary binary classification of privileges could be made on the basis of the relationship between the holder of the privilege and the other communicant. The first class or group of privileges includes those in which a professional counseling relationship exists between the holder of the privilege and the "other." Privileges of this sort include the well-recognized ones of lawyer-client, physician-patient, and communications-to-clergy and the generally unrecognized ones of accountant-client, social worker, and stockbroker. The most obvious purpose of recognizing these privileges is to foster the effective rendering of the professional service offered by the counselor.

The second group of privileges includes those that are designed simply to throw a veil of secrecy around specific zones of privacy in order to protect individual autonomy and human dignity. No professional relationship is involved and no furthering of any service need be demonstrated. Examples of these privileges include the marital privilege and the privilege against self-incrimination.

These categories necessarily overlap. The reporter's privilege is one example of a privilege that falls into both categories, and there may be others. Nonetheless, it may be helpful to try to sort the privileges in this fashion to see whether more than one test should be applied to determine if a putative privilege should be recognized. For example, perhaps only the privileges in the first group—those based on the existence of a professional relationship—should be subjected to an instrumentalist or pragmatic test; those in the second group may not be susceptible to the same analysis. If this is true, then on what basis might they be justified? And why do these justifications fail to justify privileges for communications between "best friends" and "grandma-grandson" as well?

Despite all the effort that has been devoted to rationalizing the law of privileges, it is possible that neither the instrumentalist-utilitarian approach nor the humanistic approach can justify either the present system of privileges as a whole or even any particular privilege. For the professional privileges, for example, what data would suffice to prove that the utilitarian calculus justifies the various privileges? Is it possible to obtain such data? What data justify the nonprofessional privileges? How would a social scientist go about testing the assumptions or assertions that underlie most thinking about these privileges? If it is not possible to demonstrate under either the utilitarian or humanistic approach that the various established privileges should exist and that other asserted privileges should not, what else explains the present system of privileges?

Does an alternate thesis that privileges rest on relative power and influence exercised by certain segments of society better explain the present system of privileges? After all, we are talking about *privilege*.

IN RE FARBER (STATE v. JASCALEVICH)
78 N.J. 259, 394 A.2d 330, cert. denied, 439 U.S. 997 (1978)

MOUNTAIN, J. In these consolidated appeals The New York Times Company and Myron Farber, a reporter employed by the newspaper, challenge judgments entered against them in two related matters — one a proceeding in aid of a litigant (civil contempt), the other for criminal contempt of court. The proceedings were instituted in an ongoing murder trial now in its seventh month, as a result of the appellants' failure to comply with two subpoenas duces tecum, directing them to produce certain documents and materials compiled by one or both of these appellants in the course of Farber's investigative reporting of certain allegedly criminal activities. Farber's investigations and reporting are said to have contributed largely to the indictment and prosecution of Dr. Mario E. Jascalevich for murder. Appellants moved unsuccessfully before Judge William J. Arnold, the trial judge in State v. Jascalevich, to quash the two subpoenas; an order was entered directing that the subpoenaed material be produced for in camera inspection by the court. . . .

Impelled by appellants' persistent refusal to produce the subpoenaed materials for in camera inspection, Judge Arnold issued an order returnable before Judge Theodore W. Trautwein, directing appellants to show cause why they should not be deemed in contempt of court. . . .

Judge Trautwein determined that both appellants had wilfully contemned Judge Arnold's order directing that materials be produced for in camera inspection and found them guilty as charged. A fine of $100,000 was imposed on The New York Times and Farber was ordered to serve six months in the Bergen County jail and to pay a fine of $1,000. Additionally, in order to compel production of the materials subpoenaed on behalf of Jascalevich, a fine of $5,000 per day for every day that elapsed until compliance with Judge Arnold's order was imposed upon The Times; Farber was fined $1,000 and sentenced to confinement in the county jail until he complied with the order. . . .

I. THE FIRST AMENDMENT

Appellants claim a privilege to refrain from revealing information sought by the subpoenas duces tecum essentially for the reason that were they to divulge this material, confidential sources of such information would be made public. Were this to occur, they argue, newsgathering and the dissemination of news would be seriously impaired, because much information would never be forthcoming to the news media unless the persons who were the sources of such information could be entirely certain that their identities would remain secret. The final result, appellants claim, would be a substantial lessening in the supply of available news on a variety of important and sensitive issues, all to the detriment of the public interest. They contend further that this privilege to remain silent with respect to confidential information and the sources of such information emanates from the "free speech" and "free press" clauses of the First Amendment.

In our view the Supreme Court of the United States has clearly rejected this claim and has squarely held that no such First Amendment right exists. In Branzburg v. Hayes, 408 U.S. 665 (1972), three news media representatives argued that, for the same reason here advanced, they should not be required to appear and testify before grand juries, and that this privilege to refrain from divulging information, asserted to have been received from confidential sources, derived from the First Amendment. Justice White, noting that there was no common law privilege, stated the issue and gave the Court's answer in the first paragraph of his opinion:

"The issue in these cases is whether requiring newsmen to appear and testify before state or federal grand juries abridges the freedom of speech and press guaranteed by the First Amendment. We hold that it does not." Branzburg v. Hayes, supra, 408 U.S. at 667 (1972).

In that case one reporter, from Frankfort, Kentucky, had witnessed individuals making hashish from marijuana and had made a rather comprehensive survey of the drug scene in Frankfort. He had written an article in the Louisville Courier-Journal describing this illegal activity. Another, a newsman-photographer employed by a New Bedford, Massachusetts television station, had met with members of the Black Panther movement at the time that certain riots and disorders occurred in New Bedford. The material he assembled formed the basis for a television program that followed. The third investigative reporter had met with members of the Black Panthers in northern California and had written an article about the nature and activities of the movement. In each instance there had been a commitment on the part of the media representative that he would not divulge the source of his article or story.

By a vote of 5 to 4 the Supreme Court held that newspaper reporters or other media representatives have no privilege deriving from the First Amendment to refrain from divulging confidential information and the sources of such information when properly subpoenaed to appear before a grand jury. The three media representatives were directed to appear and testify. The holding was later underscored and applied directly to this case by Justice White in a brief opinion filed in this cause upon the occasion of his denial of a stay sought by these appellants. He said,

"There is no present authority in this Court either that newsmen are constitutionally privileged to withhold duly subpoenaed documents material to the prosecution or defense of a criminal case or that a defendant seeking the subpoena must show extraordinary circumstances before enforcement against newsmen will be had." New York Times and Farber v. Jascalevich, 439 U.S. 1317, 1322 (1978). . . .

[A]mong the many First Amendment protections that may be invoked by the press, there is not to be found the privilege of refusing to reveal relevant confidential information and its sources to a grand jury which is engaged in the fundamental governmental function of "[f]air and effective law enforcement aimed at providing security for the person and property of the individual. . . ." 408 U.S. at 690. The reason this is so is that a majority of the members of the United States Supreme Court have so determined. . . .

Thus we do no weighing or balancing of societal interests in reaching our determination that the First Amendment does not afford appellants the privilege they claim. The weighing and balancing has been done by a higher court. Our conclusion that appellants cannot derive the protection they seek from the First Amendment rests upon the fact that the ruling in *Branzburg* is binding upon us and we interpret it as applicable to, and clearly including, the particular issue framed here. It follows that the obligation to appear at a criminal trial on behalf of a defendant who is enforcing his Sixth Amendment rights is at least as compelling as the duty to appear before a grand jury.

II. THE SHIELD LAW[2]

In Branzburg v. Hayes, supra, the Court dealt with a newsman's claim of privilege based solely upon the First Amendment. As we have seen,

2. The term "shield law" is commonly and widely applied to statutes granting newsmen and other media representatives the privilege of declining to reveal confidential sources of information. The New Jersey shield law reads as follows:

"Subject to Rule 37, a person engaged on, engaged in, connected with, or employed by news media for the purpose of gathering, procuring, transmitting, compiling, editing or disseminating news for the general public or on whose behalf news is so gathered, procured, transmitted, compiled, edited or disseminated has a privilege to refuse to disclose, in any legal or quasi-legal proceeding or before any investigative body, including, but not limited to, any court, grand jury, petit jury, administrative agency, the Legislature or legislative committee, or elsewhere:

"a. The source, author, means, agency or persons from or through whom any information was procured, obtained, supplied, furnished, gathered, transmitted, compiled, edited, disseminated, or delivered; and

"b. Any news or information obtained in the course of pursuing his professional activities whether or not it is disseminated. . . .

"Unless a different meaning clearly appears from the context of this act, as used in this act:

"a. 'News media' means newspapers, magazines, press associations, news agencies, wire services, radio, television or other similar printed, photographic, mechanical or electronic means of disseminating news to the general public.

"b. 'News' means any written, oral or pictorial information gathered, procured,

this claim of privilege failed. In *Branzburg* no shield law was involved. Here we have a shield law, said to be as strongly worded as any in the country.

We read the legislative intent in adopting this statute in its present form as seeking to protect the confidential sources of the press as well as information so obtained by reporters and other news media representatives to the greatest extent permitted by the Constitution of the United States and that of the State of New Jersey. It is abundantly clear that appellants come fully within the literal language of the enactment. . . .

III. THE SIXTH AMENDMENT AND ITS NEW JERSEY COUNTERPART

Viewed on its face, considered solely as a reflection of legislative intent to bestow upon the press as broad a shield as possible to protect against forced revelation of confidential source materials, this legislation is entirely constitutional. Indeed, no one appears to have attacked its facial constitutionality.

It is, however, argued, and argued very strenuously, that if enforced under the facts of this case, the Shield Law violates the Sixth Amendment of the Federal Constitution as well as Article 1, ¶10 of the New Jersey Constitution. . . . Essentially the argument is this: The Federal and State Constitutions each provide that in all criminal prosecutions the accused shall have the right "to have compulsory process for obtaining

---

transmitted, compiled, edited or disseminated by, or on behalf of any person engaged in, engaged on, connected with or employed by a news media and so procured or obtained while such required relationship is in effect.

"c. 'Newspaper' means a paper that is printed and distributed ordinarily not less frequently than once a week and that contains news, articles of opinion, editorials, features, advertising, or other matter regarded as of current interest, has a paid circulation and has been entered at a United States post office as second class matter.

"d. 'Magazine' means a publication containing news which is published and distributed periodically, has a paid circulation and has been entered at a United States post office as second class matter.

"e. 'News agency' means a commercial organization that collects and supplies news to subscribing newspapers, magazines, periodicals, and news broadcasters.

"f. 'Press association' means an association of newspapers or magazines formed to gather and distribute news to its members.

"g. 'Wire service' means a news agency that sends out syndicated news copy by wire to subscribing newspapers, magazines, periodicals or news broadcasters.

"h. 'In the course of pursuing his professional activities' means any situation, including a social gathering, in which a reporter obtains information for the purpose of disseminating it to the public, but does not include any situation in which a reporter intentionally conceals from the source the fact that he is a reporter, and does not include any situation in which a reporter is an eyewitness to, or participant in, any act involving physical violence or property damage."

N.J.S.A. 2A:84A-21 and 21a.

witnesses in his favor." Dr. Jascalevich seeks to obtain evidence to use in preparing and presenting his defense in the ongoing criminal trial in which he has been accused of multiple murders. He claims to come within the favor of these constitutional provisions — which he surely does. Finally, when faced with the Shield Law, he invokes the rather elementary but entirely sound proposition that where Constitution and statute collide, the latter must yield. Subject to what is said below, we find this argument unassailable.

The compulsory process clause of the Sixth Amendment has never been elaborately explicated by the Supreme Court. Not until 1967, when it decided Washington v. Texas, 388 U.S. 14, had the clause been directly construed. Westen, Confrontation and Compulsory Process: A Unified Theory of Evidence for Criminal Cases, 91 Harv. L. Rev. 567, 586 (1978). In *Washington* the petitioner sought the reversal of his conviction for murder. A Texas statute at the time provided that persons charged or convicted as co-participants in the same crime could not testify for one another. One Fuller, who had already been convicted of the murder, was prevented from testifying by virtue of the statute. The record indicated that had he testified his testimony would have been favorable to petitioner. The Court reversed the conviction on the ground that petitioner's Sixth Amendment right to compulsory process had been denied. At the same time it determined that the compulsory process clause in the Sixth Amendment was binding on state courts by virtue of the due process clause of the Fourteenth Amendment. It will be seen that *Washington* is like the present case in a significant respect. The Texas statute and the Sixth Amendment could not both stand. The latter of course prevailed. So must it be here.

Quite recently, in United States v. Nixon, 418 U.S. 683 (1974), the Court dealt with another compulsory process issue. There the Special Prosecutor, Leon Jaworski, subpoenaed various tape recordings and documents in the possession of President Nixon. The latter claimed an executive privilege and refused to deliver the tapes. The Supreme Court conceded that indeed there was an executive privilege and that although "[n]owhere in the Constitution . . . is there any explicit reference to a privilege of confidentiality, yet to the extent this interest relates to the effective discharge of a President's powers, it is constitutionally based." 418 U.S. at 711. Despite this conclusion that at least to some extent a president's executive privilege derives from the Constitution, the Court nonetheless concluded that the demands of our criminal justice system required that the privilege must yield. . . .

It is important to note that the Supreme Court in this case compelled the production of privileged material — the privilege acknowledged to rest in part upon the Constitution — even though there was no Sixth Amendment compulsion to do so. The Sixth Amendment affords rights to an accused but not to a prosecutor. The compulsion to require the production of the privileged material derived from the necessities of our system of administering criminal justice.

Article I, ¶10 of the Constitution of the State of New Jersey contains, as we have seen, exactly the same language with respect to compulsory process as that found in the Sixth Amendment. There exists no authoritative explication of this constitutional provision. Indeed it has rarely been mentioned in our reported decisions. We interpret it as affording a defendant in a criminal prosecution the right to compel the attendance of witnesses and the production of documents and other material for which he may have, or may believe he has, a legitimate need in preparing or undertaking his defense. It also means that witnesses properly summoned will be required to testify and that material demanded by a properly phrased subpoena duces tecum will be forthcoming and available for appropriate examination and use.

Testimonial privileges, whether they derive from common law or from statute, which allow witnesses to withhold evidence seem to conflict with this provision. This conflict may arise in a variety of factual contexts with respect to different privileges. We confine our consideration here to the single privilege before us—that set forth in the Shield Law. We hold that Article 1, ¶10 of our Constitution prevails over this statute. . . .

IV. Procedural Mechanism

Appellants insist that they are entitled to a full hearing on the issues of relevance, materiality and overbreadth of the subpoena. We agree. The trial court recognized its obligation to conduct such a hearing, but the appellants have aborted that hearing by refusing to submit the material subpoenaed for an in camera inspection by the court to assist it in determining the motion to quash. That inspection is no more than a procedural tool, a device to be used to ascertain the relevancy and materiality of that material. Such an in camera inspection is not in itself an invasion of the statutory privilege. Rather it is a preliminary step to determine whether, and if so to what extent, the statutory privilege must yield to the defendant's constitutional rights.

Appellants' position is that there must be a full showing and definitive judicial determination of relevance, materiality, absence of less intrusive access, and need, prior to any in camera inspection. The obvious objection to such a rule, however, is that it would, in many cases, effectively stultify the judicial criminal process. It might well do so here. The defendant properly recognizes Myron Farber as a unique repository of pertinent information. But he does not know the extent of this information nor is it possible for him to specify all of it with particularity, nor to tailor his subpoena to precise materials of which he is ignorant. Well aware of this, Judge Arnold refused to give ultimate rulings with respect to relevance and other preliminary matters until he had examined the material. We think he had no other course. It is not rational to ask a judge to ponder the relevance of the unknown.

The same objection applies with equal force to the contention that the subpoena is overbroad. Appellants do not assert that the subpoena is vague and uncertain, but that the data requested may not be relevant and material. To deal effectively with this assertion it is not only appropriate but absolutely necessary for the trial court to inspect in camera the subpoenaed items so that it can make its determinations on the basis of concrete materials rather than in a vacuum. . . .

While we agree, then, that appellants should be afforded the hearing they are seeking, one procedural aspect of which calls for their compliance with the order for in camera inspection, we are also of the view that they, and those who in the future may be similarly situated, are entitled to a preliminary determination before being compelled to submit the subpoenaed materials to a trial judge for such inspection. Our decision in this regard is not, contrary to the suggestion in some of the briefs filed with us, mandated by the First Amendment; for in addition to ruling generally against the representatives of the press in *Branzburg,* the Court particularly and rather vigorously, rejected the claims there asserted that before going before the grand jury, each of the reporters, at the very least, was entitled to a preliminary hearing to establish a number of threshold issues. Branzburg v. Hayes, supra, 408 U.S. at 701-07. Rather, our insistence upon such a threshold determination springs from our obligation to give as much effect as possible, within ever-present constitutional limitations, to the very positively expressed legislative intent to protect the confidentiality and secrecy of sources from which the media derive information. To this end such a determination would seem a necessity.

PASHMAN, J., dissenting. . . .

This case is the first major test of New Jersey's new "Shield Law." There is no reason to accord this statute an unfriendly reception in any court of this State. There should be no eagerness to narrow or circumvent it. The Shield Law is not an irritation. It is an act of the Legislature.

This law was passed in the aftermath of the Supreme Court's decision in Branzburg v. Hayes, 408 U.S. 665 (1972). In *Branzburg,* the Court held that the First Amendment will not always prevent forced disclosure of a reporter's confidential sources and information. More specifically, it ruled that the reporters there involved had no privilege under the First Amendment against being compelled, on pain of contempt, to reveal such confidential data to an investigating grand jury. In its view, the resulting infringement upon the reporters' investigating abilities was outweighed by the grand jury's need to have everyman's evidence.

The Court emphasized, however, that state legislatures were not powerless to alter the result reached in *Branzburg*. As Justice White stated:

"At the federal level, Congress has freedom to determine whether a statutory newsman's privilege is necessary and desirable and to fashion standards and rules as narrow or broad as deemed necessary to deal with the evil discerned and, equally important, to refashion those rules as experience from time to time may dictate. *There is also merit in leaving state legislatures free, within First Amendment limits, to fashion their own standards in light of the conditions and problems with respect to the relations between law enforcement officials and press in their own areas.* It goes without saying, of course, that we are powerless to bar state courts from responding in their own way and construing their own constitutions so as to recognize a newsman's privilege, either qualified or absolute." [408 U.S. at 706, emphasis supplied].

The News Media Privilege Act was New Jersey's response to the Court's invitation. This Act reflects our Legislature's judgment that an uninhibited news media is more important to the proper functioning of our society than is the ability of either law enforcement agencies, the courts or criminal defendants to gain access to confidential news data. . . .

A reporter's ability to obtain sensitive information depends on his reputation for keeping confidences. Once breached—that reputation is destroyed. Potential sources of information can no longer rest secure that their identities and confidences will remain free from disclosure.

Realizing that strict confidentiality is essential to the workings of a free press, our Legislature, through the News Media Privilege Act, has granted reporters an immunity from disclosure which is both absolute and comprehensive. *Any* person connected with *any* news media for the purpose of gathering or disseminating news is granted the privilege of refusing to disclose, in *any* legal or quasi-legal proceeding or before *any* investigative body, both the source of and any information acquired.

Courts are thus given no discretion to determine on a case-by-case basis whether the societal importance of a free and robust press is "outweighed" by other assertedly compelling interests. The Legislature has done the weighing and balancing and has determined that in every case the right to non-disclosure is paramount. If a reporter falls within the ambit of the statute, he has a privilege of non-disclosure.

This privilege exists not only with respect to public disclosures; it encompasses revelations to any legal or quasi-legal body, including "any court." Even forced in camera disclosures are thus prohibited.

[A concurring opinion by Chief Judge Hughes and a dissenting opinion by Judge Handler are omitted.]

What arguments may be advanced in support of a reporter's privilege? Does a reporter's privilege satisfy Wigmore's four conditions? Can such a privilege be defended on purely utilitarian grounds or on the basis of other values extrinsic to the litigation process? What data would support a reporter's privilege on either basis? Is such data obtainable? If not, is a reporter's privilege justifiable? Do the majority and dissenting opinions in the *Farber* case reflect fundamentally different philosophical approaches to privileges in general or only different conceptions of the impact that such a privilege would have on the judicial process?

What institutional issues do you see in the *Farber* case? What are the appropriate respective roles of the legislature and the judiciary in establishing privileges? Again, does this question depend upon the approach taken to the subject of privileges — the instrumentalist-utilitarian, the humanistic, or the perquisite of power?

Problem: Clergymen, Psychiatrists, Lawyers: The Farber *Variations*

In the *Farber* case, the defendant in the criminal prosecution, Dr. Jascalevich, subpoenaed documents and solicited testimony that he alleged was relevant, material, and unavailable from any other source, including the prosecution. Dr. Jascalevich's lawyers alleged that the reporter, Myron Farber, had obtained this material in the course of his investigation into deaths in Dr. Jascalevich's hospital, which subsequently led to the reopening of the police investigation and the indictment of Dr. Jascalevich. Among the evidence sought by the defense counsel were Farber's notes and his recollections of interviews with Dr. Stanley Harris, a surgeon at the hospital where the criminal activities are said to have occurred. Dr. Harris admitted having spoken to Farber five times before the New York Times articles appeared and before his reinterview by the prosecutor's office. In his interview with the prosecutor, Dr. Harris stated that his suspicions of Dr. Jascalevich were originally aroused by the unexplained deaths of some of his patients. The defense characterized Dr. Harris as Dr. Jascalevich's principal accuser.

(1) Suppose that Dr. Harris's communications were made to his clergyman or to his psychiatrist rather than to Myron Farber. If defense counsel subpoenaed the clergyman or psychiatrist, how would the court be likely to treat a claim of privilege asserted on Dr. Harris's behalf by the clergyman or doctor under a state common law privilege for communications to clergymen or psychiatrists similar to proposed Rules 504 and 506?

(2) Suppose Dr. Harris's communications were with Martin Ferber, Esq., his attorney. If defense counsel subpoenaed Attorney Ferber, how

would the court be likely to treat a claim of privilege asserted by the lawyer on Dr. Harris's behalf under a state common law lawyer-client privilege similar to proposed Rule 503?

To the extent that you feel that the court would react differently to a claim of clergyman, psychiatrist, or lawyer-client privilege than it did to Farber's claim of reporter's privilege, what explains the difference?

B. The Lawyer-Client Privilege

Of all the privileges, the lawyer-client privilege is undoubtedly the most solidly entrenched. Not surprisingly, it is also the privilege with which lawyers—litigators and nonlitigators alike—are most often concerned. Indeed, on a daily basis, most practicing lawyers find themselves in situations in which the existence or nonexistence of the privilege is a vital consideration. Fortunately, at its core and in routine cases, the privilege is relatively easy to understand and apply. At the edges, however, for example, when the attorney is communicating with corporate employees about possible unlawful payments to public officials or is handed a smoking gun by an out-of-breath client, the privilege is both murky and controversial. For lawyers in these situations, a correct understanding of the privilege and their professional responsibilities is all that stands between them and the possibility of malpractice, contempt of court, or disciplinary sanctions.

This section takes a quick look at the basic elements of the privilege and the mechanisms for asserting it. It then focuses on two specific and very real problems that highlight the difficult policy judgments underlying the privilege:

(1) How does a lawyer handle "hot stuff"—in the business context, tax records; in the criminal law context, weapons, evidence, or contraband?

(2) How well does current privilege doctrine recognize and provide for the conflicting interests of lawyer, client, and others, especially in the context of the modern business enterprise?

Before taking on the complex policy and ethical issues that emerge at the frontiers of the privilege when these problems are considered, it may be helpful to try to formulate possible reasons for recognizing a lawyer-client privilege in the simplest case—that is, where the lawyer is explicitly retained by an individual to furnish confidential legal advice to that person concerning a lawful course of conduct contemplated or previously taken by that person. The following arguments have been advanced to support the privilege in this and more complex situations.

(1) It is necessary for the effective rendering of legal services that the client communicate every relevant detail to the lawyer. No stone can be

left unturned if the client is to receive effective legal advice. The client may not feel free to reveal damaging, embarrassing, or tentative details unless she is assured that her confidence will be protected. In the criminal context it may be asserted that the lawyer-client privilege is necessary to protect the accused's Fifth and Sixth Amendment rights to the effective assistance of counsel.

(2) Without the privilege, lawyers would become witnesses in almost every lawsuit, creating intolerable problems in the administration of trials.

(3) The adversary system and the professional role of the lawyer/counselor require that a zone of privacy surround the lawyer-client relationship.

(4) The privilege promotes justice. In fact, very little evidence is suppressed that cannot be obtained by other means. And the existence of the privilege causes information to come to the attention of the attorney that is useful in counseling the client toward the "correct" course of conduct.

Which of these arguments do you find persuasive in the simple core situation described above? Are they equally applicable in all situations to which the privilege might arguably be extended, such as communications to a corporate attorney by mid-level corporate employees or communications by an individual to an attorney concerning the location of a weapon or a body? Which of these arguments rest on untested or untestable assumptions about human behavior? What data support these assumptions? Is the case for a broad lawyer-client privilege stronger than the case for a similarly broad privilege for communications with other professionals and counselors, such as accountants, social workers, stock brokers, show business agents, trustees, partners, or other fiduciaries, or between employees or even "best friends"? As long ago as 1827, one observer was skeptical that the lawyer-client privilege could be justified on *any* basis.

J. BENTHAM, RATIONALE OF JUDICIAL EVIDENCE
from The Works of Jeremy Bentham 473-479 (Browning ed. 1842), as quoted in 8 Wigmore, Evidence §2291, pp.549-551 (McNaughton rev. 1961)

When in consulting with a law adviser, attorney or advocate, a man has confessed his delinquency, or disclosed some fact which, if stated in court, might tend to operate in proof of it, such law adviser is not to be suffered to be examined as to any such point. The law adviser is neither to be compelled, nor so much as suffered, to betray the trust thus reposed in him. Not suffered? Why not?

Oh, because to betray a trust is treachery; and an act of treachery is an immoral act.

But if such confidence, when reposed, is permitted to be violated, and if this be known, (which, if such be the law, it will be), the consequence will be, that no such confidence will be reposed. Not reposed? —Well: and if it be not, wherein will consist the mischief? The man by the supposition is guilty; if not, by the supposition there is nothing to betray: let the law adviser say every thing he has heard, every thing he can have heard from his client, the client cannot have any thing to fear from it. That it will often happen that in the case supposed no such confidence will be reposed, is natural enough: the first thing the advocate or attorney will say to his client, will be,—Remember that, whatever you say to me, I shall be obliged to tell, if asked about it. What, then, will be the consequence? That a guilty person will not in general be able to derive quite so much assistance from his law adviser, in the way of concerting a false defence, as he may do at present. . . .

. . . A rule of law which, in the case of the lawyer, gives an express license to that wilful concealment of the criminal's guilt, which would have constituted any other person an accessory in the crime, plainly declares that the practice of knowingly engaging one's self as the hired advocate of an unjust cause, is, in the eye of the law, or (to speak intelligibly) in that of the law-makers, an innocent, if not a virtuous practice. But for this implied declaration, the man who in this way hires himself out to do injustice or frustrate justice with his tongue, would be viewed in exactly the same light as he who frustrates justice or does injustice with any other instrument.

Problem: The Blackacre Fraud

(1) Action to enjoin *D* from recording a deed to Blackacre allegedly procured by fraud from the trustee of the Widow Brown Trust. While the first witness is testifying for *P* at trial, *P*'s attorney notices that *D* is whispering to his attorney. After the first witness stands down, *P*'s attorney calls *D*'s attorney and asks him to repeat his conversation with *D*. On *D*'s attorney's objection, what ruling and why?

(2) Instead of calling *D*'s attorney, *P* calls *D* to testify as to what he said to his attorney. On *D*'s attorney's objection, what ruling and why?

(3) Suppose, instead, that *D* is asked, "What did you tell the trustee of the Widow Brown Trust?" *D* replies, "I object. I just told that to my attorney." What ruling and why?

(4) Suppose that *D* is asked to hand over to *P*'s attorney notes that he has been writing to his attorney during the trial. On *D*'s objection, what ruling and why? What result if *D* is asked to produce notes and letters to his attorney sent prior to the trial?

(5) Before trial, at a preliminary hearing, *P*'s attorney moves for an order directing *D*'s attorney, if he has possession of the deed or any document purporting to be the deed, to deliver it to the clerk to be

marked as Plaintiff's Exhibit 1 for identification. *D*'s attorney objects on the grounds that the deed was given to him in private by *D*. What ruling and why?

Problem: The Eavesdropper

Action for breach of promise of marriage. At trial, *P* called *W* to testify that a few days before the action was commenced, *W* was at the office of *D*'s attorney. *W* observed *D* enter and through a closed door overheard a muted conversation between *D* and his attorney in which *D* said he was afraid a woman would sue him for breach of a promise of marriage. *D* objects to *W*'s proposed testimony on grounds of the lawyer-client privilege. What ruling and why? See the answer of the Massachusetts Supreme Court in a venerable case.

HOY v. MORRIS
79 Mass. 519 (1859)

[A]ssuming that the interview between Mr. Todd [the attorney] and the defendant was strictly of a privileged character, and that all the communications of the latter during its continuance were made by him as a client to his counsel and professional adviser, still the testimony of the witness Aldrich was admissible, and was properly allowed to be used before the jury.

The privilege of exemption from testifying to facts actually known is extended only to an attorney or legal adviser who derives his knowledge from the communications of a client who applies and makes disclosures to him in his professional character, and to those other persons whose intervention is strictly necessary to enable the parties to communicate with each other. This is the rule which . . . seems uniformly to have been recognized as a correct statement of the law upon this subject. . . . Applying this rule to the facts in the present case, the conclusion is inevitable that the statement of [defendant] to his counsel Mr. Todd was overheard and became known to Aldrich under circumstances which entitled the plaintiff to the benefit of his testimony concerning it. Aldrich was not an attorney, nor in any way connected with Mr. Todd; and certainly in no situation where he was either necessary or useful to the parties to enable them to understand each other. On the contrary, he was a mere bystander, and casually overheard conversation not addressed to him nor intended for his ear, but which the client and attorney meant to have respected as private and confidential. Mr. Todd could not lawfully have revealed it. But, in consequence of a want of proper precaution, the communications between him and his client were overheard by a mere stranger. As the latter stood in no relation of confidence to either of the parties, he was clearly not within the rule of exemption from giving testimony; and he might therefore, when summoned as a witness, be compelled to testify to what he overheard, so far as it was pertinent to the subject matter of inquiry upon the trial; this is all that was allowed by the court.

Do you agree with the Massachusetts court? Does *Hoy* reflect an objective or subjective approach to the issue of the existence of the conditions necessary for the lawyer-client privilege? Which approach would you adopt? Which approach does the proposed Federal Rule adopt?

PRICHARD v. UNITED STATES
181 F.2d 326 (6th Cir.), aff'd, 339 U.S. 974 (1950)

SIMONS, J. The appellant and his law partner, A.E. Funk, Jr., were indicted under §241, Title 18 U.S.C.A. for conspiracy to stuff ballot boxes in certain precincts of Bourbon County, Kentucky, at the general election in November, 1948, which was, of course, a national election. . . .

The principal ground for the appeal as argued and briefed, relates to the testimony of Judge Ardery as to an interview solicited from him by Prichard, and this necessitates a recital of the circumstances which led to the conversation and the status of the parties at the time. Prichard is a lawyer with a career of marked distinction. Graduated from college and with a law degree from Harvard Law School, admitted to the bar in 1939, he had been research secretary to one and probably two of the present Justices of the Supreme Court, to the Attorney General of the United States and the Secretary of the Treasury, and was, at one time, general counsel of the Democratic National Committee. Returning from Washington to Kentucky a number of years before the incidents here involved, he practiced law in the Circuit Court of his county and in the Court of Appeals of the Commonwealth of Kentucky. He became a man of great influence in the politics of his state and county. Judge Ardery is a judge of the 14th Judicial Circuit of the State of Kentucky, had known Prichard all his life, especially since Prichard had been a school mate and later a law partner of his son, Philip. At the election 254 forged ballots had been placed in the ballot boxes of a number of the precincts in Bourbon County prior to the opening of the polls. On the night that the appellant, accompanied by Philip Ardery, sought the interview with the judge, the latter had already called a grand jury to investigate election frauds in the county. The grand jury was to meet the following morning at which time Judge Ardery was expected to instruct the grand jurors as to their duties and the scope of the investigation, as required by Kentucky law.

Prichard had gone to Philip Ardery, his former law partner, on Sunday evening, November 7, 1948, for legal advice. Whatever conversation there was between them at that time was held by the district judge to be within the attorney-client relationship, so privileged, and is not here involved. Prichard and Philip Ardery, however, decided to consult Judge Ardery and drove to the judge's house, arriving there about 11 o'clock. Being advised that the interview which then transpired would be met by the claim of privilege on behalf of Prichard, the district judge heard evidence and argument in camera as to the nature of the evidence expected to be solicited from the judge, and limited interrogation with scrupulous concern for Prichard's rights. In view of Judge Ardery's official position, the duties he was then engaged upon in reference to the grand jury, the command of Kentucky statutes and the public interest, he concluded that one who seeks the advice of the judge of the court in which his case is to be tried is not entitled to the privilege accorded by law to confidential communications between an attorney and client. To allow the privilege under such circumstances would invite frustration of the administration of the courts by their duly elected and qualified judges. Such application would seem inimical to the public interest and a perversion of the purpose and spirit of the rule. He decided that Judge Ardery's testimony was admissible and would be received by the jury with caution as to its lack of bearing upon the guilt of the co-defendant.

At the preliminary hearing the judge had told the court that when Mr. Prichard appeared at his door that night he said, "Judge, I am in deep trouble and I want your advice." He then invited him into his home. To the jury the judge testified, "Mr. Prichard told me that he and two other young men prepared the ballots here in issue and put them in the ballot boxes before the election began." He said that he felt he could give Prichard legal advice and that if anything transpired later he would not sit in the case. Prichard gave him two details in regard to it. He said one of the young men wrote the names of the election officers on the ballots and that he stamped the ballot which scratched Senator Chapman. Prichard appeared greatly disturbed, both mentally and emotionally. His mind was not on the past. It was on the future, at what it might hold for him. "He asked me if I had a suggestion which would help him. I had none at that time." Asked whether Prichard had requested suggestions at any other time, the judge testified that he had on the following Wednesday. At this point the court excused the jury for the purpose of considering the competency of this additional evidence. Judge Ardery then explained, "I suggested to him that he go to his pastor and talk over the matter he had told me of. He didn't seem inclined to receive that suggestion favorably, and then I told him that in my opinion the sooner he got this question over and disposed of, the better it would be. My grand jury was then in session. . . . We understood each other as to what my words meant." While this second conversation was not permitted to go to the jury it has bearing upon the problem here involved. . . .

Judge Ardery was not merely a judge giving, as a lawyer, legal advice to a client—he was the presiding circuit judge of Bourbon County and as such had impaneled a grand jury which he was about to instruct concerning reported infractions of law upon which his advice was sought. By all standards of ethical conduct which govern the conduct of a judge it was morally, if not legally, impossible for Judge Ardery to enter into an attorney-client relationship with one whose conduct was to be investigated by a grand jury already called and about to be instructed, and this Prichard knew or must have known. It is true that no indictment against Prichard was returned by the local grand jury, but this was because the Federal Bureau of Investigation had taken over the inquiry and the state grand jury investigation was never completed. Prichard testified in camera that he knew Judge Ardery would be disqualified in sitting upon his case if an indictment against him were returned. By all the modern concepts of judicial ethics, the judge was not only disqualified from sitting on Prichard's case, but doubtless was also disqualified from organizing and instructing the grand jury once he was advised that the investigation would likely bring within the ambit of the inquest matters bearing upon the conduct of one who, upon the eve of inquiry, had already discussed with him participation in the very alleged unlawful conduct about to be investigated. . . .

While Prichard asserts he went to the judge for legal advice, and while the judge thought he might give such advice and then withdraw from any case that might result from the grand jury investigation, there is no suggestion in the record as to any advice sought or given that would constitute legal advice. Rather is there strong inference that Prichard sought the interview to ease a troubled conscience and sought it of Judge Ardery not in his professional capacity as a lawyer capable of giving legal counsel but as a wise and valued friend who had known him all his life. "I am in deep trouble and I want your advice," and so the judge seemingly interpreted it. "I suggested to him that he go to his pastor and talk over the matter he had told me of. . . . We understood each other as to what my words meant." . . .

Finally, Prichard's request for advice was robbed of the element of good faith once he knew, as know he did, that the judge was about to charge a grand jury in respect to election frauds. Whether we conceive the function of the judge in organizing and instructing a grand jury to be judicial or administrative is immaterial. In either capacity, knowledge of law violation may not be reposed in him under the cloak of privilege. As Wigmore puts it, [5 Wigmore on Evidence, 2d ed.] §2300, "A consultation with a judge, in his capacity as such, falls unquestionably outside the present privilege." Judge Ardery was currently engaged in ferreting out election frauds under the authority and command of the laws of his state. Knowledge that came to him while exercising this function could not be received by him in confidence. Whether judges of superior courts may ever enter into an attorney-client relationship, we need not presently decide, even though voicing our doubts. It is sufficient to say for purpose of present decision, that a judge circumstanced as was Judge Ardery, may not enter into such relationship with a lawyer who may not deny knowledge of accepted notions of judicial propriety. There was no error in receiving Judge Ardery's evidence.

Is the result in *Prichard* consistent with proposed Rule 503? Does the *Prichard* court utilize an objective, subjective, or strict liability approach to the question of the existence of a confidential lawyer-client relationship?

Problem: The Energetic Investigator

Action for damages for assault and battery. *D*'s attorney, Silvertongue, has been trying to arrange an interview with *P* for some time but with no success. Silvertongue sends Archie Goodwind, his private investigator, over to *P*'s counsel's office to try to arrange for an interview. Archie is cooling his heels in opposing counsel's waiting room when he observes *P* entering the office. Seizing the initiative, Archie rises to his feet and introduces himself to *P* as "a private investigator on the *P* v. *D* case." Archie explains that the lawyer is busy. At this point, *P* starts to discuss the facts of the case with Archie. Pleased with this opportunity to talk to *P* about the case, Archie directs him into an empty conference room off the waiting room, where he interrogates *P* in detail for 35 minutes.

At trial, *D* calls Archie to testify to statements made by *P* during this interview. *P*'s attorney objects on grounds of lawyer-client privilege. What ruling and why?

Problem: Tania's Tale

Patty sues Lee, an attorney who represented her in a criminal case, for malpractice after he lost her case and she was sent to jail. Her complaint alleges that Lee advised her to assert her Fifth Amendment privilege against self-incrimination as to some events with which she was charged and that this constituted malpractice because she was put in the position of frequently invoking the privilege in front of the jury. Lee counterclaims for $250,000, representing the amount allegedly still due him on his fee, which Patty has refused to pay on the grounds of incompetent assistance of counsel. At the trial of these actions, Lee takes the stand to testify to various communications between himself and Patty regarding the events about which she asserted the privilege against self-incrimination. Patty's present lawyer objects on grounds of privilege. What ruling and why?

Problem: The Evanescent Privilege

D was convicted of armed robbery. At the sentencing hearing, he told the judge that he had not committed the armed robbery but that he had been prevented from so testifying because his court-appointed counsel, Louis Bender, had advised him that all or virtually all of his extensive prior criminal record would be introduced to impeach his credibility. Under questioning by the judge, it became apparent that Mr. Bender was not completely familiar with Rule 609. In particular, it was unclear whether Mr. Bender understood that under Rule 609 some of the defendant's prior crimes could be excluded by the judge because of their prejudicial impact. The court scheduled a hearing to consider whether *D* should be granted a new trial because of incompetent assistance of counsel.

At the hearing on the motion for a new trial, *D* represented himself with the assistance of an attorney-adviser appointed by the court. Mr. Bender, who had been subpoenaed by the prosecution, was also represented by counsel. *D* called himself as his first witness. Before taking the stand, he attempted to obtain from the court a ruling limiting cross-examination to Mr. Bender's advice to him concerning the admissibility of his prior criminal record at his original trial if he had taken the stand. The court refused to so limit the scope of cross-examination.

D changed his mind and decided not to testify. Instead, he called Mr. Bender. After eliciting some preliminary testimony, *D* asked Mr. Bender to relate the substance of conversations he had with him in *D*'s prison cell and during trial concerning the admissibility of *D*'s prior criminal record. Mr. Bender objected to such questions on the ground that they were covered by the attorney-client privilege and that there was no evidence that *D* had made a knowing and intelligent waiver of the privilege. The judge stated that he had had lengthy discussions with *D* and was satisfied that *D* was making a knowing and intelligent waiver, overruled the objection, and ordered Mr. Bender to answer. Mr. Bender then related the substance of several conversations between himself and *D* concerning his advice as to the admissibility of *D*'s prior convictions at the original trial. On cross-examination, the assistant U.S. Attorney asked Mr. Bender to relate the entirety of the conversations concerning *D*'s decision whether to take the stand. Both *D* and Mr. Bender objected to this line of questioning, attempting to assert the attorney-client privilege to everything except the portions of the conversations concerning the admissibility of the prior convictions.

How should the court rule?

Problem: Name That Client

At a grand jury probe into conspiracy to commit income tax violations, the state calls three persons, each of whom is a duly licensed and practicing attorney. The purpose of calling them is to obtain the names of certain unknown conspirators who, among other things, met with the attorneys to secure representation for the named and indicted conspirators.

The U.S. Attorney asks each attorney the following questions:

(1) Did any of the named defendants employ you to represent him?

(2) Did any third party make arrangements for you to represent a named defendant? If so, who?

(3) If you posted bond for a named defendant, who furnished the bond money?

(4) If you have been paid any attorney's fees on behalf of a named defendant, who paid them?

Which, if any, of these questions may be successfully resisted on grounds of privilege? When the attorney-client privilege is asserted and contested, where does the burden of proof lie?

UNITED STATES v. PAPE
144 F.2d 778 (2d Cir. 1944)

CLARK, J. Pape appeals from a judgment of conviction under an indictment for transporting a woman in interstate commerce "for the purpose of prostitution, debauchery and other immoral purposes." . . .

[T]he attorney, Buckley, . . . appeared for the woman in Washington when she was first taken up by the police, and she was discharged in his custody. On preliminary examination the judge developed that he was retained by the accused about July 15, 1942, to represent the woman as well as the accused — for what purpose, so far as the latter was concerned, never appeared. . . . [The judge] proceeded to make his ruling explicit by saying that the lawyer could be asked who retained him to appear for the woman on the occasion in question and who paid his fee, identifying the persons if they were in court. . . . The lawyer did, therefore, testify that the accused retained him to represent the woman and paid his fee, also that he saw the defendant in Washington and that he had a Packard automobile. Of course, practically all this was merely cumulative; the court records were produced and showed that the woman was indeed released to the attorney; and the only additional fact brought out was that the accused's clearly proved interest in the woman went to the point of retaining and paying for a lawyer to secure her release.

The authorities are substantially uniform against any privilege as applied to the fact of retainer or identity of the client. The privilege is limited to confidential communications, and a retainer is not a confidential communication, although it cannot come into existence without some communication between the attorney and the—at that stage prospective—client. . . . [T]here may be situations in which so much has already appeared of the actual communications between an attorney and a client, that the disclosure of the client will result in a breach of the privilege; but nothing of the sort occurred here. . . .

It seems clear on the authorities, therefore, that the evidence actually brought out before the jury was not privileged. There seems nothing in the preliminary disclosure to the judge that the attorney was also to represent the accused to change this result. . . . Generally speaking, relevant evidence is freely admissible, except as it is privileged; and the privilege extends only so far as the policy behind it demands. Here, as Mr. Justice Shientag shows with his usual felicity, People ex rel. Vogelstein v. Warden of County Jail, 150 Misc. 714, 270 N.Y.S. at page 367, "it was not the purpose of the privilege to shield guilt. Its primary object was to secure the orderly administration of justice by insuring frank revelation by the client to the attorney without fear of a forced disclosure; in other words, to promote freedom of consultation. To be sure the exercise of the privilege may at times result in concealing the truth and allowing the guilty to escape. That is an evil, however, which is considered to be outweighed by the benefit which results to the administration of justice generally."

He adds, "There is nothing in the books to show that the privilege was to extend to the fact of the retention of counsel. No point is made that the employment of counsel should be shrouded with secrecy." Hence when the narrow exclusionary rule ceases to apply, then the more general and pervasive rule of free disclosure to ascertain the truth and prevent the guilty from escaping furnishes the governing principle.

Conviction affirmed.

L. HAND, J. (dissenting).

The evidence of the accused's guilt was so strong that I feel some compunction in voting to reverse, yet there are two errors which I think require the case to be retried. Pape retained Buckley as his own lawyer at the same time that he retained him for the woman. I agree that this retainer of an attorney for himself involved no privileged communication; I have nothing to add to, or subtract from, what my brothers say on that. Moreover, it goes without saying that Pape's retainer of Buckley for the woman would not have been privileged, had he not retained him as his own attorney. On the other hand I attach no importance to the fact that he retained him in both capacities at the same time; the case stands as it would, if he had retained him for himself first. Yet if he had done that, when he told him to appear for her, I think it was a communication between attorney and client, a step in his own defence; it may have been also a step in hers but that, I submit, is irrelevant. That direction to his own attorney in his own interest was as much a privileged communication as any direction would have been, made in the course of preparing for a trial; as much, for example, as to tell one's attorney to interview a witness. That it was an important step in connecting him with the woman's prostitution, admits of no debate.

Problem: Hit and Run

N.Y. Times, Oct. 12, 1988

WEST PALM BEACH, Fla. (AP)—The police know many facts about the hit-and-run death of Mark Baltes, whose body was dragged 60 feet when he was struck by a white Buick after midnight on March 9, 1986.

But there is one crucial fact the authorities lack: the name of the driver. The driver's lawyer had shielded the identity for more than two and a half years. This week the lawyer, Barry Krischer, may finally be ordered to divulge his secret.

In a case that challenges the sanctity of the confidential relationship between lawyer and client, a Florida district judge is considering a request by Mr. Baltes' parents to force Mr. Krischer to disclose his client's name.

The unusual struggle, which has aroused considerable interest among lawyers, began the day after the accident when the driver asked Mr. Krischer to initiate a plea bargain arrangement without disclosing his client's name to the authorities.

According to the police, Mr. Baltes, a 28-year old electrician, was struck and killed as he staggered down a road at night while drunk. Detectives used car fragments at the scene and paint chips from Mr. Baltes' skull to theorize that the vehicle was a 1984 or 1985 Buick Riviera. But hundreds of interviews and a reward failed to yield any firm suspects.

Mr. Krischer, in an attempt to block pressure to disclose the name, retained another lawyer, Scott Richardson, who opened talks with prosecutors but did not divulge Mr. Krischer's link to the case. Mr. Richardson says he never learned the name of the driver. Mr. Krischer eventually came forward but refused to identify his client.

Joseph D. Farrish, Jr., an attorney for Mr. Baltes' parents, filed a $6 million wrongful death suit against an unspecified defendant in February, naming the unknown driver Dow. He then subpoenaed Mr. Krischer to testify to the identity of his client. Mr. Krischer refused on grounds of attorney-client privilege. Mr. Farrish contends that the attorney-client privilege does not give lawyers a blanket under which to conceal the identity of a fugitive.

"To me the case is quite clear," said Mr. Farrish. "I'm ready to take it as far as they are willing to go."

Mr. Baltes' parents, who have sat quietly through hearings this month, are exasperated at efforts to learn the name. "I'm getting the lawyer-client privilege up to here," said the dead man's mother, Mildred Baltes. "It certainly doesn't help solve any cases."

Earlier this year the Balteses even agreed to allow state prosecutors to offer the driver immunity from criminal, but not civil, prosecution if the person came forward.

"If there was ever a case to test the sanctity of the attorney-client privilege, this one is it," said Prof. Andrew Kaufman of the Harvard University Law School, who is author of a book on legal ethics. "In most disputes over the attorney-client privilege, the identity is known and the contents of the conversations are not. What makes this case unique is that it is just the opposite."

N.Y. Times, Oct. 13, 1988
Article by Jeffrey Schmalz

MIAMI—In a case closely watched in legal circles nationwide, a Florida Judge ruled today that a lawyer does not have to disclose the identity of a client who may have killed a man in a hit-and-run accident two years ago. The decision will be appealed. . . .

Judge Timothy Poulton ruled that the name was protected by the attorney-client privilege. "If we fail to rule as we do in this case," Judge Poulton wrote, "the result could be the erection of a wall between the public and attorneys."

Mr. Farrish said: "I bet today this fleeing felon is laughing at the system."

———————————

Assume you are a law clerk working with a judge on the court of appeals. The judge sends you these New York Times articles and asks for your analysis.

Problem: On the Waterfront

Blumfeld, attorney for the United Importers Association, Inc., an organization of merchants who import produce from abroad, testified before the Commissioner of Investigation that a member of the association had retained him in an effort to work out certain problems he was having on the waterfront with racketeers trying to extort protection money from the importers. In response to questioning, Blumfeld also testified that this anonymous member told him that he had learned that two powerful city politicians were involved in the protection racket and shared in its proceeds. The Commissioner asked the name of the member. Blumfeld refused to give it on grounds of lawyer-client privilege and was cited for contempt. On appeal, what ruling and why?

COUCH v. UNITED STATES
409 U.S. 322 (1973)

Mr. Justice POWELL delivered the opinion of the Court.

On January 7, 1970, the Government filed a petition in the United States District Court for the Western District of Virginia, pursuant to 26 U.S.C. §§7402(b) and 7604(a), seeking enforcement of an Internal Revenue summons in connection with an investigation of petitioner's tax liability from 1964-1968. The summons was directed to petitioner's accountant for the production of:

> All books, records, bank statements, cancelled checks, deposit ticket copies, workpapers and all other pertinent documents pertaining to the tax liability of the above taxpayer.

The question is whether the taxpayer may invoke her Fifth Amendment privilege against compulsory self-incrimination to prevent the production of her business and tax records in the possession of her accountant. Both the District Court and the Court of Appeals for the Fourth Circuit held the privilege unavailable. We granted certiorari, 405 U.S. 1038.

Petitioner is the sole proprietress of a restaurant. Since 1955 she had given bank statements, payroll records, and reports of sales and expenditures to her accountant, Harold Shaffer, for the purpose of preparing her income tax returns. The accountant was not petitioner's personal employee but an independent contractor with his own office and numerous other clients who compensated him on a piecework basis. When petitioner surrendered possession of the records to Shaffer, she, of course, retained title in herself.

During the summer of 1969, Internal Revenue Agent Dennis Groves commenced an investigation of petitioner's tax returns.

Special Agent Jennings of the Intelligence Division next commenced a joint investigation with Groves to determine petitioner's correct tax liability, the possibility of income tax fraud and the imposition of tax fraud penalties, and, lastly, the possibility of a recommendation of a criminal tax violation. Jennings first introduced himself to petitioner, gave her Miranda warnings as required by IRS directive, and then issued the summons to Shaffer after the latter refused to let him see, remove, or microfilm petitioner's records.

When Jennings arrived at Shaffer's office on September 2, 1969, the return day of the summons, to view the records, he found that Shaffer, at petitioner's request, had delivered the documents to petitioner's attorney. Jennings thereupon petitioned the District Court for enforcement of the summons, and petitioner intervened, asserting that the ownership of the records warranted a Fifth Amendment privilege to bar their production.

II

The importance of preserving inviolate the privilege against compulsory self-incrimination has often been stated by this Court and need not be elaborated. Counselman v. Hitchcock, 142 U.S. 547 (1892); Malloy v. Hogan, 378 U.S. 1 (1964); Miranda v. Arizona, 384 U.S. 436 (1966). By its very nature, the privilege is an intimate and personal one. It respects a private inner sanctum of individual feeling and thought and proscribes state intrusion to extract self-condemnation. Historically, the privilege sprang from an abhorrence of governmental assault against the single individual accused of crime and the temptation on the part of the State to resort to the expedient of compelling incriminating evidence from one's own mouth. United States v. White, 322 U.S. 694, 698 (1944). The Court has thought the privilege necessary to prevent any "recurrence of the Inquisition and the Star Chamber, even if not in their stark brutality." Ullmann v. United States, 350 U.S. 422, 428 (1956).

In Murphy v. Waterfront Commn., 378 U.S. 52, 55 (1964), the Court articulated the policies and purposes of the privilege: "[O]ur unwillingness to subject those suspected of crime to the cruel trilemma of self-accusation, perjury or contempt; our preference for an accusatorial rather than an inquisitorial system of criminal justice; our fear that self-incriminating statements will be elicited by inhumane treatment and abuses; our sense of fair play which dictates 'a fair state-individual balance by requiring the government . . . in its contest with the individual to shoulder the entire load,' . . . our respect for the inviolability of the human personality and of the right of each individual 'to a private enclave where he may lead a private life.' . . ."

It is important to reiterate that the Fifth Amendment privilege is a personal privilege: it adheres basically to the person, not to information that may incriminate him. As Mr. Justice Holmes put it: "A party is privileged from producing the evidence but not from its production." Johnson v. United States, 228 U.S. 457, 458 (1913). The Constitution explicitly prohibits compelling an accused to bear witness "against him-self"; it necessarily does not proscribe incriminating statements elicited from another. Compulsion upon the person asserting it is an important element of the privilege, and "prohibition of compelling a man . . . to be witness against himself is a prohibition of the use of physical or moral compulsion to extort communications from *him,*" Holt v. United States, 218 U.S. 245, 252-253 (1910) (emphasis added). It is extortion of infor-mation from the accused himself that offends our sense of justice.

In the case before us the ingredient of personal compulsion against an accused is lacking. The summons and the order of the District Court enforcing it are directed against the accountant. He, not the taxpayer, is the only one compelled to do anything. And the accountant makes no claim that he may tend to be incriminated by the production. In-quisitorial pressure or coercion against a potentially accused person, compelling her, against her will, to utter self-condemning words or pro-duce incriminating documents is absent. In the present case, no "shadow of testimonial compulsion upon or enforced communication by the accused" is involved. Schmerber v. California, 384 U.S. 757, 765 (1966).

The divulgence of potentially incriminating evidence against peti-tioner is naturally unwelcome. But petitioner's distress would be no less if the divulgence came not from her accountant but from some other third party with whom she was connected and who possessed substan-tially equivalent knowledge of her business affairs. The basic complaint of petitioner stems from the fact of divulgence of the possibly incrimi-nating information, not from the manner in which or the person from whom it was extracted. Yet such divulgence, where it does not result from coercion of the suspect herself, is a necessary part of the process of law enforcement and tax investigation.

III

Petitioner's reliance on Boyd v. United States, 116 U.S. 616 (1886), is misplaced. In *Boyd,* the person asserting the privilege was in possession of the written statements in question. The Court in *Boyd* did hold that "any forcible and compulsory extortion of a man's own testimony or of his private papers to be used as evidence to convict him of crime," vio-lated the Fourth and Fifth Amendments. Id., at 630. That case did not, however, address or contemplate the divergence of ownership and pos-session, and petitioner concedes that court decisions applying *Boyd* have largely been in instances where possession and ownership con-joined. . . . In *Boyd,* the production order was directed against the owner of the property who, by responding, would have been forced "to pro-duce and authenticate any personal documents or effects that might incriminate him." United States v. White, 322 U.S., at 698. But we reiterate that in the instant case there was no enforced communication of any kind from any accused or potential accused.

Petitioner would, in effect, have us read *Boyd* to mark ownership, not possession, as the bounds of the privilege, despite the fact that possession bears the closest relationship to the personal compulsion forbidden by the Fifth Amendment. To tie the privilege against self-incrimination to a concept of ownership would be to draw a meaningless line. It would hold here that the business records which petitioner actually owned would be protected in the hands of her accountant, while business information communicated to her accountant by letter and conversations in which the accountant took notes, in addition to the accountant's own workpapers and photocopies of petitioner's records, would not be subject to a claim of privilege since title rested in the accountant. Such a holding would thus place unnecessary emphasis on the form of communication to an accountant and the accountant's own working methods, while diverting the inquiry from the basic purposes of the Fifth Amendment's protections. . . .

IV

Petitioner further argues that the confidential nature of the accountant-client relationship and her resulting expectation of privacy in delivering the records protect her, under the Fourth and Fifth Amendments, from their production. Although not in itself controlling, we note that no confidential accountant-client privilege exists under federal law, and no state-created privilege has been recognized in federal cases, Falsone v. United States, 205 F.2d 734 (C.A.5 1953), cert. denied, 346 U.S. 864; Gariepy v. United States, 189 F.2d 459, 463-464 (C.A.6 1951); Himmelfarb v. United States, 175 F.2d 924, 939 (C.A.9 1949), cert. denied, 338 U.S. 860; Olender v. United States, 210 F.2d 795, 806 (C.A.9 1954). Nor is there justification for such a privilege where records relevant to income tax returns are involved in a criminal investigation or prosecution. In *Boyd*, a pre-income tax case, the Court spoke of protection of privacy, 116 U.S., at 630, but there can be little expectation of privacy where records are handed to an accountant, knowing that mandatory disclosure of much of the information therein is required in an income tax return. What information is not disclosed is largely in the accountant's discretion, not petitioner's. Indeed, the accountant himself risks criminal prosecution if he willfully assists in the preparation of a false return. 26 U.S.C. §7206(2). His own need for self-protection would often require the right to disclose the information given him. Petitioner seeks extensions of constitutional protections against self-incrimination in the very situation where obligations of disclosure exist and under a system largely dependent upon honest self-reporting even to survive. Accordingly, petitioner here cannot reasonably claim, either for Fourth or

Fifth Amendment purposes, an expectation of protected privacy or confidentiality.

V

The criterion for Fifth Amendment immunity remains not the ownership of property but the "'physical or moral compulsion' exerted." [Perlman v. United States, 247 U.S. 7, 15 (1918).] We hold today that no Fourth or Fifth Amendment claim can prevail where, as in this case, there exists no legitimate expectation of privacy and no semblance of governmental compulsion against the person of the accused. It is important, in applying constitutional principles, to interpret them in light of the fundamental interests of personal liberty they were meant to serve. Respect for these principles is eroded when they leap their proper bounds to interfere with the legitimate interest of society in enforcement of its laws and collection of the revenues. . . .

[A concurring opinion by Justice Brennan and dissenting opinions by Justices Douglas and Marshall are omitted.]

Why is there no accountant-client privilege corresponding to the lawyer-client privilege? Is the claim for an accountant-client privilege significantly weaker than the claim for the lawyer-client privilege under either Wigmore's instrumental approach or the humanistic approach to privileges? Why did the client, Lillian Couch, not have a "legitimate expectation of privacy"? Does this concept have any intrinsic meaning in this context or is it a tautology?

If, after *Couch,* a client came to you for advice on how she should handle her tax records to enhance their confidentiality, how would you advise her? In *Couch,* would the taxpayer have been in a stronger position to claim a privilege if she had kept possession of the documents herself? If she had sent the documents to her attorney in the first instance and the attorney had then hired the accountant? To what extent does the nature of the thing sought to be disclosed — e.g., thoughts, business records, personal diary, weapons—affect the scope of privilege protection? To what extent is the scope of privilege protection dependent on *why* the claimant of the privilege conveyed the records to a third person, such as an accountant or lawyer?

UNITED STATES v. SCHMIDT
343 F. Supp. 444 (M.D. Pa. 1972)

SHERIDAN, C.J. . . .

On April 1, 1971, Special Agent James W. Meade, Jr., of the Internal

Revenue Service, issued an Internal Revenue summons requiring respondent, J. Donald Schmidt, a Certified Public Accountant, to appear
and to testify concerning the tax liabilities of Vincent C. McCue for the
taxable years 1966, 1967, 1968 and 1969, and with respect to the preparation of the joint tax return of Vincent C. McCue and Elizabeth A.
McCue for the taxable year 1969. Respondent, J. Donald Schmidt, refused to answer certain questions propounded to him by Special Agent
Meade; he has continued to refuse to answer, asserting both the
attorney-client privilege and the privilege against self-incrimination. Petitioners moved the court for enforcement of the summons. . . .

The sole question to which the court presently addresses itself is the
applicability of the attorney-client privilege. On the record before the
court, the uncontroverted facts are as follows: respondent-taxpayers,
Vincent C. McCue and Elizabeth A. McCue, retained respondent-
attorneys, Shumaker, Williams & Placey, in August 1969; Shumaker, Williams & Placey employed J. Donald Schmidt, a Certified Public
Accountant, on April 1, 1970, subsequent to the establishment of the
attorney-client relationship; an agreement was entered into between
said attorneys and accountant on April 1, 1970, setting forth the terms
and conditions of Schmidt's employment. Pursuant to the aforementioned agreement, all accountant's services were to be performed at the
written request of counsel; it was made explicit that Vincent and Elizabeth McCue were the clients of the law firm, and not of the accountant;
it was stated that Schmidt's services were required to facilitate an accurate and complete legal consultation between the law firm and its tax-
payer-clients in the interest of allowing counsel to furnish informed
legal advice; all bookkeeping and accounting records, work papers,
schedules and reports relating to the taxpayers were made the exclusive
property of the law firm, even if they had been prepared by the accountant and even if they were in the accountant's possession; all bill-
ings for accounting services were to be made to the law firm; all
information obtained by the accountant while performing accounting
services was to be confidential, and the accountant was prohibited from
disclosing same without the prior written consent of the law firm or an
order of court, the only exception to the confidentiality requirement
being the information which actually appeared on the tax return.

It is respondents' contention that the establishment of the foregoing is sufficient in itself to bring the subject matter of the questions
propounded to Schmidt within the scope of the attorney-client
privilege. . . .

What result and why? Have the taxpayers successfully circumvented
Couch? Why should it make any difference to the existence of a privilege

whether the taxpayer hires an accountant or hires an attorney who hires an accountant?

Is there any privilege that protects the taxpayer from forced disclosure of tax preparation material prepared by his accountant but turned over to his attorney *prior* to the issuance of any government subpoena?

FISHER v. UNITED STATES
425 U.S. 391 (1976)

Mr. Justice WHITE delivered the opinion of the Court.

In these two cases we are called upon to decide whether a summons directing an attorney to produce documents delivered to him by his client in connection with the attorney-client relationship is enforceable over claims that the documents were constitutionally immune from summons in the hands of the client and retained that immunity in the hands of the attorney.

I

In each case, an Internal Revenue agent visited the taxpayer or taxpayers and interviewed them in connection with an investigation of possible civil or criminal liability under the federal income tax laws. Shortly after the interviews — one day later in No. 74-611 and a week or two later in No. 74-18 — the taxpayers obtained from their respective accountants certain documents relating to the preparation by the accountants of their tax returns. Shortly after obtaining the documents—later the same day in No. 74-611 and a few weeks later in No. 74-18 — the taxpayers transferred the documents to their lawyers—respondent Kasmir and petitioner Fisher, respectively—each of whom was retained to assist the taxpayer in connection with the investigation. Upon learning of the whereabouts of the documents, the Internal Revenue Service served summonses on the attorneys directing them to produce documents listed therein. In No. 74-611, the documents were described as the following records of Tannebaum Bindler & Lewis [the accounting firm].

> 1. Accountant's work papers pertaining to Dr. E.J. Mason's books and records of 1969, 1970 and 1971.
> 2. Retained copies of E.J. Mason's income tax returns for 1969, 1970 and 1971.
> 3. Retained copies of reports and other correspondence between Tannebaum Bindler & Lewis and Dr. E.J. Mason during 1969, 1970 and 1971.

In No. 74-18, the documents demanded were analyses by the accountant of the taxpayers' income and expenses which had been copied by the accountant from the taxpayers' canceled checks and deposit receipts. In No. 74-611, a summons was also served on the accountant directing him to appear and testify concerning the documents to be produced by the lawyer. In each case, the lawyer declined to comply with the summons directing production of the documents, and enforcement actions were commenced by the Government under 26 U.S.C. §§7402(b) and 7604(a). In No. 74-611, the attorney raised in defense of the enforcement action the taxpayer's accountant-client privilege, his attorney-client privilege, and his Fourth and Fifth Amendment rights. In No. 74-18, the attorney claimed that enforcement would involve compulsory self-incrimination of the taxpayers in violation of their Fifth Amendment privilege, would involve a seizure of the papers without necessary compliance with the Fourth Amendment, and would violate the taxpayers' right to communicate in confidence with their attorney. In No. 74-18 the taxpayers intervened and made similar claims. . . .

II

All of the parties in these cases and the Court of Appeals for the Fifth Circuit have concurred in the proposition that if the Fifth Amendment would have excused a *taxpayer* from turning over the accountant's papers had he possessed them, the *attorney* to whom they are delivered for the purpose of obtaining legal advice should also be immune from subpoena. Although we agree with this proposition for the reasons set forth in Part III, infra, we are convinced that, under our decision in Couch v. United States, 409 U.S. 322 (1973), it is not the taxpayer's Fifth Amendment privilege that would excuse the *attorney* from production.

The relevant part of that Amendment provides:

No person . . . shall be *compelled* in any criminal case to be a *witness against himself.* (Emphasis added by the Court.)

The taxpayer's privilege under this Amendment is not violated by enforcement of the summonses involved in these cases because enforcement against a taxpayer's lawyer would not "compel" the taxpayer to do anything—and certainly would not compel him to be a "witness" against himself. The Court has held repeatedly that the Fifth Amendment is limited to prohibiting the use of "physical or moral compulsion" exerted on the person asserting the privilege. In Couch v. United States, supra, we recently ruled that the Fifth Amendment rights of a taxpayer were not violated by the enforcement of a documentary summons directed to her accountant and requiring production of the taxpayer's own records in the possession of the accountant. We did so on the ground that in such a case "the ingredient of personal compulsion against an accused is lacking." 409 U.S., at 329.

Here, the taxpayers are compelled to do no more than was the taxpayer in *Couch*. The taxpayer's Fifth Amendment privilege is therefore not violated by enforcement of the summonses directed toward their attorneys. This is true whether or not the Amendment would have barred a subpoena directing the taxpayer to produce the documents while they were in his hands.

The fact that the attorneys are agents of the taxpayers does not change this result. *Couch* held as much, since the accountant there was also the taxpayer's agent, and in this respect reflected a longstanding view. In Hale v. Henkel, 201 U.S. 43, 69-70 (1906), the Court said that the privilege "was never intended to permit [a person] to plead the fact that some third person might be incriminated by his testimony, even though he were the agent of such person. . . . [T]he Amendment is limited to a person who shall be compelled in any criminal case to be a witness against *himself*." (Emphasis in original.) "It is extortion of information from the accused himself that offends our sense of justice." Couch v. United States, supra, at 328. Agent or no, the lawyer is not the taxpayer. The taxpayer is the "accused," and nothing is being extorted from him.

Nor is this one of those situations, which *Couch* suggested might exist, where constructive possession is so clear or relinquishment of possession so temporary and insignificant as to leave the personal compulsion upon the taxpayer substantially intact. 409 U.S., at 333. In this respect we see no difference between the delivery to the attorneys in these cases and delivery to the accountant in the *Couch* case. As was true in *Couch*, the documents sought were obtainable without personal compulsion on the accused.

Respondents in No. 74-611 and petitioners in No. 74-18 argue, and the Court of Appeals for the Fifth Circuit apparently agreed that if the summons was enforced, the taxpayers' Fifth Amendment privilege would be, but should not be, lost solely because they gave their documents to their lawyers in order to obtain legal advice. But this misconceives the nature of the constitutional privilege. The Amendment protects a person from being compelled to be a witness against himself. Here, the taxpayers retained any privilege they ever had not to be compelled to testify against themselves and not to be compelled themselves to produce private papers in their possession. *This* personal privilege was in no way decreased by the transfer. It is simply that by reason of the transfer of the documents to the attorneys, those papers may be subpoenaed without compulsion on the taxpayer. The protection of the Fifth Amendment is therefore not available. "A party is privileged from producing evidence but not from its production." Johnson v. United States, [228 U.S. 457, 458 (1913)].

The Court of Appeals for the Fifth Circuit suggested that because legally and ethically the attorney was required to respect the confidences of his client, the latter had a reasonable expectation of privacy for the records in the hands of the attorney and therefore did not forfeit his Fifth Amendment privilege with respect to the records by transferring them in order to obtain legal advice. It is true that the Court has often stated that one of the several purposes served by the constitutional privilege against compelled testimonial self-incrimination is that of protecting personal privacy. . . . But the Court has never suggested that every invasion of privacy violates the privilege. Within the limits imposed by the language of the Fifth Amendment, which we necessarily observe, the privilege truly serves privacy interests; but the Court has never on any ground, personal privacy included, applied the Fifth Amendment to prevent the otherwise proper acquisition or use of evidence which, in the Court's view, did not involve compelled testimonial self-incrimination of some sort.

The proposition that the Fifth Amendment protects private information obtained without compelling self-incriminating testimony is contrary to the clear statements of this Court that under appropriate safeguards private incriminating statements of an accused may be overheard and used in evidence, if they are not compelled at the time they were uttered, and that disclosure of private information may be compelled if immunity removes the risk of incrimination. If the Fifth Amendment protected generally against the obtaining of private information from a man's mouth or pen or house, its protections would presumably not be lifted by probable cause and a warrant or by immunity. The privacy invasion is not mitigated by immunity; and the Fifth Amendment's strictures, unlike the Fourth's, are not removed by showing reasonableness. The Framers addressed the subject of personal privacy directly in the Fourth Amendment. They struck a balance so that when the State's reason to believe incriminating evidence will be found becomes sufficiently great, the invasion of privacy becomes justified and a warrant to search and seize will issue. They did not seek in still another Amendment—the Fifth—to achieve a general protection of privacy but to deal with the more specific issue of compelled self-incrimination.

We cannot cut the Fifth Amendment completely loose from the moorings of its language, and make it serve as a general protector of privacy—a word not mentioned in its text and a concept directly addressed in the Fourth Amendment. We adhere to the view that the Fifth Amendment protects against "compelled self-incrimination, not [the disclosure of] private information."

Insofar as private information not obtained through compelled self-incriminating testimony is legally protected, its protection stems from other sources—the Fourth Amendment's protection against seizures without warrant or probable cause and against subpoenas which suffer from "too much indefiniteness or breadth in the things required to be 'particularly described,'" the First Amendment, or evidentiary privileges such as the attorney-client privilege.

III

Our above holding is that compelled production of documents from an attorney does not implicate whatever Fifth Amendment privilege the taxpayer might have enjoyed from being compelled to produce them himself. . . . In this posture of the case, we feel obliged to inquire whether the attorney-client privilege applies to documents in the hands of an attorney which would have been privileged in the hands of the client by reason of the Fifth Amendment.

Confidential disclosures by a client to an attorney made in order to obtain legal assistance are privileged. 8 J. Wigmore, Evidence §2292 (McNaughton rev. 1961) (hereinafter Wigmore); McCormick §87, p.175. The purpose of the privilege is to encourage clients to make full disclosure to their attorneys. As a practical matter, if the client knows that damaging information could more readily be obtained from the attorney following disclosure than from himself in the absence of disclosure, the client would be reluctant to confide in his lawyer and it would be difficult to obtain fully informed legal advice. However, since the privilege has the effect of withholding relevant information from the factfinder, it applies only where necessary to achieve its purpose. Accordingly it protects only those disclosures — necessary to obtain informed legal advice — which might not have been made absent the privilege. This court and the lower courts have thus uniformly held that pre-existing documents which could have been obtained by court process from the client when he was in possession may also be obtained from the attorney by similar process following transfer by the client in order to obtain more informed legal advice. The purpose of the privilege requires no broader rule. Pre-existing documents obtainable from the client are not appreciably easier to obtain from the attorney after transfer to him. Thus, even absent the attorney-client privilege, clients will not be discouraged from disclosing the documents to the attorney, and their ability to obtain informed legal advice will remain unfettered. It is otherwise if the documents are not obtainable by subpoena duces tecum or summons while in the exclusive possession of the client, for the client will then be reluctant to transfer possession to the lawyer unless the documents are also privileged in the latter's hands. Where the transfer is made for the purpose of obtaining legal advice, the purposes of the attorney-client privilege would be defeated unless the privilege is applicable. "It follows, then, that *when the client himself would be privileged* from production of the documents, either as party at common law . . . or as exempt from self-incrimination, the attorney having possession of the document is not bound to produce." 8 Wigmore §2307, p.592. . . . United States v. Judson, 322 F.2d 460, 466 (C.A.9 1963). This proposition was accepted by the Court of Appeals for the Fifth Circuit below, is asserted by petitioners in No. 74-18 and respondents in No. 74-611, and was conceded by the Government in its brief and at oral argument. Where the transfer to the attorney is for the purpose of obtaining legal advice, we agree with it.

Since each taxpayer transferred possession of the documents in question from himself to his attorney in order to obtain legal assistance in the tax investigations in question, the papers, if unobtainable by summons from the client, are unobtainable by summons directed to the attorney by reason of the attorney-client privilege. We accordingly proceed to the question whether the documents could have been obtained by summons addressed to the taxpayer while the documents were in his possession. The only bar to enforcement of such summons asserted by the parties or the courts below is the Fifth Amendment's privilege against self-incrimination. . . .

IV

The proposition that the Fifth Amendment prevents compelled production of documents over objection that such production might incriminate stems from Boyd v. United States, 116 U.S. 616 (1886). *Boyd* involved a civil forfeiture proceeding brought by the Government against two partners for fraudulently attempting to import 35 cases of glass without paying the prescribed duty. The partnership had contracted with the Government to furnish the glass needed in the construction of a Government building. The glass specified was foreign glass, it being understood that if part or all of the glass was furnished from the partnership's existing duty-paid inventory, it could be replaced by duty-free imports. Pursuant to this arrangement, 29 cases of glass were imported by the partnership duty free. The partners then represented that they were entitled to duty-free entry of an additional 35 cases which were soon to arrive. The forfeiture action concerned these 35 cases. The Government's position was that the partnership had replaced all of the glass used in construction of the Government building when it imported the 29 cases. At trial, the Government obtained a court order directing the partners to produce an invoice the partnership had received from the shipper covering the previous 29-case shipment. The invoice was disclosed, offered in evidence, and used, over the Fifth Amendment objection of the partners, to establish that the partners were fraudulently claiming a greater exemption from duty than they were entitled to under the contract. This Court held that the invoice was inadmissible and reversed the judgment in favor of the Government. The Court ruled that the Fourth Amendment applied to court orders in the nature of subpoenas duces tecum in the same manner in which it applies to search warrants, id., at 622; and that the Government may not, consistent with the Fourth Amendment, seize a person's documents or other property as evidence unless it can claim a proprietary interest in the property superior to that of the person from whom the property is obtained. Id., at 623-624. The invoice in question was thus held to have been obtained in violation of the Fourth Amendment. The Court went on to hold that the accused in a criminal case or the defendant in a forfeiture action could not be forced to produce evidentiary items without violating the Fifth Amendment as well as the Fourth. More specifically, the Court declared, "a compulsory production of the private books and papers of the owner of goods sought to be forfeited . . . is compelling him to be a witness against himself, within the meaning of the Fifth Amendment to the Constitution." Id., at 634-635. Admitting the partnership invoice into evidence had violated both the Fifth and Fourth Amendments.

Among its several pronouncements, *Boyd* was understood to declare that the seizure, under warrant or otherwise, of any purely evidentiary materials violated the Fourth Amendment and that the Fifth Amendment rendered these seized materials inadmissible. That rule applied to documents as well as to other evidentiary items—"[t]here is no special sanctity in papers, as distinguished from other forms of property, to render them immune from search and seizure, if only they fall within the scope of the principles of the cases in which other property may be seized. . . ." Private papers taken from the taxpayer, like other "mere evidence," could not be used against the accused over his Fourth and Fifth Amendment objections.

Several of *Boyd*'s express or implicit declarations have not stood the test of time. The application of the Fourth Amendment to subpoenas was limited by Hale v. Henkel, 201 U.S. 43 (1906), and more recent cases. See, e.g., Oklahoma Press Pub. Co. v. Walling, 327 U.S. 186 (1946). Purely evidentiary (but "nontestimonial") materials, as well as contraband and fruits and instrumentalities of crime, may now be searched for and seized under proper circumstances, Warden v. Hayden, 387 U.S. 294 (1967). Also, any notion that "testimonial" evidence may never be seized and used in evidence is inconsistent with Katz v. United States, 389 U.S. 347 (1967); Osborn v. United States, 385 U.S. 323 (1966); and Berger v. New York, 388 U.S. 41 (1967), approving the seizure under appropriate circumstances of conversations of a person suspected of crime. See also Marron v. United States, 275 U.S. 192 (1927).

It is also clear that the Fifth Amendment does not independently proscribe the compelled production of every sort of incriminating evidence but applies only when the accused is compelled to make a *testimonial* communication that is incriminating. We have, accordingly, declined to extend the protection of the privilege to the giving of blood samples, Schmerber v. California, 384 U.S. 757, 763-764 (1966); to the giving of handwriting exemplars, Gilbert v. California, 388 U.S. 263, 265-267 (1967); voice exemplars, United States v. Wade, 388 U.S. 218, 222-223 (1967); or the donning of a blouse worn by the perpetrator, Holt v. United States, 218 U.S. 245 (1910). Furthermore, despite *Boyd,* neither a partnership nor the individual partners are shielded from compelled production of partnership records on self-incrimination grounds. Bellis v. United States, 417 U.S. 85 (1974). It would appear that under that case the precise claim sustained in *Boyd* would now be rejected for reasons not there considered.

The pronouncement in *Boyd* that a person may not be forced to produce his private papers has nonetheless often appeared as dictum in later opinions of this Court. To the extent, however, that the rule against compelling production of private papers rested on the proposition that seizures of or subpoenas for "mere evidence," including documents, violated the Fourth Amendment and therefore also transgressed the Fifth, the foundations for the rule have been washed away. In consequence, the prohibition against forcing the production of private papers has long been a rule searching for a rationale consistent with the proscriptions of the Fifth Amendment against compelling a person to give "testimony" that incriminates him. Accordingly, we turn to the question of what, if any, incriminating testimony within the Fifth Amendment's protection, is compelled by a documentary summons.

A subpoena served on a taxpayer requiring him to produce an accountant's workpapers in his possession without doubt involves substantial compulsion. But it does not compel oral testimony; nor would it ordinarily compel the taxpayer to restate, repeat, or affirm the truth of the contents of the documents sought. Therefore, the Fifth Amendment would not be violated by the fact alone that the papers on their face might incriminate the taxpayer, for the privilege protects a person only against being incriminated by his own compelled testimonial communications. Schmerber v. California, supra; United States v. Wade, supra; and Gilbert v. California, supra. The accountant's workpapers are not the taxpayer's. They were not prepared by the taxpayer, and they contain no testimonial declarations by him. Furthermore, as far as this record demonstrates, the preparation of all of the papers sought in these cases was wholly voluntary, and they cannot be said to contain compelled testimonial evidence, either of the taxpayers or of anyone else. The taxpayer cannot avoid compliance with the subpoena merely by asserting that the item of evidence which he is required to produce contains incriminating writing, whether his own or that of someone else.

The act of producing evidence in response to a subpoena nevertheless has communicative aspects of its own, wholly aside from the contents of the papers produced. Compliance with the subpoena tacitly concedes the existence of the papers demanded and their possession or control by the taxpayer. It also would indicate the taxpayer's belief that the papers are those described in the subpoena. Curcio v. United States, 354 U.S. 118, 125 (1957). The elements of compulsion are clearly present, but the more difficult issues are whether the tacit averments of the taxpayer are both "testimonial" and "incriminating" for purposes of applying the Fifth Amendment. These questions perhaps do not lend themselves to categorical answers; their resolution may instead depend on the facts and circumstances of particular cases or classes thereof. In light of the records now before us, we are confident that however incriminating the contents of the accountant's workpapers might be, the act of producing them—the only thing which the taxpayer is compelled to do—would not itself involve testimonial self-incrimination.

It is doubtful that implicitly admitting the existence and possession of the papers rises to the level of testimony within the protection of the Fifth Amendment. The papers belong to the accountant, were prepared by him, and are the kind usually prepared by an accountant working on the tax returns of his client. Surely the Government is in no way relying on the "truthtelling" of the taxpayer to prove the existence of or his access to the documents. 8 Wigmore §2264, p.380. The existence and location of the papers are a foregone conclusion and the taxpayer adds little or nothing to the sum total of the Government's information by conceding that he in fact has the papers. Under these circumstances by enforcement of the summons "no constitutional rights are touched. The question is not of testimony but of surrender." In re Harris, 221 U.S. 274, 279 (1911).

When an accused is required to submit a handwriting exemplar he admits his ability to write and impliedly asserts that the exemplar is his writing. But in common experience, the first would be a near truism and the latter self-evident. In any event, although the exemplar may be incriminating to the accused and although he is compelled to furnish it, his Fifth Amendment privilege is not violated because nothing he has said or done is deemed to be sufficiently testimonial for purposes of the privilege. This Court has also time and again allowed subpoenas against the custodian of corporate documents or those belonging to other collective entities such as unions and partnerships and those of bankrupt businesses over claims that the documents will incriminate the custodian despite the fact that producing the documents tacitly admits their existence and their location in the hands of their possessor. The existence and possession or control of the subpoenaed documents being no more in issue here than in the above cases, the summons is equally enforceable.

Moreover, assuming that these aspects of producing the accountant's papers have some minimal testimonial significance, surely it is not illegal to seek accounting help in connection with one's tax returns or for the accountant to prepare workpapers and deliver them to the taxpayer. At this juncture, we are quite unprepared to hold that either the fact of existence of the papers or of their possession by the taxpayer poses any realistic threat of incrimination to the taxpayer.

As for the possibility that responding to the subpoena would authenticate the workpapers, production would express nothing more than the taxpayer's belief that the papers are those described in the subpoena. The taxpayer would be no more competent to authenticate the accountant's workpapers or reports by producing them than he would be to authenticate them if testifying orally. The taxpayer did not prepare the papers and could not vouch for their accuracy. The documents would not be admissible in evidence against the taxpayer without authenticating testimony. Without more, responding to the subpoena in the circumstances before us would not appear to represent a substantial threat of self-incrimination. . . .

Whether the Fifth Amendment would shield the taxpayer from producing his own tax records in his possession is a question not involved here; for the papers demanded here are not his "private papers," see Boyd v. United States, 116 U.S., at 634-635. We do hold that compliance with a summons directing the taxpayer to produce the accountant's documents involved in these cases would involve no incriminating testimony within the protection of the Fifth Amendment. . . .

[Concurring opinions by Justices Brennan and Marshall are omitted.]

After *Fisher*, how would you advise a client seeking both sound tax advice and full confidentiality of his business records? Are there any arrangements that will ensure that *both* objectives are met, or must the taxpayer choose between them?

In his concurring opinion in *Fisher*, Justice BRENNAN states:

> The common-law and constitutional extension of the privilege to testimonial materials, such as books and papers, was inevitable. An individual's books and papers are generally little more than an extension of his person. They reveal no less than he could reveal upon being questioned directly. Many of the matters within an individual's knowledge may as easily be retained within his head as set down on a scrap of paper. I perceive no principle which does not permit compelling one to disclose the contents of one's mind but does permit compelling the disclosure of the contents of that scrap of paper by compelling its production. Under a contrary view, the constitutional protection would turn on fortuity, and persons would, at their peril, record their thoughts and the events of their lives. The ability to think private thoughts, facilitated as it is by pen and paper, and the ability to preserve intimate memories would be curtailed through fear that those thoughts or the events of those memories would become the subjects of criminal sanctions however invalidly imposed.

425 U.S. at 420.

Should all types of books and papers be regarded equally for purposes of privilege? For example, in an investigation into alleged fraud on the government in the furnishing of supplies, suppose the government seeks a search warrant for the premises of the target company. Assuming there is probable cause, can a warrant lawfully be executed to obtain each of the following items?

(1) A copy of the invoice allegedly used to double-bill the government for the supplies in question;

(2) A memorandum to the file by the company's president summarizing his view of the facts relevant to the investigation;

(3) The company president's personal diary; and

(4) A copy of a letter from the company's president to his attorney including a copy of the memorandum described above.

To the extent that any of these documents could be lawfully seized during a search of the company's premises, if the documents were delivered to the company's lawyer prior to the search, could the government obtain them by means of a subpoena directed to the attorney?

What advice can the attorney in a *Fisher* situation give his clients about retention of tax preparation documents? Can she advise them to destroy such documents? How do the accessory-after-the-fact and obstruction-of-justice statutes, the spoliation doctrine, and the ethical obligations of counsel limit the attorney's options?

UNITED STATES v. DOE
465 U.S. 605 (1984)

Justice POWELL delivered the opinion of the Court.

This case presents the issue whether, and to what extent, the Fifth Amendment privilege against compelled self-incrimination applies to the business records of a sole proprietorship.

I

Respondent is the owner of several sole proprietorships. In late 1980, a grand jury, during the course of an investigation of corruption in the awarding of county and municipal contracts, served five subpoenas on respondent. The first two demanded the production of the telephone records of several of respondent's companies and all records pertaining to four bank accounts of respondent and his companies. The subpoenas were limited to the period between January 1, 1977, and the dates of the subpoenas. The third subpoena demanded the production of a list of virtually all the business records of one of respondent's companies for the period between January 1, 1976, and the date of the subpoena.

The fourth subpoena sought production of a similar list of business records belonging to another company. The final subpoena demanded production of all bank statements and cancelled checks of two of respondent's companies that had accounts at a bank in the Grand Cayman Islands.

II

Respondent filed a motion in Federal District Court seeking to quash the subpoenas. The District Court for the District of New Jersey granted his motion except with respect to those documents and records required by law to be kept or disclosed to a public agency. In reaching its decision, the District Court noted that the Government had conceded that the materials sought in the subpoena were or might be incriminating. The court stated that, therefore, "the relevant inquiry is . . . whether the *act* of producing the documents has communicative aspects which warrant Fifth Amendment protection." In re Grand Jury Empanelled March 19, 1980, 541 F. Supp. 1, 3 (1981) (emphasis in original). The court found that the act of production would compel respondent to "admit that the records exist, that they are in his possession, and that they are authentic." Ibid. While not ruling out the possibility that the Government could devise a way to ensure that the act of turning over the documents would not incriminate respondent, the court held that the Government had not made such a showing.

The Court of Appeals for the Third Circuit affirmed. It first addressed the question whether the Fifth Amendment ever applies to the records of a sole proprietorship. After noting that an individual may not assert the Fifth Amendment privilege on behalf of a corporation, partnership, or other collective entity under the holding of Bellis v. United States, 417 U.S. 85 (1974), the Court of Appeals reasoned that the owner of a sole proprietorship acts in a personal rather than a representative capacity. As a result, the court held that respondent's claim of the privilege was not foreclosed by the reasoning of *Bellis.*

The Court of Appeals next considered whether the documents at issue in this case are privileged. The court noted that this Court held in Fisher v. United States, 425 U.S. 391 (1976), that the contents of business records ordinarily are not privileged because they are created voluntarily and without compulsion. The Court of Appeals nevertheless found that respondent's business records were privileged under either of two analyses. First, the court reasoned that, notwithstanding the holdings in *Bellis* and *Fisher,* the business records of a sole proprietorship are no different from the individual owner's personal records. Noting that Third Circuit cases had held that private papers, although created voluntarily, are protected by the Fifth Amendment, the court accorded the same protection to respondent's business papers. Second, it held that respondent's act of producing the subpoenaed records would have "communicative aspects of its own." The turning over of the subpoenaed documents to the grand jury would admit their existence and authenticity. Accordingly, respondent was entitled to assert his Fifth Amendment privilege rather than produce the subpoenaed documents.

The Government contended that the court should enforce the subpoenas because of the Government's offer not to use respondent's act of production against respondent in any way. The Court of Appeals noted that no formal request for use immunity under 18 U.S.C. §§6002 and 6003 had been made. In light of this failure, the court held that the District Court did not err in rejecting the Government's attempt to compel delivery of the subpoenaed records.

We granted certiorari to resolve the apparent conflict between the Court of Appeals' holding and the reasoning underlying this Court's holding in *Fisher.* We now affirm in part, reverse in part, and remand for further proceedings.

III

A

The Court in *Fisher* expressly declined to reach the question whether the Fifth Amendment privilege protects the contents of an individual's tax records in his possession. The rationale underlying our holding in that case is, however, persuasive here. As we noted in *Fisher,* the Fifth Amendment protects the person asserting the privilege only from *compelled* self-incrimination. Where the preparation of business records is voluntary, no compulsion is present. A subpoena that demands production of documents "does not compel oral testimony; nor would it ordinarily compel the taxpayer to restate, repeat, or affirm the truth of the contents of the documents sought." . . .

This reasoning applies with equal force here. Respondent does not contend that he prepared the documents involuntarily or that the subpoena would force him to restate, repeat, or affirm the truth of their contents. The fact that the records are in respondent's possession is irrelevant to the determination of whether the creation of the records was compelled. We therefore hold that the contents of those records are not privileged.

B

Although the contents of a document may not be privileged, the act of producing the document may be. A government subpoena compels the holder of the document to perform an act that may have testimonial aspects and an incriminating effect. . . . In *Fisher,* the Court explored the effect that the act of production would have on the taxpayer and determined that the act of production would have only minimal testimonial value and would not operate to incriminate the taxpayer. Unlike the Court in *Fisher,* we have the explicit finding of the District Court that the act of producing the documents would involve testimonial self-incrimination. The Court of Appeals agreed. The District Court's finding essentially rests on its determination of factual issues. Therefore, we will not overturn that finding unless it has no support in the record. Traditionally, we also have been reluctant to disturb findings of fact in which two courts below have concurred. We therefore decline to overturn the finding of the District Court in this regard, where, as here, it has been affirmed by the Court of Appeals.

IV

The Government, as it concedes, could have compelled respondent to produce the documents listed in the subpoena. Title 18 U.S.C. §§6002 and 6003 provide for the granting of use immunity with respect to the potentially incriminating evidence. The Court upheld the constitutionality of the use immunity statute in Kastigar v. United States, 406 U.S. 441 (1972).

The Government did state several times before the District Court that it would not use respondent's act of production against him in any way. But counsel for the Government never made a statutory request to the District Court to grant respondent use immunity. We are urged to adopt a doctrine of constructive use immunity. Under this doctrine, the courts would impose a requirement on the Government not to use the incriminatory aspects of the act of production against the person claiming the privilege even though the statutory procedures have not been followed.

We decline to extend the jurisdiction of courts to include prospective grants of use immunity in the absence of the formal request that the statute requires. . . . If, on remand, the appropriate official concludes that it is desirable to compel respondent to produce his business records, the statutory procedure for requesting use immunity will be available.[17]

---

17. Respondent argues that any grant of use immunity must cover the contents of the documents as well as the act of production. We find this contention unfounded. To satisfy the requirements of the Fifth Amendment, a grant of immunity need be only as broad as the privilege against self-incrimination. Murphy v. Waterfront Commn., 378 U.S. 52, 107 (1964) (White, J., concurring); see Pillsbury Co. v. Conboy, [459 U.S. 248, 253 n.8 (1983)]; United States v. Calandra, 414 U.S. 338, 346 (1974). As discussed above, the privilege in this case extends only to the act of production. Therefore, any grant of use immunity need only protect respondent from the self-incrimination that might accompany the act of producing his business records.

V

We conclude that the Court of Appeals erred in holding that the contents of the subpoenaed documents were privileged under the Fifth Amendment. The act of producing the documents at issue in this case is privileged and cannot be compelled without a statutory grant of use immunity pursuant to 18 U.S.C. §§6002 and 6003. The judgment of the Court of Appeals is, therefore, affirmed in part and reversed in part, and the case is remanded to the District Court for further proceedings consistent with this opinion.

It is so ordered.

Justice O'CONNOR, concurring.

I concur in both the result and reasoning of Justice Powell's opinion for the Court. I write separately, however, just to make explicit what is implicit in the analysis of that opinion: that the Fifth Amendment provides absolutely no protection for the contents of private papers of any kind. The notion that the Fifth Amendment protects the privacy of papers originated in Boyd v. United States, 116 U.S. 616, 630 (1886), but our decision in Fisher v. United States, 425 U.S. 391 (1976), sounded the death knell for *Boyd.* "Several of *Boyd's* express or implicit declarations [had] not stood the test of time," 425 U.S., at 407, and its privacy of papers concept "ha[d] long been a rule searching for a rationale. . . ." Id., at 409. Today's decision puts a long overdue end to that fruitless search.

Justice MARSHALL, with whom Justice BRENNAN joins, concurring in part and dissenting in part.

Contrary to what Justice O'Connor contends, I do not view the Court's opinion in this case as having reconsidered whether the Fifth Amendment provides protection for the contents of "private papers of any kind." This case presented nothing remotely close to the question that Justice O'Connor eagerly poses and answers. First, as noted above, the issue whether the Fifth Amendment protects the contents of the documents was obviated by the Court of Appeals' rulings relating to the act of production and statutory use immunity. Second, the documents at stake here are business records which implicate a lesser degree of concern for privacy interests than, for example, personal diaries.

Were it true that the Court's opinion stands for the proposition that "the Fifth Amendment provides absolutely no protection for the contents of private papers of any kind," I would assuredly dissent. I continue to believe that under the Fifth Amendment "there are certain documents no person ought to be compelled to produce at the Government's request." Fisher v. United States, 425 U.S. 391, 431-432 (1976) (Marshall, J., concurring in judgment).

[Justice Stevens filed a separate opinion, concurring in part and dissenting in part.]

Problem: Mehrens' Problem—Who's Got the Button?

(1) Wayman allegedly engaged in certain illegal activity with a minor, his daughter Sandra, in 1979. Subsequently, she left Arizona to live in California. While she was in California, Wayman wrote and mailed certain letters to her in which, assertedly, he referred to the illegal activity. Sandra later returned to her parents' home in Arizona, bringing the letters with her. She then left home again but did not take the letters with her. One week later, the criminal complaint in this case was filed. A search warrant was issued to obtain certain incriminating items from the Waymans' residence, including the letters. The letters, however, were not found in the search because prior to the search Wayman delivered the letters to Mehrens, his attorney. Mehrens had the letters in his possession when a subpoena duces tecum, issued by the Maricopa County Grand Jury, directed him to appear and bring the letters. Mehrens moved to quash the subpoena and delivered the letters under seal to the Judge.

How would you rule?

(2) The trial court granted the motion to quash the grand jury subpoena. The letters, however, remained under seal with the court. Then, at the state's request, the trial court decided to return the letters to Mehrens. It ordered him to pick up the letters at nine o'clock the following morning. Meanwhile, the state obtained a warrant to search Mehrens. As Mehrens left the court chambers after picking up the letters, police officers served him with the warrant. When Mehrens refused to comply with the warrant voluntarily, the police seized his briefcase containing the letters.

Mehrens moved for return of the letters. How would you rule?

DISTRICT OF COLUMBIA BAR COMMITTEE ON LEGAL ETHICS, Op. 119 (March 15, 1983)

((Destruction of attorney memoranda to client which may be sought in pending or future litigation.) (DR 1-102(A)(5); DR 7-102(A)(3); DR 7-102(A)(7); DR 7-109(A); DR 7-106(A); DR 7-101(A)(3); EC 7-3))

SUMMARY

Intentional destruction of attorney memoranda which the attorney knows may be the subject of discovery or subpoena in pending or imminent litigation is conduct prejudicial to the administration of justice in violation of DR 1-102(A)(5). In the absence of pending or imminent litigation, whether destruction of such memoranda violates any Disciplinary Rule depends on (1) whether there is a legal obligation to preserve the memoranda or (2) whether destruction of the memoranda would prejudice the client.

FACTS

An attorney wishes to discard legal memoranda which were prepared and presented to his client in 1977, 1978 and 1979, and which he believes are protected by the attorney-client privilege. He believes that disclosure of the contents of his advice to his client could prejudice his client's interests. In a case which has since been settled the court ordered production of the memoranda, rejecting the argument that they were protected by the attorney-client privilege. Because of the settlement the memoranda were not produced. Another case against his client raises one of the same issues as the settled case and is still pending. There has been no request for the memoranda in the course of that case, and discovery has closed. The attorney considers it possible that further cases may be filed against his client in which further requests may be made for the memoranda.

The attorney inquires whether he would violate his ethical responsibilities by failing to retain the memoranda in question.

DISCUSSION

1.   PENDING CASE

The inquiry relates to both a pending case and possible future cases. We first address the question of a lawyer discarding documents in order to avoid a potential obligation to produce them in a pending case. DR 1-102 is entitled "Misconduct." The fifth form of lawyer misconduct listed in the rule is contained in DR 1-102(A)(5): "a lawyer shall not . . . (5) engage in conduct that is prejudicial to the administration of justice." . . .

The process of discovering and presenting evidence to the court is central to our system of justice. The destruction of potential evidence strikes at the heart of the litigation process. Thus, if there were outstanding discovery requests for the memoranda, destruction would obviously be prejudicial misconduct. The inquirer emphasizes that discovery in the case has ended, but where, as here, the lawyer knows the document is potentially relevant evidence, the possibilities that discovery could be reopened or that the memoranda could be subpoenaed at trial strongly suggest a continuing threat of prejudice from destruction of these documents. Indeed, a purpose of destruction would be to avoid production in the pending case. Thus, the critical facts here are not the close of discovery but the continued pendency of the litigation, the concomitant interest of the court in evidence which may bear on the case, the attorney's intent to avoid production, and the finality of the act of destruction. Of course, the memoranda may never be requested and if requested it is possible that the court will not require their production. But so long as a case is pending, destroying a document which the lawyer knows is potential evidence removes the judge's ability to determine whether the potential evidence should be produced. Such displacement of the court's authority would prejudice the administration of justice, in violation of DR 1-102(A)(5). While a lawyer is, of course, bound to preserve confidences and secrets of a client and should zealously protect attorney work product, he or she may not unilaterally determine that a particular attorney memorandum to a client potentially discoverable in pending litigation should be destroyed in order to prevent production. The proper course is to preserve the document, while vigorously presenting the privileges as a defense to efforts to discover the document.

While DR 1-102(A)(5) is directed primarily toward pending litigation, some circumstances may be so close to pending litigation that the Rule would apply even though no pleadings have yet been filed with the Court. For example, if counsel has received notice from an aggrieved person's lawyer, stating that suit will be filed imminently, DR 1-102(A)(5) would bar the lawyer from destroying documents he or she knows are potential evidence in the anticipated litigation. There may be other instances when objective facts so strongly suggest that suit is imminent that intentional destruction of documents because they are potentially pertinent evidence would prejudice the administration of justice. The test in each instance is whether the document destruction is directed at concrete litigation, either pending or almost certain to be filed. The needs for certainty as to when the rule applies and for flexibility of action by the lawyer dictate that the rule's application be thus confined. We therefore are not prepared to say that a mere belief that a matter is likely to be litigated is sufficient under DR 1-102(A)(5) to bar otherwise permissible destruction of attorney memoranda relating to the matter. The inquiry here does not provide sufficient information to allow us to determine whether DR 1-102(A)(5) would prohibit destroying the documents in the event the one presently pending suit were terminated.

Under DR 7-102(A)(3) a lawyer "shall not . . . conceal or knowingly fail to disclose that which he is required by law to reveal." See also DR 7-109(A) ("A lawyer shall not suppress any evidence that he or his client has a legal obligation to reveal or produce"); EC 7-27; DR 7-102(A)(7) (a lawyer may not conceal or assist illegal conduct). Federal criminal law may forbid destruction of documents under certain circumstances.[4] It is also a crime in the District of Columbia for one who knows or has reason to believe an official proceeding has begun or who knows that an official proceeding is about to begin, to destroy a document with intent to impair its availability for use in the proceeding. D.C. Code §22-723 (1981 Ed.). Further, destruction of documents pertinent to pending litigation may run afoul of discovery rules having the force of law. Such rules could conceivably apply in some circumstances to future litigation as well. Thus, whether destruction of the memoranda in question would violate DR 7-102(A)(3) or (7) or DR 7-109(A) depends on the requirements of federal and D.C. law. There is a substantial body of case law under some of these statutes. However, since the Ethics Committee renders opinions only under the Code of Professional Responsibility, we offer no view as to whether destruction would violate these statutes. Rather, we note that DR 7-102(A)(3) requires that, in deciding whether to destroy the memoranda, the attorney should take reasonable steps to determine the legality of such destruction.

The question remains whether a trial court ruling that the attorney memoranda must be produced in one case creates an ethical obligation to preserve the memoranda because parties in future cases are likely to seek their production. DR 7-106(A) provides: "A lawyer shall not disregard or advise his client to disregard . . . a ruling of a tribunal made in the course of a proceeding, but he may take appropriate steps in good faith to test the validity of such rule or ruling." The obligation imposed by the rule does not extend beyond the proceeding in which the ruling was made. While the term "proceeding" may in some circumstances encompass more than one case, the discovery order here probably does not apply to future cases. The discovery order in question here was mooted by the March 1981 settlement. It presumably does not purport to govern future cases. Therefore, unless some fact not before the Committee shows that future cases are part of the same "proceeding" as the case settled in 1981, DR 7-106(A) does not prohibit destruction of the attorney memoranda.

Under DR 7-101(A)(3) "a lawyer shall not intentionally . . . prejudice or damage his client during the course of the professional relationship. . . ." While the attorney here may properly consider prejudice which may result from disclosing the memoranda, such potential prejudice would not justify violating a disciplinary rule barring destruction of evidence. . . .

---

4. See, e.g., 18 U.S.C. §401(3) (disobedience of lawful court order); 18 U.S.C. §1503 (obstruction of justice).

BRONSTON v. UNITED STATES
409 U.S. 352 (1973)

BURGER, C.J.: . . . Petitioner is the sole owner of Samuel Bronston Productions, Inc., a company that between 1958 and 1964, produced motion pictures in various European locations. For these enterprises, Bronston Productions opened bank accounts in a number of foreign countries; in 1962, for example, it had 37 accounts in five countries. As president of Bronston Productions, petitioner supervised transactions involving the foreign bank accounts.

In June 1964, Bronston Productions petitioned for an arrangement with creditors under Chapter XI of the Bankruptcy Act, 11 U.S.C. §701 et seq. On June 10, 1966, a referee in bankruptcy held a §21(a) hearing to determine, for the benefit of creditors, the extent and location of the company's assets. . . .

[A]t that bankruptcy hearing, . . . the following colloquy with a lawyer for a creditor of Bronston Productions [took place]:

Q: Do you have any bank accounts in Swiss banks, Mr. Bronston?
A: No, sir.
Q: Have you ever?
A: The company had an account there for about six months, in Zurich.
Q: Have you any nominees who have bank accounts in Swiss banks?
A: No, sir.
Q: Have you ever?
A: No, sir.

It is undisputed that for a period of nearly five years, between October 1959 and June 1964, petitioner had a personal bank account at the International Credit Bank in Geneva, Switzerland, into which he made deposits and upon which he drew checks totaling more than $180,000. It is likewise undisputed that petitioner's answers were literally truthful. (a) Petitioner did not at the time of questioning have a Swiss bank account. (b) Bronston Productions, Inc., did have the account in Zurich described by petitioner. (c) Neither at the time of questioning nor before did petitioner have nominees who had Swiss accounts.

---

(1) If you represented Bronston in the bankruptcy proceeding and were aware of the personal Swiss bank account, what would your professional obligations be upon hearing Bronston's testimony? In advance of the hearing, how would you counsel Bronston to answer questions similar to the ones actually asked? If you counseled Bronston to answer as he did, knowing it would mislead Bronston's creditors, would you be risking violation of 18 U.S.C. §1503 (the federal obstruction of justice statute), below? If you did not counsel Bronston as to how he should

answer questions to avoid disclosing what was not strictly asked for, would you risk violating your ethical and professional responsibilities as outlined in the ABA Considerations and Standards, below?

(2) What error did the creditor's lawyer make in his interrogation?

(3) Has Bronston violated 18 U.S.C. §1621, the federal perjury statute?

> Whoever, having taken an oath before a competent tribunal, officer, or person, in any case in which a law of the United States authorizes an oath to be administered, that he will testify, declare, depose, or certify truly, or that any written testimony, declaration, deposition, or certificate by him subscribes any material matter which he does not believe to be true, is guilty of perjury, and shall, except as otherwise expressly provided by law, be fined not more than $2,000 or imprisoned not more than five years, or both.

18 U.S.C. §3
Accessory After the Fact

Whoever, knowing that an offense against the United States has been committed, receives, relieves, comforts or assists the offender in order to hinder or prevent his apprehension, trial or punishment, is an accessory after the fact.

Except as otherwise expressly provided by any Act of Congress, an accessory after the fact shall be imprisoned not more than one-half the maximum term of imprisonment or fined not more than one-half the maximum fine prescribed for the punishment of the principal, or both; or if the principal is punishable by death, the accessory shall be imprisoned not more than ten years.

18 U.S.C. §1503
Obstruction of Justice

Whoever corruptly . . . influences, obstructs, or impedes, or endeavors to influence, obstruct, or impede, the due administration of justice, shall be fined not more than $5,000 or imprisoned not more than five years, or both.

AMERICAN BAR ASSOCIATION STANDARDS FOR CRIMINAL JUSTICE, THE DEFENSE FUNCTION
(2d ed. 1980)

4-1.1. The defense counsel, in protecting the rights of the defendant, may resist the wishes of the judge on some matters, and though such resistance should never lead to disrespectful behavior, defense counsel may appear unyielding and uncooperative at times. In so doing, defense counsel is not contradicting his or her duty to the administration of justice but is fulfilling a function within the adversary system. The adversary system requires defense counsel's presence and zealous professional advocacy just as it requires the presence and zealous advocacy of the prosecutor and the constant neutrality of the judge. Defense counsel should not be viewed as impeding the administration of justice simply because he or she challenges the prosecution, but as an indispensable part of its fulfillment.

The role of counsel for the accused is difficult because it is complex, involving multiple obligations. Toward the client the lawyer is a counselor and an advocate; toward the prosecutor the lawyer is a professional adversary; toward the court the lawyer is both advocate for the client and counselor to the court. The lawyer is obliged to counsel the client against any unlawful future conduct and to refuse to implement any illegal conduct. But included in defense counsel's obligations to the client is the responsibility of furthering the defendant's interest to the fullest extent that the law and the standards of professional conduct permit.

Advocacy is not for the timid, the meek, or the retiring. Our system of justice is inherently contentious, albeit bounded by the rules of professional ethics and decorum, and it demands that the lawyer be inclined toward vigorous advocacy. Nor can a lawyer be half-hearted in the application of his or her energies to a case. Once a case has been undertaken, a lawyer is obliged not to omit any essential honorable step in the defense, without regard to compensation or the nature of the appointment. . . .

The "alter ego" concept of a defense lawyer, which regards the lawyer as a "mouthpiece" for the client, is fundamentally wrong, unethical, and destructive of the lawyer's image; more important to the accused, perhaps, this pernicious idea is destructive of the lawyer's usefulness. The lawyer's value to each client stems in large part from the lawyer's independent stance, as a professional representative rather than as an ordinary agent. What the lawyer can accomplish for any one client depends heavily on his or her reputation for professional integrity. Court and opposing counsel will treat the lawyer with the respect that facilitates furthering the client's interests only if the lawyer maintains proper professional detachment and conduct in accord with accepted professional standards.

It is fundamental that in relations with the court, defense counsel must be scrupulously candid and truthful in representations of any matter before the court. This is not only a basic ethical requirement, but it is essential if the lawyer is to be effective in the role of advocate, for if the lawyer's reputation for veracity is suspect, he or she will lack the confidence of the court when it is needed most to serve the client. . . .

[The 1974 Approved Draft of this standard contained the following specific advice to defense lawyers concerning confidential communications.

He can [bring to bear on the problems of defense the skill, experience, and judgment he possess] only if he knows all that his client knows concerning the facts. The client is not competent to evaluate the relevance or significance of facts; hence the lawyer must insist on complete and candid disclosure. Secondly, he must be able to conduct the case free from interference. These two factors explain the rule of leading criminal defense lawyers that they have complete disclosure of all facts and entire control of the technical and legal aspects of the litigation.]

LAWYER-CLIENT RELATIONSHIP

4-3.1. ESTABLISHMENT OF RELATIONSHIP.

(a) Defense counsel should seek to establish a relationship of trust and confidence with the accused. The lawyer should explain the necessity of full disclosure of all facts known to the client for an effective defense, and the lawyer should explain the obligation of confidentiality which makes privileged the accused's disclosures relating to the case. . . .

4-3.2. INTERVIEWING THE CLIENT.

(a) As soon as practicable the lawyer should seek to determine all relevant facts known to the accused. In so doing, the lawyer should probe for all legally relevant information without seeking to influence the direction of the client's responses.

(b) It is unprofessional conduct for the lawyer to instruct the client or to intimate to him in any way that the client should not be candid in revealing facts so as to afford the lawyer free rein to take action which would be precluded by the lawyer's knowing of such facts.

4-3.7. ADVICE AND SERVICE ON ANTICIPATED UNLAWFUL CONDUCT.

(a) It is a lawyer's duty to advise a client to comply with the law but the lawyer may advise concerning the meaning, scope and validity of a law.

(b) It is unprofessional conduct for a lawyer to counsel a client in or knowingly assist a client to engage in conduct which the lawyer knows to be illegal or fraudulent.

(c) It is unprofessional conduct for a lawyer to agree in advance of the commission of a crime that the lawyer will serve as counsel for the defendant, except as part of a bona fide effort to determine the validity, scope, meaning or application of the law, or where the defense is incident to a general retainer for legal services to a person or enterprise engaged in legitimate activity.

(d) A lawyer may reveal the expressed intention of a client to commit a crime and the information necessary to prevent the crime; and the lawyer must do so if the contemplated crime is one which would seriously endanger the life or safety of any person or corrupt the processes of the courts and the lawyer believes such action on his or her part is necessary to prevent it.

AMERICAN BAR ASSOCIATION MODEL CODE OF PROFESSIONAL RESPONSIBILITY, ETHICAL CONSIDERATION 4-1
(1980)

Both the fiduciary relationship existing between lawyer and client and the proper functioning of the legal system require the preservation by the lawyer of confidences and secrets of one who has employed or sought to employ him. A client must feel free to discuss whatever he wishes with his lawyer and a lawyer must be equally free to obtain information beyond that volunteered by his client. A lawyer should be fully informed of all the facts of the matter he is handling in order for his client to obtain the full advantage of our legal system. It is for the lawyer in the exercise of his independent professional judgment to separate the relevant and important from the irrelevant and unimportant. The observance of the ethical obligation of a lawyer to hold inviolate the confidences and secrets of his client not only facilitates the full development of facts essential to proper representation of the client but also encourages laymen to seek early legal assistance.

Problem: The Smoking Gun

Hombre, a regular client, walks into your office with a .32 magnum Special, the barrel still smoking, and says, "I have just shot *V* and here is the gun." What parts of this transaction are privileged? What advice should you give Hombre about the gun? What are your professional responsibilities?

If Hombre tells you where he has hidden his gun, is that information privileged? If he tells you where he has hidden V's corpse, is that information privileged? What, if anything, should you do with either piece of information? Do the application of the privilege and the lawyer's professional or personal responsibilities vary depending on whether the client discloses to the lawyer evidence, instrumentalities, or fruits of the crime or information concerning them?

CLARK v. STATE
159 Tex. Cr. R. 187, 261 S.W.2d 339, cert. denied, 346 U.S. 855 (1953)

MORRISON, J. The offense is murder; the punishment, death.

The deceased secured a divorce from appellant on March 25, 1952. That night she was killed, as she lay at home in her bed, as the result of a gunshot wound. From the mattress on her bed, as well as from the bed of her daughter, were recovered bullets which were shown by a firearms expert to have been fired by a .38 special revolver having Colt characteristics. Appellant was shown to have purchased a Colt .38 Detective Special some ten months prior to the homicide.

The State relied in main upon three witnesses to establish its case. . . .

Marjorie Bartz, a telephone operator in the City of San Angelo, testified that at 2:49 in the morning of March 26, 1952, while on duty, she received a call from the Golden Spur Hotel; that at first she thought the person placing the call was a Mr. Cox and so made out the slip; but that she then recognized appellant's voice, scratched out the word "Cox" and wrote "Clark." She stated that appellant told her he wanted to speak to his lawyer, Jimmy Martin in Dallas, and that she placed the call to him at telephone number Victor 1942 in that city and made a record thereof, which record was admitted in evidence. Miss Bartz testified that, contrary to company rules, she listened to the entire conversation that ensued, and that it went as follows:

The appellant: Hello, Jimmy I went to the extremes.
The voice in Dallas: What did you do?
The appellant: I just went to the extremes.
The voice in Dallas: You got to tell me what you did before I can help.
The appellant: Well, I killed her.
The voice in Dallas: Who did you kill; the driver?
The appellant: No, I killed her.
The voice in Dallas: Did you get rid of the weapon?
The appellant: No, I still got the weapon.

The voice in Dallas: Get rid of the weapon and sit tight and don't talk
to anyone, and I will fly down in the morning.

It was stipulated that the Dallas telephone number of appellant's attorney was Victor 1942. . . .

We now discuss the question of the privileged nature of the conversation. Wigmore on Evidence (Third Edition), Section 2326, reads as
follows:

> The law provides subjective freedom for the client by assuring him of exemp-
> tion from its processes of disclosure against himself or the attorney or their agents
> of communication. This much, but not a whit more, is necessary for the main-
> tenance of the privilege. Since the means of preserving secrecy of communica-
> tion are entirely in the client's hands, and since the privilege is a derogation
> from the general testimonial duty and should be strictly construed, it would be
> improper to extend its prohibition to third persons who obtain knowledge of
> the communications.

The precise question here presented does not appear to have been
passed upon in this or other jurisdictions.

In Hoy v. Morris, 13 Gray 519, 79 Mass. 519, a conversation between
a client and his attorney was overheard by Aldrich, who was in the adjoining room. The Court therein said:

"Aldrich was not an attorney, not in any way connected with Mr.
Todd; and certainly in no situation where he was either necessary or
useful to the parties to enable them to understand each other. On the
contrary, he was a mere bystander, and casually overheard conversation
not addressed to him nor intended for his ear, but which the client and
attorney meant to have respected as private and confidential. Mr. Todd
could not lawfully have revealed it. But, in consequence of a want of
proper precaution, the communications between him and his client
were overheard by a mere stranger. As the latter stood in no relation of
confidence to either of the parties, he was clearly not within the rule of
exemption from giving testimony; and he might therefore, when summoned as a witness, be compelled to testify as to what he overheard, so
far as it was pertinent to the subject matter of inquiry upon the trial. . . ."

We hold that the trial court properly admitted the evidence of the
telephone operator. . . .

On Appellant's Motion for Rehearing

Woodley, J. We are favored with masterful briefs and arguments in
support of appellant's motion for rehearing, including amicus curiae
brief by an eminent and able Texas lawyer addressed to the question of
privileged communications between attorney and client. . . .

It is in the interest of public justice that the client be able to make a full disclosure to his attorney of all facts that are material to his defense or that go to substantiate his claim. The purpose of the privilege is to encourage such disclosure of the facts. But the interests of public justice further require that no shield such as the protection afforded to communications between attorney and client shall be interposed to protect a person who takes counsel on how he can safely commit a crime.

We think this latter rule must extend to one who, having committed a crime, seeks or takes counsel as to how he shall escape arrest and punishment, such as advice regarding the destruction or disposition of the murder weapon or of the body following a murder.

One who knowing that an offense has been committed conceals the offender or aids him to evade arrest or trial becomes an accessory. The fact that the aider may be a member of the bar and the attorney for the offender will not prevent his becoming an accessory.

Art. 77, P.C. defining an accessory contains the exception "One who aids an offender in making or preparing his defense at law" is not an accessory.

The conversation as testified to by the telephone operator is not within the exception found in Art. 77, P.C. When the Dallas voice advised appellant to "get rid of the weapon" (which advice the evidence shows was followed) such aid cannot be said to constitute aid "in making or preparing his defense at law." It was aid to the perpetrator of the crime "in order that he may evade an arrest or trial."

Is such a conversation privileged as a communication between attorney and client?

If the adviser had been called to testify as to the conversation, would it not have been more appropriate for him to claim his privilege against self-incrimination rather than that the communication was privileged because it was between attorney and client?

Appellant, when he conversed with Mr. Martin, was not under arrest nor was he charged with a crime. He had just inflicted mortal wounds on his former wife and apparently had shot her daughter. Mr. Martin had acted as his attorney in the divorce suit which had been tried that day and had secured a satisfactory property settlement. Appellant called him and told him that he had gone to extremes and had killed "her," not "the driver." Mr. Martin appeared to understand these references and told appellant to get rid of "the weapon."

We are unwilling to subscribe to the theory that such counsel and advice should be privileged because of the attorney-client relationship which existed between the parties in the divorce suit. We think, on the other hand, that the conversation was admissible as not within the realm of legitimate professional counsel and employment. . . .

Appellant's motion for rehearing is overruled.

IN RE RYDER
263 F. Supp. 360 (E.D. Va.), aff'd, 381 F.2d 713 (4th Cir. 1967)

PER CURIAM. This proceeding was instituted to determine whether Richard R. Ryder should be removed from the roll of attorneys qualified to practice before this court. Ryder was admitted to this bar in 1953. He formerly served five years as an Assistant United States Attorney. He has an active trial practice, including both civil and criminal cases.

In proceedings of this kind the charges must be sustained by clear and convincing proof, the misconduct must be fraudulent, intentional, and the result of improper motives. We conclude that these strict requirements have been satisfied. Ryder took possession of stolen money and a sawed-off shotgun, knowing that the money had been stolen and that the gun had been used in an armed robbery. He intended to retain this property pending his client's trial unless the government discovered it. He intended by his possession to destroy the chain of evidence that linked the contraband to his client and to prevent its use to establish his client's guilt.

On August 24, 1966 a man armed with a sawed-off shotgun robbed the Varina Branch of the Bank of Virginia of $7,583. Included in the currency taken were $10 bills known as "bait money," the serial numbers of which had been recorded.

On August 26, 1966 Charles Richard Cook rented safety deposit box 14 at a branch of the Richmond National Bank. Later in the day Cook was interviewed at his home by agents of the Federal Bureau of Investigation, who obtained $348 from him. Cook telephoned Ryder, who had represented him in civil litigation. Ryder came to the house and advised the agents that he represented Cook. He said that if Cook were not to be placed under arrest, he intended to take him to his office for an interview. The agents left. Cook insisted to Ryder that he had not robbed the bank. He told Ryder that he had won the money, which the agents had taken from him, in a crap game. At this time Ryder believed Cook.

Later that afternoon Ryder telephoned one of the agents and asked whether any of the bills obtained from Cook had been identified as a part of the money taken in the bank robbery. The agent told him that some bills had been identified. Ryder made inquiries about the number of bills taken and their denominations. The agent declined to give him specific information but indicated that several of the bills were recorded as bait money.

The next morning, Saturday, August 27, 1966, Ryder conferred with Cook again. He urged Cook to tell the truth, and Cook answered that a man, whose name he would not divulge, offered him $500 on the day of the robbery to put a package in a bank lockbox. Ryder did not believe this story. Ryder told Cook that if the government could trace the money in the box to him, it would be almost conclusive evidence of his guilt. He knew that Cook was under surveillance and he suspected that Cook might try to dispose of the money.

That afternoon Ryder telephoned a former officer of the Richmond Bar Association to discuss his course of action. He had known this attorney for many years and respected his judgment. The lawyer was at home and had no library available to him when Ryder telephoned. In their casual conversation Ryder told what he knew about the case, omitting names. He explained that he thought he would take the money from Cook's safety deposit box and place it in a box in his own name. This, he believed, would prevent Cook from attempting to dispose of the money. The lawyers thought that eventually F.B.I. agents would locate the money and that since it was in Ryder's possession, he could claim a privilege and thus effectively exclude it from evidence. This would prevent the government from linking Ryder's client with the bait money and would also destroy any presumption of guilt that might exist arising out of the client's exclusive possession of the evidence.

Ryder testified:

> I had sense enough to know, one, at that time that apparently the F.B.I. did have the serial numbers on the bills. I had sense enough to know, from many, many years of experience in this court and in working with the F.B.I. and, in fact, in directing the F.B.I. on some occasions, to know that eventually the bank—that the F.B.I. would find that money if I left that money in the bank. There was no doubt in my mind that eventually they would find it. The only thing I could think of to do was to get the money out of Mr. Cook's possession. . . . [T]he idea was that I assumed that if anybody tried to go into a safety deposit box in my name, the bank officials would notify me and that I would get an opportunity to come in this court and argue a question of whether or not they could use that money as evidence.

The lawyers discussed and rejected alternatives, including having a third party get the money. At the conclusion of the conversation Ryder was advised, "Don't do it surreptitiously and to be sure that you let your client know that it is going back to the rightful owners."

On Monday morning Ryder asked Cook to come by his office. He prepared a power of attorney, which Cook signed:

> KNOW YOU ALL MEN BY THESE PRESENTS, that I, CHARLES RICHARD COOK do hereby make, constitute and appoint, R.R. RYDER as my attorney at Law and in fact and do authorize my said Attorney to enter a safety deposit box rented by me at the Richmond National Bank and Trust Company, 2604 Hull Street, Richmond, Virginia, said box requiring Mosler Key Number 30 to open the same and I further authorize the said Attorney to remove the contents of

the said box and so dispose of the said contents as he sees fit and I direct the officials of the said bank to cooperate with my said attorney towards the accomplishment of this my stated purpose.

Ryder did not follow the advice he had received on Saturday. He did not let his client know the money was going back to the rightful owners. He testified about his omission:

> I prepared it myself and told Mr. Cook to sign it. In the power of attorney, I did not specifically say that Mr. Cook authorized me to deliver that money to the appropriate authorities at any time because for a number of reasons. One, in representing a man under these circumstances, you've got to keep the man's confidence, but I also put in that power of attorney that Mr. Cook authorized me to dispose of that money as I saw fit, and the reason for that being that I was going to turn the money over to the proper authorities at whatever time I deemed that it wouldn't hurt Mr. Cook.

Ryder took the power of attorney which Cook had signed to the Richmond National Bank. He rented box 13 in his name with his office address, presented the power of attorney, entered Cook's box, took both boxes into a booth, where he found a bag of money and a sawed-off shotgun in Cook's box. The box also contained miscellaneous items which are not pertinent to this proceeding. He transferred the contents of Cook's box to his own and returned the boxes to the vault. He left the bank, and neither he nor Cook returned.

Ryder testified that he had some slight hesitation about the propriety of what he was doing. Within a half-hour after he left the bank, he talked to a retired judge and distinguished professor of law. He told this person that he wanted to discuss something in confidence. Ryder then stated that he represented a man suspected of bank robbery. The judge recalled the main part of the conversation:

> . . . And that he had received from this client, under a power of attorney, a sum [of] money which he, Mr. Ryder, suspected was proceeds of the robbery, although he didn't know it, but he had a suspicion that it was; that he had placed this money in a safety deposit vault at a bank; that he had received it with the intention of returning it to the rightful owner after the case against his client had been finally disposed of one way or the other; that he considered that he had received it under the privilege of attorney and client and that he wanted responsible people in the community to know of that fact and that he was telling me in confidence of that as one of these people that he wanted to know of it.
>
> Q: Did he say anything to you about a sawed-off shotgun?
> A: I don't recall. If Mr. Ryder says he did, I would not deny it, but I do not recall it, because the—my main attention in what he was saying was certainly drawn to the fact that the money was involved, but I just cannot answer the question emphatically, but if Mr. Ryder says he told me, why, I certainly wouldn't deny it.

Ryder testified that he told about the shotgun. The judge also testified that Ryder certainly would not have been under the impression that he—the judge—thought that he was guilty of unethical conduct.

The same day Ryder also talked with other prominent persons in Richmond—a judge of a court of record and an attorney for the Commonwealth. Again, he stated that what he intended to say was confidential. He related the circumstances and was advised that a lawyer could not receive the property and if he had received it he could not retain possession of it.

On September 7, 1966 Cook was indicted for robbing the Varina Branch of the Bank of Virginia. A bench warrant was issued and the next day Ryder represented Cook at a bond hearing. Cook was identified as the robber by employees of the bank. He was released on bond. Cook was arraigned on a plea of not guilty on September 9, 1966.

On September 12, 1966 F.B.I. agents procured search warrants for Cook's and Ryder's safety deposit boxes in the Richmond National Bank. They found Cook's box empty. In Ryder's box they discovered $5,920 of the $7,583 taken in the bank robbery and the sawed-off shotgun used in the robbery.

On September 23, 1966 Ryder filed a motion to suppress the money obtained from Cook by the agents on August 26, 1966. The motion did not involve items taken from Ryder's safety deposit box. The motion came on to be heard October 6, 1966. Ryder called Cook as a witness for examination on matters limited to the motion to suppress. The court called to Ryder's attention papers pertaining to the search of the safety deposit boxes. Ryder moved for a continuance, stating that he intended to file a motion with respect to the seizure of the contents of the lockbox.

On October 14, 1966 the three judges of this court removed Ryder as an attorney for Cook; suspended him from practice before the court until further order; referred the matter to the United States Attorney, who was requested to file charges within five days; set the matter for hearing November 11, 1966; and granted Ryder leave to move for vacation or modification of its order pending hearing.

The United States Attorney charged Ryder with violations of Canons 15 and 32 of the Canons of Professional Ethics of the Virginia State Bar. Ryder did not move for vacation or modification of the order, and the case was heard as scheduled by the court en banc. After the transcript was prepared and the case briefed, the court heard the argument of counsel on December 27, 1966.

At the outset, we reject the suggestion that Ryder did not know the money which he transferred from Cook's box to his was stolen. We find that on August 29 when Ryder opened Cook's box and saw a bag of money and a sawed-off shotgun, he then knew Cook was involved in the bank robbery and that the money was stolen. The evidence clearly establishes this. Ryder knew that the man who had robbed the bank used a sawed-off shotgun. He disbelieved Cook's story about the source of the money in the lockbox. He knew that some of the bills in Cook's possession were bait money.

Judge Learned Hand observed in United States v. Werner, 160 F.2d 438, 441 (2d Cir. 1947):

"The defendants ask us to distinguish between 'knowing' that goods are stolen and merely being put upon an inquiry which would have led to discovery; but they have misconceived the distinction which the decisions have made. The receivers of stolen goods almost never 'know' that they have been stolen, in the sense that they could testify to it in a court room."

Judge Hand then went on to say (160 F.2d 442): "But that the jury must find that the receiver did more than infer the theft from the circumstances has never been demanded, so far as we know; and to demand more would emasculate the statute. . . ."

In Melson v. United States, 207 F.2d 558, 559 (4th Cir. 1953), the court said: "It is well settled that knowledge that goods have been stolen may be inferred from circumstances that would convince a man of ordinary intelligence that this is the fact."

We also find that Ryder was not motivated solely by certain expectation the government would discover the contents of his lockbox. He believed discovery was probable. In this event he intended to argue to the court that the contents of his box could not be revealed, and even if the contents were identified, his possession made the stolen money and the shotgun inadmissible against his client. He also recognized that discovery was not inevitable. His intention in this event, we find, was to assist Cook by keeping the stolen money and the shotgun concealed in his lockbox until after the trial. His conversations, and the secrecy he enjoined, immediately after he put the money and the gun in his box, show that he realized the government might not find the property.

We accept his statement that he intended eventually to return the money to its rightful owner, but we pause to say that no attorney should ever place himself in such a position. Matters involving the possible termination of an attorney-client relationship, or possible subsequent proceedings in the event of an acquittal, are too delicate to permit such a practice.

We reject the argument that Ryder's conduct was no more than the exercise of the attorney-client privilege. The fact that Cook had not been arrested or indicted at the time Ryder took possession of the gun and money is immaterial. Cook was Ryder's client and was entitled to the protection of the lawyer-client privilege. . . .

It was Ryder, not his client, who took the initiative in transferring the incriminating possession of the stolen money and the shotgun from

Cook. Ryder's conduct went far beyond the receipt and retention of a confidential communication from his client. Counsel for Ryder conceded, at the time of argument, that the acts of Ryder were not within the attorney-client privilege. . . .

The money in Cook's box belonged to the Bank of Virginia. The law did not authorize Cook to conceal this money or withhold it from the bank. His larceny was a continuing offense. Cook had no title or property interest in the money that he lawfully could pass to Ryder. The Act of Assembly authorizing the promulgation of the Canons of Ethics in Virginia forbids inconsistency with §18.1-107 Code of Virginia, 1950, which provides:

> If any person buy or receive from another person, or aid in concealing, any stolen goods or other thing, knowing the same to have been stolen, he shall be deemed guilty of larceny thereof, and may be proceeded against, although the principal offender be not convicted.

No canon of ethics or law permitted Ryder to conceal from the Bank of Virginia its money to gain his client's acquittal.

Cook's possession of the sawed-off shotgun was illegal. 26 U.S.C. §5851. Ryder could not lawfully receive the gun from Cook to assist Cook to avoid conviction of robbery. Cook had never mentioned the shotgun to Ryder. When Ryder discovered it in Cook's box, he took possession of it to hinder the government in the prosecution of its case, and he intended not to reveal it pending trial unless the government discovered it and a court compelled its production. No statute or canon of ethics authorized Ryder to take possession of the gun for this purpose.

Canon 15 states in part:

> [T]he great trust of the lawyer is to be performed within and not without the bounds of law. The office of attorney does not permit, much less does it demand of him for any client, violation of law or any manner of fraud or chicane. He must obey his own conscience and not that of his client.

In helping Cook to conceal the shotgun and stolen money, Ryder acted without the bounds of law. He allowed the office of attorney to be used in violation of law. The scheme which he devised was a deceptive, legalistic subterfuge — rightfully denounced by the canon [15] as chicane.

Ryder's testimony that he intended to have the court rule on the admissibility of the evidence and the extent of the lawyer-client privilege does not afford justification for his action. He intended to do this only if the government discovered the shotgun and stolen money in his lockbox. If the government did not discover it, he had no intention of submitting any legal question about it to the court. If there were no discovery, he would continue to conceal the shotgun and money for Cook's benefit pending trial.

Ryder's action is not justified because he thought he was acting in the best interests of his client. To allow the individual lawyer's belief to determine the standards of professional conduct will in time reduce the ethics of the profession to the practices of the most unscrupulous. Moreover, Ryder knew that the law against concealing stolen property and the law forbidding receipt and possession of a sawed-off shotgun contain no exemptions for a lawyer who takes possession with the intent of protecting a criminal from the consequences of his crime.

Canon 15 warns against the reasoning urged in support of Ryder:

> Nothing operates more certainly to create or to foster popular prejudice against lawyers as a class and to deprive the profession of that full measure of esteem and confidence which belongs to the proper discharge of its duties than does the false claim, often set up by the unscrupulous in defense of questionable transactions, that it is the duty of the lawyer to do whatever may enable him to succeed in winning his client's cause.

We find it difficult to accept the argument that Ryder's action is excusable because if the government found Cook's box, Ryder's would easily be found, and if the government failed to find both Cook's and Ryder's boxes, no more harm would be done than if the agents failed to find only Cook's. Cook's concealment of the items in his box cannot be cited to excuse Ryder. Cook's conduct is not the measure of Ryder's ethics. The conduct of a lawyer should be above reproach. Concealment of the stolen money and the sawed-off shotgun to secure Cook's acquittal was wrong whether the property was in Cook's or Ryder's possession.

There is much to be said, however, for mitigation of the discipline to be imposed. Ryder intended to return the bank's money after his client was tried. He consulted reputable persons before and after he placed the property in his lockbox, although he did not precisely follow their advice. Were it not for these facts, we would deem proper his permanent exclusion from practice before this court. In view of the mitigating circumstances, he will be suspended from practice in this court for eighteen months effective October 14, 1966. . . .

HITCH v. ARIZONA
146 Ariz. 588, 708 P.2d 72 (1985)

CAMERON, J.

This is a special action brought by defendant from an order of the

trial court compelling defendant's attorney to deliver potentially inculpatory, physical evidence to the state and requiring that the attorney
withdraw from representation. . . .

We must decide three questions:

1.   Does a defense attorney have an obligation to turn over to the
     state potentially inculpatory, physical evidence obtained from a
     third party?
2.   If so, in what manner may this be done?
3.   Must he then withdraw as attorney for the defendant?

The essential facts are not in dispute. Defendant was indicted for first
degree murder and is currently awaiting trial on that charge. In the
course of their investigation, the police interviewed defendant's girlfriend, Diane Heaton, who told them that the victim was in possession
of a certain wristwatch shortly before his death. Subsequently, an investigator for the Pima County Public Defender's Office contacted Ms.
Heaton and she informed him that she had found a wristwatch in defendant's suit jacket. She also stated that she did not want to turn the
evidence over to the police. The investigator contacted defendant's attorney who told him to take possession of the watch and bring it to the
attorney's office. The attorney indicated that he did this for two reasons.
First, he wanted to examine the watch to determine whether it was the
same one that Ms. Heaton had described to the police. Second, he was
afraid that she might destroy or conceal the evidence. Shortly thereafter, defendant informed the police that he had taken a watch from the
victim. The police were, however, unaware of the location of that watch.

On 11 June 1984, defendant's attorney filed a petition with the Ethics
Committee of the Arizona State Bar, requesting an opinion concerning
his duties with respect to the wristwatch. The Ethics Committee informed the attorney that he had a legal obligation to turn over the watch
to the state and that he also might be compelled to testify as to the
original location and source of the evidence.

Defendant's attorney informed the Respondent Judge of the Committee's decision. Judge Veliz ordered that the watch be turned over to
the state and that the attorney withdraw from the case. He also stayed
the order to allow the filing of this petition for special action. . . .

I.   MUST DEFENDANT'S ATTORNEY TURN THE EVIDENCE
     OVER TO THE STATE?

We have previously held that an attorney need not turn over physical
evidence obtained from his client if the evidence was such that it could
not be obtained from the client against the client's will, State v. Superior

Court, 128 Ariz. 253, 625 P.2d 316 (1981). We have not, however, ruled as to physical evidence obtained from a third party. . . .

Of course, if the physical evidence is contraband, the attorney may be required to turn over the property even if he obtained that evidence from his client. For example, in a case where the attorney obtained from his client the money taken in a bank robbery and a sawed-off shotgun used in the crime, the attorney was required to turn the property over to the state. In re Ryder, 381 F.2d 713 (4th Cir. 1967). See Comment, The Right of a Criminal Defense Attorney to Withhold Physical Evidence Received from his Client, 38 U. Chi. L. Rev. 211 (1970); Note, An Attorney in Possession of Evidence Incriminating His Client, 25 Wash. and Lee L. Rev. 133 (1968).

At issue is the conflict between a defense attorney's obligation to his client and to the court. As the Preamble to the Rules of Professional Conduct notes, a lawyer is both "a representative of [his] clients, an officer of the legal system and a public citizen having special responsibility for the quality of justice." As a representative of his client, a lawyer must act as a zealous advocate, demonstrating loyalty to his client and giving him the best legal advice possible within the bounds of the law. As part of this zealous representation, the lawyer is admonished not to reveal information relating to representation of his client. . . . Because clients are aware that their lawyers will not repeat their communications, they feel that they may make both full and honest disclosure. Trial counsel is thus better able to evaluate the situation and prepare a proper defense. Thus, it has been said that "it is in the interest of public justice that the client be able to make full disclosure." Clark v. State, 159 Tex. Crim. App. 187, 199, 261 S.W.2d 339, 346, cert. denied, 346 U.S. 855 (1953).

We note also that the lawyer's role as a zealous advocate is an important one, not only for the client but for the administration of justice. We have chosen an adversary system of justice in which, in theory, the state and the defendant meet as equals — "strength against strength, resource against resource, argument against argument." United States v. Bagley, 473 U.S. 667, 671 n.2, 105 S. Ct. 3375, 3390 n.2 (1985) (Marshall, J., dissenting). In order to close the gap between theory and practice and thereby ensure that the system is working properly, a defendant must have an attorney who will fight against the powerful resources of the state. It is only when this occurs that we can be assured that the system is functioning properly and only the guilty are convicted.

Balanced against the attorney's obligation to his client is the attorney's obligation as an officer of the court, which requires him "[to aid] in determining truth whenever possible." Note, Ethics, Law and Loyalty: The Attorney's Duty to Turn Over Incriminating Evidence, 32 Stan. L. Rev. 977, 992 (1980). Both sides must have equal access to the relevant information. As the American Bar Association has noted: "[w]here the necessary evaluation and preparation are foreclosed by lack of information, the trial becomes a pursuit of truth and justice only by chance rather than by design, and generates a diminished respect for the criminal justice system, the judiciary and the attorney participants." II ABA Standards for Criminal Justice, comment to Standard 11-1.1(a) (2nd ed. 1982). . . . Thus, in order to aid the truth determining process an attorney must refrain from impeding the flow of information to the state. The defendant's attorney can neither assist nor obstruct the prosecution in its efforts to discover evidence.

Defendant asks us, in balancing these competing interests, to hold that there is "no affirmative duty on the part of defense counsel to disclose possible inculpatory evidence obtained by counsel during the course of his representation of the client." Defendant maintains that to hold otherwise would cause irreparable harm to the attorney-client relationship.

The National Legal Aid and Defender Association in its amicus brief agrees with defendant that there should be no "absolute affirmative duty rule" requiring defendant's attorney to routinely disclose all physical evidence discovered during investigation of a case. The National Legal Aid and Defender Association suggests that we adopt the "Ethical Standard to Guide [A Lawyer] Who Receives Physical Evidence Implicating His Client in Criminal Conduct," proposed by the Criminal Justice Section's Ethics Committee. This standard reads as follows:

> (a) A lawyer who receives a physical item under circumstances implicating a client in criminal conduct shall disclose the location of or shall deliver that item to law enforcement authorities only: (1) if such is required by law or court order, or (2) as provided in paragraph (d).
>
> (b) Unless required to disclose, the lawyer shall return the item to the source from whom the lawyer receives it, as provided in paragraphs (c) and (d). In returning the item to the source, the lawyer shall advise the source of the legal consequences pertaining to possession or destruction of the item.
>
> (c) A lawyer may receive the item for a period of time during which the lawyer: (1) intends to return it to the owner; (2) reasonably fears that return of the item to the source will result in destruction of the item; (3) reasonably fears that return of the item to the source will result in physical harm to anyone; (4) intends to test, examine, inspect or use the item in any way as part of the lawyer's representation of the client; or (5) cannot return it to the source. If the lawyer retains the item, the lawyer shall do so in a manner that does not impede the lawful ability of law enforcement to obtain the item.
>
> (d) If the item received is contraband, or if in the lawyer's judgment the lawyer cannot retain the item in a way that does not pose an unreasonable risk of physical harm to anyone, the lawyer shall disclose the location of or shall deliver the item to law enforcement authorities.
>
> (e) If the lawyer discloses the location of or delivers the item to law enforcement authorities under paragraphs (a) or (d), or to a third party under para-

graph (c)(1), the lawyer shall do so in the way best designed to protect the client's interest.

29 Cr. L. Rep. 2465-66 (26 August 1981).

We agree with defendant that any requirement that the defendant's attorney turn over to the prosecutor physical evidence which may aid in the conviction of the defendant may harm the attorney-client relationship. We do not believe, however, that this reason, by itself, is sufficient to avoid disclosure. We have stated that "[t]he duty of an attorney to a client . . . is subordinate to his responsibility for the due and proper administration of justice. In case of conflict, the former must yield to the latter." State v. Kruchten, 101 Ariz. 186, 191, 417 P.2d 510, 515 (1966). Thus, although we respect the relationship as an important one, we believe it must sometimes be subordinate to the free flow of information, upon which our adversary system is based. . . . Consistent with this philosophy, we feel that the potential damage to the adversary system is greater, and in need of greater protection, than the attorney-client relationship. We do not wish to create a situation in which counsel is made a repository for physical evidence — a serious and inevitable problem once clients become aware that evidence given to their attorneys, even by friends, may never be turned over to the state.

We, therefore, adopt essentially the ethical standard proposed by the Ethics Committee of the Section on Criminal Justice of the American Bar Association with regards to inculpatory evidence delivered to the attorney by a third party. Our holding is as follows: first, if the attorney reasonably believes that evidence will not be destroyed, he may return it to the source, explaining the laws on concealment and destruction. Second, if the attorney has reasonable grounds to believe that the evidence might be destroyed, or if his client consents, he may turn the physical evidence over to the prosecution. Applying this test to the instant facts, the trial court was correct in ordering the wristwatch to be turned over to the state.

II. How Should the Evidence be Returned

Having decided that the evidence must be turned over to the prosecution, we must determine how this can best be done without further prejudice to the defendant. The Ethics Committee's proposed standards provide that when this is done "the lawyer shall do so in [a] way best designed to protect the client's interest." *Standards*, supra.

Amicus National Legal Aid and Defender Association suggests that if the lawyer decides to disclose the item he should do so by delivering the evidence to an agent who would then deliver it to the police without disclosing the source of the item or the case involved. Defendant, however, suggests that the procedure followed in the District of Columbia be considered. According to defendant, inculpatory evidence is delivered to the District of Columbia's bar counsel for subsequent delivery to law enforcement officials. Defendant urges that this Court adopt a system whereby an attorney could anonymously deliver evidence to State Bar counsel, or presidents of local county bar associations, in a sealed package which indicates that it is being delivered due to the affirmative disclosure requirement.

We disagree with both suggestions. Not all items have evidentiary significance in and of themselves. In this case, for instance, the watch is not inculpatory per se; rather, it is the fact that the watch was found in defendant's jacket that makes the watch material evidence. By returning the watch anonymously to the police, this significance is lost. Assuming investigating officials are even able to determine to what case the evidence belongs, they may never be able to reconstruct where it was originally discovered or under what circumstances. Cf. People v. Meredith, 29 Cal. 3d 682, 175 Cal. Rptr. 612, 631 P.2d 46 (1981) ("to bar admission of testimony concerning the original condition and location of the evidence . . . permits the defense to 'destroy' critical information; it is as if . . . the wallet in this case bore a tag bearing the words 'located in the trash can by Scott's residence,' and the defense, by taking the wallet, destroyed this tag." Id. at 691, 175 Cal. Rptr. at 617, 631 P.2d at 53.

We believe it is simpler and more direct for defendant's attorney to turn the matter over to the state as long as it is understood that the prosecutor may not mention in front of the jury the fact that the evidence came from the defendant or his attorney. As the Michigan Court of Appeals explained:

> [P]ermitting the prosecutor to show that defendant's attorney had such evidence in his possession invites the jury to infer that defendant gave the evidence to her attorney. The prosecution should not be allowed to accomplish by inference what he is clearly prohibited from doing by direct proof.

People v. Nash, 110 Mich. App. 428, 447, 313 N.W.2d 307, 314 (1981).

If a defendant is willing to enter a stipulation concerning the chain of possession, location or condition of the evidence, then the evidence may be admitted without the jury becoming aware of the source of the evidence. Cf. People v. Meredith, supra, at 695 n.8, 175 Cal. Rptr. at 620 n.8, 631 P.2d at 54 n.8. Under these circumstances, the attorney need not be called as a witness.

III. MUST THE ATTORNEY WITHDRAW AS COUNSEL?

Under these procedures, the attorney need not withdraw as counsel. If the attorneys can stipulate as to the chain of possession and no reference is made to the fact that the defendant's attorney turned the matter over to the prosecution, then there is no need for the attorney to withdraw as counsel for the defendant. There may be some cases where the client will believe that his attorney no longer has his best interest in mind. In such a case, it may be wise for the attorney to ask to withdraw. Such requests should be liberally granted by the court. Where, however, the client does not object, there is no need for the attorney to withdraw from the case.

DISPOSITION

As to the instant case, we find that defense counsel was forced to take possession of the evidence because of a reasonable fear that to do otherwise would result in its destruction. Because the source was a nonclient, and because he had reason to believe that the witness (source) would conceal or destroy the evidence, the attorney had an obligation to disclose the item and its source to the prosecution. . . .

FELDMAN, J., dissenting.

I dissent both because I disagree with some of the majority's conclusions and because I fear that the court's opinion leaves many unanswered questions. Ordinarily, judicial discretion requires that we avoid questions not directly raised by the case before us. However, the opinion of the court affects vital areas of practice with which prosecutors and defense counsel must deal on a day-to-day basis. Under these circumstances I think it is important to emphasize some points only touched upon in the court's opinion and address some the court did not reach at all.

The court fails to consider the full scope of the role of defense counsel. The opinion indicates that defense counsel acts both as an advocate for the defendant and an officer of the court. I believe that the role of defense counsel has an even more profound dimension. The adversary feature of the criminal justice system evolved as a control on governmental absolutism and is, therefore, a fundamental component of political liberty. Hazard, Ethics in the Practice of Law, 120-122 (1978). Viewed in this framework, the role of defense counsel goes beyond assisting in the search for truth or helping to convict the guilty and acquit the innocent. Beside these two functions, defense counsel also must maintain the integrity of our personal rights by assuring that the government meet the constitutional requirements that it both prove its case and give the defendant due process of law. These are rights which may be invoked by all defendants, not just the innocent. The constitutional guarantee of due process of law extends to all, even those whose innocence is subject to doubt and those whose guilt is certain. The system was designed to restrain governmental power and protect all citizens from tyranny. See generally Hamilton, Madison and Jay, The Federalist (Scott ed. 1894) Nos. 8, 41-45, 70-78; Dworkin, Taking Rights Seriously.

In my view, therefore, defense counsel should never be put in the position of helping the government prove its case. Of course, counsel may not mislead, tamper with evidence, lie or promote such acts. To do so would violate his duty as an officer of a court which seeks to ascertain the truth. On the other hand, because defense counsel is neither an assistant to nor an investigator for the prosecutor, his function is neither to gather nor preserve inculpatory evidence for the prosecution. If he engages in such conduct, how can he then put the government to its proof? How can he be a zealous advocate for the defendant when at the same time he is likely to make himself a star witness for the prosecution?

I am led to the inevitable conclusion that defense counsel has no obligation to take possession of inculpatory evidence from third parties. Further, caution and common sense dictate that as a general rule he should never actively seek to obtain such evidence and should refuse possession even if it is offered to him. His guiding principle should be to leave things as they are found. If counsel has reasonable grounds to believe that evidence is in danger of being tampered with or destroyed by a third party, his obligations are satisfied by cautioning that person against such conduct. The majority opinion is ambiguous on this issue, but I believe that we should make it clear to the defense bar that the general rule to be followed in connection with inculpatory evidence is "hands off."

Of course, there are limited exceptions to that general rule. The defense lawyer is justified in obtaining possession of evidence where necessary to test, examine or inspect that evidence in order to determine whether it is exculpatory. Also, the lawyer may expect to use the evidence in the representation of the client. Such limited circumstances are recognized in the standard proposed by the Ethics Committee of the Criminal Justice Section of the American Bar Association and referred to in the majority opinion. Nothing in that standard indicates that defense counsel should otherwise actively seek to obtain inculpatory evidence.

Although the court purports "essentially" to adopt the standard, I believe it misconstrues it. The standard permits defense counsel to give inculpatory evidence to the prosecution only if it is required by court order or rule, if the item received is contraband or if it poses "an unreasonable risk of physical harm to anyone." (See subsec. (a) and (d).) No provision is made for delivery of inculpatory evidence to the prosecution simply because defense counsel fears that it may be destroyed if given back to its source.

In fact, the standard does cover the situation posed by this case. One of the reasons which prompted defense counsel to take the watch from Ms. Heaton was the need to examine it to determine whether it was the watch involved in the burglary. Subsection (c) of the Standard indicates that this is a legitimate purpose for obtaining the evidence. It also indicates that when lawyers have received evidence which proves to be inculpatory it shall be returned to the source "from whom the lawyer receives it" and enjoins the lawyer to "advise the source of the legal consequences pertaining to possession or destruction of the item."

In my view, therefore, the standard clearly contemplates that the defense lawyer shall not obtain or take possession of evidence without good reason; but if he does receive it, when finished with it he must return it to its source and restore everything to the *status quo ante*. It is only if he finds that he is in possession of contraband or an item which may cause serious physical injury to others that the standard permits counsel to deliver inculpatory evidence to the prosecution. Nor does the standard contemplate that the lawyer make himself a repository for the evidence. In fact, the standard indicates that the lawyer may retain evidence only: (1) if he fears that return to the source will result in its destruction; (2) if he believes that on return it may cause serious harm to others; (3) because he intends to test, examine or use the evidence in his representation; or, (4) because he cannot return it to the source. Only under these limited circumstances may the lawyer retain the item "in a manner that does not impede the lawful ability of law enforcement to obtain the item."

Properly interpreted, therefore, the standard would instruct us as follows in the present case: if defense counsel had a legitimate reason to obtain the evidence, such as examination or testing, then it was proper to receive it from the third person who had possession. When so received, it was proper for defense counsel to retain the item while he examined it or had it tested. When he had finished with it and had discovered that he would not need it for trial, it was his duty to return it to the source with instructions as to the consequences of tampering or destruction. If he had a good faith belief that return to the source would result in damage to or destruction of the evidence, then it was his duty to retain the evidence in his possession "in a manner that [did] not impede the lawful ability of law enforcement to obtain the item."

Thus, I believe the majority is incorrect in holding that defense counsel should turn the evidence over to the prosecution. This holding has not only made defense counsel an assistant to the prosecutor's investigator but also an important witness for the prosecution. The future consequences of such a confusion of roles is bound to damage a system which, despite what we are told during periods of hysteria, has survived the test of time.

SMITH v. SUPERIOR COURT (ABBOTT FORD)
151 Cal. App. 3d 491, 198 Cal. Rptr. 829 (1984)

[The text of this opinion appears in Chapter I.]

C.   The Lawyer-Client Privilege in the Corporate Context

Problem: The Corporate Client

Class action for injuries allegedly resulting when tires negligently manufactured by the *D* Tire Company blew out. Prior to trial, *D*'s attorney interviewed several company employees in connection with the case. Employees interviewed included the chairman of the board, the executive vice-president, the chief of operations, the director of quality control, the foreman of the afternoon tire-molding shift gang, and an employee in the tire-molding crew. The class action's lawyer seeks to discover what was said in these interviews. *D* claims the talks were privileged. What ruling and why?

Problem: The Assiduous Attorney

A bus owned and operated by the *D* Bus Company hits and injures pedestrian *P*. Fearing a lawsuit, *D*'s in-house counsel, Fleegal, interviews the driver of the bus, *C*, and the only eyewitness to the accident, *W*. *C* describes the relevant events to Fleegal, who takes notes, goes back to his office, and files them. *W* describes the relevant events to Fleegal, who has his secretary take down *W*'s comments verbatim and transcribe them in typewritten form. *W* signs the transcript, and Fleegal files it.

Fleegal also has his associate, Cratchet, gather up all the maintenance and driver records and other pertinent *D* Company documents. Fleegal has Cratchet prepare a memorandum analyzing these records and an index to them, all of which he files. Fleegal also reviews a memorandum he had Cratchet prepare some time ago on *D*'s maintenance and driver-training programs and has that filed with the other material.

P sues the *D* Bus Company. During discovery, *P*'s attorney files an FRCP 34 Request for Production of Documents asking for production of "all books, documents, papers, records, reports and things pertinent to, relating to or mentioning the subject accident, the maintenance of Company buses or its training of operating personnel."

What response should Fleegal make to this request? If *P* sends interrogatories to *D* pursuant to FRCP 33 seeking to elicit facts about the accident that Fleegal learned only from *C, W,* and Cratchet, what response should Fleegal make?

See the *Hickman* case, FRCP 26, and the *Radiant Burners* and *Upjohn* cases, which follow.

HICKMAN v. TAYLOR
329 U.S. 495 (1947)

Mr. Justice MURPHY delivered the opinion of the Court.

This case presents an important problem under the Federal Rules of Civil Procedure as to the extent to which a party may inquire into oral and written statements of witnesses, or other information, secured by an adverse party's counsel in the course of preparation for possible litigation after a claim has arisen. Examination into a person's files and records, including those resulting from the professional activities of an attorney, must be judged with care. It is not without reason that various safeguards have been established to preclude unwarranted excursions into the privacy of a man's work. At the same time, public policy supports reasonable and necessary inquiries. Properly to balance these competing interests is a delicate and difficult task.

On February 7, 1943, the tug "J.M. Taylor" sank while engaged in helping to tow a car float of the Baltimore & Ohio Railroad across the Delaware River at Philadelphia. The accident was apparently unusual in nature, the cause of it still being unknown. Five of the nine crew members were drowned. Three days later the tug owners and the underwriters employed a law firm, of which respondent Fortenbaugh is a member, to defend them against potential suits by representatives of the deceased crew members and to sue the railroad for damages to the tug.

A public hearing was held on March 4, 1943, before the United States Steamboat Inspectors, at which the four survivors were examined. This testimony was recorded and made available to all interested parties. Shortly thereafter, Fortenbaugh privately interviewed the survivors and took statements from them with an eye toward the anticipated litigation; the survivors signed these statements on March 29. Fortenbaugh also interviewed other persons believed to have some information relating to the accident and in some cases he made memoranda of what they told him. At the time when Fortenbaugh secured the statements of the survivors, representatives of two of the deceased crew members had been in communication with him. Ultimately claims were presented by representatives of all five of the deceased; four of the claims, however, were settled without litigation. The fifth claimant, petitioner herein, brought suit in a federal court under the Jones Act on November 26,

1943, naming as defendants the two tug owners, individually and as partners, and the railroad.

One year later, petitioner filed 39 interrogatories directed to the tug owners. The 38th interrogatory read:

> State whether any statements of the members of the crews of the Tugs "J.M. Taylor" and "Philadelphia" or of any other vessel were taken in connection with the towing of the car float and the sinking of the Tug "John M. Taylor." Attach hereto exact copies of all such statements if in writing, and if oral, set forth in detail the exact provisions of any such oral statements or reports.

Supplemental interrogatories asked whether any oral or written statements, records, reports or other memoranda had been made concerning any matter relative to the towing operation, the sinking of the tug, the salvaging and repair of the tug, and the death of the deceased. If the answer was in the affirmative, the tug owners were then requested to set forth the nature of all such records, reports, statements or other memoranda.

The tug owners, through Fortenbaugh, answered all of the interrogatories except No. 38 and the supplemental ones just described. While admitting that statements of the survivors had been taken, they declined to summarize or set forth the contents. They did so on the ground that such requests called "for privileged matter obtained in preparation for litigation" and constituted "an attempt to obtain directly counsel's private files." It was claimed that answering these requests "would involve practically turning over not only the complete files, but also the telephone records and, almost, the thoughts of counsel."

In connection with the hearing on these objections, Fortenbaugh made a written statement and gave an informal oral deposition explaining the circumstances under which he had taken the statements. But he was not expressly asked in the deposition to produce the statements. The District Court for the Eastern District of Pennsylvania, sitting en banc, held that the requested matters were not privileged. 4 F.R.D. 479. The court then decreed that the tug owners and Fortenbaugh, as counsel and agent for the tug owners, forthwith

> answer Plaintiff's 38th interrogatory and supplementary interrogatories; produce all written statements of witnesses obtained by Mr. Fortenbaugh, as counsel and agent for Defendants; state in substance any fact concerning this case which Defendants learned through oral statements made by witnesses to Mr. Fortenbaugh whether or not included in his private memoranda and produce Mr. Fortenbaugh's memoranda containing statements of fact by witnesses or to submit these memoranda to the Court for determination of those portions which should be revealed to Plaintiff.

Upon their refusal, the court adjudged them in contempt and ordered them imprisoned until they complied. . . .

The pre-trial deposition-discovery mechanism established by Rules 26 to 37 is one of the most significant innovations of the Federal Rules of Civil Procedure. Under the prior federal practice, the pre-trial functions of notice-giving, issue-formulation and fact-revelation were performed primarily and inadequately by the pleadings. Inquiry into the issues and the facts before trial was narrowly confined and was often cumbersome in method. The new rules, however, restrict the pleadings to the task of general notice-giving and invest the deposition-discovery process with a vital role in the preparation for trial. . . .

We agree, of course, that the deposition-discovery rules are to be accorded a broad and liberal treatment. No longer can the time-honored cry of "fishing expedition" serve to preclude a party from inquiring into the facts underlying his opponent's case. Mutual knowledge of all the relevant facts gathered by both parties is essential to proper litigation. To that end, either party may compel the other to disgorge whatever facts he has in his possession. The deposition-discovery procedure simply advances the stage at which the disclosure can be compelled from the time of trial to the period preceding it, thus reducing the possibility of surprise. But discovery, like all matters of procedure, has ultimate and necessary boundaries. As indicated by Rules 30(b) and (d) and 31(d), limitations inevitably arise when it can be shown that the examination is being conducted in bad faith or in such a manner as to annoy, embarrass or oppress the person subject to the inquiry. And as Rule 26(b) provides, further limitations come into existence when the inquiry touches upon the irrelevant or encroaches upon the recognized domains of privilege.

We also agree that the memoranda, statements and mental impressions in issue in this case fall outside the scope of the attorney-client privilege and hence are not protected from discovery on that basis. It is unnecessary here to delineate the content and scope of that privilege as recognized in the federal courts. For present purposes, it suffices to note that the protective cloak of this privilege does not extend to information which an attorney secures from a witness while acting for his client in anticipation of litigation. Nor does this privilege concern the memoranda, briefs, communications and other writings prepared by counsel for his own use in prosecuting his client's case; and it is equally unrelated to writings which reflect an attorney's mental impressions, conclusions, opinions or legal theories.

But the impropriety of invoking that privilege does not provide an answer to the problem before us. Petitioner has made more than an ordinary request for relevant, non-privileged facts in the possession of his adversaries or their counsel. He has sought discovery as of right of oral and written statements of witnesses whose identity is well known and whose availability to petitioner appears unimpaired. He has sought production of these matters after making the most searching inquiries of his opponents as to the circumstances surrounding the fatal accident, which inquiries were sworn to have been answered to the best of their information and belief. Interrogatories were directed toward all the events prior to, during and subsequent to the sinking of the tug. Full and honest answers to such broad inquiries would necessarily have included all pertinent information gleaned by Fortenbaugh through his interviews with the witnesses. Petitioner makes no suggestion, and we cannot assume, that the tug owners or Fortenbaugh were incomplete or dishonest in the framing of their answers. In addition, petitioner was free to examine the public testimony of the witnesses taken before the United States Steamboat Inspectors. We are thus dealing with an attempt to secure the production of written statements and mental impressions contained in the files and the mind of the attorney Fortenbaugh without any showing of necessity or any indication or claim that denial of such production would unduly prejudice the preparation of petitioner's case or cause him any hardship or injustice. For aught that appears, the essence of what petitioner seeks either has been revealed to him already through the interrogatories or is readily available to him direct from the witnesses for the asking.

The District Court, after hearing objections to petitioner's request, commanded Fortenbaugh to produce all written statements of witnesses and to state in substance any facts learned through oral statements of witnesses to him. Fortenbaugh was to submit any memoranda he had made of the oral statements so that the court might determine what portions should be revealed to petitioner. All of this was ordered without any showing by petitioner, or any requirement that he make a proper showing, of the necessity for the production of any of this material or any demonstration that denial of production would cause hardship or injustice. The court simply ordered production on the theory that the facts sought were material and were not privileged as constituting attorney-client communications.

In our opinion, neither Rule 26 nor any other rule dealing with discovery contemplates production under such circumstances. That is not because the subject matter is privileged or irrelevant, as those concepts are used in these rules. Here is simply an attempt, without purported necessity or justification, to secure written statements, private memoranda and personal recollections prepared or formed by an adverse party's counsel in the course of his legal duties. As such, it falls outside the arena of discovery and contravenes the public policy underlying the orderly prosecution and defense of legal claims. Not even the most liberal of discovery theories can justify unwarranted inquiries into the files and the mental impressions of an attorney.

Historically, a lawyer is an officer of the court and is bound to work for the advancement of justice while faithfully protecting the rightful interests of his clients. In performing his various duties, however, it is essential that a lawyer work with a certain degree of privacy, free from unnecessary intrusion by opposing parties and their counsel. Proper preparation of a client's case demands that he assemble information, sift what he considers to be the relevant from the irrelevant facts, prepare his legal theories and plan his strategy without undue and needless interference. That is the historical and the necessary way in which lawyers act within the framework of our system of jurisprudence to promote justice and to protect their clients' interests. This work is reflected, of course, in interviews, statements, memoranda, correspondence, briefs, mental impressions, personal beliefs, and countless other tangible and intangible ways—aptly though roughly termed by the Circuit Court of Appeals in this case as the "work product of the lawyer." Were such materials open to opposing counsel on mere demand, much of what is now put down in writing would remain unwritten. An attorney's thoughts, heretofore inviolate, would not be his own. Inefficiency, unfairness and sharp practices would inevitably develop in the giving of legal advice and in the preparation of cases for trial. The effect on the legal profession would be demoralizing. And the interests of the clients and the cause of justice would be poorly served.

We do not mean to say that all written materials obtained or prepared by an adversary's counsel with an eye toward litigation are necessarily free from discovery in all cases. Where relevant and non-privileged facts remain hidden in an attorney's file and where production of those facts is essential to the preparation of one's case, discovery may properly be had. Such written statements and documents might, under certain circumstances, be admissible in evidence or give clues as to the existence or location of relevant facts. Or they might be useful for purposes of impeachment or corroboration. And production might be justified where the witnesses are no longer available or can be reached only with difficulty. Were production of written statements and documents to be precluded under such circumstances, the liberal ideals of the deposition-discovery portions of the Federal Rules of Civil Procedure would be stripped of much of their meaning. But the general policy against invading the privacy of an attorney's course of preparation is so well recognized and so essential to an orderly working of our system of legal procedure that a burden rests on the one who would invade that privacy to establish adequate reasons to justify production through a subpoena or court order. That burden, we believe, is necessarily implicit in the rules as now constituted.

Rule 30(b), as presently written, gives the trial judge the requisite discretion to make a judgment as to whether discovery should be allowed as to written statements secured from witnesses. But in the instant case there was no room for that discretion to operate in favor of the petitioner. No attempt was made to establish any reason why Fortenbaugh should be forced to produce the written statements. There was only a naked, general demand for these materials as of right and a finding by the District Court that no recognizable privilege was involved. That was insufficient to justify discovery under these circumstances and the court should have sustained the refusal of the tug owners and Fortenbaugh to produce.

But as to oral statements made by the witnesses to Fortenbaugh, whether presently in the form of his mental impressions or memoranda, we do not believe that any showing of necessity can be made under the circumstances of this case so as to justify production. Under ordinary conditions, forcing an attorney to repeat or write out all that witnesses have told him and to deliver this account to his adversary gives rise to grave dangers of inaccuracy and untrustworthiness. No legitimate purpose is served by such production. The practice forces the attorney to testify as to what he remembers or what he saw fit to write down regarding witnesses' remarks. Such testimony could not qualify as evidence; and to use it for impeachment or corroborative purposes would make the attorney much less an officer of the court and much more an ordinary witness. The standards of the profession would thereby suffer.

Denial of production of this nature does not mean that any material, non-privileged facts can be hidden from the petitioner in this case. He need not be unduly hindered in the preparation of his case, in the discovery of facts or in his anticipation of his opponents' position. Searching interrogatories directed to Fortenbaugh and the tug owners, production of written documents and the statements upon a proper showing and direct interviews with the witnesses themselves all serve to reveal the facts in Fortenbaugh's possession to the fullest possible extent consistent with public policy. Petitioner's counsel frankly admits that he wants the oral statements only to help prepare himself to examine witnesses and to make sure that he has overlooked nothing. That is insufficient under the circumstances to permit him an exception to the policy underlying the privacy of Fortenbaugh's professional activities. If there should be a rare situation justifying production of these matters, petitioner's case is not of that type.

We fully appreciate the wide-spread controversy among the members of the legal profession over the problem raised by this case. It is a problem that rests on what has been one of the most hazy frontiers of the discovery process. But until some rule or statute definitely prescribes otherwise, we are not justified in permitting discovery in a situation of this nature as a matter of unqualified right. When Rule 26 and the other discovery rules were adopted, this Court and the members of the bar in general certainly did not believe or contemplate that all the files and mental processes of lawyers were thereby opened to the free scrutiny of their adversaries. And we refuse to interpret the rules at this time so as to reach so harsh and unwarranted a result.

We therefore affirm the judgment of the Circuit Court of Appeals. Affirmed.

RADIANT BURNERS v. AMERICAN GAS ASSOCIATION
207 F. Supp. 771 (N.D. Ill. 1962), rev'd, 320 F.2d 314 (7th Cir. 1963)

CAMPBELL, C.J. . . . [H]aving after much study and consideration personally come to the point of questioning the application of the attorney-client privilege to a corporate client, I now suggest to the profession and adopt as the law of this case that a corporation is not entitled to make claim to the privilege for the following reasons.

The attorney-client privilege, analogous to the privilege against self-incrimination, is historically and fundamentally personal in nature. Both privileges have their genesis in the common law, and both still exist independently of statute. (The 5th Amendment to the Constitution merely guarantees the self-incrimination privilege against legislative action.) Although at earliest common law the attorney-client privilege was solely that of the attorney, since the eighteenth century, and as it now exists, the privilege rests entirely with the client. It logically follows that this personal privilege of the client must, as in the case of the personal privilege against self-incrimination, be claimed only by natural individuals and not by mere corporate entities. As to denying corporations the privilege against self-incrimination see Wilson v. United States, 221 U.S. 361; and Essgee Co. v. United States, 262 U.S. 151. A fortiori, a corporation which is a mere creature of the state and not a natural entity should not, without legislation, be afforded a privilege historically created only for natural persons.

Still another reason exists for denying the attorney-client privilege to corporations. One of the fundamental, universally accepted and most generally stated common law elements necessarily required properly to claim the attorney-client privilege is that the communication be completely confidential between the attorney and the client. Accordingly, if any of the attorney's or client's documents or verbal statements are subject to being disclosed to third parties, anyone other than the attorney or the client, then those documents or statements can no longer be regarded as confidential, the confidence having in the language of the common law been "profaned" and the privilege terminated. Such "profanity" could occur either at the source or point of origin of the information, or, it could take place at the intended repository of the information, should at either place a third party stranger have access to it.

Were we to assume, as obviously many of us have heretofore, that a corporation may claim the privilege, then we are immediately presented with the anomalous situation of determining what persons within the corporate structure hold its confidence and may properly be considered as its alter ego and therefore the "client." In making such a determination should we include within the scope of the term "client" the corporation's president? What then of other officers, members of the board of directors, executive committee members, supervisory personnel, office workers, or for that matter any employee, and finally what about the individual stockholders? If an individual is not permitted to make an agent of still another individual, or more accurately of large groups of individuals, and thus increase the scope of the protection afforded to him through the attorney-client privilege and "profane" its confidence why permit a corporation to do the same thing through normal corporate operations? Clearly, even at common law the client's necessity and the attorney's of having immediate office personnel permitted access to documents without destroying their confidential nature is accepted and approved. (The solicitor or the barrister's clerk for example.) However, it is obvious that there is no comparison between this accepted extension of the scope of the terms "attorney" and "client," and an attempted extension of the term to encompass all those persons who constitute a corporate entity. This is well illustrated by considering the boards of directors and executive committees of most large corporations. Such groups are often made up of dominant and influential individuals of other corporations and organizations, with many of which the corporation has business dealings. . . . Information from or in the hands of these individuals would unquestionably be information from or in the hands of persons outside the scope of the term "client," as this term is intended with reference to the attorney-client privilege. It is most unrealistic to presume that such communications are made with the intention of confidentiality or could possibly avoid the "profanation" so clearly condemned by the Rule as created at common law. As Wigmore states (Sec. 2291), "It (the attorney-client privilege) ought to be strictly confined within the narrowest possible limits consistent with the logic of its principle." Another and later commentary is in my opinion salient to this issue:

> Where corporations are involved, with their large number of agents, masses of documents and frequent dealings with lawyers, the zone of silence grows large. Few judges — or legislators either, for that matter — would long tolerate any common law privilege that allowed corporations to insulate all their activities by discussing them with legal advisors.

Simon, "The Attorney-Client Privilege As Applied to Corporations," 65 Yale L.J. 953, 955 (1956).

It seems to me that the corporate entity is best exemplified for the purpose of claiming this privilege by those who actually share in its ownership, the shareholders, it being only for their benefit that a corporation could make claim to the privilege. Since, then, the privilege is being asserted for their benefit it would seem that they best qualify as the "client." Thus the term "client" is in many instances extended to include literally thousands of persons in a single corporation. Both at common law, and in many instances also by statute the shareholders have the right always to inspect corporate files and records. As owners they of course have the right to inspect property held by their agents. Although some jurisdictions might place minor restrictions aimed at protecting the interest of other owners upon it, the basic right to reasonable inspection always exists and cannot be abrogated even by the articles of incorporation. Once again it becomes apparent that the confidential nature of communications and documents so vital an element of the attorney-client privilege could never exist when such documents and information are readily available to so many thousand persons, whose qualifications for the most part are solely a monetary interest. Indeed, since all of the activities of every corporation are only for the common or group interest, it can never assert a reasonable or proper claim of secrecy. The Supreme Court has recently alluded to this fact in citing the members' right to inspect as grounds for denying a union the privilege against self-incrimination. United States v. White, 322 U.S. 694, 699-700.

An additional third party or "stranger" to a corporation "profaning" any possible confidential nature of corporate books and records is its State of incorporation with its proper visitatorial power over such records. Once a group of individuals elect to form a corporate entity there can be no overriding desire of secrecy, and the circumstances would argue against any desire to keep documents confidential from all others excluding themselves. Wilson v. United States, 221 U.S. 361. One of the prices one pays for the limitation of personal liability through incorporation is the loss of personal privileges one might otherwise have in individual business transactions.

The basic rationale of the attorney-client privilege and the reason prompting its creation apparently is the compelling desire to promote genuine freedom of communication between an individual and his attorney. In its historic genesis in the common law it is so intimately entwined with its great partner the privilege against self incrimination that a person reading its history begins to doubt that two separate privileges ever were originally intended. Rather the one seems to be but an extension and outgrowth of the other, both being limited to a purely personal application and both being restricted as obviously is the one, solely to the field of criminal law. Usage thereafter however has definitely established at common law the application of the attorney-client privilege to civil litigation although always retaining its purely personal character.

Although the same basic rationale would in my opinion warrant extending a similar privilege to a corporation dealing with its attorney this is impossible at common law because of the secrecy element of the privilege as heretofore pointed out herein. Thus nowhere can a corporation's right to the privilege be found in the common law. Neither can I find any legislative or judicial fiat extending the privilege beyond its historic common law limitations.

Since the primary element of secrecy essential to any claim of the attorney-client privilege is not possible in the case of a corporation and since in any event the privilege is purely personal, I hold that it is not available to any of the corporate parties to this suit.

I should point out in conclusion that, although not yet placed in issue here, certain valid claims of privilege do exist and may properly be asserted to protect a corporation against unbridled discovery. See Wigmore on Evidence, Volume VII, Sections 2212, 2219 and 2219(c) in re "trade secrets" and "statutory protections." Another claim of privilege exists—that of an attorney to protect his "work product" from discovery. In many instances this and the attorney-client privilege seem to overlap, their cognate natures often causing basic misapplications. My finding that the attorney-client privilege cannot be claimed by these corporations has no relation to any possible withholding of documents from the plaintiff in light of the "work product" privilege.

The attorney "work product" privilege, to be distinguished from the attorney-client privilege, is historically and traditionally a privilege of the attorney and not that of the client. Its rationale is based upon the right of lawyers to enjoy privacy in the course of their preparations for suit. Consequently, the fact that the client is a corporation would in no way affect the claim of an attorney to his "work product" privilege. . . .

UPJOHN CO. v. UNITED STATES
449 U.S. 383 (1981)

Mr. Justice REHNQUIST delivered the opinion of the Court.

I

Petitioner Upjohn manufactures and sells pharmaceuticals here and abroad. In January 1976 independent accountants conducting an audit of one of petitioner's foreign subsidiaries discovered that the subsidiary made payments to or for the benefit of foreign government officials in order to secure government business. The accountants so informed Mr. Gerard Thomas, petitioner's Vice-President, Secretary, and General

Counsel. Thomas is a member of the Michigan and New York bars, and has been petitioner's General Counsel for 20 years. He consulted with outside counsel and R.T. Parfet, Jr., petitioner's Chairman of the Board. It was decided that the company would conduct an internal investigation of what were termed "questionable payments." As part of this investigation the attorneys prepared a letter containing a questionnaire which was sent to "all foreign general and area managers" over the Chairman's signature. The letter began by noting recent disclosures that several American companies made "possibly illegal" payments to foreign government officials and emphasized that the management needed full information concerning any such payments made by Upjohn. The letter indicated that the Chairman had asked Thomas, identified as "the company's General Counsel," "to conduct an investigation for the purpose of determining the nature and magnitude of any payments made by the Upjohn Company or any of its subsidiaries to any employee or official of a foreign government." The questionnaire sought detailed information concerning such payments. Managers were instructed to treat the investigation as "highly confidential" and not to discuss it with anyone other than Upjohn employees who might be helpful in providing the requested information. Responses were to be sent directly to Thomas. Thomas and outside counsel also interviewed the recipients of the questionnaire and some 33 other Upjohn officers or employees as part of the investigation.

On March 26, 1976, the company voluntarily submitted a preliminary report to the Securities and Exchange Commission on Form 8-K disclosing certain questionable payments. A copy of the report was simultaneously submitted to the Internal Revenue Service, which immediately began an investigation to determine the tax consequences of the payments. Special agents conducting the investigation were given lists by Upjohn of all those interviewed and all who had responded to the questionnaire. On November 23, 1976, the Service issued a summons pursuant to 26 U.S.C. §7602 demanding production of:

> All files relative to the investigation conducted under the supervision of Gerard Thomas to identify payments to employees of foreign governments and any political contributions made by the Upjohn Company or any of its affiliates since January 1, 1971 and to determine whether any funds of the Upjohn Company had been improperly accounted for on the corporate books during the same period.
>
> The records should include but not be limited to written questionnaires sent to managers of the Upjohn Company's foreign affiliates, and memoranda or notes of the interviews conducted in the United States and abroad with officers and employees of the Upjohn Company and its subsidiaries.

The company declined to produce the documents specified in the second paragraph on the grounds that they were protected from disclosure

by the attorney-client privilege and constituted the work product of attorneys prepared in anticipation of litigation. On August 31, 1977, the
United States filed a petition seeking enforcement of the summons under 26 U.S.C. §§7402(b) and 7604(a) in the United States District Court
for the Western District of Michigan. That court adopted the recommendation of a magistrate who concluded that the summons should be
enforced. Petitioner appealed to the Court of Appeals for the Sixth
Circuit which rejected the magistrate's finding of a waiver of the attorney-client privilege, 600 F.2d 1223, 1227, n.12, but agreed that the privilege did not apply "to the extent the communications were made by
officers and agents not responsible for directing Upjohn's actions in
response to legal advice . . . for the simple reason that the communications were not the 'client's.'" Id., at 1225. The court reasoned that
accepting petitioner's claim for a broader application of the privilege
would encourage upper-echelon management to ignore unpleasant
facts and create too broad a "zone of silence." Noting that petitioner's
counsel had interviewed officials such as the Chairman and President,
the Court of Appeals remanded to the District Court so that a determination of who was within the "control group" could be made. In a
concluding footnote the court stated that the work-product doctrine "is
not applicable to administrative summonses issued under 26 U.S.C.
§7602." Id., at 1228, n.13.

II

Federal Rule of Evidence 501 provides that "the privilege of a witness
. . . shall be governed by the principles of the common law as they may
be interpreted by the courts of the United States in light of reason and
experience." The attorney-client privilege is the oldest of the privileges
for confidential communications known to the common law. 8 Wigmore, Evidence §2290 (McNaughton rev. 1961). Its purpose is to encourage full and frank communication between attorneys and their
clients and thereby promote broader public interests in the observance
of law and administration of justice. The privilege recognizes that sound
legal advice or advocacy serves public ends and that such advice or advocacy depends upon the lawyer being fully informed by the client. As
we stated last Term in Trammel v. United States, 445 U.S. 40, 51 (1980),
"The attorney-client privilege rests on the need for the advocate and
counselor to know all that relates to the client's reasons for seeking
representation if the professional mission is to be carried out." And in
Fisher v. United States, 425 U.S. 391, 403 (1976), we recognized the
purpose of the privilege to be "to encourage clients to make full disclosures to their attorneys." This rationale for the privilege has long been
recognized by the Court, see Hunt v. Blackburn, 128 U.S. 464, 470
(1888) (privilege "is founded upon the necessity, in the interest and

administration of justice, of the aid of persons having knowledge of the law and skilled in its practice, which assistance can only be safely and readily availed of when free from the consequences or the apprehension of disclosure"). Admittedly complications in the application of the privilege arise when the client is a corporation, which in theory is an artificial creature of the law, and not an individual; but this Court has assumed that the privilege applies when the client is a corporation, United States v. Louisville & Nashville R. Co., 236 U.S. 318, 336 (1915), and the Government does not contest the general proposition.

The Court of Appeals, however, considered the application of the privilege in the corporate context to present a "different problem," since the client was an inanimate entity and "only the senior management, guiding and integrating the several operations, . . . can be said to possess an identity analogous to the corporation as a whole." 600 F.2d at 1226. The first case to articulate the so-called "control group test" adopted by the court below, City of Philadelphia v. Westinghouse Electric Corp., 210 F. Supp. 483, 485 (E.D. Pa.), petition for mandamus and prohibition denied, General Electric Company v. Kirkpatrick, 312 F.2d 742 (C.A.3 1962), cert. denied, 372 U.S. 943 (1963), reflected a similar conceptual approach: "Keeping in mind that the question is, Is it the corporation which is seeking the lawyer's advice when the asserted privileged communication is made?, the most satisfactory solution, I think, is that if the employee making the communication, of whatever rank he may be, is in a position to control or even to take a substantial part in a decision about any action which the corporation may take upon the advice of the attorney, . . . then, in effect, *he is (or personifies) the corporation* when he makes his disclosure to the lawyer and the privilege would apply." (Emphasis supplied by the Court.) Such a view, we think, overlooks the fact that the privilege exists to protect not only the giving of professional advice to those who can act on it but also the giving of information to the lawyer to enable him to give sound and informed advice. See *Trammel,* 445 U.S., at 51; *Fisher,* 425 U.S., at 403. The first step in the resolution of any legal problem is ascertaining the factual background and sifting through the facts with an eye to the legally relevant. See ABA Code of Professional Responsibility, Ethical Consideration 4-1:

> A lawyer should be fully informed of all the facts of the matter he is handling in order for his client to obtain the full advantage of our legal system. It is for the lawyer in the exercise of his independent professional judgment to separate the relevant and important from the irrelevant and unimportant. The observance of the ethical obligation of a lawyer to hold inviolate the confidences and secrets of his client not only facilitates the full development of facts essential to proper representation of the client but also encourages laymen to seek early legal assistance.

See also Hickman v. Taylor, 329 U.S. 495, 511 (1947).

In the case of the individual client the provider of information and the person who acts on the lawyer's advice are one and the same. In the corporate context, however, it will frequently be employees beyond the control group as defined by the court below—"officers and agents . . . responsible for directing [the company's] actions in response to legal advice"—who will possess the information needed by the corporation's lawyers. Middle-level—and indeed lower-level—employees can, by actions within the scope of their employment, embroil the corporation in serious legal difficulties, and it is only natural that these employees would have the relevant information needed by corporate counsel if he is adequately to advise the client with respect to such actual or potential difficulties. This fact was noted in Diversified Industries, Inc. v. Meredith, 572 F.2d 596 (C.A.8 1978) (en banc):

"In a corporation, it may be necessary to glean information relevant to a legal problem from middle management or non-management personnel as well as from top executives. The attorney dealing with a complex legal problem is thus faced with a 'Hobson's choice.' If he interviews employees not having 'the very highest authority' their communications to him will not be privileged. If, on the other hand, he interviews *only* those employees with the 'very highest authority,' he may find it extremely difficult, if not impossible, to determine what happened." Id., at 608-609 (quoting Weinschel, Corporate Employee Interviews and the Attorney-Client Privilege, 12 B.C. Ind. & Comm. L. Rev. 873, 876 (1970)).

The control group test adopted by the court below thus frustrates the very purpose of the privilege by discouraging the communication of relevant information by employees of the client to attorneys seeking to render legal advice to the client corporation. The attorney's advice will also frequently be more significant to noncontrol group members than to those who officially sanction the advice, and the control group test makes it more difficult to convey full and frank legal advice to the employees who will put into effect the client corporation's policy. See, e.g., Duplan Corp. v. Deering Milliken, Inc., 397 F. Supp. 1146, 1164 (D.S.C. 1974) ("After the lawyer forms his or her opinion, it is of no immediate benefit to the Chairman of the Board or the President. It must be given to the corporate personnel who will apply it.").

The narrow scope given the attorney-client privilege by the court below not only makes it difficult for corporate attorneys to formulate sound advice when their client is faced with a specific legal problem but also threatens to limit the valuable effort of corporate counsel to ensure their client's compliance with the law. In light of the vast and complicated array of regulatory legislation confronting the modern corporation, corporations, unlike most individuals, "constantly go to lawyers to find out how to obey the law," Burnham, The Attorney-Client Privilege in the Corporate Arena, 24 Bus. Law. 901, 913 (1969), particularly since compliance with the law in this area is hardly an instinctive matter, see, e.g., United States v. United States Gypsum Co., 438 U.S. 422, 440-441 (1978) ("the behavior proscribed by the [Sherman] Act is often difficult to distinguish from the gray zone of socially acceptable and economically justifiable business conduct").[2] The test adopted by the court below is difficult to apply in practice, though no abstractly formulated and unvarying "test" will necessarily enable courts to decide questions such as this with mathematical precision. But if the purpose of the attorney-client privilege is to be served, the attorney and client must be able to predict with some degree of certainty whether particular discussions will be protected. An uncertain privilege, or one which purports to be certain but results in widely varying applications by the courts, is little better than no privilege at all. The very terms of the test adopted by the court below suggest the unpredictability of its application. The test restricts the availability of the privilege to those officers who play a "substantial role" in deciding and directing a corporation's legal response. Disparate decisions in cases applying this test illustrate its unpredictability.

The communications at issue were made by Upjohn employees[3] to counsel for Upjohn acting as such, at the direction of corporate superiors in order to secure legal advice from counsel. As the magistrate found, "Mr. Thomas consulted with the Chairman of the Board and outside counsel and thereafter conducted a factual investigation to determine the nature and extent of the questionable payments *and to be in a position to give legal advice to the company with respect to the payments.*" (Emphasis supplied.) Information, not available from upper-echelon management, was needed to supply a basis for legal advice concerning compliance with securities and tax laws, foreign laws, currency regulations, duties to shareholders, and potential litigation in each of these areas. The communications concerned matters within the scope of the employees' corporate duties, and the employees themselves were sufficiently aware that they were being questioned in order that the corporation could obtain legal advice. The questionnaire identified Thomas as "the company's General Counsel" and referred in its opening sen-

2. The Government argues that the risk of civil or criminal liability suffices to ensure that corporations will seek legal advice in the absence of the protection of the privilege. This response ignores the fact that the depth and quality of any investigations, to ensure compliance with the law would suffer, even were they undertaken. The response also proves too much, since it applies to all communications covered by the privilege: an individual trying to comply with the law or faced with a legal problem also has strong incentive to disclose information to his lawyer, yet the common law has recognized the value of the privilege in further facilitating communications.

3. Seven of the 86 employees interviewed by counsel had terminated their employment with Upjohn at the time of the interview. Petitioner argues that the privilege should nonetheless apply to communications by these former employees concerning activities during their period of employment. Neither the District Court nor the Court of Appeals had occasion to address this issue, and we decline to decide it without the benefit of treatment below.

tence to the possible illegality of payments such as the ones on which information was sought. A statement of policy accompanying the questionnaire clearly indicated the legal implications of the investigation. The policy statement was issued "in order that there be no uncertainty in the future as to the policy with respect to the practices which are the subject of this investigation." It began "Upjohn will comply with all laws and regulations," and stated that commissions or payments "will not be used as a subterfuge for bribes or illegal payments" and that all payments must be "proper and legal." Any future agreements with foreign distributors or agents were to be approved "by a company attorney" and any questions concerning the policy were to be referred "to the company's General Counsel." This statement was issued to Upjohn employees worldwide, so that even those interviewees not receiving a questionnaire were aware of the legal implications of the interviews. Pursuant to explicit instructions from the Chairman of the Board, the communications were considered "highly confidential" when made, and have been kept confidential by the company. Consistent with the underlying purposes of the attorney-client privilege, these communications must be protected against compelled disclosure.

The Court of Appeals declined to extend the attorney-client privilege beyond the limits of the control group test for fear that doing so would entail severe burdens on discovery and create a broad "zone of silence" over corporate affairs. Application of the attorney-client privilege to communications such as those involved here, however, puts the adversary in no worse position than if the communications had never taken place. The privilege only protects disclosure of communications; it does not protect disclosure of the underlying facts by those who communicated with the attorney:

"The protection of the privilege extends only to *communications* and not to facts. A fact is one thing and a communication concerning that fact is an entirely different thing. The client cannot be compelled to answer the question, 'What did you say or write to the attorney?' but may not refuse to disclose any relevant fact within his knowledge merely because he incorporated a statement of such fact into his communication to his attorney." City of Philadelphia v. Westinghouse Electric Corp., 205 F. Supp. 830, 831 (E.D. Pa. 1962). See also *Diversified Industries,* 572 F.2d, at 611; State v. Circuit Court, 34 Wis. 2d 559, 580, 150 N.W.2d 387, 399 (1967) ("the courts have noted that a party cannot conceal a fact merely by revealing it to his lawyer"). Here the Government was free to question the employees who communicated with Thomas and outside counsel. Upjohn has provided the IRS with a list of such employees, and the IRS has already interviewed some 25 of them. While it would probably be more convenient for the Government to secure the results of petitioner's internal investigation by simply subpoenaing the questionnaires and notes taken by petitioner's attorneys, such considerations of convenience do not overcome the policies served by the attorney-client privilege. As Justice Jackson noted in his concurring opinion in Hickman v. Taylor, 329 U.S., at 516: "Discovery was hardly intended to enable a learned profession to perform its functions . . . on wits borrowed from the adversary." . . .

III

Our decision that the communications by Upjohn employees to counsel are covered by the attorney-client privilege disposes of the case so far as the responses to the questionnaire and any notes reflecting responses to interview questions are concerned. The summons reaches further, however, and Thomas has testified that his notes and memoranda of interviews go beyond recording responses to his questions. To the extent that the material subject to the summons is not protected by the attorney-client privilege as disclosing communications between an employee and counsel, we must reach the ruling by the Court of Appeals that the work-product doctrine does not apply to summonses issued under 26 U.S.C. §7602.

The Government concedes, wisely, that the Court of Appeals erred and that the work-product doctrine does apply to IRS summonses. . . .

While conceding the applicability of the work-product doctrine, the Government asserts that it has made a sufficient showing of necessity to overcome its protections. The magistrate apparently so found. The Government relies on the following language in *Hickman:* "We do not mean to say that all written materials obtained or prepared by an adversary's counsel with an eye toward litigation are necessarily free from discovery in all cases. Where relevant and nonprivileged facts remain hidden in an attorney's file and where production of those facts is essential to the preparation of one's case, discovery may properly be had . . . [a]nd production might be justified where the witnesses are no longer available or may be reached only with difficulty." 329 U.S., at 511. The Government stresses that interviewees are scattered across the globe and that Upjohn has forbidden its employees to answer questions it considers irrelevant. The above-quoted language from *Hickman,* however, did not apply to "oral statements made by witnesses . . . whether presently in the form of [the attorney's] mental impressions or memoranda." Id., at 512. As to such material the Court did "not believe that any showing of necessity can be made under the circumstances of this case so as to justify production. . . . If there should be a rare situation justifying production of these matters petitioner's case is not of that type." Id., at 512-513. Forcing an attorney to disclose notes and memoranda of witnesses' oral statements is particularly disfavored because it tends to reveal the attorney's mental processes, 329 U.S., at 513 ("what he saw fit to write down regarding witnesses' remarks"); id., at 516-517 ("the statement would be his [the attorney's] language, permeated with his inferences") (Jackson, J., concurring).[8]

Rule 26 accords special protection to work product revealing the attorney's mental processes. The Rule permits disclosure of documents and tangible things constituting attorney work product upon a showing of substantial need and inability to obtain the equivalent without undue hardship. This was the standard applied by the magistrate. Rule 26 goes on, however, to state that "[i]n ordering discovery of such materials when the required showing has been made, the court shall protect against disclosure of the mental impressions, conclusions, opinions or legal theories of an attorney or other representative of a party concerning the litigation." Although this language does not specifically refer to memoranda based on oral statements of witnesses, the *Hickman* court stressed the danger that compelled disclosure of such memoranda would reveal the attorney's mental process. It is clear that this is the sort of material the draftsmen of the Rule had in mind as deserving special protection. See Notes of Advisory Committee on 1970 Amendment to Rules, reprinted in 48 F.R.D. 487, 502 ("The subdivision . . . goes on to protect against disclosure the mental impressions, conclusions, opinions, or legal theories . . . of an attorney or other representative of a party. The *Hickman* opinion drew special attention to the need for protecting an attorney against discovery of memoranda prepared from recollection of oral interviews. The courts have steadfastly safeguarded against disclosure of lawyers' mental impressions and legal theories. . . .").

Based on the foregoing, some courts have concluded that *no* showing of necessity can overcome protection of work product which is based on oral statements from witnesses. Those courts declining to adopt an absolute rule have nonetheless recognized that such material is entitled to special protection.

We do not decide the issue at this time. It is clear that the magistrate applied the wrong standard when he concluded that the Government had made a sufficient showing of necessity to overcome the protections of the work-product doctrine. The magistrate applied the "substantial need" and "without undue hardship" standard articulated in the first part of Rule 26(b)(3). The notes and memoranda sought by the Government here, however, are work product based on oral statements. If they reveal communications, they are, in this case, protected by the attorney-client privilege. To the extent they do not reveal communications, they reveal the attorneys' mental processes in evaluating the com-

---

8. Thomas described his notes of the interviews as containing "what I consider to be the important questions, the substance of the responses to them, my beliefs as to the importance of these, my beliefs as to how they related to the inquiry, my thoughts as to how they related to other questions. In some instances they might even suggest other questions that I would have to ask or things that I needed to find elsewhere."

munications. As Rule 26 and *Hickman* make clear, such work product cannot be disclosed simply on a showing of substantial need and inability to obtain the equivalent without undue hardship.

While we are not prepared at this juncture to say that such material is always protected by the work-product rule, we think a far stronger showing of necessity and unavailability by other means than was made by the Government or applied by the magistrate in this case would be necessary to compel disclosure. . . .

Is application of the lawyer-client privilege to communications from corporate employees justified under the Wigmore formula for privileges or on humanistic grounds?

What data does the Court cite to support the proposition that the "control group" test discourages the communication of relevant information by employees of the client to the corporation's attorneys? Is this claim logically persuasive in the abstract? Is this "relevant information" protected by any privilege that would prevent the government or a private party in a civil action from forcing its disclosure directly from the employees? What data supports the hypothesis that the quality of corporate compliance investigations will suffer unless the lawyer-client privilege is extended to communications from lower-level employees?

Could any of the Upjohn employees who responded to the company's "questionable payments questionnaire" or who furnished interviews to the outside counsel claim the lawyer-client privilege with respect to those questionnaires or interviews? Could they claim their Fifth Amendment privilege against self-incrimination?

If consulted independently, how would you advise a corporate employee facing an "*Upjohn* interview" concerning the privileged nature of his communications to the investigating outside counsel? How should investigating outside counsel advise corporate employees concerning the privileged nature of their interview? What ethical obligations do counsel in this situation have to warn the employees of a possible conflict of interest?

If outside counsel does not warn an employee that the employee has no privilege to prevent disclosure of the information imparted in the interview, could the employee's subjective belief that a privilege *does* exist nonetheless bring the privilege into existence for the employee? If so, what effect will this "rabbit-under-the-hat" privilege have on the ability of outside counsel to disseminate the results of its investigation to corporate officers, the board of directors, or enforcement agencies?

In this respect, consider American Bar Association Standards for Criminal Justice, The Defense Function 4.56 (2d ed. 1980):

4-4.3 Relations with Prospective Witnesses. . . .

(b) It is not necessary for the lawyer or the lawyer's investigator, in interviewing a prospective witness, to caution the witness concerning possible self-incrimination and the need for counsel.

Given the holding of *Upjohn* that the lawyer-client privilege applies to communications between lower-level employees and corporate counsel, should the privilege cover communication between counsel and *former* employees concerning activities during their period of employment? See footnote 3 of the Court's opinion.

Problem: Hickman *Meets* Upjohn

On the night of February 11, 1987, a tugboat named the "Benoit" sank mysteriously in Boston Harbor. Eight of the nine crewmen aboard were lost. The following morning, the Coast Guard found the ninth crewman, Richard Rothwell, clinging to a piece of floating debris. Rothwell was in shock and unable to speak.

The Benoit was owned by the Brot Company, of which Manny Brot was the CEO. Manny called Sheila Counts, the company's lawyer, as soon as he heard about the loss of the Benoit. He said, "Lawsuits against the company because of the sinking of the Benoit are inevitable. I want you to defend the company zealously in everything connected with the Benoit. I want your advice about how the company should proceed at every point."

Counts asked if she would have full cooperation within the company. "Absolutely," said Manny.

Rothwell regained effective consciousness at 10 A.M. on February 13. His family spoke with him first. When they asked him what happened, he told them that he was not ready to talk about it yet.

Sheila Counts and Manny Brot then spoke with him. Manny first introduced Counts to Rothwell. Counts then explained to Rothwell that this meeting was important to the company and asked if Rothwell objected to it being tape-recorded. Rothwell said he had no objection. Counts turned on a tape recorder and asked Rothwell to say, on tape, that he had no objection to the recording. Rothwell complied.

Manny then read a letter he had written to Rothwell at Counts's suggestion. After reading the letter to Rothwell, Manny handed it to Rothwell and left the room.

In the letter, Manny, speaking as CEO, asked Rothwell, as an employee of the Brot Company, to communicate candidly and confidentially with Sheila Counts as the company's lawyer, in order to help her represent and defend the company in connection with any future litigation relating to the sinking of the Benoit.

Sheila Counts, alone with Rothwell, said: "In my role as lawyer for the Brot Company, I request that you give me a written statement of everything that happened in connection with the sinking of the Benoit."

Rothwell replied with a question: "Will I be communicating with you in confidence?"

Counts replied, "Yes. The company will have an attorney-client privilege with respect to your communications to me about the sinking of the Benoit. That means that the company has the option of keeping your communications secret or disclosing them."

Rothwell inquired further: "What control do I have?"

Counts replied: "Legally speaking, you have none. The company is my client and the holder of the privilege of keeping your communication with me secret. I advise you that, although you are an employee of the Brot Company, you may also have interests adverse to the company in connection with the sinking of the Benoit. You may have a claim against the company. You may, therefore, not want to tell me what happened. The choice is entirely yours."

"You talk just like a lawyer," said Rothwell. "Thank you for advising me so carefully. I fully understand my position. I am a loyal employee of the Brot Company and will cooperate with you fully. Please turn off the tape recorder while I write out my statement."

Counts turned off the tape recorder at that point. Rothwell wrote out a nine-page statement.

When Rothwell completed his statement he read it over. Before signing it, Counts turned on the tape recorder again and asked two nurses to witness Rothwell signing it. Rothwell signed and dated his statement in their presence. Without reading the statement each nurse signed the statement beneath Rothwell's signature as witnesses to his signature. These actions are reflected on the tape.

Counts took the written statement to her office, where it has remained since.

That evening Rothwell died as the result of a massive stroke. Soon thereafter Brot made a substantial payment to Rothwell's wife (who was also Rothwell's executor and heir) in settlement of all claims.

A year later the next of kin of eight of the Benoit crewmen, other than Rothwell, sued Brot Company. In discovery the plaintiffs requested disclosure of Rothwell's written statement. Counts refused the request, claiming an absolute attorney-client privilege. She also claimed a work-product privilege, asserting in an affidavit that as Rothwell hesitated every once in a while in writing out his statement, she asked him various questions that helped him frame his statement, questions that she says clearly reflected her thoughts about the case. Counts is joined in opposition to disclosing Rothwell's statement by Rothwell's wife, to the extent that she may be considered the holder of any privilege.

Plaintiffs have moved to compel disclosure. They contend that without Rothwell's statement they may have no way to prove what caused the Benoit to sink.

Analyze the issues presented by the motion and recommend a decision.

COMMODITY FUTURES TRADING COMMISSION v. WEINTRAUB
471 U.S. 343 (1985)

Justice MARSHALL delivered the opinion of the Court.

The question here is whether the trustee of a corporation in bankruptcy has the power to waive the debtor corporation's attorney-client privilege with respect to communications that took place before the filing of the petition in bankruptcy. . . .

[John K. Notz was appointed receiver and later trustee for the bankrupt corporation Chicago Discount Commodity Brokers (CDCB). When the Commodity Futures Trading Commission investigated CDCB for suspected misappropriation of funds and other fraudulent practices, Notz waived CDCB's attorney-client privilege over the objections of Gary Weintraub, CDCB's former attorney.]

II

It is by now well established, and undisputed by the parties to this case, that the attorney-client privilege attaches to corporations as well as to individuals. Upjohn Co. v. United States, 449 U.S. 383 (1981). Both for corporations and individuals, the attorney-client privilege serves the function of promoting full and frank communications between attorneys and their clients. It thereby encourages observance of the law and aids in the administration of justice.

The administration of the attorney-client privilege in the case of corporations, however, presents special problems. As an inanimate entity, a corporation must act through agents. A corporation cannot speak directly to its lawyers. Similarly, it cannot directly waive the privilege when disclosure is in its best interest. Each of these actions must necessarily be undertaken by individuals empowered to act on behalf of the corporation. In *Upjohn Co.*, we considered whether the privilege covers only communications between counsel and top management, and decided that, under certain circumstances, communications between counsel and lower-level employees are also covered. Here, we face the related question of which corporate actors are empowered to waive the corporation's privilege.

The parties in this case agree that, for solvent corporations, the power to waive the corporate attorney-client privilege rests with the corporation's management and is normally exercised by its officers and directors. The managers, of course, must exercise the privilege in a manner consistent with their fiduciary duty to act in the best interests of the corporation and not of themselves as individuals.

The parties also agree that when control of a corporation passes to new management, the authority to assert and waive the corporation's attorney-client privilege passes as well. New managers installed as a result of a takeover, merger, loss of confidence by shareholders, or simply normal succession, may waive the attorney-client privilege with respect to communications made by former officers and directors. Displaced managers may not assert the privilege over the wishes of current managers, even as to statements that the former might have made to counsel concerning matters within the scope of their corporate duties.

The dispute in this case centers on the control of the attorney-client privilege of a corporation in bankruptcy. The Government maintains that the power to exercise that privilege with respect to prebankruptcy communications passes to the bankruptcy trustee. In contrast, respondents maintain that this power remains with the debtor's directors.

III

As might be expected given the conflict among the courts of appeals, the Bankruptcy Code does not explicitly address the question before us. . . .

IV

In light of the lack of direct guidance from the Code, we turn to consider the roles played by the various actors of a corporation in bankruptcy to determine which is most analogous to the role played by the management of a solvent corporation. Because the attorney-client privilege is controlled, outside of bankruptcy, by a corporation's management, the actor whose duties most closely resemble those of management should control the privilege in bankruptcy, unless such a result interferes with policies underlying the bankruptcy laws.

A

The powers and duties of a bankruptcy trustee are extensive. Upon the commencement of a case in bankruptcy, all corporate property passes to an estate represented by the trustee. The trustee is "account-able for all property received," and has the duty to maximize the value of the estate. He is directed to investigate the debtor's financial affairs, and is empowered to sue officers, directors, and other insiders to re-cover, on behalf of the estate, fraudulent or preferential transfers of the debtor's property. Subject to court approval, he may use, sell, or lease property of the estate.

Moreover, in reorganization, the trustee has the power to "operate the debtor's business" unless the court orders otherwise. Even in liqui-dation, the court "may authorize the trustee to operate the business" for a limited period of time. In the course of operating the debtor's business, the trustee "may enter into transactions, including the sale or lease of property of the estate" without court approval.

As even this brief and incomplete list should indicate, the Bankruptcy Code gives the trustee wide-ranging management authority over the debtor. In contrast, the powers of the debtor's directors are severely limited. Their role is to turn over the corporation's property to the trustee and to provide certain information to the trustee and to the creditors. Congress contemplated that when a trustee is appointed, he assumes control of the business, and the debtor's directors are "com-pletely ousted."

In light of the Code's allocation of responsibilities, it is clear that the trustee plays the role most closely analogous to that of a solvent cor-poration's management. Given that the debtor's directors retain virtu-ally no management powers, they should not exercise the traditional management function of controlling the corporation's attorney-client privilege, unless a contrary arrangement would be inconsistent with pol-icies of the bankruptcy laws.

B

We find no federal interest that would be impaired by the trustee's control of the corporation's attorney-client privilege with respect to pre-bankruptcy communications. On the other hand, the rule suggested by respondents—that the debtor's directors have this power—would frus-trate an important goal of the bankruptcy laws. In seeking to maximize the value of the estate, the trustee must investigate the conduct of prior management to uncover and assert causes of action against the debtor's officers and directors. It would often be extremely difficult to conduct this inquiry if the former management were allowed to control the cor-poration's attorney-client privilege and therefore to control access to the corporation's legal files. To the extent that management had wrong-fully diverted or appropriated corporate assets, it could use the privilege as a shield against the trustee's efforts to identify those assets. The

Code's goal of uncovering insider fraud would be substantially defeated if the debtor's directors were to retain the one management power that might effectively thwart an investigation into their own conduct.

Respondents contend that the trustee can adequately investigate fraud without controlling the corporation's attorney-client privilege. They point out that the privilege does not shield the disclosure of communications relating to the planning or commission of ongoing fraud, crimes, and ordinary torts. The problem, however, is making the threshold showing of fraud necessary to defeat the privilege. Without control over the privilege, the trustee might not be able to discover hidden assets or looting schemes, and therefore might not be able to make the necessary showing.

In summary, we conclude that vesting in the trustee control of the corporation's attorney-client privilege most closely comports with the allocation of the waiver power to management outside of bankruptcy without in any way obstructing the careful design of the Bankruptcy Code.

V

Respondents do not seriously contest that the bankruptcy trustee exercises functions analogous to those exercised by management outside of bankruptcy, whereas the debtor's directors exercise virtually no management functions at all. Neither do respondents seriously dispute that vesting control over the attorney-client privilege in the trustee will facilitate the recovery of misappropriated corporate assets.

Respondents argue, however, that the trustee should not obtain control over the privilege because, unlike the management of a solvent corporation, the trustee's primary loyalty goes not to shareholders but to creditors, who elect him and who often will be the only beneficiaries of his efforts. Thus, they contend, as a practical matter bankruptcy trustees represent only the creditors.

We are unpersuaded by this argument. First, the fiduciary duty of the trustee runs to shareholders as well as to creditors. Second, respondents do not explain why, out of all management powers, control over the attorney-client privilege should remain with those elected by the corporation's shareholders. Perhaps most importantly, respondents' position ignores the fact that bankruptcy causes fundamental changes in the nature of corporate relationships. One of the painful facts of bankruptcy is that the interests of shareholders become subordinated to the interests of creditors. In cases in which it is clear that the estate is not large enough to cover any shareholder claims, the trustee's exercise of the corporation's attorney-client privilege will benefit only creditors, but there is nothing anomalous in this result; rather, it is in keeping with the hierarchy of interests created by the bankruptcy laws.

Respondents also ignore that if a debtor remains in possession—that is, if a trustee is not appointed—the debtor's directors bear essentially the same fiduciary obligation to creditors and shareholders as would the trustee for a debtor out of possession. Indeed, the willingness of courts to leave debtors in possession "is premised upon an assurance that the officers and managing employees can be depended upon to carry out the fiduciary responsibilities of a trustee." Surely, then, the management of a debtor-in-possession would have to exercise control of the corporation's attorney-client privilege consistently with this obligation to treat all parties, not merely the shareholders, fairly. By the same token, when a trustee is appointed, the privilege must be exercised in accordance with the trustee's fiduciary duty to all interested parties.

To accept respondents' position would lead to one of two outcomes: (1) a rule under which the management of a debtor-in-possession exercises control of the attorney-client privilege for the benefit only of shareholders but exercises all of its other functions for the benefit of both shareholders and creditors, or (2) a rule under which the attorney-client privilege is exercised for the benefit of both creditors and shareholders when the debtor remains in possession, but is exercised for the benefit only of shareholders when a trustee is appointed. We find nothing in the bankruptcy laws that would suggest, much less compel, either of these implausible results. . . .

VII

For the foregoing reasons, we hold that the trustee of a corporation in bankruptcy has the power to waive the corporation's attorney-client privilege with respect to prebankruptcy communications. We therefore conclude that Notz, in his capacity as trustee, properly waived CDCB's privilege in this case. The judgment of the Court of Appeals for the Seventh Circuit is accordingly reversed.

It is so ordered.

UNITED STATES v. ZOLIN
491 U.S. 554 (1989)

Justice BLACKMUN delivered the opinion of the Court.

I

In the course of its investigation, the IRS sought access to 49 documents that had been filed with the Clerk of the Los Angeles County Superior Court in connection with a case entitled Church of Scientology of California v. Armstrong, No. C420 153. The *Armstrong* litigation involved, among other things, a charge by the Church that one of its former members, Gerald Armstrong, had obtained by unlawful means documentary materials relating to Church activities, including two tapes. Some of the documents sought by the IRS had been filed under seal.

The District Court and the Court of Appeals found that the tapes at issue in this case recorded attorney-client communications and that the privilege had not been waived when the tapes were inadvertently given to Armstrong. 809 F.2d, at 1417 (noting that Armstrong had acquired the tapes from L. Ron Hubbard's personal secretary, who was under the mistaken impression that the tapes were blank). These findings are not at issue here. Thus, the remaining obstacle to respondents' successful assertion of the privilege is the IRS' contention that the recorded attorney-client communications were made in furtherance of a future crime or fraud.

A variety of questions may arise when a party raises the crime-fraud exception. The parties to this case have not been in complete agreement as to which of these questions are presented here. In an effort to clarify the matter, we observe, first, that we need not decide the quantum of proof necessary ultimately to establish the applicability of the crime-fraud exception. Cf. [Clark v. United States, 289 U.S. 1, 15 (1933), quoting O'Rourke v. Darbishire, [1920] A.C. 581, 604 (P.C.);] S. Stone & S. Liebman, Testimonial Privileges §1.65, p.107 (1983). Rather, we are concerned here with the *type* of evidence that may be used to make that ultimate showing. Within that general area of inquiry, the initial question in this case is whether a district court, at the request of the party opposing the privilege, may review the allegedly privileged communications in camera to determine whether the crime-fraud exception applies. If such in camera review is permitted, the second question we must consider is whether some threshold evidentiary showing is needed before the district court may undertake the requested review. Finally, if a threshold showing is required, we must consider the type of evidence the opposing party may use to meet it: i.e., in this case, whether the partial transcripts the IRS possessed may be used for that purpose.

A

We consider first the question whether a district court may *ever* honor the request of the party opposing the privilege to conduct an in camera review of allegedly privileged communications to determine whether those communications fall within the crime-fraud exception. We conclude that no express provision of the Federal Rules of Evidence bars such use of in camera review, and that it would be unwise to prohibit it in all instances as a matter of federal common law.

(1)

At first blush, two provisions of the Federal Rules of Evidence would appear to be relevant. Rule 104(a) provides: "Preliminary questions concerning the qualification of a person to be a witness, *the existence of a privilege,* or the admissibility of evidence shall be determined by the court. . . . In making its determination it is not bound by the rules of evidence *except those with respect to privileges*" (emphasis added). Rule 1101(c) provides: "The rule with respect to privileges applies at all stages of all actions, cases, and proceedings." Taken together, these Rules might be read to establish that in a summons-enforcement proceeding, attorney-client communications cannot be considered by the district court in making its crime-fraud ruling: to do otherwise, under this view, would be to make the crime-fraud determination without due regard to the existence of the privilege.

Even those scholars who support this reading of Rule 104(a) acknowledge that it leads to an absurd result.

> Because the judge must honor claims of privilege made during his preliminary fact determinations, many exceptions to the rules of privilege will become "dead letters," since the preliminary facts that give rise to these exceptions can never be proved. For example, an exception to the attorney-client privilege provides that there is no privilege if the communication was made to enable anyone to commit a crime or fraud. There is virtually no way in which the exception can ever be proved, save by compelling disclosure of the contents of the communication; Rule 104(a) provides that this cannot be done.

21 C. Wright & K. Graham, Federal Practice & Procedure: Evidence §5055, p.276 (1977) (footnote omitted).

We find this Draconian interpretation of Rule 104(a) inconsistent with the Rule's plain language. The Rule does not provide by its terms that all materials as to which a "clai[m] of privilege" is made must be excluded from consideration. In that critical respect, the language of Rule 104(a) is markedly different from the comparable California evidence rule, which provides that "the presiding officer may not require disclosure of information *claimed to be privileged* under this division in order to rule on the claim of privilege." Cal. Evidence Code §915(a) (West 1966 & Supp. 1989) (emphasis added). There is no reason to read Rule 104(a) as if its text were identical to that of the California rule.

We see no basis for holding that the tapes in this case must be deemed privileged under Rule 104(a) while the question of crime or fraud remains open. Indeed, respondents concede that "if the *proponent* of the privilege is able to sustain its burden only by submitting the communications to the court" for in camera review, Brief for Respondents 14-15 (emphasis in original), the court is not required to avert its eyes (or close its ears) once it concludes that the communication would be privileged, if the court found the crime-fraud exception inapplicable. Rather, respondents acknowledge that the court may "then consider the same communications to determine if the opponent of the privilege has established that the crime-fraud exception applies." Id., at 15.

(2)

Having determined that Rule 104(a) does not prohibit the in camera review sought by the IRS, we must address the question as a matter of the federal common law of privileges. See Rule 501. We conclude that a complete prohibition against opponents' use of in camera review to establish the applicability of the crime-fraud exception is inconsistent with the policies underlying the privilege.

We begin our analysis by recognizing that disclosure of allegedly privileged materials to the district court for purposes of determining the merits of a claim of privilege does not have the legal effect of terminating the privilege. Indeed, this Court has approved the practice of requiring parties who seek to avoid disclosure of documents to make the documents available for in camera inspection, see Kerr v. United States District Court, 426 U.S. 394, 404-405, 96 S. Ct. 2119, 2124-25, 48 L. Ed. 2d 725 (1976), and the practice is well established in the federal courts. See, e.g., In re Antitrust Grand Jury, 805 F.2d 155, 168 (CA6 1986); In re Vargas, 723 F.2d 1461, 1467 (CA10 1983); United States v. Lawless, 709 F.2d 485, 486, 488 (CA7 1983); In re Grand Jury Witness, 695 F.2d 359, 362 (CA9 1982). Respondents do not dispute this point: they acknowledge that they would have been free to request in camera review to establish the fact that the tapes involved attorney-client communications, had they been unable to muster independent evidence to serve that purpose. Brief for Respondents 14-15.

Once it is clear that in camera review does not destroy the privileged nature of the contested communications, the question of the propriety of that review turns on whether the policies underlying the privilege and its exceptions are better fostered by permitting such review or by prohibiting it. In our view, the costs of imposing an absolute bar to consideration of the communications in camera for purpose of establishing the crime-fraud exception are intolerably high.

B

We turn to the question whether in camera review at the behest of the party asserting the crime-fraud exception is *always* permissible, or, in contrast, whether the party seeking in camera review must make some threshold showing that such review is appropriate. In addressing this question, we attend to the detrimental effect, if any, of in camera review on the policies underlying the privilege and on the orderly administration of justice in our courts. We conclude that some such showing must be made. . . .

We think that the following standard strikes the correct balance. Before engaging in in camera review to determine the applicability of the crime-fraud exception, "the judge should require a showing of a factual basis adequate to support a good faith belief by a reasonable person," Caldwell v. District Court, 644 P.2d 26, 33 (Colo. 1982), that in camera review of the materials may reveal evidence to establish the claim that the crime-fraud exception applies.

Once that showing is made, the decision whether to engage in in camera review rests in the sound discretion of the district court. The court should make that decision in light of the facts and circumstances of the particular case, including, among other things, the volume of materials the district court has been asked to review, the relevant importance to the case of the alleged privileged information, and the likelihood that the evidence produced through in camera review, together with other available evidence then before the court, will establish that the crime-fraud exception does apply. The district court is also free to defer its in camera review if it concludes that additional evidence in support of the crime-fraud exception may be available that is *not* allegedly privileged, and that production of the additional evidence will not unduly disrupt or delay the proceedings. . . .

D

In sum, we conclude that a rigid independent evidence requirement does not comport with "reason and experience," Fed. Rule Evid. 501, and we decline to adopt it as part of the developing federal common law of evidentiary privileges. We hold that in camera review may be used to determine whether allegedly privileged attorney-client communications fall within the crime-fraud exception. We further hold, however, that before a district court may engage in in camera review at the request of the party opposing the privilege, that party must present evidence sufficient to support a reasonable belief that in camera review may yield evidence that establishes the exception's applicability.

It is so ordered.

Problem: Common Defense

Action against *D* Company and *E* Company for infringement of a *P* Company patent by a machine manufactured by *D* and used by *E*. *D*'s attorney submits a report to the *D* Company Executive Committee analyzing the patent and pertinent prior art and setting forth the strengths and weaknesses of *D*'s defense. May *D*'s lawyer share this and other privileged memoranda with *E*'s lawyer without waiving the privilege?

D.   The Psychotherapist-Patient Privilege

A privilege for statements by a patient to a physician or psychotherapist is of much more recent origin than the attorney-client privilege. Such a privilege was not generally recognized at common law. Over the years prior to the enactment of the Federal Rules of Evidence, statutory privileges were adopted by many states, often in connection with statutes licensing physicians and, later, psychotherapists, social workers, guidance counselors, and other mental health professionals. These statutory privileges vary in their coverage and effect. Many of them include provisions authorizing the court to require disclosure on a showing of "good cause" or other special necessity.

The version of the Federal Rules of Evidence originally promulgated by the Supreme Court included a psychotherapist-patient privilege for communications to psychologists and physicians engaged in the treatment of mental or emotional conditions. As indicated above, Congress, in its wisdom, declined to adopt any privileges by rule, thus relegating further developments in this area to the common law.

Problem: Confidential Counseling

Llewellan has come to you for advice on how to respond to a subpoena issued by the Federal Grand Jury for the District of Ames. The subpoena commands Llewellan to appear and give sworn testimony concerning the embezzlement of funds from the Ames National Bank. The subpoena also requires Llewellan to produce his records relating to James Saunders.

Llewellan tells you that he is licensed as a counselor under the law of Ames and practices as a "personal and family counselor." He has always assumed that all communications and records are confidential and has told that to his clients. He also discloses to you that for the last year James Saunders, recently resigned head teller of the Ames National Bank, has counselled privately with him on a weekly basis. He wants to know whether he has to obey the subpoena, whether he has to produce any records, and how he should conduct himself under the circumstances.

What do you tell Llewellan? What additional information do you need?

JAFFEE v. REDMOND
518 U.S. 1 (1996)

Justice STEVENS delivered the opinion of the Court.

After a traumatic incident in which she shot and killed a man, a police officer received extensive counseling from a licensed clinical social worker. The question we address is whether statements the officer made to her therapist during the counseling sessions are protected from compelled disclosure in a federal civil action brought by the family of the deceased. Stated otherwise, the question is whether it is appropriate for federal courts to recognize a "psychotherapist privilege" under Rule 501 of the Federal Rules of Evidence.

I

Petitioner is the administrator of the estate of Ricky Allen. Respondents are Mary Lu Redmond, a former police officer, and the Village of Hoffman Estates, Illinois, her employer during the time that she served on the police force. Petitioner commenced this action against respondents after Redmond shot and killed Allen while on patrol duty.

On June 27, 1991, Redmond was the first officer to respond to a "fight in progress" call at an apartment complex. As she arrived at the scene, two of Allen's sisters ran toward her squad car, waving their arms and shouting that there had been a stabbing in one of the apartments. Redmond testified at trial that she relayed this information to her dispatcher and requested an ambulance. She then exited her car and walked toward the apartment building. Before Redmond reached the building, several men ran out, one waving a pipe. When the men ignored her order to get on the ground, Redmond drew her service revolver. Two other men then burst out of the building, one, Ricky Allen chasing the other. According to Redmond, Allen was brandishing a butcher knife and disregarded her repeated commands to drop the weapon. Redmond shot Allen when she believed he was about to stab the man he was chasing. Allen died at the scene. Redmond testified that before other officers arrived to provide support, "people came pouring out of the buildings," App. 134, and a threatening confrontation between her and the crowd ensued.

Petitioner filed suit in Federal District Court alleging that Redmond had violated Allen's constitutional rights by using excessive force during the encounter at the apartment complex. The complaint sought dam-

ages under Rev. Stat. §1979, 42 U.S.C. §1983 and the Illinois wrongful
death statute. . . . At trial, petitioner presented testimony from members
of Allen's family that conflicted with Redmond's version of the incident
in several important respects. They testified, for example, that Redmond drew her gun before exiting her squad car and that Allen was
unarmed when he emerged from the apartment building.

During pretrial discovery petitioner learned that after the shooting
Redmond had participated in about 50 counseling sessions with Karen
Beyer, a clinical social worker licensed by the State of Illinois and employed at that time by the Village of Hoffman Estates. Petitioner sought
access to Beyer's notes concerning the sessions for use in cross-examining Redmond. Respondents vigorously resisted the discovery. They
asserted that the contents of the conversations between Beyer and Redmond were protected against involuntary disclosure by a psychotherapist-patient privilege. The district judge rejected this argument. Neither
Beyer nor Redmond, however, complied with his order to disclose the
contents of Beyer's notes. At depositions and on the witness stand both
either refused to answer certain questions or professed an inability to
recall details of their conversations.

In his instructions at the end of the trial, the judge advised the jury
that the refusal to turn over Beyer's notes had no "legal justification"
and that the jury could therefore presume that the contents of the notes
would have been unfavorable to respondents. The jury awarded petitioner $45,000 on the federal claim and $500,000 on her state-law claim.

The Court of Appeals for the Seventh Circuit reversed and remanded
for a new trial. Addressing the issue for the first time, the court concluded that "reason and experience," the touchstones for acceptance
of a privilege under Rule 501 of the Federal Rules of Evidence, compelled recognition of a psychotherapist-patient privilege. . . . "Reason
tells us that psychotherapists and patients share a unique relationship,
in which the ability to communicate freely without the fear of public
disclosure is the key to successful treatment." . . . As to experience, the
court observed that all 50 States have adopted some form of the psychotherapist-patient privilege. . . . The court attached particular significance to the fact that Illinois law expressly extends such a privilege to
social workers like Karen Beyer. . . . The court also noted that, with one
exception, the federal decisions rejecting the privilege were more than
five years old and that the "need and demand for counseling services
has skyrocketed during the past several years." . . .

The Court of Appeals qualified its recognition of the privilege by
stating that it would not apply if "in the interests of justice, the evidentiary need for the disclosure of the contents of a patient's counseling
sessions outweighs that patient's privacy interests." Balancing those conflicting interests, the court observed, on the one hand, that the evidentiary need for the contents of the confidential conversations was

diminished in this case because there were numerous eyewitnesses to the shooting, and, on the other hand, that Officer Redmond's privacy interests were substantial. . . . Based on this assessment, the court concluded that the trial court had erred by refusing to afford protection to the confidential communications between Redmond and Beyer.

The United States courts of appeals do not uniformly agree that the federal courts should recognize a psychotherapist privilege under Rule 501. . . . Because of the conflict among the courts of appeals and the importance of the question, we granted certiorari. . . .

II

Rule 501 of the Federal Rules of Evidence authorizes federal courts to define new privileges by interpreting "common law principles . . . in the light of reason and experience." . . . The Senate Report accompanying the 1975 adoption of the Rules indicates that Rule 501 "should be understood as reflecting the view that the recognition of a privilege based on a confidential relationship . . . should be determined on a case-by-case basis." . . . The Rule thus did not freeze the law governing the privileges of witnesses in federal trials at a particular point in our history, but rather directed federal courts to "continue the evolutionary development of testimonial privileges." Trammel v. United States, 445 U.S. 40, 47 (1980). . . .

The common-law principles underlying the recognition of testimonial privileges can be stated simply. "'For more than three centuries it has now been recognized as a fundamental maxim that the public . . . has a right to every man's evidence. When we come to examine the various claims of exemption, we start with the primary assumption that there is a general duty to give what testimony one is capable of giving, and that any exemptions which may exist are distinctly exceptional, being so many derogations from a positive general rule.'" . . . Exceptions from the general rule disfavoring testimonial privileges may be justified, however, by a "public good transcending the normally predominant principle of utilizing all rational means for ascertaining the truth." . . .

Guided by these principles, the question we address today is whether a privilege protecting confidential communications between a psychotherapist and her patient "promotes sufficiently important interests to outweigh the need for probative evidence. . . ." Both "reason and experience" persuade us that it does.

III

Like the spousal and attorney-client privileges, the psychotherapist-patient privilege is "rooted in the imperative need for confidence and trust." Treatment by a physician for physical ailments can often proceed successfully on the basis of a physical examination, objective information supplied by the patient, and the results of diagnostic tests. Effective psychotherapy, by contrast, depends upon an atmosphere of confidence and trust in which the patient is willing to make a frank and complete disclosure of facts, emotions, memories, and fears. Because of the sensitive nature of the problems for which individuals consult psychotherapists, disclosure of confidential communications made during counseling sessions may cause embarrassment or disgrace. For this reason, the mere possibility of disclosure may impede development of the confidential relationship necessary for successful treatment.[1] . . .

By protecting confidential communications between a psychotherapist and her patient from involuntary disclosure, the proposed privilege thus serves important private interests.

Our cases make clear that an asserted privilege must also "serv[e] public ends." . . . Thus, the purpose of the attorney-client privilege is to "encourage full and frank communication between attorneys and their clients and thereby promote broader public interests in the observance of law and administration of justice." Ibid. And the spousal privilege, as modified in *Trammel,* is justified because it "furthers the important public interest in marital harmony," . . . the psychotherapist privilege serves the public interest by facilitating the provision of appropriate treatment for individuals suffering the effects of a mental or emotional problem. The mental health of our citizenry, no less than its physical health, is a public good of transcendent importance.

In contrast to the significant public and private interests supporting recognition of the privilege, the likely evidentiary benefit that would result from the denial of the privilege is modest. If the privilege were rejected, confidential conversations between psychotherapists and their patients would surely be chilled, particularly when it is obvious that the circumstances that give rise to the need for treatment will probably result in litigation. Without a privilege, much of the desirable evidence to which litigants such as petitioner seek access—for example, admissions against interest by a party—is unlikely to come into being. This unspoken "evidence" will therefore serve no greater truth-seeking function than if it had been spoken and privileged.

That it is appropriate for the federal courts to recognize a psychotherapist privilege under Rule 501 is confirmed by the fact that all 50 States and the District of Columbia have enacted into law some form of psychotherapist privilege. We have previously observed that the policy decisions of the States bear on the question whether federal courts should recognize a new privilege or amend the coverage of an existing

---

1. See studies and authorities cited in the Brief for American Psychiatric Association et al. as Amici Curiae 14-17, and the Brief for American Psychological Association as Amicus Curiae 12-17.

one. . . . Because state legislatures are fully aware of the need to protect the integrity of the factfinding functions of their courts, the existence of a consensus among the States indicates that "reason and experience" support recognition of the privilege. In addition, given the importance of the patient's understanding that her communications with her therapist will not be publicly disclosed, any State's promise of confidentiality would have little value if the patient were aware that the privilege would not be honored in a federal court. Denial of the federal privilege therefore would frustrate the purposes of the state legislation that was enacted to foster these confidential communications.

It is of no consequence that recognition of the privilege in the vast majority of States is the product of legislative action rather than judicial decision. Although common-law rulings may once have been the primary source of new developments in federal privilege law, that is no longer the case. In Funk v. United States, 290 U.S. 371 (1933), we recognized that it is appropriate to treat a consistent body of policy determinations by state legislatures as reflecting both "reason" and "experience." . . . That rule is properly respectful of the States and at the same time reflects the fact that once a state legislature has enacted a privilege there is no longer an opportunity for common-law creation of the protection. . . .

The uniform judgment of the States is reinforced by the fact that a psychotherapist privilege was among the nine specific privileges recommended by the Advisory Committee in its proposed privilege rules. . . .

Because we agree with the judgment of the state legislatures and the Advisory Committee that a psychotherapist-patient privilege will serve a "public good transcending the normally predominant principle of utilizing all rational means for ascertaining truth," we hold that confidential communications between a licensed psychotherapist and her patients in the course of diagnosis or treatment are protected from compelled disclosure under Rule 501 of the Federal Rules of Evidence.

IV

All agree that a psychotherapist privilege covers confidential communications made to licensed psychiatrists and psychologists. We have no hesitation in concluding in this case that the federal privilege should also extend to confidential communications made to licensed social workers in the course of psychotherapy. The reasons for recognizing a privilege for treatment by psychiatrists and psychologists apply with equal force to treatment by a clinical social worker such as Karen Beyer. Today, social workers provide a significant amount of mental health treatment. . . . Their clients often include the poor and those of modest means who could not afford the assistance of a psychiatrist or psychologist, but whose counseling sessions serve the same public goals. Perhaps in recognition of these circumstances, the vast majority of States explicitly extend a testimonial privilege to licensed social workers. We therefore agree with the Court of Appeals that "[d]rawing a distinction between the counseling provided by costly psychotherapists and the counseling provided by more readily accessible social workers serves no discernible public purpose." . . .

We part company with the Court of Appeals on a separate point. We reject the balancing component of the privilege implemented by that court and a small number of States. Making the promise of confidentiality contingent upon a trial judge's later evaluation of the relative importance of the patient's interest in privacy and the evidentiary need for disclosure would eviscerate the effectiveness of the privilege. As we explained in *Upjohn,* if the purpose of the privilege is to be served, the participants in the confidential conversation "must be able to predict with some degree of certainty whether particular discussions will be protected. An uncertain privilege, or one which purports to be certain but results in widely varying applications by the courts, is little better than no privilege at all." . . .

These considerations are all that is necessary for decision of this case. A rule that authorizes the recognition of new privileges on a case-by-case basis makes it appropriate to define the details of new privileges in a like manner. Because this is the first case in which we have recognized a psychotherapist privilege, it is neither necessary nor feasible to delineate its full contours in a way that would "govern all conceivable future questions in this area." . . .

V

The conversations between Officer Redmond and Karen Beyer and the notes taken during their counseling sessions are protected from compelled disclosure under Rule 501 of the Federal Rules of Evidence. The judgment of the Court of Appeals is affirmed.

It is so ordered.

Justice SCALIA, with whom The Chief Justice joins as to Part III, dissenting. . . .

I

The case before us involves confidential communications made by a police officer to a state-licensed clinical social worker in the course of psychotherapeutic counseling. Before proceeding to a legal analysis of the case, I must observe that the Court makes its task deceptively simple by the manner in which it proceeds. It begins by characterizing the issue as "whether it is appropriate for federal courts to recognize a 'psychotherapist privilege,'" ante, at 1925, and devotes almost all of its opinion to that question. Having answered that question (to its satisfaction) in the affirmative, it then devotes less than a page of text to answering in the affirmative the small remaining question whether "the federal privilege should also extend to confidential communications made to licensed social workers in the course of psychotherapy,". . . .

Of course the prototypical evidentiary privilege analogous to the one asserted here — the lawyer-client privilege — is not identified by the broad area of advice-giving practiced by the person to whom the privileged communication is given, but rather by the professional status of that person. Hence, it seems a long step from a lawyer-client privilege to a tax advisor-client or accountant-client privilege. But if one recharacterizes it as a "legal advisor" privilege, the extension seems like the most natural thing in the world. That is the illusion the Court has produced here: It first frames an overly general question ("Should there be a psychotherapist privilege?") that can be answered in the negative only by excluding from protection office consultations with professional psychiatrists (i.e., doctors) and clinical psychologists. And then, having answered that in the affirmative, it comes to the only question that the facts of this case present ("Should there be a social worker-client privilege with regard to psychotherapeutic counseling?") with the answer seemingly a foregone conclusion. At that point, to conclude against the privilege one must subscribe to the difficult proposition, "Yes, there is a psychotherapist privilege, but not if the psychotherapist is a social worker."

Relegating the question actually posed by this case to an afterthought makes the impossible possible in a number of wonderful ways. For example, it enables the Court to treat the Proposed Federal Rules of Evidence developed in 1972 by the Judicial Conference Advisory Committee as strong support for its holding, whereas they in fact counsel clearly and directly against it. The Committee did indeed recommend a "psychotherapist privilege" of sorts; but more precisely, and more relevantly, it recommended a privilege for psychotherapy conducted by "a person authorized to practice medicine" or "a person licensed or certified as a psychologist," Proposed Rule of Evidence 504, . . . which is to say that it recommended against the privilege at issue here. That condemnation is obscured, and even converted into an endorsement, by pushing a "psychotherapist privilege" into the center ring. The Proposed Rule figures prominently in the Court's explanation of why that privilege deserves recognition and is ignored in the single page devoted to the sideshow which happens to be the issue presented for decision. . . .

III

Of course this brief analysis — like the earlier, more extensive, discussion of the general psychotherapist privilege — contains no explanation of why the psychotherapy provided by social workers is a public good of such transcendent importance as to be purchased at the price of occasional injustice. Moreover, it considers only the respects in which social workers providing therapeutic services are similar to licensed psychiatrists and psychologists; not a word about the respects in which they are different. A licensed psychiatrist or psychologist is an expert in psychotherapy — and that may suffice (though I think it not so clear that this Court should make the judgment) to justify the use of extraordinary means to encourage counseling with him, as opposed to counseling with one's rabbi, minister, family or friends. One must presume that a social worker does not bring this greatly heightened degree of skill to bear, which is alone a reason for not encouraging that consultation as generously. Does a social worker bring to bear at least a significantly heightened degree of skill — more than a minister or rabbi, for example? I have no idea, and neither does the Court. The social worker in the present case, Karen Beyer, was a "licensed clinical social worker" in Illinois, a job title whose training requirements consist of "master's degree in social work from an approved program," and "3,000 hours of satisfactory, supervised clinical professional experience." . . . It is not clear that the degree in social work requires any training in psychotherapy. The "clinical professional experience" apparently will impart some such training, but only of the vaguest sort, judging from the Illinois Code's definition of "[c]linical social work practice," viz., "the providing of mental health services for the evaluation, treatment, and prevention of mental and emotional disorders in individuals, families and groups based on knowledge and theory of psychosocial development, behavior, psychopathology, unconscious motivation, interpersonal relationships, and environmental stress." . . . But the rule the Court announces today — like the Illinois evidentiary privilege which that rule purports to respect, . . . is not limited to "licensed clinical social workers," but includes all "licensed social workers." "Licensed social workers" may also provide "mental health services" as described in §20/ 3(5), so long as it is done under supervision of a licensed clinical social worker. And the training requirement for a "licensed social worker" consists of either (a) "a degree from a graduate program of social work" approved by the State, or (b) "a degree in social work from an undergraduate program" approved by the State, plus "3 years of supervised professional experience." . . . With due respect, it does not seem to me that any of this training is comparable in its rigor (or indeed in the precision of its subject) to the training of the other experts (lawyers) to whom this Court has accorded a privilege, or even of the experts (psychiatrists and psychologists) to whom the Advisory Committee and this Court proposed extension of a privilege in 1972. Of course these are only Illinois' requirements for "social workers." Those of other States, for all we know, may be even less demanding. Indeed, I am not even sure there is a nationally accepted definition of "social worker," as there is of psychiatrist and psychologist. It seems to me quite irresponsible to extend the so-called "psychotherapist privilege" to all licensed social workers, nationwide, without exploring these issues.

Another critical distinction between psychiatrists and psychologists, on the one hand, and social workers, on the other, is that the former professionals, in their consultations with patients, do nothing but psychotherapy. Social workers, on the other hand, interview people for a multitude of reasons. . . . Thus, in applying the "social worker" variant of the "psychotherapist privilege," it will be necessary to determine whether the information provided to the social worker was provided to him in his capacity as a psychotherapist, or in his capacity as an administrator of social welfare, a community organizer, etc. Worse still, if the privilege is to have its desired effect (and is not to mislead the client), it will presumably be necessary for the social caseworker to advise, as the conversation with his welfare client proceeds, which portions are privileged and which are not. . . .

First — and utterly conclusive of the irrelevance of this supposed consensus to the question before us — the majority of the States that accord a privilege to social workers do not do so as a subpart of a "psychotherapist" privilege. The privilege applies to all confidences imparted to social workers, and not just those provided in the course of psychotherapy. . . .

Second, the Court does not reveal the enormous degree of disagreement among the States as to the scope of the privilege. . . .

Thus, although the Court is technically correct that "the vast majority of States explicitly extend a testimonial privilege to licensed social workers," . . . that uniformity exists only at the most superficial level. No State had adopted the privilege without restriction; the nature of the restrictions varies enormously from jurisdiction to jurisdiction; and 10 States, I reiterate, effectively reject the privilege entirely. It is fair to say that there is scant national consensus even as to the propriety of a social-worker psychotherapist privilege, and none whatever as to its appropriate scope. In other words, the state laws to which the Court appeals for support demonstrate most convincingly that adoption of a social-worker psychotherapist privilege is a job for Congress.

The question before us today is not whether there should be an evidentiary privilege for social workers providing therapeutic services. Perhaps there should. But the question before us is whether (1) the need for that privilege is so clear, and (2) the desirable contours of that privilege are so evident, that it is appropriate for this Court to craft it in common-law fashion, under Rule 501. Even if we were writing on a clean slate, I think the answer to that question would be clear. But given our extensive precedent to the effect that new privileges "in derogation of the search for truth" "are not lightly created," United States v. Nixon, 418 U.S. at 710, . . . the answer the Court gives today is inexplicable.

In its consideration of this case, the Court was the beneficiary of no fewer than 14 amicus briefs supporting respondents, most of which came from such organizations as the American Psychiatric Association, the American Psychoanalytic Association, the American Association of State Social Work Boards, the Employee Assistance Professionals Association, Inc., the American Counseling Association, and the National Association of Social Workers. Not a single amicus brief was filed in support of petitioner. That is no surprise. There is no self-interested organization out there devoted to pursuit of the truth in the federal courts. The expectation is, however, that this Court will have that interest prominently — indeed, primarily — in mind. Today we have failed that expectation, and that responsibility. . . . I respectfully dissent.

Many kinds of mental health professionals have statutory obligations of confidentiality concerning communications from and the records of their clients. Sometimes these obligations are contained in the ethical precepts or regulatory provisions governing their professional activities. What happens when one of these statutory "privileges" threatens to collide with a criminal defendant's access to information potentially relevant to one or more defenses to the crime charged?

COMMONWEALTH v. FULLER
423 Mass. 216, 667 N.E.2d 847 (1996)

GREANEY, J. A judge in the Superior Court found the executive director of the Rape Crisis Center of Central Massachusetts, Inc. (center), in contempt for failure to turn over to the court for in camera inspection the rape counselling records of Jane Doe. Doe is the complainant in this case in which the defendant, David Fuller, has been charged with two indictments of rape, . . . one indictment charging indecent exposure . . . and one indictment charging lewd and lascivious behavior. . . . In connection with the preparation of his defense, the defendant sought production of Doe's counselling records from the center. The center refused production on the basis that the records were absolutely privileged under G. L. c. 233, §20J (1994 ed.), the statute protecting from disclosure the records of a victim's counselling sessions with a sexual assault counsellor. A single justice of the Appeals Court stayed the judgment of contempt pending appeal by the center, and we transferred the case to this court on our own motion. Although the judge sought to follow and apply the procedures set forth in Commonwealth v. Bishop, 416 Mass. 169, 181-183, 617 N.E.2d 990 (1993), we conclude that the order calling for the production of Doe's records was erroneously entered, and we vacate the judgment of contempt. As a general matter, we continue to adhere to the procedure set forth in the *Bishop* decision for the handling of motions seeking in camera judicial examinations of privileged records. In reliance on our statement in *Bishop*, that a judge should take into account the nature of the privilege claimed, we take this opportunity to modify the procedure to be followed in the consideration of such motions and the standard which a defendant must meet when a motion seeks access to a complainant's rape counselling records. As will be discussed, we shall include in the standard the requirement of materiality as established in our cases.

1. The testimony at the probable cause hearing on the charges may be summarized as follows. On July 11, 1995, the defendant and Doe met in a bar in Grafton. Doe agreed to accompany the defendant in his automobile for a drink at another establishment. Instead of driving to the other establishment, the defendant pulled into the parking lot of the North Grafton post office. There, the defendant made sexually explicit comments which the complainant viewed as threatening. In the next fifteen minutes, the complainant alleges, the defendant forced her to engage in [sexual activity]. When, in response to a telephone call made by a neighbor, Officer Wayne Tripp and other officers arrived at the scene, the defendant was standing outside of the automobile with his genitals exposed. The defendant claimed that he had stopped to urinate, a claim that was at first supported by the complainant. Officer Tripp, who was known to the complainant, observed that she was upset. He asked if she would like to speak to a female officer. She answered in the affirmative, and, at the police station, gave a statement generally similar to her probable cause testimony. The defendant maintains that any sexual contact between himself and the complainant was consensual.

Through a pretrial agreement, the prosecution disclosed to the defendant that Doe had sought counselling from the center following the incident, and also that she had received similar counselling in 1991 and 1992, after a sexual assault in 1991 involving a different perpetrator. In response to a motion filed by the defendant, which had not been served on the center, a judge in the Superior Court ordered the center to produce all records of Doe's counselling in its possession, in a sealed envelope with an attached letter asserting any privileges which the center claimed. The center's executive director declined to produce the records, and advised the judge that the records were absolutely privileged under G. L. c. 233, §20J, and that Doe declined to waive her privilege.

General Laws c. 233, §20J (1994 ed.), provides, in pertinent part, as follows:

> "A sexual assault counsellor shall not disclose such confidential communication, without the prior written consent of the victim; provided, however, that nothing in this chapter shall be construed to limit the defendant's right of cross-examination of such counsellor in a civil or criminal proceeding if such counsellor testifies with such written consent.
>
> "Such confidential communications shall not be subject to discovery and shall be inadmissible in any criminal or civil proceeding without the prior written consent of the victim to whom the report, record, working paper or memorandum relates."

A "confidential communication" is defined in the statute as "information transmitted in confidence by and between a victim of sexual assault and a sexual assault counsellor by a means which does not disclose the information to a person other than a person present for the benefit of the victim, or to those to whom the disclosure of such information is reasonably necessary to the counseling and assisting of such victim. The term includes all information received by the sexual assault counsellor which arises out of and in the course of such counseling and assisting, including, but not limited to reports, records, working papers or memoranda."

The defendant filed another motion seeking access to the records, asserting, in an affidavit filed by counsel, that "there is a likelihood of exculpatory evidence in the counseling records since [Doe] was allegedly raped in 1991 and puts herself in a similar situation in 1995." In a second affidavit filed in connection with the motion, counsel asserted that "consent is at issue in the present case," and that the "facts of the present case are very similar to those involved in an incident occurring in 1991." Both affidavits indicated that the defendant's counsel had spoken with "at least two independent witnesses who state that when [Doe] drinks she frequently leaves the premises with men [whom] she has just met in a bar." In connection with a hearing on the motion, the defendant's counsel filed a third affidavit in which he stated that "the alleged victim expressed feelings of embarrassment over being discovered in the parking lot with [the defendant] by [Officer] Tripp at the probable cause hearing." On that basis, defense counsel asserted that "such embarrassment may have provided [Doe] with a motive to lie," and, as a result, "there is a probability that evidence which is relevant to the issue will appear in the counseling records of [Doe]."

The prosecutor opposed the defendant's motion for the production of Doe's counselling records on the ground that the 1991 sexual assault was "wholly irrelevant," particularly because the perpetrator involved in that incident had entered guilty pleas to all charges, and had been incarcerated. The prosecution also argued with respect to all the records that the defendant had not made an adequate showing to support his assertion that the privilege conferred by §20J should be pierced.

In a written memorandum of decision, the judge ordered the center to produce a complete copy of its records concerning Doe from 1991 through the present. The judge stated that the records might show that Doe "may have been too embarrassed to tell [Officer] Tripp that she [had] consented to oral sex with the defendant," and that the records of counselling related to the 1991 incident "may be relevant to show [Doe's] propensity to lie." The judge concluded that "the defendant has shown a legitimate need for access to the records regarding [Doe's] unreliability as a witness" and that, based on the *Bishop* case, an in camera review of the records was appropriate. The center's executive director refused to comply with the production order. The judgment holding her in contempt, and this appeal, followed.

The center argues that the absolute privilege conferred by §20J is based on a constitutionally protected privacy interest "in avoiding disclosure of personal matters." . . . The center argues, first, that disclosure of such records should be foreclosed in all circumstances. In the alternative, the center calls for a "strict scrutiny analysis" which would require a defendant credibly to demonstrate that (1) the witness whose privileged material is at stake has undertaken intentionally to distort the truth-finding process, and (2) the defendant has a compelling need for access to particular information.

Victims of rape are encouraged by sexual assault counsellors to explore their personal feelings and perceptions about a form of physical violation which, by its nature, is unusually traumatic to a victim's psyche. . . . We may reasonably assume that the Legislature's choice to afford in §20J an absolute privilege for records of such counselling reflects, among other considerations, the personal and intimate nature that records of sexual assault counselling will almost certainly possess. Moreover, "revelation of privileged information adversely affects the purposes underlying the need for the confidential relationship and serves as a disincentive to the maintenance of such relationships." . . . If clients cannot be given a reasonable assurance of confidentiality, they may not feel able to make full disclosure to a counsellor, or they may forgo altogether the benefits of counselling.

By its terms, the privilege clearly promotes two important interests. First, it encourages victims of the brutal and degrading crime of rape to seek professional assistance to alleviate the psychological scarring caused by the crime, which may be more damaging than the physical invasion itself. Second, the privilege supports the reporting of rapes, which, as the note below indicates, occur in considerable numbers, but frequently are not disclosed, because the victim may feel shame about the assault and may not be able to face the grueling nature of the adversary process that occurs at trial.

. . . As this court observed in *Bishop,* supra at 177, our (elusive) goal in cases of this general nature has been to articulate a standard that will, to the extent possible, result in the abrogation of a privilege only "in those cases in which there is a reasonable risk that nondisclosure may result in an erroneous conviction." . . .

Here, for example, . . . the judge concluded that the absolute character of the privilege conferred by §20J required him to consider whether the defendant had demonstrated a "legitimate need" for records related to the complainant's sexual assault counselling. Nonetheless, his determination that an in camera review was warranted appears also to depend on a finding, presumably made under the *Bishop* standard, that the material in the records is "likely to be relevant to an issue in the case."

In our view, the decision in *Bishop* . . . plainly indicates that this court intended the *Bishop* standard and protocol to apply when a defendant seeks access to any privileged records, including those protected by §20J. It was not our intention, however, to establish a standard and protocol that would result in virtually automatic in camera inspection for an entire class of extremely private and sensitive privileged material. To do so would make the privilege no privilege at all, and would substitute an unwarranted judicial abridgment of a clearly stated legislative goal.

During sexual assault counselling, a client may be encouraged to discuss the facts of the assault. In camera review, while less intrusive than public disclosure or disclosure to a defendant's attorney, is nonetheless a substantial invasion of the privacy of a complaining witness. . . . We conclude, for these reasons, that the "likely to be relevant" standard is too broad and flexible when applied to records protected by §20J.

In considering what alternative standard might better balance a complainant's privacy concerns against a defendant's need for exculpatory information, we start with the presumption, buttressed by the demonstrated legislative concern for the inviolability of the privilege, that disclosure, even in the limited form of an in camera inspection, should not become the general exception to the rule of confidentiality. As has been previously noted, the purpose of sexual assault counselling is not to gather evidence for prosecution, but to mend a damaged psyche. Unlike some other kinds of records, rape counselling records are not particularly likely to contain information relevant and material to the question of an accused's innocence or guilt that will not be available from another source, such as a complainant's statement to the police. Nonetheless, it would appear, from the record in this case, that defense counsel routinely seek in camera review of a complainant's rape counselling records on the theory that the records may contain information that will be useful in preparing a defense, and that requests for these records are filed with other criminal discovery motions at the outset of a case. Rape counselling records should not be summonsed to the court . . . until a defendant has filed a written motion seeking their production and explaining in detail his reasons for doing so, and a judge has ruled on the motion in the defendant's favor. A motion for the production of rape counselling records should be the last step in a defendant's pretrial discovery, premised on defense counsel's analysis of the Commonwealth's case and counsel's own investigation of the matter and a showing that the material is not available elsewhere.

A judge should undertake an in camera review of records privileged under §20J, only when a defendant's motion for production of the records has demonstrated a good faith, specific, and reasonable basis for believing that the records will contain exculpatory evidence which is relevant and material to the issue of the defendant's guilt. By "material evidence" we mean evidence which is not only likely to meet criteria of admissibility, but which also tends to create a reasonable doubt that might not otherwise exist. . . . For example, a credible showing that a complainant previously had fabricated allegations of sexual assault, see Commonwealth v. Bohannon, 376 Mass. 90, 92-96, . . . or a showing of bias against the defendant, or credible information tending to suggest that the complainant has difficulty distinguishing fantasy from reality, might warrant in camera inspection of a complainant's rape counselling records. We emphasize, however, that there is to be no "unrestrained foray into confidential records in the hope that the unearthing of some unspecified information would enable [the defendant] to impeach the witness." . . .

We turn, finally, to the propriety of the judge's order in this case. As justification for in camera review of the records of Doe's counselling in the wake of the 1991 assault, the defendant pointed to certain similarities between her account of the assault in 1991 and her allegations in 1995. He sought access to Doe's 1995 counselling records on the ground that embarrassment at being discovered in a compromising situation by someone she knew (Officer Tripp) might have given her a motive to lie about a consensual sexual encounter. The records (presumably those from 1995), he suggested, might "contain relevant evidence concerning the feelings of embarrassment, humiliation and low self-esteem [Doe] experienced as a result of 'getting caught.'" The judge's order justified in camera review on the ground that the defendant had identified a credible motive for fabrication by the complainant, and the 1991-1992 records, as well as the records related to the defendant's alleged assault, might "be relevant to show [Doe's] propensity to lie." In our view, this threshold showing was not sufficient to warrant in camera inspection of Doe's counselling records.

The Commonwealth established in its submission in opposition to the defendant's motion for access to the records that the perpetrator in the 1991 incident pleaded guilty and was incarcerated for his assault on Doe. It follows that Doe's statements about this assault were credible. . . . As a general matter, it is difficult to conceive what could be revealed in records of counselling for an earlier incident that would be relevant and material to a second allegation of rape, by a different perpetrator, four years later. To the extent it is suggested that details from the earlier incident may have colored Doe's account of the defendant's conduct in 1995, the police reports of the 1991 and 1995 incidents furnish an adequate basis for framing this contention.

The defendant's justification for in camera inspection of the 1995 records was also clearly insufficient. The defendant may have shown that the complainant had a motive to lie (although that showing is not very persuasive), but he has not shown that records of Doe's counselling are likely to contain information on this point that is not available in her statement to the police and her testimony at the probable cause hearing. In every case in which consent is raised as the defense, a defendant will be able to assert that the complainant's records may contain information bearing on a motive to lie. If this were treated as a sufficient showing to justify in camera inspection, no assurance of confidentially could be offered to any complainant who alleged rape. The Federal and State Constitutions do not mandate this result, nor could the Legislature have intended it. We conclude that the judge should not have ordered production of any of Doe's records on this showing.

. . . The order for production of Doe's records is vacated. The order adjudging the executive director of the center in contempt, and the judgment of contempt, are vacated.

The creation of a privilege also requires the carving out of its exceptions. The following case is an example of the common law process of crafting evidence doctrine at work.

IN RE GRAND JURY PROCEEDINGS (GREGORY P. VIOLETTE)
183 F.3d 71 (1st Cir. 1999)

SELYA, Circuit Judge. This matter presents an issue of first impression: whether the nascent psychotherapist-patient privilege encompasses a so-called "crime-fraud exception," parallel to that which we previously have recognized anent the attorney-client privilege. We hold that the privilege entails such an exception and that the exception applies here. We therefore affirm the district court's order enforcing grand jury subpoenas served upon a pair of psychiatrists.

I. BACKGROUND

To protect the secrecy of ongoing grand jury proceedings, we limit our review of the facts to the bare essentials. Since at least October 1997, Gregory P. Violette has been the target of a federal grand jury investigation focused on possible bank fraud and related crimes. The government says that Violette made false statements to financial institutions (presumably in violation of 18 U.S.C. §1014) for the purpose of obtaining loans and credit disability insurance; that he trumped up an array of disabilities, which he communicated to selected health-care providers; and that he caused information from these providers to be transmitted to the companies that had underwritten the credit disability policies (presumably in violation of 18 U.S.C. §1341), thus fraudulently inducing payments.

In February 1999, the United States subpoenaed two licensed psychiatrists, Dr. Carol M. Spencer LeMay and Dr. Epiphanes K. Balian, to appear before the grand jury and provide evidence relating to Violette. The doctors appeared in March and asserted the psychotherapist-patient privilege on Violette's behalf. The government promptly sought enforcement of the subpoenas and buttressed its effort with an affidavit of the case agent, Michael Kelly, filed under seal. Violette countered by moving to intervene and to secure access to all the investigative information, or, alternatively, to Kelly's affidavit.

The district court allowed Violette to intervene but denied the motion for access. Violette then opposed enforcement of the subpoenas. After hearing argument, the district court enforced both subpoenas. Violette appeals, alleging: (1) that the denial of access to the investigative materials violates due process; and (2) that there is no crime-fraud exception to the psychotherapist-patient privilege, or, alternatively, that the evidence sought by the government falls outside the scope of any such exception.

Because the grand jury term is set to expire in early September and because additional delay threatens to exacerbate statute-of-limitations problems, we granted the government's request for expedited review. We consider Violette's claims in reverse order inasmuch as the analysis underlying our resolution of the second claim informs our resolution of the first.

II. THE PSYCHOTHERAPIST-PATIENT PRIVILEGE

The Supreme Court recently recognized the psychotherapist-patient privilege as a matter of federal common law, holding "that confidential communications between a licensed psychotherapist and her patients in the course of diagnosis or treatment are protected from compelled disclosure." Jaffee v. Redmond, 518 U.S. 1, 15, 135 L. Ed. 2d 337, 116

S. Ct. 1923 (1996). The Court left the exact parameters of the privilege
to future cases. See id. at 18. We assume that mantle, mindful that Federal Rule of Evidence 501 authorizes federal courts to develop the common law of privileges "in the light of reason and experience."

As a general matter, a party asserting a privilege has the burden of
showing that the privilege applies. . . . To do so, the proponent of the
privilege must set forth facts sufficient to establish all the elements of
the claimed privilege. . . . Hence, a party asserting the psychotherapist-
patient privilege must show that the allegedly privileged communications were made (1) confidentially (2) between a licensed
psychotherapist and her patient (3) in the course of diagnosis or treatment. See *Jaffee*, 518 U.S. at 15.

The first two of these requirements are not in dispute here. The
district court found that the information to which the subpoenas related
was confidential, and the government does not now challenge that finding.[2] Nor does the government question the credentials of the two psychotherapists. The battleground thus narrows to the privilege's third
fulcrum.

The district court found that the communications to which the subpoenas related were not made in the course of diagnosis or treatment,
and that a crime-fraud exception applied. The court's implicit rationale
appears to have been that because the communications were made in
furtherance of fraud, they could not have served a bona fide therapeutic
purpose.

We find the district court's logic compelling on the rather extreme
facts of this case. We nonetheless are constrained to note that the court
blurred two distinct bases for enforcing the subpoenas. The court might
have reached that result either by concluding that the communications
in question do not satisfy the requirements of the privilege or by concluding that the communications satisfy the requirements of both the
privilege and an exception thereto. Such blurring is understandable
and, in this instance, unimportant. . . . The facts set forth in Kelly's affidavit afford a basis not only for concluding that the communications
were made outside the course of genuine diagnosis or treatment, cf. In
re Doe, 711 F.2d 1187, 1193 (2d Cir. 1983) (holding that the psychotherapist-patient privilege did not protect the records of a sham medical
clinic that served as a front for the illegal sale of drugs, based in large
part on a finding that no genuine therapy took place), but also that the
crime-fraud exception, if applicable to this privilege, extended to these
facts.

We will not dwell unduly on this largely epistemological conundrum.

_____

2. The government previously had questioned the confidentiality of the material by asserting that voluntary disclosure to insurers effectively waived the privilege. The United States
Attorney has abandoned this argument on appeal, however, and we do not consider its merits.

In this appeal, the government offers only the crime-fraud rationale. For simplicity's sake, we therefore assume (without deciding) that Violette's communications can be said to have been made presumptively in the course of diagnosis or treatment. On this assumption, Violette established the essential elements of the privilege and the communications are protected unless an exception pertains. It is to this question that we now turn.

III. THE CRIME-FRAUD EXCEPTION

The government urges wholesale importation of the crime-fraud exception, as delineated in the context of the attorney-client privilege, into the emerging jurisprudence of the psychotherapist-patient privilege. Violette, in contrast, exhorts us to refuse to recognize such an exception.

The *Jaffee* Court did not envision the psychotherapist-patient privilege as absolute or immutable. Rather, the Court suggested the possibility of exceptions to the operation of the privilege and prophesied that the details would emerge on a case-by-case basis. See *Jaffee,* 518 U.S. at 18 & n.19. To our knowledge, no court since *Jaffee* has determined whether the privilege is subject to a crime-fraud exception. We hold that the crime-fraud exception applies to the psychotherapist-patient privilege.

We start our exploration of this virgin terrain with a methodological point. When a court is called upon to consider modifying a privilege or adopting a new exception to it, the appropriate inquiry is whether protecting a particular class of confidential communications "promotes sufficiently important interests to outweigh the need for probative evidence." Trammel v. United States, 445 U.S. 40, 51, 63 L. Ed. 2d 186, 100 S. Ct. 906 (1980). Common sense suggests, and the Evidence Rules make explicit, that this type of judgment must be made in light of "reason and experience." Fed. R. Evid. 501. In this area of the law, then, it is incumbent upon courts to hold the often delicate balance between competing interests steady and true. Justice Cardozo made this point well:

> The recognition of a privilege does not mean that it is without conditions or exceptions. The social policy that will prevail in many situations may run foul in others of a different social policy, competing for supremacy. It is then the function of a court to mediate between them, assigning, so far as possible, a proper value to each, and summoning to its aid all the distinctions and analogies that are the tools of the judicial process.

Clark v. United States, 289 U.S. 1, 13, 77 L. Ed. 993, 53 S. Ct. 465 (1933).

In considering whether to recognize a previously unannounced privilege, "a court must first decide whether a qualified privilege exists or

should exist before deciding how to apply it to a particular case." In re
Grand Jury (Granite Purchases), 821 F.2d 946, 955 (3d Cir. 1987). We
believe that the task of articulating the scope of an existing privilege
calls for a similar approach. An inquiring court should first decide
whether a potentially relevant exception exists. If not, the court's inquiry ends. If, however, the exception exists, the court then must define
its parameters sufficiently to ascertain whether the specific facts of the
case fit within its confines.

Against this methodological backdrop, we ponder the proposed
crime-fraud exception. This exception grew up in the shadow of the
attorney-client privilege. It ensures that the attorney-client privilege will
"not extend to communications made for the purpose of getting advice
for the commission of a fraud or crime." United States v. Reeder, 170
F.3d 93, 106 (1st Cir. 1999). . . . "Thus, the attorney-client privilege is
forfeited inter alia where the client sought the services of the lawyer to
enable or aid the client to commit what the client knew or reasonably
should have known to be a crime or fraud." United States v. Rakes, 136
F.3d 1, 4 (1st Cir. 1998).

To bring the crime-fraud exception to bear, the party invoking it must
make a prima facie showing: (1) that the client was engaged in (or was
planning) criminal or fraudulent activity when the attorney-client communications took place; and (2) that the communications were intended by the client to facilitate or conceal the criminal or fraudulent
activity. See United States v. Jacobs, 117 F.3d 82, 87-89 (2d Cir. 1997).
It is sometimes suggested that the exception follows as a matter of logic
from the principle that motivates the privilege itself. After all, the Supreme Court has stated that the purpose of the attorney-client privilege
is "to encourage full and frank communication between attorneys and
their clients and thereby promote broader public interests in the observance of law and administration of justice." Upjohn Co. v. United
States, 449 U.S. 383, 389, 66 L. Ed. 2d 584, 101 S. Ct. 677 (1981). Using
the privilege to hinder proof of fraudulent or criminal activity would,
the suggestion goes, undermine this core purpose. . . .

We caution, however, that stating the justification for the crime-fraud
exception in this almost syllogistic fashion is potentially misleading.
There is more at work than a simple dichotomy between crime or fraud,
on the one hand, and justice, on the other. We think that it is essential
to clarify the rationale behind the crime-fraud exception before considering transplantation of the exception into new soil.

In the attorney-client environment, this court has justified the crime-
fraud exception on the ground that protecting communications made
in furtherance of crime or fraud withholds relevant information from
the factfinder. See *Reeder*, 170 F.3d at 106. Of course, privileges almost
always have this exclusionary effect. Hence, the rationale for the exception must be that the systemic benefits of protecting this category of

communications are outweighed by the costs of forgoing probative evidence of criminal activity. The essential building block in the justification of the exception, then, is the judgment that statements made in furtherance of a crime or fraud have relatively little (if any) positive impact on the goal of promoting the administration of justice. This understanding is fully consistent with the balancing approach that governs privilege analysis generally. See *Trammel*, 445 U.S. at 50-51.

To summarize, the attorney-client privilege exists as matter of policy, not as a matter of logic. The benefits of full and frank communication between clients and attorneys generally have been deemed to outweigh the costs of probative evidence forgone. The balance shifts, however, when a client communicates for the purpose of advancing a criminal or fraudulent enterprise. Because such communications do not create a net benefit to the system, the rationale that underpins the privilege vanishes (or, at least, diminishes markedly in force).

This is not say that courts delude themselves into thinking that the effects of the crime-fraud exception on the administration of justice are unambiguously positive. It surely can be argued that if the veil of secrecy were totally opaque, lawyers might have more opportunities to discourage illegal behavior. But the crime-fraud exception reflects a policy judgment that this potential discouragement does not justify the costs of shielding highly probative evidence of antisocial conduct from the factfinders' eyes.

This brings us full circle. The *Jaffee* Court justified the psychotherapist-patient privilege in terms parallel to those used for the attorney-client privilege. Indeed, the Court embarked on its examination of the privilege by noting that, "like the spousal and attorney-client privileges, the psychotherapist-patient privilege is 'rooted in the imperative need for confidence and trust.'" *Jaffee*, 518 U.S. at 10 (quoting *Trammel*, 445 U.S. at 51). "Effective psychotherapy," the Court explained, "depends upon an atmosphere of confidence and trust in which the patient is willing to make a frank and complete disclosure of facts, emotions, memories, and fears." Id. But the private interests of psychotherapists and patients, while entitled to weight, do not suffice to justify a privilege; that justification depends on a showing that the privilege also serves the public interest. See 518 U.S. at 11. The Court, again likening the situation to the attorney-client privilege, found such a public good in the psychotherapist-patient context because psychotherapy promotes mental health. See id.

As the Supreme Court has framed the issues, the parallels are striking. The attorney-client privilege and the psychotherapist-patient privilege both exist to foster the confidence and trust required for effective counseling relationships (legal and psychiatric, respectively). The private interests served by these relationships, however, do not justify a privilege. Rather, we customarily respect the confidentiality of communications made in the course of these relationships because, on balance, doing so serves the public weal. The attorney-client privilege promotes "the observance of law and administration of justice," *Upjohn*, 449 U.S. at 389, just as the psychotherapist-patient privilege promotes "the mental health of our citizenry," *Jaffee*, 518 U.S. at 11.

This sense of parity carries over to the crime-fraud exception. In the attorney-client context, we exclude from the privilege communications made in furtherance of crime or fraud because the costs to truth-seeking outweigh the justice-enhancing effects of complete and candid attorney-client conversations. In the psychotherapist-patient context, we likewise should exclude from the privilege communications made in further-ance of crime or fraud because the mental health benefits, if any, of protecting such communications pale in comparison to "the normally predominant principle of utilizing all rational means for ascertaining truth." *Trammel*, 445 U.S. at 50 (quoting Elkins v. United States, 364 U.S. 206, 234, 4 L. Ed. 2d 1669, 80 S. Ct. 1437 (1960) (Frankfurter, J., dis-senting)). Several thoughts inform this conclusion.

First, it is difficult to conjure up a case in which both mental health and criminal or fraudulent purposes might simultaneously be advanced. In our view, communications that are intended to further a crime or fraud will rarely, if ever, be allied with bona fide psychotherapy and, thus, protecting such communications will not promote mental health. In this regard, it is important to emphasize that the crime-fraud excep-tion will apply only when the patient's purpose is to promote a particular crime or fraud. Cf. *Jacobs*, 117 F.3d at 87-89. Thus, for example, a career criminal's confessions to his psychotherapist will not fall within the ex-ception even though the therapy may generally increase the patient's professional productivity. Only when communications are intended di-rectly to advance a particular criminal or fraudulent endeavor will their privileged status be forfeited by operation of this exception. Conse-quently, the slit we cut today in the shroud of psychotherapist-patient secrecy will be slight and will not chill much, if any, clinically relevant speech. . . .

On the other side of the balance, we believe that the potential for abuse of the psychotherapist-patient privilege, absent the engrafting of a crime-fraud exception, is a matter of substantial concern. Psychother-apists could use the privilege to deflect investigations into health insur-ance fraud. . . . Similarly, fraudulent personal injury cases could find effective refuge under the umbrella of the privilege. See In re Grand Jury Subpoena, 710 F. Supp. at 1014. Indeed, our quest for examples need not take us so far afield: the government's version of the facts in the case at hand vividly illustrates the potential for abuse should we recognize the privilege but not the concomitant exception.

In campaigning for reversal of the district court's ukase, Violette as-cribes great significance to the absence of a crime-fraud exception from

Rule 504 of the proposed Uniform Rules of Evidence. In support of this argument by negative implication, he points to proposed Rule 503(d)(1), the crime-fraud exception to the attorney-client privilege. It is true that courts sometimes look to the proposed rules for guidance, see, e.g., *Jaffee*, 518 U.S. at 14-15, but Violette offers nothing to show that the drafters ever considered (let alone rejected) a crime-fraud exception to the psychotherapist-patient privilege. Indeed, the drafters may have thought it self-evident that communications made for the purpose of furthering a crime or fraud would not be deemed to be "made for the purposes of diagnosis or treatment." Unif. R. Evid. 504(b). In all events, the sockdolager is that Congress rejected Rule 504 in favor of the common law approach of Rule 501 (discussed supra). . . . When reason and experience lead us in a different direction than a rejected provision in the proposed rules, we are bound by law to follow the former.

IV. APPLYING THE CRIME-FRAUD EXCEPTION

Having concluded that an exception to the privilege exists, we next mull its applicability here. As explained above, a party invoking the crime-fraud exception must make a prima facie showing that the exception applies. The Supreme Court has described the required quantum of evidence as "something to give colour to the charge . . . that has some foundation in fact." *Clark*, 289 U.S. at 15 (citation omitted).

Although we have not had occasion to flesh out this rather sketchy standard, other courts of appeals have offered varying interpretations. Compare, e.g., In re Grand Jury Proceedings, 87 F.3d 377, 381 (9th Cir. 1996) ("reasonable cause"), with In re Antitrust Grand Jury, 805 F.2d 155, 165-66 (6th Cir. 1986) ("probable cause"), with In re Feldberg, 862 F.2d 622, 625-26 (7th Cir. 1988) (evidence sufficient to require an explanation by the party asserting the privilege, which the court describes as less than a preponderance), with Haines v. Liggett Group Inc., 975 F.2d 81, 95-96 (3d Cir. 1992) (evidence which, if believed, would be sufficient to support a finding that the elements of the crime-fraud exception were satisfied), with In re Grand Jury Proceedings, 641 F.2d 199, 203 (5th Cir. 1981) (same, except that evidence to the contrary is to be disregarded). This case presents no occasion to pick and choose among these sundry formulations of the standard. On the facts before us, the district court's determination that the government carried its burden is unassailable, regardless of which version of the standard applies.

We review the district court's determination that particular communications come within the crime-fraud exception for abuse of discretion. See *Reeder*, 170 F.3d at 106. Kelly's affidavit contains a wealth of evidence indicating that Violette's communications to Drs. LeMay and Balian, respectively, were made as part of a scheme to defraud lenders and/or disability insurers. Thus, the lower court's determination that the government established the key ingredients of the crime-fraud exception — that Violette was engaged in or was planning illegal and fraudulent conduct, and that he obtained assistance from the two doctors in furtherance of this activity, . . . was not an abuse of discretion.

Violette's fallback position is that the district court erred in applying the crime-fraud exception because the psychiatrists were not coconspirators, but at most unwitting pawns. The argument appears to be that since the psychiatrists believed at the time that they were engaged in the professional treatment of an authentic patient, the privilege should remain inviolate. It is true that the doctors' innocence distinguishes this case from In re Grand Jury Subpoena, 710 F. Supp. at 1001, on which the district court relied—but this is a distinction bereft of a meaningful difference. The case law dealing with the crime-fraud exception in the attorney-client context makes it transparently clear that the client's intentions control. See, e.g., *Clark,* 289 U.S. at 15 ("The attorney may be innocent, and still the guilty client must let the truth come out."); . . . We see no credible basis for applying a different rule in the psychotherapist-patient context. . . .

We need go no further. For the reasons stated, we hold that the psychotherapist-patient privilege, like the attorney-client privilege, is subject to a crime-fraud exception; that the district court did not abuse its discretion either in finding the crime-fraud exception applicable to the subpoenaed evidence or in enforcing the subpoenas issued to the two psychiatrists; and that Violette's due process rights have not been abridged by denying him access to the records of an ongoing grand jury investigation.

The orders appealed from are affirmed. Mandate shall issue forthwith.

E. The Husband-Wife Privilege

The husband-wife privilege takes many forms in many jurisdictions. As set forth in the Supreme Court's opinion in *Trammel,* below, what is now referred to as a husband-wife began at common law as an absolute disqualification. More recently the privilege can be found in various American jurisdictions as:

(a)   a disqualification at the instance of the party spouse,
(b)   a disqualification at the instance of the witness spouse,

(c)   a privilege against disclosure of confidential inter-spousal communications which can be invoked by the party spouse, and

(d)   a privilege against disclosure of confidential inter-spousal communications which can be invoked by the witness spouse.

Should the federal courts recognize an inter-spousal privilege? If so,
what kind of a privilege should be recognized? Should the scope of the
privilege depend on the context in which the testimony is sought?

Problem: The Eternal Triangle

H and *W* have been married for seven years, but lately the grapes
have begun to wither on the vine. In fact, *W* believes (correctly) that *H*
is having an affair with *V*. *W* decides she must erase *V* from the picture.
On the night of May 1, with the secret intention of confronting *V* about
the affair, *W* tells *H* she is stepping out for a few hours to go to a friend's
house. The next day, *V*'s body is found in a muddy field near her apartment. The body is riddled with stab wounds. An autopsy indicates *V* was
killed the previous night.

At *W*'s trial for first-degree murder of *V*, *W* asserts that she was home
during the night of the crime. The prosecution then calls *H* to testify
that *W* had gone out alone that night and returned two hours later with
a torn blouse and muddy shoes.

(1) Suppose *H* is more than happy to testify because he believes that
W killed the woman he loves. The trial takes place in a jurisdiction that
has adopted Proposed Rule 505. *W* objects to *H*'s testifying against her.
What ruling and why? What rule of privilege would you favor in this
situation? What social policies are involved in formulating a privilege
rule for husband-wife testimony?

(2) Suppose the jurisdiction has adopted a spousal privilege that
places the privilege in the hands of the witness spouse. Again, *H* is happy
to testify. Does this change the result? What social policies militate for
and against placing the privilege in the hands of the witness spouse
rather than the accused? In this connection, see Trammel v. United
States, which follows.

TRAMMEL v. UNITED STATES
445 U.S. 40 (1980)

Mr. Chief Justice BURGER delivered the opinion of the Court.

We granted certiorari to consider whether an accused may invoke
the privilege against adverse spousal testimony so as to exclude the vol-

untary testimony of his wife. This calls for re-examination of Hawkins v. United States, 358 U.S. 74 (1958).

I

On March 10, 1976, petitioner Otis Trammel was indicted with two others, Edwin Lee Roberts and Joseph Freeman, for importing heroin into the United States from Thailand and the Philippine Islands and for conspiracy to import heroin in violation of 21 U.S.C. §§952(a), 962(a), and 963. The indictment also named six unindicted co-conspirators, including petitioner's wife Elizabeth Ann Trammel.

According to the indictment, petitioner and his wife flew from the Philippines to California in August 1975, carrying with them a quantity of heroin. Freeman and Roberts assisted them in its distribution. Elizabeth Trammel then travelled to Thailand where she purchased another supply of the drug. On November 3, 1975, with four ounces of heroin on her person, she boarded a plane for the United States. During a routine customs search in Hawaii, she was searched, the heroin was discovered, and she was arrested. After discussions with Drug Enforcement Administration agents, she agreed to cooperate with the Government.

Prior to trial on this indictment, petitioner moved to sever his case from that of Roberts and Freeman. He advised the court that the Government intended to call his wife as an adverse witness and asserted his claim to a privilege to prevent her from testifying against him. At a hearing on the motion, Mrs. Trammel was called as a Government witness under a grant of use immunity. She testified that she and petitioner were married in May 1975 and that they remained married.[1] She explained that her cooperation with the Government was based on assurances that she would be given lenient treatment.[2] She then described, in considerable detail, her role and that of her husband in the heroin distribution conspiracy.

After hearing this testimony, the District Court ruled that Mrs. Trammel could testify in support of the Government's case to any act she observed during the marriage and to any communication "made in the presence of a third person"; however, confidential communications between petitioner and his wife were held to be privileged and inadmissible. The motion to sever was denied.

At trial, Elizabeth Trammel testified within the limits of the court's pretrial ruling; her testimony, as the Government concedes, constituted virtually its entire case against petitioner. He was found guilty on both

1. In response to the question whether divorce was contemplated, Mrs. Trammel testified that her husband had said that "I would go my way and he would go his."

2. The Government represents to the Court that Elizabeth Trammel has not been prosecuted for her role in the conspiracy.

the substantive and conspiracy charges and sentenced to an indeterminate term of years pursuant to the Federal Youth Corrections Act, 18 U.S.C. §5010(b).

In the Court of Appeals petitioner's only claim of error was that the admission of the adverse testimony of his wife, over his objection, contravened this Court's teaching in Hawkins v. United States, supra, and therefore constituted reversible error. The Court of Appeals rejected this contention. It concluded that *Hawkins* did not prohibit "the voluntary testimony of a spouse who appears as an unindicted co-conspirator under grant of immunity from the Government in return for her testimony." 583 F.2d 1166, 1168 (C.A.10 1978).

II

The privilege claimed by petitioner has ancient roots. Writing in 1628, Lord Coke observed that "it hath beene resolved by the Justices that a wife cannot be produced either against or for her husband." 1 E. Coke, A Commentarie upon Littleton 6b (1628). See, generally, 8 J. Wigmore, Evidence §2227 (McNaughton rev. 1961). This spousal disqualification sprang from two canons of medieval jurisprudence: first, the rule that an accused was not permitted to testify in his own behalf because of his interest in the proceeding; second, the concept that husband and wife were one, and that since the woman had no recognized separate legal existence, the husband was that one. From those two now long-abandoned doctrines, it followed that what was inadmissible from the lips of the defendant husband was also inadmissible from his wife.

Despite its medieval origins, this rule of spousal disqualification remained intact in most common-law jurisdictions well into the 19th century. See, 8 Wigmore, §2333. . . . [I]t was deemed so well established a proposition as to "hardly requir[e] mention." Indeed, it was not until 1933, in Funk v. United States, 290 U.S. 371, that this Court abolished the testimonial disqualification in the federal courts, so as to permit the spouse of a defendant to testify in the defendant's behalf. *Funk,* however, left undisturbed the rule that either spouse could prevent the other from giving adverse testimony. Id., at 373. The rule thus evolved into one of privilege rather than one of absolute disqualification. See J. Maguire, Evidence, Common Sense and Common Law, 78-92 (1947).

The modern justification for this privilege against adverse spousal testimony is its perceived role in fostering the harmony and sanctity of the marriage relationship. Notwithstanding this benign purpose, the rule was sharply criticized. Professor Wigmore termed it "the merest anachronism in legal theory and an indefensible obstruction to truth in practice." 8 Wigmore, §2228, at 221. The Committee on the Improvements in the Law of Evidence of the American Bar Association called for its abolition. 63 American Bar Association Reports, at 594-595

(1938). In its place, Wigmore, and others suggested a privilege protecting only private marital communications, modeled on the privilege between priest and penitent, attorney and client, and physician and patient. See 8 Wigmore, §2332 et seq.[5]

These criticisms influenced the American Law Institute, which, in its 1942 Model Code of Evidence advocated a privilege for marital confidences, but expressly rejected a rule vesting in the defendant the right to exclude all adverse testimony of his spouse. See American Law Institute, Model Code of Evidence, Rule 215 (1942). In 1953 the Uniform Rules of Evidence, drafted by the National Conference of Commissioners on Uniform State Laws, followed a similar course; it limited the privilege to confidential communications and "abolishe[d] the rule, still existing in some states, and largely a sentimental relic, of not requiring one spouse to testify against the other in a criminal action." See Rule 23(2) and comments. Several state legislatures enacted similarly patterned provisions into law.

In Hawkins v. United States, 358 U.S. 74 (1958), this Court considered the continued vitality of the privilege against adverse spousal testimony in the federal courts. There the District Court had permitted petitioner's wife, over his objection, to testify against him. With one questioning concurring opinion, the Court held the wife's testimony inadmissible; it took note of the critical comments that the common-law rule had engendered, id., at 76, and n.4, but chose not to abandon it. Also rejected was the Government's suggestion that the Court modify the privilege by vesting it in the witness-spouse, with freedom to testify or not independent of the defendant's control. The Court viewed this proposed modification as antithetical to the widespread belief, evidenced in the rules then in effect in a majority of the States and in England, "that the law should not force or encourage testimony which might alienate husband and wife, or further inflame existing domestic differences." Id., at 79.

Hawkins, then, left the federal privilege for adverse spousal testimony where it found it, continuing "a rule which bars the testimony of one spouse against the other unless both consent." Id., at 78. Accord, Wyatt v. United States, 362 U.S. 525, 528 (1960).[7] However, in so doing, the

5. This Court recognized just such a confidential marital communications privilege in Wolfle v. United States, 291 U.S. 7 (1934), and in Blau v. United States, 340 U.S. 332 (1951). In neither case, however, did the Court adopt the Wigmore view that the communications privilege be substituted in place of the privilege against adverse spousal testimony. The privilege as to confidential marital communications is not at issue in the instant case; accordingly, our holding today does not disturb Wolfle and Blau.

7. The decision in Wyatt recognized an exception to Hawkins for cases in which one spouse commits a crime against the other. 362 U.S., at 526. This exception, placed on the ground of necessity, was a longstanding one at common law. See Lord Audley's Case, 123 Eng. Rep. 1140 (1931); 8 Wigmore §2239. It has been expanded since then to include crimes against the

Court made clear that its decision was not meant to "foreclose whatever changes in the rule may eventually be dictated by 'reason and experience.'" 358 U.S., at 79.

III

A

The Federal Rules of Evidence acknowledge the authority of the federal courts to continue the evolutionary development of testimonial privileges in federal criminal trials "governed by the principles of the common law as they may be interpreted . . . in the light of reason and experience." Fed. Rul. Evid. 501. Cf. Wolfle v. United States, 291 U.S. 7, 12 (1934). The general mandate of Rule 501 was substituted by the Congress for a set of privilege rules drafted by the Judicial Conference Advisory Committee on Rules of Evidence and approved by the Judicial Conference of the United States and by this Court. That proposal defined nine specific privileges, including a husband-wife privilege which would have codified the *Hawkins* rule and eliminated the privilege for confidential marital communications. See proposed Fed. Rule Evid. 505. In rejecting the proposed rules and enacting Rule 501, Congress manifested an affirmative intention not to freeze the law of privilege. Its purpose rather was to "provide the courts with the flexibility to develop rules of privilege on a case-by-case basis," 120 Cong. Rec. 40891 (1974) (statement of Rep. Hungate), and to leave the door open to change.

Although Rule 501 confirms the authority of the federal courts to reconsider the continued validity of the *Hawkins* rule, the long history of the privilege suggests that it ought not to be casually cast aside. That the privilege is one affecting marriage, home, and family relationships —already subject to much erosion in our day—also counsels caution. At the same time, we cannot escape the reality that the law on occasion adheres to doctrinal concepts long after the reasons which gave them birth have disappeared and after experience suggests the need for change. This was recognized in *Funk* where the Court "decline[d] to enforce . . . ancient rule[s] of the common law under conditions as they now exist." 290 U.S., at 382. For, as Mr. Justice Black admonished in another setting, "[w]hen precedent and precedent alone is all the argument that can be made to support a court-fashioned rule, it is time

---

spouse's property, see Herman v. United States, 220 F.2d 219, 226 (C.A.4 1955), and in recent years crimes against children of either spouse. United States v. Allery, 526 F.2d 1362 (C.A.8 1975). Similar exceptions have been found to the confidential marital communications privilege. See 8 Wigmore, §2338.

for the rule's creator to destroy it." Francis v. Southern Pacific Co., 333 U.S. 445, 471 (1948) (dissenting opinion).

B

Since 1958, when *Hawkins* was decided, support for the privilege against adverse spousal testimony has been eroded further. Thirty-one jurisdictions, including Alaska and Hawaii, then allowed an accused a privilege to prevent adverse spousal testimony, 358 U.S., at 81, n.3 (Stewart, J., concurring). The number has now declined to 24. In 1974, the National Conference on Uniform State Laws revised its Uniform Rules of Evidence, but again rejected the *Hawkins* rule in favor of a limited privilege for confidential communications. See Uniform Rules of Evidence, Rule 504. That proposed rule has been enacted in Arkansas, North Dakota, and Oklahoma — each of which in 1958 permitted an accused to exclude adverse spousal testimony. The trend in state law toward divesting the accused of the privilege to bar adverse spousal testimony has special relevance because the laws of marriage and domestic relations are concerns traditionally reserved to the states. See Sosna v. Iowa, 419 U.S. 393, 404 (1975). Scholarly criticism of the *Hawkins* rule has also continued unabated.

C

Testimonial exclusionary rules and privileges contravene the fundamental principle that "the public . . . has a right to every man's evidence." United States v. Bryan, 339 U.S. 323, 331 (1950). As such, they must be strictly construed and accepted "only to the very limited extent that permitting a refusal to testify or excluding relevant evidence has a public good transcending the normally predominant principle of utilizing all rational means for ascertaining truth." Elkins v. United States, 364 U.S. 206, 234 (1960) (Frankfurter, J., dissenting). Accord, United States v. Nixon, 418 U.S. 683, 709-710 (1974). Here we must decide whether the privilege against adverse spousal testimony promotes sufficiently important interests to outweigh the need for probative evidence in the administration of criminal justice.

It is essential to remember that the *Hawkins* privilege is not needed to protect information privately disclosed between husband and wife in the confidence of the marital relationship — once described by this Court as "the best solace of human existence." Stein v. Bowman 13 Pet., at 223. Those confidences are privileged under the independent rule protecting confidential marital communications. Blau v. United States, 340 U.S. 332 (1951); see n.5, supra. The *Hawkins* privilege is invoked, not to exclude private marital communications, but rather to exclude evidence of criminal acts and of communications made in the presence of third persons.

No other testimonial privilege sweeps so broadly. The privileges between priest and penitent, attorney and client, and physician and patient limit protection to private communications. These privileges are rooted in the imperative need for confidence and trust. The priest-penitent privilege recognizes the human need to disclose to a spiritual counselor, in total and absolute confidence, what are believed to be flawed acts or thoughts and to receive priestly consolation and guidance in return. The lawyer-client privilege rests on the need for the advocate and counselor to know all that relates to the client's reasons for seeking representation if the professional mission is to be carried out. Similarly, the physician must know all that a patient can articulate in order to identify and to treat disease; barriers to full disclosure would impair diagnosis and treatment.

The *Hawkins* rule stands in marked contrast to these three privileges. Its protection is not limited to confidential communications; rather it permits an accused to exclude all adverse spousal testimony. As Jeremy Bentham observed more than a century and a half ago, such a privilege goes far beyond making "every man's house his castle," and permits a person to convert his house into "a den of thieves." 5 Rationale of Judicial Evidence 340 (1827). It "secures, to every man, one safe and unquestionable and every ready [*sic*] accomplice for every imaginable crime." Id., at 338.

The ancient foundations for so sweeping a privilege have long since disappeared. Nowhere in the common-law world—indeed in any modern society—is a woman regarded as chattel or demeaned by denial of a separate legal identity and the dignity associated with recognition as a whole human being. Chip by chip, over the years those archaic notions have been cast aside so that "[n]o longer is the female destined solely for the home and the rearing of the family, and only the male for the marketplace and the world of ideas." Stanton v. Stanton, 421 U.S. 7, 14, 15 (1975).

The contemporary justification for affording an accused such a privilege is also unpersuasive. When one spouse is willing to testify against the other in a criminal proceeding—whatever the motivation—their relationship is almost certainly in disrepair; there is probably little in the way of marital harmony for the privilege to preserve. In these circumstances, a rule of evidence that permits an accused to prevent adverse spousal testimony seems far more likely to frustrate justice than to foster family peace. Indeed, there is reason to believe that vesting the privilege in the accused could actually undermine the marital relationship. For example, in a case such as this the Government is unlikely to offer a wife immunity and lenient treatment if it knows that her husband can prevent her from giving adverse testimony. If the Government is dissuaded from making such an offer, the privilege can have the unto- ward effect of permitting one spouse to escape justice at the expense of the other. It hardly seems conducive to the preservation of the marital relation to place a wife in jeopardy solely by virtue of her husband's control over her testimony.

IV

Our consideration of the foundations for the privilege and its history satisfy us that "reason and experience" no longer justify so sweeping a rule as that found acceptable by the Court in *Hawkins*. Accordingly, we conclude that the existing rule should be modified so that the witness spouse alone has a privilege to refuse to testify adversely; the witness may be neither compelled to testify nor foreclosed from testifying. This modification—vesting the privilege in the witness-spouse—furthers the important public interest in marital harmony without unduly burdening legitimate law enforcement needs.

Here, petitioner's spouse chose to testify against him. That she did so after a grant of immunity and assurances of lenient treatment does not render her testimony involuntary. Cf. Bordenkircher v. Hayes, 434 U.S. 357 (1978). Accordingly, the District Court and the Court of Appeals were correct in rejecting petitioner's claim of privilege, and the judgment of the Court of Appeals is affirmed.

Affirmed.

What justifications for the discarded *Hawkins* rule of spousal exclu- sion can you articulate that are not discussed by the Court in *Trammel*? Are they persuasive enough to support retention of the *Hawkins* rule? Should the Court have gone further and abolished completely the tes- timonial spousal privilege, rather than merely shifting it to the witness spouse, thus limiting the spousal privilege to one covering confidential communications?

Should the husband-wife testimonial privilege be expanded to em- brace other members of the family? When, if ever, should a father be forced to testify against his child, for example? What values support the privilege recognized in *Trammel*? What is their generative power? Should the *Trammel* privilege be extended to common law marriages, same-sex relationships, and best friends?

Problem: Home, Sweet Home

Leo and Mickie have been living together in Beverly Hills for ten years. They have a seven-year-old daughter, Elissa. Leo is charged with assault and battery on Elissa on June 1. On June 30 Leo and Mickie are married by a justice of the peace in Las Vegas, Nevada. At Leo's trial on July 30 the state calls Mickie to testify as to what she witnessed on June 1.

(1) Leo objects. Under proposed Rule 505, what ruling and why?

(2) Mickie objects. Under *Trammel*, what ruling and why?

Problem: Private Communications

Charge: murder of *V*, *D*'s father-in-law, on June 1. M.O.: bludgeoning with a blunt instrument, dismemberment with a sharp one, and burial in the backyard of her home. The jurisdiction's spousal privilege states that "in every case, the husband or wife of either party shall be deemed a competent witness, provided that neither shall be permitted to disclose any private communication made to him or her by the other during their marriage, except on trials of petitions for divorce between them or trials between them involving their respective property rights."

(1) At trial, the district attorney proposes that *D*'s husband, *H*, testify for the prosecution, over *D*'s objection, that he asked *D* on June 2 where his father was and *D* said, "I killed him and chopped him up into a hundred pieces." Admissible?

(2) *H* testifies that *D*, in response to his question, "Where is Poppa?" showed *H* the 100 pieces of his father that *D* had hidden in a trunk. Admissible?

(3) *H* testifies that on June 1 he was reading in the living room. *D* carried a trunk up from the basement, said "Hi, dear," proceeded to drag the trunk through the living room and out to the backyard, and buried it. Admissible?

(4) *H* testifies that he was asleep in bed the night of June 1. He woke up and noticed that *D* was not beside him. He got out of bed and as he passed the bedroom window saw *D* in the moonlight furtively digging in the backyard. *H* got back into bed and pretended he was asleep. About a half-hour later, *D* crept back to bed. *D* never mentioned the matter to *H*, and *H* never raised it with *D*. Admissible?

Problem: The Set-Up

Section 2054 of State *S*'s penal code prohibits carrying concealed weapons unless one reasonably fears an attack from an enemy. *D* is charged with violating §2054 by carrying a derringer pistol. At trial, *D* proposes to testify that *W*, his wife, told him confidentially before he armed himself that she was having an affair with *X* who loved her so much he was going to kill *D*.

The prosecution objects to *D*'s testimony. *W*, in court, objects as well. Is the testimony admissible?

Problem: Big Brother Is Watching You

A federal grand jury is conducting an investigation into racketeering, loan-sharking, and drug trafficking in the Miami area. A primary target of the inquiry is Mickey "Squeeky" Ratón. The grand jury is investigating a series of activities of Ratón and his associates, including alleged murders, extortions, kidnapping, smuggling, gambling, and drug sales and distribution.

Ratón and his three children, Huey, Duey, and Luey, were subpoenaed to appear and testify before the grand jury. Attorneys for the Ratóns moved to quash the subpoenas, claiming a family or parent-child privilege to refuse to testify. The Assistant United States Attorney submitted an affidavit to the trial judge who is hearing the motions to quash the subpoenas. It outlined the general nature of the grand jury's investigation and the prosecution's interest in the Ratóns. The affidavit further stated:

(1) Huey is 28 years old. He lives in a separate household with his own family. The prosecution believes that Huey is centrally involved in the illegal activities of Mickey Ratón and "that he has knowledge relevant to the grand jury investigation of illegal activities planned and carried out by Mickey Ratón by virtue of his (Huey's) observation of such activities and discussions with Mickey Ratón concerning such activities."

(2) Duey is 22 years old. He attends college at the University of Florida where he lives in an on-campus residence hall. The prosecution does not allege that Duey is involved in any illegal activities himself. It believes that he has knowledge relevant to the investigation by virtue of private conversations with Mickey and other private conversations with Huey, which the prosecution would like to ask him about before the grand jury.

(3) Luey is 15 years old and lives at home with his parents. The prosecution does not allege that Luey is involved in any criminal activities himself. Rather, it believes that he has knowledge relevant to the investigation by virtue of his observations of the comings and goings of Ratón and others at the Ratón home, which the prosecution would like to ask him about before the grand jury.

(4) The prosecution would also like to ask Mickey Ratón questions about Huey's activities and about conversations that Mickey had with Huey that are relevant to the grand jury's investigation of Huey's illegal activities.

Should any of the motions to quash be granted?

THREE JUVENILES v. COMMONWEALTH
390 Mass. 357, 455 N.E.2d 1203 (1983), cert. denied, 465 U.S. 1068 (1984)

WILKINS, J.

We are presented for the first time with the question whether a minor child may be compelled to appear and to testify, over the objection of both the child and the child's parents, before a grand jury that is investigating the possible murder of a nonfamily member by the child's father. We conclude that, in these circumstances, a minor child has no privilege to refuse to appear. Further, the child has no privilege to refuse to testify as to what he may have seen or heard, except perhaps as to confidential communications between the child and the parents, a question we need not decide on this record.

The plaintiffs, twelve, fourteen, and fifteen years of age, live with their parents. The children were subpoenaed to appear on April 4, 1983, to testify before a grand jury that was investigating the possible murder of a missing woman. The woman was an acquaintance of their father, and the investigation had focused on him. Neither the children nor their parents wish the children to appear or to testify. On April 4, the children moved to quash the subpoenas, claiming a family or parent-child privilege not to testify. A judge of the Superior Court denied the motion, but stayed the appearance of the children before the grand jury until April 14.

On April 13, the children filed a petition under G.L. c.211, §3, in the Supreme Judicial Court for the county of Suffolk seeking reversal of the denial of their motion. A single justice allowed the parents to intervene. The Commonwealth submitted an affidavit to the single justice in support of its contention that the children's expected testimony would be relevant to the grand jury investigation. The affidavit, which has been impounded, states in part that,

> there is reason to believe that [the missing woman] was murdered on the evening of March 5 . . . and that an examination by the Grand Jury of the above mentioned children . . . as to their observations of the comings and goings of their parents and in particular [the father and the missing woman] during this critical period of time, as well as any conversations they may have witnessed between them could . . . provide further evidence pertaining to her murder.

The single justice further stayed the witnesses' appearances, and reserved and reported the case, without decision, for determination by the full court. . . .

Testimonial privileges "are exceptions to the general duty imposed on all people to testify." Commonwealth v. Corsetti, 387 Mass. 1, 5 (1982); Matter of Pappas, 358 Mass. 604, 607-609 (1971), aff'd sub nom.

Branzburg v. Hayes, 408 U.S. 665 (1972). Such privileges diminish the evidence before the court (Commonwealth v. Corsetti, supra), and contravene the fundamental principle that "the public . . . has a right to every man's evidence." United States v. Bryan, 339 U.S. 323, 331 (1950), quoting 8 J. Wigmore, Evidence §2192, at 64 (3d ed. 1940). As such, they must be strictly construed (see Commonwealth v. Corsetti, supra), and accepted "only to the very limited extent that permitting a refusal to testify or excluding relevant evidence has a public good transcending the normally predominant principle of utilizing all rational means for ascertaining truth." Elkins v. United States, 364 U.S. 206, 234 (1960) (Frankfurter, J., dissenting). Except for the privilege against self-incrimination (Branzburg v. Hayes, 408 U.S. 665, 689-690 [1972]; Matter of Roche, 381 Mass. 624, 634 n.11 [1980]), and a limited "executive privilege" (United States v. Nixon, 418 U.S. 683, 709-710 [1974]), testimonial privileges have generally not been based on a constitutional right. The question "we must decide [is] whether the privilege against adverse [parent-child] testimony promotes sufficiently important interests to outweigh the need for probative evidence in the administration of criminal justice." Trammel v. United States, 445 U.S. 40, 51 (1980). See Matter of Pappas, supra at 609, quoting Professor Edmund M. Morgan in his preface to the American Law Institute's Model Code of Evidence.

We are, of course, free to identify a privilege of a child not to testify against his or her parent. Such a privilege could be based on common law or constitutional principles. In recent years, however, courts have tended to leave the creation of evidentiary privileges to legislative determination.

We have recognized common law testimonial privileges, as a matter of public policy, such as the attorney-client privilege (Foster v. Hall, 12 Pick. 89, 97 [1832]), and the government informer privilege (Worthington v. Scribner, 109 Mass. 487, 489, 493 [1872]). Some members of this court have expressed a willingness to consider recognizing a news reporter's privilege. See Matter of Roche, 381 Mass. 624, 638-640 (1980). The Legislature has also recognized certain testimonial privileges. See G.L. c.233, §20A (certain communications to a clergyman); G.L. c.233, §20B (certain communications between a psychotherapist and a patient); G.L. c.112, §135 (certain communications to a social worker). All these statutory and common law privileges involve communications made in confidential circumstances. They do not involve disqualifications from testifying.

The Legislature has recognized a testimonial disqualification as to certain private conversations between spouses. G.L. c.233, §20, clause First. It has granted one spouse the right to elect not to testify against the other spouse in a criminal proceeding (except in a proceeding relating to child abuse or in an action for nonsupport). G.L. c.233, §20, clause Second, as appearing in St. 1983, c.145. There is, however, no privilege for a spouse not to testify against the other spouse in a civil action, even if that testimony may be highly destructive of the marital relationship. The Legislature has not chosen to establish a parent-child testimonial privilege or disqualification. It has, however, been willing to recognize problems presented to family members by criminal conduct of another family member. See G.L. c.274, §4 (exemption of certain family members from criminal liability as accessories after the fact for harboring a family member after his commission of a felony).

In our order of August 4, 1983, we expressly declined to rule on the question of a privilege as to "alleged confidential communications between the parents and their children." We adhere to that determination. Although there is limited support for a testimonial privilege to protect confidential communications from child to parent, the weight of authority is against it.[4] Because a parent does not need the advice of a minor child in the same sense that a child may need the advice of a parent, the case for a testimonial privilege as to confidential communications from parent to child seems weaker than the case as to such a communication from child to parent. We are aware of no State that, through legislation or by a decision of its court of last resort, has recognized any privilege that would protect a child from testifying against a parent concerning the parent's confidential communications to the child. In any event, the case before us does not currently involve, and may never involve, the question of confidential communications between parent and child.

A clear majority of the courts that have considered whether there is a general privilege of a child not to testify against his or her parent have found no such privilege. Understandably, there should be no privilege when a parent is charged with physically abusing the child (Hunter v. State, 172 Ind. App. 397, 410, cert. denied, 434 U.S. 906 [1977]), or where a family member may otherwise be the victim of wrongdoing. Where the focus of inquiry involves the conduct of a parent, courts have almost universally declined to recognize a privilege. See United States v. Jones, 683 F.2d 817, 818-819 (4th Cir. 1982); United States v. Penn,

---

4. An intermediate appellate court in New York has said that parents have a right of privacy under the Constitution of the United States to decline to disclose information told to them by their minor child "in the context of the familial setting for the purpose of obtaining support, advice or guidance," if the child does not want that information disclosed. Matter of A & M, 61 A.D.2d 426, 433-434 (N.Y. 1978). See Matter of Mark G., 65 A.D.2d 917 (N.Y. 1978) (mem.). One judge in New York has said that the right of a parent and child to prevent disclosure of confidential communications from the child to the parent is founded on both the Federal and New York Constitutions and is broad enough to encompass confidential statements made to his father by a twenty-three-year-old son who was not living at home. People v. Fitzgerald, 101 Misc. 2d 712, 716, 718 (N.Y. County Ct. 1979). On the other hand, several courts have rejected the idea of a privilege to exclude confidential communications to a parent from a child. In re Terry W., 59 Cal. App. 3d 745, 748-749 (1976). Cissna v. State, 170 Ind. App. 437, 439-440 (1976). Matter of Grand Jury Subpoena Served Upon Kinoy, 326 F. Supp. 400, 406 (S.D.N.Y. 1970).

647 F.2d 876, 885 (9th Cir. 1980) ("There is no judicially or legislatively recognized general 'family' privilege"); In re Grand Jury Proceedings, 647 F.2d 511, 512-513 (5th Cir. 1981) (per curiam); State v. Gilroy, 313 N.W.2d 513, 516 (Iowa 1981). We are aware of only one opinion that has recognized not only a privilege of a child not to testify against his father as to confidential communications but also a privilege not to testify against his father at all in a criminal proceeding. In re Grand Jury Proceedings Witness: Agosto, 553 F. Supp. 1298 (D. Nev. 1983). This prolix opinion of a single Federal judge demonstrates the judge's concern for the preservation of the American family but cites no authority or persuasive policy reason for such an extreme position. It is this extreme position — an absolute privilege not to testify at all — that we reject.[6]

In the last analysis, the question comes down to a balancing of the public's interest in obtaining every person's testimony against public policy considerations in favor of erecting a testimonial privilege in the circumstances. We have put to one side the question of confidential communications between parent and child and thus are concerned here only with what the children may have seen and heard in nonconfidential circumstances. Confidential communications aside, we see no basis for concluding that a constitutional right of privacy requires that the children and their parents be given a testimonial privilege. Neither Congress nor the Legislature of any State has seen fit to adopt a rule granting a privilege to one family member not to testify against another (except between spouses) or even to grant a privilege not to testify as to confidential communications between family members (again, except as to spouses). Courts have been generally reluctant to identify any such privilege, and, as far as we can tell from reported decisions, only one judge in this country has found an absolute privilege of a child not to testify against a parent as to nonconfidential matters. Society's interest in the preservation of the family does not require such a broad rule, either as a matter of common law privilege or constitutional right. The

---

6. In recent years, perhaps because of the increased application of traditional constitutional and other rights in juvenile proceedings, the subject of establishing a parent-child privilege has received favorable attention. See Coburn, Child-Parent Communications: Spare the Privilege and Spoil the Child, 74 Dick. L. Rev. 599 (1969); Stanton, Child-Parent Privilege for Confidential Communications: An Examination and Proposal, 16 Fam. L.Q. 1 (1982); Comment, From the Mouths of Babes: Does the Constitutional Right of Privacy Mandate a Parent-Child Privilege?, 1978 B.Y.U.L. Rev. 1002; Comment, The Child-Parent Privilege: A Proposal, 47 Fordham L. Rev. 771 (1979); Comment, Confidential Communication Between Parent and Child: A Constitutional Right, 16 San Diego L. Rev. 811 (1979); Note, Recognition of a Parent-Child Testimonial Privilege, 23 St. Louis U.L.J. 676 (1979). Contra, Note: Questioning the Recognition of a Parent-Child Testimonial Privilege, 45 Alb. L. Rev. 142 (1980). However, although these various commentators have almost universally favored adoption of a testimonial privilege as to confidential communications from a minor child to his or her parent, none has argued for a privilege as to communications made by a parent to a child and none has espoused establishing a child's privilege not to testify against his parent at all.

exclusion of testimony concerning the parents' nonconfidential words and deeds would not promote "sufficiently important interests" so as "to outweigh the need for probative evidence in the administration of criminal justice." Trammel v. United States, 445 U.S. 40, 50-51 (1980). In the circumstances of this case, the Commonwealth's interest in obtaining all relevant information concerning the disappearance of a young woman who may have been murdered must predominate over generalizations favoring the preservation of the American family through barring a child from testifying about nonconfidential matters involving his or her parent.

O'CONNOR, J. (dissenting, with whom HENNESSEY, C.J., and LYNCH, J., join).

The court has declined to create a testimonial privilege that would protect unemancipated minor children from being coerced by the State to appear and to testify, over the objection of the children and their parents, before a grand jury that is investigating the possible murder of a nonfamily member by the children's father. The court reaches this conclusion despite its acknowledgment that it is "of course, free to identify a privilege of a child not to testify against his or her parent."

Correctly recognizing that its task is to balance the public's interest in obtaining every person's testimony against public policy considerations in favor of erecting such a testimonial privilege, the court concludes that in the circumstances presented by this case a minor child has no privilege to refuse to appear before a grand jury or to refuse to testify as to what he or she may have seen or heard, except perhaps as to confidential communications between the child and the parents. The court reasons that erecting the privilege "would not promote 'sufficiently important interests' so as 'to outweigh the need for probative evidence in the administration of criminal justice.' Trammel v. United States, 445 U.S. 40, 50-51 (1980)." I respectfully, but firmly, disagree with the court's reasoning and with its conclusion. The violence done to the child, the damage to family unity, and the consequent injury to society that may result from the State's coercing an unemancipated minor to testify against a parent in the circumstances of this case are too high a price to pay for the enforcement of our criminal laws.

Although the court reasons that the privilege would not promote sufficiently important interests to warrant depriving the Commonwealth of evidence that might aid its investigation, the opinion fails to compare adequately the values that compete for protection by the court. Legitimate concerns about the impact of the court's determination on children, families, and society are summarily dismissed. Instead, the court relies on what it perceives to be the weight of authority against judicial creation of a parent-child testimonial privilege, and the lack of substantial precedent favoring such a privilege. . . . There is little helpful precedent. Such precedent as there is provides no justification for the court's failure to create a parent-child testimonial privilege in this case. A proper balancing of the values that are involved yields the conclusion that the privilege for which the plaintiffs contend should have been granted.

The court has ruled that a child must appear before a grand jury and may be required to testify in the circumstances of this case. The significance of the court's decision, however, would appear not to be limited to the circumstances of this case. The fair import of the decision is that, with the possible exception of confidential communications between parents and their children, and in the absence of concerns about self-incrimination, this Commonwealth does not recognize the right of a child to refuse to testify before a grand jury against his or her parent with respect to observations made inside or outside the home, having possible bearing on any kind of crime, violent or nonviolent, "white collar" or otherwise.

The State should not make unrealistic demands on its citizens, especially its children. A requirement that an unemancipated minor child, living with his or her parents, must incriminate one or both of them is an unrealistic demand, at least when a family member is not a victim of the crime under investigation. The demand is unrealistic because it is insensitive to the needs of children, and to the nature of the normal relationship between children and their parents, involving, as it does, love, trust, loyalty, and dependency. This court should recognize a public policy against imposing on the conscience of a child responsibility for incriminating his or her parent. Society's interest in its children should be recognized as sufficiently important to outweigh the need for probative evidence in the administration of criminal justice in the circumstances presented by this case.

Not only does society have an interest in children's being free from unreasonable public demands, but society also has an interest in fostering the unity of the family. "[T]he institution of the family is deeply rooted in this Nation's history and tradition." Moore v. East Cleveland, Ohio, 431 U.S. 494, 499, 503-504 (1977). The Massachusetts Legislature has declared that "the policy of the commonwealth [is] to direct its efforts . . . to the strengthening and encouragement of family life." G.L. c.119, §1, as amended by St. 1972, c.785, §5. The Legislature has granted one spouse the right not to testify against the other spouse in a criminal proceeding except in child abuse and nonsupport cases. G.L. c.233, §20. General Laws c.274, §4, exempts specified family members from criminal liability as accessories after the fact to the commission of a felony by other members of the same family. These statutes demonstrate a legislative awareness that there are basic human instincts to protect the members of one's family, even from the State, and that the State should respect those instincts, despite the possible adverse effect on law enforcement. These statutes also demonstrate a legislative judgment that in some circumstances the important interests of society in obtaining every person's evidence must give way to the recognition and protection of marital and family integrity. If society's interest in the enhancement of the marriage relationship justifies a spouse's privilege not to testify against a spouse in a criminal proceeding a corresponding interest in family integrity must justify, with at least equal force, an unemancipated minor's privilege not to testify in the circumstances presented by this case. Furthermore, if public policy dictates that family members should be protected from criminal liability for shielding other family members from apprehension for felonious conduct, all the more does public policy call for the grant to a child of a privilege not to testify against his or her parent in the circumstances of this case.

That the Legislature has not seen fit to grant such a privilege is not an adequate answer. It may be that the necessity for such legislation has not come to the Legislature's attention. Perhaps prosecutors have heretofore refrained from forcing the issue. In any event, this court has the power to create testimonial privileges in appropriate circumstances. For the reasons I have stated, and for the additional reason that the enforceability of a rule requiring a child to testify against his or her parent is very doubtful, I believe that the court's order was erroneous.

I comment briefly on the precedents cited by the court. Nearly all of the cases which have rejected claims of a parent-child privilege can be distinguished from this case. The courts that decided In re Terry W., 59 Cal. App. 3d 745 (1976), Cissna v. State, 170 Ind. App. 437 (1976), followed by Hunter v. State, 172 Ind. App. 397, cert. denied, 434 U.S. 906 (1977), and State v. Gilroy, 313 N.W.2d 513 (Iowa 1981), reasoned that only the Legislature, and not the court, was authorized to grant testimonial privileges. In this Commonwealth, however, there is no bar to the creation of a common law privilege in appropriate circumstances, so those cases give us no assistance whatsoever.

Cases in which the court has considered and rejected a general common law privilege of a child not to testify against his or her parent are significantly distinguishable on their facts from the present case. In Matter of a Grand Jury Subpoena Served Upon Kinoy, 326 F. Supp. 400 (S.D.N.Y. 1970), the family member about whom the grand jury sought information was not a target of the grand jury investigation, but was sought in connection with an investigation of another individual. Also the parent and child did not live together. That is unlike the present case in which the grand jury investigation has focused on the father, with whom the children live. In United States v. Jones, 683 F.2d 817, 819 (4th Cir. 1982), the court held that "[u]nder the circumstances, namely an emancipated, adult child's testimony which only arguably would be adverse to his father, limited to questions unrelated to his familial association with his parent, and involving no communication between father and son, we are satisfied that there simply is no privilege such as Jones has asserted. See In re Kinoy, 326 F. Supp. 400, 406 (S.D.N.Y. 1970)." In United States v. Penn, 647 F.2d 876 (9th Cir. 1980), a majority of the Court of Appeals, sitting en banc, reversed a Federal District Court order granting the defendant's motion to suppress a jar of heroin taken from the defendant's backyard. The Court of Appeals held that the conduct of the police in offering the defendant's five year old son $5 if he would show them the location of the heroin did not violate due process, and that the seizure of the heroin did not violate the Fourth Amendment to the Constitution of the United States. At the conclusion of its opinion, the court considered the defendant's claim of privilege. It stated simply: "There is no judicially or legislatively recognized general 'family' privilege . . . and we decline to create one here." Id. at 885. That case did not involve a child's compelled testimony against a parent. In In re Grand Jury Proceedings, 647 F.2d 511 (5th Cir. 1981), the opinion does not reveal whether the daughter, called as a witness, was a minor, was emancipated, or was living with her parents.

The court fails to cite a single case in which a court that has recognized its authority to grant testimonial privileges has undertaken a comparison of the competing values presented by a case such as this one, and concluded that the interest of the State in obtaining evidence is entitled to priority over the interests of children, families, and society that would be served by granting the privilege for which the plaintiffs contend. However, there is one recent case in which the court did balance the competing interests, and held that, as a matter of constitutional law, a child of any age may claim the parent-child privilege and refuse to appear and give any testimony whatsoever against his or her parent in any criminal proceeding. See In re Grand Jury Proceedings Witness: Agosto, 553 F. Supp. 1298 (D. Nev. 1983). The court reasoned that the government's interest in presenting all relevant evidence in criminal proceedings was outweighed by the individual's interest in the privacy of family communications and the family's interest in its integrity and inviolability. Maintaining the harmony and privacy of the family relationship, the court concluded, was just as compelling a goal as maintaining the harmony and privacy of the marriage relationship, which is protected by the husband-wife privilege. Id. at 1325. The court emphasized that placing a child in the position of being "scorned and branded as disloyal if he does testify and jailed if he does not" would undermine the unity of the family and would risk grave psychological harm to the child. Id. at 1326. I do not consider that opinion unpersuasive here, although it goes beyond the necessities of the case before us. I would have ruled in this case that unemancipated minor children, living with their parents, should not be compelled either to appear or to testify before a grand jury that is investigating the possible murder by their father of a nonfamily member.

CHAPTER VIII

Opinions, Scientific Proof, and Expert Testimony

Expert opinion poses special problems for courts because it deals with problems of factual inquiry that exceed the ordinary competence of the tribunal and therefore threaten its credibility and control. But as long as our system depends on lay juries and judges, the use of experts will require nonexperts to judge experts and define the boundaries of their expertise.

This chapter presents the range of issues that this problem raises. First, the specificity with which a lay witness must testify is examined. How far may lay witnesses go in presenting their observations in the form of conclusions? Next examined are the questions of what makes a subject appropriate for expert testimony and what makes a witness an expert in the subject. New fields of expertise such as polygraphy (lie detection), spectrography (voiceprint identification), and hypnotic memory enhancement pose serious conceptual and practical problems for courts and juries. Next, the problem of examining expert witnesses is addressed—how they may testify on direct and what weapons may be used against them on cross. Unlike other witnesses, experts are teachers; there is art in being a good teacher, and art in destroying one. The chapter ends with a discussion of court-appointed experts, a remarkably underutilized instrument of judicial administration considering the tremendous problems that adversarial experts pose for factfinders.

How well suited is our court system to the task of resolving disputes involving complex technical or scientific issues, given its present focus on adversarial presentation to lay jurors and judges? What reforms would you suggest to promote efficiency, fairness, and rationality in the resolution of such cases? What damages lurk in increased use of experts at trial?

A.   Lay Opinions

NOTE: THE CONVERGENCE OF FACT AND OPINION

Rule 701 of the Federal Rules of Evidence codifies the long-standing common law practice of favoring specific "factual" testimony by lay witnesses over testimony in the form of opinions and conclusions. Note that Rule 701 does not require a lay witness to limit himself to statements of fact, as opposed to statements of opinion or inference. The following excerpt from W. King and D. Pillinger, Opinion Evidence in Illinois 3-4 (1942), a book that was highly influential with the draftsmen, explains why.

When you look at the object on which you are sitting and say "chair" the sound "chair" is obviously not the object "chair." You can't sit on the noise "chair." The word is only your . . . response to the pressure of the object on your buttocks and the light beams from the object upon your optic nerves when you look down at it. The word "chair" isn't the fact "chair."

You can perceive a simple thing like a chair in many aspects. You can see it as a piece of furniture constituting with other pieces the furnishings in your room, or as an article of wood and upholstering designed to accommodate a person in a sitting position. A close examination might disclose to the expert that it was a Grand Rapids chair made since 1910. A microscopic examination would disclose the cellular character of the material from which it was made and possibly the locality where that wood was grown, the age of the trees from which it was cut, and (if you were sufficiently interested) the particular tools which have been used in cutting it and which have left their marks upon it. In a sense, however, the ultimate reality of this chair is far beyond your perceptions even with a microscope. Submicroscopically, you know from what science has told you that this chair consists of a mad dance of electrons which you cannot see just as you cannot see the blades of your electric fan when it is running. But which of these various perceptions of the chair is The Fact? Obviously any one of them is just as much (and just as little) a fact as the others. Each of us sees different "facts" in everything we look at. We are surrounded by a world of objective reality which we call facts. But as soon as we try to translate any part of that world into language it ceases to be facts and becomes thoughts.

So, when our judge instructs the witness to state the facts it is as though we demanded that the witness fly by flapping his arms. The witness can't state facts and neither can the judge — facts are unspeakable and unstatable. We can't reproduce in language either reality or our perception of reality. All statements in language are statements of opinion, i.e., statements of mental processes or perceptions. So-called "statements of fact" are only more specific statements of opinion. What the judge means to say, when he asks the witness to state the facts, is: The nature of this case requires you to be more specific, if you can, in your description of what you saw.

Just how specific a judge should require a witness to be will depend greatly on how central the matter about which the witness is testifying is to the resolution of the case:

> Ordinarily, in a law suit, you would be permitted to testify that this object was a chair. But if the suit were an action to collect a tax on chairs, if the kernel of the controversy was whether the object was a chair, your statement that this was a chair would be rejected as your opinion and you would be asked to "state the facts" regarding the object. In other words, the legal concept of what is a statement of fact and what is a statement of opinion varies with the issues in the case.

Id.

The rule, then, is meant to encourage witnesses to speak in a natural way at a level of specificity helpful to the factfinder. For example, witnesses anxious not to overstate their testimony often qualify what they are saying by adding, "I think" or "I believe." Does this indicate that their statements are impermissible opinions under Rule 701 or not based on first-hand knowledge as required by Rule 602? The question cannot be answered dogmatically. As the rule indicates, the judge must decide whether the witness is speaking from personal knowledge, and whether the testimony, as qualified, will be helpful. As Dean Ladd states:

> Closely associated with expression of facts in terms of inference is the statement of facts as the impression of the witness. Illustrative of these expressions are, "I think," "I believe," "my impression is," "I cannot be positive, but I think," "to the best of my recollection," or "it is my understanding." The admissibility of testimony accompanied by such limitations involves the same fundamental issue to be considered when permitting the witness to testify in terms of inference, namely, is the witness speaking from his personal knowledge or is his testimony only a mental speculation. Not infrequently such precautionary statements may strengthen the testimony because they indicate that the witness does not want to overstate the facts. On the other hand, such statements may indicate that his recollection is poor which would weaken the testimony but not exclude it. Only when it appears that the witness has not personally perceived the matter about which he testifies will the testimony be excluded.

Ladd, Expert and Other Opinion Testimony, 40 Minn. L. Rev. 437, 440 (1956). See 3 Weinstein and Berger, Weinstein's Evidence 701-15 to 701-18 at ¶710[02] (1981).

The following case demonstrates one judge's disgust with the majority's willingness to unquestioningly accept the opinion of a lay witness.

COMMONWEALTH v. HOLDEN
390 Pa. 221, 134 A.2d 868 (1957)

MUSMANNO, Justice (dissenting).

The Majority Opinion fails to discuss a very important matter raised by the defendant Charles Holden in his appeal to this Court for a new trial.

On December 31, 1955, between 5:15 and 6:40 A.M., Cora Smith was killed in her home as the result of being struck over the head. The defendant, Charles Holden, was accused, tried, and convicted of her murder. He maintained in his defense that he was innocent since he was not in the victim's home at the time of the brutal attack.

At the time of Holden's arrest, he was taken by the police to the home of a Ralph Jones who had been with Holden for several hours prior to the killing. In Holden's presence, Jones was questioned by the police. The matter of this questioning became a subject for inquiry at the later trial. The assistant district attorney representing the Commonwealth asked Jones if, at the time he was being quizzed by the police in Holden's presence, Holden did anything that was unusual. Jones replied:

> "Well, during the period of time that the detectives were questioning me in his presence, I believe one of them noticed him to sort of wink or something."

The assistant district attorney then asked Jones what Holden meant, and Jones replied:

> "I didn't rightfully know whether it was a wink or something that was in his eye."

The prosecuting attorney's question was a flagrant violation of the rules of evidence and should not have been permitted. What Jones may have thought that Holden meant by the wink, if it was a wink, was entirely speculative. The prosecuting attorney might just as well have asked: "What was Holden thinking of at the time?" In fact, the question imported that very type of query because obviously the eye, no matter how eloquent it is supposed to be in the minds of poets, novelists, and dreamers, is still not capable, by a blink, to telegraph complicated messages, unless, of course, the blinker and the blinkee have previously agreed upon a code.

When Jones replied that he did not know whether Holden had actually winked or had been troubled by a foreign substance in his eye, the Commonwealth's attorney asked him about a statement he had made to the police some time following the winking incident. On January 11th, a few days after the blinking affair, Captain Flynn of the City Detective Bureau asked Jones: "What did you take this wink to be?" and Jones replied:

> "I think he was trying to get me to make an alibi for him to cover up some of his actions and I don't know nothing about any of his actions."

Commonwealth's counsel sought to introduce this statement at the trial and defense counsel properly objected, explaining:

> "We object to that. Whatever it was, it wasn't made in the presence of the defendant, Charles Holden."

The objection was overruled and the jury was thus informed that the defendant endeavored to have Jones frame an alibi for him. On what evidence was this information based? On a wink.

And what did the wink say? I repeat:

> "I think he was trying to get me to make an alibi for him to cover up some of his actions and I don't know nothing about any of his actions."

It will be noted that the stupendous and compendious wink not only solicited the fabrication of a spurious alibi but specified that it was "to cover up some of his actions." One movement of the eyelid conveyed a message of 21 words. Not even the most abbreviated Morse code could say so much with such little expenditure of muscular and mechanical power.

Although the statement of the interpretation of the wink is preposterous on its face, I can see how it could be made to seem very informative and convincing to the jury, since it was given to the jury with the Court's approval. If Holden had actually spoken to Jones the words which Jones related in his interpretation of the wink, no more effective admission of guilty knowledge could be imagined. Jones and Holden had been together prior to the killing. Holden tells Jones to make up an alibi so that Jones can extend their companionship of the evening to an hour including and beyond the time of the killing. And then Jones not only refuses to do what Holden asks him to do, but relates the criminal attempt on the part of Holden to suborn perjury.

But the fact of the matter is that Holden did not ask Jones to fabricate an alibi. He did not ask him to "cover up some of his actions." All that Holden did was to wink. No one knows whether he was trying to convey a message, whether he was attempting to shut out a strong ray of light, or whether a bit of dust troubled him at the moment. The Court, however, allowed the jury to believe that the wink was a semaphoric signal to Jones to commit perjury.

Was ever more ridiculous evidence presented in a murder trial? What is to happen to our rules of evidence in criminal trials if they can be breached so glaringly, without reproof or criticism by this Court?

Holden was convicted and sentenced to life imprisonment. He might have been sentenced to death. On a wink.

And the Majority does not consider the matter of sufficient importance even to mention it.

If a witness is to be allowed to state what he believes a wink said, why should he not be allowed to interpret a cough? Or a sneeze? Or a grunt? Or a hiccough? Why should he indeed not be empowered to testify as to what is passing through an accused's brain? Why not permit mind readers to read a defendant's mind, and thus eliminate the jury system completely because who knows better than the defendant himself whether or not he committed the crime of which he stands accused?

The refusal of this Court to grant a new trial, with so momentous a violation of the defendant's rights, duly noted and excepted to on the record, would suggest that here the law has not only winked but closed both eyes.

Problem: Mrs. Jones's Baby

W testifies, "I saw Mrs. Jones about three hundred yards away walking with her baby in her arms." Opposing counsel objects on the grounds of opinion testimony. What ruling and why? Would the ruling be any different if *W* were unavailable at trial and her statement were offered through another witness under an applicable exception to the hearsay rule, such as Rule 804(b)(1) (former testimony)?

Problem: Presidential Debate

Suppose that you were asked to watch and then testify about a presidential debate. What could you say about how each candidate looked and sounded without violating Rule 701?

Problem: Murder at the Hotel Thoreau

Action by *P*, executor of *M*'s estate, against *D* Insurance Company, to recover on *M*'s life insurance policy. At trial evidence is introduced to show that *M* was behind in his premium payments and the policy was due to lapse at midnight, May 31. *M*'s body was found in shallow waters of the Concord River the morning of June 1. The crucial issue at trial is the time of *M*'s death.

(1) *P* calls *W*, the night clerk at the Hotel Thoreau, an inn near the Concord River. *W* testifies that *M* checked in on May 31 at 10 P.M., went to his room, and reappeared in the lobby at 11 P.M. The following dialogue then ensues:

Q: Did you observe *M*'s expression?
A: Yes.
Q: What was it?
A: An expression of ineffable sadness.
By defense counsel: Objection. Move to strike. The witness is giving an opinion.
Court: Denied.
Q: Did you observe *M*'s conduct at that time?
A: Yes.
Q: What was it?
A: *M* acted disoriented.
By defense counsel: Objection. Move to strike. The witness is giving an opinion.
Court: Sustained.
Q: What did *M* do?
A: He paced up and down the room, twirled the revolving door, went out, and walked up and down the sidewalk several times, bumping into two or three people when they came by.

How can you reconcile the two rulings by the court?

(2) *Y* is called by *D* and testifies to discovering *M*'s body at 7 A.M. on June 1. The following dialogue then ensues:

Q: Please describe the appearance of the body when you found it.
A: The stomach was bloated, the skin blue, there was blood coming from the nose and froth coming from the mouth. The whole body was stiff as a board.
Q: How long would you say the person had been dead?
A: About eight hours.
By plaintiff's counsel: Objection. Move to strike. The witness is giving an opinion.

What ruling and why?

What is the boundary between the kinds of opinion that may be admitted as lay opinions under Rule 701 and those that are "expert opinions" subject to Rule 702?

UNITED STATES OF AMERICA v. FIGUEROA-LOPEZ
125 F.3d 1241 (9th Cir. 1997)

TROTT, Circuit Judge:

OVERVIEW

Raul Figueroa-Lopez ("Lopez") appeals his jury conviction and sentence for possession of cocaine with intent to distribute, in violation of 21 U.S.C. §841(a)(1). Lopez contends that the district court erred by: 1) admitting damaging opinion testimony from law-enforcement officers, who the Government did not qualify as experts, that Lopez's behavior was consistent with that of an experienced drug trafficker;

BACKGROUND

I. THE UNDERLYING OFFENSE

At the end of May 1994, federal agents arrested Darryl Storm. Storm and others were charged with conspiracy to distribute cocaine and marijuana, and with money laundering.

Storm agreed to cooperate with the government and provided agents with a list of names of narcotics traffickers known to him. This list included Lopez, although at that time Storm only knew him as "Raul." At the instruction of DEA Agent Sam Larsen, Storm contacted Lopez to explore whether Lopez would sell him some narcotics. Storm met with Lopez on February 1, 1995. Agents attempted to record this meeting, but the audiotape malfunctioned. According to Storm, Storm told Lopez that he wanted to buy 5-10 kilograms of cocaine.

On March 24, 1995, Storm taped a telephone conversation with Lopez, during which Lopez offered to sell Storm ten kilograms of cocaine for $170,000. Lopez and Storm used oblique terminology borrowed from the construction industry to refer to the type, quantity, and price of the drugs.

On March 27, 1995, Storm again met with Lopez. This meeting was not recorded because the recording device malfunctioned again. Lopez gave Storm a sample of cocaine.

During the next month, Storm and Lopez spoke by telephone several times about the impending cocaine deal. These conversations were recorded. On May 25, 1995, Storm called Lopez and arranged to meet later that day to complete the cocaine transaction. Before meeting with Storm, Lopez drove in circles around the parking lot in a Monte Carlo. Storm and Lopez then met in the parking lot. Lopez drove away from Storm and parked next to a silver Nissan Sentra. Lopez entered the Nissan, bent down for several minutes, and then returned to the Monte Carlo.

Lopez returned to Storm's location and showed Storm a kilogram package of cocaine. Storm gave the arrest signal, and agents arrested Lopez. In the Monte Carlo, the agents found the keys to the Nissan and one kilogram of cocaine on the floor below the front seat. In the Nissan, the agents found nine kilograms of cocaine concealed in the car's door panels.

II. THE TRIAL

A. OPINION TESTIMONY

Throughout the trial, the Government presented opinion testimony by law-enforcement witnesses as to how Lopez's conduct, as observed by the agents, conformed to the methods and techniques of experienced drug dealers. Lopez objected to this testimony, claiming that it was "improper opinion testimony," hearsay, lacking foundation, and speculative. He also argued that it was improper expert testimony because the Government had not given prior notice as required by Federal Rule of Criminal Procedure 16(a)(1)(E). The district court overruled all of Lopez's objections and admitted the testimony as *lay* opinion testimony, presumably pursuant to Federal Rule of Evidence 701. The court ruled that the testimony regarding the way Lopez was driving—from which the agent inferred that Lopez was behaving as an "experienced narcotics trafficker"—was admissible notwithstanding Lopez's objections because the officer was a "percipient witness."

The court also overruled without explanation Lopez's objections to Agent Larsen's testimony that: 1) Lopez's actions were "countersurveillance" and "a common practice for narcotics dealers"; and 2) the use of a rental car was "indicative of an experienced narcotics trafficker." In response to Lopez's objection to an agent's opinion as to the street value of the cocaine found in the Nissan, the district court stated that "the Court has repeated over and over that the witness is giving testimony relating to matters in which he has participated and which he personally observed, and his testimony may incorporate his knowledge and his observations, so on that basis, it will be admitted." Agents repeatedly referred to Lopez's actions as consistent with an "experienced narcotics trafficker." The prosecution relied on this testimony in its closing arguments.

B. LOPEZ'S TESTIMONY

Lopez testified at trial that, before his arrest on May 25, 1995, he worked as a forklift operator for $10 per hour. He had never been arrested or convicted of any offense. He was 26 years old. In late 1993 or early 1994, Lopez was introduced to an "auto salesman," Tony Sagoo, who took Lopez to an auto auction. Later that day, Lopez gave Sagoo $5,000 to purchase a minivan they had seen. Lopez borrowed much of this money from family members.

Sagoo was unable to purchase the minivan, but he failed to return the $5,000 over the next several months. Sagoo introduced Lopez to Storm and told Lopez that Storm would repay the debt. Lopez was "shocked" by Storm's suggestion that they engage in a narcotics transaction as a way to repay the debt. Initially, Lopez refused Storm's suggestions. Eventually, however, Lopez felt pressured and realized that the only way he would get his $5,000 was to complete the drug deal. He therefore agreed to sell cocaine to Storm.

According to Lopez, when Storm asked Lopez for a sample of cocaine, Lopez contacted a friend named "Manny," whom he had met five to six years before in a bar. Lopez got the cocaine from Manny and gave Storm a sample.

Storm continued to pressure Lopez to conduct the transaction, and Lopez acted as a middleman between Storm and Manny. According to Lopez, Manny arranged all the details of the transaction, including the meeting place, the use of two cars, the secret panels, and the price of the ten kilograms. . . .

The district court overruled Lopez's hearsay and relevance objections to the out-of-court statements of Sagoo and his mother. Lopez requested and submitted a limiting instruction to advise the jury that all of this testimony was not admissible for the truth of the matters asserted. The district court refused to give this or any other limiting instruction.

DISCUSSION

I.   THE LAW-ENFORCEMENT OPINION TESTIMONY

A.   *The Error*

Lopez contends that the district court abused its discretion by admitting without a proper foundation opinion testimony of law-enforcement officers that Lopez's actions were consistent with those of an experienced drug trafficker. Specifically, Lopez contends that the testimony improperly "profiled" him as a drug trafficker and was not the proper subject of lay opinion testimony.

As detailed above, at numerous points throughout Lopez's trial, law-enforcement officers testified:

- that Lopez was engaging in countersurveillance driving;
- that certain terms used by Lopez and informant Storm were code words for a drug deal, a common practice of narcotics dealers;
- that Lopez's use of a rental car was consistent with the practices of an experienced drug trafficker;
- that the manner of hiding the cocaine was consistent with the practices of experienced drug traffickers; and

- that the large quantity and high purity of the cocaine indicated that Lopez was close to the source of the cocaine.

Lopez vigorously objected throughout this testimony.

A district court's evidentiary rulings during trial are reviewed for an abuse of discretion. United States v. Sarno, 73 F.3d 1470, 1488 (9th Cir. 1995), cert. denied, 135 L. Ed. 2d 1073, 116 S. Ct. 2555 (1996).

If "specialized knowledge will assist the trier of fact to understand the evidence or to determine a fact in issue," a qualified expert witness may provide opinion testimony on the issue in question. Fed. R. Evid. 702. The rule recognizes that an intelligent evaluation of the facts by a trier of fact is "often difficult or impossible without the application of some . . . specialized knowledge." Fed. R. Evid. 702 (advisory comm. n.). In this light, we have held that "drug enforcement *experts* may testify that a defendant's activities were consistent with a common criminal modus operandi." United States v. Webb, 115 F.3d 711, 713-14 (9th Cir. 1997) (emphasis added) (citing cases). This testimony "helps the jury to understand complex criminal activities, and alerts it to the possibility that combinations of seemingly innocuous events may indicate criminal behavior." United States v. Johnson, 735 F.2d 1200, 1202 (9th Cir. 1994). "Further, we even allow modus operandi expert testimony in cases that are not complex." *Webb,* 115 F.3d at 714 (internal quotation and citation omitted).

The testimony in the instant case is similar to *expert* testimony properly admitted in other drug cases. See, e.g., United States v. Cordoba, 104 F.3d 225, 229-30, amended, 1997 WL 54578 (9th Cir. 1997) (allowing expert testimony that a sophisticated drug dealer would not entrust large quantities of cocaine to an unknowing dupe); United States v. Espinosa, 827 F.2d 604, 611-12 (9th Cir. 1987) (allowing expert testimony regarding the use of apartments as "stash pads" for drugs and money); United States v. Patterson, 819 F.2d 1495, 1507 (9th Cir. 1987) (allowing expert testimony on how criminal narcotics conspiracies operate); United States v. Maher, 645 F.2d 780, 783 (9th Cir. 1981) (per curiam) (permitting expert testimony that defendant's actions were consistent with the modus operandi of persons transporting drugs and engaging in countersurveillance).

In the above cases, the testimony was necessary to inform the jury of the techniques employed by drug dealers in their illegal trade, techniques with which an ordinary juror would most probably be unfamiliar. Thus, the testimony in the instant case could have been admitted as *expert opinion* testimony to inform the jury about the methods and techniques used by experienced drug dealers, *if* the law-enforcement agents had been called as experts and properly qualified as such pursuant to Rule 104 of the Federal Rules of Evidence. In fact, Special Agent Larsen began his testimony with a recitation of his extensive training and experience with the DEA. It appears virtually certain that had the Government opted to do so, Larsen could have been formally qualified as an expert witness on the dispositive issue of whether Lopez's behavior suggested that he was an "experienced"—as contrasted with a fledgling—drug trafficker. However, this routine process did not occur. The testimony was neither offered nor admitted as *expert* testimony, but rather as *lay opinion* testimony. The Government concedes that it made no effort properly to qualify the witnesses as having the knowledge, experience, training, or education to render their testimony admissible under Rule 702.

The Government contends that "the same analysis applies whether the witness is testifying as an expert or as a lay witness." In support of its argument, the Government relies primarily on two cases, United States v. Fleishman, 684 F.2d 1329, 1335-36 (9th Cir. 1982), and United States v. VonWillie, 59 F.3d 922, 929 (9th Cir. 1995). The Government's reliance is misplaced.

In *Fleishman*, a DEA agent testified as a lay witness that the defendant was acting as a "lookout." *Fleishman*, 684 F.2d at 1335. A thorough foundation was laid that the agent had extensive training and experience in recognizing whether a person was performing countersurveillance. Id. On appeal, the Government argued that the agent's testimony was permissible lay witness testimony under Federal Rule of Evidence 701. The court never directly addressed this argument, stating rather that "whether lay or expert," the testimony was admissible. Id. at 1335.

In *VonWillie*, an agent testified "as a lay witness about the nexus between drug trafficking and the possession of weapons." *VonWillie*, 59 F.3d at 929. Specifically, he testified that in his experience with the Drug Enforcement Bureau, (1) it was common for drug traffickers to possess and use weapons in order to protect their drugs and to intimidate buyers; (2) the MK-11, one of the guns found in VonWillie's bedroom, was a particularly intimidating gun and he knew of drug dealers who used that specific weapon; and (3) drug traffickers commonly kept a weapon near their drugs. Id. The court concluded that "these observations are common enough and require such a limited amount of expertise, if any, that they can, indeed, be deemed lay witness opinion." Id.

Fleishman and *VonWillie* remain good law, but both are distinguishable from the instant case. First, Lopez's case involved several agents testifying that Lopez's actions "were consistent with those of an experienced narcotics trafficker." In fact, Agent Larsen alone testified more than *seven* times to this effect as to various aspects of Lopez's activity. In *Fleishman* and *VonWillie*, only one agent gave an opinion on very limited issues.

Second, the agents' observations in the instant case are not "common enough" to "require such a limited amount of expertise." *VonWillie*, 59

F.3d at 929. Here, the agents testified that the following behaviors were consistent with an *experienced* drug trafficker: 1) countersurveillance driving; 2) use of code words to refer to drug quantities and prices; 3) use of a third-person lookout when attending a narcotics meeting; 4) use of a rental car to make the drug delivery; 5) hiding the cocaine in the door panels of a car; and 6) dealing in large amounts of very pure cocaine. These "observations" require demonstrable expertise; in fact, several times, the Government instructed the witness to answer questions "based upon your training and experience." Additionally, one agent testified that his familiarity with the fact that narcotics traffickers sometimes speak in code is based upon the training that he had at the DEA Academy.

However, part of the testimony in this case does provide us with a clear example of when a witness may give his lay opinion as to the implications of his observations. INS Special Agent Rapp testified that the movements of the Monte Carlo were "suspicious." Under *Von Willie* and *Fleishman,* such testimony related to matters "common enough" to qualify as lay opinion testimony.

The Government's argument simply blurs the distinction between Federal Rules of Evidence 701 and 702. Lay witness testimony is governed by Rule 701, which limits opinions to those "rationally based on the perception of the witness." Rule 702, on the other hand, governs admission of *expert* opinion testimony concerning *"specialized* knowledge." The testimony in this case is precisely the type of "specialized knowledge" governed by Rule 702. A holding to the contrary would encourage the Government to offer all kinds of specialized opinions without pausing first properly to establish the required qualifications of their witnesses. The mere percipience of a witness to the facts on which he wishes to tender an opinion does not trump Rule 702. Otherwise, a layperson witnessing the removal of a bullet from a heart during an autopsy could opine as to the cause of the decedent's death. Surely a civilian bystander, or for that matter a raw DEA recruit would not be allowed to interpret for the jury Lopez's behavior in the parking lot on May 25, 1995 as that of an "experienced" trafficker merely because that person was an eyewitness to the same.

In addition, the Government's argument subverts the requirements of Federal Rule of Criminal Procedure 16(a)(1)(E). Rule 16 requires the Government to "disclose to the defendant a written summary of [expert] testimony the government intends to use . . . during its case in chief." The Rule "is intended to minimize surprise that often results from unexpected testimony, reduce the need for continuances, and to provide the opponent with a fair opportunity to test the merit of the expert's testimony through focused cross-examination." Fed. R. Evid. 16(a)(1)(E) (advisory committee's note).

In sum, rather than testimony "based on the perceptions of the witness"—as the district court described it when overruling Lopez's objections—the bulk of the above opinion testimony is properly characterized as testimony based on the perceptions, education, training, and experience of the witness. It requires precisely the type of "specialized knowledge" of law enforcement governed by Rule 702. Trial courts must ensure that experts are qualified to render their opinions and that the opinions will assist the trier of fact. This careful analysis was absent in this case. See also *Webb*, 115 F.3d at 714 (recognizing that "the expert was particularly qualified" to give his opinion). As judges who have heard such testimony many times, we must not forget that *our* familiarity with it does not bring it within Rule 701, especially given the purpose of Rule 16(a)(1)(E). . . .

Rule 701 was amended effective December 1, 2000, to limit admissibility under Rule 701 to opinions or inferences "not based on scientific, technical, or other specialized knowledge within the scope of Rule 702." How specialized is "specialized"? It may require a large number of decisions to give reasonable definition to the boundary between Rules 701 and 702.

B. Law Opinions

MARX & CO., INC. v. DINERS CLUB, INC.
550 F.2d 505 (2d Cir. 1977)

GURFEIN, J.D. This appeal by the Diners' Club, Inc. and Diners/Fugazy Travel, Inc. (collectively "Diners") arises out of a series of transactions whereby the Fugazys sold the assets of their company, Fugazy Travel Bureau, Inc. ("Fugazy Travel") to Diners Club in return for unregistered stock in the latter company. The Fugazys, plaintiffs below, allege that the defendants fraudulently induced the sale, in violation of §10(b) of the Securities Exchange Act of 1934 and Rule 10b-5 thereunder, by representing that defendant Continental Corporation was about to "take over" Diners and that the failure of Diners to use its best efforts to make effective a registration of plaintiffs' shares was part of a manipulative device to induce the plaintiffs not to offer their shares for sale from October 10, 1967 to February 6, 1970. The court ultimately submitted to the jury whether Diners breached *its contractual obligation* to use its best efforts to register the plaintiffs' stock. . . .

The jury found against Diners on these contentions. We agree with Judge Ward that there was sufficient evidence to support the verdict. -

. . . The crucial issue, sufficiently posed by objection below, is whether, notwithstanding the general discretion allowed to trial judges respecting expert testimony, the admission of the testimony of a securities law expert, Stanley Friedman, was, in the circumstances, an error of law and highly prejudicial. His testimony construed the contract, as a matter of law, and includes his opinion that the defenses of Diners were unacceptable as a matter of law. . . .

We hold that the District Court erred in permitting Friedman, an expert witness called by plaintiffs, to give his opinion as to the legal obligations of the parties under the contract. . . . Friedman was qualified as an expert in securities regulation, and therefore was competent to explain to the jury the step-by-step practices ordinarily followed by lawyers and corporations in shepherding a registration statement through the SEC. Indeed, Friedman had done so as an expert witness on previous occasions. . . .

In the case at bar, however, witness Friedman's objectionable testimony did *not* concern only the customary practices of a trade or business. Rather, he gave his opinion as to the legal standards which he believed to be derived from the contract and which should have governed Diners' conduct. He testified not so much as to common practice as to what was necessary "to fulfill the covenant" [of the contract]. For example, over the objection of defense counsel, he said that:

> I construe "best efforts" in the context of a covenant to register shares as the assumption on the part of the person who gives the covenant *an absolute, unconditional responsibility,* to set to work promptly and diligently to do everything that would have to be done to make the registration statement effective . . . (emphasis added).

Counsel made timely objection — "that's a legal conclusion." Similarly, the witness opined that "the best efforts obligations requires you to pursue the registration statement unless there is cause beyond your control." This testimony did not concern practices in the securities business, on which Friedman was qualified as an expert, but were rather legal opinions as to the meaning of the contract terms at issue. It was testimony concerning matters outside his area of expertise. See Federal Rule of Evidence 702. Moreover, it would not have been possible to render this testimony admissible by qualifying Friedman as an "expert in contract law." It is not for witnesses to instruct the jury as to applicable principles of law, but for the judge. As Professor Wigmore has observed, expert testimony on law is excluded because "the tribunal does not need the witness' judgment. . . . [T]he *judge* (or the jury as instructed by the judge) can determine equally well. . . ." The special legal knowledge of the judge makes the witness' testimony superfluous. VII Wigmore on Evidence §1952, at 81. . . .

Not only did Friedman construe the contract, but he also repeatedly gave his conclusions as to the legal significance of various facts adduced at trial. He testified on direct examination that, pursuant to its contractual obligation, Diners Club "should have" filed its registration on or about June 20, 1969, and not at the end of August, and therefore concluded that Diners Club did *not* use its best efforts promptly to file. He asserted that it would not be a *legal* excuse (1) that Diners' employees may have been occupied in other activities, or (2) that the parties to the contract were simultaneously attempting to renegotiate the contract, — "Therefore, I don't see that it excuses performance" . . . or (3) that plaintiffs had failed to advance one-half of the costs of the registration. He also gave it as his legal opinion that the fact that the parties were exploring alternatives was not a *legal* waiver by the plaintiffs of the requirement that Diners go forward.

Friedman was also permitted to testify, over objection, that correspondence between the litigants relating to the payment of one-half the cost of registration by the plaintiffs, including a letter to plaintiff Marx dated July 15, was irrelevant "because the registration statement would have been filed by approximately June 20th and therefore this question comes up very much after the fact." His conclusion that Diners Club had no *legal* excuses for nonperformance was based merely on his examination of documents and correspondence, which were equally before the judge and jury. Thus Friedman's opinion testimony was superfluous. See VII Wigmore on Evidence, §1918. As Professor McCormick notes, such testimony "amounts to no more than an expression of the [witness'] general belief as to how the case should be decided." McCormick on Evidence, §12 at 26-27. The admission of such testimony would give the appearance that the court was shifting to witnesses the responsibility to decide the case. McCormick on Evidence §12, at 27. It is for the jury to evaluate the facts in the light of the applicable rules of law, and it is therefore erroneous for a witness to state his opinion on the law of the forum. Loeb v. Hammond, [407 F.2d 779 (1969).] . . . The applicable law, not being foreign law, could, in no sense, be a question of fact to be decided by the jury.

The limits of expert testimony in securities cases should not be too difficult to draw. While the able trial judge below recognized that "testimony in the form of an opinion or inference otherwise admissible is not objectionable because it embraces an ultimate issue to be decided by the trier of fact," Fed. R. Ev. 704, he failed, in our view, sufficiently to emphasize "otherwise admissible." With the growth of intricate securities litigation over the past forty years, we must be especially careful not to allow trials before juries to become battles of paid advocates posing as experts on the respective sides concerning matters of domestic law.

The basis of expert capacity, according to Wigmore (§555), may "be summed up in the term 'experience.'" But experience is hardly a qualification for construing a document for its legal effect when there is a knowledgeable gentleman in a robe whose exclusive province it is to instruct the jury on the law. The danger is that the jury may think that the "expert" in the particular branch of the law knows more than the judge—surely an inadmissible inference in our system of law.

Recognizing that an expert may testify to an ultimate fact, and to the practices and usage of a trade, we think care must be taken lest, in the field of securities law, he be allowed to usurp the function of the judge. In our view, the practice of using experts in securities cases must not be permitted to expand to such a point, and hence we must reluctantly conclude that the leeway allowed Friedman was highly prejudicial to the appellant.

If jurors are regarded as capable of determining conflicts in expert testimony in all other recognized areas of knowledge—e.g., medicine, statistics, literature, physics—why should law be different? The *Marx* court says: "The danger is that the jury may think that the 'expert' in the particular branch of the law knows more than the judge—surely an inadmissible inference in our system of law." Why is the inference inadmissible? Whom is the court kidding?

Problem: Wolfman's Law

Consider the facts of the following case, drawn from Sharp v. Coopers & Lybrand, 457 F. Supp. 879 (E.D. Pa. 1978):

> Plaintiffs, investors in an oil drilling venture, alleged in this class action that the defendant, a major accounting firm, is liable to them for misstatements in several opinion letters which advised them as to the supposed tax consequences of those investments. . . .
>
> We certified a class consisting of all persons who purchased these securities after July 22, 1971, 70 F.R.D. 544 (E.D. Pa. 1976). There ensued an apparent novelty in our jurisprudence: a jury trial of issues common to the class under the Rule 10b-5, §20(a) and pendent claims. These issues included foreseeability of damages, the exercise of reasonable care, whether there were misrepresentations and omissions and, if so, their materiality and scienter, and whether the defendant controlled an employee for §20(a) purposes and adequately supervised him. . . .
>
> Plaintiffs are persons who purchased limited partnership interests in oil wells to be drilled in Kansas and Ohio, of which Westland Minerals Corporation (WMC) was general partner and promoter. As a result of criminal fraud by WMC, many of these wells were never drilled and much of the invested money was diverted to WMC's own use. Economic Concepts, Inc. (ECI), the selling agent

for these limited partnerships, and WMC sought to engage in April 1971 the services of defendant in rendering opinions as to the federal income tax consequences of these limited partnerships. In July the defendant [agreed to draft the opinion letters. An] opinion letter signed by a Coopers & Lybrand partner in its name [stated] that "based solely on the facts contained [in the Limited Partnership Agreement] and without verification by us" a limited partner who contributed $65,000 in cash could deduct approximately $128,000 on his 1971 tax return. . . . The letter was written specifically for the use of one Muhammed Ali, a potential WMC investor, with regard to reducing the amount of taxes that would be withheld from a fight purse. . . .

The jury found that the . . . letter contained both material misrepresentations and material omissions, and that Higgins [a tax supervisor employed by Coopers & Lybrand who worked "directly under the supervision of four partners of defendant"] acted either recklessly or with intent to defraud in preparing the letters. Much of the evidence concerning those misrepresentations and omissions and their recklessness came from plaintiffs' expert witness, Professor Bernard Wolfman of the Harvard Law School, a specialist in federal income taxation. Most of his testimony was not rebutted by the defendant. Professor Wolfman explained the principles behind this tax shelter: a taxpayer who in 1971 contributed $25,000 to a partnership involved in a bona fide oil drilling venture, which then obtained for each $25,000 contribution an additional $25,000 bona fide bank loan that was fully secured by partnership property (the as yet undrilled wells) and then expended all of that $50,000 for drilling, could under the law applicable in 1971 deduct the full $50,000 from his taxable income. The effect would be to accelerate the tax deduction available to the investor in 1971. Professor Wolfman's expert testimony in concert with other evidence provided the basis for the jury's findings that the . . . letter misrepresented or omitted to state material facts in at least three ways. . . .

Professor Wolfman testified that writing such a letter was reckless on its face in that it omitted to state that the non-recourse loan which the letter assumed lending institutions would make to WMC, the value of which loan would be deductible by the taxpayer according to the opinion letter, would have to be secured by collateral (i.e., the oil wells) whose value was equal to or greater than the amount of that loan. Non-recourse loans of the type contemplated by the opinion letter (i.e., with no personal liability to the limited partners) are very rarely entered into by banks for oil drilling ventures, according to Professor Wolfman, because it is hard to secure them fully by undrilled wells, whose value is not known. Unless the value of the property used by the partnership to secure the loan were equal to the amount of the loan, Professor Wolfman explained, the amount of the loan would not be deductible to the limited partner under §752(c) of the Internal Revenue Code. To assume this unlikely fact that the loans would be thus secured without stating the assumption was itself reckless, he said.

(1) Should Professor Wolfman have been allowed to testify as he did?

(2) Suppose the case were criminal. Should the prosecutor be allowed to call Professor Wolfman to explain to the jury why what the defendant did was criminal? (That sort of "explanation" is called "teaching" in Professor Wolfman's regular line of work.)

(3) Would it make more sense for Professor Wolfman to be called as a court-appointed expert under Rule 706?

(4) If Wolfman is allowed to testify, what sort of evidence should the defendant be allowed to introduce to counter it? Who resolves any conflicts between Wolfman's testimony and the rebuttal evidence?

(5) Would it be better for judges simply to instruct jurors on the law after considering the arguments of counsel on proposed instructions?

C.   Expert Testimony, Scientific Proof, and Junk Science

Many of the issues arising in present-day civil and criminal cases concern matters clearly outside the common experience of virtually all of the trial participants. Very few judges, jurors, or, for that matter, attorneys, are conversant with such matters as comminuted compression fractures of the L-2 vertebra, reduction of the I-Plane in microwave transmission by horn reflector antennas, an in vitro radioimmunoassay for allergen-specific IgE, or the relationship between Bendectin and birth defects. How can the judge and jury decide factual issues involving subject matters of which they have no background, knowledge, or experience?

One solution to this dilemma is to equip the tribunal with sufficient expertise so that the deciders will be able to understand and adjudicate the esoteric scientific or technical issues with which they are faced. The adjudication of many legal conflicts involving technical issues has been confided to administrative agencies such as Public Utilities Commissions, the Securities and Exchange Commission, the Patent Office, Workers Compensation Commissions, all of which have members possessing specialized expertise in specific areas.

In other countries the use of specialized courts for special matters may be more widespread. For instance in Germany, there are specialized courts to hear labor, administrative, social welfare, tax and patent claims.

However, many if not most "ordinary" cases these days involve specialized issues beyond the ken of judge or jury. Even the most routine of personal injury case is likely to involve issues of medical causation or impairment that are not within the experience of most lay people. It is scarcely feasible to provide specialized adjudicators for every kind of issue that may be unfamiliar to the ordinary judge or jury.

The traditional "solution" to the problem of deciding issues outside the knowledge and experience of the trial participants is to permit the parties to call "expert witnesses" with knowledge and experience pertinent to the issues at hand. The role of the expert is to educate the jury on the expert's area of expertise and to express opinions on how the esoteric issues should be resolved. The jury's job is to make use of the information provided by the expert (including the opinions proffered) to resolve the issues in the case. In many cases, the jury will have to select between differing opinions offered by opposing experts or to decide how far they will go along with an expert's controversial view. Whether lay jurors are qualified to make these choices reputably is an issue about which there is considerable debate.

Rule 702 of the Federal Rules of Evidence authorizes "a witness qualified as an expert by knowledge, skill, experience, training or education" to "assist the trier of fact to understand the evidence or to determine a fact in issue" "in the form of an opinion or otherwise." This formulation leaves three questions open:

(1) Is the nature of the issue one on which scientific, technical, etc. expertise will be helpful? Is the issue really one outside the ken of the jury?

(2) Is the scientific, technical, etc. knowledge or expertise of a quality that will be of assistance to the jury? Bogus pseudoscience will not be of any help.

(3) Is the person who is appearing sufficiently versed in this science or technical knowledge to apply that knowledge or expertise to the issues in this case?

And, most important, who will answer these threshold questions, the judge or the jury, and by what standard—Rule 104(a) or 104(b)?

The original and most widely used standard for the admissibility of expert testimony and scientific evidence is found in Frye v. United States, a 1923 decision of the U.S. Court of Appeals for the District of Columbia Circuit. In *Frye,* the court upheld the exclusion of results of a primitive form of polygraph test that was offered by the defense in a murder trial.

FRYE v. UNITED STATES
293 F. 1013 (D.C. Cir. 1923)

VAN ORSDEL, J. Appellant, defendant below, was convicted of the crime of murder in the second degree, and from the judgment prosecutes this appeal.

A single assignment of error is presented for our consideration. In the course of the trial counsel for defendant offered an expert witness to testify to the result of a deception test made upon defendant. The test is described as the systolic blood pressure deception test. It is asserted that blood pressure is influenced by change in the emotions of the witness, and that the systolic blood pressure rises are brought about by nervous impulses sent to the sympathetic branch of the autonomic nervous system. Scientific experiments, it is claimed, have demonstrated that fear, rage, and pain always produce a rise of systolic blood pressure, and that conscious deception or falsehood, concealment of facts, or guilt of crime, accompanied by fear of detection when the person is under examination, raises the systolic blood pressure in a curve, which corresponds exactly to the struggle going on in the subject's mind, between fear and attempted control of that fear, as the examination touches the vital points in respect of which he is attempting to deceive the examiner.

In other words, the theory seems to be that truth is spontaneous, and comes without conscious effort, while the utterance of a falsehood requires a conscious effort, which is reflected in the blood pressure. The rise thus produced is easily detected and distinguished from the rise produced by mere fear of the examination itself. In the former instance, the pressure rises higher than in the latter, and is more pronounced as the examination proceeds, while in the latter case, if the subject is telling the truth, the pressure registers highest at the beginning of the examination, and gradually diminishes as the examination proceeds.

Prior to the trial defendant was subjected to this deception test, and counsel offered the scientist who conducted the test as an expert to testify to the results obtained. The offer was objected to by counsel for the government, and the court sustained the objection. Counsel for defendant then offered to have the proffered witness conduct a test in the presence of the jury. This also was denied.

Counsel for defendant, in their able presentation of the novel question involved, correctly state in their brief that no cases directly in point have been found. The broad ground, however, upon which they plant their case, is succinctly stated in their brief as follows:

> The rule is that the opinions of experts or skilled witnesses are admissible in evidence in those cases in which the matter of inquiry is such that inexperienced persons are unlikely to prove capable of forming a correct judgment upon it, for the reason that the subject-matter so far partakes of a science, art, or trade as to require a previous habit or experience or study in it, in order to acquire a knowledge of it. When the question involved does not lie within the range of common experience or common knowledge, but requires special experience or special knowledge, then the opinions of witnesses skilled in that particular science, art, or trade to which the question relates are admissible in evidence.

Numerous cases are cited in support of this rule. Just when a scientific principle or discovery crosses the line between the experimental and demonstrable stages is difficult to define. Somewhere in this twilight zone the evidential force of the principle must be recognized, and while courts will go a long way in admitting expert testimony deduced from a well-recognized scientific principle or discovery, the thing from which the deduction is made must be sufficiently established to have gained general acceptance in the particular field in which it belongs.

We think the systolic blood pressure deception test has not yet gained such standing and scientific recognition among physiological and psychological authorities as would justify the courts in admitting expert testimony deduced from the discovery, development, and experiments thus far made.

The judgment is affirmed.

According to Giannelli, The Admissibility of Novel Scientific Evidence: Frye v. United States, A Half-Century Later, 80 Colum. L. Rev. 1197 (1980), on which the following discussion is based, the *Frye* test originally envisioned a process whereby the admissibility of a scientific technique would be decided by reference to the stages of its evolution. The technique, after being invented or discovered within a particular field, would be first subjected to rigorous analysis by the scientific community during its "experimental stage." Only after this community "agreed" that the technique was valid ("demonstrable") would evidence of its use be admissible in court. Thus, the way in which the *Frye* test determined when evidence had reached the point of admissibility was to see if the technique was generally accepted by the relevant scientific community. In the last half century the *Frye* test was used for determining the admissibility of many types of scientific evidence besides the polygraph. For example, the test was used with voice prints,[1] neutron activation,[2] gunshot residue tests,[3] bitemark comparisons,[4] sodium pentothal,[5] ion microprobic analysis,[6] and blood grouping tests.[7] See Giannelli, supra, at 1205-1206.

According to Giannelli, the primary argument raised in favor of the *Frye* test is that it "assures that those most qualified to assess the general validity of a scientific method will have the determinative voice." United States v. Addison, 498 F.2d 741, 743-744 (D.C. Cir. 1974). Thus, the *Frye* test assigns to experts the task of determining a test's reliability.

> It is therefore best to adhere to a standard which in effect permits the experts who know the most about a procedure to experiment and to study it. In effect, they form a kind of technical jury, which must first pass on the scientific status of a procedure before the lay jury utilizes it in making its findings of fact.

People v. Barbara, 400 Mich. 352, 405, 255 N.W.2d 171, 194 (1977).

Courts have also cited less substantive rationales for the *Frye* test: The

---

1. See, e.g., Reed v. State, 283 Md. 374, 386, 391 A.2d 364, 381 (1978).
2. See, e.g., United States v. Stifel, 433 F.2d 431, 436, 438, 441 (6th Cir. 1970).
3. See, e.g., State v. Smith, 50 Ohio App. 2d 183, 193, 362 N.E.2d 1239, 1246 (1976).
4. See, e.g., People v. Slone, 76 Cal. App. 3d 611, 623, 143 Cal. Rptr. 61, 68 (1978).
5. See, e.g., Lindsey v. United States, 237 F.2d 893, 896 (9th Cir. 1956).
6. See, e.g., United States v. Brown, 557 F.2d 541, 556-557, 558 (6th Cir. 1977).
7. See, e.g., People v. Alston, 79 Misc. 2d 1077, 1085, 362 N.Y.S.2d 356, 362 (Sup. Ct. 1974).

"general acceptance standard" guarantees that "a minimal reserve of experts exists who can critically examine the validity of a scientific determination in a particular case." United States v. Addison, supra, 498 F.2d at 744. By requiring general acceptance by the relevant scientific community, *Frye* implicitly requires that such a community exists. Another court has suggested that the *Frye* test "may well promote a degree of uniformity of decision," People v. Kelly, 17 Cal. 3d 24, 31 (1976), because "[i]ndividual judges whose particular conclusions may differ regarding the reliability of particular scientific evidence, may discover substantial agreement and consensus in the scientific community." Id. Another has suggested that "[w]ithout the *Frye* test or something similar, the reliability of an experimental scientific technique is likely to become a central issue in each trial in which it is introduced, as long as there remains serious disagreement in the scientific community over its reliability." Reed v. State, 283 Md. 374, 388, 391 A.2d 364, 371-372 (1978). Finally, some courts have used the "general acceptance" standard as a check against new techniques because "scientific proof may in some instances assume a posture of mystic infallibility in the eyes of a jury of laymen." United States v. Addison, supra, 498 F.2d at 741; United States v. Wilson, 361 F. Supp. 510, 513 (D. Md. 1973).

J.R. TYBOR, PERJURY CASE GOES TO DOGS AFTER SHADOW CAST ON WITNESS

The National Law Journal, Sept. 14, 1980, p.4

CHICAGO—Government attorneys would do better to quit star-gazing and talk to the animals, according to a recent appellate opinion here.

After listening to what one clerk said was some of the most "entertaining" oral argument it ever heard, the 7th U.S. Circuit Court of Appeals reversed a perjury conviction based on the expert testimony of an astronomer. The forensic skywatcher attempted to determine the date of a family photo by measuring the angle of shadow cast by a pet dog named Jerry.

The case stemmed from the purchase with a phony $5 bill of what the court described as "two so-called Burger King 'Whoppers'" on Mothers' Day, May 12, 1974.

Stanley Tranowski was convicted of passing the phony bill and sentenced to six years in prison.

At Stanley's trial, however, Walter Tranowski, his brother, testified that he was in the defendant's presence for much of the day in question and insisted that Stanley couldn't have committed the crime.

To support his testimony, Walter produced at trial a family photo he said was taken in his mother's backyard between 2 P.M. and 3 P.M. that day—not long before Stanley was alleged to have bought the burgers with the funny money. It showed Stanley, their mother, Cecilia Knie-busch, and Jerry the dog.

The jury rejected Stanley's alibi defense, however, and found him guilty on Dec. 16, 1977.

Then Walter was indicted for perjury on June 29, 1979.

At the perjury trial, the government's key witness was an astronomer, Larry Ciupik, of the Adler Planetarium here. He said he measured from an enlargement of the photo the shadows cast by the dog and by the chimney at the rear of the house and made mathematical and astronomical calculations using a sun chart that ordinarily is used to measure "lunar mountains."

Based on these calculations, Mr. Ciupik testified that the photo could only have been taken on the morning of one of two days—April 13 or Aug. 31, 1974.

In an opinion written by Senior Judge John R. Bartels of the Eastern District of New York, who was sitting by designation, the majority decision described Mr. Ciupik's testimony as "a novel application of untested mathematical and astronomical theories" and said that the "trial court should not be used as a testing ground for theories supported neither by prior control experiments nor by calculations with [necessary] indicia of reliability." U.S. v. Tranowski, 80-1413.

It reversed Walter's perjury conviction outright without remand for a new trial.

Problem: Frye *and the Defense*

Charge: murder. Defense: self-defense. The state's version is that *D* had his knife in his hand when he approached *V. D*'s version is that he did not draw the knife until *V* wrapped his belt around his hand with the buckle dangling and approached *D*. There is a conflict over who struck the first blow. *D*'s credibility is crucial to his defense.

At trial, *D* offers the testimony of a polygraph examiner to testify that he administered a lie-detector test to *D*. Tendered questions and answers from the test were to the effect that *D* did not intend to use his knife when he stopped his car near *V,* that he did not pull his knife before he got out of the car, that *V* had his belt in his hand when *D* pulled his knife, and that *V* struck the first blow. The polygraph examiner would have testified that *D* was telling the truth when he gave these answers.

The trial judge finds that the polygraph examiner is trained, experienced, and qualified and that the test was well conducted under controlled circumstances and therefore generally reliable. However, the trial judge sustains the state's objection to the polygraph examiner's testimony on the grounds that polygraphy "has not gained sufficient

standing and scientific recognition among physiological and psychological authorities and therefore has not gained general acceptance in the
particular field in which it belongs."

D is convicted and sentenced to death. Have his constitutional rights
been violated?

Problem: The Dowser

To determine whether there is water within 400 feet of the surface
of a piece of land, *P* offers a dowser to testify that she has dowsed the
land and that there is no water. Is the testimony admissible?

Problem: Good Buddy

P wants to show that the load in the back of a truck shifted when the
truck going 30 MPH hit a bump in the road. *W* is offered to testify that
he is a trucker who often drives the type of truck in question, that he
drove over the bump at 30 MPH, and that the bump was big enough to
cause a load to shift. Is his testimony admissible? How should the judge
decide whether to rule under 701 or 702? Does it matter?

Problem: Abortion or Manslaughter?

P calls *W*, a pathologist, to give his medical opinion that based on his
examination of slides of fetal tissue, the fetus drew a breath of air before
it died. Is *D* entitled to cross-examine *W* about his qualifications as a
pathologist before he gives his opinion? What is the material issue to
which such examination would be directed? Would *D* be entitled, before
the doctor gave his opinion, to call witnesses of his own to prove that
the doctor is not qualified?

UNITED STATES v. JOHNSON
575 F.2d 1347 (5th Cir. 1978), cert. denied, 440 U.S. 907 (1979)

CLARK, Circuit Judge. [Defendant was charged with conspiracy to import marijuana.]

The next appellant, Dennis Lipper, raises four points in his brief on
appeal. He first argues that it was improper to permit de Pianelli to
testify as an expert concerning the origin of the marijuana. Appellants
concede that the substance with which they were dealing was marijuana.
They contend, however, that there was no objective evidence showing

that the marijuana was imported from outside the customs territory of the United States. Since no marijuana was ever seized, the only non-hearsay evidence concerning the origin of this marijuana came from de Pianelli. When de Pianelli was first asked to state whether the marijuana had come from Colombia, counsel for defendants objected. The jury was then excused and de Pianelli was examined on voir dire and cross-examined by defense counsel. During voir dire, he admitted that he had smoked marijuana over a thousand times and that he had dealt in marijuana as many as twenty times. He also said that he had been asked to identify marijuana over a hundred times and had done so without making a mistake. He based his identification upon the plant's appearance, its leaf, buds, stems, and other physical characteristics, as well as upon the smell and the effect of smoking it. On cross-examination he stated that he had been called upon to identify the source of various types of marijuana. He explained that characteristics such as the packaging, the physical appearance, the smell, the taste, and the effect could all be used in identifying the source of the marijuana. It was stipulated that he had no special training or education for such identification. Instead, his qualifications came entirely from "the experience of being around a great deal and smoking it." He also said that he had compared Colombian marijuana with marijuana from other places as many as twenty times. Moreover, he had seen Colombian marijuana that had been grown in the United States and had found that it was different from marijuana grown in Colombia.

After the voir dire examination, the defendants objected to de Pianelli's expertise for lack of authentication that he had actually smoked it, touched it, or correctly identified it. Despite the objection, the trial court permitted de Pianelli to give opinion evidence. Before the jury he related his experiences with marijuana and explained that he had tested a sample of marijuana from each importation and had verified that it came from Colombia.

Lipper contends that the source of marijuana is not a matter requiring expert opinion and that there was no foundation for de Pianelli's testimony. Lipper further contends that it was an error to qualify de Pianelli as an expert because he had never been to South America and, of course, had never smoked marijuana there or seen it growing in South America. Finally, Lipper contends that de Pianelli's testimony was conclusively rebutted by an associate professor of biological science at Florida State University, Loren C. Anderson.

In Crawford v. Worth, 447 F.2d 738, 740-41 (5th Cir. 1971), we stated the principle which guides appellate review of trial court determinations concerning expert testimony:

"The federal rule regarding review standards of trial court rulings on expert opinion evidence is stringent. . . . '[T]he trial judge has broad discretion in the matter of the admission or exclusion of expert evi-

dence, and his action is to be sustained unless manifestly erroneous.'
Salem v. United States Lines Co., 370 U.S. 31. In this Circuit's terms:
'The expert qualification of a witness is a question for the trial judge,
whose discretion is conclusive unless clearly erroneous as a matter of
law.' United States v. 41 Cases, More or Less, 420 F.2d 1126 (5th Cir.
1970). . . ."

Here the subject of the inference, the source of the marijuana, is
related to the occupation of selling illegal drugs and to the science of
botany, neither of which is likely to be within the knowledge of an average juror. For the government to obtain a conviction it was necessary
that it prove that the marijuana came from outside the customs territory
of the United States. See 21 U.S.C. §952. Testimony which would identify the source of the marijuana would be of obvious assistance to the
jury. It was therefore proper for the trial court to consider whether de
Pianelli was qualified to provide such testimony.

Rule 702 of the Federal Rules of Evidence provides that expertise
may be obtained by experience as well as from formal training or education. De Pianelli's testimony during voir dire revealed that his substantial experience in dealing with marijuana included identification of
Colombian marijuana. In light of that testimony, the trial court was
within its discretion in deciding to admit the testimony for the jury's
consideration.

The introduction of testimony from an expert witness does not foreclose the issue from consideration by the jury, which need not accept
the expert's testimony. A defendant is free to introduce his own expert
to challenge the prosecution's witness. Here the defense introduced the
testimony of Professor Anderson, who said that it was impossible to determine the origin of a particular sample of marijuana by examining its
physical characteristics. The trial court instructed the jury in general
terms concerning the weight it should give to testimony. In addition, it
specifically instructed the jury regarding expert witnesses and concluded with this admonition: "You should consider such expert opinion
received in this case and give it such weight as you think it deserves."
Thus the conflict between the experts was correctly presented to the
jury for resolution. . . .

The only remaining challenge to de Pianelli's status as an expert is
the argument that no one can acquire the skill which he professed to
have. That objection may be rephrased in the words of this court in
International Paper Company v. United States, 227 F.2d 201, 205 (5th
Cir. 1955): "an opinion is no better than the hypothesis or the assumption upon which it is based." If the hypothesis is proved to be flawed,
the witness should not be allowed to testify. This type of objection would
be directed at, for example, the testimony of someone purporting to
tell the color of a person's hair from fingerprints or the use of a testing
device that had not been generally accepted by the scientific commu-

nity. For a discussion of the latter problem, see United States v. Brown, 557 F.2d 541, 554-59 (6th Cir. 1977). Neither at trial nor on appeal have the appellants directly argued that no one can distinguish marijuana that has been grown in Colombia from other marijuana. They have, however, done so implicitly; and we believe that they tried to do so through the testimony of Professor Anderson. We shall therefore briefly consider that objection as well. Cf. United States v. Brown, supra, 557 F.2d at 557 n.17.

On the record before us we cannot say that the claim of an ability to identify Colombian marijuana is so inherently implausible that, as a matter of law, a jury should not be permitted to hear testimony on the identification. De Pianelli claimed that he could identify Colombian marijuana. Professor Anderson disputed that claim. But Professor Anderson admitted that climatological differences could produce differences in the marijuana plants. Professor Anderson's testimony was based upon the lack of scientific tests which would demonstrate that marijuana grown in Colombia differed from that grown elsewhere. Tests had shown, however, that marijuana grown in Canada differed from marijuana grown in other locations. Thus, there was some ambiguity in Professor Anderson's testimony. The issue was one that could have been resolved by the jury. In allowing the jury to consider the question and to hear the same arguments counsel now make to us, the court did not err.

NOTE: THE BASES OF EXPERT OPINIONS

The presentation of an expert opinion involves not only the applicability and quality of the expertise and the knowledge and experience of the expert, but also the factual data relevant to the particular case which the expert uses in formulating the testimony. Traditionally at common law it was thought that the expert could base an opinion rendered in court only on facts already admitted in evidence in that case whether through the expert's own testimony (e.g., physical examination of an injured person), or through other witnesses and evidence (e.g., testimony about the accident, medical records, etc.). This requirement led to the use of elaborate "hypothetical questions" in which the lawyer would incorporate all of the relevant facts upon which the opinion was to be based.

By the time of the original adoption of the Federal Rules of Evidence, the traditional common law practice had liberalized. Rule 703 recognizes four distinct ways for an expert to acquire the data on which he bases his opinion: (1) by supposition at the trial (the hypothetical question); (2) by listening to the testimony of other witnesses at trial; (3) by personal experience before the trial, as in the case of a doctor testifying about a patient whom she has treated personally; or (4) by being informed of data by others before the trial (hearsay).

Hypothetical Questions. The hypothetical question has the potential for carefully delineating the basis of an expert's opinion and for allowing precisely formed cross-examination. The question typically takes a form such as:

Q: Doctor, assume that the following facts are true: fact A, fact B, . . . fact N. (Counsel poses all the relevant facts of *his* case as facts to be assumed.) Now, doctor, based on those assumed facts, do you have an opinion whether . . . ?
A: Yes.
Q: What is your opinion?
A: My opinion is that. . . .

On cross-examination opposing counsel can then test the opinion by changing one or more facts, or adding or deleting facts, and asking how (or whether) the doctor's opinion is affected. For example:

Q: Doctor, assume that the car was travelling at 10 MPH instead of 30 MPH at the moment of impact. What then would be your opinion as to . . . ?

One problem with hypothetical questions is that while they may be used constructively, they also may be abused. With each statement of a hypothetical question counsel has an opportunity to reiterate the facts of his case, order them, and indicate their significance — in effect, to make a closing argument. Another problem is their potential complexity. One hypothetical question consumed nearly one hundred pages of transcript. What are the chances that the jury understood the question, or even kept awake through it?

Do the Federal Rules leave the option with counsel to use or not to use hypothetical questions? If so, have the rules failed to deal with the problem of abuse? What power does a federal trial judge have to stop a lawyer from using hypothetical questions in a manner that the judge considers abusive?

Other Witnesses. The difficulties with this method of data acquisition are both practical and theoretical. To acquire data by listening to other witnesses requires the expert to sit in court while the others testify, an expensive proposition. Moreover, if there is any conflict or ambiguity in the testimony of the other witnesses, the expert's data base will be ambiguous and will require clarification.

Personal Experience. This, typically, is the most effective basis for testimony. A ballistics expert will be most effective if he has test-fired the weapon himself and made microscopic photos of the resulting grooves and comparison photos with the bullet. The problem is that with some forms of expertise it is neither efficient nor sensible for the expert to perform all tests or analyses himself. Unless the expert could rely on the work of others, those who actually performed the tests would have to be called to testify before the expert could give his opinion based on the tests. This problem led to recognition of hearsay as a fourth legitimate form of data base.

Hearsay. As indicated by the Advisory Committee's notes to Rule 703, the most radical extension of this rule is its authorization for experts to rely on facts or data "made known to him" before the hearing — e.g., hearsay. The hearsay must be of a type reasonably relied upon by experts in the particular field in forming opinions or inferences upon the subject; but who is to make *this* determination and how?

Would the following reformulation of Rule 703 be an improvement on the present version or an unwise retreat from a useful reform?

> An expert's opinion may be based on a hypothetical question, facts or data perceived by the expert at or before the hearing, or facts or data in evidence. If of a type reasonably and customarily relied upon by experts in the particular field in forming opinions upon the subject, the underlying facts or data shall be admissible without testimony from the primary source.

Problem: Engineer's Investigation

(1) *P* offers an engineer to give her opinion that the steering wheel of *P*'s car was defective prior to the accident. She bases her opinion on her post-accident examination of the wreck and on the statement of the driver, reported to the engineer, that the auto lost its steering control before it crashed. How should the trial judge decide whether the engineer's opinion is admissible?

(2) Could the engineer state her opinion without revealing the information on which she based it? If so, how would opposing counsel probe to find out what the basis of the opinion was and what would happen if and when the arguably impermissible basis for the opinion emerged?

(3) Would the situation be materially different if the case were criminal instead of civil?

Problem: Pediatric Poison

In January, *P* gives birth to a child five weeks prematurely. The child is blue, weak, and sickly. By February 22, the child shows little improvement and little weight gain and is even more fretful. On March 1, *P*'s pediatrician prescribes a mild dosage of elixir of phenobarbital, one teaspoon every six hours. The prescription is delivered to pharmacist D. D fills a bottle with a solution, labels it, and puts on the label instructions to give the child one teaspoon every six hours. On March 2, the prescription is delivered to P. P gives the child one teaspoon of the medicine. Two hours later, the child suffers convulsions and dies. An examination of the contents of the bottle reveals that it contained morphine acetate in a one-thirtieth of a grain solution rather than phenobarbital. P sues D for wrongful death of her child caused by D's negligence in filling the doctor's prescription. D admits all of the above facts but denies that his negligence proximately caused the child's death. At trial, P offers to prove that section 904 of Taylor's Medical Jurisprudence (a concededly standard treatise) states that for infants less than one year of age, the maximum safe dosage of morphine acetate is one-fortieth of a grain per teaspoon every six hours and that any greater concentration is likely to cause convulsions and death. D objects. What ruling and why at common law?

Suppose D's objection to P's offer of section 904 is sustained. P then calls Dr. Kildare to the witness stand. Through questioning, P adduces Dr. Kildare's education, internship, professional affiliations, and practice as an expert endocrinologist with 12 years on the staff of a major metropolitan hospital. P then examines Dr. Kildare as follows:

Q: Doctor, what in your opinion is the maximum safe dosage of morphine acetate for an infant less than one year?
A: One-fortieth of a grain per teaspoon every six hours.
Q: That is all. Thank you, Dr. Kildare.

The cross-examination is as follows:

Q: Doctor, have you ever prescribed morphine acetate?
A: No.
Q: Have you ever observed a patient under the influence of morphine acetate?
A: No.
Q: Doctor, have you ever taken morphine acetate yourself?
A: No.
Q: Your opinion, then, is simply a guess, isn't it?
A: No. It is based on section 904 of Taylor's Treatise on Medical Jurisprudence.

D moves to strike Dr. Kildare's entire testimony, including the direct examination. P responds, citing Finnegan v. Fall River Gas Works Co., 159 Mass. 311, 312-313, 34 N.E. 523 (1893) (Holmes, J.):

> Although it might not be admissible merely to repeat what a witness had read in a book not itself admissible, still, when one who is competent on the general

"Is this really necessary, Your Honor? I'm an expert."

Drawing by Levin. Copyright © 1979 by The New Yorker Magazine, Inc.

subject accepts from his reading as probably true a matter of detail which he has not verified, the fact gains an authority which it would not have had from the printed page alone, and, subject perhaps to the exercise of some discretion, may be admitted.

Do you agree with Holmes? What should be the limits, if any, to the license given experts to base their opinions on inadmissible hearsay?

STATE v. SALDANA
324 N.W.2d 227 (Minn. 1982)

Scott, J.

Camilo Saldana appeals from his conviction of criminal sexual conduct in the first degree in violation of Minn. Stat. §609.342(e)(i) (1980).

At trial appellant admitted that sexual intercourse had occurred but claimed it was consensual. To rebut appellant's claim, the state presented an expert witness who described the typical post-rape symptoms and behavior of rape victims, and gave her opinion that the complainant was a victim of rape and had not fabricated her allegations. We find that the admission of such testimony requires the reversal of appellate's conviction, and we remand for a new trial.

Our concern is directed toward the testimony of Lynn Dreyer, a counselor for sexual assault victims, who testified for the state. Dreyer, the director of the Victim Assistance Program in Mankato, holds a bachelor's degree in psychology and social work. Dreyer testified that she met Martha Fuller, the complainant, 10 days after the alleged rape and that she counseled Fuller for approximately a 10-week period. In her testimony, Dreyer explained the stages that a rape victim typically goes through and discussed typical behavior of victims after a rape. She then described Fuller's reactions as she had observed them. In response to a question, Dreyer testified that it was not unusual that Fuller did not report the incident until the following day and that many rape victims never report a rape. Dreyer stated that Fuller was the victim of "acquaintance rape," that she definitely believed Fuller was a victim of sexual assault and rape, and that she did not think Fuller fantasized or "made it up."

The issue is whether admission of testimony concerning typical post-rape symptoms and behavior of rape victims, opinions that Fuller was a victim of rape, and an opinion that Fuller did not fantasize the rape was reversible error.

To be admissible, expert testimony must be helpful to the jury in reaching its decision. . . . If the jury is in as good a position to reach a decision as the expert, expert testimony would be of little assistance to the jury and should not be admitted. Expert testimony may also be excluded if its probative value is substantially outweighed by the danger of unfair prejudice, confusion, or misleading the jury. Minn. R. Evid. 403. Under this test of admissibility, we must examine each segment of Dreyer's testimony.

Dreyer's discussion of the stages a rape victim typically goes through was essentially an explanation of "rape trauma syndrome,"[1] although she did not so label it. On the facts of the case before us, such testimony is of no help to the jury and produces an extreme danger of unfair prejudice. The factual question to be decided by the jury is whether the

---

1. Ann Burgess and Lydia Holmstrom coined the term in their semiannual 1974 article to describe the recurring pattern of post-rape symptoms. Burgess & Holmstrom, Rape Trauma Syndrome, 131 Am. J. Psychiatry 981 (1974). For a discussion of rape trauma syndrome, see In re Pittsburgh Action Against Rape, 494 Pa. 15, 428 A.2d 126, 138-40 (1981) (Larsen, J., dissenting).

alleged criminal conduct occurred. It is not necessary that Fuller react in a typical manner to the incident. Fuller need not display the typical post-rape symptoms and behavior of rape victims to convince the jury that her view of the facts is the truth.

Rape trauma syndrome is not the type of scientific test that accurately and reliably determines whether a rape has occurred. The characteristic symptoms may follow any psychologically traumatic event. At best, the syndrome describes only symptoms that occur with some frequency, but makes no pretense of describing every single case. The jury must not decide this case on the basis of how most people react to rape or on whether Fuller's reactions were the typical reactions of a person who has been a victim of rape. Rather, the jury must decide what happened in *this case,* and whether the elements of the alleged crime have been proved beyond a reasonable doubt.

The scientific evaluation of rape trauma syndrome has not reached a level of reliability that surpasses the quality of common sense evaluation present in jury deliberations. As we stated in refusing to permit introduction of "battering parent" syndrome, the evidence may not be introduced "until further evidence of the scientific accuracy and reliability of syndrome or profile diagnoses can be established." State v. Leobach, 310 N.W.2d 58, 64 (Minn. 1981). Permitting a person in the role of an expert to suggest that because the complainant exhibits some of the symptoms of rape trauma syndrome, the complainant was therefore raped, unfairly prejudices the appellant by creating an aura of special reliability and trustworthiness. Since jurors of ordinary abilities are competent to consider the evidence and determine whether the alleged crime occurred, the danger of unfair prejudice outweighs any probative value. To allow such testimony would inevitably lead to a battle of experts that would invade the jury's province of fact-finding and add confusion rather than clarity.

Rape trauma syndrome is not a fact-finding tool, but a therapeutic tool useful in counseling. Because the jury need be concerned only with determining the facts and applying the law, and because evidence of reactions of other people does not assist the jury in its fact-finding function, we find the admission of expert testimony on rape trauma syndrome to be error.

The second segment of Dreyer's testimony of questionable admissibility is her opinion that Fuller was raped.[4] The issue is whether the

---

4. The prosecutor elicited the following testimony from Dreyer:

Q: Can you explain to the jury the stages that Martha Fuller went through since the date of this incident?

[Objection overruled.]

A: . . . She has went through a lot because her rape is what we call acquaintance rape, where it involves someone that they know, and she's gone through a lot of feelings of guilt and internalizing the pain, because it is a friend and a personal friend of her husband. . . .

state may introduce expert testimony in a rape prosecution that, in the expert's opinion, a rape in fact occurred.

The primary criterion for admissibility is the helpfulness requirement as discussed above. An expert witness may testify in the form of an opinion, Minn. R. Evid. 702, and opinion testimony is not objectionable merely because it embraces an ultimate issue to be decided by the jury, Minn. R. Evid. 704. However, according to the Advisory Committee Comment to Rule 704, opinions involving a legal analysis or mixed questions of law and fact are deemed to be of no use to the jury.

A majority of the courts that have considered the issue have held that admission of a doctor's opinion that rape or sexual assault had occurred is error.[5] A few courts in other jurisdictions have permitted a doctor who has physically examined the complaining witness shortly after the alleged rape to give an opinion that sexual intercourse was not voluntary.[6]

The admission of Dreyer's testimony constitutes error under the majority rule. Furthermore, because Dreyer is not a physician, never physically examined Martha Fuller and did not meet Fuller until 10 days after the alleged rape, the admission of Dreyer's testimony constitutes error even under the minority rule.

We conclude that the admission of Dreyer's testimony was error. Because the jurors were equally capable of considering the evidence and determining whether a rape occurred, Dreyer's opinion was not helpful. Her testimony was a legal conclusion which was of no use to the jury. Furthermore, the danger of unfair prejudice outweighed any probative value. Dreyer's testimony "gave a stamp of scientific legitimacy to the truth of the complaining witness's factual testimony." People v. Izzo, 90 Mich. App. 727, 730, 282 N.W.2d 10, 11 (1979).

Q: From your professional involvement with Martha Fuller, do you have an opinion Miss Dreyer, as to whether or not this incident actually took place?
A: I definitely believe that Martha was a victim of assault.
Q: Of a sexual assault?
A: Sexual assault and rape.

5. See, e.g., Farley v. State, 324 So. 2d 662 (Fla. App. 1975); Commonwealth v. Gardner, 350 Mass. 664, 216 N.E.2d 558 (1966); People v. McGillen, 392 Mich. 278, 220 N.W.2d 689 (1974) (dictum); State v. Castore, R.I., 435 A.2d 321 (1981); Cartera v. Commonwealth, 219 Va. 516, 248 S.E.2d 784 (1978). The examining physician may of course testify to observations of physical and emotional conditions, examinations and tests performed, and medical conclusions reached.

6. See, e.g., State v. Miller, 254 Iowa 545, 117 N.W.2d 447 (1962) (no reversible error in admitting examining physician's opinion that intercourse was not voluntary where jury did not convict of rape); People v. LaPorte, 103 Mich. App. 443, 303 N.W.2d 222 (1981) (no error in admitting attending physician's expert opinion, based upon the victim's physical and emotional conditions shortly after the incident, that there had been penetration against the will of the complainant); State v. Ring, 54 Wash. 2d 250, 339 P.2d 461 (1959) (no error in permitting physicians who examined prosecuting witness shortly after the episode to state that her physical condition could not have been the result of "ordinary normal sexual intercourse," because it involved a question of medical science).

The final segment of Dreyer's testimony was her opinion that Fuller had not fantasized the rape. Once a witness is deemed competent, expert opinions concerning the witness's reliability in distinguishing truth from fantasy are generally inadmissible because such opinions invade the jury's province to make credibility determinations. Expert testimony should be received only in "unusual cases." United States v. Barnard, 490 F.2d 907, 913 (9th Cir. 1973), cert. denied, 416 U.S. 959 (1974). An example of such an unusual case is a sexual assault case where the alleged victim is a child or mentally retarded. See Commonwealth v. Carter, 9 Mass. App. 680, 403 N.E.2d 1191 (1980), aff'd, 417 N.E.2d 438 (Mass. 1981) (examining pediatrician may give opinion relating to the ability of a retarded child to differentiate between reality and fantasy but not concerning whether the child was telling the truth about an alleged sexual assault).

The admission of Dreyer's testimony that Martha Fuller did not fantasize or fabricate her story was erroneous. First, there are no unusual circumstances in this case which warrant the admission of expert testimony concerning the credibility of Fuller, who is an adult with at least average intelligence. Second, Dreyer, who had no medical education or training, was unqualified to determine whether a person could differentiate between reality and fantasy or to detect whether a person was telling the truth or fabricating a story. Finally, the question and answer did not concern Fuller's general tendency to fantasize or fabricate but whether she fantasized or fabricated the particular facts at issue. Dreyer was simply stating her opinion that Fuller was telling the truth. Because credibility is the sole province of the jury, admission of the testimony was erroneous. . . .

We hold that in this prosecution for criminal sexual conduct where the defendant claimed consent it was reversible error for an expert to testify concerning typical post-rape symptoms and behavior of rape victims and give opinions that the complainant was a victim of rape and had not fantasized the rape. Our holding is necessary in order to assure accuracy in the truth-seeking process and to guarantee fairness to the accused. . . .

Reversed and remanded.*

State v. Saldahna represents a traditional and relatively conservative approach to a kind of evidence that is becoming of greater significance. Traditionally, such issues as "normal" psychology (even under stress), and the credibility of testifying witnesses have been considered matters within the common ken of the jury for which expert testimony was neither necessary nor helpful. Modern social science research has disclosed

---

*See People v. Bledsoe, 189 Cal. Rptr. 726 (Cal. Ct. App. 1983) for a contrasting approach. — [EDS].

that specialized expertise can make important contributions to the understanding of the jury even on such mundane matters as the percipience of an eye-witness. In many states at least some of the testimony excluded in *Saldahna* would now be admissible.

STATE v. CHAPPLE
135 Ariz. 281, 660 P.2d 1208 (1983)

FELDMAN, Justice.

Dolan Chapple was convicted on three counts of first degree murder, one count of unlawfully transporting marijuana and one count of conspiring to unlawfully transport marijuana. . . . The defendant appealed from this judgment and sentence. . . .

FACTS

The instigator of this bizarre drama was Mel Coley, a drug dealer who resided in Washington, D.C., but who was also connected with dealers in Kansas City. Coley had a history of dealing with a supplier named Bill Varnes, who lived near Phoenix.

Coley had made a large number of drug deals through Malcolm Scott, a "middle-man" who lived near Phoenix. . . .

Coley telephoned in early December 1977 and told Scott that he was interested in purchasing approximately 300 pounds of marijuana. He asked Scott to act as middleman in the transaction. Scott was to get $700 for his efforts. Scott testified that he called one or two of the Arizona suppliers . . . and found they could not supply the necessary quantity. He then called his sister, Pamela Buck. . . . Scott asked Buck to contact her friend Varnes and see whether he could handle the sale. Buck talked to Varnes and reported to her brother that Varnes could supply the necessary amount of marijuana at an agreed upon price. Scott relayed this information to Coley. Scott instructed Buck not to tell Varnes that Coley or anyone from Washington, D.C. was involved in the deal.

On the evening of December 10 or the early morning of December 11, 1977, Coley arrived at the Phoenix airport from Washington, D.C. Scott met him at the airport and found that Coley was accompanied by two strangers who were introduced as "Dee" and "Eric." Scott drove the three men to a trailer located at his parents' farm near Higley in Pinal County, Arizona. . . .

Coley, Dee and Eric spent the night at the trailer, while Scott returned to his residence in Mesa. The next morning Scott returned to the farm and took Coley to the airport where they picked up a brown leather bag. Back at the trailer, Scott observed Coley, Eric and Dee take four guns from the bag and clean them. Scott examined and handled one of the guns. Buck had also arrived at the trailer in Higley, and she and Dee were dispatched to Varnes' trailer in order to purchase a sample of the marijuana. . . .

That evening, Scott and his sister met at the trailer with Coley, Eric and Dee. Varnes arrived with two companions, Eduardo Ortiz and Carlos Elsy. Ortiz and Elsy began to unload the marijuana and put it in the trailer. Buck was in the trailer with Coley, Eric and Dee at this time. Scott was some distance away, sitting on the porch of his parents' house. Buck was told by Dee or Coley that after the marijuana was unloaded she should lock herself in the bathroom.

After Ortiz and Elsy had finished unloading the marijuana and stacking it in the living room of the trailer, Dee suggested to Varnes that they go in the bedroom and "count the money." They started toward the bedroom and Buck went into the bathroom. A few moments later, Buck heard several shots, opened the bathroom door and ran out. Scott heard the shots while he was on the porch and saw a door of the trailer open. Elsy ran out, pursued by either Eric or Dee. After seeing Buck run out of the door at the other end of the trailer, Scott went back to the trailer and found Varnes dead in the bedroom of a gunshot wound to the head and Ortiz in the living room dead of a gunshot wound to the body. Subsequent ballistic tests showed they had been shot with different weapons. Elsy was outside, dead from a blow to the back of the head.

Dee and Eric then removed the marijuana from the trailer and loaded it into a car. . . . Scott, Eric and Dee loaded the three bodies into the trunk of Varnes' car. That car was driven out to the desert, doused with gasoline and set afire. The trailer was cleaned to remove evidence of the crime and the carpet in the trailer was burned. The parties then left the scene of the crime and returned to Scott's house in Mesa. . . . Coley gave Scott and Buck $500 each. . . . Scott returned to the trailer and completed the cleanup. Fear or remorse, or both, drove Scott to seek the aid of a lawyer, who succeeded in negotiating an immunity deal for Scott and in getting him to surrender to the sheriff.

Defendant does not contest any of the foregoing facts. Defendant is accused of being "Dee." He denies this. At his extradition hearing in Illinois, seven witnesses placed him in Cairo, Illinois during the entire month of December 1977, three of them testifying specifically to his presence in that town on December 11, the day of the crime. The same witnesses testified for him in the trial at which he was convicted. No direct or circumstantial evidence of any kind connects defendant to the crime, other than the testimony of Malcolm Scott and Pamela Buck, neither of whom had ever met the defendant before the crime and neither of whom saw him after the crime except at the trial. Defendant was apprehended and tried only because Malcolm Scott and Pamela Buck picked his photograph out of a lineup more than one year after the date of the crime; he was convicted because they later identified both the photographs and defendant himself at trial.

The State's position was that the identification was correct, while the defendant argued at trial that the identification was erroneous for one of two reasons. The first reason advanced by defendant is that Scott and Buck were lying to save themselves by "fingering" him. To buttress this contention, defendant established that Scott and Buck had made a "deal" with the State whereby they were granted complete immunity for their part in the crime unless the facts showed that they had knowingly participated in the killings. . . .

Defendant further argued at trial, and urges here, that even if Scott and Buck are not lying, their identification was a case of mistaken identity. The argument is that Scott and Buck picked the wrong picture out of the photographic lineup and that their subsequent photographic and in-court identifications were part of the "feedback phenomenon" and are simply continuations or repetitions of the same mistake. To support this contention of mistaken identification, defendant offered expert testimony regarding the various factors that affect the reliability of identification evidence. For the most part, that testimony was rejected by the trial court as not being within the proper sphere of expert testimony.

EXPERT TESTIMONY REGARDING EYEWITNESS IDENTIFICATION

. . . The detectives . . . showed Scott and Buck various photographs and lineups containing pictures of known acquaintances of Mel Coley. . . . One of the photographic lineups displayed to Scott, but not to Buck, contained a picture of the defendant, Dolan Chapple, but Scott did not identify him as Dee. . . .

The police continued to show the witnesses photographic lineups in an attempt to obtain an identification of Dee. Police efforts were successful on January 27, 1979, when Scott was shown a nine-picture photo lineup. For the first time, this lineup included photos of both Eric Perry, who had already been tentatively identified by Scott and Buck, and of the defendant. . . . Upon seeing this lineup, Scott immediately recognized Eric's picture again. About ten minutes later, Scott identified defendant's picture as Dee. Scott was then shown the picture of defendant he had failed to identify at a previous session and asked to explain why he had not previously identified it. He stated that he had no recollection of having seen it before. After Scott had identified Dee and before he could talk to his sister, the police showed Buck the same lineup. Buck identified the defendant as Dee and then re-identified Eric.

Defendant argues that the jury could have found the in-court identification unreliable for a variety of reasons. The defendant argues that the identification of Dee from photographic lineups in this case was unreliable because of the time interval which passed between the occurrence of the event and the lineup and because of the anxiety and tension inherent in the situation surrounding the entire identification process.[9] The defendant also argues that since Scott and Buck had smoked marijuana on the days of the crime, their perception would have been affected, making their identification through photographs less reliable. Further, defendant claims the January 27, 1979 identification of Dee by Scott and Buck from the photographic lineup was the product of an unconscious transfer. Defendant claims that Scott picked the picture of Dolan Chapple and identified it as Dee because he remembered that picture from the previous lineup (when he had not been able to identify defendant's picture). Defendant urges that the in-court identifications were merely reinforcements of the initial error. Defendant also argues that Eric's presence in the lineup heightened the memory transfer and increased the chance of an incorrect photographic identification. . . . Further, defendant claims that the identification was made on the basis of subsequently acquired information which affected memory. Finally, defendant argues that the confidence and certainty which Scott and Buck displayed in making their in-court identification at trial had no relation whatsoever to the accuracy of that identification and was, instead, the product of other factors.

It is against this complicated background, with identification the one issue on which the guilt or innocence of defendant hinged, that defense counsel offered the testimony of an expert on eyewitness identification in order to rebut the testimony of Malcolm Scott and his sister, Pamela Buck. The witness called by the defense was Dr. Elizabeth Loftus, a professor of psychology at the University of Washington. Dr. Loftus specializes in an area of experimental and clinical psychology dealing with perception, memory retention and recall. Her qualifications are unquestioned, and it may fairly be said that she "wrote the book" on the subject. The trial court granted the State's motion to suppress Dr. Loftus' testimony. Acknowledging that rulings on admissibility of expert testimony are within the discretion of the trial court, defendant contends that the court erred and abused its discretion in granting the motion to suppress Dr. Loftus' testimony.

The admissibility of expert testimony is governed by Rule 702, Ariz. R. of Evid. That rule states:

> If scientific, technical, or other specialized knowledge will assist the trier of
> fact to understand the evidence or to determine a fact in issue, a witness qualified

---

9. Buck and Scott both said they were frightened for their lives during the events. Since they are the only witnesses, one might assume they were also frightened and apprehensive during the time period when Eric and Dee were both at liberty.

as an expert by knowledge, skill, experience, training, or education, may testify thereto in the form of an opinion or otherwise.

In what is probably the leading case on the subject, the Ninth Circuit affirmed the trial court's preclusion of expert evidence on eyewitness identification in United States v. Amaral, 488 F.2d 1148 (9th Cir. 1973). In its analysis, however, the court set out four criteria which should be applied in order to determine the admissibility of such testimony. These are: (1) qualified expert; (2) proper subject; (3) conformity to a generally accepted explanatory theory; and (4) probative value compared to prejudicial effect. Id. at 1153. We approve this test and find that the case at bar meets these criteria.

We recognize that the cases that have considered the subject have uniformly affirmed trial court rulings denying admission of this type of testimony. However, a careful reading of these cases reveals that many of them contain fact situations which fail to meet the *Amaral* criteria or are decided on legal principles which differ from those we follow in Arizona.

Applying the *Amaral* test to the case at bench, we find from the record that the State has conceded that the expert was qualified and that the question of conformity to generally accepted explanatory theory is not raised and appears not to be a question in this case. The two criteria which must therefore be considered are (1) determination of whether the probative value of the testimony outweighs its possible prejudicial effect and (2) determination of whether the testimony was a proper subject.

(1) PROBATIVE VALUE VS. PREJUDICE

The State argues that there would have been little probative value to the witness' testimony and great danger of unfair prejudice. The latter problem is claimed to arise from the fact that Loftus' qualifications were so impressive that the jury might have given improper weight to her testimony. We do not believe that this raises the issue of *unfair* prejudice. The contention of lack of probative value is based on the premise that the offer of proof showed that the witness would testify to general factors which were applicable to this case and affect the reliability of identification, but would not express any opinion with regard to the accuracy of the specific identification made by Scott and Buck and would not express an opinion regarding the accuracy percentage of eyewitness identification in general.

We believe that the "generality" of the testimony is a factor which favors admission. Witnesses are permitted to express opinions on ultimate issues but are not required to testify to an opinion on the precise questions before the trier of fact.

Most of the literature assumes that experts testify only in the form of opinions. The assumption is logically unfounded. [Rule 702] accordingly recognizes that an expert on the stand may give a dissertation or exposition of scientific or other principles relevant to the case, leaving the trier of fact to apply them to the facts. Since much of the criticism of expert testimony has centered upon the hypothetical question, it seems wise to recognize that opinions are not indispensable and to encourage the use of expert testimony in non-opinion form when counsel believes the trier can itself draw the requisite inference.

Fed. R. of Evid. 702 advisory committee note.

(2) PROPER SUBJECT

The remaining criterion at issue is whether the offered evidence was a proper subject for expert testimony. Ariz. R. of Evid. 702 allows expert testimony if it "will assist the trier of fact to understand the evidence or to determine a fact in issue." Put conversely, the test "is whether the subject of inquiry is one of such common knowledge that people of ordinary education could reach a conclusion as intelligently as the witness. . . ." State v. Owens, 112 Ariz. 223, 227, 540 P.2d 695, 699 (1975). Furthermore, the test is not whether the jury could reach some conclusion in the absence of the expert evidence, but whether the jury is qualified without such testimony "to determine intelligently and to the best possible degree the particular issue without enlightenment from those having a specialized understanding of the subject. . . ." Fed. R. Evid. 702 advisory committee note (quoting Ladd, Expert Testimony, 5 Vand. L. Rev. 414, 418 (1952)).

In excluding the evidence in the case at bench, the trial judge stated:

I don't find anything that's been presented in the extensive discussions that I have read in your memorandum with regard to the fact that this expert is going to testify to anything that isn't within the common experience of the people on the jury, that couldn't really be covered in cross-examination of the witnesses who made the identification, and probably will be excessively argued in closing arguments to the jury.

This basis for the view that eyewitness identification is not a proper subject for expert testimony is the same as that adopted in United States v. Amaral, supra, and in the great majority of cases which have routinely followed Amaral. . . .

However, after a careful review of these cases and the record before us, we have concluded that although the reasons cited by the trial judge would correctly permit preclusion of such testimony in the great majority of cases, it was error to refuse the testimony in the case at bench. In reaching this conclusion, we have carefully considered the offer of proof made by the defense in light of the basic concept of "proper subject" underlying Rule 702. . . .

Even assuming that jurors of ordinary education need no expert testimony to enlighten them to the danger of eyewitness identification, the offer of proof indicated that Dr. Loftus' testimony would have informed the jury that there are many specific variables which affect the accuracy of identification and which apply to the facts of this case. For instance, while most jurors would no doubt realize that memory dims as time passes, Dr. Loftus presented data from experiments which showed that the "forgetting curve" is not uniform. Forgetting occurs very rapidly and then tends to level out; immediate identification is much more trustworthy than long-delayed identification. . . .

Another variable in the case is the effect of stress upon perception. Dr. Loftus indicated that research shows that most laymen believe that stressful events cause people to remember "better" so that what is seen in periods of stress is more accurately related later. However, experimental evidence indicates that stress causes inaccuracy of perception with subsequent distortion of recall.

Dr. Loftus would also have testified about the problems of "unconscious transfer," a phenomenon which occurs when the witness confuses a person seen in one situation with a person seen in a different situation. Dr. Loftus would have pointed out that a witness who takes part in a photo identification session without identifying any of the photographs and who then later sees a photograph of one of those persons may relate his or her familiarity with the picture to the crime rather than to the previous identification session.

Another variable involves assimilation of post-event information. Experimental evidence, shown by Dr. Loftus, confirms that witnesses frequently incorporate into their identifications inaccurate information gained subsequent to the event and confused with the event. An additional problem is the "feedback factor." We deal here with two witnesses who were related and . . . engaged in discussions with each other about the identification of Dee. . . . Dr. Loftus would have explained that through such discussions identification witnesses can reinforce their individual identifications. Such reinforcement will often tend to heighten the certainty of identification. The same may be said of the continual sessions that each witness had with the police in poring over large groups of photographs.[13]

The last variable in this case concerns the question of confidence and

---

13. We do not suggest that the police attempted to prejudice the identification procedure. The facts show that the police were careful to avoid the possibility of prejudice. However, as Dr. Loftus pointed out, it is not possible to discuss identification of photographs with witnesses on seven different occasions, comprising a total of over 200 pictures, without giving the witness some "feedback" with respect to what the officers anticipate or expect the witness to find.

its relationship to accuracy. Dr. Loftus' testimony and some experimental data indicate that there is no relationship between the confidence which a witness has in his or her identification and the actual accuracy of that identification. Again, this factor was specifically tied to the evidence in the case before us since both Scott and Buck indicated in their testimony that they were absolutely sure of their identification. Evidently their demeanor on the witness stand showed absolute confidence.[14]

We cannot assume that the average juror would be aware of the variables concerning identification and memory about which Dr. Loftus was qualified to testify.

> Depriving [the] jurors of the benefit of scientific research on eyewitness testimony force[d] them to search for the truth without full knowledge and opportunity to evaluate the strength of the evidence. In short, this deprivation prevent[ed] [the] jurors from having "the best possible degree" of "understanding the subject" toward which the law of evidence strives.

Note, [Did Your Eyes Deceive You? Expert Psychological Testimony on the Unreliability of Eyewitness Identification, 29 Stan. L. Rev. 969, 1017-1018 (1977)]. Thus, . . . we believe that Dr. Loftus' offered evidence was a proper subject for expert testimony and should have been admitted.

Of course, the test is not whether we believe that under these facts the evidence was admissible, but whether the trial court abused its discretion in reaching the contrary conclusion. . . . As indicated above, the key to this issue is whether the testimony might assist the jury to resolve the issues raised by the facts. In making this determination, the trial court must first consider those contentions of ultimate fact raised by the party offering the evidence and supported by evidentiary facts in the record. It must then determine whether the expert testimony will assist in resolving the issues.

. . . In effect, the trial judge ruled that all of the information necessary to resolve the conflicting factual contentions on these issues was within the common experience of the jurors and could be covered in cross-examination of the identification witnesses and argued to the jury.

It is difficult to support this conclusion. For instance, while jurors are aware that lapse of time may make identification less reliable, they are almost certainly unaware of the forgetting curve phenomenon and the resultant inference that a prompt tentative identification may be much more accurate than later positive identification. Similarly, cross-examination is unlikely to establish any evidentiary support for argument that eyewitnesses who have given similar nonfactual descriptions of the crim-

---

14. We base this conclusion on statements the prosecutor made in closing argument and in defense counsel's attempts to argue that the jurors should not be misled by the confidence which the witnesses displayed in their identification testimony.

inal may have been affected by the feedback phenomenon. Again, experimental data provides evidentiary support to arguments which might otherwise be unpersuasive because they seem contrary to common "wisdom."

Thus, while we have no problem with the usual discretionary ruling that the trier of facts needs no assistance from expert testimony on the question of reliability of identification, the unusual facts of this case compel the contrary conclusion. The preclusion ruling here was based upon a determination that the jury would not be assisted by expert testimony because the subjects embraced by that testimony could be elicited on cross-examination and argued without the evidentiary foundation. Preclusion here was not predicated upon a balancing of conflicting factual contentions or equitable considerations; it was based upon the court's own conclusion that scientific theory regarding the working of human memory could be developed on cross-examination and effectively argued without evidentiary foundation. The examples listed above demonstrate that under the facts here this conclusion was incorrect; there were a number of substantive issues of ultimate fact on which the expert's testimony would have been of significant assistance. Accordingly, we hold that the order precluding the testimony was legally incorrect and was unsupported by the record. It was, therefore, an abuse of discretion.

In reaching this conclusion, we do not intend to "open the gates" to a flood of expert evidence on the subject. We reach the conclusion that Dr. Loftus should have been permitted to testify on the peculiar facts of this case and have no quarrel with the result reached in the vast majority of cases which we have cited above. The rule in Arizona will continue to be that in the usual case we will support the trial court's discretionary ruling on admissibility of expert testimony on eyewitness identification. Nor do we invite opinion testimony in even the most extraordinary case on the likelihood that a particular witness is correct or mistaken in identification or that eyewitness identification in general has a certain percentage of accuracy or inaccuracy.

The judgment below is reversed and the case remanded for a new trial.

HOLOHAN, C.J., GORDON, V.C.J., and CAMERON, J., concur.

HAYS, Justice, concurring in part and dissenting in part:

I cannot agree with the majority's position that the trial court abused its discretion in excluding the testimony of an expert witness on eyewitness identification. With a view to preserving the integrity of the jury as finders of fact, I dissent in part.

It is the jury's task to determine the weight and credibility of a witness' testimony. What this court addresses is whether it is appropriate to have that determination put before the jury on the basis of expert witness testimony. Rule 704, Arizona Rules of Evidence, permits opinion testimony which embraces an ultimate issue if that testimony is otherwise admissible. However, rule 704 does *not* resolve all worry about invading the province of the jury. Testimony which is of such common knowledge that persons of ordinary education and background could reach as intelligent a conclusion as the expert shall be excluded. State v. Williams, 132 Ariz. 153, 644 P.2d 889, 896 (1982).

Courts have consistently held that expert testimony relating to eyewitness identification constitutes an invasion of the jury's province. While I recognize the problems in eyewitness testimony, I am unable to distinguish the case at bench from the wealth of cases where identification is in issue.

Identification of a criminal defendant is always crucial, notwithstanding the number of issues in a case. The fact that identification was defendant Chapple's sole defense should not compel us to carve out an exception to our rule against such testimony.

Our rules of evidence provide that a witness shall be impeached through cross-examination. "It is the responsibility of counsel during cross-examination to inquire into the witness' opportunity for observation, his capacity for observation, his attention and interest and his distraction or division of attention." United States v. Amaral, 488 F.2d 1148, 1153 (9th Cir. 1973). A defense attorney can properly expose through cross-examination of the witness the time interval which passed between the occurrence of the event and the line-up and, through probing questions, the effects of stress and drugs on the witness' perception. Allowing an expert to testify on the factors affecting the reliability of identification by an eyewitness is merely a guise for impeaching that witness. We cannot permit an expert to disparage the memory of a witness in order to impeach him. The ability of a person to make accurate observations is to be considered by the jury when assessing that witness' credibility.

I also disagree with the majority's conclusion that the average juror does not know that immediate identification is much more trustworthy than long-delayed identification. The average juror may not know the technical terms for this phenomenon, but that is not relevant to his ability to assess a witness' credibility.

My concern here goes beyond the borders of this case. Once we have opened the door to this sort of impeaching testimony, what is to prevent experts from attacking any real or supposed deficiency in every other mental faculty? The peculiar risk of expert testimony with its scientific aura of trustworthiness and the possibility of undue prejudice should be respected. I have great reluctance to permit academia to take over the fact-finding function of the jury. Although clothed in other guise, that will be the practical effect. With little to distinguish this case from the general rule against admitting expert testimony on eyewitness identification, we are left with no guidelines to decide the deluge of similar issues which are sure to result.

I dissent in part.

The adoption of the Federal Rules in 1975 raised the question of whether the new rules had changed the *Frye* "general acceptance" standard for the admissibility of expert testimony. Rule 702 said nothing about "general acceptance" as a prerequisite for expert testimony. On the other hand, neither the Rules nor the Advisory Committee Note specifically stated an intent to overrule *Frye*. For 20 years in which science marched forward, and ever more frequently into the courtroom, the law in the federal courts remained unclear. One extreme position was that *Frye* was unaffected by the promulgation of the Federal Rules, and that "general acceptance" was still the standard by which proffered expertise was to be measured. An example of this position is Barrel of Fun, Inc. v. State Farm Fire and Casualty Co., 739 F.2d 1028 (5th Cir. 1984) in which the Fifth Circuit sustained the exclusion of results of an improved form of polygraph test on the ground that polygraphy had not achieved the level of "general acceptance" necessary to render it admissible under *Frye*. On the other hand, in United States v. Downing, 753 F.2d 1224 (3rd Cir. 1985) the Third Circuit concluded that the Federal Rules of Evidence "neither incorporate nor repudiate" the *Frye* test and that "a particular degree of acceptance of a scientific technique within the scientific community is neither a necessary nor a sufficient condition for admissibility: it is, however, one factor that a district court normally should consider in deciding whether to admit evidence based upon the technique."

Meanwhile, courts in states which had adopted evidence rules based on the Federal Rules of Evidence were applying those rules to various forms of expert testimony and deciding whether the *Frye*-type analysis survived the rules in their jurisdictions.

STATE v. WILLIAMS
388 A.2d 500 (Me. 1978)

WERNICK, J. On May 26, 1976, defendant Thomas Williams was indicted in the Superior Court (Kennebec County) for the offense of terrorizing, in violation of 17-A M.R.S.A. §210. A jury found defendant guilty as charged, and he has appealed from the judgment of conviction entered on the verdict.

We deny the appeal.

On May 20, 1976, an unidentified person made a telephone call to a dispatcher at the Augusta Police Department and stated that a bomb was going to go off at the Augusta State Airport. While the call was in process, the Augusta police recorded it on magnetic tape. Thereafter, Officer Richard Gary Judkins of the Augusta Police Department listened to the tape recording and recognized the voice of the person telephoning as the voice of defendant. Later that day, at the request of the police, defendant came to the Augusta police station and read aloud a rough transcript of the threatening telephone call previously received and recorded at the police station. With defendant's agreement, a tape recording was made of defendant's reading. The police thereafter submitted both the tape recording of the threatening telephone call and of defendant's reading to Dr. Oscar Tosi of Michigan State University and Lieutenant Lonnie Smrkovski of the Michigan Department of State Police, each to make a voice identification analysis through the use of a speech spectrograph.

At trial, Dr. Tosi gave preliminary testimony as to the nature, reliability and scientific acceptance of the "scientific" voice identification process known as speech spectrography or "voiceprint" analysis. Dr. Louis J. Gertsman, of City College in New York, and Faulsto Poza, a consultant to the Stanford Research Institute, testified, preliminarily, in opposition to allowing in evidence testimony as to voice identification achieved by the use of speech spectrography.

At the conclusion of the extensive preliminary testimony the presiding Justice ruled, over defendant's objection, that adequate foundation had been shown to satisfy him that (1) voiceprint identification has such scientific acceptance and reliability as warrants its admissibility in evidence, (2) the experts whose opinions were here being sought as evidence were qualified to assist the jury in its determinations.

Thereafter, Dr. Tosi and Lt. Smrkovski testified that through use of a speech spectrograph each of them had independently analyzed the voices recorded on the two tapes and had independently made a "positive identification" that the unknown voice from the telephone call and the known voice of the defendant belonged to the same person. Officer Judkins then testified that he had recognized defendant's voice when he had listened to the recording of the bomb threat.

Defendant's position on appeal is that it was error to admit the speech spectrograph evidence because the scientific community has not generally accepted the speech spectrograph as a scientifically reliable method of voice identification. Defendant further contends that in any event speech spectrograph voice identification evidence is unreliable in forensic situations.

The threshold question we confront is to determine what standard, under the law of evidence, governs *admissibility* in relation to the type of evidence here involved.

The preliminary evidence of record shows that the process of voice identification used by Dr. Tosi and Lt. Smrkovski consists of an aural comparison of two recorded voices and a visual comparison of graphic representations or "spectrograms" of the recorded voices. The spectrograms used in the visual comparison process are plotted by a machine known as a spectrograph. The spectrograph separates the sounds of a voice into elements of time, frequency and intensity and plots these variables on electronically sensitive paper. Since the spectrograms of the voice of a person often vary over time and under a variety of conditions and circumstances, the accuracy of the spectrogram voice identification process is largely dependent on the ability, experience and judgmental consistency of the examiner. There is no dispute that for most of the 20th century the sound spectrograph has been widely resorted to for the analysis and classification of human speech sounds, but it had not been used to identify individual human voices until the early 1960's when Lawrence Kersta, a scientist with the Bell Telephone Laboratories, undertook such projects. Thereafter, Dr. Tosi conducted a number of significant experiments in individual voice identification with the use of the speech spectrograph. The publication in 1971 and 1972 of the results of these experiments and expert testimony given in cases by Dr. Tosi and his associates have induced many courts to allow as evidence individual voice identifications made by use of speech spectrographs.

Defendant argues that speech spectrograph voice identification rests on new developments in the application of scientific principles and therefore its admissibility as evidence should be governed by a special standard, as set forth in Frye v. United States, 54 App. D.C. 46, 47, 293 F. 1013, 1014 (1923):

> "Just when a scientific principle or discovery crosses the line between the experimental and demonstrable stages is difficult to define. Somewhere in this twilight zone the evidential force of the principle must be recognized, and while courts will go a long way in admitting expert testimony deduced from a well-recognized scientific principle or discovery, the thing from which the deduction is made must be sufficiently established to have gained general acceptance in the particular field in which it belongs."

Prior to the adoption of the Maine Rules of Evidence in 1976, the law of Maine was unclear about the evidentiary rules governing the admissibility of evidence involving the new ascertainment, or application, of scientific principles. In State v. Knight, 43 Me. 11, 133, 134 (1857), the Court upheld the admissibility of scientific testimony as to the properties and appearance of human blood and animal blood. *Knight* gave the following rationale:

> The history of the development of scientific principles by actual experiments, within a few of the last years, [shows] us that many things which were once

regarded generally as incredible, are now admitted universally to be established facts. And as long as the existence of facts, which are the result of experiments, made by those versed in the department of science to which they pertain, are received as evidence, it would be legally erroneous for the court to determine that the absurdity of such facts was so great as to require their exclusion."

(43 Me., at 133, 134)

It is questionable from this language whether *Knight* was suggesting a special standard, such as is stated in *Frye*, supra, to govern the admissibility of expert testimony resting on newly ascertained, or applied, scientific principles. More recently, this Court may have given stronger indication of following the *Frye* rule in regard to evidence of the results of lie detector or polygraph tests. Holding polygraph evidence generally inadmissible, this Court in State v. Casale, 150 Me. 310, 320, 110 A.2d 588 (1954) resorted to language contained in the Nebraska opinion in Boeche v. State, 151 Neb. 368, 37 N.W.2d 593, 597 (1949), as follows:

"'It is apparent from the foregoing authorities that the scientific principle involved in the use of such polygraph has not yet gone beyond the experimental and reached the demonstrable stage, and that it has not yet received general scientific acceptance.'"

. . . The reference to a special standard of admissibility in *Casale*, however, was occasioned by the peculiarly special nature of lie detector tests as evidence. Lie detector evidence directly and pervasively impinges upon that function which is so uniquely the prerogative of the jury as fact-finder: to decide the credibility of witnesses. The admissibility of lie detector evidence therefore poses the serious danger that a mechanical device, rather than the judgment of the jury, will decide credibility. State v. Casale, 150 Me. 310, 320, 110 A.2d 588 (1954). For this reason, it remains questionable whether this Court by its language in *Casale* was purporting to establish a specially restrictive standard regarding the admissibility of *any* type of expert testimony which may rest on new, or new applications of, scientific principles.

The Maine Rules of Evidence adopted in 1976 do not purport to establish a special standard to govern the admissibility of testimony involving newly ascertained, or applied, scientific principles. Under the Rules of Evidence all "relevant" evidence is admissible

"except as limited by constitutional requirements or as otherwise provided by statute or by . . . rules applicable in the courts of this state."

Rule 402, M.R.Evid.

In Rule 702, specific reference is made to the admissibility of scientific testimony:

"If scientific, technical, or other specialized knowledge will assist the trier of fact to understand the evidence or to determine a fact in issue, a witness qualified as an expert by knowledge, skill, experience, training, or education, may testify thereto in the form of an opinion or otherwise."

As also potentially affecting a case of this nature, Rule 403 provides a general limitation on the admissibility of relevant evidence:

"Although relevant, evidence may be excluded if its probative value is substantially outweighed by the danger of unfair prejudice, confusion of the issues, or misleading the jury, or by considerations of undue delay, waste of time, or needless presentation of cumulative evidence."

Defendant's argument relies on the fact that the Rules of Evidence do not deal *specifically* with the admissibility problem as it may arise by virtue of newness in the development, or application, of scientific principles. Defendant asks us to fill this gap by establishing an additional precondition of admissibility as applicable *specially* to the situation in which proffered expert testimony will rest on a new ascertainment, or new application, of scientific principles — this further condition to be that there must be "general acceptance" of such newly discovered scientific principle, or new application of scientific principle, in the relevant scientific field.

We refuse to take the course for which defendant argues. We believe it would be at odds with the fundamental philosophy of our Rules of Evidence, as revealed more particularly in Rules 402 and 702, generally favoring the *admissibility* of expert testimony whenever it is relevant and can be of assistance to the trier of fact.[4] As stated in McCormick on Evidence §203 at 491 (2d ed. 1972):

"'General scientific acceptance' is a proper condition for taking *judicial notice* of scientific *facts*, but not a criterion for the *admissibility* of scientific *evidence*. Any relevant conclusions which are supported by a qualified expert witness should be received unless there are other reasons for exclusion. Particularly, probative value may be overborne by the familiar dangers of prejudicing or misleading the jury, and undue consumption of time." (emphasis supplied)

In accordance with the provisions, and basic spirit, of our Rules of Evidence in regard to the admissibility of expert testimony, we conclude

___

4. We reach this conclusion, too, because of the difficulties experienced by courts in applying the *Frye* rule. As explained in McCormick on Evidence §203 at 490 (2d ed. 1972): "The difficulty of determining how to distinguish scientific evidence from other expert testimony, of deciding what is the particular field of science to which the evidence belongs, and of settling what is general acceptance, has led to an application of the . . . [*Frye*] test which is highly selective, although not enlightening as to its details."

that there is no justifiable distinction in principle arising because such expert testimony may happen to involve newly ascertained or newly applied scientific principles. The controlling criteria regarding the admissibility of expert testimony, so long as the proffered expert is qualified and probative value is not substantially outweighed by the factors mentioned in Rule 403, are whether in the sound judgment of the presiding Justice the testimony to be given is relevant and will assist the trier of fact to understand the evidence or to determine a fact in issue.

In particular cases where the expert testimony proffered rests on newly ascertained, or applied, scientific principles, a stronger showing may become necessary before the presiding Justice is satisfied that the preconditions of admissibility, in terms of relevance and helpfulness to the fact-finder, have been met. Thus, in the particular circumstances of a given case the presiding Justice may see fit to place greater emphasis on the consideration whether or not the scientific matters involved in the proffered testimony have been generally accepted or conform to a generally accepted explanatory theory. Cf. United States v. Baller, 519 F.2d 463, 466 (4th Cir. 1975) and United States v. Brown, 557 F.2d 541, 556 (6th Cir. 1977). The Justice may believe this appropriate either (1) to avoid prejudice which might arise because the assertion that the principle, or technique, has a "scientific" basis may import an objectivity which could unduly influence the jury as a lay fact-finder or (2) to assist the presiding Justice in his responsibility to determine relevance, within the definition of Rule 401 M.R.Evid., i.e., whether the proffered testimony is likely to make the existence of any fact or consequence more probable or less probable than it would be without the evidence.

This, however, is not the same as saying, as does the *Frye* rule, that the presiding Justice is *bound* by an additional, *independently controlling* standard which exists over and above relevance (Rule 401 M.R.Evid.) and the capability of the expert testimony to assist the trier of fact (Rule 702 M.R.Evid.). On the approach we adopt the presiding Justice will be allowed a latitude, which the *Frye* rule denies, to hold admissible in a particular case proffered evidence involving newly ascertained, or applied, scientific principles which have not yet achieved general acceptance in whatever might be thought to be the applicable scientific community, if a showing has been made which satisfies the Justice that the proffered evidence is sufficiently reliable to be held relevant. Cf. United States v. Franks, 511 F.2d 25, 33 (6th Cir. 1975).

With the criteria of admissibility thus decided, we address whether the presiding Justice committed error, here, by admitting the spectrograph testimony in evidence.

Dr. Tosi's testimony related to the nature of the human voice and the spectrograph process, the results of his experiments and the reliability of the spectrograph voice identification process. Simultaneously, however, Dr. Tosi was careful to explain that the spectrograph voice identification process is not infallible. According to Dr. Tosi, the reliability of the spectrograph voice identification method is highly dependent on the experience, ability and judgment of the person who makes the spectrograph comparisons.

Testimony was also given by acoustical scientists who oppose the use of spectrograph as evidence. In their view, (1) the examiners of spectrographic data cannot maintain firm and stable criteria of decision; (2) they may tend to relax their threshold standards for making a "positive identification", in particular where only a single sample voice exemplar is presented for comparison with the known voice; and (3) the spectrograph experiments generally have not accounted for many variables such as telephone recordings, disguised voices, noncontemporaneous recordings, background noise and voices of persons under psychological stress.

Yet, none of the acoustical scientists who testified questioned as facts that recordings of different human voices vary more in time, frequency and intensity than recordings of the same voice and that the spectrograph can accurately plot these variables. The opposition experts focused only on the difficulties of comparison and the exercise of judgment and the failure of the spectrograph experiments to account for many real world variables.

In view of the evidence of reliability presented by Dr. Tosi, we conclude that it was not error for the presiding Justice to admit the expert voice identification testimony in this case. The Justice was justified in finding that the spectrograph principle was sufficiently reliable to qualify as "relevant" within the definition of Rule 401 M.R.Evid., and that the qualified expert testimony based on it could be of assistance to the jury as fact-finder.

The issue raised by defendant regarding the application of the spectrograph process to forensic situations concerns the weight, not the admissibility, of the evidence[5] and was exclusively for the jury's determination.

5. A number of courts in other jurisdictions have admitted spectrograph evidence either on the basis of the general acceptability test of *Frye* or on the basis of some type of reliability standard. See, e.g., United States v. Jenkins, 525 F.2d 819 (6th Cir. 1975) United States v. Baller, 519 F.2d 463 (4th Cir. 1975); United States v. Franks, 511 F.2d 25 (6th Cir. 1975). United States v. Sample, 378 F. Supp. 44 (E.D. Pa.1974) (probation revocation proceeding); United States v. Wright, 17 U.S.C.M.A. 183, 37 C.M.R. 447 (1967); Hodo v. Superior Court, 30 Cal.App.3d 778, 106 Cal.Rptr. 547 (1973); Worley v. State, 263 So.2d 613 (Fla.App.1972); Alea v. State, 265 So.2d 96 (Fla.App.1972); Reed v. State, 35 Md.App. 472, 372 A.2d 243 (1977); Commonwealth v. Lykus, 367 Mass., 191, 327 N.E.2d 671 (1975); State ex rel. Trimble v. Hedman, 291 Minn., 442, 192 N.W.2d 432 (1971) (probable cause hearing); People v. Rogers, 86 Misc.2d 868, 385 N.Y.S.2d 228 (1976); State v. Olderman, 44 Ohio App.2d 130, 336 N.E.2d 442 (1975). Some courts, relying primarily on the *Frye* rule, have excluded spectrograph evidence because of the substantial opposition to it of many acoustical scientists. See, e.g., United States v. Addison, 162 U.S. App.D.C. 199, 498 F.2d 741 (1974) (but see United States v. McDaniel, 176 U.S. App.D.C. 60, 538 F.2d 408 (1976) where the Court noted that it may be time to reexamine *Addison*); People v. Kelly, 17 Cal.3d 24, 130 Cal.Rptr. 144, 549 P.2d 1240

The entry is:
Appeal denied. Judgment affirmed.

NICHOLS, J., (Concurring in the judgment)

I concur in the judgment. I cannot, however, join in the opinion of the Court this day because I believe it retreats too far from the position often taken — and well taken — by this Court that before we recognize the evidential force of new applications of scientific principles, these should have attained general acceptance in the scientific community.

This standard of "general acceptance" was recognized by the Court of Appeals of the District of Columbia in Frye v. United States, 54 App.D.C. 46, 47, 293 F. 1013, 1014 (1923), in which a systolic blood pressure deception test was held to have been properly excluded from evidence.

When our Court had occasion to reject evidence of a polygraph test in State v. Casale, 150 Me. 310, 320, 110 A.2d 588 (1954); it quoted from the opinion of the Nebraska court in Boeche v. State, 151 Neb. 368, 37 N.W.2d 593 (1949). There the Nebraska court had expressly relied upon *Frye.*

When eight years later our Court in State v. Mottram, 158 Me. 325, 329, 184 A.2d 225 (1962) reaffirmed that evidence of the results of "lie detector tests" was inadmissible, the lack of general acceptance of the results of such tests was again the determinative factor.

Even more recently when in State v. Mower, Me., 314 A.2d 840, 841 (1974) our Court ruled that evidence of the defendant's willingness to take a polygraph test was properly excluded, it reiterated the language of *Mottram.*

Such was the state of the law in this jurisdiction when in 1976 the Maine Rules of Evidence, modeled after the Federal Rules of Evidence, were promulgated. Rule 702 M.R.Evid., relates generally to testimony by experts without addressing specifically the question of new application of scientific principles. This rule was regarded by the Advisers, not as relaxing the standards of admissibility, but as declaratory of Maine law. Advisers' Note, M.R.Evid. 702. A rule intended as a codification of existing law, however, is today being employed to change that law.

We should continue to adhere to the *Frye* standard. It is not merely because such has been the law in this jurisdiction. It is not merely because the *Frye* standard continues to be applied in many federal courts notwithstanding the promulgation of Federal Rules of Evidence. United States v. McDaniel, 176 U.S.App.D.C. 60, 65, 538 F.2d 408, 413 (1976); United States v. Brown, 557 F.2d 541, 557 (6th Cir., 1977); United States

---

(1976); People v. Law, 40 Cal.App.3d 69, 114 Cal.Rptr. 708 (1974) (disguised voices); People v. King, 266 Cal.App.2d 437, 72 Cal.Rptr. 478 (1968); People v. Tobey, 401 Mich. 141, 257 N.W.2d 537 (1977); State v. Cary, 56 N.J. 16, 264 A.2d 209 (1970) (but see State v. Andretta, 61 N.J. 544, 296 A.2d 644 (1972) where the Court suggested that reconsideration of *Cary* was appropriate in view of new developments in speech spectrography); Commonwealth v. Topa, 471 Pa. 223, 369 A.2d 1277 (1977).

v. Kilgus, 571 F.2d 508 (9th Cir., 1978). Rather, it is because there are good reasons why each new scientific technique should not become the basis for expert testimony as quickly as the expert can persuade the court that it will assist the trier of fact to understand the evidence or to determine a fact in issue.

To adhere to the *Frye* standard of requiring general — but not universal — acceptance within the scientific community will enhance the fairness of the trial, especially in criminal cases. It will avoid the difficulty of rebutting the expert's opinion except by other experts or by cross-examination grounded upon a thorough acquaintance with the novel application of scientific principles. This burden of rebuttal is generally borne in these criminal cases by defendants without the economic means to marshal scientific witnesses for a battle of the experts.

As was observed in United States v. Brown, supra, 557 F.2d at 556, the fate of a defendant should not hang on his ability to successfully rebut scientific evidence when the expert may be testifying upon the basis of an unproved hypothesis arrived at in an isolated experiment. It is far better that the expert first expose his new ideas to the critical review of his peers. The courtroom, after all, is not a laboratory. Id.

Furthermore, adherence to the *Frye* standard would result in more uniformity within our trial courts than if scientific evidence may come in whenever the trial judge decides it is relevant and concludes it will help to determine a factual issue.

Moreover, the litigants would be protected by a clearer standard of review.

Finally, it would avoid the risk that, by announcing a lesser standard, the door may inadvertently be opened to pseudo-scientific expertise.

As acknowledged by the majority, a number of courts have admitted spectrographic evidence without abandoning the *Frye* standard. E.g., United States v. Baller, 519 F.2d 463, 465-466 (4th Cir.) cert. den. 423 U.S. 1019, 96 S. Ct. 456, 46 L. Ed. 2d 391 (1975); Commonwealth v. Lykus, 367 Mass. 191, 327 N.E.2d 671, 674-676 (1975). There is sufficient basis in those cases to uphold the admission of spectrograph evidence in the trial of the instant case without abandoning the important protections which *Frye* affords.

. . . For our Court as well, I submit that such adherence to the *Frye* standard would be the better course.

———————

In criminal cases does the constitutional guarantee of due process erect some kind of minimum standard of quality of expert testimony used against the defendant? Here is the answer of the United States Supreme Court.

BAREFOOT v. ESTELLE
463 U.S. 880 (1983)

Justice WHITE delivered the opinion of the Court.

We have two questions before us in this case: whether the District Court erred on the merits in rejecting the petition for habeas corpus filed by petitioner, and whether the Court of Appeals for the Fifth Circuit correctly denied a stay of execution of the death penalty pending appeal of the District Court's judgment.

I

On November 14, 1978, petitioner was convicted of the capital murder of a police officer in Bell County, Tex. A separate sentencing hearing before the same jury was then held to determine whether the death penalty should be imposed. Under Tex. Code Crim. Proc. Ann., Art. 37.071 (Vernon 1981),[6] two special questions were to be submitted to the jury: whether the conduct causing death was "committed deliberately and with reasonable expectation that the death of the deceased or another would result"; and whether "there is a probability that the defendant would commit criminal acts of violence that would constitute a continuing threat to society." The State introduced into evidence petitioner's prior convictions and his reputation for lawlessness. The State also called two psychiatrists, John Holbrook and James Grigson, who, in response to hypothetical questions, testified that petitioner would probably commit further acts of violence and represent a continuing threat to society. The jury answered both of the questions put to them in the affirmative, a result which required the imposition of the death penalty.

On appeal to the Texas Court of Criminal Appeals, petitioner urged, among other submissions, that the use of psychiatrists at the punish-

---

6. Texas Code Crim. Proc. Ann., Art. 37.071 (Vernon 1981), provides:

"(a) Upon a finding that the defendant is guilty of a capital offense, the court shall conduct a separate sentencing proceeding to determine whether the defendant shall be sentenced to death or life imprisonment. The proceeding shall be conducted in the trial court before the trial jury as soon as practicable. In the proceeding, evidence may be presented as to any matter that the court deems relevant to sentence. This subsection shall not be construed to authorize the introduction of any evidence secured in violation of the Constitution of the United States or of the State of Texas. The state and the defendant or his counsel shall be permitted to present argument for or against sentence of death.

"(b) On conclusion of the presentation of the evidence, the court shall submit the following issues to the jury:

"(1) whether the conduct of the defendant that caused the death of the deceased was committed deliberately and with the reasonable expectation that the death of the deceased or another would result;

"(2) whether there is a probability that the defendant would commit criminal acts of violence that would constitute a continuing threat to society; and

"(3) if raised by the evidence, whether the conduct of the defendant in killing the deceased was unreasonable in response to the provocation, if any, by the deceased.

"(c) The state must prove each issue submitted beyond a reasonable doubt, and the jury shall return a special verdict of 'yes' or 'no' on each issue submitted."

The question specified in (b)(3) was not submitted to the jury.

ment hearing to make predictions about petitioner's future conduct was unconstitutional because psychiatrists, individually and as a class, are not competent to predict future dangerousness. Hence, their predictions are so likely to produce erroneous sentences that their use violated the Eighth and Fourteenth Amendments. It was also urged, in any event, that permitting answers to hypothetical questions by psychiatrists who had not personally examined petitioner was constitutional error. The court rejected all of these contentions and affirmed the conviction and sentence on March 12, 1980, Barefoot v. State, 596 S. W. 2d 875; rehearing was denied on April 30, 1980.

[Discussion of other issues omitted]. . . .

III

Petitioner's merits submission is that his death sentence must be set aside because the Constitution of the United States barred the testimony of the two psychiatrists who testified against him at the punishment hearing. There are several aspects to this claim. First, it is urged that psychiatrists, individually and as a group, are incompetent to predict with an acceptable degree of reliability that a particular criminal will commit other crimes in the future and so represent a danger to the community. Second, it is said that in any event, psychiatrists should not be permitted to testify about future dangerousness in response to hypothetical questions and without having examined the defendant personally. Third, it is argued that in the particular circumstances of this case, the testimony of the psychiatrists was so unreliable that the sentence should be set aside. As indicated below, we reject each of these arguments.

A

The suggestion that no psychiatrist's testimony may be presented with respect to a defendant's future dangerousness is somewhat like asking us to disinvent the wheel. In the first place, it is contrary to our cases. If the likelihood of a defendant's committing further crimes is a constitutionally acceptable criterion for imposing the death penalty, which it is, Jurek v. Texas, 428 U.S. 262 (1976), and if it is not impossible for even a lay person sensibly to arrive at that conclusion, it makes little sense, if any, to submit that psychiatrists, out of the entire universe of persons who might have an opinion on the issue, would know so little about the subject that they should not be permitted to testify. In *Jurek*, seven Justices rejected the claim that it was impossible to predict future behavior and that dangerousness was therefore an invalid consideration in imposing the death penalty. Justices STEWART, POWELL, and STEVENS responded directly to the argument, id., at 274-276:

"It is, of course, not easy to predict future behavior. The fact that such a determination is difficult, however, does not mean that it cannot be made. Indeed,
prediction of future criminal conduct is an essential element in many of the
decisions rendered throughout our criminal justice system. The decision
whether to admit a defendant to bail, for instance, must often turn on a judge's
prediction of the defendant's future conduct. Any sentencing authority must
predict a convicted person's probable future conduct when it engages in the
process of determining what punishment to impose. For those sentenced to
prison, these same predictions must be made by parole authorities. The task that
a Texas jury must perform in answering the statutory question in issue is thus
basically no different from the task performed countless times each day throughout the American system of criminal justice. What is essential is that the jury have
before it all possible relevant information about the individual defendant whose
fate it must determine. Texas law clearly assures that all such evidence will be
adduced."

Although there was only lay testimony with respect to dangerousness
in *Jurek*, there was no suggestion by the Court that the testimony of
doctors would be inadmissible. To the contrary, the joint opinion announcing the judgment said that the jury should be presented with all
of the relevant information. Furthermore, in Estelle v. Smith, 451 U.S.
454, 473 (1981), in the face of a submission very similar to that presented in this case with respect to psychiatric testimony, we approvingly
repeated the above quotation from *Jurek* and went on to say that we
were in "no sense disapproving the use of psychiatric testimony bearing
on future dangerousness." See also California v. Ramos, post, at 1005-
1006, 1009-1010, n. 23; Gregg v. Georgia, 428 U.S. 153, 203-204 (1976)
(joint opinion) (desirable to allow open and far-ranging argument that
places as much information as possible before the jury).

Acceptance of petitioner's position that expert testimony about future dangerousness is far too unreliable to be admissible would immediately call into question those other contexts in which predictions of
future behavior are constantly made. For example, in O'Connor v. Don-
aldson, 422 U.S. 563, 576 (1975), we held that a nondangerous mental
hospital patient could not be held in confinement against his will. Later,
speaking about the requirements for civil commitments, we said:

"There may be factual issues in a commitment proceeding, but the factual aspects
represent only the beginning of the inquiry. Whether the individual is mentally
ill and dangerous to either himself or others and is in need of confined therapy
turns on the *meaning* of the facts which must be interpreted by expert psychiatrists and psychologists." Addington v. Texas, 441 U.S. 418, 429 (1979).

In the second place, the rules of evidence generally extant at the
federal and state levels anticipate that relevant, unprivileged evidence
should be admitted and its weight left to the factfinder, who would have
the benefit of cross-examination and contrary evidence by the opposing

party. Psychiatric testimony predicting dangerousness may be countered not only as erroneous in a particular case but also as generally so unreliable that it should be ignored. If the jury may make up its mind about future dangerousness unaided by psychiatric testimony, jurors should not be barred from hearing the views of the State's psychiatrists along with opposing views of the defendant's doctors.[5]

Third, petitioner's view mirrors the position expressed in the amicus brief of the American Psychiatric Association (APA). As indicated above, however, the same view was presented and rejected in Estelle v. Smith. We are no more convinced now that the view of the APA should be converted into a constitutional rule barring an entire category of expert testimony. We are not persuaded that such testimony is almost entirely unreliable and that the factfinder and the adversary system will not be competent to uncover, recognize, and take due account of its shortcomings.

The amicus does not suggest that there are not other views held by members of the Association or of the profession generally.[7] Indeed, as this case and others indicate, there are those doctors who are quite

5. In this case, no evidence was offered by petitioner at trial to contradict the testimony of Doctors Holbrook and Grigson. Nor is there a contention that, despite petitioner's claim of indigence, the court refused to provide an expert for petitioner. In cases of indigency, Texas law provides for the payment of $500 for "expenses incurred for purposes of investigation and expert testimony." Tex. Code Crim. Proc. Ann., Art. 26.05(d) (Vernon Supp. 1982).

7. At trial, Dr. Holbrook testified without contradiction that a psychiatrist could predict the future dangerousness of an individual, if given enough background information about the individual. Tr. of Trial (T. Tr.) 2072-2073. Dr. Grigson obviously held a similar view. See id., at 2110, 2134. At the District Court hearing on the habeas petition, the State called two expert witnesses, Dr. George Parker, a psychologist, and Dr. Richard Koons, a psychiatrist. Both of these doctors agreed that accurate predictions of future dangerousness can be made if enough information is provided; furthermore, they both deemed it highly likely that an individual fitting the characteristics of the one in the *Barefoot* hypothetical would commit future acts of violence. Tr. of Hearing (H. Tr.) 183-248.

Although Barefoot did not present any expert testimony at his trial, at the habeas hearing he called Dr. Fred Fason, a psychiatrist, and Dr. Wendell Dickerson, a psychologist. Dr. Fason did not dwell on the general ability of mental health professionals to predict future dangerousness. Instead, for the most part, he merely criticized the giving of a diagnosis based upon a hypothetical question, without an actual examination. He conceded that, if a medical student described a patient in the terms of the Barefoot hypothetical, his "highest order of suspicion," to the degree of 90%, would be that the patient had a sociopathic personality. Id., at 22. He insisted, however, that this was only an "initial impression," and that no doctor should give a firm "diagnosis" without a full examination and testing. Id., at 22, 29-30, 36. Dr. Dickerson, petitioner's other expert, was the only person to testify who suggested that no reliable psychiatric predictions of dangerousness could ever be made.

We are aware that many mental health professionals have questioned the usefulness of psychiatric predictions of future dangerousness in light of studies indicating that such predictions are often inaccurate. For example, at the habeas hearing, Dr. Dickerson, one of petitioner's expert witnesses, testified that psychiatric predictions of future dangerousness were wrong two out of three times. Id., at 97, 108. He conceded, however, that, despite the high error rate, one "excellently done" study had shown "some predictive validity for predicting violence." Id., at 96, 97. Dr. John Monahan, upon whom one of the State's experts relied as "the leading thinker on this issue," id., at 195, concluded that "the 'best' clinical research currently in existence indicates that *psychiatrists and psychologists are accurate in no more than one*

willing to testify at the sentencing hearing, who think, and will say, that
they know what they are talking about, and who expressly disagree with
the Association's point of view. Furthermore, their qualifications as experts are regularly accepted by the courts. If they are so obviously wrong
and should be discredited, there should be no insuperable problem in
doing so by calling members of the Association who are of that view and
who confidently assert that opinion in their amicus brief. Neither petitioner nor the Association suggests that psychiatrists are always wrong
with respect to future dangerousness, only most of the time. Yet the
submission is that this category of testimony should be excised entirely
from all trials. We are unconvinced, however, at least as of now, that the
adversary process cannot be trusted to sort out the reliable from the
unreliable evidence and opinion about future dangerousness, particularly when the convicted felon has the opportunity to present his own
side of the case.

We are unaware of and have not been cited to any case, federal or
state, that has adopted the categorical views of the Association.[8] Certainly it was presented and rejected at every stage of the present proceeding. After listening to the two schools of thought testify not only
generally but also about the petitioner and his criminal record, the
District Court found:

"The majority of psychiatric experts agree that where there is a pattern of repetitive assaultive and violent conduct, the accuracy of psychiatric predictions of

---

*out of three predictions of violent behavior over a several-year period among institutionalized populations
that had both committed violence in the past . . . and who were diagnosed as mentally ill."* J. Monahan,
The Clinical Prediction of Violent Behavior 47-49 (1981) (emphasis in original). However,
although Dr. Monahan originally believed that it was impossible to predict violent behavior,
by the time he had completed his monograph, he felt that "there may be circumstances in
which prediction is both empirically possible and ethically appropriate," and he hoped that
his work would improve the appropriateness and accuracy of clinical predictions. Id., at v.
   All of these professional doubts about the usefulness of psychiatric predictions can be called
to the attention of the jury. Petitioner's entire argument, as well as that of Justice BLACKMUN's
dissent, is founded on the premise that a jury will not be able to separate the wheat from the
chaff. We do not share in this low evaluation of the adversary process.
   8. Petitioner relies on People v. Murtishaw, 29 Cal. 3d 733, 631 P. 2d 446 (1981). There
the California Supreme Court held that in light of the general unreliability of such testimony,
admitting medical testimony concerning future dangerousness was error in the context of a
sentencing proceeding under the California capital punishment statutes. The court observed
that "the testimony of [the psychiatrist was] not relevant to any of the listed factors" which the
jury was to consider in deciding whether to impose the death penalty. Id., at 771-772, 631 P.
2d, at 469. The court distinguished cases, however, where "the trier of fact is required by
statute to determine whether a person is 'dangerous,'" in which event "expert prediction,
unreliable though it may be, is often the only evidence available to assist the trier of fact."
Ibid. Furthermore, the court acknowledged that "despite the recognized general unreliability
of predictions concerning future violence, it may be possible for a party in a particular case
to show that a reliable prediction is possible. . . . A reliable prediction might also be conceivable
if the defendant had exhibited a long-continued pattern of criminal violence such that any
knowledgeable psychiatrist would anticipate future violence." Id., at 774, 631 P. 2d, at 470.
Finally, we note that the court did not in any way indicate that its holding was based on
constitutional grounds.

future dangerousness dramatically rises. The accuracy of this conclusion is re-affirmed by the expert medical testimony in this case at the evidentiary hearing. . . . It would appear that Petitioner's complaint is not the diagnosis and prediction made by Drs. Holbrook and Grigson at the punishment phase of his trial, but that Dr. Grigson expressed extreme certainty in his diagnosis and prediction. . . . In any event, the differences among the experts were quantitative, not qualitative. The differences in opinion go to the weight [of the evidence] and not the admissibility of such testimony. . . . Such disputes are within the province of the jury to resolve. Indeed, it is a fundamental premise of our entire system of criminal jurisprudence that the purpose of the jury is to sort out the true testimony from the false, the important matters from the unimportant matters, and, when called upon to do so, to give greater credence to one party's expert witnesses than another's. Such matters occur routinely in the American judicial system, both civil and criminal." App. 13-14 (footnote omitted).

Petitioner also relies on White v. Estelle, 554 F. Supp. 851 (SD Tex. 1982). The court in that case did no more than express "serious reservations" about the use of psychiatric predictions based on hypotheticals in instances where the doctor has had no previous contact with the defendant. Id., at 858. The actual holding of the case, which is totally irrelevant to the issues here, was that the testimony of a doctor who *had* interviewed the defendant should have been excluded because, prior to the interview, the defendant had not been given *Miranda* warnings or an opportunity to consult with his attorney, as required by Estelle v. Smith, 451 U.S. 454 (1981).

We agree with the District Court, as well as with the Court of Appeals' judges who dealt with the merits of the issue and agreed with the District Court in this respect.

B

Whatever the decision may be about the use of psychiatric testimony, in general, on the issue of future dangerousness, petitioner urges that such testimony must be based on personal examination of the defendant and may not be given in response to hypothetical questions. We disagree. Expert testimony, whether in the form of an opinion based on hypothetical questions or otherwise, is commonly admitted as evidence where it might help the factfinder do its assigned job. As the Court said long ago in Spring Co. v. Edgar, 99 U.S. 645, 657 (1879):

"Men who have made questions of skill or science the object of their particular study, says Phillips, are competent to give their opinions in evidence. Such opinions ought, in general, to be deduced from facts that are not disputed, or from facts given in evidence; but the author proceeds to say that they need not be founded upon their own personal knowledge of such facts, but may be founded upon the statement of facts proved in the case. Medical men, for example, may give their opinions not only as to the state of a patient they may have visited, or as to the cause of the death of a person whose body they have examined, or as to the nature of the instruments which caused the wounds they have examined, but also in cases where they have not themselves seen the patient, and have only heard the symptoms and particulars of his state detailed by other witnesses at the trial. Judicial tribunals have in many instances held that medical works are not admissible, but they everywhere hold that men skilled in science, art, or particular trades may give their opinions as witnesses in matters pertaining to their professional calling."

See also Dexter v. Hall, 15 Wall. 9, 26-27 (1873); Forsyth v. Doolittle, 120 U.S. 73, 78 (1887); Bram v. United States, 168 U.S. 532, 568-569 (1897).

Today, in the federal system, Federal Rules of Evidence 702-706 provide for the testimony of experts. The Advisory Committee Notes touch on the particular objections to hypothetical questions, but none of these caveats lends any support to petitioner's constitutional arguments. Furthermore, the Texas Court of Criminal Appeals could find no fault with the mode of examining the two psychiatrists under Texas law:

> "The trial court did not err by permitting the doctors to testify on the basis of the hypothetical question. The use of hypothetical questions in the examination of expert witnesses is a well-established practice. 2 C. McCormick and R. Ray, Texas Evidence, §1402 (2d ed. 1956). That the experts had not examined appellant went to the weight of their testimony, not to its admissability."

596 S. W. 2d, at 887.

Like the Court of Criminal Appeals, the District Court, and the Court of Appeals, we reject petitioner's constitutional arguments against the use of hypothetical questions. Although cases such as this involve the death penalty, we perceive no constitutional barrier to applying the ordinary rules of evidence governing the use of expert testimony.

C

As we understand petitioner, he contends that even if the use of hypothetical questions in predicting future dangerousness is acceptable as a general rule, the use made of them in his case violated his right to due process of law. For example, petitioner insists that the doctors should not have been permitted to give an opinion on the ultimate issue before the jury, particularly when the hypothetical questions were phrased in terms of petitioner's own conduct;[9] that the hypothetical

---

9. There is support for this view in our cases, United States v. Spaulding, 293 U.S. 498, 506 (1935), but it does not appear from what the Court there said that the rule was rooted in the

questions referred to controverted facts;[10] and that the answers to the questions were so positive as to be assertions of fact and not opinion.[11] These claims of misuse of the hypothetical questions, as well as others, were rejected by the Texas courts, and neither the District Court nor the Court of Appeals found any constitutional infirmity in the application of the Texas Rules of Evidence in this particular case. We agree.

In sum, we affirm the judgment of the District Court. There is no doubt that the psychiatric testimony increased the likelihood that petitioner would be sentenced to death, but this fact does not make that evidence inadmissible, any more than it would with respect to other relevant evidence against any defendant in a criminal case. At bottom, to agree with petitioner's basic position would seriously undermine and in effect overrule Jurek v. Texas, 428 U.S. 262 (1976). Petitioner conceded as much at oral argument. Tr. of Oral Arg. 23-25. We are not inclined, however, to overturn the decision in that case.

The judgment of the District Court is
Affirmed.

[Dissent by Justice MARSHALL omitted]

Justice BLACKMUN, with whom Justice BRENNAN and Justice MARSHALL join as to Parts I-IV, dissenting.

. . .

Last, the prosecution called Doctors Holbrook and Grigson, whose testimony extended over more than half the hearing. Neither had examined Barefoot or requested the opportunity to examine him. In the presence of the jury, and over defense counsel's objection, each was qualified as an expert psychiatrist witness. Doctor Holbrook detailed at length his training and experience as a psychiatrist, which included a position as chief of psychiatric services at the Texas Department of Corrections. He explained that he had previously performed many "criminal evaluations," . . . and that he subsequently took the post at the

---

Constitution. In any event, we note that the Advisory Committee Notes to Rule 704 of the Federal Rules of Evidence state as follows:

> "The basic approach to opinions, lay and expert, in these rules is to admit them when helpful to the trier of fact. In order to render this approach fully effective and to allay any doubt on the subject, the so-called 'ultimate issue' rule is abolished by the instant rule." 28 U. S. C. App., p. 571.

10. Nothing prevented petitioner from propounding a hypothetical to the doctors based on his own version of the facts. On cross-examination, both Drs. Holbrook and Grigson readily admitted that their opinions might change if some of the assumptions in the State's hypothetical were not true.

11. The more certain a State's expert is about his prediction, the easier it is for the defendant to impeach him. For example, in response to Dr. Grigson's assertion that he was "100% sure" that an individual with the characteristics of the one in the hypothetical would commit acts of violence in the future, Dr. Fason testified at the habeas hearing that if a doctor claimed to be 100% sure of something without examining the patient, "we would kick him off the staff of the hospital for his arrogance." H. Tr. 48. Similar testimony could have been presented at Barefoot's trial, but was not.

Department of Corrections to observe the subjects of these evaluations so that he could "be certain those opinions that [he] had were accurate at the time of trial and pretrial." . . . He then informed the jury that it was "within [his] *capacity as a doctor of psychiatry* to predict the future dangerousness of an individual within a *reasonable medical certainty,*" . . . (emphasis supplied), and that he could give "*an expert medical opinion* that would be *within reasonable psychiatric certainty* as to whether or not that individual would be dangerous to the degree that there would be a probability that that person would commit criminal acts of violence in the future that would constitute a continuing threat to society," . . . (emphasis supplied).

Doctor Grigson also detailed his training and medical experience, which, he said, included examination of "between thirty and forty thousand individuals," including 8,000 charged with felonies, and at least 300 charged with murder. . . . He testified that with enough information he would be able to "give *a medical opinion within reasonable psychiatric certainty* as to the psychological or psychiatric makeup of an individual," . . . (emphasis supplied), and that this skill was "particular to the field of psychiatry and not to the average layman." . . .

Each psychiatrist then was given an extended hypothetical question asking him to assume as true about Barefoot the four prior convictions for nonviolent offenses, the bad reputation for being law-abiding in various communities, the New Mexico escape, the events surrounding the murder for which he was on trial and, in Doctor Grigson's case, the New Mexico arrest. On the basis of the hypothetical question, Doctor Holbrook diagnosed Barefoot "within a reasonable [psychiatric] certainty," as a "criminal sociopath." . . . He testified that he knew of no treatment that could change this condition, and that the condition would not change for the better but "may become accelerated" in the next few years. . . . Finally, Doctor Holbrook testified that, "within reasonable psychiatric certainty, " there was "a probability that the Thomas A. Barefoot in that hypothetical will commit criminal acts of violence in the future that would constitute a continuing threat to society," and that his opinion would not change if the "society" at issue was that within Texas prisons rather than society outside prison. . . .

Doctor Grigson then testified that, on the basis of the hypothetical question, he could diagnose Barefoot "within reasonable psychiatric certainty" as an individual with "a fairly classical, typical, sociopathic personality disorder." . . . He placed Barefoot in the "most severe category" of sociopaths (on a scale of one to ten, Barefoot was "above ten"), and stated that there was no known cure for the condition. . . . Finally, Doctor Grigson testified that whether Barefoot was in society at large or in a prison society there was a *"one hundred percent and absolute"* chance that Barefoot would commit future acts of criminal violence that would constitute a continuing threat to society. . . . (emphasis supplied).

On cross-examination, defense counsel questioned the psychiatrists about studies demonstrating that psychiatrists' predictions of future dangerousness are inherently unreliable. Doctor Holbrook indicated his familiarity with many of these studies but stated that he disagreed with their conclusions. Doctor Grigson stated that he was not familiar with most of these studies, and that their conclusions were accepted by only a "small minority group" of psychiatrists—"[it's] not the American Psychiatric Association that believes that." . . .

After an hour of deliberation, the jury answered "yes" to the two statutory questions, and Thomas Barefoot was sentenced to death.

II

A

The American Psychiatric Association (APA), participating in this case as amicus curiae, informs us that "[the] unreliability of psychiatric predictions of long-term future dangerousness is by now an established fact within the profession." . . . The APA's best estimate is that *two out of three* predictions of long-term future violence made by psychiatrists are wrong, . . . The Court does not dispute this proposition, . . . and indeed it could not do so; the evidence is overwhelming. For example, the APA's Draft Report of the Task Force on the Role of Psychiatry in the Sentencing Process (1983) (Draft Report) states that "[considerable] evidence has been accumulated by now to demonstrate that long-term prediction by psychiatrists of future violence is an extremely inaccurate process." . . . John Monahan, recognized as "the leading thinker on this issue" even by the State's expert witness at Barefoot's federal habeas corpus hearing, . . . , concludes that "the 'best' clinical research currently in existence indicates that psychiatrists and psychologists are accurate in no more than one out of three predictions of violent behavior," even among populations of individuals who are mentally ill and have committed violence in the past. . . . Neither the Court nor the State of Texas has cited a single reputable scientific source contradicting the unanimous conclusion of professionals in this field that psychiatric predictions of long-term future violence are wrong more often than they are right.

The APA also concludes, . . . as do researchers that have studied the issue, that psychiatrists simply have no expertise in predicting long-term future dangerousness. A layman with access to relevant statistics can do at least as well and possibly better; psychiatric training is not relevant to the factors that validly can be employed to make such predictions, and psychiatrists consistently err on the side of overpredicting violence. Thus, while Doctors Grigson and Holbrook were presented by the State and by self-proclamation as experts at predicting future dangerousness, the scientific literature makes crystal clear that they had no expertise whatever. Despite their claims that they were able to predict Barefoot's future behavior "within reasonable psychiatric certainty," or to a "one hundred percent and absolute" certainty, there was in fact no more than a one in three chance that they were correct. . . . A death sentence cannot rest on highly dubious predictions secretly based on a factual foundation of hearsay and pure conjecture. . . .

B

It is impossible to square admission of this purportedly scientific but actually baseless testimony with the Constitution's paramount concern for reliability in capital sentencing. Death is a permissible punishment in Texas only if the jury finds beyond a reasonable doubt that there is a probability the defendant will commit future acts of criminal violence. The admission of unreliable psychiatric predictions of future violence, offered with unabashed claims of "reasonable medical certainty" or "absolute" professional reliability, creates an intolerable danger that death sentences will be imposed erroneously. . . .

. . . The Court all but admits the obviously prejudicial impact of the testimony of Doctors Grigson and Holbrook; granting that their absolute claims were more likely to be wrong than right, . . . the Court states that "[there] is no doubt that the psychiatric testimony increased the likelihood that petitioner would be sentenced to death," ante, at 905.

Indeed, unreliable scientific evidence is widely acknowledged to be prejudicial. The reasons for this are manifest. "The major danger of scientific evidence is its potential to mislead the jury; an aura of scientific infallibility may shroud the evidence and thus lead the jury to accept it without critical scrutiny." Giannelli, The Admissibility of Novel Scientific Evidence: Frye v. United States, a Half-Century Later, 80 Colum. L. Rev. 1197, 1237 (1980) (Giannelli, Scientific Evidence).[11] Where the public

11. There can be no dispute about this obvious proposition:

"Scientific evidence impresses lay jurors. They tend to assume it is more accurate and objective than lay testimony. A juror who thinks of scientific evidence visualizes instruments capable of amazingly precise measurement, of findings arrived at by dispassionate scientific tests. In short, in the mind of the typical lay juror, a scientific witness has a special aura of credibility." Imwinkelried, Evidence Law and Tactics for the Proponents of Scientific Evidence, in Scientific and Expert Evidence 33, 37 (E. Imwinkelried ed. 1981).

See 22 C. Wright & K. Graham, Federal Practice and Procedure §5217, p. 295 (1978) ("Scientific . . . evidence has great potential for misleading the jury. The low probative worth can often be concealed in the jargon of some expert . . ."). This danger created by use of scientific evidence frequently has been recognized by the courts. Speaking specifically of psychiatric predictions of future dangerousness similar to those at issue, one District Court has observed that when such a prediction "is proffered by a witness bearing the title of 'Doctor,' its impact on the jury is much greater than if it were not masquerading as something it is not." White v. Estelle, 554 F. Supp. 851, 858 (SD Tex. 1982). See Note—People v. Murtishaw: Applying the Frye Test to Psychiatric Predictions of Dangerousness in Capital Cases, 70 Calif. L. Rev. 1069,

holds an exaggerated opinion of the accuracy of scientific testimony, the prejudice is likely to be indelible. . . . There is little question that psychiatrists are perceived by the public as having a special expertise to predict dangerousness, a perception based on psychiatrists' study of mental disease. . . . It is this perception that the State in Barefoot's case sought to exploit. Yet mental disease is not correlated with violence, ... and the stark fact is that no such expertise exists. Moreover, psychiatrists, it is said, sometimes attempt to perpetuate this illusion of expertise, . . . and Doctors Grigson and Holbrook—who purported to be able to predict future dangerousness "within reasonable psychiatric certainty," or absolutely—present extremely disturbing examples of this tendency. The problem is not uncommon. . . . .

III

A

Despite its recognition that the testimony at issue was probably wrong and certainly prejudicial, the Court holds this testimony admissible because the Court is "unconvinced . . . that the adversary process cannot be trusted to sort out the reliable from the unreliable evidence and opinion about future dangerousness." . . . One can only wonder how juries are to separate valid from invalid expert opinions when the "experts" themselves are so obviously unable to do so. Indeed, the evidence suggests that juries are not effective at assessing the validity of scientific evidence. . . .

As if to suggest that petitioner's position that unreliable expert testimony should be excluded is unheard of in the law, the Court relies on the proposition that the rules of evidence generally "anticipate that relevant, unprivileged evidence should be admitted and its weight left to the factfinder, who would have the benefit of cross-examination and contrary evidence by the opposing party." . . . But the Court simply ignores hornbook law that, despite the availability of cross-examination and rebuttal witnesses, "opinion evidence is not admissible if the court believes that the state of the pertinent art or scientific knowledge does not permit a reasonable opinion to be asserted." E. Cleary, McCormick on Evidence §13, p. 31 (2d ed. 1972). Because it is feared that the jury will overestimate its probative value, polygraph evidence, for example, almost invariably is excluded from trials despite the fact that, at a con-

---

1076–1077 (1982). In United States v. Addison, 162 U. S. App. D. C. 199, 202, 498 F.2d 741, 744 (1974), the court observed that scientific evidence may "assume a posture of mystic infallibility in the eyes of a jury of laymen." Another court has noted that scientific evidence "is likely to be shrouded with an aura of near infallibility, akin to the ancient oracle of Delphi." United States v. Alexander, 526 F.2d 161, 168 (CA8 1975). See United States v. Amaral, 488 F.2d 1148, 1152 (CA9 1973); United States v. Wilson, 361 F. Supp. 510, 513 (Md. 1973); People v. King, 266 Cal. App. 2d 437, 461, 72 Cal. Rptr. 478, 493 (1968).

servative estimate, an experienced polygraph examiner can detect truth or deception correctly about 80 to 90 percent of the time.[12] ... In no area is purportedly "expert" testimony admitted for the jury's consideration where it cannot be demonstrated that it is correct more often than not. "It is inconceivable that a judgment could be considered an 'expert' judgment when it is less accurate than the flip of a coin." ... The risk that a jury will be incapable of separating "scientific" myth from reality is deemed unacceptably high.

B

The Constitution's mandate of reliability, with the stakes at life or death, precludes reliance on cross-examination and the opportunity to present rebuttal witnesses as an antidote for this distortion of the truth-finding process. Cross-examination is unlikely to reveal the fatuousness of psychiatric predictions because such predictions often rest, as was the case here, on psychiatric categories and intuitive clinical judgments not susceptible to cross-examination and rebuttal. ... Psychiatric categories have little or no demonstrated relationship to violence, and their use often obscures the unimpressive statistical or intuitive bases for prediction. ... The APA particularly condemns the use of the diagnosis employed by Doctors Grigson and Holbrook in this case, that of sociopathy:

> "In this area confusion reigns. The psychiatrist who is not careful can mislead the judge or jury into believing that a person has a major mental disease simply on the basis of a description of prior criminal behavior. Or a psychiatrist can mislead the court into believing that an individual is devoid of conscience on the basis of a description of criminal acts alone. ... The profession of psychiatry has a responsibility to avoid inflicting this confusion upon the courts and to spare the defendant the harm that may result. ... Given our uncertainty about the implications of the finding, the diagnosis of sociopathy ... should not be used to justify or to support predictions of future conduct. There is no certainty in this area."

Draft Report 30.

... Nor is the presentation of psychiatric witnesses on behalf of the defense likely to remove the prejudicial taint of misleading testimony

12. Other purportedly scientific proof has met a similar fate. See, e. g., United States v. Kilgus, 571 F.2d 508, 510 (CA9 1978) (expert testimony identifying aircraft through "forward looking infrared system" inadmissible because unreliable and not generally accepted in scientific field to which it belongs); United States v. Brown, 557 F.2d 541, 558-559 (CA6 1977) (expert identification based on "ion microprobic analysis of human hair" not admissible because insufficiently reliable and accurate, and not accepted in its field); United States v. Addison, 162 U. S. App. D. C., at 203, 498 F.2d, at 745 (expert identification based on voice spectrogram inadmissible because not shown reliable); United States v. Hearst, 412 F. Supp. 893, 895 (ND Cal. 1976) (identification testimony of expert in "psycholinguistics" inadmissible because not demonstrably reliable), aff'd on other grounds, 563 F.2d 1331 (CA9 1977).

by prosecution psychiatrists.[12] No reputable expert would be able to predict with confidence that the defendant will *not* be violent; at best, the witness will be able to give his opinion that all predictions of dangerousness are unreliable. Consequently, the jury will not be presented with the traditional battle of experts with opposing views on the ultimate question. Given a choice between an expert who says that he can predict with certainty that the defendant, whether confined in prison or free in society, will kill again, and an expert who says merely that no such prediction can be made, members of the jury charged by law with making the prediction surely will be tempted to opt for the expert who claims he can help them in performing their duty, and who predicts dire consequences if the defendant is not put to death.[13] . . .

IV

In *Smith*, the psychiatric testimony at issue was given by the same Doctor Grigson who confronts us in this case, and his conclusions were disturbingly similar to those he rendered here. . . . The APA, appearing as amicus curiae, argued that all psychiatric predictions of future dangerousness should be excluded from capital sentencing proceedings. The Court did not reach this issue, because it found Smith's death sentence invalid on narrower grounds: Doctor Grigson's testimony had violated Smith's Fifth and Sixth Amendment rights. Contrary to the Court's inexplicable assertion in this case, *Smith* certainly did not reject the APA's position. Rather, the Court made clear that "the holding in *Jurek* was guided by recognition that the inquiry [into dangerousness] mandated by Texas law does *not* require resort to medical experts." . . .

12. For one thing, although most members of the mental health professions believe that such predictions cannot be made, defense lawyers may experience significant difficulties in locating effective rebuttal witnesses. Davis, Texas Capital Sentencing Procedures: The Role of the Jury and the Restraining Hand of the Expert, 69 J. Crim. L. & Criminology 300, 302 (1978). I presume that the Court's reasoning suggests that, were a defendant to show that he was unable, for financial or other reasons, to obtain an adequate rebuttal expert, a constitutional violation might be found.

13. "Although jurors may treat mitigating psychiatric evidence with skepticism, they may credit psychiatric evidence demonstrating aggravation. Especially when jurors' sensibilities are offended by a crime, they may seize upon evidence of dangerousness to justify an enhanced sentence." . . . Thus, the danger of jury deference to expert opinions is particularly acute in death penalty cases. Expert testimony of this sort may permit juries to avoid the difficult and emotionally draining personal decisions concerning rational and just punishment. . . . Doctor Grigson himself has noted both the superfluousness and the misleading effect of his testimony:

> "'I think you could do away with the psychiatrist in these cases. Just take any man off the street, show him what the guy's done, and most of these things are so clearcut he would say the same things I do. But I think the jurors feel a little better when a psychiatrist says it—somebody that's supposed to know more than they know.'"

Bloom, Killers and Shrinks, Texas Monthly 64, 68 (July 1978) (quoting Doctor Grigson).

If *Jurek* and *Smith* held that psychiatric predictions of future dangerousness are admissible in a capital sentencing proceeding as the Court claims, this guiding recognition would have been irrelevant. . . .

Our constitutional duty is to ensure that the State proves future dangerousness, if at all, in a reliable manner, one that ensures that "any decision to impose the death sentence be, and appear to be, based on reason rather than caprice or emotion." . . . Texas' choice of substantive factors does not justify loading the factfinding process against the defendant through the presentation of what is, at bottom, false testimony.

V

I would vacate petitioner's death sentence, and remand for further proceedings consistent with these views.

The late 1970s and 1980s saw an increase in personal injury litigation based on exposure to toxic substances in consumer products, at the workplace, and in the environment. Often these cases were brought as class actions against the manufacturers and distributors of the substances or products claimed to be responsible for the plaintiff's injuries or illnesses. Manufacturers of asbestos-containing products, pharmaceutical firms manufacturing and selling DES, Bendectin, and silicon breast implants were also sued. Some claimed that there had been a "litigation explosion" and pled for "tort reform" to curb the litigation initiatives of plaintiffs and their attorneys or cap the ability of juries to respond to those initiatives.

Many claims for injury or illness from toxic substances faced the challenge of proof of causation. That is, did the drug, toxic substance, or other product in question, whether or not negligently manufactured, distributed or handled, actually cause the plaintiff's condition? This question almost always required an expert to answer.

IN RE AGENT ORANGE PRODUCT LIABILITY LITIGATION (LILLEY)

611 F. Supp. 1267 (E.D.N.Y. 1985), aff'd, 818 F.2d 187 (2d Cir.), petition for cert. filed sub nom. Lombardi v. Dow Chem. Co., 56 U.S.L.W. 3249 (No. 87-436, Dec. 15, 1987)

WEINSTEIN, C.J.: Anna Lilley sues on behalf of her deceased husband John Lilley, a Vietnam veteran. (The Lilleys are sometimes individually and jointly referred to as "plaintiff.") Defendants are seven chemical companies that manufactured the herbicide Agent Orange for use in Vietnam. They have moved to dismiss and for summary judgment. As in the cases of the other veterans who opted out of the class, summary judgment of dismissal must be granted. See In re "Agent Orange" Product Liability Litigation, 611 F. Supp. 1223 (E.D.N.Y. 1985).

I. Introduction

Based on all the information available in this case and in the related MDL litigation, we can assume the plaintiff might establish that the government as well as the defendant chemical companies knew that Agent Orange contained dioxin. The government and defendants undoubtedly knew before the spraying began that dioxin was a highly toxic chemical that might pose dangers to those exposed. Plaintiff can probably show that defendants knew that Agent Orange was to be sprayed in higher concentrations than recommended by the manufacturers for safe commercial use of similar herbicides, creating additional dangers to those on the ground. Plaintiff could also convince a trier that defendants were aware that packaging Agent Orange in drums without warnings was likely to lead to handling in ways contrary to safe usage, such as spillage on personnel and failure to wash and change clothing promptly after exposure.

There is also reason to believe that plaintiff could adduce evidence lending support to a contention that neither the government nor the chemical companies met a responsibility to conduct proper experiments and tests before production and use, to reveal promptly the dangers and to take adequate precautions by warnings and the like. In this respect the case arguably resembles the asbestos litigation where substantial contentions of cover-up and carelessness have been made. See P. Brodeur, "Annals of Law—Asbestos," The New Yorker (June 10, 17, 24, July 1, 1985).

Finally, on the basis of the record, there is evidence of plaintiff's exposure to Agent Orange. It occurred while he was in Vietnam.

Thus plaintiff could establish enough to withstand a motion for summary judgment directed to the first leg of any tort claim—defendant's wrongful act violating a right of plaintiff. Whether the rule is couched in terms of traditional negligence or strict liability we may assume for the purposes of this motion that defendants violated an obligation they owed to plaintiff.

Plaintiff's difficulty is with establishing the second leg of a tort claim —damage to plaintiff caused by defendants' wrongful conduct. Causation cannot be established on the basis of information presently available. It cannot be shown that John Lilley's illness and death were caused by exposure to Agent Orange. On the evidence available no trier could be permitted to find for the plaintiff. At this point any analogy to many of the asbestos or other toxic tort cases—where there is a clear linkage between the product and a disease—ends.

Under these circumstances, there is no need to consider whether the risks to those on the ground from spraying would have been greater than the risks from ambushes or other enemy action had Agent Orange never been used. Speculation about what the President and other high government officials would have done if they had known of the possible dangers, or what the manufacturers would or should have done if the government ordered the spraying of Agent Orange with full knowledge, becomes legally irrelevant.

Although lack of proof of causation requires that the complaint be dismissed, attorneys for plaintiffs in this and related MDL cases did not bring a frivolous suit requiring them to pay defendants' attorney fees under Rule 11 of the Federal Rules of Civil Procedure. See Eastway v. City of New York, 762 F.2d 242 (2d Cir. 1985). The plaintiffs' attorneys in this multidistrict litigation have made a valuable contribution by discovering and revealing evidence supporting the first leg of their claim —defendants' and the government's knowledge of the dangers in using Agent Orange and their failure to take reasonable precautions. That the scientific studies completed after they brought suit failed to support their theories of causation is hardly a reason for punishing the lawyers.

As a result of this litigation, future members of the armed forces may be protected by "sunshine" legislation, Defense Department regulations, and manufacturers' practice requiring disclosure of new and dangerous chemical processes. The importance of this and related Agent Orange litigation to veterans and to the public argues strongly against denominating the complaint in this case frivolous and burdening counsel with Rule 11 sanctions.

A long latency period may ultimately reveal some causal relationship between exposure to Agent Orange and adverse health effects in those exposed and in their children. If and when such a connection is shown the issue of compensation should be addressed by the government. This court must decide the case on the evidence presently available.

II.   Procedural Background

Plaintiff opted out of the class previously certified by this court in a suit against the defendant chemical companies. In re "Agent Orange" Product Liability Litigation, 506 F. Supp. 762, 787-792 (E.D.N.Y. 1980), modified, 100 F.R.D. 718 (E.D.N.Y. 1983), mandamus denied, 725 F.2d 858 (2d Cir.), cert. denied, 465 U.S. 1067, 104 S. Ct. 1417 (1984). After settling with members of the class on May 7, 1984, defendants moved on July 24, 1984 for summary judgment in the opt-out cases and a number of cases brought by civilians.

The court granted the opt-out plaintiffs repeated adjournments and opportunities for discovery to obtain evidence in opposition to the motion. On December 10, 1984, the court heard oral argument on defendants' motions. Defendants offered overwhelming proof that no causal connection exists between exposure to Agent Orange and development of miscarriages or birth defects. In response, the veterans' wives and children produced no evidence sufficient to create an issue of material fact on causation. See also In re "Agent Orange" Product Liability Litigation, 603 F. Supp. 239 (E.D.N.Y. 1985) (dismissing claims of wives and children against government). The court adjourned consideration of the majority of the opt-out veterans' claims to enable counsel to produce additional evidence of causation.

Counsel for the opt-out plaintiffs submitted materials by Doctors Samuel S. Epstein and Barry M. Singer. Oral argument was heard on April 15, 1985. The court issued an opinion granting defendants' motion for summary judgment on May 8, 1985. In re "Agent Orange" Product Liability Litigation, 611 F. Supp. 1223 (E.D.N.Y. 1985).

In the Lilley case, plaintiff produced the affidavit of Dr. Bertram Warren Carnow on October 18, 1984. On December 10, 1984, the court denied summary judgment. Defendants' motion to reargue was granted on February 6, 1985. Expedited discovery occurred and oral argument was heard on April 15, 1985.

On May 14, 1985, the court issued an order granting plaintiff an added thirty days to submit additional proof of exposure and additional medical evidence. Plaintiffs' counsel submitted the affidavit of Mrs. Lilley's brother-in-law John Comeaux on June 12, 1985. Defendants' counsel submitted John Comeaux's supplemental affidavit and an accompanying memorandum of law on June 13, 1985.

III.   FACTS

More discovery has occurred in the Lilley case than in any other opt-out case. Still, as the deposition of plaintiff Anna Lilley demonstrates, little is known about John Lilley's medical background and exposure history. Plaintiff's expert, Dr. Bertram Carnow, relies on information supplied by Mrs. Lilley, some of Mr. Lilley's medical records, and studies of animal and industrial exposure to dioxin. He concludes that Agent Orange caused John Lilley's illness and death. Defendants contest causation, relying primarily on epidemiologic studies, the depositions of Mrs. Lilley, the affidavits of John Comeaux and the affidavits of two experts.

A.   INFORMATION ON JOHN LILLEY

John Lilley grew up in western Pennsylvania. He entered what subsequently became the Air Force in 1947 at the age of seventeen. According to Mrs. Lilley, her husband received specialized training in the use of chemicals and gas and instruction on how to be an airplane mechanic. During his years in the service, John Lilley worked primarily as an airplane mechanic. He "tore engines apart." Mr. Lilley's main workplace was Andrews Air Force Base, and he commuted home on weekends.

He had several tours of duty abroad, including service in Germany, England, Japan, Korea, and Vietnam. He worked as a cargo inspector in Vietnam from April 1966 through April 1967. There he inventoried cargo and assisted in loading and unloading it onto airplanes.

Dr. Carnow states that Mr. Lilley "was not exposed to any spraying nor did he handle any chemicals" other than in Vietnam. Mrs. Lilley's deposition makes clear that she would not have been aware of her husband's exposure to chemicals. According to Mrs. Lilley, whatever John Lilley's assignment, "he would be . . . on top secret . . . [and] never knew where he was going until he boarded the plane and opened the envelope."

Dr. Carnow also states that Mr. Lilley told Mrs. Lilley "that he did handle drums of Agent Orange extensively and that he did get some of the chemical on him from ruptured or defective containers." Mrs. Lilley, on the other hand, repeatedly stated that "he could never tell me what was in the containers."

Mrs. Lilley testified at her deposition that she first learned that Agent Orange may have been in the containers her husband handled some-time after his death. She was told this by her brother-in-law, who had worked with John Lilley in Vietnam. There are indications in Mrs. Lilley's deposition that the chemicals handled by her husband and her brother-in-law included chemicals other than Agent Orange ("[t]he boys never knew what they were handling, all they knew it was chemicals . . . supposed to kill the mosquitos or something over there"); (describing "red, green, blue" seals on barrels); ("chemicals my husband [used] . . . to spray for the bugs").

The affidavit of Mrs. Lilley's brother-in-law, John C. Comeaux, is more explicit about the material John Lilley handled in Vietnam. Mr. Comeaux served as a flight engineer and cargo inspector in Vietnam, frequently working with John Lilley.

Mr. Comeaux "cannot clearly recall the color of the various bands used" on the barrels he and Mr. Lilley handled. They emptied the 55-gallon drums into larger aircraft tanks for use on C-123 aircraft as part of Operation Ranch Hand. The material in the drums, which Mr. Comeaux "understood . . . to be for defoliating the jungle, killing the tall grasses and occasionally for destroying enemy crops," "was constantly spilling" on Mr. Comeaux and Mr. Lilley. A film of what Mr. Comeaux believes to have been Agent Orange developed on the water when it rained. Rainwater flooded the barracks and Mr. Lilley and Mr. Comeaux were forced to wade in it. Mr. Comeaux concludes that "John Lilley was exposed to Agent Orange *and possibly other herbicides*" (emphasis supplied). John Comeaux's supplemental affidavit filed at the request of defendant Monsanto states that he has "no personal knowledge of the contents of the barrels we handled" and that he does "not know . . . whether the barrels in fact contained the herbicide known as Agent Orange."

Dr. Carnow notes that after returning from Vietnam, Mr. Lilley had blister-like lesions on both lower legs which were then diagnosed as shingles. He also complained of a red rash which would later result in brownish patches on his skin. He had difficulty holding a hammer because of numbness in his hands. Finally, he had a cough and sore throat, which were apparently cured by a tonsillectomy.

Mr. Lilley retired from the Air Force after twenty years of service in August 1967. Upon returning to civilian life he worked for Aircraft Armaments Company, a manufacturer of grenades, machine guns and shells. Dr. Carnow states that during his subsequent occupation, Mr. Lilley "never handled any toxic chemicals including solvents or pesticides." This conclusion is presumably based on Mrs. Lilley's statement that "[t]hey didn't have chemicals down there." While employed at Aircraft Armaments, Mr. Lilley replaced light bulbs and fixed air conditioners.

With respect to Mr. Lilley's personal habits, Dr. Carnow states that, according to Mrs. Lilley, Mr. Lilley did not smoke or drink. Mrs. Lilley's deposition reads:

Q: At any time since you have known your husband, did he ever smoke?
A: Well, I don't know what he did. He started one time and went back off of it and broke himself of it.
Q: Was he ever advised by a doctor in the military to stop smoking?
A: I don't know. He never told me.

Mr. Lilley, however, "admitted to smoking 1 pack per day for the last 30 years. . . ."

Dr. Carnow relies on information from Mrs. Lilley to conclude that Mr. Lilley never contracted hepatitis or infectious mononucleosis and did not take any medications regularly. She gave Dr. Carnow an abbreviated family history: Mr. Lilley's father died of a stroke in his 50s or 60s. His mother had cancer of the uterus or cervix. He has five sisters, all of whom are alive and well. There is no history of any leukemias or other cancers in the family.

Mrs. Lilley notes that she had a stillbirth after five months' gestation in 1969. She became pregnant again several months later and after a full-term pregnancy gave birth to an eight pound, five ounce baby. The boy has developed rashes on about 13 occasions, diagnosed as Scarlet Fever, German Measles, and other infectious diseases. The child also suffers from a lung disorder.

After Mr. Lilley's return from Vietnam, he received medical attention twice; once in April 1966 for a boil on his scrotum, and once for a sore throat in May 1967. His retirement examination in August 1967 showed a normal electrocardiogram, no significant findings on the physical examination, and no complaints. He was 6 feet tall and weighed 180 pounds. His blood pressure was 120/84 and he was thought to be in excellent health.

In September 1970 at the age of 40, Mr. Lilley was diagnosed as having poorly differentiated lymphocytic lymphoma, nodular type. He was treated with various medications and told that he had only six months to live — although fortunately he lived longer. He had a spleenectomy in 1970 after the diagnosis of lymphosarcoma was made.

Dr. Carnow notes that the progression of Mr. Lilley's disease was from poorly differentiated lymphocytic lymphoma, nodular type, to mixed histiocytic-lymphocytic, nodular type, to lymphosarcomatous leukemia. Mr. Lilley died on January 28, 1976. According to Dr. Carnow, the autopsy report shows a lymphosarcomatous leukemia with various other findings, all related to the cancer diagnosis.

A hospital discharge summary dated February 17, 1975 shows that Mr. Lilley had just suffered a myocardial infarction. He had had a previous myocardial infarction in 1973. Dr. Carnow concludes that Mr. Lilley's lymphosarcoma was caused by exposure to Agent Orange during his tour of duty in Vietnam. He further states that John Lilley's myocardial infarction "was also the result of absorption of these chemicals into his body and the development of chronic chemical intoxication as a result." Cf. Tr. at 183 (Hearings March 5, 1985) ("medical evidence would suggest that if somebody had occluded arteries, that person did not die from Agent Orange exposure") (remarks of Plaintiff's Management Committee member David Dean).

Assuming, based on the Comeaux affidavits, that Mr. Lilley was in fact exposed to Agent Orange, there is insufficient evidence to support Dr. Carnow's opinion that such exposure caused Mr. Lilley's lymphosarcoma and myocardial infarctions. Dr. Carnow relies on insufficient information about Mr. Lilley's background and personal habits. What little information is available makes clear that Mr. Lilley was exposed to a wide variety of carcinogens during his lifetime. The only medical records submitted make no mention of Agent Orange. The inapposite scientific studies described by Dr. Carnow do not support the claim of causation.

B.   REVIEW OF SCIENTIFIC LITERATURE

To reach his conclusion that Agent Orange caused Mr. Lilley's lymphosarcoma and myocardial infarctions, Dr. Carnow relies primarily on a number of studies conducted on animals and workers exposed to dioxin.

1. STUDIES RELIED UPON BY DR. CARNOW

These studies, previously submitted by plaintiffs, have been discussed in the court's prior opt-out opinion. In re "Agent Orange" Product Liability Litigation, 611 F. Supp. 1223 (E.D.N.Y. 1985). Many of the studies involved laboratory animals subjected to extreme exposures with unknown human significance; some, such as the Swedish studies by Hardell and his colleagues, have never been replicated, and involved chemicals in addition to the constituents of Agent Orange. See, e.g., L. Hardell, et al., "Malignant Lymphoma and Exposure to Chemicals, Especially Organic Solvents, Chlorophenols and Phenoxy Acids: A Case-Control Study," Br. J. Cancer (1981). Others involved chronic or acute industrial exposures different from the exposures in Vietnam.

The studies cited by Dr. Carnow do not establish any cause and effect relationship. For example, Dr. Carnow relies heavily on three animal studies—Van Miller, Lalich, et al., 1977, Kociba, et al., 1978, and Toth et al., 1979—that he states "have demonstrated the carcinogenicity of TCDD in rats and mice." The Van Miller study, however, concludes that more research is necessary into the mechanisms of TCDD's action before any conclusions can be drawn as to the carcinogenicity of TCDD even in laboratory animals. See Van Miller, et al., "Increased Incidence of Neoplasms in Rats Exposed to Low Levels of 2,3,7,8-Tetrachlorodibenzo-p-Dioxin," 9 Chemosphere 537, 543 (1979).

As the Toth study concludes, the results of animal studies cannot be extrapolated to humans:

> Until more is known about the people who have been exposed to them, the carcinogenicity of 2,4,5-T and structurally related chemicals in humans cannot be evaluated.

Toth, et al., "Carcinogenicity testing of herbicide 2,4,5-trichlorophenoxyethanol containing dioxin and of pure dioxin in Swiss mice" 549 (1979).

In the Kociba study, neoplasms were found only in those animals fed sufficient quantities of the chemical to cause severe, acute toxic effects. The study concluded:

> In summary, data collected in the study reported herein indicate that doses sufficient to induce severe toxicity increased the incidence of some types of neoplasms in rats, while reducing the incidence of other types. No increase in neoplasms occurred in rats receiving sufficient TCDD during the 2-year study to induce slight or no manifestations of toxicity.

Kociba, et al., "Results of a Two-Year Chronic Toxicity and Oncogenicity

Study of 2-3-7-8-Tetrachlorodibenzino-p-Dioxin in Rats," 46 Toxicology and Applied Pharmacology 279, 302 (1978).

Dr. Carnow's discussion of human studies avoids any mention of the epidemiologic studies conducted on Vietnam veterans actually exposed to Agent Orange and their offspring. Instead, he relies on studies involving industrial exposure, small cohorts and different chemical compounds. He does mention Sarma and Jacobs, who reported in 1981 three cases of soft-tissue sarcomas in veterans presumed to have been exposed to Agent Orange. Sarma and Jacobs concluded that more studies are needed:

> Soft-tissue sarcomas are rare neoplasms. If there is a true risk of these neoplasms in veterans who served in Vietnam, follow-up studies should be able to define it. If there is an increased risk of malignant disease in these veterans, then a more critical question that has to be addressed is: Are the defoliants causative, or is some other unidentified environmental factor responsible, acting alone or in concert with the defoliants?

Sarma and Jacobs, "Thoracic Soft-Tissue Sarcoma in Vietnam Veterans Exposed to Agent Orange" 1109 (letter to the editor). . . .

In sum, the various studies discussed by Dr. Carnow do not support his firm conclusion that exposure to Agent Orange caused John Lilley's lymphosarcoma. The authors of these studies acknowledge that more research is necessary and that no more than a suggestion or vague association may be hypothesized at present. Dr. Carnow does not discuss the directly relevant epidemiologic studies conducted on exposed Vietnam veterans.

2.   STUDIES OF RELEVANT POPULATION GROUP

The epidemiologic studies conducted on veterans exposed to Agent Orange in Vietnam have been extensively discussed in prior opinions. See, e.g., In re "Agent Orange" Product Liability Litigation, 597 F. Supp. 740 (E.D.N.Y. 1984) (fairness of settlement); In re "Agent Orange" Product Liability Litigation, 611 F. Supp. 1223 (E.D.N.Y. 1985) (granting summary judgment against plaintiffs who opted out of the class action). This research was designed to determine the direct effects of exposure on servicepersons and the indirect effects of exposure on spouses and children of servicepersons. No acceptable study to date of Vietnam veterans and their families concludes that there is a causal connection between exposure to Agent Orange and the serious adverse health effects claimed by plaintiff.

Chloracne and porphyria cutanea tarda are the only two diseases that have been recognized by Congress as having some possible connection to Agent Orange exposure. Arguably there has been some proof that this plaintiff suffered from chloracne on his return from Vietnam. . . . This is, however, a death action and chloracne has not been claimed to be a precursor of the cancer and heart disease from which plaintiff allegedly died. At most it is evidence of exposure to Agent Orange, a fact that may be assumed for purposes of this motion.

The studies have been negative with respect to effects on veterans' health. The Air Force study is one of the most extensive examinations to date of the effect of Agent Orange on exposed veterans. See Air Force Health Study, An Epidemiologic Investigation of Health Effects in Air Force Personnel Following Exposure to Herbicides (February 24, 1984) (Ranch Hand II Study—1984 Report). This study utilized 1,024 matched pairs of men for analysis. Essentially all those who had participated in the fixed wing spraying and who could be located were studied. The conclusion was negative. In summary,

> This baseline report concludes that there is insufficient evidence to support a cause and effect relationship between herbicide exposure and adverse health in the Ranch Hand group at this time.

Significantly, "no cases of chloracne were diagnosed clinically or by biopsy."

The small Ranch Hand sample and other factors, particularly the length of time it takes for some cancers to develop, support the conclusion that more work is needed before any firm conclusion can be reached respecting morbidity. The authors suggest a 20-year mortality follow-up study.

The Ranch Hand Study authors state that "[i]n full context, the baseline study results should be viewed as reassuring to the Ranch Handers and their families at this time." Even if we assume that plaintiff was part of the Ranch Hand operation, this study offers no help to him in establishing causation. It is at best inconclusive. . . .

C. EXPERT AFFIDAVITS SUBMITTED BY DEFENDANTS

In support of their motion for summary judgment, defendants submitted affidavits from Dr. Edmund H. Sonnenblick and Dr. Edward A. Smuckler. Dr. Sonnenblick, who is Chief of the Cardiology Department at Albert Einstein Medical School, addresses the question of whether John Lilley's myocardial infarctions resulted from exposure to Agent Orange.

A review of Mr. Lilley's medical records, Dr. Carnow's testimony and sources, and the scientific literature convinces him that the infarction was unrelated to Agent Orange. John Lilley was a member of an age, race and sex group that was at risk for myocardial infarction. In addition, John Lilley's medical history includes several known risk factors

for myocardial infarction: a 30-year history of cigarette smoking, hyper-
cholesterolemia, and parental stroke. Even Dr. Carnow acknowledges
that these factors may enhance the risk of heart disease.

Dr. Sonnenblick notes that no scientific study has found an association between coronary artery disease and exposure to Agent Orange,
2,3,7,8-tetrachlorodibenzo-p-dioxin or any other form of dioxin. According to Dr. Sonnenblick, the "list of scientific materials which support the opinions of plaintiffs' experts" does not include any reference
to literature that addresses this purported association. The Ranch Hand
Mortality and Morbidity Studies did not find any increased incidence
of coronary artery disease or myocardial infarction among persons exposed to Agent Orange in Vietnam.

Dr. Sonnenblick states that:

> [w]ithout studies demonstrating an excess incidence of myocardial infarction
> among persons of John Lilley's age group who were exposed to Agent Orange,
> there is no basis for the opinion that John Lilley's myocardial infarction was more
> probably than not caused by his exposure to Agent Orange, since there would
> be no basis for distinguishing his condition from the "background" incidence of
> such disease.

Given the lack of an increased incidence of heart disease in veterans
exposed to Agent Orange and the existence of risk factors in John Lilley's own background, Dr. Sonnenblick concludes that Dr. Carnow's
opinion lacks any "scientific, factual or logical basis."

Dr. Smuckler addresses the claim that Agent Orange exposure caused
John Lilley's lymphoma. Dr. Smuckler is Chairman of the Department
of Forensic Pathology at the University of California at San Francisco
Medical School. His areas of research and publication include chemi-
cally-induced cancer and the effects of exposure to chlorinated dioxins
and related compounds.

Dr. Smuckler has also reviewed the records, documents and testimony submitted by plaintiffs. He notes that according to the Third National Cancer Survey: Incidence Data, National Cancer Institute
Monograph 41, March 1975, attached as Exhibit B to his affidavit, for
every 100,000 white males aged 40-44, 4.1 new cases of lymphocytic lymphoma occur each year. The prevalence of the disease is higher. Although the etiology of lymphomas is "largely unknown," "[t]here are
certain recognized associations that have been established between
some agents and the development of lymphomas in humans and
animals."

Dr. Smuckler states that one agent recognized as increasing risk of
lymphoma is benzene. Mr. Lilley is likely to have been exposed to benzene in his many years as a flight engineer and airplane mechanic. Dr.
Smuckler points out that there is an established link between this oc-

cupation and an increased incidence of lymphoma and leukemia. Exhibit C contains articles on the increased incidence of lymphoma among those exposed to benzene and "An Occupation Health Survey of Selected Airports" conducted by the Centers for Disease Control. This survey warns that airplane maintenance employees risk exposure to a number of toxic substances: carbon monoxide, aluminum oxide, stoddard solvent, kerosene, nonflammable halogenated solvents, alkaline solutions, cleaners, vapor degreasers containing chlorinated hydrocarbons, metal oxide fumes and phosgene (from welding), x-radiation (from electron beam welding), metal and nitrogen oxides (from metal spraying), benzene (from paint stripping), and a variety of other potentially hazardous substances. . . .

Dr. Smuckler concludes that

> [c]onsidering the following uncontroverted facts:
>
> a. there is no established association between exposure to Agent Orange and increased incidence of lymphoma;
> b. there is no evidence of an excess incidence of lymphoma in Vietnam veterans;
> c. lymphoma is a neoplastic disease that occurs in the general United States population;
> d. the etiology of lymphomas is largely unknown; and
> e. John Lilley's medical and occupational history demonstrates other risk factors for cancer generally and lymphoma/leukemia specifically;
>
> there is no scientific, factual or logical basis to permit or support the conclusion that it is more probable than not that John Lilley's malignancy was caused by his alleged exposure to Agent Orange in Vietnam.

IV. LAW

Defendants assert a number of legal grounds for dismissal. All defendants claim that plaintiff has not created an issue of material fact regarding causation, that plaintiff has failed to show who caused the harm alleged, and that the government contract defense bars recovery. In addition, defendant Monsanto moves to dismiss claiming that the applicable statute of limitations bars recovery.

A. EVIDENCE OF LACK OF CAUSATION

To prevail defendants must show that there can be no genuine issue of material fact regarding exposure to Agent Orange as a cause of John Lilley's disease. In re "Agent Orange" Product Liability Litigation, 611 F. Supp. 1223 (E.D.N.Y. 1985). Plaintiff must rebut with competent, nonconclusory evidence. Fed. R. Civ. Proc. 56(e).

1. Epidemiologic Studies

The epidemiological studies conducted by the federal, state and Australian governments are admissible under Federal Rule of Evidence 803(8)(C), the public records and reports exception to the hearsay rule. As previously pointed out, the Ranch Hand, Australian and other studies "alone demonstrate that on the basis of present knowledge there is no question of fact: Agent Orange cannot now be shown to have caused plaintiff's numerous illnesses." In re "Agent Orange" Product Liability Litigation, supra, at 1241.

The Ranch Hand study is particularly relevant to the instant case. John Lilley allegedly worked in Vietnam as part of Operation Ranch Hand. He was associated with the very group considered in the Ranch Hand study. No increase was found in lymphosarcoma, lymphoma or myocardial infarction among former Ranch Handers.

2. Dr. Carnow's Affidavit

Plaintiff attempts to overcome the unavailability of any general evidence of causation with "particularistic" proof in the form of Dr. Carnow's affidavit. Dr. Carnow concludes that "Agent Orange is the likely cause of [John Lilley's] malignancy and death at well above the '50 percent certainty level.'" This opinion must be considered in light of Federal Rules of Evidence 403, 702 and 703. . . .

(a) Rule 702

Rule 702 of the Federal Rules of Evidence provides for opinion testimony by experts "if scientific, technical or other specialized knowledge will assist the trier of fact to determine a fact in issue" and the witness is "qualified as an expert by knowledge, experience, training or education. . . ." The court must first determine whether the expert is sufficiently qualified in his or her field to be allowed to testify. Frazier v. Continental Oil Co., 568 F.2d 378, 383 (5th Cir. 1978). Doubts about whether the proffered evidence is helpful to the trier should be resolved in favor of admissibility. In re Japanese Electronic Products Antitrust Litigation, 723 F.2d 238, 279 (3d Cir. 1983), cert. granted, 471 U.S. 1002 (1985). Finally, courts must assess the admissibility of testimony based on a novel scientific technique by balancing the relevance, reliability, and helpfulness of the evidence against the likelihood of waste of time, confusion, and prejudice.

In their motion for reargument and other papers, defendants urge that Dr. Carnow is unqualified to testify because he has allegedly given contradictory testimony in various cases involving the effects of exposure to dioxin on humans and because of his general lack of credibility. There has been no dispositive proof that Dr. Carnow has committed perjury in the course of the present case. Defendants also cite Dr. Carnow's opening remark at his deposition — "I have just one statement. I'd like to know who is going to take care of my fees in this case"—as rendering him unqualified under the Federal Rules.

Defendants' arguments address the weight of Dr. Carnow's testimony and not its admissibility. The Federal Rules of Evidence assume that rigorous cross-examination will alleviate concern about expert testimony that is contradictory or overly influenced by the prospect of monetary gain. The jury, not the judge, decides whether these considerations have so tainted an expert's opinion as to make it unworthy of belief.

Under Rule 702, the court must merely determine whether Dr. Carnow is sufficiently qualified to testify. He received his degree in medicine from the Chicago Medical School, is board certified in occupational medicine and has extensive professional experience in occupational and environmental medicine. Dr. Carnow belongs to a number of professional organizations and writes for professional journals. Defendants' contention that Dr. Carnow has on several occasions failed the internal medicine board examination does not preclude him from testifying. He will be considered an expert.

The other elements of Rule 702 analysis — helpfulness and appropriate methodology — are equally satisfied by Dr. Carnow's testimony. His opinion is directed toward one of the most important issues in this protracted litigation — causation — and would therefore assist the trier of fact. Dr. Carnow's general scientific technique of inference from animal and other studies is acceptable.

Compliance with Rule 702 does not suffice. Rule 703 also must be considered.

(b)   Rule 703

Rule 703 of the Federal Rules of Evidence limits the "facts" and "data" upon which an expert may rely to those "reasonably relied" upon "by experts in the field." It provides:

> The facts or data in the particular case upon which an expert bases an opinion or inference may be those perceived by or made known to him at or before the hearing. If of a type reasonably relied upon by experts in the particular field in forming opinions or inferences upon the subject, the facts or data need not be admissible in evidence.

Dr. Carnow does not base his conclusion about the cause of John Lilley's death on observation. Instead, the doctor relies on anecdotal information from Mrs. Lilley and on some medical records. Under Rule 703, the court must determine whether such reliance is "reasonable."

The cases interpreting this requirement have already been discussed in detail. In re "Agent Orange" Product Liability Litigation, 611 F. Supp. 1223, 1243-1244 (E.D.N.Y. 1985).

The reasonable reliance requirement means that an expert may not base his or her testimony on hearsay that would not be used by other experts in the field. In re Swine Flu Immunization Products Liability Litigation, 508 F. Supp. 897, 904 (D. Colo. 1981), aff'd sub nom. Lima v. United States, 708 F.2d 502 (10th Cir. 1983).

Dr. Carnow has never examined John Lilley. Instead, he relies almost exclusively on hearsay information about Mr. Lilley's symptoms, personal habits and medical background. The confused recollection of Mrs. Lilley about the few things she believes Mr. Lilley told her before his death is not the kind of information physicians customarily rely upon in diagnosing illness. See Slaughter v. Abilene State School, 561 S.W.2d 789, 791 (Tex. 1977) (doctor's testimony predicated upon both hearsay and personal knowledge admissible); Smith v. Tennessee Life Insurance Co., 618 S.W.2d 829, 832 (Tex. Civ. App. 1981) ("report of private investigators is not . . . the type of hearsay data that a doctor can rely upon in forming his expert opinion"). We do not have the kind of reliable statements about direct observation of actions, contemporaneous statements and symptoms usually related by a spouse. Cf. Fed. R. Ev., Rules 803(1), (2), (3), (4), 805. Mrs. Lilley had little or no contact with her husband for long periods of time and made no direct observations about his work or its effects upon him.

While perhaps less self-serving than the plaintiff checklists rejected in the previous opt-out opinion, see In re "Agent Orange" Product Liability Litigation, 611 F. Supp. 1223 (E.D.N.Y. 1985), Mrs. Lilley's recollections about John Lilley's past statements are insufficiently trustworthy to form the basis of an expert opinion. Plaintiff has not submitted evidence that Dr. Carnow or any other physician would rely on similar information in rendering a diagnosis.

Dr. Carnow asserts that he also relied in forming his opinion on John Lilley's medical records during Air Force Service, hospital discharge summaries and the autopsy report. Use of medical records to corroborate the "patient's" statements could alleviate the problem of unreliable hearsay. O'Gee v. Dobbs Houses, Inc., 570 F.2d 1084, 1089 (2d Cir. 1978). . . . The only medical records available to the court were submitted by the defendants. They fail to enhance the basis of Dr. Carnow's opinion.

These records nowhere mention "Agent Orange" or chloracne. One record indicates that John Lilley admitted to smoking a pack of cigarettes daily for thirty years, which suggests the unreliability of Dr. Carnow's information that Mr. Lilley was a nonsmoker. Moreover, plaintiffs' expert in the related opt-out cases has stressed that quitting smoking is the "most effective single action you can take" to avoid developing cancer. S. Epstein, The Politics of Cancer 473 (Anchor Press ed. 1979). . . . The fact that a family history of lymphosarcoma is not recorded in the medical records does not show the nonexistence of such a family history. Mr. Lilley's mother had cervical or uterine cancer.

Thus, Dr. Carnow's reference to medical records does not serve to make his reliance on Mrs. Lilley's statements about her husband reasonable. Given the difficulty of establishing which of the myriad potentially hazardous substances that John Lilley probably was exposed to during his life that may have caused his cancer, precise information about his exposure history, personal habits and medical history is crucial in forming an accurate opinion. Since there is no record supporting his theory, Dr. Carnow's proposed testimony lacks any basis in fact. See In re "Agent Orange" Product Liability Litigation, 611 F. Supp. 1223, 1248 (E.D.N.Y. 1985) (cases interpreting this aspect of Federal Rule of Evidence 703).

Courts excluding expert opinion for lack of adequate basis often note that it is speculative or without any factual foundation. Merit Motors, Inc. v. Chrysler Corp., 569 F.2d 666, 671-73 (D.C. Cir. 1977) ("To hold that Rule 703 prevents a court from granting summary judgment against a party who relies solely on an expert's opinion that has no more basis in or out of the record than [this expert's] . . . would seriously undermine the policies of Rule 56."). . . .

Most important, Dr. Carnow fails to consider the relevant epidemiologic studies conducted on Vietnam veterans. This omission is particularly incomprehensible in Mr. Lilley's case, since he was allegedly associated with the very group considered in the Ranch Hand Study. As already noted, the Air Force Study found no increased incidence of lymphosarcoma among Ranch Handers. Dr. Carnow's claim that Agent Orange exposure caused Mr. Lilley's myocardial infarction is similarly without support. . . .

Dr. Carnow states that the incidence rate for deaths from lymphosarcomatous leukemia in the population at large "in white males age 40 years in the period 1959-1969 was 2 to 3 per 100,000" which he concludes is "relatively rare." Aff. at 4. He further notes that certain factors — geographic location, familial history, exposure to radiation, and immuno-suppression—increase the risk of developing lymphosarcoma.

Dr. Carnow's data is generally borne out by the literature. See M.M. Wintrobe, G.R. Lee, D.R. Boggs, T.C. Bithell, J. Foerster, J.W. Athens, J.N. Lukens, Clinical Hematology, 1449-83 (1981) (cause of lymphoma or leukemia unknown, but time-space clustering, environmental factors, familial disease and ethnic differences important). A more recent survey finds a higher incidence than does Dr. Carnow of the disease for Mr. Lilley's age group—4.1 per 100,000. See "Third National Cancer Survey: Incidence Data," National Cancer Institute Monograph 41, March 1975. In contrast to the association Dr. Carnow finds between exposure to Agent Orange and lymphosarcoma, "with the exception of gamma irradiation and benzene and related hydrocarbons, no firm relationship of such factors to disease has been established." Wintrobe, et al., supra, at 1477; J. Aleksandrowicz & A. Skotnicki, Leukemia Ecology: Ecological

Prophylaxis of Leukemia 47-69 (1982) (ionizing radiation and benzene are leukemogenic agents).

Commentators stress what Dr. Carnow ignores—that the etiology of leukemia and lymphosarcoma is unknown. See, e.g., Wintrobe, supra, at 1471....

The uncertainty surrounding the etiology of lymphosarcoma underscores the central problem with Dr. Carnow's testimony: he applies a causal hypothesis without any scientific support and excludes other potential causes without any factual basis for doing so. John Lilley's long career "tearing engines apart" makes it far more likely that exposure to benzene or radiation from contaminated aircraft caused his lymphosarcoma. See J.L. Kulp & J.L. Dick, "The Radiation Hazard from Contaminated Aircraft," 4 Health Physics 133-56 (1960). It is impossible to pinpoint which of the many personal, familial and environmental factors—alone or in combination—is responsible. See Aleksandrowicz & Skotnicki, supra, at 72-85 (arguing that naturally occurring carcinogens such as mycotoxins may play a role in leukemia).

In conclusion, there are no facts that rationally support Dr. Carnow's opinion. The only information available on John Lilley is sketchy and unreliable. Dr. Carnow's assumption that Mr. Lilley was exposed to no toxic substances other than Agent Orange during his lifetime is baseless. Dr. Carnow's information about Mr. Lilley's family history and personal habits is suspect. The only relevant epidemiologic studies, which were conducted on the very group with whom John Lilley apparently served, are entirely negative.... Dr. Carnow's resort to inappropriate studies of animals and workers exposed during industrial accidents, see supra III.B.1, cannot redeem his unfounded opinion. The conclusions set forth in the Carnow affidavit would be excluded at trial under Rule 703 of the Federal Rules of Evidence....

(c)   Rule 403

Federal Rule of Evidence 403 requires the court to exclude relevant evidence "if its probative value is substantially outweighed by the danger of unfair prejudice, confusion of the issues, or misleading the jury...." A determination to exclude such evidence lies within the trial court's discretion.

The unfounded assumptions and speculations underlying Dr. Carnow's testimony reduce its probative value to a point approaching zero. Establishing the testimony's low probative value would embroil the jury in a protracted and fruitless inquiry into complex issues. The false aura of scientific infallibility surrounding Dr. Carnow's opinion makes the court particularly reluctant to admit it. The likelihood that admitting Dr. Carnow's opinion would waste the trier's time is particularly disturbing in a litigation that has already dragged on for many years. On balance, then, Dr. Carnow's testimony would be excluded under Rule 403 even if it were competent under Rule 703.

3. Defendants' Affidavits

The affidavits of Doctors Smuckler and Sonnenblick confirm the unreliability of plaintiff's expert testimony. As discussed supra IIIC, defendants' experts support the conclusion that the scientific literature to date offers no basis for concluding that exposure to Agent Orange caused John Lilley's lymphosarcoma and coronary artery disease. The doctors further suggest that John Lilley's smoking, high cholesterol, family history and occupational exposure to benzene and radiation are more likely causes of Mr. Lilley's illness and death.

The opinions of Doctors Smuckler and Sonnenblick would be admissible at trial. They are reputable physicians with a high degree of expertise in their respective areas. Fed. R. Ev. 702. In contrast to Dr. Carnow, they take into account the entire body of relevant scientific literature, including the Ranch Hand and other studies of exposed veterans. While obviously not plaintiff's treating physicians (who, if they are available, have not been relied upon by plaintiff or defendants), defendants' experts have considered the relevant medical records, which are submitted as exhibits to their affidavits.

B. APPROPRIATENESS OF GRANTING SUMMARY JUDGMENT

The court has scrutinized all of the evidence relevant to John Lilley's claim with great care. See In re "Agent Orange" Product Liability Litigation, 611 F. Supp. 1223, 1260 (E.D.N.Y. 1985). . . . Defendants have met their burden of showing that no genuine issue of fact exists.

For purposes of deciding this motion, the court has assumed, based on John Comeaux's affidavit, that Mr. Lilley was exposed to Agent Orange in Vietnam. The rash and subsequent discoloration that John Lilley developed on his legs upon returning from Vietnam *may* have been chloracne. See S.L. Moschella & H.J. Hurley, 2 Dermatology 1714-15 (2d ed. 1985). . . . Chloracne is a fairly reliable indicator of exposure since it appears shortly after contact with the suspected chemical (even though it tends to disappear thereafter). In re "Agent Orange" Product Liability Litigation, 597 F. Supp. 740, 794-95 (E.D.N.Y. 1984).

Plaintiff's lawsuit, however, does not rest on damage from chloracne. . . . It rests on the far more serious diseases of lymphosarcoma and myocardial infarction. The epidemiologic studies and affidavits relied upon by defendants make clear that no rational jury could conclude that exposure to Agent Orange caused John Lilley's illness and death.

Plaintiff's attempt to create a material issue of fact with conclusory allegations and inadmissible expert testimony must fail. Fed. R. Civ.

Proc. 56(e). It is well-settled that a litigant opposing summary judgment "'may not rest upon mere conclusory allegations or denials' as a vehicle for obtaining a trial." Quinn v. Syracuse Model Neighborhood Corp., 613 F.2d 438, 445 (2d Cir. 1980). . . .

Summary judgment is even more appropriate here than in the other opt-out cases because extensive discovery has been conducted in the Lilley case and it is highly unlikely that any new evidence of substance can be obtained. The court granted plaintiff every reasonable opportunity to present a case by granting adjournments and requesting additional information. It has taken into consideration all the evidence from all related M.D.L. cases that could possibly support plaintiff's causal hypothesis.

Considering all of the evidence and potential evidence, there is no question that a directed verdict will be entered at the close of plaintiff's case. It is uncontroverted that John Lilley was a member of the general population at risk of contracting the diseases that he did, that no study of veterans exposed to Agent Orange in Vietnam shows an increased incidence of these diseases, and that no treating physician linked John Lilley's illness to Agent Orange exposure. Under the circumstances, defendants are entitled to judgment as a matter of established tort law.

Granting summary judgment in this case does not involve issues of credibility or demeanor. The documents and studies submitted to the court establish that there can be no question of fact as to whether Agent Orange caused plaintiff's illness and death.

C.   OTHER GROUNDS FOR GRANTING THE MOTION

Even if plaintiff could show a causal link between Agent Orange and John Lilley's illness, several other legal difficulties preclude recovery. These include the Maryland statute of limitations, see In re "Agent Orange" Product Liability Litigation, 597 F. Supp. 740, 800-816 & Appendix E (E.D.N.Y. 1984), the inability to demonstrate which defendant caused harm, id. at 819-833, and the government contract defense. In view of the court's finding on causation, there is no need to further explore these issues. See the discussion in In re "Agent Orange" Product Liability Litigation, 611 F. Supp. 1223 (E.D.N.Y. 1985).

V.   CONCLUSION

Summary judgment is granted. The complaint is dismissed without costs, disbursements or attorneys' fees. This memorandum constitutes a final judgment.

So ordered.

The problem with expert testimony does not end with its admission. If the testimony is controverted by other expert testimony, how is the jury (or the judge, for that matter) to determine which expert testimony is correct, or at least more correct?

WELLS BY MAIHAFER v.
ORTHO PHARMACEUTICAL CORP.
615 F. Supp. 262 (N.D. Ga. 1985), modified, 788 F.2d 741 (11th Cir.),
cert. denied, 479 U.S. 950 (1986)

SHOOB, J.

Plaintiffs—Mary Maihafer and Gary S. Wells, on behalf of their infant daughter Katie Laurel Wells, and Mary Maihafer, individually—brought this products liability action against defendant Ortho Pharmaceutical Corporation to recover damages arising from multiple birth defects suffered by Katie Wells. The central issues that emerged at trial were (1) whether Ortho-Gynol Contraceptive Jelly, a spermicide manufactured and marketed by defendant and allegedly used by plaintiff Mary Maihafer several months before and several weeks after Katie Wells was conceived, proximately caused these birth defects; and (2) whether defendant negligently failed to warn plaintiff Mary Maihafer that an increased risk of birth defects accompanied the use of its product.

At the parties' request, the case was tried before the Court without a jury. After an exhaustive two-week trial with competent and well-prepared counsel for each side, the Court's decision was not an easy one. The medical and scientific evidence presented was in direct conflict. Still, the Court recognized then, and reiterates now, that its task was not to presume the expertise to resolve, once and for all, the dispute within the scientific community about the safety of spermicides. Rather, the Court's function was to render a legal decision, not a medical one. That is, the Court's duty was to weigh carefully the evidence that *these* parties presented to *this* Court in the trial of *this* case and to determine with reference to the facts of the case at hand whether plaintiffs had satisfied their burden of proving that they were entitled to the relief sought.

At trial the key evidence was the testimony of highly qualified expert witnesses and various medical and scientific studies. In considering this evidence, the Court kept in mind plaintiffs' burden of proof: plaintiffs could not recover if the Court found that there was only a "bare possibility" that the spermicide caused these birth defects or that other theories of causation were equally plausible. Rather, to authorize recovery plaintiff's evidence must have shown to a "reasonable degree of medical certainty" that defendant's product was responsible.

The testimony of plaintiffs' and defendant's experts conflicted on several crucial points. Experts on each side testified that, to a reasonable degree of medical certainty, their side's theory of the case was correct. Attempting to resolve these direct conflicts in the experts' opinions, throughout the trial the Court regularly examined daily transcripts of much of the expert testimony and spent an entire weekend reviewing the studies introduced. Although some of the studies suggested a connection between spermicides and birth defects, overall the studies failed to show conclusively whether or not the spermicide caused any or all of the birth defects suffered by Katie Wells. The Court emphasizes, however, that plaintiffs' ultimate burden was not to produce an unassailable scientific study which proves that spermicides have caused birth defects in rats, rabbits, or members of a large group health plan, but rather to show from *all* the evidence presented, to a reasonable degree of medical certainty, that the spermicide caused some or all of *Katie Wells'* birth defects.

The Court's decision, therefore, turned on the oral testimony of a variety of expert witnesses whose opinions often were diametrically opposed on the major issues presented in the case. In assessing the credibility of these witnesses, the Court considered each expert's background, training, experience, and familiarity with the circumstances of this particular case; and the Court evaluated the rationality and internal consistency of each expert's testimony in light of all the evidence presented. The Court paid close attention to each expert's demeanor and tone. Perhaps most important, the Court did its best to ascertain the motives, biases, and interests that might have influenced each expert's opinion.

With few exceptions, the Court found the testimony of plaintiffs' experts generally to be competent, credible, and directed to the specific circumstances of this case. The testimony of defendant's experts, in contrast, often indicated bias or inconsistency. Primarily because the Court found plaintiffs' expert testimony to be far more credible than defendant's, at the conclusion of trial the Court announced that plaintiffs had carried their burden of proving that the spermicide proximately caused some, but not all, of Katie Wells' birth defects and that defendant had been negligent in failing to warn plaintiff Mary Maihafer of this danger. As a result, the Court awarded damages to plaintiffs Katie Wells and Mary Maihafer. The following discussion explains in detail how the Court arrived at this decision from the evidence presented at trial and sets forth the Court's findings of fact and conclusion of law in accordance with Rule 52, Fed. R. Civ. P.

PLAINTIFFS' CONTENTIONS

Plaintiff Mary Maihafer, the mother of plaintiff Katie Wells, is a thirty-two year old college instructor who, plaintiffs contended, has no family history of birth defects and who in 1979 gave birth to a child with no birth defects. According to plaintiffs, Gary S. Wells, the father of Katie Wells, also has no family history of birth defects and is the father of a child born in 1974 without birth defects.

In July 1980, Ms. Maihafer obtained from her gynecologist a prescription for a diaphragm to be used for contraception and a sample tube of Ortho-Gynol Contraceptive Jelly ("the Product"). At that time, plaintiffs contended, a nurse instructed her on the proper use of the diaphragm and spermicidal jelly, and Ms. Maihafer read the "Directions for Using Ortho-Gynol Contraceptive Jelly," which accompanied the Product.

Plaintiffs alleged that Ms. Maihafer had used the diaphragm and Ortho-Gynol Contraceptive Jelly in accordance with these instructions every time she had sex with Gary Wells from the time the diaphragm was prescribed in late July 1980 until mid-November 1980. Notwithstanding these precautions, Ms. Maihafer missed her menstrual period that was due to occur around November 1, 1980, and later discovered that she had become pregnant in October 1980.

On July 1, 1981, Ms. Maihafer gave birth to plaintiff Katie Wells, who was born with the following birth defects: (1) a cleft lip; (2) an abnormal formation and shortening of her right hand; (3) the absence of the distal joint of her right ring finger; (4) the complete lack of a left arm; and (5) only partial development of the left clavicle and shoulder. Later Katie Wells was diagnosed as also suffering from hypoplasia of the right optic nerve, which according to plaintiffs has made her almost ninety percent blind in that eye.

Plaintiffs filed this action on September 2, 1982, seeking to recover for damages to both Katie Wells and Mary Maihafer. The complaint stated causes of action for negligence, strict products liability, intentional tort, and breach of warranty. Plaintiffs asserted that the spermicide's active ingredient, a non-ionic surfactant that works to break down sperm cell membranes, caused these birth defects through one of the following "mechanisms":

(1) injury to a sperm that ultimately fertilizes an egg;
(2) injury to an unfertilized egg;
(3) injury to a fertilized egg or zygote; or
(4) injury to the developing fetus, either by direct contact with the fetus or by absorption by the mother.

Moreover, plaintiffs alleged that, at the time Mary Maihafer purchased and used the Product, defendant knew or should have known of certain studies that were available to the scientific community linking the use of spermicides to birth defects in the children of mothers who used spermicides around the time of conception.

According to plaintiffs, defendant's actual or constructive knowledge of this increased risk imposed on defendant a duty to warn health professionals and prospective users of this risk by placing a warning on the Product. Plaintiffs argued that defendant's failure to warn constituted a defect in the Product and thus established defendant's liability under a strict products liability theory. Further, plaintiffs maintained that the failure to warn was also a basis for finding defendant negligent. Finally, plaintiffs maintained that they were entitled to punitive damages because defendant's failure to warn was part of a conscious decision to protect its market share.

DEFENDANT'S CONTENTIONS

Defendant vehemently denied any association between the use of Ortho-Gynol Contraceptive Jelly and birth defects. Defendant pointed out that the Product's active ingredient, a non-ionic surfactant called p-diisobutylphenoxypolyethoxyethanol or octoxynol-9, is almost identical to non-ionic surfactants used by other manufacturers of spermicides. Since 1950, defendant has sold the Product in its present form to millions of women.

Defendant maintained that the Product is safe and effective when properly used. Defendant suggested that Ms. Maihafer may not have used the spermicide in strict accordance with the instructions. Defendant also pointed out that the Product carried a warning that no form of birth control is one hundred percent effective.

According to defendant, no additional warning was or is necessary. Defendant argued that at the time of Katie Wells' conception in the fall of 1980, no published reports or studies had concluded that spermicides cause birth defects; further, according to defendant, it had received no other complaints nor had access to any other evidence suggesting a link between its Product and birth defects.

Defendant argued that, on the contrary, "[t]he overwhelming weight of the credible scientific evidence has established that use of such products does not cause birth defects." Defendant criticized studies relied on by plaintiffs' experts as "flawed" and "not scientifically reliable." According to defendant, numerous respected scientists have conducted extensive testing and critical review of non-ionic surfactants and have concluded that the Product is safe and effective. Defendant pointed out that at least one select panel appointed by the government has concluded that the Product should carry no warning that it might cause birth defects.

Finally, defendants argued that even if plaintiffs succeeded in proving a causal link between the Product and Katie Wells' birth defects, defendant had no duty to place a warning on the Product in 1980 because of the absence of any reliable information at that time connecting spermicides and birth defects. Thus, according to defendant, the Product was not defective, defendant had not been negligent, and the failure to provide any such warning was not the result of a conscious marketing decision that might support a claim for punitive damages.

THE EVIDENCE AT TRIAL

A.   MARY MAIHAFER

Plaintiff Mary Maihafer testified on direct examination consistently with plaintiffs' theory of the case outlined above. Ms. Maihafer testified positively that she had used the diaphragm and spermicidal jelly according to the instructions every time she and Gary Wells had sex from late July until mid-November 1980. She further stated that she had continued to use the Product for one to two weeks after she missed her menstrual period of November 1, 1980. Ms. Maihafer also mentioned that several months into this pregnancy she had used the prescription drug Decadron for bronchitis and some prescribed antibiotics for an ear infection. In addition, she testified that after Katie Wells' birth, she interrupted her college teaching career for two years to take care of the child. On cross-examination, Ms. Maihafer admitted that she had known, at the time she obtained the diaphragm and spermicide, that diaphragms are not one hundred percent effective in preventing conception.

B.   GARY WELLS

Gary Wells testified that, to his knowledge, Mary Maihafer used the diaphragm and spermicide every time they had sex from the time she obtained it until mid-November 1980. Counsel for both sides questioned him about his use of drugs. He testified that he had used LSD once in 1971, amphetamines three or four times in 1979, and methaqualone in two or three doses in 1979. Further, he stated that he had smoked marijuana on infrequent occasions from 1969-72 and that he may have smoked marijuana once or twice in 1980 during the time he dated Mary Maihafer.

C.   DR. BRUCE BUEHLER

Plaintiffs' primary expert witness was Dr. Bruce Buehler, who is an associate professor of pediatrics and pathology at the University of Nebraska Medical Center, the director of the Center for Human Genetics, and the director and dean of the Meyer Children's Rehabilitation Institute. Dr. Buehler is board-certified in pediatrics, chemical genetics, and biochemical and metabolic genetics. His research area is biochemical teratology, the study of the effects of drugs and environmental agents on developing fetuses. The list of Dr. Buehler's credentials is long and impressive.

Dr. Buehler testified that the Meyer Children's Rehabilitation Institute each year handles approximately 25,000 visits by handicapped persons from birth through age sixty. The Institute, which employs an estimated ninety professionals who work with handicapping disorders, has a national reputation that attracts patients from all over the country.

Dr. Buehler had examined Katie Wells in person, as opposed to merely viewing her medical records. Before testifying about his findings in the examination and his conclusions that followed, Dr. Buehler explained what a geneticist looks for in an examination to determine the cause of birth defects, and he demonstrated with Katie Wells in court certain aspects of the examination.

The doctor testified that in examining patients with birth defects, a geneticist attempts to determine at what stage of fetal development the defects or abnormalities occurred. He stated that because genetic problems "tend to do their dirty work" from the moment of conception, they result in abnormalities in the body that are symmetrical. On the other hand, Dr. Buehler explained, birth defects tend to be asymmetrical when they are caused by the environment, drugs, and a few genetic problems. Thus, in examining Katie Wells, Dr. Buehler testified that he and a colleague spent much time studying the symmetry of her body and the placement and size of her body parts.

Dr. Buehler explained his findings as he re-enacted portions of the examination in court with Katie Wells. What the doctor found most significant, and what the Court partially observed, was the condition of Katie's left shoulder: the shoulder was totally smooth, the shoulder blade and scapula were half their normal size, and the size of the muscles was normal. Dr. Buehler testified that although most limb deficiencies show some attempt at making an arm or finger — such as a hand or piece of tissue attached to the shoulder — the complete smoothness of this shoulder was rare and suggested total disruption of the limb bud. He also found surprising the normal musculature of a shoulder with no arm.

Although Dr. Buehler testified definitively that vascular disruption had caused the birth defects of Katie Wells' shoulder and hand, he would not attribute her other defects to the same cause. He testified that although he could not rule out the possibility of vascular disruption, he did not have "enough data to make a cleft lip a vascular accident as I do with limb deformities." With respect to the hypoplasia of the optic nerve, Dr. Buehler stated as follows:

> It is much easier to explain eye formation and optic nerve formation on a vascular basis than it would be for me for a cleft [lip]. That is not what I ruled out or ruled

in. I have not included that in my opinion because I have focused on the arms, which are the most comfortable to me.

That Dr. Buehler was careful in limiting his opinion to matters within his area of expertise greatly enhanced his credibility in the view of the Court. . . .

The Court found Dr. Buehler to be the most credible of all the witnesses presented in this case. His credentials and experience in biochemical teratology were impressive. Unlike defendant's experts, he had personally examined Katie Wells. His uncontradicted testimony was that he formed no opinion until after this examination. His opinion at trial was the same as the opinion that he previously had offered at his deposition, which defense counsel conducted within an hour of his examination of Katie Wells. That Dr. Buehler limited his testimony to the area of his expertise — limb defects — and would not say that all Katie Wells' defects were caused by the spermicide, made his opinion even more believable. His detailed explanation of how he had ruled out other possible causes demonstrated that his opinion was the product of a careful, methodical reasoning process, not mere speculation. His demeanor as a witness was excellent: he answered all questions fairly and openly in a balanced manner, translating technical terms and findings into common, understandable language, and he gave no hint of bias or prejudice. In short, this witness could hardly have been more credible. . . .

As discussed above, plaintiffs carried their burden of proof regarding causation. The Court found that plaintiffs had presented competent and credible medical and scientific evidence that showed to a reasonable degree of medical certainty that the Product proximately caused the birth defects of Katie Wells' left arm and shoulder and right hand.

SUMMARY

The Court . . . directs that judgment be entered in favor of plaintiffs in the following amounts:

(1) Katie Wells
    (a) loss of future earnings $415,000
    (b) future medical expenses $1,200,000
    (c) past and future pain and suffering $3,000,000

(2) Mary Maihafer
    (a) medical expenses of Katie Wells $30
    (b) loss of earnings $36,000
    (c) mental distress $500,000

The Court further directs that plaintiffs shall recover their costs of this action from defendant.

FEDERAL JUDGES v. SCIENCE
N.Y. Times, Dec. 27, 1986, p.22, col. 1

Katie Wells was born in 1981 with serious birth defects. Her parents attributed them to a contraceptive jelly and sued the maker, Ortho Pharmaceutical. Judge Marvin Shoob of the U.S. District Court in Georgia ruled they had proved their case and assessed $5 million in damages against Ortho. The Court of Appeals declined to overturn the judgment and last month the Supreme Court refused to intervene. What is wrong with that?

First, the facts. Scientific experts often differ and the courts generally decide, with some skill, which to believe. But with spermicides like Ortho's, there is no serious difference among experts. After reviewing some 20 epidemiological studies, an expert committee advised the Food and Drug Administration in 1983 that the preponderance of available evidence "indicates no association" between spermicides and birth defects.

How then could Judge Shoob have ruled otherwise? Despite the written evidence of the scientific literature, he focused on the oral testimony given in his court, and says he "paid close attention to each expert's demeanor and tone." Ortho's witnesses included prominent epidemiologists but were gravely deficient in the demeanor department.

One had impressive credentials, Judge Shoob conceded, yet "lacked credibility." Of another, the judge said "his overall demeanor and manner indicated a degree of bias." He cited objective grounds for doubting one main witness, who had not disclosed that he consulted with Ortho before participating in the Federal review of the jelly's safety.

Judge Shoob, who sat without a jury, chose instead to believe the plaintiff's main witnesses, three pharmacologists and an expert in birth defects, none of whom had any expertise in epidemiology, the science of determining the causes of disease. Typically their demeanor was—in the judge's words— "excellent." He ruled they had shown Ortho's jelly caused Katie Wells's birth defects.

Science's finest achievement is finding methods to raise objective evidence above the merely anecdotal. Judge Shoob was not moved by the preponderance of scientific evidence—and neither was the Appeals Court. It espoused the fiction that there had been a battle of experts, even though no scientist would consider pharmacologists expert in a matter of epidemiology. The Court of Appeals explicitly rejected scientific standards of proof; "What matters," the court declared, "is that [Judge Shoob] found sufficient evidence of causation in a legal sense in this particular case, and that that finding is not clearly erroneous."

Ortho argued in vain that the Court of Appeals should have held Judge Shoob's reasoning to a higher standard than "not clearly erroneous." The Supreme Court refused to hear the case. Thus the Federal judiciary has placed itself opposite the best judgment of the scientific community.

As is noted in The New England Journal of Medicine, "The Wells v. Ortho decisions are of great concern to the medical community because they indicate that the courts will not be bound by reasonable scientific standards of proof."

The practical consequences of the Ortho decision could be profound. Spermicides are used by some three million women, particularly by teenagers, who can buy them without a prescription. Profits are small. Ortho makes $3 million a year on its product and a few more such suits will drive spermicides off the market, like intrauterine devices before them. Contraceptive choice for all women will be further narrowed.

In their different ways, both law and science seek after truth. That Judge Shoob and the appellate judges ignored the best scientific evidence is an intellectual embarrassment. The practical result is that many citizens may suffer.

Concern about the "litigation explosion" and the role being played by expert testimony in it led to proposals to amend Rule 702 to incorporate a requirement that expert testimony be "reasonably reliable" and that it "substantially assist" the factfinder. This amendment was in the rules promulgation process in the early 1990s when the Supreme Court finally granted certiorari on the issue of the standard of quality for expert testimony under FRE 702.

DAUBERT v. MERRELL DOW PHARMACEUTICALS, INC.
509 U.S. 579 (1993)

Justice BLACKMUN delivered the opinion of the Court.

In this case we are called upon to determine the standard for admitting expert scientific testimony in a federal trial.

I

Petitioners Jason Daubert and Eric Schuller are minor children born with serious birth defects. They and their parents sued respondent in California state court, alleging that the birth defects had been caused by the mothers' ingestion of Bendectin, a prescription anti-nausea drug marketed by respondent. Respondent removed the suits to federal court on diversity grounds.

After extensive discovery, respondent moved for summary judgment, contending that Bendectin does not cause birth defects in humans and that petitioners would be unable to come forward with any admissible evidence that it does. In support of its motion, respondent submitted an affidavit of Steven H. Lamm, physician and epidemiologist, who is a well-credentialed expert on the risks from exposure to various chemical substances. Doctor Lamm stated that he had reviewed all the literature on Bendectin and human birth defects—more than 30 published studies involving over 130,000 patients. No study had found Bendectin to be a human teratogen (i.e., a substance capable of causing malformations in fetuses). On the basis of this review, Doctor Lamm concluded that maternal use of Bendectin during the first trimester of pregnancy has not been shown to be a risk factor for human birth defects.

Petitioners did not (and do not) contest this characterization of the published record regarding Bendectin. Instead, they responded to respondent's motion with the testimony of eight experts of their own, each of whom also possessed impressive credentials. These experts had concluded that Bendectin can cause birth defects. Their conclusions were based upon "in vitro" (test tube) and "in vivo" (live) animal studies that found a link between Bendectin and malformations; pharmacological studies of the chemical structure of Bendectin that purported to show similarities between the structure of the drug and that of other substances known to cause birth defects; and the "reanalysis" of previously published epidemiological (human statistical) studies.

The District Court granted respondent's motion for summary judgment. The court stated that scientific evidence is admissible only if the principle upon which it is based is "'sufficiently established to have general acceptance in the field to which it belongs.'" 727 F. Supp. 570, 572 (S.D. Cal. 1989), quoting United States v. Kilgus, 571 F.2d 508, 510 (CA9 1978). The court concluded that petitioners' evidence did not meet this standard. Given the vast body of epidemiological data concerning Bendectin, the court held, expert opinion which is not based on epidemiological evidence is not admissible to establish causation. Thus, the animal-cell studies, live-animal studies, and chemical-structure analyses on which petitioners had relied could not raise by themselves a reasonably disputable jury issue regarding causation. Petitioners' epidemiological analyses, based as they were on recalculations of data in previously published studies that had found no causal link between the drug and birth defects, were ruled to be inadmissible because they had not been published or subjected to peer review.

The United States Court of Appeals for the Ninth Circuit affirmed. 951 F.2d 1128 (1991). Citing Frye v. United States, 54 App. D.C. 46, 293 F. 1013, 1014 (1923), the court stated that expert opinion based on a scientific technique is inadmissible unless the technique is "generally accepted" as reliable in the relevant scientific community. 951 F.2d at 1129-1130. The court declared that expert opinion based on a methodology that diverges "significantly from the procedures accepted by recognized authorities in the field . . . cannot be shown to be 'generally accepted as a reliable technique.'" Id., at 1130, quoting United States v. Solomon, 753 F.2d 1522, 1526 (CA9 1985).

The court emphasized that other Courts of Appeals considering the risks of Bendectin had refused to admit reanalyses of epidemiological studies that had been neither published nor subjected to peer review. Those courts had found unpublished reanalyses "particularly problematic in light of the massive weight of the original published studies supporting [respondent's] position, all of which had undergone full scrutiny from the scientific community." Id., at 1130. Contending that reanalysis is generally accepted by the scientific community only when it is subjected to verification and scrutiny by others in the field, the Court of Appeals rejected petitioners' reanalyses as "unpublished, not subjected to the normal peer review process and generated solely for use in litigation." Id., at 1131. The court concluded that petitioners' evidence provided an insufficient foundation to allow admission of expert testimony that Bendectin caused their injuries and, accordingly, that petitioners could not satisfy their burden of proving causation at trial.

We granted certiorari in light of sharp divisions among the courts regarding the proper standard for the admission of expert testimony.

II

A

In the 70 years since its formulation in the *Frye* case, the "general acceptance" test has been the dominant standard for determining the admissibility of novel scientific evidence at trial. See E. Green & C. Nesson, Problems, Cases, and Materials on Evidence 649 (1983). Although under increasing attack of late, the rule continues to be followed by a majority of courts, including the Ninth Circuit.

The *Frye* test has its origin in a short and citation-free 1923 decision concerning the admissibility of evidence derived from a systolic blood pressure deception test, a crude precursor to the polygraph machine. In what has become a famous (perhaps infamous) passage, the then Court of Appeals for the District of Columbia described the device and its operation and declared: "Just when a scientific principle or discovery crosses the line between the experimental and demonstrable stages is difficult to define. Somewhere in this twilight zone the evidential force of the principle must be recognized, and while courts will go a long way in admitting expert testimony deduced from a well-recognized scientific principle or discovery, the thing from which the deduction is made must be sufficiently established to have gained general acceptance in the particular field in which it belongs." 54 App. D.C. at 47. Because the deception test had "not yet gained such standing and scientific recognition among physiological and psychological authorities as would justify the courts in admitting expert testimony deduced from the discovery, development, and experiments thus far made," evidence of its results was ruled inadmissible. Ibid.

The merits of the *Frye* test have been much debated, and scholarship on its proper scope and application is legion. Petitioners' primary attack, however, is not on the content but on the continuing authority of the rule. They contend that the *Frye* test was superseded by the adoption of the Federal Rules of Evidence. We agree.

We interpret the legislatively-enacted Federal Rules of Evidence as we would any statute. Rule 402 provides the baseline: "All relevant evidence is admissible, except as otherwise provided by the Constitution of the United States, by Act of Congress, by these rules, or by other rules prescribed by the Supreme Court pursuant to statutory authority. Evidence which is not relevant is not admissible." "Relevant evidence" is defined as that which has "any tendency to make the existence of any fact that is of consequence to the determination of the action more probable or less probable than it would be without the evidence." Rule 401. The Rule's basic standard of relevance thus is a liberal one.

Frye, of course, predated the Rules by half a century. In United States v. Abel, 469 U.S. 45 (1984), we considered the pertinence of background common law in interpreting the Rules of Evidence. We noted that the Rules occupy the field but, quoting Professor Cleary, the Reporter, explained that the common law nevertheless could serve as an aid to their application: "In principle, under the Federal Rules no common law of evidence remains. 'All relevant evidence is admissible, except as otherwise provided. . . .' In reality, of course, the body of common law knowledge continues to exist, though in the somewhat altered form of a source of guidance in the exercise of delegated powers." Id., at 51-52. We found the common-law precept at issue in the *Abel* case entirely consistent with Rule 402's general requirement of admissibility, and considered it unlikely that the drafters had intended to change the rule. In Bourjaily v. United States, 483 U.S. 171 (1987), on the other hand, the Court was unable to find a particular common-law doctrine in the Rules, and so held it superseded.

Here there is a specific Rule that speaks to the contested issue. Rule 702, governing expert testimony, provides: "If scientific, technical, or other specialized knowledge will assist the trier of fact to understand the evidence or to determine a fact in issue, a witness qualified as an expert by knowledge, skill, experience, training, or education, may testify thereto in the form of an opinion or otherwise." Nothing in the text of this Rule establishes "general acceptance" as an absolute prerequisite to admissibility. Nor does respondent present any clear indication that Rule 702 or the Rules as a whole were intended to incorporate a "general acceptance" standard. The drafting history makes no mention of *Frye*, and a rigid "general acceptance" requirement would be at odds with the "liberal thrust" of the Federal Rules and their "general approach of relaxing the traditional barriers to 'opinion' testimony." Beech Aircraft Corp. v. Rainey, [488 U.S. 153, 169 (1988)]. Given the

Rules' permissive backdrop and their inclusion of a specific rule on expert testimony that does not mention "general acceptance," the assertion that the Rules somehow assimilated *Frye* is unconvincing. *Frye* made "general acceptance" the exclusive test for admitting expert scientific testimony. That austere standard, absent from and incompatible with the Federal Rules of Evidence, should not be applied in federal trials.

B

That the *Frye* test was displaced by the Rules of Evidence does not mean, however, that the Rules themselves place no limits on the admissibility of purportedly scientific evidence. Nor is the trial judge disabled from screening such evidence. To the contrary, under the Rules the trial judge must ensure that any and all scientific testimony or evidence admitted is not only relevant, but reliable.

The primary locus of this obligation is Rule 702, which clearly contemplates some degree of regulation of the subjects and theories about which an expert may testify. "If scientific, technical, or other specialized knowledge will assist the trier of fact to understand the evidence or to determine a fact in issue" an expert "may testify thereto." The subject of an expert's testimony must be "scientific . . . knowledge." The adjective "scientific" implies a grounding in the methods and procedures of science. Similarly, the word "knowledge" connotes more than subjective belief or unsupported speculation. The term "applies to any body of known facts or to any body of ideas inferred from such facts or accepted as truths on good grounds." Webster's Third New International Dictionary 1252 (1986). Of course, it would be unreasonable to conclude that the subject of scientific testimony must be "known" to a certainty; arguably, there are no certainties in science. But, in order to qualify as "scientific knowledge," an inference or assertion must be derived by the scientific method. Proposed testimony must be supported by appropriate validation—i.e., "good grounds," based on what is known. In short, the requirement that an expert's testimony pertain to "scientific knowledge" establishes a standard of evidentiary reliability.

Rule 702 further requires that the evidence or testimony "assist the trier of fact to understand the evidence or to determine a fact in issue." This condition goes primarily to relevance. "Expert testimony which does not relate to any issue in the case is not relevant and, ergo, nonhelpful." 3 Weinstein & Berger ¶702[02], p.702-18. See also United States v. Downing, 753 F.2d 1224, 1242 (CA3 1985) ("An additional consideration under Rule 702 — and another aspect of relevancy — is whether expert testimony proffered in the case is sufficiently tied to the facts of the case that it will aid the jury in resolving a factual dispute"). The consideration has been aptly described by Judge Becker as one of "fit." Ibid. "Fit" is not always obvious, and scientific validity for one purpose is not necessarily scientific validity for other, unrelated purposes. The study of the phases of the moon, for example, may provide valid scientific "knowledge" about whether a certain night was dark, and if darkness is a fact in issue, the knowledge will assist the trier of fact. However (absent creditable grounds supporting such a link), evidence that the moon was full on a certain night will not assist the trier of fact in determining whether an individual was unusually likely to have behaved irrationally on that night. Rule 702's "helpfulness" standard requires a valid scientific connection to the pertinent inquiry as a precondition to admissibility.

That these requirements are embodied in Rule 702 is not surprising. Unlike an ordinary witness, see Rule 701, an expert is permitted wide latitude to offer opinions, including those that are not based on first-hand knowledge or observation. See Rules 702 and 703. Presumably, this relaxation of the usual requirement of first-hand knowledge — a rule which represents "a 'most pervasive manifestation' of the common law insistence upon 'the most reliable sources of information,' " Advisory Committee's Notes on Fed. Rule Evid. 602 — is premised on an assumption that the expert's opinion will have a reliable basis in the knowledge and experience of his discipline.

C

Faced with a proffer of expert scientific testimony, then, the trial judge must determine at the outset, pursuant to Rule 104(a), whether the expert is proposing to testify to (1) scientific knowledge that (2) will assist the trier of fact to understand or determine a fact in issue.[11] This entails a preliminary assessment of whether the reasoning or methodology underlying the testimony is scientifically valid and of whether that reasoning or methodology properly can be applied to the facts in issue. We are confident that federal judges possess the capacity to undertake this review. Many factors will bear on the inquiry, and we do not presume to set out a definitive checklist or test. But some general observations are appropriate.

Ordinarily, a key question to be answered in determining whether a theory or technique is scientific knowledge that will assist the trier of fact will be whether it can be (and has been) tested. "Scientific methodology today is based on generating hypotheses and testing them to

11. Although the *Frye* decision itself focused exclusively on "novel" scientific techniques, we do not read the requirements of Rule 702 to apply specially or exclusively to unconventional evidence. Of course, well-established propositions are less likely to be challenged than those that are novel, and they are more handily defended. Indeed, theories that are so firmly established as to have attained the status of scientific law, such as the laws of thermodynamics, properly are subject to judicial notice under Fed. Rule Evid. 201.

see if they can be falsified; indeed, this methodology is what distinguishes science from other fields of human inquiry." [Green, Expert Witnesses and Sufficiency of Evidence in Toxic Substances Litigation: The Legacy of Agent Orange and Bendectin Litigation, 86 Nw. U.L. Rev. 643, 645 (1992).]

Another pertinent consideration is whether the theory or technique has been subjected to peer review and publication. Publication (which is but one element of peer review) is not a sine qua non of admissibility; it does not necessarily correlate with reliability, and in some instances well-grounded but innovative theories will not have been published. Some propositions, moreover, are too particular, too new, or of too limited interest to be published. But submission to the scrutiny of the scientific community is a component of "good science," in part because it increases the likelihood that substantive flaws in methodology will be detected. The fact of publication (or lack thereof) in a peer-reviewed journal thus will be a relevant, though not dispositive, consideration in assessing the scientific validity of a particular technique or methodology on which an opinion is premised.

Additionally, in the case of a particular scientific technique, the court ordinarily should consider the known or potential rate of error, see, e.g., United States v. Smith, 869 F.2d 348, 353-354 (CA7 1989) (surveying studies of the error rate of spectrographic voice identification technique), and the existence and maintenance of standards controlling the technique's operation. See United States v. Williams, 583 F.2d 1194, 1198 (CA2 1978) (noting professional organization's standard governing spectrographic analysis), cert. denied, 439 U.S. 1117 (1979).

Finally, "general acceptance" can yet have a bearing on the inquiry. A "reliability assessment does not require, although it does permit, explicit identification of a relevant scientific community and an express determination of a particular degree of acceptance within that community." United States v. Downing, 753 F.2d, at 1238. See also 3 Weinstein & Berger ¶702[03], pp.702-41 to 702-42. Widespread acceptance can be an important factor in ruling particular evidence admissible, and "a known technique that has been able to attract only minimal support within the community," Downing, supra, at 1238, may properly be viewed with skepticism.

The inquiry envisioned by Rule 702 is, we emphasize, a flexible one. Its overarching subject is the scientific validity—and thus the evidentiary relevance and reliability—of the principles that underlie a proposed submission. The focus, of course, must be solely on principles and methodology, not on the conclusions that they generate.

Throughout, a judge assessing a proffer of expert scientific testimony under Rule 702 should also be mindful of other applicable rules. Rule 703 provides that expert opinions based on otherwise inadmissible hearsay are to be admitted only if the facts or data are "of a type reasonably relied upon by experts in the particular field in forming opinions or inferences upon the subject." Rule 706 allows the court at its discretion to procure the assistance of an expert of its own choosing. Finally, Rule 403 permits the exclusion of relevant evidence "if its probative value is substantially outweighed by the danger of unfair prejudice, confusion of the issues, or misleading the jury. . . ." Judge Weinstein has explained: "Expert evidence can be both powerful and quite misleading because of the difficulty in evaluating it. Because of this risk, the judge in weighing possible prejudice against probative force under Rule 403 of the present rules exercises more control over experts than over lay witnesses." [Weinstein, Rule 702 of the Federal Rules of Evidence Is Sound; It Should Not Be Amended, 138 F.R.D. 631, 632 (1991).]

III

We conclude by briefly addressing what appear to be two underlying concerns of the parties and amici in this case. Respondent expresses apprehension that abandonment of "general acceptance" as the exclusive requirement for admission will result in a "free-for-all" in which befuddled juries are confounded by absurd and irrational pseudoscientific assertions. In this regard respondent seems to us to be overly pessimistic about the capabilities of the jury, and of the adversary system generally. Vigorous cross-examination, presentation of contrary evidence, and careful instruction on the burden of proof are the traditional and appropriate means of attacking shaky but admissible evidence. See Rock v. Arkansas, 483 U.S. 44, 61 (1987). Additionally, in the event the trial court concludes that the scintilla of evidence presented supporting a position is insufficient to allow a reasonable juror to conclude that the position more likely than not is true, the court remains free to direct a judgment, Fed. Rule Civ. Proc. 50(a), and likewise to grant summary judgment, Fed. Rule Civ. Proc. 56. . . . These conventional devices, rather than wholesale exclusion under an uncompromising "general acceptance" test, are the appropriate safeguards where the basis of scientific testimony meets the standards of Rule 702.

Petitioners and, to a greater extent, their amici exhibit a different concern. They suggest that recognition of a screening role for the judge that allows for the exclusion of "invalid" evidence will sanction a stifling and repressive scientific orthodoxy and will be inimical to the search for truth. It is true that open debate is an essential part of both legal and scientific analyses. Yet there are important differences between the quest for truth in the courtroom and the quest for truth in the laboratory. Scientific conclusions are subject to perpetual revision. Law, on the other hand, must resolve disputes finally and quickly. The scientific project is advanced by broad and wide-ranging consideration of a multitude of hypotheses, for those that are incorrect will eventually be shown to be so, and that in itself is an advance. Conjectures that are probably wrong are of little use, however, in the project of reaching a quick, final, and binding legal judgment—often of great consequence — about a particular set of events in the past. We recognize that in practice, a gatekeeping role for the judge, no matter how flexible, inevitably on occasion will prevent the jury from learning of authentic insights and innovations. That, nevertheless, is the balance that is struck by Rules of Evidence designed not for the exhaustive search for cosmic understanding but for the particularized resolution of legal disputes.[13]

IV

To summarize: "general acceptance" is not a necessary precondition to the admissibility of scientific evidence under the Federal Rules of Evidence, but the Rules of Evidence—especially Rule 702—do assign to the trial judge the task of ensuring that an expert's testimony both rests on a reliable foundation and is relevant to the task at hand. Pertinent evidence based on scientifically valid principles will satisfy those demands.

The inquiries of the District Court and the Court of Appeals focused almost exclusively on "general acceptance," as gauged by publication and the decisions of other courts. Accordingly, the judgment of the Court of Appeals is vacated and the case is remanded for further proceedings consistent with this opinion.

It is so ordered.

Chief Justice REHNQUIST, with whom Justice STEVENS joins, concurring in part and dissenting in part.

The petition for certiorari in this case presents two questions: first, whether the rule of Frye v. United States remains good law after the enactment of the Federal Rules of Evidence; and second, if *Frye* remains valid, whether it requires expert scientific testimony to have been subjected to a peer-review process in order to be admissible. The Court concludes, correctly in my view, that the *Frye* rule did not survive the enactment of the Federal Rules of Evidence, and I therefore join Parts I and II-A of its opinion. The second question presented in the petition for certiorari necessarily is mooted by this holding, but the Court nonetheless proceeds to construe Rules 702 and 703 very much in the abstract, and then offers some "general observations."

"General observations" by this Court customarily carry great weight with lower federal courts, but the ones offered here suffer from the flaw

---

13. This is not to say that judicial interpretation, as opposed to adjudicative factfinding, does not share basic characteristics of the scientific endeavor: "The work of a judge is in one sense enduring and in another ephemeral. . . . In the endless process of testing and retesting, there is a constant rejection of the dross and a constant retention of whatever is pure and sound and fine." B. Cardozo, The Nature of the Judicial Process 178, 179 (1921).

common to most such observations—they are not applied to deciding whether or not particular testimony was or was not admissible, and therefore they tend to be not only general, but vague and abstract. This is particularly unfortunate in a case such as this, where the ultimate legal question depends on an appreciation of one or more bodies of knowledge not judicially noticeable, and subject to different interpretations in the briefs of the parties and their amici. Twenty-two amicus briefs have been filed in the case, and indeed the Court's opinion contains no less than 37 citations to amicus briefs and other secondary sources.

The various briefs filed in this case are markedly different from typical briefs, in that large parts of them do not deal with decided cases or statutory language — the sort of material we customarily interpret. Instead, they deal with definitions of scientific knowledge, scientific method, scientific validity, and peer review—in short, matters far afield from the expertise of judges. This is not to say that such materials are not useful or even necessary in deciding how Rule 703 should be applied; but it is to say that the unusual subject matter should cause us to proceed with great caution in deciding more than we have to, because our reach can so easily exceed our grasp.

But even if it were desirable to make "general observations" not necessary to decide the questions presented, I cannot subscribe to some of the observations made by the Court. In Part II-B, the Court concludes that reliability and relevancy are the touchstones of the admissibility of expert testimony. Federal Rule of Evidence 402 provides, as the Court points out, that "[e]vidence which is not relevant is not admissible." But there is no similar reference in the Rule to "reliability." The Court constructs its argument by parsing the language "[i]f scientific, technical, or other specialized knowledge will assist the trier of fact to understand the evidence or to determine a fact in issue . . . an expert . . . may testify thereto. . . ." Fed. Rule Evid. 702. It stresses that the subject of the expert's testimony must be "scientific . . . knowledge," and points out that "scientific" "implies a grounding in the methods and procedures of science," and that the word "knowledge" "connotes more than subjective belief or unsupported speculation." From this it concludes that "scientific knowledge" must be "derived by the scientific method." Proposed testimony, we are told, must be supported by "appropriate validation." . . .

Questions arise simply from reading this part of the Court's opinion, and countless more questions will surely arise when hundreds of district judges try to apply its teaching to particular offers of expert testimony. Does all of this dicta apply to an expert seeking to testify on the basis of "technical or other specialized knowledge"—the other types of expert knowledge to which Rule 702 applies—or are the "general observations" limited only to "scientific knowledge"? What is the difference between scientific knowledge and technical knowledge; does Rule 702 actually contemplate that the phrase "scientific, technical, or other specialized knowledge" be broken down into numerous subspecies of expertise, or did its authors simply pick general descriptive language covering the sort of expert testimony which courts have customarily received? The Court speaks of its confidence that federal judges can make a "preliminary assessment of whether the reasoning or methodology underlying the testimony is scientifically valid and of whether that reasoning or methodology properly can be applied to the facts in issue." The Court then states that a "key question" to be answered in deciding whether something is "scientific knowledge" "will be whether it can be (and has been) tested." Following this sentence are three quotations from treatises [deleted], which speak not only of empirical testing, but one of which states that "the criterion of the scientific status of a theory is its falsifiability, or refutability, or testability."

I defer to no one in my confidence in federal judges; but I am at a loss to know what is meant when it is said that the scientific status of a theory depends on its "falsifiability," and I suspect some of them will be, too.

I do not doubt that Rule 702 confides to the judge some gatekeeping responsibility in deciding questions of the admissibility of proffered expert testimony. But I do not think it imposes on them either the obligation or the authority to become amateur scientists in order to perform that role. I think the Court would be far better advised in this case to decide only the questions presented, and to leave the further development of this important area of the law to future cases.

———————————

It is one thing for the United States Supreme Court to announce the definitive construction of Rule 702 to establish a standard of scientific reliability and relevance to govern the admission of expert testimony. It is another for the courts to apply this new standard to the flow of cases.

A virtue of the *Frye* test was the trial judge was not required to understand much about the proffered expertise. The judge could merely determine from secondary indicia whether the expertise had gained a level of general acceptance. What was the count of articles, experts, court decisions for and against the new expertise?

Daubert, on the other hand, required the trial judge to look harder at the expertise itself. Is it science? Is it good science? Is the methodology scientific? Are the results tested? Lawyers and hence judges are often individuals who shunned science from an early age. It is no wonder that they did not greet with unbridled joy the new adjudicatory responsibilities entrusted to them by the Supreme Court in *Daubert.* Compare the approaches taken by the 9th Circuit in *Daubert* itself on remand and the 6th Circuit in Glaser v. Thompson Medical Co., 32 F. 3d 969 (6th Cir. 1994) immediately following.

DAUBERT v. MERRELL DOW PHARMACEUTICALS, INC.
(on remand)
43 F.3d 1311 (9th Cir. 1995)

KOZINSKI, Circuit Judge.

On remand from the United States Supreme Court, we undertake "the task of ensuring that an expert's testimony both rests on a reliable foundation and is relevant to the task at hand." Daubert v. Merrell Dow Pharmaceuticals, Inc. (1993).

I

A.   BACKGROUND

Two minors brought suit against Merrell Dow Pharmaceuticals, claiming they suffered limb reduction birth defects because their mothers had taken Bendectin, a drug prescribed for morning sickness to about 17.5 million pregnant women in the United States between 1957 and 1982. This appeal deals with an evidentiary question: whether certain expert scientific testimony is admissible to prove that Bendectin caused the plaintiffs' birth defects.

For the most part, we don't know how birth defects come about. We do know they occur in 2-3% of births, whether or not the expectant mother has taken Bendectin. See Jose F. Cordero & Godfrey P. Oakley, Jr., Drug Exposure During Pregnancy: Some Epidemiologic Considerations, 26 Clinical Obstetrics & Gynecology 418, 424-25 (June 1983). Limb defects are even rarer, occurring in fewer than one birth out of every 1000. But scientists simply do not know how teratogens (chemicals known to cause limb reduction defects) do their damage: They cannot reconstruct the biological chain of events that leads from an expectants mother's ingestion of a teratogenic substance to the stunted development of a baby's limbs. Nor do they know what it is about teratogens that causes them to have this effect. No doubt, someday we will have this knowledge, and then we will be able to tell precisely whether and how Bendectin (or any other suspected teratogen) interferes with limb development; in the current state of scientific knowledge, however, we are ignorant.

Not knowing the mechanism whereby a particular agent causes a particular effect is not always fatal to a plaintiff's claim. Causation can be proved even when we don't know precisely how the damage occurred, if there is sufficiently compelling proof that the agent must have caused the damage somehow. One method of proving causation in these circumstances is to use statistical evidence. If 50 people who eat at a restaurant one evening come down with food poisoning during the night, we can infer that the restaurant's food probably contained something unwholesome, even if none of the dishes is available for analysis. This inference is based on the fact that, in our health-conscious society, it is highly unlikely that 50 people who have nothing in common except that they ate at the same restaurant would get food poisoning from independent sources.

It is by such means that plaintiffs here seek to establish that Bendectin is responsible for their injuries. They rely on the testimony of three groups of scientific experts. One group proposes to testify that there is a statistical link between the ingestion of Bendectin during pregnancy and limb reduction defects. These experts have not themselves conducted epidemiological (human statistical) studies on the effects of Bendectin; rather, they have reanalyzed studies published by other scientists, none of whom reported a statistical association between Bendectin and birth defects. Other experts proffered by plaintiffs propose to testify that Bendectin causes limb reduction defects in humans because it causes such defects in laboratory animals. A third group of experts sees a link between Bendectin and birth defects because Bendectin has a chemical structure that is similar to other drugs suspected of causing birth defects.

The opinions proffered by plaintiffs' experts do not, to understate the point, reflect the consensus within the scientific community. The FDA—an agency not known for its promiscuity in approving drugs—continues to approve Bendectin for use by pregnant women because "available data do not demonstrate an association between birth defects and Bendectin." U.S. Department of Health and Human Services News, No. P80-45 (Oct. 7, 1980). Every published study here and abroad—and there have been many—concludes that Bendectin is not a teratogen. In fact, apart from the small but determined group of scientists testifying on behalf of the Bendectin plaintiffs in this and many other cases, there doesn't appear to be a single scientist who has concluded that Bendectin causes limb reduction defects.

It is largely because the opinions proffered by plaintiffs' experts run counter to the substantial consensus in the scientific community that we affirmed the district court's grant of summary judgment the last time the case appeared before us. The standard for admissibility of expert testimony in this circuit at the time was the so-called *Frye* test: Scientific evidence was admissible if it was based on a scientific technique generally accepted as reliable within the scientific community. We found that the district court properly applied this standard, and affirmed. The Supreme Court reversed, holding that *Frye* was superseded by Federal Rule of Evidence 702, and remanded for us to consider the admissibility of plaintiffs' expert testimony under this new standard. . . .

II

A.   BRAVE NEW WORLD

Federal judges ruling on the admissibility of expert scientific testimony face a far more complex and daunting task in a post-*Daubert* world than before. The judge's task under *Frye* is relatively simple: to determine whether the method employed by the experts is generally accepted in the scientific community. Under *Daubert,* we must engage in a difficult, two-part analysis. First, we must determine nothing less than whether the experts' testimony reflects "scientific knowledge," whether their findings are "derived by the scientific method," and whether their work product amounts to "good science." Second, we must ensure that the proposed expert testimony is "relevant to the task at hand," i.e., that it logically advances a material aspect of the proposing party's case. The Supreme Court referred to this second prong of the analysis as the "fit" requirement.

The first prong of *Daubert* puts federal judges in an uncomfortable position. The question of admissibility only arises if it is first established that the individuals whose testimony is being proffered are experts in a particular scientific field; here, for example, the Supreme Court waxed eloquent on the impressive qualifications of plaintiffs' experts. Yet something doesn't become "scientific knowledge" just because it's uttered by a scientist; nor can an expert's self-serving assertion that his conclusions were "derived by the scientific method" be deemed conclusive, else the Supreme Court's opinion could have ended with footnote two. As we read the Supreme Court's teaching in *Daubert,* therefore, though we are largely untrained in science and certainly no match for any of the witnesses whose testimony we are reviewing, it is our responsibility to determine whether those experts' proposed testimony amounts to "scientific knowledge," constitutes "good science," and was "derived by the scientific method."

The task before us is more daunting still when the dispute concerns matters at the very cutting edge of scientific research, where fact meets theory and certainty dissolves into probability. As the record in this case illustrates, scientists often have vigorous and sincere disagreements as to what research methodology is proper, what should be accepted as sufficient proof for the existence of a "fact," and whether information derived by a particular method can tell us anything useful about the subject under study.

Our responsibility, then, unless we badly misread the Supreme Court's opinion, is to resolve disputes among respected, well-credentialed scientists about matters squarely within their expertise, in areas where there is no scientific consensus as to what is and what is not "good science," and occasionally to reject such expert testimony because it was not "derived by the scientific method." Mindful of our position in the hierarchy of the federal judiciary, we take a deep breath and proceed with this heady task.

B. DEUS EX MACHINA

The Supreme Court's opinion in *Daubert* focuses closely on the language of Fed. R. Evid. 702, which permits opinion testimony by experts as to matters amounting to "scientific . . . knowledge." The Court recognized, however, that knowledge in this context does not mean absolute certainty. Rather, the Court said, "in order to qualify as 'scientific knowledge,' an inference or assertion must be derived by the scientific method." Elsewhere in its opinion, the Court noted that Rule 702 is satisfied where the proffered testimony is "based on scientifically valid principles." Our task, then, is to analyze not what the experts say, but what basis they have for saying it.

Which raises the question: How do we figure out whether scientists have derived their findings through the scientific method or whether their testimony is based on scientifically valid principles? Each expert proffered by the plaintiffs assures us that he has "utiliz[ed] the type of data that is generally and reasonably relied upon by scientists" in the relevant field, and that he has "utilized the methods and methodology that would generally and reasonably be accepted" by people who deal in these matters. The Court held, however, that federal judges perform a "gatekeeping role," to do so they must satisfy themselves that scientific evidence meets a certain standard of reliability before it is admitted. This means that the expert's bald assurance of validity is not enough. Rather, the party presenting the expert must show that the expert's findings are based on sound science, and this will require some objective, independent validation of the expert's methodology.

While declining to set forth a "definitive checklist or test," the Court did list several factors federal judges can consider in determining whether to admit expert scientific testimony under Fed. R. Evid. 702: whether the theory or technique employed by the expert is generally accepted in the scientific community; whether it's been subjected to peer review and publication; whether it can be and has been tested; and whether the known or potential rate of error is acceptable.[3] We read these factors as illustrative rather than exhaustive; similarly, we do not deem each of them to be equally applicable (or applicable at all) in every case. Rather, we read the Supreme Court as instructing us to de-

---

3. These factors raise many questions, such as how do we determine whether the rate of error is acceptable, and by what standard? Or, what should we infer from the fact that the methodology has been tested, but only by the party's own expert or experts? Do we ask whether the methodology they employ to test their methodology is itself methodologically sound? Such questions only underscore the basic problem, which is that we must devise standards for acceptability where respected scientists disagree on what's acceptable.

termine whether the analysis undergirding the experts' testimony falls within the range of accepted standards governing how scientists conduct their research and reach their conclusions.

One very significant fact to be considered is whether the experts are proposing to testify about matters growing naturally and directly out of research they have conducted independent of the litigation, or whether they have developed their opinions expressly for purposes of testifying. That an expert testifies for money does not necessarily cast doubt on the reliability of his testimony, as few experts appear in court merely as an eleemosynary gesture. But in determining whether proposed expert testimony amounts to good science, we may not ignore the fact that a scientist's normal workplace is the lab or the field, not the courtroom or the lawyer's office.

That an expert testifies based on research he has conducted independent of the litigation provides important, objective proof that the research comports with the dictates of good science.

See Peter W. Huber, Galileo's Revenge: Junk Science in the Courtroom 206-09 (1991) (describing how the prevalent practice of expert-shopping leads to bad science). For one thing, experts whose findings flow from existing research are less likely to have been biased toward a particular conclusion by the promise of remuneration; when an expert prepares reports and findings before being hired as a witness, that record will limit the degree to which he can tailor his testimony to serve a party's interests. Then, too, independent research carries its own indicia of reliability, as it is conducted, so to speak, in the usual course of business and must normally satisfy a variety of standards to attract funding and institutional support. Finally, there is usually a limited number of scientists actively conducting research on the very subject that is germane to a particular case, which provides a natural constraint on parties' ability to shop for experts who will come to the desired conclusion. That the testimony proffered by an expert is based directly on legitimate, preexisting research unrelated to the litigation provides the most persuasive basis for concluding that the opinions he expresses were "derived by the scientific method."

We have examined carefully the affidavits proffered by plaintiffs' experts, as well as the testimony from prior trials that plaintiffs have introduced in support of that testimony, and find that none of the experts based his testimony on preexisting or independent research. While plaintiffs' scientists are all experts in their respective fields, none claims to have studied the effect of Bendectin on limb reduction defects before being hired to testify in this or related cases.

If the proffered expert testimony is not based on independent research, the party proffering it must come forward with other objective, verifiable evidence that the testimony is based on "scientifically valid principles." One means of showing this is by proof that the research and analysis supporting the proffered conclusions have been subjected to normal scientific scrutiny through peer review and publication. Huber, Galileo's Revenge at 209 (suggesting that "[t]he ultimate test of [a scientific expert's] integrity is her readiness to publish and be damned").

Peer review and publication do not, of course, guarantee that the conclusions reached are correct; much published scientific research is greeted with intense skepticism and is not borne out by further research. But the test under *Daubert* is not the correctness of the expert's conclusions but the soundness of his methodology. That the research is accepted for publication in a reputable scientific journal after being subjected to the usual rigors of peer review is a significant indication that it is taken seriously by other scientists, i.e., that it means at least the minimal criteria of good science. . . . If nothing else, peer review and publication "increase the likelihood that substantive flaws in methodology with be detected."

Bendectin litigation has been pending in the courts for over a decade, yet the only review the plaintiffs' experts' work has received has been by judges and juries, and the only place their theories and studies have been published is in the pages of federal and state reporters. None of the plaintiffs' experts has published his work on Bendectin in a scientific journal or solicited formal review by his colleagues. Despite the many years the controversy has been brewing, no one in the scientific community — except defendant's experts — has deemed these studies worthy of verification, refutation or even comment. It's as if there were a tacit understanding within the scientific community that what's going on here is not science at all, but litigation.

Establishing that an expert's proffered testimony grows out of pre-litigation research or that the expert's research has been subjected to peer review are the two principal ways the proponent of expert testimony can show that the evidence satisfies the first prong of Rule 702.[10] Where such evidence is unavailable, the proponent of expert scientific testimony may attempt to satisfy its burden through the testimony of its own experts. For such a showing to be sufficient, the experts must explain precisely how they went about reaching their conclusions and point to some objective source—a learned treatise, the policy statement

10. This showing would not, of course, be conclusive. Proffering scientific testimony and making an initial showing that it was derived by the scientific method enables a party to establish a prima facie case as to admissibility under Rule 702. The opposing party would then be entitled to challenge that showing. This it could do by presenting evidence (including expert testimony) that the proposing party's expert employed unsound methodology or failed to assiduously follow an otherwise sound protocol. Where the opposing party thus raises a material dispute as to the admissibility of expert scientific evidence, the district court must hold an in limine hearing (a so-called *Daubert* hearing) to consider the conflicting evidence and make findings about the soundness and reliability of the methodology employed by the scientific experts. . . .

of a professional association, a published article in a reputable scientific journal or the like — to show that they have followed the scientific method, as it is practiced by (at least) a recognized minority of scientists in their field. See United States v. Rincom, 28 F.3d 921, 924 (9th Cir. 1994) (research must be described "in sufficient detail that the district court [can] determine if the research was scientifically valid").[11]

Plaintiffs have made no such showing. As noted above, plaintiffs rely entirely on the experts' unadorned assertions that the methodology they employed comports with standard scientific procedures. In support of these assertions, plaintiffs offer only the trial and deposition testimony of these experts in other cases. While these materials indicate that plaintiffs' experts have relied on animal studies, chemical structure analyses and epidemiological data, they neither explain the methodology the experts followed to reach their conclusions nor point to any external source to validate that methodology. We've been presented with only the experts' qualifications, their conclusions and their assurances of reliability. Under *Daubert,* that's not enough.

This is especially true of Dr. Palmer—the only expert willing to testify "that Bendectin did cause the limb defects in each of the children." In support of this conclusion, Dr. Palmer asserts only that Bendectin is a teratogen and that he has examined the plaintiffs' medical records, which apparently reveal the timing of their mothers' ingestion of the drug. Dr. Palmer offers no tested or testable theory to explain how, from this limited information, he was able to eliminate all other potential causes of birth defects, nor does he explain how he alone can state as a fact that Bendectin caused plaintiffs' injuries. We therefore agree with the Sixth Circuit's observation that "Dr. Palmer does not testify on the basis of the collective view of his scientific discipline, nor does he take issue with his peers and explain the grounds for his differences. Indeed, no understandable scientific basis is stated. Personal opinion, not science, is testifying here." For this reason, Dr. Palmer's testimony is inadmissible as a matter of law under Rule 702.

The failure to make any objective showing as to admissibility under the first prong of Rule 702 would also fatally undermine the testimony of plaintiffs' other experts, but for the peculiar posture of this case. Plaintiffs submitted their experts' affidavits while *Frye* was the law of the

---

11. This underscores the difference between *Daubert* and *Frye.* Under *Frye,* the party proffering scientific evidence had to show it was based on the method generally accepted in the scientific community. The focus under *Daubert* is on the reliability of the methodology, and in addressing that question the court and the parties are not limited to what is generally accepted; methods accepted by a minority in the scientific community may well be sufficient. However, the party proffering the evidence must explain the expert's methodology and demonstrate in some objectively verifiable way that the expert has both chosen a reliable scientific method and followed it faithfully. Of course, the fact that one party's experts use a methodology accepted by only a minority of scientists would be a proper basis for impeachment at trial.

circuit and, although they've not requested an opportunity to augment their experts' affidavits in light of *Daubert,* the interests of justice would be disserved by precluding plaintiffs from doing so. Given the opportunity to augment their original showing of admissibility, plaintiffs might be able to show that the methodology adopted by some of their experts is based on sound scientific principles. For instance, plaintiffs' epidemiologists might validate their reanalyses by explaining why they chose only certain of the data that was available, or the experts relying on animal studies might point to some authority for extrapolating human causation from teratogenicity in animals.

Were this the only question before us, we would be inclined to remand to give plaintiffs an opportunity to submit additional proof that the scientific testimony they proffer was "derived by the scientific method." *Daubert,* however, establishes two prongs to the Rule 702 admissibility inquiry. We therefore consider whether the testimony satisfies the second prong of Rule 702: Would plaintiffs' proffered scientific evidence "assist the trier of fact to . . . determine a fact in issue"? Fed. R. Evid. 702.

C.   NO VISIBLE MEANS OF SUPPORT

In elucidating the second requirement of Rule 702, *Daubert* stressed the importance of the "fit" between the testimony and an issue in the case: "Rule 702's 'helpfulness' standard requires a valid scientific connection to the pertinent inquiry as a precondition to admissibility." Here, the pertinent inquiry is causation. In assessing whether the proffered expert testimony "will assist the trier of fact" in resolving this issue, we must look to the governing substantive standard, which in this case is supplied by California tort law.

Plaintiffs do not attempt to show causation directly; instead, they rely on experts who present circumstantial proof of causation. Plaintiffs' experts testify that Bendectin is a teratogen because it causes birth defects when it is tested on animals, because it is similar in chemical structure to other suspected teratogens, and because statistical studies show that Bendectin use increases the risk of birth defects. Modern tort law permits such proof, but plaintiffs must nevertheless carry their traditional burden; they must prove that their injuries were the result of the accused cause and not some independent factor. In the case of birth defects, carrying this burden is made more difficult because we know that some defects — including limb reduction defects — occur even when expectant mothers do not take Bendectin, and that most birth defects occur for no known reason.

California tort law requires plaintiffs to show not merely that Bendectin increased the likelihood of injury, but that it more likely than not caused their injuries. See Jones v. Ortho Pharmaceutical Corp., 163

Cal. App. 3d 396, 403, 209 Cal. Rptr. 456 (1985). In terms of statistical proof, this means that plaintiffs must establish not just that their mothers' ingestion of Bendectin increased somewhat the likelihood of birth defects, but that it more than doubled it—only then can it be said that Bendectin is more likely than not the source of their injury. Because the background rate of limb reduction defects is one per thousand births, plaintiffs must show that among children of mothers who took Bendectin the incidence of such defects was more than two per thousand.

None of plaintiffs' epidemiological experts claims that ingestion of Bendectin during pregnancy more than doubles the risk of birth defects. To evaluate the relationship between Bendectin and limb reduction defects, an epidemiologist would take a sample of the population and compare the frequency of birth defects in children whose mothers took Bendectin with the frequency of defects in children whose mothers did not. The ratio derived from this comparison would be an estimate of the "relative risk" associated with Bendectin. See generally Joseph L. Fleiss, Statistical Methods for Rates and Proportions (2d ed. 1981). For an epidemiological study to show causation under a preponderance standard, "the relative risk of limb reduction defects arising from the epidemiological data . . . will, at a minimum, have to exceed '2'." That is, the study must show that children whose mothers took Bendectin are more than twice as likely to develop limb reduction birth defects as children whose mothers did not. While plaintiffs' epidemiologists make vague assertions that there is a statistically significant relationship between Bendectin and birth defects, none states that the relative risk is greater than two. These studies thus would not be helpful, and indeed would only serve to confuse the jury, if offered to prove rather than refute causation. A relative risk of less than two may suggest teratogenicity, but it actually tends to disprove legal causation, as it shows that Bendectin does not double the likelihood of birth defects.

With the exception of Dr. Palmer, whose testimony is inadmissible under the first prong of the Rule 702 analysis, the remaining experts proffered by plaintiffs were equally unprepared to testify that Bendectin caused plaintiffs' injuries; they were willing to testify only that Bendectin is "capable of causing" birth defects. Plaintiffs argue "these scientists use the words 'capable of causing' meaning that it does cause. This is an ambiguity of language. . . . If something is capable of causing damage in humans, it does." But what plaintiffs must prove is not that Bendectin causes some birth defects, but that it caused their birth defects. To show this, plaintiffs' experts would have had to testify either that Bendectin actually caused plaintiffs' injuries (which they could not say) or that Bendectin more than doubled the likelihood of limb reduction birth defects (which they did not say).

As the district court properly found below, "the strongest inference to be drawn for plaintiffs based on the epidemiological evidence is that Bendectin could possibly have caused plaintiffs' injuries." The same is true of the other testimony derived from animal studies and chemical structure analyses — these experts "testify to a possibility rather than a probability." Plaintiffs do not quantify this possibility, or otherwise indicate how their conclusions about causation should be weighted, even though the substantive legal standard has always required proof of causation by a preponderance of the evidence. Unlike these experts' explanation of their methodology, this is not a shortcoming that could be corrected on remand; plaintiffs' experts could augment their affidavits with independent proof that their methods were sound, but to augment the substantive testimony as to causation would require the experts to change their conclusions altogether. Any such tailoring of the experts' conclusions would, at this stage of the proceedings, fatally undermine any attempt to show that these findings were "derived by the scientific method." Plaintiffs' experts must, therefore, stand by the conclusions they originally proffered, rendering their testimony inadmissible under the second prong of Fed. R. Evid. 702.

CONCLUSION

The district court's grant of summary judgment is affirmed.

GLASER v. THOMPSON MEDICAL CO.
32 F.3d 969 (6th Cir. 1994)

MERRITT, Chief Judge.

Plaintiffs appeal the district court's grant of summary judgment for the defendant on the single issue of causation in this product liability action. Plaintiffs allege negligence and breach of warranty in defendant-pharmaceutical company's manufacture and distribution of the diet pill "Dexatrim." Specifically, the complaint alleges that plaintiff Bryan Glaser's ingestion of one capsule of Dexatrim caused him to suffer acute hypertension which in turn caused him to suffer a stroke or intracranial bleed. That stroke caused him to fall, hit his head, and suffer further severe injuries. In granting defendant's motion for summary judgment on this single issue, the district court ruled that the evidence proffered by plaintiffs on causation was insufficient to go to the jury. The issue before us is essentially a factual one: Is the evidence offered below consisting primarily of the deposition testimony of plaintiffs' expert sufficient to create a dispute of material fact? We believe there is a genuine dispute of material fact regarding causation and therefore reverse. This holding carries no implications regarding the other facets of plaintiffs' claims of negligence and breach of warranty.

I

The evidence offered by plaintiff on summary judgment is as follows: Twenty-year-old Bryan Glaser began daily ingestion of one or two extra-strength Dexatrim diet pills around Thanksgiving, 1987. On Sunday, January 3, 1988, Bryan complained that he felt ill: his ears were ringing, and he experienced hot and cold flashes and other flu-like symptoms. He cancelled plans for that evening in order to rest. Early the next morning while Bryan was still asleep, Bryan's sister Jodi noticed an un-opened foil package containing one capsule of Dexatrim on Bryan's dresser in his bedroom along with a glass of water and other vitamin pills. Although no one ever observed Bryan ingest the capsule, Jodi tes-tified that the package had been opened and the capsule and other vitamins were no longer on the dresser later that morning. Bryan left home around noon on Monday and went to the Medstop walk-in medi-cal clinic. Medical records indicate that he complained of hot and cold flashes, ringing in his ears and fatigue. His blood pressure was within normal range (128/82) and the treating physician, Dr. Baubie, diag-nosed Bryan with post-viral syndrome and fatigue. Dr. Baubie did not know that Bryan was taking Dexatrim.

After leaving the clinic, Bryan went to the bank, where he stood in line for approximately 20 minutes before reaching teller Jaqueline Kul-chycki's window. Kulchycki's testimony is important. She testified that it was obvious to her that Bryan was not feeling well: he was squinting, holding his head as if he had a severe headache, and was flushed and sweating. As she turned away from her station, Bryan collapsed to the floor and hit his head. Emergency medical personnel were called and they transported Bryan to Detroit Macomb Hospital for treatment. He was diagnosed with an intracerebral bleed on the left frontal lobe of his brain, a skull fracture and a subdural hematoma. Emergency room doc-tors never attempted to diagnose the cause of his fall, but rather as-sumed that all of his injuries resulted from the fall.

The plaintiffs filed this lawsuit asserting that the fall was caused by the intracranial bleed found on the left frontal lobe of Bryan's brain, and that this bleed had been caused by ingestion of Dexatrim. After extensive discovery, the defendant filed motions for summary judgment, arguing that the scientific literature did not support a conclusion that one capsule of Dexatrim could cause an acute hypertensive reaction, that there was no evidence that an intracranial bleed preceded the fall, and that there was no evidence that Dexatrim caused such a reaction in Bryan. The district court assumed in its opinion that the scientific evidence was sufficient to support the conclusion that one capsule of Dexatrim can cause an acute hypertensive reaction serious enough to induce intracranial bleeding. The district court held, however, that the opinion of Dr. Zaloga, plaintiff's medical expert, was merely consistent with the known facts and conditions of the case, but was not based on a logical sequence of cause and effect. On that basis, the court granted summary judgment in favor of the defendants. . . .

The propriety of summary judgment in this case hinges on three causation questions:

1. Whether one capsule of Dexatrim is capable of causing hypertension severe enough to cause an intracranial bleed.

2. Whether Bryan suffered the intracranial bleed on the left frontal lobe of his brain prior to his fall.

3. Whether the bleed was caused by ingestion of Dexatrim. . . .

A

The defendant first challenges the scientific basis for Dr. Zaloga's conclusion that Dexatrim can cause severe hypertension. It argues that the medical studies proffered by the plaintiffs as support for Zaloga's conclusions actually support the defendant's position that Dexatrim cannot cause significant elevations in blood pressure and further that because there is no basis for the expert's opinion, the court should not allow a jury to decide the causation issue.

The testimony of plaintiff's expert is admissible. The Supreme Court, in Daubert v. Merrell Dow Pharmaceuticals, Inc., set forth the standard for admission of expert scientific testimony, holding that Rule 702 of the Federal Rules of Evidence governs the admissibility of such expert testimony. Rule 702 admits expert testimony if the evidence will assist the trier of fact and if the witness is qualified as an expert. . . . *Daubert* explained that Rule 702 must be read in the context of the liberal thrust of the Federal Rules of Evidence and must be interpreted consistently with the "general approach of relaxing the traditional barriers to 'opinion' testimony." The Court also cautioned in its opinion that even under these liberal requirements, trial judges must ensure that scientific testimony is not only relevant, but reliable. A court must determine:

> whether the expert is proposing to testify to (1) scientific knowledge that (2) will assist the trier of fact to understand or determine a fact in issue. This entails a preliminary assessment of whether the reasoning or methodology underlying the testimony is scientifically valid and of whether that reasoning or methodology properly can be applied to the facts in issue.

In assessing scientific validity, the Court provided a non-exclusive list of factors to assist the trial courts: (1) whether a theory or technique can be (and has been) tested, (2) whether the theory or technique has been subjected to peer review and publication, (3) the known or potential rate of error in using a particular scientific technique and the existence and maintenance of standards controlling the technique's operation, and (4) whether the theory or technique has been generally accepted in the particular scientific field. The inquiry must be a flexible one whose "overarching subject is the scientific validity—and thus the evidentiary relevance and reliability—of the principles that underlie a proposed submission."

If a court concludes that the evidence supporting the expert's position is insufficient to allow a reasonable juror to conclude that the position more likely than not is true, then the court remains free to prohibit the case from proceeding to the jury. "[A]lthough judges should respect scientific opinion and recognize their own limited scientific knowledge, nevertheless courts have a duty to inspect the reasoning of qualified scientific experts to determine whether a case should go to a jury." Turpin v. Merrell Dow Pharmaceuticals, Inc., 959 F.2d 1349 (6th Cir. 1992) (calling for a "hard look" by courts at the basis of scientific opinion).

A thorough review of all of the literature submitted by both parties and of Dr. Zaloga's testimony convinces us that sufficient, valid, peer-reviewed scientific evidence, along with Dr. Zaloga's own clinical and research experience, provide a solid foundation upon which Dr. Zaloga bases his conclusion that the 75 milligrams of phenylpropanolamine (PPA), the active ingredient in one capsule of Dexatrim, caused acute hypertension. Dr. Zaloga testified during his deposition that his opinion was based on the five studies he published on the topic, the published articles of other medical researchers, case reports, his experience treating patients who had ingested PPA-containing compounds, his clinical experience with PPA in other studies, and his experience directing endocrine and obesity clinics.

The medical literature upon which Dr. Zaloga relies includes five studies which he coauthored and two other published research papers on the subject of PPA's effect on blood pressure. . . .

Zaloga also relies on at least two other studies to support his conclusion. . . .

Finally, Zaloga relies to a lesser extent on the Horowitz paper. It summarizes a study done on the effects of single doses of PPA-containing compounds. . . .

These studies, together with Dr. Zaloga's extensive experience and work in this area, provide sufficient, reliable scientific data upon which Dr. Zaloga may base his conclusion. All of these papers have clearly explained, solid scientific methodologies upon which they have tested their theories, and all have been peer-reviewed and published in reputable medical journals, including The American Journal of Medicine, the Lancet, The Journal of Clinical Pharmacology, and Neuropsychopharmacology. The error rates are published and their impact on the studies explained. These factors, as outlined in *Daubert* and *Bonds*, indicate the reliability of the foundation upon which Dr. Zaloga rests his opinion.

Finally, Dr. Zaloga and the plaintiffs concede readily that there are other studies that disagree with Dr. Zaloga's conclusion. Dr. Zaloga distinguishes many of them and points to flaws in their methods and data reporting techniques which led him to rely on the above-outlined works in reaching his conclusions. Such differences in opinions among medical experts do not invalidate Dr. Zaloga's opinion, but rather create material issues of fact which must be resolved by the jury. . . . In sum, we believe that sufficient, reliable evidence exists upon which Dr. Zaloga may testify that one capsule of Dexatrim (75 mg PPA) is capable of causing acute hypertension. Such testimony creates material issues of fact and precludes summary judgment on the question. . . .

We therefore reverse the district court's grant of summary judgment in favor of the defendant and remand the case for further proceedings.

[Dissenting opinion by Boggs, Circuit Judge, omitted.]

Daubert relied heavily on the word "scientific" in its construction of Rule 702 to require a preliminary determination of scientific reliability for expert testimony. However, much expertise is not "scientific." What does this mean for "technical or other specialized knowledge"? Does the trial judge have a role in requiring a minimum quality or substance to expert testimony of this kind? Compare the approach taken by the Supreme Court of the United States in construing and applying Rule 702 in *Daubert* with that taken by the Maine Supreme Court in construing and applying identical Maine Rule 702 in *Williams*. Which makes better conceptual, better practical sense?

KUMHO TIRE COMPANY, LTD. v. CARMICHAEL
526 U.S. 137 (1999)

Justice BREYER delivered the opinion of the Court.

In Daubert v. Merrll Dow Pharmaceuticals, Inc., 509 U.S. 579, 125 L. Ed. 2d 469, 113 S. Ct. 2786 (1993), this Court focused upon the admissibility of scientific expert testimony. It pointed out that such testimony is admissible only if it is both relevant and reliable. And it held that the Federal Rules of Evidence "assign to the trial judge the task of ensuring that an expert's testimony both rests on a reliable foundation and is relevant to the task at hand." Id. at 597. The Court also discussed certain more specific factors, such as testing, peer review, error rates, and "acceptability" in the relevant scientific community, some or all of which might prove helpful in determining the reliability of a particular scientific "theory or technique." Id. at 593-594.

This case requires us to decide how *Daubert* applies to the testimony of engineers and other experts who are not scientists. We conclude that *Daubert*'s general holding—setting forth the trial judge's general "gate-keeping" obligation—applies not only to testimony based on "scientific" knowledge, but also to testimony based on "technical" and "other specialized" knowledge. See Fed. Rule Evid. 702. We also conclude that a trial court *may* consider one or more of the more specific factors that *Daubert* mentioned when doing so will help determine that testimony's reliability. But, as the Court stated in *Daubert,* the test of reliability is "flexible," and *Daubert*'s list of specific factors neither necessarily nor exclusively applies to all experts or in every case. Rather, the law grants a district court the same broad latitude when it decides *how* to determine reliability as it enjoys in respect to its ultimate reliability determination. See General Electric Co. v. Joiner, 522 U.S. 136, 143, 139 L. Ed. 2d 508, 118 S. Ct. 512 (1997) (courts of appeals are to apply "abuse of discretion" standard when reviewing district court's reliability determination). Applying these standards, we determine that the District Court's decision in this case—not to admit certain expert testimony—was within its discretion and therefore lawful.

I

On July 6, 1993, the right rear tire of a minivan driven by Patrick Carmichael blew out. In the accident that followed, one of the passengers died, and others were severely injured. In October 1993, the Carmichaels brought this diversity suit against the tire's maker and its distributor, whom we refer to collectively as Kumho Tire, claiming that the tire was defective. The plaintiffs rested their case in significant part upon depostition testimony provided by an expert in tire failure analysis, Dennis Carlson, Jr., who intended to testify in support of their conclusion.

Carlson's depositions relied upon certain features of tire technology that are not in dispute. A steel-belted radial tire like the Carmichaels' is made up of a "carcass" containing many layers of flexible cords, called "plies," along which (between the cords and the outer tread) are laid steel strips called "belts." Steel wire loops, called "beads," hold the cords together at the plies' bottom edges. An outer layer, called the "tread," encases the carcass, and the entire tire is bound together in rubber, through the application of heat and various chemicals. See generally, e.g., J. Dixon, Tires, Suspension and Handling 68-72 (2d ed. 1996). The bead of the tie sits upon a "bead seat," which is part of the wheel assembly. That assembly contains a "rim flange," which extends over the bead and rests against the side of the tire. See M. Mavrigian, Performance Wheels & Tires 81, 83 (1998)....

Carlson's testimony also accepted certain background facts about the tire in question. He assumed that before the blowout the tire had traveled far. (The tire was made in 1988 and had been installed some time before the Carmichaels bought the used minivan in March 1993; the Carmichaels had driven the van approximately 7,000 additional miles in the two months they had owned it.) Carlson noted that the tire's tread depth, which was 11/32 of an inch when new, App. 242, had been worn down to depths that ranged from 3/32 of an inch along some parts of the tire, to nothing at all along others. Id. at 287. He conceded that the tire tread had at least two punctures which had been inadequately repaired. Id. at 258-261, 322.

Despite the tire's age and history, Carlson concluded that a defect in its manufacture or design caused the blowout. He rested this conclusion in part upon three premises which, for present purposes, we must assume are not in dispute. First, a tire's carcass should stay bound to the inner side of the tread for a significant period of time after its tread depth has worn away. Id. at 208-209. Second, the tread of the tire at issue had separated from its inner steel-belted carcass prior to the accident. Id. at 336. Third, this "separation" caused the blowout. Ibid.

Carlson's conclusion that a defect caused the separation, however, rested upon certain other propositions, several of which the defendants strongly dispute. First, Carlson said that if a separation is *not* caused by a certain kind of tire misuse called "overdeflection" (which consists of underinflating the tire or causing it to carry too much weight, thereby generating heat that can undo the chemical tread/carcass bond), then, ordinarily, its cause is a tire defect. Id. at 193-195, 277-278. Second, he said that if a tire has been subject to sufficient overdeflection to cause separation, it should reveal certain physical symptoms. These symptoms include (a) tread wear on the tire's shoulder that is greater than the tread wear along the tire's center, id. at 211; (b) signs of a "bead groove," where the beads have been pushed too hard against the bead seat on the inside of the tire's rim, id. at 196-197; (c) sidewalls of the tire with physical signs of deterioration, such as discoloration, id. at 212; and/or (d) marks on the tire's rim flange, id. at 219-220. Third, Carlson said that where he does not find *at least two* of the four physical signs just mentioned (and presumably where there is no reason to suspect a less common cause of separation), he concludes that a manufacturing or design defect caused the separation. Id. at 223-224.

Carlson showed that he had inspected the tire in question. He conceded that the tire to a limited degree showed greater wear on the shoulder than in the center, some signs of "bead groove," some discoloration, a few marks on the rim flange, and inadequately filled puncture holes (which can also cause heat that might lead to separation). Id. at 256-257, 258-261, 277, 303-304, 308. But, in each instance, he testified that the symptoms were not significant, and he explained why he believed that they did not reveal overdeflection. For example, the extra shoulder wear, he said, appeared primarily on one shoulder, whereas an overdeflected tire would reveal equally abnormal wear on both shoulders. Id. at 277. Carlson concluded that the tire did not bear at least two of the four overdeflection symptoms, nor was there any less obvious cause of separation; and since neither overdeflection nor the punctures caused the blowout, a defect must have done so.

Kumho Tire moved the District Court to exclude Carlson's testimony on the ground that his methodology failed Rule 702's reliability requirement. The court agreed with Kumho that it should act as a *Daubert*-type reliability "gatekeeper," even though one might consider Carlson's testimony as "technical," rather than "scientific." See Carmichael v. Samyang Tires, Inc., 923. F. Supp. 1514, 1521–1522 (SD Ala. 1996). The court then examined Carlson's methodology in light of the reliability-related factors that *Daubert* mentioned, such as a theory's testability, whether it "has been a subject of peer review or publication," the "known or potential rate of error," and the "degree of acceptance . . . within the relevant scientific community." 923 F. Supp. at 1520 (citing *Daubert*, 509 U.S. 579 at 592-594). The District Court found that all those factors argued against the reliability of Carlson's methods, and it granted the motion to exclude the testimony (as well as the defendants' accompanying motion for summary judgment).

The plaintiffs, arguing that the court's application of the *Daubert* factors was too "inflexible," asked for reconsideration. And the Court granted that motion. Carmichael v. Samyang Tires, Inc., Civ. Action No. 93-0860-CB-S (SD Ala., June 5, 1996), App. to Pet. for Cert. 1c. After reconsidering the matter, the court agreed with the plaintiffs that *Daubert* should be applied flexibly, that its four factors were simply illustrative, and that other factors could argue in favor of admissibility. It conceded that there may be widespread acceptance of a "visual-inspection method" for some relevant purposes. But the court found insufficient indications of the reliability of

> "the component of Carlson's tire failure analysis which most concerned the Court, namely, the methodology employed by the expert in analyzing the data obtained in the visual inspection, and the scientific basis, if any, for such an analysis." Id. at 6c.

It consequently affirmed its earlier order declaring Carlson's testimony inadmissible and granting the defendants' motion for summary judgment.

The Eleventh Circuit reversed. See Carmichael v. Samyang Tire, Inc., 131 F.3d 1433 (1997). It "reviewed . . . *de novo*" the "district court's legal decision to apply *Daubert*." 131 F.3d at 1435. It noted that "the Supreme

Court in *Daubert* explicitly limited its holding to cover only the 'scientific context,'" adding that "a *Daubert* analysis" applies only where an expert relies "on the application of scientific principles," rather than "on skill- or experience-based observation." Id. at 1435-1436. It concluded that Carlson's testimony, which it viewed as relying on experience, "falls outside the scope of *Daubert*," that "the district court erred as a matter of law by applying *Daubert* in this case," and that the case must be remanded for further (non-*Daubert*-type) consideration under Rule 702. Id. at 1436.

Kumho Tire petitioned for certiorari, asking us to determine whether a trial court "may" consider *Daubert*'s specific "factors" when determining the "admissibility of an engineering expert's testimony." Pet. for Cert. i. We granted certiorari in light of uncertainty among the lower courts about whether, or how, *Daubert* applies to expert testimony that might be characterized as based not upon "scientific" knowledge, but rather upon "technical" or "other specialized" knowledge. Fed. Rule Evid. 702. . . .

II

A

In *Daubert*, this Court held that Federal Rule of Evidence 702 imposes a special obligation upon a trial judge to "ensure that any and all scientific testimony . . . is not only relevant, but reliable." 509 U.S. at 589. The initial question before us is whether this basic gatekeeping obligation applies only to "scientific" testimony or to all expert testimony. We, like the parties, believe that it applies to all expert testimony. . . .

For one thing, Rule 702 itself says:

"If scientific, technical, or other specialized knowledge will assist the trier of fact to understand the evidence or to determine a fact in issue, a witness qualified as an expert by knowledge, skill, experience, training, or education, may testify thereto in the form of an opinion or otherwise."

This language makes no relevant distinction between "scientific" knowledge and "technical" or "other specialized" knowledge. It makes clear that any such knowledge might become the subject of expert testimony. In *Daubert*, the Court specified that it is the Rule's word "knowledge," not the words (like "scientific") that modify that word, that "establishes a standard of evidentiary reliability." 509 U.S. at 589-590. Hence, as a matter of language, the Rule applies its reliability standard to all "scientific," "technical," or "other specialized" matters within its scope. We concede that the Court in *Daubert* referred only to "scientific" knowledge. But as the Court there said, it referred to "scientific" testimony "because that was the nature of the expertise" at issue. Id. at 590, n. 8.

Neither is the evidentiary rationale that underlay the Court's basic *Daubert* "gatekeeping" determination limited to "scientific" knowledge. *Daubert* pointed out that Federal Rules 702 and 703 grant expert witnesses testimonial latitude unavailable to other witnesses on the "assumption that the expert's opinion will have a reliable basis in the knowledge and experience of his discipline." Id. at 592 (pointing out that experts may testify to opinions, including those that are not based on firsthand knowledge or observation). The Rules grant that latitude to all experts, not just to "scientific" ones.

Finally, it would prove difficult, if not impossible, for judges to administer evidentiary rules under which a gatekeeping obligation depended upon a distinction between "scientific" knowledge and "technical" or "other specialized" knowledge. There is no clear line that divides the one from the others. Disciplines such as engineering rest upon scientific knowledge. Pure scientific theory itself may depend for its development upon observation and properly engineered machinery. And conceptual efforts to distinguish the two are unlikely to produce clear legal lines capable of application in particular cases. Cf. Brief for National Academy of Engineering as *Amicus Curiae* 9 (scientist seeks to understand nature while the engineer seeks nature's modification); Brief for Rubber Manufacturers Association as *Amicus Curiae* 14-16 (engineering, as an "applied science," relies on "scientific reasoning and methodology"); Brief for John Allen et al. as *Amici Curiae* 6 (engineering relies upon "scientific knowledge and methods").

Neither is there a convincing need to make such distinctions. Experts of all kinds tie observations to conclusions through the use of what Judge Learned Hand called "general truths derived from . . . specialized experience." Hand, Historical and Practical Considerations Regarding Expert Testimony, 15 Harv. L. Rev. 40, 54 (1901). And whether the specific expert testimony focuses upon specialized observations, the specialized translation of those observations into theory, a specialized theory itself, or the application of such a theory in a particular case, the expert's testimony often will rest "upon an experience confessedly foreign in kind to [the jury's] own." Ibid. The trial judge's effort to assure that the specialized testimony is reliable and relevant can help the jury evaluate that foreign experience, whether the testimony reflects scientific, technical, or other specialized knowledge.

We conclude that *Daubert's* general principles apply to the expert matters described in Rule 702. The Rule, in respect to all such matters, "establishes a standard of evidentiary reliability." 509 U.S. at 590. It "requires a valid . . . connection to the pertinent inquiry as a precondition to admissibility." Id. at 592. And where such testimony's factual basis, data, principles, methods, or their application are called sufficiently into question, see Part III, infra, the trial judge must determine whether the testimony has "a reliable basis in the knowledge and experience of [the relevant] discipline." 509 U.S. at 592.

B

The petitioners ask more specifically whether a trial judge determining the "admissibility of an engineering expert's testimony" *may* consider several more specific factors that *Daubert* said might "bear on" a judge's gatekeeping determination. These factors include:

- Whether a "theory or technique . . . can be (and has been) tested";
- Whether it "has been subjected to peer review and publication";
- Whether, in respect to a particular technique, there is a high "known or potential rate of error" and whether there are "standards controlling the technique's operation"; and
- Whether the theory or technique enjoys "general acceptance" within a "relevant scientific community." 509 U.S. at 592-594.

Emphasizing the word "may" in the question, we answer that question yes.

Engineering testimony rests upon scientific foundations, the reliability of which will be at issue in some cases. See, e.g., Brief for Stephen Bobo et al. as *Amici Curiae* 23 (stressing the scientific bases of engineering disciplines). In other cases, the relevant reliability concerns may focus upon personal knowledge or experience. As the Solicitor General points out, there are many different kinds of experts, and many different kinds of expertise. See Brief for United States as *Amicus Curiae* 18-19, and n.5 (citing cases involving experts in drugs terms, handwriting analysis, criminal modus operandi, land valuation, agricultural practices, railroad procedures, attorney's fee valuation, and others). Our emphasis on the word "may" thus reflects *Daubert*'s description of the Rule 702 inquiry as "a flexible one." 509 U.S. at 594. *Daubert* makes clear that the factors it mentions do *not* constitute a "definitive checklist or test." Id. at 593. And *Daubert* adds that the gatekeeping inquiry must be "tied to the facts" of a particular "case." Id. at 591 (quoting United States v. Downing, 753 F.2d 1224, 1242 (CA3 1985)). We agree with the Solicitor General that "the factors identified in *Daubert* may or may not be pertinent in assessing reliability, depending on the nature of the issue, the expert's particular expertise, and the subject of his testimony." Brief for United States as *Amicus Curiae* 19. The conclusion, in our view, is that we can neither rule out, nor rule in, for all cases and for all time the applicability of the factors mentioned in *Daubert*, nor can we now do so for subsets of cases categorized by category of expert or by kind of evidence. Too much depends upon the particular circumstances of the particular case at issue.

Daubert itself is not to the contrary. It made clear that its list of factors was meant to be helpful, not definitive. Indeed, those factors do not all necessarily apply even in every instance in which the reliability of scientific testimony is challenged. It might not be surprising in a particular case, for example, that a claim made by a scientific witness has never been the subject of peer review, for the particular application at issue may never previously have interested any scientist. Nor, on the other hand, does the presence of *Daubert*'s general acceptance factor help show that an expert's testimony is reliable where the discipline itself lacks reliability, as, for example, do theories grounded in any so-called generally accepted principles of astrology or necromancy.

At the same time, and contrary to the Court of Appeals' view, some of *Daubert*'s questions can help to evaluate the reliability even of experience-based testimony. In certain cases, it will be appropriate for the trial judge to ask, for example, how often an engineering expert's experience-based methodology has produced erroneous results, or whether such a method is generally accepted in the relevant engineering community. Likewise, it will at times be useful to ask even of a witness whose expertise is based purely on experience, say, a perfume tester able to distinguish among 140 odors at a sniff, whether his preparation is of a kind that others in the field would recognize as acceptable.

We must therefore disagree with the Eleventh Circuit's holding that a trial judge may ask questions of the sort *Daubert* mentioned only where an expert "relies on the application of scientific principles," but not where an expert relies "on skill- or experience-based observations." 131 F.3d at 1435. We do not believe that Rule 702 creates a schematism that segregates expertise by type while mapping certain kinds of questions to certain kinds of experts. Life and the legal cases that it generates are too complex to warrant so definitive a match.

To say this is not to deny the importance of *Daubert*'s gatekeeping requirement. The objective of that requirement is to ensure the reliability and relevancy of expert testimony. It is to make certain that an expert, whether basing testimony upon professional studies or personal experience, employs in the courtroom the same level of intellectual rigor that characterizes the practice of an expert in the relevant field. Nor do we deny that, as slated in *Daubert,* the particular questions that it mentioned will often be appropriate for use in determining the reliability of challenged expert testimony. Rather, we conclude that the trial judge must have considerable leeway in deciding in a particular case how to go about determining whether particular expert testimony is reliable. That is to say, a trial court should consider specific factors identified in *Daubert* where they are reasonable measures of the reliability of expert testimony.

C

The trial court must have the same kind of latitude in deciding *how* to test an expert's reliability, and to decide whether or when special briefing or other proceedings are needed to investigate reliability, as it enjoys when it decides *whether* that expert's relevant testimony is reliable.

Our opinion in *Joiner* makes clear that a court of appeals is to apply an abuse-of-discretion standard when it "reviews a trial court's decision to admit or exclude expert testimony." 522 U.S. at 138-139. That standard applies as much to the trial court's decisions about how to determine reliability as to its ultimate conclusion. Otherwise, the trial judge would lack the discretionary authority needed both to avoid unnecessary "reliability" proceedings in ordinary cases where the reliability of an expert's methods is properly taken for granted, and to require appropriate proceedings in the less usual or more complex cases where cause for questioning the expert's reliability arises. Indeed, the Rules seek to avoid "unjustifiable expense and delay" as part of their search for "truth" and the "just determination" of proceedings. Fed. Rule Evid. 102. Thus, whether *Daubert*'s specific factors are, or are not, reasonable measures of reliability in a particular case is a matter that the law grants the trial judge broad latitude to determine. See *Joiner,* supra, at 143. And the Eleventh Circuit erred insofar as it held to the contrary.

III

We further explain the way in which a trial judge "may" consider *Daubert*'s factors by applying these considerations to the case at hand, a matter that has been briefed exhaustively by the parties and their 19 *amici.* The District Court did not doubt Carlson's qualifications, which included a masters degree in mechanical engineering, 10 years' work at Michelin America, Inc., and testimony as a tire failure consultant in other tort cases. Rather, it excluded the testimony because, despite those qualifications, it initially doubted, and then found unreliable, "the methodology employed by the expert in analyzing the data obtained in the visual inspection, and the scientific basis, if any, for such an analysis." Civ. Action No. 93-0860-CB-S (SD Ala., June 5, 1996), App. to Pet. for Cert. 6c. After examining the transcript in "some detail," 923 F. Supp. at 1518-519, n.4, and after considering respondents' defense of Carlson's methodology, the District Court determined that Carlson's testimony was not reliable. It fell outside the range where experts might reasonably differ, and where the jury must decide among the conflicting views of different experts, even though the evidence is "shaky." *Daubert,* 509 U.S. at 596. In our view, the doubts that triggered the District Court's initial inquiry here were reasonable, as was the court's ultimate conclusion.

For one thing, and contrary to respondents' suggestion, the specific issue before the court was not the reasonableness *in general* of a tire expert's use of a visual and tactile inspection to determine whether overdeflection had caused the tire's tread to separate from its steel-belted carcass. Rather, it was the reasonableness of using such an approach, along with Carlson's particular method of analyzing the data thereby obtained, to draw a conclusion regarding *the particular matter to which the expert testimony was directly relevant.* That matter concerned the likelihood that a defect in the tire at issue caused its tread to separate from its carcass. The tire in question, the expert conceded, had traveled far enough so that some of the tread had been worn bald; it should have been taken out of service; it had been repaired (inadequately) for punctures; and it bore some of the very marks that the expert said indicated, not a defect, but abuse through overdeflection. See supra, at 3-5; App. 293-294. The relevant issue was whether the expert could reliably determine the cause of *this* tire's separation. Nor was the basis for Carlson's conclusion simply the general theory that, in the absence of evidence of abuse, a defect will normally have caused a tire's separation. Rather, the expert employed a more specific theory to establish the existence (or absence) of such abuse. Carlson testified precisely that in the absence of *at least two* of four signs of abuse (proportionally greater tread wear on the shoulder; signs of grooves caused by the beads; discolored sidewalls; marks on the rim flange) he concludes that a defect caused the separation. And his analysis depended upon acceptance of a further implicit proposition, namely, that his visual and tactile inspection could determine that the tire before him had not been abused despite some evidence of the presence of the very signs for which he looked (and two punctures).

For another thing, the transcripts of Carlson's depositions support both the trial court's initial uncertainty and its final conclusion. Those transcripts cast considerable doubt upon the reliability of both the explicit theory (about the need for two signs of abuse) and the implicit proposition (about the significance of visual inspection in this case). Among other things, the expert could not say whether the tire had traveled more than 10, or 20, or 30, or 40, or 50 thousand miles, adding that 6,000 miles was "about how far" he could "say with any certainty." Id. at 265. The court could reasonably have wondered about the reliability of a method of visual and tactile inspection sufficiently precise to ascertain with some certainty the abuse-related significance of minute shoulder/center relative tread wear differences, but insufficiently precise to tell "with any certainty" from the tread wear whether a tire had traveled less than 10,000 or more than 50,000 miles. And these concerns might have been augmented by Carlson's repeated reliance on the "subjectiveness" of his mode of analysis in response to questions seeking specific information regarding how he could differentiate between a tire that actually had been overdeflected and a tire that merely looked as though it had been. Id. at 222, 224-225, 285-286. They would have been further augmented by the fact that Carlson said he had inspected the tire itself for the first time the morning of his first deposition, and then only for a few hours. (His initial conclusions were based on photographs.) Id. at 180.

Moreover, prior to his first deposition, Carlson had issued a signed report in which he concluded that the tire had "not been . . . overloaded or underinflated," not because of the absence of "two of four" signs of abuse, but simply because "the rim flange impressions . . . were normal." Id. at 335-336. That report also said that the "tread depth remaining was 3/32 inch," id. at 336, though the opposing expert's (apparently undisputed) measurements indicate that the tread depth taken at various positions around the tire actually ranged from .5/32 of an inch to 4/32 of an inch, with the tire apparently showing greater wear along *both* shoulders than along the center, id. at 432-433.

Further, in respect to one sign of abuse, bead grooving, the expert seemed to deny the sufficiency of his own simple visual-inspection methodology. He testified that most tires have some bead groove pattern, that where there is reason to suspect an abnormal bead groove he would ideally "look at a lot of [similar] tires" to know the grooving's significance, and that he had not looked at many tires similar to the one at issue. Id. at 212-213, 214, 217.

Finally, the court, after looking for a defense of Carlson's methodology as applied in these circumstances, found no convincing defense. Rather, it found (1) that "none" of the *Daubert* factors, including that of "general acceptance" in the relevant expert community, indicated that Carlson's testimony was reliable, 923 F. Supp. at 1521; (2) that its own analysis "revealed no countervailing factors operating in favor of admissibility which could outweigh those identified in *Daubert*," App. to Pet. for Cert. 4c; and (3) that the "parties identified no such factors in their briefs," ibid. For these three reasons *taken together,* it concluded that Carlson's testimony was unreliable.

Respondents now argue to us, as they did to the District Court, that a method of tire failure analysis that employs a visual/tactile inspection is a reliable method, and they point both to its use by other experts and to Carlson's long experience working for Michelin as sufficient indication that that is so. But no one denies that an expert might draw a conclusion from a set of observations based on extensive and specialized experience. Nor does anyone deny that, as a general matter, tire abuse may often be identified by qualified experts through visual or tactile inspection of the tire. See Affidavit of H. R. Baumgardner 1-2, cited in Brief for National Academy of Forensic Engineers as *Amici Curiae* 16 (Tire engineers rely on visual examination and process of elimination to analyze experimental test tires). As we said before, supra, at 14, the question before the trial court was specific, not general. The trial court had to decide whether this particular expert had sufficient specialized knowledge to assist the jurors "in deciding the particular issues in the case." 4 J. McLaughlin, Weinstein's Federal Evidence P702.05[1], p. 702-33 (2d ed. 1998); see also Advisory Committee's Note on Proposed Fed. Rule Evid. 702, Preliminary Draft of Proposed Amendments to the Federal Rules of Civil Procedure and Evidence: Request for Comment 126 (1998) (stressing that district courts must "scrutinize" whether the "principles and methods" employed by an expert "have been properly applied to the facts of the case").

The particular issue in this case concerned the use of Carlson's two-factor test and his related use of visual/tactile inspection to draw conclusions on the basis of what seemed small observational differences. We have found no indication in the record that other experts in the industry use Carlson's two-factor test or that tire experts such as Carlson normally make the very fine distinctions about, say, the symmetry of comparatively greater shoulder tread wear that were necessary, on Carlson's own theory, to support his conclusions. Nor, despite the prevalence of tire testing, does anyone refer to any articles or papers that validate Carlson's approach. Compare Bobo, Tire Flaws and Separations, in Mechanics of Pneumatic Tires 636-637 (S. Clark ed. 1981); C. Schnuth et al., Compression Grooving and Rim Flange Abrasion as Indicators of Over-Deflected Operating Conditions in Tires, presented to Rubber Division of the American Chemical Society, Oct. 21-24, 1997; J. Walter & R. Kiminecz, Bead Contact Pressure Measurements at the Tire-Rim Interface, presented to Society of Automotive Engineers, Feb. 24-28, 1975. Indeed, no one has argued that Carlson himself, were he still working for Michelin, would have concluded in a report to his employer that a similar tire was similarly defective on grounds identical to those upon which he rested his conclusion here. Of course, Carlson himself claimed that his method was accurate, but, as we pointed out in *Joiner,* "nothing in either *Daubert* or the Federal Rules of Evidence requires a district court to admit opinion evidence that is connected to existing data only by the ipse dixit of the expert." 522 U.S. at 146.

Respondents additionally argue that the District Court too rigidly applied *Daubert's* criteria. They read its opinion to hold that a failure to satisfy any one of those criteria automatically renders expert testimony inadmissible. The District Court's initial opinion might have been vulnerable to a form of this argument. There, the court, after rejecting respondents' claim that Carlson's testimony was "exempted from *Daubert*-style scrutiny" because it was "technical analysis" rather than "scientific evidence," simply added that "none of the four admissibility criteria outlined by the *Daubert* court are satisfied." 923 F. Supp. at 1522. Subsequently, however, the court granted respondents' motion for reconsideration. It then explicitly recognized that the relevant reliability inquiry "should be 'flexible,'" that its "'overarching subject [should be] ... validity' and reliability," and that "*Daubert* was intended neither to be exhaustive nor to apply in every case." App. to Pet. for Cert. 4c (quoting *Daubert,* 509 U.S. at 594-595). And the court ultimately based its decision upon Carlson's failure to satisfy either *Daubert's* factors *or any other* set of reasonable reliability criteria. In light of the record as developed by the parties, that conclusion was within the District Court's lawful discretion.

In sum, Rule 702 grants the district judge the discretionary authority, reviewable for its abuse, to determine reliability in light of the particular facts and circumstances of the particular case. The District Court did not abuse its discretionary authority in this case. Hence, the judgment of the Court of Appeals is

Reversed.

Justice SCALIA, with whom Justice O'CONNOR and Justice THOMAS join, concurring.

I join the opinion of the Court, which makes clear that the discretion it endorses — trial-court discretion in choosing the manner of testing expert reliability—is not discretion to abandon the gatekeeping function. I think it worth adding that it is not discretion to perform the function inadequately. Rather, it is discretion to choose among *reasonable* means of excluding expertise that is *fausse* and science that is junky. Though, as the Court makes clear today, the *Daubert* factors are not holy writ, in a particular case the failure to apply one or another of them may be unreasonable, and hence an abuse of discretion.

Justice STEVENS, concurring in part and dissenting in part.

The only question that we granted in certiorari to decide is whether a trial judge "may . . . consider the four factors set out by this Court in Daubert v. Merrell Dow Pharmaceuticals, Inc., 509 U.S. 579, 125 L. Ed. 2d 469, 113 S. Ct. 2786 (1993), in a Rule 702 analysis of admissibility of an engineering expert's testimony." Pet. for Cert. i. That question is fully and correctly answered in Parts I and II of the Court's opinion, which I join.

Part III answers the quite different question whether the trial judge abused his discretion when he excluded the testimony of Dennis Carlson. Because a proper answer to that question requires a study of the record that can be performed more efficiently by the Court of Appeals than by the nine Members of this Court, I would remand the case to the Eleventh Circuit to perform that task. There are, of course, exceptions to most rules, but I firmly believe that it is neither fair to litigants nor good practice for this Court to reach out to decide questions not raised by the certiorari petition. See General Electric Co. v. Joiner, 522 U.S. 136, 150-151, 139 L. Ed. 2d 508, 118 S. Ct. 512 (1997) (STEVENS, J., concurring in part and dissenting in part).

Accordingly, while I do not feel qualified to disagree with the well-reasoned factual analysis in Part III of the Court's opinion, I do not join that Part, and I respectfully dissent from the Court's disposition of the case.

———————————

Another question left unanswered by *Daubert* was the standard of appellate review of a trial judge's determination of the admissibility or non-admissibility of expert testimony based on the *Daubert* criteria. In many cases, the *Daubert* issue arises not during trial, but on a motion for summary judgment. If the case is one where causation or some other element of the case must be demonstrated by expert testimony, a ruling that the plaintiff's expert will not be allowed to testify can make it impossible for the plaintiff to sustain its burden of proof and can result in summary dismissal of the entire case. The evidentiary ruling thus can become, in practical effect, a ruling on the merits.

GENERAL ELECTRIC COMPANY v. JOINER
522 U.S. 136 (1997)

Chief Justice REHNQUIST delivered the opinion of the Court.

We granted certiorari in this case to determine what standard an appellate court should apply in reviewing a trial court's decision to admit or exclude expert testimony under Daubert v. Merrell Dow Pharmaceuticals, Inc., 509 U.S. 579, 113 S. Ct. 2786, 125 L. Ed. 2d 469 (1993). We hold that abuse of discretion is the appropriate standard. We apply this standard and conclude that the District Court in this case did not abuse its discretion when it excluded certain proffered expert testimony.

I

Respondent Robert Joiner began work as an electrician in the Water & Light Department of Thomasville, Georgia (City) in 1973. This job required him to work with and around the City's electrical transformers, which used a mineral-based dielectric fluid as a coolant. Joiner often had to stick his hands and arms into the fluid to make repairs. The fluid would sometimes splash onto him, occasionally getting into his eyes and mouth. In 1983 the City discovered that the fluid in some of the transformers was contaminated with polychlorinated biphenyls (PCBs). PCBs are widely considered to be hazardous to human health. Congress, with limited exceptions, banned the production and sale of PCBs in 1978.

Joiner was diagnosed with small cell lung cancer in 1991. He sued petitioners in Georgia state court the following year. Petitioner Monsanto manufactured PCBs from 1935 to 1977; petitioners General Electric and Westinghouse Electric manufactured transformers and dielectric fluid. In his complaint Joiner linked his development of cancer to his exposure to PCBs and their derivatives, polychlorinated dibenzofurans (furans) and polychlorinated dibenzodioxins (dioxins). Joiner had been a smoker for approximately eight years, his parents had both been smokers, and there was a history of lung cancer in his family. He was thus perhaps already at a heightened risk of developing lung cancer eventually. The suit alleged that his exposure to PCBs "promoted" his cancer; had it not been for his exposure to these substances, his cancer would not have developed for many years, if at all.

Petitioners removed the case to federal court. Once there, they moved for summary judgment. They contended that (1) there was no evidence that Joiner suffered significant exposure to PCBs, furans, or dioxins, and (2) there was no admissible scientific evidence that PCBs promoted Joiner's cancer. Joiner responded that there were numerous disputed factual issues that required resolution by a jury. He relied largely on the testimony of expert witnesses. In depositions, his experts had testified that PCBs alone can promote cancer and that furans and dioxins can also promote cancer. They opined that since Joiner had been exposed to PCBs, furans, and dioxins, such exposure was likely responsible for Joiner's cancer.

The District Court ruled that there was a genuine issue of material fact as to whether Joiner had been exposed to PCBs. But it nevertheless granted summary judgment for petitioners because (1) there was no genuine issue as to whether Joiner had been exposed to furans and dioxins, and (2) the testimony of Joiner's experts had failed to show that there was a link between exposure to PCBs and small cell lung cancer. The court believed that the testimony of respondent's experts to the contrary did not rise above "subjective belief or unsupported speculation." 864 F.Supp. 1310, 1326 (N.D. Ga.1994). Their testimony was therefore inadmissible.

The Court of Appeals for the Eleventh Circuit reversed. 78 F.3d 524 (1996). It held that "[b]ecause the Federal Rules of Evidence governing expert testimony display a preference for admissibility, we apply a particularly stringent standard of review to the trial judge's exclusion of expert testimony." Id. at 529. Applying that standard, the Court of Appeals held that the District Court had erred in excluding the testimony of Joiner's expert witnesses. The District Court had made two fundamental errors. First, it excluded the experts' testimony because it "drew different conclusions from the research than did each of the experts." The Court of Appeals opined that a district court should limit its role to determining the "legal reliability of proffered expert testimony, leaving the jury to decide the correctness of competing expert opinions." Id. at 533. Second, the District Court had held that there was no genuine issue of material fact as to whether Joiner had been exposed to furans and dioxins. This was also incorrect, said the Court of Appeals, because testimony in the record supported the proposition that there had been such exposure.

We granted petitioners' petition for a writ of certiorari, 520 U.S.—, 117 S. Ct. 1243, 137 L. Ed. 2d 325 (1997), and we now reverse.

II

Petitioners challenge the standard applied by the Court of Appeals in reviewing the District Court's decision to exclude respondent's experts' proffered testimony. They argue that that court should have applied traditional "abuse of discretion" review. Respondent agrees that abuse of discretion is the correct standard of review. He contends, however, that the Court of Appeals applied an abuse of discretion standard in this case. As he reads it, the phrase "particularly stringent" announced no new standard of review. It was simply an acknowledgement that an appellate court can and will devote more resources to analyzing district court decisions that are dispositive of the entire litigation. All evidentiary decisions are reviewed under an abuse of discretion standard. He argues, however, that it is perfectly reasonable for appellate courts to give particular attention to those decisions that are outcome-determinative.

We have held that abuse of discretion is the proper standard of review of a district court's evidentiary rulings. Old Chief v. United States, 519 U.S. 172, —n.1, 117 S. Ct. 644, 647 n.1, 136 L. Ed. 2d 574 (1997), United States v. Abel, 469 U.S. 45, 54, 105 S. Ct. 465, 470, 83 L. Ed. 2d 450 (1984). Indeed, our cases on the subject go back as far as Spring Co. v. Edgar, 99 U.S. 645, 658, 25 L. Ed. 487 (1878) where we said that "cases arise where it is very much a matter of discretion with the court whether to receive or exclude the evidence; but the appellate court will not reverse in such a case, unless the ruling is manifestly erroneous." The Court of Appeals suggested that *Daubert* somehow altered this general rule in the context of a district court's decision to exclude scientific evidence. But *Daubert* did not address the standard of appellate review for evidentiary rulings at all. It did hold that the "austere" *Frye* standard of "general acceptance" had not been carried over into the Federal Rules of Evidence. But the opinion also said:

> "That the *Frye* test was displaced by the Rules of Evidence does not mean, however, that the Rules themselves place no limits on the admissibility of purportedly scientific evidence. Nor is the trial judge disabled from screening such evidence. To the contrary, under the Rules the trial judge must ensure that any and all scientific testimony or evidence admitted is not only relevant, but reliable."

509 U.S., at 589, 113 S.Ct., at 2794-2795 (footnote omitted).

Thus, while the Federal Rules of Evidence allow district courts to admit a somewhat broader range of scientific testimony than would have been admissible under *Frye*, they leave in place the "gatekeeper" role of the trial judge in screening such evidence. A court of appeals applying "abuse of discretion" review to such rulings may not categorically distinguish between rulings allowing expert testimony and rulings which disallow it. Compare Beech Aircraft Corp. v. Rainey, 488 U.S. 153, 172, 109 S. Ct. 439, 451, 102 L. Ed. 2d 445 (1988) (applying abuse of discretion review to a lower court's decision to exclude evidence) with United States v. Abel, supra, at 54, 105 S. Ct., at 470 (applying abuse of discretion review to a lower court's decision to admit evidence). We likewise reject respondent's argument that because the granting of summary judgment in this case was "outcome determinative," it should have been subjected to a more searching standard of review. On a motion for summary judgment, disputed issues of fact are resolved against the moving party—here, petitioners. But the question of admissibility of expert testimony is not such an issue of fact, and is reviewable under the abuse of discretion standard.

We hold that the Court of Appeals erred in its review of the exclusion of Joiner's experts' testimony. In applying an overly "stringent" review to that ruling, it failed to give the trial court the deference that is the hallmark of abuse of discretion review. See, e.g., Koon v. United States, 518 U.S. 81, ——, 116 S. Ct. 2035, 2046-2047, 135 L. Ed. 2d 392 (1996).

III

We believe that a proper application of the correct standard of review here indicates that the District Court did not abuse its discretion. Joiner's theory of liability was that his exposure to PCBs and their derivatives "promoted" his development of small cell lung cancer. In support of that theory he proffered the deposition testimony of expert witnesses. Dr. Arnold Schecter testified that he believed it "more likely than not that Mr. Joiner's lung cancer was causally linked to cigarette smoking and PCB exposure." App. at 107. Dr. Daniel Teitelbaum testified that Joiner's "lung cancer was caused by or contributed to in a significant degree by the materials with which he worked." Id. at 140.

Petitioners contended that the statements of Joiner's experts regarding causation were nothing more than speculation. Petitioners criticized the testimony of the experts in that it was "not supported by epidemiological studies . . . [and was] based exclusively on isolated studies of laboratory animals." Joiner responded by claiming that his experts had identified "relevant animal studies which support their opinions." He also directed the court's attention to four epidemiological studies on which his experts had relied.

The District Court agreed with petitioners that the animal studies on which respondent's experts relied did not support his contention that exposure to PCBs had contributed to his cancer. The studies involved infant mice that had developed cancer after being exposed to PCBs. The infant mice in the studies had had massive doses of PCBs injected directly into their peritoneums or stomachs. Joiner was an adult human being whose alleged exposure to PCBs was far less than the exposure in the animal studies. The PCBs were injected into the mice in a highly concentrated form. The fluid with which Joiner had come into contact generally had a much smaller PCB concentration of between 0-500 parts per million. The cancer that these mice developed was alveologenic adenomas; Joiner had developed small-cell carcinomas. No study demonstrated that adult mice developed cancer after being exposed to PCBs. One of the experts admitted that no study had demonstrated that PCBs lead to cancer in any other species.

Respondent failed to reply to this criticism. Rather than explaining how and why the experts could have extrapolated their opinions from these seemingly far-removed animal studies, respondent chose "to proceed as if the only issue [was] whether animal studies can ever be a proper foundation for an expert's opinion." Joiner, 864 F. Supp., at 1324. Of course, whether animal studies can ever be a proper foundation for an expert's opinion was not the issue. The issue was whether these experts' opinions were sufficiently supported by the animal studies on which they purported to rely. The studies were so dissimilar to the facts presented in this litigation that it was not an abuse of discretion for the District Court to have rejected the experts' reliance on them.

The District Court also concluded that the four epidemiological studies on which respondent relied were not a sufficient basis for the experts' opinions. The first such study involved workers at an Italian capacitor plant who had been exposed to PCBs. Bertazzi, Riboldi, Pesatori, Radice, & Zocchetti, Cancer Mortality of Capacitor Manufacturing Workers, 11 American Journal of Industrial Medicine 165 (1987). The authors noted that lung cancer deaths among ex-employees at the plant were higher than might have been expected, but concluded that "there were apparently no grounds for associating lung cancer deaths (although increased above expectations) and exposure in the plant." Id. at 172. Given that Bertazzi et al. were unwilling to say that PCB exposure had caused cancer among the workers they examined, their study did not support the experts' conclusion that Joiner's exposure to PCBs caused his cancer.

The second study followed employees who had worked at Monsanto's PCB production plant. J. Zack & D. Munsch, Mortality of PCB Workers at the Monsanto Plant in Sauget, Illinois (Dec. 14, 1979) (unpublished report), 3 Rec., Doc. No. 11. The authors of this study found that the incidence of lung cancer deaths among these workers was somewhat higher than would ordinarily be expected. The increase, however, was not statistically significant and the authors of the study did not suggest a link between the increase in lung cancer deaths and the exposure to PCBs.

The third and fourth studies were likewise of no help. The third involved workers at a Norwegian cable manufacturing company who had been exposed to mineral oil. Ronneberg, Andersen, Skyberg, Mortality and Incidence of Cancer Among Oil-Exposed Workers in a Norwegian Cable Manufacturing Company, 45 British Journal of Industrial Medicine 595 (1988). A statistically significant increase in lung cancer deaths had been observed in these workers. The study, however, (1) made no mention of PCBs and (2) was expressly limited to the type of mineral oil involved in that study, and thus did not support these experts' opinions. The fourth and final study involved a PCB-exposed group in Japan that had seen a statistically significant increase in lung cancer deaths. Kuratsune, Nakamura, Ikeda, & Hirohata, Analysis of Deaths Seen Among Patients with Yusho — A Preliminary Report, 16 Chemosphere, Nos. 8/9, 2085 (1987). The subjects of this study, however, had been exposed to numerous potential carcinogens, including toxic rice oil that they had ingested.

Respondent points to *Daubert*'s language that the "focus, of course, must be solely on principles and methodology, not on the conclusions that they generate." 509 U.S., at 595, 113 S. Ct., at 2797. He claims that because the District Court's disagreement was with the conclusion that the experts drew from the studies, the District Court committed legal error and was properly reversed by the Court of Appeals. But conclusions and methodology are not entirely distinct from one another. Trained experts commonly extrapolate from existing data. But nothing in either *Daubert* or the Federal Rules of Evidence requires a district court to admit opinion evidence which is connected to existing data only by the ipse dixit of the expert. A court may conclude that there is simply too great an analytical gap between the data and the opinion proffered. See Turpin v. Merrell Dow Pharmaceuticals, Inc., 959 F.2d 1349, 1360 (C.A.6), cert. denied, 506 U.S. 826, 113 S. Ct. 84, 121 L. Ed. 2d 47 (1992). That is what the District Court did here, and we hold that it did not abuse its discretion in so doing.

We hold, therefore, that abuse of discretion is the proper standard by which to review a district court's decision to admit or exclude scientific evidence. We further hold that, because it was within the District Court's discretion to conclude that the studies upon which the experts relied were not sufficient, whether individually or in combination, to support their conclusions that Joiner's exposure to PCBs contributed to his cancer, the District Court did not abuse its discretion in excluding their testimony. These conclusions, however, do not dispose of this entire case.

Respondent's original contention was that his exposure to PCBs, furans, and dioxins contributed to his cancer. The District Court ruled that there was a genuine issue of material fact as to whether Joiner had been exposed to PCBs, but concluded that there was no genuine issue as to whether he had been exposed to furans and dioxins. The District Court accordingly never explicitly considered if there was admissible evidence on the question whether Joiner's alleged exposure to furans and dioxins contributed to his cancer. The Court of Appeals reversed the District Court's conclusion that there had been no exposure to furans and dioxins. Petitioners did not challenge this determination in their petition to this Court. Whether Joiner was exposed to furans and dioxins, and whether if there was such exposure, the opinions of Joiner's experts would then be admissible, remain open questions. We accordingly reverse the judgment of the Court of Appeals and remand this case for proceedings consistent with this opinion. It is so ordered.

Justice BREYER, concurring.

The Court's opinion, which I join, emphasizes *Daubert*'s statement that a trial judge, acting as "gatekeeper," must "'ensure that any and all scientific testimony or evidence admitted is not only relevant, but reliable.'" Ante, at 517 (quoting Daubert v. Merrell Dow Pharmaceuticals, Inc., 509 U.S. 579, 589, 113 S. Ct. 2786, 2795, 125 L. Ed. 2d 469 (1993)). This requirement will sometimes ask judges to make subtle and sophisticated determinations about scientific methodology and its relation to the conclusions an expert witness seeks to offer — particularly when a case arises in an area where the science itself is tentative or uncertain, or where testimony about general risk levels in human beings or animals is offered to prove individual causation. Yet, as amici have pointed out, judges are not scientists and do not have the scientific training that can facilitate the making of such decisions. See, e.g., Brief for Trial Lawyers for Public Justice as Amicus Curiae 15; Brief for The New England Journal of Medicine et al. as Amici Curiae 2 ("Judges . . . are generally not trained scientists").

Of course, neither the difficulty of the task nor any comparative lack of expertise can excuse the judge from exercising the "gatekeeper" duties that the Federal Rules impose—determining, for example, whether particular expert testimony is reliable and "will assist the trier of fact," Fed. Rule Evid. 702, or whether the "probative value" of testimony is substantially outweighed by risks of prejudice, confusion or waste of time. Fed. Rule Evid. 403. To the contrary, when law and science intersect, those duties often must be exercised with special care.

Today's toxic tort case provides an example. The plaintiff in today's case says that a chemical substance caused, or promoted, his lung cancer. His concern, and that of others, about the causes of cancer is understandable, for cancer kills over one in five Americans. See U.S. Dept. of Health and Human Services, National Center for Health Statistics, Health United States 1996-97 and Injury Chartbook 117 (1997) (23.3% of all deaths in 1995). Moreover, scientific evidence implicates some chemicals as potential causes of some cancers. See, e.g., U.S. Dept. of Health and Human Services, Public Health Service, National Toxicology

Program, 1 Seventh Annual Report on Carcinogens, pp. v-vi (1994). Yet modern life, including good health as well as economic well-being, depends upon the use of artificial or manufactured substances, such as chemicals. And it may, therefore, prove particularly important to see that judges fulfill their *Daubert* gatekeeping function, so that they help assure that the powerful engine of tort liability, which can generate strong financial incentives to reduce, or to eliminate, production, points towards the right substances and does not destroy the wrong ones. It is, thus, essential in this science-related area that the courts administer the Federal Rules of Evidence in order to achieve the "end[s]" that the Rules themselves set forth, not only so that proceedings may be "justly determined," but also so "that the truth may be ascertained." Fed. Rule Evid. 102.

I therefore want specially to note that, as cases presenting significant science-related issues have increased in number, see Judicial Conference of the United States, Report of the Federal Courts Study Committee 97 (Apr. 2, 1990) ("Economic, statistical, technological, and natural and social scientific data are becoming increasingly important in both routine and complex litigation"), judges have increasingly found in the Rules of Evidence and Civil Procedure ways to help them overcome the inherent difficulty of making determinations about complicated scientific or otherwise technical evidence. Among these techniques are an increased use of Rule 16's pretrial conference authority to narrow the scientific issues in dispute, pretrial hearings where potential experts are subject to examination by the court, and the appointment of special masters and specially trained law clerks. See J. Cecil & T. Willging, Court-Appointed Experts: Defining the Role of Experts Appointed Under Federal Rule of Evidence 706, pp. 83-88 (1993); J. Weinstein, Individual Justice in Mass Tort Litigation 107-110 (1995); cf. Kaysen, In Memoriam: Charles E. Wyzanski, Jr., 100 Harv. L. Rev. 713, 713-715 (1987) (discussing a judge's use of an economist as a law clerk in United States v. United Shoe Machinery Corp., 110 F. Supp. 295 (D. Mass.1953), aff'd, 347 U.S. 521, 74 S. Ct. 699, 98 L. Ed. 910 (1954)).

In the present case, the New England Journal of Medicine has filed an amici brief "in support of neither petitioners nor respondents" in which the Journal writes:

> "[A] judge could better fulfill this gatekeeper function if he or she had help from scientists. Judges should be strongly encouraged to make greater use of their inherent authority . . . to appoint experts. . . . Reputable experts could be recommended to courts by established scientific organizations, such as the National Academy of Sciences or the American Association for the Advancement of Science."

Brief for The New England Journal of Medicine 18-19; cf. Fed. Rule
Evid. 706 (court may "on its own motion or on the motion of any party"
appoint an expert to serve on behalf of the court, and this expert may
be selected as "agreed upon by the parties" or chosen by the court); see
also Weinstein, supra, at 116 (a court should sometimes "go beyond the
experts proffered by the parties" and "utilize its powers to appoint independent experts under Rule 706 of the Federal Rules of Evidence").
Given this kind of offer of cooperative effort, from the scientific to the
legal community, and given the various Rules-authorized methods for
facilitating the courts' task, it seems to me that Daubert's gatekeeping
requirement will not prove inordinately difficult to implement; and that
it will help secure the basic objectives of the Federal Rules of Evidence;
which are, to repeat, the ascertainment of truth and the just determination of proceedings. Fed. Rule Evid. 102.

Justice STEVENS, concurring in part and dissenting in part.
    The question that we granted certiorari to decide is whether the
Court of Appeals applied the correct standard of review. That question
is fully answered in Parts I and II of the Court's opinion. Part III answers
the quite different question whether the District Court properly held
that the testimony of plaintiff's expert witnesses was inadmissible. Because I am not sure that the parties have adequately briefed that question, or that the Court has adequately explained why the Court of
Appeals' disposition was erroneous, I do not join Part III. Moreover,
because a proper answer to that question requires a study of the record
that can be performed more efficiently by the Court of Appeals than by
the nine members of this Court, I would remand the case to that court
for application of the proper standard of review.
    One aspect of the record will illustrate my concern. As the Court of
Appeals pointed out, Joiner's experts relied on "the studies of at least
thirteen different researchers, and referred to several reports of the
World Health Organization that address the question of whether PCBs
cause cancer." 78 F.3d 524, 533 (C.A.11 1996). Only one of those studies
is in the record, and only six of them were discussed in the District Court
opinion. Whether a fair appraisal of either the methodology or the conclusions of Joiner's experts can be made on the basis of such an incomplete record is a question that I do not feel prepared to answer.
    It does seem clear, however, that the Court has not adequately ex-
plained why its holding is consistent with Federal Rule of Evidence 702,
as interpreted in Daubert v. Merrell Dow Pharmaceuticals, Inc., 509 U.S.
579, 113 S. Ct. 2786, 125 L. Ed. 2d 469 (1993). In general, scientific
testimony that is both relevant and reliable must be admitted and testimony that is irrelevant or unreliable must be excluded. Id., at 597, 113
S. Ct., at 2798-2799. In this case, the District Court relied on both
grounds for exclusion.

The relevance ruling was straightforward. The District Court correctly reasoned that an expert opinion that exposure to PCBs, "furans" and "dioxins" together may cause lung cancer would be irrelevant unless the plaintiff had been exposed to those substances. Having already found that there was no evidence of exposure to furans and dioxins, 864 F. Supp. 1310, 1318-1319 (N.D. Ga.1994), it necessarily followed that this expert opinion testimony was inadmissible. Correctly applying *Daubert,* the District Court explained that the experts' testimony "manifestly does not fit the facts of this case, and is therefore inadmissible." 864 F. Supp., at 1322. Of course, if the evidence raised a genuine issue of fact on the question of Joiner's exposure to furans and dioxins—as the Court of Appeals held that it did—then this basis for the ruling on admissibility was erroneous, but not because the district judge either abused her discretion or misapplied the law.

The reliability ruling was more complex and arguably is not faithful to the statement in *Daubert* that "[t]he focus, of course, must be solely on principles and methodology, not on the conclusions that they generate." . . . Joiner's experts used a "weight of the evidence" methodology to assess whether Joiner's exposure to transformer fluids promoted his lung cancer. They did not suggest that any one study provided adequate support for their conclusions, but instead relied on all the studies taken together (along with their interviews of Joiner and their review of his medical records). The District Court, however, examined the studies one by one and concluded that none was sufficient to show a link between PCBs and lung cancer. 864 F. Supp., at 1324-1326. The focus of the opinion was on the separate studies and the conclusions of the experts, not on the experts' methodology. Id., at 1322 ("Defendants . . . persuade the court that Plaintiffs' expert testimony would not be admissible . . . by attacking the conclusions that Plaintiffs' experts draw from the studies they cite").

Unlike the District Court, the Court of Appeals expressly decided that a "weight of the evidence" methodology was scientifically acceptable. To this extent, the Court of Appeals' opinion is persuasive. It is not intrinsically "unscientific" for experienced professionals to arrive at a conclusion by weighing all available scientific evidence—this is not the sort of "junk science" with which *Daubert* was concerned. After all, as Joiner points out, the Environmental Protection Agency (EPA) uses the same methodology to assess risks, albeit using a somewhat different threshold than that required in a trial. Brief for Respondents 40-41 (quoting EPA, Guidelines for Carcinogen Risk Assessment, 51 Fed. Reg. 33992, 33996 (1986)). Petitioners' own experts used the same scientific approach as well. And using this methodology, it would seem that an expert could reasonably have concluded that the study of workers at an Italian capacitor plant, coupled with data from Monsanto's study and other studies, raises an inference that PCBs promote lung cancer.

The Court of Appeals' discussion of admissibility is faithful to the dictum in *Daubert* that the reliability inquiry must focus on methodology, not conclusions. Thus, even though I fully agree with both the District Court's and this Court's explanation of why each of the studies on which the experts relied was by itself unpersuasive, a critical question remains unanswered: when qualified experts have reached relevant conclusions on the basis of an acceptable methodology, why are their opinions inadmissible?

Daubert quite clearly forbids trial judges from assessing the validity or strength of an expert's scientific conclusions, which is a matter for the jury. Because I am persuaded that the difference between methodology and conclusions is just as categorical as the distinction between means and ends, I do not think the statement that "conclusions and methodology are not entirely distinct from one another," ante, at 519, is either accurate or helps us answer the difficult admissibility question presented by this record.

In any event, it bears emphasis that the Court has not held that it would have been an abuse of discretion to admit the expert testimony. The very point of today's holding is that the abuse of discretion standard of review applies whether the district judge has excluded or admitted evidence. Ante, at 517. And nothing in either *Daubert* or the Federal Rules of Evidence requires a district judge to reject an expert's conclusions and keep them from the jury when they fit the facts of the case and are based on reliable scientific methodology.

Accordingly, while I join Parts I and II of the Court's opinion, I do not concur in the judgment or in Part III of its opinion.

Do you find the Supreme Court's resolution of the expert testimony quandary in *Daubert, Kumho,* and *Joiner* ultimately satisfying? Are unschooled judges and even less schooled jurors ultimately qualified to render satisfactory decisions of controversies beyond their own knowledge and experience, with or without the help of expert witnesses? *Daubert* and its progeny may have provided us with some useful guidance about when to admit expert testimony, but they have not given us much help on how to choose between competing experts to make the ultimate decision.

UNITED STATES OF AMERICA v. JOHN RAY BONDS ET AL.
12 F.3d 540 (6th Cir. 1993)

ALICE M. BATCHELDER, Circuit Judge:

On February 27, 1988, David Hartlaub was gunned down in his van as he stopped at a bank near the Sandusky Mall in Perkins Township, Ohio, where he planned to make a night deposit of cash from the music store he helped manage. The killers apparently had no interest in robbery; police found the deposit bag containing some four thousand dollars on the seat of the van. Three individuals—Wayne Yee, Mark Verdi and John Ray Bonds — were indicted in connection with the crime, tried, and convicted on federal firearms offenses, in violation of 26 U.S.C. §5861(d) and 18 U.S.C. §922(g)(1), and conspiracy in violation of 18 U.S.C. §371. At trial, the Government's theory for the shooting was that the gunmen, members of the Hell's Angels motorcycle gang, had mistaken Mr. Hartlaub's yellow van for an identical van driven by a local member of a rival motorcycle gang, the Outlaws, whom the gunmen had allegedly planned to "hit" in retaliation for the shooting of a Hell's Angels member by an Outlaw the previous year in Joliet, Illinois. The defendants also claim that this is a case of mistaken identity—theirs —and challenge their convictions, claiming the Government's evidence to be either flawed, circumstantial, or both. Among the issues we must confront in this appeal is an issue of first impression for this court: whether the district court erred in admitting expert testimony concerning deoxyribonucleic acid (DNA) evidence in the trial of these defendants. For the reasons set forth below, we affirm the defendants' convictions.

I. FACTS

No bystanders saw the shooting. However, Douglas Waratuke, another music store employee, had followed Mr. Hartlaub to the bank and saw Mr. Hartlaub lying on the ground next to the van when Waratuke arrived at the bank. When Waratuke went to get out of his car, however, a man ran up and put a gun to Waratuke's head through the half-open window and ordered him to stay in the car. Based on Mr. Waratuke's description of the gunman as 25-27 years old, 5' 11", 165 pounds, with a "lanky build" and a "Hispanic appearance," the police made a sketch. Four other bystanders saw the same man and gave similar descriptions. One, Elizabeth Graf, also saw the getaway car, which she described to the police as a cream or tan color Buick, four door, dirty but in good condition.

After the Hispanic-looking man ran away, apparently heading for a nearby hotel, Mr. Waratuke saw an arm reach out of the van and close the door; the occupant then drove off with the van. Police later found the van abandoned behind the hotel with its engine still running and lights on. The gun used in the shooting, a MAC-11 9-mm semi-automatic pistol fitted with a homemade silencer and a multi-round clip with a plastic garbage bag taped on to catch the spent cartridges, lay on the floor between the seats. The gun's serial number had been obliterated;

however, the FBI was later able to "raise" the serial number. The gun turned out to have been owned previously by Donald Myers, a former roommate of defendant Yee, who had owned two such guns and testified that they had been stolen from his car when it was parked outside their apartment.

Both the gun and the van's carpet were spattered with blood. Serology tests showed that the blood was not Mr. Hartlaub's, but rare enzymes identified in the spattered blood, which only appear in about 1% of caucasian males, matched those found in Mr. Bonds's blood. Most of the blood in the van had dripped between the front seats; shortly after the murder Mr. Bonds wore his right arm in a sling, and it was later established that he had a serious ricochet wound which evidently bled between the seats as he drove the van that night. . . .

In Yee's car, which the agents tracked down a few days later, the agents found, among other things, spent shell casings which experts later determined came from the murder weapon, and blood in the back seat which the FBI eventually matched with John Bonds's blood sample by DNA identification. A hair found in the back seat of the Yee car also matched Bonds's hair. Fibers found in the car also matched fibers from a green glove found three weeks after the murder on the side of the road (Route 2) connecting Cleveland and Sandusky. With the glove was found Mr. Hartlaub's van registration and title, an empty box of 9-mm cartridges of the type used in the murder and found in Yee's car (this box was later shown to have been bought at a gun shop near Mr. Yee's apartment), and a loaded revolver. A hair found on the glove matched Mr. Bonds's hair. Fibers found on the glove matched the carpeting in the van; the fibers of the glove itself matched fibers stuck to the tape attaching the cartridge-catcher bag to the murder weapon and also matched fibers found on the shirt seized from Mr. Verdi's home.

On March 16, the grand jury issued a subpoena ordering Mr. Bonds to submit to fingerprints and photographs; he complied. On April 20, another subpoena ordered him to appear for photographs of his bare arms, legs and torso, to see if he showed wounds consistent with those thought to have caused the blood stains in the van. On April 25, Bonds refused to comply, invoking his Fourth and Fifth Amendment rights. After a hearing before a district court judge, Bonds was ordered to comply by the morning of April 27 or be held in contempt. On April 27, Bonds was held to be in contempt and was taken into custody in the Cleveland Federal Courthouse. That evening, Bonds was taken to a jail in Toledo; the plan was to take him to a federal prison in Michigan the next day.

Agents prepared an affidavit seeking to obtain a search warrant for blood and hair samples from Mr. Bonds, which was brought before a federal magistrate judge in Toledo on April 28. The magistrate was satisfied with the reliability of the information and issued the warrant based on a finding of probable cause. The agents seized the samples from Bonds. These samples were the basis for evidence introduced at trial, including evidence that the DNA in Bonds's blood matched the DNA from the blood found in the back seat of Yee's car. Bonds was subsequently indicted, but fled before he could be brought to trial; he was a fugitive for several months before being discovered in Kentucky.

All three defendants were eventually tried to a jury and convicted; Messrs. Verdi and Yee were each sentenced to a total of fifteen years and Mr. Bonds was sentenced to a total of twenty five years.

II. ADMISSIBILITY OF THE DNA EVIDENCE

We first address whether the district court committed reversible error in admitting expert testimony concerning the DNA evidence obtained from the blood sample of defendant Bonds. Although several federal courts have ruled on the admissibility of forensic DNA testimony and evidence, . . . as have numerous state courts, . . . this is a case of first impression for the Sixth Circuit. We find that the district court did not err in admitting the expert testimony in this case.

A. BACKGROUND OF DNA TESTING

Deoxyribonucleic acid (DNA) is the molecule, found in the nucleus of nearly every cell of every living thing, that houses genetic information. The structure of this molecule in a human provides a unique genetic code for that person; only genetic twins have identical DNA. In some regions of the DNA molecule, scientists have found segments called variable number tandem repeats (VNTRs), which vary greatly among individuals. Accordingly, VNTR genes are called *polymorphic* because they appear in different forms, called *alleles,* in different individuals. It is these VNTR genes that are analyzed to determine whether biological material found in body fluid of a known individual can be linked to the DNA found in a body fluid sample of an unidentified crime-scene specimen. The greater the number of matching alleles detected in the crime-scene blood and a suspect's blood, the more probable it is that the suspect is the source of the crime-scene sample. DNA has been heralded because DNA markers—VNTRs—vary much more from individual to individual than do traditional blood serology markers —blood type and enzymes. Therefore, a detailed examination of DNA theoretically can yield a positive association between a suspect's sample and a crime-scene sample.

The technique used by the FBI laboratory in this case involves the use of a molecular biology technique called restriction fragment length polymorphism (RFLP). The RFLP procedure isolates DNA in a blood sample so that scientists can locate the VNTRs in that DNA. Using this technique, molecular biologists can detect differences in DNA by analyzing size and length variations between the VNTR alleles of the suspect's blood and of the crime-scene sample blood. They then compare visually and with a computer program the resulting sizes of the DNA band patterns. Finally, they attempt to determine whether there is a "match" by analyzing whether it is likely or unlikely that a known sample and an unknown sample come from the same source, or whether the results are inconclusive.

After the RFLP procedure is completed and a match is found, the lab makes a statistical estimate of the rarity of the pattern of DNA bands found in the suspect's sample. By conducting DNA studies on FBI agents, the FBI has developed a table of DNA allele frequencies for each of three racial groups—caucasian, black and hispanic—using a "fixed-bin method," in which the lab divides up the size of the alleles into bins. Although these population studies are broken down by racial groups, they are not further divided into ethnic subpopulation within these groups, such as (within the caucasian group) Polish or Italian. The forensic scientist uses these tables to determine the frequency of each allele in the particular suspect's sample. To estimate the frequency of a suspect's overall DNA pattern, the individual allele frequencies are multiplied together, using a multiplication or product rule, to compute an aggregate estimate of the probability that this combination of alleles in the suspect's DNA sample would be encountered in a particular racial population. This comparison highlights the significance of a DNA "match" by determining the frequency with which the particular genetic traits, or alleles, of the suspect are observed in a particular racial population.

B.   USE OF DNA EVIDENCE IN THIS CASE

On April 7, 1989, the FBI's DNA laboratory submitted a report stating that there was a "match" of DNA profiles from a bloodstain found in victim David Hartlaub's car and the DNA profiles derived from the blood of defendant Bonds. The FBI then calculated a probability of 1 in 270,000 that an unrelated individual selected randomly from the caucasian population would have a DNA profile matching that of Bonds. In May of 1990, the FBI revised its probability figure to 1 in 35,000. This revised probability estimate was presented to the jury in this case.

Defendants filed a motion to suppress the DNA evidence, and the Government filed a motion to admit the evidence. Because at that time the FBI test results had not yet been published in a peer review journal explaining the FBI's methods and offering data to support the results, defendants moved to discover the predicate data underlying the FBI's unpublished DNA studies and records of the internal proficiency tests that the FBI had conducted. The magistrate judge granted most of the discovery requests. See United States v. Yee, 129 F.R.D. 629, 631 (N.D. Ohio 1990). The magistrate judge then conducted a six-week *Frye* hearing[7] to determine whether the proposed experts' trial testimony about the DNA evidence was based on principles generally accepted in the scientific community. During the hearing, the Government called six expert witnesses, the defendants called five expert witnesses, and the court called Dr. Eric Lander as the court's witness. More than 200 exhibits were introduced relating to the FBI's methods of testing.

At the conclusion of the hearing, Magistrate Judge Carr issued a comprehensive 120-page report and recommendation (R&R), recommending that the Government's motion to admit the DNA evidence be granted and that the defendants' motion to suppress be denied. The district court adopted the magistrate's R&R, United States v. Yee, 134 F.R.D. 161 (N.D. Ohio 1991), specifically addressing the three issues raised by defendants in their objections to the R&R: consensus and general acceptance, reliability, and Federal Rule of Evidence 403. The district court found that the Rule 403 argument must be raised at trial.

Before trial, defendants moved for an in limine hearing to resolve the Rule 403 ground for exclusion and to expand the *Frye* hearing. The trial court denied the motion for exclusion of the evidence and for another evidentiary hearing, again holding that the Rule 403 challenge must be addressed at trial. At trial, the district court admitted the testimony over the Rule 403 challenge. The district court's orders denying the motion to suppress are now before us on appeal.

C. CONSIDERATION OF NRC REPORT

We address first the Government's motion to strike the references in defendants' appellate brief to the report by the National Research Committee (NRC) of the National Academy of Sciences (NAS), entitled "DNA Technology in Forensic Science" (hereinafter NRC Report). Defendants ask us to take judicial notice of this report for purposes of this appeal. We grant the Government's motion to strike, deny the motion to take judicial notice, and find that we cannot consider this report for purposes of this appeal.

The *Frye* hearing before the magistrate began in June of 1990; the magistrate issued his R&R in October of 1990. The district court adopted the R&R in January of 1991. Defendants were convicted and sentenced, and filed their notices of appeal in 1991. On April 16, 1992,

---

7. This circuit has used the test for admissibility of scientific expert testimony established in Frye v. United States, 54 App. D.C. 46, 293 F. 1013 (D.C. Cir. 1923), which requires that the testimony be based on a theory that has "gained general acceptance in the particular field in which it belongs." Id. at 1014. Thus, until recently, district courts conducted "*Frye* hearings" prior to trial to determine if certain scientific expert testimony would be based on generally accepted theories and procedures. In a recent ruling, Daubert v. Merrell Dow Pharmaceuticals, Inc., 125 L. Ed. 2d 469, 113 S. Ct. 2786 (1993), the Supreme Court held that the *Frye* test was superseded by Federal Rule of Evidence 702. See discussion infra part II.E.

nearly two years after the *Frye* hearing and more than a year after the convictions, the NAS issued the NRC Report. On June 8, 1992, defendants filed their brief on appeal, urging reversal and relying heavily on the report's findings.

The NRC Report examines the FBI's method of declaring DNA matches and of calculating the statistical probability of a suspect's pattern of DNA occurring in a particular population. The report was authored by a committee of scientists in population and molecular genetics, forensic scientists, legal academicians, ethicists, and a federal judge, including Dr. Eric Lander, the court's witness at the *Frye* hearing. Dr. Caskey, a Government witness, was a former member of the committee, and Dr. Kidd and Dr. Budowle, two of the Government's witnesses, were among those who made presentations to the committee and whose views are reflected in the report. The report cites to the published works in the field, including documents discussed at the *Frye* hearing. The report, which was peer-reviewed by a group other than the authors, questions a number of the FBI's procedures. Most significantly, it contends that the FBI's multiplication rule (the rule of multiplying the frequency of the alleles by one another to compute a composite frequency of a suspect's particular DNA pattern) distorts the probability estimates because the rule does not take into account the possibility of "population substructure," a view that racial populations contain ethnic subpopulations (e.g., Italian, Polish, etc.) that have distinct DNA allele frequencies. The report proposes an interim method, called the ceiling method, for performing probability calculations in a way that would compensate for population substructure. Under this proposed ceiling method, defendants argue that the probability of Bonds's DNA pattern being found in the caucasian population in this case would be 1 in 17, not 1 in 35,000 as reported by the FBI. The Government responds that even under the ceiling method, the figure would be 1 in 6,200.

In its motion to strike, the Government argues that this NRC Report was issued more than a year after defendants' convictions and was not part of the record in the district court. The defendants counter that although the report was not part of the district court record, this Court can take judicial notice of this scientific report in determining if scientific testimony is "generally accepted." See People v. Reilly, 196 Cal. App. 3d 1127, 242 Cal. Rptr. 496, 501 (Cal. Ct. App. 1987) (overview of literature outside record can reveal consensus and end case-by-case general acceptance decision).

We grant the Government's motion to strike the NRC Report because this report was not available to the magistrate judge at the *Frye* hearing and was not before the magistrate judge or the district court judge when they ruled on the motion to suppress. We cannot consider a report that is not part of the record. See Fed. R. App. P. 10(a) (record on appeal consists of "original papers and exhibits filed in the district court, the transcript of proceedings, if any, and a certified copy of the docket entries"); see also United States v. Allen, 522 F.2d 1229, 1235 (6th Cir. 1975) (court will not consider material in brief that is not in record), cert. denied, 423 U.S. 1072, 96 S. Ct. 854, 47 L. Ed. 2d 82 (1976). As a panel of this Court stated in Sovereign News Co. v. United States, 690 F.2d 569 (6th Cir. 1982), cert. denied, 464 U.S. 814, 104 S. Ct. 69, 78 L. Ed. 2d 83 (1983), "A party may not bypass the fact-finding process of the lower court and introduce new facts in its brief on appeal." *Id.* at 571. Although this case differs from *Sovereign News* in that this is a criminal appeal, appellate courts hearing criminal matters also have refused to take judicial notice of, or supplement the record with, evidence that was not before the district court. . . .

While defendants' request that we merely take judicial notice of this report pursuant to Federal Rules of Evidence 201(f) and 104(a) has a certain facial appeal, Federal Rule 201 permits a court to take judicial notice only of facts "not subject to reasonable dispute. . . ." Fed. R. Evid. 201(b). There is no dispute that the NRC Report exists, but there is considerable dispute over the significance of its contents. We acknowledge that several appellate courts have considered the NRC Report retroactively, asked the parties to brief the significance of the report, or remanded for consideration of it. See, e.g., United States v. Porter, 618 A.2d 629 (D.C. 1992) (remand in part for consideration of NRC Report, which was issued during appeal process); State v. Anderson, 115 N.M. 433, 853 P.2d 135 (N.M. Ct. App.) (considering NRC Report issued while case on appeal), cert. granted, 848 P.2d 531 (N.M. 1993); New Hampshire v. Vandebogart, 136 N.H. 365, 616 A.2d 483 (N.H. 1992) (using NRC Report to conclude that probability methods are not generally accepted); People v. Barney, 8 Cal. App. 4th 798, 10 Cal. Rptr. 2d 731 (1992). However, we do not agree with those courts that have considered the NRC Report retroactively or remanded for consideration of it, and we decline to take judicial notice of an article published a year after defendants' convictions were handed down.

As the Government points out, if we were to take judicial notice of this article, the Government would be precluded from rebutting the report with expert testimony, as both sides were permitted to do for the reports and articles submitted to the magistrate judge at the *Frye* hearing. We in essence would be bypassing the fact-finding function of the district court and overriding the requirement that all pertinent evidence be admitted at the evidentiary hearing. Most importantly, if we were to look at new scientific data available to us but not available to the district court that made the admissibility determination, we would not be confining ourselves to *reviewing* the district court's admissibility ruling, but would be making a de novo determination based on post-conviction developments or articles. This is not the function of an appellate court.

This scientific report is evidence just as the other scientific reports and exhibits introduced at the *Frye* hearing are evidence; it is not judicial precedent that we must consider retroactively up until the date the decision in this case is handed down. Thus, as noted below, in addressing the admissibility of the DNA evidence presented at trial, we find that the key is whether the testimony met the requirements of Federal Rule of Evidence 702 at the time of the district court's admissibility determination, not whether subsequent events provide evidence that contradicts or calls into question the district court's view at the time of its admissibility ruling.

In any case, we note that the substance of the criticisms in the NRC Report, including the possibility of ethnic substructure, is before us in the form of the testimony from defendants' expert witnesses. Thus, we do consider the substance of the NRC Report's criticisms; we do not consider only the collective opinion of the NRC and the NAS and the synopsis of these criticisms in the report itself.

D.   STANDERS USED IN ADMISSIBILITY DETERMINATION

For the reasons outlined below, we affirm the district court's admission of the DNA testimony and evidence, although for reasons in addition to those stated by the district court, because the Supreme Court, subsequent to the district court's order, held that the *Frye* test is no longer controlling and that Rule 702 now governs.

1.   Standard of Review

We review the trial court's admission of testimony and other evidence under the abuse of discretion standard. Mitroff v. Xomox Corp., 797 F.2d 271, 275 (6th Cir. 1986). Even if the trial court abuses its discretion, a new trial is not required unless "substantial rights" of a party are affected. Fed. R. Crim. P. 52(a); Rye v. Black & Decker Mfg. Co., 889 F.2d 100, 103 (6th Cir. 1989). Thus, an abuse of discretion that does not affect substantial rights is harmless error and is to be disregarded. Fed. R. Crim. P. 52(a). Specifically, the admissibility of expert testimony "has been traditionally left to the sound discretion of the trial court." United States v. Green, 548 F.2d 1261, 1268 (6th Cir. 1977). The scope of this discretion has been broadly construed, and the trial court's actions are to be sustained "unless manifestly erroneous." Id.

2.   New Standard for Admission of Expert Testimony

In determining the admissibility of novel scientific evidence, this circuit, like the majority of other circuits, has utilized the *Frye* test, set out in Frye v. United States, 54 App. D.C. 46, 293 F. 1013 (D.C. Cir. 1923).

The court in *Frye* created a "general acceptance" test for the admissibility of testimony about scientific evidence, holding:

> While courts will go a long way in admitting expert testimony deduced from a well-recognized scientific principle or discovery, the thing from which the deduction is made must be sufficiently established to have gained *general acceptance in the particular field in which it belongs.*

Id. at 1014 (emphasis added).[11] We latched onto and tried to define this general acceptance test in a long line of cases. See, e.g., United States v. Brown, 557 F.2d 541 (6th Cir. 1977).

The Supreme Court in Daubert v. Merrell Dow Pharmaceuticals, Inc., 125 L. Ed. 2d 469, 113 S. Ct. 2786 (1993), has now rejected *Frye*'s general acceptance test as the exclusive test and has redefined the standard for the admission of expert scientific testimony. The Supreme Court found that the *Frye* test was superseded by Federal Rule of Evidence 702, which makes expert testimony admissible if the scientific or specialized knowledge will assist the trier of fact and if the witness is qualified as an expert. Specifically, that rule states:

> If scientific, technical, or other specialized knowledge will assist the trier of fact to understand the evidence or to determine a fact in issue, a witness qualified as an expert by knowledge, skill, experience, training, or education, may testify thereto in the form of an opinion or otherwise.

Fed. R. Evid. 702. The Supreme Court explained that "a rigid 'general acceptance' requirement would be at odds with the 'liberal thrust' of the Federal Rules and their 'general approach of relaxing the traditional barriers to "opinion" testimony.' " Id. at 2794 (quoting Beech Aircraft Corp. v. Rainey, 488 U.S. 153, 169, 102 L. Ed. 2d 445, 109 S. Ct. 439 (1988)). The Court concluded that the "austere" general acceptance standard, "absent from and incompatible with the Federal Rules of Evidence, should not be applied in federal trials." Id.

The Court explained that even under these liberal Federal Rules, the trial judge must ensure that scientific testimony is "not only relevant but reliable." Id. at 2795. The "relevance" requirement stems from Rule 702's requirement that the testimony "assist the trier of fact to understand the evidence or to determine a fact in issue." Thus, there must be a "fit" between the inquiry in the case and the testimony, and expert testimony that does not relate to any issue in the case is not relevant

---

11. Several courts have adopted other tests for determining the admissibility of scientific evidence. See United States v. Williams, 583 F.2d 1194, 1198 (2d Cir. 1978) (admissible if probativeness, materiality, and reliability outweigh its tendency to mislead, prejudice, and confuse the jury), . . . United States v. Jakobetz, 955 F.2d 786, 794 (2d Cir.1992) . . . ; People v. Castro, 144 Misc. 2d 956, 545 N.Y.S.2d 985 (N.Y. Sup. Ct. 1989) (*Frye* test with additional layer for DNA cases); United States v. Two Bulls, 918 F.2d 56 (8th Cir.) (adopting *Castro* test), . . . ; People v. Atoigue, No. CR 91-95 A, 1992 WL 245628 (D. Guam. App. Div. Sept. 11, 1992) (applying California's *Kelly-Frye* test).

and therefore not helpful. Id. The "reliability requirement" is based on Rule 702's requirement that the subject of an expert's testimony be "scientific . . . knowledge." Id. The Court defined "scientific" as having "a grounding in the methods and procedures of science" and defined "knowledge" as "connoting more than subjective belief or unsupported speculation" and "'applying to any body of known facts or to any body of ideas inferred from such facts or accepted as truths on good grounds.'" Id. (quoting Webster's Third New International Dictionary 1252 (1986)). The Court noted that the subject of scientific testimony need not be known to a certainty, but that an inference or assertion must be "derived by the scientific method" and "be supported by appropriate validation—i.e., 'good grounds,' based on what is known." In other words, "scientific knowledge" is that which is known based upon sound reasoning within the framework of the scientific method. In finding that this "scientific knowledge" requirement was a reliability check, the Court indicated that by "reliability" it meant "evidentiary reliability" or "trustworthiness," and that in turn "evidentiary reliability" means "scientific validity."

Thus, the trial judge must determine at the outset "whether the expert is proposing to testify to (1) scientific knowledge that (2) will assist the trier of fact to understand or determine a fact in issue." Id. at 2796. "This entails a preliminary assessment of whether the reasoning or methodology underlying the testimony is scientifically valid and of whether the reasoning or methodology properly can be applied to the facts in issue."

While the *Daubert* Court did not explicitly define scientific validity or apply its new teaching to the evidence at issue in that case, it did begin to draw the parameters of this inquiry by providing the following nonexclusive list of factors: (1) whether a theory or technique can be (and has been) tested, (2) whether the theory or technique has been subjected to peer review and publication, (3) the known or potential rate of error in using a particular scientific technique and the existence and maintenance of standards controlling the technique's operation, and (4) whether the theory or technique has been generally accepted in the particular scientific field. See id. at 2796-97. The Court emphasized that "the inquiry envisioned by Rule 702 is . . . a flexible one. Its overarching subject is the scientific validity—and thus the evidentiary relevance and reliability—of the principles that underlie a proposed submission. The focus, of course, must be solely on principles and methodology, not on the conclusions that they generate." Id. at 2797.

Finally, the Court noted that in assessing a proffer of expert scientific testimony under Rule 702, the trial court also must consider other applicable rules, including: (1) Rule 703 (providing that expert opinions based on otherwise inadmissible hearsay are to be admitted only if the facts or data are of a type reasonably relied upon by experts in the field),

(2) Rule 706 (allowing the court to call an expert of its own choosing), and (3) Rule 403 (permitting the exclusion of expert evidence if its probative value is substantially outweighed by the danger of unfair prejudice). Id. at 2797-98.

We believe that by defining evidentiary reliability in terms of scientific validity, by couching almost the entire discussion of admissibility of scientific evidence in terms of scientific validity, and by requiring that the inquiry be focused solely on the methodology and principles underlying the proffered scientific expert testimony, the *Daubert* Court has instructed the courts that they are not to be concerned with the reliability of the conclusions generated by valid methods, principles and reasoning. Rather, they are only to determine whether the principles and methodology underlying the testimony itself are valid. If the principles, methodology and reasoning are scientifically valid then it follows that the inferences, assertions and conclusions derived therefrom are scientifically valid as well. Such reliable evidence is admissible under Rule 702, so long as it is relevant.

E.   APPLYING RULE 702 TO THE EXPERT TESTIMONY
      IN THIS CASE

1.   *Rulings of the Magistrate Judge and the District Court*

We note that although the findings of the magistrate judge and the district court were based only on the pre-*Daubert–Frye* hearing and the general acceptance test, these findings are relevant to our examination under a *Daubert* analysis, first because, as the district court noted, neither the defendants nor the Government challenge the magistrate judge's findings regarding the substance of the expert testimony presented at the *Frye* hearing or his characterization of the testimony, and second, because general acceptance is still one factor the Supreme Court has said can impact on a court's scientific validity determination and the defendants' arguments on appeal focus on these findings and their general acceptance determination.

After a thorough review of the record, we hold that these findings are not clearly erroneous, and we adopt the magistrate's findings as conclusive, . . . We briefly summarize those findings below.

The magistrate judge issued exhaustive findings on the DNA evidence. He began with a discussion of DNA technology and the procedures used in the FBI's DNA lab to come up with matches, he proceeded through a very thorough overview of the experts' testimony at the *Frye* hearing, and he discussed the *Frye* standard in this Circuit and the general acceptance test, concluding that the Government must show that the principles and procedures used in formulating the DNA evidence are generally accepted or that they are in conformity with generally accepted explanatory theories. The magistrate found that the pertinent scientific community was molecular biologists and population geneticists, that the burden of proof to meet general acceptance is a preponderance of the evidence, and that the judge's role is limited to determining whether the procedures and principles are generally accepted and does not extend to determining the reliability or validity of the results. The magistrate then defined general acceptance by stating what general acceptance is not—it does not require unanimity or consensus, or certainty, or approval by other courts. He cited factors to consider in determining general acceptance and noted that this Circuit has found the absence of general acceptance only where the evidence "has been manifestly unsupported outside the proponent's own laboratory." Relying on the government witnesses' stature, Dr. Caskey's acceptance of the protocol, the other witnesses' belief that the protocol is generally accepted, other labs' acceptance of the protocol, and the more persuasive testimony of the Government's experts, the magistrate concluded that disputes over the reliability of results went only to the weight of the evidence and that the Government had met its burden of showing that the FBI's protocol and procedures were accepted by "the general scientific community."

The magistrate went on to make alternative findings on the merits of the disputes about the reliability of the results, in the event that a reviewing court disagreed with him that reliability disputes go to weight, not admissibility. He found that the FBI was able to produce reliable results, despite some flaws in the protocol relating to such matters as quasi-continuous allele systems, validation studies, environmental insult studies, proficiency testing, and ethidium bromide use. Notably, he concluded that the prospect of ethnic substructure did not impact on the reliability of results, but went to the weight of the evidence. Finally, the magistrate concluded that he could not make a Rule 403 ruling because this was a fact-specific inquiry for the trial court.

The defendants objected to the R&R on three grounds: (1) that the magistrate's definition of "general acceptance" was flawed and his finding that a consensus is not needed was erroneous; (2) that the magistrate's findings on reliability were flawed; and (3) that the magistrate failed to consider the Rule 403 argument. The district court, in an opinion that thoroughly reviewed the magistrate's report, found no merit in defendants' objections and adopted the report and recommendation.

Although the magistrate judge and the district court in admitting the DNA testimony focused on the general acceptance test that has now been superseded by the Supreme Court's recent *Daubert* decision, we still may affirm the district court on other grounds. . . . We need not ask the parties to rebrief the issues or remand this case to the district court for reconsideration since we have a complete record before us, and, as we shall demonstrate hereinafter, it is clear from this record that the DNA evidence and testimony would have met the more liberal Rule 702 test adopted by the Supreme Court.

2. Daubert's *Prongs*

a. Relevance Requirement

We hold that the expert testimony meets the "relevance" prong of the admissibility test: that the evidence or testimony "assist the trier of fact to understand the evidence or to determine a fact in issue." This requirement merely looks at whether the evidence and testimony is relevant to any issue in the case. *Daubert*, 113 S. Ct. at 2795. The testimony must be "'sufficiently tied to the facts of the case that it will aid the jury in resolving a factual dispute.'" Id. at 2796 (quoting United States v. Downing, 753 F.2d 1224, 1242 (3d Cir. 1985)). The evidence that Bonds's DNA matched at least to some extent the DNA found in the crime-scene sample clearly is relevant to whether defendant Bonds was present in the victim's van on the night of the murder. Thus, the DNA evidence was helpful to the jury in determining whether defendants were guilty of the charges.

b. Evidentiary Reliability Requirement

Daubert requires that a preliminary assessment of the proffered testimony be made to determine whether the principles, methodology and reasoning underlying the testimony are scientifically valid. It is important to note that what is being challenged here by the defendants is not the general principle that individuals can be identified by their DNA, the principle that there are tests that can be performed to make these identifications, or the methodology of performing comparative testing by analyzing size and length variations among VNTR alleles in blood samples and calculating the statistical probabilities of a "match." In fact, the defendants presented considerable evidence at the *Frye* hearing about how these tests should have been performed. What the defendants challenge is the particular application of that methodology by the FBI in performing those tests and the results reached by the FBI. Their challenge is essentially that had the tests been performed differently, using a different database for the calculation of the statistical probabilities of the match, and using different materials in performing the test or using a different multiplication rule, the results would have been more accurate and perhaps different. Defendants also challenge the way the methodology was tested, arguing that the reliability of the results would have been greater had a different method of testing been employed. Defendants do not challenge the fact that the specific application of the methodology used by the FBI generated *some probability* that the DNA sample that "matched" Bonds's sample in fact came from

Bonds; they only challenge the precision of that probability estimate. *Daubert* requires only scientific validity for admissibility, not scientific precision.

With this in mind, we now turn to the four factors that the Supreme Court observed would bear on a determination of whether the testimony pertains to scientific knowledge that will assist the trier of fact: (1) whether a theory or technique can be or has been tested; (2) whether the theory or technique has been subjected to peer review and publication; (3) the known or potential rate of error in using a particular scientific technique and the standards controlling the technique's operation; and (4) whether the theory or technique has been generally accepted in the particular scientific field. We note that the first two—can it be or has it been tested? and has it been peer reviewed? —are integral to the former general acceptance analysis and the magistrate judge made specific findings regarding them. The third factor— the known or potential rate of error and the existence and maintenance of standards controlling the technique's operation — is also encompassed in the peer review and testing factors and is implicit in the magistrate's general acceptance findings. The fourth factor is, of course, general acceptance, and the magistrate made explicit findings as to this. Thus, we can look to the magistrate's findings in making our determination.

i.   Testing of theory or technique

The *Daubert* Court found that a "key question" is whether the theory or technique can be and has been tested. . . . Evidence credited by the district court establishes that the theory behind matching DNA and calculating probabilities, and the particular technique employed by the FBI lab, can in fact be tested by comparing the results generated from one set of samples with the results reached after repeating the matching and probability estimate process on control samples. It is irrelevant that there are other methods for DNA matching that could also be or have been tested.

Furthermore, the FBI's principles and methodology have in fact been tested. The FBI performed internal proficiency testing as well as validation studies and environmental insult studies to determine whether the lab could produce reliable, reproducible results from samples that had been mixed with contaminants or subjected to environmental insults such as sun. In his report and recommendation, the magistrate made alternative findings on reliability and found that the FBI could reliably determine a match. Specifically, the magistrate addressed the criticisms raised about the FBI's validation studies, finding that the defects in the validation studies "did not affect [the FBI's] ability reliably to make accurate determinations of matches and avoid false positives." The magistrate also addressed the criticisms of the FBI's mixed body fluid and environmental insult studies, and of the "Repeat Caucasian

Database," and concluded that these too did not present a significant risk of false matches. The magistrate considered as well the FBI's failure to implement a "comprehensive" or "meaningful" program of effective proficiency testing, and found that the FBI did have a proficiency testing program — although one with serious deficiencies — and that this dispute was merely a dispute over technique. Therefore, it is clear that the FBI's theories, principles, methods, and techniques can be tested and have in fact been tested.

Finally, it seems clear that this first *Daubert* factor is not really in dispute. The *Daubert* Court found that "'the criterion of the scientific status of a theory is its . . . refutability.'" Id. at 2797 (quoting K. Popper, Conjectures and Refutations: The Growth of Scientific Knowledge 37 (5th ed. 1989)). Defendants vociferously dispute the accuracy of the match results and the adequacy of the testing done, and in refutation have presented evidence about deficiencies in both the results and the testing of the results. Thus, it appears that by attempting to refute the FBI's theory and methods with evidence about deficiencies in both the results and the testing of the results, the defendants have conceded that the theory and methods can be tested. The dispute between the Government and the defendants is over *how* the results have been tested, not over *whether* the results can be or have been tested.

ii.   Peer review

The Supreme Court has observed that peer review and publication is another consideration in determining whether scientific evidence is admissible under Rule 702. The Court noted that publication—just one element of peer review—is not essential for admissibility or synonymous with reliability.

> In some instances well-grounded but innovative theories will not have been published. Some propositions, moreover, are too particular, too new, or of too limited interest to be published. But submission to the scrutiny of the scientific community is a component of "good science," in part because it increases the likelihood that substantive flaws in methodology will be detected. The fact of publication (or lack thereof) in a peer-reviewed journal thus will be a relevant, though not dispositive, consideration in assessing the scientific validity of a particular technique or methodology on which an opinion is premised.

The key here is that the theory and procedures have been submitted to the scrutiny of the scientific community, in part to "increase[ ] the likelihood that substantive flaws in methodology will be detected." It is important, however, to note that "flaws in methodology" uncovered by peer review do not necessarily equate to a lack of scientific validity, since the methods may be based on scientific principles and the alleged flaws go merely to the weight, not the admissibility, of the evidence and the testimony. Instead, peer review and publication should be viewed as evidence that the theory and methodology are scientific knowledge capable of being scrutinized and have in fact been scrutinized by the scientific community.

Here, the FBI's procedures certainly have received "at least some exposure within the scientific peerage to which [they] belong[ ]." United States v. Kozminski, 821 F.2d 1186, 1201 (6th Cir. 1987) (en banc), aff'd, 487 U.S. 931, 108 S. Ct. 2751, 101 L. Ed. 2d 788 (1988). In fact, at the *Frye* hearing, the Government introduced articles on the FBI's techniques, including the FBI's statistical estimates. See Government's Exhibit §9. . . . And the theory behind "matching" DNA itself and the general procedures used to come up with the forensic results clearly have received peer evaluation. In addition, the magistrate in this case anticipated *Daubert* by concluding that expert testimony from experts outside the proponents' lab and acceptance of the proponent's writings in professional journals—in essence peer evaluation or review—were factors to consider in determining general acceptance and thus admissibility. The magistrate concluded that the FBI's methods had received ample acceptance outside the FBI lab.

iii.   Rate of error

The *Daubert* Court also observed that the trial court "ordinarily should consider the known or potential rate of error" and "the existence and maintenance of standards controlling the technique's operation." *Daubert*, 113 S. Ct. at 2797. The FBI did conduct *internal* proficiency tests to determine a rate of error and calculated a rate of error, although the magistrate found these proficiency tests to have "serious deficiencies." Defendants argued at the *Frye* hearing and on appeal that the scientific community considers indispensable *external blind* proficiency tests to account for laboratory error.

The deficiencies in calculating the rate of error and the failure to conduct external blind proficiency tests are troubling. We find troubling as well the lack of specific references to the rate of error in the Joint Appendix provided to this Court by the parties. Although we find that on the basis of the record before us the rate of error is a negative factor in the analysis of whether the FBI's procedures are scientifically valid, the error rate is only one in a list of nonexclusive factors that the *Daubert* Court observed would bear on the admissibility question. In addition, as noted in the next subsection, we find that the district court did not err in finding that the FBI's principles and procedures for declaring matches and calculating probabilities are generally accepted by the scientific community; because the magistrate judge's findings underlying general acceptance encompass the "existence and maintenance of standards controlling the technique's operations," id., it is implicit that the rate of error is acceptable to the scientific community as well.

iv.   General acceptance

Finally, the *Daubert* Court indicated that the scientific validity analysis "does not require, although it does permit," us to consider the degree to which the FBI's principles and methodology are generally accepted in the relevant scientific community. *Daubert* noted that "widespread acceptance can be an important factor in ruling particular evidence admissible, and 'a known technique that has been able to attract only minimal support within the community' may properly be viewed with skepticism." Id. (quoting *Downing*, 753 F.2d at 1238).

The concept of examining the "general acceptance" of a particular scientific theory and procedure stems from Frye v. United States, 54 App. D.C. 46, 293 F. 1013 (D.C. Cir. 1923), where the D.C. Circuit held:

> While courts will go a long way in admitting expert testimony de-duced from a well-recognized scientific principle or discovery, *the thing from which the deduction is made* must be sufficiently established to have gained *general acceptance in the particular field in which it belongs.*

Id. at 1014 (emphasis added). Before *Daubert,* the *Frye* general accep-tance test was the exclusive test in this and several other circuits for determining whether testimony about scientific evidence was admissi-ble. Post-*Daubert*, general acceptance is but one of at least four factors that we may consider in determining whether testimony is admissible under Rule 702. Since the defendants argue extensively that the DNA testimony was not based on generally accepted procedures, since this was the focus of both the magistrate's *Frye* hearing and the district court's ruling, and since the *Frye* test utilizes to some extent at least two of the *Daubert* factors, we address general acceptance in some detail.

(a)   Elements of general acceptance

Under our pre-*Daubert* case law, general acceptance exists when a substantial portion of the pertinent scientific community accepts the theory, principles, and methodology underlying scientific testimony be-cause they are grounded in valid scientific principles. . . . The cases dis-cuss general acceptance in terms of "reliability" but refer only to the reliability of the procedures and process, not the reliability of the results of the procedures. . . .

. . . In examining "general acceptance" and in addressing the parties' arguments, we are confronted in this case with the question of what exactly must be generally accepted: whether only the theory of DNA profiling needs to be generally accepted or whether the FBI's meth-odology for conducting DNA testing need also to be generally accepted. The cases out of this circuit have not been entirely consistent in ad-dressing what needs to be generally accepted.

We find that general acceptance encompasses both. See *Brown*, 557 F.2d at 556 ("'There must be a *demonstrable, objective procedure* for reach-ing the opinion and qualified persons who can either duplicate the result or criticize the means by which it was reached.'" (emphasis added) (quoting United States v. Baller, 519 F.2d 463, 466 (4th Cir. 1975). . . . This view is consistent with *Daubert*'s requirement that we determine whether the "reasoning or methodology underlying the testimony is scientifically valid," *Daubert*, 113 S. Ct. at 2796, and its acknowledgement that a "known technique that has been able to attract only minimal support in the scientific community may properly be viewed with skepticism," id.

Having defined *what* must be generally accepted, we now must review the defendants' arguments that the magistrate judge and the district court erred in defining general acceptance. The magistrate concluded that general acceptance does not require that there be "unanimity, or consensus within the scientific community concerning such acceptability." He noted, however, that although "neither consensus nor certainty" is needed, an absence of consensus is not immaterial. The district court concurred in the magistrate judge's conclusion. The defendants strenuously object, arguing that a consensus is necessary and that the FBI's procedure is not supported by such a consensus.

A careful review of the case law in this circuit persuades us that the "consensus" question is a red herring. "Consensus" is simply not a term that has been used in this circuit to determine whether the *Frye* general acceptance test has been met. Rather, our precedent demonstrates that while ordinarily the principles and procedures must be accepted by a majority of those in the pertinent scientific community, the absence of a majority does not necessarily rule out general acceptance. The general acceptance test is designed only to uncover whether there is a general agreement of scientists in the field that this scientific data is not based on a novel theory or procedure that is "mere speculation or conjecture." *Brown*, 557 F.2d at 559. In some instances, there may be several different theories or procedures used concerning one type of scientific evidence, all of which are generally accepted. None may have the backing of the majority of scientists, yet the theory or procedure can still be generally accepted. And even substantial criticism as to one theory or procedure will not be enough to find that the theory/procedure is not generally accepted. Only when a theory or procedure does not have the acceptance of most of the pertinent scientific community, and in fact a substantial part of the scientific community disfavors the principle or procedure, will it not be generally accepted. See, e.g., Novak v. United States, 865 F.2d 718, 725 (6th Cir. 1989) (theories were neither "widely accepted" or "generally accepted" in the medical community).

Accordingly, we find that the magistrate judge's definition of consensus and his holding in regard to consensus thus defined are immaterial to the resolution of this issue. What is material is that the magistrate judge's findings clearly indicate that the degree of acceptance in the scientific community of the theory of DNA profiling and of the basic

procedures used by the lab in this case is sufficient to meet the requirements in this circuit for general acceptance. The Government's experts,
some of whom were from outside the FBI lab, clearly indicated that the
FBI's DNA procedures were generally accepted. Despite their rebuttal
criticism, the defendants' experts did not in fact show that the procedures were not generally accepted; they only showed a substantial controversy over whether the results produced were reliable and accurate.

Defendants argue that the magistrate judge erred in stating that questions about the reliability of the results are not relevant to the general
acceptance determination but are only factors for the jury to weigh in
considering the evidence at trial. We hold that questions about the accuracy of results are matters of weight, not admissibility.

The decision whether to admit the expert testimony in the first place
is a matter of law for the trial judge. *Stifel*, 433 F.2d at 438. Once a court
admits the testimony, "then it is for the jury to decide whether any, and
if any what, weight is to be given to the testimony." Id. In the context
of scientific evidence, this means that "conflicting testimony concerning
the conclusions drawn by experts, so long as they are based on a generally accepted and reliable scientific principle, ordinarily go to the
weight of the testimony rather than its admissibility." *Brown*, 557 F.2d at
556. The *Daubert* Court made it explicit that in determining the scientific validity and thus the "evidentiary reliability" of scientific evidence,
"the focus, of course, must be solely on principles and methodology,
not on the conclusions that they generate." *Daubert*, 113 S. Ct. at 2797.
Questions about the certainty of the scientific results are matters of
weight for the jury. For example, in discussing the fact that a hair sampling technique only showed similarities between the hairs and could
not show a match with certainty, "the lack of certainty went to the weight
to be assigned to the testimony of the expert, not its admissibility, and
defense counsel did a creditable job of arguing to the jury that it should
be assigned little weight." United States v. Brady, 595 F.2d 359, 363 (6th
Cir. 1979). And, in general, criticisms touching on whether the lab
made mistakes in arriving at its results are for the jury. As the Court in
United States v. Jakobetz, 955 F.2d 786 (2d Cir.1992). . . . stated:

> The district court should focus on whether accepted protocol was adequately
> followed in a specific case, but the court, in exercising its discretion, should be
> mindful that this issue should go more to the weight than to the admissibility of
> the evidence. Rarely should such a factual determination be excluded from jury
> consideration. With adequate cautionary instructions from the trial judge, vig-
> orous cross-examination of the government's experts, and challenging testimony
> from defense experts, the jury should be allowed to make its own factual deter-
> mination as to whether the evidence is reliable.

Id. at 800 (discussing *Williams* standard but noting it would meet *Frye*
as well).

Accordingly, we hold that general acceptance is required as to the principles and methodology employed. The assessment of the validity and reliability of the conclusions drawn by the expert is a jury question; the judge may only examine whether the principles and methodology are scientifically valid and generally accepted.

Thus in this case, the criticisms about the specific application of the procedure used or questions about the accuracy of the test results do not render the scientific theory and methodology invalid or destroy their general acceptance. These questions go to the weight of the evidence, not the admissibility.

With this in mind, we turn to address the defendants' arguments that the FBI's DNA procedures are not generally accepted by population geneticists and molecular biologists.

(b) Defendants' contentions

Defendants make several arguments to support their contention that the FBI's procedures for making statistical probability estimates are not generally accepted by population geneticists. These arguments focus on the FBI's methods of computing the 1 in 35,000 probability that a caucasian person other than defendant Bonds would have the same DNA pattern that Bonds has.

Defendants first argue that the magistrate's projections that the FBI's statistical method would be generally accepted turned out to be wrong because the NRC Report later showed the FBI's statistical basis to be invalid. Because, as we noted above, we cannot consider the NRC Report, this argument is irrelevant and we do not consider it. However, the particular complaints that defendants have as to erroneous projections by the magistrate judge are addressed below in the context of their objections to the magistrate judge's overall general acceptance finding.

Defendants next argue that general acceptance was not established because the FBI's methods were not published in peer-reviewed journals. As the *Daubert* Court noted, publication is but one element of peer review, is not a sine qua non of admissibility, *Daubert,* 113 S. Ct. at 2797, and is not prerequisite to a finding of scientific validity. As noted above in our discussion of the second *Daubert* factor, we believe that the FBI's procedures have received some peer review. Any shortcomings in the peer review of the FBI's procedures are not sufficient to overcome the other strong evidence that the FBI's principles and procedures were both generally accepted and scientifically valid.

Defendants' strongest criticism of the FBI's procedures for declaring DNA matches and estimating probabilities is that the database used by the FBI to make a probability estimate of the DNA pattern found in Bonds's blood failed to take into account ethnic substructure. Defendants' argument is based on the fact that the blood samples of the 225

FBI agents which make up the database used in this case were not divided into ethnic subgroups within the caucasian group, such as Polish and Italian. Defendants' experts testified that without accounting for ethnic substructure, the statistics indicating the frequencies with which certain DNA alleles appear in each racial group are exaggerated when the individual allele frequencies are multiplied together using the product or multiplication rule. According to these experts, the FBI should have used a more conservative method of estimating the frequencies of the alleles to take into account the possibility of ethnic substructure.

This substructure argument involves a dispute over the accuracy of the probability results, and thus this criticism goes to the weight of the evidence, not its admissibility. . . . Defendants' experts indicated that the FBI's methods were flawed because they did not take into account ethnic substructure. However, the Government's witnesses indicated that the results were not distorted by the possibility of ethnic substructure because the Government's methods of estimating frequencies were still conservative. Significantly, the defense witnesses could only speculate about the effect of ethnic substructure because there is no positive evidence that ethnic substructure in fact exists.

The district court correctly found that it could not examine this dispute going to the accuracy of the results, but could only examine whether the testimony was based on generally accepted (and scientifically valid) theories and procedures. The evidence and testimony presented at this *Frye* hearing demonstrate that the DNA evidence was not based on untested or unacceptable theories or procedures. Because the DNA results were based on scientifically valid principles and derived from scientifically valid procedures, it is not dispositive that there are scientists who vigorously argue that the probability estimates are not accurate or reliable because of the possibility of ethnic substructure. The potential of ethnic substructure does not mean that the theory and procedures used by the FBI are not generally accepted; it means only that there is a dispute over whether the results are as accurate as they might be and what, if any, weight the jury should give those results.

Besides their contention that the FBI's statistical procedures are not generally accepted among population geneticists, defendants also argue that the FBI's methods for declaring matches and interpreting autorads are not generally accepted among molecular biologists. Defendants allege a number of flaws in these methods including that the FBI's environmental insult studies and match criterion were flawed, that the FBI used ethidium bromide in analytic gels, and that the FBI was unable to type the same DNA samples reliably and reproducibly in its repeat caucasian database.

We addressed some of these concerns in discussing *Daubert* factors number one (can it be tested?) and number three (what is the known or potential rate of error?). We reiterate here that the magistrate and the district court did not err in finding that these flaws in the methods for declaring matching and interpreting autorads were issues of weight and did not pose the risk that the results were based on unaccepted principles or procedures.

Thus, we find that *Daubert* factor number four argues in favor of admissibility because the principles and procedures on which the DNA testimony was based are generally accepted by the relevant scientific communities.

(c)   Conclusion as to *Daubert* prongs

When reviewed in light of the four *Daubert* factors (testing, peer review, rate of error, and general acceptance), we find that the underlying principles and methodology used by the FBI to declare matches and make statistical probabilities are scientifically valid. The methodology was valid in that it "resulted from sound and cogent reasoning," Bert Black, A Unified Theory of Scientific Evidence, 56 Ford. L. Rev. 595, 599 (1988), and was "'well grounded or justifiable [and] applicable to the matter at hand,'" id. at 599 n.9 (quoting Webster's Unabridged 2529-30). Thus, the methodology clearly had "a grounding in the methods and procedures of science" and was based on "more than subjective belief or unsupported speculation." *Daubert,* 113 S. Ct. at 2795.

Daubert sets out a "flexible" and more lenient test that favors the admission of any scientifically valid expert testimony. "Vigorous cross-examination, presentation of contrary evidence, and careful instruction on the burden of proof are the traditional and appropriate means of attacking shaky but admissible evidence." Id. The Court added that if the trial court concludes that the scintilla of evidence supporting a position is insufficient to allow a reasonable juror to conclude that the position is more likely than not true, the court can direct a judgment or grant summary judgment. Id. "These conventional devices, rather than wholesale exclusion under an uncompromising 'general acceptance' test, are the appropriate safeguards where the basis of scientific testimony meets the standards of Rule 702." Id. Thus, it is irrelevant that the FBI's DNA matching and statistical techniques are still being refined or that the results produced may not be wholly accurate since, as the Supreme Court noted, "it would be unreasonable to conclude that the subject of scientific testimony must be 'known' to a certainty; arguably, there are no certainties in science." Id. at 2795. The results of the DNA testing were clearly derived from tests based on methods and procedures of science and not based merely on speculation, and were supported by sound and cogent reasoning, even if these methods and procedures are not perfected.

Daubert requires only that the evidence be scientifically valid to have evidentiary reliability. We have found that the underlying methodology and reasoning are scientifically valid, and it is undisputed that the general principle that individuals can be identified by DNA is scientifically valid. Therefore, we need not examine that issue further. Having found as well that the evidence meets the relevance requirement of being "helpful to the trier of fact," we hold that the testimony proffered by the Government about the DNA matching and probabilities easily met the *Daubert* standard and was admissible under Rule 702.

F.   OTHER APPLICABLE RULES

The *Daubert* Court stated that, throughout this analysis of the admission of scientific data, a judge assessing a proffer of expert scientific testimony under Rule 702 "should also be mindful of other applicable rules," such as Federal Rules of Evidence 703, 706, and 403. Thus, we must review the admission of the DNA testimony in light of these rules as well.

1.   Rule 703

Defendants argue that the FBI's method for calculating the probability of a coincidental match of Bonds's DNA should have been excluded under Fed. R. Evid. 703 because it was not based on the type of data reasonably relied upon by experts in the field. Ordinarily, we would find defendants had waived this Rule 703 argument for appeal because they failed to raise it in the district court in their objections to the R&R or in the *Frye* hearing. See United States v. Ushery, 968 F.2d 575, 582 n.2 (6th Cir.1992) (failure to raise issue in district court is waiver), . . . However, because the *Daubert* Court requires that trial judges be mindful of this rule in admitting scientific evidence, we address this rule as well in reviewing the admission of the testimony.

The trial court is to use "great liberality" in determining the basis of an expert's opinions, and the trial court may not decide whether the opinion itself should be accepted. Mannino v. International Mfg. Co., 650 F.2d 846, 852 (6th Cir. 1981). Rule 703 permits experts to testify without personal knowledge of the underlying facts or data and permits them to testify on the basis of hearsay or unadmitted evidence, as long as the evidence is of a kind "reasonably relied upon by experts in the particular field." Coal Resources Inc. v. Gulf & W. Indus., Inc., 954 F.2d 1263, 1272 (6th Cir. 1992). The rule has been interpreted as merely requiring that experts' scientific knowledge be based on sound methodology. Ambrosini v. Labarraque, 296 U.S. App. D.C. 183, 966 F.2d 1464 (D.C. Cir. 1992).

We find that the Government experts' testimony was based on data and facts reasonably relied upon by experts in molecular biology and population genetics. Our finding that the FBI's theory and procedures are "scientifically valid" under Rule 702 indicates that the experts' testified about scientific knowledge that was based on "sound methodology." In addition, in finding that the principles and procedures have been "generally accepted" in the pertinent scientific communities, we cannot help but find that the evidence is "of a type reasonably relied upon by experts in the particular field in forming opinions or inferences upon the subject." Fed. R. Evid. 703.

2.   Rule 706

Federal Rule of Evidence 706 permits the court on its own to appoint an expert witness. Here, the magistrate appointed Dr. Eric Lander as its expert witness. In its R&R, the magistrate recognized the "preeminent status" of Dr. Lander, took into account his reservations about the FBI's procedures, but concluded that other experts' assessments were "more likely to reflect an accurate understanding of the view of the scientific community than that of Dr. Lander [alone]." Thus, the magistrate relied on the testimony of Dr. Lander as well as that of the parties' experts to conclude that the DNA testimony was admissible. The court's appointment of its own expert witness counsels in favor of affirming the admission of the DNA testimony.

3.   Rule 403 Challenge

In addition to the mandate from *Daubert* that we consider the admission of scientific testimony in light of Rule 403, defendants at trial and in their brief also made an argument that the Government's expert testimony did not meet Rule 403, which requires that the probative value of the scientific expert testimony not be substantially outweighed by any unfair and prejudicial effect of the testimony. We find that the district court did not err in finding that the prejudice from the testimony about the DNA evidence did not substantially outweigh its probative value.

The district court's Rule 403 balancing is an evidentiary ruling that we may review only for an abuse of discretion. . . .

For a Rule 403 violation to occur, the admitted evidence must result in "unfair prejudice" in that "the evidence must suggest a decision on an impermissible basis." United States v. Schrock, 855 F.2d 327, 333 (6th Cir. 1988). Unfair prejudice "'does not mean the damage to a defendant's case that results from the legitimate probative force of the evidence; rather it refers to evidence which tends to suggest decision on an improper basis.'" Id. at 335 . . . Here, the evidence and the testimony were clearly probative because they linked Bonds to the murder scene when no direct evidence existed to do so. The aura of reliability surrounding DNA evidence does present the prospect of a decision based on the perceived infallibility of such evidence, especially in a case such as this where the evidence is largely circumstantial. However, the damaging nature of the DNA evidence to defendants and the potential prejudice does not require exclusion. We have found that the theory of matching DNA patterns and the FBI's procedures were scientifically valid. Defendants had an opportunity to cross examine all of the Government's witnesses to show why the results were unreliable, the procedures flawed, and the DNA evidence not infallible. And, defendants' concern that the jury relied unduly on this circumstantial DNA evidence cannot be resolved by excluding the evidence under Rule 403. Their concern is accommodated through a Rule 29 motion for judgment of acquittal to assure that the Government produced enough evidence, circumstantial or direct, to support a jury verdict. See *Daubert*, 113 S. Ct. at 2798 ("the court remains free to direct a judgment and likewise to grant summary judgment") (citations omitted); United States v. Reifsteck, 841 F.2d 701, 703 (6th Cir. 1988). Therefore, the district court did not abuse its discretion in finding that the probative value outweighed any prejudice.

G. CONCLUSION

Thus, because the theory, methodology, and reasoning used by the FBI lab to declare matches of DNA samples and to estimate statistical probabilities are scientifically valid and helpful to the trier of fact, we affirm the district court's conclusion that they are admissible under Rule 702. In addition, we affirm the admission of the testimony based on the DNA evidence in light of the other rules of evidence. Our conclusion is not altered by the fact that there are numerous substantive, heated disputes over the procedures that the FBI used and over the accuracy of the results that these procedures produced. We find that the DNA testimony easily meets the more liberal test set out by the Supreme Court in *Daubert.* . . .

IX. CONCLUSION

United States v. Bonds is not only an early case attempting to apply the new standard set by *Daubert.* It is also an example of the friendly reception given to DNA evidence when offered by the prosecution as evidence of identity. The court indicates that potential inaccuracies in the DNA analysis from errors in technique go to the weight, not the admissibility of this evidence. Is the jury in any position, with or without expert testimony, to make a reasoned judgment of the effect of errors in technique on the reliability of a DNA identification?

D.   Court-Appointed Experts

Problem: Medical Malpractice

In 1979, *P,* a 61-year-old man, is operated on by Dr. *D* for removal of his appendix and gall bladder. On February 18, 1979, *P* suffers severe abdominal pains. An X-ray taken that day reveals a hemostat inside *P*'s side. *P* dies February 22, 1979. Doctors *A* and *B* perform an autopsy on *P* prior to interment. *P*'s executor sues Dr. *D* for malpractice and wrongful death. Dr. *D*'s negligence is conceded, but the cause of death is contested. *A* testifies for the plaintiff that the hemostat killed *P. B* testifies for the defendant that *D* died of other causes. What is the role of the experts, judge, and jury in this situation?

NOTE: NEUTRAL EXPERTS

Use of court-appointed experts is a highly desirable method of assisting juries in cases in which they would otherwise be confused by a barrage of contradictory expert opinions. In addition to assisting the jury in choosing between conflicting opinions, the neutral expert may "exert a sobering effect on the expert witness of a party. . . ." Advisory Committee Notes to Rule 706. Yet many judges have been reluctant to appoint experts. They fear that the court-appointed expert acquires an "aura of infallibility," id., and becomes too dominant. Despite the fact that the trial judge had "unquestioned inherent power," id., even before the adoption of Rule 706, to appoint a neutral expert, a survey of all federal district judges reveals that few have done so.

Rule 706 is designed to encourage greater use of court-appointed experts. In an effort to dispel qualms about the expert's dominance, Judge Weinstein writes:

> The fact of the appointment need not be divulged to the jury if the court fears it would be overimpressed by the status of the witness; the judge may ask the parties for their recommendations and act upon them; a court expert's lack of neutrality can be readily exposed because the parties must be furnished with his report and have an absolute right to call their own experts, thus enabling them to prepare for cross-examination; provision is made for compensation; and many procedural aspects surrounding the use of expert testimony are consolidated.

3 Weinstein and Berger, Weinstein's Evidence 706-11-102 (1981).

When should the court exercise its power to appoint an expert? In addition to the more obvious instances in which the appointment of a neutral expert seems appropriate, such as in criminal cases where the prosecution offers novel scientific evidence and the defense is without resources to mount an adversary examination of its reliability, see, for example, Rule 28, F.R. Crim. P. Professor Green has suggested that the court should consider appointing a neutral expert early in a complex civil case where the crucial issue is highly technical. Green believes that a court-appointed expert in such cases may have a powerful dispute-narrowing and settling influence. Under his proposal, the parties would be encouraged to nominate and select a mutually acceptable neutral expert to be appointed by the court. The expert would then conduct an inquiry into the issues within the scope of his appointment. This inquiry could include examination of documents, inspections, experiments, and interviews with witnesses, including the parties' own experts. Green goes so far as to suggest that in certain cases the court-appointed neutral expert conduct a "mini-trial" among the parties and their experts on the crucial technical issues. Green, Expanded Use of the Mini-Trial, Private Judging, Neutral-Expert Fact-Finding, Patent Arbitration and Industry Self-Regulation, Dispute Management (1981).

In many cases, Green suggests, this process will result in a narrowing of the disputed issues and sometimes in complete settlement of the dispute. If the case does not settle during the expert's inquiry, the neutral expert would then "advise the parties of his findings" by submitting to them his written report, as provided in Rule 706. Green argues that since the expert may testify at trial with the imprimatur of the court, the expert's findings will have a persuasive influence on the parties and very often facilitate informal resolution. The danger with this use of neutral experts is that a party may feel unduly coerced by the prospect of a court-appointed expert's adverse testimony. Some critics of this proposal take the position that the deliberate use of a court-appointed expert for this purpose would violate the parties' rights to trial by jury. Green counters that the expert's opinion is "just coercive enough" and that the parties' rights to a fair trial are fully protected by their right to call their own witnesses, including experts, and to cross-examine the court-appointed expert. What do you think?

E. GREEN, THE COMPLETE COURTHOUSE, IN DISPUTE RESOLUTION DEVICES IN A DEMOCRATIC SOCIETY
44-51 (1985 Roscoe Pound ATLA Foundation, Washington, D.C.)

COURT-APPOINTED NEUTRAL EXPERTS

Cases involving complex scientific, sociological, technical, economic, and business issues pose particularly difficult problems for our adversarial adjudicatory structure. This category includes litigation where the issues are, for example, the infringement and validity of a patent on a computer-based algorithmic model or on a life form; conformance of a product, say an electronic component, to the specifications of a contract or standards of the industry; the cause of the collapse of a bridge; the scope of the relevant market and the defendant's control of that market; and whether the defendant's accounting practices and other actions amounted to violations of the securities laws. It also includes environmental disputes about the actual level of pollution, the short- and long-term health effects of contamination, and the costs of remedying the situation; medical malpractice; and toxic tort or product liability personal injury cases where the issue is whether a particular product is capable of causing certain types of harm and whether that harm was caused by the product in a specific instance. Utility ratemaking cases and other administrative appeals also fall within this category. Such cases make up an increasing percentage of the workload of federal and state courts.

Several factors set such disputes apart from other forms of legal combat. First, their resolution usually requires appraisal of data and analysis of information outside most everyday experience. Indeed, the dispute often turns on an issue that only a person with highly specialized and advanced training or experience can understand. Second, in these cases the "truth" about a key issue—such as the degree of harm likely to be caused over an extended period by a contaminant—may itself be in a state of flux or nearly impossible to determine without years of empirical investigation. Here any decision must be made under conditions of uncertainty that are much greater or are qualitatively different than those faced in other kinds of litigation. Third, developing and presenting proof on the scientific issues is likely to be enormously difficult, time-consuming, and expensive and thus apt to exacerbate the inherent deficiencies and opportunities for abuse present in the adversarial process generally.[102] Fourth, the scientists, engineers, or other experts who will

---

102. With regard to the difference between the process of factfinding in law and in science, see F. Pollack & F. Maitland, The History of English Law 670-71 (2d ed. 1968), quoted in Resnik, Managerial Judges, 96 Harv. L. Rev. 374 (1982).

> The behaviour which is expected of a judge in different ages and by different systems of law seems to fluctuate between two poles. At one of these the model is the conduct of the man of science who is making researches . . . and will use all appropriate methods for the solution of problems and the discovery of truth. At the other stands the umpire of our English games, who is there . . . merely to see that the rules of the game are observed.

See also Hart & McNaughton, Evidence and Inference in the Law, in Evidence and Inference 48, 50-51 (Lerner ed. 1959); Russell, On Induction, in The Problems of Philosophy 60-69 (1912).

See M. Saks & R. Van Duizend, The Use of Scientific Evidence in Litigation (1983); Nyhart & Heaton, Proceedings of the Task Force Workshop on Disputes Involving Science and Technology, in Corporate Dispute Management 389, 390 (1982). Nyhart and Heaton point out that "crucial concepts like truth, fact, and probability, hold different meanings for each culture, and each set of persons [lay and scientific] may be threatened."

be called to testify live in their own cultures and bring their own languages, values, and modes of thought with them. This makes communications among witnesses, lawyers, judge, and jury difficult. Finally, the experts called to testify are likely to be carefully selected and prepared to present only the testimony most favorable to the party that called them. This means that in most cases, the factfinder will be faced with conflicting expert opinion and technical evidence that by definition was beyond the understanding of the factfinder in the first place.

As courts increasingly become the forum where major public policy decisions are resolved, there is a pressing need to develop a method of resolving cases raising complex scientific, sociological, technical, economic, and business issues that eliminates or reduces the deficiencies and abuses of the present system. Increased use of court-appointed neutral experts is one approach. The neutral expert can promote accurate factfinding by assessing the facts objectively and often is a person of higher caliber than is available on a partisan basis. The neutral expert can also serve as a disincentive to strategic manipulation of the litigation process and, most important, promote fast, fair, and efficient settlement.[105]

Since the adoption of the federal rules in 1975, Rule 706 of the Federal Rules of Evidence is the most likely mechanism for court appointment of a neutral expert. Rule 706, however, is not the only source of such authority. Under Rule 53 of the Federal Rules of Civil Procedure, the court can appoint a master "to report . . . upon particular issues or to do or perform particular acts or to receive and report evidence." References to masters are limited by the rule to situations in which "exceptional conditions require it" (nonjury cases) or only "when the issues are complicated" (jury cases). The "exceptional" case requirement has limited the cases in which masters have been appointed, but

---

105. On the common law use of neutral experts generally and the early use of court-appointed medical experts pursuant to rules or statutes, see Sink, The Unused Power of a Federal Judge to Call His Own Expert Witness, 29 So. Cal. L. Rev. 195, 197 (1956); Morgan, Suggested Remedy for Obstructions to Expert Testimony by Rules of Evidence, 10 U. Cal. L. Rev. 285, 293 (1943); Schuck, Techniques for Proof of Complicated Scientific and Economic Facts, 40 F.R.D. 38 (1967); Wick & Kightlinger, Impartial Medical Testimony Under the Federal Civil Rules: A Tale of Three Doctors, 34 Ins. Counsel J. 115, 131 (1967); Levy, Impartial Medical Testimony—Revisited, 34 Temple L.Q. 416, 424-25 (1961); Van Dusen, The Impartial Medical System: The Judicial Point of View, 34 Temple L.Q. 386, 396-397 (1961); De Parq, Law, Science, and the Expert Witness, 24 Tenn. L. Rev. 166, 171 (1956).

See also 3 J. Weinstein & M. Berger, Weinstein's Evidence at pp.706-8 (1985), tracing the development of the present evidence rules from the Uniform Expert Testimony Act in 1937 through the Model Code of Evidence (Rules 403-410), and the 1953 draft of the Uniform Rules of Evidence (Rules 59-61) into Rule 28 of the Federal Rules of Criminal Procedure and Rule 706 of the Federal Rules of Evidence. Prior to adoption of Rule 706 in 1975, the only rules authorizing the appointment of an expert in federal cases were contained in local rules. See 3 Weinstein's Evidence at pp.706-8 n.6. In 1952, New York adopted a neutral expert rule for impartial medical testimony in personal injury cases. New York Impartial Expert Testimony Plan, §550.11(1), Rules for the Supreme Court of New York and Bronx Counties. See P. Rothstein, Federal Rules of Evidence 300-306 (student ed. 1979).

where they have, masters have exercised extraordinary powers over pre-trial and trial-stage proceedings. In appointing masters and experts, in addition to Rule 53 federal courts have relied on their "inherent authority" over the administration of justice and on the consent of the parties.

The characteristics that make Rule 706 particularly suitable as an alternative dispute resolution device are that:

1. *It does not require the agreement of the parties.* The court may appoint an expert on its own motion or at the request of one party.
2. *It provides for the parties to participate in selecting the expert and in forming the instructions.* The court may appoint any expert witnesses agreed on by the parties or its own selection. The expert is informed of his duties in writing by the court or at a conference in which the parties "shall have opportunity to participate."
3. *The expert advises the parties of his findings.* This presents an opportunity for the expert to play a mediation/conciliation role. The expert's deposition may also be taken by any party.
4. *The procedure is coercive but nonbinding.* The expert's opinion is admissible but it is not conclusive. Jury trial rights are preserved. Cross-examination and the calling of retained experts is permitted, but the court may tell the jury when an expert was court-appointed.
5. *The expert is entitled to "reasonable compensation."* Costs are apportioned in the court's discretion, and may be taxable like other litigation costs to the parties.
6. *Appointment at any phase of the proceeding is allowed.*

Similar neutral expertise can also be applied to complex disputes in other ways. For example, parties can agree privately, outside the litigation process, to retain a neutral expert to advise them on disputed complex issues. Disputants could agree to hire a neutral expert even before litigation begins. There seem to be no barriers that would prevent a privately appointed neutral expert from performing any of the functions specified in Rule 706: conducting research, advising the parties of his findings, giving his deposition, and testifying in court. Although the expert would not be identified to the jury as court-appointed, the parties could agree to disclose to the jury that the expert was jointly selected and retained.

A privately-appointed neutral expert may be able to do much more than an expert appointed under Rule 706. For example, if the parties agree, the privately-appointed expert could investigate documents, persons, and things, and perform experiments and testing. The authority of the Rule 706 expert to conduct such discovery is unclear. Carrying this procedure to its logical conclusion, the parties could agree to submit the dispute to a neutral expert for *binding* resolution. This, of course, is arbitration or reference under a statute and rule providing for a general order of reference. Private referral of a dispute to a neutral expert for a *nonbinding* opinion or assistance might be a form of mediation or minitrial. The important distinctions between these other forms of neutral assistance and Rule 706 are that they require the parties' consent, and their purposes generally do not include neutral fact-finding for trial presentation.

To understand how the appointment of a neutral expert will affect the settlement process, it is necessary to understand how litigants decide to settle cases. The factors influencing the decision whether and when to settle a dispute include "rational" factors intrinsic and extrinsic to the dispute, such as the likely outcome and the litigants' resources, needs, averseness to risk, and staying power, and "nonrational" factors such as the litigants' emotional condition. . . .

. . . In complex scientific and technical cases, disparity in the parties' estimates of the plaintiff's probability of success are usually caused by sincere and strongly held divergent views on how a crucial technical issue will be decided. Often each side's high estimate of its probability of success is based principally on the opinions and assurances of its experts. Unless some additional information causes the parties to reevaluate their experts' confidence in their opinions or the parties' confidence in their experts' opinions, the disparity between the estimates of success will prevent settlement.

The most effective piece of additional information can be the opinion of a neutral expert on a key technical issue. Indeed, the mere possibility that a court-appointed neutral expert will testify at trial may be enough to cause the parties to reassess their pretrial estimates of success.

Appointment of a neutral expert may have several other settlement-inducing side-effects. Although Rule 706 does not specify how the expert shall conduct his inquiry and formulate his opinions, contact between the expert and the parties is not prohibited and, except where the court directs that all communication between the expert and the parties pass through the court, is indeed likely. In "instructing" the expert as to his duties, the court, certainly when the parties consent and possibly even when they do not, may instruct the expert to inspect people, places, and things. This may well include discussions with the parties through their lawyers and experts, whether from highly unstructured and informal ex parte discussions or highly structured on-the-record hearings.

Departing from the "pure" neutral-expert role in this manner, during the course of his investigations there may be many opportunities for the neutral expert to assume a mediational role between the adversaries' own experts. Thus, the expert may find himself assuming some or all of the functions of other kinds of third-party intervenors to a dispute.

While this creates danger for an inexperienced or overly ambitious neutral expert, it also provides significant dispute resolution opportunities. In formulating instructions to the neutral expert, the court and parties should clearly delineate the expert's functions, duties, and range of activities. In this way the court can minimize the danger that the neutral expert will overstep his role and destroy his effectiveness, while at the same time maximizing the possibilities for successful intervention.

If neutral experts are such a readily available palliative to the excesses of adversariness in complex cases, why are they not used more often?[120] Besides just plain lack of knowledge about the potential benefits, their underutilization may be the result of ingrained conceptions about the adjudicatory process and the unease of judges and lawyers who believe that introducing neutral experts will threaten their roles in the process. The most common criticism of the use of neutral experts is that they will influence the jury excessively. It is unclear what "excessively" means here. If the case involves subject matter on which expert testimony is admissible, then expert testimony *should* influence the jury. Further,

---

120. The use of neutral experts by federal judges is sufficiently uncommon that their exceptional use is noticeable. Judge Finesilver employed a panel of five medical experts in In re Swine Flu Immunization Products Liability Litigation, 495 F. Supp. 1185, with good results. Judge Zampano has reported successful use of court-appointed experts in over a hundred cases over a twenty-year span in cases ranging from backsprains to complex commercial cases. He finds them very effective in construction cases. See Green, Proceedings of the Intercorporate Disputes Task Force Conference, in Corporate Dispute Management, at 333 (1982).

To ascertain more precisely how often neutral experts are appointed in civil cases, in 1980 I surveyed all federal trial judges. I asked them:

1. Whether they had ever appointed a neutral expert under Rule 706 or any other provision in civil cases over which they have presided (other than personal injury cases).
2. Other than in personal injury cases, whether they had ever used their power to appoint a neutral expert deliberately to promote settlement, and, if so, in what kinds of cases and with what results.
3. Whether they believed that the use of a neutral expert had significantly furthered settlement in any of their cases; and if so, how often.
4. In what kinds of cases they believed the early use of a court-appointed expert other than a medical panel in personal injury cases, could help the parties settle the case themselves.
5. What problems they experienced in using court-appointed experts, specifically focusing on increased delay, increased costs, selection of the expert(s), and excessive influence of the expert(s).

Of the 568 judges in the sample, only nine reported any significant use of neutral experts or enthusiasm for the practice. Of the 308 judges who responded, 212 had no experience with the concept, 8 rejected the idea in principle, and 54 indicated they had some moderate interest in or incidental experience with the concept. Of the judges who had appointed a neutral expert, only four had done so deliberately to promote settlement, although a much larger number of the respondents stated that they thought a neutral expert would have a positive effect on the settlement process. The types of cases most frequently mentioned as candidates for the appointment of a neutral expert to promote settlement were patent infringement, condemnation, and antitrust cases. The most frequently mentioned problems experienced by the judges related to increased costs—"getting the expert paid," one judge put it, and difficulty of selection. Inquiry of the Administrative Office of the United States court turned up no additional experiences with the use of neutral experts in civil cases for settlement purposes.

when there is a clash of testimony from the parties' experts, the opinion of a nonpartisan expert should receive important consideration from the jury because it is at least free from adversarial bias. "Excessive influence" in this context must mean "giving the evidence more weight than it deserves," but the procedures of Rule 706 and the traditional tools of the adversary process are available to control the impact of the neutral expert's testimony on the jury. There is no evidence that these procedures are insufficient to limit the impact of neutral expert testimony to its proper level.

What judges (and lawyers) may really be concerned about is the power that they fear the neutral expert will take away from them. In our system, the judge and parties control the adversary process. There is only one neutral in the courtroom and that neutral is the judge. The only experts are leashed to the parties' lawyers. Bringing a neutral expert into the process destroys the judge's monopoly on neutrality and the parties' control of the expert information and opinion. But in the face of strong evidence that the lawyers' lock on the levers regarding expert testimony can retard accurate fact-finding and hinder settlement, some adjustments seem appropriate. The traditional roles of judges and lawyers should give way slightly if adjustments will rationalize the adjudicatory process, making it fairer and more efficient.

For a view of the expert problem from a European perspective, consider the following:

LANGBEIN, THE GERMAN ADVANTAGE IN CIVIL PROCEDURE
52 U. Chi. L. Rev. 823, 836-841 (1985) (most footnotes omitted)

IV. EXPERTS

The European jurist who visits the United States and becomes acquainted with our civil procedure typically expresses amazement at our witness practice. His amazement turns to something bordering on disbelief when he discovers that we extend the sphere of partisan control to the selection and preparation of experts. In the Continental tradition experts are selected and commissioned by the court, although with great attention to safeguarding party interests. In the German system, experts are not even called witnesses. They are thought of as "judges' aides."

Perverse incentives. At the American trial bar, those of us who serve as expert witnesses are known as "saxophones." This is a revealing term, as slang often is. The idea is that the lawyer plays the tune, manipulating the expert as though the expert were a musical instrument on which the lawyer sounds the desired notes. I sometimes serve as an expert in trust and pension cases, and I have experienced the subtle pressures to join the team — to shade one's views, to conceal doubt, to overstate nuance, to downplay weak aspects of the case that one has been hired to bolster. Nobody likes to disappoint a patron; and beyond this psychological pressure is the financial inducement. Money changes hands upon the rendering of expertise, but the expert can run his meter only so long as his patron litigator likes the tune. Opposing counsel undertakes a similar exercise, hiring and schooling another expert to parrot the contrary position. The result is our familiar battle of opposing experts. The more measured and impartial an expert is, the less likely he is to be used by either side.

At trial, the battle of experts tends to baffle the trier, especially in jury courts. If the experts do not cancel each other out, the advantage is likely to be with the expert whose forensic skills are the more enticing. The system invites abusive cross-examination. Since each expert is party-selected and party-paid, he is vulnerable to attack on credibility regardless of the merits of his testimony. A defense lawyer recently bragged about his technique of cross-examining plaintiffs' experts in tort cases. Notice that nothing in his strategy varies with the truthfulness of the expert testimony he tries to discredit:

> A mode of attack ripe with potential is to pursue a line of questions which, by their form and the jury's studied observation of the witness in response, will tend to cast the expert as a "professional witness." By proceeding in this way, the cross-examiner will reap the benefit of a community attitude, certain to be present among several of the jurors, that bias can be purchased, almost like a commodity.

Thus, the systematic incentive in our procedure to distort expertise leads to a systematic distrust and devaluation of expertise. Short of forbidding the use of experts altogether, we probably could not have designed a procedure better suited to minimize the influence of expertise.

The Continental tradition. European legal systems are, by contrast, expert-prone. Expertise is frequently sought. The literature emphasizes the value attached to having expert assistance available to the courts in an age in which litigation involves facts of ever-greater technical difficulty. The essential insight of Continental civil procedure is that credible expertise must be neutral expertise. Thus, the responsibility for selecting and informing experts is placed upon the courts, although with important protections for party interests.

Selecting the expert. German courts obtain expert help in lawsuits the way Americans obtain expert help in business or personal affairs. If you need an architect, a dermatologist, or a plumber, you do not commission a pair of them to take preordained and opposing positions on your problem, although you do sometimes take a second opinion. Rather, you take care to find an expert who is qualified to advise you in an objective manner; you probe his advice as best you can; and if you find his advice persuasive, you follow it.

When in the course of winnowing the issues in a lawsuit a German court determines that expertise might help resolve the case, the court selects and instructs the expert. The court may decide to seek expertise on its own motion, or at the request of one of the parties. The code of civil procedure allows the court to request nominations from the parties —indeed, the code requires the court to use any expert upon whom the parties agree—but neither practice is typical. In general, the court takes the initiative in nominating and selecting the expert.

The only respect in which the code of civil procedure purports to narrow the court's discretion to choose the expert is a provision whose significance is less than obvious: "If experts are officially designated for certain fields of expertise, other persons should be chosen only when special circumstances require." One looks outside the code of civil procedure, to the federal statutes regulating various professions and trades, for the particulars on official designation. For the professions, the statutes typically authorize the official licensing bodies to assemble lists of professionals deemed especially suited to serve as experts. In other fields, the state governments designate quasi-public bodies to compile such lists. For example, under section 36 of the federal code on trade regulation, the state governments empower the regional chambers of commerce and industry (Industrie- and Handelskammern) to identify experts in a wide variety or commercial and technical fields. That statute directs the empowered chamber to choose as experts persons who have exceptional knowledge of the particular specialty and to have these persons sworn to render professional and impartial expertise. The chamber circulates its lists of experts, organized by specialty and subspecialty, to the courts. German judges receive sheaves of these lists as the various issuing bodies update and recirculate them.

Current practice. In 1984 I spent a little time interviewing judges in Frankfurt about their practice in selecting experts. My sample of a handful of judges is not large enough to impress statisticians, but I think the picture that emerges from serious discussion with people who operate the system is worth reporting. Among the judges with whom I spoke, I found unanimity on the proposition that the most important factor predisposing a judge to select an expert is favorable experience with that expert in an earlier case. Experts thus build reputations with the bench. Someone who renders a careful, succinct, and well-substantiated report and who responds effectively to the subsequent questions of the court and the parties will be remembered when another case arises in his specialty. Again we notice that German civil procedure tracks the patterns of decision-making in ordinary business and personal affairs: If you get a plumber to fix your toilet and he does it well, you incline to hire him again.

When judges lack personal experience with appropriate experts, I am told, they turn to the authoritative lists described above. If expertise is needed in a field for which official lists are unavailing, the court is thrown upon its own devices. The German judge then gets on the

phone, working from party suggestions and from the court's own research, much in the fashion of an American litigator hunting for expertise. In these cases there is a tendency to turn, first, to the bodies
that prepare expert lists in cognate areas; or, if none, to the universities
and technical institutes.

If enough potential experts are identified to allow for choice, the
court will ordinarily consult party preferences. In such circumstances a
litigant may ask the court to exclude an expert whose views proved
contrary to his interests in previous litigation or whom he otherwise
disdains. The court will try to oblige the parties' tastes when another
qualified expert can be substituted. Nevertheless, a litigant can formally
challenge an expert's appointment only on the narrow grounds for
which a litigant could seek to recuse a judge.

Preparing the expert. The court that selects the expert instructs him, in
the sense of propounding the facts that he is to assume or to investigate,
and in framing the questions that the court wishes the expert to address.
In formulating the expert's task, as in other important steps in the conduct of the case, the court welcomes adversary suggestions. If the expert
should take a view of premises (for example, in an accident case or a
building-construction dispute), counsel for both sides will accompany
him.

Safeguards. The expert is ordinarily instructed to prepare a written
opinion. When the court receives that report, it is circulated to the
litigants. The litigants commonly file written comments, to which the
expert is asked to reply. The court on its own motion may also request
the expert to amplify his views. If the expert's report remains in contention, the court will schedule a hearing at which counsel for a dissatisfied litigant can confront and interrogate the expert.

The code of civil procedure reserves to the court the power to order
a further report by another expert if the court should deem the first
report unsatisfactory. A litigant dissatisfied with the expert may encourage the court to invoke its power to name a second expert. The code
of criminal procedure has a more explicit standard for such cases, which
is worth noticing because the literature suggests that courts have similar
instincts in civil procedure. The court may refuse a litigant's motion to
engage a further expert in a criminal case, the code says,

> If the contrary of the fact concerned has already been proved through the
> former expert opinion; this [authority to refuse to appoint a further expert]
> does not apply if the expertise of the former is doubted, if his report is
> based upon inaccurate factual presuppositions, if the report contains contradic-
> tions, or if the new expert has available means of research that appear superior
> to those of a former expert.

When, therefore, a litigant can persuade the court that an expert's
report has been sloppy or partial, that it rests upon a view of the field

that is not generally shared, or that the question referred to the expert is exceptionally difficult, the court will commission further expertise.

A litigant may also engage his own expert, much as is done in the Anglo-American procedural world, in order to rebut the court-appointed expert. The court will discount the views of a party-selected expert on account of his want of neutrality, but cases occur in which he nevertheless proves to be effective. Ordinarily, I am told, the court will not in such circumstances base its judgment directly upon the views of the party-selected expert; rather, the court will treat the rebuttal as ground for engaging a further court-appointed expert (called an *Oberexperte,* literally an "upper" or "superior" expert), whose opinion will take account of the rebuttal.

To conclude: In the use of expertise German civil procedure strikes an adroit balance between nonadversarial and adversarial values. Expertise is kept impartial, but litigants are protected against error or caprice through a variety of opportunities for consultation, confrontation, and rebuttal.

The American counterpart. It may seem curious that we make so little use of court-appointed experts in our civil practice, since "[t]he inherent power of a trial judge to appoint an expert of his own choosing is virtually unquestioned" and has been extended and codified in the Federal Rules of Evidence and the Uniform Rules of Evidence (Model Expert Testimony Act). The literature displays both widespread agreement that our courts virtually never exercise this authority, and a certain bafflement about why.

While "simple inertia" doubtless accounts for much (our judges "are accustomed to presiding over acts initiated by the parties"), comparative example points to a further explanation. The difficulty originates with the locktight segmentation of our procedure into pretrial and trial compartments, and with the tradition of partisan domination of the pretrial. Until lately, it was exceptional for the judge to have detailed acquaintance with the facts of the case until the parties presented their evidence at trial. By then the adversaries would have engaged their own experts, and time would no longer allow a court-appointed expert to be located and prepared. Effective use of court-appointed experts as exemplified in German practice presupposes early and extensive judicial involvement in shaping the whole of the proofs. It seems possible that the rise of managerial judging (discussed below in Part VIII) may at last achieve that precondition for effective use of court-appointed experts in our system.

Does the use of a neutral court-appointed expert witness solve the fundamental problem of expert testimony? A legal philosopher thinks not.

BREWER, SCIENTIFIC EXPERT TESTIMONY AND INTELLECTUAL DUE PROCESS

107 Yale L.J., 1535, 1673-1679 (1998) (most footnotes omitted)

. . .

A. EPISTEMIC NONARBITRARINESS AS A PRACTICAL CONSTRAINT ON LEGITIMATE EPISTEMIC DEFERENCE

My goal for the present section is to explicate some of the overall normative aims in the "practical point of view" from which a legal system ought to evaluate the transfer of scientific information from scientific experts to nonexpert judges and jurors. The normative aims that are such an important element in the practical point of view of a legal system are articulated and relied upon in many decisions by courts dealing in one way or another with the rationality of legal decisionmaking in cases to which complex scientific information is rationally pertinent. I discuss a few such cases to help explicate what those normative aims are.

The central idea animating these practical norms is that certain rule-of-law values require epistemic nonarbitrariness in factfinding reasoning, as in other types of reasoning. Thus, if the nonexpert cannot acquire scientific beliefs from competing experts in a way that is nonarbitrary, from an epistemic point of view, those beliefs will therefore not be legitimate from the practical legal point of view. That is, according to this practical rule-of-law norm, at least in cases in which life, liberty, or property is at stake, epistemic nonarbitrariness in the process of "finding" scientifically discerned facts is a necessary condition of the practical legitimacy of a decision that relies on that factfinding.

One finds respect for and recognition of this norm in both philosophical and legal materials. John Rawls, for example, has long maintained that among those "guidelines intended to preserve the integrity of the judicial process" are the requirements that courts undertake conscientiously to determine whether an infraction has taken place. . . . Thus a legal system must . . . contain rules of evidence that guarantee rational procedures of inquiry. While there are variations in these procedures, the rule of law requires some form of due process: that is, a process reasonably designed to ascertain the truth, in ways consistent with the other ends of the legal system, as to whether a violation has taken place and under what circumstances.

Rawls's point applies no less to the integrity of the judicial process in civil cases than it does to the integrity of that process in criminal cases. A reflection of this same basic rule-of-law value, articulated in the setting of a civil antitrust action, is found in a prominent federal appellate case. In In re Japanese Electronic Products Antitrust Litigation,[428] several U.S.

---

428. 631 F.2d 1069 (3d Cir. 1980).

electronics manufacturers brought an antitrust action against several Japanese manufacturers. When the U.S. plaintiffs made a motion for jury trial, the defendant Japanese companies countered, claiming among other things that the economic and technical issues were too conceptually complex for the jury to understand, even with the help of expert testimony. The case was on appeal from a federal district court on the sole question whether the plaintiffs had a right to a jury trial even when the issues and evidence involved would be acutely complex. In effect, the court considered whether there was (what has come to be referred to as) a "complexity exception" to the Seventh Amendment right to jury trial under the U.S. Constitution. The district judge had held that there was no such "complexity exception." In what appears to be an unprecedented decision in the federal courts, the appellate court overturned the district court judgment. The appellate court agreed with the defendant, vacated the district court's pretrial order, and held that, despite the normative force of the Seventh Amendment right to jury trial, the Fifth Amendment due process right to have a rational and fair adjudication outweighed the Seventh Amendment right. The court concluded that the Fifth Amendment narrows the scope of the Seventh Amendment by means of a complexity exception.

In its cogently articulated opinion, the appellate court specified the kind of complexity that might trump the right to jury trial as follows:

> A suit is too complex for a jury when circumstances render the jury unable to decide in a proper manner. The law presumes that a jury will find facts and reach a verdict by rational means. It does not contemplate scientific precision but does contemplate a resolution of each issue on the basis of a fair and reasonable assessment of the evidence and a fair and reasonable application of the relevant legal rules. A suit might be excessively complex as a result of any set of circumstances which singly or in combination render a jury unable to decide in the foregoing rational manner. Examples of such circumstances are an exceptionally long trial period and conceptually difficult factual issues.

The court concludes that "due process precludes trial by jury when a jury is unable to perform this task with a reasonable understanding of the evidence and the legal rules." The court went on to elucidate the connection between this right to rational comprehension by the legal decisionmaker and rule-of-law values like predictability and notice:

> The due process objections to jury trial of a complex case implicate values of fundamental importance. If judicial decisions are not based on factual determinations bearing some reliable degree of accuracy, legal remedies will not be applied consistently with the purposes of the laws. There is a danger that jury verdicts will be erratic and completely unpredictable, which would be inconsistent with evenhanded justice. Finally, unless the jury can understand the evidence and the legal rules sufficiently to rest its decision on them, the objective of most rules of evidence and procedure in promoting a fair trial will be lost

entirely. We believe that when a jury is unable to perform its decisionmaking task with a reasonable understanding of the evidence and legal rules, it undermines the ability of a district court to render basic justice.

The court also addressed the question of what values the legal system might injure in cases to which the complexity exception applied by choosing not to allow the kind of community input that the constitutional jury trial right was designed to secure. The central values often mentioned in connection with the jury trial right — values powerful enough, in the district court's judgment, to lead it to reject the idea of a complexity exception — are the jury's function as a check on judicial power, and the jury's ability to modify and conform the law to, and suffuse the law with, community values (so-called jury equity), thereby lending the law a communitarian legitimacy it might not otherwise have. Assessing these countervailing values reflected in the Seventh Amendment, the court of appeals delivered something of a coup de grace debater's point:

> In the context of a lawsuit of the complexity that we have posited, however, these features [of the jury system] do not produce real benefits of substantial value. The function of "jury equity" may be legitimate when the jury actually modifies the law to conform to community values. However, when the jury is unable to determine the normal application of the law to the facts of a case and reaches a verdict on the basis of nothing more than its own determination of community wisdom and values, its operation is indistinguishable from arbitrary and unprincipled decisionmaking. Similarly, the "line-drawing" function is difficult to justify when the jury cannot understand the evidence or legal rules relevant to the issue of where to draw a line.
>
> ... A jury unable to understand the evidence and legal rules is hardly a reliable and effective check on judicial power. Our liberties are more secure when judicial decisionmakers proceed rationally, consistently with the law, and on the basis of evidence produced at trial. If the jury is unable to function in this manner, it has the capacity of becoming itself a tool of arbitrary and erratic judicial power.

In In re Japanese Electronic Products Antitrust Litigation, one thus finds a powerful articulation of the legal system's commitment to practical norms in the family of rule-of-law values that are specifically addressed to the epistemic cogency of juridical factfinding. In various ways, one finds a similar commitment to these epistemically oriented rule of law values in many other judicial opinions, state and federal. Thus, one state supreme court declared:

> One cogent reason for overturning the verdict of a jury is that the verdict is based on conclusions that are physically impossible. "[A] verdict should be set aside 'where testimony is thus in conflict with indisputable physical facts, the facts demonstrate that the testimony is either intentionally or unintentionally untrue,

and leave no real question of conflict of evidence for the jury concerning which reasonable minds could reasonably differ.' . . ."

Scientific evidence is relevant to a determination of what is physically impossible. In Roma v. Thames River Specialties Co., this court held that the trial judge "would have failed in his duty" if he had not set aside the verdict when "the laws of mechanics, as testified to and uncontradicted, tended to prove [the claimant's] story impossible." In Jump v. Ensign-Bickford Co. the trial court properly set aside the verdict when expert scientific testimony indicated that it was physically impossible for a fuse to burn as fast as the claimant had alleged, and this court could "find in the evidence no reasonable ground which would have justified the jury in disregarding that evidence."[436]

Similarly, in an opinion perhaps signaling that the U.S. Supreme Court may be amenable to something like a complexity exception, Justice Souter declared that, when a case requires the legal decision-maker to interpret and comprehend complex technical patents, the decision is to be made by the judge, not the jury. He reasoned:

> In the main, we expect, any credibility determinations will be subsumed within the necessarily sophisticated analysis of the whole document, required by the standard construction rule that a term can be defined only in a way that comports with the instrument as a whole. Thus, in these cases a jury's capabilities to evaluate demeanor, to sense the "mainsprings of human conduct," or to reflect community standards . . . are much less significant than a trained ability to evaluate the testimony in relation to the overall structure of the patent. The decision-maker vested with the task of construing the patent is in the better position to ascertain whether an expert's proposed definition fully comports with the specification and claims and so will preserve the patent's internal coherence.[438]

These cases suggest a strong commitment among leading jurists to the idea that factfinding, including factfinding regarding matters that are the special epistemic province of expert scientists, must be conducted in a coherent and rational manner in order that this epistemic process meet the normative requirements of a legal system that operates to grant or deprive people of life, liberty, and property. Reflecting on these and other such statements by judges and other jurists, we may sense a commitment, imminent in the broad materials that constitute authoritative law (U.S. law, at least), to what we may call the practical norm of intellectual due process. In re Japanese Electronic Products Antitrust Litigation is especially fertile here, with its suggestion that the epistemic process of comprehension of theoretical complexities is a

---

436. State v. Hammond, 604 A.2d 793, 795 (Conn. 1992) (citations omitted).

438. Markman v. Westview Instruments, Inc., 116 S. Ct. 1384, 1396 (1996) (citations omitted). From an epistemic point of view, Markman's solution suffers from the same problem that afflicts In Re Japanese Products Antitrust Litigation: A technically nonexpert judge is not in a decisively better position than a technically nonexpert jury.

mandate of the decidedly practical norm of the Due Process Clause. Though there are, to be sure, many features of due process that do not specifically "sound" epistemic, that case reveals that some distinctively practical norms do have meaningful epistemic consequences. Much philosophical work remains to be done to explicate this emerging rule-of-law norm. Recognition of intellectual due process as a practical norm in the family of rule-of-law norms has only just begun—partly because the startling advances in scientific methods—coupled with the striking increases in the technological complexity of society and the laws that arise to govern and guide it, is also a relatively recent socio-epistemic phenomenon.

A great deal of work remains in explicating the scope and criteria of "intellectual due process," but this much seems clear even now: A reasoning process that is epistemically arbitrary is incapable of producing a legitimate decision, for such a reasoning process is "indistinguishable from arbitrary and unprincipled decisionmaking." If I am right that practical epistemic deference to expert scientists is doomed, on average, to generate in nonexpert judges and jurors beliefs that are only accidentally and arbitrarily true at best and thus are not epistemically justified beliefs, then this process perforce does not produce legally legitimate decisions.

B.   Consequences for Doctrinal and Institutional Design: "Two-Hat" Solutions and Intellectual Due Process

What is to be done? Detailed analysis of the consequences of this analysis for institutional and doctrinal revision and transformation are beyond the scope of my current project. A few conclusions do emerge, however. If legal systems are to endorse and aspire to satisfy the intellectual due process norms (and other related rule-of-law norms), they would be well advised to move toward a "two-hat" model of legal decisionmaking in areas to which scientific results are rationally pertinent. On this model, the system seeks to ensure that one and the same decisionmaker has both legal legitimacy (by being duly elected or appointed by a legitimate elective or appointing authority) and epistemic competence with the basic formal tools of scientific analysis. A useful heuristic analogy might be that of a mathematician or physicist who has practical decisionmaking authority as a voting member of his department (wearing one hat), and epistemic competence that informs the practical judgment (wearing the other), or similarly, a physicist voting on who should receive a physics prize for the most important contribution to his field. Many jurists have already begun to consider different paths on this broad avenue of reform, and various proposals consistent with the "two-hat solution" satisfy it. These include turning over many decisions currently made by private litigation to public administrative agencies staffed with trained scientists, relying on blue ribbon scientifically trained juries, scientific expert magistrate judges, or even special science courts staffed by scientifically trained judges. Already in the wake of *Daubert*'s increased demands on federal trial court judges, special workshops on scientific theory and method have become available to train them.

A further word about *Daubert*'s gatekeeping solution is in order. Both *Daubert* and In re Japanese Electronic Products Antitrust Litigation rely on the underlying assumption that a judge is in a decisively better epistemic position than a jury to assess rationally the merits of competing scientific testimony, even when the underdetermination condition is satisfied. My analysis of the legitimacy of epistemic deference gives reason to be skeptical about that assumption, for the analysis applies no less to a nonexpert judge than it does to a nonexpert jury. It is for this reason that the distinction between the threshold question of the admissibility of evidence, on the one hand, and the question of the weight of the evidence, on the other, is not particularly important in my analysis. *Daubert* and (implicitly) In re Japanese Electronic Products Antitrust Litigation treat this distinction as very important, for they both assume that a judge is in a significantly better epistemic position to decide whether proffered scientific evidence is sufficiently reliable to be admissible in a trial before a nonexpert jury, which could then weigh the suitably screened evidence. I have argued that we have good reason to doubt that assumption and, indeed, to be quite skeptical about the idea of solving problems of selection, competition, and underdetermination by taking decisions about expert testimony away from nonexpert juries and giving them to nonexpert judges.

It is important not to overstate my argument here. Early in the Article, I noted that epistemic competence is a matter of degree—that not all experts are equally epistemically competent and not all nonexperts are equally epistemically incompetent. This means that it is certainly conceptually possible that a trial judge is significantly more epistemically competent than a jury in assessing the scientific merits of expert scientific testimony, even when the underdetermination condition is satisfied. That is, it is conceptually possible that the underlying assumption of *Daubert*, In re Japanese Electronic Products Antitrust Litigation, Markman, and many other state and federal cases, is accurate as to some judges. Nor is this a bare conceptual possibility. It is not unreasonable to suppose that some judges, who are repeatedly and predictably faced with proffers of scientific evidence, may find and take the time and energy required to become decently competent in manipulating the aims, methods, and results of some of the specific sciences that are likely to come into their courts. Perhaps some autodidactic judges even become sufficiently competent to satisfy the demands of intellectual due process. The plausible possibility that this is true of some judges raises the largely empirical question about what percentage of judges in state or federal systems are in fact in this happy—from the point of view of intellectual due process—state.

Still, though I have not done the kind of empirical work required cogently to answer that question, the norm of intellectual due process itself places the burden of empirical proof on those who would maintain that a large enough percentage of judges are or will in the near future be in that state. That is, the burden is on the person who claims, along with the *Daubert* Court, that, by and large, trial judges already wear, or soon will wear, the required "two hats." The burden is on the person who claims that the requirements of intellectual due process can be satisfied on a large scale by taking the decisions out of the hands of nonexpert juries and leaving them in the hands of judges. Carrying that burden of proof would of course call for a procedure significantly different from that of *Daubert* itself, for *Daubert* is still willing to turn over many ultimate decisions, even in cases in which the underdetermination condition is satisfied, to nonexperts whom we have no reason to believe are sufficiently competent in the expert discipline to meet the requirements of intellectual due process.

I have spoken of remaining empirical questions and of burdens of empirical proof. There are also important conceptual details that remain to be worked out for the two-hat solution. What kind of training should the experts—or expertly trained judges—get? One can get a clear sense of the training required to have basic competence in biology, genetics, statistics, economics, or epidemiology, but how scientifically specialized is it feasible to allow the two-hat-wearing legal decisionmaker to be? Even the heuristic analogy of the mathematician may break down, since that field, like virtually all fields in the empirical and demonstrative sciences, is becoming intensely specialized. Will scientific discipline become so specialized that it ceases to make sense to talk about general epistemic competence even within a discipline? And if that problem looms for singular disciplines, what hope is there for resolving problems of extra-disciplinary competition in a manner consistent with the suasions of intellectual due process? Still another question is, how much training is enough? To the level of a Ph.D? An M.A.? Are formal degrees good signals at all? Still another question involves the democratic legitimacy of the two-hat solution. Rule by technocrat-kings has its dangers, just as does rule by epistemically unruly mobs. Is there a feasible and meaningful way in which a responsible polity can deliberate and endorse the training programs and institutional schemes that would implement the "two-hat" solution and achieve a reasonable degree of intellectual due process?

These are deep and difficult questions. But few topics, I hazard to say, will be more important to the health of the polity and its citizens than the close investigation of how the law ought—from legal, moral, and other closely related practical points of view — to keep up with science.

VIII. CONCLUSION

Though its steps have been long, the argument presented in this Article is not too difficult to summarize. I have argued that there is a structured reasoning process that a nonexpert judge or jury must use in an effort to take account of scientific expert testimony in the course of reaching a legal decision about liability (in the civil setting) or guilt (in the criminal setting). When one attends carefully to the precise steps of the reasoning process, one sees that there are crucial steps that a nonexpert judge or jury is, in a great many instances, not capable of performing in an epistemically nonarbitrary manner. Specifically, when competing scientific experts are, for all the nonexpert knows, fairly evenly matched in credentials, reputation, and demeanor, and when no generally accessible rational criteria (such as self-contradiction by an expert witness) break the "tie" (i.e., when what I have called the "underdetermination condition" is satisfied), then a nonexpert is not capable of choosing among the competing experts in an epistemically nonarbitrary way. I have also sought to show that epistemic nonarbitrariness is a necessary condition of legitimacy, as expressed in the norm of intellectual due process. This norm, an emerging rule-of-law norm, immanent in both decided cases and various analyses of jurists and philosophers, will be increasingly important as scientific expert testimony comes to be used in a greater and greater percentage of cases. When the conditions of this norm are not satisfied, decisions by nonexperts, even in light of relevant scientific expert testimony, lack epistemic legitimacy, and therefore lack the kind of practical-cum-moral legitimacy that legal systems do and ought to demand.

What is to be done if the relevance of scientific information to legal decisions continues to grow, while nonexperts are so often incapable of legitimately incorporating that information into their decisions? Nothing in this Article suggests that a nonexpert judge cannot become sufficiently epistemically competent, even without the formal training of a scientist. Perhaps some judges, by virtue of background or repeat "on the bench" experience with scientific evidence, will become sufficiently epistemically competent to render decisions about scientific expert testimony that are epistemically legitimate and that meet the demands of intellectual due process. *Daubert* itself calls upon judges to be more active as "gatekeepers" in screening out unreliable science. But *Daubert*'s solution to the problem of legitimately assessing expert scientific testimony seems a poor one. First, given the press of other judicial business, it seems unlikely that a significant percentage of judges either already have, or will find the time to acquire, the kind of scientific competence that legitimate, intellectually "duly processed" decisionmaking requires. That is, unless judges are routinely and systematically trained in scientific theories and methods, *Daubert* does not offer a promising overall solution to the problem. Also, under *Daubert*, even when a judge is sufficiently competent, that competence could yield a duly processed, legitimate decision only when the judge decides not to admit some proffered scientific testimony. But in a great many other cases, the judge will admit competing scientific evidence, and allow the nonexpert, noncompetent jury to make the decision—the quintessential circumstance, as this Article has argued, in which failures of intellectual due process occur.

Nor can the expedient emphasized by Justice Breyer in the *Joiner* decision—the Supreme Court's next major treatment of an issue concerning scientific evidence after *Daubert*—resolve the problem. Justice Breyer rightly highlighted the epistemic problem judges have in attempting to fulfill *Daubert*'s requirements:

> This requirement will sometimes ask judges to make subtle and sophisticated determinations about scientific methodology and its relation to the conclusions an expert witness seeks to offer—particularly when a case arises in an area where the science itself is tentative or uncertain, or where testimony about general risk levels in human beings or animals is offered to prove individual causation. Yet. . . judges are not scientists and do not have the scientific training that can facilitate the making of such decisions.[442]

In Justice Breyer's view, given this challenge, judges should more actively solicit scientific information in order to perform their *Daubert*-mandated role of "gatekeepers" vigilant against junk science, for example by using court appointed experts, appointing special masters or specially trained law clerks, or using pretrial conferences to narrow the scientific issues. But, for reasons suggested above, this solution also fails to meet the needs of intellectual due process for any judge who is himself not epistemically competent in scientific methods and theories. For the judge is not capable of making an epistemically legitimate decision about which special master, law clerk, or court-appointed expert to consult.

The only solution (actually, it is a family of solutions) I see requires that one and the same legal decisionmaker wear two hats, the hat of epistemic competence and the hat of practical legitimacy. That is, whether it is a scientifically trained judge or juror or agency adminis-

---

442. Id. *Joiner* held that, even under *Daubert*, the proper standard of review for decisions about the admissibility of scientific evidence was "abuse of discretion," regardless of whether the district judge's decision was to admit or exclude the evidence, and regardless of whether that decision was "outcome determinative." See id. at 515 (majority opinion).

trator, the same person who has legal authority must also have epistemic competence in relevant scientific disciplines. In an age in which culture will increasingly take advantage of the massive intellectual power of science, this is not too high a price for the legal system to pay to satisfy its own just intellectual aspirations.

CHAPTER IX

Authentication and Identification: Writings, Photographs, Voices, and Real Evidence

Much of the material in the previous chapters has dealt with the most frequent type of evidence encountered — live, in-court witness testimony. Often, however, facts can be proved more easily or powerfully through the introduction of a document, photograph, or object. Special rules of evidence apply to such proof, and a careful understanding of these rules is essential not only for the trial lawyer, but also for the lawyer who never intends to see the inside of a courtroom — today's contract is tomorrow's "Exhibit A." This chapter deals with the rules that apply to various kinds of exhibits — what Wigmore called "autoptic profferance"—with a special emphasis on writings.

A document is a particularly powerful piece of evidence. In contrast to the testimony of an in-court witness that is developed through interrogation, subject to change upon further interrogation and dependent throughout on the credibility of the witness, documentary proof generally predates the litigation, is permanent, and is not dependent on the perceived credibility of a witness. Once authenticated (the documentary corollary to credibility), a document speaks directly to the trier of fact and may travel into the jury room.

A document is also a versatile piece of evidence. In the hands of a skilled trial lawyer, the same document may be used to refresh a witness's memory (Rule 612); to impeach a witness's testimony (Rule 613); as the basis for expert opinion (Rule 703); as recorded recollection or as a business, public, or similar type of record (Rule 803(5) to (18)). Yet a document may be no more reliable than testimonial evidence and much more difficult to discredit.

Appreciation of the great persuasive potential of documents, photographs, and real evidence has led to the creation of special rules of evidence for this type of proof, especially documents. One group of rules implements the foundational requirement of authentication or identification. Another set of rules specifies whether the original of a document will be required or if a copy or another form of proof will be accepted as a substitute for the original; this is the so-called best evidence rule.

The "digital revolution" and the widespread use of electronic communication and "electronic writings" such as e-mail raises new issues about "writings" as evidence. At the time the Rule of Evidence were adopted, the state of technology of written communication on paper gave documents a kind of permanence and reliability. It was difficult to alter a written document without leaving traces of the alteration. Handwritten signatures had unique characteristics, which enabled recognition of particular documents. Electronic documents can be altered at will without leaving any trace of the alteration. E-mails are typically "signed" by characters easy to duplicate. It is hard to have the same confidence in the origin or integrity of an electronic document that prior generations could have in a deed, letter, or will. How our rules on authentication will adapt to these developments in technology remains yet to be seen.

This chapter is organized around the concepts of authentication and best evidence, but it should be kept in mind that effective use of documents and real evidence in trial requires an appreciation of the many ways in which this kind of evidence can be used and an understanding of all the rules that apply to it.

A. Authentication

Treatment of the authentication of documents and identification of real evidence formerly comprised a major portion of a course in evidence. At common law, the foundational requirements for admitting a document or a physical object into evidence were complex and unforgiving. The Advisory Committee Notes to the Federal Rules on authentication (Rules 901 to 903) incorporate the scholarly criticism that the common law approach reflected an "attitude of agnosticism" that "departs sharply from men's customs in ordinary affairs" and presents "only a slight obstacle to the introduction of forgeries in comparison to the time and expense devoted to proving genuine writings which correctly show their origin on their face." Advisory Committee Notes to Rule 901, quoting McCormick, Cases on Evidence 388 n.4 (3d ed. 1956), and McCormick, Evidence §185, pp. 395-396.

The Federal Rules greatly simplify the foundational requirements. Authentication and identification are treated as "a special aspect of relevancy" and "an inherent logical necessity." Advisory Committee Notes to Rule 901(a), quoting Michael and Adler, Real Proof, 5 Vand. L. Rev. 344, 362 (1952), and 7 Wigmore, Evidence §2129, p. 564. Thus, the Committee Notes take the position that "the requirement of showing authenticity or identity falls into the category of relevancy dependent upon fulfillment of a condition of fact and is governed by the procedure set forth in Rule 104(b)."

In implementing this approach, the Federal Rules contain a general provision that the requirement of authentication or identification is satisfied "by evidence sufficient to support a finding that the matter in question is what its proponent claims." Rule 901(a). This single provision is supplemented—"by way of illustration only"—with ten examples of authentication or identification conforming with the requirements of the rule. Rule 901(b). These ten examples may be classified into three general categories:

1. Testimony of a witness with knowledge — in the case of a document, either the writer or an observer;
2. Testimony of an expert; and
3. Circumstantial proof.

The general provision of Rule 901 is also supplemented by ten categories of "self-authenticated" evidence for which "extrinsic evidence of authenticity as a condition precedent to admissibility is not required." Rule 902. Finally, as the Advisory Committee Notes make clear, at least in civil cases, modern procedural devices such as requests for admission, F.R. Civ. P. 36, and pretrial conferences, F.R. Civ. P. 16, obviate the need for much proof of authenticity at trial.

Despite the attempt by the Federal Rules to simplify and modernize the common law approach, many difficult authentication questions remain. For example, may inadmissible evidence (such as hearsay) be used to authenticate a document? Do the Federal Rules retain the common law chain-of-custody requirement? Does Rule 901 require a showing that an offered document tends to prove the issue on which it is offered, or only that the offered document is "genuine"? Beyond the examples listed in 901(b), what other types of proof will satisfy Rule 901(a)'s general provision? How does Rule 901 relate to Rule 703, which permits an expert to base her opinion on facts or data reasonably relied on by experts in that field? Should voice identification be treated more like eyewitness identification or authentication of handwriting?

More generally, what rationale justifies the distinction between the categories of self-authenticated evidence in Rule 902 and all other evidence subject to Rule 901's authentication requirement? What are the operative effects of self-authentication? For example, may the opposing party contest the authenticity of a self-authenticated item of evidence? How may it do this? If self-authenticated evidence is challenged, how is the issue resolved and by whom?

Problem: Blackacre

Action to determine title to Blackacre. P traces her title through an unrecorded 1982 deed from G, now dead. D claims by adverse possession for more than 21 years. P and D dispute the validity of the other's claim. At trial, how may the following evidence be authenticated by the proponent:

(1)　The unrecorded deed from G to P?
(2)　The 1954 recorded deed from G's grantor to G?
(3)　A list of expenditures and receipts relating to the upkeep of Blackacre, going back to 1965, offered by D?
(4)　A copy of the local newspaper from July 5, 1978, describing a Fourth of July picnic at "D's ranch, Blackacre," offered by D?
(5)　Tax records and receipts offered by D?
(6)　Cancelled checks by D for utilities for Blackacre over the past 25 years?
(7)　A letter from G to D, offered by D, that states, "In reply to your letter of March 3, 1986, I have not executed any deeds to Blackacre."
(8)　A telephone conversation a witness allegedly had with G on November 10, 1983, in which G reportedly denied making any deeds to Blackacre?

Problem: The Problematic Promissory Note

Charge: income tax evasion for the year 1996. Using the net worth method, the government seeks to prove that D substantially understated his income in 1996 and owed approximately $13,000 more in taxes than he paid. In defense, D offers in evidence a 1995 promissory note signed by his brother, B, to prove that part of the unreported income the government claims he received was actually a nontaxable loan repayment. What foundational proof will suffice to admit the note:

(1) Testimony of a witness that he was familiar with B's handwriting and that the signature on the note appeared to be B's?

(2) Testimony of a witness that he had represented B for several years, had seen him sign hundreds of documents, was able to recognize B's handwriting, and identified the signature on the note as B's?

(3) Testimony of D that he had seen B sign the note?

(4) Testimony of a witness that, in preparation for the trial, he had examined several exemplars of *B*'s signature, conceded to be valid, and that in his opinion the note was signed by *B*?

(5) An offer by *D*'s attorney to submit the note and the concededly valid exemplars to the jury for its comparison?

Suppose the authenticity of the exemplars of *B*'s signature was challenged. Who resolves the issue of their admissibility and on what basis? If none of the above testimony is offered, may the note nonetheless be admitted? Before the note is admissible, must *D* offer testimony by the maker, the payee, or someone who prepared the note to testify as to the transaction of which it was a part?

Problem: The International Bank of Commerce Mail Scam

Charge: 11 counts of mail fraud and 2 counts of use of wire communications to defraud. At trial, the government seeks to introduce over *D*'s objection 22 letters that on their face purported to come from *D*, "President and Senior Counsel of the International Bank of Commerce," with an address at 8 Creswell Road, Worcester, Massachusetts, and a telephone number of (617) 754-5000. *D* contends that there is no direct evidence that he signed or authorized the sending of any of the documents that purported to come from him. In support of its offer of proof, the government introduces evidence that (1) *D* had a residence at 8 Creswell Road and a telephone number of 754-5000, (2) *D* received, retained, and used at trial replies from 7 of the 22 addressees of these letters, and (3) all 22 letters were on the same stationery, referred to the same type of transaction, and otherwise indicated a common authorship.

Should the letters be admitted?

Problem: Viva Card

Collection action against *D* by Bank *P*, owner of the Viva Card credit service. Viva Card's computerized billing service billed *D* on his January statement for $75 for two tickets to an Opera Company December 18 production of *Rigoletto*. *D* denies ordering the tickets. At trial, *P* offers proof through the opera's business manager that the opera's ticket office contains a computer terminal connected to a data-storage system, that telephone charge orders for tickets are taken by operators in the ticket office, and that the operators enter the caller's credit-card number into the computer terminal, causing that number and the amount of the charge to be recorded on tape in the data-storage system. This tape is then sent to *P*, which runs it through its computer system, thereby picking up the opera's charges on its central file of account charges. Each month this central file, containing all charges at any location in that month for all card holders, is "unloaded" to create the monthly statements sent to each card holder. *P* offers:

(1) A printout of Opera Company's December tape;

(2) A printout of the portion of *P*'s central file tape showing *D*'s December account; and

(3) A copy of *D*'s January statement produced for trial by *P* by causing the central file tape for December for his account to be reprinted in statement format.

How may such evidence be authenticated?

Problem: Offer and Acceptance

Sam Brown, of Hartford Surplus Products, sends an e-mail to his list of 30 customers of surplus electronic products as follows:

"We offer 500 Toshiba 6Gb hard drives, Model 1863, for $40 each for immediate acceptance."

Within an hour of dispatch of the message, Joe Green, of Green Computer Sales, e-mails the reply address on Brown's e-mail, "We accept your offer of 500 Toshiba hard drives @$40. Please ship to our warehouse at 12 Page Street, St. Louis.

Later that day Brown sells the hard drives to White. Green sues Brown for breach of contract. Green has a printout from his computer of the e-mail he received from Brown and the e-mail he sent in reply. As Green's counsel how would you authenticate these two e-mails? What problems would you anticipate in getting the e-mail communications admitted in evidence?

Problem: The Cudia City Wash

Action by a group of Phoenix, Arizona, homeowners against the Salt River Valley Water Users' Association when their homes were damaged by water escaping from the Arizona Canal. The Arizona Canal is operated by the association as agent for the Salt River Valley Agricultural Improvement and Power District.

The canal traverses the valley in which the homeowners live and intersects at least four major natural washes, including the Cudia City Wash. During normal rainfall, surface runoff collects in these washes and then flows through the canal. However, during extremely severe storms, the washes overflow and flood the surrounding ground. When a storm is anticipated, the association follows storm-control procedures designed to enable the canal system to accept and safely carry off as much excess runoff as possible. Ordinarily, these procedures are sufficient to prevent dangerous overflow. However, several of the valley's brief, high-intensity summer storms have been severe enough to cause major breaches in the canal. The records of the association showed that in 1939 and 1943 a desert storm produced runoff that broke the canal banks in several places.

On June 22, 1998, a severe rainstorm occurred in the Cudia City Wash area. The storm was one having a 100-year return frequency, that is, a storm so severe that it could be expected to occur, on the average, only once in 100 years. During the storm, the association went into its storm-control procedures. Nonetheless, when the water from the Cudia City Wash hit the canal, there was so much water in the canal and the wash that it created a backflow, causing water in the canal to flow upstream, overtopping the south bank of the canal, eroding the bank in three places, and causing a wall of water to hit the area in which the plaintiffs reside. The water traveled swiftly, carrying great amounts of mud and debris and possessing sufficient kinetic force to knock down houses and carry away automobiles and horses. The flood waters caused serious damage to the plaintiffs' homes and other property.

Plaintiffs' complaint alleged that the association owed the home owners a duty to use reasonable care in operating the canal to minimize the destructive effect of desert storms and that the association was negligent in designing and following procedures in the event of severe storms.

At trial, plaintiffs seek to introduce a two-page document that purports to show in graph form the amounts of rain that fell at various points in the Salt River Valley during the storms of 1939 and 1943. This document was found in the association's files and was produced upon plaintiffs' request. The purpose of offering this document is to show that the association knew, or should have known, that storms similar to the June 1993 storm have occurred with some frequency in the valley. The document is unsigned and undated. Is the document admissible?

THREADGILL v. ARMSTRONG WORLD INDUSTRIES, INC.
928 F.2d 1366 (3d Cir. 1991)

MANSMANN, Circuit Judge.

This appeal requires that we resolve an evidentiary dispute arising in the context of a personal injury action alleging negligence and conspiracy on the part of various manufacturers and distributors of asbestos-containing products. The plaintiffs appeal the district court's denial of their motion for a new trial following a jury verdict in favor of the defendants, contending that the district court erred in excluding certain exhibits, well-known in asbestos litigation, as the "Sumner Simpson documents," on authenticity grounds. The district court declined to review the disputed documents and based its ruling of inadmissibility on a prior decision involving essentially the same documents rendered by another district judge in an unrelated case in the same district. Because we conclude that the district court erred in excluding the documents on the basis of authenticity, we will reverse the order of the district court and remand the case for a new trial.

On March 18, 1988, the widow and children of Walter Threadgill filed suit in the United States District Court for the District of Delaware against multiple defendants. The plaintiffs contended that as a result of the defendants' negligent failure to warn of health hazards associated with asbestos, and conspiracy to conceal those hazards, Walter Threadgill was exposed to asbestos, contracted mesothelioma, and died. Prior to trial, all of the defendants except the Manville Corporation Asbestos Disease Compensation Fund ("the Fund"), were dismissed on limitations grounds.

In anticipation of trial, the parties filed witness and exhibit lists. Among the documents listed by the plaintiffs were some of the approximately 6,000 so-called "Sumner Simpson documents." These documents, which have been considered with some frequency in the context of asbestos litigation, consist primarily of correspondence among a former president of Raybestos-Manhattan Sumner Simpson, Johns-Manville's former in-house counsel Vandiver Brown, and others. The documents, originally produced by Raybestos-Manhattan in the course of nation-wide asbestos litigation, have been offered by various plaintiffs in other asbestos-related actions in an attempt to show that as early as the 1930's, asbestos manufacturers knew of the health hazards associated with asbestos and knowingly concealed those dangers. While many courts considering these documents have admitted them, others, responding to various defense objections, have not. . . .

The history of the Sumner Simpson documents can be traced through a summary of the original deposition testimony of William Simpson, Sumner Simpson's son.

The William Simpson deposition establishes that Sumner Simpson was the president of Raybestos-Manhattan, Inc. from the 1930's until his death in the 1950's. William Simpson, who spent his career at Raybestos-Manhattan and also served as president, testified that he was personally aware of the fact that Sumner Simpson had stored personal files in the Raybestos-Manhattan vault. The vault, in which William Simpson had seen documents filed, was secured by a combination lock, with access prior to 1969 limited to Sumner Simpson, William Simpson, two secretaries and the security guards. William Simpson never received reports of theft or tampering.

In 1969, the box containing the papers at issue was moved to William Simpson's Bridgeport, Connecticut office where it remained secure in a closet until 1974. In 1974, the box was delivered to Raybestos-

Manhattan's Director of Environmental Affairs, John Marsh. At some point between 1974 and 1977, Marsh told Simpson that the papers were relevant to asbestos disease and, in 1977, the papers were transferred to lawyers for Raybestos-Manhattan pursuant to a document production request in a then pending lawsuit.

While the original documents remain in the possession of Raymark (the successor to Raybestos-Manhattan), copies were produced during discovery in this matter. The plaintiffs contend that the documents show that Johns-Manville had knowledge of health-related asbestos hazards and conspired with Raybestos-Manhattan to suppress information regarding these risks. Brief excerpts from these documents illustrate why the plaintiffs desire to have them admitted.

In a letter dated September 25, 1935, written on "Asbestos" magazine letterhead and signed "A.S. Rossiter," Rossiter wrote to Sumner Simpson at Raybestos-Manhattan asking whether Simpson would object to "Asbestos" printing an article on the company's dust control procedures. The letter included the following:

> You may recall that we have written you on several occasions concerning the publishing of information, or discussion of, asbestosis and the work which has been and is being done, to eliminate or at least reduce it.

> Always you have requested that for certain obvious reasons we publish nothing, and naturally your wishes have been respected.

A carbon copy of an October 1, 1935 letter from Bridgeport, Connecticut (Raybestos headquarters), to Vandiver Brown, general counsel for Johns-Manville, indicates that the Rossiter letter was enclosed. The copy, while unsigned, contains the word "President" beneath the signature line. The initials "SS-G" appear in the bottom left-hand corner of the copy. The letter, presumed to have been written or dictated by Sumner Simpson, and typed by Miss Garvey reads in part:

> As I see it personally, we would be just as well off to say nothing about it until our survey is complete. I think the less said about asbestosis, the better off we are, but at the same time, we cannot lose track of the fact that there have been a number of articles on asbestos dust control and asbestosis in the British trade magazines. The magazine "Asbestos" is in the business to publish articles affecting the trade and they have been very decent about not re-printing the English articles.

Vandiver Brown apparently received the Sumner Simpson letter as, on October 3, 1935, Brown wrote a letter to Simpson on Johns-Manville letterhead. This letter acknowledged receipt of the September 25th Rossiter letter and read as follows:

I quite agree with you that our interests are best served by having asbestosis receive the minimum of publicity. Even if we should eventually decide to raise no objection to the publication of an article on asbestosis in the magazine in question, I think we should warn the editors to use American data on the subject, rather than English. Dr. Lanza has frequently remarked, to me personally and in some of his papers, that the clinical picture presented in North American localities where there is an asbestos dust hazard is considerably milder than that reported in England and South Africa.

The plaintiffs contend that these documents indicate that certain asbestos manufacturers knew of the health hazards posed by asbestos and acted in concert to conceal those hazards. . . .

Our review of the district court's exclusion of the Sumner Simpson documents requires that we focus on the issue of authentication. Federal Rule of Evidence 901(a) provides that "[t]he requirement of authentication . . . as a condition precedent to admissibility is satisfied by evidence sufficient to support a finding that the matter in question is what its proponent claims." We have stated the standard to be applied in authenticating a document under Rule 901 as follows:

[The] showing of authenticity is not on a par with more technical evidentiary rules, such as hearsay exceptions governing admissibility. Rather, there need be only a prima facie showing, to the court, of authenticity, not a full argument on admissibility. Once a prima facie case is made, the evidence goes to the jury and it is the jury who will ultimately determine the authenticity of the evidence. The only requirement is that there has been substantial evidence from which they could infer that the document was authentic.

United States v. Goichman, 547 F.2d 778, 784 (3d Cir. 1976). Where the authenticity of the Summer Simpson documents has been challenged, the documents have most often been analyzed under Federal Rule of Evidence 901(b)(8), the ancient document provision. Under the ancient document provision, a document is admissible if it "(A) is in such condition as to create no suspicion concerning its authenticity, (B) was in a place where it, if authentic, would likely be, and (C) has been in existence 20 years or more at the time it is offered." Once a document qualifies as an ancient document, it is automatically excepted from the hearsay rule under Fed. R. Evid. 803(16).

While the ancient documents provision has not been a subject of frequent discussion in reported opinions, those cases which do address the provision establish that the point of a Rule 901(b)(8) inquiry is to determine whether the documents in question are, in fact, what they appear to be. "Although the rule requires that the document be free of suspicion, that suspicion does not go to the content of the document but rather to whether the document is what it purports to be. . . ."

United States v. Kairys, 782 F.2d 1374, 1379 (7th Cir.), cert. denied, 476 U.S. 1153, 106 S. Ct. 2258, 90 L. Ed. 2d 703 (1986). Questions as to the documents' content and completeness bear upon the weight to be accorded the evidence and do not affect the threshold question of authenticity. Id. The determination that a set of documents are, indeed, prima facie authentic in no way precludes counsel from challenging the content of the documents or from arguing that missing documents subject the contents to a different interpretation. . . .

Having reviewed the Sumner Simpson documents originally contained on the plaintiffs' exhibit list and the relevant portions of the original William Simpson deposition, we are convinced that on the basis of these materials alone, the plaintiffs have met their burden of establishing the prima facie authenticity of the documents. The Simpson deposition indicates to us that the manner of retaining the Sumner Simpson documents was consistent with what might have been expected.

> In view of this clear and unsuspicious history of custody . . . the papers are authentic under the standard of 901(b)(8). Defendants cannot put forward so much as a hint that these documents have been tampered with in any way. Nor in [our] perusal of the transcripts of the argument on similar motions in other asbestos litigation have [we] found any serious suggestion that the documents are fake or that they have been altered.

Parsons v. Celotex Corporation, C.A. No. CV 478-319, slip op. at 3 (S.D. Ga. Aug. 27, 1980). We conclude that the district court's exclusion of the Sumner Simpson documents . . . was not consistent with the sound exercise of judicial discretion and that the ultimate determination of the authenticity of these documents was a question for the jury.

We have concluded that the district court's . . . conclusions . . . [are] not consistent with a sound exercise of discretion and that the error was not harmless. Thus we will reverse the order of the district court and remand this matter for a new trial on the counts of negligence and conspiracy.

UNITED STATES v. STONE
604 F.2d 922 (5th Cir. 1979)

THORNBERRY, J. In this appeal from a conviction for possession of stolen mail we must decide whether the government violated the hearsay rule and the defendant's right of confrontation when the government used an affidavit instead of live testimony for the purpose of explaining how an official record demonstrated that the Treasury Department mailed a check that the defendant later had in his possession. . . .

I

Stone was convicted in a jury trial under 18 U.S.C. §1708 for possession of an item, in this case a United States Treasury check, stolen from the mails. . . .

To prove that the check was in the mail, the government presented as a witness Gwendolyn G. Howard, the payee of the check in question. Howard testified that she was employed by a Veterans Administration Hospital in Florida during 1975, and that she received her paycheck in the mail every two weeks at her residence. She identified a check dated June 30, 1975 as her payroll check for that period, and testified that she never received it. When she failed to receive her check in the mail on June 30, 1975, she obtained a duplicate check at the hospital. Her original check dated June 30, 1975, and numbered 69,137,606 was found to have been in Stone's possession, and was introduced into evidence.

The government also presented a progress sheet from the Treasury Department's Regional Disbursing Center in Austin, Texas, for the purpose of showing that the check had been placed in the mail. The sheet was an official disbursement form that was marked in part as follows: "payment date: 6-30-75," "object: salary," and "agency: va: composite-bulk-direct." The sheet specified that 99,625 "checks or bonds" were disbursed on that date in a total amount of $65,751,002.39. Checks or bonds numbered 69,108,660 to 69,205,121 were under the category "Direct." The sheet was marked to show the various stages of processing checks. In particular, the checks were marked "mailed or delivered" and "Date and time released: 6/27/75 4:00." The government authenticated this document by attaching an affidavit from staff assistant Alan Ford, the officer with legal custody and direct supervision of the progress sheets. Ford's affidavit identified his position in the first paragraph, then stated that

> I further certify that the attached document is a true copy of Treasury Department disbursing records related to check number 69,137,626, dated June 30, 1975, payable to Gwendolyn G. Howard, 2120 E University AV, NO 14, Gainesville, FL 32601, in the amount of $219.91, issued by G. Clark, Regional Disbursing Officer, over symbol 2205. It consists of a photographic copy of the Progress Sheet used to control the issuance and mailing of the check indicating that such check was individually inserted in an envelope and was mailed on June 27, 1975 with a group of other individually enclosed checks bearing the serial numbers 69,019,681 to 69,205,121.

Counsel for Stone made proper objections against the admission of the affidavit with these explanatory sentences. The judge overruled the objections, and allowed the full affidavit into evidence. Neither the government nor Stone called Ford to testify in person, although no evidence suggests he was unavailable for the trial. The hearsay and confrontation issues are the only points raised on appeal.

Stone does not challenge the admissibility of the progress sheet itself. This sheet was properly admitted under the hearsay exceptions in Fed. R. Evid. 803(6) for records of regularly conducted activity and Fed. R. Evid. 803(8) for public records and reports. The sheet was properly authenticated under Fed. R. Evid. 902(4) by Ford's attached affidavit.

Stone challenges the admission only of the extraneous explanatory statements in Ford's affidavit. To satisfy the requirements of Fed. R. Evid. 902(4), Ford's authenticating affidavit needed only to identify his position of authority and to state that the copy was correct. Ford's affidavit includes these items. Ford's affidavit goes on, however, to explain in detail that the progress sheet refers to Howard's particular check, and that the sheet shows that Howard's check was actually placed in the mail, although the sheet itself only states that certain numbered checks were "mailed or delivered." The admission of these statements without Ford's actual testimony prevented Stone from cross-examining Ford about his explanation of the form.

At oral argument counsel for the government displayed little concern for Stone's need to cross-examine Ford. Government counsel asserted that they typically use such ex parte affidavits to explain the meaning of office records in litigation. The government's frequent and flagrant use of this method for proving an essential element of a crime does not justify its impropriety. When an ex parte affidavit presents evidence beyond the simple authentication requirements of Fed. R. Evid. 902(4), the extraneous portions of the affidavit constitute inadmissible hearsay under Fed. R. Evid. 801. The government relied upon Whiteside v. United States, 346 F.2d 500 (8 Cir. 1965), cert. denied, 384 U.S. 1023 (1966), to show that an affidavit and progress sheet can be used to prove that a check was mailed under 18 U.S.C. §1708. In Whiteside, however, the regional disbursing officer actually appeared and testified in the case; the defendant's right to cross-examine the witness was preserved.

The government contends that Ford's statements in the affidavit should be admissible under the hearsay exception for public reports in Fed. R. Evid. 803(8)(A). . . . This hearsay exception is designed to allow admission of official records and reports prepared by an agency or government office for purposes independent of specific litigation. This exception for an agency's official records does not apply to Ford's personal statements prepared solely for purposes of this litigation. Ford's statements are likely to reflect the same lack of trustworthiness that prevents admission of litigation-oriented statements in cases such as Palmer v. Hoffman, 318 U.S. 109 (1943).

The trial judge erred in not striking out those portions of Ford's affidavit that exceed the simple authentication requirements of Fed. R. Evid. 902(4). This error does not require reversal of Stone's conviction, however, because under the circumstances of this case the hearsay violation was harmless. . . .

Stone contends that the admission of Ford's hearsay statement violates his sixth amendment right to confront the witness against him. Although a violation of the evidentiary hearsay rule does not establish that the constitutional right of confrontation has been denied, prevention of ex parte affidavits, like the extraneous statements in Ford's affidavit, is the primary purpose for the constitutional right of confrontation. California v. Green, 399 U.S. 149, 156-59 (1970). When the government introduced into evidence the explanatory statements in Ford's affidavit, and did not present Ford as a witness or show that he was unavailable, Stone's sixth amendment right of confrontation was denied. Although the government's method of presenting testimony cannot be justified, we find that, under the circumstances of this case, the error was harmless beyond a reasonable doubt, and that the conviction should be affirmed according to Chapman v. California, 386 U.S. 18 (1967). Howard's testimony that she always received her paychecks in the mail and the language on the progress sheet itself provide such overwhelming proof of mailing that the denial of Stone's confrontation right is harmless beyond a reasonable doubt. See Harrington v. California, 395 U.S. 250 (1969) (denial of confrontation rights constitutes error harmless beyond a reasonable doubt on record showing overwhelming evidence of guilt). . . .

We hold that the admission into evidence of explanatory statements on an authenticating affidavit constitutes inadmissible hearsay when the person making the statements is available, but does not testify at the trial. Because the defendant had no opportunity to cross-examine the person making the statement, admission of the explanatory statements also violates the defendant's sixth amendment right to confront the witnesses against him. The government's practice of using explanatory affidavits as a substitute for live testimony cannot be tolerated. We find in this case, however, that the admission of these statements was not a substantial influence upon the result, and was harmless beyond a reasonable doubt. For this reason, we affirm appellant's conviction in the court below.

Affirmed.

Could the admissibility of the progress sheet be attacked on confrontational grounds? Is Rule 902(4) constitutional when applied in criminal cases to authenticate an important item of inculpatory evidence?

Problem: The Unregistered Gun

D is charged with violating the National Firearms Act by possessing an unregistered firearm in violation of U.S.C.A. §5861(d). At trial, the government offers the testimony of *W*, a special agent of the Alcohol, Tobacco, and Firearms Division of the Internal Revenue Service. Through *W*, the government then seeks to introduce a document bearing a government seal and the signature of the assistant chief of the division's Operations-Coordination Section, stating that the assistant chief has custody of the National Firearms Registration and Transfer Record and that after a diligent search of said record she has found no evidence that the gun seized from *D* was registered. *D* objects on the grounds of Rules 901 to 902, the Sixth Amendment to the Constitution, and Rule 27 of the Federal Rules of Criminal Procedure.

What ruling and why?

Problem: "Reach Out, Reach Out and Touch Someone"

D was charged on two counts of violating 26 U.S.C. §7203 by failing to file timely income tax returns for the calendar years 1996 and 1997. At trial, an agent of the Internal Revenue Service was called to testify that in September of 1998 she obtained *D*'s telephone number from *D*'s husband and that pursuant to the agent's routine practice, she attempted to contact *D* by telephone. The agent further testified that when she called the telephone number given her by *D*'s husband, *D* stated that the income tax returns for 1996 and 1997 had been filed, which was false. This evidence was offered on the theory that a defendant's false, out-of-court, exculpatory statements may be taken as evidence of guilt. *D* objected to the introduction of this evidence on the grounds that the telephone conversation was not properly authenticated.

What ruling and why?

Problem: The Set-Up

D is charged with ten counts of possession of U.S. Treasury checks stolen from the mails in violation of 18 U.S.C. §1708. The prosecution's evidence indicates that postal inspector Wilson was approached by an informant who arranged a "check buy" from *D*. Wilson arranged to meet the informant and *D* at a restaurant. After preliminary discussions, *D* left briefly, returning with ten U.S. Treasury checks made out to various payees. Five of the checks had forged endorsements, and five were unendorsed. Wilson offered to pay *D* 25 percent of the face value of the checks. *D* accepted this offer. Wilson then left, presumably to obtain the cash, and government agents arrested *D*, feigning the arrest of Wilson and the informant.

At trial, *D* acknowledges that he sold Treasury checks to Wilson but claims that his arrest was a product of entrapment. He asserts that he had met the informant, "Jimmy," at the home of a friend and that Jimmy asked him if he "did checks" or "could get checks." *D* testifies that he told Jimmy that he was not interested but that Jimmy was not satisfied with this initial rebuff and continued to pursue him both by visiting and telephoning him on numerous occasions. *D* asserts that he obtained checks solely in order to pass them on to Jimmy and satisfy him. *D* also testifies that when Jimmy told him about the proposed check buy, *D* protested but finally agreed to go ahead with the deal only under duress.

D seeks to introduce the testimony of his co-defendant's mother that she received several telephone calls from someone named "Jimmy" who said that he was looking for *D*. The proposed witness was not acquainted with the informant and there was no evidence offered that she could recognize his voice at the time. Is the evidence admissible?

Would it make a difference if the witness testified that although she did not recognize Jimmy's voice at the time, after hearing the informant testify at trial she recognized the voice on the telephone as belonging to him?

Problem: Four Unknown, Named Narcotics Agents

P brought an action for damages pursuant to 42 U.S.C. §1983 alleging that the defendants, four New York City police officers, violated his civil rights by falsely arresting him, beating him, and failing to provide him with prompt and adequate medical care.

At trial, *P* testified that he had assisted several officers of the narcotics division of the New York City Police Department in investigating narcotics trafficking in Jamaica, Queens, and that he had applied to become a paid informer. On March 4, 1988, the date of the events in question, at approximately 10:00 P.M., *P* entered a vacant building in Jamaica, which he knew to be a drug "shooting gallery," in an effort to obtain information. While he was there, he observed two hypodermic needles abandoned on the floor and a person receiving a drug injection from the operator of the shooting gallery. Moments later, a contingent of police officers arrived, causing the other people at the scene to flee the premises. *P* testified that he was seized, arrested, and handcuffed, and then placed in an unmarked car with the four defendants. During the ride to the station house, he attempted to convince the officers that he was a police informant and that he had been on the premises attempting to collect information for the police. *P* further testified that if allowed to make a telephone call he could clear up the misunderstanding but that the defendants reacted by punching him in the face with their fists and a hand-held police radio until he lost consciousness, bleeding from his mouth, the left side of his face, and his left ear. At the precinct house he was booked on charges of burglary in the second degree, unlawful possession of a hypodermic needle, and resisting arrest.

P's second witness at trial was New York City Detective Wayne Carrington, who had worked with *P* prior to the incident. Carrington testified that he had asked *P* to gather information concerning drug trafficking in the city and that at the time of *P*'s arrest, he was processing *P*'s application to become a paid informer. Carrington also testified that when he learned of *P*'s arrest, he visited him in the detention center and that *P* told him that the defendants had beaten him after placing him under arrest. Carrington then testified that he contacted the assistant district attorney handling the case to ask if he could check the records to see exactly what the officers said compared to what *P* said. The following colloquy then took place:

Q: Now, after you spoke to the Assistant District Attorney, what did you do if anything next in regard to the case?
A: I attempted to contact the arresting officer.
Q: And how did you do that?
A: I called Mr. Meel.
Q: What happened when you made that phone call? What command are you talking about?
A: I believe it was the Street Crime Unit.
Q: When you called the Street Crime Unit, what happened?
A: I asked for the arresting officer, and he wasn't available, and whoever answered the phone said they'd put me in contact with his partner and I spoke to—
Defendants' counsel: Objection.
Q: Did you seek [*sic*] his partner?
A: I—
Court: Sustained.
Q: Did you seek [*sic*] his partner?
Court: Yes, or no. That is all.
Defendants' counsel: Objection.
Court: Just yes or no whether he spoke to him or not.
Q: Did you speak to his partner? Would you please answer that yes or no?
Defendants' counsel: Objection.
Court: I didn't hear that last part.

Plaintiff's counsel: He objected to what you said. I asked—I asked if he
    spoke to his partner, yes or no.
Court: He may answer it only yes or no. Period. Nothing else.
A: I don't know.
Q: Well did somebody take the phone call—the person—when they
    said they were going to put you in touch with his partner, did they
    transfer you to another officer?
A: Another officer got on the phone.
Q: Did that officer tell you he was his partner?
A: Yes, he did.
Q: And did you ask that officer if he was present on the night of the
    arrest of *P* at the scene?
A: Yes, I did.
Q: What did he say?
Defendants' counsel: Objection. May we approach the bench?

(Whereupon, the following discussion was held at the side bar:)

Defendants' counsel: Your honor, we contend that any of this—
Court: None of this is relevant.
Plaintiff's counsel: Your honor, can I say one thing? I can't say it?
Court: The only issue in this case is whether the policemen were there,
    had probable cause or reasonable cause to make the arrest and
    believed that a crime had been committed. That is it. That is where
    we are at, not what he thinks or what he said or what somebody
    told him.
Plaintiff's counsel: Can I say one thing, your honor? He stated his officer
    told him he was the partner of the arresting officer, and he was
    present at the arrest which makes him one of the defendants in
    this case.
Court: No it doesn't.
Defendants' counsel: No foundation.
Court: It does not help.
Plaintiff's counsel: That was my point. Then there is an admission. I am
    going to ask him about that. That was my point.
Court: Is he a defendant in this case?
Plaintiff's counsel: I beg your pardon?
Court: Is he a defendant in this case?
Plaintiff's counsel: I beg your pardon?
Court: Is he a defendant in this case?
Defendants' counsel: Who?
Plaintiff's counsel: Yes, that is my contention.
Defendants' counsel: There has been no foundation for the question.
Court: Yes.

Plaintiff's counsel: Respectfully except.
Court: Okay.

Defendants contend that the exclusion of the conversation was proper because *P* failed to satisfy the authentication or identification requirements of Rule 901(a). Was the trial judge's ruling correct?

Problem: "Joe Sent Me"

Charge: conspiracy to transport in interstate commerce obscene films and magazines concerning and involving children in violation of 18 U.S.C. §1465.

At the trial of *D,* former president of J-E, Inc., of California, *K,* the owner-operator of Kip's Discount, a West Virginia retail outlet dealing in sexually explicit matter, testified that in 1997 he had placed an order for kiddi-porn in a telephone conversation with "Joe" at J-E's place of business in California. Following the telephone conversation, the items of child pornography mentioned in the indictment, consisting of magazines and films, were shipped from J-E in California to Kip's Discount in West Virginia by Greyhound bus. Upon receipt, *K* turned them over to an agent of the FBI.

D contended that he could not be guilty of the charges because during the period in question he was not involved extensively enough in or with J-E's business operations to have been implicated in, or even aware of, those violations if they did in fact occur. *D* admitted incorporating J-E and being its president until 1996 but alleged that he resigned in that year to attend to other business and was succeeded by others who continued to manage and operate J-E.

D objected to permitting the witness to testify to the contents of the telephone conversations, arguing that since the witness had never met him, he could not identify him as the person with whom he had spoken at J-E. The witness testified that he had communicated by telephone with J-E on at least four occasions, always speaking with "Joe," concerning ordering, pricing, and shipping adult materials and kiddi-porn, some of those conversations having been initiated by him and some by J-E. The witness could not pinpoint the exact dates upon which he talked with "Joe" but identified and dated two of the J-E invoices forwarded to Kip's Discount, several of which corresponded to merchandise actually received by Kip's Discount and found to be child pornography. An FBI agent testified that during a search of J-E's premises shortly after these telephone calls, he saw a sign on the door of *D*'s office reading "Joe Espinoza." Are the telephone conversations admissible?

If the criminal action were against J-E, Inc., and *K* still could not identify the voice of "Joe," would the case for admission be stronger or weaker than in the criminal action against *D*?

Problem: The Case of the Nosy Neighbor

Charge: assault with a deadly weapon. Weapon: baseball bat. M.O.: aiming and swinging the baseball bat at Nosy Neighbor's head.

At *D*'s jury trial the prosecution calls Nosy Neighbor as its first witness. Neighbor testifies to certain background facts, that *D* came up behind him and swung a baseball bat at him, but that he managed to duck just in time to avoid disaster. At this point, the judge announces that it is time for the court's lunch recess. Upon reconvening at 2:30 P.M., the district attorney produces a 32-inch Louisville slugger, Roberto Clemente model baseball bat, has the clerk tag the bat for identification as People's Exhibit A, and tenders the bat in evidence as the weapon involved in the assault. Defendant objects. What ruling and why?

Problem: The Case of the Careless Cop

Section 909 of the penal code of state *S* provides that it is unlawful to possess in a motor vehicle any alcoholic beverage except those contained in bottles sealed with unbroken state tax stamps. On June 1, State Police Officer Obie stopped *D* for speeding. While writing out the ticket, Obie saw on the seat a half-full bottle of Old Redneck 100 proof sour-mash bourbon with fragments of a torn state tax stamp around the neck of the bottle. Obie confiscated the bottle, and shortly thereafter *D* was charged with violation of Section 909 of the Penal Code.

At *D*'s trial, Obie is the star witness. On direct examination, Obie testifies to the facts set forth above. The D.A. then produces a half-full bottle of Old Redneck, has the clerk tag the bottle as People's Exhibit A for identification, and asks Obie if he recognizes it. Obie says that he recognizes the bottle as the bottle confiscated from *D* on June 1. The D.A. then offers the bottle into evidence. Defense counsel asks the court for permission to take the witness on voir dire for the purpose of making an objection to the admission of the bottle. The court grants defense counsel's request. On voir dire counsel shows Obie three other identical half-full bottles of Old Redneck (which secretly contain iced tea) and asks Obie how he distinguishes between the offered exhibit and the three other bottles presented to him.

What mistake in police administration has Obie made? What principle of evidence relating to the handling of real evidence has Obie violated?

UNITED STATES v. MAHECHA-ONOFRE
936 F.2d 623 (1st Cir.), cert. denied, 112 S. Ct. 648 (1991)

BREYER, Chief Judge.

Luis Mahecha-Onofre appeals his conviction and 146 month prison sentence for unlawfully bringing cocaine into the United States. . . .

First, Mahecha says that the evidence was not sufficient to support the convictions, in particular the conviction for possessing cocaine with intent to distribute it to others. The evidence shows, however, that, on July 27, 1989, Mahecha was a passenger on Iberia Airlines flight 910, which stopped in Puerto Rico on its way from Bogota, Colombia, to Madrid, Spain. Customs officials, examining passenger luggage, found two odd (especially heavy and hard) suitcases that had a strong chemical odor and screws instead of rivets. They scratched the sides of the suitcases and performed a field test that indicated the suitcases themselves were made of cocaine. Later testing showed that the suitcases contained about 2.5 kilograms of cocaine bonded chemically with the acrylic suitcase material. Customs agent Carlos Ruiz testified that the suitcases had name tags with Mahecha's name and two baggage tags with numbers that matched claim checks on Mahecha's airline ticket. Mahecha admitted the suitcases were his, but he said he was a legitimate businessman, on his way to Spain to look for parts for machines which produce polyethylene and to establish a wholesale shawl distributing system. He added that he had bought the suitcases in April at a warehouse that sold stolen goods in Bogota.

This evidence, in our view, is more than sufficient to sustain a conviction. The jury might have disbelieved Mahecha's testimony. It might have thought it most unlikely that a legitimate businessman would set out for Spain knowing as few details about machines which produce polyethylene or the shawl industry as Mahecha's testimony suggests he knew. It might have questioned that Mahecha was on a business trip when the company he allegedly represented did not pay for his airline ticket or give him money (or a letter of credit or otherwise authorize him) to buy the equipment Mahecha said he thought was available in Spain. It might have thought it most unlikely that one could buy suitcases made of cocaine at a Bogota warehouse. It might have thought (to mention one detail) that Mahecha pasted old Eastern Airlines stickers all over the suitcases to make them look used and less suspicious since Mahecha testified that he had never in fact flown on Eastern Airlines. And, it might then have concluded that a person carrying suitcases with about 5 pounds of cocaine chemically bonded with the suitcase material was part of a professional drug smuggling operation. We cannot say that a reasonable juror could not reason in this way; or that such a juror must have a reasonable doubt about the conclusion. That being so, we must find the evidence sufficient.

Second, Mahecha says that the Government did not properly authenticate the suitcases that it introduced into evidence at his trial. That is to say, it did not show that the suitcases introduced at trial were both 1) the suitcases that customs officials seized at the airport and 2) the suitcases that Drug Enforcement Agency chemists in Miami found contained the cocaine. As the federal rules of evidence point out, however, the "authentication [requirement is] . . . satisfied by evidence sufficient to support a finding that the matter in question is what its proponent claims." Fed. R. Evid. 901(a). And, here the evidence was more than sufficient. The record shows that the two bags introduced into evidence at trial were black, made of a cocaine/acrylic mixture, were oddly shaped and unusually hard, had scratched upon them the initials of customs agents, that they had several blue scratches where they had been field tested for cocaine, that they had Eastern Airlines tags pasted on them, and that they had each had a baggage tag tied to the handle, one with the number 004501 and the other with the number 004502. A customs official, Carlos Ruiz, testified at trial that the bags that he seized at the airport matched this description, that he had scratched his initials on them, and that his testing them at the airport for cocaine involved scratching them and exposing them to a chemical that (in the presence of cocaine) turned them blue. The customs agent also noted that the suitcases contained unusual rivets, which were handmade. A DEA agent, Victor Ayala, also testified at trial that the suitcases admitted into evidence were the same ones which he took to the DEA laboratory in Miami. In addition, Mahecha testified at trial that the bags introduced into evidence were his. Finally, the chemist from the Miami laboratory identified the bags at trial as the ones he had tested. He said that he had placed a special laboratory seal on the bags he had tested and he identified that seal as the one placed on the bags. There is no evidence of any tampering with the suitcases from the time they left the airport until the time they arrived in the courtroom. Consequently, authentication was legally proper. . . .

MILLER v. PATE
386 U.S. 1 (1967)

Mr. Justice STEWART delivered the opinion of the Court.

On November 26, 1955, in Canton, Illinois, an eight-year-old girl died as the result of a brutal sexual attack. The petitioner was charged with her murder.

Prior to his trial in an Illinois court, his counsel filed a motion for an order permitting a scientific inspection of the physical evidence the prosecution intended to introduce. The motion was resisted by the prosecution and denied by the court. The jury trial ended in a verdict of guilty and a sentence of death. On appeal the judgment was affirmed by the Supreme Court of Illinois. On the basis of leads developed at a subsequent unsuccessful state clemency hearing, the petitioner applied to a federal district court for a writ of habeas corpus. After a hearing, the court granted the writ and ordered the petitioner's release or prompt retrial. The Court of Appeals reversed, and we granted certiorari to consider whether the trial that led to the petitioner's conviction was constitutionally valid. We have concluded that it was not.

There were no eyewitnesses to the brutal crime which the petitioner was charged with perpetrating. A vital component of the case against him was a pair of men's underwear shorts covered with large, dark, reddish-brown stains — People's Exhibit 3 in the trial record. These shorts had been found by a Canton policeman in a place known as the Van Buren Flats three days after the murder. The Van Buren Flats were about a mile from the scene of the crime. It was the prosecution's theory that the petitioner had been wearing these shorts when he committed the murder, and that he had afterwards removed and discarded them at the Van Buren Flats.

During the presentation of the prosecution's case, People's Exhibit 3 was variously described by witnesses in such terms as the "bloody shorts" and "a pair of jockey shorts stained with blood." Early in the trial the victim's mother testified that her daughter "had type 'A' positive blood." Evidence was later introduced to show that the petitioner's blood "was of group 'O.'"

Against this background the jury heard the testimony of a chemist for the State Bureau of Crime Identification. The prosecution established his qualifications as an expert, whose "duties include blood identification, grouping and typing both dry and fresh stains," and who had "made approximately one thousand blood typing analyses while at the State Bureau." His crucial testimony was as follows:

> I examined and tested "People's Exhibit 3" to determine the nature of the staining material upon it. The result of the first test was that this material upon the shorts is blood. I made a second examination which disclosed that the blood is of human origin. I made a further examination which disclosed that the blood is of group "A."

The petitioner, testifying in his own behalf, denied that he had ever owned or worn the shorts in evidence as People's Exhibit 3. He himself referred to the shorts as having "dried blood on them."

In argument to the jury the prosecutor made the most of People's Exhibit 3:

> Those shorts were found in the Van Buren Flats, with blood. What type blood? Not "O" blood as the defendant has, but "A" — type "A."

And later in his argument he said to the jury:

> And, if you will recall, it has never been contradicted the blood type of Janice May was blood type "A" positive. Blood type "A." Blood type "A" on these shorts. It wasn't "O" type as the defendant has. It is "A" type, what the little girl had.

Such was the state of the evidence with respect to People's Exhibit 3 as the case went to the jury. And such was the state of the record as the judgment of conviction was reviewed by the Supreme Court of Illinois. The "blood stained shorts" clearly played a vital part in the case for the prosecution. They were an important link in the chain of circumstantial evidence against the petitioner,[8] and, in the context of the revolting crime with which he was charged, their gruesomely emotional impact upon the jury was incalculable.[9]

So matters stood with respect to People's Exhibit 3, until the present habeas corpus proceeding in the Federal District Court.[10] In this proceeding the State was ordered to produce the stained shorts, and they were admitted in evidence. It was established that their appearance was the same as when they had been introduced at the trial as People's Exhibit 3. The petitioner was permitted to have the shorts examined by a chemical microanalyst. What the microanalyst found cast an extraordinary new light on People's Exhibit 3. The reddish-brown stains on the shorts were not blood, but paint.

The witness said that he had tested threads from each of the 10 reddish-brown stained areas on the shorts, and that he had found that all of them were encrusted with mineral pigments ". . . which one commonly uses in the preparation of paints." He found "no traces of human blood."[11] The State did not dispute this testimony, its counsel contenting himself with prevailing upon the witness to concede on cross-examination that he could not swear that there had never been any blood on the shorts.[12] . . . .

In argument at the close of the habeas corpus hearing, counsel for the State contended that "[e]verybody" at the trial had known that the

8. In affirming the petitioner's conviction, the Supreme Court of Illinois stated that "it was determined" that the shorts "were stained with human blood from group A," and referred to the petitioner's "bloody shorts." 13 Ill. 2d, at 89 and 106, 148 N.E.2d, at 458 and 467.

9. People's Exhibit 3 was forwarded here as part of the record, and we have accordingly had an opportunity to see it with our own eyes.

10. At the state clemency hearing, some additional evidence was adduced to show that the shorts had not belonged to the petitioner.

11. There were two other discolored areas on the shorts, one black and the other "a kind of yellowish color." A thread from the first of these areas contained material "similar to a particle of carbon." "[N]o particulates showed up" on the thread taken from the other.

12. The witness pointed out, however, that "blood substances are detectable over prolonged periods. That is, there are records of researches in which substances extracted from Egyptian mummies have been identified as blood."

shorts were stained with paint. That contention is totally belied by the record. The microanalyst correctly described the appearance of the shorts when he said, "I assumed I was dealing . . . with a pair of shorts which was heavily stained with blood. . . . [I]t would appear to a layman . . . that what I see before me is a garment heavily stained with blood." The record of the petitioner's trial reflects the prosecution's consistent and repeated misrepresentation that People's Exhibit 3 was, indeed, "a garment heavily stained with blood." The prosecution's whole theory with respect to the exhibit depended upon that misrepresentation. For the theory was that the victim's assailant had discarded the shorts *because* they were stained with blood. A pair of paint-stained shorts, found in an abandoned building a mile away from the scene of the crime, was virtually valueless as evidence against the petitioner.[15] The prosecution deliberately misrepresented the truth. . . .

The judgment of the Court of Appeals is reversed, and the case is remanded for further proceedings consistent with this opinion.

It is so ordered.

What does this case reveal about defense counsel's function when confronted with an item of "real" evidence? What opportunities and options do the Federal Rules provide in these situations? Who has the burden of raising an issue as to the authenticity of an item of real evidence? Who has the burden of proving that an exhibit is authentic?

Problem: Where the Rubber Meets the Road

You represent *P* in a consumer's action for damages arising out of an alleged breach of warranty on two new automobile tires purchased by your client from *D* Tire Company. The alleged defects are loose treads and bulges in the sidewalls of the tires. At trial, your first witness is *P*. Draft a short examination of *P* sufficient to establish your case-in-chief.

Problem: Live Exhibits

Action for support payments. The complaint alleges that *D* had sexual intercourse with *P* two years ago and that nine months later *P* gave birth to a boy, Snookins, of whom *D* is the father. *D* admits the intercourse but denies paternity.

During her preparation of the case *P*'s lawyer observes that Snookins bears a striking resemblance to *D* and decides that she would like the

---

15. The petitioner was not a painter but a taxi driver.

jury to see this with their own eyes. How can she do this? What kind of evidence is involved? If the case is appealed, how could the evidence be transferred to an appellate court for review? When should such evidence be admitted in paternity cases? What procedures should be followed? What instructions should be given?

Problem: The Case of the Spite Fence

Action for abatement of an alleged spite fence erected by *D* on his property, which abuts and faces *P*'s property. The complaint alleges that *D* has erected a spite fence as defined by Property Code §2022. Section 2022 defines a spite fence as any fence exceeding 15 feet in height or a fence of less than 15 feet that is constructed or decorated in a manner not conforming to prevailing standards.

The case is tried to a jury, and the crucial question is whether the fence erected by *D* is a spite fence within the meaning of the Code. On this issue, *P* testifies as to his ownership of his property and that *D* erected a fence on *D*'s adjoining property that faces *P*'s house. On *P*'s motion and on order of the court, the jury takes a view and observes the fence. In some spots the fence is 15 feet high, but in other spots it is less than 15 feet. However, along the entire length of the fence on the side facing *P*'s property are paintings that are repulsive by any standard. When court reconvenes, *P* rests.

D moves for a nonsuit. Should it be granted? On what rationale?

In many cases, the factfinder is taken to "view" scenes of accidents or crimes or relevant objects that are too large to be brought into the courtroom and offered as exhibits. Traditionally, views were not considered as evidence, but merely as a means to assist the jury to understand the evidence. At the time of taking the view, the jurors were instructed that they could not base their verdict on what they observed in the view. This seemingly curious rule was likely based on the fact that at least up until recently it was not possible accurately to preserve the view and make it a part of the record on appeal. If the jury was permitted to decide based on this view, there would be no way for a reviewing court to determine what they based their decision on. Although this view on views seems anomalous in this day of videotape and similar recording technology, it remains the rule in most, if not all, American jurisdictions.

The American rule on views is directly contrary to that prevailing in Europe, where proof by view is considered an important kind of evidence. The salient points observed are noted for the record at the time by the judge. The judge must also identify and describe anything in the view which is of importance in the decision.

Taking a view even under the American rules presents a number of potential problems. For example, must a court reporter be present at the view? Must the judge? Must counsel be present? What safeguards should be taken to ensure that only the right objects are viewed, that conditions are substantially the same at the time of the view as the time of the occurrence in issue, and that no hearsay or other unsworn evidence is obtained by the viewers at the scene? What if conditions have changed since the time of the incident? Must the accused in a criminal case be present at a view? May a view be taken beyond the jurisdiction of the trial court? Does a defendant in a criminal case have a constitutional or other right to demand that the jury take a view of the scene of the crime or other relevant place? If some members of the jury take an unauthorized view of the scene of the crime, what effect does it have on the defendant's rights?

Problem: The Spite Fence—A Reprise

Suppose that in the previous problem *P* testifies to ownership of his property and other background matters. Instead of having the jury take a view of the fence, however, on direct examination *P*'s counsel shows *P* a photograph marked Plaintiff's Exhibit A for identification. In response to counsel's questions, *P* states that he recognizes the photograph as a fair and accurate representation of *D*'s fence as it appears from the living room of *P*'s house. *P*'s counsel offers the photograph into evidence as Exhibit A. *D* moves to examine the witness on voir dire for the purpose of making an objection to this exhibit. The court allows the examination. On voir dire the following colloquy takes place:

Q: Did you take Exhibit A?
A: No.
Q: Do you know who did?
A: No.
Q: Well, did you develop or print it?
A: No.
Q: Do you know who did?
A: No.
Q: Have you ever seen this picture before?
A: No.

Defense counsel objects to the photograph on grounds of inadequate foundation. What result and why? What are the general conditions of admissibility of photographic evidence?

After offering the photograph, Plaintiff rests. Defendant moves for a nonsuit. What result? What is the status of a photograph introduced as an exhibit? Is it evidence in and of itself? Is everything it reveals evidence?

ADAMCZUK v. HOLLOWAY
338 Pa. 263, 13 A.2d 2 (1940)

MAXEY, J. Plaintiffs brought an action in trespass against defendants for personal injuries and property damage arising out of a collision between a car owned and operated by plaintiff, Jack J. Adamczuk, and a car owned by defendant, Morris Cohen, and driven by defendant, Elmer Holloway. . . .

The jury returned a verdict for defendants. Plaintiffs' motion for a new trial was refused and these appeals followed.

The assignment of error which appellant stresses is based upon the refusal of the court to admit in evidence a certain photograph of the locus of the accident and the approach to it on Highway Route 6.

When plaintiff, Jack Adamczuk, was on the stand, he was shown "Exhibit No. 3" and he identified the roads and buildings appearing in the picture and stated, in answer to his counsel, that "the conditions represented by that picture truly represent the conditions of the crossing at the time of this accident except for the fact of daylight or dark." Then the exhibit was offered in evidence. On cross-examination it was disclosed that the witness did not know who took the picture or when it was taken. He stated that when the picture was taken the location of the camera was on route 6 but he did not know at what distance from the intersection. He had no experience in photography. He said he did not know whether the photographer tilted the camera up or down when the picture was taken, and he did not know whether the photographer "endeavored to accentuate certain parts of the picture." The court then sustained the objection to the picture's introduction.

It was offered in evidence again when Herbert C. Dillard, Civil Engineer and County Surveyor, was on the stand. He was asked on cross-examination by defendant's counsel: "If you were taking a picture, and wanted to accentuate the curve of route six to the west, you could accomplish that by taking the picture farther away from the intersection, that is, farther to the east of the intersection, could you not?" He answered: "I think you could, yes." This witness was asked if he took photographs and developed them. He answered: "Very little."

At the close of plaintiff's case the picture was again offered in evidence and was objected to and the objection sustained, and court saying: "There is some mystery about exhibit number three, which is not clear to the court. There is no proof of who took it, or any identity as to the picture, other than the physical view thereon; it isn't shown where the camera was standing, under what conditions it was taken, and whether it was taken with a view to distorting it or not." The court then commented on the fact that plaintiff had two days "since adjournment last Friday, to procure the original taker of this photograph and thus establish it in the legal way with the right of cross-examination to defendants' counsel of the photographer."

The rule is well settled that a photograph may be put in evidence if relevant to the issue and if verified. It does not have to be verified by the taker. Its verification depends on the competency of the verifying witness and as to that the trial judge must in the first instance decide, subject to reversal for substantial error.

Wigmore on Evidence (2d ed.), Vol. 2, sec. 792, p.97, says:

> The objection that a photograph may be so made as to misrepresent the object is genuinely directed against its testimonial soundness; but it is of no validity. It is true that a photograph can be deliberately so taken as to convey the most false impression of the object. But so also can any witness lie in his words. A photograph can falsify just as much and no more than the human being who takes it or verifies it. The fallacy of the objection occurs in assuming that the photograph can come in testimonially without a competent person's oath to support it. If a qualified observer is found to say, "This photograph represents the fact as I saw it," there is no more reason to exclude it than if he had said, "The following words represent the fact as I saw it," which is always in effect the tenor of a witness's oath. If no witness has thus attached his credit to the photograph, then it should not come in at all, any more than an anonymous letter should be received as testimony.

Section 793:

> The map or photograph must first, to be admissible, be made a part of some qualified person's testimony. Someone must stand forth as its testimonial sponsor; in other words, it must be verified. There is nothing anomalous or exceptional in this requirement of verification; it is simply the exaction of those testimonial qualities which are required equally of all witnesses; the application merely takes a different form.

In other words, if a witness is familiar with the scene photographed and is competent to testify that the photograph correctly represents it, it should, if relevant, be admitted. . . .

What are the theoretical underpinnings of the pictorial testimony rule advocated by Wigmore (2d ed.), above, and followed by the court in this case? Is it broad enough to cover all cases where photographs should be admitted? Is it too broad?

Problem: The Case of the Hidden Camera

Action for alleged conversion of negotiable bearer bonds. M.O.: rifling *P*'s safe in the wall of her study by turning the combination lock.

At trial, *P* is the first witness. She testifies that during May she noticed that cash and jewels were apparently being pilfered from her safe. On June 1 she engaged a Pinkerton's detective to install a hidden camera in the wall of her study that would be triggered by the opening of the safe and that would clandestinely take a picture of whoever was opening the safe. *P* further testified that on June 1, when the camera was installed, 100,000 Big Mac bonds were safely ensconced in her safe and that she did not open the safe thereafter until June 15. *P* further testifies that on June 15 she noticed that the camera had been triggered. When she opened the safe, the bonds were missing. *P* removed the film from the camera and turned it over to Pinkerton's. The Pinkerton's detective was the next witness. She testified to her expertise and experience with the camera, the operation of the camera and the triggering mechanism, the development of the film, and the chain of custody of the film. The detective then identified a print of the photograph taken by the camera as Plaintiff's Exhibit A for identification. It is a photograph of *D*. *P* offered this exhibit into evidence.

Is Exhibit A admissible? Should it be? What basis of proof should suffice for admission of photographs generally when no witness can sponsor the photograph?

SISK v. STATE
232 Md. 155, 192 A.2d 108 (1963)

PRESCOTT, J. After conviction of, and sentence for, obtaining money by means of a false pretense under Code (1962 Cum. Supp.), Article 27, §140, James T. Sisk appeals.

The questions involved are whether a Regiscope photograph was properly admitted into evidence, and if not, was its admission prejudicial.

At the trial below, the State offered a Mr. William Sraver, chief investigator for the Protection Department of Montgomery Ward Company, Inc. (the Company). He stated that his "record" showed that a check was cashed in "our store" on August 1st, 1962, drawn by Talbott & Hanson, Inc., made payable to Charles A. Neubert, Jr., dated August 1st, drawn on the Maryland Trust Company, and signed by Frank G. Hanson and Anna P. Myers. The check was endorsed "Charles A. Neubert, Jr." It was not honored, but returned to the Company.

Sraver explained that when cash is requested for a check, the Company takes a picture with a Regiscope machine. These machines operate in the following manner. A number stamp places numbers in sequence on the checks. After a number is stamped on a check, a picture is taken of the check, the identification used by the person having the check cashed and the individual cashing the check, simultaneously. This is accomplished by means of a two-lens camera, located in the cashier's cage, which takes two pictures at one time, one straight down at the check and identification, and the other pointing out, taking a picture of the individual cashing the check. When five hundred films have been used or there is current need for a picture, whichever first occurs, the film is removed from the camera by Sraver, and sent by mail to the Regiscope Company in Fairfax, Virginia. Upon request, the films are developed and the pictures of individual transactions are sent to the Company. Sraver was not present when the photograph in the instant case was taken by a cashier, or when the film was developed by Regiscope. He, therefore, stated that he was not "in a position to say whether the picture [was] a correct likeness of what was in front of the camera" at the time the picture was taken. He also stated that he supposed it was "within the realm of possibility" that the same check could have been exposed with six different persons in front of the camera, from time to time, if the cashier had so desired. The appellant admitted to the police that the individual on the photograph was he, but he denied cashing the check. Without further authentication, the photograph of appellant, the check he allegedly cashed and the identification purportedly used by him was admitted over his objection. And this was all the evidence produced against him, except, as noted above, his admission to the police that he was the individual pictured on the exhibit.

Although the taking of a picture by the Regiscope operation is more complicated than the taking of an ordinary photograph, we see no reason why the admissibility of a picture taken by such an operation should not be governed by the same principles as those governing ordinary pictures. A photograph, like a map or diagram, is the witness' pictured expression of the data observed by him and therein communicated to the tribunal more accurately than by words says Professor Wigmore. 3 Wigmore, Evidence (3 Ed.) §792. Generally, a photograph's admissibility as evidence is left to the discretion of the trial court, but it is obvious, even if we take at full value appellant's admission that the individual was he, that the portion of the picture taken straight down had no testimonial sponsor. And the rule that the admissibility of photographs is ordinarily left to the discretion of the trial court does not come into play until there is competent extrinsic evidence showing the photograph to be a true representation of the scene or object which it purports to represent at the time when the appearance of such scene or object is relevant to the inquiry in connection with which the photograph is offered. . . . At no time was the exhibit shown by extrinsic evidence to be a fair representation of the scene that it purported to represent; hence it should not have been admitted. And there can be little doubt that its admission was prejudicial. As we pointed out above in our statement of the facts, it was the only evidence that connected him with the alleged offense. Of course, it may be possible for the State in the new trial ordered to authenticate it properly.

STATE v. TATUM
360 P.2d 754 (Wash. 1961)

DONWORTH, J. Ralph Tatum (hereinafter called appellant) was convicted of the crime of first degree forgery and was sentenced to life imprisonment as an habitual criminal.

The essential facts of the case are summarized as follows:

One William Tousin, of Pasco, received monthly welfare checks from the state of Washington. In February, 1960, Tousin did not receive his check (the checks were generally mailed to a rooming house in Pasco where Tousin resided). The mail was normally left on a window ledge in the hallway of the rooming house. Appellant resided at the same place. Tousin's February check for $28.90 was endorsed and cashed at Sherman's Food Store in Pasco by someone other than the payee, Tousin.

An employee of the store, Caroline Pentecost, testified that, although she could not specifically recall the above-mentioned transaction, the initials appearing on the face of the check were hers. She also testified that whenever a check was presented to her for payment at the store, the store manager had instructed her to initial it and then insert it into a "Regiscope" machine. This machine is designed to simultaneously photograph, through two separate lenses, both the check and the person facing the machine.

When it was discovered that the endorsement of the payee was a forgery, the Regiscope film of the transaction was sent to the Regiscope distributor in Portland to be developed. The processed film shows both the check and the person of appellant (from his waist up) with the food store in the background. Upon the trial, both the negative and the print therefrom were admitted in evidence, over appellant's objection. . . .

Were the Regiscope films (the negative and the print) authenticated sufficiently to warrant their admission into evidence? . . .

At the outset, with respect to the question of the admissibility of the Regiscope films, it should be noted that this court has for many years encouraged the admission and use of demonstrative evidence, including photographs. There is equally well-established precedent for the proposition that the admission or rejection of photographs as evidence lies within the sound discretion of the trial court. . . . We have also held that the trial court's discretion extends to the sufficiency of identification.

What quantum of authentication do courts require before a photograph may be admissible in evidence? It is simply this—that some witness (not necessarily the photographer) be able to give some indication as to when, where, and under what circumstances the photograph was taken, and that the photograph accurately portray the subject or subjects illustrated. The photograph need only be sufficiently accurate to be helpful to the court and the jury.

Witness Pentecost testified that she recognized the background shown in the picture as that of the food store, and, as mentioned previously, she also testified as to the store's standard procedure of "regiscoping" each individual who cashed a check at the store. Phillip Dale testified at length concerning the Regiscope process. The testimony of these two witnesses taken together amounted to a sufficient authentication to warrant the admission of the photograph (both the print and the negative) into evidence.

The authentication supplied by the testimony summarized above, of course, did not preclude appellant from attempting to prove that the individual portrayed was someone other than appellant, that the photograph was inaccurate in one or more respects, the appellant was somewhere else at the moment the photograph was taken, or any other such defense. But these arguments go to the weight rather than to the admissibility of the exhibits in question. In our opinion, the Regiscope exhibits, coupled with the other evidence produced by the state, sufficed to establish a prima facie case of first degree forgery. . . .

The judgment of the trial court is affirmed.

Do the *Sisk* and *Tatum* courts apply the same standards to the Regiscope pictures? Do they seem to proceed from the same theoretical basis respecting pictorial evidence? Do they apply the same rules regarding what foundation must be laid for introduction of this type of evidence? Can the cases be reconciled? With which case do you agree?

Do these cases suggest any shortcomings in the "pictorial testimony" theory advocated by Wigmore and followed by the *Adamczuk* court? Under this pictorial testimony theory, would X-rays be admissible? What about a chance picture of a crowd that on close examination shows the commission of a crime not seen by anyone at the time? Or a picture taken with a telescopic lens?

PEOPLE v. BOWLEY
59 Cal. 2d 855, 31 Cal. Rptr. 471, 382 P.2d 591 (1963)

PETERS, J. Defendant appeals from a judgment of conviction entered upon a jury verdict finding him guilty of a violation of Penal Code section 288a,[1] and of a prior felony conviction.

----

1. That section provides, in part: "Any person participating in an act of copulating the mouth of one person with the sexual organ of another is punishable by imprisonment in the state prison. . . ."

The only witness who testified for the prosecution[2] was a woman named Joan. She testified that in April of 1960 the defendant's brother employed her to play a part in a motion picture to be filmed in a San Francisco studio; that she went to the studio; that the picture was taken; that in making this picture . . . she voluntarily engaged in . . . [several sexual activities with the defendant].

A film purporting to show these activities was produced by the prosecution. Joan testified that she had seen portions of the film, and that those portions accurately represented what took place during the making of the film. Over objection, it was introduced into evidence and was shown to the jury. In response to the question: "Is that the film of the events in which you participated on this particular date at the Beaumont Studio," Joan said "yes." She also testified that the defendant was the male in the film whose face was covered with a coat of dark grease, whose hair was covered with a cloth turban, and with whom frequent acts in violation of Penal Code section 288a were shown.

Joan was, of course, an accomplice. As such her testimony must be corroborated.[3] This is a strict requirement, much stricter than found in many other states. It is based on the fear that an accomplice may be motivated to falsify his testimony in the hope of securing leniency for himself. . . .

Defendant's main contention is that the film may not be used to corroborate Joan's testimony because its admission into evidence rests solely upon her foundation testimony. Under these circumstances, it is argued, the film is not "other evidence" within the meaning of Penal Code section 1111.

According to Professor Wigmore, a photograph is no more than the nonverbal expression of the witness upon whose foundation testimony its authenticity rests. (3 Wigmore, Evidence (3d ed. 1940) §790, pp.174-175; ibid. §792, p.178; ibid. §793, p.186.) It is merely that witness' testimony in illustrated form; a "pictorial communication of a qualified witness who uses this method of communication instead of or in addition to some other method." (3 Wigmore, Evidence (3d ed. 1940) §793, p.186.) If this theory were accepted, it would necessarily follow that the film in this case does not fulfill the corroboration requirement. An accomplice cannot, of course, corroborate his own testimony.

Other authorities disagree. They urge that once a *proper foundation* has been established as to the accuracy and authenticity of a photo-

---

2. Defendant did not testify, nor did he offer any evidence in his defense.

3. Section 1111 of the Penal Code provides in part: "A conviction can not be had upon the testimony of an accomplice unless it be corroborated by such other evidence as shall tend to connect the defendant with the commission of the offense; and the corroboration is not sufficient if it merely shows the commission of the offense or the circumstances thereof."

graph, "it speaks with a certain probative force in itself." (Scott, Photographic Evidence (1942) §601, p.476.)

> [P]hotographs may, under proper safeguards, not only be used to illustrate testimony, but also as photographic or silent witnesses who speak for themselves. . . . [A] picture taken with adequate equipment under proper conditions by a skilled photographer is itself substantive evidence to be weighed by the jury. (Gardner, The Camera Goes to Court, (1946) 24 N.C.L. Rev. 233, 245). . . .

Until now, this court has not been called upon to state the theory upon which photographs are admitted into evidence. In doing so we recognize that photographs are useful for different purposes. When admitted merely to aid a witness in explaining his testimony they are, as Wigmore states, nothing more than the illustrated testimony of that witness. But they may also be used as probative evidence of what they depict. Used in this manner they take on the status of independent "silent" witnesses.

An example of a photograph which is probative in itself is found in People v. Doggett, 83 Cal. App. 2d 405, 188 P.2d 792, in which convictions of violating Penal Code section 288a were affirmed. The only evidence of the crime was a photograph showing the defendants committing an act of sexual perversion. This photograph was introduced into evidence although there was no testimony by any eyewitness that it accurately depicted what it purported to show. There was, however, other evidence of when, in point of time, the picture was taken, the place where it was taken and that the defendants were the persons shown in the picture. Furthermore, there was testimony by a photographic expert that the picture was not a composite and had not been faked but was a true representation of a "pure" negative. Upon this foundation, it was held that the photograph was admissible in evidence.

Since no eyewitness laid the foundation for the picture's admission into evidence in the Doggett case, the picture necessarily was allowed to be a silent witness; to "speak for itself." It was not illustrating the testimony of a witness. This seems to be a sound rule. Similarly, X-ray photographs are admitted into evidence although there is no one who can testify from direct observation inside the body that they accurately represent what they purport to show.[5]

There is no reason why a photograph or film, like an X-ray, may not,

---

5. Wigmore recognizes the apparent inconsistency between his pictorial testimony theory of photographs and the introduction of X-rays. He reasons, however, that once the instrument or process is known to be trustworthy, as is the case with X-rays, "it follows that a photograph of its images would always be receivable like any other photograph." (3 Wigmore, Evidence (3d ed. 1940) §795, p.190.) Other writers have not been convinced by this analysis, however, and refer to the admission of X-rays as an example of a photograph speaking for itself. (See Scott, Photographic Evidence (1942) §601, p.476; Gardner, The Camera Goes to Court (1946) 24 N.C.L. Rev. 233, 243-245.)

in a proper case, be probative in itself. To hold otherwise would illogi-
cally limit the use of a device whose memory is without question more
accurate and reliable than that of a human witness. It would exclude
from evidence the chance picture of a crowd which on close examination shows the commission of a crime that was not seen by the photographer at the time. It would exclude from evidence pictures taken with
a telescopic lens. It would exclude from evidence pictures taken by a
camera set to go off when a building's door is opened at night. We hold,
therefore, that a photograph may, in a proper case, be admitted into
evidence not merely as illustrated testimony of a human witness but as
probative evidence in itself of what it shows.

But because the film was properly admitted into evidence, and because that film, if properly authenticated is of itself evidence of what it
depicts, it does not follow that the film can corroborate the testimony
of the sole authenticating witness when she is an accomplice. To satisfy
the requirement of Penal Code section 1111,

> [T]he corroborative evidence . . . must be considered without the aid of the
> testimony which is to be corroborated and . . . it is not sufficient if it requires the
> interpretation and direction of such testimony in order to give it value.

In other words, the section requires evidence apart from that of the
accomplice which tends to instill trust in the inherently suspect testimony of the accomplice.[6] The film in the instant case can fulfill this
function only if it is assumed to be authentic. Since the film cannot
"speak for itself" as to its own authenticity, reliance must first be placed
in the veracity of Joan that it is accurate before it can supply any corroboration. This is the very reliance which section 1111 tells us cannot
be assumed but reason for which must be found elsewhere.

No photograph or film has any value in the absence of a proper
foundation. It is necessary to know when it was taken and that it is
accurate and truly represents what it purports to show. It becomes probative only upon the assumption that it is relevant and accurate. This
foundation is usually provided by the testimony of a person who was
present at the time the picture was taken, or who is otherwise qualified
to state that the representation is accurate. In addition, it may be pro-

---

6. If it were necessary for Joan to identify the male participant in the film as the defendant,
this test would not have been satisfied and no further discussion of the point would be necessary. But as already pointed out, the disguise was not effective. Comparing the height, weight,
build and visible facial features of the man portrayed in the film with those of the defendant,
the members of the jury could reasonably make the identification for themselves. In fact, the
record shows that the jury relied heavily upon their independent identification of the male in
the film. After deliberating for over two hours, the jury requested that the defendant stand
before them without his glasses. Following 45 minutes more deliberation, they requested a
second viewing of part of the film. It then required only eight minutes more to decide upon
a verdict of guilty.

vided by the aid of expert testimony, as in the *Doggett* case, although there is no one qualified to authenticate it from personal observation. When authenticated by a witness from personal observation its admission into evidence presumes confidence in that witness' veracity. Although Penal Code section 1111 does not bar the use of accomplice testimony for purposes of admitting the film into evidence, it does fix a stringent standard for purposes of the sufficiency of the evidence to sustain a conviction. Just as we do not question the competency of an accomplice to testify, we do not question his competency to lay the foundation for the admission of a photograph into evidence. But as Penal Code section 1111 prohibits conviction upon the testimony of an accomplice, so it also prohibits conviction upon evidence the foundation for which was supplied by an accomplice. For a photograph to qualify for admission into evidence the source of the authentication is immaterial. But section 1111 requires that to sustain a conviction the source of the authentication of the corroborating evidence must be independent of the accomplice. To hold otherwise would allow the prosecution to pull itself up by its own bootstraps.

It follows that although the film is sufficient corroboration if authenticated by a source independent of the accomplice, it cannot here be used to corroborate Joan's testimony. Since its value rests upon the testimony of the accomplice, it is not "other evidence" within the meaning of Penal Code section 1111. This result is compelled by the code section. The judgment must therefore be reversed.

The judgment is reversed.

Is the California court's approach to photographic evidence an improvement on Wigmore's pictorial testimony theory? Should a photograph be admitted as probative evidence in and of itself, even without a testimonial sponsor to vouch that the picture accurately depicts what she saw? What are the foundational requirements for photographic evidence under the Federal Rules?

Problem: Digital Doubts *

Charge: first-degree murder. Defendant: *D,* the assistant managing director of Tempura, Ltd., the owner and sole occupant of the Tempura Tower office building. M.O.: strangulation after luring *V* to a deserted conference room on the 37th floor of the Tempura Tower. Time of death: between 9:00 and 11:00 P.M., June 28. Defense: alibi. At trial, *D* offers a videotape cassette that *D* claims was tape recorded from 8 P.M.

---

* With thanks to Michael Crichton, Rising Sun (1992).

to midnight on June 28 by the hidden automatic security system camera trained on the 37th floor conference room. The police learned of the security system and videotapes at 2:00 P.M. on June 29 and by 5:00 P.M. had obtained a warrant and seized 12 videotapes from the security office, including the tape in question.

The videotape offered by *D* shows side and back glimpses of a person obviously not *D* entering the 37th floor conference room with *V* at 10:17 P.M. and leaving alone at 10:28 P.M. The prosecutor objects to introduction of the tape on grounds of authentication and reliability, particularly that it is "virtually impossible" to detect whether the videotape has been altered digitally by sophisticated optical digital equipment.

What ruling and why? What safeguards or foundational requirements should be required before such evidence is admitted? Returning to the problem Spite Fence—A Reprise above, would the foundation required for admission of the photograph be different if it appeared that the photograph had been taken with a digital camera?

B.   The "Best Evidence" Rule

One of the larger questions raised by the Anglo-American system of evidence is who should be responsible for selecting the evidence to be presented to the trier of fact. The range of possible answers to this question is very broad. At one end of the spectrum, the rules could dictate very rigidly that certain types of evidence will not be accepted in lieu of other types of available "superior" evidence. For example, in a dispute over a defective auto part, there could be rules of evidence that provide that, if available, the part must be produced and that photographs of the part or in-court witness testimony describing the part are inadmissible. One could justify such a system with the argument that (1) reliability is the primary concern of the factfinding process, (2) certain kinds of evidence (e.g., "real" evidence) are inherently more reliable than other kinds (e.g., testimonial evidence), and (3) the rules of evidence should specify evidentiary choices so as to promote reliability. If one accepted all three parts of this argument, it might be possible to construct a detailed typology of kinds of evidence, from the most to the least favored variety, to apply to all situations. If nothing else, such a catalogue would provide an easily accessible guide to the advocate planning a litigation strategy and to judges ruling on objections at trial. Indeed, Professor Dale Nance believes that the "best evidence principle" was the crucial organizing concept motivating the rationalistic common law judges during the formative era of Anglo-American jurisprudence. See Nance, The Best Evidence Principle, 73 Iowa L. Rev. 227 (1988).

At the other end of the spectrum would be a system in which there were no rules limiting the kinds of evidence the parties may present at trial. Under this approach, the decision to offer real evidence, documents, in-court witness testimony, views, photographs, affidavits, or what-have-you would be left to the parties. The justification for this approach would be that it is impossible to construct a typology of evidence along reliability lines that is valid for all situations and that it is preferable to permit the parties to select the evidence that they feel best proves their case. An obvious advantage of this "free market" approach is its greater flexibility. Another advantage is that the court need not decide whether in the particular case before it an item of evidence is the best available type of evidence according to the relevant ranking of evidence. On the other hand, if there is no control over the kind of proof offered, might not accuracy in factfinding suffer? Somewhat, perhaps, but probably not a great deal. To the extent that the most *reliable* evidence is also the most *persuasive,* applying the free market approach ordinarily should result in the use of the most reliable evidence. The tendency to utilize the best evidence is reinforced by the adversarial nature of our justice system. If the best available evidence is not offered, the opposing party is permitted to draw the attention of the jury or judge to the fact that a particular item of evidence has *not* been introduced and to suggest that this was done for strategic reasons. Nonetheless, there may still be situations in which a party deliberately chooses a less reliable and possibly unfair type of evidence. Judicial discretion to exclude in these circumstances would be a necessary component of the free market approach. Professor Edward Imwinkelried, in sharp contrast to Professor Nance, points out that a generalized "best evidence principle," applicable beyond proof of the contents of a writing, was rejected by the post-Gilbert common law evidence scholars such as William Evans, S.M. Phillips, and the great debunker, Jeremy Bentham, as not having any explanatory force at all. Imwinkelried, perhaps tongue-in-cheek, finds more force in a "worst evidence principle" that has as its objective the prevention of perjury, fraud, and deliberate falsehood in court. Imwinkelried, The Worst Evidence Principle: The Best Hypothesis as to the Logical Structure of Evidence Law, 46 U. Miami L. Rev. 1069 (1992).

Civil law systems are split on the issue. In some European countries there are statutory preferences for certain kinds of written evidence as well as rules for the relative weights to be afforded different kinds of written evidence and oral testimony. On the other hand, with few special exceptions, in systems based on the German civil law system there is "free evaluation of proof" by the judge, who is to give the evidence such weight as circumstance and experience would indicate.

What kind of system do we have? A look at the Federal Rules reveals a mixed approach. In the main, the free-market approach dominates. There are very few restrictions on what kinds of proof parties must offer.

By and large, parties are free to prove their case with whatever evidence they choose, so long as the foundational requirements are satisfied. On the other hand, as discussed in Chapter II, the categorical rules of exclusion found in Rules 404 to 412 can be seen as expressing preferences for certain kinds of proof as well as reflecting social policy. Also, the rule against hearsay and its exceptions, especially those of Rule 804, may be seen as incorporating a rule of preference for live, in-court testimony whenever the truth of an assertion is in issue. In addition, the lay-opinion rule (Rule 701) operates as a preference rule, forcing more specific testimony. But aside from these rules (usually justified on different grounds), with one major exception there are no master lists arranging evidence in hierarchical fashion from the "best" to the "next best" and down through the "worst," and no rules dictating that the best available evidence be offered.

The exception is the rule that requires that in certain cases the original of a document be produced and that other forms of proof of its contents, such as copies or witness testimony, be excluded. This is the so-called best evidence rule of Rules 1001 to 1008—"so-called" because its familiar appellation implies an application far broader than its terms. Examination of the rule reveals that it does not apply to all evidence but only to "writings" and similar things, such as photographs and recordings. Also, it applies only when the proponent is seeking to prove the "contents" of a writing.

The material in this section explores what "writing" means in this context (Rule 1001) and when the "contents" of a writing are being proved (Rule 1002). Next, the problems and cases examine the issue of what is an "original" for purposes of the rule (Rule 1001) and when a "duplicate" is admissible in lieu of the original (Rule 1003). Finally, the material addresses the acceptable excuses for not producing the original or a duplicate (Rule 1004) and the use of public records (Rule 1005), admissions (Rule 1007), and summaries (Rule 1006). In considering each of these issues, the problems also examine the respective roles of judge and jury in this particular area (Rule 1008).

The mechanics of complying with the requirements of this rule have been greatly simplified by the Federal Rules and by modern discovery and pretrial procedures. Yet the flow of cases under the Federal Rules indicates that many problems remain. Students should consider whether, on balance, the rule requiring the production of original documents is worth preserving as one corner of the system of evidence in which the "best evidence" is supposedly required.

Problem: Whiteacre

Action of ejectment to recover possession of Whiteacre. *P* claims to be the owner entitled to possession. *D* admits *P*'s possession but denies

P's ownership. At trial, *P* proposes to testify that *D* executed a deed by which he conveyed title in fee simple absolute to *P*. *D* objects on best evidence grounds.

What ruling and why? What is so special about writings that there exists a special rule of preference for them?

Problem: Sparkplugs

P, the owner and operator of a Piper Cub airplane, placed an order with *D*, the owner and operator of an airport service station, to fill the fuel tank of her plane with gas. *D* filled the tank, and *P* took off. After being airborne for a short time, *P*'s airplane experienced motor failure, requiring a crash landing. *P* sues *D* for property damage and personal injuries, alleging that *D* put automotive rather than aviation gas in the plane, causing the motor failure.

At trial, *P*'s first witness is an aeronautics expert who testifies that one can tell the type of gasoline used in an airplane by the appearance of the sparkplugs and describes the appearance of sparkplugs when automotive gas has been used. *P* then testifies that following the crash landing she removed the sparkplugs and kept them in her safe deposit box, where they now repose. *P*'s attorney asks her to describe the appearance of the plugs. *D* objects on grounds of the best evidence rule.

What ruling and why?

Problem: Accident Report Forms

(1) Action for personal injuries arising out of an automobile accident. *D* fills out an accident report form. At trial, *P* objects to *D*'s testifying to the details of the collision on the grounds that the accident report form exists and that *D* is testifying to the contents of a document in violation of Rule 1002. What ruling and why?

(2) On cross-examination, *D* is charged with recent fabrication. On redirect, *D* is asked what he said on the accident report form. *P* objects. What ruling and why?

UNITED STATES v. CARROLL
860 F.2d 500 (1st Cir. 1988)

Acosta, District Judge.

Richard A. Carroll ("appellant") appeals the District Court's denial of his motion for a new trial. He was convicted by a jury for violations of the Hobbs Act. 18 U.S.C. §1951. We affirm the judgment. . . .

The government charged that appellant, who was the Chairman of the Water Supply Board of the City of Providence, Rhode Island, and DiSanto, who was the Director of the Department of Public Works, demanded and received kickbacks from the owner of a plumbing company in return for a $79,000 contract to replace a boiler at the Board's offices. The contract was awarded in 1979 and the work was completed in 1980.

The star witness for the prosecution was Robert J. Riccitelli ("Riccitelli") the owner and operator of Elaine Plumbing and Heating Company, Inc. ("Elaine").

Riccitelli testified that he started to attend local political functions in order to improve his chances of obtaining government contracts. As part of this strategy, he purchased tickets to the Sixth Ward "Republican Italian Night" fund-raising function at Caruso's Restaurant in Providence. While there, DiSanto "caught [Riccitelli's] eye and asked [him] to come over to where he [DiSanto] was standing with Mr. Carroll." DiSanto asked Riccitelli whether or not he would be interested in a "large job" for the Water Supply Board, to which he replied affirmatively. While appellant silently stood at arms-length near the bar at Caruso's, DiSanto explained the kickback scheme, which Riccitelli described at trial as follows:

> Okay. At this point, Mr. DiSanto had told me that it was a large job, and if I wanted it I could have it, and with conditions that if I accepted, that there would be a kickback on the job. It was a 15 or 20 percent for the job, I forgot, to make me low, and 50 percent for any extras, that I would have to determine what they would be. He agreed to that, and then I accepted it.

In other words: the contractor had to pay a bribe to get the contract, fifteen percent (15%) of the contract amount if he *was* the low bidder, and twenty percent (20%) if appellant and DiSanto had *to make* him the low bidder; plus fifty percent (50%) of the charges for the so-called "extras," i.e., work not contemplated in the original contract. Riccitelli demanded and received the right to determine what the extras would be, and thereafter he accepted the arrangement.

Later, in a meeting at his city hall office, DiSanto told Riccitelli that a bid in the eighty to ninety thousand dollar range would probably get him the job.

During a conversation with either appellant or DiSanto, Riccitelli was told that the matter of a required performance bond, which he had been unable to obtain, "would be taken care of." The contract was signed and no bond was ever demanded although it was normally required on such contracts.

Some time thereafter, Riccitelli called appellant to ask about a "progress payment," i.e., partial payment for work already completed on the contract. Riccitelli requested about $30,000 in order to pay for labor and materials costs actually incurred, but appellant told him to request more so he (appellant) could get his bribe money. A few days later, appellant called Riccitelli to ask when he (Riccitelli) would deliver the kickback money to appellant. Riccitelli advised appellant it would be delivered in a few days. Shortly thereafter, Riccitelli received a $45,000 check from the city of Providence which he deposited in Elaine's checking account. Riccitelli then obtained $11,000 in cash and delivered the kickback money to appellant at his place of business, a jewelry store in Providence.

Riccitelli then made up an inflated bill for extra work and submitted the pertinent invoice to the City in the amount of $18,425. Later, Riccitelli called appellant requesting payment. Some time after that, the city paid Riccitelli in full even though the architect who had done the design work for the job reviewed the invoice and told appellant that he "was being ripped off" by the contractor. Soon after he had received the money for the extras, appellant called Riccitelli to ask when the fifty percent kickback would be paid. Riccitelli again replied that he would deliver the money in a few days. Several days later, Riccitelli delivered $9,212.00 in cash to appellant's store.

The kickback scheme was uncovered when Riccitelli was subpoenaed by a Grand Jury investigating corruption in the Providence City government. In 1984, he testified before a Grand Jury under a grant of "use immunity." Riccitelli's testimony at trial was also given under a grant of full immunity.

The mishandling of Elaine's funds, the doctoring of its financial records,[7] as well as Riccitelli's tax evasion conviction became important issues at appellant's trial for the following reasons: (1) Riccitelli's testimony about pay-offs to appellant was supported by introducing copies of several checks into evidence, and (2) the defense argued that Riccitelli made up the kickback scheme in order to cover up conversions of moneys from Elaine's account to his personal use.

Two of the checks, Exhibits 7 and 8, were prints of the microfilm records of the bank from which they were issued. There were two checks for $4,606.00 paid to "cash" for a total of $9,212.00. Riccitelli testified that these checks were used to generate the cash for appellant's kickback on the extras ($9,212.00 is approximately half of the $18,425 that the City paid for extras).

A bank custodian of records presented the prints and described them as true and accurate copies of records kept in the regular course of business, i.e., microfilm copies of all checks drawn from their customer's accounts. The checks were first admitted into evidence contingent upon their being properly identified by the person who wrote and cashed

---

7. It appears that the Riccitelli brothers and their brother-in-law used creative bookkeeping to evade taxes. Riccitelli allowed Martin to handle the financial records of Elaine in return for writing checks to himself when he needed money. Martin would often write checks signing Riccitelli's name, with the latter's approval.

them. When Riccitelli testified that he could not say whether the signature on the checks was written by him or by Martin (since either one of them signed Elaine checks using Riccitelli's name), the judge excluded the exhibits and instructed the jury as follows:

> ... [Exhibits] 7 and 8, you were shown those two checks earlier in the day. You're shaking your head[s in the affirmative]. . . . Those checks are stricken from this record. The exhibits, as exhibits, are stricken from the record. They have proven to have no relevancy, no nexus, no connection with the testimony in this case and play no part in the evidence that you are to consider at the conclusion of this trial. Do all understand me clearly? I don't even want those checks as being discussed at anytime, because they just simply are no part of this case and have nothing to do with this case. They're stricken from the record, is that clear? Okay.

However, after further testimony and argument on the matter, the trial judge ruled that the evidence was admissible under the Federal Rules of Evidence. He first found that the checks were what they purported to be, i.e., checks drawn on Elaine's bank account, and that the jury would decide the question of how the funds obtained through those checks were used. The judge then ruled that the checks were relevant and that their probative value was not substantially outweighed by the possibility of unfair prejudice to appellant. On the question of authentication of Exhibits 7 and 8, the judge ruled that testimony by Riccitelli as well as by a handwriting expert would meet the requirements of Rule 901(a).[9]

Appellant's counsel then joined DiSanto's attorney in moving for a mistrial because of the purportedly prejudicial effect of the admission-exclusion-admission of these exhibits. The trial judge took the motion under advisement.

Thereafter, Martin testified that he wrote the two checks, gave one to Riccitelli, cashed the other one and gave the money to Riccitelli; but he could not identify which of the two checks he had endorsed and cashed. The judge denied the motion for a mistrial and announced to the jury that he had reversed himself on the admissibility of these exhibits by stating:

> I want to advise you that earlier in this trial I told you to disregard two checks. I don't know the numbers. I think they're 13 — no, 7 and 8, I think were the numbers, am I correct, Gentlemen? Exhibits 7 and 8. Those checks are in evidence now, and are part of the evidence in the case, which together with all the evidence in the case you are to weigh in your deliberations. My rulings were based purely on legal principles and legal concepts, and when you make rulings on law, it's a developing thing as the trial goes on. The legal premise for admissibility or exclusion may change, may take on a different posture as the facts

9. . . . This evidence was apparently never presented.

develop or as the case develops, but it has no significance as far as you are concerned. You under no circumstances must ask yourselves, well why did that ruling change, or why did the Government rule in favor—or why did the Court rule in favor of the Government, or why did the Court rule in favor of the defendant. That's why I've told you so many times that I excuse you from the courtroom when we have legal arguments for fear that the legal arguments which we have, and which are in most instances freewheeling arguments, could possibly affect your thinking. But for those legal arguments that do take place in your presence, and those legal arguments as a result of which you have become aware of [sic], nevertheless, must be disregarded by you. They're of no significance at all and no invasion of your province, because of rulings of law that I make. Do you understand? It does not in any way emphasize that evidence, it does not in any way diminish that evidence. As far as you're concerned, it's the evidence, period, and you don't weigh what I did in deciding the significance of that evidence and the weight that you will give to that evidence when you commence your deliberations. Does anyone have any problems with that? No? Okay. . . .

Following this instruction, Riccitelli was again called to testify and he identified the two exhibits as the checks used to generate the fifty-percent kickback. On cross-examination he admitted that he could not tell who had endorsed and cashed the checks, but added that it must have been either him or Martin.

After further testimony, the case was given to the jury which, following three hours and forty minutes of deliberations, returned verdicts of guilty on both counts against appellant, and not guilty on both counts as to DiSanto. . . .

Appellant argues that the so-called "best evidence rule" requires that the original checks or at least the original microfilm should have been admitted because of the possibility of alteration by Riccitelli or his employees and, alternatively, that the checks were unfairly highlighted because of the roundabout way in which they were finally allowed into evidence. We disagree on both counts.

The originals[13] of these checks were returned to Elaine and were not available for use at trial.[14] Nonetheless, copies of the checks generated from microfilm records kept by the bank were produced.

"To prove the content of a writing . . . the original writing . . . . is required, except as otherwise provided in [the Federal Rules of Evidence]." Rule 1002, Fed. R. Evid. However, "[a] duplicate is admissible to the same extent as an original unless (1) a genuine question is raised as to the authenticity of the original or (2) in the circumstances it would

13. Rule 1001(3), Fed. R. Evid., defines "[a]n 'original' of a writing or recording [as] the writing or recording itself or any counterpart intended to have the same effect by a person executing or issuing it." Therefore, the originals of the checks used by Riccitelli and Martin to generate the cash amount of the bribe are the checks themselves.

14. Appellant's counsel tried to establish that they were unavailable because Riccitelli and Martin had destroyed records in order to protect themselves from the tax evasion charges.

be unfair to admit the duplicate in lieu of the original." Rule 1003, Fed. R. Evid.

The Federal Rules of Evidence define a "duplicate" as follows:

> A "duplicate" is a counterpart produced by the same impression as the original, or from the same matrix, or by means of photography, including enlargements and miniatures, or by mechanical or electronic re-recording, or by chemical reproduction, or by other equivalent techniques which accurately reproduces the original.

Rule 1001(4). Under the facts of this case, the microfilm copy of a check is a "duplicate" as defined by this rule.[15] Additionally, the fact that what was actually admitted into evidence was technically a duplicate of a duplicate, i.e., a print made from the microfilm does not affect our analysis. In a pre-rules case in which the evidence had been admitted pursuant to the Federal Business Records Act, 28 U.S.C. §1732, a Circuit Court held that "when satisfactorily identified[,] the microfilm and re-production therefrom become equally competent as the original check[,]" and their introduction into evidence did not violate the common law Best Evidence Rule. Williams v. United States, 404 F.2d 1372, 1373 (5th Cir. 1968), cert. denied, 394 U.S. 992, 89 S. Ct. 1482, 22 L. Ed. 2d 768 (1969). We think that this rule is the proper one under the new rules of evidence. Consequently, we hold that when a print of a microfilm copy of bank checks, kept by the bank in the regular course of business, is properly identified by a custodian of records as a complete and accurate reproduction thereof — as were the materials here when the bank custodian of records authenticated them — such prints are "duplicates" under the Federal Rules of Evidence and the microfilm itself need not be produced.

The remaining issue is whether these duplicates may be admitted in lieu of the missing original checks, which requires us to study the possibility of alteration of the original or of the unfairness of admitting the duplicates. We find that admission of these duplicates is not barred by either exception to Rule 1003.

While Martin acknowledged that he altered checks and check stubs *after* he received the cancelled checks from the bank, and the alteration of Elaine's financial records was fully explored before the judge and the jury, there is no evidence that there was any alteration *before* the checks got to the bank. Nor did appellant argue that there was any alteration

15. The Notes of the Advisory Committee on the Proposed Rules indicate that

a bank's microfilm record of checks cleared is the original as a record. However, a print [of the microfilm] offered as a copy of a check whose contents are in controversy is a duplicate. This result is substantially consistent with 28 U.S.C. §1732(b) [The Federal Business Records Act].

at the bank level. Thus, the authenticated print of the microfilm *provided by the bank* is just as good as the check itself under the facts of this case.[16]

The checks also pass the last hurdle of the Best Evidence Rule. In relevant part, Rule 1004 states:

> The original is not required, and other evidence of the contents of a writing, recording, or photograph is admissible if—
>
> (1) . . . [a]ll originals are lost or have been destroyed, unless the proponent lost or destroyed them in bad faith;

The record reflects that the originals were either lost or destroyed by Riccitelli or Martin, and there are strong suggestions that this was done in bad faith (i.e., in order to hamper the tax-evasion investigation). However, the proponent of the evidence, i.e., the government, had nothing to do with their disappearance and repeatedly requested the original checks through subpoenas duces tecum. Thus we find that admission of the legitimate duplicates of the checks was permissible because the originals were either lost or destroyed through no fault of the proponent.

We would also note that these microfilm prints are precisely what their proponent claims they are: authenticated copies of the checks actually used to obtain $9,212 in cash from Elaine's account with the bank. Thus, the microfilm would alternatively be admissible as the record of the cash transaction from Elaine's account with the bank. Whether or not the money was actually used to bribe appellant was a question of fact properly decided by the jury. The admissibility of the exhibits into evidence is a separate matter and the judge's ruling on it was appropriate.

Lastly, we do not find that the exhibits received unfair prominence because of the way in which they were admitted. During his opening instructions, the trial judge carefully advised the jury that he would decide all issues of law, including evidentiary problems. When the exhibits were removed from the record, he again told the jury that he had merely made a ruling on their admission and gave a curative instruction. Finally, when the items were re-admitted the judge gave a carefully worded instruction explaining the situation. Jurors are assumed to follow the instructions of the court, and we hold that in the context of this long trial the treatment of these exhibits was not unfairly prejudicial to appellant.

---

16. In fact, under the circumstances of this case, the bank's records would appear to be the most reliable source for the checks given the self-serving handling of Elaine's financial records by Riccitelli and Martin.

Problem: No Ticket, No Laundry

(1) *D* owns and operates a hand laundry. *P* brings seven shirts to the laundry for cleaning ("boxed, no starch"). *D* fills out a laundry slip and after negotiations with *P* marks on the slip, "Pick-up Tuesday the 12th," and gives the slip to *P*. Later, *P* sues *D* for breach of contract, alleging that the shirts were not ready until Friday the 15th. The first witness is *P*, who attempts to testify to the terms of the contract. *D* objects. What ruling and why?

(2) Suppose *D* used a laundry ticket book that contained a series of two identically numbered slips separated by carbon papers. *D* would write up the order and due date and give the carbon to the customer. If *P* offers the carbon and *D* objects, what ruling and why?

Problem: Barnyard Justice

Civil action for libel. The complaint alleges that *P* is a general surgeon and *D* is a photographer specializing in novelty photos. *D* refused to pay *P* for plastic surgery after the incision went awry when *P* sneezed. In addition, *D* threatened other retaliatory measures, and when *P* returned to his office in downtown Philadelphia one day, he was greeted by a huge photograph on a billboard depicting a barnyard scene that included *P*'s head attached to the body of a jackass. At trial, *P* is the first witness. He is asked to describe the photograph. *D* objects.

What ruling and why?

Problem: The Dangerous Druggist

Action against *D*, a druggist, for the alleged negligent filling of a prescription. At trial, *P*'s first witness is *W*, her family physician. *W* testifies that on January 1, in response to a call from *P*, she phoned *D* and prescribed for *P* a solution of paraldehyde, $C_6H_6O_3$, as a sedative and hangover relief. Unfortunately, *D* delivered a solution of formaldehyde, $HCHO$, a colorless compound used to manufacture fertilizers, dyes, embalming fluids, preservatives, and disinfectants. Formaldehyde is highly toxic to humans, and *P* was badly hurt when she gulped down half the bottle delivered by *D*.

In defense, *D* claims that *W* ordered formaldehyde. On cross-examination, *D* is asked whether he made a written record of the order. *D* replies that he did but that he threw it away. *P*'s counsel moves to strike *D*'s direct testimony.

What ruling and why?

Problem: Arson Interrogation

Charge: arson. At trial the prosecution calls the arresting officer, *A,* to testify that after *D* was read his *Miranda* rights at the station, *D* told *A* that he "knew they had him" and that he wanted to tell *A* the whole story. *A* stopped *D* only long enough to find a secretary to transcribe *D*'s statement. The prosecution then asks *A* to relate the essence of *D*'s statement.

D objects to *A*'s testimony on grounds that the transcript of *D*'s statement must be introduced as the "best evidence." What ruling and why? Does it make any difference if *D*'s statement is signed? Is your analysis the same (1) if a tape recording instead of a written transcription of *D*'s statement is available, or (2) if *D* never delivers his statement orally but transcribes it himself and asks *A* to read it?

MEYERS v. UNITED STATES
171 F.2d 800 (D.C. Cir.), cert. denied, 336 U.S. 912 (1949)

[In *Meyers,* an appeal from a perjury conviction, the Court of Appeals for the District of Columbia upheld the trial court's admission of a witness's testimony of his recollection of proceedings for which a written transcript was available, against a challenge that it was not the "best evidence." Judge Miller, writing for the court, noted that:]

As applied generally in federal courts, the [best evidence] rule is limited to cases where the contents of a writing are to be proved. Here there was no attempt to prove the contents of a writing; the issue was what [the defendant] had said, not what the transcript contained. The transcript made from shorthand notes of his testimony was, to be sure, evidence of what he had said, but it was not the only admissible evidence concerning it. [The witness's] testimony was equally competent, and was admissible whether given before or after the transcript was received in evidence. Statements alleged to be perjurious may be proved by any person who heard them, as well as by a reporter who recorded them in shorthand.

[Judge Prettyman delivered a lengthy dissent:]

The testimony given by Lamarre before the Senate Committee was presented to the jury upon the trial in so unfair and prejudicial a fashion as to constitute reversible error. . . .

When the trial began, the principal witness called by the Government . . . was asked by the United States Attorney, "Now, will you tell the Court and the jury in substance what the testimony was that the defendant Lamarre gave before the Committee concerning the Cadillac automobile?" . . .

The court at once called counsel to the bench and said to the prosecutor: "Of course, technically, you have the right to proceed the way you are doing. . . . I do not think that is hearsay under the hearsay rule, but it seems to me . . . that, after all, when you have a prosecution based on perjury, and you have a transcript of particular testimony on which the indictment is based, that you ought to lay a foundation for it or ought to put the transcript in evidence, instead of proving what the testimony was by someone who happens to be present, who has to depend on his memory as to what was said."

Counsel for the defense, objecting, insisted that the procedure was "preposterously unfair." The trial judge said that it seemed to him that the transcript ought to be made available to defense counsel. That was then done, but the prosecutor insisted upon proceeding as he had planned with the witness.

Mr. Rogers then testified: "I will try to give the substance of the testimony. . . . I am sure your Honor appreciates that I do not remember exactly the substance of the testimony. The substance of testimony was this. . . ."

The notable characteristics of this testimony of Rogers are important. In each instance, the "substance" was a short summation, about half a printed page in length. The witness did not purport to be absolute in his reproduction but merely recited his unrefreshed recollection, and his recollection on each of the three matters bears a striking resemblance to the succinct summations of the indictment. It is obvious that what the witness gave as "substance" was an essence of his own distillation and not an attempt to reproduce the whole of Lamarre's testimony. . . .

The difference between the presentation of elemental facts and the piecing of them together so as to reach a conclusion is basic. One is evidence and the other argument. The principle runs through much of the law of evidence.

I doubt that anyone would say that the prosecutor could first have put into evidence the transcript of Lamarre's testimony and thereafter have produced Rogers to give to the jury from the witness box his own summation of it. He would have been met with a ruling that "the transcript speaks for itself." Indeed, exactly that developed. The prosecutor first produced the oral summation, and it was admitted. Then he produced the transcript. Then, when defense counsel attempted to cross-examine as to "the substance," he was blocked because of the presence of the transcript. Can a prosecutor do by so simple and obvious a maneuver that which the law otherwise forbids as unfair? Can he thus transform into sworn evidence from the box that which is otherwise only argument from the rail? I do not think so. In the presence of the unimpeached transcript, even though it was temporarily on counsel table and not yet in the clerk's hands, summation and interpretation was argument and not evidence.

Nor was the prejudice cured by the availability of the transcript to defense counsel for cross-examination. If that were so in this case, the same doctrine would admit in evidence any opinion, or description, or summation of elemental facts otherwise provable in precise accuracy. The impression given by a succinct summation by a live witness on the stand cannot be corrected or offset by the later reading of a long, cold record. It is my view that for this exceedingly practical reason the reception of Rogers' summation in evidence was not permissible. . . .

The rationale of the so-called "best evidence rule" requires that a party having available evidence which is relatively certain may not submit evidence which is far less certain. The law is concerned with the true fact, and with that alone; its procedures are directed to that objective, and to that alone. It should permit no procedure the sole use of which is to obscure and confuse that which is otherwise plain and certain. . . .

To be sure, the writing may be attacked for forgery, alteration or some such circumstance. But absent such impeachment, the writing is immutable evidence from the date of the event, whereas human recollection is subject to many infirmities and human recitation is subject to the vices of prejudice and interest. Presented with that choice, the law accepts the certain and rejects the uncertain. The repeated statement in cases and elsewhere that the best evidence rule applies only to documents is a description of practice and not a pronouncement of principle. The principle is that as between human recollections the law makes no conclusive choice; it makes a conclusive choice only as between evidence which is certain and that which is uncertain. . . .

In my view, the court iterates an error when it says that the best evidence rule is limited to cases where the contents of a writing are to be proved. The purpose of offering in evidence a "written contract" is not to prove the contents of the writing. The writing is not the contract; it is merely evidence of the contract. The contract itself is the agreement between the parties. Statutes such as the statute of frauds do not provide that a contract be in writing; they provide that the contract be evidenced by a writing, or that a written memorandum of it be made. The writing is offered as evidence of an agreement, not for the purpose of proving its own contents. A deed to real estate is different, being actually the instrument of conveyance, although there is authority that it too is merely evidence of the agreement between the parties.

The doctrine that stenographic notes are not the best evidence of testimony was established when stenography was not an accurate science. . . .

But we have before us no such situation. Stenographic reporting has become highly developed, and official stenographic reports are relied upon in many of the most important affairs of life. Even as early as 1909, a court referred to "Experience having demonstrated the impartiality

and almost absolute accuracy of the notes of court stenographers" as
the reason for legislation making admissible as evidence a court stenographer's report. In the present instance, at least, no one has disputed
the correctness of the transcript.

From the theoretical point of view, the case poses this question: Given
both (1) an accurate stenographic transcription of a witness' testimony
during a two-day hearing and (2) the recollection of one of the
complainants as to the substance of that testimony, is the latter admissible as evidence in a trial of the witness for perjury? I think not. To say
that it is, is to apply a meaningless formula and ignore crystal-clear ac-
tualities. The transcript is, as a matter of simple, indisputable fact, the
best evidence. The principle and not the rote of the law ought to be
applied. . . .

Problem: The Tapes Case

D and others are charged under the federal gambling statute with
running a bookmaking operation that took bets on sporting events,
primarily over the telephone. The evidence used to secure the indictment was derived from court-ordered electronic surveillance of some
3,000 telephone calls. The statute requires, among other things, a volume of at least $2,000 per day. At the trial an FBI agent with consider-
able experience in telephone interceptions testifies as to the mechanics
of the wiretaps, the accuracy of the equipment, and the training of the
monitoring agents. The prosecution then offers the testimony of an
expert to the effect that the total daily dollar volume based on an analysis of the 3,000 calls was $899,855, with the lowest daily total being
$8,395. *D* objects on best evidence grounds, arguing that it is necessary
to play the tapes to the jury.

What ruling and why?

Problem: The Unlisted Number

Charge: knowingly transporting in interstate commerce a stolen vehicle in violation of 18 U.S.C. §2312. At trial, *D* concedes that the automobile was stolen at the time of interstate transport but denies that
he knew it was stolen. The government's first witness, *W*, an FBI agent,
testified that at the time of arrest, *D* told him that he had bought the
automobile from "Bill Holt" of "Bill Holt's Body Shop" on the west side
of Chicago. The agent also attempted to testify that he had checked the
Chicago telephone directory for the area and that there was no listing
for "Bill Holt," "Bill Holt's Body Shop," "Bill Holdt," "Bill Hult," or any
other reasonable spelling variation of those names. *D* objected to the
agent's testimony on grounds of Rule 1002. The court ruled that the

rule does not apply to testimony that books or records have been examined and found *not* to contain any reference to a designated matter. Is the court's ruling correct?

Recall the Unregistered Gun problem. Would a best evidence rule objection lie to oral testimony or the introduction of an affidavit that a search of the National Firearms Registration and Transfer Record did not reveal any registration of the defendant's firearm? How does the evidence in that problem differ from the evidence of no telephone number in this case?

UNITED STATES v. RATLIFF
623 F.2d 1293 (8th Cir.), cert. denied, 449 U.S. 876 (1980)

PER CURIAM. Malcolm Eugene Ratliff was convicted pursuant to a jury trial in the United States District Court for the Eastern District of Arkansas of five counts of an eight-count indictment. The jury convicted Ratliff of four counts of making false statements to a bank in violation of 18 U.S.C. §1014 (1976) and of one count of conspiracy to make false statements in violation of 18 U.S.C. §371 (1976). Ratliff misrepresented the collateral value and history of pre-World War II German corporate bonds in order to obtain bank loans. . . .

Ratliff challenges the admission into evidence of the expert testimony of a German banker and bond examiner, Mintken, with regard to the value of the bonds. Ratliff claims Mintken's testimony was hearsay, in violation of the best evidence rule and of Ratliff's constitutional right to compulsory process. The District Court fully considered this issue in its post-trial memorandum. The question presented was whether the unavailability of a master list of redeemable bonds,[7] compiled by the German government after the war, precluded Mintken's testimony of his valuation of the bonds supplied by Ratliff. The District Court admitted Mintken's testimony, finding:

"The primary factor in this Court's decision to admit Mr. Mintken's testimony despite the absence of the master list is the unique relation-

---

7. The bonds were issued and sold prior to the outbreak of World War II. These bonds were due and payable in 1950, but prior to World War II many of the bonds had been purchased by or on behalf of the issuer and held for conservation. During the war, the New York selling agent was precluded from cancelling the German obligations. The German authorities, however, repurchased a considerable amount of the bonds. These uncancelled bonds were stored, among others, in the Reichsbank until they would be redeemed by the issuing corporation. When Berlin was invaded at the end of the war, the Russians plundered the bank, resulting in the recirculation of the bonds. The German government set up an examining system to determine which bonds were valid and redeemable. Only a relative few of the bonds (29 with face value of $29,000) were valid and outstanding obligations as of the date of this trial. The bonds now are redeemable only in Germany. Proof of source, right to possession, and validity must be supplied by those seeking redemption. Mintken is the examiner for the issue of bonds involved in Ratliff's case.

ship of the list, Mr. Mintken's conclusions regarding potential validity, and the value of the bonds. The issue in the case is the value of the bonds—not their value in some abstract sense, but the value they have in a normal commercial context. It is the Court's perception that the value is determined by Mr. Mintken's conclusions as to underlying validity, not by investigation of the master list or other background records. . . .

"This perception leads the Court to conclude that the relevant inquiry concerning a bond's validity ends with a thorough investigation of Mr. Mintken's conclusion and the processes behind it, which may be accomplished by his cross-examination without production of the master list. In this case, . . . the witness who testified to his conclusions was vigorously cross-examined about the background and process behind his conclusions, as well as about the reliability and accuracy of the master list and other records. His testimony regarding background was relevant to the weight and credibility assigned by the jury to his testimony regarding his conclusions, but it did not undermine the admissibility of that testimony. . . ."

We agree with the District Court that Mintken's testimony was not a mere reiteration that Ratliff's bonds were not included on the master list as being valid and outstanding. To the extent that Mintken did testify to the bonds' status on the list, the testimony was admissible under the "catch-all" exception to the hearsay rule. See Fed. R. Evid. 803(24); United States v. Friedman, 593 F.2d 109, 118-19 (9th Cir. 1979). Mintken was subjected to extensive cross-examination, thus satisfying Ratliff's constitutional right of cross-examination.

Ratliff also contends that the District Court erred in not striking Mintken's testimony on the basis that it violated the best evidence rule. See Fed. R. Evid. 1002. Since Mintken did not attempt to "prove the content of a writing [the master list]" the rule does not apply herein. In addition, the District Court found the list to be "unavailable" and "not amenable to court processes in this country."[8] The best evidence rule does not apply to the list under these conditions. See Fed. R. Evid. 1004(2).

Affirmed.

Problem: The Electronic Scrivener

Action for breach of contract, the terms of which are allegedly contained in an e-mail from buyer *D* to seller *P*. *D* refused to go through

---

8. On appeal, Ratliff does not challenge this factual finding. He does claim that the court erred in not ruling on whether the list was privileged. Whether the master list was privileged or not is but one possible reason for its unavailability. Ratliff has not demonstrated that it is the only reason. The court, in fact, believed that it had no subpoena power over the documents in Germany. In the absence of such a demonstration, we cannot find the court's finding to be clearly erroneous.

with the deal when a dispute arose over the price and number of units ordered.

At trial, *P* offers as Plaintiff's Exhibit 1 a copy of the e-mail printed from plaintiff's computer. *D* disputes the accuracy of the e-mail and objects to the introduction of the copy under Rule 1003.

Is the printout admissible? Would it make a difference if the copy were printed by the computer or printed by a photocopy machine from a printout? Who decides, judge or jury? In what situations would it be "unfair to admit the duplicate in lieu of the original"?

Problem: The Guarantor

(1) Action for breach of contract. *P* Bank contends that the alleged contract was contained in a typewritten letter from *D* to the bank authorizing the bank to pay checks to *X*, which *D* would cover. *D* admits sending the letter but disputes the terms.

At trial, the bank's attorney calls *C*, the head cashier, to testify that he received the letter, read it, and filed it but that a new file clerk, *S*, mistakenly threw out the file during a regular purge of old files. *C* is asked what the letter said. *D* objects. What ruling and why?

(2) As part of his rebuttal case, *D* attempts to testify to the terms of the letter. *P* objects. On voir dire it is disclosed that *D* made a longhand copy of the letter before he sent it and that this copy is in his office in Chicago. *D* testifies that he did not bring it with him to the trial because he thought that *P* would bring its original. What ruling and why?

Problem: The Cocaine Connection

Charge: conspiracy to distribute a controlled substance, to wit, cocaine. At *D*'s trial, the government calls *W*, an FBI agent, to testify to the contents of a piece of paper with a telephone number on it found in *D*'s possession at the time of arrest. The agent testified that she had lost the paper and had no independent recollection of the telephone number but that she had accurately transcribed the number onto a telephone company form at the time of arrest. The court overruled *D*'s objection on grounds of hearsay, citing Rule 803(5) (recorded recollection).

Does *D* have other grounds to object to *W*'s testimony? How do Rule 803(5) and the rules governing the admissibility of writings relate?

UNITED STATES v. MARCANTONI
590 F.2d 1324 (5th Cir.), cert. denied, 441 U.S. 937 (1979)

TJOFLAT, J. [Defendant was charged with armed bank robbery.] . . . On Friday, August 6, 1976, at approximately 9:10 A.M., a white male, standing 5′9″-5′10″, weighing 170-180 pounds, and wearing a motorcycle helmet with tinted brown sun visor, entered the Tampa Federal Savings & Loan Association (the Bank), Tampa, Florida, and went to the only teller window open at that time. The teller, Tina Brown, looked up into the barrel of a shotgun, screamed and ducked to the floor. The head teller, Debra Beckerink, realizing the situation, walked to Ms. Brown's window and began pulling bills of small denominations out of the money drawer and placing them in a bag. The gunman nervously commanded Beckerink to "give [him] the big bills." She complied, supplying him in the process with $3,791.00, including ten $10 bills of bait money.[2] The gunman then ran out of the Bank, firing a shot at the sidewalk as he left, and jumped into the back seat of a waiting getaway car being driven by a white, blond-haired female. The getaway car and its occupants were observed by various witnesses. When the Tampa police arrived on the scene moments later, the witnesses gave the officers a description of the vehicle, a 1966 light green Rambler station wagon with luggage racks on the top, and its Florida license tag number. A search of the Florida vehicle registration records disclosed that the tag had been issued to Helen Suzanne Tune Marcantoni for a 1966 Rambler station wagon. . . .

The following Monday morning, August 9, 1976, Charlie Marcantoni consented to and assisted in a search of his Rogers Avenue residence by the Tampa police. During the search, Detective Edward Brodesser examined several hundred dollars in currency and recorded the serial numbers from the faces of the $10 bills he found, but he did not seize the bills. . . .

On August 13, 1976, Detective Brodesser returned to the Marcantoni residence on Rogers Avenue with a search warrant authorizing the seizure of any of the bait money that might be there. Following his August 9 search of the residence Brodesser had learned that the serial numbers he had recorded from two of the $10 bills he had uncovered during the search matched the serial numbers of two $10 bills on the Bank's list of the bait money taken in the robbery. Brodesser was unable to find these bills on August 13, however, when he returned with the search warrant. Six days later the Marcantonis were indicted. . . .

---

2. Bait money was kept in each teller's money drawer. When the bait money in question was removed, a silent alarm to the Tampa Police Department activated. The denominations, serial numbers, series years, and the bank of issue of each bait money bill had been recorded by the Bank.

The argument advanced by the Marcantonis in the court below and on appeal in support of their objection to Detective Brodesser's testimony concerning the two $10 bills has been articulated inartfully at best. Giving the Marcantonis the benefit of every doubt, we read their argument as posing alternative objections to admissibility: (1) Detective Brodesser's testimony was irrelevant because it lacked probative value; (2) his testimony violated the best evidence policy embraced by Fed. R. Evid. 1004.

When Brodesser copied the serial numbers of the two $10 bills, he neglected to record all of the essential identifying data printed on the face of each of the bills—he omitted the series year. Knowledge of the series year was necessary, according to the Government's expert from the Bureau of Printing and Engraving, William Holland, to resolve any possible doubt whether the two bills Brodesser saw were bait money. Holland explained that each of the serial numbers Brodesser copied from the bills had been used by the Bureau on $10 bills in three separate series or years: series 1934A, 1950A, and 1969C. The $10 bills used as bait money were of the 1969C series.

The Marcantonis first objected to Brodesser's testimony about the serial numbers he had seen on the ground that the testimony would prove absolutely nothing; without the series year, they claimed, the jury could not find that either of the $10 bills found at their residence actually came from the Bank. The Government's response to this attack lies in the balance of Holland's testimony, considered in the unique circumstances of this case. Holland explained that the average life of a $10 bill is three and one-half years; thus there is very little chance that any of the series 1934A or 1950A bills were in circulation at the time of the robbery. He further pointed out that series 1934A bills are so rare that they are worth four to five times their face value and are collectors' items, making it extremely unlikely that any of those bills were still in active circulation in 1976. And chances are not much better that any of the series 1950A bills were then in circulation either. Holland's opinion was, therefore, that the two $10 bills Detective Brodesser uncovered were of the 1969C series and part of the Bank's bait money. He reinforced his opinion by observing that the odds are "extremely remote" that a $10 bill from the 1934A or 1950A series with the same serial number as one of the bait bills could have found its way to the Tampa Bay area at the same time as the bait bills; the odds were "hundreds of times greater" that two sets of such bills could have been in the Tampa Bay vicinity at once. Given Holland's opinion and the independent evidence establishing that Charlie Marcantoni left the Bank with bait money of the same serial numbers and denominations as those found in his home a short time later, the trial judge properly concluded that Brodesser's testimony concerning the serial numbers had probative value.

The Marcantonis' alternative objection to the reception of Brodesser's testimony is that rule 1004 required the Government to introduce the two bills in evidence. Brodesser's testimony, they argue, was secondary evidence of the contents of the bills and not admissible because the Government failed to establish any of the conditions to the admissibility of secondary evidence specified by Fed. R. Evid. 1004. . . .

The Government made no formal attempt to qualify Brodesser's recital of the incriminating serial numbers as secondary evidence admissible under the rule. First, as the Government concedes, it did not undertake to show that the two bills were lost or destroyed. Second, it was not established that the Marcantonis were served notice that the contents of the bills would be a subject of proof at trial, and no process was directed to them to produce the bills in court. Finally, the Government did not, and in our opinion could not, contend that the evidence was "not closely related to a controlling issue."

There was little if anything in the argument of counsel that even addressed the qualifications of rule 1004 or, much less, whether they had been met in this instance. In overruling the Marcantonis' objection, the trial judge, quite understandably we think, gave no reasons for his decision. Consequently, we cannot determine whether the court treated Brodesser's statements about the serial numbers as secondary evidence,[4] and, if so, which of the conditions to admissibility prescribed by the rule it found to be fulfilled.

If, in truth, the court considered Brodesser's testimony to be secondary evidence, we must assume that the court was satisfied that at least one of those conditions had been established. It should have been obvious after Detective Brodesser's return to the Marcantoni residence with a search warrant failed to produce the two $10 bills in question that the bills would not be available to the prosecution for trial. We have no difficulty in concluding that, under the circumstances of this case, the trial judge would have been authorized to find, under section (1) of the rule, that the two bills were "lost or [had] been destroyed." Surely, the Marcantonis could not have contended that the unavailability of the bills was the product of Government "bad faith." The trial judge could also have found, under section (2) of the rule, that "[n]o original [could] be obtained by any available judicial process or procedure." Even assuming that the Marcantonis were amenable to a subpoena directing the production of the bills at trial,[5] we think it unrealistic to expect that they would have readily produced the two instruments that

---

4. It is conceivable that the court viewed Brodesser's statements as present recollection refreshed or as past recollection recorded. Fed. R. Evid. 803(5).

5. We think it fairly debatable whether the Marcantonis could have been compelled, in the face of the fifth amendment privilege against self-incrimination, to produce the two $10 bills for use by the prosecution at trial. See generally Bellis v. United States, 417 U.S. 85 (1974); United States v. Hankins, 565 F.2d 1344 (5th Cir. 1978).

would have made the Government's case against them complete. In short, the Government was not required to go through the motion of having a subpoena issued, served and returned unexecuted in order to establish, under section (2), that the bills were unobtainable.

As for section (3) of the rule, a legitimate argument can be made on this record that the Marcantonis were "put on notice" that the serial numbers of the two $10 bills "would be a subject of proof" at the trial, and that, having not produced them at trial, the Marcantonis could not object to the use of Brodesser's notes. In sum, although the trial judge, in overruling the Marcantonis' best evidence objection, should have announced the predicate to admissibility he found to have been established under rule 1004, his decision to receive the evidence was correct.[6]

Problem: Burning Romeo

Action for libel. *P* testifies that on the day before his wedding his fiancee showed him the allegedly libelous letter written to her by *D* but that the letter is now unavailable because *P* burned it. *P*'s counsel asks him to testify to the contents of the letter. *D* objects.

What ruling and why?

This problem was inspired by the nineteenth century antics of "The Count Joannes," born "George Jones" in 1810. In the course of his career, Joannes instituted at least 16 libel suits, gained a conviction for barratry in Boston and admission to the Bar in New York, and played

---

6. An argument can be advanced that the admissibility of Detective Brodesser's statements about the serial numbers is not controlled by rule 1004. Although these statements have all the indicia of mere secondary evidence, it might be said that they constitute something more; Brodesser was testifying about what he had observed first hand during the course of his search of the Marcantoni residence. Whether he was testifying from present recollection refreshed or past recollection recorded, see Fed. R. Evid. 803(5), however, cannot be determined with certainty from the record. In questioning Brodesser about the serial numbers on direct examination, the prosecutor did not undertake to establish, as a preliminary matter, whether the witness was actually able to remember the precise serial numbers he had noted on the two $10 bills in issue; instead, he went straight to the heart of the matter, simply asking Brodesser to repeat the serial numbers he had seen and recorded. The likelihood is, of course, that even with the benefit of his notes, Brodesser could not recall the precise serial numbers and that his testimony was strictly a recital of what he had recorded.

We think it not far fetched to say that Brodesser's notes constituted, in the language of rule 803(5), "[a] memorandum or record concerning a matter about which a witness once had knowledge but now has insufficient recollection to enable him to testify fully and accurately, shown to have been made . . . by the witness when the matter was fresh in his memory and to reflect that knowledge correctly." We should point out, however, that if Rule 803(5) is considered the sole basis of admissibility, the notes themselves, as distinguished from a recital thereof, should not have been received as an evidentiary exhibit in the Government's case-in-chief. As the rule states, "[i]f admitted, the memorandum or record may be read into evidence but may not itself be received as an exhibit unless offered by an adverse party."

the role of Romeo a number of times, both on and off stage. The Count, who believed that his power of speech gained him in "one hour with a lady ... [what took] three months with mere clods of humanity," brought his first libel suit pro se (Joannes v. Bennett, 87 Mass. (5 Allen) 169 (1862)):

> [The Count] was apparently paying court to an eligible widow of the city. She was living with her parents, and both she and they were active in the church, she singing soprano in the church choir. Her name remains unknown, but her minister's name was Bennett. Apparently having no high opinion of the Count's qualifications as a son-in-law, her parents appealed to this minister for help and, concurring in their view, the latter undertook to write the lady in question attempting to dissuade her from the match. She promptly turned the letter over to her suitor, who just as promptly sued the Rev. Mr. Bennett for libel, the first gun in a salvo of litigation that was to continue for a dozen years or more.
>
> The Count appeared as his own counsel, although there is no indication that he had ever been admitted to the Massachusetts Bar. His case was considerably weakened by the fact that he had destroyed the letter and was unable to produce it in court. His damages were also considerably mitigated due to the circumstance that despite the remonstrance of her parents and the Rev. Bennett, he subsequently married the lady. A more serious obstacle than even their disapproval, however, would appear to be the continued existence of Mrs. Melinda Jones, still legally his wife; but fortunately this was known neither to the lady, her parents, the court, nor the Rev. Bennett, but only to the Count, who chose not to reveal it, and Melinda, who was not present. In any event, the jury returned a verdict in his favor for $2,000.00.
>
> On appeal the case was reversed and a new trial ordered, on the ground that the Count, having destroyed the letter under unexplained circumstances, should not have been permitted to introduce secondary evidence of its contents. The outcome of the second trial does not appear. . . .

Armstrong, The Count Joannes: A Vindication of a Much-Maligned Man, 36 A.B.A.J. 829 (1956).

Problem: Close Enough for Government Work?

Action by the government against *D* for collection of unpaid taxes. *D* asserts the statute of limitations as a defense. The government contends that *D* is estopped from pleading the statute of limitations because she executed a written waiver of the limitations period, as specifically authorized by 26 U.S.C. §§6501(c)(4) and 6502(a)(2). *D* denies having executed the waiver.

At trial, the government cannot produce the written waiver. *W*, an IRS agent, is called to testify that the waiver was destroyed according to standard IRS procedure. The government also offers evidence of the normal practice of the IRS, which, it contends, establishes the likelihood that *D* did execute a waiver. *D* objects to *W*'s testimony and to the introduction of the government's other evidence.

What ruling and why?

UNITED STATES v. TAYLOR
648 F.2d 565 (9th Cir. 1981)

ELY, J. Taylor and Dennis B. Wittman were jointly indicted for their part in the assertedly fraudulent acquisition of a substantial loan from the Continental Bank of Texas ("Continental"), in Houston, Texas. During the period of time covered by the indictment, late 1974 to early 1975, Taylor was a vice-president of the real estate department of Home Federal Savings and Loan Association ("Home Federal"), located in San Diego, California. The fraudulent "scheme or artifice" alleged by the Government was that Taylor and Wittman, who was a principal in several San Diego real estate development entities, had induced Continental to make a $1.97 million loan to a corporation run by Wittman, on the basis of their false representations of several material facts. In a January 16, 1975 letter signed by Taylor and containing an initialed postscript, Taylor and Wittman blatantly misrepresented to Continental that Home Federal held a first lien on certain California real property. This letter was telecopied from San Diego to Houston, where Wittman received it, photocopied it, and delivered the photocopy to a loan officer of Continental. The photocopy tendered to Continental, which was the copy of the letter Continental relied on in approving the loan, was admitted into evidence at Taylor's trial as Government Exhibit "24." On January 23, 1975, Taylor signed a letter agreement with Continental purporting to confirm Home Federal's first lien commitment. After Taylor signed the letter agreement, without authorization, in his capacity as an officer of Home Federal, Continental funded the $1.97 million loan.

In July 1975, Wittman's corporation defaulted on the loan. Taylor and Wittman were indicted in June 1977. . . .

An issue at trial critical to the jurisdictional element of the crime charged[2] was whether Taylor had already signed the fraudulent letter dated January 16, 1975 (the predecessor of Exhibit "24") when it was telecopied from California to Texas, or whether Taylor had signed it after its transmission to Texas. Neither the "original" nor the telecopy was ever produced at trial. Instead, the Government introduced Exhibit "24," which was either a photocopy of the telecopy or a more remote reproduction.[3] While Exhibit "24" did reflect Taylor's signature, it was

---

2. 18 U.S.C. §1343 (1976) requires that the "scheme or artifice to defraud" involve the transmission "by means of wire, radio, or television communication in interstate or foreign commerce, any writings, signs, signals, pictures, or sounds for the purpose of executing such scheme or artifice."

3. An argument can be made that the "original" letter typed in San Diego is not the original, legally operative document for purposes of "best evidence" analysis because the officer of the

never conclusively established that the exhibit was a direct copy of the telecopy, leaving open the possibility that the signature was not affixed prior to interstate communication. Taylor's counsel at trial objected to the admission of this potentially spurious document on the basis of the "best evidence rule." The trial court ultimately admitted Exhibit "24" as secondary evidence, relying on the Government's claim that the original document had been unsuccessfully subpoenaed from the relevant parties, i.e., Continental, Home Federal, and Wittman's corporation.

In the course of the District Court's probe of the prosecuting attorney on the subpoena issue, Taylor's trial counsel made a qualified stipulation to the admission of the exhibit based on the truth of the Government's representations.[5]

---

defrauded Texas bank made the loan in reliance of either the telecopy or a photocopy of the telecopy. Under this view, the latter documents, rather than the "original" typed letter, must be treated as legally operative originals. See United States v. Gerhart, 538 F.2d 807, 810 n.4 (8th Cir. 1976); 5 J. Weinstein & M. Berger, Weinstein's Evidence ¶1001(3)[01] to [02] (1978 & Supp. 1979). Because we decide the admissibility issue on other grounds, we need not rule on this rationale.

5. At trial, the following colloquy between the district judge, defense counsel, and prosecutor took place:

The Court: Well, now, here's my ruling. I understand your point. I am going to overrule your objection to the admissibility, and the evidence in the case will have to be whatever it is concerning what [Exhibit "24"] purports to be—ultimately turns out to be.

Mr. Shenas [Defense Counsel]: Is that ruling based on a representation that the original of this letter has been subpoenaed from [Continental], from [Wittman's corporation], and from Home Federal by the Government?

The Court: Yes.

Mr. Shenas: Thank you.

The Court: Now do you want something—and that's a representation you are willing to rely on?

Mr. Shenas: Your Honor, I don't know if that's true or not. If counsel will tell me that's true, I will believe it. He hasn't said that—anything.

Mr. Kelton [Prosecuting Attorney]: What?

Mr. Shenas: That the original of that document was subpoenaed by the Government from [Continental], [Wittman's corporation], and Home Federal.

Mr. Kelton: When the Grand Jury investigation was—

The Court: Now, can't you answer that question directly?

Mr. Kelton: When the Grand Jury investigation was initiated—

The Court: Can't you answer "yes" or "no"?

Mr. Kelton: Yes.

The Court: Is that the answer, "Yes"? All right. Now, this is important when you come down to make a representation of that kind.

Mr. Kelton: Judge, I must say for the record that there's no original that could be located. But I am making this statement after subpoenaes, after speaking to the attorneys, after speaking to everybody involved in this transaction, and I really object to Mr. Shenas' implication that somebody has tampered with this evidence.

The Court: Just a minute. I am the person who is asking the question, whether [Wittman's corporation] has been subpoenaed, Home Federal has been subpoenaed, and the bank in Texas has been subpoenaed for the production of the original letter of January 16, 1975—which was Telexed to Texas.

Mr. Kelton: Yes, they have, and I would also say this, your Honor: There is no way that the original letter could have been in Texas because it was Telexed. That's the point.

The Court: Well, it would then show up with Home Federal, wouldn't it?

Mr. Kelton: Home Federal does not have it.

The Court: All right. It's been subpoenaed there. That's the only thing I am asking about,

Exhibit "24" proved to be a vital piece of evidence for the Government. It was used to rebut Taylor's contention that a fraudulent scheme did not exist at the time of the transmission of the January 16, 1975 letter; it was used to corroborate in important respects the testimony of the prosecution's key witness, Continental loan officer Michael Wells; and, most importantly, it provided evidence of an essential element of the charged offense—interstate communication to execute a fraud.

The jury rendered a guilty verdict on March 29, 1978. Taylor was sentenced to a term of one year and a day. . . . The most significant allegation of error was that the District Court erred in the admission of Exhibit "24" because, inter alia, the copy was improper under the "best evidence rule" of the Federal Rules of Evidence. In his direct appeal Taylor did not impugn the veracity of the Government's statements concerning the inability of the subpoena power to uncover the original document, since resolution of that matter necessarily involved matters outside the trial record. Taylor made a personal request for proof of the subpoenas. Unfortunately, the Government did not respond with such proof. . . .

Taylor raises several claims of error in his direct appeal, the most serious of which is that the District Court erred in admitting Exhibit "24" into evidence. Having determined that these claims are without merit, we affirm Taylor's conviction.

Taylor argues that because Exhibit "24" is at best a photocopy of the telecopied January 16, 1975 letter, it was improperly admitted into evidence. Federal Rule of Evidence 1002, Taylor correctly asserts, requires the production of the "original" writing to prove the contents thereof, "except as otherwise provided." Taylor contends that since Exhibit "24" is neither an "original" under Rule 1002 nor a "duplicate" within the exception of Rule 1003, it should not have been admitted into evidence. Taylor's argument overlooks the state of the trial record and the clear application of the exception of Rule 1004(2), which allows the admission of secondary evidence when the "original" cannot be obtained by

---

and you said it has been. So that's enough. That's what you have said and we needn't have any more explanation.

And on that basis, I will accept this in evidence.

Now, you know the responsibility you are assuming when you say it's been subpoenaed. Don't look so disheartened.

Mr. Kelton: I'm not disheartened, Judge. The only point I am trying to make is that I made a good faith offer of proof to the Court—

The Court: I am not suggesting you didn't make it in good faith. I am asking about a foundation for it, for my accepting in evidence secondary evidence.

Mr. Kelton: I would just like to put my position on the record, your Honor. It would take one second. That is this: That all I have to do to lay that foundation through this witness is establish a record that that was kept in the ordinary course of business at [Wittman's corporation], and that they do not have the original available. And that is my position under the Federal Rules. And I think I have made that clear.

The Court: All right. I will admit the document on the basis of secondary evidence because of your inability through subpoena power to produce the originals.

#R.T., Vol. V, at 51-54 (emphasis added).

available judicial procedures. When Exhibit "24" was offered for introduction into evidence at trial, the Government represented to the District Court that subpoenas requesting the "original" letter—i.e., the one typed in San Diego—had been served on the parties and that the "original" was not produced. In reliance on this representation, the District Court admitted Exhibit "24" into evidence. Taylor's counsel did not object to the exhibit's admission. Because Taylor's counsel failed to object to the admission of Exhibit "24," and even stipulated to the unavailability of the "original" letter, the record on direct appeal compels that we reject Taylor's "best evidence" argument.

We have carefully considered Taylor's remaining claims and find that the District Court did not abuse its discretion, that the jury was properly instructed, and that the evidence was adequate to support the jury verdict. Therefore, Taylor's conviction of wire fraud in the District Court is affirmed. . . .

AMOCO PRODUCTION CO. v. UNITED STATES
619 F.2d 1383 (10th Cir. 1980)

McKay, J. In 1942, the Federal Farm Mortgage Corporation (FFMC) conveyed by special warranty deed a fee simple interest in certain land in Summit County, Utah, to Hyrum and Florence Newton. The original deed and all copies other than a recorded version kept in the Summit County Recorder's Office are apparently no longer in existence. The parties dispute the exact contents of the original 1942 deed. Appellants claim that the deed reserved to the FFMC a one-half mineral interest in the property. As recorded, however, the deed contains no such reservation.

In 1957, the FFMC conveyed by quitclaim deed to the United States all of its mineral interest in various tracts of property, including the Newtons' property. The United States subsequently leased its claimed one-half mineral interest to the other appellants in this case.

In 1960, the Newtons conveyed their entire interest in the property to a family corporation, the Hyrum J. Newton & Sons Sheep Company (Newton Company). Beginning in 1971, this family corporation leased the entire mineral interest in the property to the appellees.

Appellees brought suit on January 21, 1976, under 28 U.S.C. §2409a to quiet title to the disputed mineral rights. . . . [The appellees moved for summary judgment.]

[T]he district court was faced with two alternative approaches to resolve the merits of the dispute. The court could have determined whether the Newton Company or any of its successors in interest was a bona fide purchaser sufficient to cut off any interest in the appellants. The court selected, however, to decide first whether FFMC conveyed the disputed mineral interest to the Newtons in the 1942 deed, or whether it reserved the interest to itself. If the original 1942 deed contained no mineral reservation clause, the appellants obviously have no mineral interest in the property.

Because appellees brought this quiet title action, they have the burden of establishing their title to the disputed interest. By introducing the recorded version of the deed, which showed that they received the entire interest in the property, appellees established a prima facie right to relief. See Utah Code Ann. §78-25-3 (1953). The burden then shifted to the appellants to introduce evidence of the invalidity or inaccuracy of the recorded version of the deed. In granting summary judgment, the court excluded all of the evidence proffered by appellants.

ROUTINE PRACTICE

The appellants offered evidence in an attempt to show that the routine practice of the FFMC was to reserve a one-half mineral interest in all property transferred during the relevant period. The court excluded this evidence on the ground that under Rule 1005 of the Federal Rules of Evidence, the availability of a properly recorded version of the 1942 deed precluded admission of any other evidence of the contents of the deed. We believe the court misinterpreted the purpose and effect of Rule 1005. . . .

The notes of the Advisory Committee on the proposed rules of evidence help explain the purpose of this rule:

> Public records call for somewhat different treatment. Removing them from their usual place of keeping would be attended by serious inconvenience to the public and to the custodian. As a consequence judicial decisions and statutes commonly hold that no explanation need be given for failure to produce the original of a public record. . . . This blanket dispensation from producing or accounting for the original would open the door to the introduction of every kind of secondary evidence of contents of public records were it not for the preference given certified or compared copies. Recognition of degrees of secondary evidence in this situation is an appropriate quid pro quo for not applying the requirement of producing the original.

Rule 1005 authorizes the admission of certified copies of records and documents filed and stored in public offices. The purpose of the rule is to eliminate the necessity of the custodian of public records producing the originals in court. This purpose is not furthered by extending the rule to encompass documents not filed and stored in public offices.

Rule 1005, by its terms, extends to "a document authorized to be recorded or filed and actually recorded or filed." This language encompasses deeds, mortgages and other documents filed in a county recorder's office. However, it is the actual record maintained by the public office which is the object of Rule 1005, not the original deed from which the record is made. If the original deed is returned to the parties after it is recorded, it is not a public record as contemplated by Rule 1005.

Applying Rule 1005 to exclude all other evidence of the contents of a deed is especially troublesome in a case such as this one. We cannot embrace an interpretation of the Rule which would exclude all evidence of the original deed other than the recorded version when the very question in controversy is whether the original deed was correctly transcribed onto the recorded version. Rule 1004(1), which authorizes the admission of other evidence of the contents of a writing if all originals are lost or destroyed, rather than Rule 1005, is applicable to the 1942 deed.[6] Accordingly, assuming it is otherwise admissible, evidence of a routine practice of the FFMC is relevant to prove conduct under Rule 406, and is admissible in lieu of the original under Rule 1004(1). Even if the evidence is not extremely probative, as indicated by the court, it is sufficient to create a question of fact and render summary judgment improper. Accordingly, the case must be remanded for the district court to consider admissibility of the evidence under a proper interpretation of Rules 1004 and 1005.

BLM FILE COPY

The appellants offered into evidence a photocopy of what is purportedly a conformed copy of the 1942 deed. The copy was found in a case file of the Bureau of Land Management (BLM). In excluding the file copy, the court indicated that it was "apparently incapable of being properly authenticated," and, in any event, admission would be "unfair" under Rule 1003 of the Federal Rules of Evidence.

Documentary evidence introduced in federal courts must be authenticated under the provisions of Rules 901 or 902 of the Federal Rules of Evidence. Specifically, the proponent of such evidence must produce evidence "sufficient to support a finding that the matter in question is what its proponent claims." Fed. R. Evid. 901(a). The district court did not decide that the file copy could not be properly authenticated, but rather that it was "apparently incapable" of proper authentication. On remand, the appellants should be given the opportunity to properly authenticate the file copy under the provisions of Rule 901.[7]

---

6. The court properly applied Rule 1005 in admitting a certified copy of the deed as recorded by the county recorder. Furthermore, because such a certified copy was available, the court should properly exclude any other proffered evidence of the contents of the recorded version of the deed. However, Rule 1005 does not preclude the admission of other evidence of the contents of the original 1942 deed. That deed is not a public record and Rule 1005 does not apply to it.

7. Appellants urge that the file copy can be authenticated as a public record under Rules 901(b)(7) or 902(4). However, the mere fact that a document is kept in a working file of a governmental agency does not automatically qualify it as a public record for purposes of au-

The court also excluded the file copy on the ground that it would be "unfair to admit the duplicate in lieu of the original" under Rule 1003.[8] The trial court felt that admission of the file copy would be unfair because the most critical part of the original conformed copy (the reservation clause) is not completely reproduced in the "duplicate." We find no abuse of discretion in this holding.

In determining that admission of the file copy would be "unfair," the court was apparently considering admission for purposes of proving the contents of the original conformed copy (and ultimately, the original 1942 deed). However, the appellants also urge admissibility of the file copy for other purposes. They argue that the file copy supports their claim that the original 1942 deed was prepared on standard form 657, that it bears the same identification number as the county recorder's copy and the Federal Land Bank ledger, and that it demonstrates the physical length of the land description, supporting the theory that a flapped attachment was used on the 1942 deed. Even if admission of the file copy is unfair for the purpose of proving the contents of the original conformed copy, it may not be unfair for other purposes. Assuming the appellants can satisfactorily authenticate the file copy, on remand the district court should consider admissibility for these purposes.

BLM PLAT AND INDEX

The appellants urge that the district court improperly failed to consider an official BLM land office plat and a historical index which reflect the government's retained mineral interest. The court did not rule on this evidence, but said in a footnote: "[D]efendants allege that certain official land office plats or indexes reflect a mineral reservation in the federal government. The court, however, has seen no evidence supporting this allegation or the inference defendants wish to be drawn therefrom."

In fact, the evidence was before the court. The index and plat were submitted by some of the appellants as exhibits to a July 6, 1976, motion for summary judgment. Furthermore, they were specifically mentioned in the appellants' memorandum in opposition to the appellees' motion for summary judgment. Accordingly, on remand the district court should consider this evidence.[9]

---

thentication or hearsay. Although the recorded version of a deed is a public record, a copy of a deed deposited in a working file of the BLM is not, by that fact alone, a public record.

8. Although the BLM file copy is not a "duplicate" of the original 1942 deed, see Rule 1001(4), it is apparently a duplicate of the original conformed copy of the deed. As such, it is admissible to the same extent as the original conformed copy unless the trial court exercises its discretion under Rule 1003 to exclude it as "unfair."

9. Unlike the file copy which is not a public record simply by virtue of its presence in a BLM working file, the BLM land office plat and historical index appear to be official records of a governmental agency and may qualify as "public records" under the federal rules.

OTHER EVIDENCE

The appellants also offered other evidence including a blank standard deed form 657, a copy of the 1957 quitclaim deed and certain working files of the BLM. On remand, the court should consider the admissibility of such evidence. The blank standard deed form would be relevant upon sufficient showing that the 1942 deed was prepared on a similar form. The 1957 quitclaim deed is not a "nullity" as suggested by the court. Rather, it represents a valid transfer of all interest retained by the FFMC, if any, to the United States. However, the appellants must show that it is relevant to issues in this case and otherwise admissible. The working files of the BLM, although not necessarily admissible as public records, may be admissible to show the practice of the agency and the manner in which deeds with lengthy descriptions were constructed. . . .

Reversed and remanded.

Problem: The Thunderbird Valley Scam

Charge: mail fraud. The government charged defendants with an elaborate land sale fraud involving Thunderbird Valley corporation, of which the defendants were stockholders, officers, and directors. The essence of the case against defendants was that they had double assigned mortgages to defraud investors and lenders. Defendants claimed they were unaware of any improprieties and that the defalcations shown by the government were inadvertent.

At trial, the government offered the testimony of W, a postal inspector, that he had made a summary of records seized from the offices of Thunderbird Valley corporation that established 80 double assignments out of 260 files of transactions perused.

Is W's testimony admissible? What foundation must the government lay before this evidence is admitted? Must the government show it would be impossible, difficult, or simply inconvenient to produce the 260 files? Must the government show that the underlying, summarized documents are admissible? May W testify to what the summary shows, or must the summary itself be produced? Is the actual summary admissible as an exhibit? Does this make any difference to the jury? Does it make any difference if W is qualified as an expert? Must W be qualified as an expert? Is the government required to give advance notice to defendants that they intend to rely on a summary? Does notice obviate any of the necessary foundational requirements? Is there a Sixth Amendment problem in the use of summaries in criminal cases?

UNITED STATES v. SCALES
594 F.2d 558 (6th Cir.), cert. denied, 441 U.S. 946 (1979)

TAYLOR, J. John E. Scales has appealed his conviction on nine counts of unlawfully converting to his own use assets of Local 423 of the Laborer's International Union in violation of 29 U.S.C. §501(c) and one count of conspiracy in violation of 18 U.S.C. §371. He was acquitted on the six remaining counts, which included three charges under Section 501(c), two charges for conversion of funds from an employee insurance fund in violation of 18 U.S.C. §664, and one charge of mail fraud in violation of 18 U.S.C. §1341. He was given an aggregate sentence of ten years.

From 1968 through 1977, appellant was the business manager of Local 423 of the Laborer's International Union, a labor organization as that term is used in 29 U.S.C. §§401-531. Count I of the indictment charged him with conspiracy to embezzle and misapply the funds of Local 423 and the Ohio Laborer's District Council—Ohio Contractor's Association Insurance Fund. A number of overt acts were alleged in furtherance of the conspiracy including receiving double payments for expenses, receiving payment for expenses not incurred, using Local 423 funds for personal expenses of no benefit to the members of the Union and receiving interest free loans made for fraudulent purposes from union funds. All but one of the substantive counts upon which appellant was convicted were also charged as overt acts. Count XV involved similar self dealing with union funds.

At trial, the Government introduced 161 exhibits, consisting of thousands of pages of documents, and the testimony of eight co-conspirators who had previously pleaded guilty to conspiring with appellant to embezzle union funds. Seventeen other witnesses, also testified, including FBI Agent Charles A. Tosi, who prepared Government's summary exhibit, Exhibit 145. The trial lasted eight days.

Appellant question[s] on appeal . . . whether the trial judge erred prejudicially in admitting Government Exhibit 145 and in admitting the testimony of Special Agent Tosi of the FBI in connection with said exhibit. . . .

GOVERNMENT EXHIBIT 145 AND RELATED TESTIMONY

Appellant contends that the trial judge erred in allowing Government Exhibit 145 to be admitted into evidence as well as in permitting Special Agent Charles Tosi to testify concerning the exhibit. Appellant argues that the exhibit was inadmissible and prejudicial because it summarized the indictment and part of the Government's proof, thereby constituting conclusion and argument, and that Agent Tosi's testimony contained improper conclusions and argument.

Exhibit 145 consisted of a series of large charts. The first chart summarized all the charges contained in the indictment. Each of the remaining charts summarized a count or an overt act, or both, by reproducing, or making reference to, some of the documentary proof already in evidence. The only references in Exhibit 145 that were not to documents admitted previously into evidence were several statements in the charts that union records did not contain certain information. The charts were authenticated by Agent Tosi.

There was no prejudicial error committed by the admission of Exhibit 145. In regard to the summary of the indictment, the rule is clear that the trial judge has discretion to submit the indictment to the jury in a criminal case as long as limiting instructions are given to the effect that the indictment is not to be considered as evidence of the guilt of the accused. Such a charge was given in this case. Indeed, the actual indictment was submitted to the jury in this case, and appellant raises no objection in that regard.

Nor can appellant claim that he was prejudiced by this chart because it was a summary rather than a copy of the full indictment. Not only was the Government's summary not inflammatory or prejudicially worded, the summary contained only enough description of the charges to remind the jury of the substance of each count. The trial judge carefully charged the jury as to all of the elements necessary for conviction on each count. The summary of the indictment clearly was intended to aid the jury in organizing the proof and no rights of appellant were prejudiced by its admission into evidence.

The remainder of Exhibit 145 consisted of a summary of some of the objective proof relating to a number of the counts and overt acts charged. The Government argues that the exhibit was admissible under Fed. R. Evid. 1006. . . .

Insofar as Exhibit 145 contained summaries of other exhibits in evidence, appellant contends that Rule 1006 does not apply because each document listed could have been, and was, examined at the time of its admission. There is no requirement in Rule 1006, however, that it be literally impossible to examine the underlying records before a summary or chart may be utilized. All that is required for the rule to apply is that the underlying "writings" be "voluminous" and that in-court examination not be convenient. With 161 exhibits, involving facts relevant to sixteen counts and twenty-one overt acts, comprehension of the exhibits would have been difficult, and certainly would have been inconvenient, without the charts utilized by the Government.

Exhibit 145 also contained written statements that union records did not contain certain information, primarily authorization for travel. Appellant argues that this information is not covered by Rule 1006 because this is information that records *do not* contain, and thus is not a summary of their contents as required by the rule.

Appellant admits that the underlying union records could have been introduced to prove the nonoccurrence of the relevant matters under Fed. R. Evid. 803(7). If the records themselves could have been admitted to show what their contents did not include, there appears to be no reason why Rule 1006 would not apply to a summary of their contents. It is true that in such an instance the content of the records is negative, but that does not render the fact of omission any less an accurate summary of the content of the records. The Court is strengthened in this conclusion by the similar view of 4 Wigmore, Evidence §1230 (Chadbourn rev. 1972):

> [T]estimony, by one who has examined records, that *no record* of a specific tenor is there contained is receivable instead of producing the entire mass for perusal in the courtroom.

(Emphasis in original). . . .

Of course even under Rule 1006, the summary or chart must be accurate, authentic and properly introduced before it may be admitted in evidence. In this regard appellant urges in general terms that Exhibit 145 is replete with characterizations and conclusions, and is deceptive. After a careful examination of Exhibit 145, the Court is unable to find any misleading or conclusory references. Exhibit 145 appears to present merely an organization of some of the undisputed objective evidence in terms of the relevant counts of the indictment.

Appellant also complains that the charts were too large and that the authenticating testimony was insufficient because Agent Tosi was not an expert. Size alone does not render inadmissible an exhibit containing otherwise unobjectionable objective evidence. Given the nature of Exhibit 145, it is difficult to see how Agent Tosi's lack of expertise could have prejudiced appellant. The chart did not contain complicated calculations that would require an expert for accuracy. In order to authenticate Exhibit 145 it was necessary only that Agent Tosi had properly catalogued the exhibits previously admitted and had knowledge of the analysis of the union records referred to in the exhibit. Neither of these requirements necessitated any special expertise. As the one who supervised the compilation of Exhibit 145, Agent Tosi was the proper person to attest to the authenticity and accuracy of the chart.

Entirely aside from Rule 1006, there would still be ample authority for the admission of Exhibit 145 into evidence. There is an established tradition, both within this circuit and in other circuits, that permits a summary of evidence to be put before the jury with proper limiting instructions. Some cases allow the summary of purely testimonial evidence, so strictly speaking, such summaries cannot be said to come within the requirements of Rule 1006. The purpose of the summaries in these cases is simply to aid the jury in its examination of the evidence already admitted. Authority for such summaries is not usually cited, but would certainly exist under Fed. R. Evid. 611(a).

The danger of permitting presentation of a summary of some of the evidence in a criminal case is plain. The jury might rely upon the alleged facts in the summary as if these facts had already been proved, or as a substitute for assessing the credibility of witnesses. This danger has led to the requirement of "guarding instructions" to the effect that the chart is not itself evidence but is only an aid in evaluating the evidence. Even with such instructions, a summary may still be considered as too conclusory or as emphasizing too much certain portions of the Government's case, or as presenting incompetent facts. Trial courts may take care that such unfair summaries are not presented to juries.

Despite the danger, however, most summaries are routinely admitted. In fact, not only are the summaries themselves admitted, but computations and evaluations are often permitted on the basis of such summaries.

In contrast to such extensive use, this appeal presents a very limited utilization of an evidence summary. The facts of the case were complex. Thus the summary was likely to have been very helpful to the jury. The facts summarized were entirely objective, and, for all that appears from this appeal, uncontested. No issue of credibility was presented. The exhibit was in no sense conclusory, but stated the facts shown in a neutral way. The facts summarized did not even directly undermine appellant's theory of the case. Finally, the trial judge did instruct the jury as to the limited purpose that such a summary could serve.[3]

Appellant's final argument is that the trial court improperly permitted Agent Tosi to deliver a closing argument during his authentication of the summary. Ultimately the trial court accepted appellant's objection and limited Agent Tosi's testimony. Because Exhibit 145 was essentially a presentation of objective material which aided the jury in remembering portions of the evidence and sorting out the charges, there was really no need for Agent Tosi to restate the portions of the evidence contained in Exhibit 145. Under these circumstances, it would perhaps have been preferable had the trial judge ruled from the start of Agent Tosi's testimony that Exhibit 145 was essentially self-explanatory. The Court need not decide this issue, however, because the early portion of Agent Tosi's testimony consisted of an accurate recounting

---

3. Appellant has not specifically raised the issue of permitting such a summary to go to the jury during deliberations. As it appears that Exhibit 145 did accompany the jury, appellant's objection to this course may be viewed as implicit. It is certainly not unusual for such demonstrative evidence to go to the jury. In most cases, however, once the summary is considered properly admitted, the issue of its going to the jury is not separately raised. It appears generally that when such summaries are kept from the jury, it is either because they were not properly offered into evidence, or because the summary was considered unfair or unreliable for the reasons listed above. For essentially the same reasons we rule that this exhibit was properly admitted, we conclude that no right of appellant was prejudiced by its submission to the jury.

of certain objective evidence already before the jury. No rights of appellant could have been prejudiced by such a recital.

For the foregoing reasons, the judgment of the trial court is affirmed.

Problem: Diagrams

Personal Injury Case. Plaintiff Raymond Cluney sues for injuries when the car in which he was riding as a passenger collided with a car driven by the defendant, Albert Borak, at the intersection of Wood and Vale Streets. During his direct examination Plaintiff is asked if use of the blackboard in the courtroom would help him to illustrate his testimony. Upon his affirmative response, he is invited to step down from the witness stand and draw the intersection of Wood and Vale Streets on the blackboard, and then draw in the locations of the two cars after the crash and other pertinent details.

During the direct examination of the defendant, Albert Borak, the witness is shown a pre-drawn diagram of an intersection on a large white easel tablet, which has been marked for identification as Exhibit 1. The examination goes as follows:

Q: Do you recognize what has been marked as Exhibit 1 for Identification?
A: Yes . . .
Q: Does Exhibit 1 for Identification fairly and accurately depict the intersection of Wood and Vale Streets as it existed at the time of the accident?
A: It looks like it.
Q: We offer Exhibit 1 for Identification in evidence as Exhibit 1.
Other lawyer: Objection!

What ruling and why?

Q: Can you indicate on Exhibit 1 where your car was just before the accident?
A: It was here — (drawing).
Q: We offer Exhibit 1 for Identification in evidence.
Other lawyer: Objection!

What ruling and why?

_____

The status of diagrams and other graphic illustrations of a witness's verbal testimony is somewhat uncertain in many jurisdictions. There is no Federal Rule that specifically addresses the use of graphic "illustrative aids" to enhance a witness's oral testimony. Among the various states, there are wide variations in treatment of this media. In some states, illustrations of a witness's testimony such as diagrams, models, and computer simulations are treated as visual testimony. They are not considered "real evidence" and they are not sent to the jury room for use by the jurors during their deliberations. In the New England states, such diagrams are often referred to as "chalks" deriving from their historical development out of the in-court chalkboard. In other states, this kind of media is considered as "demonstrative evidence" and is admitted as a special category of evidence, sometimes with a limiting instruction to the effect that the diagram should be given no greater weight than the supporting witness's testimony. In some states, diagrams seem to be treated as ordinary tangible evidence.

Increasing sophistication in the use of visual aids in all teaching settings, whether classroom, salesroom, or courtroom, and the opportunities offered by electronic technology for handsome and persuasive visuals have made trials into multimedia events. How can counsel and the court detect and control distortion and subtle messages in fancy computer simulations, charts, and illustrations? Does Rule 403, which applies to material actually offered in evidence, also give the court the power to regulate the use of diagrams and other material developed and used merely to illustrate concededly admissible verbal testimony? Does the sometimes high cost of these aids increase the effect of disparate economic resources on judicial outcomes? What kinds of advance notice and access should be afforded opposing parties? Can parties "mark up" or even spoil the opponent's chart during the course of cross-examination or argument? Some states have started to try to experiment with regulations governing the use of "illustrative aids" in court. See, e.g., Maine Rule of Evidence 616.

CHAPTER X

Allocation, Inference, Burdens, and Presumptions

More than any other aspect of evidence, burdens of proof and presumptions pose the deep epistemological question, What does it mean to prove something? As a result, evidence scholars over the years have been fascinated with presumptions. More than a few have set out to solve their mysteries, only to become lost in philosophical and operational details. In approaching this material we are well aware of Professor Morgan's warning, "Every writer of sufficient intelligence to appreciate the difficulty of the subject matter has approached the topic of presumptions with a sense of hopelessness and has left it with a feeling of despair." Morgan, Presumptions, 12 Wash. L. Rev. 255 (1937).

The problem may be that we have been asking the wrong questions about presumptions. As John Hart Ely has said in another context, "No answer is what the wrong question begets." Ely, Democracy and Distrust 72 (1980). We believe that the right question to ask about presumptions is, What is their *function*? Since presumptions are commonly justified as procedural tools, they can be truly understood only by understanding their function.

The functional theory of presumptions on which this chapter is based assumes that presumptions work to create the epistemological phenomenon of coming to a conclusion (a belief) about the happening of a disputed past event. This may be contrasted with the more common—and seemingly more rationalistic—approach of justifying presumptions on the grounds that they yield an acceptable probability statement assessing the odds that the disputed past event occurred. Choosing between these two approaches requires one to speculate about the role that these two quite different states of mind play in the process of judicial proof. In the realist world of twentieth-century American legal thought, the second approach has predominated, bolstered by the tendency on the part of many jurists and scholars to incorporate in law the quantification techniques of the scientific method. We believe, however, that overemphasis on the probabilistic-based approach obscures the ways in which presumptions work to bridge the gap between doubt and proof at individual trials and, on a broader scale, between doubt and faith in the justice system. Thinking about presumptions in terms of their contribution to belief-formation illuminates these functions. It also reveals the connections between presumptions and allocations of burdens of proof, inferential reasoning, and choices of substantive rules of law. Seeing these connections tends to lend some coherence to what otherwise appears to be a chaotic mixture of rules and doctrines.

Congress was not troubled by these larger concerns when adopting the Federal Rules. The Advisory Committee Notes reveal little in the way of deep structure in this area. Nor have the courts concerned themselves with epistemology in interpreting the presumption rules. Nonetheless, we commend the theoretical inquiry to you. It is interesting for its own sake and even if the theoretical approach suggested here does not fully convince you, it provides a practical framework for understanding not only the rules relating to presumptions but also how they fit within the broader subject of judicial proof.

We begin by addressing the problem of allocation of burdens of proof in civil and criminal cases. This subject is sometimes treated in courses in civil procedure, torts, contracts, and property but not always in connection with presumptions, inferences, judicial comment, and choices of substantive rules of law. As the following sections indicate, these subjects are all parts of the same machine and must fit together for the machine to work properly. Thinking about burdens of proof inevitably involves consideration of the use of probabilistic and mathematical proof, a subject already touched on in Chapter II.

Our discussion of presumptions in civil cases is organized around three ways ("strategies") in which they and other devices can bridge the gap between speculation (which is unacceptable in court) and inference (acceptable). This approach is not explicit in the Federal Rules or in the cases. Indeed, the series of federal court cases dealing with presumptions that we have included in this chapter reveal a tendency to confuse these three strategies in most instances. In addition to pointing out various problems courts have in applying Rule 301, these cases demonstrate the continuing validity of Professor Morgan's nearly half-century-old warning. The *Sindell* case from the California Supreme Court, which concludes the section on presumptions in civil cases, is an interesting example of one of the three described strategies in disguise. The *Hinds* case illustrates one court's effort to define the "weight" to be given a presumption faced with contrary evidence.

The section on presumptions in criminal cases again focuses on the connection between the initial allocation of burdens of proof and presumptions. To what extent can the legislature constitutionally shift burdens of proof through reallocation of elements *or* by the use of presumptions? Does it make any difference in which manner the burden of proof is shifted? A series of problems and cases and a lengthy dialogue between Professor Nesson and Professor Allen raise these and a host of other thorny constitutional and policy issues.

A. Allocation in Civil Cases

E. CLEARY, PRESUMING AND PLEADING: AN ESSAY ON JURISTIC IMMATURITY
12 Stan. L. Rev. 5-14 (1959)

THE SUBSTANTIVE LAW

Since all are agreed that procedure exists only for the purpose of putting the substantive law effectively to work, a preliminary look at the nature of substantive law, as viewed procedurally, is appropriate.

Every dog, said the common law, is entitled to one bite. This result was reached from reasoning that man's best friend was not in general dangerous, and hence the owner should not be liable when the dog departed from his normally peaceable pursuits and inflicted injury. Liability should follow only when the owner had reason to know of the dangerous proclivities of his dog, and the one bite afforded notice of those proclivities. So the formula for holding a dog owner liable at common law is: + *ownership* + *notice of dangerous character* + *biting*.

This rule of law becomes monotonous to postmen. Hence the postmen cause to be introduced in the legislature a bill making owners of dogs absolutely liable, i.e., eliminating notice from the formula for liability. At the hearing on the bill, however, the dog lovers appear and, while admitting the justness of the postmen's complaint, point out that a dog ought at least to be entitled to defend himself against human aggression. Then the home owners' lobby points out the usefulness of dogs in guarding premises against prowlers. Balancing these factors, there emerges a statute making dog owners liable for bites inflicted except upon persons tormenting the dog or unlawfully on the owner's premises. The formula for liability now becomes: + *ownership* + *biting* − *being tormented* − *unlawful presence on the premises*.

So in any given situation, the law recognizes certain elements as material to the case, and the presence or absence of each of them is properly to be considered in deciding the case. Or, to rephrase in somewhat more involved language, rules of substantive law are "statements of the specific factual conditions upon which specific legal consequences depend. . . . Rules of substantive law are conditional imperatives, having the form: *If* such and such *and* so and so, *etc.* is the case, *and unless* such and such *or unless* so and so, *etc.* is the case, *then* the defendant is liable.

. . ." Now obviously the weighing and balancing required to determine what elements ought to be considered material cannot be accomplished by any of the methodologies of procedure. The result is purely a matter of substantive law, to be decided according to those imponderables which travel under the name of jurisprudence.

This view of the substantive law may seem unduly Euclidean, yet some system of analysis and classification is necessary if the law is to possess a measure of continuity and to be accessible and usable.

PRIMA FACIE CASE AND DEFENSE

Under our adversary method of litigation a trial is essentially not an inquest or investigation but rather a demonstration conducted by the parties.

Since plaintiff is the party seeking to disturb the existing situation by inducing the court to take some measure in his favor, it seems reasonable to require him to demonstrate his right to relief. How extensive must this demonstration be? Should it include every substantive element, which either by its existence or nonexistence may condition his right to relief? If the answer is "yes," then plaintiff under our dog statute would be required to demonstrate each of the elements in the formula: + *ownership* + *biting* − *tormenting* − *illegal presence on the premises.*

In the ordinary dog case this would not be unduly burdensome, but if the suit is on a contract and we require plaintiff to establish the existence or nonexistence, as may be appropriate, of every concept treated in Corbin and Williston, then the responsibility of plaintiff becomes burdensome indeed and the lawsuit itself may include a large amount of unnecessary territory. Actually, of course, the responsibility for dealing with every element is not placed on plaintiff. Instead we settle for a "prima facie case" or "cause of action," consisting of certain selected elements which are regarded as sufficient to entitle plaintiff to recover, *if* he proves them and *unless* defendant in turn establishes other elements which would offset them. Thus in a simple contract case, by establishing + *offer* + *acceptance* + *consideration* + *breach,* plaintiff is entitled to recover, unless defendant establishes + *accord and satisfaction* or + *failure of consideration* or + *illegality* or − *capacity to contract,* and so on.

Observe that the plus and minus signs change, in accord with proper mathematical rules, when we shift elements to the defendant's side of the equation as "defenses." For example, if plaintiff were required to deal with capacity to contract, it would become + *capacity to contract* as a part of his case, rather than the − *capacity to contract* of defendant's case.

Defenses, too, may be prima facie only and subject to being offset by further matters produced by plaintiff, as in the case of the defense of release, offset by the further fact of fraud in the inducement for the release. The entire process is the familiar confessing and avoiding of the common law.

ALLOCATING THE ELEMENTS

The next step to be taken is the determination whether a particular material element is a part of plaintiff's prima facie case or a defense. Or, referring back to the statement that rules of substantive law are "conditional imperatives, having the form: *If* such and such *and* so and so, *etc.,* is the case . . . *then* the defendant is liable," should the element in question be listed as an *if* or as an *unless?*

In some types of situations, the test has been purely mechanical, with the mechanics in turn likely to be accidental and casual. Thus, in causes of action based on statute, if an exception appears in the enacting clause, i.e., the clause creating the right of action, then the party relying on the statute must show that the case is not within the exception; otherwise the responsibility for bringing the case within an exception falls upon the opposite party. The principle is widely recognized, but the vagaries of statutory draftsmanship detract largely from its certainty of application. Returning to our dogs, two statutes will serve as illustrations.

> If any dog shall do any damage to either the body or property of any person, the owner . . . shall be liable for such damage, unless such damage shall have been occasioned to the body or property of a person who, at the time such damage was sustained, was committing a trespass or other tort, or was teasing, tormenting or abusing such dog. Mass. Ann. Laws ch. 140, §155 (1950).
>
> Every person owning or harboring a dog shall be liable to the party injured for all damages done by such dog; but no recovery shall be had for personal injuries to any person when they [*sic*] are upon the premises of the owner of the dog after night, or upon the owner's premises engaged in some unlawful act in the day time. Ky. Laws 1906, ch. 10, at 25, Ky. Stats. 1936, §68a-5.

The Massachusetts statute was construed as imposing on a two and one quarter year old plaintiff the burden of establishing that he was not teasing, tormenting or abusing the dog, while under the Kentucky statute a plaintiff was held to have stated a prima facie case by alleging only that he was bitten by a dog owned by defendant, leaving questions of presence on the premises at night or unlawful activities in the day time to be brought in as defenses. The difference in result can scarcely be regarded as calculated but is typical. Unfortunately, the statute which states in so many words the procedural effects of its terms is a rarity.

Exceptions in contracts receive similar treatment. If the words of promising are broad, followed by exceptions, the general disposition is to place on defendant the responsibility of invoking the exception. Of course, many of the cases involve insurance policies, with all that implies. In Munro, Brice & Co. v. War Risks Assn., during World War I one underwriter insured plaintiffs' ship against loss due to hostilities and another underwriter insured it against perils of the sea except consequences of hostilities. The ship was lost, and plaintiffs sued on both policies. The King's Bench Division held that as regards the first policy plaintiffs must show the loss to have been due to hostilities, but that under the second policy merely establishing the loss was sufficient, leaving it to the underwriter to bring in loss by hostilities as a defense. Since evidence of the cause of loss was wholly lacking, the loss fell on the second underwriter.

Julius Stone commented as follows: "Every qualification of a class can equally be stated without any change of meaning as an exception to a class not so qualified. Thus the proposition 'All animals have four legs except gorillas,' and the proposition 'all animals which are not gorillas have four legs,' are, so far as their meanings are concerned, identical. . . .

"If the distinction between an element of the rule and an exception to it does not represent any distinction in meaning, it may still remain a valid distinction for legal purposes. In that case, however, it must turn upon something other than the meaning of the propositions involved. It may turn, for instance, merely upon their relative form or order."

So in a few kinds of cases the answer to the question of allocation is found in the structure of a statute or contract, perhaps with some tenuous reference to intent, either of the legislature or of the contracting parties. But what of the great bulk of the cases, involving neither exception in a statute nor limitation upon words of promising? What general considerations should govern the allocation of responsibility for the elements of the case between the parties?

Precedent may settle the manner in a particular jurisdiction, but precedent as such does nothing for the inquiring mind. Thayer was of the view that questions of allocation were to be referred to the principles of pleading, or perhaps to analysis of the substantive law, and "one has no right to look to the law of evidence for a solution of such questions as these. . . ." Books about pleading, however, have not been numerous in recent years, except for the local practice works; and aside from a brief but provocative treatment by Judge Clark they offer slight assistance. The substantive law texts, when they deal with the matter at all, tend to describe results rather than reasons.

Despite Thayer's strictures, his descendants in the field of writing about evidence, by assuming to deal with problems of burden of proof as an aspect of the law of evidence, have found themselves inevitably enmeshed in the problems of allocation and have contributed most of the literature on the subject, although in an introductory and incidental fashion.

Before trying to establish some bench marks for allocation, let us note, though only for the purpose of rejecting them, two which are sometimes suggested. (a) That the burden is on the party having the affirmative; or, conversely stated, that a party is not required to prove a negative. This is no more than a play on words, since practically any proposition may be stated in either affirmative or negative form. Thus a plaintiff's exercise of ordinary care equals absence of contributory negligence, in the minority jurisdictions which place this element in plaintiff's case. In any event, the proposition seems simply not to be so. (b) That the burden is on the party to whose case the element is essential. This does no more than restate the question.

Actually the reported decisions involving problems of allocation rarely contain any satisfying disclosure of the ratio decidendi. Implicit, however, seem to be considerations of policy, fairness and probability. None affords a complete working rule. Much overlap is apparent, as sound policy implies not too great a departure from fairness, and probability may constitute an aspect of both policy and fairness. But despite the vagueness of their generality, it is possible to pour enough content into these concepts to give them some real meaning.

(1) POLICY

As Judge Clark remarks, "One who must bear the risk of getting the matter properly set before the court, if it is to be considered at all, has to that extent the dice loaded against him." While policy more obviously predominates at the stage of determining what elements are material, its influence may nevertheless extend into the stage of allocating those elements by way of favoring one or the other party to a particular kind of litigation. Thus a court which is willing to permit a recovery for negligence may still choose to exercise restraints by imposing on plaintiff the burden of freedom from contributory negligence, as a theoretical, though perhaps not a practical, handicap. Or the bringing of actions for defamation may in some measure be discouraged by allocating untruth to plaintiff as an element of his prima facie case, rather than by treating truth as an affirmative defense. And it must be apparent that a complete lack of proof as to a particular element moves allocation out of the class of a mere handicap and makes it decisive as to the element, and perhaps as to the case itself. In Summers v. Tice plaintiff was hunting with two defendants and was shot in the eye when both fired simultaneously at the same bird. The court placed on each defendant the burden of proving that his shot did not cause the injury. To discharge this burden was impossible, since each gun was loaded with identical shot. In Munro, Brice & Co. v. War Risks Assn. the absence of proof of the cause of the ship's loss meant that the party on whom that burden was cast lost the case. In these cases the admonition of Julius Stone is particularly apt: "the Courts should not essay the impossible task of making the bricks of judge-made law without handling the straw of policy."

(2) FAIRNESS

The nature of a particular element may indicate that evidence relating to it lies more within the control of one party, which suggests the fairness of allocating that element to him. Examples are payment, discharge in bankruptcy, and license, all of which are commonly treated as affirmative defenses. However, caution in making any extensive generalization is indicated by the classification of contributory negligence, illegality, and failure of consideration also as affirmative defenses, despite the fact that knowledge more probably lies with plaintiff. Certainly in the usual tort cases, knowledge of his own wrongdoing rests more intimately in defendant, though the accepted general pattern imposes this burden on plaintiff.

(3) PROBABILITY

A further factor which seems to enter into many decisions as to allocation is a judicial, i.e., wholly nonstatistical, estimate of the probabilities of the situation, with the burden being put on the party who will be benefited by a departure from the supposed norm.

The probabilities may relate to the type of situation out of which the litigation arises or they may relate to the type of litigation itself. The standards are quite different and may produce differences in result. To illustrate: If it be assumed that most people pay their bills, the probabilities are that any bill selected at random has been paid; therefore, a plaintiff suing to collect a bill would be responsible for nonpayment as an element of his prima facie case. If, however, attention is limited to bills upon which suit is brought, a contrary conclusion is reached. Plaintiffs are not prone to sue for paid bills, and the probabilities are that the bill is unpaid. Hence payment would be an affirmative defense. Or again, "guest" statutes prohibit nonpaying passengers from recovering for the negligence of the driver. If most passengers are nonpaying, then the element of compensation for the ride would belong in the prima facie case of the passenger-plaintiff. If, however, most passengers in the litigated cases ride for compensation, then absence of compensation would be an affirmative defense. In the payment-of-a-bill situation the probabilities are estimated with regard to the litigated situation, payment being regarded generally as an affirmative defense, while in the guest situation they are estimated with regard to such situations generally and not limited to those which are litigated, status as a nonguest being a part of plaintiff's prima facie case. No reason for the shift is apparent, and it may be unconscious. The litigated cases would seem to furnish the more appropriate basis for estimating probabilities.

Matters occurring after the accrual of the plaintiff's right are almost always placed in the category of affirmative defenses. Examples are payment, release, accord and satisfaction, discharge in bankruptcy, and limitations. A plausible explanation is that a condition once established is likely to continue; hence the burden ought to fall on the party benefited by a change.

In the cases of complete absence of proof, a proper application of the probability factor is calculated to produce a minimum of unjust results, and the same is true, though less impressively, even if proof is available.

Problem: Civil Allocation in Idylia

In the past Idylia operated without an adversary system of justice. All civil disputes were brought to the Tribunal of Inquiry, which thoroughly investigated and reached factual conclusions about each and every element that the Idylia legislature specified as essential to recovery. In some cases the Tribunal of Inquiry would remain uncertain even after exhaustive investigation. These cases would be decided by coin flip. The system was enormously expensive and the results unsatisfying, particularly in the coin-flip cases.

You are commissioned to allocate the proof of elements between plaintiff and defendant in contract suits and to provide a coherent theoretical justification for your allocation

The elements for breach of contract in Idylia are as follows: agreement, consideration, breach, and absence of mistake. Records of the Tribunal of Inquiry show that in the last year (consider it representative) there were 3,000 disputed contracts. Estimates are that this is approximately 5 percent of all contracts. Damages were awarded in 1,000 cases.

	Number of cases in which the element was the major disputed issue	Number of cases in which Tribunal decided for recovery	Number of cases in which decision was for no recovery	Number of cases in which Tribunal wound up uncertain and flipped a coin
Agreement	850	325	275	250
Consideration	400	200	150	50
Breach	1,700	440	970	290
Absense of mistake	50	35	5	10
	3,000	1,000	1,400	600*

What do you recommend, and why?

*300 of these came out for the plaintiff.

B.   Inference and Speculation: What Is the Difference Between "Reasoning" and "Guessing"?

Problem: Big-Time Charlie

D, prosecuted for passing counterfeit money, admits that he bought drinks at a bar for himself and two friends and paid for the drinks with a counterfeit $20 bill but claims ignorance that the bill was counterfeit. The only evidence against him on the issue of knowledge is testimony that while in the company of his two friends, *D* lit a cigar with a $20 bill. *D* moves for a directed verdict. How should the judge rule?

Problem: Prison Yard

Reconsider the Prison Yard problem in Chapter I. If you conclude that a directed verdict of acquittal is appropriate in the first instance in that problem but not the second, then consider the following.

C. NESSON, REASONABLE DOUBT AND PERMISSIVE INFERENCE: THE VALUE OF COMPLEXITY
92 Harv. L. Rev. 1187, 1194 (1979)

Why should it be that the high likelihood but starkly numerical case is thrown out of court while the cases based on self-serving testimony or additional circumstantial evidence will be put to the jury? The question becomes truly puzzling when one considers that even a case in which the quantifiable likelihood of guilt was much lower — for example, where originally only two prisoners were in the yard—might be allowed to go to the jury as long as the prosecutor's case was bolstered by additional circumstantial evidence or by other evidence distinguishing the defendant.

Why should evidence which generates a clear-cut mathematical statement of the likelihood of guilt be considered insufficient, even when the probability of guilt is high, while other evidence of a testimonial or circumstantial nature is much more readily considered by the courts to be sufficient to sustain a prosecutor's case? Do we actually consider the jury to be accurate in assessing the credibility of witnesses and the strength of circumstantial evidence? Or are some risks of inaccurate verdicts more acceptable than others?

Is the problem of speculation limited to criminal cases? If the prison yard case were a civil action by the estate of the murdered guard against prisoner #1, would the analysis of issues be different?

In a civil case, is it useful to think in terms of odds or wagers when considering admissibility or sufficiency of evidence? Consider the following.

L. COHEN, THE PROBABLE AND THE PROVABLE §30
(1977)

The inapplicability of betting odds. Another commonly invoked criterion for the assignment of a mathematical probability is the acceptance or acceptability of appropriate betting odds within a coherent betting policy. So perhaps well-behaved jurors, who are fully self-conscious in their reasoning, should be supposed to measure the strength of their belief in the correctness of a particular verdict by reference to the odds they would accept if wagering on its correctness? This measure, the betting quotient, would be the ratio of the favourable figure to the sum of the two figures, and would have the structure of a mathematical probability. Odds of 4 to 1 on the plaintiff's case, say, would give a betting quotient or mathematical probability of .8. It would then apparently be possible for judges or legislators to stipulate a degree of mathematical probability that could be taken as putting the guilt of an accused person beyond reasonable doubt and a lower degree of mathematical probability that would suffice for the decision of civil cases.

But in fact such a procedure would be grossly fallacious. A reasonable man's betting practice is subject to two additional constraints, besides his knowledge of relevant data.

One constraint is that he only wagers on discoverable outcomes. Bets must be settlable. In each case the outcome must be knowable otherwise than from the data on which the odds themselves are based. When the horse-race is finally run, the winner is photographed as he passes the winning-post. When the football match is finally played, each goal is seen as it is kicked. Consequently wagers on past events or on the truth of scientific generalizations over an unbounded domain, or on any issue where the whole truth cannot be directly observed, are only intelligible in a context of total or partial ignorance about the relevant data. Knowing nothing, or only a little, about the local archaeological evidence I can wager you, on the basis of experience elsewhere, that there was no Roman settlement at Banbury; and to settle the bet we can excavate and see. But, if all the appropriate excavations have already been done, and we know their results, there is nothing to wager about. Similarly, to request a juryman to envisage a wager on a past event, when, ex hypothesi, he normally already knows all the relevant evidence that is likely to be readily obtainable, is to employ the concept of a wager in a context to which it is hardly appropriate. There is no time machine to take us back into the past. So there is no sure way of discovering whether the accused is guilty, or the plaintiff's statement of claim is true, except by looking at the relevant evidence. If one asks a juryman to envisage a wager in such a context, one is hardly entitled to expect a rational response.

Perhaps it will be objected that since people do sometimes wager sensibly about past events, as on the existence of a Roman settlement at Banbury, they can reasonably be assumed to have a general technique for assigning betting-quotient probabilities to past events on given evidence. Why then cannot a jury employ such a technique for the solution of its own special problems about probabilities? The answer to this objection is that it still does not succeed in attaching significance to the conception of judicial probabilities as betting quotients. The argument against a betting-quotient analysis of judicial probability is not that there is no sufficiently general technique for devising betting-quotients: the argument is rather that in certain situations the operational acceptance of a betting quotient is irrational. So talk about assigning probabilities, when probabilities are understood in the proposed way, involves the absurdity of talk about accepting reasonable bets on unsettlable issues.

Moreover, another constraint on rational betting practice has to be mentioned here. No one bothers about odds unless the amounts at stake are of some consequence. Only the very poor bet seriously in pennies. But when the amounts at stake begin to rise a prudent man tends to be more and more cautious about the odds he will accept for a given size of stake. Bookmakers shorten the odds on a horse not only when they hear of its latest wins elsewhere but also when they begin to be concerned about how much they would lose if it won the current race. So there is little sense in asking a man what odds he would accept on a certain outcome unless the value of the units wagered is also specified. Every juryman would have to be instructed separately by the judge, in accordance with the judge's estimate of what would be an appropriate sum of money for that juryman to envisage wagering. Consequently every accused would be at risk not only in relation to the evidence, but also in relation to the judge's estimates of how much importance each juryman attaches to the gain or loss of this or that sum of money. Such a system certainly does not yet exist anywhere, and its institution seems scarcely likely to promote the ends of justice.

C.   Strategies for Bridging the Gap

Faced with a gap between speculation and inference courts have the obvious choice of directing the verdict against the plaintiff. This is what happened in Smith v. Rapid Transit (see page 103) and probably would happen in the hypothetical Prisoners and Blue Bus cases (see pages 107 and 105). In some cases, however, the evidence may be circumstantial and thin, posing the same kind of uncertainty about what happened as the Rapid Transit, Blue Bus, and Prisoners cases did, and yet in these cases a directed verdict against the plaintiff might not be the best result. There will be *recurrent* types of cases where imposition of the burden of displacing uncertainty on the class of plaintiffs is deemed undesirable. For example, at the turn of the century people often were killed at railroad crossings. Their next of kin would bring suit but be unable to prove that the railroad was negligent (no witnesses—just a body by the crossing). One can well imagine concluding (1) that the defendant might be able to add to knowledge about what happened and that a procedure to elicit this knowledge should be adopted, or (2) that cases that result in uncertainty on the negligence issue should be resolved against the railroad, perhaps on a deep-pocket or easy-to-spread-the-loss theory, or (3) that the case should be decided on the basis of the kind of safety device at the crossing. Each of these approaches would allow us to reach a judgment for the plaintiff without having obviously to jump to a conclusion. These approaches are worth abstracting and naming.

1. *The Explanation Seeker.* Fill in the gap with more information. Specifically, impose a burden on the defendant to come forward with an explanation for the suggestive but not sufficient circumstantial evidence and authorize an inference to be drawn from his failure to do so. If he comes forward with more information, the gap will have been bridged. If he does not and it appears to the factfinder that the defendant was in a position to come forward with an explanation favorable to himself, had there been one, then an inference can be drawn from his failure that will help bridge the gap. If it appears that the defendant is not in such a position, then this strategy will not help.

2. *The Allocation Shifter.* Bridge the gap by changing the starting assumption on the troublesome issue. Once the suggestive but insufficient circumstance is proved, a rule could be devised that changes the starting assumption on the issue in question, shifting the burden of displacing uncertainty to the defendant. As the rule stands today, if the case continues in an uncertain state the defendant will lose.

3. *The Issue Switcher.* The gap could be bridged by forsaking the initial troublesome issue altogether once it appears unresolvable and switching to another (not necessarily related) issue as a basis for resolving the controversy.

In the following problems, which strategy would you suggest to bridge the gap?

Problem: Family Car

A recurrent problem arises in auto accident cases in which the party at fault is a minor driving a car owned by a parent. The plaintiff sues the parent-owner, but to recover the plaintiff must prove that the minor was driving the car with the parent-owner's permission. Typically, the plaintiff has no proof of this beyond proof of the relationship between the parent and the driver.

What procedural strategies would make sense for resolving these cases?

Problem: Post Office

P sues *D* for breach of contract. *P* proves that he mailed his acceptance of *D*'s offer to *D* at *D*'s proper address. *D* claims that he never received it. How should the issue be decided?

Problem: Last Carrier

P ships a crate of parts from Boston to Phoenix by rail. The crate is in good shape when sent but arrives damaged. Three different rail companies, *D1, D2,* and *D3,* have handled the goods along the route of shipment. *P* has no way of knowing which one damaged the crate. *P* sues *D1, D2,* and *D3.* How should the case be resolved?

D. Civil Presumptions and Rule 301

The tremendous confusion that has characterized the law of civil presumptions stems primarily from a concept known as the "bursting bubble" theory of presumptions. The bursting bubble approach comes close to embodying the explanation-seeking strategy but misses. Under the bursting bubble theory, the only effect of a presumption is to shift a burden of producing evidence regarding the presumed fact. If evidence is produced by the adversary to meet that burden, the presumption disappears — the bubble bursts. The effect of a bursting bubble presumption is to create a burden of coming forward on the party on whom it is imposed. If the party meets this burden, the presumption has done its job; it is spent; the "bubble bursts" and the case is then decided according to the original allocation of burdens. Many problems have been associated with the bursting bubble approach:

(1) The burden of production imposed by this form of presumption has been thought to carry with it the risk of losing by directed verdict if the burden of production is not discharged.

(2) There has been much difference of opinion over the appropriate standard for determining whether the burden has been discharged: Can it be discharged by an offer of a "scintilla" of evidence or must the evidence offered to discharge the burden be sufficient to support a finding?

(3) Since the question of whether the burden has been discharged is for the judge to decide, it is possible that the presumption will be made to disappear on the basis of evidence that the jury will wholly discredit. This seems to give the presumption "too slight and evanescent" an effect (note the language of the FRE Advisory Committee Note).

This criticism spurred the other major presumption theories (presumptions as evidence and burden-shifting presumptions). See Rule 301 as originally proposed and as amended by the House. The following case represents a pre-Rules attempt of one court to determine the "weight" that should be accorded a presumption when the presumption is in conflict with evidence.

HINDS v. JOHN HANCOCK MUTUAL LIFE INSURANCE CO.
155 Me. 349, 155 A.2d 721 (1959)

WEBBER, J. Plaintiff is beneficiary of an insurance policy covering the life of his late father, Donald Hinds. The policy provides for payment of a death benefit of $9,000 and, in addition thereto, of a like sum in the event the death of the assured should be due to bodily injuries sustained solely through "violent, external and accidental means." Suit was brought in behalf of plaintiff, a minor, by Emily Hinds, his mother and legal guardian. It is not disputed that the death of the assured being shown, the plaintiff is entitled to recover the ordinary death benefit of $9,000. The jury, however, awarded double indemnity as reflected by a verdict of $18,000. Issues are raised both by general motion and exceptions.

At the outset it was stipulated that an analysis of the blood of the decedent, Donald Hinds, made shortly after his death, disclosed an alcoholic content of .267% by weight. During the presentation of the plaintiff's case, it was shown by competent medical and other testimony that the assured was found slumped unconscious in a chair at his kitchen table late in the evening; that he was removed to a hospital and died there without regaining consciousness; that the cause of death was a gunshot wound inflicted by a revolver fired while in contact with the skin in the region of the right temple; that the bullet pursued approximately a horizontal course through the head from right to left; that decedent was a "big man" over six feet tall and weighing about 200 pounds; that he was fifty years old and apparently in good health; that on a table at his right side were a revolver and an opened package of bullets; that there were present no cloths or other gun cleaning paraphernalia; that there were no outward or visible signs of any violent scuffle, quarrel or other disturbance on the premises; and that there were empty whiskey bottles near the decedent's body. The family physician, first to arrive at the scene, found Emily Hinds holding her husband's head. He described her as appearing confused and in a state of shock. Social and business friends gave testimony tending to negative any apparent motive for suicide. A medical expert stated that one in the decedent's state of intoxication would be confused, with his reactions markedly slow and his pain sensation diminished; that he would be unable to think clearly but would not be unconscious and would be able to "navigate" although not very steadily. Not one of the witnesses had ever before seen the decedent in this stage of intoxication. Emily Hinds, although inferentially an eye witness to the tragedy, was not called by the plaintiff.

On this posture of the evidence, as will be shown, the plaintiff at the close of his main case had by no means offered sufficient proof of death by "accidental means." However, no request was made to the court to direct a verdict and we are satisfied that the election by counsel for the defendant to go forward with evidence stemmed largely from the uncertainty heretofore existing in this jurisdiction as to the evidentiary status of presumptions. We will have occasion to discuss this problem later in the opinion. Attention should first be given, however, to the evidence offered by the defendant.

The witness first called in defense was Emily Hinds. At the very beginning of her examination, she was asked if she was the widow of Donald Joseph Hinds. She then replied, "I refuse to *testify*, on the advice of counsel, on my constitutional right that it might tend to incriminate me." (Emphasis supplied.) She was then asked, "Do you consider that you would be incriminated by being the wife of Donald Joseph Hinds?" At this point the jury was ordered to retire and colloquy then ensued which resulted in a ruling by the presiding justice that the pending question and all further questions of this witness were *excluded* because of her claim of privilege. Defendant's counsel took no exception nor did he pursue the matter further with this witness. He next called a police officer who had investigated the death on the evening of its occurrence. This witness identified the gun which he had observed on the kitchen table as being a 22 caliber automatic pistol, designed to fire long rifle bullets. He testified that the broken box of ammunition scattered about the table contained short rifle bullets. The full box originally contained 50 cartridges, all of which were accounted for. The officer counted 47 cartridges on the table and found three in the gun, one of which had been fired. He further noted what appeared to be a few business papers scattered on the table. He noted the presence on the floor beside the table of two empty bottles, each designed to contain a fifth of a gallon of whiskey. He was permitted to testify that on the evening in question he had a conversation with Emily Hinds as to the events leading up to the shooting of her husband but, upon objection by the plaintiff, was not allowed to state the substance of that conversation. Thereupon, in the absence of the jury, the defendant made an offer to prove by the witness that Emily Hinds freely and voluntarily described to him the events of the evening which culminated when the decedent held the gun against his right temple and pulled the trigger. This proffered evidence was rejected by the court as hearsay. At this point the evidence on both sides was closed and the case submitted to the jury, with what result we have already noted.

In the case of Cox v. Life Insurance Co., 139 Me. 167, 28 A.2d 143, involving suit on a policy covering accidental death, our court recognized that the burden of proving accident rested upon the claimant throughout the trial and never shifted. The distinction is clearly made in Watkins v. Prudential Insurance Co. (1934), 315 Pa. 497, 173 A. 644, 95 A. L. R. 869, 875, as "between suits on insurance policies like the one here sued on, which insure against 'death as a result of bodily injuries effected solely through external, violent and accidental means' and suits on those policies which insure against death but which contain a proviso avoiding the policy if the insured dies by his own act." As the court there pointed out, in the former situation the plaintiff has the unremitting burden of proof as to accident, whereas in the latter situation the plaintiff need only prove death while the defendant has from the inception the burden of proof as to suicide which is there raised as an affirmative defense. So in the case before us, the death of the insured person by violent and external means was conceded. The defendant by its pleadings having raised the issue, it remained for the plaintiff to prove by a fair preponderance of the whole evidence that those means were also accidental. . . .

The plaintiff in the first instance was aided by the so-called presumption against suicide. This presumption stems from and is raised by our common knowledge and experience that most sane men possess a natural love of life and an instinct for self-protection which effectively deter them from suicide or the self-infliction of serious bodily injury. It is commonly recognized that there is an affirmative presumption of death by accidental means which arises under appropriate circumstances from the negative presumption against suicide. Whether and to what extent the presumption persists in the face of contrary evidence is a matter of great and even decisive importance in the instant case.

Although a small minority of states adhere to an opposite view, it is now almost universally held that disputable presumptions are not themselves evidence nor are they entitled to be weighed in the scales as evidence. Rather are they recognized as "rules about evidence." They may be distinguished from inferences in that an inference is *permissible*, whereas a presumption is *mandatory*. They compel a finding of the presumed fact in the absence of contrary evidence. They perform the office of locating the burden of going forward with evidence, but having performed that office they *disappear* in the face of countervailing evidence. [Citing cases.]

The minority view that the presumption is itself evidence or has evidentiary weight has its adherents among the courts, some of which have felt constrained to that result by judicial interpretation of applicable statutes. [Citing cases.] No statute exists in Maine declaring that disputable presumptions are themselves evidence.

Although our own court has never found it necessary to contribute any extended academic discussion to the plethora of words which have been written on this controversial subject, we find no satisfactory indication from the language used, confusing though it may be, that our court has accepted the principle that presumptions are themselves evidence. . . . We now hold unequivocally that presumptions serve their allotted procedural purpose but are not themselves evidence.

A far more difficult and troublesome question arises, however, in determining what quantum or quality of evidence is required to cause a rebuttable presumption to disappear. Conversely, to what extent will such a presumption persist in the face of contrary evidence? And who is to evaluate that evidence, the trial judge or the jury? It is at this point that courts have gone their several ways and too often semantics have been substituted for logic. On the one hand is the risk that the jury may be confused by instructions relating to presumptions and may misapply them, especially by according to presumptions artificial evidentiary weight in the scales which they do not possess. On the other hand is the concern expressed by many writers of opinion and texts that if the presumption be regarded purely as a procedural tool *in the hands of the trial judge*, he will have in effect usurped the province of the jury as factfinder in determining the weight and credibility of such evidence as tends to negative the presumed fact. Efforts to reconcile these two desirable objectives have produced both compromise and confusion.

Many courts have adopted what is usually referred to as the Thayer theory of rebuttal which provides that disputable presumptions (other than the presumption of legitimacy) fall as a matter of law when evidence has been introduced which would support a finding of the non-existence of the presumed fact. This rule has the virtue of uniformity and won approval in the American Law Institute, Model Code of Evidence, Rules 703 and 704. In the foreword of the Model Code, Professor Edmund M. Morgan, the reporter and a recognized authority in the field of evidence and procedure, makes this excellent analysis of the several views (page 55):

"As to the other consequences of the establishment of the basic fact, save only the basic fact of the presumption of legitimacy, the opinions reveal at least eight variant views, of which the following are the most important:

1. The existence of the presumed fact must be assumed unless and until evidence has been introduced *which would justify a jury in finding the non-existence of the presumed fact.* When once such evidence has been introduced, the existence or non-existence of the presumed fact is to be determined exactly as if no presumption had ever been operative in the action; indeed, as if no such concept as a presumption had ever been known to the courts. *Whether the judge or the jury believes or disbelieves the opposing evidence thus introduced is entirely immaterial.* In other words, the sole effect of the presumption is to cause the establishment of the basic fact to put upon the party asserting the non-existence of the presumed fact the risk of the non-introduction of evidence which would support a finding of its non-existence. This may be called the *pure Thayerian rule,* for if he did not invent it, he first clearly expounded it.

2. The existence of the presumed fact must be assumed unless and until evidence has been introduced which would justify a jury in finding the non-existence of the presumed fact. When such evidence has been introduced, the existence or non-existence of the presumed fact is a question for the jury unless and until *substantial evidence of the non-existence of the presumed fact has been introduced. When such substantial evidence has been introduced, the existence or non-existence of the presumed fact is to be decided as if no presumption had ever been operative in the action.* Thus if the basic fact, by itself or in connection with other evidence, would rationally support a finding of the presumed fact, the existence or non-existence of the presumed fact is a question for the jury; if the basic fact is the only evidence of the presumed fact and would not rationally justify a finding of the presumed fact, the judge directs the jury to find the non-existence of the presumed fact. *Unfortunately the cases which support this rule do not define substantial evidence: it is certainly more than enough to justify a finding; sometimes it seems to be such evidence as would ordinarily require a directed verdict.*

3. The existence of the presumed fact must be assumed *unless and until the evidence of its non-existence convinces the jury that its non-existence is at least as probable as its existence.* This is sometimes expressed as requiring evidence which balances the presumption.

4. The existence of the presumed fact must be assumed unless and until the jury finds *that the non-existence of the presumed fact is more probable than its existence.* In other words the presumption puts upon the party alleging the non-existence of the presumed fact both the burden of producing evidence and *the burden of*

persuasion of its non-existence. This is sometimes called the Pennsylvania rule." (Emphasis supplied.)

Professor Morgan and his distinguished colleague, Professor John M. Maguire, have never concealed their preference for some form of the fourth of the foregoing variants which would involve the shifting of the burden of *persuasion* at least as to certain classifications of presumptions, if not as to all. . . . This concept was finally approved by both the American Bar Association and the American Law Institute in 1954 and appears as Rule 14 of the Uniform Rules of Evidence promulgated by the National Conference of Commissioners on Uniform State Laws. That rule is as follows:

> "Rule 14. *Effect of Presumptions.* Subject to Rule 16, and except for presumptions which are conclusive or irrefutable under the rules of law from which they arise, (a) if the facts from which the presumption is derived have any probative value as evidence of the existence of the presumed fact, the presumption continues to exist *and the burden of establishing the non-existence of the presumed fact* is upon the party against whom the presumption operates, (b) if the facts from which the presumption arises have no probative value as evidence of the presumed fact, the presumption does not exist when evidence is introduced *which would support a finding of the non-existence of the presumed fact,* and the fact which would otherwise be presumed shall be determined from the evidence exactly as if no presumption was or had ever been involved." (Emphasis supplied.)

Jones on Evidence, 5th Ed., Vol. 4, page 1903 (see Comment, page 1904).

It will be noted that the proposed rule classifies presumptions, applying the Thayerian Rule to those situations where the presumption is raised out of expediency and the basic facts have no tendency to prove the presumed fact, and applying the so-called Pennsylvania Rule to those situations where the basic facts have probative value as evidence of the presumed fact. Thus far, obviously, the rule remains virtually untried and we have no adequate information available as to the extent to which it may have found favor with the courts. . . .

If we have, as we believe, because of the conflicting expressions and the lack of any definitive announcement in our own opinions, some freedom in determining what procedural effect we will assign to disputable presumptions, some examination of the cases which have employed the several variants may be helpful. . . .

It has frequently been stated that a disputable presumption disappears in the face of "substantial countervailing evidence" and the case is thereafter in the hands of the jury free of any presumption. As previously noted, what is meant by "substantial," however, is not always clear. In Alpine Forwarding Co. v. Penn. R. Co. (1932), 60 F.2d 734, another case which has been often cited, L. Hand, J. held that the determination as to whether the evidence contrary to the presumed fact is "substantial" is always and solely for the trial judge, and that in a properly conducted trial the presumption will never be mentioned to the jury at all. The same writer, speaking for a divided court in Pariso v. Towse (1930), 45 F.2d 962, although satisfied that the unqualified denials of the presumed fact by the defendant and her somewhat interested nephew should cause the presumption to disappear as a matter of law, felt constrained by his interpretation of applicable New York law to hold in effect that the denials of a party corroborated by an interested witness are not such "substantial" evidence as will cause the disappearance of the presumption as a matter of law. The credibility of these defense witnesses therefore became an issue for the jury. . . .

Reaching an opposite conclusion, however, at least with respect to certain classes of presumptions, are such cases as O'Dea v. Amodeo (1934), 118 Conn. 58, 170 A. 486; Koops v. Gregg (1943), 130 Conn. 185, 32 A.2d 653; and United States v. Tot (1942), 131 F.2d 261, 267, which seem to require that the requisite contrary evidence must be in fact believed and any question of veracity raises an issue for the fact-finder. The latter opinion voices the criticism which has often been made of the pure Thayerian rule that a presumption should not fall merely because words are uttered which nobody believes. "A gentle tapping on a window pane will not break it; so a mere attempt to refute a presumption should not cause it to vanish, if it is of any value at all." Hildebrand v. Chicago, B. & Q. R. R. (1933), 17 P.2d 651, 657. See Anno. 5 A. L. R. (2nd) 196 and cases cited reflecting the diversity of opinion on this subject.

O'Dea v. Amodeo, supra, established an elaborate classification of disputable presumptions with a prescribed rebuttal requirement for each classification. It does not appear that this method of approach has won any substantial following, perhaps because of the practical difficulties which might arise in applying the rule on a case by case basis in the trial courts.

Amid so much confusion there is the natural temptation toward oversimplification. Nevertheless, if the presumption is to be a useful procedural tool in the hands of the trial court, relative simplicity is a desirable goal. In the article in 47 Harvard Law Review 59 already cited, Professor Morgan has made a thorough and helpful analysis of this troublesome problem. As he points out, rebuttable presumptions have been created "(a) to furnish an escape from an otherwise inescapable dilemma or to work a purely procedural convenience, (b) to require the litigant to whom information as to the facts is the more easily accessible to make them known, (c) to make more likely a finding in accord with the balance of probability, or (d) to encourage a finding consonant with the judicial judgment as to sound social policy." Although the purposes for which presumptions are raised might properly and logically affect the method of their rebuttal, the writer, while suggesting that they should be permitted to shift the burden of persuasion, sees no serious or insurmountable objection to the establishment of a single procedural rule that a disputable presumption persists until the contrary evidence persuades the factfinder that the balance of probabilities is in equilibrium, or, stated otherwise, until the evidence satisfies the jury or factfinder that it is as probable that the presumed fact does not exist as that it does exist. We view the adoption of such a rule as a practical solution of a confusing procedural problem. In establishing the vanishing point for presumptions, it provides more certainty than do the varying definitions of "substantial countervailing evidence." It has also the virtue of reserving to the factfinder decisions as to veracity, memory and weight of testimony whenever they are in issue. In essence, the proposed rule recognizes that when an inference has hardened into a presumption compelling a finding in the absence of contrary evidence, it has achieved a status which should not vanish at the first "tapping on the window pane." It recognizes that "surely the courts do not raise such a presumption merely for the purpose of making the opponent of the presumption cause words to be uttered." We agree with Mr. Morgan that our objective should be to devise a "simple, sensible and workable" plan for the procedural use of disputable presumptions and are satisfied that the suggested rule achieves that end.

Such a rule gives to the presumption itself maximum coercive force short of *shifting the burden of persuasion*. Although we are keenly aware that there is severe criticism by respected authority of the widely accepted rule that the burden of persuasion on an issue never shifts, that rule has been thoroughly imbedded in the law of this state. An unbroken line of judicial pronouncements to this effect are to be found in our opinions. We would be most reluctant to make a radical change in the accepted rule unless forced to do so by some compelling logic. We feel no such compulsion here. Logic compels the conclusion that a mere procedural device is not itself evidence. But beyond that there seems to be a certain amount of judicial latitude which permits the court to determine how a disputable presumption, necessarily artificial in its nature, can best perform a useful function in forwarding the course of a trial. As already noted, it seems pointless to create a presumption and endow it with coercive force, only to allow it to vanish in the face of evidence of dubious weight or credibility. Neither does it seem to us necessary, in order to bring some order out of chaos, to overrule all precedent and permit the presumption to shift the burden of persuasion from him who first proposes the issue and seeks to change the *status quo*. These considerations prompt us to adopt the foregoing rule which seems to us a satisfactory middle course.

In our review of many opinions on this subject, we have discovered no more careful or accurate an analysis than is contained in a dissenting opinion by Mr. Justice Traynor appearing in Speck v. Sarver, supra, at page 19. Endorsing the view which we take of the effect of rebuttable presumptions as the "sounder one," he states: "Once such evidence (contrary to the presumed fact) is produced and believed, the jury should weigh it against any evidence introduced in support of the facts presumed and decide in favor of the party against whom the presumption operates if it believes that the non-existence of the facts is as probable as their existence. Nothing need be said about weighing the presumption as evidence."

With respect to the presumption against suicide in particular, Mr. Justice Taft concurring in Carson v. Metropolitan Life Ins. Co., supra, said: "There may be instances where the only evidence produced or introduced to rebut the presumption against suicide is evidence which the jury may quite properly disbelieve in exercising its function as trier of the facts and judge of the credibility of the witnesses. In such an instance, if the rule is as broadly stated as is suggested . . . then incredible evidence or evidence having no weight whatever could be effective in making the presumption against suicide disappear. Obviously, that would be unreasonable.

"There may therefore be instances where it will be necessary for the trial court to mention the presumption against suicide in charging a jury, even though it is erroneous to advise the jury . . . that that presumption may be weighed as evidence."

The rule for which we have expressed preference does not, as we interpret it, mean that the persistence or disappearance of a disputable presumption may never be resolved as a matter of law. Whenever no countervailing evidence is offered or that which is offered is but a scintilla, or amounts to no more than speculation and surmise, the presumed fact will stand as though proven and the jury will be so instructed. On the other hand, when the contrary evidence comes from such sources and is of such a nature that rational and unprejudiced minds could not reasonably or properly differ as to the non-existence of the presumed fact, the presumption will disappear as a matter of law. Where proof of the presumed fact is an essential element of the plaintiff's case, he would suffer the consequence of a directed verdict. Such would ordinarily be the result, for example, when evidence effectively rebutting the presumption is drawn from admissions by the plaintiff, evidence from witnesses presented and vouched for by the plaintiff, or from uncontroverted physical or documentary evidence.

Regardless of the view taken of the procedural effect of the presumption of death by accidental means, courts have not failed to be impressed by undisputed evidence of physical facts negativing accident. In Mitchell v. New England Mut. Life Ins. Co. (1941), 123 F.2d 246, the court, noting a contact wound and the horizontal course of the shot, concluded that "the nature of the wound itself bars any reasonable hypothesis of accident." . . .

Bearing in mind the sage admonition of Chief Justice Clark, dissenting in McDowell v. Norfolk S. R. Co. (1923), 186 N.C. 571, 120 S.E. 205, that too much technical and procedural "hair splitting" may impede the orderly course of litigation, let us turn to the facts before us. Applying the above stated rules of law to the facts of the instant case, it becomes at once apparent that the verdict of the jury was erroneous. As has been noted, the plaintiff undertook to satisfy his burden of proof, that is, the risk of nonpersuasion, that the death was caused by violent, external and accidental means. In the initial stages of the presentation of the plaintiff's case, there was undisputed and conclusive evidence that the means of death were both violent and external. Momentarily, as to the required proof of accidental means, the plaintiff was aided by the presumption, and the burden of going forward with evidence (as distinguished from the burden of proof) on this element of the case at once shifted to the defendant. This burden, however, could be as well satisfied by evidence adduced from plaintiff's witnesses as from those produced by the defendant. As the presentation of the plaintiff's main case proceeded, evidence of physical facts, emanating from the plaintiff's own witnesses and never disputed, clearly depicted an intentional, self-inflicted injury resulting in death. This evidence must be assessed in the light of inherent probabilities. Most significant is the fact that this was a *contact* wound at the right temple. Moreover, the course of the bullet on a horizontal plane through the head conclusively completes the picture of a fatal shot fired from a revolver held at and against the right temple and in a horizontal position. It is apparent that this evidence tends effectively to rule out any reasonable likelihood that there was an accidental discharge of the firearm while being cleaned or handled by either the decedent or his wife. The only reasonable inference is that the decedent placed a loaded revolver against his right temple and pulled the trigger. It matters not whether in so doing he intended to take his own life or was performing a grossly negligent and dangerous act reasonably calculated to produce grievous bodily harm or death. Where a shooting is the natural and probable consequence of the acts of the decedent, the result which should have been anticipated can hardly be termed an accident. . . . Whatever the thought processes of the decedent may have been when he placed a loaded revolver at right angles against his temple and pulled the trigger, the tragic results of that act can hardly be said to have been unusual, unexpected or unforeseen.

We note the negative evidence suggesting the absence of any apparent motive for self-destruction. The explanation of the decedent's conduct may well lie in his state of voluntary intoxication. Whatever may have been the reason for his act, we are satisfied that apparent absence of motive *alone* will not suffice under circumstances such as these to support a plaintiff's verdict or even to take the case to the jury. This is so because men without apparent motive do commit suicide and what prompts a man suddenly to succumb or appear to succumb to an access of depression or despair is usually a secret locked in the recesses of his mind. Evidence tending either to demonstrate or negative any motive for self-destruction is always properly received in a case of this sort, but as already noted cannot *alone* suffice against undisputed physical evidence all pointing toward a voluntary act, the natural consequence of which was self-destruction. See N. Y. Life Ins. Co. v. Trimble (1934), 69 F.2d 849, 851; Pilot Life Ins. Co. v. Boone (1956), 236 F.2d 457, 463; Inghram v. National Union (1897), 103 Iowa 395, 72 N.W. 559.

The evidence offered by the defendant did no more than to bolster the evidence of physical facts which, uncontradicted and unexplained, conclusively destroyed any presumption against the intentional self-infliction of the fatal wound. The plaintiff failed to offer any further evidence tending to show that the decedent met his death other than by his own hand, even though the burden of going forward with evidence on this element of the case had shifted back again to him. Having lost the benefit of the presumption, he was left with nothing to support his theory of accident but the merest surmise and conjecture conjuring up the most unlikely possibilities. Such speculation will not suffice for evidence. With the evidence complete, there was then but one possible verdict which the jury could properly return, and that for the defendant as to the claim for double indemnity.

Why then did the jury reach a verdict so obviously contrary to the evidence? We think the explanation may be found at least in part in the sequel of unusual developments which started when Mrs. Hinds first claimed the privilege against self-incrimination. As these events occurred, two exceptions were noted by the defendant which are now before us, and since this case may be retried, some discussion of the rather novel issues raised may be profitable.

It must be noted at the outset that the witness made her claim of privilege, not as to the particular question then asked, but as to giving any testimony whatever. As previously emphasized, she declined to "*testify*." When another question was asked, after some colloquy with the court, the pending question and *all further questions* of the witness were excluded. The questions, when viewed as cross-examination, were entirely proper. The witness, although not technically a party to the suit, was so identified in interest with the minor plaintiff, her son and ward for whom she had instigated the action, that her hostility to the defendant could fairly be assumed. The ruling when such privilege is claimed should not be to *exclude* the question if it is otherwise proper and admissible, but merely to grant or refuse the request that the witness not be compelled to answer. See Gendron v. Burnham, 146 Me. 387, 407. 58, 82 A.2d 773. Am. Jur. 54, Sec. 53, states the applicable rule. "The mere fact that the answer to a question might incriminate the witness does not render the question improper, because it is the privilege of the witness to refuse to answer it." Such a request will be honored by the court only when it is satisfied that the danger is real and not fancied or fabricated by the witness, and that the answer, if given, might tend to incriminate the witness. The court must be satisfied that the claim of privilege is made in good faith. 58 Am. Jur. 70, Sec. 81. The witness should not be accorded the privilege as to all further testimony but may properly be expected to claim the privilege on a question by question basis. As was said in Rogers v. U.S. (1950), 340 U.S. 367, 71 S. Ct. 438, 442, 95 L. Ed. 344: "As to each question to which a claim of privilege is directed, the court must determine whether the answer *to that particular question* would subject the witness to a real danger of . . . crimination." (Emphasis supplied.) Only thus can the examining counsel be afforded a fair opportunity to draw from the witness answers and information which can be given without any incriminating effect whatever. See Apodaca v. Viramontes (1949), 53 N.M. 514, 212 P.2d 425. Such a process may sometimes be tedious and time consuming, but fortunately the claim of privilege is infrequently made in the trial of civil cases.

Some latitude must be afforded to opposing counsel to show evidence of bad faith on the part of a witness claiming privilege, and the court must be vigilant to pursue any indications of bad faith before granting the privilege. This great constitutional safeguard against self-incrimination was never intended to be used as a means of avoiding the disclosure of the truth by witnesses who only pretend a fear of proving themselves guilty of crime. As stated in 58 Am. Jur. 53, Sec. 50: "It is essential to the existence of the right not to testify that the danger to be apprehended be real and appreciable, with reference to the ordinary operation of law, in the ordinary course of things, not a danger of an imaginary and unsubstantial character, having reference to some extraordinary and barely possible contingency, so improbable that no reasonable man would suffer it to influence his conduct. The law does not permit a witness arbitrarily to hide behind a fancied or intangible danger to himself." In the instant case the questions asked were seemingly innocuous. By claiming the privilege when she did, the witness suggested a fear of self-incrimination as to some crime involving her marital status. She was merely asked if she was the wife of the decedent. The fact that she then requested privilege not to testify at all suggests that she may have been making the claim prematurely and without particular reference to the pending question. It may well be that an explanation by the court of the nature of the privilege might have allayed her fears, if indeed any existed, as to the possible results of revealing whether or not she was the wife of the decedent. This would seem to have been a proper case for discreet and cautious examination by the court to ascertain whether any "real danger" of incrimination actually existed.

As has been noted, counsel for the defendant mistook his remedy and abandoned his right to ask further questions of the witness. Instead, he proffered the evidence of the police officer to whom Mrs. Hinds had related the events of the evening. This he did on the theory that since the best evidence was not available to him, he had a right to resort to secondary hearsay evidence. No case has been called to our attention which recognizes the right to introduce hearsay evidence under such circumstances as these. Whether a valid argument could be made in support of such a position need not be decided here. The defendant had laid no proper basis for the introduction of such evidence in any event. He at no time asked the witness to relate the events of that evening and it cannot now be known with certainty whether or not she would have claimed any privilege as to such a question. If the court erroneously ruled in advance that defendant was precluded from asking such a question, the defendant took no exception to such ruling. We can see at once that if such a question had been asked and a claim of privilege then asserted, the testimony of the officer might properly have been received by the court in the absence of the jury on the issue of the good faith of the witness in claiming privilege. The narrative of events which she gave to the officer suggested no wrongful act on her part. The proffered testimony of the officer, however, would have thrown no light on the good or bad faith of the witness in refusing to answer a question relating only to her marital status. We must constantly bear in mind that no other questions were asked of the witness. Since no proper basis was laid for the introduction of the excluded portion of the officer's testimony, the two exceptions taken in connection with that exclusion must be overruled.

Returning now to the developments in this trial which may have confused the jury, we note the situation which existed when the evidence closed. The jury had heard the only apparent eye witness to the tragedy refuse to "testify," claiming the protection of Art. I, Sec. 6 of the Constitution of Maine. They had seen that action apparently sustained by the court and acceded to by the defendant. They had no knowledge of the contents of the offer of proof made by the defendant in connection with the proffered testimony of the officer. It is not unreasonable to suppose that the jury may have mistaken these developments for evidence and may have somehow drawn the erroneous inference that Mrs. Hinds had shot her husband. Although no such inference could properly be drawn from her refusal to answer, the impression that such an inference might be raised could easily have been created in the minds of the jury by one of the instructions given by the court. After reminding the jury that a witness had claimed privilege, the court said: "Now such an invocation of the constitutional provision against self-incrimination

1046 X. Allocation, Inference, Burdens, and Presumptions

is not to be taken lightly and a person who invokes that privilege must be assumed to do so in good faith." No further explanatory instructions were given in this connection. Without more, the jury might have understood that they were free to draw such inferences as they chose from the act of the witness in claiming privilege. Obviously it would not have been proper for the jury to have speculated or conjectured that the witness had committed any particular crime, or especially that the witness had shot her husband.

The presiding justice gave the jury to understand that in claiming the privilege, the witness was presumed to have done so in good faith. We know of no such presumption. So many persons have claimed the privilege in recent years for reasons based upon political convictions or upon their personal philosophy as to the proper scope of inquiry and examination rather than upon any honest fear of self-incrimination, that the probabilities that might otherwise have tended to support such a presumption have been greatly diminished. In fact, resort to this great constitutional heritage has been so abused and misused that the claim of privilege is now too often popularly and vulgarly referred to as "taking the fifth." If we are to preserve this safeguard for posterity, courts will do well to make no assumptions but rather to make proper inquiry to ascertain as nearly as may be in each case whether or not the privilege is sought in good faith. Doubtless, in this case, the court below had in mind the rule that the acts of men outside the courtroom are ordinarily presumed to have been performed in good faith. This rule, however, has no application to the events of a trial which takes place in the presence of court and jury. The jury is itself witness to the acts and demeanor of those who appear before it and needs the aid of no presumption in determining whether a witness as a participant in the trial is acting in good faith. . . . The instruction certainly suggested to the jury that the act of claiming privilege was itself a piece of evidence for their consideration. Although no exception was taken to the instruction as given, we think it tended to mislead the jury into drawing the erroneous inference that since Mrs. Hinds claimed the privilege against self-incrimination, she must have shot her husband. We can conceive of no other theory which the jury might have entertained which could rationally explain a verdict so manifestly wrong. . . .

In conclusion, then, the plaintiff had the burden of persuasion throughout to prove death by violent, external and accidental means. At the close of all the evidence there was an uncontradicted showing by strong evidence of physical facts drawn from disinterested witnesses presented by the plaintiff that death was self-inflicted and non-accidental. The plaintiff, not the defendant, needed the aid of supporting testimony from Mrs. Hinds if he was to satisfy his burden of proof. The plaintiff was left with no proof of accident whatever. Only one verdict was possible and that for the plaintiff in the sum of $9,000.

The entry will be *Exceptions overruled. Motion for new trial overruled if plaintiff within 30 days from filing of this mandate remit all of the verdict in excess of $9,000; otherwise motion sustained and new trial granted.*

Problem: Conflicting Presumptions

You have brought a diversity case in Federal Court against Sun Life Insurance Company of Canada in behalf of Miranda Brown, beneficiary of a $100,000 "double indemnity" life insurance policy insuring the life of her husband, Alex Brown. The policy requires the company to pay twice the face amount upon the death of the insured "by sudden, violent, and accidental means." Applicable state law recognizes a presumption of continuing life (for seven years after unexplained disappearance) and a presumption against suicide. Here is the evidence.

(1) Alex Brown, a contractor by occupation, and a pilot by hobby, disappeared with his 1988 Cessna 172 single-engine airplane on July 12, 1998 and has not been seen or heard from since.

(2) On July 12 a commercial fisherman working near Matinicus Island (about 60 miles from Alex's house and airstrip) heard on his radio (which was tuned to the aircraft Unicom frequency) an unidentified male voice exclaim, "I am going in!"

(3) On July 29 a nosewheel of a Cessna washed up on Matinicus Island. It came from a Cessna of the same model as Alex's. This model had been manufactured from 1982-1992.

(4) On July 12 Miranda Brown came home from work and found an envelope lying in the middle of the dining room table. On the front of the envelope in Alex's handwriting were the words, "To my wife, with Love." Inside the envelope was the Sun Life Insurance policy on which suit was brought.

At the conclusion of the evidence both parties move for a directed verdict. What ruling and why? Does it depend on the "weight" to be afforded the applicable presumptions under state law? See Rule 302. If the motions are denied, how should the jury be instructed?

Rule 301 as ultimately enacted appears to be an adaptation of the bursting bubble approach and certainly is a rejection of the burden-shifting and presumptions-as-evidence approaches. What it actually is, as we shall see, remains somewhat unclear. Apparently the Senate Committee thought that the burden of production described by Rule 301, if unmet, would *not* result in a directed verdict. The Senate report says that "it would be inappropriate under this rule to instruct the jury that the inference they are to draw is conclusive." But what did the drafters think the jury should be told? Here the legislative history offers up gibberish:

> If the adverse party offers no evidence contradicting the presumed fact, the court will instruct the jury that if it finds the basic facts, it *may presume* the existence of the presumed fact. If the adverse party does offer evidence contradicting the presumed fact, the court cannot instruct the jury that it *may presume* (emphasis in the original) the existence of the presumed fact from proof of the basic facts. The court may, however, instruct the jury that it *may infer* the existence of the presumed fact from proof of the basic facts.

Do the drafters presume that jurors know the difference between "presume" and "infer"?

Suppose a juror who is told that he "may presume" a fact says, "Well, I understand that I *may* do so, but by what criteria do I decide whether I *should* do so?"

Suppose a judge wanted to use Rule 301 as an explanation-seeker? How would he instruct the jury? And would the instructions be consistent with the legislative history of 301?

TEXAS DEPARTMENT OF COMMUNITY AFFAIRS v. BURDINE
450 U.S. 248 (1981)

Justice POWELL delivered the opinion of the Court.

This case requires us to address again the nature of the evidentiary burden placed upon the defendant in an employment discrimination suit brought under Title VII of the Civil Rights Act of 1964, 42 U.S.C. §2000e et seq. The narrow question presented is whether, after the plaintiff has proved a prima facie case of discriminatory treatment, the burden shifts to the defendant to persuade the court by a preponderance of the evidence that legitimate, nondiscriminatory reasons for the challenged employment action existed.

I

Petitioner, the Texas Department of Community Affairs (TDCA), hired respondent, a female, in January 1972, for the position of accounting clerk in the Public Service Careers Division (PSC). PSC provided training and employment opportunities in the public sector for unskilled workers. When hired, respondent possessed several years' experience in employment training. She was promoted to Field Services Coordinator in July 1972. Her supervisor resigned in November of that year, and respondent was assigned additional duties. Although she applied for the supervisor's position of Project Director, the position remained vacant for six months.

PSC was funded completely by the United States Department of Labor. The Department was seriously concerned about inefficiencies at PSC. In February, 1973, the Department notified the Executive Director of TDCA, B.R. Fuller, that it would terminate PSC the following month. TDCA officials, assisted by respondent, persuaded the Department to continue funding the program, conditioned upon PSC reforming its operations. Among the agreed conditions were the appointment of a permanent Project Director and a complete reorganization of the PSC staff.

After consulting with personnel within TDCA, Fuller hired a male from another division of the agency as Project Director. In reducing the PSC staff, he fired respondent along with two other employees, and retained another male, Walz, as the only professional employee in the division. It is undisputed that respondent had maintained her application for the position of Project Director and had requested to remain with TDCA. Respondent soon was rehired by TDCA and assigned to another division of the agency. She received the exact salary paid to the Project Director at PSC, and the subsequent promotions she has received have kept her salary and responsibility commensurate with what she would have received had she been appointed Project Director.

Respondent filed this suit in the United States District Court for the Western District of Texas. She alleged that the failure to promote and the subsequent decision to terminate her had been predicated on gender discrimination in violation of Title VII. After a bench trial, the District Court held that neither decision was based on gender discrimination. The court relied on the testimony of Fuller that the employment decisions necessitated by the commands of the Department of Labor were based on consultation among trusted advisors and a nondiscriminatory evaluation of the relative qualifications of the individuals involved. He testified that the three individuals terminated did not work well together, and that TDCA thought that eliminating this problem would improve PSC's efficiency. The court accepted this explanation as rational and, in effect, found no evidence that the decisions not to promote and to terminate respondent were prompted by gender discrimination.

The Court of Appeals for the Fifth Circuit reversed in part. 608 F.2d 563 (1979). The court held that the District Court's "implicit evidentiary finding" that the male hired as Project Director was better qualified for that position than respondent was not clearly erroneous. Accordingly, the court affirmed the District Court's finding that respondent was not discriminated against when she was not promoted. The Court of Appeals, however, reversed the District Court's finding that Fuller's testimony sufficiently had rebutted respondent's prima facie case of gender discrimination in the decision to terminate her employment at PSC. The court reaffirmed its previously announced views that the defendant in a Title VII case bears the burden of proving by a preponderance of the evidence the existence of legitimate nondiscriminatory reasons for the employment action and that the defendant also must prove by objective evidence that those hired or promoted were better qualified than the plaintiff. The court found that Fuller's testimony did not carry either of these evidentiary burdens. It, therefore, reversed the judgment of the District Court and remanded the case for computation of backpay. Because the decision of the Court of Appeals as to the burden of proof borne by the defendant conflicts with interpretations of our precedents adopted by other courts of appeals, we granted certiorari, 447 U.S. 920 (1980). We now vacate the Fifth Circuit's decision and remand for application of the correct standard.

II

In McDonnell Douglas Corp. v. Green, 411 U.S. 792 (1973), we set forth the basic allocation of burdens and order of presentation of proof in a Title VII case alleging discriminatory treatment. First, the plaintiff has the burden of proving by the preponderance of the evidence a prima facie case of discrimination. Second, if the plaintiff succeeds in proving the prima facie case, the burden shifts to the defendant "to articulate some legitimate, nondiscriminatory reason for the employee's rejection." Id., at 802. Third, should the defendant carry this burden, the plaintiff must then have an opportunity to prove by a preponderance of the evidence that the legitimate reasons offered by the defendant were not its true reasons, but were a pretext for discrimination. Id., at 804.

The nature of the burden that shifts to the defendant should be understood in light of the plaintiff's ultimate and intermediate burdens. The ultimate burden of persuading the trier of fact that the defendant intentionally discriminated against the plaintiff remains at all time with the plaintiff. See Board of Trustees of Keene State College v. Sweeney, 439 U.S. 24, 25, n.2 (1979); id., at 29 (Stevens, J., dissenting). See generally 9 Wigmore, Evidence §2489 (3d ed. 1940) (the burden of persuasion "never shifts"). The *McDonnell Douglas* division of intermediate evidentiary burdens serves to bring the litigants and the court expeditiously and fairly to this ultimate question.

The burden of establishing a prima facie case of disparate treatment is not onerous. The plaintiff must prove by a preponderance of the evidence that she applied for an available position, for which she was qualified, but was rejected under circumstances which give rise to an inference of unlawful discrimination. The prima facie case serves an important function in the litigation: it eliminates the most common nondiscriminatory reasons for the plaintiff's rejection. As the Court explained in Furnco Construction Co. v. Waters, 438 U.S. 567, 577 (1978), the prima facie case "raises an inference of discrimination only because we presume these acts, if otherwise unexplained, are more likely than not based on the consideration of impermissible factors." Establishment of the prima facie case in effect creates a presumption that the employer unlawfully discriminated against the employee. If the trier of fact believes the plaintiff's evidence, and if the employer is silent in the face of the presumption, the court must enter judgment for the plaintiff because no issue of fact remains in the case.

The burden that shifts to the defendant, therefore, is to rebut the presumption of discrimination by producing evidence that the plaintiff was rejected, or someone else was preferred, for a legitimate, nondiscriminatory reason. The defendant need not persuade the court that it was actually motivated by the proffered reasons. It is sufficient if the defendant's evidence raises a genuine issue of fact as to whether it discriminated against the plaintiff. To accomplish this, the defendant must clearly set forth, through the introduction of admissible evidence, the reasons for the plaintiff's rejection. The explanation provided must be legally sufficient to justify a judgment for the defendant. If the defendant carries this burden of production, the presumption raised by the prima facie case is rebutted,[10] and the factual inquiry proceeds to a new level of specificity. Placing this burden of production on the defendant thus serves simultaneously to meet the plaintiff's prima facie case by presenting a legitimate reason for the action and to frame the factual issue with sufficient clarity so that the plaintiff will have a full and fair opportunity to demonstrate pretext. The sufficiency of the defendant's evidence should be evaluated by the extent to which it fulfills these functions.

The plaintiff retains the burden of persuasion. She now must have the opportunity to demonstrate that the proffered reason was not the true reason for the employment decision. This burden now merges with the ultimate burden of persuading the court that she has been the victim of intentional discrimination. She may succeed in this either directly by persuading the court that a discriminatory reason more likely motivated the employer or indirectly by showing that the employer's proffered explanation is unworthy of credence. See *McDonnell Douglas*, supra, at 804-805. . . .

---

10. See generally J. Thayer, Preliminary Treatise on Evidence 346 (1898). In saying that the presumption drops from the case, we do not imply that the trier of fact no longer may consider evidence previously introduced by the plaintiff to establish a prima facie case. A satisfactory explanation by the defendant destroys the legally mandatory inference of discrimination arising from the plaintiff's initial evidence. Nonetheless, this evidence and inferences properly drawn therefrom may be considered by the trier of fact on the issue of whether the defendant's explanation is pretextual. Indeed, there may be some cases where the plaintiff's initial evidence, combined with effective cross-examination of the defendant, will suffice to discredit the defendant's explanation.

IV

In summary, the Court of Appeals erred by requiring the defendant to prove by a preponderance of the evidence the existence of nondiscriminatory reasons for terminating the respondent and that the person retained in her stead had superior objective qualifications for the position. When the plaintiff has proved a prima facie case of discrimination, the defendant bears only the burden of explaining clearly the nondiscriminatory reasons for its actions. The judgment of the Court of Appeals is vacated and the case is remanded for further proceedings consistent with this opinion.

It is so ordered.

ST. MARY'S HONOR CENTER v. HICKS
509 U.S. 502 (1993)

Justice SCALIA delivered the opinion of the Court.

We granted certiorari to determine whether, in a suit against an employer alleging intentional racial discrimination in violation of §703(a)(1) of Title VII of the Civil Rights Act of 1964, the trier of fact's rejection of the employer's asserted reasons for its actions mandates a finding for the plaintiff.

I

Petitioner St. Mary's Honor Center (St. Mary's) is a halfway house operated by the Missouri Department of Corrections and Human Resources (MDCHR). Respondent Melvin Hicks, a black man, was hired as a correctional officer at St. Mary's in August 1978 and was promoted to shift commander, one of six supervisory positions, in February 1980.

In 1983 MDCHR conducted an investigation of the administration of St. Mary's, which resulted in extensive supervisory changes in January 1984. Respondent retained his position, but John Powell became the new chief of custody (respondent's immediate supervisor) and petitioner Steve Long the new superintendent. Prior to these personnel changes respondent had enjoyed a satisfactory employment record, but soon thereafter became the subject of repeated, and increasingly severe, disciplinary actions. He was suspended for five days for violations of institutional rules by his subordinates on March 3, 1984. He received a letter of reprimand for alleged failure to conduct an adequate investigation of a brawl between inmates that occurred during his shift on March 21. He was later demoted from shift commander to correctional officer for his failure to ensure that his subordinates entered their use of a St. Mary's vehicle into the official log book on March 19, 1984.

Finally, on June 7, 1984, he was discharged for threatening Powell during an exchange of heated words on April 19.

Respondent brought this suit in the United States District Court for the Eastern District of Missouri, alleging that petitioner St. Mary's violated §703(a)(1) of Title VII of the Civil Rights Act of 1964, and that petitioner Long violated Rev. Stat. §1979, 42 U.S.C. §1983, by demoting and then discharging him because of his race. After a full bench trial, the District Court found for petitioners. 756 F. Supp. 1244 (E.D. Mo. 1991). The United States Court of Appeals for the Eighth Circuit reversed and remanded, and we granted certiorari, 113 S. Ct. 954 (1993).

II

Section 703(a)(1) of Title VII of the Civil Rights Act of 1964 provides in relevant part:

> It shall be an unlawful employment practice for an employer—
> (1) . . . to discharge any individual, or otherwise to discriminate against any individual with respect to his compensation, terms, conditions, or privileges of employment, because of such individual's race. . . .

With the goal of "progressively . . . sharpen[ing] the inquiry into the elusive factual question of intentional discrimination," Texas Dept. of Community Affairs v. Burdine, 450 US. 248, 255, n.8, 101 S. Ct. 1089, 1094, n.8, 67 L. Ed. 2d 207 (1981), our opinion in McDonnell Douglas Corp. v. Green, 411 U.S. 792, 93 S. Ct. 1817, 36 L. Ed. 2d 668 (1973), established an allocation of the burden of production and an order for the presentation of proof in Title VII discriminatory-treatment cases. The plaintiff in such a case, we said, must first establish, by a preponderance of the evidence, a "prima facie" case of racial discrimination. Petitioners do not challenge the District Court's finding that respondent satisfied the minimal requirements of such a prima facie case by proving (1) that he is black, (2) that he was qualified for the position of shift commander, (3) that he was demoted from that position and ultimately discharged, and (4) that the position remained open and was ultimately filled by a white man.

Under the McDonnell Douglas scheme, "[e]stablishment of the prima facie case in effect creates a presumption that the employer unlawfully discriminated against the employee." To establish a "presumption" is to say that a finding of the predicate fact (here, the prima facie case) produces "a required conclusion in the absence of explanation" (here, the finding of unlawful discrimination). Thus, the McDonnell Douglas presumption places upon the defendant the burden of producing an explanation to rebut the prima facie case—i.e., the burden of "producing evidence" that the adverse employment actions were taken "for a legitimate, nondiscriminatory reason." "[T]he defendant must clearly set forth, through the introduction of admissible evidence," reasons for its actions which, if believed by the trier of fact, would support a finding that unlawful discrimination was not the cause of the employment action. It is important to note, however, that although the *McDonnell Douglas* presumption shifts the burden of production to the defendant, "[t]he ultimate burden of persuading the trier of fact that the defendant intentionally discriminated against the plaintiff remains at all times with the plaintiff." In this regard it operates like all presumptions, as described in Rule 301 of the Federal Rules of Evidence:

> In all civil actions and proceedings not otherwise provided for by Act of Congress or by these rules, a presumption imposes on the party against whom it is directed the burden of going forward with evidence to rebut or meet the presumption, but does not shift to such party the burden of proof in the sense of the risk of nonpersuasion, which remains throughout the trial upon the party on whom it was originally cast.

Respondent does not challenge the District Court's finding that petitioners sustained their burden of production by introducing evidence of two legitimate, nondiscriminatory reasons for their actions: the severity and the accumulation of rules violations committed by respondent. Our cases make clear that at that point the shifted burden of production became irrelevant: "If the defendant carries this burden of production, the presumption raised by the prima facie case is rebutted," and "drops from the case." The plaintiff then has "the full and fair opportunity to demonstrate," through presentation of his own case and through cross-examination of the defendant's witnesses, "that the proffered reason was not the true reason for the employment decision," and that race was. He retains that "ultimate burden of persuading the [trier of fact] that [he] has been the victim of intentional discrimination."

The District Court, acting as trier of fact in this bench trial, found that the reasons petitioners gave were not the real reasons for respondent's demotion and discharge. It found that respondent was the only supervisor disciplined for violations committed by this subordinates; that similar and even more serious violations committed by respondent's coworkers were either disregarded or treated more leniently; and that Powell manufactured the final verbal confrontation in order to provoke respondent into threatening him. It nonetheless held that respondent had failed to carry his ultimate burden of proving that his race was the determining factor in petitioners' decision first to demote and then to dismiss him. In short, the District Court concluded that "although [respondent] has proven the existence of a crusade to terminate him, he has not proven that the crusade was racially rather than personally motivated."

The Court of Appeals set this determination aside on the ground that "[o]nce [respondent] proved all of [petitioners'] proffered reasons for the adverse employment actions to be pretextual, [respondent] was entitled to judgment as a matter of law." The Court of Appeals reasoned:

> Because all of defendants' proffered reasons were discredited, defendants were in a position of having offered no legitimate reason for their actions. In other words, defendants were in no better position than if they had remained silent, offering no rebuttal to an established inference that they had unlawfully discriminated against plaintiff on the basis of his race.

That is not so. By producing evidence (whether ultimately persuasive or not) of nondiscriminatory reasons, petitioners sustained their burden of production, and thus placed themselves in a "better position than if they had remained silent."

In the nature of things, the determination that a defendant has met its burden of production (and has thus rebutted any legal presumption of intentional discrimination) can involve no credibility assessment. For the burden-of-production determination necessarily precedes the credibility-assessment stage. At the close of the defendant's case, the court is asked to decide whether an issue of fact remains for the trier of fact to determine. None does if, on the evidence presented, (1) any rational person would have to find the existence of facts constituting a prima facie case, and (2) the defendant has failed to meet its burden of production — i.e., has failed to introduce evidence which, taken as true, would permit the conclusion that there was a nondiscriminatory reason for the adverse action. In that event, the court must award judgment to the plaintiff as a matter of law under Federal Rule of Civil Procedure 50(a)(1) (in the case of jury trials) or Federal Rule of Civil Procedure 52(c) (in the case of bench trials). If the defendant has failed to sustain its burden but reasonable minds could differ as to whether a preponderance of the evidence establishes the facts of a prima facie case, then a question of fact does remain, which the trier of fact will be called upon to answer.

If, on the other hand, the defendant has succeeded in carrying its burden of production, the *McDonnell Douglas* framework—with its presumptions and burdens — is no longer relevant. To resurrect it later, after the trier of fact has determined that what was "produced" to meet the burden of production is not credible, flies in the face of our holding in *Burdine* that to rebut the presumption "[t]he defendant need not persuade the court that it was actually motivated by the proffered reasons." The presumption, having fulfilled its role of forcing the defendant to come forward with some response, simply drops out of the picture. The defendant's "production" (whatever its persuasive effect) having been made, the trier of fact proceeds to decide the ultimate question: whether plaintiff has proven "that the defendant intentionally discriminated against [him]" because of his race. The factfinder's disbelief of the reasons put forward by the defendant (particularly if disbelief is accompanied by a suspicion of mendacity) may, together with the elements of the prima facie case, suffice to show intentional discrimination. Thus, rejection of the defendant's proffered reasons, will permit the trier of fact to infer the ultimate fact of intentional discrimination, and the Court of Appeals was correct when it noted that, upon such rejection, "[n]o additional proof of discrimination is required." But the Court of Appeals' holding that rejection of the defendant's proffered reasons compels judgment for the plaintiff disregards the fundamental principle of Rule 301 that a presumption does not shift the burden of proof, and ignores our repeated admonition that the Title VII plaintiff at all times bears the "ultimate burden of persuasion."

III

Only one unfamiliar with out case-law will be upset by the dissent's alarum that we are today setting aside "settled precedent," "two decades of stable law in this Court," "a framework carefully crafted in precedents as old as 20 years," which "Congress is [aware]" of and has implicitly approved. Panic will certainly not break out among the courts of appeals, whose divergent views concerning the nature of the supposedly "stable law in this Court" are precisely what prompted us to take this case—a divergence in which the dissent's version of "settled precedent" cannot remotely be considered the "prevailing view." [Citations omitted.] We mean to answer the dissent's accusations in detail, by examining our cases, but at the outset it is worth noting the utter implausibility that we would ever have held what the dissent says we held.

As we have described, Title VII renders it unlawful "for an employer . . . to fail or refuse to hire or to discharge any individual, or otherwise to discriminate against any individual with respect to his compensation, terms, conditions, or privileges of employment, because of such individual's race, color, religion, sex, or national origin." Here (in the context of the now-permissible jury trials for Title VII causes of action) is what the dissent asserts we have held to be a proper assessment of liability for violation of this law: Assume that 40% of a business' work force are members of a particular minority group, a group which comprises only 10% of the relevant labor market. An applicant, who is a member of that group, applies for an opening for which he is minimally qualified, but is rejected by a hiring officer of that same minority group, and the search to fill the opening continues. The rejected applicant files suit for racial discrimination under Title VII, and before the suit comes to trial, the supervisor who conducted the company's hiring is fired. Under *McDonnell Douglas*, the plaintiff has a prima facie case, and under the dissent's interpretation of our law not only must the company come forward with some explanation for the refusal to hire (which it will have to try to confirm out of the mouth of its now antagonistic former employee), but the jury must be instructed that, if they find that explanation to be incorrect, they must assess damages against the company, whether or not they believe the company was guilty of racial discrimination. The disproportionate minority makeup of the company's work force and the fact that its hiring officer was of the same minority group as the plaintiff will be irrelevant, because the plaintiff's case can be proved "indirectly by showing that the employer's proffered explanation is unworthy of credence." Surely nothing short of inescapable prior holdings (the dissent does not pretend there are any) should make one assume that this is the law we have created.

We have no authority to impose liability upon an employer for alleged discriminatory employment practices unless an appropriate factfinder determines, according to proper procedures, that the employer has unlawfully discriminated. We may, according to traditional practice, establish certain modes and orders of proof, including an initial rebuttable presumption of the sort we described earlier in this opinion, which we believe *McDonnell Douglas* represents. But nothing in law would permit us to substitute for the required finding that the employer's action was the product of unlawful discrimination, the much different (and much lesser) finding that the employer's explanation of its action was not believable. The dissent's position amounts to precisely this, unless what is required to establish the *McDonnell Douglas* prima facie case is a degree of proof so high that it would, in absence of rebuttal, require a directed verdict for the plaintiff (for in that case proving the employer's rebuttal noncredible would leave the plaintiff's directed-verdict case in place, and compel a judgment in his favor). Quite obviously, however, what is required to establish the *McDonnell Douglas* prima facie case is infinitely less than what a directed verdict demands. The dissent is thus left with a position that has no support in the statute, no support in the reason of the matter, no support in any holding of this Court (that is not even contended), and support, if at all, only in the dicta of this Court's opinions. It is to those that we now turn — begrudgingly, since we think it generally undesirable, where holdings of the Court are not at issue, to dissect the sentences of the United States Reports as though they were the United States Code. . . .

IV

We turn, finally, to the dire practical consequences that the respondents and the dissent claim our decision today will produce. What appears to trouble the dissent more than anything is that, in its view, our rule is adopted "for the benefit of employers who have been found to have given false evidence in a court of law," whom we "favo[r]" by "exempting them from responsibility for lies." As we shall explain, our rule in no way gives special favor to those employers whose evidence is disbelieved. But initially we must point out that there is no justification for assuming (as the dissent repeatedly does) that those employers whose evidence is disbelieved are perjurers and liars. . . . Even if these were typically cases in which an individual defendant's sworn assertion regarding a physical occurrence was pitted against an individual plaintiff's sworn assertion regarding the same physical occurrence, surely it would be imprudent to call the party whose assertion is (by a mere preponderance of the evidence) disbelieved, a perjurer and a liar. And in these Title VII cases, the defendant is ordinarily not an individual but a company, which must rely upon the statement of an employee — often a relatively low-level employee — as to the central fact; and that central fact is not a physical occurrence, but rather that employee's state of mind. To say that the company which in good faith introduces such testimony, or even the testifying employee himself, becomes a liar and a perjurer when the testimony is not believed, is nothing short of absurd.

Undoubtedly some employers (or at least their employees) will be lying. But even if we could readily identify these perjurers, what an extraordinary notion, that we "exempt them from responsibility for their lies" unless we enter Title VII judgments for the plaintiffs! Title VII is not a cause of action for perjury; we have other civil and criminal remedies for that. The dissent's notion of judgment-for-lying is seen to be not even a fair and even-handed punishment for vice, when one realizes how strangely selective it is: the employer is free to lie to its heart's content about whether the plaintiff ever applied for a job, about how long he worked, how much he made — indeed, about anything and everything except the reason for the adverse employment action. And the plaintiff is permitted to lie about absolutely everything without losing a verdict he otherwise deserves. This is not a major, or even a sensible, blow against fibbery.

The respondent's argument based upon the employer's supposed lying is a more modest one: "A defendant which unsuccessfully offers a 'phony reason' logically cannot be in a better legal position [i.e., the position of having overcome the presumption from the plaintiff's prima facie case] than a defendant who remains silent, and offers no reasons at all for its conduct." But there is no anomaly in that, once one recognizes that the *McDonnell Douglas* presumption is a procedural device, designed only to establish an order of proof and production. The books are full of procedural rules that place the perjurer (initially, at least) in a better position than the truthful litigant who makes no response at all. A defendant who fails to answer a complaint will, on motion, suffer a default judgment that a deceitful response could have avoided. A defendant whose answer fails to contest critical averments in the complaint will, on motion, suffer a judgment on the pleadings that untruthful denials could have avoided. And a defendant who fails to submit affidavits creating a genuine issue of fact in response to a motion for summary judgment will suffer a dismissal that false affidavits could have avoided. In all of those cases, as under the *McDonnell Douglas* framework, perjury may purchase the defendant a chance at the factfinder — though there, as here, it also carries substantial risks.

The dissent repeatedly raises a procedural objection that is impressive only to one who mistakes the basic nature of the *McDonnell Douglas* procedure. It asserts that "the Court now holds that the further enquiry [i.e., the injury that follows the employer's response to the prima facie case] is wide open, not limited at all by the scope of the employer's proffered explanation." The plaintiff cannot be expected to refute "reasons not articulated by the employer, but discerned in the record by the factfinder." He should not "be saddled with the tremendous disadvantage of having to confront not the defined task of proving the employer's stated reasons to be false, but the amorphous requirement of disproving all possible nondiscriminatory reasons that a factfinder might find lurking in the record." "Under the scheme announced today, any conceivable explanation for the employer's actions that might be suggested by the evidence, however unrelated to the employer's articulated reasons, must be addressed by [the plaintiff]." These statements imply that the employer's "proffered explanation," his "stated reasons," his "articulated reasons," somehow exist apart from the record — in some pleading, or perhaps in some formal, nontestimonial statement made on behalf of the defendant to the factfinder. ("Your honor, pursuant to *McDonnell Douglas* the defendant hereby formally asserts, as its reason for the dismissal at issue here, incompetence of the employee.") Of course it does not work like that. The reasons the defendant sets forth are set forth "through the introduction of admissible evidence." In other words, the defendant's "articulated reasons" themselves are to be found "lurking in the record." It thus makes no sense to contemplate "the employer who is caught in a lie, but succeeds in injecting into the trial an unarticulated reason for its actions." There is a "lurking-in-the-record" problem, but it exists not for us but for the dissent. If, after the employer has met its preliminary burden, the plaintiff need not prove discrimination (and therefore need not disprove all other reasons suggested, no matter how vaguely, in the record) there must be some device for determining which particular portions of the record represent "articulated reasons" set forth with sufficient clarity to satisfy *McDonnell Douglas* — since it is only that evidence which the plantiff must refute. But of course our *McDonnell Douglas* framework makes no provision for such a determination, which would have to be made not at the close of the trial but in medias res, since otherwise the plaintiff would not know what evidence to offer. It makes no sense.

Respondent contends that "[t]he litigation decision of the employer to place in controversy only . . . particular explanations eliminates from further consideration the alternative explanations that the employer chose not to advance." The employer should bear, he contends, "the responsibility for its choices and the risk that plaintiff will disprove any pretextual reasons and therefore prevail." It is the "therefore" that is problematic. Title VII does not award damages against employers who cannot prove a nondiscriminatory reason for adverse employment action, but only against employers who are proven to have taken adverse employment action by reason of (in the context of the present case) race. That the employer's proffered reason is unpersuasive, or even obviously contrived, does not necessarily establish that the plaintiff's proffered reason of race is correct. That remains a question for the factfinder to answer, subject, of course, to appellate review — which should be conducted on remand in this case under the "clearly erroneous" standard of Federal Rule of Civil Procedure 52(a).

Finally, respondent argues that it "would be particularly ill-advised" for us to come forth with the holding we pronounce today "just as Congress has provided a right to jury trials in Title VII" cases. . . . We think quite the opposite is true. Clarity regarding the requisite elements of proof becomes all the more important when a jury must be instructed concerning them, and when detailed factual findings by the trial court will not be available upon review.

We reaffirm today what we said in *Aikens*:

> [T]he question facing triers of fact in discrimination cases is both sensitive and difficult. The prohibitions against discrimination contained in the Civil Rights Act of 1964 reflect an important national policy. There will seldom be "eyewitness" testimony as to the employer's mental processes. But none of this means that trial courts or reviewing courts should treat discrimination differently from other ultimate questions of fact. Nor should they make their injury even more difficult by applying legal rules which were devised to govern "the basic allocation of burdens and order of presentation of proof" in deciding this ultimate question.

The judgment of the Court of Appeals is reversed, and the case is remanded for further proceedings consistent with this opinion.

It is so ordered.

[Dissenting opinion by Justice Souter omitted.]

WARDS COVE PACKING CO. v. ATONIO
490 U.S. 642 (1989)

Justice WHITE delivered the opinion of the Court.

Title VII of the Civil Rights Act of 1964, 78 Stat. 253, as amended, 42

U.S.C. §2000e et seq., makes it an unfair employment practice for an employer to discriminate against any individual with respect to hiring or the terms and condition of employment because of such individual's race, color, religion, sex, or national origin; or to limit, segregate, or classify his employees in ways that would adversely affect any employee because of the employee's race, color, religion, sex, or national origin. §2000e-2(a). Griggs v. Duke Power Co., 401 U.S. 424, 431 (1971), construed Title VII to proscribe "not only overt discrimination but also practices that are fair in form but discriminatory in practice." Under this basis for liability, which is known as the "disparate-impact" theory and which is involved in this case, a facially neutral employment practice may be deemed violative of the Title VII without evidence of the employer's subjective intent to discriminate that is required in a "disparate-treatment" case.

I

The claims before us are disparate-impact claims, involving the employment practices of petitioners, two companies that operate salmon canneries in remote and widely separated areas of Alaska. The canneries operate only during the salmon runs in the summer months. They are inoperative and vacant for the rest of the year. In May or June of each year, a few weeks before the salmon runs begin, workers arrive and prepare the equipment and facilities for the canning operation. Most of these workers possess a variety of skills. When salmon runs are about to begin, the workers who will operate the cannery lines arrive, remain as long as there are fish to can, and then depart. The canneries are then closed down, winterized, and left vacant until the next spring. During the off-season, the companies employ only a small number of individuals at their headquarters in Seattle and Astoria, Oregon, plus some employees at the winter shipyard in Seattle.

The length and size of salmon runs vary from year to year, and hence the number of employees needed at each cannery also varies. Estimates are made as early in the winter as possible; the necessary employees are hired, and when the time comes, they are transported to the canneries. Salmon must be processed soon after they are caught, and the work during the canning season is therefore intense. For this reason, and because the canneries are located in remote regions, all workers are housed at the canneries and have their meals in company-owned mess halls.

Jobs at the canneries are of two general types: "cannery jobs" on the cannery line, which are unskilled positions; and "noncannery jobs," which fall into a variety of classifications. Most noncannery jobs are classified as skilled positions. Cannery jobs are filled predominantly by nonwhites: Filipinos and Alaska Natives. The Filipinos are hired through, and dispatched by, Local 37 of the International Longshoremen's and Warehousemen's Union pursuant to a hiring hall agreement with the local. The Alaska Natives primarily reside in villages near the remote cannery locations. Noncannery jobs are filled with predominantly white workers, who are hired during the winter months from the companies' offices in Washington and Oregon. Virtually all of the noncannery jobs pay more than cannery positions. The predominantly white noncannery workers and the predominantly nonwhite cannery employees live in separate dormitories and eat in separate mess halls.

In 1974, respondents, a class of nonwhite cannery workers who were (or had been) employed at the canneries, brought this Title VII action against petitioners. Respondents alleged that a variety of petitioners' hiring/promotion practices—e.g., nepotism, a rehire preference, a lack of objective hiring criteria, separate hiring channels, a practice of not promoting from within — were responsible for the racial stratification of the work force and had denied them and other nonwhites employment as noncannery workers on the basis of race. Respondents also complained of petitioners' racially segregated housing and dining facilities. All of respondents' claims were advanced under both the disparate-treatment and disparate-impact theories of Title VII liability. . . .

II

It is clear to us that the Court of Appeals' acceptance of the comparison between the racial composition of the cannery work force and that of the noncannery work force, as probative of a prima facie case of disparate impact in the selection of the latter group of workers, was flawed for several reasons. Most obviously, with respect to the skilled noncannery jobs at issue here, the cannery work force in no way reflected "the pool of *qualified* job applicants" or the "*qualified* population in the labor force." Measuring alleged discrimination in the selection of accountants, managers, boat captains, electricians, doctors, and engineers — and the long list of other "skilled" noncannery positions found to exist by the District Court, see App. to Pet. for Cert. I-56 to I-58—by comparing the number of nonwhites occupying these jobs to the number of nonwhites filling cannery worker positions is nonsensical. If the absence of minorities holding such skilled positions is due to a dearth of qualified nonwhite applicants (for reasons that are not petitioners' fault), petitioners' selection methods or employment practices cannot be said to have had a "disparate impact" on nonwhites. . . .

The Court of Appeals also erred with respect to the unskilled noncannery positions. Racial imbalance in one segment of an employer's work force does not, without more, establish a prima facie case of disparate impact with respect to the selection of workers for the employer's other positions, even where workers for the different positions may have somewhat fungible skills (as is arguably the case for cannery and un-skilled noncannery workers). As long as there are no barriers or prac-tices deterring qualified nonwhites from applying for noncannery positions, if the percentage of selected applicants who are nonwhite is not significantly less than the percentage of qualified applicants who are nonwhite, the employer's selection mechanism probably does not operate with a disparate impact on minorities. Where this is the case, the percentage of nonwhite workers found in other positions in the employer's labor force is irrelevant to the question of a prima facie statistical case of disparate impact. As noted above, a contrary ruling on this point would almost inexorably lead to the use of numerical quotas in the workplace, a result that Congress and this Court have rejected repeatedly in the past. . . .

Consequently, we reverse the Court of Appeals' ruling that a com-parison between the percentage of cannery workers who are nonwhite and the percentage of noncannery workers who are nonwhite makes out a prima facie case of disparate impact. Of course, this leaves unre-solved whether the record made in the District Court will support a conclusion that a prima facie case of disparate impact has been estab-lished on some basis other than the racial disparity between cannery and noncannery workers. This is an issue that the Court of Appeals or the District Court should address in the first instance.

III

Since the statistical disparity relied on by the Court of Appeals did not suffice to make out a prima facie case, any inquiry by us into whether the specific challenged employment practices of petitioners caused that disparity is pretermitted, as is any inquiry into whether the disparate impact that any employment practice may have had was justified by business considerations. Because we remand for further proceedings, however, on whether a prima facie case of disparate impact has been made in defensible fashion in this case, we address two other challenges petitioners have made to the decision of the Court of Appeals.

A

First is the question of causation in a disparate-impact case. The law in this respect was correctly stated by Justice O'Connor's opinion last Term in Watson v. Fort Worth Bank & Trust, 487 U.S., at 994:

> [W]e note that the plaintiff's burden in establishing a prima facie case goes beyond the need to show that there are statistical disparities in the employer's work force. The plaintiff must begin by identifying the specific employment prac-tice that is challenged. . . . Especially in cases where an employer combines sub-

jective criteria with the use of more rigid standardized rules or tests, the plaintiff is in our view responsible for isolating and identifying the specific employment practices that are allegedly responsible for any observed statistical disparities.

Cf. also id., at 1000 (Blackmun, J., concurring in part and concurring in judgment).

Indeed, even the Court of Appeals—whose decision petitioners assault on this score—noted that "it is . . . essential that the practices identified by the cannery workers be linked causally with the demonstrated adverse impact." 827 F.2d, at 445. Notwithstanding the Court of Appeals' apparent adherence to the proper inquiry, petitioners contend that that court erred by permitting respondents to make out their case by offering "only [one] set of cumulative comparative statistics as evidence of the disparate impact of each and all of [petitioners' hiring] practices." Brief for Petitioners 31.

Our disparate-impact cases have always focused on the impact of *particular* hiring practices on employment opportunities for minorities. Just as an employer cannot escape liability under Title VII by demonstrating that, "at the bottom line," his work force is racially balanced (where particular hiring practices may operate to deprive minorities of employment opportunities), see Connecticut v. Teal, 457 U.S., at 450 [(1982)], a Title VII plaintiff does not make out a case of disparate impact simply by showing that, "at the bottom line," there is racial *imbalance* in the work force. As a general matter, a plaintiff must demonstrate that it is the application of a specific or particular employment practice that has created the disparate impact under attack. Such a showing is an integral part of the plaintiff's prima facie case in a disparate-impact suit under Title VII.

Here, respondents have alleged that several "objective" employment practices (e.g., nepotism, separate hiring channels, rehire preferences), as well as the use of "subjective decision making" to select noncannery workers, have had a disparate impact on nonwhites. Respondents base this claim on statistics that allegedly show a disproportionately low percentage of nonwhites in the at-issue positions. However, even if on remand respondents can show that nonwhites are underrepresented in the at-issue jobs in a manner that is acceptable under the standards set forth in Part II, supra, this alone will *not* suffice to make out a prima facie case of disparate impact. Respondents will also have to demonstrate that the disparity they complain of is the result of one or more of the employment practices that they are attacking here, specifically showing that each challenged practice has a significantly disparate impact on employment opportunities for whites and nonwhites. To hold otherwise would result in employers being potentially liable for "the myriad of innocent causes that may lead to statistical imbalances in the composition of their work forces." Watson v. Fort Worth Bank & Trust, supra, at 992.

Some will complain that this specific causation requirement is unduly burdensome on Title VII plaintiffs. But liberal civil discovery rules give plaintiffs broad access to employers' records in an effort to document their claims. Also, employers falling within the scope of the Uniform Guidelines on Employee Selection Procedures, 29 CFR §1607.1 et seq. (1988), are required to "maintain ... records or other information which will disclose the impact which its tests and other selection procedures have upon employment opportunities of persons by identifiable race, sex, or ethnic group[s]." See §1607.4(A). This includes records concerning "the individual components of the selection process" where there is a significant disparity in the selection rates of whites and non-whites. See §1607.4(C). Plaintiffs as a general matter will have the benefit of these tools to meet their burden of showing a causal link between challenged employment practices and racial imbalances in the work force; respondents presumably took full advantage of these opportunities to build their case before the trial in the District Court was held.

Consequently, on remand, the courts below are instructed to require, as part of respondents' prima facie case, a demonstration that specific elements of the petitioners' hiring process have a significantly disparate impact on nonwhites.

B

If, on remand, respondents meet the proof burdens outlined above, and establish a prima facie case of disparate impact with respect to any of petitioners' employment practices, the case will shift to any business justification petitioners offer for their use of these practices. This phase of the disparate-impact case contains two components: first, a consideration of the justifications an employer offers for his use of these practices; and second, the availability of alternative practices to achieve the same business ends, with less racial impact. See, e.g., Albemarle Paper Co. v. Moody, 422 U.S., at 425 [(1975)]. We consider these two components in turn.

(1)

Though we have phrased the query differently in different cases, it is generally well established that at the justification stage of such a disparate-impact case, the dispositive issue is whether a challenged practice serves, in a significant way, the legitimate employment goals of the employer. See, e.g., Watson v. Fort Worth Bank & Trust, 487 U.S., at 997-999; New York City Transit Authority v. Beazer, 440 U.S., at 587,

n.31 [(1979)]; Griggs v. Duke Power Co., 401 U.S., at 432. The touchstone of this inquiry is a reasoned review of the employer's justification
for his use of the challenged practice. A mere insubstantial justification
in this regard will not suffice, because such a low standard of review
would permit discrimination to be practiced through the use of spurious, seemingly neutral employment practices. At the same time, though,
there is no requirement that the challenged practice be "essential" or
"indispensable" to the employer's business for it to pass muster: this
degree of scrutiny would be almost impossible for most employers to
meet, and would result in a host of evils. . . .

In this phase, the employer carries the burden of producing evidence
of a business justification for his employment practice. The burden of
persuasion, however, remains with the disparate-impact plaintiff. To the
extent that the Ninth Circuit held otherwise in its en banc decision in
this case, see 810 F.2d, at 1485-1486, or in the panel's decision on remand, see 827 F.2d, at 445, 447—suggesting that the persuasion burden
should shift to petitioners once respondents established a prima facie
case of disparate impact—its decisions were erroneous. "[T]he ultimate
burden of proving that discrimination against a protected group has
been caused by a specific employment practice remains with the plaintiff
at all times." *Watson,* supra, at 997 (O'Connor, J.) (emphasis added).
This rule conforms with the usual method for allocating persuasion and
production burdens in the federal courts, see Fed. Rule Evid. 301, and
more specifically, it conforms to the rule in disparate-treatment cases
that the plaintiff bears the burden of disproving an employer's assertion
that the adverse employment action or practice was based solely on a
legitimate neutral consideration. See Texas Dept. of Community Affairs
v. Burdine, 450 U.S. 248, 256-258 (1981). We acknowledge that some
of our earlier decisions can be read as suggesting otherwise. See *Watson,*
supra, at 1006-1008 (Blackmun, J., concurring). But to the extent that
those cases speak of an employer's "burden of proof" with respect to a
legitimate business justification defense, see, e.g., Dothard v. Rawlinson,
433 U.S. 321, 329 (1977), they should have been understood to mean
an employer's production — but not persuasion — burden. Cf., e.g.,
NLRB v. Transportation Management Corp., 462 U.S. 393, 404, n.7
(1983). The persuasion burden here must remain with the plaintiff, for
it is he who must prove that it was "because of such individual's race,
color," etc., that he was denied a desired employment opportunity. See
42 U.S.C. §2000e-2(a).

(2)

Finally, if on remand the case reaches this point, and respondents
cannot persuade the trier of fact on the question of petitioners' business
necessity defense, respondents may still be able to prevail. To do so,

respondents will have to persuade the factfinder that "other tests or selection devices, without a similarly undesirable racial effect, would also serve the employer's legitimate [hiring] interest[s]"; by so demonstrating, respondents would prove that "[petitioners were] using [their] tests merely as a 'pretext' for discrimination." *Albemarle Paper Co.,* supra, at 425; see also *Watson,* 487 U.S., at 998 (O'Connor, J.); id., at 1005-1006 (Blackmun, J., concurring in part and concurring in judgment). If respondents, having established a prima facie case, come forward with alternatives to petitioners' hiring practices that reduce the racially disparate impact of practices currently being used, and petitioners refuse to adopt these alternatives, such a refusal would belie a claim by petitioners that their incumbent practices are being employed for non-discriminatory reasons.

Of course, any alternative practices which respondents offer up in this respect must be equally effective as petitioners' chosen hiring procedures in achieving petitioners' legitimate employment goals. Moreover, "[f]actors such as the cost or other burdens of proposed alternative selection devices are relevant in determining whether they would be equally as effective as the challenged practice in serving the employer's legitimate business goals." *Watson,* supra, at 998 (O'Connor, J.). "Courts are generally less competent than employers to restructure business practices," Furnco Construction Corp. v. Waters, 438 U.S. 567, 578 (1978); consequently, the judiciary should proceed with care before mandating that an employer must adopt a plaintiff's alternative selection or hiring practice in response to a Title VII suit.

IV

For the reasons given above, the judgment of the Court of Appeals is reversed, and the case is remanded for further proceedings consistent with this opinion. It is so ordered.

[Dissents omitted.]

SINDELL v. ABBOTT LABORATORIES
26 Cal. 3d 588, 163 Cal. Rptr. 132, 607 P.2d 924 (1980)

MOSK, J. This case involves a complex problem both timely and significant; may a plaintiff, injured as the result of a drug administered to her mother during pregnancy, who knows the type of drug involved but cannot identify the manufacturer of the precise product, hold liable for her injuries a maker of a drug produced from an identical formula?

Plaintiff Judith Sindell brought an action against eleven drug companies and Does 1 through 100, on behalf of herself and other women similarly situated. The complaint alleges as follows:

Between 1941 and 1971, defendants were engaged in the business of manufacturing, promoting, and marketing diethylstilbestrol (DES), a drug which is a synthetic compound of the female hormone estrogen. The drug was administered to plaintiff's mother and the mothers of the class she represents,[1] for the purpose of preventing miscarriage. In 1947, the Food and Drug Administration authorized the marketing of DES as a miscarriage preventative, but only on an experimental basis, with a requirement that the drug contain a warning label to that effect.

DES may cause cancerous vaginal and cervical growths in the daughters exposed to it before birth, because their mothers took the drug during pregnancy. The form of cancer from which these daughters suffer is known as adenocarcinoma, and it manifests itself after a minimum latent period of 10 or 12 years. It is a fast-spreading and deadly disease, and radical surgery is required to prevent it from spreading. DES also causes adenosis, precancerous vaginal and cervical growths which may spread to other areas of the body. The treatment for adenosis is cauterization, surgery, or cryosurgery. Women who suffer from this condition must be monitored by biopsy or colposcopic examination twice a year, a painful and expensive procedure. Thousands of women whose mothers received DES during pregnancy are unaware of the effects of the drug. . . .

Defendants demurred to the complaint. While the complaint did not expressly allege that plaintiff could not identify the manufacturer of the precise drug ingested by her mother, she stated in her points and authorities in opposition to the demurrers filed by some of the defendants that she was unable to make the identification, and the trial court sustained the demurrers of these defendants without leave to amend on the ground that plaintiff did not and stated she could not identify which defendant had manufactured the drug responsible for her injuries. Thereupon, the court dismissed the action. This appeal involves only five of ten defendants named in the complaint. . . .

This case is but one of a number filed throughout the country seeking to hold drug manufacturers liable for injuries allegedly resulting from DES prescribed to the plaintiffs' mothers since 1947. According to a note in the Fordham Law Review, estimates of the number of women who took the drug during pregnancy range from 1½ million to 3 million. Hundreds, perhaps thousands, of the daughters of these women suffer from adenocarcinoma, and the incidence of vaginal adenosis among them is 30 to 90 percent. (Comment, DES and a Proposed Theory of Enterprise Liability (1978) 46 Fordham L. Rev. 963, 964-967 [hereafter Fordham Comment].) Most of the cases are still pending.

1. The plaintiff class alleged consists of "girls and women who are residents of California and who have been exposed to DES before birth and who may or may not know that fact or the dangers" to which they were exposed. Defendants are also sued as representatives of a class of drug manufacturers which sold DES after 1941.

With two exceptions, those that have been decided resulted in judgments in favor of the drug company defendants because of the failure of the plaintiffs to identify the manufacturer of the DES prescribed to their mothers. The same result was reached in a recent California case. (McCreery v. Eli Lilly & Co. (1978) 87 Cal. App. 3d 77, 82-84, 150 Cal. Rptr. 730.) The present action is another attempt to overcome this obstacle to recovery.

We begin with the proposition that, as a general rule, the imposition of liability depends upon a showing by the plaintiff that his or her injuries were caused by the act of the defendant or by an instrumentality under the defendant's control. . . .

There are, however, exceptions to this rule. Plaintiff's complaint suggests several bases upon which defendants may be held liable for her injuries even though she cannot demonstrate the name of the manufacturer which produced the DES actually taken by her mother. The first of these theories, classically illustrated by Summers v. Tice (1948) 33 Cal. 2d 80, 199 P.2d 1, places the burden of proof of causation upon tortious defendants in certain circumstances. The second basis of liability emerging from the complaint is that defendants acted in concert to cause injury to plaintiff. There is a third and novel approach to the problem, sometimes called the theory of "enterprise liability," but which we prefer to designate by the more accurate term of "industry-wide" liability, which might obviate the necessity for identifying the manufacturer of the injury-causing drug. We shall conclude that these doctrines, as previously interpreted, may not be applied to hold defendants liable under the allegations of this complaint. However, we shall propose and adopt a fourth basis for permitting the action to be tried, grounded upon an extension of the *Summers* doctrine.

I

Plaintiff places primary reliance upon cases which hold that if a party cannot identify which of two or more defendants caused an injury, the burden of proof may shift to the defendants to show that they were not responsible for the harm. This principle is sometimes referred to as the "alternative liability" theory.

The celebrated case of Summers v. Tice, supra, 33 Cal. 2d 80, 199 P.2d 1, a unanimous opinion of this court, best exemplifies the rule. In *Summers,* the plaintiff was injured when two hunters negligently shot in his direction. It could not be determined which of them had fired the shot which actually caused the injury to the plaintiff's eye, but both defendants were nevertheless held jointly and severally liable for the whole of the damages. We reasoned that both were wrongdoers, both were negligent toward the plaintiff, and that it would be unfair to require plaintiff to isolate the defendant responsible, because if the one pointed out were to escape liability, the other might also, and the plaintiff-victim would be shorn of any remedy. In these circumstances, we held, the burden of proof shifted to the defendants, "each to absolve himself if he can." (Id., p.86, 199 P.2d p.4.) . . .

In *Summers*, we relied upon Ybarra v. Spangard (1944) 25 Cal. 2d 486, 154 P.2d 687. There, the plaintiff was injured while he was unconscious during the course of surgery. He sought damages against several doctors and a nurse who attended him while he was unconscious. We held that it would be unreasonable to require him to identify the particular defendant who had performed the alleged negligent act because he was unconscious at the time of the injury and the defendants exercised control over the instrumentalities which caused the harm. Therefore, under the doctrine of res ipsa loquitur, an inference of negligence arose that defendants were required to meet by explaining their conduct. . . .

Defendants assert that these principles are inapplicable here. First, they insist that a predicate to shifting the burden of proof under *Summers-Ybarra* is that the defendants must have greater access to information regarding the cause of the injuries than the plaintiff, whereas in the present case the reverse appears.

Plaintiff does not claim that defendants are in a better position than she to identify the manufacturer of the drug taken by her mother or, indeed, that they have the ability to do so at all, but argues, rather, that *Summers* does not impose such a requirement as a condition to the shifting of the burden of proof. In this respect we believe plaintiff is correct. . . .

Here, as in *Summers*, the circumstances of the injury appear to render identification of the manufacturer of the drug ingested by plaintiff's mother impossible by either plaintiff or defendants, and it cannot reasonably be said that one is in a better position than the other to make the identification. Because many years elapsed between the time the drug was taken and the manifestation of plaintiff's injuries she, and many other daughters of mothers who took DES, are unable to make such identification. Certainly there can be no implication that plaintiff is at fault in failing to do so—the event occurred while plaintiff was in utero, a generation ago.

On the other hand, it cannot be said with assurance that defendants have the means to make the identification. In this connection, they point out that drug manufacturers ordinarily have no direct contact with the patients who take a drug prescribed by their doctors. Defendants sell to wholesalers, who in turn supply the product to physicians and pharmacies. Manufacturers do not maintain records of the persons who take the drugs they produce, and the selection of the medication is made by the physician rather than the manufacturer. Nor do we conclude that the absence of evidence on this subject is due to the fault of defendants. While it is alleged that they produced a defective product with delayed effects and without adequate warnings, the difficulty or impossibility of identification results primarily from the passage of time rather than from their allegedly negligent acts of failing to provide adequate warnings. . . .

It is important to observe, however, that while defendants do not have means superior to plaintiff to identify the maker of the precise drug taken by her mother, they may in some instances be able to prove that they did not manufacture the injury-causing substance. In the present case, for example, one of the original defendants was dismissed from the action upon proof that it did not manufacture DES until after plaintiff was born. . . . Nevertheless, plaintiff may not prevail in her claim that the *Summers* rationale should be employed to fix the whole liability for her injuries upon defendants, at least as those principles have previously been applied. There is an important difference between the situation involved in *Summers* and the present case. There, all the parties who were or could have been responsible for the harm to the plaintiff were joined as defendants. Here, by contrast, there are approximately 200 drug companies which made DES, any of which might have manufactured the injury-producing drug.

Defendants maintain that, while in *Summers* there was a 50 percent chance that one of the two defendants was responsible for the plaintiff's injuries, here since any one of 200 companies which manufactured DES might have made the product which harmed plaintiff, there is no rational basis upon which to infer that any defendant in this action caused plaintiff's injuries, nor even a reasonable possibility that they were responsible.

These arguments are persuasive if we measure the chance that any one of the defendants supplied the injury-causing drug by the number of possible tortfeasors. In such a context, the possibility that any of the five defendants supplied the DES to plaintiff's mother is so remote that it would be unfair to require each defendant to exonerate itself. There may be a substantial likelihood that none of the five defendants joined in the action made the DES which caused the injury, and that the offending producer not named would escape liability altogether. While we propose, infra, an adaptation of the rule in *Summers* which will substantially overcome these difficulties, defendants appear to be correct that the rule, as previously applied, cannot relieve plaintiff of the burden of proving the identity of the manufacturer which made the drug causing her injuries. . . .

III

A [further] theory upon which plaintiff relies is the concept of industry-wide liability, or according to the terminology of the parties, "enterprise liability." This theory was suggested in Hall v. E.I. DuPont de Nemours & Co., Inc. (E.D.N.Y. 1972) 345 F. Supp. 353. In that case, plaintiffs were 13 children injured by the explosion of blasting caps in 12 separate incidents which occurred in 10 different states between 1955 and 1959. The defendants were six blasting cap manufacturers, comprising virtually the entire blasting cap industry in the United States, and their trade association. There were, however, a number of Canadian blasting cap manufacturers which could have supplied the caps. The gravamen of the complaint was that the practice of the industry of omitting a warning on individual blasting caps and of failing to take other safety measures created an unreasonable risk of harm, resulting in the plaintiffs' injuries. The complaint did not identify a particular manufacturer of a cap which caused a particular injury.

The court reasoned as follows: there was evidence that defendants, acting independently, had adhered to an industry-wide standard with regard to the safety features of blasting caps, that they had in effect delegated some functions of safety investigation and design, such as labelling, to their trade association, and that there was industry-wide cooperation in the manufacture and design of blasting caps. In these circumstances, the evidence supported a conclusion that all the defendants jointly controlled the risk. Thus, if plaintiffs could establish by a preponderance of the evidence that the caps were manufactured by one of the defendants, the burden of proof as to the causation would shift to all the defendants. The court noted that this theory of liability applied to industries composed of a small number of units, and that what would be fair and reasonable with regard to an industry of five or ten producers might be manifestly unreasonable if applied to a decentralized industry composed of countless small producers.

Plaintiff attempts to state a cause of action under the rationale of *Hall.* She alleges joint enterprise and collaboration among defendants in the production, marketing, promotion and testing of DES, and "concerted promulgation and adherence to industry-wide testing, safety, warning and efficacy standards" for the drug. We have concluded above that allegations that defendants relied upon one another's testing and promotion methods do not state a cause of action for concerted conduct to commit a tortious act. Under the theory of industry-wide liability, however, each manufacturer could be liable for all injuries caused by DES by virtue of adherence to an industry-wide standard of safety. . . .

We decline to apply this theory in the present case. At least 200 manufacturers produced DES; *Hall,* which involved 6 manufacturers representing the entire blasting cap industry in the United States, cautioned against application of the doctrine espoused therein to a large number of producers. (345 F. Supp. at p.378.) Moreover, in *Hall,* the conclusion that the defendants jointly controlled the risk was based upon allegations that they had delegated some functions relating to safety to a trade association. There are no such allegations here, and we have concluded above that plaintiff has failed to allege liability on a concert of action theory. . . .

IV

If we were confined to the theories of *Summers* and *Hall,* we would be constrained to hold that the judgment must be sustained. Should we require that plaintiff identify the manufacturer which supplied the DES used by her mother or that all DES manufacturers be joined in the action, she would effectively be precluded from any recovery. As defendants candidly admit, there is little likelihood that all the manufacturers who made DES at the time in question are still in business or that they are subject to the jurisdiction of the California courts. There are, however, forceful arguments in favor of holding that plaintiff has a cause of action. . . .

The most persuasive reason for finding plaintiff states a cause of action is that advanced in *Summers:* as between an innocent plaintiff and negligent defendants, the latter should bear the cost of the injury. Here, as in *Summers,* plaintiff is not at fault in failing to provide evidence of causation, and although the absence of such evidence is not attributable to the defendants either, their conduct in marketing a drug the effects of which are delayed for many years played a significant role in creating the unavailability of proof.

From a broader policy standpoint, defendants are better able to bear the cost of injury resulting from the manufacture of a defective product. As was said by Justice Traynor in [Escola v. Coca Cola Bottling, 24 Cal. 2d 453, 150 P.2d 436 (1944),] "[t]he cost of an injury and the loss of time or health may be an overwhelming misfortune to the person injured, and a needless one, for the risk of injury can be insured by the manufacturer and distributed among the public as a cost of doing business." The manufacturer is in the best position to discover and guard against defects in its products and to warn of harmful effects; thus, holding it liable for defects and failure to warn of harmful effects will provide an incentive to product safety. (Cronin v. J.B.E. Olson Corp. (1972) 8 Cal. 3d 121, 129, 104 Cal. Rptr. 433, 501 P.2d 1153; Beech Aircraft Corp. v. Superior Court (1976) 61 Cal. App. 3d 501, 522-523, 132 Cal. Rptr. 541.) These considerations are particularly significant where medication is involved, for the consumer is virtually helpless to protect himself from serious, sometimes permanent, sometimes fatal, injuries caused by deleterious drugs.

Where, as here, all defendants produced a drug from an identical formula and the manufacturer of the DES which caused plaintiff's injuries cannot be identified through no fault of plaintiff, a modification of the rule of *Summers* is warranted. As we have seen, an undiluted *Summers* rationale is inappropriate to shift the burden of proof of causation to defendants because if we measure the chance that any particular manufacturer supplied the injury-causing product by the number of producers of DES, there is a possibility that none of the five defendants in this case produced the offending substance and that the responsible manufacturer, not named in the action, will escape liability.

But we approach the issue of causation from a different perspective: we hold it to be reasonable in the present context to measure the likelihood that any of the defendants supplied the product which allegedly injured plaintiff by the percentage which the DES sold by each of them for the purpose of preventing miscarriage bears to the entire production of the drug sold by all for that purpose. Plaintiff asserts in her briefs that Eli Lilly and Company and 5 or 6 other companies produced 90 percent of the DES marketed. If at trial this is established to be the fact, then there is a corresponding likelihood that this comparative handful of producers manufactured the DES which caused plaintiff's injuries, and only a 10 percent likelihood that the offending producer would escape liability.

If plaintiff joins in the action the manufacturers of a substantial share of the DES which her mother might have taken, the injustice of shifting the burden of proof to defendants to demonstrate that they could not have made the substance which injured plaintiff is significantly diminished. While 75 to 80 percent of the market is suggested as the requirement . . . , we hold only that a substantial percentage is required.

The presence in the action of a substantial share of the appropriate market also provides a ready means to apportion damages among the defendants. Each defendant will be held liable for the proportion of the judgment represented by its share of that market unless it demonstrates that it could not have made the product which caused plaintiff's injuries. In the present case, as we have seen, one DES manufacturer was dismissed from the action upon filing a declaration that it had not manufactured DES until after plaintiff was born. Once plaintiff has met her burden of joining the required defendants, they in turn may cross-complain against other DES manufacturers, not joined in the action, which they can allege might have supplied the injury-causing product.

Under this approach, each manufacturer's liability would approximate its responsibility for the injuries caused by its own products. Some minor discrepancy in the correlation between market share and liability is inevitable; therefore, a defendant may be held liable for a somewhat different percentage of the damage than its share of the appropriate market would justify. It is probably impossible, with the passage of time, to determine market share with mathematical exactitude. But just as a jury cannot be expected to determine the precise relationship between fault and liability in applying the doctrine of comparative fault (Li v. Yellow Cab Co. (1975) 13 Cal. 3d 804, 119 Cal. Rptr. 858, 532 P.2d 1226) or partial indemnity (American Motorcycle Assn. v. Superior Court

(1978) 20 Cal. 3d 578, 146 Cal. Rptr. 182, 578 P.2d 899), the difficulty of apportioning damages among the defendant producers in exact relation to their market share does not seriously militate against the rule we adopt. As we said in *Summers* with regard to the liability of independent tortfeasors, where a correct division of liability cannot be made "the trier of fact may make it the best it can." (33 Cal. 2d at p.88, 199 P.2d at p.5.)

We are not unmindful of the practical problems involved in defining the market and determining market share, but these are largely matters of proof which property cannot be determined at the pleading stage of these proceedings. Defendants urge that it would be both unfair and contrary to public policy to hold them liable for plaintiff's injuries in the absence of proof that one of them supplied the drug responsible for the damage. Most of their arguments, however, are based upon the assumption that one manufacturer would be held responsible for the products of another or for those of all other manufacturers if plaintiff ultimately prevails. But under the rule we adopt, each manufacturer's liability for an injury would be approximately equivalent to the damages caused by the DES it manufactured.

The judgments are reversed.

BIRD, C.J., and NEWMAN and WHITE, J.J., concur.

E. Allocation and Presumptions in Criminal Cases

Problem: Criminal Allocation in Idylia

The Idylia constitution, like our own, is interpreted to require the prosecution in criminal cases to prove each and every element of a criminal offense beyond reasonable doubt. See In re Winship, 397 U.S. 358 (1970). But what is an "element" to which this mandate applies?

Idylia has adopted a criminal statute that defines the offense of first-degree touching. The elements of this offense, to be proved by the prosecution beyond reasonable doubt, are (1) a touching, (2) lack of consent of the victim, and (3) intent. Conviction of first-degree touching carries a penalty of life imprisonment. The defendant may present various affirmative defenses, as follows:

(1) The touching was not premeditated (this reduces the offense to second degree, with a maximum penalty of 20 years);

(2) The touching did not result in the victim's death (this reduces the offense to third degree, with a maximum penalty of 10 years); and

(3) The touching did not result in serious bodily harm (this reduces the offense to fourth degree, with a maximum penalty of one year).

Is this statute constitutional? Could Idylia have gone even further and made consent to the touching a defense? Consider these questions in light of the next two cases and the commentary that follows.

MULLANEY v. WILBUR
421 U.S. 684 (1975)

Mr. Justice POWELL delivered the opinion of the Court.

The State of Maine requires a defendant charged with murder to prove that he acted "in the heat of passion on sudden provocation" in order to reduce the homicide to manslaughter. We must decide whether this rule comports with the due process requirement, as defined in In re Winship, 397 U.S. 358, 364 (1970), that the prosecution prove beyond a reasonable doubt every fact necessary to constitute the crime charged. . . .

Petitioners, the warden of the Maine Prison and the State of Maine, argue that . . . Winship should not be extended to the present case. They note that as a formal matter the absence of the heat of passion on sudden provocation is not a "fact necessary to constitute the *crime*" of felonious homicide in Maine. In re Winship, 397 U.S., at 364 (emphasis supplied). This distinction is relevant, according to petitioners, because in Winship the facts at issue were essential to establish criminality in the first instance, whereas the fact in question here does not come into play until the jury already has determined that the defendant is guilty and may be punished at least for manslaughter. . . . In short, petitioners would limit Winship to those facts which, if not proved, would wholly exonerate the defendant.

This analysis fails to recognize that the criminal law of Maine, like that of other jurisdictions, is concerned not only with guilt or innocence in the abstract but also with the degree of criminal culpability. Maine has chosen to distinguish those who kill in the heat of passion from those who kill in the absence of this factor. Because the former are less "blameworth[y]," State v. Lafferty, 309 A.2d, at 671, 673 (concurring opinion), they are subject to substantially less severe penalties. By drawing this distinction, while refusing to require the prosecution to establish beyond a reasonable doubt the fact upon which it turns, Maine denigrates the interests found critical in Winship.

The safeguards of due process are not rendered unavailing simply because a determination may already have been reached that would stigmatize the defendant and that might lead to a significant impairment of personal liberty. The fact remains that the consequences resulting from a verdict of murder, as compared with a verdict of manslaughter, differ significantly. Indeed, when viewed in terms of the potential difference in restrictions of personal liberty attendant to each conviction, the distinction established by Maine between murder and manslaughter may be of greater importance than the difference between guilt or innocence for many lesser crimes.

Moreover, if *Winship* were limited to those facts that constitute a crime as defined by state law, a State could undermine many of the interests that decision sought to protect without effecting any substantive change in its law. It would only be necessary to redefine the elements that constitute different crimes, characterizing them as factors that bear solely on the extent of punishment. . . .

Winship is concerned with substance rather than this kind of formalism. . . .

PATTERSON v. NEW YORK
432 U.S. 197 (1977)

Mr. Justice WHITE delivered the opinion of the Court.

The question here is the constitutionality under the Fourteenth Amendment's Due Process Clause of burdening the defendant in a New York State murder trial with proving the affirmative defense of extreme emotional disturbance as defined by New York law. . . .

We decline to adopt as a constitutional imperative, operative countrywide, that a State must disprove beyond a reasonable doubt every fact constituting any and all affirmative defenses related to the culpability of an accused. Traditionally, due process has required that only the most basic procedural safeguards be observed; more subtle balancing of society's interests against those of the accused have been left to the legislative branch. We therefore will not disturb the balance struck in previous cases holding that the Due Process Clause requires the prosecution to prove beyond a reasonable doubt all of the elements included in the definition of the offense of which the defendant is charged. Proof of the non-existence of all affirmative defenses has never been constitutionally required; and we perceive no reason to fashion such a rule in this case and apply it to the statutory defense at issue here.

This view may seem to permit state legislatures to reallocate burdens of proof by labeling as affirmative defenses at least some elements of the crimes now defined in their statutes. But there are obviously constitutional limits beyond which the States may not go in this regard. "[I]t is not within the province of a legislature to declare an individual guilty or presumptively guilty of a crime." McFarland v. American Sugar Rfg. Co., 241 U.S. 79, 86 (1916). The legislature cannot "validly command that the finding of an indictment, or mere proof of the identity of the accused, should create a presumption of the existence of all the facts essential to guilt." Tot v. United States, 319 U.S. 463, 469 (1943). . . .

It is urged that Mullaney v. Wilbur necessarily invalidates Patterson's conviction. In *Mullaney* the charge was murder, which the Maine statute defined as the unlawful killing of a human being "with malice aforethought, either express or implied." The trial court instructed the jury that the words "malice aforethought" were most important because "malice aforethought is an essential and indispensable element of the crime of murder." Malice, as the statute indicated and as the court instructed, could be implied and was to be implied from "any deliberate, cruel act committed by one person against another suddenly . . . or without a considerable provocation," in which event an intentional killing was murder unless by a preponderance of the evidence it was shown that the act was committed "in the heat of passion, on sudden provocation." The instructions emphasized that "'malice aforethought and heat of passion on sudden provocation are two inconsistent things'; thus, by proving the latter the defendant would negate the former." 421 U.S., at 686-687. . . .

Mullaney's holding, it is argued, is that the State may not permit the blameworthiness of an act or the severity of punishment authorized for its commission to depend on the presence or absence of an identified fact without assuming the burden of proving the presence or absence of that fact, as the case may be, beyond a reasonable doubt. In our view, the *Mullaney* holding should not be so broadly read. . . .

Mullaney surely held that a State must prove every ingredient of an offense beyond a reasonable doubt, and that it may not shift the burden of proof to the defendant by presuming that ingredient upon proof of the other elements of the offense. This is true even though the State's practice, as in Maine, had been traditionally to the contrary. Such shifting of the burden of persuasion with respect to a fact which the State deems so important that it must be either proved or presumed is impermissible under the Due Process Clause.

It was unnecessary to go further in *Mullaney*. The Maine Supreme Judicial Court made it clear that malice aforethought, which was mentioned in the statutory definition of the crime, was not equivalent to premeditation and that the presumption of malice traditionally arising in intentional homicide cases carried no factual meaning insofar as premeditation was concerned. Even so, a killing became murder in Maine when it resulted from a deliberate, cruel act committed by one person against another, "suddenly without any, or without a considerable provocation." State v. Lafferty, [309 A.2d] at 665. Premeditation was not within the definition of murder; but malice, in the sense of the absence of provocation, was part of the definition of that crime. Yet malice, i.e., lack of provocation, was presumed and could be rebutted by the defendant only by proving by a preponderance of the evidence that he acted with heat of passion upon sudden provocation. In *Mullaney* we held that however traditional this mode of proceeding might have been, it is contrary to the Due Process Clause as construed in *Winship.*

As we have explained, nothing was presumed or implied against Patterson; and his conviction is not invalid under any of our prior cases. The judgment of the New York Court of Appeals is affirmed.

Mr. Justice REHNQUIST took no part in the consideration or decision of this case.

Mr. Justice POWELL, with whom Mr. Justice BRENNAN and Mr. Justice MARSHALL join, dissenting.

In the name of preserving legislative flexibility, the Court today drains In re Winship, 397 U.S. 358 (1970), of much of its vitality. Legislatures do require broad discretion in the drafting of criminal laws, but the Court surrenders to the legislative branch a significant part of its responsibility to protect the presumption of innocence. . . .

Mullaney held invalid Maine's requirement that the defendant prove heat of passion. The Court today, without disavowing the unanimous holding of *Mullaney,* approves New York's requirement that the defendant prove extreme emotional disturbance. The Court manages to run a constitutional boundary line through the barely visible space that separates Maine's law from New York's. It does so on the basis of distinctions in language that are formalistic rather than substantive.

This result is achieved by a narrowly literal parsing of the holding in *Winship:* "[T]he Due Process Clause protects the accused against conviction except upon proof beyond a reasonable doubt of every fact necessary to constitute the crime with which he is charged." 397 U.S., at 364. The only "facts" necessary to constitute a crime are said to be those that appear on the face of the statute as a part of the definition of the crime. Maine's statute was invalid, the Court reasons, because it "defined [murder] as the unlawful killing of a human being 'with malice aforethought, either express or implied.'" Ante. "[M]alice," the Court reiterates, "in the sense of the absence of provocation, was part of the definition of that crime." Ante. *Winship* was violated only because this "fact" — malice — was "presumed" unless the defendant persuaded the jury otherwise by showing that he acted in the heat of passion. New York, in form presuming no affirmative "fact" against Patterson, and blessed with a statute drafted in the leaner language of the 20th century, escapes constitutional scrutiny unscathed even though the effect on the defendant of New York's placement of the burden of persuasion is exactly the same as Maine's.

This explanation of the *Mullaney* holding bears little resemblance to the basic rationale of that decision. But this is not the cause of greatest concern. The test the Court today establishes allows a legislature to shift, virtually at will, the burden of persuasion with respect to any factor in a criminal case, so long as it is careful not to mention the nonexistence of that factor in the statutory language that defines the crime. The sole requirement is that any references to the factor be confined to those sections that provide for an affirmative defense. . . .

With all respect, this type of constitutional adjudication is indefensibly formalistic. A limited but significant check on possible abuses in the criminal law now becomes an exercise in arid formalities. What *Winship* and *Mullaney* had sought to teach about the limits a free society places on its procedures to safeguard the liberty of its citizens becomes a rather simplistic lesson in statutory draftsmanship. Nothing in the Court's opinion prevents a legislature from applying this new learning to many of the classical elements of the crimes it punishes. It would be preferable, if the Court has found reason to reject the rationale of *Winship* and *Mullaney,* simply and straightforwardly to overrule those precedents.

The Court understandably manifests some uneasiness that its formalistic approach will give legislatures too much latitude in shifting the burden of persuasion. And so it issues a warning that "there are obviously constitutional limits beyond which the States may not go in this regard." Ante. The Court thereby concedes that legislative abuses may occur and that they must be curbed by the judicial branch. But if the State is careful to conform to the drafting formulas articulated today, the constitutional limits are anything but "obvious." This decision simply leaves us without a conceptual framework for distinguishing abuses from legitimate legislative adjustments of the burden of persuasion in criminal cases. . . .

R. ALLEN, STRUCTURING JURY DECISIONMAKING IN CRIMINAL CASES: A UNIFIED CONSTITUTIONAL APPROACH TO EVIDENTIARY DEVICES
94 Harv. L. Rev. 321, 338-353 (1980)

[T]he superficially distinct evidentiary devices employed in criminal trials—affirmative defenses, placement of burdens of production and the concomitant possibility of a directed verdict on an issue, judicial comment on the evidence, and instructions on presumptions and inferences—are actually very similar. Their primary unifying trait is that they all modify the evidentiary relationship of the parties at trial by manipulating burdens of persuasion. Affirmative defenses and burdens of production manipulate the relative burden of persuasion explicitly, while the other devices do so implicitly.

Moreover, these devices cannot be distinguished on the basis of the magnitude of their effect on the burden of persuasion, for that effect unmistakably varies within each category. Comments on the evidence, or presumptive instructions, may be very influential with a jury, and thus have a great impact on the relative burden of persuasion, or may have little influence and little or no effect on the relative burden. Similarly, one affirmative defense may be much easier to establish than another, even though the formal burden of persuasion is the same in both cases. Moreover, instructions that comment on the evidence, either explicitly or implicitly, involve essentially the same problems of ensuring the accuracy of the comment. Both explicit judicial comment and presumptive instructions may enhance the likelihood of a correct outcome; but both may also do just the opposite, thereby unconstitutionally abridging the defendant's right to have the state prove its case against him beyond a reasonable doubt.

Finally, the detrimental impact on the defendant does not adequately distinguish any of these evidentiary devices. Compare, for example, shifts in burdens of "persuasion" and "production." As a rule, it may be more damaging to a defendant to have to prove something by a preponderance of the evidence instead of to some lower degree. If, however, the defendant has access to little or no convincing evidence on an issue, he will not be able to meet either standard. Similarly, the prevailing view that shifts in burdens of persuasion are more damaging than instructions on inferences seems erroneous. A shift in the explicit burden of persuasion conceivably may have no impact upon the outcome. If, for example, after all the evidence is in, the jury would conclude that there is a sixty-five percent chance that the defendant committed a homicide in the heat of passion, then the result will be the same—mitigation to manslaughter—regardless of whether the state has to prove the absence of provocation beyond reasonable doubt or the defendant has to establish it by a preponderance of the evidence. By contrast, judicial comment on that evidence conceivably could cause the same jury to find that provocation has been disproven beyond reasonable doubt.

The actual effect in a particular case of any of the evidentiary devices discussed above is an empirical question that probably is not subject to very satisfactory empirical investigation, but the devices all share the function of allocating burdens of persuasion to the state and to the defendant. Consequently, they all raise essentially the same two issues, despite the diversity of their manifestations in the current case law. The first issue is the compatibility of the devices with In re Winship's imposition of the reasonable doubt standard as a constitutional mandate. The second is the effect of the devices on our conception of the right to a jury trial.

Because of the functional similarity of these devices, a unified analysis of their constitutionality can be developed. . . .

Such a framework can be constructed by asking three fundamental questions. The first two questions respond specifically to *Winship*'s requirement of proof beyond a reasonable doubt, and the last relates to both *Winship* and the right to a jury trial. First, we must determine whether the evidentiary device has a favorable or unfavorable effect on the defendant's case, since there is no danger of the state's burden being lowered and therefore no question of constitutionality if the effect is favorable. Second, if the effect is unfavorable, we must establish whether the device affects a fact that the state is constitutionally required to demonstrate as an element of criminality. This step is a necessary part of the analysis because imposing a constitutional standard of proof makes sense *only* if it is linked to a theory that indicates what facts constitutionally must be proved under the standard; otherwise, the standard could be circumvented by a state choosing to redefine the factual elements constituting a crime. The third step of this analysis, which applies if the fact affected is one that the state cannot constitutionally remove from its definition of the crime in question, is to ask whether the device amounts to an accurate judicial comment on the evidence. Manipulations of the burden of persuasion are permitted *only* if the device moves the jury toward a more rational, accurate result. This last inquiry guards against undermining the jury's fact-finding role, and ensures that the jury does not reach its conclusion on the basis of inaccurate commentary that would lower the state's burden of proof.

A.   A FAVORABLE EFFECT

The first standard applicable to the evidentiary devices is obvious and requires no extended discussion. If a state employs an evidentiary device that is favorable to a defendant, it should not be struck down on constitutional grounds. "Favorable" in this context means only that the explicit burden of persuasion on the issue involved remains with the government at least to the level of beyond reasonable doubt, and that the comment, whether accurate or not, tends to dispose the jury more in favor of the defendant on that issue than the jury would have been without the comment. Under such circumstances, a defendant has no basis for complaint. The constitutionally required burden of persuasion has been maintained, and the jury's evaluation of the factual issue will be at least as fair as he has a right to expect.

B.   THE CONSTITUTIONAL NECESSITY OF PROVING THE FACT IN ISSUE

In the second step of the analysis, the nature of a particular fact in issue is examined to determine whether it is one that the state is required by the Constitution to prove beyond a reasonable doubt. Because forcing a defendant to bear the burden of persuasion in proving facts that establish a defense is functionally the same as requiring the state to prove the absence of those facts, constitutional analysis must not depend upon whether a state legislature chose to label a factual issue a defense or an "element of the offense." Without some substantive re-striction on a legislature's discretion to define crime, *Winship* may be eviscerated. Therefore, step two inquires whether the state has increased the defendant's relative burden of persuasion with respect to an issue that is critical to culpability. . . .

Commentators who advocate the substantive due process test argue that "in evaluating the constitutionality of an affirmative defense, the ultimate question should be whether the issue is so critical to culpability that it would offend 'the deepest notions of what is fair and right and just' to obtain a conviction where a reasonable doubt remains as to that issue." To say that a fact "so critical to culpability" has not been proven beyond reasonable doubt, however, is simply another way of saying that the conditions for imposing punishment have not been satisfied. To subject a person to substantial punishment when such a critical fact has not been proven beyond reasonable doubt would distort the relation-ship between what the defendant has been proven to have done and what the state does to him. Unmistakably, this "due process" test is yet another manifestation of the concern that a proper relationship be-tween crime and punishment be maintained, and thus is simply a vari-ation on the theme of maintaining proportionate punishment. . . .

If the Constitution does not limit a state's ability simply to remove a particular element from the definition of criminality, there is no point in attempting to limit the state's power to shift the burden as to that element by creating an affirmative defense; nor, for that matter, is there any point in forbidding jury instructions that permit an element to be "presumed" on the basis of some other fact that lacks a rational rela-tionship with that element. . . . [I]t seems to me that if a state limits its manipulation of burdens of persuasion to issues that need not be proved under the eighth amendment's proportionality standard or principles of substantive fairness imposed by due process, then whatever the state does should be acceptable. If, by contrast, the state manipulates a bur-den on an issue that constitutionally it must establish, then it must do so in a way that either favors the defendant or amounts to accurate judicial comment.

C.   ACCURATE JUDICIAL COMMENT

Judicial comment on the evidence may be either accurate or inac-curate. Comment that is accurate enhances the jury's conception of reality, and permits the jury to deliberate in a more accurate and real-istic factual matrix. Inaccurate comment also changes the factual matrix within which the jury operates, but it skews the decisionmaking process away from reality. . . . [I]naccurate judicial comment detrimental to the defendant, on an issue that constitutionally must be included in a state's definition of a crime, violates the mandate of In re Winship by effectively lowering the state's burden of proving guilt beyond a reasonable doubt. In fact, inaccurate comment on an issue is tantamount to creating an affirmative defense since the defendant is forced to show the existence of more than a reasonable doubt on the issue. Accurate comment, on the other hand, can prevent an erroneous verdict when the jury is unable to appreciate the implications of certain facts proven at trial. Certainly a state should be permitted to fill in gaps in the jury's knowledge. Since accurate judicial comment serves this important function without undercutting the reasonable doubt standard, it should be constitutionally permissible—as should its functional equivalents—so long as the comment does not violate the right to a jury trial. Accordingly, the impact of judicial comment on that right must be examined.

The effect of judicial comment on the right to a jury trial raises three questions that may generate constitutional problems: first, does the right to a jury trial limit the manner in which the jury may acquire information; second, how constrained may a jury be made to feel concerning the content of the comment; and third, what is the significance of ambiguity or incoherence in the comment?

1. THE MANNER OF PRESENTING INFORMATION TO
   THE JURY

The first difficulty results from the very nature of judicial comment. Judicial comment is, in essence, a method of presenting evidence to the jury. Legislative investigation[105] or judicial experience[106] may result in the conclusion that certain facts usually present themselves in a certain relationship, a relationship that may not be known by the jury. One method of communicating the substance of that relationship is by judicial comment, which is precisely the dynamic the Supreme Court was referring to when it commented that "a valid presumption may . . . be created upon a view of relation broader than that a jury might take in a specific case."[107]

There are alternatives to comment, however. The facts that the comment is based upon could be presented to the jury. Prosecutorial argument on the basis of those data and the other evidence in the case may often be sufficient. Nonetheless, there does not seem to be any constitutional basis for preferring these procedures to judicial comment. Since the Constitution does not dictate a specific method of introducing evidence, accurate judicial comment does not contravene any constitutional command.

---

105. See, e.g., Turner v. United States, 396 U.S. 398, 410 & n.10 (1970).
106. See, e.g., Barnes v. United States, 412 U.S. 837 (1973).
107. Tot v. United States, 319 U.S. 463, 468 (1943) (footnote omitted).

2. JURY INDEPENDENCE FROM JUDICIAL COMMENT

Though judicial comment is a permissible method of presenting evidence, it still raises problems with respect to the right to an independent evaluation of the evidence by a jury, which is implicit in the constitutional right to a jury trial. To be permissible, judicial comment must not convey to the jury a sense that it is bound by the content of the comment. The comment must be in permissive language and make very clear that the jury is simply being presented with another matter for its consideration. Obviously, the jury may be influenced by the comment, but if the comment is accurate, it ought to be influential. It ought to be influential, however, only to its degree of accuracy as determined by the jury, which raises the third problem with judicial comment.

3. AMBIGUITY IN JUDICIAL COMMENT

The judge is quite likely to be viewed with some respect by the jurors, and there will surely be a strong inclination to accept what he says as true. Accordingly, he must be careful to make sure that his comment is clear and coherent. Thus, instructions that say only that a jury "may but need not" infer or presume one fact from another should be struck down on the ground that they lead to irrational jury decisionmaking in contravention of the right to a trial by jury. The judge should be required to elaborate on what the word "may" means—what is the basis for concluding that one fact implies another, how close does the relationship seem to be, what are the levels of confidence that the data possess? These questions, of course, prompted the development of the "rational relationship" test in the first place. This test was created in order to ensure that a reasonable connection exists between an "inferred fact" and one proved at trial so that an instruction on the inference would not skew the jury's deliberations away from reality. However, the rational relationship test is, at best, only a crude guarantor of jury rationality because the instructions on inferences and presumptions are usually so ambiguous that it is difficult to assess their impact on the jury's inferential process. The goal of the test would be accomplished better by requiring thorough, cautious comment in place of current instructions.

C. NESSON, RATIONALITY, PRESUMPTIONS, AND JUDICIAL COMMENT: A RESPONSE TO PROFESSOR ALLEN
94 Harv. L. Rev. 1574, 1576-1583 (1981)

. . . Allen's approach is flawed in that it only tests for the accuracy and rationality of judicial comment *after* finding that the issue affected is constitutionally essential to culpability.

Restricting his test in this way is problematic for two reasons. First, Allen fails to appreciate how limited and difficult the application of a substantive limitation theory will be, and therefore does not realize that his approach would virtually eliminate the requirement of rationality in instructing jurors. Second, rationality is a necessary, albeit not sufficient, condition for the constitutionality of every criminal presumption, whether or not the presumed fact is a constitutionally essential element of a crime.

A. THE IMPRACTICALITY OF SUBSTANTIVE LIMITATION THEORY

Allen's analysis begins with In re Winship and the puzzle that it posed. *Winship* announced the constitutional requirement that a state prove every "element" of a criminal offense beyond a reasonable doubt. That holding raised doubts about any use of affirmative defenses. If the statutory definition of a particular crime recognizes an affirmative defense, then it is possible to see the absence of that defense as an element that the state must prove beyond a reasonable doubt. Such a reading of *Winship* gained currency in Mullaney v. Wilbur. In *Mullaney,* the Court struck down a statute allowing the prosecution to rely on a presumption to prove malice, a statutorily prescribed element of homicide. The effect of the presumption was to impose on the defendant the burden of rebutting it (in order to mitigate the crime) by showing that the act was committed in the heat of passion.

Two years later, however, in Patterson v. New York, the Court adopted a narrow reading of *Mullaney.* The Court upheld a statute that shifted the burden to the defendant, not by a presumption as in *Mullaney,* but by a requirement that the defendant prove an affirmative defense. The Court took as its starting point the strict legislative definition of the offense: Only if the state expressly defined malice as an "element" of the crime would *Winship* require the prosecution to prove it beyond a reasonable doubt, unaided by any presumptions. Apparently, the state would be permitted to undercut the force of *Winship* merely by shifting elements from the prosecution to the defense.

Abhorrence of *Patterson*'s arid formalism stimulated a wave of commentary, including a fine article by Professors Jeffries and Stephan. Jeffries and Stephan* rejected the purely formalistic approach that would have left the *Winship* issue up to state definition. However, they found equally untenable a reading of *Mullaney* that would require the state to prove beyond a reasonable doubt each and every issue affecting stigma or penalty. Such an approach would effectively eliminate all evidentiary

---

*Jeffries and Stephan, Defenses, Presumptions, and Burden of Proof in the Criminal Law, 88 Yale L.J. 1325 (1979).

devices, including affirmative defenses, by forcing the state to choose between two extremes. Either it must require the prosecution to prove an element beyond reasonable doubt, or it must eliminate it altogether from the definition of the crime. Jeffries and Stephan could find no substantive or procedural justification for this Hobson's choice. Indeed, putting states to such a choice might lead to harsher, less discriminating definitions of crimes. Further, it would be paradoxical to deny states the opportunity to use moderating measures (such as affirmative defenses and presumptions) to shift the burden on an element of an offense, but to allow them to eliminate the element altogether.

Attempting to cut between the two extreme solutions to the *Winship* puzzle, Jeffries and Stephan confronted the need for a constitutional jurisprudence defining the elements a state must prove to convict someone of a crime. Drawing on classic common law notions of actus reus and mens rea, as well as on the eighth amendment's prohibition of cruel and unusual punishment, they attempted to sketch out substantive constitutional limitations on the minimum definition of crime and on the maximum punishment that can be imposed for a particular offense.

Although Jeffries and Stephan presented their ideas of substantive limitation merely as directions for analysis, Allen seizes the theory, without developing it further, and makes it the keystone of his integrated test. . . . [S]ubstantive limitation embodies requirements of act, intent, and proportionality of punishment. It is difficult, however, to give content to these components. The "act" requirement is intended to guard against the possibility that the state would punish mere intention or status, an important but obviously limited protection given the minimal nature of the act necessary to meet the requirement.[31] The "intent" requirement is meant to ensure that a defendant's conduct is morally blameworthy, but its content too is both limited and obscure. Some crimes, for example, require no showing of intent at all.[32] As to proportionality, Jeffries and Stephan recognize that there is "no way to calculate exact relationships between wrong done and punishment earned, for the perception of good and bad and harm and blame flows from normative judgments that defy precise quantification."[33] The Con-

---

31. Consider, for example, the act requirement associated with the crime of conspiracy, see, e.g., Yates v. United States, 354 U.S. 298 (1957), the act of an alcoholic in being publicly drunk, see, e.g., Powell v. Texas, 392 U.S. 514 (1968), and the "act" of nonfeasance, see Jones v. United States, 308 F.2d 307, 310 & nn. 8-11 (D.C. Cir. 1962).

32. See, e.g., United States v. Park, 421 U.S. 658 (1975) (interstate shipment of contaminated food); United States v. Dotterweich, 320 U.S. 277 (1943) (interstate shipment of adulterated food and mislabeled drugs).

33. Jeffries & Stephan, supra.

stitution would at most require "some rough sense of proportion in the assignment of sanctions."[34] Because any finer honing of a proportionality standard would require articulation of a coherent theory of punishment, the authors in effect suggest that the test apply only when punishment is excessive in light of all possible justifications.

B. RATIONALITY: AN INDEPENDENT CONSTITUTIONAL REQUISITE

Allen's test demands accuracy and rationality of evidentiary devices only in cases running afoul of a substantive limitation theory. The problem that this poses is illustrated by Tot v. United States,[49] in which the defendant was convicted for violating a federal prohibition against possession of firearms by a felon. Tot's conviction was in part based on a statutory presumption authorizing the jury to infer from mere possession of a firearm that the firearm had been obtained in an interstate transaction. The Court invalidated the presumption, finding no "rational connection" between possession and interstate transport. Despite this irrationality, Professor Allen's theory leads to the conclusion that the case was wrongly decided, unless he were to argue that movement of the gun in interstate commerce was an issue constitutionally essential to culpability (as opposed to federal jurisdiction) under his proportionality analysis.

Allen ... fails to recognize that rationality serves an independent constitutional value. The authority and integrity of courts rest to a significant degree on the extent to which society perceives them to be fair and rational arbiters of justice. It is one thing for the courts to tolerate a legislature's being ambiguous or arbitrary in defining a crime or establishing sentencing limits, and quite another to permit a legislature to insist on judicial arbitrariness in adjudicating criminal prosecutions. A legislatively established presumption that lacks a rational connection between predicate and conclusion makes the court administering it appear to be arbitrary. The very statement of the contrary proposition suggests Gilbert and Sullivan rules of procedure: "Jurors, you may presume A from proof of B, even though there is no rational connection between the two." One need not look further for the roots of the rational connection test. It does not depend on any theory of clear legislative statement or substantive due process, but rather on the notion that the legitimacy of judicial process requires that issues to be proved in court be proved rationally.

34. Id. at 1377.
49. 319 U.S. 463 (1943).

F. Criminal Presumptions: Are There Problems with the Fifth Amendment and the Presumption of Innocence?

The Federal Rules of Evidence as originally proposed for adoption by the United States Supreme Court included a Proposed Rule 303 providing that in criminal cases a presumption would authorize submission of the presumed fact to the jury upon proof of the basic fact provided that a reasonable jury could find the presumed fact on all the evidence. The jury would be instructed that they could, but would not be required to, regard proof of the basic fact as sufficient proof of the presumed fact. The Advisory Committee deleted this rule because the subject of presumptions in criminal cases was to be addressed in revisions to the federal criminal code. What would a judge, using this presumption, say to a jury?

Problem: Moonshine

D is prosecuted for operating an illegal whiskey still. The prosecution's only proof is that *D* was found at the site of an illegal whiskey still. Is that a sufficient basis for inferring that *D* was operating the still? Can the jury take into account the fact that *D* offered no alternative explanation of what he was doing at the site of the still?

Does it help if based upon the state legislature's adoption of a presumption the trial judge gives the jury the following instruction?

> Under a statute enacted by the Legislature, when the defendant is shown to have been present at the site of the still such presence shall be deemed sufficient evidence to authorize conviction, unless the defendant explains such presence to the satisfaction of the jury.

How is the problem different if instead of the instruction above, the judge gives the following instruction?

> If you find that the defendant was present at the still, then that fact should be highly significant in your consideration whether the defendant was operating the still. You should consider that fact together with all the other facts of the case—the time of day, what the defendant was seen doing, what he was wearing, the equipment in his car—in deciding whether you are convinced beyond reasonable doubt that he was operating the still. This is a case based on circumstantial evidence. The fact that I leave it to you jurors to decide means that in my judgment it would be reasonable and legally supportable for you to reach a conclusion of guilt. It would also be reasonable and legally supportable for you to reach a conclusion of not guilty. It is up to you to decide whether, on consid-

ering all the facts and the defendant's explanation or lack of explanation, you are convinced beyond reasonable doubt that the defendant was operating the still.

Does it make any difference that the only way *D* can put forward an explanation is by testifying himself? How do the next two cases, Yee Hem v. United States and Griffin v. California, relate to these questions and to each other?

YEE HEM v. UNITED STATES
268 U.S. 178 (1925)

Mr. Justice SUTHERLAND delivered the opinion of the Court.

Plaintiff in error was convicted in the court below of the offense of concealing a quantity of smoking opium after importation, with knowledge that it had been imported in violation of the Act of February 9, 1909, c.100, 35 Stat. 614, as amended by the Act of January 17, 1914, c.9, 38 Stat. 275. Sections 2 and 3 of the act as amended are challenged as unconstitutional, on the ground that they contravene the due process of law and the compulsory self-incrimination clauses of the Fifth Amendment of the federal Constitution.

Section 1 of the act prohibits the importation into the United States of opium in any form after April 1, 1909, except that opium and preparations and derivatives thereof, other than smoking opium or opium prepared for smoking, may be imported for medicinal purposes only, under regulations prescribed by the Secretary of the Treasury. Section 2 provides, among other things, that if any person shall conceal or facilitate the concealment of such opium, etc., after importation, knowing the same to have been imported contrary to law, the offender shall be subject to fine or imprisonment or both. It further provides that whenever the defendant on trial is shown to have, or to have had, possession of such opium, etc., "such possession shall be deemed sufficient evidence to authorize conviction unless the defendant shall explain the possession to the satisfaction of the jury." Section 3 provides that on and after July 1, 1913, "all smoking opium or opium prepared for smoking found within the United States shall be presumed to have been imported after the first day of April, nineteen hundred and nine, and the burden of proof shall be on the claimant or the accused to rebut such presumption."

The plaintiff in error, at the time of his arrest in August, 1923, was found in possession of and concealing a quantity of smoking opium. The lower court overruled a motion for an instructed verdict of not guilty, and, after stating the foregoing statutory presumptions, charged the jury in substance that the burden of proof was on the accused to rebut such presumptions; and that it devolved upon him to explain that he was rightfully in possession of the smoking opium—"at least explain it to the satisfaction of the jury." The court further charged that the defendant was presumed to be innocent until the government had satisfied the minds of the jurors of his guilt beyond a reasonable doubt; that the burden to adduce such proof of guilt beyond the existence of a reasonable doubt rested on the government at all times and throughout the trial; and that a conviction could not be had "while a rational doubt remains in the minds of the jury." . . .

We think it is not an illogical inference that opium, found in this country more than four years (in the present case, more than fourteen years) after its importation had been prohibited, was unlawfully imported. Nor do we think the further provision, that possession of such opium in the absence of a satisfactory explanation shall create a presumption of guilt, is "so unreasonable as to be a purely arbitrary mandate." By universal sentiment, and settled policy as evidenced by state and local legislation for more than half a century, opium is an illegitimate commodity, the use of which, except as a medicinal agent, is rigidly condemned. Legitimate possession, unless for medicinal use, is so highly improbable that to say to any person who obtains the outlawed commodity, "since you are bound to know that it cannot be brought into this country at all, except under regulation for medicinal use, you must at your peril ascertain and be prepared to show the facts and circumstances which rebut, or tend to rebut, the natural inference of unlawful importation, or your knowledge of it," is not such an unreasonable requirement as to cause it to fall outside the constitutional power of Congress.

Every accused person, of course, enters upon his trial clothed with the presumption of innocence. But that presumption may be overcome, not only by direct proof, but, in many cases, when the facts standing alone are not enough, by the additional weight of a countervailing legislative presumption. If the effect of the legislative act is to give to the facts from which the presumption is drawn an artificial value to some extent, it is no more than happens in respect of a great variety of presumptions not resting upon statute. See . . . Wilson v. United States, 162 U.S. 613, 619. In the *Wilson* case the accused, charged with murder, was found, soon after the homicide, in possession of property that had belonged to the dead man. This Court upheld a charge of the trial court to the effect that such possession required the accused to account for it, to show that as far as he was concerned the possession was innocent and honest, and that if not so accounted for it became "the foundation for a presumption of guilt against the defendant."

The point that the practical effect of the statute creating the presumption is to compel the accused person to be a witness against himself may be put aside with slight discussion. The statute compels nothing. It does no more than to make possession of the prohibited article prima facie evidence of guilt. It leaves the accused entirely free to testify or not as he chooses. If the accused happens to be the only repository of the facts necessary to negative the presumption arising from his possession, that is a misfortune which the statute under review does not create but which is inherent in the case. The same situation might present itself if there were no statutory presumption and a prima facie case of concealment with knowledge of unlawful importation were made by the evidence. The necessity of an explanation by the accused would be quite as compelling in that case as in this; but the constraint upon him to give testimony would arise there, as it arises here, simply from the force of circumstances and not from any form of compulsion forbidden by the Constitution.

Judgment affirmed.

GRIFFIN v. CALIFORNIA
380 U.S. 609 (1965)

Mr. Justice DOUGLAS delivered the opinion of the Court.

Petitioner was convicted of murder in the first degree after a jury trial in a California court. He did not testify at the trial on the issue of guilt. . . . The trial court instructed the jury on the issue of guilt, stating that a defendant has a constitutional right not to testify. But it told the jury:

> As to any evidence or facts against him which the defendant can reasonably be expected to deny or explain because of facts within his knowledge, if he does not testify or if, though he does testify, he fails to deny or explain such evidence, the jury may take that failure into consideration as tending to indicate the truth of such evidence and as indicating that among the inferences that may be reasonably drawn therefrom those unfavorable to the defendant are the more probable.

It added, however, that no such inference could be drawn as to evidence respecting which he had no knowledge. It stated that failure of a defendant to deny or explain the evidence of which he had knowledge does not create a presumption of guilt nor by itself warrant an inference of guilt nor relieve the prosecution of any of its burden of proof.

Petitioner had been seen with the deceased the evening of her death, the evidence placing him with her in the alley where her body was found. The prosecutor made much of the failure of petitioner to testify:

> The defendant certainly knows whether Essie Mae had this beat up appearance at the time he left her apartment and went down the alley with her.
> What kind of a man is it that would want to have sex with a woman that beat up if she was beat up at the time he left?
> He would know that. He would know how she got down the alley. He would know how the blood got on the bottom of the concrete steps. He would know how long he was with her in that box. He would know how her wig got off. He would know whether he beat her or mistreated her. He would know whether he walked away from that place cool as a cucumber when he saw Mr. Villasenor because he was conscious of his own guilt and wanted to get away from that damaged or injured woman.
> These things he has not seen fit to take the stand and deny or explain.
> And in the whole world, if anybody would know, this defendant would know.
> Essie Mae is dead, she can't tell you her side of the story. The defendant won't.

The death penalty was imposed and the California Supreme Court affirmed. 60 Cal. 2d 182, 383 P.2d 432. The case is here on a writ of certiorari which we granted, 377 U.S. 989, to consider whether comment on the failure to testify violated the Self-Incrimination Clause of the Fifth Amendment which we made applicable to the States by the Fourteenth in Malloy v. Hogan, 378 U.S. 1, decided after the Supreme Court of California had affirmed the present conviction. . . .

If this were a federal trial, reversible error would have been committed. Wilson v. United States, 149 U.S. 60, so holds. It is said, however, that the *Wilson* decision rested not on the Fifth Amendment, but on an Act of Congress, now 18 U.S.C. §3481. That indeed is the fact, as the opinion of the Court in the *Wilson* case states. And see Adamson v. California, 332 U.S. 46, 50, n.6; Bruno v. United States, 308 U.S. 287, 294. But that is the beginning, not the end, of our inquiry. The question remains whether, statute or not, the comment rule, approved by California, violates the Fifth Amendment. . . .

We think it does. It is in substance a rule of evidence that allows the State the privilege of tendering to the jury for its consideration the failure of the accused to testify. No formal offer of proof is made as in other situations; but the prosecutor's comment and the court's acquiescence are the equivalent of an offer of evidence and its acceptance. The Court in the *Wilson* case stated: ". . . the act was framed with a due regard also to those who might prefer to rely upon the presumption of innocence which the law gives to every one, and not wish to be witnesses. It is not every one who can safely venture on the witness stand though entirely innocent of the charge against him. Excessive timidity, nervousness when facing others and attempting to explain transactions of a suspicious character, and offenses charged against him, will often confuse and embarrass him to such a degree as to increase rather than remove prejudices against him. It is not every one, however honest, who would, therefore, willingly be placed on the witness stand. The statute, in tenderness to the weakness to those who from the causes mentioned might refuse to ask to be a witness, particularly when they may have been in some degree compromised by their association with others, declares that the failure of the defendant in a criminal action to request to be a witness shall not create any presumption against him." 149 U.S., p.66.

If the words "Fifth Amendment" are substituted for "act" and for "statute," the spirit of the Self-Incrimination Clause is reflected. For comment on the refusal to testify is a remnant of the "inquisitorial system of criminal justice," Murphy v. Waterfront Commn., 378 U.S. 52, 55, which the Fifth Amendment outlaws. It is a penalty imposed by courts for exercising a constitutional privilege. It cuts down on the privilege by making its assertion costly. It is said, however, that the inference of guilt for failure to testify as to facts peculiarly within the accused's knowledge is in any event natural and irresistible, and that comment on the failure does not magnify that inference into a penalty for asserting a constitutional privilege. People v. Modesto, 62 Cal. 2d 436, 452-453, 398 P.2d 753, 762-763. What the jury may infer, given no help from the court, is one thing. What it may infer when the court solemnizes the silence of the accused into evidence against him is quite another. That the inference of guilt is not always so natural or irresistible is brought out in the *Modesto* opinion itself:

"Defendant contends that the reason a defendant refuses to testify is that his prior convictions will be introduced in evidence to impeach him ([Cal.] Code Civ. Proc. §2051) and not that he is unable to deny the accusations. It is true that the defendant might fear that his prior convictions will prejudice the jury, and therefore another possible inference can be drawn from his refusal to take the stand." Id., p.453, 398 P.2d, p.763.

We said in Malloy v. Hogan, supra, p.11, that "the same standards must determine whether an accused's silence in either a federal or state proceeding is justified." We take that in its literal sense and hold that the Fifth Amendment, in its direct application to the Federal Government, and in its bearing on the States by reason of the Fourteenth Amendment, forbids either comment by the prosecution on the accused's silence or instructions by the court that such silence is evidence of guilt.

Reversed.

The CHIEF JUSTICE took no part in the decision of this case. Mr. Justice HARLAN concurred. Justices STEWART and WHITE dissented.

C. NESSON, REASONABLE DOUBT AND PERMISSIVE INFERENCES: THE VALUE OF COMPLEXITY
92 Harv. L. Rev. 1187, 1208-1213 (1979)

LACK OF SATISFACTORY EXPLANATION

It should be clear by this point that the concept of reasonable doubt is inconsistent with a procedure that permits an otherwise unassisted leap from aggregate likelihood to a conclusion of guilt in a specific case. There is, however, a frequent limitation on permissive inferences which, to some, has appeared to solve the problem: the factfinder typically is only allowed to infer the requisite conclusion from the predicate fact if there is a lack of satisfactory explanation. In *Gainey*, for example [the case from which the Moonshine problem was drawn, United States v. Gainey, 380 U.S. 63 (1965)], the jury was told that it was permitted to infer from the presence of the defendant at the still that he was operating the still, "unless the defendant . . . explains such presence to the satisfaction of the jury." The statute unsuccessfully challenged in [Turner v. United States, 396 U.S. 398 (1970)] placed a similar qualification on the jury's authority to infer importation and knowledge from possession of heroin. If an inference can legitimately be drawn from a failure to explain a suggestive circumstance, that additional datum could bridge the gap between aggregate likelihood and a conclusion beyond reasonable doubt in the specific case. Moreover, if a defendant understands that an adverse inference will be drawn from the lack of a satisfactory explanation, the conclusion that there is no innocent explanation becomes more logical when he fails to offer one. Indeed, the statutory declaration of the permissive inference may be seen as notifying the defendant of the circumstances in which his passivity in defending will be counted against him. This, however, presents an obvious fifth amendment problem: is it constitutional to draw an inference against the defendant from his refusal to defend?

The fifth amendment is not a guarantee of acquittal. If the prosecution has offered proof which is sufficient to warrant a conclusion of guilt beyond reasonable doubt, a defendant may feel considerable pressure to take the stand and dispute the prosecution's case. Practically speaking, it may be his only chance for acquittal. The "compulsion" which the defendant feels in such a case is the natural consequence of the prosecution's presentation of a strong case, and clearly does not result in any violation of the fifth amendment.

But the situation created by permissive inferences is different. If proof of the predicate fact is sufficient to warrant a conclusion beyond reasonable doubt, then the case is no different from other cases in which the prosecution survives a motion for a directed verdict and puts to the defendant the strategic choice of testifying or not. If, on the other hand, proof of the predicate fact alone is not sufficient to warrant a conclusion of guilt beyond reasonable doubt, then the permissive inference instruction, by requiring the defendant to put forward a satisfactory explanation, significantly changes the situation. Now it is not simply the force of the prosecution's proof which warrants a verdict and puts pressure on the defendant to testify. The defendant's decision not to explain himself becomes an essential part of the prosecution's case, and the pressure to testify now comes from the statutory inference which the jury is invited to draw from the lack of any satisfactory explanation.

This fifth amendment problem implicit in permissive inferences was first raised before the Supreme Court in 1925, in Yee Hem v. United States. The case involved a prosecution for concealing imported opium. The trial judge had instructed the jury in the terms typical of the federal narcotics presumption: whenever the defendant is shown to have possessed opium, "such possession shall be deemed sufficient evidence to authorize conviction [i.e., for the jury to find knowledge and importation] unless the defendant shall explain the possession to the satisfaction of the jury." Yee Hem challenged this permissive inference on the grounds that the "satisfactory explanation" clause made the permissive inference an unconstitutional burden on his right to remain silent.

The Supreme Court, by its own admission, "put aside" the question "with slight discussion." The permissive inference, said the Court, "compels nothing":

> It leaves the accused entirely free to testify or not as he chooses. If the accused happens to be the only repository of the facts necessary to negative the presumption arising from his possession, that is a misfortune which the statute under review does not create but which is inherent in the case. The same situation might present itself if there were no statutory presumption and a prima facie case of concealment with knowledge of unlawful importation were made by the evidence. . . . [T]he constraint upon him to give testimony would arise there, as it arises here, simply from the force of circumstances and not from any form of compulsion forbidden by the Constitution.

There are two basic flaws in this reasoning. First, it ignores the question which this Article poses: can the prosecution be considered to have offered a prima facie case of knowledge and importation merely by proving possession? The Court in Yee Hem merely assumed an affirmative answer. Second, even if proof of mere possession could constitute a prima facie case, and thus constitutionally impel the defendant to explain his possession, it does not follow that the jury may be told that it can supplement the prosecution's case with an inference based on the defendant's silence. In Griffin v. California, the Court examined the difference between a conviction based on the strength of the prosecution's case and one based on the prosecution's case supplemented by an inference drawn from the defendant's decision not to testify, and held that neither prosecutor nor judge may urge the jury to draw an adverse inference from a defendant's silence.

The Court's language in the latter case is particularly germane here. The remarks of the prosecutor and the judge in *Griffin* were held to violate the privilege against self-incrimination because the California rule permitting comment upon the defendant's silence by the prosecutor was "in substance a rule of evidence that allows the State the privilege of tendering to the jury for its consideration the failure of the accused to testify." *Griffin* held that "when the court solemnizes the silence of the accused into evidence against him," the state is in practical effect exercising that compulsion which the fifth amendment forbids.

If one accepts the proposition that the aggregate likelihood presupposed by the permissive inference is not itself enough to sustain a verdict beyond reasonable doubt, then any attempt to draw additional strength for the permissive inference from the defendant's lack of explanation means necessarily that the defendant's silence is functioning as an added piece of "evidence," "solemnized" by the statute and the jury instruction. *Griffin* thus suggests that permissive inferences must stand or fall on the strength of the inference to be drawn from the predicate fact, unaided by any inference from the lack of satisfactory explanation.

The best defense of the "lack of satisfactory explanation" language against fifth amendment challenge is not to deny that an inference is being drawn from the lack of a satisfactory explanation, but to argue that the explanation could have come from witnesses other than the defendant, and therefore that no inference is being drawn from the *defendant's* failure to testify. This argument, however, conveniently glosses over the fact that the defendant is the obvious person from whom the jury would expect explanation, particularly so in cases involving issues of intent and knowledge, issues which permissive inferences often address. The "unless satisfactorily explained" instruction, however phrased, is thus likely to be *understood by jurors* as an invitation to draw an inference from the *defendant's* silence. This in itself might be considered enough to invalidate it.

But there is a more fundamental weakness in the argument: it assumes that it is constitutional to require a defendant to put on a defense. A defendant cannot be constitutionally required to come forward with a defense unless the prosecution has first met its burden of proof. As Wigmore long ago explained, the presumption of innocence is merely a corollary of the rule that the prosecution must adduce evidence and produce persuasion beyond reasonable doubt; and by reason of this rule, the accused "may remain inactive and secure, until the prosecution has taken up its burden and produced evidence and effected persuasion."[84] The question, then, of whether any inference may be drawn

---

84. 9 J. Wigmore on Evidence §2511, at 407.

from a defendant's failure to provide a satisfactory explanation, even if he might be able to do so by calling witnesses other than himself, depends upon whether the prosecution has first discharged its burden of production. But if the analysis so far presented in this Article is credited, the proof of the predicate fact of a permissive inference cannot by itself meet that burden, and therefore cannot provide a constitutional basis for authorizing an inference to be drawn against the defendant who fails to come forward with a defense. If the prosecution can only overcome the presumption of innocence by meeting its burden of persuasion, then allowing the prosecution to discharge this burden by means of any inference based on the defendant's failure to defend is inconsistent with the presumption of innocence.

G.   Criminal Presumptions and Rationality

UNITED STATES v. DUBE
520 F.2d 250 (1st Cir. 1975)

Before COFFIN, C.J., McENTEE and CAMPBELL, J.J.

McENTEE, J. Defendant Dube was tried on an indictment charging him with robbery of a federally insured bank. He did not deny that he committed the robbery, but introduced the testimony of a psychiatrist and a psychologist that he was insane when he committed the offense. The prosecution did not present expert opinion evidence but relied instead on cross-examination and the lay testimony of two bank tellers and Dube's accomplice to rebut his case. Dube moved for a judgment of acquittal on the ground that the prosecution had failed as a matter of law to sustain its burden of proving his sanity beyond a reasonable doubt, but the motion was denied. The jury returned a verdict of guilty and Dube appeals.

A criminal defendant is presumed sane, but the introduction of evidence of insanity dispels the presumption and subjects the prosecution to the burden of proving sanity beyond a reasonable doubt. Beltran v. United States, 302 F.2d 48, 52 (1st Cir. 1962). . . . There is no general principle that the prosecution must counter defendant's expert medical evidence with expert testimony of its own. The expert testimony is not conclusive even where uncontradicted; its weight and credibility are for the jury to determine, and it may be rebutted in various ways apart from the introduction of countervailing expert opinion.[1]

---

1. In Mims v. United States, 375 F.2d 135, 143-44 (5th Cir. 1967), the court stated that expert testimony may be rebutted "by showing the incorrectness or inadequacy of the factual

We do not think the evidence in this case was such that a reasonable man must necessarily have entertained doubts as to defendant's sanity. Both Dr. Voss, the psychiatrist, and Dr. Bishop, the psychologist, testified that in their opinion defendant was a schizophrenic and substantially incapable of conforming his conduct to the requirements of the law at the time of the crime. They arrived at those diagnoses nearly five months after the robbery and only a week before trial. Dr. Voss's opinion was based on two hours of interviews and Dr. Bishop's on a one-hour interview and three hours of intelligence and personality testing. . . .

Most importantly, Dr. Voss's diagnosis was based almost entirely on the subjective history narrated by defendant and his counsel, see United States v. Ingman, 426 F.2d 973 (9th Cir. 1970), and Dr. Bishop undoubtedly interpreted the test results in light of the history he received. Both testified that they were able to detect malingering and that defendant could not fabricate a history suggesting schizophrenia, but of course a jury would not be bound to believe these assertions. Id. Indeed the factual assumptions they derived from Dube's narrative, on which they predicated their conclusions, did not comport with the testimony at trial. On the basis of defendant's statements, both regarded the robbery as compulsive and irrational, but the testimony of Mrs. Kyllonen, the accomplice, furnished abundant evidence of a carefully planned and executed crime. The experts' testimony also seemed to rest in part on the notion that bank robbery is an irrational activity in the first place, making the competence of a bank robber at least suspect. Both concluded that defendant was shy, a "loner," unable to form emotional attachments to others, but Mrs. Kyllonen testified that she was in love with defendant, that they had lived together for as long as three weeks before the robbery and that they had arranged to get back together after defendant disposed of some stolen checks in New York. She also testified that during the period immediately after the robbery she did not notice anything peculiar about defendant's activities. . . .

We agree with our concurring brother that the prosecution was remiss in not offering psychiatric testimony of its own. However, on all

---

assumptions upon which the opinion is based, 'the reasoning by which he progresses from his material to his conclusion,' the interest or bias of the expert, inconsistencies or contradiction in his testimony as to material matters, material variations between the experts themselves, and defendant's lack of co-operation with the expert. Also in cases involving opinions of medical experts, the probative force of that character of testimony is lessened where it is predicated on subjective symptoms, or where it is based on narrative statements to the expert as to past events not in evidence at the trial. In some cases, the cross-examination of the expert may be such as to justify the trier of facts in not being convinced by him. One or more of these factors may, depending on the particular facts of each case, make a jury issue as to the credibility and weight to be given to the expert testimony . . ." (footnotes omitted). See also United States v. McGraw, 515 F.2d 758 (9th Cir. 1975), holding that defendant's expert testimony may be rebutted by cross-examination or evidence from which the jury could infer that the defendant's expert testimony depended upon an incorrect view of the facts.

the evidence we think the court correctly allowed the case to go to the jury. See United States v. Coleman, [501 F.2d 342 (10th Cir. 1974)].

Affirmed.

CAMPBELL, J. (concurring).

I find this a difficult case to analyze though, on the facts, I concur in the result. The court dwells on the inadequacy of the psychiatrist's and psychologist's diagnoses. While in certain respects I think it is overly critical, I agree that the jury was entitled to be skeptical of opinions of insanity based upon relatively brief examinations made several months after the crime and at a time when Dube had everything to gain from a finding of insanity. . . .

Still it is not simple to identify the affirmative evidence from which the jury could find defendant sane *beyond a reasonable doubt.* Certain conclusions, could, it is true, be drawn from Dube's girl friend's description of his conduct before and after the crime. She had lived with Dube for several weeks and was in his company when he fled. While the defense argues that by selecting a bank to rob on the spur of the moment, Dube behaved in a bizarre manner, this behavior does not necessarily compel an inference of mental abnormality; and his conduct during and after the robbery, including precautions to avoid detection such as discarding the gun and driving to a city where he felt the police were less likely to be on the lookout, seems rational enough. The two tellers, who saw him briefly during the robbery, observed nothing bizarre, and the jury was able to add to this evidence its own observations of Dube while in the courtroom. Thus, there was evidence that Dube at certain times had behaved in a way which, to the average eyes, might seem normal. Still one wonders by what standard the fleeting glimpses of behavior transmitted by Dube's girl friend and the tellers allowed a finding of sanity beyond a reasonable doubt.* Dr. Voss, the psychiatrist, testified that the girl friend's version of Dube's behavior was consistent with a diagnosis of schizophrenia. Whether or not that is so, it is questionable whether her association with Dube was extensive enough, and her behavioral testimony detailed enough, to permit a positive diagnosis of sanity either by a layman or an expert.

Yet not without some hesitation I think the jury was entitled to receive

---

* Our approach is not easily reconciled with that taken in Beltran v. United States, 302 F.2d 48 (1st Cir. 1962), in which Judge Aldrich wrote, 302 F.2d at 52,

"The introduction of evidence of insanity places a burden on the government of proving sanity beyond a reasonable doubt. . . . This burden cannot be spirited away by the simple method proposed by the government of the court's saying it does not believe the evidence, therefore there is no evidence, therefore there is no burden. . . . [S]uch thinking would render the whole principle meaningless. Rather, the record must be looked at as a whole, with the burden on the government to overcome any reasonable doubt." . . .

help from another quarter. In Davis v. United States, 160 U.S. 469 (1895), the Supreme Court did not characterize the presumption of sanity as belonging to that category of presumption which vanishes once the defense shows evidence of insanity. Instead, it stated, "If the whole evidence, *including that supplied by the presumption of sanity,* does not exclude beyond a reasonable doubt the hypothesis of insanity, of which some proof is adduced, the accused is entitled to an acquittal. . . ." 160 U.S. at 488 [Emphasis supplied].

Except for the quoted reference in *Davis* (which was the case that established the federal rule requiring the prosecution to prove sanity beyond a reasonable doubt) there has been little attention paid in federal cases to whether the presumption of sanity, once questioned, continues to have evidentiary force. Some courts, like the court here, see it as a presumption that evaporates once evidence of insanity is introduced. Yet viewed as a common sense inference that a person without marked symptoms to the contrary is likely to be sane, I think the presumption is entitled to be given reasonable weight in determining whether on all the evidence the Government gets to a jury. . . .

In the present case, given the evidence of an ability to function normally, and an absence of evidence of abnormal behavior, I think the jury could summon assistance from the inference, or presumption, that Dube was sane. Evidence bearing upon insanity has never been restricted to expert evidence. Conduct, lay observations and even lay opinions have traditionally been given much weight. 2 J. Wigmore, Evidence, §§227 et seq. (3d ed. 1940). And the jury could add to factors such as the reasonableness of Dube's conduct before and after the crime and his apparent lack of any history of mental disturbance, an inference of sanity drawn from its common experience that most people (at least those without marked outward symptoms) are sane. With the aid of this inference it could reach the conclusion that he was sane beyond a reasonable doubt. I recognize that this rationale is not without its difficulties, but it seems more satisfying than to pretend that the Government's meager evidence of Dube's conduct established, or could establish, by itself, much of anything.

Had there been somewhat less evidence of ordinary behavior, or slightly stronger evidence of abnormality, reversal might be in order. But without condoning the Government's failure to call an expert or otherwise bolster its case I think the issue was properly submitted to the jury.

Does *Dube* present a problem of allocation or presumption? Suppose the court had recognized that a burden of persuasion could have been placed on the defendant *without* altering the degree of certainty to which the insanity issue had to be proved; that is, suppose that the court had imposed on the defendant the burden of persuading the jury that there was at least a doubt about his sanity? Would that approach have solved the problem here? Would it have been constitutional?

Recall that the major historical debate with civil presumptions has been between the "bursting bubble" and the "shifting burden" approaches, with the first criticized for producing too slight an effect and the second for producing too great an effect. Would a workable middle ground be an approach that keeps the degree of certainty fixed but simply changes the direction from which the parties come at it? It seems to be so in the criminal context but not in the civil. The reciprocal of the plaintiff proving that an element is more probable than not would seem to be the defendant proving that the element is "as likely as not." But how does this differ from total ignorance?

See Eule, The Presumption of Sanity: Bursting the Bubble, 25 U.C.L.A. L. Rev. 637 (1978).

COUNTY COURT OF ULSTER CITY v. ALLEN
442 U.S. 140 (1979)

Mr. Justice STEVENS delivered the opinion of the Court.

A New York statute provides that, with certain exceptions, the presence of a firearm in an automobile is presumptive evidence of its illegal possession by all persons then occupying the vehicle. The United States Court of Appeals for the Second Circuit held that respondents may challenge the constitutionality of this statute in a federal habeas corpus proceeding and that the statute is "unconstitutional on its face." 568 F.2d 998, 1009. We granted certiorari to review these holdings and also to consider whether the statute is constitutional in its application to respondents. 439 U.S. 815.

Four persons, three adult males (respondents) and a 16-year-old girl (Jane Doe, who is not a respondent here), were jointly tried on charges that they possessed two loaded handguns, a loaded machinegun, and over a pound of heroin found in a Chevrolet in which they were riding when it was stopped for speeding on the New York Thruway shortly after noon on March 28, 1973. The two large-caliber handguns, which together with their ammunition weighed approximately six pounds, were seen through the window of the car by the investigating police officer. They were positioned crosswise in an open handbag on either the front floor or the front seat of the car on the passenger side where Jane Doe was sitting. Jane Doe admitted that the handbag was hers. The machinegun and the heroin were discovered in the trunk after the police pried it open. The car had been borrowed from the driver's brother earlier that day; the key to the trunk could not be found in the car or on the person of any of its occupants, although there was testimony that two of the occupants had placed something in the trunk before embarking in the borrowed car. The jury convicted all four of possession of the handguns and acquitted them of possession of the contents of the trunk.

Counsel for all four defendants objected to the introduction into evidence of the two handguns, the machinegun, and the drugs, arguing that the State had not adequately demonstrated a connection between their clients and the contraband. The trial court overruled the objection, relying on the presumption of possession created by the New York statute. Tr. 474-483. Because that presumption does not apply if a weapon is found "upon the person" of one of the occupants of the car, . . . the three male defendants also moved to dismiss the charges relating to the handguns on the ground that the guns were found on the person of Jane Doe. Respondents made this motion both at the close of the prosecution's case and at the close of all evidence. The trial judge twice denied it, concluding that the applicability of the "upon the person" exception was a question of fact for the jury. . . .

At the close of the trial, the judge instructed the jurors that they were entitled to infer possession from the defendants' presence in the car. He did not make any reference to the "upon the person" exception in his explanation of the statutory presumption, nor did any of the defendants object to this omission or request alternative or additional instructions on the subject. . . .

In this case, the Court of Appeals undertook the task of deciding the constitutionality of the New York statute "on its face." Its conclusion that the statutory presumption was arbitrary rested entirely on its view of the fairness of applying the presumption in hypothetical situations—situations, indeed, in which it is improbable that a jury would return a conviction, or that a prosecution would ever be instituted. We must accordingly inquire whether these respondents had standing to advance the arguments that the Court of Appeals considered decisive. An analysis of our prior cases indicates that the answer to this inquiry depends on the type of presumption that is involved in the case.

Inferences and presumptions are a staple of our adversary system of factfinding. It is often necessary for the trier of fact to determine the existence of an element of the crime — that is, an "ultimate" or "elemental" fact—from the existence of one or more "evidentiary" or "basic" facts. E.g., Barnes v. United States, 412 U.S. 837, 843-844; Tot v. United States, 319 U.S. 463, 467; Mobile, J. & K.C.R. Co. v. Turnipseed, 219 U.S. 35, 42. The value of these evidentiary devices, and their validity under the Due Process Clause, vary from case to case, however, depending on the strength of the connection between the particular basic and elemental facts involved and on the degree to which the device curtails the factfinder's freedom to assess the evidence independently. Nonetheless, in criminal cases, the ultimate test of any device's constitutional validity in a given case remains constant: the device must not undermine the factfinder's responsibility at trial, based on evidence adduced by the State, to find the ultimate facts beyond a reasonable doubt. See In re Winship, 397 U.S. 358, 364; Mullaney v. Wilbur, 421 U.S., at 702-703, n.31.

The most common evidentiary device is the entirely permissive inference or presumption, which allows—but does not require—the trier of fact to infer the elemental fact from proof by the prosecutor of the basic one and which places no burden of any kind on the defendant. See, e.g., Barnes v. United States, supra, at 840 n.3. In that situation the basic fact may constitute prima facie evidence of the elemental fact. See, e.g., Turner v. United States, 396 U.S. 398, 402 n.2. When reviewing this type of device, the Court has required the party challenging it to demonstrate its invalidity as applied to him. Because this permissive presumption leaves the trier of fact free to credit or reject the inference and does not shift the burden of proof, it affects the application of the "beyond a reasonable doubt" standard only if, under the facts of the case, there is no rational way the trier could make the connection permitted by the inference. For only in that situation is there any risk that an explanation of the permissible inference to a jury, or its use by a jury, has caused the presumptively rational factfinder to make an erroneous factual determination.

A mandatory presumption is a far more troublesome evidentiary device. For it may affect not only the strength of the "no reasonable doubt" burden but also the placement of that burden; it tells the trier that he or they *must* find the elemental fact upon proof of the basic fact, at least unless the defendant has come forward with some evidence to rebut the presumed connection between the two facts. In this situation, the Court has generally examined the presumption on its face to determine the extent to which the basic and elemental facts coincide. To the extent that the trier of fact is forced to abide by the presumption, and may not reject it based on an independent evaluation of the particular facts presented by the State, the analysis of the presumption's constitutional validity is logically divorced from those facts and based on the presumption's accuracy in the run of cases. It is for this reason that the Court had held it irrelevant in analyzing a mandatory presumption, but not in analyzing a purely permissive one, that there is ample evidence in the record other than the presumption to support a conviction.

Without determining whether the presumption in this case was mandatory, the Court of Appeals analyzed it on its face as if it were. In fact, it was not, as the New York Court of Appeals had earlier pointed out. 40 N.Y.2d, at 510-511, 354 N.E.2d, at 840.

The trial judge's instructions make it clear that the presumption was merely a part of the prosecution's case, that it gave rise to a permissive inference available only in certain circumstances, rather than a mandatory conclusion of possession, and that it could be ignored by the jury even if there was no affirmative proof offered by defendants in rebuttal. The judge explained that possession could be actual or constructive, but that constructive possession could not exist without the intent and ability to exercise control or dominion over the weapons. He also carefully instructed the jury that there is a mandatory presumption of innocence in favor of the defendants that controls unless it, as the exclusive trier of fact, is satisfied beyond a reasonable doubt that the defendants possessed the handguns in the manner described by the judge. In short, the instructions plainly directed the jury to consider all the circumstances tending to support or contradict the inference that all four occupants of the car had possession of the two loaded handguns and to decide the matter for itself without regard to how much evidence the defendants introduced.

Our cases considering the validity of permissive statutory presumption such as the one involved here have rested on an evaluation of the presumption as applied to the record before the Court. None suggests that a court should pass on the constitutionality of this kind of statute "on its face." It was error for the Court of Appeals to make such a determination in this case.

III

As applied to the facts of this case, the presumption of possession is entirely rational. Notwithstanding the Court of Appeals' analysis, respondents were not "hitchhikers or other casual passengers," and the guns were neither "a few inches in length" nor "out of [respondents'] sight." . . . The argument against possession by any of the respondents was predicated solely on the fact that the guns were in Jane Doe's pocketbook. But several circumstances — which, not surprisingly, her counsel repeatedly emphasized in his questions and his argument — made it highly improbable that she was the sole custodian of those weapons.

Even if it was reasonable to conclude that she had placed the guns in her purse before the car was stopped by police, the facts strongly suggest that Jane Doe was not the only person able to exercise dominion over them. The two guns were too large to be concealed in her handbag. The bag was consequently open, and part of one of the guns was in plain view, within easy access of the driver of the car and even, perhaps, of the other two respondents who were riding in the rear seat.

Moreover, it is highly improbable that the loaded guns belonged to Jane Doe or that she was solely responsible for their being in her purse. As a 16-year-old girl in the company of three adult men she was the least likely of the four to be carrying one, let alone two, heavy handguns. It is far more probable that she relied on the pocketknife found in her brassiere for any necessary self-protection. Under these circumstances, it was not unreasonable for her counsel to argue and for the jury to infer that when the car was halted for speeding, the other passengers in the car anticipated the risk of a search and attempted to conceal their weapons in a pocketbook in the front seat. The inference is surely more likely than the notion that these weapons were the sole property of the 16-year-old girl.

Under these circumstances, the jury would have been entirely reasonable in rejecting the suggestion—which, incidentally, defense counsel did not even advance in their closing arguments to the jury—that the handguns were in the sole possession of Jane Doe. Assuming that the jury did reject it, the case is tantamount to one in which the guns were lying on the floor or the seat of the car in the plain view of the three other occupants of the automobile. In such a case, it is surely rational to infer that each of the respondents was fully aware of the presence of the guns and had both the ability and the intent to exercise dominion and control over the weapons. The application of the statutory presumption in this case therefore comports with the standard laid down in Tot v. United States, 319 U.S., at 467, and restated in Leary v. United States, 395 U.S., at 36. For there is a "rational connection" between the basic facts that the prosecution proved and the ultimate fact presumed, and the latter is "more likely than not to flow from" the former.

Respondents argue, however, that the validity of the New York presumption must be judged by a "reasonable doubt" test rather than the "more likely than not" standard employed in *Leary*. Under the more stringent test, it is argued that a statutory presumption must be rejected unless the evidence necessary to invoke the inference is sufficient for a rational jury to find the inferred fact beyond a reasonable doubt. See Barnes v. United States, 412 U.S., at 842-843. Respondents' argument again overlooks the distinction between a permissive presumption on which the prosecution is entitled to rely as one not necessarily sufficient part of its proof and a mandatory presumption which the jury must accept even if it is the sole evidence of an element of the offense.

In the latter situation, since the prosecution bears the burden of establishing guilt, it may not rest its case entirely on a presumption unless the fact proved is sufficient to support the inference of guilt beyond a reasonable doubt. But in the former situation, the prosecution may rely on all of the evidence in the record to meet the reasonable-doubt standard. There is no more reason to require a permissive statutory presumption to meet a reasonable-doubt standard before it may be permitted to play any part in a trial than there is to require that degree of probative force for other relevant evidence before it may be admitted. As long as it is clear that the presumption is not the sole and sufficient basis for a finding of guilt, it need only satisfy the test described in *Leary*.

The permissive presumption, as used in this case, satisfied the *Leary* test. And, as already noted, the New York Court of Appeals has concluded that the record as a whole was sufficient to establish guilt beyond a reasonable doubt.

The judgement is reversed.

Mr. Justice POWELL, with whom Mr. Justice BRENNAN, Mr. Justice STEWART, and Mr. Justice MARSHALL join, dissenting.

I agree with the Court that there is no procedural bar to our considering the underlying constitutional question presented by this case. I am not in agreement, however, with the Court's conclusion that the presumption as charged to the jury in this case meets the constitutional requirements of due process as set forth in our prior decisions. On the contrary, an individual's mere presence in an automobile where there is a handgun does not even make it "more likely than not" that the individual possesses the weapon.

I

In the criminal law, presumptions are used to encourage the jury to find certain facts, with respect to which no direct evidence is presented, solely because other facts have been proved.[1] See, e.g., Barnes v. United States, 412 U.S. 837, 840 n.3; United States v. Romano, 382 U.S. 136, 138 (1965). The purpose of such presumptions is plain: Like certain other jury instructions, they provide guidance for jurors' thinking in considering the evidence laid before them. Once in the juryroom, jurors necessarily draw inferences from the evidence—both direct and circumstantial. Through the use of presumptions, certain inferences are commended to the attention of jurors by legislatures or courts.

Legitimate guidance of a jury's deliberations is an indispensable part of our criminal justice system. Nonetheless, the use of presumptions in criminal cases poses at least two distinct perils for defendants' constitutional rights. The Court accurately identifies the first of these as being the danger of interference with "the factfinder's responsibility at trial, based on evidence adduced by the State, to find the ultimate facts beyond a reasonable doubt." If the jury is instructed that it must infer some ultimate fact (that is, some element of the offense) from proof of other facts unless the defendant disproves the ultimate fact by a pre-

---

1. Such encouragement can be provided either by statutory presumptions, see, e.g., 18 U.S.C. §1201(b), or by presumptions created in the common law. See, e.g., Barnes v. United States, 412 U.S. 837 (1973). Unless otherwise specified, "presumption" will be used herein to refer to "permissible inferences," as well as to "true" presumptions. See F. James, Civil Procedure §7.9 (1965).

ponderance of the evidence, then the presumption shifts the burden of proof to the defendant concerning the element thus inferred.[2]

But I do not agree with the Court's conclusion that the only constitutional difficulty with presumptions lies in the danger of lessening the burden of proof the prosecution must bear. As the Court notes, the presumptions thus far reviewed by the Court have not shifted the burden of persuasion; instead they either have required only that the defendant produce some evidence to rebut the inference suggested by the prosecution's evidence, see Tot v. United States, 319 U.S. 463 (1943), or merely have been suggestions to the jury that it would be sensible to draw certain conclusions on the basis of the evidence presented. See Barnes v. United States, supra, 412 U.S. at 840 n.3. Evolving from our decisions, therefore, is a second standard for judging the constitutionality of criminal presumptions which is based—not on the constitutional requirement that the State be put to its proof—but rather on the due process rule that when the jury is encouraged to make factual inferences, those inferences must reflect some valid general observation about the natural connection between events as they occur in our society.

This due process rule was first articulated by the Court in Tot v. United States, supra, in which the Court reviewed the constitutionality of §2(f) of the Federal Firearms Act. That statute provided in part that "possession of a firearm or ammunition by any . . . person [who has been convicted of a crime of violence] shall be presumptive evidence that such firearm or ammunition was shipped or transported [in interstate or foreign commerce]." As the Court interpreted the presumption, it placed upon a defendant only the obligation of presenting some exculpatory evidence concerning the origins of a firearm or ammunition, once the Government proved that the defendant had possessed the weapon and had been convicted of a crime of violence. Noting that juries must be permitted to infer from one fact the existence of another essential to guilt, "if reason and experience support the inference," id., at 467, the Court concluded that under some circumstances juries may be guided in making these inferences by legislative or common-law presumptions, even though they may be based "upon a view of relation broader than that a jury might take in a specific case," 319 U.S., at 468. To provide due process, however, there must be at least "a rational

---

2. The Court suggests that presumptions that shift the burden of persuasion to the defendant in this way can be upheld provided that "the fact proved is sufficient to support the inference of guilt beyond a reasonable doubt." As the present case involves no shifting of the burden of persuasion, the constitutional restrictions on such presumptions are not before us, and I express no views on them.

It may well be that even those presumptions that do not shift the burden of persuasion cannot be used to prove an element of the offense, if the facts proved would not permit a reasonable mind to find the presumed fact beyond a reasonable doubt. My conclusion in Part II, infra, makes it unnecessary for me to address this concern here.

connection between the facts proved and the fact presumed"—a connection grounded in "common experience." Id., at 467. In *Tot,* the
Court found that connection to be lacking.

Subsequently, in Leary v. United States, 395 U.S. 6 (1969), the Court
reaffirmed and refined the due process requirement of *Tot* that inferences specifically commended to the attention of jurors must reflect
generally accepted connections between related events. At issue in *Leary*
was the constitutionality of a federal statute making it a crime to receive,
conceal, buy, or sell marihuana illegally brought into the United States,
knowing it to have been illegally imported. The statute provided that
mere possession of marihuana "shall be deemed sufficient evidence to
authorize conviction unless the defendant explains his possession to the
satisfaction of the jury." After reviewing the Court's decisions in Tot v.
United States, supra, and other criminal presumption cases, Mr. Justice
Harlan, writing for the Court, concluded "that a criminal statutory presumption must be regarded as 'irrational' or 'arbitrary,' and hence unconstitutional, unless it can be said with substantial assurance that the
presumed fact is more likely than not to flow from the proved fact on
which it is made to depend." 395 U.S., at 36 (footnote omitted). The
Court invalidated the statute, finding there to be insufficient basis in
fact for the conclusion that those who possess marihuana are more likely
than not to know that it was imported illegally.[5]

Most recently, in Barnes v. United States, supra, we considered the
constitutionality of a quite different sort of presumption—one that suggested to the jury that "[p]ossession of recently stolen property, if not
satisfactorily explained, is ordinarily a circumstance from which you may
reasonably draw the inference . . . that the person in possession knew
the property had been stolen." Id., 412 U.S. at 840 n.3. After reviewing
the various formulations used by the Court to articulate the constitutionally required basis for a criminal presumption, we once again found
it unnecessary to choose among them. As for the presumption suggested
to the jury in *Barnes,* we found that it was well founded in history, common sense, and experience, and therefore upheld it as being "clearly
sufficient to enable the jury to find beyond a reasonable doubt" that
those in the unexplained possession of recently stolen property know it
to have been stolen. Id., at 845.

In sum, our decisions uniformly have recognized that due process
requires more than merely that the prosecution be put to its proof.[6] In

---

5. Because the statute in Leary v. United States, 395 U.S. 6 (1969), was found to be unconstitutional under the "more likely than not" standard, the Court explicitly declined to consider
whether criminal presumptions also must follow "beyond a reasonable doubt" from their premises, if an essential element of the crime depends upon the presumption's use. Id., at 36 n.64.
See supra n.2. The Court similarly avoided this question in Turner v. United States, 396 U.S.
398 (1970).

6. The Court apparently disagrees, contending that "the factfinder's responsibility . . . to

addition, the Constitution restricts the court in its charge to the jury by requiring that, when particular factual inferences are recommended to the jury, those factual inferences be accurate reflections of what history, common sense, and experience tell us about the relations between events in our society. Generally this due process rule has been articulated as requiring that the truth of the inferred fact be more likely than not whenever the premise for the inference is true. Thus, to be constitutional a presumption must be at least more likely than not true.

II

In the present case, the jury was told that,

> Our Penal Law also provides that the presence in an automobile of any machine gun or of any handgun or firearm which is loaded is presumptive evidence of their unlawful possession. In other words, [under] these presumptions or this latter presumption upon proof of the presence of the machine gun and the hand weapons, you may infer and draw a conclusion that such prohibited weapon was possessed by each of the defendants who occupied the automobile at the time when such instruments were found. The presumption or presumptions is effective only so long as there is no substantial evidence contradicting the conclusion flowing from the presumption, and the presumption is said to disappear when such contradictory evidence is adduced.

Undeniably, the presumption charged in this case encouraged the jury to draw a particular factual inference regardless of any other evidence presented: to infer that respondents possessed the weapons found in the automobile "upon proof of the presence of the machine gun and the hand weapon" and proof that respondents "occupied the automobile at the time such instruments were found." I believe that the presumption thus charged was unconstitutional because it did not fairly reflect what common sense and experience tell us about passengers in automobiles and the possession of handguns. People present in automobiles where there are weapons simply are not "more likely than not" the possessors of those weapons.

Under New York law, "to possess" is "to have physical possession or otherwise to exercise dominion or control over tangible property." N.Y. Penal Law §10.00(8). Plainly the mere presence of an individual in an automobile—without more—does not indicate that he exercises "dominion or control over" everything within it. As the Court of Appeals noted, there are countless situations in which individuals are invited as guests into vehicles the contents of which they know nothing about, much less have control over. Similarly, those who invite others into their

---

find the ultimate facts beyond a reasonable doubt" is the only constitutional restraint upon the use of criminal presumptions at trial.

automobile do not generally search them to determine what they may have on their person; nor do they insist that any handguns be identified and placed within reach of the occupants of the automobile. Indeed, handguns are particularly susceptible to concealment and therefore are less likely than are other objects to be observed by those in an automobile.

In another context, this Court has been particularly hesitant to infer possession from mere presence in a location, noting that "[p]resence is relevant and admissible evidence in a trial on a possession charge; but absent some showing of the defendant's function at [the illegal] still, its connection with possession is too tenuous to permit a reasonable inference of guilt—'the inference of the one from proof of the other is arbitrary. . . .' Tot v. United States, 319 U.S. 463, 467." United States v. Romano, 382 U.S. 136, 141 (1965). We should be even more hesitant to uphold the inference of possession of a handgun from mere presence in an automobile, in light of common experience concerning automobiles and handguns. Because the specific factual inference recommended to the jury in this case is not one that is supported by the general experience of our society, I cannot say that the presumption charged is "more likely than not" to be true. Accordingly, respondents' due process rights were violated by the presumption's use.

As I understand it, the Court today does not contend that in general those who are present in automobiles are more likely than not to possess any gun contained within their vehicles. It argues, however, that the nature of the presumption here involved requires that we look, not only to the immediate facts upon which the jury was encouraged to base its inference, but to the other facts "proved" by the prosecution as well. The Court suggests that this is the proper approach when reviewing what it calls "permissive" presumptions because the jury was urged "to consider all the circumstances tending to support or contradict the inference."

It seems to me that the Court mischaracterizes the function of the presumption charged in this case. As it acknowledges was the case in *Romano,* supra, the "instruction authorized conviction even if the jury disbelieved all of the testimony except the proof of presence" in the automobile.[7] The Court nevertheless relies on all of the evidence intro-

---

7. In commending the presumption to the jury, the court gave no instruction that would have required a finding of possession to be based on anything more than mere presence in the automobile. Thus, the jury was not instructed that it should infer that respondents possessed the handguns only if it found that the guns were too large to be concealed in Jane Doe's handbag; that the guns accordingly were in the plain view of respondents; that the weapons were within "easy access of the driver of the car and even, perhaps, of the other two respondents who were riding in the rear seat"; that it was unlikely that Jane Doe was solely responsible for the placement of the weapons in her purse; or that the case was "tantamount to one in which the guns were lying on the floor or the seat of the car in the plain view of the three other occupants of the automobile."

duced by the prosecution and argues that the "permissive" presumption could not have prejudiced defendants. The possibility that the jury disbelieved all of this evidence, and relied on the presumption, is simply ignored.

I agree that the circumstances relied upon by the Court in determining the plausibility of the presumption charged in this case would have made it reasonable for the jury to "infer that each of the respondents was fully aware of the presence of the guns and had both the ability and the intent to exercise dominion and control over the weapons." But the jury was told that it could conclude that respondents possessed the weapons found therein from proof of the mere fact of respondents' presence in the automobile. For all we know, the jury rejected all of the prosecution's evidence concerning the location and origin of the guns, and based its conclusion that respondents possessed the weapons solely upon its belief that respondents had been present in the automobile.[8] For purposes of reviewing the constitutionality of the presumption at issue here, we must assume that this was the case.

The Court's novel approach in this case appears to contradict prior decisions of this Court reviewing such presumptions. Under the Court's analysis, whenever it is determined that an inference is "permissive," the only question is whether, in light of all of the evidence adduced at trial, the inference recommended to the jury is a reasonable one. The Court has never suggested that the inquiry into the rational basis of a permissible inference may be circumvented in this manner. Quite the contrary, the Court has required that the "evidence *necessary to invoke the inference* [be] sufficient for a rational juror to find the inferred fact. . . ." Barnes v. United States, 412 U.S. 843 (1973) (emphasis supplied). See Turner v. United States, 396 U.S. 398, 407 (1970). Under the presumption charged in this case, the only evidence necessary to invoke the inference was the presence of the weapons in the automobile with respondents—an inference that is plainly irrational.

In sum, it seems to me that the Court today ignores the teaching of our prior decisions. By speculating about what the jury may have done with the factual inference thrust upon it, the Court in effect assumes away the inference altogether, constructing a rule that permits the use of any inference — no matter how irrational in itself — provided that

---

8. The Court is therefore mistaken in its conclusion that, because "respondents were not 'hitch-hikers or other casual passengers,' and the guns were neither 'a few inches in length' nor 'out of [respondents'] sight,'" reference to these possibilities is inappropriate in considering the constitutionality of the presumption as charged in this case. To be sure, respondents' challenge is to the presumption as charged to the jury in this case. But in assessing its application here, we are not free, as the Court apparently believes, to disregard the possibility that the jury may have disbelieved all other evidence supporting an inference of possession. The jury may have concluded that respondents — like hitchhikers — had only an incidental relationship to the auto in which they were traveling, or that, contrary to some of the testimony at trial, the weapons were indeed out of respondents' sight.

otherwise there is sufficient evidence in the record to support a finding of guilt. Applying this novel analysis to the present case, the Court upholds the use of a presumption that it makes no effort to defend in isolation. In substance, the Court—applying an unarticulated harmless error standard — simply finds that the respondents were guilty as charged. They may well have been but rather than acknowledging this rationale, the Court seems to have made new law with respect to presumptions that could seriously jeopardize a defendant's right to a fair trial. Accordingly, I dissent.

Do you agree with the majority's characterization of the device involved in *Ulster City* as a "permissive inference"? If the factfinder's responsibility is to find the ultimate facts beyond a reasonable doubt based on evidence presented by the prosecution, how can the court apply *any* standard other than the "beyond-a-reasonable-doubt-rational-connection test" to this device, regardless of how it is characterized? Has the majority applied a standard even lower than the preponderance standard, i.e., "not-irrational"? Is the majority correct in considering all the evidence in the case in deciding whether the presumption passes constitutional muster? Is the dissent correct in insisting that the presumption be judged solely on the basis of the relationship between the basic fact and the presumed fact? Did the device in this case operate to shift the burden of production to the defendant? Is this constitutional? Is the decision in this case consistent with proposed Rule 303?

MEDINA v. CALIFORNIA
509 U.S. 502 (1992)

Justice KENNEDY delivered the opinion of the Court.

It is well established that the Due Process Clause of the Fourteenth Amendment prohibits the criminal prosecution of a defendant who is not competent to stand trial. Drope v. Missouri, 420 U.S. 162 (1975); Pate v. Robinson, 383 U.S. 375 (1966). The issue in this case is whether the Due Process Clause permits a State to require a defendant who alleges incompetence to stand trial to bear the burden of proving so by a preponderance of the evidence.

I

In 1984, petitioner Teofilo Medina, Jr. stole a gun from a pawn shop in Santa Ana, California. In the weeks that followed, he held up two gas stations, a drive-in dairy, and a market, murdered three employees of those establishments, attempted to rob a fourth employee, and shot at two passersby who attempted to follow his getaway car. Petitioner was apprehended less than one month after his crime spree began and was charged with a number of criminal offenses, including three counts of first-degree murder. Before trial, petitioner's counsel moved for a competency hearing under Cal. Pen. Code Ann. §1368 (West 1982), on the ground that he was unsure whether petitioner had the ability to participate in the criminal proceedings against him.

Under California law, "[a] person cannot be tried or adjudged to punishment while such person is mentally incompetent." Cal. Pen. Code Ann. §1367 (West 1982). A defendant is mentally incompetent "if, as a result of mental disorder or developmental disability, the defendant is unable to understand the nature of the criminal proceedings or to assist counsel in the conduct of a defense in a rational manner." Ibid. The statute establishes a presumption that the defendant is competent, and the party claiming incompetence bears the burden of proving that the defendant is incompetent by a preponderance of the evidence. §1369(f) ("It shall be presumed that the defendant is mentally competent unless it is proved by a preponderance of the evidence that the defendant is mentally incompetent").

The trial court granted the motion for a hearing and the preliminary issue of petitioner's competence to stand trial was tried to a jury. Over the course of the six-day hearing, in addition to lay testimony, the jury heard conflicting expert testimony about petitioner's mental condition. The Supreme Court of California gives this summary: "Dr. Gold, a psychiatrist who knew defendant while he was in the Arizona prison system, testified that defendant was a paranoid schizophrenic and was incompetent to assist his attorney at trial. Dr. Echeandia, a clinical psychologist at the Orange County jail, doubted the accuracy of the schizophrenia diagnosis, and could not express an opinion on defendant's competence to stand trial. Dr. Sharma, a psychiatrist, likewise expressed doubts regarding the schizophrenia diagnosis and leaned toward a finding of competence. Dr. Pierce, a psychologist, believed defendant was schizophrenic, with impaired memory and hallucinations, but nevertheless was competent to stand trial. Dr. Sakurai, a jail psychiatrist, opined that although defendant suffered from depression, he was competent, and that he may have been malingering. Dr. Sheffield, who treated defendant for knife wounds he incurred in jail, could give no opinion on the competency issue." 51 Cal. 3d 870, 880 (1990). During the competency hearing, petitioner engaged in several verbal and physical outbursts. On one of these occasions, he overturned the counsel table.

The trial court instructed the jury in accordance with §1369(f) that "the defendant is presumed to be mentally competent and he has the burden of proving by a preponderance of the evidence that he is mentally incompetent as a result of mental disorder or developmental disability." The jury found petitioner competent to stand trial. A new jury was impanelled for the criminal trial, and petitioner entered pleas of not guilty and not guilty by reason of insanity. At the conclusion of the guilt phase, petitioner was found guilty of all three counts of first-degree murder and a number of lesser offenses. He moved to withdraw his insanity plea, and the trial court granted the motion. Two days later, however, petitioner moved to reinstate his insanity plea. Although his counsel expressed the view that reinstatement of the insanity plea was "tactically unsound," the trial court granted petitioner's motion. A sanity hearing was held, and the jury found that petitioner was sane at the time of the offenses. At the penalty phase, the jury found that the murders were premeditated and deliberate, and returned a verdict of death. The trial court imposed the death penalty for the murder convictions, and sentenced petitioner to a prison term for the remaining offenses.

On direct appeal to the California Supreme Court, petitioner did not challenge the standard of proof set forth in §1369(f), but argued that the statute violated his right to due process by placing the burden of proof on him to establish that he was not competent to stand trial. In addition, he argued that §1369(f) violates due process by establishing a presumption that a defendant is competent to stand trial unless proven otherwise. The court rejected both of these contentions. Relying upon our decision in Leland v. Oregon, 343 U.S. 790 (1952), which rejected a due process challenge to an Oregon statute that required a criminal defendant to prove the defense of insanity beyond a reasonable doubt, the court observed that "the states ordinarily have great latitude to decide the proper placement of proof burdens." 51 Cal. 3d, at 884. In its view, §1369(f) "does not subject the defendant to hardship or oppression," because "one might reasonably expect that the defendant and his counsel would have better access than the People to the facts relevant to the court's competency inquiry." Id., at 885. The court also rejected petitioner's argument that it is "irrational" to retain a presumption of competence after sufficient doubt has arisen as to a defendant's competence to warrant a hearing, and "decline[d] to hold as a matter of due process that such a presumption must be treated as a mere presumption affecting the burden of production, which disappears merely because a preliminary, often undefined and indefinite, 'doubt' has arisen that justifies further inquiry into the matter." Id., at 885. We granted certiorari and now affirm.

II

Petitioner argues that our decision in Mathews v. Eldridge, 424 U.S. 319 (1976), provides the proper analytical framework for determining whether California's allocation of the burden of proof in competency hearings comports with due process. We disagree. In *Mathews*, we articulated a three-factor test for evaluating procedural due process claims which requires a court to consider "[f]irst, the private interest that will be affected by the official action; second, the risk of an erroneous deprivation of such interest through the procedures used, and the probable value, if any, of additional or substitute procedural safeguards; and finally, the Government's interest, including the function involved and the fiscal and administrative burdens that the additional or substitute procedural requirement would entail." Id., at 335. In our view, the *Mathews* balancing test does not provide the appropriate framework for assessing the validity of state procedural rules which, like the one at bar, are part of the criminal process. . . .

The proper analytical approach, and the one that we adopt here, is that set forth in Patterson v. New York, 432 U.S. 197 (1977), which was decided one year after *Mathews.* In *Patterson,* we rejected a due process challenge to a New York law which placed on a criminal defendant the burden of proving the affirmative defense of extreme emotional disturbance. Rather than relying upon the *Mathews* balancing test, however, we reasoned that a narrower inquiry was more appropriate: "It goes without saying that preventing and dealing with crime is much more the business of the States than it is of the Federal Government, Irvine v. California, 347 U.S. 128 (1954) (plurality opinion), and that we should not lightly construe the Constitution so as to intrude upon the administration of justice by the individual States. Among other things, it is normally 'within the power of the State to regulate procedures under which its laws are carried out, including the burden of producing evidence and the burden of persuasion,' and its decision in this regard is not subject to proscription under the Due Process Clause unless 'it offends some principle of justice so rooted in the traditions and conscience of our people as to be ranked as fundamental.'" . . .

Based on our review of the historical treatment of the burden of proof in competency proceedings, the operation of the challenged rule, and our precedents, we cannot say that the allocation of the burden of proof to a criminal defendant to prove incompetence "offends some principle of justice so rooted in the traditions and conscience of our people as to be ranked as fundamental." Patterson v. New York, supra, 432 U.S., at 202. . . .

Under California law, the allocation of the burden of proof to the defendant will affect competency determinations only in a narrow class of cases where the evidence is in equipoise; that is, where the evidence that a defendant is competent is just as strong as the evidence that he is incompetent. Our cases recognize that a defendant has a constitutional right "not to be tried while legally incompetent," and that a State's "failure to observe procedures adequate to protect a defendant's right not to be tried or convicted while incompetent to stand trial deprives him of his due process right to a fair trial." Drope v. Missouri, 420 U.S., at 172. Once a State provides a defendant access to procedures for making a competency evaluation, however, we perceive no basis for holding that due process further requires the State to assume the burden of vindicating the defendant's constitutional right by persuading the trier of fact that the defendant is competent to stand trial.

Petitioner relies upon federal and state-court decisions which have said that the allocation of the burden of proof to the defendant in these circumstances is inconsistent with the rule of Pate v. Robinson, supra, 383 U.S., at 384, where we held that a defendant whose competence is in doubt cannot be deemed to have waived his right to a competency hearing. Because "'it is contradictory to argue that a defendant may be incompetent, and yet knowingly or intelligently "waive" his right to have the court determine his capacity to stand trial,'" it has been said that it is also "contradictory to argue that a defendant who may be incompetent should be presumed to possess sufficient intelligence that he will be able to adduce evidence of his incompetency which might otherwise be within his grasp." United States v. DiGilio, [538 F.2d 972, 988 (CA3 1976), cert. denied, 429 U.S. 1038 (1977), quoting Pate v. Robinson, supra, 383 U.S. at 384].

In our view, the question whether a defendant whose competence is in doubt may waive his right to a competency hearing is quite different from the question whether the burden of proof may be placed on the defendant once a hearing is held. The rule announced in *Pate* was driven by our concern that it is impossible to say whether a defendant whose competence is in doubt has made a knowing and intelligent waiver of his right to a competency hearing. Once a competency hearing is held, however, the defendant is entitled to the assistance of counsel, and psychiatric evidence is brought to bear on the question of the defendant's mental condition. Although an impaired defendant might be limited in his ability to assist counsel in demonstrating incompetence, the defendant's inability to assist counsel can, in and of itself, constitute probative evidence of incompetence, and defense counsel will often have the best-informed view of the defendant's ability to participate in his defense. While reasonable minds may differ as to the wisdom of placing the burden of proof on the defendant in these circumstances, we believe that a State may take such factors into account in making judgments as to the allocation of the burden of proof, and we see no basis for concluding that placing the burden on the defendant violates the principle approved in *Pate*.

Petitioner argues that psychiatry is an inexact science, and that placing the burden of proof on the defendant violates due process because it requires the defendant to "bear the risk of being forced to stand trial as a result of an erroneous finding of competency." . . . Consistent with our precedents, it is enough that the State affords the criminal defendant on whose behalf a plea of incompetence is asserted a reasonable opportunity to demonstrate that he is not competent to stand trial.

Petitioner further contends that the burden of proof should be placed on the State because we have allocated the burden to the State on a variety of other issues that implicate a criminal defendant's constitutional rights. The decisions upon which petitioner relies, however, do not control the result here, because they involved situations where the government sought to introduce inculpatory evidence obtained by virtue of a waiver of, or in violation of, a defendant's constitutional rights. In such circumstances, allocating the burden of proof to the government furthers the objective of "deterring lawless conduct by police and prosecution." No such purpose is served by allocating the burden of proof to the government in a competency hearing.

In light of our determination that the allocation of the burden of proof to the defendant does not offend due process, it is not difficult to dispose of petitioner's challenge to the presumption of competence imposed by §1369(f). Under California law, a defendant is required to make a threshold showing of incompetence before a hearing is required and, at the hearing, the defendant may be prevented from making decisions that are normally left to the discretion of a competent defendant. Petitioner argues that, once the trial court has expressed a doubt as to the defendant's competence, a hearing is held, and the defendant is deprived of his right to make determinations reserved to competent persons, it is irrational to retain the presumption that the defendant is competent.

In rejecting this contention below, the California Supreme Court observed that "[t]he primary significance of the presumption of competence is to place on defendant (or the People, if they contest his competence) the burden of rebutting it" and that, "[b]y its terms, the presumption of competence is one which affects the burden of proof." 51 Cal. 3d, at 885. We see no reason to disturb the California Supreme Court's conclusion that, in essence, the challenged presumption is a restatement of the burden of proof, and it follows from what we have said that the presumption does not violate the Due Process Clause. . . .

The judgment of the Supreme Court of California is affirmed.

Justice O'CONNOR, with whom Justice SOUTER joins, concurring in the judgment.

I concur in the judgment of the Court, but I reject its intimation that the balancing of equities is inappropriate in evaluating whether state criminal procedures amount to due process. . . . The balancing of equities that Mathews v. Eldridge outlines remains a useful guide in due process cases. . . .

In determining whether the placement of the burden of proof is fundamentally unfair, relevant considerations include: whether the Government has superior access to evidence; whether the defendant is capable of aiding in the garnering and evaluation of evidence on the matter to be proved; and whether placing the burden of proof on the Government is necessary to help enforce a further right, such as the right to be presumed innocent, the right to be free from self-incrimination, or the right to be tried while competent.

After balancing the equities in this case, I agree with the Court that the burden of proof may constitutionally rest on the defendant. As the dissent points out, the competency determination is based largely on the testimony of psychiatrists. The main concern of the prosecution, of course, is that a defendant will feign incompetence in order to avoid trial. If the burden of proving competence rests on the Government, a defendant will have less incentive to cooperate in psychiatric investigations, because an inconclusive examination will benefit the defense, not the prosecution. A defendant may also be less cooperative in making available friends or family who might have information about the defendant's mental state. States may therefore decide that a more complete picture of a defendant's competence will be obtained if the defense has the incentive to produce all the evidence in its possession. The potentially greater overall access to information provided by placing the burden of proof on the defense may outweigh the danger that, in close cases, a marginally incompetent defendant is brought to trial. Unlike the requirement of a hearing or a psychiatric examination, placing the burden of proof on the Government will not necessarily increase the reliability of the proceedings. The equities here, then, do not weigh so much in petitioner's favor as to rebut the presumption of constitutionality that the historical toleration of procedural variation creates.

As the Court points out, the other cases in which we have placed the burden of proof on the government are distinguishable. See Colorado v. Connelly, 479 U.S. 157 (1986) (burden of proof on Government to show waiver of rights under Miranda v. Arizona, 384 U.S. 436 (1966)); Nix v. Williams, 467 U.S. 431, 444-445, n.5 (1984) (burden on Government to show inevitable discovery of evidence obtained by unlawful means); United States v. Matlock, 415 U.S. 164, 177-178, n.14 (1974) (burden on Government to show voluntariness of consent to search); Lego v. Twomey, 404 U.S. 477, 489 (1972) (burden on Government to show voluntariness of confession). In each of these cases, the Government's burden of proof accords with its investigatory responsibilities. Before obtaining a confession, the Government is required to ensure that the confession is given voluntarily. Before searching a private area without a warrant, the Government is generally required to ensure that the owner consents to the search. The Government has no parallel responsibility to gather evidence of a defendant's competence.

Justice BLACKMUN, with whom Justice STEVENS joins, dissenting.

Teofilo Medina, Jr., may have been mentally incompetent when the State of California convicted him and sentenced him to death. One psychiatrist testified he was incompetent. Another psychiatrist and a psychologist testified he was not. Several other experts testified but did not express an opinion on competence. Instructed to presume that petitioner Medina was competent, the jury returned a finding of competence. For all we know, the jury was entirely undecided. I do not believe a Constitution that forbids the trial and conviction of an incompetent person tolerates the trial and conviction of a person about whom the evidence of competency is so equivocal and unclear. I dissent. . . .

As an initial matter, I believe the Court's approach to this case effectively asks and answers the wrong doctrinal question. Following the lead of the parties, the Court mistakenly frames its inquiry in terms of whether to apply a standard it takes to be derived from language in Patterson v. New York, 432 U.S. 197 (1977), or a standard based on the functional balancing approach of Mathews v. Eldridge, 424 U.S. 319 (1976). The Court is not put to such a choice. Under *Drope* and *Pate,* it need decide only whether a procedure imposing the burden of proof upon the defendant is "adequate" to protect the constitutional prohibition against trial of incompetent persons.

The Court, however, chooses the *Patterson* path, announcing that there is no violation of due process unless placing the burden of proof of incompetency upon the defendant "'offends some principle of justice so rooted in the traditions and conscience of our people as to be ranked as fundamental.'" Separating the primary right (the right not to be tried while incompetent) from the subsidiary right (the right not to bear the burden of proof of incompetency), the Court acknowledges the primary right to be fundamental in "our common-law heritage," but determines the subsidiary right to be without a "settled tradition" deserving of constitutional protection. This approach is mistaken, because it severs two integrally related procedural rights that cannot be examined meaningfully in isolation. The protections of the Due Process Clause, to borrow the second Justice Harlan's words, are simply not "a series of isolated points pricked" out in terms of their most specific level of historic generality. Poe v. Ullman, 367 U.S. 497 (1961) (dissenting opinion). Had the Court taken the same historical-categorical approach in *Pate* and *Drope,* it would not have recognized that a defendant has a right to a competency hearing, for in neither of those cases was there any showing that the mere denial of a hearing where there is doubt about competency offended any deeply rooted traditions of the American people.

In all events, I do not interpret the Court's reliance on *Patterson* to undermine the basic balancing of the government's interests against the individual's interest that is germane to any due process inquiry.

While unwilling to discount the force of tradition and history, the Court in *Patterson* did not adopt an exclusively tradition-based approach to due process analysis. Relying on Morrison v. California, 291 U.S. 82 (1934), the Court in *Patterson* looked to the "convenience" to the government and "hardship or oppression" to the defendant in forming its allocation of the burden of proof. 432 U.S., at 203, n.9, and 210. "'The decisions are manifold that within limits of reason and fairness the burden of proof may be lifted from the state in criminal prosecutions and cast on a defendant. The limits are in substance these, that the state shall have proved enough to make it just for the defendant to be required to repel what has been proved with excuse or explanation, or at least that upon a balancing of convenience or of the opportunities for knowledge the shifting of the burden will be found to be an aid to the accuser without subjecting the accused to hardship or oppression. Cf. Wigmore, Evidence, Vol. 5, §§2486, 2512, and cases cited.'" Id., at 203, n.9, quoting Morrison v. California, 291 U.S., at 88-89. . . .

The Court suggests that "defense counsel will often have the best-informed view of the defendant's ability to participate in his defense." There are at least three good reasons, however, to doubt the Court's confidence. First, while the defendant is in custody, the State itself obviously has the most direct, unfettered access to him and is in the best position to observe his behavior. In the present case, Medina was held before trial in the Orange County jail system for more than a year and a half prior to his competency hearing. During the months immediately preceding the competency hearing, he was placed several times for extended periods in a padded cell for treatment and observation by prison psychiatric personnel. While Medina was in the padded cell, prison personnel observed his behavior every 15 minutes.

Second, a competency determination is primarily a medical and psychiatric determination. Competency determinations by and large turn on the testimony of psychiatric experts, not lawyers. . . . While the testimony of psychiatric experts may be far from infallible, it is the experts and not the lawyers who are credited as the "best-informed," and most able to gauge a defendant's ability to understand and participate in the legal proceedings affecting him.

Third, even assuming that defense counsel has the "best-informed view" of the defendant's competency, the lawyer's view will likely have no outlet in, or effect on, the competency determination. Unlike the testimony of medical specialists or lay witnesses, the testimony of defense counsel is far more likely to be discounted by the factfinder as self-interested and biased. Defense counsel may also be discouraged in the first place from testifying for fear of abrogating an ethical responsibility or the attorney-client privilege. By way of example from the case at hand, it should come as little surprise that neither of Medina's two attorneys was among the dozens of persons testifying during the six days of competency proceedings in this case.

Like many psychological inquiries, competency evaluations are "in the present state of the mental sciences . . . at best a hazardous guess however conscientious." Solesbee v. Balkcom, 339 U.S., at 23 (Frankfurter, J., dissenting). This unavoidable uncertainty expands the range of cases where the factfinder will conclude the evidence is in equipoise. The Court, however, dismisses this concern on grounds that "'[d]ue process does not require that every conceivable step be taken, at whatever cost, to eliminate the possibility of convicting an innocent person.'" Yet surely the Due Process Clause requires some conceivable steps be taken to eliminate the risk of erroneous convictions. I search in vain for any guiding principle in the Court's analysis that determines when the risk of a wrongful conviction happens to be acceptable and when it does not.

The allocation of the burden of proof reflects a societal judgment about how the risk of error should be distributed between litigants. . . . "The individual should not be asked to share equally with society the risk of error when the possible injury to the individual is significantly greater than any possible harm to the state." Addington v. Texas, [441 U.S. 418, 427 (1979)]. The costs to the State of bearing the burden of proof of competency are not at all prohibitive. The Court acknowledges that several States already bear the burden, and that the allocation of the burden of proof will make a difference "only in a narrow class of cases where the evidence is in equipoise." In those few difficult cases, the State should bear the burden of remitting the defendant for further psychological observation to ensure that he is competent to defend himself. . . .

Table of Cases

Table of Authorities

Books and Treatises

Appleman, Insurance Law and Practice (1962), 166
Ayer, A. J., Probability and Evidence (1972), 17-20
Bentham, J., Rationale of Judicial Evidence (1842), 619-620
Brownmiller, S., Against our Will (1975), 292
Cohen, L. J., The Probable and the Provable (1977), 105-106, 1029-1030
Copi, I. M., Introduction to Logic (1972), 22
Ely, J.H., Democracy and Distrust (1982), 1019
Estrich, S., Real Rape (1987), 274-284, 292
Fairstein, L. A., Sexual Violence: Our War Against Rape (1993), 292-293, 297-299, 303-304
Field & Murray, Maine Evidence (4th ed.), 134
Field & Murray, Maine Evidence (2000 ed.), 319
Green, E., The Complete Courthouse, in Dispute Resolution Devices in a Democratic Society (1985), 923-929
Green, Expanded Use of the Mini-Trial, Private Judging, Neutral-Expert Fact-Finding, Patent Arbitration and Industry Self-Regulation, Dispute Management (1981), 923
Hart, H. & J. McNaughton, Evidence and Inference in the Law (1959), 16-17
Holdsworth, A History of English Law (1926), 408
King, W. & D. Pillinger, Opinion Evidence in Illinois (1942), 754-755
MacKinnon, C., Toward a Feminist Theory of the State (1989), 292
Maguire, J., J. Weinstein, J. Chadbourn & J. Mansfield, Evidence (1973), 334
McCormick, Cases on Evidence, 946
McCormick, Evidence (2d ed.1972), 166, 168, 267, 946
McKenna, J., J. Cecil, & P. Coukos, Reference Manual on Scientific Evidence (1994), 114-123
National Research Council, DNA Technology in Forensic Science (1992), 124, 129-130
Phillimore, J. G., History and Principles of the Law of Evidence (1850), 408
Russell, B., Problems of Philosophy (1912), 20-21
Stephen, J., A History of the Criminal Law of England (1883), 408
Thayer, J., Preliminary Treatise on Evidence (1898), 1-2, 50
Tillers, P. & E. Green, Probability and Inference in the Law of Evidence (1988), 103
Weinstein, J. & M. Berger, Weinstein's Evidence (1981), 755, 922
Westin, A., Privacy and Freedom (1967), 604
Wigmore, J., Evidence (Chadbourn rev. 1974), 560
Wigmore, J., Evidence (McNaughton rev. 1961), 602
Wigmore, J., A Student's Textbook on the Law of Evidence (1935), 2
Wigmore, J., Wigmore on Evidence (1940), 973

Articles

Allen, R., Structuring Jury Decisionmaking in Criminal Cases: A Unified Constitutional Approach to Evidentiary Devices (1980), 1080-1085
Althouse, A., Beyond King Solomon's Harlots: Women in Evidence (1992), 5-6

Rules

Miscellaneous

Index